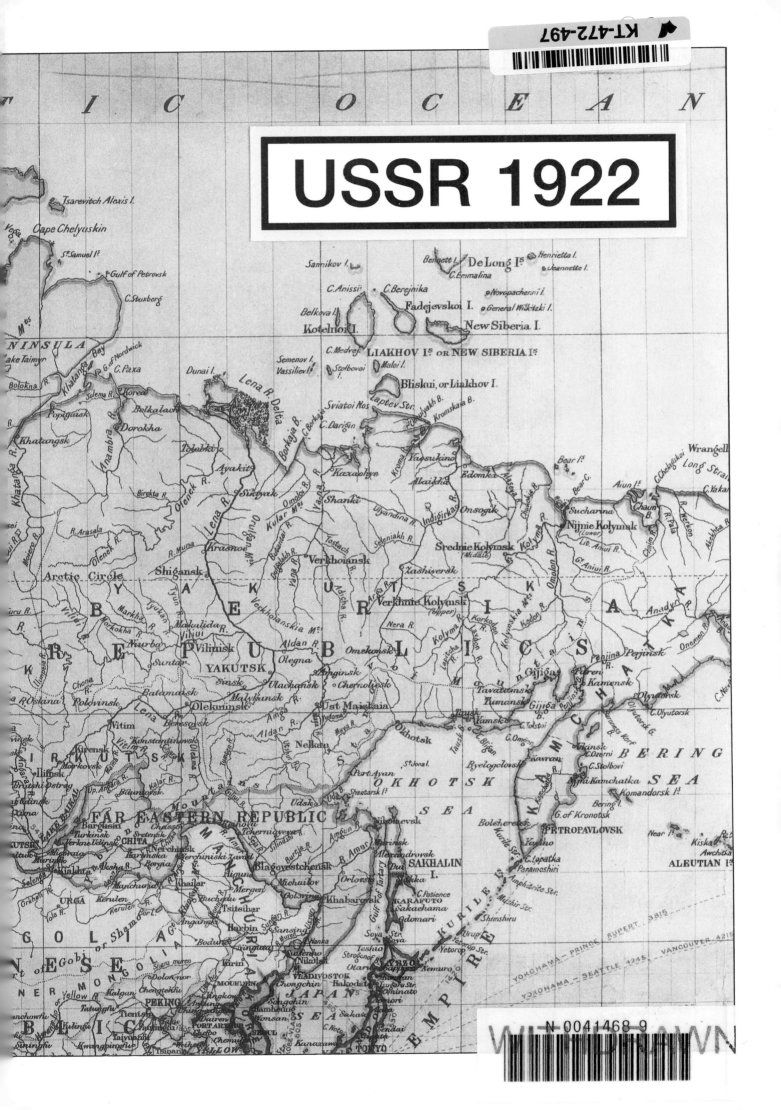

A BIOGRAPHICAL
DICTIONARY OF THE
SOVIET UNION 1917–1988

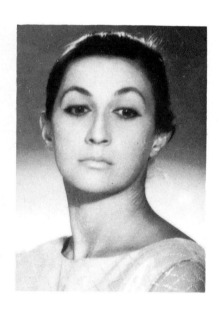  

Top line left to right: Mikhail Tukhachevskii (1893–1937), Solomon Gol'din (1887–   ), Iosef Stalin (1879–1953). Middle line left to right: Lev Kopelev (1912–   ), Tikhon, Patriarch of Moscow (1865–1925), Vatslav Nizhinskii (1889?–1950). Bottom line left to right: Sofiko Chiaureli (1937–   ), Peter Struve (1870–1944), Marina Tsvetaeva (1892–1941).

A BIOGRAPHICAL DICTIONARY OF THE SOVIET UNION 1917–1988

BY JEANNE VRONSKAYA

WITH VLADIMIR CHUGUEV

1989

K · G · Saur

London · Edinburgh · Munich · New York

Singapore · Sydney · Toronto · Wellington

PORTRAITS ON FRONT COVER

Top row, left to right: Karl Radek (1885–1939), Nadezhda Plevitskaia (1884–1940), Sergei Diaghilev (1872–1929).

Bottom row, left to right: Andrei Vlasov (1900–1946), Valentina Tereshkova (1937–   ), Mikhail Gorbachev (1931–   ).

Cover design by iNHOUSE/Calverts Press.

The two maps of the Soviet Union on the end papers are reproduced from the collection in the Royal Geographical Society. They are from *Stanford's General Map of the World* (1922) and the *Daily Telegraph Map of the World*, published by Geographia (1976).

British Library Cataloguing in Publication Data
Vronskaya, Jeanne
   Biographical dictionary of the Soviet Union 1917–1988.
   1. Soviet Union—Biographies—Collections
   I. Title   II. Chuguev, Vladimir
   920′.047
   ISBN 0–86291–470–1

Library of Congress Cataloguing-in-Publication Data
Vronskaya, Jeanne.
   A biographical dictionary of the Soviet Union,
   1917–1988/ by Jeanne Vronskaya with Vladimir Chuguev.
   545p. 29.5 cm.
   Includes index.
   ISBN 0–86291–470–1: £128.00
   1. Soviet Union—Biography—Dictionaries.   I. Chuguev, Vladimir.
II. Title.
CT1213.V76 1988
920′.047—dc19   88-39417
                                                       CIP

K. G. Saur is an imprint of Butterworth & Co. (Publishers) Ltd., Borough Green, Sevenoaks, Kent, TN15 8PH.

Printed in Great Britain
at the University Printing House, Oxford

Contents

Preface

In the aftermath of 1917, a 'mass society' began to emerge in Russia. The old order, in which a small, educated elite dominated a vast peasant mass, was replaced by a more differentiated system, based on a rapidly growing urban workforce and more highly diversified, educated, professional, technical, scientific and cultural intelligentsia. Early Soviet directories in Russian, though few in number, yielded much valuable biographical information on political figures, particularly on the Bolsheviks themselves. But official policy imposed an increasingly distorted selection. In fields such as the armed forces, the arts and sciences, the well-known names vanished as biographical writing itself became a fruitless and ultimately hazardous human endeavour. This process continued from the early 1930s, when Stalin's lethal sifting of the various elites began, to the middle of the 1980s, when the new establishment began to shrug off the burden of the past by lifting the veil on previously taboo subjects. As 'non-persons' are resurrected, their biographies will be revised.

The picture in English has been much improved by recent reference works on current figures, such as Saur's *Who's Who in the Soviet Union,* but a survey such as the present volume, which includes 5000 biographies covering all fields over the whole Soviet period, holds a special attraction for the professional user, whether researcher or journalist. For at a time when the quantity, quality and range of information from the Soviet Union is growing at an unprecedented rate, a universal Biographical Dictionary needs little justification. The Soviet media are devoting increasing space to hitherto unspoken topics of recent history, the periodical press itself is expanding, ambitious plans are afoot to translate Soviet journals, or materials from them, into English on a regular basis, and meanwhile current translated sources teem with new names. The stage of Soviet public life is becoming more crowded. Russian language activity has also received an infusion of fresh supplies beyond the Soviet border, especially since the large-scale emigration of the 1970s. In this situation, to be able to reach for a guide with so many entries on personalities in all walks of Soviet and emigré life over the entire Soviet period from 1917 is to have an invaluable additional tool at hand.

Harold Shukman
Director of the Russian and East European Centre
St Antony's College, Oxford

Author's note

Some time in the early 1970s, when I was starting as a writer and journalist, I thought it would be a good idea to have a single basic source of information on Russian personalities, and I began to collect biographies from whatever sources I could find. The resulting dictionary provides a wealth of detail on the lives of Soviet/Russian people from all walks of life. Of the 5,000 biographies included, about half are of historical figures who died after 1 January 1917: I and my fellow researcher and co-author Vladimir Chuguev have covered a whole range of people who were born as early as 1831 and who were active from about 1850. We decided to disregard the question of whether such activity took place on Russian territory or outside it in order to include people who emigrated, defected or moved for any other reason, and even those who were born abroad of Russian parentage if their activity involved them closely in Russian life.

The research preceding – and accompanying – the preparation of the book involved work in many libraries and archives, as well as digging into thousands of publications – books, magazines and newspapers, Soviet, emigré, American, English, French and German. Many of the sources are given in the biographical entries. Important sources were *Sovremennye Zapiski* (Contemporary Notes), *Illustrirovannaia Rossiia* (La Russie Illustrée), *Vozrozhdenie* (La Renaissance), *Grani* (Facets), the Paris weekly *Russkaia Mysl'* (La Pensée Russe), the New York daily *Novoe Russkoe Slovo* (New Russian Word), *Novyi Zhurnal* (New Magazine), and of course the Soviet press. We often had serious difficulties establishing the manner of death and other 'negative' aspects of people's lives during the Stalin terror period, the famous blank pages of history which are being so passionately discussed in the Soviet Union now. Special attention was given to people who disappeared 'suddenly' between 1933 and 1953.

In addition to published sources, I derived material for many of the biographies from personal enquiries and interviews. My previous specialisation in Russian films facilitated the treatment of Russian film-makers, many of whom I have known personally.

At the request of the publishers, the spelling of names follows Library of Congress transliteration – for example, Vassilchikov is spelt Vasil'chikov, and Yutkevich becomes Iutkevich. Alternative spellings, married names, maiden names, nicknames and pen-names are given in brackets after the main heading. We decided to leave in their more familiar form internationally-known names such as Chagall, Chaliapin, Meyerhold and Trotsky, and non-Russian names such as Wrangel, Lieven, Hackel and Moutafian.

Research was completed by the time of the party and government leadership reshuffle in October 1988, but last minute amendments have been incorporated up to the end of December.

Jeanne Vronskaya
January 1989, London

Acknowledgments

I owe special thanks to Vladimir Chuguev who, apart from being the author of all the biographies of philosophers and the clergy, provided me with remarkable research into some political and literary figures of the 1920s, advised me on many prominent emigrés between the wars, and undertook the tiring task of preparing a final draft for publication.

I also received great assistance from Prince Leonid Lieven and Princess Dina Lieven who supplied me with information about several members of the Lieven and Anrep families; Prince George Vassiltchikov furnished details of the Vassiltchikov family; Boris Gold gave me the opportunity to meet and speak with his father, Solomon; Jenifer Middleton showed me her family albums and a remarkable book which described the work and life in Russia of her mother-in-law, Lady Sybil Middleton; Gerard Tallack drew my attention to some important economists and defectors, and helped me with the time-consuming work of preparing the Index.

I want also to thank the following for information and assistance: Prince Dominik Lieven, Prince George Galitzine and Princess Jean Galitzine, Princess Elena Alekseevna (Helena) Moutafian, Pamela de Meo (Mrs Brian Synge), Baron Alexis Wrangel, Baron Bob de Zoubowitch, Archpriest Sergei Hackel, actor Boris Isarov, and actress Eileen Benskin (Mrs Boris Isarov).

Information was also kindly offered by the artists Edouard Zelenine, Oleg Tselkov, Valentina Kropivnitskaya, Oscar Rabin and Gari Faif, the art collector George Costakis, Soviet film directors Georgy Shengelaya and Emil Lotianu, the Moscow theatre critic of *Moskovskaya Kultura* Aleksandr Svobodin, Soviet film director Aleksandr Mitta, Soviet stage designer Aleksei Porai-Koshits, Soviet writer Fazil Iskander, sculptor and art editor Igor Shelkovsky, Soviet actor-director Oleg Efremov, Professor Efim Etkind, economist Nikolai Czugunow-Schmitt, journalist and writer Mark Popovsky, writer Anatoly Gladilin, writer Mikhail Rozanov, ballet critic Georgy Shapovalenko, Professor of gynaecology Dr Mikhail Tsyriulnikov, artist and publisher Nikolai Dronnikov, historian and writer Abdurakhman Avtorkhanov, Soviet actor Suimenkul Chokmorov, writer Lev Kopelev.

Several of my informants died while I was collecting material for this book. They are: producer and personal friend Michel Salkind, Soviet writer in exile Viktor Nekrasov, Soviet film director Andrei Tarkovsky, artist Vasily Sitnikov, writer and dear friend Anatoly Kuznetsov, colonel Konstantin Kromiadi, Soviet writer and film director Vasilii Shukshin.

List of Abbreviations and Terms

Agitprop	*Agitatsionnaia propaganda* (Agitation and propaganda)
AKHRR	*Assotsiatsiia Khudozhnikov Revolutsionnoi Rossii* (Association of the Artists of Revolutionary Russia)
Apr.	April
ASSR	*Avtonomnaia sovetskaia sotsialisticheskaia respublika* (Autonomous Soviet Socialist Republic)
Aug.	August
b.	born
BO	*Boevaia Organizatsiia* (SR terrorist organization)
BUND	Jewish Socialist Democratic Party
cand.	candidate
CD	Cadets, Constitutional Democrats, Liberal Party
Cen. Cttee.	*Tsentral'nyi Komitet*
Cheka	*Chrezvychainaia Kommissiia po Bor'be s Kontr-revoliutsiei i Sabotazhem* (Extraordinary Commission for the Fight Against Counter-Revolution and Sabotage), Soviet secret police
Col.	Colonel
COMECON	Council for Mutual Economic Aid
Cominform	Communist Information Bureau, successor to Comintern
Comintern	Communist International
CP	Communist party
CPSU	Communist Party of the Soviet Union
Dec.	December
DOSAAF	*Vsesoiuznoe Dobrovol'noe Obshchestvo Sodeistviia Armii, Aviatsii i Flotu* (All-Union Voluntary Society of Cooperation with Army, Aviation and Navy)
DP	Displaced Person
Dr. Sc.	Doctor of Sciences
DSO	*Dobrovol'noe Sportivnoe Obshchestvo* (Voluntary Sports Society)
Exec. Cttee.	Executive Committee
Feb.	February
FEKS	*Fabrika Ekstsentricheskogo Aktera* (Slapstick Actors' Workshop)
FZU	*fabrichno-zavodskoe uchilishche* (Factory school)
Gen.	General
GLAVLIT	*Glavnoe Upravlenie po Okhrane Gosudarstvennykh Tain v Pechati* (Chief Directorate for Protection of State Secrets in the Press), censorship office
Glavpromstroi	*Glavnoe Promyshlennoe Stroitel'stvo* (Chief Industrial Construction Committee)
Glavsevmorput'	*Glavnyi Severo-morskoi Put'* (Chief Northern Sea Way)
Glavvoenstroi	*Glavnoe Voennoe Stroitel'stvo* (Chief Military Construction Committee)
GOELRO	*Gosudarstvennaia Eletrofikatsiia Rossii* (State Plan for the Electrification of Russia)
gorproletkult	*Gorodskaia proletarskaia kul'tura* (City proletarian culture)
Gosagroprom	*Gosudarstvennaia sel'skokhoziaistvennaia promyshlennost'* (State Agricultural Committee)
Gosizdat	*Gosudarstvennoe Izdatel'stvo* (State Publishing House)
Goskino	*Gosudarstvennoe Kino* (State Cinema)
Goskinprom	*Gosudarstvennaia Kinopromyshlennost'* (State Film Industry)
GOSPLAN	*Gosudarstvennoe Planirovanie* (State Planning Committee)
Gouvt.	*guberniia* (Gouvernement, administrative district in pre-revolutionary Russia)
GPU	*Gosudarstvennoe Politicheskoe Upravleniie* (State Political Directorate), Soviet secret police
GRU	*Gosudarstvennoe Razvedovatel'noe Upravleniie* (Military Intelligence Directorate)
Gubpolitprosvet	*Gubernskoe politicheskoe prosveshchenie* (Governmental political education)
Gulag	*Gosudarstvennoe Upravlenie Lagerei* (Chief Administration of Camps)
HQ	headquarters
INKHUK	*Institut Khudozhestvennoi Kul'tury* (Institute of Artistic Culture), 1920–24.
Ispolkom	*Ispolnitel'nyi Komitet* (Executive Committee)
Jan.	January
KB	*Konstruktorskoe Biuro* (Design Bureau)
KGB	*Komitet Gosudarstvennoi Bezopasnosti* (Committee of State Security), Soviet secret police
kolkhoz	*kollektivnoe khoziaistvo* (collective farm)
Komsomol	*Kommunisticheskii soiuz molodezhi* (Young Communists League)
KONR	*Komitet Osvobozhdeniia Narodov Rossii* (Committee of Liberation of the People's of Russia), Vlasov's movement in Germany during WWII
Krai	Administrative region in the USSR

LEF	*Levyi Front* (Left Front of Arts)
lt.	lieutenant
m.	married
magnitizdat	unofficial recording and distribution of tapes and cassettes
MGB	*Ministerstvo Gosudarstvennoi Bezopasnosti* (Ministry of State Security), Soviet secret police
MGIMO	*Moskovskii Gosudarstvennyi Institut Mezhdunarodnykh Otnoshenii* (Institute of International Relations in Moscow)
MID	*Ministerstvo Inostrannykh Del* (Ministry of Foreign Affairs)
MKHAT or MHAT	*Moskovskii Khudozhestvennyi Akademicheskii Teatr* (Moscow Arts Theatre)
MOLKH	*Moskovskoe Obshchestvo Liubitelei Khudozhestv* (Moscow Society of Amateurs of Arts)
Mossovet	*Moskovskii Sovet* (Moscow Soviet)
Mossukno	*Moskovskoe Sukno* (Moscow Cloth Industry)
MSK	*Moskovskaia Simfonicheskaia Kapella* (Moscow Symphonic Capella)
MTKH	*Moskovskoe Tovarishchestvo Khudozhnikov* (Moscow Association of Artists)
MVD	*Ministerstvo Vnutrennikh Del* (Ministry of Internal Affairs)
Narkompros	*Narodnyi Kommissariat Prosveshcheniia* (People's Commissariat for Education), Ministry of Education
Narkomzdrav	*Narodnyi Kommissariat Zdravookhraneniia* (People's Commissariat for Health Service), Ministry of Health Service
NEP	*Novaia Ekonomicheskaia Politika* (New Economic Policy)
NKVD	*Narodnyi Kommissariat Vnutrennikh Del* (People's Commissariat of Internal Affairs), Soviet secret police
NS	*Narodnye Sotsialisty* (People Socialists), right wing socialists
NTS	*Narodno-Trudovoi Soiuz* (Popular Labour Alliance) known as Russian Solidarists, an anti-Soviet, very active organization
nomenklatura	nomenclature, the top layer of the ruling class in the USSR, senior party members, decision-makers
Nov.	November
oblast'	administrative unit in the USSR
obkom	*oblastnoi komitet* (party regional committee)
Oblispolkom	*Oblastnoi Ispolnitel'nyi Komitet* (District Executive Committee)
Oct.	October
OKHR	*Ob'edinenie Khudozhnikov Realistov* (Association of Artists-Realists)
OMKH	*Ob'edinenie Moskovskikh Khudozhnikov* (Association of Moscow Artists)
Orgburo	*Organizatsionnoe Biuro* (Organizing Bureau or Committee)
PERSIMFAMS	*Pervyi Simfonicheskii Ansambl' Mossoveta* (First Symphonic Ensemble of the Mossovet)
pomgol	*pomoshch' golodaiushchim* (Aid to Starving)
prodotriady	*prodovol'stvennye otriady* (military and Cheka food requisitions detachments)
prodrazverstka	*prodovol'stvennaia razverstka* (requisitioning of agricultural products from peasants by the State)
PROKOLL	*Proizvodstvennyi Kollektiv Studentov-Kompozitorov Moskovskoi Konservatorii* (Working Collective of Composers-Students of Moscow Conservatory)
Proletkult	*Proletarskaia Kul'tura* (Workers' Organization for Culture)
rabfak	*rabochii fakul'tet* (Workers' Faculty), a 2-year higher education course for adults of proletarian background
RAPP	*Rabochaia Assotsiatsiia Proletarskikh Pisatelei* (Workers' Association of Proletarian Writers)
Revkom	*Revoliutsionnyi komitet* (Revolutionary Committee)
RKKA	*Raboche-krest'ianskaia krasnaia armiia* (Workers' and Peasants' Red Army)
RMO	*Russkoe Muzykal'noe Obshchestvo* (Russian Music Society)
ROA	*Russkaia Osvoboditel'naia Armiia* (Russian Liberation Army) during WWII, General Vlasov's army
ROSTA	*Rossiiskoe Telegrafnoe Agentstvo* (Russian Telegraph Agency)
ROVS	*Russkii Obshche-Voinskii Soiuz* (Russian All-Military Union), organization of White army veterans in exile
RSDRP	*Rossiiskaia sotsial-demokraticheskaia rabochaia partiia* (Russian Social-Democratic Workers Party), Russian Marxists, later split into Bolshevik and Menshevik wings
RSFSR	Russian Soviet Federative Socialist Republic
RSKHD	*Russkoe Khristianskoe Studencheskoe Dvizhenie* (Russian Christian Students Movement)
samizdat	self-publishing
SD	Social Democrats, marxist socialists
Sel'khoztekhnika	*Sel'sko-khoziaistvennaia tekhnika* (Agricultural equipment organization)

Sept.	September
SMERSH	*Smert' shpionam* (Death to the Spies) Directorate of the Soviet secret police connected with military intelligence and terror in the Soviet Union and abroad during WWII
Sovinformburo	*Sovetskoe informatsionnoe biuro* (Soviet Information Bureau)
sovkhoz	*sovetskoe khoziaistvo*, state farm
Sovnarkhoz	*Sovet Narodnogo Khoziaistva* (Council of National Economy)
Sovnarkom	*Sovet Narodnykh Komissarov* (Council of People's Commissars)
SR	Socialist revolutionaries, Russian non-Marxist socialists
SRKH	*Soiuz Russkikh Khudozhnikov* (Union of Russian Painters)
TASS	*Telegrafnoe Agentstvo Sovetskogo Soiuza* (Soviet News Agency)
TSAGI	*Tsentral'nyi Aero-Gidrodinamicheskii Institut* (Central Aero-Dynamics Institute)
Tsentrobalt	Central Baltic sailors Committee
Tsentrosibir'	Central Siberia
Tsentrosoiuz	Central Union
TSIK	*Tsentral'nyi Ispolnitel'nyi Komitet* (Central Executive Committee)
UN	United Nations
UPA	*Ukrainskaia Povstancheskaia Armiia* (Ukrainian Partisans' army)
UPDK	*Upravlenie Obsluzhivaniia Diplomaticheskogo Korpusa* (Directorate for Services to Diplomatic Corps), an organization run by KGB
VGIK	*Vsesoiuznyi Gosudarstvennyi Institut Kinematografii* (State Film School in Moscow)
VKHUTEIN	*Vysshii Khudozhestvenno-tekhnicheskii Institut* (Higher Technical Art Institute)
VKHUTEMAS	*Vysshie Khudozhestvenno-tekhnicheskie Masterskie* (Higher Technical Art Workshops)
VKP(b)	*Vsesoiuznaia kommunisticheskaia partiia bol'shevikov* All-Union Communist Party of Bolsheviks
VOKHR	*Voennizirovannaia Okhrana* (Armed Security)
Vsevobuch	*Vsesoiuznoe voennoe obuchenie* (All-union Military Education)
VSNKH	*Vysshii Sovet Narodnogo Khoziaistva* (Supreme Council of National Economy)
VTO	*Vsesoiuznoe Teatral'noe Obshchestvo* (All-Union Theatre Society)
VTSIK	*Vsesoiuznyi Tsentral'no-Ispolnitel'nyi Komitet* (All-Union Central Executive Committee)
VUFKU	All-Ukrainian Foto-Film Administration
WWI	First World war
WWII	Second World War
WCC	World Council of Churches
ZAGS	*Zapis' aktov grazhdanskogo sostoianiia* (Registry Office of marriages, birth and death)
Zek	prisoner in the Gulag
Zemstvo	Pre-revolutionary rural local administration

A

Abakumov, Viktor Semenovich

1894–18.12.1954. Minister of state security, head of SMERSH.

Rose through the state security system during the Stalin purges of the 1930s. Member of Stalin's personal secretariat. Sent to control the NKVD in Rostov-on-Don. Became known by his exceptional brutality. One of Beria's deputies. During WWII head of SMERSH, 1942–46, the special terror network devoted to the complete liquidation of all enemies of Stalin. In the post-WWII years, practically the head of the whole Soviet spying and terror network abroad, united by Stalin under the name of Komitet Informatsii (KI). Tortured prisoners at Lubianka with his own hands. With Beria, involved in abducting young girls for orgies. Minister of State Security (MGB), 1950–51, in charge of the Leningrad Affair, a post-WWII purge, leading to the execution and imprisonment of several thousand people. Removed by Stalin, who became suspicous of Beria, and replaced by Ignat'ev, 1951. In 1952 failed to believe in the so-called doctors' plot and was arrested on Stalin's orders. Released immediately after Stalin's death by Beria in spring 1953 and returned to work in the state security system, but soon re-arrested in summer 1953 after Beria's fall. Tried in Leningrad for his part in the Leningrad Affair. On 24 Dec. 1954 *Pravda* reported his execution a week earlier.

Abdulbekov, Zagalav Abdulbekovich

29.12.1945–   . Athlete.

Born in a Caucasian village, in the Daghestan ASSR. Graduated from the Daghestan Pedagogical Institute, 1968. Olympic champion (free-style wrestling), 1972. Many times USSR champion, 1966–73.

Abel, Rudolf Ivanovich (Fischer, William)

2.7.1902–1971. Intelligence officer.

Little is known of Abel's life and work before WWII. A GRU agent in Nazi Germany during the war. It is believed that his father was a German communist who took his family to the Soviet Union in the 1930s. In 1947, entered Canada as a German national and went from there to the

USA using a false Canadian passport. Provided by the US Communist Party with the birth certificate of a dead child. Surfaced in Brooklyn where he set up a photographic studio. Also known as a good musician, artist and craftsman. Multilingual and a first-class radio engineer. Under the name of Emil Robert Goldfus, operated a large network of Soviet agents throughout America. Recalled to Moscow, but soon sent to Finland where his mission was to eliminate anti-communist Russians living there. Married a Finnish woman although at the time already married to a Russian woman in Moscow. In 1952, returned to America with his Finnish wife. Arrested by the FBI when another GRU agent, who had defected to the USA, exposed him. Tried and sentenced to 30 years in prison in 1957. After only 5 years, in Feb. 1962, exchanged in East Berlin for Gary Powers, who had been shot down when flying his U-2 plane over Soviet territory. Promoted to General in Moscow and appointed head of the Anglo-American network, working from his Lubianka office. His private life was very quiet. Visited at his dacha, outside Moscow, by a small circle of friends and colleagues including K. Khenkin who later published memoirs about him.
See: Kiril Khenkin, *Okhotnik Vverkh Nogami,* Frankfurt on Main, 1970; Louise Bernikow, *Abel,* USA, 1970; Ronald Seth, *Encyclopaedia of Espionage*, London, 1972.

Abesadze, Otar Davidovich

1934–5.11.1980. Film director.

Born in Georgia. Graduated from the Moscow VGIK (State Film School). First two short films: *The Reed* and *From House to House,* both 1960. Full-length feature film: *The Spring Will Come Soon* (1969) produced by Georgia Film Studio in Tbilisi. Worked closely with Otar Eseliani, a major Georgian director, who wrote the script.

Abovin-Egides, Petr Markovich

1917–   . Editor, dissident.

Born in Kiev. Grew up in an orphanage. Studied at the Moscow Institute of Philosophy, Literature and History. Participant in WWII. Arrested in 1942, sentenced to 7 years

in the Vorkuta camps. Released, chairman of a kolkhoz, 1953–59. Engaged in dissident activity at the end of the 1960s. Arrested for the samizdat manuscript, *Edinstvennyi Vykhod.* Spent three years in a psychiatric hospital. Editor of the samizdat magazine, *Poiski.* Emigrated, 1980. Lives in France. Editor of *Poiski,* Paris.

Abramov, Fedor Aleksandrovich

29.2.1920–   . Author.

Born in Verkola, Arkhangelsk Oblast'. Graduated from Leningrad University Faculty of Philology in 1948. Prof. of Soviet literature at the Leningrad University in the 1950s. From the late 1950s became widely known through his novels, showing realistically the hardships of rural life in the USSR. Forerunner of the rural writers school.
Main works: *Brothers and Sisters, Bezotsovshchina, Vokrug da Okolo, Pelageia.*

Abuladze, Tengiz Evgen'evich

31.1.1924–   . Film director.

Born in Georgia. Educated at the Tbilisi Railway School, 1943. Studied at a theatrical institute in Tbilisi. Entered the director's faculty of the Moscow VGIK (State Film School). Studied under Sergei Iutkevich and Mikhail Romm. First feature film, *Magdan's Donkey* (1955, with Revaz Chkheidze), was well received both in the Soviet Union and abroad. Awarded a prize in the category of short films at the 1956 Cannes Film Festival. His next film, *Someone Else's Children* (1958), brilliantly depicted life in Tbilisi. Other films: *Me, Grandma, Iliko and Illarion* (1963) (very popular in the Soviet Union); *A Necklace For My Beloved* (1972); and *The Tree of Wishes,* a film version of Georgii Leonidze's tales about pre-revolutionary country life. In 1987 made a sensation with *Repentance,* which deals with the repressions of the Stalin era. Competed in 1984 and shelved, but released eventually. Became a major box office success all over the country. Tickets were sold out for two months ahead in all cinemas, an unprecedented event in Soviet cultural life.

1

Adamashin, Anatolii Leonidovich
11.10.1934– . Diplomat.
Born in Kiev. Graduated from Moscow University, 1957. Member of the CPSU, 1965. Worked at the Ministry of Foreign Affairs (MID), 1957–59. Attaché, 3rd then 2nd secretary at USSR Embassy in Italy, 1959–65. 2nd, then 1st secretary, councillor and consultant in the 1st European Dept. of the MID, 1965–71. Senior councillor. Head of the Administration for Planning of Foreign Policy Measures in the MID, 1973–78. Head of the 1st European Dept., 1978–86. Deputy Foreign Minister of the USSR from May 1986.

Adamov, Arkadii Grigor'evich
1920– . Author.
Best-selling Soviet author specializing in crime stories. His first book, *Delo Pestrykh*, published in the magazine *Iunost'* was a huge success. Since then he has written some 30 books, nearly all of which have been filmed. Known as the Soviet Agatha Christie.

Adamovich, Evgenia Nikolaevna
1872–1938. Revolutionary.
Involved with revolutionary circles, 1892. Member of the SD Party, 1898. Close to M. Ulianova (Lenin's sister). After the October Revolution 1917, member of the State Cttee. for Education. Took part in the Civil War, 1918–19.

Adamovich, Georgii Viktorovich (Pengs)
1894–21.2.1972. Literary critic.
Born in Moscow. Graduated from Petersburg University. Began writing as a poet, 1916. At first close to the Acmeists. Emigrated after the October Revolution. Settled in Paris, became one of the most influential literary critics in the Russian emigré press between the world wars. Main supporter of the so-called Parizhskaia Nota in Russian 20th century poetry, based on *l'art pour l'art* principles. Had famous literary feuds with Tsvetaeva and Nabokov. After WWII, gave lectures on Russian literature at Manchester University and broadcast talks on Radio Liberty in Munich. Wrote a biography of V. Maklakov. Died in France.

Adomaitis, Regimantas Vaitekovich
31.1.1937– . Film actor.
Born in Lithuania. Graduated from the Faculty of Physics and Mathematics at the University of Vilnius, then from the Vilnius Conservatory as an actor. Worked at the Vilnius Drama Theatre. First film: *The Chronicle of One Day,* 1963. One of the leading actors in Lithuanian cinema. Worked with the outstanding director Grigorii Kozintsev on *King Lear,* made by Lenfilm in 1971. Other films: *No One Wanted to Die,* 1965; *Feelings,* 1970; *That Sweet Word Freedom,* 1973; *Stone Upon Stone,* 1973; *They Made Him a Criminal,* 1979 (dir. by G. Chukhrai, made in Italy).

Adrianov, Sergei Aleksandrovich
1871–1941. Literary critic, lawyer.
Assistant editor of the newspaper *Russkaia Molva.* Extremely popular at the beginning of the 20th century. Died, largely forgotten, during the Stalin epoch.

Adzhemov, Konstantin Khristoforovich
21.3.1911– . Pianist, music critic.
Born in Moscow. Pupil of K. Igumnov and A. Gedike. Taught at the Moscow Conservatory (Chamber Ensemble) and at the Gnesin Pedagogical Institute for Music (piano).

Adzhemov, Moisei Sergeevich
1878–1950. Politician.
Member of the Cen. Cttee of the CD Party. Member of the Duma. In 1917, together with Vinaver and Nabokov, argued for immediate peace with Germany. Emigrated after the Bolshevik take-over.

Afanas'ev, Georgii Dmitrievich
4.3.1906– . Geologist.
Worked at the Institute of Petrography in Leningrad. Chief editor of the magazine, *Geologia,* 1956. Deputy chief scientific secretary of the Academy of Sciences. Specializes in studies of Caucasus rock strata and questions of petrogenesis.

Afanas'ev, Iurii
1932– . Politician, historian.
Supporter of Gorbachev. In 1985 appointed Rector of the Institute of Historic Archives in Moscow. His team has faced opposition in carrying out the monumental task of removing some of the Stalinist distortions in Soviet history. Gave a speech on this subject at the Institute to a professional audience (published by the weekly, *Moscow News*). Has been viciously attacked by four old-guard historians accusing him of being influenced by Western scholars. The extracts of the speech published pointed at the selectivity of history under Stalin's rule and blank pages in important chapters. Suggested a detailed study of the biographies of many leaders whose activities were far from being glorious. Quoted as saying: 'Stalin did not need historians since he destroyed history as a science in our country.'

Afanas'ev, Sergei Aleksandrovich
1918– . Party official.
Graduated from the Moscow Bauman Technical College, 1941. Joined the Communist Party, 1941. Worked in the munitions industry, 1946–57, first as an engineer, then as deputy chief. Deputy Chairman of Leningrad Economic Council, 1957–58. Chairman, 1958–61. Chairman of the Economic Council of the RSFSR, 1961–65. Member of the Cen. Cttee. of the CPSU from 1961. Minister of Heavy Transport and Engineering throughout the 1980s. Removed from his post, July 1987.

Afanas'ev, Viktor Grigor'evich
1922– . Politician, journalist.
Member of the CPSU from 1943. Graduated from the State Pedagogical Institute in Chita, in the Far East, 1950. Teacher, 1953–54. Deputy Director and Professor of Philosophy at the same institute, 1954–59. Professor, Chair of Scientific Communism at the Academy of Sociology of the Cen. Cttee. of the CPSU, 1960–68. Deputy and first deputy chief editor of *Pravda,* 1968–74 and *Communist,* the monthly journal, 1974–76. From 1976 member of the Cen. Cttee. of the CPSU. In 1976 took over editorship of *Pravda.* Dr.Phil. Sc., 1964. Corresponding member of the USSR Academy of Sciences, 1972. Regarded as one of the Soviet Union's most influential journalists. Supports Gorbachev's glasnost policy. Was quoted as saying that 'restricted zones are still facing the Soviet media in their reporting.'

Afanas'eva, Anna Stepanovna
1892–1981. Revolutionary.
Joined the Bolshevik Party, 1915. Took part in the Bolshevik take-over in Moscow, 1917. Worked in the Secretariat of the Cen. Cttee. of the Bolshevik Party from 1919. Joined the Marx-Engels Institute, 1923–25. One of the organizers of the V.Lenin Museum.

Afanasii (Sakharov), Bishop of Kovrov
2.7.1887–1962. Russian Orthodox clergyman.
Educated at Vladimir Seminary, 1902–08. Graduated from the Moscow Theological Academy in 1912. Monk, 1912. Taught at Poltava and Vladimir seminaries, 1912–18. Bishop of Kovrov, 1921. Arrested for the first time in 1922. One of the leaders of the catacomb church, which opposed the official church policy of submission to the orders of communist state officials. This part of the Orthodox church existed secretly and was ruthlessly persecuted. Endured almost constant prison and camp sentences from the early 1920s until Stalin's death, 1953. Left a concise list of his imprisonments, which reads like a modern martyrium.

Agababov, Sergei Artem'evich
25.10.1926–23.10.1959. Composer.
Born in Makhachkala, Daghestan. Used Daghestani themes in his compositions which included songs, a piano and violin suite, and pieces for children. Died in an air crash.

Agadzhanova-Shutko, Nina Ferdinandovna
8.11.1889–14.12.1974. Security services officer, scriptwriter.
Studied at teachers' courses in Ekaterinodar. From 1911–16 active party worker. Several short arrests. During the Civil War, in the Cheka. Official at the Soviet Embassy, Prague, 1921–22 and at the Soviet Embassy in Latvia, 1934–38. Active intelligence work in both countries. Retired from the security services and entered the film industry, 1924. Her script, *1905 God*, became the basis of S.Eisenstein's *The Battleship Potemkin*. Specialized in revolutionary subjects. Assisted Lev Kuleshov in his film *Dva Bul'di Dva*, 1930. Co-scriptwriter of V. Pudovkin's film,

Dezertir. Taught at the VGIK, 1945–52.

Agafangel (Preobrazhenskii, Aleksandr Lavrent'evich), Metropolitan of Iaroslavl' and Rostov
27.9.1854–16.10.1928. Russian Orthodox clergyman.
Born in Tula Gouvt. Son of a priest. Graduated from Moscow Theological Academy, 1881. Monk, 1885. Head of Irkutsk seminary, 1888. Bishop of Kirensk, 1889. Bishop of Tobolsk, 1893. Bishop of Riga, 1897. Archbishop of Wilno, 1910. Archbishop of Iaroslavl', 1913. Metropolitan of Iaroslavl' in 1917. Appointed locum tenens by Patriarch Tikhon in 1922, in the case of the latter's death or inability to discharge his duties. Was in exile when Tikhon was arrested and so was not able to prevent Metropolitan Sergii (Stragorodskii) taking over with the help of the state authorities. Died in Kineshma.

Agal'tsov, Filipp Aleksandrovich
1900–1980. Marshal of aviation.
Joined the Bolsheviks and the Red Army, 1919. Took part in the Civil War. Graduated from the Military-Political Academy, 1932. Qualified as a pilot, 1934. Political officer in the air force. Sent to Spain during the Civil War, 1936–39. Air force regiment commander, 1941. Head of the Air Force School in Tambov, 1941–43. Deputy Commander of the Air Force, 1949–62. Commander of Soviet strategic air force (long range bombers), 1962.

Aganbegian, Abel Gezevich
8.11.1932–   Politician, economist.
Born in Tbilisi. Armenian. Graduated from the Moscow State Institute of Economics in 1955. Joined the Communist Party in 1956. From 1955–61 worked for the USSR State Cttee of the Council of Ministers on problems of labour and wages. Head of the Laboratory of the Institute of Economics and Organization of Industrial Production of the Siberian Section of the Academy of Sciences of the USSR, 1961. Appointed its director in 1966. Corresponding member of the Academy of Sciences since 1964. Author of many works. Gorbachev's chief adviser on econo-

mic matters. Insisted on removing state subsidies, on which the Soviet economy is based, from everything except education, health, care for the elderly and book-publishing. Created in 1987 the New Economic Mechanism, a three-year plan for the complete reform of the Soviet economy (perestroika).

Aganov, Sergei Khristoforovich
1917–   . Marshal of military engineers.
Joined the Soviet Army, 1938. Educated at the Military Engineers' School in Moscow, 1940. Took part in the Soviet-Finnish war, 1939–40. With military engineers' army units from 1942. Graduated from the Frunze Military Academy, 1950. Commander of Soviet military engineers, 1950–60. Later professor and head of military engineers' education establishments. Head of the Engineering Army department in the Ministry of Defence, 1975.

Ageev, Nikolai Vladimirovich
17.6.1903–   . Metallurgist.
Graduated from the Leningrad Polytechnical Institute, 1926. Worked at the Institute of Metallurgy of the Academy of Sciences, 1951. Chief editor of the magazine, *Metallurgy Abstracts*, 1956. Specialist on metallic alloys.

Agishev, Odelsha Aleksandrovich
10.8.1939–   . Scriptwriter.
Tartar. Important scriptwriter of the 1960–70s. Worked with every director of note in Soviet Asia's film studios. Initially graduated from the Suvorov Military School (Suvorovets), then from the VGIK (Moscow Film School) as a scriptwriter.
Scripts: *Storm Over Asia* (1964 with K. Iarmatov), *Tenderness* (1966), *The White White Storks* (1966), *In Love* (1969).

Agoshkov, Mikhail Ivanovich
30.10.1905–   . Mining expert.
Graduated from Vladivostok Polytechnic Institute, 1931. Deputy director of the Institute of Mining of the Academy of Sciences, 1952. Chief scientific secretary of the Presidium of the Academy of Sciences, 1962. Works on the exploitation of ore deposits.

3

Agreneva-Slavianskaia, Ol'ga Khristoforovna (b. Pozdniakova)
1847–20.12.1920. Folklorist, ethnographer.
Born in the village of Makarino, Kostroma Gouvt. Wife and collaborator of D. Agrenev-Slavianskii. Wrote on folk poetry and songs. Died in Yalta, Crimea.

Agurskii, Mikhail (Melib) Samuilovich
1933– . Author, historian, dissident.
Born in Moscow. Son of a founder of the Communist Party of America, who returned to Russia in 1917. Graduated from the Machine-Tool Institute, Moscow. Candidate of Technical Science, 1969. Became actively involved in the human rights movement from the early 1970s. Emigrated to Israel, 1975. Doctor of Slavic Studies, Ecole des Hautes Etudes, Paris. Author of many books and articles. Works include: *Ideologiia Natsional Bolshevizma*, Paris, 1980; *Sovetskii Golem*, London, 1983.

Aigi, Gennadii Nikolaevich
1934– . Poet.
Born in the village of Shamurzino in Chuvashia. Graduated from the Moscow Gorkii Literary Institute. Became known as a talented modernist poet, circulating his work in samizdat. Considered a classic of Chuvash literature. Collections of his verse (in Russian) have been published in West Germany and France.

Aikhenvald, Iulii Isaevich (Eichenwald)
1872–1928. Literary critic.
Before WWI, travelled all over Russia giving tremendously popular lectures on literary subjects. The texts of his lectures were later published in several volumes under the title *Siluety Russkikh Pisatelei*, giving charming impressionistic vignettes of many Russian literary figures. Understandable to the uninitiated, and somewhat overloaded by quotations, the lectures are by no means without deeper insight (e.g. a realistic appraisal of Gorkii at the time when he was at the peak of his success, or his judgment on Gumilev, when he was still not widely known). Emigrated after the Bolshevik take-over. Settled in Berlin. Became the main literary critic of the Russian right-of-centre newspaper, *Rul'*. Died in an accident (run over by a tram).

Aikhenvald, Iurii Aleksandrovich
1928– . Author.
Son of a communist official, who perished in the Gulag. Arrested, 1949. Inmate of a special psychiatric clinic in Leningrad, 1951–55. Taught literature in high schools, 1957–68. Took part in protests against the trials of dissidents Ginzburg and Galanskov. Poems and literary criticism (*Don Kikhot na Russkoi Pochve*. 2 vols) published in the West.

Aini (Said-Murodzoda, Sadriddin)
27.4.1878–15.7.1954. Tadzhik author.
Born in Soktare, near Gizhduvan. Educated at Medrese (Moslem religious school), Bukhara. Participant in revolution in Bukhara in 1920. One of the founders of Tadzhik and Uzbek Soviet literature. Deputy of the USSR Supreme Soviet. First President of the Tadzhik Academy of Sciences, 1951. Wrote a trilogy of novels in the late 1920–30s, depicting the life of the Tadzhiks over a one hundred year period. Early 1950s, *Autobiography,* 4 vol., showing the transformation of the Bukhara Khanate into a Soviet republic. Died in Dushanbe.

Airikian, Paruir
1950– . Dissident.
Involved in the Armenian nationalist movement since the 1960s. Arrested, 1969, sentenced to 4 years in prison. Released, March 1973, re-arrested, Feb. 1974. Sentenced to 7 years in prison and 3 years exile. Played an active role in the 1988 mass demonstrations in Armenia demanding the transfer of the Nagorno-Karabakh Autonomous Region from Azerbaidzhan to Armenia. Held a press conference in Moscow on the events in Sumgait. Accused of inciting national unrest and re-arrested 25 March 1988. Released and expelled, July 1988.

Aitmatov, Chingiz
1928– . Author.
Born in Kirghizia. Writes in both Russian and Kirghiz. His first short stories attracted the critics' attention. Several of his books have been made into films. Works: *Dzhamilia,* 1958; *Verbliuzhii Glaz,* 1961; *Pervyi Uchitel',* 1963; *Belyi Parokhod,* 1970.

Akakii, (Kuznetsov, Andrei) monk
17.10.1874–30.1.1984. Russian Orthodox clergyman.
Son of a peasant. Born near Vologda. Monk at Solovetskii Monastery, later of the Pechenga (Petsamo) Monastery, which after the Civil War was on Finnish territory. Last survivor of the monks in his monastery. Moved to New Valaam (Valamo) Monastery, where he died peacefully as the last surviving Russian monk of the older generation, having reached the age of 110 years. Buried at the monastery cemetery of New Valaam in Finland.

Akhmadulina, Bella Akhatovna (Evtushenko, Nagibina)
1937– . Poetess.
Born in Moscow. Graduated from the Moscow Gorkii Literary Institute. In the early 1960s considered one of the best young modern poetesses in the Soviet Union. Became known as a member of the group which consisted of Evtushenko, Voznessenskii and others (oboima). Married Evtushenko. Later divorced and remarried to the well-known Soviet writer, Iu. Nagibin. Remained a distinctive neo-classical voice in modern Russian poetry, though her early promise faded somewhat over the years.

Akhmatova, Anna Andreevna (Gorenko)
23.6.1889–5.3.1966. Poetess.
Born at Bolshoi Fontan near Odessa. Daughter of a naval engineer. Brought to Tsarskoe Selo in 1890, where she grew up. Educated at a secondary school in Tsarskoe Selo. Moved to Kiev in 1907. Married Nikolai Gumilev in 1910. Visited Paris. Moved to Petersburg. Started to write and published her first poems in 1912. Very soon acknowledged as a fine poetess, became the darling of the silver age of Russian poetry. Originally member of the Acmeists (Gumilev's group), later created her own original style of restrained and lyrical classicism. After the October Revolution 1917, worked as a librarian at the Agronomical Institute in Petrograd. Stressing her common experience with

the people, became in a very personal way the voice of the victims of a tragic epoch (*Requiem, Poem without a Hero*), her impact accentuated by her personal experience: Gumilev was shot, her son, Lev Gumilev, spent many years in the Gulag camps, WWI, the Civil War and the terror, WWII and the Leningrad siege (which she escaped from at the last moment), and the post-war persecutions. All this found expression in her work. During WWII lived in Tashkent and returned to Leningrad in 1944. Became the main target (along with Zoshchenko) of a vicious attack by Zhdanov (Stalin's literature expert) in 1946. Expelled from the Writers' Union, for a long time unable to publish her work. Turned to translation and became a serious Pushkin scholar. In the mid-1960s made visits to Britain, Italy and France (awarded an Oxford doctorate in the spring of 1965). In her later years, surrounded by immense prestige in the Soviet Union as a major literary figure.

Works: *Stikhotvoreniia i poemy*, Moscow, 1976; *Collected Works*, USA, 3 vol.

Akhmetov, Nizametdin
1948– .Dissident.
Muslim. One of the longest serving prisoners of conscience in the Soviet Union. Spent 18 years in labour camps and mental hospitals. One of the activists in the Crimean Tartars movement for their return to the Crimea, their ancestral homeland, from which they were deported by Stalin in 1944. First conflict with the authorities, 1966. Sentenced to 2 years imprisonment. Not released after having served his term. Put in solitary confinement and given another 7 years for anti-Soviet agitation to be followed by another 5 years in exile. In prison protested with other prisoners about the appalling conditions. Sentenced to 5 more years for having written on his cell wall 'The USSR is a Prison of the Peoples'. In 1979 a letter from him was published in West Germany. Became a celebrated international case (see Bernard Levin, 'Two Men Under Tyranny', printed in *The Times*, 1987). Another letter from him was smuggled to the Madrid sessions of the Helsinki Conference. Severely beaten up in prison. Sent to a psychiatric hospital in Kazakhstan, later moved to another such hospital in Cheliabinsk in the Urals. Following international pressure released in July 1987. Received permission to go for medical treatment to West Germany.

Akhromeev, Sergei Fedorovich
5.5.1923– . Marshal.
Son of a peasant. Member of the CPSU from 1943. Graduated from the Military Academy of Tank Troops in 1952 and the Military Academy of the General Staff in 1967. With the Soviet Army from 1940. Commander at various fronts, 1941–45, Chief-of-staff of a regiment, regiment commander, division commander, 1946–64. Senior military commanding posts, 1967–72. Chief of Administration in the USSR Ministry of Defence, 1974–79. 1st Deputy Chief of the General Staff of the USSR Armed Forces from 1979. Candidate member of the Cen. Cttee. from 1981. Full member, 1983. Marshal, 1983. Succeeded Marshal Ogarkov as Chief-of-staff, Sept. 1984. First Deputy Minister of Defence, 1984.

Akhron, Iosif Iul'evich
13.5.1886–29.4.1943. Violinist, composer.
Born in Lodz. Brother of Isidore Akhron, pianist and composer. Pupil of L. Auer. Emigrated, 1922. In the USA from 1925. His works include a suite for chamber orchestra, music for violin and piano, and a string quartet. Died in Hollywood.

Akhsharumov, Dmitrii Vladimirovich
20.9.1864–after 1936. Violinist, conductor.
Born in Odessa. Organized the RMO (Russian Musical Society) and the Symphony Orchestra in Poltava. Made guest appearances with his orchestra all over Russia. Died in Central Asia.

Akimenko, Fedor Stepanovich (Iakimenko)
20.2.1876–8.1.1945. Composer, pianist, musicologist.
Born in Khar'kov. Brother of Ia. Stepovoi. Professor at the Petrograd Conservatory. Emigrated. Lived in Paris from 1923 until his death.

Akimov, Anatolii Ivanovich
15.11.1947– . Athlete.
Born in Moscow. Master of Sports, 1972. European champion (water polo), 1970. Champion of the USSR, 1965–75. Olympic champion, 1972.

Akimova, Sofia Vladimirovna
27.3.1887–1947? Singer (soprano).
Born in Tiflis (Tbilisi). Pupil of M. Slavina and S. Mirovich. Wife of I. Ershov. Soloist with the Mariinskii Theatre, Petrograd, 1913–29. Professor at the Leningrad Conservatory.

Akselrod, Liubov Ivanovna (penname–Orthodox)
1868–5.2.1946. Philosopher, art critic.
As a young girl in 1884, joined the revolutionary movement. Lived abroad, 1887–1906. Graduated from Bern University in 1900. Joined the SD Party. Close to Plekhanov. Criticized Lenin's philosophical essays. Menshevik after the split of the SDs, 1903. Member of the Cen. Cttee. of the Menshevik Party, 1917. Lecturer at the Institute of Red Professors (courses for the education of the new intelligentsia, true to Communist principles), 1921–23. Later specialized in sociological problems of the arts. Represented Marxist thought among the Russian intelligentsia, before Marxist dogma took over under Stalin.

Akselrod, Pavel Borisovich
1850–1928. Politician.
Studied at Kiev University. In the 1870s became a populist (narodnik), later Marxist, 1883. In the late 1880s founded (with Plekhanov and Zasulich) Liberation of Labour (Osvobozhdenie Truda), the group which was the precursor of the RSDRP. One of the editors of *Iskra*, 1900. After the split of the SDs, became the leader of the Mensheviks, 1903, and one of the main opponents of Lenin. Suggested a Workers Congress in 1905. Member of the Executive Committee of the Petrograd Soviet, 1917. Supported the Provisional Government. Veteran revolutionary, consistent in his rejection of Bolshevik tendencies, first within his own party (the SDs), later within Russia, and thereafter within the international socialist movement. Emigrated after the October Revolu-

tion 1917. One of the leaders of the 2nd (Socialist) International. Died in Berlin.

Aksenov, Vasilii Pavlovich
1932–   . Author.
For a time, in the 1960s, the star writer of the Soviet Union. Born in Kazan' where his father was mayor. His parents were arrested and taken to a labour camp, when he was aged 4. Taken to an orphanage for children of the enemies of the people by train in a sealed compartment with a KGB nurse. Rescued by a brave uncle who had already lost his job. Grew up with his grandmother. Reunited with his mother, Evgenia Ginzburg, the writer and journalist, when he was 16. Lived together with his mother in internal exile in Magadan in Siberia. In 1956 graduated from the Leningrad Medical Institute. Worked as a doctor in the Far North, 1956–60. Moved to Karelia. Doctor in Karelia and Leningrad Commercial Ports, later at a Moscow TB clinic. His first novel, *Kollegi*, became an instant bestseller in 1960. His next book, *Zvezdnyi Bilet*, 1961, confirmed his reputation as a modern Soviet writer. Criticized by Soviet critics for his 'bad language' (which is in fact the slang of modern Soviet youth). Other books: *Na Polputi k Lune* (1962), *Apelsiny Iz Marokko* (1963). Emigrated, after difficulties with authorities, being unable to publish his work, 1980. Lives in California and teaches Russian literature at American universities.

Aladzhalov, Manuil Khristoforovich
1862–1934. Artist.
Studied at the Moscow School of Painting, Sculpture and Architecture, 1880–91, under A. Savrasov, V. Makovskii, I. Prianishnikov and E. Sorokin. Landscape painter. Took part in exhibitions: as a student, 1882–85 and 1887–91; 36 Artists, 1901–02 and 1902–03; Mir Iskusstva, 1903; 2nd State Exhibition, Moscow, 1918–19; The Zhar-Tsvet Society; 1925; the Association of Realist Artists, Moscow, 1927–28.

Alafuzov, Vladimir Antonovich
1901–1966. Admiral.
Joined the Red Navy, 1918. Took part in the Civil War. Graduated from the Naval Academy, 1932. Sent to Spain during the Civil War, 1936–39. Deputy Chief-of-staff of the Soviet Navy, 1938. Chief-of-staff of the Soviet Pacific fleet, 1943. In the Gulag, 1948–53. Head, 1945–48, and Deputy Head, 1953–58, of the Naval Academy.

Alchevskii, Ivan Alekseevich
27.12.1876–10.5.1917. Singer (tenor).
Born in Kharkov. Trained by his brother, Grigorii Alchevskii (1866–1920). With the Mariinskii Theatre, Petersburg, 1901–05, the Paris Grand Opera, 1908–10, and the Moscow Bolshoi Theatre, 1910–14. Appeared in chamber concerts. Died in Baku.

Aldan, Andrei Georgievich (Nerianin)
1902–1957. Colonel.
Born in the Urals, son of a worker. Red Army soldier in the Civil War. Graduated from the Frunze Military Academy, 1934, and from the Academy of the General Staff, 1939. During WWII Chief-of-staff of the 22nd Army. Taken prisoner by the Germans. Joined Vlasov's army, the ROA, Deputy Chief-of-staff, 1945. One of the few who escaped SMERSH, May 1945–47. Escaped from a US POW camp in Germany. Lived in DP camps, 1945–48. Wrote memoirs, published in the USA, about the Vlasov army – *Armiia Obrechennykh*. Active in Vlasov veterans' organizations in Western Europe. Moved to the USA, 1953, where he lectured on Soviet armed forces in the Pentagon. Died in Washington.

Aldan-Semenov (Semenov, Andrei Ignat'evich)
1908–   . Author.
Began writing as a poet in 1926. First volume of poetry published in 1934. Arrested during the purges in 1937. Inmate of the Gulag camps, 1938–53, (sentenced to forced labour – gold digging, fishing and tree-felling). Rehabilitated after Stalin's death. Wrote books on workers in Siberia and the North. Remained faithful to communism despite his personal sufferings.

Aldanov, Mark Aleksandrovich (Landau)
7.11.1889–25.2.1957. Author.
Born in Kiev. Trained as a scientist. Emigrated to France in 1918. Work- ed as a chemical engineer. During WWII moved to the USA. Became well known between the wars for a 4-volume historical work *The Thinker* (Myslitel') (*Deviatoe Termidora*, *Chertov Most*, *Sviataia Elena* and *Zagovor* published by Slovo in Berlin between 1923–27). His work is marked by meticulous research, historical detail and a remarkably elegant style. His books have been translated into English but are completely unknown in the Soviet Union because of his total rejection of dictatorship. Other books: *Istoki*, 2 vol, Paris, 1950, *Punshevaia Vodka*, Paris, 1940, *Ogon' i Dym*, Paris, 1922, *Desiataia Simfoniia*, Paris, 1931, *Portrety*, Berlin, 1931, *Zemlia i Liudi*, Berlin, 1932, *Sovremenniki*, Berlin, 1932, *Samoubiistvo*, Paris, 1977. Founded in the USA the magazine *Novyi Zhurnal*. First publication in the USSR, *Deviatoe Termidora*, 1988. Died in France.

Alekhin, Aleksandr Aleksandrovich
1.11.1892–24.3.1946. Chess player.
Born in Moscow. Son of a nobleman. Emigrated, 1920. Settled in France, 1921. Graduated in law from the Sorbonne. Became a French citizen. Regarded as one of the greatest chess players of all times. World champion for almost two decades, 1927–46 (with one year interval in 1936). Died in Portugal, buried in Paris.

Alekin, Oleg Aleksandrovich
23.8.1908–   . Hydrochemist.
Graduated from Leningrad University, 1938. Worked at the Hydrological Institute in Leningrad, 1929–51. Director of the Hydrochemical Institute, 1951–61. Author of studies on the chemical analysis of water and on hydrological condition of rivers and lakes.

Aleksandr, Archbishop of Dmitrov
8.8.1941–   . Russian Orthodox clergyman.
Born in Teikovo, son of a worker. On military service, 1963–66. Graduated from Moscow Theological Academy, 1971. Monk, 1971. Lecturer at the Moscow Theological Academy, 1973, professor, 1981. Dean of the Moscow Theological Academy and Seminary, 1982. Archbishop, 1986. Chairman of the Education Cttee of the Holy Synod, Sept. 1986.

Aleksandr Mikhailovich (Romanov, Sandro)
1866–1933. Grand Duke.
Married the sister of Nicholas II, Ksenia. Father-in-law of Prince F. Iusupov, who murdered Rasputin. Head of the merchant fleet administration before WWI. President of the Naval Museum in Petersburg. During the Revolution stayed in the Crimea, and later emigrated on a British warship. Wrote interesting memoirs. See: *Kniga Vospominanii*, 1932, reprint, 1979, Paris.

Aleksandra Fedorovna (Romanova, b. Alix Victoria Helene Louise Beatrice, Princess of Hesse-Darmstadt)
6.6.1872–17.7.1918. Last Empress of Russia.
Born in Darmstadt, daughter of Grand-Duke Louis of Hesse and Princess Alice of England. From the age of 6 (after her mother's early death) lived in England with her grandmother Queen Victoria and became her favourite grand-child (nicknamed 'Sunshine'). Travelled to Russia in 1884, when her elder sister Elizabeth married Grand-Duke Sergei (brother of Aleksander III). Met the heir to the throne, Nicholas, who later fell in love with her and, despite the opposition of his parents, married her (26 Nov. 1894, one week after the funeral of his father, Aleksander III). Originally protestant, she changed to Orthodoxy before the marriage and coronation. Later became a victim of extreme mysticism caused by isolation from the Romanov dynasty and personal difficulties (though enjoying throughout her life the complete trust and devotion of her husband). Longed for many years for a male heir, and after four girls at last had a boy, suffering from haemophilia, transmitted through her from Queen Victoria. Turned for solace to miracle healers, religion and holy men, including the Siberian peasant, Rasputin. Never able to acquire popularity in her adopted country, vilified as a German during WWI (despite active charity work) and disliked by society as an adviser to the Tsar and patron of Rasputin. Thus she unwittingly helped to create a vacuum around the monarch. After the February Revolution 1917, under guard at Tsarskoe Selo (with her family). Exile to England was prevented by Lloyd George's intervention. On Kerenskii's orders the family was sent to Tobolsk, and disappeared in July 1918 in Ekaterinburg, where they had been held under Bolshevik guard at the Ipat'ev house. Their fate aroused considerable controversy. Some charred remains and jewellery was found in summer 1918 in disused mines near Ekaterinburg by the White forces, and it was assumed that the bodies of Aleksandra, her husband, son, four daughters and a small group of staff had been burnt. See: *Great Soviet Encyclopedia*, 3rd ed., which states that the Tsarina was shot.

Aleksandrov, Aleksandr
1943–   . Cosmonaut, flight engineer.
In July 1987 joined Iurii Romanenko in space replacing A. Laveikin. Returned to earth on 29 Dec. 1987. Became a national hero.

Aleksandrov, Aleksandr Danilovich
4.8.1912–   . Mathematician.
Dean of Leningrad University in the 1960s. Founder of the Soviet school of geometry. Carried out research into the intrinsic geometry of general surfaces.

Aleksandrov, Aleksandr Petrovich
17.12.1906–   . Politician, engineer.
Born in the village Khotilitsy near Pskov. Educated at the Central Asian Road-Building Institute in Tashkent, 1933. Worked on the constructrion of the Volga-Don Canal (built by slave labour), 1948. Chief Soviet expert at the building of the Aswan Dam on the Nile, 1962–66. Deputy Minister of Energetics and Electrification of the USSR, 1966.

Aleksandrov, Aleksandr Vasil'evich
13.4.1883–8.7.1946. Composer, conductor.
Born in the village of Plakhino, Riazan' Gouvt. Studied music at the Imperial Chapel in St. Petersburg, and at the Conservatory (under Liadov and Glazunov). Founded a musical school in Tver' (now Kalinin), 1913–16. From 1918 taught choral singing at the Moscow Conservatory. Founded the Red Army Ensemble of Song and Dance, 1928. Wrote the music for the Soviet anthem. Died in Berlin.

Aleksandrov, Anatolii Nikolaevich
25.5.1888–16.4.1982. Composer.
Born in Moscow. Received early musical training from his mother. First compositions at the age of eight. Studied musical theory at Moscow University under N. Zhiliaev and S. Taneev, 1907–10. Graduated from the Moscow Conservatory 1916. Gold medallist. Appeared in concerts playing his own works till 1974. Worked with Narkompros, 1918–20. Conductor and editor with a broadcasting station, 1922–23. Taught from 1923. Professor at the Moscow Conservatory, 1926–56. Among his many pupils was N. Budashkin. For several years headed the children's section of the Union of Composers of the USSR. Produced a wide range of piano and vocal compositions. Died in Moscow.

Aleksandrov, Anatolii Petrovich
13.2.1903–   . Nuclear scientist.
Born in Taraschi near Kiev. Graduated from Kiev University, 1930. From 1946 one of the leading nuclear scientists in the Soviet Union, working on many military and civilian projects. Head of the Kurchatov Institute of Nuclear Energy, 1960. Member of the Communist Party, 1962. Member of the Cen. Cttee of the CPSU, 1966. Highly decorated, 5 times laureate of the State Prize (Lenin Prize).

Aleksandrov, Boris Aleksandrovich
4.8.1905–   . Composer, conductor.
Born in Bologoe. Son of the composer A. Aleksandrov, founder of the Red Army Choir and Dance Ensemble. After the death of his father, 1946, became the head of the Ensemble, conducting it on the same lines. Colonel. Wrote several operettas.

Aleksandrov, Boris Viktorovich
13.11.1955–   . Athlete.
Born in Ust'-Kamenogorsk. Master of Sports (ice hockey), 1976. From 1979 with the Spartak team. Graduated from the Ust'-Kamenogorskii Pedagogical Institute, 1978. USSR champion, 1975, 1977–78. Olympic champion, 1976.

Aleksandrov, Georgii Fedorovich
4.4.1908–21.7.1961. Philosopher.
Born in Petersburg. Graduated from
the Institute of Red Professors. Head
of the Department of Agitation and
Propaganda of the Cen. Cttee of the
CPSU, 1940–47. Director of the
Institute of Philosophy of the USSR
Academy of Sciences, 1947–54. Attacked by Zhdanov for his history of
Western philosophy (for acknowledging Marx as a *Western* philosopher), 1947, but soon recovered his
reputation. Minister of Culture of the
USSR, 1954–55. Member of the
Institute of Philosophy in Minsk,
1955–61. Died in Moscow.
Main works: *Istoriia Zapadno-Evrop-
eiskoi Filosofii* (1946), *Istoriia Sot-
siologii, Kak Nauki* (1958).

**Aleksandrov, Grigorii Vasil'evich (real
name – Mormonenko)**
23.1.1903–16.12.1983. Film director.
Started as an assistant costume and
stage designer in the Ekaterinburg
Opera Theatre. After the October
Revolution 1917 held various jobs in
several governmental art departments. Studied at the same time on
directors' courses. From 1921 actor
at the Proletkult Workers Theatre.
Met Sergei Eisenstein, and acted in
his plays. Assisted him in the making
of *Stachka*, 1924, *Bronenosets Potemkin*, 1924, *Oktiabr*, 1927, and
Staroe i Novoe, 1929. From 1929–32
with Eisenstein, and the cameraman
E. Tisse, toured the USA, Mexico
and Europe. In 1934 made his own
film, *Veselye Rebiata* (with his wife,
L. Orlova, in the lead), shown with
great success at the Venice Film
Festival. Worked with Eisenstein on
his unfinished film, *Da Zdravstvuet
Meksika!* His own films, *Veselye
Rebiata* (with L.Utesov), *Tsirk,* and
Volga-Volga, enjoyed a huge success
due to L. Orlova's remarkable talent
as a comedienne. His films in the late
1930–40s, especially *Vstrecha Na
Elbe*, 1949 (Stalin Prize, 1950), were
basically propaganda works. In 1983,
with E. Mikhailova, filmed the
documentary, *Liubov' Orlova.* From
1950–57 taught at the VGIK. Died in
Moscow.

Aleksandrov, Ivan Gavrilovich
1857–1936. Politician, engineer,
economist.
Born in Moscow. Graduated from
the Higher Technical School (now

Bauman Higher Technical School),
Moscow, also from the School of
Railway Engineering. Worked as an
eingeer and consultant. One of the
chief engineers with the GOELRO
Electrification Plan. One of the heads
of GOSPLAN, 1921–24. Chief engineer with the Dneproges Power
Station, 1921–27, and the Central
Asia Electrification Plan, 1928. In
charge of various irrigation and
economic projects during the 1930s,
using Gulag prisoners as a source of
cheap labour. Member of the Academy of Sciences, 1932. Head of the
Transport Department, Head of the
cttee. in charge of the Central Asian
university project in Tashkent. One
of the main representatives of the old
technocratic intelligentsia. Attacked
for his reactionary views.

Aleksandrov, Pavel Sergeevich
7.5.1896–after 1970. Mathematician.
Graduated from Moscow University,
1917. Member of the Moscow Mathematical Society, 1921. Professor of
Moscow University, 1929. President
of the Moscow Mathematical Society, 1932. Member of many international scientific bodies. Academician, 1953. Founder of the Soviet
school of topology, and originator of
the theory of Bi-compact spaces.
World authority on basic laws of
duality.

**Aleksandrov, Veniamin
Veniaminovich**
18.4.1937–   . Athlete.
Born in Moscow. Master of Sports
(ice hockey), 1963. Graduated from
the RSFSR Central School of
Coaches, 1971. Olympic champion,
1964, 1968. Bronze medal, Olympic
Games, 1960. World champion,
1963–68. European champion, 1958–
60, 1963–68. Champion of the USSR,
1956, 1958–61, 1963–66, 1968.

Aleksandrovich, Mikhail Davydovich
1914–   . Singer.
Born in a Latvian village. Made his
singing debut in Riga, 1923. Sang as a
cantor in synagogues in Manchester
and Kaunas. After the Soviet annexation of Lithuania in 1940 his fame
spread to the Soviet Union. Made
many records but was not allowed to
perform in the West. Emigrated to
the USA, 1971. Wrote *Ia Pomniu,*
Munich, 1985 (Memoirs).

Alekseev, Aleksandr Emel'ianovich
27.11.1891–after 1969. Designer of
electric machinery.
Worked at an electric plant in
Petersburg, 1908–19. Graduated
from the Leningrad Electrotechnical
Institute, 1925. Professor at the
Leningrad Institute of Railroad Engineers, 1936. Joined the Institute of
Electromechanics of the Academy of
Sciences, 1953. Supervised the design
of the first Soviet electric traction
machines.

Alekseev, Gleb Vasil'evich
1892–1938. Author, journalist.
In 1909 worked with the newspaper
Kopeika (which became *Izvestia* after
the 1917 Revolution). In the 1910s
worked for one of the largest
newspapers, *Russkoe Slovo.* Front
correspondent during WWI, twice
wounded. After the 1917 Revolution,
emigrated, travelled in the Balkans,
served as a sailor on a British ship,
settled on a Dalmatian island. Moved
to Berlin. 1922. Wrote novels and
became known as a writer. Suddenly
returned to the Soviet Union, Nov.
1923. Allowed to publish new works
in the Soviet Union in the late 1920s
and early 1930s. Close to the
influential Cheka official, Agranov.
Arrested during the Stalin purges,
perished in the Gulag, circumstances
of death unknown.

Alekseev, Mikhail Nikolaevich
1918–   . Author, editor, journalist.
Born in Monastyrskoe, Saratov
Oblast'. Son of a peasant. Graduated
from the High Literary Courses of
the Writers' Union, 1957. Member of
the CPSU, 1942. His first novel,
Soldaty, 1951–53, was marked by its
humanity and frankness. Editor-in-
chief of the literary journal *Moskva*
from 1968. At a meeting between M.
Gorbachev and top editors and
artists in 1987, he complained loudly
about the Soviet media's treatment of
Soviet history. Considered one of the
most hopeful editors to emerge out of
Gorbachev's glasnost.

Alekseev, Mikhail Pavlovich
5.6.1896–1960? Musicologist.
Born in Kiev. Professor at Leningrad
University. Academician, 1958.
Author of works on Russian musical

culture of the 18th and first half of the 19th centuries. Compiled a bibliography of Russian writings on Beethoven and Schubert.

Alekseev, Mikhail Vasil'evich
15.11.1857–25.9.1918. General.
Born in Viaz'ma. Son of an officer. Educated at Moscow Military School, 1876. Took part in Russo-Turkish war, 1877. Professor of the Academy of the General Staff, 1898. Took part in Russo-Japanese war, 1904–05, Major-general. During WWI a very efficient Chief-of-staff of the Russian armies (under the Tsar as supreme commander), Aug. 1915. In Feb. 1917 circulated a report from the chairman of the Duma, Rodzianko, on the revolutionary situation in Petrograd to the army commanders. The measure was intended as an information exercise, but was taken by Nicholas II as a sort of opinion poll of the army leadership and led directly to the abdication of the monarch. Appointed Supreme Commander, Feb. 1917 but dismissed by Kerenskii after criticizing anarchy, March 1917. Moved to the Don area and became the first organizer of the White armies Alekseev Organization, Dobrovolcheskaia Armiia. Handed over command to Kornilov, Jan. 1918. Died of pneumonia in Ekaterinodar.

Alekseev, N. N.
1879–1964. Politician, lawyer.
Professor of law at Moscow University before WWI. Professor of Tavricheskii University and the Law Institute at Sebastopol during the Civil War, 1919. Evacuated with the White Army to Constantinople, where he tried to organize a Russian university for refugees. Moved to Prague, lectured at the Russian Law Institute, founded by P. Novgorodtsev. Moved to Berlin, 1922. Became a prominent member of the Eurasian movement in the mid-1920s.

Alekseev, Nikolai Nikolaevich
1914–1980. Marshal.
Joined the Soviet Army, 1953. Graduated from the Military Electrotechnical Academy, 1940. Took part in the Soviet Finnish war, 1939–40. During WWII in the Air Defence staff, 1942; later head of the

supply system of the Western and Northern Air Defences. Chairman of the Scientific-Technical Commission of the General Staff, 1960. Deputy Defence Minister, 1970.

Alekseev, Rostislav Evgen'evich
1916– . Ship-builder.
Graduated from the Polytechnical Institute in Gorkii, 1941. Started work as an engineer, and rose to become Chief Designer in the KB (Design Bureau) of the Zhdanov Krasnoe Sormovo Works which was one of the main suppliers of T-34 tanks during WWII. Designer of fast military boats. Member of the CPSU, 1950. Stalin Prize, 1951. Lenin Prize, 1962. Attached to the Ministry of Defence as a consultant.

Alekseeva, Galina Sergeevna (Kreft)
14.3.1950– . Athlete.
Born in Leningrad. Master of Sports, 1976. Studied at the Leningrad Institute of Physical Culture. Olympic champion with N. Gopova (canoe), 1976.

Alekseeva, Liudmila Mikhailovna
1927– . Dissident.
Born in Evpatoria in the Crimea. Graduated in history from Moscow University. Editor at the Nauka Publishing House, Moscow. Became involved in dissident activity in the early 1960s. Member of the Moscow Helsinki Group, 1976. Lost her job after that and was harassed by the KGB. Emigrated to the USA, 1977. Works: *Soviet Dissent,* 1985, USA.

Alekseevskii, Nikolai Evgen'evich
1912– . Physicist.
Graduated from the Leningrad Polytechnical Institute, 1936. During WWII X-ray technician at military hospitals. Subsequently in the physics faculty of Moscow University, 1947–60. Carried out research into low temperature physics.

Aleksei (Romanov, Aleksei Nikolaevich), Tsarevich
1904–17.7.1918. The last heir to the Russian throne.
Suffered from haemophilia (a disease inherited from his ancestor, Queen Victoria, through his mother, Aleksandra). In Feb. 1917 Nicholas II abdicated, not only by himself, but

also on his son's behalf, in order not to be separated from him. Aleksei remained with his parents and sisters first under house arrest in Tsarskoe Selo, and later in exile in the Urals. Shot, in the arms of his father, in the Ipat'ev house in Ekaterinburg (Sverdlovsk).

Aleksii (Ridiger, Aleksei Mikhailovich, Ruediger), Metropolitan of Leningrad and Novgorod
23.2.1929– . Russian Orthodox clergyman.
Born in Tallinn. Educated at Leningrad Seminary, 1949. Graduated from the Leningrad Theological Academy, 1953. Priest in Tartu, 1957. Archpriest, 1958. Monk, 1961. Archbishop, 1964. Chairman of the Commission for Christian Unity and Inter-Church Relations, 1963–79. Metropolitan, 1968. Member of the Cen. Cttee. of the World Council of Churches, 1961–68. Metropolitan of Leningrad and Novgorod, July 1986.

Aleksii (Simanskii, Sergei Vladimirovich), Patriarch of Moscow
27.10.1877–1970. Russian Orthodox clergyman.
Born in Moscow. Educated at the Moscow Nicholas Lycée. Graduated from Moscow University in law, 1899. Served in Samogitskii Grenadier Regiment, 1899–1900. Studied at Moscow Theological Academy, 1900–04. Monk, 1902. Rector of Tula seminary, Archimandrite, 1906. Rector of Novgorod seminary, 1911. Bishop of Tikhvin, 1913. In charge of the Petrograd Diocese (after the execution of Metropolitan Veniamin), 1922. In charge of the Novgorod diocese, 1926. Metropolitan of Novgorod and Staraia Russa, 1932. Metropolitan of Leningrad, 1933. Stayed in Leningrad during the siege in WWII. With Sergii (Stragorodskii) and Nikolai (Iarushevich) took part in a meeting with Stalin, at which the re-establishment of the Patriarchate was allowed in return for assurance of a subservient position of the church towards the state authorities, 1943. Patriarch of Moscow, Feb. 1945–Apr. 1970. During his long reign kept to the line established during WWII: subservience and passivity in the USSR and active support

of Soviet government initiatives on the international scene. During Stalin's time this was rewarded by comparative leniency in the post-war period, which gave way to a renewed vicious persecution campaign under Khrushchev, somewhat moderated after the latter's fall. During his reign the Russian Orthodox Church became a member of the World Council of Churches, 18 July 1961. Died in Moscow.

Aleksinskii, Grigorii Alekseevich
1879–1968? Politician.
Involved in revolutionary activity as a teenager. Prominent member of the SD Party, close to the Bolsheviks during the 1905 Revolution. Member of the 2nd Duma (SD faction). Moved to right wing socialism (in the group Vpered). Opponent of Lenin during WWI. Member of the Menshevik group Edinstvo within the SD Party, 1917. In July 1917 publicly accused Lenin of accepting financial subsidy from the German government. After the Bolshevik take-over emigrated, 1918. As a political emigré published anti-Bolshevik articles in Burtsev's newspaper *Obshchee Delo* and other publications.

Aleshin, Ivan Ivanovich
1901–1944. Political commissar, partisan commander.
Joined the Bolshevik Party, 1920. Political commissar in the Red Army, 1922–33. During WWII Secretary of the Cen. Cttee. of the Moldavian Communist Party. Commander of Soviet partisans in Moldavia. Killed in action.

Aleshkovskii, Iuz Efimovich
1929– . Author.
Widely known in the 1960s in samizdat for his poem, *Tovarishch Stalin, Vy Bolshoi Uchenyi* (Comrade Stalin, You are a Great Scientist), also for his short stories *Nikolai Nikolaevich* and *Maskirovka* (published later in the USA, 1980). Became famous in America, to where he emigrated in the early 1970s, for his stories *Ruka* (Hand, 1981) and *Kenguru*, 1981. Contributor to the Moscow almanac *Metropol* together with V. Aksenov, A. Bitov and others. Lives in Connecticut.
Source: P. Vail, A. Genis, *Sovremennaia Russkaia Proza*, USA, 1982.

Alferov, Zhores Ivanovich
1930– . Physicist, academician.
Graduated from the Leningrad Electro-technical Institute, 1952. Member of the CPSU from 1965. Doctoral degree in physical-mathematical sciences, 1971. Professor, 1972. Corresponding member of the USSR Academy of Sciences, 1972. Began his career in 1953 as an engineer, then senior research assistant, 1964–67, and finally Section Chief of the Physico-Technical Institute of the USSR Academy of Sciences, 1967. In the 1980s appointed leader of a group of researchers at the Ioffe Physics Institute in Leningrad, responsible for space and agricultural projects. Also in charge of a project which possibly could soon meet the present electricity demands of the Soviet Union.

Aliakrinskii, Petr Aleksandrovich
1892–1961. Artist.
Graphic artist, lithographer, illustrator, poster artist. Studied at the Moscow School of Painting, Sculpture and Architecture, 1909–10, under S. Ivanov and A. Vasnetsov. Graduated from A.L. Shaniavskii City University, Moscow, 1911–15. Exhibitions: the All-Union Polygraphic, Moscow, 1927; Soviet Illustration for Five Years, Moscow, 1936; the All-Union, 1945, 1947, 1949–50, 1957; the Soviet Russia Exhibition, Moscow, 1960.

Alianskii, Samuil Mironovich
1891–1971? Publisher.
Founder and owner of the publishing house, Alkonost, which during the NEP period continued the traditions of the Russian pre-revolutionary Symbolist publishing houses. Published A. Blok, among others, and also wrote about him in his memoirs. Emigrated after 1917 Revolution.

Aliev, Geldar Ali Rza ogly
10.5.1923– . Politician, state security official.
Azerbaidzhanian. At the age of 18 entered the security service (NKVD) in Azerbaidzhan. In 1945 joined the CP. In 1957 graduated from Azerbaidzhan State University. Various senior positions in the local security service (KGB). Deputy Chairman, 1964–67, Chairman, 1967–69, Major-general, candidate member of the

Cen. Cttee. of the Azerbaidzhan CP, 1966–71. 1st Secretary and member of the Bureau of the Cen. Cttee. of the Azerbaidzhan CP, 1969–82. Member of the Cen. Cttee. of the CPSU from 1971. Candidate member of the Politburo, 1976–82. Full member from 1982. 1st Deputy Chairman of the USSR Council of Ministers from Dec. 1982. One of two non-Slavs in the Politburo. Taken ill on 11 May 1987 while at work. Believed to have suffered a major heart attack. Closely identified with the Brezhnev era, opponent of Gorbachev's line. Excluded from the Politburo, 21 Aug. 1987.

Alikhan'ian, Artemii Isaakovich
24.7.1908– . Physicist.
Brother of Abram Alikhanov. Graduated from Leningrad University, 1931. Participated with his brother in nuclear physics and cosmic ray research. Instrumental in establishing a cosmic ray station on Mount Aragats, 1945. Director of the Institute of Physics of the Armenian Academy of Sciences, 1961.

Alikhanov, Abram Isaakovich
4.3.1904– . Nuclear physicist.
Graduated from the Leningrad Polytechnical Institute, 1931. Worked at the Physico-Technical Institute, 1927, Director of the Power Engineering Laboratories of the Institute. Research into X-rays, cosmic rays and nuclear research. Built the first heavy water reactor in the Soviet Union, 1949. Director of the Institute of Theoretical and Experimental Physics.

Alimarin, Ivan Pavlovich
11.9.1903– . Chemist.
Worked at the Institute of Mineral Raw Materials, 1923, and the Institute of Geochemistry, 1949. Professor at Moscow University, 1953. Works on analytical chemistry of rare elements, microchemistry and radiochemical analysis.

Alksnis, Iakov Ivanovich (Astrov)
26.1.1897–29.7.1938. Commissar, air force commander.
Born in Latvia. Son of a peasant. Educated at Odessa military school, 1917. Bolshevik propagandist at the front during WWI. Joined the Red Army, 1919. Fought during the Civil War in the Red Latvian detachments

(elite fighting and terror forces of the Red Army). Graduated from the Frunze Military Academy, 1924. Organizer of the Soviet Air Force, 1926–31. Commander of the Soviet Air Force, 1931. Arrested, 1937. Shot on Stalin's orders.

Alliluev, Sergei Iakovlevich
7.10.1866–2.7.1945. Revolutionary.
Born in the village of Ramoni, now Voronezh Oblast'. The son of a peasant, became a factory worker. Bolshevik-propagandist, who was active in Russian provincial towns and in the Caucasus (1908) where he met Stalin, his future son-in-law. During 1907–18 lived and worked in Petersburg, where his flat was constantly used for secret party meetings. After the defeat of the attempted Bolshevik uprising in July 1917, sheltered Lenin. An active participant in the October Revolution. Fought as a Red Army officer in the Civil War. Died in Moscow.

Allilueva, Nadezhda Sergeevna (m. Dzhugashvili, Stalin)
1902–9.11.1932. Party worker.
Daughter of the Bolshevik, Sergei Alliluev, and a Georgian mother. Married Iosif Stalin at the age of 17. Worked in Lenin's Secretariat. After the birth of her second child, Vasilii, she entered the Moscow Industrial Academy. In the opinion of all who knew her, she was an intelligent, kind woman who suffered from her husband's cruelty. Her sudden death remains a mystery (suicide?)
Source: Lev Trotsky, *Portrety*, USA, 1984.

Allilueva, Svetlana Iosifovna (Stalin, Singh, Lana Peters)
1926– . Stalin's daughter, author.
Born in Moscow. Daughter of Joseph Stalin and his second (Russian) wife, Nadezhda Sergeevna Allilueva. Defected to the West in March 1967 from India, where she had been allowed to go with the ashes of her second husband, the Indian communist, Bradegh Singh. At the time her defection caused a sensation both in the West and in the Soviet Union. Burned her Soviet passport. Condemned the Soviet authorities in a series of TV and newspaper interviews. Settled in Princeton, New Jersey. Wrote two books – *Twenty Letters to a Friend*, and *Only One Year*. Disclosed her father's private life, and that of his entourage in the Kremlin. Fell in love with Louis Fischer, a writer on Soviet affairs, a known womaniser and 30 years her senior (died in 1970). After the break-up with Fischer, went through a period of depression and loneliness. In 1970 married the US architect William Wesley Peters and gave birth to a daughter, Olga, a year later. The marriage broke up in 1972. Moved to Cambridge, England in 1982 in order to send Olga to a local Quaker boarding school. Felt very lonely and disillusioned with the West. In Aug. 1984 returned to the Soviet Union, causing a second sensation. Took with her Olga, who spoke no Russian. Was welcomed with enthusiasm by the Soviet authorities. Her Soviet citizenship was restored instantly. Soon discovered that her son's letters to her were sent under KGB instructions. Was made to live in the small Georgian town of Gori, her father's birthplace, and not in Moscow where she had been born. Clashed with the Soviet authorities once more. Probably after Gorbachev's personal intervention, was allowed to go back to America in Nov. 1986. Settled in Wisconsin, USA, Nov. 1987.

Alloi, Vladimir Efimovich
1946– . Editor, journalist.
Born in Leningrad. Graduated in philology from Leningrad University. Emigrated, 1975, settled in France. Actively involved in Russian language publishing in Paris. Director of the YMCA-Press, 1976–81, La Presse Libre, 1982–84, and Atheneum publishing house, 1986. Publisher of the historical almanac *Minuvshee*.

Al'metov, Aleksandr Davletovich
18.1.1940– . Athlete.
Born in Kiev. Master of Sports (ice hockey), 1963. Olympic champion, 1964. Bronze medal at the Olympic Games, 1960. World champion, 1963–67. European champion, 1960–67. USSR champion, 1959–66.

Alpatov, Mikhail Vladimirovich
27.11.1902– . Art scholar.
Born in Moscow. Graduated from Moscow University, 1921. Taught at many famous art schools in the 1920s (VKHUTEMAS, VKHUTEIN). Taught philosophy of art at Moscow University. Professor of the Surikov Art School in Moscow. Wrote many monographs, on icons, the Italian Renaissance, Aleksander Ivanov, and a 3-volume-history of world art.

Alpert, Maks Vladimirovich
1899–1980. Photographer.
Born in Simferopol. The son of an artisan. In 1914 moved to Odessa where he was apprenticed to a photographer. In 1919 joined the Red Army as a volunteer. In 1924 came to Moscow and worked as a photographer on *Rabochaia Gazeta*. Specialized exclusively in current news reporting. Took pictures of prominent communists and public figures such as Clara Zetkin, the military commander M. Frunze, Maksim Gorkii and others. 1928, picture editor of *Pravda*. Became a prominent photo journalist. From 1931 worked for the *USSR in Construction* magazine. His most important photographs were of industrial scenes and of the Fergana Canal in particular. Considered an expert photographer and influenced many young photographers in the USSR. During WWII, war correspondent for TASS, the Soviet Information Office and the Novosti Press Agency.
See: *Soviet Photography, 1917–40*, London, 1984.

Altfater, Vasilii Mikhailovich (Altvater)
1883–1919. Admiral.
Graduated from the Naval Academy, 1908. Took part in WWI, vice-admiral, 1917. Joined the Red Navy, 1918, commander of the naval forces of the republic, Oct. 1918–1919. Killed in action.

Amal'rik, Andrei Alekseevich
1938–1980. Author, dissident.
Born in Moscow. Expelled from Moscow University, 1963. His plays and essays circulated in samizdat, 1953–65. In 1965 arrested for parasitism. Sentenced to 2½ years exile in Siberia. In 1970 re-arrested for his book, *Prosushchestvuet li Sovetskii Soiuz do 1984 Goda?* published in the West in 1969. Sentenced to 3 years in the camps, then another 3 years. Released in 1976 as a result of international protests. Left the USSR.

Lived in Paris. Killed in a car crash going to the Madrid International Conference on Human Rights.
See: *Zapiski Dissidenta,* USA, 1982.

Amarantov, Boris
1947–1987. Mime artist.
Famous solo performer in theatres and concert halls in the 1960–70s. Tried unsuccessfully to emigrate to America in the late 1970s. Became the focus of an international campaign. Western celebrities sent letters to the Soviet government in his support. Eventually allowed to go to New York where he made a very successful debut in Carnegie Hall. Performed in various cities throughout America but soon was forgotten and unable to get a job. After several years of struggling, in complete despair, began asking the Soviet Embassy for permission to return to the USSR. By this time he had developed a psychiatric disorder. After some deliberate bureaucratic delays was put in with a group of re-emigrants. Arrived in Moscow but soon discovered that he was not allowed to work. Became seriously ill. Early in 1987 it was reported from Moscow that he had committed suicide.

Amashukeli, Goudji
1941–   . Silversmith, sculptor.
Born and studied art in Georgia. Emigrated, 1974. Settled in Paris where he works at his studio in Montmartre. Major exhibition in January 1988 at the ASB Gallery in London. *Art Review*'s editor-in-chief likened him to Fabergé with less commercial tendencies. His work is based on Georgian and Russian traditions.

Ambartsumian, Viktor Amazaspovich
18.9.1908–   . Astrophysicist.
Born in Tiflis. Educated at Leningrad University and taught there until 1944. Thereafter professor at Erevan University. Founder and director of Biurakan Observatory, 1946. Member of the USSR Academy of Sciences and member and president of the Armenian Academy of Sciences. Vice-president of the International Astronomical Union, 1948–55. President of the International Astronomical Union, 1961–64.

Member of many international scientific bodies, widely known as an outstanding modern specialist in astronomy and astrophysics. Published important research work on stellar and galactic cosmogony.

Amfiteatrov, Aleksandr Valentinovich
1862–1938. Author.
Born in Kaluga. Graduated from Moscow University in law, 1885. Exiled to Minusinsk for his political pamphlet on the Romanovs (*Gospoda Obmanovy*), 1902. Became a well known writer before WWI. Emigrated, 1920. Settled in Italy. Died in Levanto.

Amiranashvili, Petr (Petre) Varlamovich
16.11.1911–   . Singer (baritone).
Born in the village of Nigoiti, in the Kutaisi Gouvt. Pupil of O.A. Bakhutashvili-Shul'gina. Soloist with the Tbilisi Theatre of Opera and Ballet from 1931. His daughter Medea, born 1931, is a singer (lyrical soprano), and soloist with the same theatre.

Amiraslanov, Ali Agamaly ogly
12.1900–16.10.1962. Geologist.
Graduated from the Moscow Mining Academy, 1900. Worked at the Geological Gold Survey Institute. Chief geologist of the USSR Geological Survey Directorate at the Ministry of Non-Ferrous Metals. Taught at the Moscow Geological Survey Institute, 1931–55. Specialized in non-ferrous and rare metal deposits.

Amosova, Zinaida Stepanovna
12.1.1950–   . Athlete.
Born in the village of Krupskoe, Kazakhstan. Graduated from the Novosibirsk High School of Physical Culture, 1970. Taught skiing at Sverdlovsk Trud. Olympic champion (sprinting), 1976.

Anastasii (Gribanovskii), Metropolitan, Russian Church in Exile
1873–1964. Russian Orthodox clergyman.
Son of a priest. Graduated from the Moscow Theological Academy, 1897. Monk, 1898. Bishop, 1906. During the Civil War emigrated in 1919. Presiding Bishop of the Russian Church in Exile (which broke away from the Moscow Patriarchate after

the death of Patriarch Tikhon), 1936–1964. Consistently taking an anti-communist line, was involved in the attempts to create an anti-Stalin movement in Germany (KONR) during WWII, and after the war, in the resettlement of Russian refugees from Europe overseas, mainly to the USA, where he moved the administration of his church. Died and buried at St. Trinity Monastery, Jordanville, USA.
Selected works, USA, 1948.

Anatolii (Gisiuk, Andrei Grigor'evich), Metropolitan of Odessa and Kherson
20.8.1880–10.1.1938. Russian Orthodox clergyman.
Born in Volhynia (Ukraine). Graduated from the Kiev Theological Academy, 1904. Bishop of Samara, 1922. Archbishop, 1923. Arrested and sent to the Solovki concentration camp with a group of church leaders, 1924–27. Bishop of Odessa, 1928. Metropolitan, 1932. Rearrested in 1936. A well known preacher and religious author. Died in Odessa.

Anders, Wladyslaw
1892–12.5.1970. General.
Born in Poland. Educated at Warsaw High School. Studied at Riga Technical Institute. Son of the manager of the Prince Vasil'chikov estates in the Baltic. Officer in the Russian Army Cavalry during WWI. Joined the Polish corps of Dowbor-Musnicki with the Russian Army, 1917, fought the Red Army with this corps (Bobruisk). After Polish independence joined the Polish Army. Cavalry regimental commander during the Soviet-Polish War. Head of the Polish Olympic horse-riding team (first prize at the international event at Nice, 1925). General, 1934. Cavalry commander in Wolhynia, involved also in cultural work. In 1939 fought both the German and Soviet invading forces. Wounded, taken prisoner by the Red Army near Lvov. Imprisoned at the Lubianka. This saved him from the fate of about 15,000 other POW Polish officers, murdered by the NKVD at Katyn' and other places. After the German invasion of the Soviet Union given the task of creating a Polish army out of Polish POWs in the USSR. Insisted on transferring his force to the Western front, instead of fighting together with the Red Army. Left with his

soldiers through Iran. Took part in military operations in the Middle East and North Africa. The main achievement of his forces was the storming of Monte Cassino in Italy, 1944. After WWII, together with most of his soldiers, remained as a political refugee in the West. Considered the figurehead of Polish emigrés. Lived and died in London. Buried at the Polish military cemetery at Monte Cassino. Wrote memoirs and a clear, concise description of WWII on the Eastern front (*Hitler's Defeat*).

Andolenko, Sergei Pavlovich
26.6.1907–27.8.1973. General, military historian.
Born at Volochisk in the Ukraine. Emigrated with his parents during the Civil War. Educated in France. Graduated from the St. Cyr Military Academy. Joined the Foreign Legion, served in Africa and Syria. During WWII fought under de Gaulle. Many awards for bravery, including Commander of the Legion d'Honneur. With the French occupation forces in Germany, 1949–52. On the staff of the Paris military district, 1952–55. Commander of a regiment of the Foreign Legion during the Algerian war, 1956–58. Deputy Inspector of the Foreign Legion, 1959–60. French military attaché in Vienna, 1961–63. Wrote (in French) many books on military history, including his *History of the Russian Army*, 1967. Organized a unique department of the Imperial Russian Army at the French Military Museum in Paris (Hotel des Invalides). Active member of the Society of Russian Military History in France. In the 1960s published (in Russian) an anthology of military poetry (*Stokrat Svyashchen Soiuz Mecha i Liry*).

Andreas-Salome, Lou (Louise)
1861–1937. Author.
Born at Petersburg. Daughter of a Russian general of Huguenot descent. Educated at a protestant school at Petersburg. Lived mostly in Germany, became a well-known member of the intellectual elite before WWI. In her youth was the great love of Nietzsche, keeping the prophet of the *Uebermensch* practically in bondage. Married Professor Andreas in a wholly platonic relationship. In middle age became the mentor and

lover of R.M. Rilke, when he was a very young and completely unknown student in Munich, and visited Russia (and L. Tostoy) with him twice before WWI. In later years became a pupil and inspiration of Sigmund Freud, helped him in his research work and wrote on psychoanalysis. Memoirs of her life in Russia, *Rodinka*, published in Germany. Posthumously inspired a number of biographies in different countries. Died in Germany.

Andreenko, Mikhail Fedorovich
10.1.1895–1969? Artist.
Born in Kherson. Studied art under Roerich, Bilibin, and Rylov at the School of the Society for the Encouragement of Arts in St. Petersburg. Worked as a stage designer from 1915. Most of his theatre work was done after 1917. For a time lived in Bucharest, then Prague. From 1924 lived in Paris. Later turned to abstract painting.

Andreev, Andrei Andreevich
30.10.1895–late 1970s? Politician.
Born in the village of Kuznetsovo near Smolensk. During WWI worker at an ammunition works in Petrograd. Bolshevik activist, one of the organizers of the Metal Workers' Trade Union. Took part in the October Revolution 1917. Secretary of the VTSSPS (Soviet Trade Union Council), 1920–22. Secretary of the Cen. Cttee of the Bolshevik Party, 1924–25. Head of the Railway Workers' Trade Union, 1922–27. Minister of Transport of the USSR, 1931–35. Veteran Stalinist member of the Politburo, 1932–52. Chairman of the Supreme Soviet, 1938–45. Minister of Agriculture, 1943–46. Adviser to the Presidium of the Supreme Soviet from July 1962. Not mentioned in official political publications after Apr. 1970.

Andreev, Boris Fedorovich
9.2.1915–   . Actor.
Born in Saratov. Graduated from the Saratov Drama School in 1936. Worked in the Film Actor's Studio Theatre, and with Ivan Pyr'ev, Mikhail Kalatozov, Igor Savchenko. Mark Donskoi, Boris Barnet and many other distinguished directors. His first film was a popular comedy *The Tractor Drivers* (director Ivan

Pyr'ev) produced by Mosfilm in 1939. Became famous for his acting in this film although it is now regarded as a classic example of Stalinist cinema. Made over 50 films. Best in comedies.

Andreev, Daniil Leonidovich
1906–1959. Poet, philosopher.
Born in Moscow. Son of the writer L. Andreev. Arrested and sentenced to 25 years, 1948. After Stalin's death, released and rehabilitated, 1955. His poems have been published in the Soviet Union and abroad but his major philosophical work *Roza mira* is still unpublished.

Andreev, Leonid Nikolaevich
21.8.1871–12.9.1919. Author.
Born in Orel. Graduated from Moscow University in law in 1897. Became a well known writer in the 1900s. His pessimistic, irrational and expressionist style made him very influential in the period between the revolutions, 1905–17. Appalled by the violence of the October Revolution, moved to Finland. Remained till his death a resolute opponent of communist dictatorship. Died in Neivala near Mustamiaki, Finland.
Main works: *Bergamot i Garaska, The Red Laughter, Story of the Seven Hanged, Life of a Man, Days of our Life, The One who gets Slapped.*

Andreev, Nikolai Efremovich
1908–1982. Literary scholar, historian.
Left Russia with his parents after the Bolshevik take-over. Lived and studied in Prague. Moved to Great Britain. For many decades one of the most influential Slavists in Cambridge, educating several generations of British scholars, specializing in Russian history and literature.

Andreev, Nikolai Nikolaevich
1880–1970. Scientist.
Graduated from Basel University, 1909. Member of the Academy of Sciences of the USSR, 1953. One of the founders of the Hydroacoustics Institute of the Academy. World authority on hydroacoustics and piezo-electricity.

Andreev, Pavel Zakharovich
9.3.1874–15.9.1950. Singer (bass-baritone).
Born in the village of Os'mino, in the Petersburg Gouvt. Pupil of S.Gabel. Soloist with the Mariinskii Theatre in Petersburg from 1900. Professor at the Leningrad Conservatory. Died in Leningrad.

Andreev, Vadim Leonidovich (Osokin, Sergei)
1903–1976. Author, poet.
Son of the writer Leonid Andreev. Lived in France between WWI and WWII. After 1945 contributed to the pro-Soviet Parisian newspaper *Sovetskii Patriot.* Returned to the Soviet Union. Later worked with the UN in Geneva.

Andreev, Vasilii Vasil'evich
26.1.1861–26.12.1918. Musician.
Born near Bezhetsk, Tula Gouvt. Balalaika virtuoso and the greatest authority on this instrument. Founder of the first Orchestra of Russian Folk Instruments in Petersburg in 1886. Many tours in Russia and abroad with his orchestra. Composed music for the balalaika. Died in Petrograd.

Andreeva, Maria Fedorovna (Iurkovskaia, Phenomen, Zheliabuzhskaia)
1868–8.12.1953. Actress.
Born in Petersburg. Began to act 1894. Later a well-known MKHAT actress, 1898–1905. Joined the Bolsheviks, 1904. During the 1905 Revolution, official publisher of the Bolshevik newspaper *Novaia Zhizn'.* Married a high ranking official, Zheliabuzhskii, but later became the common law wife of Maksim Gorkii. Emigrated with him, 1906. Their visit to the USA created a scandal, because they were living together without being married officially. Personal friend of V. Lenin. Returned to Russia, 1913. Resumed acting. After the Bolshevik take-over active in various cultural organizations of the Soviet government. Died in Moscow.

Andreeva, Zoia Anan'evna
1899–1982. Politician.
Village teacher, 1917–25. Joined the Bolshevik Party, 1928. Social Security Minister of the Chuvash ASSR in the 1930s. President of the Chuvash ASSR, 1937–55, Vice-president of the RSFSR, 1958–59.

Andreevskii, Sergei Arkad'evich
1847–1920. Lawyer, literary critic.
One of the best known lawyers in late 19th century Russia. One of the first modern critics of Dostoevskii, Baratynskii and other classics of Russian literature.

Andrianov, Konstantin Aleksandrovich
16.2.1910–   . Sports official.
Born in Moscow. Member of the CPSU, 1931. Graduated from the Higher Party School of the Cen. Cttee, 1950. Deputy Chairman of the Olympic Cttee. from 1975. Senior executive of the Organizational Cttee. of the Olympic Games in 1980 in Moscow.

Andrianov, Kuz'ma Andrianovich
28.12.1904–   . Chemist.
Graduated from Moscow University, 1930. Taught at various Moscow scientific institutes. Highly decorated (three state awards). Works on high molecular compounds, especially silicon-organic polymers.

Andrianov, Nikolai Efimovich
14.11.1952–   . Athlete.
Born in Vladimir. Studied at the Vladimir Pedagogical Institute. Master of Sports (gymnastics), 1972. Olympic champion, 1972, 1976. USSR champion, 1972–74. European champion, 1975. World champion, 1978.

Andronik (Nikolskii, Vladimir), Archbishop of Perm' and Solikamsk
1.8.1870–4.6.1918. Russian Orthodox clergyman.
Son of a deacon. Graduated from the Moscow Theological Academy, 1895. Bishop of Kyoto (Japan), 1906. Moved to Kholm in 1907, in charge of the diocese, when Bishop Eulogy was elected member of the Duma. Archbishop of Perm' and Solikamsk, 1915–18. Killed during the revolution in Perm'.

Andropov, Iurii Vladimirovich
15.6.1914–9.2.1984. Politician, state security official.
Born in the village of Nagutskaia near Stavropol. Son of a railway worker. Worked as a telegraph worker, film projectionist, seaman, 1930–32. Graduated from the Rybinsk Technical School for Water-

way Transport. Education at Petrozavodsk University interrupted during WWII. Komsomol activist at a shipyard. Joined the Communist Party in 1939. Secretary, then 1st Secretary of the Cen. Cttee. of the Karelian Komsomol during WWII. Probably already then connected with the security services since he did not serve at the front but was involved with the control of partisans in Karelia (normally the task of the security organs). 1st Secretary of Petrozavodsk City Cttee., 1944–47. 2nd Secretary of the Cen. Cttee. of the Karelian CP, 1947–51. USSR Ambassador to Hungary, 1953–57, supervised the crushing of the Hungarian uprising in 1956. Thereafter Chief of the Cen. Cttee. Liaison Department for Communist and Workers' Parties of Socialist Countries, 1957–67. From 1962 member of the Foreign Affairs Cttee. of the USSR Supreme Soviet, 1962–67. Member of the Cen. Cttee. from 1961. Secretary of the Cen. Cttee., 1962–67. Chairman of the State Security Cttee. (Head of the KGB), 1967–82. Elected successor to Brezhnev as General Secretary of the Cen. Cttee. in 1982, aged 68. Under his rule the KGB systematically silenced human rights activists including Dr. Andrei Sakharov. The use of psychiatry for political purposes was widely introduced. International terrorism received KGB support. Terrorist acts committed abroad were linked by observers to the KGB (Markov's murder in London, the shooting of Pope John Paul II in Rome, etc). Considered highly intelligent, knew some English and had a taste for art collecting. In Sept. 1977 went on Soviet TV to give his opinion on dissidents, an unprecedented step for a KGB chief. During his rule as General Secretary of the CPSU tried to fight the entrenched Brezhnevites in the Cen. Ctte., and introduced some economic reforms but without much success. Contracted a kidney disease which was kept secret and described as a cold. Never recovered and after a long illness died in Moscow.

Andzhaparidze, Zurab Ivanovich
12.4.1928–   . Singer (tenor).
Born in Kutaisi, Georgia. Pupil of D. Andguladze. Soloist with the Tbilisi Theatre of Opera and Ballet, 1952–59. With the Bolshoi Theatre from 1959.

Angelina, Praskov'ia Nikitichna
12.1.1913–21.1.1959. Tractor driver.
Born in Starobeshevo, Donetsk Oblast. One of the first women to complete a tractor driver course, 1929. Organized a women's tractor driver brigade. Figure head of a Stalinist campaign for the technical education of women. Member of the CPSU, 1937. Signed a proclamation—*Hundred thousand women friends take to the tractor,* 1938. Graduated from Moscow Agricultural Academy, 1940. Wrote a book on kolkhoz activists, 1948. A typical Stalinist propaganda hero of the 1930s. Died in Moscow.

Anichkov, Nikolai Nikolaevich
3.11.1885–7.12.1964. Pathomorphologist.
Graduated from the Military Medical Academy, 1909. Professor at the same Academy, 1920–46. President of the Academy of Medical Sciences, 1946–53. Worked on the pathology of blood vessels, atherosclerosis, lipid exchange and contagious diseases.

Anikeev, Serafim Mikhailovich
6.3.1904–26.8.1962. Actor.
Born in Voronezh. Appeared in plays, variety shows and operettas from 1923. With the Moscow Operetta Theatre from 1930. Died in Moscow.

Anikin, Nikolai Petrovich
25.1.1932–   . Athlete, coach.
Born in Ishim, Tiumen' Oblast', Siberia. Master of Sports (skiing), 1956. USSR honorary coach, 1976. Olympic champion (long distance relay-race, 4×10km), 1956. USSR champion (relay-race, 4 × 10km), 1957.

Anikst, Aleksandr Abramovich
16.7.1910–   . Literary scholar.
Born in Zurich. Literary scholar and art historian. The foremost authority on English and American literature in the Soviet Union. His main interests are Shakespeare and Shaw. Also wrote many articles on the modern theatre and cinema.

Anisfeld, Boris (Ber) Izrailevich
14.10.1879–1973. Stage designer.
Born in Beltsy, Bessarabia. Studied at the Odessa Art School, and at the Petersburg Academy of Arts, 1900–09. A pupil of Il'ia Repin. Took part in exhibitions of the *Mir Iskusstva* and the Union of Russian Artists. Stage designer with Mikhail Fokin's productions. Worked closely with A. Benois, A. Golovin and Leon Bakst for the Ballets Russes. Worked for Anna Pavlova. From 1918 lived in the USA. Stage designer and teacher of stage design in Chicago and New York. Died in New York.

Anisimov, Nikolai Petrovich
1899–1977. General.
Joined the Red Army in 1918, and the Bolshevik Party in 1919. Specialist in supply organization. Deputy Commander of the Rear, 1962–68.

Anisimova, Nina Aleksandrovna
27.1.1909–23.9.1979. Ballerina.
Born in Petersburg. Graduated from the Leningrad Choreographic School, 1926. Pupil of A. Vaganova. Began her career at the Leningrad Malyi Theatre. Moved to the Kirov Ballet Theatre in 1927. Soloist at the Kirov Ballet Theatre. From 1935 choreographer. Taught ballet at the Leningrad Conservatory, 1963–74.

Annenkov, Boris Vladimirovich
9.2.1889–25.9.1927. Cossack general.
Educated at the Aleksandrovskoe Military School, 1908. Active service during WWI. Head of partisan detachments of the Siberian Cossack army at the front, 1915. After the October Revolution 1917 returned with his detachments to Siberia, and refused to acknowledge the Soviet authorities at Omsk. Organized a Cossack partisan division (White), 1918. Fought against Red forces in West Siberia, Kazakhstan, later in Semirech'e. Appointed head of the Semirechenskaia Army by Admiral Kolchak, 1919. After the defeat of Kolchak fled to China, 1920. Kidnapped by Soviet agents there in 1926 and brought back by train to Moscow. Condemned to death and shot in Semipalatinsk.

Annenkov, Iurii Pavlovich (Temiriazev, Boris)
23.7.1889–12.7.1974. Painter, stage designer, author.
Born in Petropavlovsk-Kamchatskii while his father was exiled there for revolutionary activity. Later brought back by his parents to Petersburg, where he grew up. Wanted to become a painter. Studied with Stieglitz and graduated in law from Petersburg University, 1909–11. Studied with Valloton in Paris, 1911–12. Became famous for his portraits and stage and cinema designs. One of the prominent avant-garde artists in the 1920s (illustrator of Blok's *The Twelve*), designer of early revolutionary jubilee demonstrations (storming of the Winter Palace) and official appearances of revolutionary leaders (Lenin, Trotsky). Professor of Academy of Art, 1920. Commissioned by the first Soviet government to draw portraits of revolutionary leaders, including Lenin. Especially patronized by L. Trotsky. Sent as a designer to Soviet exhibitions in Western Europe and stayed in France in 1924. Celebrated member of the Russian art élite in exile in Paris, 1920–60s, designer in French and American film productions (over 60 films). His memoirs, *Dnevniki Moikh Vstrech*, 2 vol. encyclopaedia of the 1920–30s, give very interesting descriptions of many artists, writers and politicians (Akhmatova, L. Pasternak, Mayakovsky and others). Died in France.

Anokhin, Andrei Viktorovich
1874–31.8.1931. Musician, ethnographer.
Born in Biisk. Studied the music of the Turkoman peoples. Collected about 800 songs. Composed music on folkloristic themes. Died in Kuium, in the Oirotskaia Oblast'.

Anokhin, Petr Fedorovich
3.6.1891–10.5.1922. Politician.
Born in Petrozavodsk. Son of a worker. Communist leader of railway workers in Petrozavodsk, 1917. Participated in the Civil War in Northern Russia and Siberia. Killed during the Civil War by the Whites near Chita.

Anokhin, Petr Kuzmich
26.1.1898–1982? Physiologist.
Born in Tsaritsyn (now Volgograd). Educated at the Leningrad Medical Institute, 1926. In the 1920s worked with Bekhterev and Pavlov. Head of the Neurophysiological Institute of the Academy of Medical Sciences of the USSR, 1950. Specialist on brain functions and biological aspects of cybernetics. Many theoretical works published.

Anoshchenko, Nikolai Dmitrievich
1894–1974. Aviator.
One of the pioneers of aviation in Russia. Military service during WWI and the Civil War. Head of the first Soviet Scientific Aviation Institute, 1920. Made over 100 flights in hot-air balloons.

Anosov, Nikolai Pavlovich
18.2.1900–2.12.1962. Conductor.
Born in Borisoglebsk. Professor at the Moscow Conservatory. Father of the internationally known conductor, Gennadii Rozhdestvenskii. Died in Moscow.

Anpilogov, Aleksandr Semenovich
18.1.1954–   . Athlete.
Born in Tbilisi. Honoured Master of Sports (handball), 1976. Olympic champion, 1976. Graduated from the Georgian Polytechnical Institute, 1979.

Anrep, Boris Vasil'evich (Boris von)
1885–6. 1969. Mosaic pavement artist.
Born in St. Petersburg. Son of Vasilii von Anrep and Praskov'ia Zatsepina. Graduated in law from St Petersburg University. Became interested in mosaics. Gave up his professorship and began travelling throughout Russia, the Middle East, Italy and France studying mosaics. In 1908 enrolled at the Académie Julien, Paris. Studied painting techniques at the Edinburgh College of Art during the winter of 1910–11 and eventually moved to London. Met and became close to Augustus John and Henry Lamb. John gave him his first encouragement. Became a friend of Lytton Strachey and Roger Fry. In 1912 responsible for the selection of Russian works for Fry's important second Post-Impressionist Exhibition at the Grafton Galleries, and wrote that section of the catalogue. Met Clive Bell, who was responsible for the selection of English works for Fry, and whom he later portrayed on a National Gallery pavement. During WWI sailed to Arkhangelsk as a reserve cavalry officer in the Russian Army. Fought in the Carpathian Campaign, 1914–16. Returned to London as a military secretary and assistant legal adviser to the Russian Government Committee. Met Maynard Keynes with whom later he also became friends. Returned to Russia but soon left again for London and began making mosaics. First commissioned by Miss Ethel Sands in 1917 to execute a floor for her entrance hall. Three years later made mural decorations for her house in the same style. Made a floor mosaic for Sir William and Lady Jowitt for their Queen Anne house, and also the Blake Room floor in the Tate Gallery, 1923. Became a fashionable artist for British high society but left London for Paris in 1926 when his wife Helen Ann Maitland left him for Roger Fry. From his Paris studio executed a series of commissions on a monumental scale for public places. Portrayed Bertrand Russell (for the National Gallery floor), Anna Akhmatova (whom he knew when they were students in Russia), Greta Garbo, and Edith Sitwell among many other prominent personalities. Decorated the Bank of England, St Anne's Chapel, the Greek Church of St Sophia (on Moscow Road, Bayswater), the Memorial Chapel in the Church of the Royal Military College, Sandhurst, and Westminster Cathedral. Died in London.
Work: *Russian Ikons*, 1930. Sources: *Works by Boris Anrep* exhibition at Chenil Gallery, Chelsea, Oct. 1913, foreword by Roger Fry; Roger Fry, 'Modern Mosaic and Boris Anrep', *Burlington Magazine*, June 1923; Herbert Furst, *Boris Anrep and His Mosaics*, 1929; Wendy Baron, *Miss Sands and Her Circle*, 1947.

Anrep, Gleb Vasil'evich (Gleb von)
10.8.1889–11.1.1955. Doctor of medicine, professor.
Born in St. Petersburg. Younger son of Vasilii von Anrep and brother of the artist Boris von Anrep. Graduated from St. Petersburg University in medicine. Pupil of Professor Ivan Pavlov. Professor of Physiology at the University of Cairo. Member of the Royal Society. Naturalized British subject. In Cambridge met Kapitsa, the future Soviet academician, and became his close friend. Went to Egypt to work as professor in the Medical Faculty of Cairo University. Died in Cairo.

Antikainen, Toivo
8.6.1898–4.10.1941. Politician.
Born in Helsingfors (Helsinki). Son of a worker. After the October Revolution an organizer of young communists in Finland, 1918, and member of the Finnish Red Guards. After the defeat of the Finnish communists, fled to the Soviet Union. Took part in the Russian Civil War, participated in the action against the Kronstadt sailors, 1921. Leader of the Finnish communists in exile in the Soviet Union, and underground in Finland in the 1920s and 1930s. Arrested in Finland, 1934. After Soviet demands was sent to the Soviet Union, 1940. During WWII killed during a Soviet attack on Finland.

Antipenko, Nikolai Aleksandrovich
1901–   . General.
Joined the Red Army, 1920. Graduated from the Frunze Military Academy, 1940. During WWII commander of the rear of the Soviet army. After WWII head of the construction department of the Soviet armed forces.

Antipov, Nikolai Kirillovich
15.12.1894–24.8.1941. Politician, state security official.
Born near Staraia Russa. Son of a peasant. Metal worker in Petrograd. Joined the Bolsheviks, 1912. Communist worker organizer in Oct 1917. Chairman of the Petrograd Cheka, 1918. In the 1920s held many prominent party post (Moscow City Cttee, Ural obkom, Leningrad gubkom). Minister of Post and Communications of the USSR, 1928–31.

Antonian, Musheg Misakovich
1916–   . Artist.
Genre and portrait painter. Born in Erevan, Armenia. Studied at the Erevan Art Technical School, 1932–36, and at the Moscow School of Painting, Sculpture and Architecture,

1937–43, under S. Gerasimov, V. Karev, R. Frents. Member of the Iaroslavl' Union of Artists. Exhibitions: Moscow, 1945–60, Iaroslavl and Gorkii.

Antonii (Bartoshevich, Andrei Georgievich), Archbishop of Geneva and Western Europe
1917–   . Russian Orthodox clergyman.
Emigrated as a child with his parents after the Civil War, 1924. Settled in Yugoslavia. Graduated from the Theological Faculty of Belgrade University. Archimandrite, 1945. Taught at the Cadet School in Belaia Tserkov' until 1949. Emigrated to Switzerland. Bishop, 21 Apr. 1957 (Russian Church in Exile), in Geneva. Archbishop, 1965. Active in child and youth welfare work, and in supplying Christian literature to Russia.

Antonii (Blum, Andrei Borisovich), Metropolitan of Surozh (residence in London)
19.6.1914–   . Russian Orthodox clergyman.
Born in Lausanne. Son of a diplomat. Moved with his parents to Persia, 1915. Educated at a private school in Vienna. Graduated from the medical faculty of Paris University in 1943. During WWII involved with the French Resistance. Secretly took Holy Orders. Worked as a surgeon. Priest, 1948. Head of the Russian Orthodox London parish (Moscow patriarchate), 1958. Bishop, 30 Nov. 1958. Exarch of the Patriarch of Moscow in Western Europe, 1963–74. Widely known both in the USSR and in the West as an outstanding modern theologian through his books, sermons and broadcasts.
Main works (in English): *Living Prayer, School for Prayer, God and Man, Meditation on a Theme.*

Antonii, (Grabbe, Count) archimandrite
1928?–   . Russian Orthodox clergyman.
Head of Mission of the Russian Orthodox Church in Exile in Palestine, in charge of the considerable properties of the Church. Left his post after some misunderstandings with his superiors. Left the Russian Church in Exile and joined the Greek Church in America. Lives in the USA.

Antonii (Khrapovitskii, Aleksei Pavlovich), Metropolitan of Kiev and Galich
17.3.1863–10.8.1936. Russian Orthodox clergyman.
Born at Vatagino, Novgorod Gouvt. Educated at Petersburg High School. Graduated from Petersburg Theological Academy in 1885. Monk, 1885. Rector of Moscow Theological Academy, 1890–94 Rector of Kazan Theological Academy, 1894–1900. Bishop of Ufa, 1900. Bishop of Volhynia, 1902. Elected Metropolitan of Kiev and Galich, 1917. Member of the Holy Synod. Candidate for Patriarch at the Council, 1917. The most outstanding churchman of his generation. During the Civil War left Russia (through Poland and Rumania). Abroad became the main founder and leader of the Russian Orthodox Church in Exile, which broke with the Moscow Patriarchate after the death of Patriarch Tikhon. Main works: *Collected works*, 7 vols, NY, 1963–69.

Antonii (Mel'nikov, Anatolii Sergeevich), Metropolitan of Leningrad and Novgorod
19.2.1924–29.5.1986. Russian Orthodox clergyman.
Born in Moscow. Deacon with Aleksii (Simanskii), 1944–50. Graduated from the Moscow Theological Academy, 1950. Monk, 1950. Worked in the Odessa, Saratov and Minsk seminaries, 1950–64. Bishop, 1964. Archbishop of Minsk and Belorussia, 1965, Metropolitan, 1975. Metropolitan of Leningrad and Novgorod, 1978–86. Active in theological work and international relations of the Russian Orthodox church. Died and buried at Leningrad.

Antonov, Aleksandr Stepanovich
1885?–1922. Anti-Bolshevik guerilla leader.
Took part in the 1905 Revolution. Member of the Socialist Revolutionary Party. Arrested by Tsarist police and sentenced to 8 years exile. After the revolution became head of the local militia in Kirsanov, Tambov Gouvt. 1917–18. Went underground in Aug. 1920, and started a peasant revolt in the Tambov region (Antonovshchina). The revolt gained strength because of the dissatisfaction of the peasants with the Bolshevik government's measures concerning the confiscation of grain (prodrazverstka). In Jan. 1921, his army consisted of some 50,000 men, mainly peasants and deserters from the Red Army. They killed in action some 2000 Bolshevik officials. After a year of fighting, regular Red Army detachments under Tukhachevskii and Uborevich defeated them. Survived for another year with a small group of followers. Killed in action in June 1922.

Antonov, Aleksei Innokent'evich
15.9.1896–18.6.1962. General.
Born in Grodno. Son of an officer. Educated at the Pavlovskoe Military School, 1916. Took part in WWI. Joined the Red Army, 1919, as a staff officer. Graduated from the Frunze Military Academy, 1931, and the Academy of the General Staff, 1937. Became well known during WWII as an efficient staff officer, serving in Stalin's HQ from 1942. Took part in the Yalta and Potsdam conferences. From 1955 Chief-of-staff of the Warsaw Pact. Died in Moscow, buried at Red Square.

Antonov, D.A. (Broide-Trepper, Edgar Leopoldovich)
1936–   . Author.
Born in Moscow. Son of the chief of the Red Orchestra Soviet spy network in West Europe during WWII, Leopold Trepper. Graduated from Moscow University. Emigrated, 1971. Settled in West Germany. Published a number of novels on contemporary subjects stressing the Chekhov approach to life.

Antonov, Oleg Konstantinovich
7.2.1906–1984. Aircraft designer.
Born in the village of Troitskoe, now Moskovskaia Oblast'. Son of a building engineer. Graduated from the Leningrad Polytechnical Institute, 1930. Began his career as an engineer, then chief of a KB (Design Bureau), and then chief designer in a glider factory, 1930–62. Member of the CPSU, 1945. Doctor of Technical Science, 1960. From 1938 designer at

the A. Iakovlev Aviation KB. From 1943 Deputy Chief Designer, and Chief Designer, from 1946, of Ant(onov)-10, Ant–22, and Ant–24 aircraft. Corresponding member of the Academy of Sciences of the Ukrainian SSR, 1964. Stalin Prize, 1952. Lenin Prize, 1962. During the post-war years Senior Designer with the USSR Ministry of Aviation (until 1963). Has written over 50 works on glider and aircraft design.
Publications: *Na Kryl'iakh Iz Dereva i Polotna*, 1962; *Dlia Vsekh I Dlia Sebia*, 1965.

Antonov-Ovseenko, Anton Vladimirovich
1920–   . Historian, author, dissident.
Son of the old Bolshevik and revolutionary, V.A. Antonov-Ovseenko. (After the arrest of his father, his mother, as a 'wife of the enemy of the people', was arrested and commited suicide in a prison in Khanty-Mansiisk.) Arrested for the first time in 1940, but soon set free. Rearrested in 1941. Spent WWII in prison camps in Turkmenia and in the Saratov region. After the war, released and allowed to live in Moscow. In 1948 arrested again for anti-Soviet agitation, sent to Vorkuta and Pechora labour camps. Released in 1956, returned to Moscow. Rehabilitated in 1957. In 1967 (together with 43 old Bolsheviks who had survived Stalin's purges) he addressed the Kremlin protesting against the attempt to rehabilitate Stalin and his crimes. In 1983 the Khronika-Press (USA) published his historical research *The Portrait of the Tyrant* about his father's fate under Stalin with especially valuable details of the mystery of Kirov's murder. Harassed by the KGB. Became nearly blind and was put under home arrest under the close supervision of the KGB. In Nov. 1984 was arrested again and accused of anti-Soviet agitation and propaganda. Removed from Moscow.

Antonov-Ovseenko, Vladimir Aleksandrovich (revolutionary name – Shtyk; pen name –A. Galskii)
21.3.1883–1939. Revolutionary, party and state official.
Born in Chernigov, son of a military officer. An active revolutionary from 1901, joined the Social Democratic Labour Party Menshevik wing in 1903. Graduated from military school in Petersburg, 1904. During the 1905 Revolution tried to organize military revolts in Poland and Sebastopol. Sentenced to death, commuted to 20 years' imprisonment. Escaped from prison and continued revolutionary activity. Emigrated to France, 1910. Returned to Russia after the February Revolution 1917 and supported Trotsky. Joined the Bolshevik Party. One of the chief organizers of the October coup, personally led the siege of the Winter Palace and arrested the ministers of the Provisional Government. One of the three men in charge of military and naval affairs. During the Civil War commander of the Red forces fighting the Don Cossacks under Kaledin and the anti-Bolshevik Ukrainians. Head of VTSIK. Head of the Political Administration of the Red Army. In charge of the repression of the peasant revolt in Tambov Gouvt., 1921. Dismissed after the defeat of Trotsky in 1925. Acknowledged Stalin's supremacy, 1928. Soviet Ambassador to Czechoslovakia, Lithuania, Poland, 1924–30. Attorney-General of the RSFSR, 1934. During the Spanish Civil War Soviet General Consul at Barcelona (where most Soviet military shipments arrived), 1936–37. Recalled to Moscow, arrested 1938, disappeared during the Great Purge. Moscow dissident historian Roy Medvedev in the Russian edition of *They Surrounded Stalin* says that 'Mikoian at the 20th Congress of CPSU regretted the loss of many outstanding communists, among them Antonov-Ovseenko'. Died imprisoned, presumably executed in 1939.

Antropov, Oleg Petrovich
4.11.1947–   . Athlete.
Born in the village of Novyi, Chimkent Oblast'. Studied at the Riga Medical Institute. Honoured Master of Sports (volleyball), 1962. Coach. Member of the CPSU, 1977. Olympic champion, 1968. USSR champion, 1969.

Antsiferov, Aleksei Nikolaevich
1867–1943. Economist.
Born in Voronezh. Son of a mathematics professor. Graduated in law from Moscow University, 1890. Became known as an authority on the cooperation movement and statistics. Lecturer later professor at Kharkov University, 1903. Took part in the European agricultural cooperation movement before WWI. During the Civil War emigrated and settled in Paris. Chairman of the Russian Academic Group in France. Died in France.

Antson, Ants Arturovich
11.11.1938–   . Athlete.
Born in Tallinn. Graduated from the Tallinn Pedagogical Institute, 1975. Honoured Master of Sports (skating) 1964. Olympic champion, 1964 (1,500 metres). European champion, 1964. USSR champion, 1964, 1967, 1968. World champion, 1964, (3,000 metres).

Anuchin, Dmitrii Nikolaevich
1843–1923. Geographer, publicist.
Organizer of an anthropological exhibition in Moscow in 1879. Professor at Moscow University. The driving force behind the All-Russian Geographical Exhibition in 1892 in Moscow. Founder and editor-in-chief of the geographical magazine, *Zemlevedenie*. Also on the editorial board of the newspaper *Russkie Vedomosti*. One of the few prominent members of the old Russian intelligentsia who co-operated with the Soviet government.

Anvelt, Ian Ianovich
1884–1937. Politician.
Joined the Bolshevik Party, 1907. Estonian communist leader. Graduated in law from Petersburg University, 1912. Active in Estonia during the October Revolution 1917. Chairman of the government of the (abortive) Estonian Soviet Republic, 1918. Political commissar in the Red Army, 1919–21. Underground communist leader in independent Estonia, 1921–25. Returned to the USSR, 1925. Worked as a high ranking political officer in the Soviet armed forces, later active in the Comintern. Liquidated by Stalin.

Aptekman, Osip Vasil'evich
30.3.1849–8.7.1926. Revolutionary, historian.
Born in Petersburg. Studied at Kharkov University and Petersburg Medical Academy. While a student

became a populist (narodnik), 'went to the people' (distributed revolutionary propaganda) in Pskov and Penza Gouvt., 1874–75. Worked as a junior country doctor, took part in revolutionary activity, 1877–79. One of the founders of the purist wing of the populist movement (Chernyi Peredel), Black Repartition, which parted company with the terrorist wing (Narodnaia Volia), 1879. Arrested in 1880, exiled to Iakutia for 5 years. After exile studied medicine in Munich, 1887–89. Doctor in the provinces from the 1890s. Became sympathetic to the SD Party in 1895. Participant in the 1905 Revolution in Wilno. Emigrated to Switzerland in 1906. Became close to the Mensheviks. Returned to Russia in 1917. Worked in the Historico-Revolutionary Archive in Petrograd. His books and articles are a valuable source of information on the populist movement.

Arakishvili, Dmitrii Ignat'evich (Arakchiev)
23.2.1873–13.8.1953. Composer, conductor, musical ethnologist.
Born in Vladikavkaz (now Ordzhonikidze). Graduated from the Musical Drama School of the Moscow Philharmonic Society, 1901. Pupil of A. Il'inskii (composition) and V.Kes (conducting). Perfected training as composer under A. Grechaninov, 1910–11. Graduated from the Moscow Archaeological Institute, 1917. Influenced by S. Taneev and others. Contributed to the Moscow People's Conservatory, and free music classes in Arbatskii Square, 1906. Edited the Moscow periodical *Musyka i Zhizn'*, 1908–12. Travelled in Georgia studying and recording folk music. Moved to Tiflis, 1918. Founded the second conservatory there, 1921 (amalgamated with the Tiflis Conservatory, 1923). Founded, at the same time, the Muzykalnyi Rabfak (music school for workers). Professor at the Conservatory from 1919 (subjects: History of Music, Theory, Georgian Folk Music). Director of the Conservatory and dean of the Faculty of Composition, 1926–29. Doctorate in musical history, 1943. Member of the Academy of Sciences of the GSSR, 1950. One of the founders of professional Georgian music, creating a classical Georgian lyrical style. Died in Tbilisi.

Araminas, Al'girdas
1937–   . Cameraman, director.
One of the best Lithuanian cameramen turned director. Graduated from the VGIK (Moscow Film School). First tried his hand as a cameraman in 1959. Shot one episode from the important film *Living Heroes*. Other films as a cameraman: *Strangers* (1962), *The Chronicle of One Day* (1963). As a director-cameraman: *Nights Without Lodging* (1967), *Find Me* (1968), *When I Was Young* (1969). Works at the Lithuanian Film Studio in Vilnius.

Aranovich, Iurii Mikhailovich
13.5.1932–   . Conductor.
Born in Leningrad. Chief conductor with the symphony orchestra of the Iaroslavl' Philharmonic, 1957–64. Conductor and artistic director of the All-Union Radio and Television Symphony Orchestra.

Arbatov, Georgii Arkad'evich
1923–   . Politician, foreign affairs adviser, journalist.
Graduated from the Moscow Institute of International Relations in 1949. Member of the CPSU from 1943. Served in the Soviet Army, 1941–44. Editor and later Senior Editor of *Voprosy Filosofii, Novoe Vremia and Kommunist*, 1949–60. Editorial columnist of *Problemy Mira i Sotsializma*, 1960–62. Section chief of the Institute of World Economics and International Relations of the USSR Academy of Sciences, 1962–64. Adviser on foreign policy to the Cen. Cttee. of the CPSU, 1964–67. From 1967 Director of the Institute of US and Canadian Studies of the USSR Academy of Sciences. Candidate member of the Cen. Cttee, 1976–81, full member of the Cen. Cttee. of the CPSU, 1981. Has been directly involved with Soviet foreign policy from the late 1960s. Personal adviser on foreign affairs (especially American) to Gorbachev.

Arbuzov, Aleksandr Erminingel'dovich
30.8.1877–22.1.1968. Organic chemist.
Graduated from Kazan' University, 1900. Professor at Kazan' University, 1911–30. Research on phosphorous-organic compounds. Wrote on the history of chemistry. Died in Kazan'.

Arbuzov, Boris Aleksandrovich
22.10.1903–   . Organic chemist.
Son of the famous chemist, A.E. Arbuzov. Graduated from the Kazan' Institute of Agriculture and Forestry, 1926. Professor of Kazan' University, 1938. Research on terpenes, diene compounds and the application of physical methods for the study of organic compounds.

Ardamatskii, Vasilii Ivanovich
8.9.1911–   . Author, journalist.
Writer of crime stories with political overtones. Wrote novels using Cheka archives (on Savinkov and Reilly). Worked in the cinema. Often appears in *Literaturnaia Gazeta*. Considered an expert on legal and state security matters.

Arends, Andrei (Genrikh) Fedorovich
14.3.1855–27.4.1924. Conductor, composer.
Born in Moscow. Chief conductor with the Ballet of the Bolshoi Theatre, 1900–24. Composed an opera, ballet, symphony and concerto for voice and orchestra. Died in Moscow.

Argunov, A.A.
1867–1939. Politician.
Member of the SR Party, close to the Trudovik group. Editor of *Revolutsionnaia Rossia* in 1917. Member of the Directorium in Ufa during the Civil War. Emigrated, lived in Prague. Contributed to Russian emigré publications. Published memoirs.

Arinbasarova, Natal'ia Utevlevna
24.9.1946–   . Film actress.
Born in Kirghizia. Trained as a ballerina. Graduated from the Moscow Choreographic School, 1964, and from the VGIK, 1971. Played the leading role in A. Mikhalkov-Konchalovskii's film, *The First Teacher* (Pervyi Uchitel'), which received a prize at the Venice Film Festival. At the age of 19 married Mikhalkov-Koncholovskii. Gave birth to a son. The marriage broke up subsequently.

Aristov, Averkii Borisovich
1903–7.1973. Politician.
Joined the Bolshevik Party, 1921. Party secretary of several Siberian and Ural obkoms, 1943–52. Member

of the Cen. Cttee., 1952, and of the Presidium of the Cen. Cttee., 1952–53, and 1957–61. Secretary of the Cen. Cttee., 1955–60. Ambassador in Warsaw, 1961.

Arkanov, Arkadii Mikhailovich
1933– . Writer.
One of the leading writers of the club of the Twelve Chairs, the humour section of *Literaturnaia Gazeta.* Wrote plays (with Gorin): *Blanket,* 1967, *Svad'ba na Vsiu Evropu,* 1966. Has published humorous short stories (also with Gorin). In 1979 published two short stories in the almanac, *Metropol.* Lives in Moscow.
Source: P. Vail, A. Genis, *Sovremennaia Russkaia Proza,* USA, 1982.

Arkhangel'skii, Aleksandr Andreevich
23.10.1846–16.11.1924. Composer of religious music, conductor.
Born in the village of Bolshoe Tezikovo, near Penza. Son of a priest. Educated at the Penza seminary, 1870. Showed early interest in church music. Studied in Petersburg at the Medical Academy, later at the Technological Institute. Had to leave studies because of poverty, became a civil servant. Later became a choir master at the Court Choir capella. Choir master at Guards regiments. Organized his own choir, 1880. Organized concerts very successfully in Russia and abroad. Re-awakened the interest in old Russian church singing. Became the outstanding master of Russian church music in modern times. Lived at Petersburg and composed church music for over half a century. Died in Prague while on tour, later re-buried at the Aleksandro-Nevskaia Lavra at Petrograd.

Arkhangel'skii, Aleksei Petrovich
18.3.1872–1950? General.
In 1917 worked in the War Ministry. Continued to serve the new government after the Bolshevik take-over. Secretly organized transport for all officers who volunteered to serve in the White armies in the South. In 1919 he himself left to join Denikin's forces, and served with the Whites until the end of the Civil War in the Crimea. Evacuated and settled in France. Became chairman of ROVS (the organization of White veterans of the Civil War), 1938.

Arkhipenko, Aleksandr
1887–2.1964. Sculptor, painter.
Born in Kiev. Moved to Paris in 1908. Became one of the best known modernist sculptors (under the influence of cubism). In the early 1920s lived and worked in Berlin. Later moved to the USA. Regarded as the founder of the post-Rodin era in sculpture. Remained a typical representative of the 1920s. Died in the USA.

Arkhipov, Abram Efimovich
27.8.1862–25.9.1930. Artist.
Born in the village of Egorovo, Riazan Gouvt. Studied at the Moscow School of Painting, Sculpture and Architecture, 1877–83, 1886–88 under V. Perov, V. Makovskii, A. Savrasov, V. Polenov and I. Prianishnikov. Also studied at the Petersburg Academy of Arts, 1884–86, under B.Villevalde, K.Venig and P. Chistiakov. Landscape and genre painter. People's artist of the RSFSR, 1927. Member of the Tovarishchestvo Peredvizhnykh Khudozhestvennykh Vystavok from 1891. Member of the Union of Russian Painters from 1904. Took part in the following exhibitions: All-Russian Exhibition, Nizhnii Novgorod, 1896; 36 Artists, 1902–03; Mir Iskusstva, 1903; the Red Army Exhibition, Moscow, 1923; Ten Years of the RKK, 1928. One-man exhibitions: 1927, 1949, Moscow. Taught at the Moscow School of Painting, Sculpture and Architecture, 1894–1918, then in the State-Free Art Shops, 1918–20 and at the VKHUTEMAS, 1922–24. Died in Moscow.

Arkhipov, Ivan Vasil'evich
1907– . State official.
Operator in various railroad workshops, 1921–24. Joined the Communist Party in 1928. In 1932, working as a senior foreman, graduated from the Moscow Machine Tools Institute. Worked at various metallurgical plants until 1938. 1st secretary of Krivoi Rog City Cttee, of the Ukrainian CP, 1938–39. Moved to Moscow. Worked in the Cen. Cttee. apparatus, 1939–43. Deputy USSR Minister of Nonferrous Metallurgy, 1943–57. Chief Soviet economic adviser in China at the time of their first five-year plan. Deputy Chairman of the State Cttee. on

Foreign Economic Relations of the USSR Council of Ministers, 1958–59. 1st Deputy Chairman, 1959–74. Deputy Chairman of the USSR Council of Ministers, 1974–80. 1st Deputy Chairman, 1980. Member of the Cen. Cttee. of the CPSU from 1976. In the late 1980s was the highest-ranking Kremlin official to visit China for 15 years. Signed a 1986–90 trade pact with China.

Arkhipova, Irina Konstantinovna
2.1.1925– . Singer (mezzo soprano).
Born in Moscow. Pupil of L. Savranskii. Soloist with the Bolshoi Theatre from 1956. Guest appearances all over the world.

Arkhuzen, Robert Ivanovich
16.12.1844–20.1.1920. Guitar maker.
Born in Petersburg. Son of the guitar maker, Iogann (Iohann), Ivan Arkhuzen, under whom he studied. His guitars are especially valued on the international market. Died in Moscow.

Armand, Inessa Theodorovna (Elizaveta Fedorovna; b. Steffen; pen name–Elena Blonina)
26.4.1874–24.9.1920. Revolutionary, politician.
Born in Paris, daughter of an actor. Orphaned, brought up by an aunt (a governess with the factory-owning family of Armand) in Moscow. Married a son of the Armand family (4 children), later married his younger brother (1 child). Took part in the 1905 Revolution, connected with the SRs in Moscow. Arrested and exiled. Emigrated to Paris, and met Lenin (who was a political exile) in 1909. The only romantic attachment of Lenin's life, she remained close to him till her death. Lectured at the Longjumeau party school, translated Lenin's works into French. Returned secretly to Russia (on party business) in 1912, arrested, but soon released. During WWI lived in Switzerland. Bolshevik representative at Kienthal and Zimmerwald. Returned with Lenin to Russia in 1917. After the October Revolution 1917, chairwoman of Moscow Gouvt. Sovnarkhoz, active at the 2nd Congress of the Comintern, head of the women's section of the Cen. Cttee. of the Bolshevik Party, organizer of the 1st

Conference of International Women Communists on 1920 in Moscow. Buried in Red Square with John Reed and others.

Arnshtam, Aleksandr Martynovich
1881–1961? Painter.
Considered one of the best graphic artists of his time. Became widely known for his satirical cartoons in the magazine *Signal* during the 1905 Revolution. Lived in Petersburg, 1919. Edited Pushkin's works. Arrested by the Cheka, 1919–20. Wrote a diary of his prison experiences. Moved to Moscow, 1920. Illustrated books by Pushkin, Briusov, Lunacharskii and others. Moved to Berlin, 1920, active in the flourishing Russian publishing business in that city in the 1920s.

Aronson, Grigorii Iakovlevich
1892?–1968. Politician.
Active member of the Menshevik Party. Before WWI, actively involved in revolutionary work. After the Bolshevik take-over in October 1917, many arrests, several terms in prison and exile. Left the USSR, settled in the USA. Author of *Kniga o Russkom Evreistve* (2 vol). Regular and prolific contributor to the Russian language magazines *Sotsialisticheskii Vestnik* and *Novyi Zhurnal*. Wrote memoirs concerning the revolutionary years. In 1959 was first to write publicly about the influence of masonic lodges in Russia in the early 20th century and during the revolutionary years. Died in the USA.

Arosev, Aleksandr Iakovlevich
1890–1938. Revolutionary, author, politician.
Early involvement in revolutionary activity, member of the SRs. Changed to the Bolsheviks, 1907. Active in the Bolshevik take-over in Moscow, 1917. Became a Soviet diplomat and started writing in the early 1920s. Secretary of the Soviet Embassy in Riga, 1922. Head of the All-Union Society for Cultural Relations with Foreign Countries in the 1930s. In 1936, with Bukharin and Adoratskii, conducted negotiations with the Menshevik, Nikolaevskii, in Paris about the acquisition of the archives of German Socialists (saved by Nikolaevskii from the Nazis). Arrested

during the Stalin purges, perished in the Gulag.

Arsen'ev, Konstantin Konstantinovich
5.2.1837–22.3.1919. Editor, lawyer, lexicographer.
Born in Petersburg. Editor of the long established magazine *Vestnik Evropy* (European Herald), 1909. One of the main editors of the best Russian pre-revolutionary reference work, the Brockhaus-Efron Encyclopaedia, from 1891. Editor of *Novyi Entsiklopedicheskii Slovar*, from 1911. Leader of the Party of Democratic Reforms, 1906–07. Died in Petrograd.

Arsen'ev, Nikolai Sergeevich
16.5.1888–1983? Author, philosopher, theologian, poet.
Born in Stockholm. Son of a diplomat. Graduated from Moscow University, 1910. Lecturer at Moscow University, 1914. Professor of Western European literature at Saratov University, 1918. Fled to Poland in 1920. Lived in Berlin. Professor at Koenigsberg University (Eastern Prussia), 1921. Gave frequent lectures at Warsaw University, Riga, and many other European cities. Authority on Orthodoxy, Russian cultural traditions, and later highly respected participant of the oecumenical movement. After WWII in DP camps in Germany. Moved to the USA. Professor at St. Vladimir seminary, NY, and Montreal University, from 1948. Died in USA.
Main works: *The Thirst for True Existence, Mysticism and the Eastern Church, The Russian Cultural Tradition, Gifts and Meetings on the Path of Life* (memoirs).

Arsen'ev, Vladimir Klavdievich
10.9.1872–4.9.1930. Explorer, author.
Born in Petersburg. From 1902 till mid–1920s almost continually engaged in exploring the Russian Far East (the Ussuri river, Kamchatka and the Commodore Islands). Became the leading authority in the world on this region. Published many scientific reports on his travels, as well as autobiographical sketches and novels, including the now classic *Dersu Uzala*, about the friendship of an explorer with a local hunter (filmed for Mosfilm by Akira Kurosawa). Taught in schools in the Soviet

Far East. In Gorkii's words Arsen'ev was the 'Russian Brehm and Fenimore Cooper'. Other works: *Po Ussuriiskomu Kraiu*, 1921, *V Gorakh Sikhote- Alinia*, 1937.

Arsenii (Zhadanovskii), Bishop of Serpukhov
1874–1945. Russian Orthodox clergyman.
Born in Kharkov Gouvt. Graduated from Moscow Theological Academy in 1903. Bishop of Serpukhov, 1914. Led the moderate opposition against state measures to impose its will upon the church (Danilovtsy). Arrested in 1929, inmate of Gulag camps till his death.

Artem (Sergeev, Fedor Andreevich)
19.3.1883–24.7.1921. Revolutionary.
Born in Glebovo, Kursk Gouvt., son of a peasant. Joined the Bolshevik Party in 1901. Emigrated to Paris in 1902. Took part in 1905 Revolution in Kharkov. Arrested in 1906, but escaped. Bolshevik leader in Perm. Arrested and sentenced to life exile to Eastern Siberia in 1907. Fled in 1910 through Korea and China to Australia where he worked as a farm hand, 1911. Returned to Russia in 1917, leader of the Kharkov Soviet. Took part in the Civil War, organizer of the Red detachments in Donbass in the Ukraine. Member of the Cen. Cttee. of the Bolshevik Party, 1920. Occupied many important party posts. Chairman of the miners' trade union, 1921. Died in an accident.

Artem'ev, Pavel Artem'evich
1897–1979. General, state security officer.
Joined the Red Army, 1918. Member of the Bolshevik Party, 1920. Graduated from the Frunze Military Academy, 1938. Made his career in special state security detachments. Divisional commander of NKVD troops, 1938. Commander of NKVD troops, 1941, and at the same time commander of the Moscow defence zone, 1941–43.

Artem'ev, Viacheslav Pavlovich
27.8.1903–   . Colonel.
Born in Moscow. Graduated from the Frunze Military Academy. Commander of a cavalry regiment, taken prisoner by the Germans, 1943. In

June 1944 joined the Vlasov army (anti-Stalinist Russians in Germany financed by the Germans). Appointed commander of the 2nd regiment of the ROA. Eyewitness of the intervention of the ROA on the side of the Czechs in Prague, 1945 (the last military action of WWII), and of the end of the Vlasov army. Valuable memoirs published in 1974 (*Pervaia divizia ROA*). Managed to escape from SMERSH and forcible repatriation after WWII. Lectured on Soviet military affairs in US army establishments.

Artobolevskii, Ivan Ivanovich
26.9.1905–   . Engineer.
Graduated from Timiriazev Agricultural Academy, 1926. Professor at Moscow University and the Zhukovskii Air Force Academy, 1932. Academician, 1946. Works on the kinematic analysis of mechanisms and the theory and practice of automation.

Artsimovich, Lev Andreevich
25.2.1909–   . Nuclear physicist, academician.
Born in Moscow. Graduated from the Belorussian University, 1928. Member of the USSR Academy of Sciences, 1953. Member of the Presidium of the USSR Academy of Sciences from 1957. Worked at the Moscow Institute of Atomic Energy from 1944, one of the founders of nuclear science in the USSR. Member of the USA Academy of Art and Science from 1966. Awarded seven Orders of Lenin.

Artsybashev, Mikhail Petrovich
5.11.1878–3.3.1927. Author.
Born in Kharkov Gouvt. First appeared in print at the age of 23. His sexually explicit novel *Sanin* made him a fashionable best selling writer before WWI. At the time considered very immoral. Criticized the revolutionary zeal of the Russian intelligentsia in his work *U Poslednei Cherty*. Emigrated in 1917. Died in Warsaw.

Artuzov (Frauchi), Artur Khristianovich
2.1891–7.1943. Secret police official.
Born in Ustinovo, Tver Gouvt. Son of a Swiss-Italian. Graduated from Petrograd Polytechnic in 1917. Active during the Civil War as a Cheka official. From 1919 one of the chiefs of the Cheka-GPU. Carried out many secret operations abroad, including the operations leading to the eventual arrest of Boris Savinkov. Liquidated by Stalin.

Arutiunian, Aleksandr Grigor'evich
23.9.1920–   . Composer.
Born in Erevan, Armenia. Graduated in composition and piano from the Erevan Conservatory, 1941. Pupil of V. Talian, S. Barkhudarian and O.Babasian. Perfected his art at the Moscow Dom Kultury. Performed his own works as a soloist. Artistic director of the Armenian Philharmonic from 1954. Taught composition at the Erevan Conservatory from 1964. Professor, 1971. Work characterized by the use of Armenian folk melodies.

Arvatov, Boris Ignat'evich
1896–1940. Literary critic, author.
Wrote *Sotsiologicheskaia Poetika*, Moscow, 1928, (foreword by Osip Brik.) Member of LEF. One of the theoreticians of the so-called 'proizvodstvennoe iskusstvo'.

Asaf'ev, Boris Vladimirovich (Glebov, Igor)
29.7.1884–27.1.1949. Composer, musicologist.
Born in Petersburg. Graduated from Petersburg University in 1908, and from Petersburg Conservatory in 1910. Pupil of Liadov. Musical director of the Mariinskii Ballet in 1910. Active as a music critic. Professor of Leningrad Conservatory in 1925. Moved to Moscow in 1943. Professor of Moscow Conservatory. Consultant at the Bolshoi Theatre. Elected Chairman of the Union of Composers in 1948. Composed music for the ballets *Flame of Paris*, *Fountain of Bakhchisarai*, *The Captive of the Caucasus*. Gained the reputation of a musical scholar with very wide interests. Published many books on musical subjects from operas to symphonies, to chamber music and songs. Died in Moscow. *Collected Works*, 5 vol.

Asatiani, Nugzar Platonovich
1.7.1937–   . Athlete.
Born in a village in Kutaisi district, Georgia. Graduated from the Tbilisi Institute of Physical Culture, 1960, then from Tbilisi University in law, 1968. Worked as a lawyer and taught physical culture. Honoured Master of Sports (fencing) 1964. With Tbilisi Dynamo from 1960. Olympic champion, 1964. World champion, 1965. USSR champion, 1961.

Aseev, Nikolai Nikolaevich
9.7.1889–16.7.1963. Poet.
Born in Lvov. Educated at Moscow Commercial Institute, 1909–12. Studied at Moscow and Kharkov universities. First book of poems published in 1913 shows the influence of the Symbolist movement. Turned to Khlebnikov and later became a close friend of Mayakovsky. During the Civil War in the Far East, from 1922 in Moscow. Member of LEF, 1923. Became an orthodox communist poet and literary official much praised during his life time, but since forgotten. Died in Moscow.

Ashenbrenner, Mikhail Iul'evich (Aschenbrenner)
21.9.1842–11.11.1926. Revolutionary.
Born in Moscow. Son of an officer. In the early 1880s organized a number of revolutionary groups among army officers, connected with the populist terrorists (Narodnaia Volia). Arrested, 1883, sentenced to death, commuted to life imprisonment, 1884. Spent 20 years in solitary confinement in Schlüsselburg prison, 1884–1904. In 1924 received the honorary title of First Red Army Soldier (pervyi krasnoarmeets). Died in Moscow.

Ashkenazi, Vladimir
1937–   . Musician, pianist, conductor.
Born in Gorkii. Attended the Central Music School, Moscow, aged 8. Moscow debut, 1954. Second prize in the Chopin Competition in Warsaw, 1955. Student of Moscow Conservatory. Gold medal in the Queen Elizabeth Competition, Brussels, 1956. The next year made his debut in the United States and Canada. Joint first prize in the Tchaikovskii Competition, Moscow, 1962. Debut in London, 1963. Announced his desire to settle in the West with his Icelandic wife and their child (17 Apr. 1963),

but returned to Moscow in May of the same year. Left again for London two months later. Toured Japan, 1965. Settled in Iceland, 1968. Conductor of the Iceland Symphony Orchestra, 1969. Conducted the Royal Liverpool Philharmonic Orchestra, 1976. Conductor with the New Philharmonic Orchestra, 1977. Moved to Lucerne, Switzerland, for tax reasons, 1978. Recorded the Mozart piano concerto cycle, Chopin's solo piano works etc., 1978. Concerts in China, 1979. In 1981 appointed Principal Guest Conductor of the Philharmonia Orchestra. In 1983 conducted the Cleveland Orchestra. Relinquished his Philharmonia post. In 1984, made a new recording of the Beethoven piano concertos.

Ashrafi, Mukhtar Ashrafovich
11.6.1912–19.12.1975. Composer, conductor.
Born in Bukhara, Central Asia. Graduated from the Bukhara Higher School of Music, 1928 and from the Samarkand Institute of Music and Choreography, 1928–30. Studied composition at the Moscow Conservatory under S. Vasilenko and B. Shekhter, 1934–37. Continued his studies at the Leningrad Conservatory under M.Steinberg, 1941–43. Graduated as conductor from the Leningrad Conservatory, 1948. Began composing and conducting in 1930. Artistic director of Samarkand Radio, 1929–30. Musical director, 1930–47 (with intervals). Director of the Uzbek Theatre of Opera and Ballet (Navoi Bolshoi Akademicheskii Teatr UzSSR). Director of operatic training at the Tashkent Conservatory, 1947–62. Chief conductor with Tashkent Opera and Ballet Theatre. Professor in 1953. Director, artistic director and chief conductor of the Samarkand Theatre of Opera and Ballet, 1964–66. Director, artistic director and chief conductor of the Tashkent Bolshoi Theatre. Director of the Tashkent Conservatory from 1971. Died in Tashkent.

Askoldov, Sergei Aleksandrovich (Alekseev)
1871–1945. Philosopher.
Son of the philosopher Kozlov. Close friend of the philosopher Losskii. Graduated from Petersburg University. Professor of philosophy at Petrograd University, 1916–19. Lecturer of chemical technology at Leningrad Technical Institute 1919–25. Arrested and sent to the Gulag camps in 1928. Released in 1940. At the end of WWII among Russian refugees in Germany. Died in Potsdam.

Asmolov, Aleksei Nikitich
31.3.1906–1981. Secret police official. Born in Saratov Gouvt., son of a peasant. Joined the Soviet Army in 1928. Graduated from Frunze Military Academy in 1939. Member of the CPSU from 1932. Intelligence officer in charge of partisan operations near Leningrad, 1941–43. Later transferred by the GRU to control partisan operations in Czechoslovakia, 1944–45. After WWII, became a high ranking MGB (KGB) officer. Retired in 1956 at the age of 50 after Khrushchev's speech at the 20th Party Congress about the crimes of Stalin's Gulag. Active in the Soviet Cttee. of War Veterans in the 1960s.

Asmus, Valentin Ferdinandovich
30.12.1894–5.6.1975. Philosopher, literary scholar.
Born in Kiev. Graduated from Kiev University in 1919. Professor of Moscow University, 1939. Member of the Institute of Philosophy of the Academy of Science, 1968. Author of many works on Western philosophers and writers.

Aspasia (Rosenberg, Elsa; m. Rainis)
16.3.1868–5.11.1943. Poetess.
Born in Dauknas, Latvia. Classic of turn of the century Latvian poetry. Married the poet, Y.Rainis. After the 1905 Revolution emigrated with Rainis to Switzerland. Continued to publish poetry in exile. Returned to independent Latvia, 1920. Died in Dubulty during the German occupation of Latvia.

Asratian, Ezras Akratovich
31.5.1903–   . Physiologist.
Graduated from Erevan University, 1930. Professor of the Leningrad Institute of Pedagogy, 1938. Director of the Higher Neuroactivity Institute, 1950. Director of the Institute of Neurophysiology of the Academy of Sciences, 1961. Worked on the problems of regeneration in damaged organisms. Carried out research based on Pavlov's theories. Developed an anti-shock liquid, used at the front during WWII.

Astaf'eva, Serafima Aleksandrovna
1876–13.9.1934. Ballerina, ballet teacher.
Graduated from the Petersburg Theatre School, 1895. Soloist at the Mariinskii Theatre until 1905. With Diaghilev in the Ballets Russes, 1910–11. In 1914 set up a ballet school in London. Choreographer. Among her pupils were M. Fonteyn, A. Markova and A. Dolin. Died in London.

Astakhova, Polina Grigor'evna
30.10.1936–   . Athlete.
Born in Donetsk. Honoured Master of Sports (gymnastics), 1960. Graduated from the Kiev Institute of Physical Culture, 1969. Olympic champion, 1960 and 1964 (parallel bars). World champion, 1958 and 1962. European champion, 1959 and 1961. USSR champion, 1959–65. International referee from 1973.

Astankova, Elizaveta Vasil'evna
1900–1981. Revolutionary, politician. Joined the Bolshevik Party, 1917. One of the organizers of Red partisans in Siberia during the Civil War. Fought against Kolchak. In the 1920s party functionary in Siberia, from 1926 party work in Moscow.

Astaurov, Boris Lvovich
27.10.1904–   . Biologist.
Graduated from Moscow University, 1927. Specialist in the breeding of silkworms. Worked on this problem in Tashkent, 1930–35.

Astra, Gunar
28.12.1931–6.4.1988. Dissident.
One of the best known representatives of the human rights movement in Latvia. First conflict with the authorities in 1961 for communicating with Latvian emigrés. Spent 15 years in the Gulag. Distributed samizdat. Also accused of translating into Latvian, and distributing the Molotov-Ribbentrop pact. Arrested, Sept. 1983. Received a 7 year camp sentence and subsequent 5 years in exile. Released, 1 Feb. 1988 follow-

ing demonstrations in Riga. Died in Leningrad hospital after a heart operation.

Astrov, Nikolai Ivanovich
1868–1934. Politician.
Member of the Cen. Cttee. of the CD Party. One of the founders of the All-Russian Union of Towns. Mayor of Moscow, 1917. During the Civil War with the army of Denikin, member of the civilian administration of the Whites. After the defeat of the Whites, emigrated to France. Wrote memoirs on Moscow life before the Revolution.

Asylmuratova, Altynai
1962– . Ballerina.
One of the stars to have emerged from the Kirov Opera and Ballet Theatre. Graduated from the Vaganova Ballet School, Leningrad, 1980. Met with critical acclaim in 1982 in Paris. Attracted a lot of attention from the press while on tour in the USA and Canada. On 27 Nov. 1987 performed *Swan Lake* (with F. Ruzimatov) with great success.

Atarbekov, Georgii Aleksandrovich (Atarbekian)
14.12.1892–22.3.1925. Secret police official.
Born in Echmiadzin, Armenia. Joined the Bolshevik Party in 1908. Studied at Moscow University, 1910–11. During the 1917 Revolution a Bolshevik agitator among soldiers in the Caucasus. From 1918 in high positions in the Cheka (northern Caucasus, and Caspian Front). Head of the Cheka in Astrakhan in 1919. Cheka work at the Southern Front (Kuban', Black Sea). Head of the Cheka in Baku in 1920. Died in an aircrash in Tbilisi.

Avdeenko, Aleksandr Aleksandrovich
25.5.1937– . Ballet critic.
Born in Makeevka, Don Oblast'. Graduated in journalism from Moscow University, 1959. Editor in the Dept. of Literature and Art of the Moscow weekly, *Nedelia*, 1971–79. From 1979 editor and senior member of the editorial board of *Sovetskaia Kultura*. Author of many articles on ballet productions. Also wrote the script of the documentary *Bolshoi Theatre, Yesterday and Today*, 1976,

and the TV documentary, *A Life in Dance*, 1979. Author of several books about ballet personalities.

Averbakh, Leopold Leonidovich
1903–14.8.1939. Literary critic.
Leader of the militant communists in 1930s Russian literature, theorist of the On Guard and RAPP groups. Brother-in-law of Iagoda, the secret police chief. Tried to impose the dictatorship of his group on the literary scene, especially on the fellow travellers, who, proclaiming general agreement with communist demands, tried nevertheless to retain some degree of individuality. With the establishment of the official unified dogma of socialist realism, Stalin found it expedient to get rid of the excessive zeal of the Averbakh group. He was arrested during the purges.

Averchenko, Arkadii Timofeevich
1881–12.3.1925. Author, humorist.
Born in Sebastopol. Son of a merchant. Became one of the best known Russian satirists before the revolution. Contributor to, and later editor of the magazine *Satirikon* (the Russian *Punch*). Emigrated after the October Revolution, wrote satirical attacks on communism. Died in Prague. Remains (with Zoshchenko) the best known and most popular humorist in modern Russian literature.
Main works: *Stories*, 3 vol., *A Dozen Knives into the Back of the Revolution*.

Averichkin, Fedor Stepanovich
1889–1933. Sailor, politician.
Joined the Bolsheviks, 1917. One of the leaders of revolutionary sailors in the Baltic, Tsentrobalt. During the October Revolution 1917 in Petrograd, one of three sailors, who took control of the Navy. During the Civil War commander of revolutionary sailor detachments, which together with the Latvian regiments were the main force of the Bolsheviks at that time. Political commissar in the Red Navy in the Baltic and in the Caspian Sea.

Avilov, Nikolai Viktorovich
6.8.1948– . Athlete.
Born in Odessa. Master of Sports, 1972. Graduated from Odessa Uni-

versity, 1974. Olympic champion (decathlon), 1972. USSR champion, 1972.

Avksentiev, Nikolai Dmitrievich
1878–1943. Politician.
Member of the Cen. Cttee. of the Socialist Revolutionary Party, and leader of its right wing. Opposed SR involvement in terrorism, pleaded for legal political activity. Defended the war effort during WWI. Member of the Executive Committee of Petrograd Soviet in 1917. Chairman of the All-Russian Congress of Peasants' Deputies. Minister of the Interior in the Provisional Government, July-Aug. 1917 and chairman of the Pre-Parliament, 1917. Organized anti-Bolshevik resistance in the Volga region and Siberia in 1918. Member of the Ufa Directory which was abolished by right-wing officers who made a successful coup in favour of Admiral Kolchak. Emigrated at the end of 1918, lived in Paris. Co-editor of the most important emigré magazine of its time, *Annales Contemporaines*. Active opponent of the Soviet government until his death.

Avsiuk, Grigorii Aleksandrovich
1906– . Glaciologist.
Graduated from the Moscow Geodesic Institute, 1930. Worked at the Institute of Geography of the Academy of Sciences. Involved in preparing and publishing maps of remote regions of the USSR.

Avtorkhanov, Abdurrakhman Genazovich
1908– . Historian, author.
Born in Chechnia in the Caucasus. Left home after a family row. Involved in the Komsomol after 1917. Member of the Communist Party, 1927–37. Graduated from the Institute of Red Professors, 1937. Arrested, 1937. Imprisoned until 1942. Taken prisoner by the Germans during WWII. After the war in DP camps in Germany. Graduated from a German university. For 30 years taught Russian and Soviet history. Wrote several important studies of modern Soviet history, including, *Tekhnologiia Vlasti*, 1976, Frankfurt/ Main, which was re-issued in the Soviet Union by samizdat, and by the

special publishing house for Communist Party apparatchiks. Lives in West Germany.

Azar, Vladimir Nikolaevich

1920–1984. Publisher.
Grew up in Yugoslavia. During WWII joined the ROA as a junior officer. After WWII moved to the USA. Founded the Russian publishing house, Globus, in San Francisco, which published in Russian many unique works, mainly on the Russian anti-Stalin movement during WWII. Died of cancer in San Francisco.

Azef, Evno Fishelevich (code-names –Raskin, Neumayer, Aleksander)

1869–24.4.1918. Politician, revolutionary, police agent.
Born in the town of Lyskovo, into a poor Jewish tailor's family. In 1899 joined the Northern Union of the Socialist Revolutionary Party and became one of its leaders. Led the SR terrorist operations from 1903. Masterminded the assassinations of the Interior Minister Pleve, 1904, and of Grand-Duke Sergei Aleksandrovich (the Tsar's uncle), governor-general of Moscow, 1905. At the same time worked for Zubatov, the chief of the Tsarist police, (the Okhrana) from March 1892. In 1901 gave Zubatov a list of participants at the underground congress of the SR Party in Kharkov, and in 1905 gave him a further list of active members of the SR Party. In 1908, seven members of the group were hanged after his denunciations. Unmasked by V. Burtsev, 1908. The Cen. Cttee. of the SR Party sentenced him to death in absentia. Escaped abroad. Lived in hiding in Berlin until arrested by the German police in 1915 as a dangerous anarchist. Interned during WWI. Released, 1917. Died in Berlin.
See: M. Aldanov, *Azef*, Paris, 1931.

Azin, Vladimir Martinovich (Mikhailovich)

1895–1920. Revolutionary.
Revolutionary activist in the army. Joined the Bolsheviks, 1918. In the Red Army, 1918, commander of a Latvian detachment, (Cheka) in Kazan', 1918 and on other fronts during the Civil War. Taken prisoner by the Whites and shot.

B

Babadzhanian, Amazasp Khachaturovich

18.2.1906–1977. Marshal.
Born in the village of Chardakhly, Azerbaidzhan. Son of an Armenian peasant. Joined the Soviet Army, 1925. Participated in the Soviet–Finnish war, 1939–40. Became known as a talented tank forces commander during WWII. Head of the Soviet Tank armies, 1969–77.

Babadzhanian, Arno Arutiunovich

22.1.1921–   . Composer, pianist.
Born in Erevan, Armenia. Studied at the Gnesin Music School, Moscow. Pupil of E. Gnesina and V. Shebalin, then at Moscow and Erevan Conservatories. Graduated in composition from the Erevan Conservatory, 1947. Pupil of V. Tal'ian. Graduated from the Moscow Conservatory, 1948. Pupil of K. Igumnov. Taught at the Erevan Conservatory from 1950. Lecturer from 1956. Compositions (largely song music) characterised by a sense of modernity and a variety of genres. Composed also for films.

Babakin, Georgii Nikolaevich

1914–1971. Space technology designer.
Top space scientist in the post-WWII years. Head of the team which designed the Soviet automatic lunar vehicle Lunokhod-1 and the automatic devices for the exploration of the solar system Mars-2 and Mars-3.

Babel', Isaak Emmanuilovich

13.7.1894–17.3.1941. Writer.
Born in Odessa, son of a Jewish merchant. Until the age of 16 spoke only Yiddish. Graduated from the Nikolaevskoe Commercial School, 1915. Began writing at this time. In 1916 met Gorkii, who became his mentor. First publication of short stories in *Letopis*, edited by Gorkii, 1916. From 1917 until 1924 made several changes of direction in his life — was a Rumanian soldier, Cheka soldier, then joined Iudenich in the White Army, later in the Red Cavalry, First Konnaia Army, under Budennyi, a Soviet official at Odessa, then a newspaper reporter in Petersburg and Tiflis. In 1924 published in Mayakovsky's *LEF* the short stories *Sol'*, *Pis'mo*, *Korol'* and others. These

stories appeared later in the book *Konnaia Armiia*. Took part in the International Congress of Writers, Paris, 1935. Mastered many foreign languages. One of his most distinguished books is *Istoriia Moei Golubiatni*, 1926, about Jewish life in Odessa, and also *Odesskie Rasskazy*, 1931. Wrote plays, *Zakat* and *Mariia*. Considered a master of the short story. Very influential during his lifetime, all but banned later until his books were republished three decades after his death. Disappeared in the late 1930s. A victim of the Gulag.

Babich, Evgenii Makarovich

7.1.1921–11.6.1972. Athlete.
Born in Moscow. Honoured Master of Sports (ice hockey), 1953. Graduated from the Military Institute of Physical Culture, 1957. Member of the CPSU, 1957. Olympic champion, 1956. World champion, 1954, 1956. European champion, 1954–56. USSR champion, 1948–53, 1955–56. Died in Moscow.

Babinov, Sergei Panteleimonovich

11.7.1955–   . Athlete.
Born in Cheliabinsk. Honoured Master of Sports (ice hockey), 1979. Studied at the Moscow Institute of Physical Culture. Olympic champion, 1976. World and European champion, 1979. USSR champion, 1978–79.

Bachaev, Mordekhai (Mukhib)

1911–   . Author, editor.
Active in Jewish circles in Bukhara. Wrote on Jewish subjects in central Asian publications, 1929–38. Arrested, 1938, and accused of Zionism and anti-Soviet propaganda. Gulag inmate, 1938–43. In exile, 1943–57. Rehabilitated, 1957. Editor of the Tadzhik state publishing house and the *Tadzhik Encyclopaedia*, 1954–71. Emigrated to Israel, 1973. Prominent member of the Bukhara Jews in Israel. Published several works of poetry and prose. Wrote memoirs of his time in the Gulag.

Badaev, Aleksei Egorovich

4.2.1883–3.11.1951. Politician.
Born in the village of Iur'evo near Orel. Son of a peasant. Became a railway-worker in Petersburg, joined the Bolsheviks, 1904. In 1912 elected to the 4th Duma where he read

Lenin's speeches sent from abroad. Official publisher of *Pravda* before WWI. During WWI arrested with other Bolshevik members of the Duma and exiled to Turukhansk, 1914. Returned to Petrograd after the February Revolution 1917. Participated in the October Revolution 1917. In Petrograd appointed commissar for food supplies. Chairman of Tsentrosoiuz, 1930. Chairman of the Presidium of the Supreme Soviet of the RSFSR, 1938–43, and Deputy Chairman of the Presidium of the Supreme Soviet of the USSR. Died in Moscow.

Badanov, Vasilii Mikhailovich
1895–1971. Lt.-general.
Joined the Red Army and the Bolshevik Party, 1919. Took part in the Civil War. In the 1920s in Cheka and GPU military units. During WWII commander of tank detachments. Head of tank training schools, 1944. After WWII worked in the USSR Ministry of Defence. Retired after Khrushchev's revelations about Stalin's crimes, 1953.

Badridze, David (Datiko) Georgievich
4.4.1899–   . Singer (tenor).
Born in Kutaisi. Pupil of E. Vronskii. With the Tbilisi and Sverdlovsk Operas. Soloist with The Bolshoi Theatre, 1944–48. Taught at the Gnesin Pedagogical Institute of Music, Moscow, 1952–61.

Bagirov, M.D.
1905?–1953. Politician, state security officer.
First Secretary of the Cen. Cttee. of the Communist Party of Azerbaidzhan. Non-voting member of the Presidium of the Cen. Cttee. of the CPSU. A close friend and associate of Beria, arrested and executed with him.

Bagramian, Ivan Khristoforovich
2.12.1897–21.9.1982. Marshal.
Born in Elizavetpol in Azerbaidzhan. Son of a worker. Joined the army, 1915. From 1920 in the Red Army, took part in the Civil War. Graduated from the Frunze Military Academy, 1934, and from the Academy of the General Staff, 1938. Became known as a successful front com-

mander during WWII (Kursk, the Baltic, and Köenigsberg). After WWII commander of the Baltic military district. Deputy Defence Minister, 1954. Chief inspector of the Ministry of Defence, and Commander of the rear of the army. Member of the Cen. Cttee. of the CPSU, 1961.

Bagritskii, Eduard Georgievich (Dziuba)
3.11.1895–16.2.1934. Poet.
Born in Odessa. During the Civil War, in Cheka detachments. In the 1920s and 1930s became widely known for his poems glorifying the revolutionary struggle (*Duma pro Opanasa,* etc). Considered a classic of Soviet revolutionary romanticism. Died in Moscow.

Bagrov, Lev Semenovich (Leo)
5.7.1881–9.8.1957. Historian, editor.
Born in Solikamsk. Graduated from Petersburg University, 1903. Professor of navigation in the Petrograd Technical Institute, later at the Geographical Institute in Petrograd. Emigrated to Germany, 1918. Moved to Sweden, 1945. Founded and edited the famous historical and geographical international magazine *Imago Mundi,* 1935–57. Wrote on cartography. Died in the Hague.

Baibakov, Nikolai Konstantinovich
1911–   . State official.
Graduated from the Azerbaidzhan Petroleum Institute, 1932. Director of an oilfield, 1932–37. Member of the CPSU, 1939. Head of the Eastern Oil Drilling Association, Kuibyshev. Head of the Central Eastern Oil Extraction Board, 1937–40. USSR Deputy People's Commissar, then People's Commissar of the Oil Industry, 1946–48. USSR Minister of the Petroleum Industry, 1948–55. Member of the Central Committee of the CPSU, 1952–61, and 1966. Chairman of GOSPLAN, 1955–57. 1st Deputy Chairman of the RSFSR Council of Ministers, 1957–58. Chairman of the Krasnodar Economic Council, and later of the Northern Caucasian Economic Council, 1958–63. Chairman of the GOSPLAN State Committee for Chemistry, then of the Chemical and Petroleum Industry with the rank of Minister of the USSR, 1963–64. Chairman of the GOSPLAN State Committee for the

Petroleum Industry 1964–65. Deputy Chairman of the USSR Council of Ministers and Chairman of GOSPLAN, Oct. 1965 until Nov. 1985. Retired.

Bakaev, Viktor Grigor'evich
21.11.1902–   . Engineer, politician.
Born in Bezhitsa near Briansk. Metal worker, 1913. Educated at the Moscow Institute of Transport Engineers, 1929, later specialized in water transport. During WWII in charge of the sea deliveries of war supplies from Britain to Murmansk, 1943–45. Minister of Soviet Commercial Fleets, 1954–69. Retired, 1970.

Bakaleinikov, Vladimir Romanovich
3.10.1885–5.11.1953. Viola player, conductor.
Born in Moscow. Brother of the flautist Nikolai Bakaleinikov. Member of the Mecklenburg Quartet, 1910–20, and the Stradivarius Quartet, 1920–24. Conductor with the Teatr Muzykal'noi Dramy (Theatre of Musical Drama), 1914–16, and with the MKHAT Music Studio, 1920–27. Professor in Petrograd, 1917–20, and with the Moscow Conservatory, 1920–24. Emigrated, 1925. In the USA from 1927. Died in Pittsburg.
Works: *Notes of a Musician,* NY, 1943.

Bakatin, Aleksandr
1922–1977. Athlete.
Honoured Master of Sports (diving). Won 7th place at the XVth Olympic Games.

Bakhirev, Viacheslav Vasil'evich
1916–   . State official.
Graduated from Moscow State University in 1941. Engineer-constructor, deputy head, later head of a construction bureau. Chief constructor, chief engineer of a plant, 1941–60. Director of a machine-building factory in Vladimir Oblast', 1960–65. 1st Deputy Minister of the Defence Industry, 1965–68. USSR Minister for the Engineering Industry until June 1987. Retired.

Bakhmetev, Boris Aleksandrovich
1880–1951. Engineer, diplomat.
Professor of mechanics. Early in-

volvement in revolutionary activity. At first a Menshevik, later a Cadet. Appointed head of the Russian commission sent to the USA for the purchase of military technology, 1916. Appointed Russian ambassador to the USA by the Provisional Government. Was against both Whites and Reds during the Civil War, promoted the idea of a revolutionary, democratic Russia. Published in English in the USA an informative volume on the history of Russian revolutionary movements, including the period of the February Revolution 1917 (*The Birth of Russian Democracy*). Refused to recognize the Soviet government. Retained the status of ambassador to the USA until 1922. From former Embassy funds created the Bakhmetev Foundation, which played a large part in preserving Russian cultural and historical heritage in the USA, mainly in the large university libraries and archives.

Bakhrakh, Aleksandr Vasil'evich
1902–1985. Journalist, author.
Emigrated after the Civil War. Became known as a journalist and literary critic in the 1920s. Settled in Germany, and later in France. During WWII was hidden by Ivan Bunin from the Germans at his villa in Southern France. In the 1950s–60s worked at Radio Liberty in Munich. Wrote memoirs describing the literary life of Russian emigrés in the West. Died in Israel.

Bakhrushin, Aleksei Aleksandrovich
31.1.1865–7.6.1929. Art collector.
Born in Moscow. Son of a merchant, from a well-known Moscow merchant dynasty (leather industry, later bankers), famous for their charity work (hospitals, homes for the poor and elderly). Representative of the Russian merchant princes (Tretiakov, Morozov) whose capital, artistic taste and passion made possible the amazing flowering of art in late 19th-early 20th century Russia. Collected an extremely rich museum of dramatic art, 1894. Donated his museum to the Russian Academy of Sciences, 1913. The Bakhrushin Theatre Museum in Moscow still remains a unique showcase of theatrical art. Died in Gorkii.

Bakhrushin, Iurii Alekseevich
27.1.1896–4.8.1973. Ballet critic, teacher.
Born in Moscow. Son of Aleksei Bakhrushin, the founder of the Bakhrushin Theatre Museum in Moscow. Worked at the Bolshoi Theatre as a props manager, 1918–24. Head of Productions and Scripts at the Moscow Stanislavskii Opera Theatre, 1924–39. Ballet critic and author of several books about Russian ballet. Died in Moscow.
Books: *Bolshoi Theatre Ballet*, 1947, *History of Russian Ballet*, 1965.

Baklanov, Georgii Andreevich (real name–Bakkis)
4.1.1881–6.12.1938. Singer (baritone).
Born in Riga. Pupil of M. Pets and I. Prianishnikov. Soloist with the Bolshoi Theatre, 1905–09. Guest performances in Western Europe and the USA from 1909. Guest appearances on the Russian stage. Lived abroad from 1915. Died in Basel.

Baksheev, Vasilii Nikolaevich
24.12.1862–28.9.1958. Artist.
Born in Moscow. Studied at the Moscow School of Painting, Sculpture and Architecture, 1878–88 under V. Perov, A. Savrasov, V. Makovskii, V. Polenov. Landscape and genre painter. Member of the Tovarishchestvo Peredvizhnykh Khudozhestvennykh Vystavok from 1896. From 1922 member of the AKHRR, (Association of Artists of Revolutionary Russia). Took part in the following exhibitions: the All-Russian Exhibition, Nizhnii Novgorod, 1896; Mir Iskusstva, 1901; 36 Artists, 1901–03; the 15 Years Anniversary of the RKKA, Moscow, 1933. One-man exhibitions: 1937, 1943, 1947, 1952. Died in Moscow.

Bakst, Leon (Rosenberg, Lev Samoilovich)
8.2.1866–27.12.1924. Painter, stage designer.
Born in Grodno in Belorussia. St. Petersburg in 1909 as a Jew of Arts, 1883–87, and in Paris, 1893. Member of the World of Art group. Worked as a portraitist and book illustrator. Leading stage designer with Diaghilev's Ballets Russes. Left St. Petersburg in 1909 as a Jew without a residence permit. Lived mostly in Paris. With his extremely colourful, exotic and erotic art, became a major influence on world stage design in the 1910s and 1920s. Worked for Ida Rubinstein. Died in Paris.

Bakulev, Aleksandr Nikolaevich
7.12.1890–31.3.1967. Surgeon.
Born in the village of Nevenikovskaia near Viatka. Graduated in medicine from Saratov University, 1915. Specialist in neurosurgery. Became famous during WWII by creating a new school of surgery which specialized in coronary operations. The Moscow Coronary Medical Institute is named after him. Academician, 1958. President of the Academy of Medical Sciences of the USSR, 1953–60. Died in Moscow.

Balanchine, George (Balanchivadze, Georgii Melitonovich)
22.1.1904–1983. Choreographer.
Born in Petersburg. Son of the composer, M. Balanchivadze. Studied at the Petersburg Conservatory. From 1914–21 studied at the Mariinskii (now Kirov) Theatrical School in Petrograd. Choreographer from 1923. Emigrated from Russia, 1924. Worked as a choreographer with Diaghilev until his death in 1929. In 1933 moved to the USA and became the first artistic director of the New York City Ballet, 1948, and a major influence on the development of American ballet after WWII (and American culture in general). Ballets include *Firebird* (1950) and *Don Quixote* (1965). Also choreographed for films and stage musicals.

Balanchivadze, Andrei Melitonovich
1.6.1906–   . Composer.
Born in Petersburg. Brother of George Balanchine. Graduated from the Tbilisi Conservatory, 1927 and Leningrad Conservatory, 1931. Musical director at several theatres in Tbilisi, 1931–34. From the late 1930s one of the best known Georgian composers. Wrote music for many Georgian ballet productions. From 1935 taught at the Tbilisi Conservatory. From 1942 professor at the same conservatory. Chairman, 1953, and First Secretary, 1956–61 and 1968–72, of the Union of Composers of the Georgian SR.

Balanchivadze, Meliton Antonovich
24.12.1862–21.11.1937. Composer.
Born in a village near Tskhaltubo, Georgia. Father of George Balanchine and Andrei Balanchivadze. Early musical training at the Tiflis Seminary, 1877–79. Studied singing under V. Aushev. Operatic singer from 1880. Collected and edited folk songs. Organized an ethnographic choir, 1882. Studied at the Petersburg Conservatory from 1889. Pupil of N. Rimskii-Korsakov and I. Iogansen. Gave Georgian concerts in Petersburg and other Russian cities, in Poland, the Baltic Provinces and Georgia, 1895-1917. After the October Revolution 1917 concentrated on the social aspects of musical life in Georgia. Founded the School of Music in Kutaisi, 1918 (now called after him). With Z. Paliashvili and D. Arakishvili, laid the foundation of classical Georgian music. Composed the first Georgian opera, *Daredzhan Tsbieri*, 1897. Died in Kutaisi.

Balandin, Aleksei Aleksandrovich
8.12.1898–22.5.1967. Organic chemist.
Graduated from Moscow University, 1923. Professor at the University, 1934. Academician, 1946. Research concerning the multiple theory of catalysis. Specialist in the kinetics of organic catalytic reactions.

Balboshin, Nikolai Fedorovich
8.6.1949– . Athlete.
Born in Potsdam, GDR, son of an officer in the Soviet army of occupation. Honoured Master of Sports (wrestling), 1973. Studied at the Moscow Institute of Physical Culture. Olympic champion, 1976 (light-heavy weight). World, European and USSR champion, 1973–79.

Baldycheva, Nina Viktorovna (Fedorova)
18.7.1947– . Athlete.
Born in the village of Travino, Pskov Oblast'. Graduated from the Leningrad High School of Physical Culture, 1972. Honoured Master of Sports (skiing), 1970. Olympic champion, 1976. World champion, 1970, 1974. USSR champion, 1969–76.

Balmont, Konstantin Dmitrievich
16.6.1867–23.12.1942. Poet.
Born in the village of Gumnishchi, Vladimir Gouvt. Son of a landowner. Studied at Moscow University, expelled for revolutionary activity, 1887. Started to write verse in the narodnik vein, 1890, but soon became an early and most influential symbolist poet, 1895, especially with the book *Budem, Kak Solntse*, 1903. Gained a very fashionable reputation with his extremely sonorous and exotic verse. At one time the most popular poet in Russia. Travelled around the world, translated poetry from many languages into Russian. After the revolution emigrated, 1920, settled in France. Continued to write and publish verse, but gradually lost his popularity. Now remembered more as a facile versifier, than as a true poet, though some of his later work in exile rings with true suffering and deep emotion. Died near Paris. Main works: *Collected Works*, 10 vol., Moscow, 1908–13.

Baltrushaitis, Iurgis Kazimirovich (Baltrusaitis, Jurgis)
2.5.1873–3.1.1944. Poet.
Born near Kovno (Kaunas) in Lithuania. Symbolist poet, wrote in Russian and Lithuanian. Printed his works in the Symbolist magazine, *Vesy*, collaborator in the publishing house Skorpion. Close to Briusov. Employed by Narkompros (Ministry of Education), 1918–20. At the end of 1920 was appointed Lithuanian Ambassador to the Soviet Union. In this exalted position was able to help many of his former friends and colleagues. Moved to Western Europe 1939, settled in France, where he lived and died as a political exile.

Baltsvinik, Mikhail Abramovich
2.2.1931–13.4.1980. Journalist.
Born in Leningrad. Son of a doctor. During WWII evacuated with his parents to Tashkent, 1941–45. Studied journalism at Leningrad University, 1949–54. Worked in provincial newspapers in Kirghizia and Chuvashia. Returned to Leningrad, 1957. Became one of the most influential representatives of the Leningrad underground culture. Collected a unique literary and photographic archive. Persecuted by the KGB in the 1960s and 1970s. Committed suicide.

Balukhatyi, Sergei Dmitrievich
24.3.1893–2.4.1945. Literary scholar.
Born in Feodosia. Professor of Samara University, 1919–23, professor of Leningrad University, 1923–45. Researcher at the Institute of Russian Literature of the Soviet Academy of Sciences (Pushkinskii dom). Died in Leningrad.

Bandera, Stepan Andreevich (Popiel)
1.1.1909–15.10.1959. Ukrainian nationalist leader.
Born in Ugryniv Staryi, West Ukraine (then in the Austro-Hungarian Empire). Son of a Greek-Catholic priest. After WWI became involved in underground Ukrainian nationalist youth groups (directed against the Polish authorities in Galicia). Studied in the agricultural department of the technical college in Lvov (then Poland), 1928. Chairman of the Executive of the OUN (Organization of Ukrainian Nationalists) in the Ukraine, 1933. Organized the assassination of the Polish Minister of the Interior, Pieracki, in Warsaw, June 1934. Arrested 1934, and sentenced to death. Sentence commuted to life imprisonment. After the collapse of Poland at the beginning of WWII, released. Elected leader of the OUN in the Ukraine and abroad, 1941. At the beginning of German-Soviet hostilities, supporters of Bandera in Lvov proclaimed Ukrainian independence, 30 June 1941, but soon thereafter he was arrested by the Germans, brought to a prison in Berlin, and later to Sachsenhausen concentration camp (his two brothers died at Auschwitz). At the end of 1944 he and other Ukrainian nationalist leaders were released by the Germans. After WWII resumed control of the Ukrainian partisans (now fighting the Soviet army) from abroad, while living under an assumed name in Munich. Assassinated by a KGB agent on the personal instructions of the head of the KGB Shelepin by a special poison bullet (his murder was later described in detail by the murderer himself, Bohdan Stashynskyi, who defected to West Germany in 1961). Buried in Munich.

Banionis, Donatas Iuozovich
28.4.1924– . Film actor.
At the age of 14 joined the theatre of

the Lithuanian town of Panavezhis. Studied under the director Miltinis, a pupil of Charles Dullen. Became an actor at the same theatre in 1941. Worked mainly with the leading Lithuanian director Zhalakiavichius. First film of note was *No One Wanted to Die* (1966 by Zhalakiavichius) with which he won a prize at the Karlovy Vary Film Festival. Became known as the Duke of Albany in Grigorii Kozintsev's *King Lear*. Played Kris Kelvin in Andrei Tarkovskii's *Solaris*. Other films: *The Red Tent* (director M. Kalatozov, Mosfilm, 1969), *Goya* (Konrad Wolf, Soviet-GDR co-production, 1972), *Captain Jack* (Riga Film Studios, 1973). Winner of a USSR State Prize in 1974.

Barabanov, Evgenii Viktorovich
1943–   . Historian, dissident.
Born in Leningrad. Graduated in history from Moscow University. Essays on historical, cultural and religious subjects circulated in samizdat. Some were published in the West, including one in Solzhenitsyn's collection of articles, *Iz pod glyb*, Paris, 1974.

Barabash, Tat'iana Borisovna (Averina)
25.6.1950–   . Athlete.
Born in Gorkii. Graduated from the Moscow Institute of Physical Culture, 1976. Honoured Master of Sports (skating), 1976. Coach from 1977. Member of the CPSU, 1977. Olympic champion, 1976 (1,000 metres and 3,000 metres). World champion, 1978 (1,000 and 1,500 metres). USSR champion, 1979.

Baranov, Petr Ionovich
22.9.1892–5.9.1933. Politician.
Born in Petersburg. Son of a worker. Joined the Bolsheviks, 1912. During WWI in the army, sentenced to 8 years of exile for revolutionary propaganda, 1916. Released after the February Revolution 1917. Active Bolshevik agitator. Joined the Red Army, 1918. Several high positions as commander or commissar during the Civil War. Commander of the Red tank detachments, 1923. Commander of the Red Air Force, 1924. Head of the Soviet aviation industry, 1932. Died in an aircrash. Buried in Moscow at the Kremlin wall.

Baranov, Vladimir Mikhailovich
1901–   . Artist.
Miniature and icon painter. Studied at the Safonov's Icon Art School in Palekh, the centre of miniature and icon art in Russia and the Soviet Union. Exhibitions: The Art of Palekh, Moscow, 1939; Art Works of Applied Folk Art and Art Industry, Moscow, 1952; Thirty Years of the Art of Palekh, Moscow, 1955. Produced many Palekh boxes which are on sale all over the world.

Baranova, Liubov Vladimirovna (Kozyreva)
27.8.1929–   . Athlete.
Born in the village of Bugrym, Leningrad Oblast'. Graduated from the Leningrad Institute of Physical Culture, 1958. Honoured Master of Sports (skiing), 1954. Coach, Leningrad, 1957. Member of the CPSU, 1976. Olympic champion, 1956. World champion, 1954. USSR champion, 1950–58.

Baranovskaia, Vera Fedorovna
1885–7.12.1935. Film actress.
Remembered for her leading role in V. Pudovkin's film, *Mother* (Mat'), 1926. Actress in the theatre until 1915. Trained at the MKHAT. Acted in V. Pudovkin's *The End of St Petersburg* (Konets Peterburga), 1927. From 1928 lived in Prague. Moved to Paris where she died. She became a 'non-person' after her emigration, despite her powerful performance in *Mother*. After Stalin's death her name began to be mentioned again in the Soviet press.

Baranskii, Nikolai Nikolaevich
26.7.1881–29.11.1963. Geographer.
Studied at Tomsk University, expelled for revolutionary activity, 1901. During the 1905 Revolution Bolshevik organizer in Irkutsk. Graduated from the Moscow Commercial Institute, 1914. Prepared text books and university courses on economic geography.

Baratov, Leonid Vasil'evich
1.4.1895–22.7.1964. Conductor, theatrical producer.
Born in Moscow. Professor at the A. V. Lunacharskii Institute of Dramatic Art. Producer at the Bolshoi Theatre from 1943. Chief pro-

ducer with the K. S. Stanislavskii and V. I. Nemirovich-Danchenko Theatre from 1950. Died in Moscow.

Barinov, Aleksandr Ivanovich
1884–1960. Major-general.
Active participant in the Civil War. Took part in the conquest of Bukhara by the Red Army. Graduated from the Frunze Military Academy, 1936. Later professor at this academy. Head of the Military Pedagogical Institute, 1941–46.

Barinov, Valerii
1945–   . Musician.
Christian rock musician. Composed the rock musical *Trubnyi zov*. Came into conflict with the KGB. Served two and a half years in a labour camp. Became a focus of international pressure on the Soviet authorities. The British Prime Minister, Margaret Thatcher, passed a letter from Barinov to Gorbachev when she visited the Soviet Union. Released, 1987, and emigrated to Britain.

Barinova, Galina Vsevolodovna
20.10.1910–   . Violinist.
Born in Petersburg. Daughter of M.N. Barinova. Pupil of V. Zavetnovskii and J. Thibaud. Teacher at the Moscow Conservatory. State Prize, 1949.

Barinova, Maria Nikolaevna
30.3.1878–18.10.1956. Pianist.
Born in Petersburg. Pupil of F. Busoni. Taught at the Petersburg/Leningrad Conservatory, 1907–29. Professor from 1911. Author of works on piano methodology. Memoirs: *Vospominaniia o I. Gofmane i F. Busoni*, Moscow, 1964. Died in Leningrad.

Bark, Petr Lvovich
18.4.1869–16.1.1937. Banker, statesman.
Born in Ekaterinoslav. Graduated from Petersburg University, 1892. Director of several large Russian banks. Last Imperial Finance Minister, 1914–17. Member of the State Council (Upper Chamber). Emigrated to Britain after the Bolshevik takeover. Continued his banking career as a director of a London bank. Died in London.

Barkalov, Aleksei Stepanovich
18.2.1946– . Athlete.
Born in the village of Vvedenka, Chuguev district, Kharkov Oblast'. Honoured Master of Sports (water polo), 1970. With Kiev Dynamo, 1972. Graduated from Kharkov Polytechnical Institute, 1972. Electrical engineer. Olympic champion, 1972. Silver medal (Olympic Games), 1968. World champion, 1975. European champion, 1970. USSR champion, 1971.

Barkhudarov, Stepan Grigor'evich
7.3.1894–1970? Linguistic scholar.
Born in Baku. Professor at Leningrad University, 1932. Author of many works on Russian linguistics. Editor of the 17 volume *Dictionary of Contemporary Literary Russian Language,* 1948–65.

Barkova, Anna Aleksandrovna
1901–1976. Journalist.
Born in Ivanovo-Voznessensk. Published a book of verse, *Zhenshchina,* in the 1920s. Became the secretary of A. Lunacharskii. Arrested, 1934, inmate of Gulag for 6 years. Re-arrested in 1947, and sentenced to 10 years. After Stalin's death, released and rehabilitated, 1955. Again arrested for alleged anti-Soviet verse and diaries, 1957. Released and rehabilitated for a second time in 1965. Lived thereafter in Moscow.

Barmin, Aleksandr Grigor'evich
1899–1987. Diplomat.
Rose through the ranks of the Red Army to Brigadier-general. Consul at Reshd in Persia. In 1935, 1st Secretary at the Soviet Legation in Athens. In 1937 fled to Paris. Denounced Stalin. Appealed for action to save the lives of other Soviet diplomats. In 1940 moved to the USA. Served as a private in the US Army. Married President Roosevelt's granddaughter, Edith. Contributed to *Readers Digest* and *Saturday Evening Post,* and to the Russian Service of Voice of America. In 1951, denounced the Head of Section as a Russian spy, and 2 years later secured the post for himself. Died in the USA.

Barnet, Boris Vasil'evich
18.6.1902–8.1.1965. Film director.
His grandfather was Thomas Barnet, an Englishman who settled in Russia in the 19th century, and started a printing business. Graduated from the Higher Military School of Physical Education. Once appeared in a boxing ring. Studied at the State Technical School of Cinematography under Lev Kuleshov. Appeared as an actor in Kuleshov's films. His first film was *Miss Mend,* 1926, (with F. Otsep). Two comedies followed, *Girl with the Hatbox,* and *House on Trubnaia Square,* 1927–28. He made three films in the 1930s: *Thaw, Outskirts* (in which he experimented with sound and music), and *The Bluest of Seas.* During the Stalinist period when films were tightly controlled, he did virtually nothing. Became very depressed, which led to alcoholism. Committed suicide. His earlier films became internationally recognized classics of the early and best period of experimental Soviet cinema. During his life, remained in total obscurity in his own country and was unknown in the West. Rediscovered in the late 1970s. Two major seasons of his films took place in the UK in 1979 and 1980. Rediscovered at last in his own country. Several books have since been written about his work in the USSR.

Baron, Krishianis Iur'evich
31.10.1835–8.3.1923. Writer, politician.
Published a monumental collection of Latvian folk songs in 6 volumes, 1894–1915. Published in Petersburg the first left-wing Latvian newspaper, *Peterburgas Avizes,* 1862–65. Early Latvian nationalist leader. After 1917 lived in Latvia. Died in Riga.

Baronova, Irina
13.3.1919– . Ballerina.
Born in Petrograd. Moved with her family to France after the October Revolution 1917. Pupil of O. Preobrazhenskaia in Paris. With Les Ballets Russes de Monte Carlo, 1932, and the Ballet Theatre, 1941–42. Soloist in Leonid Miasin's productions, and also with Bronislava Nizhinskaia and Mikhail Fokin. Performed with Ballets Russes High Lights, 1945 and the Original Ballet Russe, 1946. Starred in films and musicals, 1942–46. Member of the Royal Academy of Dance, London.

Barshai, Rudolf Borisovich
28.9.1924– . Viola player, conductor.
Born in the Krasnodarsk district. Pupil of V. Borisovskii. Organiser and director of the Moscow Chamber Orchestra, 1956. Defected, 1970s. Principal conductor of the Bournemouth Symphony Orchestra.

Barsova, Valeria Vladimirovna (real name–Vladimirova)
13.6.1892–13.12.1967. Singer (soprano).
Born in Astrakhan'. Pupil of her sister, V. Vladimirova, and of U. Mazetti. Soloist with the Bolshoi Theatre, 1920–48. People's Artist of the USSR, 1937. State (Stalin) Prize, 1941. Stalin's favourite singer at the Bolshoi. Died in Sochi.

Barsukov, Evgenii Zakharovich
1866–1957. Major-general.
Studied at the Academy of the General Staff, 1895. During WWI on active service, as Major-general in the artillery. Joined the Red Army, 1918. Commander of the (Red) Minsk military district during the Civil War, 1918–19. Wrote a 4 vol. history of Russian artillery, *Artilleriia Russkoi Armii.*

Bart, Viktor Sergeevich
20.4.1887–27.5.1954. Artist.
Born in the village of Velichaevo near Stavropol'. Studied at the St. Petersburg Academy of Fine Arts. In 1919 emigrated to Paris. Took part in several exhibitions of Russian painters. In 1936 returned to Moscow. Worked as a book illustrator. Died in Moscow.

Bartini, Robert Ludvigovich
1897–1974. Aircraft designer, scientist.
Born in Italy. Member of the Italian Communist Party, 1921. Came to the Soviet Union, 1923. Designed 10 experimental types of aircraft (the arctic exploration plane Stal' and others). Has published books on aerodynamics, and theoretical physics.

Barvinskii, Vasilii Aleksandrovich
20.2.1888–9.6.1963. Composer, pianist.
Born in Tarnopol'. Director of the N.

V. Lysenko Institute for Higher Musical Studies, 1915–39. Director of and professor at the Lvov Conservatory (piano and composition), 1939–48. Suffered illegal arrest and was a Gulag inmate, 1948–58. Accused of Ukrainian nationalism. Returned to Lvov, 1958. Died in Lvov.

Barysheva, Olga Fedorovna
24.8.1954– . Athlete.
Born in Sverdlovsk. Honoured Master of Sports (basket-ball), 1976. Studied at the Sverdlovsk Pedagogical Institute. Olympic champion, 1976. World champion, 1975. European champion, 1974, 1976.

Baryshnikov, Mikhail
1948– . Ballet dancer, choreographer.
Son of a Soviet Army colonel who disapproved of his son's profession. His mother committed suicide when he was a child. In 1974, defected while on tour with the Kirov Ballet in Canada. Settled in America. Joined the American Ballet Theatre. Resigned in 1978. Joined the New York City Ballet, then run by the ailing George Balanchine. Danced 22 new roles. In 1979 returned to the ABT as an artistic director. Was accused of choosing bad ballets, surrounding himself with mediocrities, alienating many fine performers and ducking responsibilities. Occasionally acted in films and TV productions (*The Gershwin Years*, BBC2, July 1987). Has a daughter, Aleksandra, whose mother is the American actress Jessica Lange. Considered now as one of the finest male ballet dancers in the world.

Baryshnikov, Vladimir Arkhipovich
1889–1919. Worker, revolutionary.
Born in Orekhovo-Zuevo. Revolutionary organizer of textile workers in his home town. Organized a mass strike (70,000) during the 1905 Revolution. After the February Revolution 1917, mayor of Orekhovo-Zuevo. In October 1917, brought Red Guard worker groups from his town to Moscow to help the Bolsheviks. During the Civil War political commissar with the Reds. Taken prisoner by Gen. Mamontov's troops and hanged by the White Cossacks.

Basanavicius, Jonas
23.11.1851–16.2.1927. Politician, writer, historian.
Born in the village of Ozhkabalai near Vylkovyshki in Lithuania. Graduated in medicine from Moscow University, 1879. Moved to Bulgaria, where he worked as a doctor. Returned to Lithuania, 1905. Founded the first Lithuanian newspaper, *Ausra*, 1883 (published illegally in East Prussia). Director of the Ethnographical Museum in Wilno (Vilnius), 1919. Collected and published 9 volumes of Lithuanian folk songs and fairy tales. Widely respected Lithuanian nationalist leader. Died in Wilno.

Bashashkin, Anatolii Vasil'evich
23.2.1924– . Athlete.
Born in Reutovo, Moscow Oblast'. Honoured Master of Sports (football), 1955. Graduated from the Military Academy of Armoured Troops, 1963. Military mechanical engineer. Member of the CPSU, 1968. From 1953 with Spartak. Olympic champion, 1956. USSR champion, 1948, 1950–51, 1953.

Basil (Colonel de Basil; Voskresenskii, Vasilii Grigor'evich)
1888–27.7.1951. Ballet impresario.
Born in Kaunas. From 1925 one of the organizers of Russian Opera Seasons in Paris. Set up (with René Blum) Les Ballets Russes de Monte Carlo based on the Ballet Russe of the Opera Theatre of Monte Carlo and Diaghilev's Ballets Russes, 1931–36. George Balanchine and Leonid Miasin worked for the company as well as many distinguished Russian ballet stars. After the split with Blum, set up the Ballets Russes de Colonel Basil, then the Educational Ballet, the Original Ballet Russe, and the Covent Garden Ballet Russe, 1936–39. All his companies toured Europe, America and Latin America, and performed with huge success in England. Died in Paris.

Basistyi, Nikolai Efremovich
22.5.1898–1971. Admiral.
Born in the village of Iurievka near Odessa. Joined the Black Sea Navy, 1915. Fought with the Reds during the Civil War on the Volga and in the Caspian Sea, 1918–21. Received higher naval education in the 1930s.

During WWII commander in the Black Sea Navy, rising to Commander-in-chief, 1948. Deputy Commander of the Soviet Navy, 1951. Retired, 1960.

Basov, Nikolai Gennad'evich
14.12.1922– . Physicist.
Born in Voronezh. Educated at the Moscow Engineering-Technical Institute, 1950. Member of the Institute of Physics of the Academy of Sciences of the USSR, 1950. Professor at the Moscow Engineering-Technical Institute, 1963. Pioneering work in the creation of lasers. One of the foremost world authorities in this field. Nobel prize for physics, 1964.

Basova, Irina Borisovna (Zaborova)
1937– . Journalist, editor.
Born in Leningrad. Daughter of the Soviet poet B. Kornilov, who perished in the Gulag. Graduated from Moscow University. Lived in Minsk. Emigrated in 1980 with her husband, the artist B. Zaborov. Settled in France.

Batalov, Aleksei Vladimirovich
20.11.1928– . Actor, director.
Born in Vladimir. Son of the famous actor, Vladimir Batalov. His uncle was Nikolai Batalov, a very popular film actor in the 1930s. His mother, Nina Ol'shevskaia, was an actress and director. Graduated from the Actors' Studio at the Moscow Arts Theatre in 1950. Acted in the Theatre of the Soviet Army, 1950–53, and in the Moscow Arts Theatre, 1953–56. First film, *The Big Family,* in 1954. Played his uncle's part of Pavel Vlasov in the Soviet classic film, *Mother* (after Maxim Gorkii's story) in 1956 directed by Mark Donskoi. Became famous in *The Cranes Are Flying* (director Mikhail Kalatozov, 1957) opposite Tat'iana Samoilova. The film received a prize at the Cannes Film Festival. Other films: *The Lady With the Little Dog* (Lenfilm, director Iosif Kheifits, 1960); *Nine Days of One Year* (director Mikhail Romm, Mosfilm, 1962), which was a sensation in the Soviet Union; *Three Fat Men* (as director, Lenfilm, 1967); *The Living Corpse* (Lenfilm, 1969); *The Flight* (Mosfilm, 1971, directors A. Alov and V. Naumov); *A Very English Murder* (Mosfilm, 1975).

Batalov, Nikolai Petrovich
6.12.1899–10.11.1937. Film actor.
Actor at the 2nd MKHAT Studio from 1916. Joined MKHAT, 1924. Entered the film industry in 1924. Acted in *Aelita*. Best known for his leading role in V. Pudovkin's classic film, *Mother*. His last film was *Putevka v Zhizn'*, 1931. The cause of his early death is not known.

Batitskii, Pavel Fedorovich
27.6.1910–17.2.1984. Marshal.
Born in Khar'kov. Son of a worker. Educated at a cavalry school, 1929. Graduated from the Frunze Military Academy, 1938. Academy of the General Staff, 1948. Took part in WWII. After the war, held high command posts in air defence and air force systems. Commander-in-chief of Air Defence and Deputy Minister of Defence, 1966. Member of Cen. Cttee. of the CPSU, 1966. According to the Soviet paper *Nedelia* (weekly supplement of *Izvestia*), Feb. 1988, he personally carried out the death sentence on the secret police chief, Beria, who begged him on his knees to spare his life.

Batiukov, Isaak Polievktovich
1863–1934. Artist.
Studied at the Moscow School of Painting, Sculpture and Architecture, 1886–1903. Also at F. Kormon's studio in Paris and the Petersburg Academy of Arts, 1899–1903. Genre painter. Taught at Iaroslavl' Art School. Exhibitions: TPKHV, 1901–03; Iaroslavl' Arts Society, 1912. A posthumous exhibition of his works was held in Iaroslavl' in 1937.

Batiushkov, Fedor Dmitrievich
1857–1920. Literary scholar.
Appointed by the Provisional Government successor to the Imperial Director of the Petersburg Theatres. After the Bolshevik takeover, Nov. 1917, replaced by Lunacharskii.

Batov, Pavel Ivanovich
1.6.1897–1985. General.
Born in the village of Filisovo, Iaroslavl' Gouvt. Son of a peasant. Joined the army, 1915. Joined the Red Army, 1918. Sent to Spain during the Civil War, wounded. Participated in the Soviet-Finnish war, 1939-40. Prominent front commander during WWII (Stalingrad, Kursk, Berlin). Deputy commander of Soviet occupation forces in East Germany. Chief-of-staff of the Warsaw Pact 1962–65. Chairman of the Soviet War Veterans Cttee, 1970–81. Highly decorated (5 Orders of Lenin). Wrote several volumes of memoirs, mainly concerning WWII.

Bauer, Evgenii Frantsevich
1865–22.7.1917. Film director.
One of the first distinguished directors of Russian silent cinema. Graduated from the Moscow School of Painting, Sculpture and Architecture. Started making films in 1912. Worked with various famous actors, such as Vera Kholodnaya, Ivan Mozzhukhin, and V. Polonskii. Films: *Sumerki Zhenskoi Dushi*, 1913; *Iamshchik Ne Goni Loshadei*, 1916; *Korol' Parizha*, 1916. His films are now considered silent classics and are kept at the State Film Archive.

Baumvol, Rakhil' Lvovna
1914– . Author.
Born in Odessa. Published books for children in the Soviet Union from the 1930s. Became involved in the human rights movement in the 1960s. Gave V. Bukovskii a job as her private secretary to protect him from accusations of parasitism, 1969. Emigrated to Israel, 1971.

Bazhan, Mykola (Nikolai Platonovich)
9.10.1904– . Poet.
Born in Kamenets-Podolskii. Began writing in the 1920s. Became a well known literary establishment figure in the Ukraine. Joined the Communist Party, 1940. Academician of the Ukrainian Academy of Sciences, 1951. Highly decorated.

Bazhanov, Boris
1900– . Politician, author.
Born in Mogilev-Podolskii in the Ukraine. Studied at Kiev University. Joined the Communist Party, 1919. Moved to Moscow. Studied at the Higher Technical School, Moscow, 1920. Worked in the administrative department of the Central Cttee. of the Bolshevik Party under Kaganovich, 1922. Was a ghost-writer for Bolshevik leaders. Wrote Kaganovich's first published article. Author of a new version of the Communist Party statute that was noticed by Stalin and published under Molotov's name, 1922. Secretary of the Orgburo, 1923. Appointed Stalin's personal secretary in Aug. 1923, and became in practice the secretary of the Politburo. As such had an opportunity to observe closely (according to his memoirs) the *mafiosi* methods of his boss in dealing with friends, comrades and enemies. Thought it wise to distance himself from this dangerous spot. Moved to two other jobs – in the High Council for Sport and in the Ministry of Finance. Editor of *Finansovaia Gazeta*, 1926. Sent himself on a business trip to Soviet Central Asia. Fled from Ashkhabad to Persia, (1 Jan. 1928). Crossed the border to Iran while the border guards were drunk after a New Year party. After an adventurous journey, managed to escape from the GPU agent Agabekov, who had been sent by Stalin to hunt him down. Eventually arrived in Simla, British India. Moved to Europe. Settled in France. After WWII lived in Britain. Published valuable historical memoirs, describing his colourful career and the internal decision-making machine in the Kremlin in the 1920s: *Vospominaniia byvshego sekretaria Stalina* (Memoirs by Stalin's Former Secretary), France, 1980.

Bazhanov, Iurii Pavlovich
23.4.1905–1975. Marshal.
Born in Kazatin near Kiev. Son of a railway worker. Joined the Red Army, 1920. Artillery officer. Made his name as a commander of Katiusha batteries in WWII, 1942–45. After WWII served as an artillery commander in the Far East.

Bazhov, Pavel Petrovich
27.1.1879–3.12.1950. Writer.
Born at Sysertskii zavod near Ekaterinburg. Educated at Perm' Seminary, 1899. Worked as a teacher in the Urals, where he gathered local folklore and made his name as a writer of stories in a quasi fairy tale, folklore style. Died in Moscow.

Bazhukov, Nikolai Serafimovich
23.7.1953–   . Athlete.
Born in the village of Troitsko-Pechersk, Komi ASSR. Honoured Master of Sports (skiing), 1976. Olympic champion, 1976 (15km race). USSR champion, 1974, 1976–78.

Bazilevich, Georgii Dmitrievich
26.1.1889–3.3.1939. Military commander.
Born in the village of Kriski near Chernigov. Son of a peasant. Educated at the Kiev Military School, 1910. Took part in WWI as a Lt-colonel. In 1917 Menshevik, later joined the Bolsheviks. Red commander during the Civil War. He defeated the White Cossacks under Nazarov, sent by Wrangel to the Northern Caucasus, 1920. In the early 1920s commanded detachments used for the confiscation of valuables belonging previously to the Crown, church or private persons. High military posts in the early 1930s. Arrested during Stalin's purge of the Red Army. Disappeared, probably shot.

Bazovskii, Vladimir Nikolaevich
1917–   . Politician, diplomat.
Began as a locksmith, and designer in various factories, 1932–41. Member of the CPSU, 1942. Served in the Soviet Army until 1946. Graduated from the Leningrad Institute of Refrigeration Engineering, 1947. Party administration posts. 1st Secretary of a raion Komsomol Cttee., Leningrad. Deputy Head of Leningrad City CPSU Cttee, Inspector, then Section Head of the Cen. Cttee. of the CPSU until 1961. 1st Secretary of Novgorod Oblast CPSU Cttee. until 1972. Candidate member, 1961–76, and full member of the Cen. Cttee. of the CPSU, 1962–74. Soviet Ambassador to Bulgaria, 1972–82. Soviet Ambassador to Hungary, 1982–86. Head of the main State Customs Control Board, 1987.

Begma, Vasilii Andreevich
14.1.1906–12.8.1965. Politician, partisan leader.
Born in Odessa. Komsomol, trade union and party posts in the 1920s and 1930s. Secretary of the underground Rovno Party Cttee. during the German occupation. Member of the Cen. Cttee. of the underground Ukrainian Communist Party. Head of the partisan detachments around Rovno, 1941–45. Several party posts after WWII. Involved in the re-stalinization of the Ukraine. Died in Kiev.

Begun, Iosif
1933–   . Dissident, Hebrew teacher.
One of the first 'refuseniks'. Tried to exercise his right to emigrate in Apr. 1971 and lost his job as a mathematician at one of the scientific research institutes of GOSPLAN, where he was employed. Pioneer of the Hebrew teaching movement in the USSR. He was arrested as a parasite and sent to Siberian labour camps. Spent 7 years in prison. Brought several libel cases against Soviet journalists and their respective papers. After a 16-year-long international campaign left the USSR for Israel in Dec. 1987.

Bei-Bienko, Grigorii Iakovlevich
7.2.1903–5.11.1971. Entomologist.
Born in Belopol'e near Kharkov. Graduated from the Omsk Agricultural Institute, 1925. Specialist in locusts and cockroaches. President of the Soviet Entomological Society, 1966.

Beibutov, Rashid Madzhid ogly
14.12.1915–   . Singer (tenor).
Born in Nagornyi Karabakh. Member of the family of the folk singer Khanende. Star singer of the variety stage, singing folk songs by Soviet and foreign composers. Has appeared in operas. Appeared in the film *Arshin Mal Alan*, 1946. His reputation grew, and Stalin personally gave him a prize, 1946.

Beilis, Mendel
1874–1934. Construction worker.
Junior manager of a brick factory in Kiev. Became the victim of an attempt by anti-Semitic circles to revive the medieval blood ritual accusation against Jews. Accused of the murder of a young boy, Andrei Iushchinskii, found with multiple stab-wounds. The Beilis trial in Kiev, 1913, attracted the best defence lawyers of the time (Maklakov, Gruzenberg, Kistiakovskii). The jury, composed of local peasants, found the accused not guilty.

Bek, Aleksandr Alfredovich
1903–1972. Author, journalist.
Born in Saratov. During the Civil War fought with the Reds. Became a well known journalist in the 1920s. WWII war correspondent, and author of novels. Editor of the almanac *Literaturnaia Moskva*. During the Khrushchev thaw, wrote an anti-Stalinist novel *Novoe Naznachenie*, which was announced for publication in the magazine *Novyi Mir* in 1965, but did not appear. It was later published in West Germany, 1971, attracting world wide attention.

Bekman-Shcherbina, Elena Aleksandrovna (Kamentseva)
12.1.1882–30.9.1951. Pianist.
Born in Moscow. Pupil of V. Safonov. Taught at the Moscow Conservatory, 1921–30, later at the Central Pedagogical Correspondence Institute for Music. Professor from 1940. Author of *Moi Vospominaniia*, Moscow, 1962. Died in Moscow.

Bek-Nazarov, Amo Ivanovich (real name – Beknazarian, Ambartsum)
31.5.1892–27.4.1965. Film director, actor, scriptwriter.
While a student at the Moscow Commercial Institute, started appearing in films as an actor under the name of Amo Bek. In 1915–19 played romantic parts in films by E. Bauer, V. Gardin, P. Chardynin, and I. Perestiani. Returned to Georgia, and in 1921 headed the film section of Narkompros in Tbilisi. Director and artistic director of Goskinprom in Georgia where he produced his first films, *U Pozornogo Stolba* and *Propavshie Sokrovishcha*, both 1924. His big success was *Namus,* 1926, followed by *Zare*, and a comedy, *Shor i Shorshor*, 1927. With Armenkino and Azgoskino, made the first Armenian revolutionary films – *Khas-Push*, 1928, and *Dom na Vulkane,* 1929. One of the founders of the Vostokkino Studio. Several of his films were made there. His major success was *Pepo*, 1935. Armenfilm Studio was renamed in 1965 in his honour.

Belavskii, Sergei Ivanovich
7.12.1883–13.10.1953. Astronomer.
Born in Petersburg. Graduated from Petersburg University, 1906. Director of Pulkovo Observatory, 1937–44.

Compiled the *Astrographical Catalogue of Stars* (which describes 11,322 stars),1947. Died in Leningrad.

Beliaev, Mikhail Alekseevich
23.2.1863–1918. General, minister.
Graduated from the Academy of the General Staff, 1893. Staff officer during the Russo-Japanese war, 1904–05. Chief of the General Staff, 1916. Representative of the Russian Army in Rumania, 1916. Last Defence Minister of the Tsarist government, Jan.-Feb. 1917. Arrested after the February Revolution 1917. Released after the October Revolution 1917, but soon re-arrested and executed.

Beliaev, Nikolai Il'ich
1903–10.1966. Politician.
Joined the Bolshevik Party, 1921. Secretary of Novosibirsk obkom, 1940–43, and of the Altai Cttee., 1943–55. Member of the Cen. Cttee., 1952–61. Member of the Presidium of the Cen. Cttee., 1957–60. 1st secretary of the Kazakhstan Cen. Cttee., 1957–60. After a bad harvest, sacked by Khrushchev, and sent as Secretary to the Stavropol Territorial Cttee., 1960. Purged in June, 1960.

Beliaev, Spartak Timofeevich
27.10.1923–   . Nuclear physicist.
Born in Moscow. Graduated from Moscow University, 1952. Worked at the Kurchatov Institute of Nuclear Energy, 1952–62. Moved to the Nuclear Physics Institute of the Siberian Department of the Academy of Sciences, 1962. Dean of Novosibirsk University, 1965.

Beliaev, Vladimir Ivanovich
7.12.1944–   . Athlete.
Born in Michurinsk, Tambov Oblast'. Honoured Master of Sports (volleyball), 1968. Graduated from the Voroshilovgrad Pedagogical Institute, 1969. Coach. Olympic champion, 1968. European and USSR champion, 1967.

Beliakov, Rostislav Appolonovich
1919–   . Aircraft designer.
Graduated from Ordzhonikidze Aviation Institute, Moscow 1941. Worked as an engineer, Deputy Chief, and Chief Designer in a KB of the Institute of Aviation Industry

attached to the Ministry of Defence. Member of the CPSU, 1944. Stalin Prize, 1952. From 1971 Chief Designer at the Mikoian Aircraft Bureau designing Soviet MIGs and other aircraft. Lenin Prize, 1972. Doctor of Technical Science, 1973. Corresponding member of the Academy of Sciences, 1974. Lives in Moscow.

Beliakov, Vladimir Timofeevich
2.1.1918–   . Athlete.
Born in Dmitrov, Moscow Oblast'. Honoured Master of Sports (gymnastics), 1947. With Moscow Dynamo. RSFSR Honoured Coach from 1960. Referee (international category), 1962. Graduated from the Moscow Institute of Physical Culture, 1951. Olympic champion, 1952. USSR champion, 1939–47.

Belinder, Shmaia
1914–   . Kremlin tailor.
Born in the Ukraine into a poor Jewish family of tailors. Educated at a Jewish school. In the Soviet Army during WWII. Leading tailor for the Stanislavskii Theatre, 1945–82. Exclusive tailor of the Kremlin VIPs. Among his clients were Iliushin, the aircraft manufacturer, all government ministers throughout three decades, as well as the artistic élite of Moscow. Won a special award for his work in the 1960s. Was named one of the 10 most popular people in the Soviet Union. In 1984 emigrated to Israel.

Belinkov, Arkadii Viktorovich
1921–14.5.1970. Literary critic.
Born in Moscow. Studied at Leningrad University (Gorkii Literary Institute). Arrested for his dissertation, sentenced to death in 1942, commuted to 8 years imprisonment in the camps. Inmate of Karaganda Gulag in the 1950s. Returned to prison and sentenced to 25 more years for three books which he had written in the camps and was trying to smuggle out. The books were destroyed before his eyes. Released in 1956. Lecturer at Gorkii Literary Institute in Moscow. Dismissed in 1958. Published a book on Iurii Tynianov, 1960. Wrote on Bulgakov, Olesha (*Sdacha i gibel sovetskogo intelligenta*, 1976), Platonov. Some of his manuscripts were circulated in samizdat. Allowed to go with his wife

to Yugoslavia, from where he defected in 1968. Settled in the USA, and taught at the universities there. One of the first Soviet dissidents. Died in New Haven, USA.

Belinkova, Natalia Aleksandrovna (Iablokova)
1930–   . Journalist, editor.
Born in Moscow. Graduated in philology from Moscow University. Married A. Belinkov, 1957. Defected with her husband in 1968. Settled in the USA. Published the works of her husband posthumously, and engaged in polemics, defending his views.

Beloborodov, Afanasii Pavlant'evich
31.1.1903–   . General.
Born in the village of Akinino near Irkutsk. During the Civil War, fought as a Red partisan in the Far East. Graduated from the Frunze Military Academy, 1936. During WWII, commander in Belorussia and East Prussia, and later against Japan. Chief of the Personnel Department of the Ministry of Defence, 1957. Commander of Moscow military district, 1963–68. Member of the Cen. Cttee. of the CPSU, 1966–71.

Beloborodov, Aleksandr Georgievich
26.10.1891–9.2.1938. Revolutionary, politician, state security officer.
Born in Perm Gouvt. Son of a worker. Worked as an electrician. Joined the Bolshevik Party in 1907. After the October Revolution, chairman of the Ural Oblast' Soviet, Jan. 1918. Signed the order of execution of Tsar Nicholas II and his family, who were held prisoners at Ekaterinburg, July 1918. (This is often used to prove that the local authorities themselves ordered the execution, but according to other accounts the order was given from Moscow by Sverdlov and Lenin). Involved in the suppression of the Cossack anticommunist rebellion on the Don, 1919. Political commissar in the Northern Caucasus, 1920. Deputy Minister of the Interior of the RSFSR, 1921–23. Minister of the Interior (State Security), 1923–27. Joined Trotsky's camp during the struggle for power with Stalin. Joined the Stalinists after Trotsky's defeat, but was nevertheless arrested, condemned to death and shot.

Belokon', Viktor
1939–   . Collective farm manager.
Improved the productivity of his farm near Odessa by unorthodox methods under Brezhnev. Arrested and imprisoned for his initiative. In Jan. 1988, an investigative TV film was made about his methods, his treatment of his work force, and what had happened to him. The party bosses in Odessa were shown to be responsible. They, in turn, banned the film, to show their opposition to Gorbachev. Still in prison in May 1988, Belokon' has become the focus of attention of Moscow legal journalists.

Belokoskov, Vasilii Evlampievich
1898–1961. Col.-general.
Joined the Red Army, 1918. Cavalry commander during the Civil War. During WWII, held several command posts in the rear administration and mechanized detachments. Deputy Commander of the Rear of the Armed Forces, 1943. Deputy Minister of Defence of the USSR, 1949–58, in charge of military building projects.

Belonogov, Aleksandr
1931–   . Diplomat, state official.
USSR Ambassador to Egypt until Aug. 1986, when he replaced Iurii Dubinin as Ambassador to the United Nations.

Belotserkovskii, Vadim Vladimirovich
1928–   . Journalist.
Born in Moscow. Son of the well-known Stalinist writer, V. Bill-Belotserkovskii. Graduated from Moscow University. Published articles in the Soviet press. Became involved in the human rights movement, defending the right to emigrate. He himself emigrated in 1972. Broadcaster with Radio Liberty, specializing in Soviet human rights subjects. Published sociological works in the West.

Belousov, Evsei Iakovlevich
9.1.1882–2.12.1945. Cellist.
Born in Moscow. Pupil of A. Glen. Shared with I. Press 2nd prize in the Cellists' Competition, Moscow, 1911. Appeared in various Russian towns. Emigrated and lived abroad from 1922. Died in New York.

Belousov, Leonid Georgievich
1909–   . Pilot.
Joined the Red Army, 1930. Graduated from fighter pilot school, 1935. On active service in the Soviet-Finnish war, 1939–40. Active during the defence of Leningrad. Had both legs amputated, but returned to active service and continued to fly fighter planes. Major, 1945. Hero of the Soviet Union, 1957.

Belousov, Vladimir Pavlovich
14.7.1946–   . Athlete.
Born in Vsevolozhsk, Leningrad Oblast'. Honoured Master of Sports (skiing), 1968. Graduated from the Leningrad Military Institute of Physical Culture, 1978. Olympic champion, 1968.

Belousov, Vladimir Vladimirovich
30.10.1907–   . Geologist.
Head of the Laboratory on Theoretical Geotectonics and Geodynamics of the Academy of Sciences. Professor at Moscow University, 1953. President of the International Union of Geodesy and Geophysics, 1960–63. Works on tectonics and tectonophysics.

Belov, Aleksandr Aleksandrovich
9.11.1951–3.10.1978. Athlete.
Born in Leningrad. Honoured Master of Sports (basket-ball, 1972, Spartak). Graduated from the Leningrad Ship-building Institute, 1978. World champion, 1974. European champion, 1969, 1971. USSR champion, 1975. Olympic champion, 1972. Died in Leningrad under suspicious circumstances, (believed to have taken dangerous steroids).

Belov, Andrei Ivanovich
1917–   . Marshal.
Joined the Soviet Army, 1938. Graduated from the Military Electrotechnical Academy, 1940. Took part in the Soviet-Finnish war, 1939–40. Commander of the ballistic rocket forces of the Soviet Army, 1960–68. Deputy Chief of the General Staff, 1977.

Belov, Iurii Sergeevich
1940–   . Dissident
Born in Kronstadt. Took part in the human rights movement in the USSR connected with the Helsinki accords. Spent 15 years in the Gulag camps and exile. First arrested in 1963, sentenced to 3 years in the labour camps. Second arrest for dissident activity, 1967, sentenced to 5 years imprisonment. Sent to a psychiatric hospital, 1972. In 1977 released and emigrated. Lives in West Germany, active in dissident and human rights groups in Western Europe. Described his camps experience in samizdat works.

Belov, Ivan Panfilovich
27.6.1893–29.7.1938. Military commander.
Born in the village of Kolinichevo, Novgorod Gouvt. Joined the army, 1913. After the February Revolution 1917, left-wing SR, chairman of a soldiers' revolutionary committee in a regiment in Tashkent. Commander of the garrison in Tashkent, 1918. Joined the Bolshevik Party, 1919, after suppressing a left-wing SR revolt in Tashkent. Commander of the army of the Turkestan Republic, 1919. Supressed the Cossack uprising in the Kuban region, 1921–22. Thereafter held several high military positions. Arrested and shot.

Belov, Konstantin
1953–   . Colonel.
Until 15 May 1988, in charge of military communications for the Kabul area in Afghanistan.

Belov, Nikolai Vasil'evich
14.12.1891–1975? Crystallographer.
Educated at the Petrograd Polytechnical Institute, 1921. Professor at Gorkii University, 1946, and Moscow University, 1953. Chairman of the Soviet Committee of Crystallographers, 1957. President of the International Union of Crystallographers, 1966.

Belov, Pavel Alekseevich
18.2.1897–3.12.1962. Col.-general.
Born in Shuia. Joined the Red Army, 1918. Took part in the Civil War. Graduated from the Frunze Military

Academy, 1933. At the beginning of WWII, commander of a cavalry corps, which was cut off by the Germans before Moscow, and for half a year fought behind German lines. Well-known commander at the front (Kursk, Dnepr, Belorussia, Vistula, Berlin). After the war, commander of several military districts. Chairman of the Cen. Cttee. of DOSAAF, 1955–60. Retired, 1960. Died in Moscow.

Belov, Sergei Aleksandrovich
23.1.1944– . Athlete.
Born in the village of Nashchekovo, Tomsk Oblast'. Honoured Master of Sports (basket-ball), 1968. Graduated from the Moscow Institute of Physical Culture, 1977. Coach. Olympic champion, 1972. Bronze medal, 1968 and 1976. World champion, 1967 and 1974. European champion, 1967, 1969, 1971, 1979. USSR champion 1969–79.

Belov, Vasilii Ivanovich
23.10.1932– . Writer.
Born in the village of Timonikha, Vologda Oblast'. Graduated from the Gorkii Literary Institute in Moscow, 1964. One of the best known modern village writers.

Belova, Elena Dmitrievna (Novikova)
28.7.1947– . Athlete.
Born in Sovetskaia Gavan', Khabarovskii Krai. Honoured Master of Sports (fencing), 1968. Graduated from the Minsk Pedagogical Institute, 1970. Member of the CPSU, 1974. Olympic champion, 1968 and 1968, 1972 and 1976 with her team. Bronze medal, 1976. World champion, 1969.

Belozerskii, Andrei Nikolaevich
29.8.1905– . Scientist.
Graduated from the University of Central Asia, 1927. Professor of Moscow University, 1946. Worked on the chemistry and biochemistry of albumen and nucleic acids.

Bel'skii, Igor Dmitrievich
28.3.1925– . Ballet dancer, choreographer.
Born in Leningrad. Graduated from the Leningrad Choreographic School in 1943 during the siege. Pupil of A.Lopukhov. Graduated from the

Moscow GITIS (Theatre School), 1957. Leading ballet dancer with the Kirov Ballet Theatre, 1943–63. From 1962, choreographer with the Leningrad Malyi Theatre. From 1973, choreographer with the Kirov Ballet Theatre. Also taught at the Leningrad Choreographic School, 1946–66 and from 1966 in the Ballet Department of the Leningrad Conservatory.

Bel'skii, Vladimir Ivanovich
1866–28.2.1946. Librettist.
Specialist in Russian antiquities and old Russian literature (legends, songs etc). Wrote the librettos for N. Rimskii-Korsakov's operas based on Russian sagas (*Skazka o tsare Saltane, Zolotoi Petushok etc*). Died in Leningrad.

Belyi, Andrei (Bugaev, Boris Nikolaevich)
26.10.1880–8.1.1934. Poet, author, literary scholar.
Born in Moscow. Son of a famous mathematician. Graduated in mathematics from Moscow University, 1903. First appeared in print with Symbolist poetry in 1901. Soon became famous with his collection of poetry *Zoloto v Lazuri*, 1904. He and his close friend A. Blok were much influenced by the philosophy of V. Solov'ev. Original poet, literary scholar, philosopher, familiar with exact sciences and mathematics, style innovator in poetry and prose, and mystic. Became one of the foremost theoreticians of Symbolism in Russia. Came under the influence of Rudolph Steiner and his anthroposophy, 1912. Went abroad and took part in the building of Steiner's Goetheanum in Switzerland. Later his friendship with Steiner turned to quarrels and bitter recriminations. Always unconventional, during WWI and the revolution, was near to mental collapse. Returned to Russia in 1916. Left for a short time after the October Revolution, 1917, but soon returned from Berlin to the Soviet Union. Subsequently wrote mostly prose, including brilliant memoirs (which, however, tried rather clumsily and in retrospect to superimpose a Marxist interpretation on his essentially mystical and satirical view of the world). Very influential during his life-time, especially through his prose works *Petersburg* and *Serebrianyi Golub'*.

After the Stalin era, again acknowledged as one of the most influential figures of 20th century Russian literature. Died in Moscow.

Belykh, Grigorii Georgievich
1906–1938. Author.
In 1927, in collaboration with L. Panteleev, wrote a story of the besprizorniki called *Respublika Shkid*, which at once became and remains a classic of children's literature in the Soviet Union. Arrested in Leningrad, 1937. According to his co-author, a group of writers wrote to Stalin asking for the transfer of Belykh to a labour camp. The answer, a refusal, arrived after he had already died of tuberculosis in the prison hospital.
See: *Novyi Mir*, 1965, Nr. 5, p. 155.

Benefelde, Ada
19.2.1887–1946? Singer (soprano).
Born in Riga. Pupil of A.Viulnar. Appeared in Germany, 1908–13. From 1913, soloist at the Riga Latyshskaia Opera. Professor at the Latvian Conservatory till 1939.

Benois, Aleksandr Nikolaevich
3.5.1870–9.2.1960. Artist, stage designer, art scholar.
Born in St.Petersburg into a well known arts dynasty (architects, painters) of French origin. Founder, leading member and chief theoretician of the Mir Isskustva (World of Art) group. In his early years, mentor of Diaghilev in art appreciation and later his constant collaborator in different ventures. Greatest achievements are in art history, book illustration and stage design. One of the most important figures in Russian cultural life during the 1900–20s. Moved to Paris, 1927. Continued to work as a stage designer and painter. Died in Paris.

Benois, Nadia
1896–1981? Artist.
Born in St.Petersburg. Studied privately under her uncle Aleksandr Benois and at the school attached to the Academy of Fine Arts in St.Petersburg. Mother of Peter Ustinov. Main works were designs for the Ballet Rambert, Sadler's Wells and other smaller companies. Settled in England.

Benois, Nikolai Aleksandrovich (Nicola)
2.5.1901–14.4.1988. Artist, stage designer.
Son of the distinguished artist, Aleksandr Benois. Born in St.Petersburg. Studied under his father. Began working as a stage designer in 1920 for the Petrograd Bolshoi Drama Theatre. Left Russia for Western Europe in 1924. In Paris met Nikita Baliev, a theatrical producer, who was the principal director of a theatre on the Champs Elysées, and began working for him. Met A.Sanin, who offered him a job as a stage designer at La Scala in Milan. Decorator and stage designer at La Scala for 40 years. Took Italian citizenship in 1937 in order to continue working and living in Italy. In 1964 went with La Scala to the Soviet Union on the invitation of the Bolshoi Theatre. Stage designer of over 200 productions.

Bensin, Vasilii Mitrofanovich
30.1.1881–2.1973. Church historian.
Educated at the Simferopol Seminary. Graduated from the Moscow Theological Academy, 1905. Sent to an Orthodox seminary in Minneapolis, 1905. Graduated from Minneapolis University in agronomy, 1910. Created special strains of wheat, which could be sown in Alaska. Wrote on theological subjects. Was the official historian of the Orthodox Church in America.

Berberova, Nina Nikolaevna
1901–   . Author, literary scholar, poet.
Daughter of a professor of the Lazarevskii Institute of Oriental Languages. Emigrated after the October Revolution 1917. Married (later divorced) the poet and critic V.Khodasevich. Her husband was close to M.Gor'kii and they often visited him on Capri. Before WWII, lived mostly in Paris. Wrote poetry, short stories and biographies (e.g. of Tchaikovskii). After WWII, worked for the Russian newspaper *Russkaia Mysl* in Paris, and reported on the Kravchenko libel case. Moved to USA, Nov. 1950. Taught Russian literature at Princeton, Yale and Columbia universities. In her memoirs, *Kursiv moi*, described the Russian literary life in the West between the wars. Published a biography of M.Budberg, close companion of Bruce Lockhart, Gor'kii and H.G. Wells (*Zheleznaia zhenshchina*) and a detailed study of Russian masonic lodges of modern times (*Liudi i lozhi*), USA, 1986.

Berdiaev, Nikolai Aleksandrovich
6.3.1874–24.3.1948. Philosopher.
Born in Kiev. Son of a nobleman. Studied law at Kiev University. Became involved in revolutionary activity and Marxist propaganda, exiled to Vologda, 1898. Went to Germany to study, and returned to Petersburg in 1904. Co-editor with Bulgakov of the philosophical magazin *Voprosy zhizni*. Became widely known as a representative of a group of thinkers who moved from Marxism towards a religious view of life. Gained the reputation of a philosopher of freedom, which he considered to be the pre-condition of all true existence. Stressed the value of personality and individual liberty. His philosophy is defined as personalism or Christian existentialism. His popularity was greatly increased by his colourful, aphoristic style, which gave little regard to logical development of thought. He himself considered his non-academic approach to philosophy a definite virtue. Taught at the private Academy of Spiritual Culture in Moscow, 1918-22. Exiled after an interview with Dzerzhinskii, 1922 (together with a large group of intellectuals sent abroad by Lenin). Went to Berlin. Settled in France, near Paris, 1925. Married L. Rapp. Very active in the emigré press as author, editor and organizer (one of the founders of the YMCA Press in Paris, which published most of the Russian thinkers living abroad after 1917). Became widely known in the 1930s, and remains the best known modern Russian philosopher in the West. Under the influence of the events of WWII, took a pro-Soviet line, and after the war took a Soviet passport, but did not return to the USSR. Received an Oxford doctorate in 1947. Died in Paris.
Main works: *The Meaning of History, Philosophy of Inequality, The New Middle Ages, Philosophy of the Free Spirit, The Origin of Russian Communism, On Slavery and Freedom of Man, The Existential dialectic of the Divine and Human, Autobiography.*

Berdiev, Iosif Konstantinovich
26.11.1924–   . Athlete.
Born in Ashkhabad. Graduated from the Leningrad Military Institute of Physical Culture, 1953. Coach. Honoured Master of Sports (gymnastics), 1955. Olympic champion, 1952. USSR champion, 1948–53, 1955.

Berdnikova, Avgusta Vasil'evna
1897–1974. Revolutionary.
Joined the Bolshevik Party, 1917. Organized communist underground cells in Siberia under Kolchak during the Civil War. Took part in the Red Army's march from Irkutsk to Vladivostok. Graduated from the Institute of Red Professors in Moscow. Party functionary in Moscow and Novosibirsk.

Beregovoi, Georgii Timofeevich
15.4.1921–   . Cosmonaut, general.
Born in the village of Fedorovka, Poltava Oblast'. Joined the army, 1938. Air force pilot during WWII. Test pilot, 1948–64. Cosmonaut, 1964. In orbit Oct. 1968. Commander of the Cosmonauts Training Centre, 1972. Lt.-gen. 1977.

Berens, Evgenii Andreevich (Behrens)
11.11.1876–7.4.1928. Naval officer, diplomat.
Born in Tiflis (Tbilisi). Educated at the Naval Corps, 1895. Took part in the Russo-Japanese war, 1905. Naval attaché in Germany, 1910–14, Italy, 1915–17. After the October Revolution joined the Bolsheviks 1917. Due to a lack of naval officers in the Red camp, appointed Commander of the Red Navy, 1919. Later on diplomatic service at the Genoa and Lausanne conferences as the Soviet representative. Again naval attaché in Britain, 1924, France, 1925. Soviet naval expert at the Geneva disarmament commission, 1927. Died in Moscow.

Berezka, Dusia
1879–1968. Ballerina, teacher.
Graduated from the Petersburg Theatre School. Pupil of P. Karsavin. Received most of her training in Zurich under Mary Wigman. Assistant to Rudolf von Laban in his Kammertanzbuehne after which she became a star. Taught in Zurich, Paris and London. After WWII

moved to London where she lived until her death.
See: R. von Laban, *Ein Leben für den Tanz,* Dresden, 1935.

Berezov, Nikolai Nikolaevich
16.5.1906–   . Ballet dancer, choreographer, ballet teacher.
Born in Kovno (Kaunas). Studied ballet in Prague, and danced there until 1930. Moved to Kaunas where he married. Father of the internationally known British ballerina Svetlana Beriozova. From 1935–38, one of the leading dancers with René Blum's Ballet Russe de Monte Carlo. From 1944, a choreographer with the International Ballet. In 1948 with the London Metropolitan Ballet, from 1950–51 with La Scala, from 1951–54 with the London Festival Ballet and from 1956 with the Ballet de Marquis de Cuevas. Chief choreographer of the Stuttgart Ballet, 1957–59. In Helsinki 1962–64, Zurich 1964–71, and Naples 1971–73, where he staged his production of *Giselle* with E. Maksimova and V. Vasiliev. Lectured at Bloomington University, Indiana, 1975–81. Continued to stage his ballet productions all over the world. Memoirs: *Zhizn' I Balet,* London, 1983.

Berezova, Anna (Galina) Alekseevna
15.6.1909–   . Ballet dancer, teacher.
Graduated from the Leningrad Choreographic School, where she was a pupil of A. Vaganova, in 1925, and from the Leningrad Conservatory, as a stage director, in 1937. Soloist, 1925–33. Assistant to A. Vaganova, 1933–37. Artistic director and chief choreographer with the Kirov Ballet Theatre, 1937–41. Choreographer at the Shevchenko Theatre, 1944–47. From 1945–66, artistic director, and from 1972, teacher at the Kiev Choreographic School.

Berezovskii, Vladimir Antonovich
1852–1917. Publisher.
Founded the first Russian publishing house for military literature, 1879. Published over four thousand titles, including an encyclopaedia of military and naval sciences, and an atlas of 19th century battles.

Berg, Aksel Ivanovich
10.11.1893–1979. Admiral, politician.
Born in Orenburg. Served on submarines during WWI and the Civil War. Graduated from the Naval Academy in Leningrad, 1925. Deputy Minister of the electrical industry 1943-44. Academician, 1946. Deputy Minister of Defence, 1953–57. Chairman of the Commission for Cybernetics of the Academy of Sciences, 1959. Editor of the Soviet Computer Encyclopaedia, 1962–65.

Berg, Lev Semenovich
14.3.1876–24.12.1950. Geographer, biologist.
Born in Bendery. Graduated from Moscow University, 1898. Professor of Petrograd University, 1916. President of the Soviet Geographical Society, 1940–50. Many geographical works, and a 3-volume reference work on fish. His name is incorporated in the Latin names of over 60 species of plants and animals. Died in Leningrad.

Berg, Raisa Lvovna
1913–   . Biologist.
Born in Moscow. Graduated from Leningrad University in biology. Head of the Department of Cytology and Genetics at the Novosibirsk Research Institute. In the 1960s, became involved with the human rights movement. Emigrated, 1973. Lives in the USA.

Bergelson, David Rafailovich
12.8.1884–12.8.1952. Writer.
Born in Okhrimovo near Kiev. Became well-known as a novelist before WWI. Emigrated to Germany, 1921. Returned to the Soviet Union, 1929. Wrote novels on the heroism of the Civil War and the October Revolution. After WWII arrested and shot together with a group of Jewish writers and poets, including Kvitko, Markish and others, during Stalin's anti-Semitic campaign.

Berggolts, Olga Fedorovna
1910–26.11.1975. Poetess.
Born in Petersburg. Graduated in philology from Leningrad University Her first book was published in 1929. Arrested briefly in 1937. Lived in Leningrad during the siege. Prolific writer and recipient of the Stalin Prize.

Berggolts, Richard Aleksandrovich
1865–1920. Artist.
Studied under A. Bogoliubov and L. Peluse in Paris. Also at Dusseldorf under E. Ducker, 1887–88. Correspondence student at the Petersburg Academy of Arts, 1888–89. Landscape painter. Exhibitions: Academy of Arts, 1887, 1893; Society of Russian Water-Colour Painters, St. Petersburg, 1893–1916; St. Petersburg Society of Artists, 1894–1903; All-Russian Exhibition, Nizhnii Novgorod, 1896; Association of Artists, 1903–16; Spring Exhibitions, Academy of Arts, 1915–16.

Beria, Lavrentii Pavlovich
29.3.1899–1953. Secret police chief, politician.
Born in the village of Merkheuli near Sukhumi in Georgia. Mingrelian (Western Georgian) by nationality. Educated at Sukhumi High School, 1915. Moved to Baku to study at a technical building college. Graduated, 1919. Became involved in SD illegal work. Joined the Bolsheviks, March 1917. During WWI, spent a few months in Rumania at the front as a conscript, active in revolutionary propaganda work. At the end of 1917, deserted and returned to Baku. During the Civil War in Azerbaidzhan, 1919–20, carried out underground Bolshevik work, but had shadowy connections with other groups (his alleged relations with the British at the time were used to brand him as a British spy three decades later). Moved to Georgia (then independent, under a Menshevik nationalist government) on illegal Bolshevik work. Arrested and expelled from Georgia. Returned to Baku. Joined the secret police, 1921. High posts in the secret police in the Caucasus, 1921–31 (Georgia and Azerbaidzhan). First Secretary of the Cen. Cttee. of the Georgian CP, 1931. One of those responsible for the rule of terror in the Caucasus where he supervised the collectivization campaign. Brought to Moscow in 1934 by Stalin who called him his promising fellow Georgian. Replaced Ezhov as head of the secret police, an appointment which was greeted with hope after the horrors of the Ezhov period. He began by liquidating some of Ezhov's aides and making some improvements to the Gulag system, but soon started a reign of terror of

his own. Remained chief of the terror system until Stalin's death, almost two decades later. During WWII, Stalin's deputy both as head of government, and as head of the State Cttee. for Defence. Marshal, 1945. Actively involved in the gigantic growth of the slave labour Gulag empire and the Stalinization of Eastern Europe in the aftermath of WWII. Stalin's daughter, in her memoirs, alleged that he had a demonic hold over her father, blaming *his* influence for the worst Stalinist excesses. Though untrue, this impression is symptomatic of the image he had in his later years. At the moment of Stalin's death he thought of himself as a likely successor. Shrewdly began at once with some liberalizing measures, stopping the investigation of the so-called Doctors' Plot. But his colleagues, on the initiative of Khrushchev, united against him. He was arrested and vanished in the summer of 1953. In the middle of July 1953, a short notice appeared saying that he had been expelled from the Politburo and the party as an enemy of the party and the people. Only in Dec. 1953 was it reported that he and a group of his close collaborators had been shot after being sentenced by the Soviet Supreme Court (no court proceedings were ever published). Subscribers to the 2nd edition of the *Great Soviet Encyclopaedia* received an extra printed page, and instructions to cut out the page containing an extremely laudatory article on Beria, and replace it with a new page dealing with the Bering Sea. The following edition of the same reference work does not mention him at all, but he is far from forgotten in the Soviet Union where his name remains one of the most hated. Stories about his rule of terror are many; for example his alleged orgies with young girls kidnapped from the streets are mentioned by several researchers and hinted at in the sensational 1987 film *Repentance* by Georgian director Abuladze. According to *Nedelia*, supplement of *Izvestia* (Feb. 1988), before his (secret) trial he went on an 11 days' hunger strike, refused to plead guilty or admit anything, but pleaded on his knees for mercy, when Marshal P. Batitsky came to execute the death sentence. According to *Nedelia*, he was shot on the spot. (For the current Soviet version of his death, see *Komsomolskaia Pravda*, 21.2.1988 and *Nedelia*, 22.2.1988).

Beritashvili, Ivan Solomonovich (real name - Beritov)
10.1.1885–1971? Physiologist.
Graduated from Petersburg University, 1910. Professor of Tbilisi University, 1919. Head of the Institute of Physiology of the Georgian Academy of Sciences, 1935–52. The Institute was later renamed in his honour. Member of the USSR Academy of Sciences, 1939, and of the Georgian Academy of Sciences, 1941. Honorary member of the New York Academy of Sciences, 1959. Carried out research into muscle and nervous system physiology.

Berkhin, Viktor
1930–7.1987. Journalist.
Courageously exposed the abuse of KGB power in the Ukrainian town of Voroshilovgrad in a series of articles in the local press, which led to his arrest. According to the Moscow *Meditsinskaia Gazeta,* the official medical journal of the USSR, he was interrogated and tortured until he lost consciousness. Never recovered after his release. His death led to an unprecedented front-page statement in *Pravda* by Viktor Chebrikov, the KGB chief, who announced the dismissal of a senior KGB officer. The party boss of Voroshilovgrad, Boris Goncharenko, was sacked when it had emerged that, together with Berkhin, the local KGB had arrested on false charges a Dr. Vadin and his brother, Igor Kreinin, from whom they had attempted to obtain statements incriminating Berkhin.

Berkov, Pavel Naumovich
14.12.1896–9.8.1969. Literary scholar.
Born in Belgorod-Dnestrovskii. Professor of Leningrad University. An authority on 18th century Russian literature. Died in Leningrad.

Berkutov, Aleksandr Nikolaevich
21.5.1933–   . Athlete.
Born in the village of Zubchaninovka, Kuibyshev Oblast'. Honoured Master of Sports (rowing), 1957. Graduated from the Moscow Institute of Oil and Gas Industry, 1957. With Moscow Dynamo. Olympic champion, 1956 (with Iu. Tiukalov). Silver medal, 1960. European champion, 1956–61. USSR champion, 1954, 1957, 1961.

Berman, Eugene (Evgenii)
4.11.1899–22.12.1972. Stage designer.
Born in Petersburg. Lived in Finland, 1920. Moved to England and then France. Studied at the Paris Academy of Arts. Stage designer for Les Ballets Russes de Monte Carlo, Sadlers Wells Ballet, the American Theatre Ballet, and the New York City Ballet. Died in Rome.

Bermont-Avalov, Pavel Rafalovich, Prince
17.3.1884–27.12.1973. Major-general.
On active service during WWI as a Cossack officer. During the Civil War, organized White forces, which fought the Reds in the Baltic countries with the help of the local German commander von der Goltz. Involved in conflicts with the local post-revolutionary governments. Defeated by Latvians, Estonians and the British Navy. Moved to Germany.

Bernandt, Grigorii Borisovich
21.4.1905–   . Music critic.
Born in Wilno. Moved to Moscow. Author of *S.I. Taneev*, Moscow–Leningrad, 1950, and *Slovar' Oper,* Moscow, 1962.

Bernshtam, Mikhail Semenovich
1940–   . Author, historian.
Graduated in history from Leningrad University. Became involved in the human rights movement. Arrested, 1973. Inmate in a mental hospital in Rostov-on-Don, released 1974. Works circulated in samizdat. Emigrated, 1976, settled in the USA. Edited valuable material in a collection by Solzhenitsyn, *INRI,* on 20th century Russian history: *Narodnoe Soprotivlenie Kommunizmu v Rossii: Nezavisimoe Rabochee Dvizhenie v 1918 Godu: Dokumenty i Materialy,* Paris, 1981.

Bernshtein, Sergei Natanovich (Bernstein)
6.3.1880–26.10.1968. Mathematician.
Born in Odessa. Graduated from the University of Paris, 1904. Doctor of mathematics at Khar'kov University, 1914. Professor of Khar'kov University, 1907–33. Professor of Leningrad University, 1934–41. Works mainly on the theory of differential equations and the theory of approximations by polynomials of functions. Created the constructive theory of functions. Died in Moscow.

Bervi-Flerovskii, Vasilii Vasil'evich (Bervi)
1829–1918. Economist.
Prominent economist of the 1870s. Involved in the populist movement. His book *Polozhenie Rabochego Klassa v Rossii,* 1869, was the first major analysis of the workers' position. Wrote memoirs, describing his revolutionary career.

Berzarin, Nikolai Erastovich
1.4.1904–16.6.1945. Col.-general.
Born in Petersburg. Son of a worker. Joined the Red Army, 1918. Took part in the Civil War. Later took part in the skirmishes with the Japanese on Lake Hassan, 1938. Became known as a WWII front commander. First Soviet commandant of Berlin, 1945. Died in a car crash in Berlin.

**Berzin, Ian Antonovich (Berzin';
Ziemelis, Pavel Vasil'evich;
Pavlovskii; Winter)**
11.10.1881–29.8.1938. Diplomat, state official.
Born in Latvia. Son of a peasant. Veteran Latvian communist leader. Joined the SDs, 1902. Emigrated, 1908. Participated in the Zimmerwald conference, 1915. Member of the Cen. Cttee. of the Latvian SD Party, 1917. Soviet Ambassador to Switzerland, 1918. Soviet Minister of Education in Latvia, 1919. Secretary of the Executive Cttee. of the Comintern, 1919–20. Soviet Ambassador to Finland, 1921. Deputy Ambassador to Britain, 1921–25. Chief of the Central Archives of the USSR and the RSFSR, 1932. Arrested, died in the Gulag.

Berzin, Ian (Jan) Karlovich (also Pavel Ivanovich. Real name —Kyuzis Peteris; party name —Papus)
25.11.1889–27.7.1938. Secret police official, first chief of the GRU.
Born in Latvia, son of a peasant. Member of the Bolshevik Party from 1905. Court-martialled for shooting a police officer in 1907, sentenced to 8 years imprisonment,which was reduced to 2 years. Re-arrested and exiled to Irkutsk in 1911. Escaped from exile in 1914. Conscripted into the army during WWI, but fled and worked in Petrograd factories in 1915. Took an active part in the February Revolution 1917. During the October Revolution 1917, member of the Vyborg and Petrograd party committees. Career in the secret police service began in 1919 as a minor Cheka official. Promoted to Deputy Commissar of the Interior in Soviet Latvia, and later occupied top security positions in the Red Army. Worked in military intelligence from 1921. First Chief of the GRU, 1924–35. One of the principal organizers of the forced labour system in the USSR. Chief of Dalstroi Industrial Combine (part of the Gulag system of concentration camps in the Far East) in 1932. Chief military adviser to the Spanish communists during the Spanish Civil War. Recalled to Moscow and arrested in 1937. Tried and shot after a year in prison.

Berzin, Reinhold Iosifovich
16.7.1888–11.11.1939. Politician, military commander.
Born in Latvia. Son of a peasant. Joined the Bolshevik Party, 1905. Factory worker, later teacher. Arrested for revolutionary work, 1911–12. Lt. during WWI. Active in Bolshevik work at the front. After the Bolshevik take-over, organized revolutionary soldiers. During the Civil War Red commander, fought Ukrainian nationalists and Poles under Dowbor-Musnicki. Commander of the Western front, 1918. Commander of the Siberian-Ural front, June 1918. High commanding posts at other fronts. After the Civil War active in armaments industry and agriculture. Arrested, 1938. Shot.

Bessmertnova, Natal'ia Igorevna
19.7.1941– . Ballet star.
Born in Moscow. Graduated from the Moscow Choreographic School, 1961. A pupil of S. Golovkina. Joined the Bolshoi Theatre and soon became one of its leading dancers. Has since performed all over the world.

Bessmertnykh, Aleksandr Aleksandrovich
10.11.1933– . Diplomat, state official.
Born in Altai Krai. Graduated from the MGIMO (Moscow State Institute of International Relations), 1957. Member of the CPSU, 1963. Attaché in the Press Dept. of the MID (Ministry of Foreign Affairs), 1957–60. Member of the Soviet Delegation at the UN, 1960–66. 2nd Secretary, and then 1st Secretary of the Secretariat of the MID, 1966–70. 1st Secretary, and councillor at the USSR Embassy in the USA under Dobrynin, 1970–83. Head of the USA Dept. in the MID, 1983–86. Deputy Foreign Minister of the USSR from May 1986.

Bestuzhev-Lada, Igor
1932?– . Historian.
Descendant of the Decembrist Bestuzhev family. Created a sensation with his two-page article in *Nedelia* (Apr. 1988), which gave a detailed account of the atrocities of the Stalin era – '50 million killed, or condemned to labour camps from which they never emerged'. He also said that dekulakization had cost 25 million peasants' lives during Stalin's collectivization campaign. Among letters received from readers was one signed by five 'veterans of WWII', which threatened to finish him off without witnesses.

Betaki, Vasilii Pavlovich
1930– . Poet, journalist, translator.
Born in Rostov-on-Don. Graduated from the Moscow Gorkii Literary Institute. Published translations of poetry and original verse. Some of his poems circulated in samizdat. Expelled from the Writers' Union, 1972. Emigrated, 1973. Lives in France.

Bezekirskii, Vasilii Vasil'evich
26.1.1835–8.11.1919. Violinist.
Born in Moscow. Father of the violinist V. Bezekirskii (1880–1960). Pupil of Iu. Leonar. Soloist with the Orchestra of the Bolshoi Theatre, Moscow, 1861–90. Professor at the School of Musical Drama attached to the Philharmonic Society, 1882–1902. K. Grigorovich was one of his pupils. Lived in the USA from 1914. Returned to Moscow, 1923. Wrote works for orchestra, arranged pieces for violin. Author of *Iz Zapisnoi Knizhki Artista*, Petersburg, 1910, *Kratkii Istoricheskii Obzor Muzykal'no-Skripichnogo Iskusstva, XVII–XVIII Vekov*, Kiev, 1913. Died in Moscow.

**Bezmenov, Iurii Aleksandrovich
(Schuman, Thomas)**
1939– . Journalist.
Born in Mytishchi, near Moscow. Graduated from Moscow University in Oriental languages. Employee of the Novosti Press Agency, later press attaché at the Soviet Embassy in India, defected, 1970. Settled in Canada. Worked in the Russian Section of Radio Canada. Gave lectures in the USA and Canada on Soviet disinformation and the KGB.

Bezredka, Aleksandr Mikhailovich
8.4.1870–28.2.1940. Immunologist.
Graduated from Odessa University, 1892. Pupil of I. Mechnikov. Joined the Mechnikov laboratory in the Pasteur Institute in Paris, 1897. Deputy head of the Pasteur Institute, 1916. Lived in France. Suggested new methods of immunization.

Bezrodnyi, Igor' Semenovich
7.5.1930– . Violinist.
Born in Tiflis, Georgia. Pupil of A. Iampol'skii. 1st prize at the J.S. Bach International Competition in Leipzig, 1950. 1st prize at the J. Kubelik Violin Competition in Prague, 1947. State Prize, 1951. Teacher at the Moscow Conservatory.

Bezymenskii, Aleksandr Il'ich
18.1.1898–2.7.1973. Poet.
Born in Zhitomir. Joined the Bolsheviks, 1916. Member of RAPP. Considered one of the best exponents of Komsomol poetry of the 1920s–30s with works such as *Komsomolia, V.I. Ulianov,* and *Feliks*.

Biakov, Ivan Ivanovich
21.9.1944– . Athlete.
Born in the village of Isakovtsy, Kirov Oblast'. Honoured Master of Sports (bi-athlon), 1972. Graduated from the Kiev Institute of Physical Culture, 1977. Coach. USSR champion, 1973. Olympic champion, 1972, 1976.

Bialik, Khaim Nakhman
1873–1934. Poet.
Jewish poet. Wrote in Hebrew and Yiddish. Emigrated, 1920. Lived in France and Germany. In 1924 moved to Palestine.
Works: *Mertvetsy Pustyni*, 1902; *Skazanie o Pogrome*, 1904.

Bialynitskii-Birulia, Vitold Kaetanovich
12.2.1872–18.6.1957. Artist.
Born in the village of Krynki, Mogilev Oblast'. Studied at the Kiev Murashko School of Graphic Art, 1885–89 and at the Moscow School of Painting, Sculpture and Architecture, 1889–97, under I. Prianishnikov, V. Makovskii, L. Pasternak, S. Korovin, and V. Polenov. Landscape painter. Exhibitions: MTKH, 1897, 1899, 1900 and 1903; MOLKH, 1897–01, 1906; TPKHV, 1899–1916, 1918. Personal exhibitions: 1936, 1943, 1947. Died in Moscow.

Bianki, Vitalii Valentinovich
1894–1959. Writer.
Popular writer of children's stories about nature and animals. Published in millions of copies. His 4-vol. *Sobranie Sochinenii* was published in 1974–75.

Bicherakhov, Georgii Fedorovich
1886?–after 1945. Military commander.
Born in Ossetia. Member of the SD Party (Menshevik). Participant in the Civil War in the Caucasus. In the summer of 1918 staged a revolt of the Terek Cossacks against the Reds. Created a provisional government of the Terek. In Nov. 1918 after his defeat by the Bolsheviks, moved to Petrovsk (Makhach-Kala), where he joined White detachments led by his brother, L. Bicherakhov.

Bicherakhov, Lazar Fedorovich
27.11.1882–1934? Colonel.
Born in Ossetia. Colonel of the Terek Cossacks, 1917. During WWI, stationed in Iran. During the Civil War in the Caucasus, pretended to accept the authority of the Baku Soviet, while establishing links with the British in Iran and the Whites under Denikin. In July 1918, let British detachments into Baku, and withdrew to Daghestan. Created a short-lived Caucasian-Caspian White government. Emigrated to Britain, 1919.

Bikhter, Mikhail Alekseevich
23.4.1881–7.5.1947. Pianist, conductor.
Born in Moscow. Pupil of A. Esipova and N. Cherepnin. Professor at the Leningrad Conservatory (chamber music). Conductor with the Musical Drama Theatre, Petrograd, 1912–17. Author of *Listki iz Knigi Vospominanii, Sovetskaia Muzyka*, 1959, No. 9, 12. Died in Leningrad.

Bilibin, Ivan Iakovlevich
16.8.1876–7.2.1942. Artist, stage designer.
Born near St. Petersburg. Studied at the St. Petersburg Academy of Fine Arts under Repin. Member of the Mir Iskusstva (World of Art) group. Created a very distinctive ornamental style suited to the fairy-tales and folk legends of Old Russia. Main speciality: book illustration and stage design. In stage design from 1907. From 1908–36 lived in Egypt, England and France. Returned to the Soviet Union shortly before WWII. Professor of Theatre Design at the Leningrad Academy of Fine Arts. Died in Leningrad during the WWII siege from cold and hunger.

Bill-Belotserkovskii, Vladimir Naumovich
9.1.1885–1.3.1970. Writer, playwright.
Born in Aleksandria, Kherson Gouvt. Worked as a seaman on Russian and British ships. Spent 7 years in the USA (window cleaner and similar jobs). Returned to Russia, 1917, joined the Communist Party. Author of many propaganda stories. Became a well-known Stalinist writer. According to some sources he expressed dissatisfaction with Stalin-

ism in his old age. Died in Moscow.

Biriukov, Pavel Ivanovich
15.11.1860–10.10.1931. Author.
Born in Ivanovskoe near Kostroma.
Became an active follower and close
friend of L. Tolstoy. One of the
organizers of the Posrednik publishing house and other tolstovtsy initiatives. Defended the Dukhobor sect,
which with L. Tolstoy's help eventually emigrated to Canada. From
the end of the 19th century lived
mostly abroad. Published a 4-vol.
biography of L.Tolstoy (1922–23).
Died in Geneva.

Biriukova, Aleksandra Pavlovna
25.2.1929–   . Party and state
official.
Graduated from the Moscow Textile
Institute, 1952. Member of the
CPSU, 1956. Began as a forewoman,
and became department head in a
Moscow factory. Responsible for
consumer goods production, food
industry and light industry. Member
of the Central Cttee. of the CPSU
since 1976. Secretary and Deputy
Chairwoman of the Central Council
of Trade Unions, 1968–85. Elected to
the Secretariat of the Central Committee of the CPSU on 6 March,
1986. Non-voting member of the
Politburo, Oct. 1988.

Biriuzov, Sergei Semenovich
21.8.1904–19.10.1964. Marshal.
Born in Skopin near Riazan'. Joined
the army, 1922. Graduated from the
Frunze Military Academy, 1937.
Staff officer during WWII. Commanded the Soviet Army, which
entered Yugoslavia at the end of
WWII. After the war, senior Soviet
officer in Bulgaria, until 1947. Commander of Soviet Air Defences, 1955.
Commander of ballistic rocket
forces, 1962. Chief of the General
Staff, Apr. 1963. Member of the Cen.
Cttee. of the CPSU, 1961. Highly
decorated (5 Lenin Orders). Died in
an air crash near Belgrade. Buried at
the Kremlin wall.

Birman, Igor Iakovlevich
1928–   . Economist.
Born in Moscow. Graduated from
the Moscow Plekhanov Institute of
Economics. Author of many articles
on the Soviet economy and history.
Left the USSR, 1974. Lives in the
USA. His work *Ekonomika Nedos-*

tach, NY, 1983, was translated into
English.

Birman, Naum Borisovich
19.5.1924–   . Film director.
Graduated from the Leningrad Institute of Theatre, Music and Cinema,
1951. Joined the Lenfilm Studios in
1965. Produced an adaptation of
Three Men in a Boat, 1979.

Bisk, Aleksandr Akimovich
29.1.1883–3.5.1973. Poet, translator.
Born in Kiev. Began to publish
poetry, 1903. Belonged to many of
the circles of the Silver Age of
Russian poetry before WWI. Lived
in Paris, where he was close to
Voloshin, Balmont and other
Russian poets. Emigrated from
Odessa, 1919. Moved to Belgium,
then Paris and later the USA. Continued to write in the emigré press.
Active in the Literaturnyi Fond (aid
to Russian writers abroad). Translated many West European poets
into Russian. Made some of the best
translations of Rilke. Died in a fire in
New York.

Bitov, Andrei Georgievich
1937–   . Writer.
Younger brother of Oleg Bitov. First
published in the early 1960s: *Bolshoi
Shar*, 1963; *Takoe Dolgoe Detstvo*,
1965; *Dachnaia Mestnost'*, 1967 etc.
One of his best works, *Pushkinskii
Dom*, was severely censored in the
Soviet Union but published in its
original form by Ardis, USA in 1978.
Participant in the almanac *Metropol*,
1979. Lives in Moscow.
See: P. Vail, A. Genis, *Sovremennaia
Russkaia Proza*, USA, 1982.

Bitov, Oleg Georgievich
1932–   . Journalist.
Journalist and one of the editors of
Literaturnaia Gazeta. Elder brother
of the writer, Andrei Bitov. Defected
during the Venice Film Festival,
1983. Asked for political asylum in
Britain. Welcomed by the West, gave
many interviews and wrote many
articles criticizing the Soviet Government. After a year in London,
reappeared under unknown circumstances in Moscow claiming he had
been kidnapped in Italy and tortured
by British intelligence. Reappeared
in *Literaturnaia Gazeta* writing hostile articles about the West.

Bitsadze, Andrei Vasil'evich
22.5.1916–   . Mathematician.
Born in Georgia. Graduated from
Tbilisi University, 1940. Professor at
the same University, 1942–47. Joined
the Mathematics Institute of the
USSR Academy of Sciences, 1948.
Works on the theory of differential
equations with partial derivatives
and singular integral equations.

Blagonravov, Anatolii Arkad'evich
1.6.1894–1975. Ballistic expert.
Born in the village of An'kovo near
Vladimir. Educated at the Petrograd
Polytechnic Institute, 1916, and the
Mikhailovskoe Artillery School,
1916. Professor at the Dzerzhinskii
Artillery Academy, 1929–46. Head
of the Commission for the Explora-
tion and Use of Space of the Soviet
Academy of Sciences, 1963.

Blanter, Matvei Isaakovich
10.2.1903–   . Composer.
Born in Pochep (now Brianskaia
Oblast'). Studied at the Kursk Music
School, 1915–19, at the Moscow
Philharmonic School, 1920–21. Pupil
of G. Konius. Musical director of the
Leningrad Teatr Satiry, of the Magnitogorsk Theatre, and of the Gorkii
Teatr Miniatiur. In the 1920s, composed mainly for the variety stage. In
the 1930s, one of the leading lyrical
soviet composers. Various wartime
songs. Postwar song compositions
till 1975. Influenced by Russian folk
music.

Blazhevich, Vladislav Mikhailovich
13.8.1881–10.4.1942. Trombone
player, conductor, composer.
Born in the Smolensk Gouvt. Professor at the Moscow Conservatory.
Organiser of the State Orchestra of
Wind Instruments, 1937. Author of
works for wind instruments, methods
for collective playing on wind instruments, and methods for playing the
trombone and tuba. Died in Moscow.

Bliakhin, Pavel Andreevich
25.12.1886–19.6.1961. Writer.
Born in the village of Verkhodym,
near Saratov. Old Bolshevik from
1903. Took part in the 1905 Revolution. In the 1920s published an
adventure story, *The Little Red Devils*
(Krasnye diavoliata), about the revolutionary exploits of a group of
children, which became immensely

popular, especially in its film adaptation. Died in Moscow.

Blinov, Iurii Ivanovich
13.1.1949– . Athlete.
Born in Moscow. Honoured Master of Sports (ice hockey), 1971. Olympic champion, 1972. USSR champion, 1968, 1970–73, 1975.

Blinov, Mikhail Fedoseevich
1892–1919. Revolutionary, military commander.
Member of the Ust'-Medveditskaia revolutionary committee. Leader of the Red Cossacks on the Don during the Civil War, first in charge of a regiment, and later as a brigade commander. Killed in action against the White Cossacks.

Blinov, Viktor Nikolaevich
1.9.1945–9.7.1968. Athlete.
Born in Omsk, Siberia. Honoured Master of Sports (ice hockey) 1968. With Moscow Spartak. Olympic champion, 1968. World and European champion, 1968. USSR champion, 1967. His premature death in Moscow was said to have been the result of his taking dangerous steroids.

Blinova, Ekaterina Nikitichna
7.12.1906– . Meteorologist.
Graduated from Rostov University. Joined the Central Institute of Weather Forecasting in Moscow, 1943. Worked out methods of long-range weather forecasting by integrating vortex equations.

Bliukher, Vasilii Konstantinovich
1.12.1890–9.11.1938. Marshal.
Born in the village of Barshchinka, Iaroslavl' Gouvt. Son of a peasant. Metal worker, involved in revolutionary activity before WW1. During WW1, conscripted into the army, private, later sergeant, wounded 1915. Took part in the Bolshevik take-over in Samara. Gained fame during the Civil War as a Red commander on the Volga and in the Urals, fighting Admiral Kolchak, later in the South against General Wrangel. In 1921–22 again in the Far East. Minister of Military Affairs of the buffer state, Far Eastern Republic. Soviet adviser to revolutionary Chinese armies in Kanton,

1924–27. Commander of the Red Army during military actions against the Chinese, 1929. Virtual military dictator of the Far Eastern Soviet provinces. During the purges of the Red Army, member of the military tribunal which sentenced Marshal Tukhachevskii and seven others to death, but this did not save him from a similar fate soon thereafter. Sentenced to death and executed. Rehabilitated during the Khrushchev years.

Bliumkin, Iakov Grigor'evich
1898–1929. Secret police official.
Member of the SR Party, 1914. Left the SRs, 1917. In Moscow on 6 July 1918 assassinated the German Ambassador, Count Mirbach, (as a protest against the terms of the Brest-Litovsk peace treaties, which the Left SRs, partners in the coalition government with the Bolsheviks, completely rejected). This served as the signal for the left wing SR uprising in Moscow, which was defeated only with difficulty by Latvian Cheka detachments. Took part in the uprising, and went underground. Maximalist SR in 1919 in the Ukraine, trying to fight the German occupation army. Soon amnestied (May 1919). Worked closely with Trotsky in the Army and Navy Ministry (People's Commissariat) and in the secret police (Cheka, GPU, under Dzerzhinskii, Menzhinskii and Trilisser). Later met Trotsky in exile in Constantinople and took a letter from him to his followers in the USSR (both facts acknowledged later by Trotsky). Arrested and executed.

Blok, Aleksandr Aleksandrovich
28.11.1880–7.8.1921. Poet.
Born in Petersburg. Son of a professor. Brought up, after his parents had separated, in the family of his maternal grandparents, the Beketovs. Graduated from Petersburg University in philology, 1906. Son-in-law of the famous chemist Mendeleev. Early influences – the liberal gentry, Russian countryside near Moscow (Shakhmatovo) and the philosophy of V. Solov'ev. First poems published, 1903. Soon became the clearest voice of symbolism in Russian poetry. Extremely gifted lyricist, whose motives of the penitent nobleman, populism, inherited culture and

apocalyptic atmosphere, coming from Solov'ev, caught the mood of the moment. Despite his shy and retiring nature, became the widest known and best loved of the poets of the Silver Age. Has retained his high reputation ever since ('the tragic tenor of the epoch', according to Akhmatova).

Explored in many articles the intelligentsia-people divide. In 1917 secretary of the Murav'ev Commission, investigating the leaders of the Tsarist regime. His basically pessimistic view of the world turned later in life, under the influence of the revolutionary events (and the left SR, Ivanov-Razumnik, the mentor of left-wing poets), to a symbolic-historical vision. His poem, *The Twelve*, is the only significant, contemporary celebration of the 1917 Revolution, although it scandalized both sides of the conflict (and surprised the author) by the comparison of twelve Red Guards with the Apostles, following a fleeting vision of Christ. As throughout his life, he defended himself by pointing to his medium-like conception of poetry. Just before his death he protested against the oppressive atmosphere under communist rule. His early death was widely understood as another symbol – of the end of the flowering of Russian culture at the beginning of the century. *Collected Works*, 12 volumes, 1932–36.

Blok, Liubov Dmitrievna (b. Mendeleeva)
29.12.1881–29.9.1939. Actress, ballet historian.
Born in Petersburg. Daughter of the chemical scientist Dmitrii Mendeleev and wife of the poet Aleksandr Blok. Graduated from the Bestuzhev School, 1906. Studied acting with A. Chitau. Actress with Vsevolod Meyerhold, 1907–22. Editor of Vaganova's *Basics of Classical Dance*. Ballet critic for several Soviet periodicals. Died in Leningrad. Her main work, *Vozniknovenie I Razvitie Tekhniki Klassicheskogo Tantsa*, 3 vol. remains unpublished (the manuscript is kept at the Bakhrushin Theatre Museum, Moscow).

Blok, Vladimir Mikhailovich
7.11.1932– . Composer.
Born in Moscow. Wrote orchestral

suites, pieces for string orchestra, and vocal cycles. Author of articles on music.

Blokhintsev, Dmitrii Ivanovich
11.1.1908–   . Physicist, Academician.
Graduated from Moscow University, 1930. Professor at the same University, 1936. Worked in the Physics Institute of the Academy of Sciences, 1935–56. Directed the construction of a Soviet nuclear power plant 1954.

Blonskii, Pavel Petrovich
26.5.1884–15.2.1941. Psychologist, educationalist.
Born in Kiev. Graduated from Kiev University, 1907. Member of the SR Party, 1903–17. Lecturer in psychology at Moscow University, 1913. After the revolution, organized the Academy of Social Education, 1919–31. Founder of pedology (childrens' psychology) in the USSR, which was very influential in the 1920s and early 1930s, taking the place of traditional pedagogy. Stressing the scientific approach, pedologists collected a lot of factual data, which reflected the chaos and misery of the social conditions of Soviet children. In July 1936 pedology was declared an anti-Marxist science and banned. Arrested with many of his colleagues and perished in the Gulag. Later partly rehabilitated. Some of his psychological works were republished in the 1960s.

Blumenfel'd, Feliks Mikhailovich
19.4.1863–21.1.1931. Pianist, conductor, composer.
Born in the Khersonskaia Gouvt. Professor at the Petersburg, Kiev and Moscow Conservatories. Director of the Kiev Conservatory, 1918–22. Conductor with the Mariinskii Theatre, Petersburg, 1898–1918. Wrote works for piano and other instruments. V. Horowitz was one of his pupils. Died in Moscow.

Boborykin, Petr Dmitrievich
27.8.1836–12.8.1921. Writer.
Born in Nizhnii Novgorod (now Gorkii). Studied at Kazan' and Derpt universities. Editor and publisher of the magazine *Biblioteka dlia chtenia* in the 1860s. From the 1890s lived mainly abroad. Chronicler of literary, political and society life for half a century. Extremely prolific writer of novels, sociological sketches, and memoirs. His 12-volume collected works were published in Petersburg, 1897. Died in Lugano.

Bobrinskii, Aleksei Aleksandrovich, Count
1852–1927. Politician, industrialist.
Descendant of Catherine the Great and Count Orlov. Member of a millionaire family which owned the world's largest sugar factories in the Ukraine. Chairman of the Council of the Union of Nobility, 1906. Senator, and member of the State Council (upper chamber), 1912. Member of the 3rd Duma. Minister of Agriculture, 1915. Emigrated, 1919.

Bobrinskii, Vladimir Alekseevich, Count
1868–1937. Politician, industrialist.
Right wing member of the Duma. Leader of the Russian nationalists. Supported Stolypin's reforms in the 3rd Duma. Opposed the Bolshevik take-over. Emigrated, 1919.

Bobrov, Evgenii Aleksandrovich
5.2.1867–1933. Philosopher.
Representative of personalism, following G. Teichmueller and A. Kozlov. Translated the works of Leibniz into Russian. Wrote a history of Russian philosophy. Published many valuable materials in his six editions of *Philosophy in Russia* (1899–1902).

Bobrov, Sergei Pavlovich
1889–1971. Poet.
Leader of the futurist group Tsentrifuga. His first poetry in print was *Vertogradari Nad Lozami*, 1913. Other works include: *Lira Lir*, 1917; *Vosstanie Mizantropov*, 1922.

Bobrov, Vsevolod Mikhailovich
1.12.1922–1.7.1979. Athlete.
Born in Morshansk, Tambov Oblast'. Honoured Master of Sports, 1948 (football, ice hockey). USSR Honoured Coach, 1967. Graduated from the N. Zhukovskii Air Force Academy, 1956, and from the Military Institute of Physical Culture, 1960. Member of the CPSU, 1952. Olympic champion, 1956. World champion, 1954, 1956. European champion, 1954–56. USSR champion, 1948–49, 1951–52, 1955–56 (ice hockey); 1945–46 (hockey). The only participant in the history of the Olympic Games to be the captain of both football (1952) and ice hockey teams (1956). Died in Moscow.
See: *Samyi Interesnyi Match*, Moscow, 1963; *Rytsari Sporta*, Moscow, 1971.

Bobrovskaia, Cecilia Samoilovna (Zelikson)
19.9.1876–6.7.1960. Revolutionary, party official.
Born in Velizh, Vitebsk Gouvt. Involved in revolutionary activity as a teenager, 1894. Member of the SD Party 1898, carrying out underground party work in many Russian and Polish towns. After the 1905 Revolution secretary of the Moscow region Bolshevik Party Cttee., 1906–7. Active participant in the Bolshevik take-over in Moscow during the October Revolution 1917. Head of the military section of the Bolshevik Moscow Cttee., 1919–20. Worked in the Comintern, 1928–40. From 1940 researcher at the Marxism-Leninism Institute of the Cen. Cttee. of the CPSU.

Bobyshev, Dmitrii Vasil'evich
1936–   . Poet.
Born in Mariupol. Graduated from the Leningrad Technological Institute. Worked as an engineer. Became known as a modernist poet in samizdat. Emigrated, 1979. Settled in the USA. Considered one of the foremost Russian modernist and absurdist poets.

Bobyshov, Mikhail Pavlovich
19.11.1885–7.7.1964. Artist, stage designer.
Born in the village of Pogoreloe, Tver' Oblast'. Studied at the Petersburg Stieglitz School of Graphic Art, 1907. Specialized in painting, then in sculpture. Pupil of V. Savitskii. At one time was influenced in his stage design by the Mir Iskusstva group. Taught at the Leningrad Academy of Arts from 1926. Professor, 1939. Stage designs for *Zolotoi Petushok* by Rimskii-Korsakov (Petrograd Malyi

Theatre), *Rigoletto* (Stanislavskii Opera Theatre), *Mednyi Vsadnik* (Kirov Theatre and Bolshoi Theatre, Moscow). Exhibited from 1911. His last exhibition was held in Moscow, 1960. Died in Leningrad.

Bocharova, Nina Antonovna
24.9.1924–   . Athlete.
Born in the village of Suprunovka, Poltava Oblast'. Graduated from the Kiev Institute of Physical Culture, 1948. Honoured Master of Sports (gymnastics), 1952. Coach. USSR champion, 1949, 1951. World champion, 1954. Olympic champion, 1952. Silver medal, 1952.

Bochkov, Feodosii Nikolaevich
1901–1952. Artist.
Born in Vologda. Genre and landscape painter. Studied first at the Vologda Art School, 1918–22, under N. Dmitrevskii, A. Karinskaia and D. Marten, then at the Moscow VKHUTEMAS, 1923–29 under N. Kupreianov and P. Lvov. Worked with the gouache technique, and water-colours. Also lithographer. Exhibitions from 1939, all in Moscow. Posthumous exhibition in Moscow, 1955.

Bochvar, Andrei Anatol'evich
26.7.1902–   . Metallographer.
Son of A. Bochvar, founder of the school of metallurgists. Graduated from the Moscow Higher Technical School, 1923. Professor at the Moscow Institute of Gold and Non-Ferrous Metals, 1934. Specialist in the structural pecularities and anomalies of alloys. Established temperature patterns of the crystallization of metals and alloys (the Bochvar law).

Bodiul, Ivan Ivanovich
1918–   . State official.
Born in Moldavia. Agronomist at a machine and tractor station. Graduated from the Veterinary Academy, 1942, and the Party Higher School of the Central Cttee. of the CPSU, 1958. Member of the CPSU from 1940. Served in the Soviet Army, 1942–46. Worked for the Moldavian Council of Ministers, 1946–51. Party posts in Moldavia. 1st Secretary of the Central Cttee. of the Moldavian CP, 1961–80. Member of the Credentials Cttee., 1962–66.

Member of the Foreign Affairs Cttee. from 1966. Deputy Chairman of the USSR Council of Ministers, from Dec. 1980 until Nov. 1985. Retired.

Bogaevskii, Afrikan Petrovich
8.1.1873–21.10.1934. Cossack general.
Son of a Don Cossack officer. Educated at the Nikolaevskoe Cavalry School, 1892. Graduated from the Academy of the General Staff, 1900. During WWI, chief-of-staff of the HQ of the Cossack armies. After the February Revolution 1917, commander of a cavalry division. Head of the Don government under Ataman Krasnov. Joined the Dobrovolcheskaia Armiia under General Denikin as commander (ataman) of the Don Cossacks. After the defeat of General Wrangel emigrated from the Crimea to France. Died in Paris.

Bogaevskii, Konstantin Fedorovich
24.1.1872–17.2.1943. Artist.
Born in Feodosia, in the Crimea. Studied at Petersburg Academy of Arts, 1891–97. Pupil of A. Kuindzhi. Member of the Mir Iskusstva group, Union of Russian Artists and the Zhar-Tsvet group. Landscape and water-colour painter. Also lithographer and etcher. Exhibitions: Higher Art School of the Petersburg Academy of Arts, 1897; Spring Exhibitions, Academy of Arts, 1898–05; the Mir Iskusstva group, 1910–13, 1915; the Zhar-Tsvet Society, 1924–26, 1928; K. Kostandi Society, Odessa, 1927. Personal exhibitions: 1926, 1927, 1928, 1936 in Feodosia and Moscow. Died in Feodosia.

Bogatkin, Vladimir Nikolaevich
1903–1956. Political officer.
Joined the Soviet Army, 1920. Graduated from the Sverdlov Communist University, 1933. Editor of the army paper *Krasnaia Zvezda*. Head of the political department of the General Staff, 1951–55.

Bogatyrchuk, Fedor Parfen'evich
14.11.1892–   . Physician, politician, chess player.
Born in Kiev. Graduated in medicine from Kiev University. On active service during WWI. Medical officer with the White Armies during the Civil War. In the 1920s–30s a pioneer

of X-ray research and a chess grandmaster of the USSR. During WWII, Head of the Ukrainian National Rada, close to General Vlasov. Signed the Prague Manifesto, 1944. After WWII, in DP camps in Germany. Defended the idea of a federal union between Russia and the Ukraine, polemicized with Ukrainian separatists. Moved to Canada, 1949. Professor of X-ray anatomy at Ottawa University, 1949–70, and one of the best known Canadian radiologists. Wrote an autobiography, *Moi Put K Prazhskomu Manifestu*, USA, 1980.

Bogatyrev, Aleksandr Iur'evich
4.5.1949–   . Ballet dancer.
Born in Tallinn. Graduated from the Moscow Choreographic School, 1968. From 1969 with the Bolshoi Theatre, where he is one of its leading ballet dancers. Has since performed all over the world.

Bogatyrev, Konstantin Petrovich
1925–1976. Poet, translator.
Born in Prague. Son of a Russian emigré, the well-known folklorist P. Bogatyrev. Studied at Moscow University. Arrested, 1948. Sentenced to death, commuted to 25 years in the Gulag camps. Released after Stalin's death. Became known for his excellent translations of Rilke and Koestler. Involved in the human rights movement. Assaulted by the KGB near his home in Moscow under unknown circumstances. Died of his injuries.
Source: *Poet-Perevodchik Konstantin Bogatyrev. Drug Nemetskoi Literatury*, compiled by W. Kosack with the participation of L. Kopelev and E. Etkind, Germany, 1982.

Bogatyrev, Semen Semenovich
15.2.1890–31.12.1960. Musicologist.
Born in Khar'kov. Professor at the Moscow Conservatory. Wrote music. Restored Tchaikovskii's Unfinished Symphony. Performed 1957. Author of *Dvoinoi Kanon*, Moscow–Leningrad, 1947, and *Obratimyi Kontrapunkt*, Moscow, 1960. Died in Moscow.

Bogdan, Ivan Gavrilovich
29.2.1928–   . Athlete.
Born in the village of Dmitrovo-Belovka, Nikolaevsk Oblast'. Hon-

oured Master of Sport (wrestling), 1960. Graduated from the Kiev Institute of Physical Culture, 1960. Coach. USSR champion, 1958–59, 1961. World champion, 1958, 1961. Olympic heavyweight champion, 1960.

Bogdanov, Aleksandr Aleksandrovich (Malinovskii; pen-names – Werner, Maksimov, Riadovoi)
22.8.1873 – 7.4.1928. Economist, medical scientist, philosopher, revolutionary.
Born in Sokolka, Grodno Gouvt. Graduated from Kharkov University in medicine, 1899. Involved in revolutionary activity, at first as a populist (narodnik), later as a Marxist. Social democrat, 1896, Bolshevik after the split of the SDs, 1903. Member of the Cen. Cttee. of the Bolshevik Party, 1905–07. Head of a Bolshevik terrorist group (with Krasin), although Marxists, in contrast to SRs, were in principle against individual terrorism (considering it useless), while approving of the concept of class war and mass terror. Organizer of the Capri party school (financed by the bestseller royalties of M. Gorkii) and similar courses at Bologna. Lenin (considering Bogdanov a rival in his philosophical works) clashed violently with him and engineered his expulsion from the party for ideological deviation, 1909. After the October Revolution 1917, member of the Communist Academy, lecturer in economics at Moscow University. Ideologist of Proletkult (proletarian culture, destined to replace bourgeois culture, i.e. all previous human culture), 1918. Continued his medical scientific work, especially in gerontology and haematology. Organized the first institute for blood transfusion in the world in Moscow, 1926, and died after conducting a risky blood transfusion experiment on himself. His colourful personality and universal interests were obscured in the USSR, first due to his quarrels with Lenin, and later by the anti-modernist atmosphere of the Stalin years. Present day researchers find in his writings some surprisingly modern concepts (e.g. cybernetics principles of backfeed and simulation), and are rediscovering his important influence, especially on the modernist approach of the 1920s.

Main works: *Revolution and Philosophy, Empiriomonism*, 3 vols, *Philosophy of the Living Experience, Tectology, Universal Organizational Science, Political Economy*, 2 vols, SF novels – *The Red Star, Engineer Manny*.

Bogdanov, Anatolii Ivanovich
1.1.1931– . Athlete.
Born in Leningrad. Graduated from the Military Political Academy, 1963. Honoured Master of Sports (shooting), 1952. Coach. Member of the CPSU, 1955. Many times European and USSR champion, 1952–59. World champion, 1954–59. Olympic champion, 1952 and 1956.
Works: *Vizhu Tsel'*, Moscow, 1971.

Bogdanov, Ivan Petrovich
1855–1932. Artist.
Studied at the Moscow School of Painting, Sculpture and Architecture, 1878–1889 under I. Prianishnikov and V. Makovskii. Genre and portrait painter. Exhibitions: Students of the Moscow School of Painting, Sculpture and Architecture, 1885–86–88–90; TPKHV, 1891–1923.

Bogdanov, Palladii Andreevich
9.12.1881– . Composer, conductor.
Born in Petersburg. Conductor of the State Academic Orchestra in Leningrad, 1903–41. Organised a children's choral school, 1934. Chief conductor of a boys' choir connected with the orchestra, until 1955. Conductor of the Municipal Ensemble of Song and Dance of the Working Reserves. Wrote a cantata, pieces for children's vocal ensembles and choral pieces.

Bogdanov, Semen Il'ich
29.8.1894–12.3.1960. Marshal.
Born in Petersburg. Metal worker. In the army from 1915. Took part in the Civil War, after which received a higher military technical education. Became a well-known tank commander during WWII. Commander of Soviet Tank Forces, 1948–54. Head of the Soviet Tank Academy, 1954–56. Retired for health reasons, 1956. Died in Moscow.

Bogdanov-Bel'skii, Nikolai Petrovich
20.12.1868–1945. Artist.
Born in the village of Shopotovo,

Smolensk Gouvt. Studied at the Troitse-Sergieva Lavra art school and the Moscow School of Painting, Sculpture and Architecture, 1884–89, under E. Sorokin, V. Makovskii, V. Polenov, and I. Prianishnikov. Also studied at the Higher Art School of the Petersburg Academy of Arts in the 1890s under I. Repin. Genre and portrait painter. After the October Revolution 1917, emigrated to Latvia, 1921. Exhibitions: MOLKH, 1889, 1894–95, 1898; TPKHV, 1890–92–94 and 1918; All-Russian Exhibition, Nizhnii Novgorod, 1896. Died in Latvia.

Bogdanov-Berezovskii, Valerian Mikhailovich
17.7.1903– . Music critic, composer.
Born in Petersburg. Author of 2 operas, 2 ballets, 2 symphonies (1940, 1945), instrumental pieces, choral works, romances, and music for plays and films. Author of articles and several books (e.g. *Sovetskii Dirizher – E. Mravinskii*, Leningrad, 1956).

Bogdanova, Nastas'ia Stepanovna (Zinov'eva)
1860?–9.4.1937. Narrator, folk singer.
Born in Zinov'evskaia, Olonetskaia Gouvt. Repertoire of ancient laments. According to the press at the time, was a rare musical folk talent. Appeared in Zaonezh'e, Petrozavodsk, where she lived from 1902, Petersburg and Moscow. Her songs have been recorded. Died in Petrozavodsk.

Bogdanovich, Aleksandr Vladimirovich
3.11.1874–6.4.1950. Singer (tenor).
Born in Smolensk. Soloist with the Bolshoi Theatre, 1906–36. One of the organisers of the Operatic Studio attached to the Bolshoi Theatre. Artistic director of the Stanislavskii Opera Theatre. Died in Moscow.

Bogdanovich, Pavel Nikolaevich
7.7.1883–6.3.1973. Colonel.
Born in Kiev. Educated at the Kiev Military School. Served in the Caucasus. Graduated from the Academy of the General Staff, 1911. Served in the Preobrazhenskii regiment.

Wounded and taken prisoner in the battle for East Prussia, 1914. Escaped to Holland. Head of the Russian Military Mission with the Russian Embassy in Paris, 1921. Founded a youth organization for Russian exiles, NORR (monarchist scouts). After WWII, moved to Argentina, 1948. Managed a large hacienda in the mountains. After a serious illness moved to Buenos Aires where he taught languages, and wrote historical novels and a valuable description of the East Prussia campaign, 1914. Died in Buenos Aires.

Bogin, Mikhail
1936– . Film director.
Born in Leningrad. Studied for 2 years at the Leningrad Polytechnical Institute. Entered the VGIK (State Film School). Graduated as a director in 1965. Assistant director to Joseph Heifitz on *The Lady with a Little Dog*. First short film, *Ten Seconds in an Hour* (documentary, student work). One of his most beautiful films is *The Two*, made in 1965 at Riga Film Studio with Viktoria Fedorova in the leading role. *The Two* is based on the love story of a young musician and a deaf-mute girl who loses her hearing during the siege of Leningrad. His next feature film, *Zosya*, was made in 1967 at the Gorkii Studios in Moscow, as was *About Love* in 1971. Emigrated to America in the mid-1970s.

Bogolepov, Aleksandr Aleksandrovich
15.1.1885–31.8.1980. Philosopher, religious historian, professor.
Educated at the Riazan' Seminary, 1906. Graduated in law from Petersburg University, 1910. Reader from 1918. Legal adviser to the Minister of Finance, 1915–17. Last elected dean of Petrograd University. Exiled by Lenin with a group of other philosophers and writers, 1922. Member of the Russian Scientific Institute, Berlin, 1923. Taught Russian language and law. Moved to West Germany in 1945. Moved to the USA, 1951. Professor of law at the St. Vladimir Orthodox Seminary. Doctor of the Orthodox Theological Institute, Paris, and Professor from 1970. Chairman and honorary member of the Russian Academic Group in the USA, 1966–70. Doctor of Theology of the St. Vladimir Orthodox Seminary, 1975. Died in the USA.

Bogoliubov, Klavdii Mikhailovich
1909– . Party official.
Director of a school in Vologda, 1930–39. Joined the Communist Party in 1938. Served in the Soviet Army, 1939–41. High party posts from 1941–63. From 1960, in the administration of the Cen. Cttee. of the CPSU. Deputy Chairman of the State Cttee. of the USSR Council of Ministers for Printing and Publishing, 1963–65. 1st Deputy Head of the General Department of the Cen. Cttee. of the CPSU. Chief assistant to Chernenko. Retired under Andropov, 1983.

Bogoliubov, Nikolai Nikolaevich
25.1.1870–4.3.1951. Opera conductor.
Born near Buguruslan, Simbirskaia Gouvt. Producer with the Mariinskii Theatre, 1911–17. After 1917 chief producer with various operas, and professor at the conservatories of Odessa, Baku, Tiflis and elsewhere. Died on a train journey while on a tour of the Soviet Union. Author of *Polveka na Opernoi Stsene*, Moscow, 1957.

Bogoliubov, Nikolai Nikolaevich
1900– . Mathematician.
Born in Nizhnii Novgorod (now Gor'kii). Moved to Kiev, 1922. Pupil of the mathematicians, D. Grave and N. Krylov. Taught at Kiev University, 1936–41, and 1945–49. Academician, 1953. Professor of Moscow University, 1959. World authority in various fields of mathematical analysis, function theory, differential equations, theory of vibrations, theory of stability and quantum field theory.

Bogomolets, Aleksandr Aleksandrovich
24.5.1881–19.7.1946. Pathologist.
Born in Kiev. Graduated from Odessa University in 1906. Professor at Saratov University, 1911–25. Professor of Moscow University, 1925–31. Director of the Institute for Haematology and Blood Transfusion, 1928–31. Vice-president of the USSR Academy of Sciences, 1942. President of the Ukrainian Academy of Sciences, 1930–46. Created a large school of pathophysiologists in the USSR. An authority on endocrinology, the nervous system and gerontology.

Bogomolov, Dmitrii Vasil'evich
1890–1937. Diplomat.
From 1929–32 counsellor at the Soviet Embassy in London, and from 1927–29 in Warsaw, where he met and befriended V. Mayakovsky. Disappeared in the Gulag.

Bogoraz, Iosif Aronovich
1896–1985. Economist.
Born in Ovrug in Volhynia. Joined the Communist Party, 1919. Lecturer in economics in Kharkov and Kiev in the 1920s and 1930s. Arrested as a Trotskyist, 1936. Spent the next 20 years in Gulag camps. Rehabilitated and re-instated in the party, 1956. Became involved in the human rights movement. His works circulated in samizdat. Resigned from the Communist Party, 1974.

Bogoraz, Larisa Iosifovna (Daniel, Marchenko)
1929– . Dissident.
Born in Khar'kov. Daughter of Iosif Bogoraz. Married the writer Iu. Daniel, 1955, who later became famous during the Daniel-Siniavskii trial. Actively involved in the human rights movement. Arrested in 1968 for participating in a demonstration against the invasion of Czechoslovakia. Several terms of exile. Later married A. Marchenko and shared his struggle with the authorities and his exile.

Bogoraz, Vladimir Germanovich (N.A. Tan)
27.4.1865–10.5.1936. Ethnographer.
Born in Ovruch, Volhynia. Involved in revolutionary activity with the populists. In exile near Kolyma, 1890–98. Became interested in the life of the local population, and after taking part in several expeditions in order to study the people of north eastern Russia (1894–96, 1900–01), became the foremost authority on their history, folklore, culture and languages. Organized the Northern Committee of the Cen. Cttee. of the CPSU and the Institute of the People

of the North. Professor at Leningrad University, 1921. One of the creators of alphabets for local Siberian languages. Died near Rostov-on-Don. Author of the classical monograph, *Chukchi*.
Main works: *Collected Works*, 10 vols, 1910–11.

Bogorov, Veniamin Grigor'evich
24.12.1904– . Oceanographer.
Graduated from Moscow University, 1926. Worked at the Institute of Oceanography from 1941. Suggested new methods for quantitative investigation of plankton and marine research.

Bogoslovskii, Nikita Vladimirovich
22.5.1913– . Composer.
Born in Petersburg. Popular and well-established modern composer. Wrote the symphony *Povest' Vasilii Terkin*, 1950, as well as music for plays and films.

Boiarskii, Vladimir Il'ich
1905?–1945. Major-general.
Took part in WWII as commander of the 41st Guards division of the Red Army. Taken prisoner by the Germmans. Joined the ROA as Deputy Chief-of-staff. During fighting between the ROA and the SS in Prague, fell into the hands of Czech communists partisans and was executed.

Boiarskikh, Klavdia Sergeevna
11.11.1939– . Athlete.
Born in Verkhniaia Pyshma, Sverdlovsk Oblast'. Graduated from the Sverdlovsk Pedagogical Institute, 1971. Honoured Master of Sports (skiing), 1964. USSR champion, 1964–67. World champion, 1966. Olympic champion, 1964 (5 and 10 km).

Bokarev, Konstantin Sergeevich
1928– . Artist.
Miniature painter. Studied at the A.M. Gorkii Art School in Palekh, 1951. Exhibitions: Thirty Years of Soviet Palekh, Moscow, 1955; RSFSR Artists, Moscow, 1955, 1957; Ivanovo Artists, Moscow, 1956; RSFSR Folk Applied and Decora-

tive Art, Moscow, 1956–57. Created many miniature objets d'art including the Ruslan and Liudmila box.

Bokii, Georgii Borisovich
26.9.1909– . Chemist.
Graduated from the Leningrad Mining Institute, 1930. Professor at Moscow University, 1944. Used crystallographic methods for the study of complex compounds.

Bokii, Gleb Ivanovich (party names – Kuzma, Diadia, Maksim Ivanovich)
3.7.1879–15.11.1937. Revolutionary, secret police official.
Born in Tiflis. Member of the SD Party from 1900. Member of the Petersburg Bolshevik Party Cttee. in 1904. Took part in the 1905 Revolution in Petersburg. Arrested several times for revolutionary activity. Member of the Military Revolutionary Cttee. in Petrograd, Apr. 1917. From 1918 one of the chiefs of the Cheka in Petrograd and at different fronts during the Civil War. From 1921 member of the Vecheka (All Union Cheka), later member of the Collegium of the GPU and NKVD. One of the most active organizers of the Gulag system. Arrested in 1937 and shot.

Bokov, Fedor Efimovich
1904–1984. Lt-general.
Joined the Red Army, 1926. Member of the Communist Party, 1927. Graduated from the Military-Political Academy, 1937. From the 1930s, political officer in the army. Professor, and later head, of the Military-Political Academy, training political commissars for the armed forces. Participated in WWII as a political officer. After WWII, had leading posts in the Soviet Occupation Forces in East Germany. Returned to the Military-Political Academy, 1956–61.

Bokov, Nikolai Konstantinovich
1945– . Writer.
Author of the short story *Pokhozhdenia Vani Chmotanova* circulated in samizdat and later published in the West, followed by the novel *Bestseller* published in Paris. Emigrated in 1975. Editor of *Kovcheg*, the emigré literary magazine. Lives in Paris.

Bokov, Viktor Fedorovich
19.9.1914– . Poet.
Born in the village of Iazvitsy near Moscow. Son of a peasant. Graduated from the Gorkii Literary Institute, 1938. Spent some time in the Gulag camps. Wrote poems about his experiences in the camps which circulated in samizdat. Writes in a simple folkloristic style, which brings him wide popularity. Several collections of verse published.

Bokun, German
1927–1978. Athlete.
Honoured Master of Sports (fencing). Member of the USSR team at the XVth Olympic Games. USSR and European champion many times.

Bolm, Adolf (Emilii) Rudolfovich
25.9.1884–16.4.1951. Ballet dancer, choreographer, teacher.
Born in Petersburg. Graduated from the Petersburg Theatre School, 1903. Pupil of P.K. Karsavin. Member of the corps de ballet of the Mariinskii Theatre. From 1905 a soloist. Partner of Anna Pavlova during her first tour abroad in 1908. Danced with Diaghilev's Ballets Russes, 1911–16. In 1916 moved to the USA, where he organized the Intimnyi Ballet. During the last years of his life, worked in Hollywood, staging dances in balletfilms. Memoirs: *Dni Tantsovshchika*, 1926. Died in Hollywood.

Boloshev, Aleksandr Aleksandrovich
12.3.1947– . Athlete.
Born in Elektrogorsk, Moscow Oblast'. Studied at the Volgograd Institute of Physical Culture. Honoured Master of Sports (basketball), 1972. European champion, 1969, 1971. World champion, 1974. Olympic champion, 1972.

Bolotnikov, Petr Grigor'evich
8.3.1930– . Athlete.
Born in the village of Zinovkino, Moldavian ASSR. Graduated from the Moscow Institute of Physical Culture, 1967. Honoured Master of Sports (athletics), 1959. With Moscow Spartak. Member of the CPSU, 1962. Olympic champion (1960, 10,000 metres race). European champion, 1962. USSR champion, 1957–62, 1964. World champion, 1960–63. Works: *Poslednii Krug*, Moscow, 1975.

Bol'shakov, Kirill Andreevich
24.12.1906– . Chemist.
Graduated from Kazan' Univesity, 1930. Worked in the Institute of Rare Metals in Moscow. Mainly concerned with physical-chemical methods of extracting rare elements.

Bol'shakov, Valerii Vasil'evich
1928– . Artist.
Miniature painter. Studied at the A.M. Gorkii Art School in Palekh. Created many miniature objets d'art specialising in papier-mâché. Exhibitions: Thirty Years of Soviet Palekh, Moscow, 1955; Ivanovo Artists, Moscow, 1956; RSFSR Folk Applied and Decorative Art, Moscow, 1956–57; Applied Art, Moscow, 1957. Many of his works are on sale in Berezka currency shops all over the world.

Bonch-Bruevich, Mikhail Aleksandrovich
21.2.1888–7.3.1940. Radio technician.
Born in Orel. Educated at the Military Electrotechnical School in Petersburg, 1914. In 1918 organized a radiotechnical laboratory in Nizhnii Novgorod. Became the main organizer of the technical side of Soviet broadcasting. Died in Leningrad.

Bonch-Bruevich, Mikhail Dmitrievich
8.3.1870–3.8.1956. General.
Born in Moscow. Graduated from the Academy of the General Staff, 1898. Staff officer. Took part in WWI. During the February Revolution 1917, commander of the Pskov garrison and member of the Pskov Soviet. Commander of the armies of the Northern Front, Aug.–Sept. 1917. Close to his brother, who was a prominent Bolshevik. One of the first generals to join the Red Army after October 1917. Chief-of-staff to the Boshevik commander-in-chief from the day of the October Revolution, 7 Nov. 1917. High military posts in the Bolshevik HQ during the Civil War. Specialist on geodesy, cartography and air photography. Died in Moscow.

Bonch-Bruevich, Vladimir Dmitrievich
28.6.1873–14.7.1955. Politician.
Born in Moscow. Member of the SD Party, 1895. Was close to Lenin during his time as a student in Zurich. Organized most of the publishing ventures of the Bolsheviks in Russia before 1917 (the publishing houses Vpered, and Zhizn' i Znanie, and the newspapers *Zvezda*, and *Pravda*). In 1917 one of the editors of *Izvestia*. Editor of the Bolshevik newspaper *Rabochii i Soldat*. Also known as an ethnographer and an authority on Russian sects. Before the revolution, wrote a special report denying that Rasputin should be considered a sectarian, thus ensuring his continued presence in public life, which proved very useful for revolutionary propaganda purposes. Took part in the Bolshevik take-over in Petrograd as first chairman of the Commission for the Struggle against Counter-revolution (later Cheka, the Soviet secret police). Supervised the move of the Soviet government from Petrograd to Moscow, 1918. Organizer of publishing during the early years of Soviet rule. Director of the State Literary Museum, 1933. Director of the Museum of History of Religion and Atheism at the Academy of Sciences in Leningrad, 1945–55. Died in Moscow.

Bondarchuk, Anatolii Pavlovich
31.5.1941– . Athlete.
Born in Starokonstantinov, in the Ukraine. Graduated from the Kamenets-Podolskii Pedagogical Institute, 1963. Honoured Master of Sports (athletics), 1972. World champion, 1969–71. USSR champion, 1969–70, 1972–73. European champion, 1969. Bronze medal at the Olympic Games, 1976. Olympic champion, 1972.

Bondarchuk, Sergei Fedorovich
25.9.1920– . Film director, actor.
Born in the village of Belozerka, Odessa Oblast'. Attended a theatrical school in Rostov-on-Don before the war. In 1946 entered the actor's faculty of the VGIK (State Film School) as a third-year student. Studied under Sergei Gerasimov. Graduated in 1948. First effort as a director was *The Fate of a Man* produced by Mosfilm in 1959. Became known as a director for his adaptation of Tolstoy's *War and Peace*. He himself played the part of Pierre Bezukhov. The original 16-hour version was re-edited and sold all over the world. Directed *Waterloo*, 1970, for Dino De Laurentis in which he also played a part. Other films: *They Fought For Their Motherland*, *The Steppe* (Chekhov adaptation). Acted in *Othello* (1955), *Serezha* (1960), Roberto Rosselini's *It Was One Night in Rome* (1960), *Uncle Vania* (1970).

Bondarenko, Petr Abramovich
4.11.1903– . Violinist.
Born in Fastov, Kiev Gouvt. Pupil of A. Iampol'skii. Professor at the Gnesin Pedagogical Institute of Music, and at the Moscow Conservatory, 1927–54. Soloist with the All-Union Radio, Moscow.

Bonner, Ruth
1900–26.12.1987. Human rights campaigner.
Daughter of a Jewish revolutionary. Mother-in-law of Dr Andrei Sakharov. Before 1917, lived with her family in Eastern Siberia. Committed socialist. Joined the Communist Party in the 1920s. Married an activist of the Armenian Communist Party. After her husband's arrest and execution in 1937, she too was arrested as a wife of the enemy of the people, and became an inmate of a prison camp in Kazakhstan, working on the excavation of a canal. Released, 1946. Lived near Leningrad. Later continued her exile in the Gorkii region. In 1954, after her husband's rehabilitation, returned to Moscow. In 1961 wrote a private letter to Khrushchev warning of the evils of nuclear weapons. In 1980 was let out of the country for a short visit to the USA. Actively campaigned from abroad for the release of the Sakharovs from their Gorkii exile. Was refused an entry visa to the USSR in 1980. Eventually returned to the USSR in June 1986. Died in Moscow.

Boreiko, Valentin Vasil'evich
7.10.1933– . Athlete.
Born in Leningrad. Graduated from the Leningrad Institute of Physical Culture, 1962. Honoured Master of Sports (rowing), 1960. Coach. USSR champion, 1959–63. Olympic champion (1960, with O. Golovanov).

Borisiak, Andrei Alekseevich
18.2.1885–21.4.1962. Cellist.
Born in Samara. Pupil of A. Verzh-

49

bilovich. Taught in Kharkov, 1913–18. In Moscow from 1919. Author of the first Soviet textbook for cello, 1949, and of other text books. Amateur astronomer. Discovered a new star in the constellation Perseus, 1901. Wrote works on methodology, 1929–47. Died in Moscow.

Borisov, Vadim Mikhailovich
1945–   . Historian.
Graduated from Moscow University in history. Specialized in church history of the 14–15th centuries. Published an article in the collection *Iz pod glyb* edited by Solzhenitsyn, Paris, 1974. Author of many articles.

Borisov, Vasilii Fedorovich
12.12.1922–   . Athlete.
Born in the village of Maiaki, Donetsk Oblast'. Graduated from the Higher School of Coaches of the Moscow Institute of Physical Culture, 1961. Honoured Master of Sports (shooting), 1955. With Moscow Dynamo. Member of the CPSU, 1955. World, European and USSR champion, 1951–65. World record holder, 1954–55. Olympic champion, 1956. Silver medal, 1956. Bronze medal, 1960.

Borisov, Vladimir Il'ich
1945–19.5.1970. Dissident.
Born in Vladimir. Early involvement in human rights movement. Founded a local group of young people striving for social democracy and progress. Published two samizdat broadsheets called *Youth* (Molodost). In spring 1969 certified insane by the infamous Serbskii Institute, acting on KGB orders. Committed suicide by hanging in his cell in the Butyrki prison in Moscow.

Borisovskii, Vadim Vasil'evich
19.1.1900–   . Viola and viola d'amore player.
Born in Moscow. Pupil of V. Bakaleinikov. Professor at the Moscow Conservatory. Member of the Beethoven State Quartet. Wrote arrangements and transcriptions for viola. R. Barshai was one of his pupils.

Borodai, Mikhail Matveevich
1853–1929. Theatrical manager.
From the late 1880s, owner of opera and drama companies in Khar'kov,

Kiev, Kazan', Saratov, Odessa, in the towns of the Urals, Siberia and elsewhere. Popularized opera in the Russian provinces. After the revolution worked in the Irkutsk Theatre. Died in Irkutsk.
See: *Iz Muzykal'nogo Proshlogo*, Moscow, 1959.

Borodin, Leonid Ivanovich
1938–   . Dissident, author.
A founder-member of the All-Russian Union for the Liberation of Russian People, active at Leningrad University during the 1960s. Served his first term in Vladimir prison, 1967–73, for membership of this student group which discussed freedom in a religious context. Wrote *The Miracle and the Grief*, 1983, a fairy tale set in Siberia, a political parody which caused his second arrest and term in a labour camp. His second book, *The Third Truth*, was translated into French, and a third book, *Partings*, was published in London in 1987. He was released 25 June 1987.

Borodin, Mikhail Markovich (Gruzenberg)
9.7.1884–29.5.1951. Politician, editor.
Involved in revolutionary activity from 1900. Member of the Bolshevik Party, 1903. Lived in Bern, 1904–05. Active in social democratic organizations in Riga, 1905–06. Emigrated to Great Britain, 1906, then lived in the USA. Active in the Socialist Party of America, 1907–18. Appointed first Soviet consul in Mexico, 1919. Worked in the Comintern, 1919–23. Arrested in Glasgow as an agent of the Comintern, 1922. After 6 months imprisonment, expelled from Britain. Invited by Sun Yat Sen as adviser to the Cen. Cttee. of the Kuomintang, 1923–27. Very active in spreading communist influence in China at this early stage. After his return from China, Deputy Minister of Labour. Chief Editor of the English language edition of *Moscow News*, 1932. Deputy Director of TASS News Agency. Chief Editor of Sovinformburo, 1941–49.

Borovik, Artem Genrikhovich
1960–   . Journalist.
Born in Moscow. Son of G. Borovik. Educated at the Moscow English

School and at New York's Dalton's School while his father was employed there by Novosti Press. Graduated from the elite MGIMO (Moscow Institute of International Relations), 1981. Speaks several languages. Trained as a diplomat. First job was at the Soviet Embassy in Peru. Turned to journalism. Reporter on the weekly magazine *Ogonek*. Sent by V. Korotich, the editor-in-chief, to Afghanistan as a war reporter. Described with frankness the horrors of the war for the Soviet soldiers. Impressed the *International Herald Tribune* which ran his story. In his interview with the *Tribune*, he told of his lifestyle, including his grand Moscow flat, fast cars and drugs.

Borovik, Genrikh Aviezerovich
1929–   . Journalist.
Prominent journalist throughout the 1960–80s. Known for his connections with government figures, and (according to the *International Herald Tribune*, 5.2.88) with the KGB. Interviewed inaccessible people all over the world, including Edward Lee Howard, the CIA defector, and Kim Philby. In the 1950s, reported for *Ogonek* from Cuba, where he interviewed Fidel Castro and Hemingway. Lived between 1966 and 1972 on Riverside Drive, New York, where he worked for the Novosti Press. At his luxurious flat in Moscow, hosted Arthur Miller, Norman Mailer, John Updike, and Hemingway's widow, Mary. Chairman of the official Soviet Peace Committee, an organization which is controlled by the KGB. His works, apart from his reports from abroad, include several books about his travels in Cuba, Buenos Aires, etc. Also wrote some scripts of journalistic rather than literary value.

Borovskii, Aleksandr Konstantinovich
18.3.1889–   . Pianist.
Born in Mitava. Pupil of A. N. Esipova. Taught at the Moscow Conservatory, 1915–20. Emigrated. Lived abroad from 1920, in the USA from 1940. First guest appearance in the USSR, 1927.

Bortkevich, Sergei Eduardovich
28.2.1877–25.10.1952. Pianist, composer.
Born in Khar'kov. Guest appearances

in many countries from 1902. Professor at the Klindvort-Sharvenka Conservatory, Berlin, 1904–14. Returned to Russia, but then emigrated to Vienna. Author of orchestral works, symphonies, suites, pieces for piano, violin, and cello. Died in Vienna.

Borzov, Anatolii Alekseevich
7.11.1928– . Dancer, teacher.
Born in the village of Vorovo, near Moscow. Graduated from the Moscow Choreographic School, 1955. Soloist with the Igor Moiseev Dance Company, 1946–69. Artistic director of the Moiseev Company in Egypt, 1966–68. Taught at the Moscow Choreographic School from 1953 and from 1969 at the Moscow GITIS. Professor, 1979.

Borzov, Ivan Ivanovich
21.10.1915–1974. Marshal.
Born in the village of Starovorovo near Moscow. Son of a peasant. Joined the navy, 1935. Spent his life in naval aviation units. Commander of the naval air force, 1962–74.

Borzov, Valerii Filipovich
20.10.1949– . Athlete.
Born in Sambor, Lvov Oblast'. Graduated from the Kiev Institute of Physical Culture, 1971. Honoured Master of Sports (athletics), 1970. With Kiev Dynamo. Coach. European and USSR champion, 1970–75. Olympic champion, 1972. (100 and 200 metres). Silver medal, 1972.

Bosh, Evgenia Bogdanovna (Gotlibovna)
23.8.1879–5.1.1925. Revolutionary, Cheka official.
Born at Ochakov into a working class family. Joined the SD Party in 1901. At the age of 16 married the son of a factory owner. Soon left him and joined the Bolshevik, Piatakov. Active in Kiev. First member and secretary of the Kiev Committee of the RSDRP, 1909–10. Arrested and exiled to Siberia in 1913. Fled with Piatakov abroad through Vladivostok. Lived in Switzerland, later in Scandinavia. After the February Revolution 1917, tried to organize the Bolshevik forces in the Ukraine against the Ukrainian Rada (Nationalist Government). Became People's Commissar of the Interior (chief of the

secret police) in the first communist Ukrainian government in Khar'kov in 1918. During the Civil War, took part in several terror missions (Penza, Astrakhan, Gomel). Commissar of the Caspian-Caucasian front. Accused of Trotskyism in 1923, arrested and committed suicide in a Moscow prison two years later.
See: A. Solzhenitsyn, *Lenin in Zurich.*

Boskin, Mikhail Vasil'evich
1875–1930. Artist.
Genre-painter. Exhibitions: MTKH, 1903–05; MOLKH, 1906; TPKHV, 1907, 1911–17; Sergiev Art Society (Klich), Sergiev, 1924; AKHRR (11th Exhibition, Iskusstvo V Massy), Moscow, 1929.

Botev, Gratsian Georgievich
13.12.1928–1981. Athlete.
Born in Luga, Leningrad Oblast'. Graduated from the Leningrad Pedagogical Higher School of Physical Culture, 1948. Honoured Master of Sport (rowing), 1957. USSR champion, 1956, 1958–60. Olympic champion (with P. Kharin 10,000 metres), 1956. Silver medal (1,000 metres), 1956.

Botvinik, Mikhail Moiseevich
17.8.1911– . Chess player, grand master.
Born in St. Petersburg. Originally trained as an electronics engineer. Was not trained as a professional chess player, but combined chess playing with his work as an engineer. His reign lasted fifteen years from 1948 until 1963, with two intervals in 1957–58 (V. Smyslov) and 1960–61 (M. Tal'). Trains young chess players.

Bovt, Violetta Trofimovna
9.5.1927– . Ballerina.
Born in Los Angeles. Graduated from the Moscow Choreographic School, 1944. Danced at the Moscow Stanislavskii and Nemirovich Danchenko Music Theatre. In the postwar years, starred with the Bolshoi Ballet.

Bozhenko, Vasilii Nazarovich
1871–1919. Revolutionary.
Joined the Bolsheviks, 1917. Active

organizer of the Red Guards and Red partisan groups in the Ukraine. During the Civil War, commanded a regiment in the Red Army.

Bragina, Liudmila Ivanovna
24.7.1943– . Athlete.
Born in Sverdlovsk. Honoured Master of Sports (track and field athletics), 1972. Graduated from the Krasnodar Pedagogical Institute, 1968. With Krasnodar Dynamo. USSR champion, 1968–74. World record holder, 1972–76 (1,500 metres and 3,000 metres). Olympic champion, 1972 (1,500 metres race). Member of the CPSU, 1976.

Brailovskii, Aleksandr
16.2.1896– . Pianist.
Born in Kiev. Pupil of V. Pukhal'skii and T. Leshetitskii. Lived abroad from 1911. Guest appearance in the USSR, 1961.

Brailovskii, Viktor
1935– . Human rights campaigner.
Trained as a cyberneticist. His career ended when he tried to emigrate in the early 1970s. Organized seminars in Moscow for refusenik scientists. Arrested in Nov. 1980 and sentenced to 5 years' internal exile. Released in 1984, and continued his fight for his right to emigrate. Became a cause célèbre and eventually was allowed to leave for Israel in 1987.

Bramson, L. M.
1869–1942. Politician.
Member of the State Duma, in the Trudovik faction. Colleague of A. Kerenskii. Member of the Petrograd Executive Committee after the February Revolution 1917.

Brandukov, Anatolii Andreevich
22.12.1856–16.2.1930. Cellist.
Born in Moscow. Pupil of V. Fittsenhagen. Lived abroad, mainly in Paris, 1878–1906. Director of the School of Musical Drama attached to the Moscow Philharmonic Society from 1906. Professor at the Moscow Conservatory from 1921. Died in Moscow.

Bratoliubov, Iurii Aleksandrovich

1893–1919. Pilot.

Took part in WWI. Served with the Red Army during the Civil War. Commander of a special aviation detachment formed to fight the White Cossack cavalry of Gen. Mamontov. His plane was shot down. Taken prisoner by the Whites and hanged.

Braudo, Evgenii Maksimovich

20.2.1882–17.10.1939. Music critic.
Born in Riga. Among other works wrote *Vseobshchaia Istoriia Muzyki*, 3 vols., Moscow, 1925–27, *Szhatyi Ocherk Istorii Musyki*, Moscow, 1928 (2 amended editions), and *Istoriia Musyki*, Moscow, 1935. Died in Moscow.

Braunstein, Aleksandr Evseevich

26.5.1902– . Biochemist.
Graduated from the Khar'kov Medical Institute, 1925. Specialist in metabolism at the Institute of Experimental Medicine, 1936. Carried out research into enzymology and nitrogen exchange of amino acids.

Bravin, Nikolai Mikhailovich (Vasiatkin)

25.10.1883–10.6.1956. Singer (baritone).
Born in Astrakhan'. Pupil of U. Mazetti. Worked in operettas from 1906. With the Moscow Operetta Theatre from 1922. Died in Moscow.

Braz, Iosif Emmanuilovich

1872–1936. Artist.
Studied at the Odessa Graphic School, and the Society of Fine Arts under K. Kostandi. Also with S. Kholloshi in Munich and at the Higher Art School of the Petersburg Academy of Arts, 1895– 96. Pupil of Il'ia Repin. Portrait and landscape painter. Exhibitions: Association of Southern-Russian Artists, Odessa, 1893–1904; MOLKH, 1896–99; Academy of Arts, 1898; Spring Exhibitions, Academy of Arts, 1898–00; Mir Iskusstva group, 1900–03, 1911–17, 1922, 1924; 36 Artists, 1901–02, 1902–03; SPKH, 1903–07; Russian portraits at Tavricheskii Palace, St Petersburg, 1905; First State Free Exhibition of Arts, 1919. Personal exhibition: Novgorod, 1926.

Brazhnikov, Maksim Viktorovich

1.4.1904– . Musicologist, paleographer.
Born in Petersburg. Wrote on ancient Russian church singing. Author of *Puti Razvitiia i Zadachi Rasshifrovki Znamennogo Raspeva XII-XVIII Vekov*, Leningrad-Moscow, 1949.

Breitbart, Ekaterina Alekseevna

1941– . Journalist, editor.
Born in Moscow. Sister of the writer V. Maksimov. Graduated from the Moscow Teachers' Institute. Emigrated to Israel, 1972. Lived in the USA, later moved to West Germany. Editor of *Grani* from 1986.

Brekhovskikh, Leonid Maksimovich

6.5.1917– . Physicist.
Graduated from Perm' University, 1939. Professor at Moscow University, 1953. Director of the Acoustics Institute, 1954. Specialist in acoustics and wave propagation, proposed the theory of a side and head waves important in seismographic surveys.

Breshko-Breshkovskaia, Ekaterina Konstantinovna

3.2.1844–12.9.1934. Revolutionary.
Born in Saratov. Daughter of a Polish nobleman. Active in the student revolutionary movement from 1873. Populist in her youth, later became one of the organizers and leaders of the SR Party. In exile 1874–96. Founded with Gershuni the Workers Party for the Liberation of Russia, 1899, which became part of the SRs in 1902. Emigrated to Switzerland, 1903, then moved to the USA, 1904. Returned to Russia and took part in the 1905 Revolution. Arrested in 1907, and sent to Siberia. Released at the beginning of the February Revolution 1917 and returned in triumph to Petrograd, affectionately greeted as 'the grandmother of the Russian revolution'. Condemned the Bolshevik take-over in October 1917. Emigrated again in 1919 to the USA, moved to Czechoslovakia in 1924, and thereafter lived mostly in France. Died near Prague.

Brezhnev, Iurii Leonidovich

1933– . Party and state official.
Son of Leonid Brezhnev. Graduated from the Dnepropetrovsk Metallurgical Institute in 1955. In 1957 joined the Communist Party. Graduated from the All-Union Academy of Foreign Trade in 1960. His first job was assistant foreman, then superintendent at the K. Liebknecht Plant in Dnepropetrovsk, 1955–57. Senior engineer, chief of a department in the USSR Trade Mission in Sweden, 1966–68. Chairman of the Foreign Trade Association, 1970–76. Deputy Minister of Foreign Trade, 1976–79. 1st Deputy Minister from 1979. Candidate member of the Cen. Cttee. of the CPSU from 1981. Dismissed by Andropov in 1983 and sent to work in the provinces.

Brezhnev, Leonid Il'ich

19.12.1906–10.11.1982. Politician, statesman.
Born in Kamenskoe (now Dneprodzerzhinsk). Started work as a land surveyor, became an agricultural administrator in the Urals. Member of the CPSU from 1931. Graduated from the Dneprodzerzhinsk Metallurgical Institute, 1935. Secretary of the Dnepropetrovsk Party Obkom, 1939. During WWII, senior political officer with the army. Subsequently engaged in party administrative work in the Ukraine. First secretary of the Cen. Cttee. of the CP of Moldavia, 1950. Member of the Cen. Cttee. of the CPSU, 1952. After Stalin's death, deputy head of the Chief Political Administration of the Armed Forces, 1953. Under Khrushchev, given the task of supervising the Virgin Land campaign in Kazakhstan. First secretary of the Cen. Cttee. of the CP of Kazakhstan, 1955. Member of the Presidium of the Cen. Cttee. of the CPSU, 1957, after the expulsion of the 'anti-party group' of old Stalinists. Supervised the development of heavy industry. Succeeded Voroshilov as head of state in 1960. Succeeded Khrushchev as leader of the party, after his retirement (dismissal) in Oct. 1964 for voluntarist deviations. Represented the 'safe' candidature of the party bureaucracy alarmed by the volatile character of Khrushchev and his erratic reforms. Remained party leader until his death. The invasion of Czechoslovakia in 1968 and the proclamation of the 'Brezhnev doctrine' of the right of interference in any country where communist rule is

under threat are connected with his name. Signed the Helsinki agreements in 1976, but through the KGB ruthlessly tried to suppress any attempts to apply the provisions of Helsinki to internal Soviet life. Allowed the use of psychiatry against dissidents (used already under Khrushchev) to develop into a system. Was awarded the highest literary prize for his wartime memoirs. In foreign affairs, cautiously advanced Soviet influence under the slogan of détente. Applied the doctrine connected with his name for the last time during the invasion of Afghanistan, leaving a difficult legacy for his successors. According to later judgement, his long years in power were marked by stagnation and corruption (epokha zastoia). Died in Moscow.

Brezhneva, Galina Leonidovna
1930–   . Circus devotee. Leonid Brezhnev's daughter.
Studied in the literature faculty of the Dnepropetrovsk Pedagogical Institute, and later moved to the philosophy department at Kishinev University. Graduated. Married Evgenii Milaev, the circus acrobat and strongman, in Kishinev, 1951. Initiated divorce proceedings 8 years later. Her second husband, whom she married in a secret ceremony in the south (probably in the Crimea), was Igor Kio, son of the famous illusionist, and head of the Kio circus dynasty, Emil Renard Kio. This marriage, to a man 15 years her junior, infuriated her father, and was annulled by militiamen sent by him. Chose as her third husband the 32-year-old lieutenant-colonel of the militia, Iurii Churbanov, who at the time was married with two children. Through her father she promoted him to the position of First Deputy Minister of the Interior. (He was later arrested and put on trial for a 4 billion-rouble cotton scandal, foreign car dealing, and numerous other offences). Soon embarrassed her father and husband through her long-time affair with a 29-year-old gypsy actor, B. Buriatse, whom she promoted into the Bolshoi Theatre. Worked at various times as a circus make-up woman when on tour abroad. Also worked at the Ministry of Foreign Affairs. It has also been suggested that she was involved in dealings on the black market in gold and diamonds. Implicated herself in a robbery from the famous animal-trainer Irina Bugrimova's registered collection of diamonds. Not prosecuted (but Buriatse was). After her father's death she lost everything. Lives virtually under house-arrest in her own dacha near Moscow.
Source: R. Medvedev, *Glasnost'*, issue 11, Moscow, 1988, reprinted in *La Pensée Russe*, Apr. 1988.

Brian, Maria Isaakovna (Schmargoner)
4.9.1886–   . Singer.
Born in Ekaterinoslav. Pupil of A. Zherebtsova-Andreeva. Soloist with the Petersburg Theatre of Musical Drama, 1912–19, with the Mariinskii Theatre from 1920. Professor at the Leningrad Conservatory, 1920–50.

Brik, Lilia Iur'evna (Lili Brik; b. Kagan)
11.11.1891–1978.
Daughter of Iurii Kagan, the Jewish lawyer, and Elena Iul'evna Berman. At the age of 13, met Osip Brik, and later married him. In the summer of 1915 met V. Mayakovsky and soon became his intimate friend. From 1926–30 lived in a ménage à trois in a flat on Gendrikovskii Pereulok. Both had affairs with others, but according to Mayakovsky's letters to her, she was one of the great loves of his life. In the autumn of 1928 after Mayakovsky had met T. Iakovleva in Paris, their relationship ended. Died in Moscow. Published 125 letters and telegrams she had received from Mayakovsky.
Source: Bengt Jangfelt, *V. V. Mayakovsky i L. Iu. Brik. Perepiska 1915–30*, Uppsala, 1982.

Brik, Osip Maksimovich
4.1.1888–22.2.1945. Playwright, editor.
Born in Moscow. Son of a wealthy Jewish businessman. Graduated from Moscow University. Became known in modernist literary groups during the revolutionary years (Opoiaz, LEF, Novyi LEF). Became a close friend of Mayakovsky, formed a famous ménage à trois, when his wife Lilia Brik became Mayakovsky's lover. Wrote together with Mayakovsky the plays *Radio Oktiabr* and *Moskva gorit*. Edited with Mayakovsky the newspaper *Iskusstvo kommuny*, 1918. An active literary theoretician of the 1920s. Wrote the script for the famous Pudovkin film *Potomok Chingiz Khana*, 1928. Died in Moscow.

Briukhanov, Nikolai Pavlovich
1878–1943. Politician.
Joined the Communist Party, 1902. Took part in the 1905 Revolution in Ufa. Active in the Bolshevik takeover in the Urals during the Civil War. People's Commissar for Food Supply in the RSFSR, 1921. Head of the Commission for Food Supply of the Red Army, 1922. USSR Minister for Food Supply, 1923–24. Finance Minister of the USSR, 1926–31.

Briusov, Valerii Iakovlevich
1.12.1873–9.10.1924. Poet, literary scholar, editor.
Born in Moscow, son of a wealthy merchant of Old Believer peasant background. Educated at Moscow high schools. Became one of the first and most active voices of fin de siècle decadence and symbolism in Russia, at first scandalizing the public who were used to simple-hearted and idealistic populist motifs, later lionized in Moscow and Petersburg. Moved more by immense ambition and diligence than talent, he nevertheless achieved remarkable results. Always trying to create his own cliques and to play the leading role, he was a successful editor of several symbolist publications (the magazine *Vesy*, Skorpion publishing house). The same restless ambition led him after October 1917, almost alone among the intelligentsia of his stature, to become a member of the Communist Party. However, his poetry of later years became pathetic propaganda, while his last job was party censor of his fellow poets and writers. From his youth, experimented with drugs, and according to several literary sources his death in Moscow was connected with his worsening drug addiction.

53

Briusova, Nadezhda Iakovlevna
19.11.1881–28.6.1951. Music critic.
Born in Moscow. Sister of the poet V. Briusov. Professor at the Moscow Conservatory. Wrote on the history and theory of music. Died in Moscow.

Brodskii, Adolf
2.4.1851–22.1.1929. Violinist.
Born in Taganrog. Taught at the Moscow Conservatory, 1875–79. Professor at the Leipzig Conservatory, 1882–93. Organized a string quartet in Leipzig. Lived in England from 1895. First interpreter of Tchaikovskii's violin concerto. Author of *Recollections of a Russian*, London, 1904. Died in Manchester.

Brodskii, Aleksandr Il'ich
19.6.1895–21.8.1969. Scientist.
Graduated from Moscow University. Director of the Institute of Physical Chemistry of the Ukrainian Academy of Sciences. Specialist in physical chemistry. Died in Kiev.

Brodskii, Iosif Aleksandrovich
1940– . Poet.
Born in Leningrad. Son of a naval officer. Left school at 15. Worked in a factory as a metal worker, a machine operator; later worked in the morgue of the local county hospital. Started writing poetry in the late 1950s. Constantly in conflict with the Soviet authorities. In 1964 imprisoned, tried and sent into internal exile. Forced to leave the country in 1972. Settled in America and became an American citizen in 1980. Teaches Russian poetry and literature in American universities. Many articles in the American press. Continues to write Russian poetry. Nobel Prize for Literature, 1987. Some of his poems were published in the Soviet Union in 1988.

Brodskii, Isaak Izrailevich
6.1.1884–14.8.1939. Painter.
Born in Sofievka in the Ukraine. Studied at the Odessa Art School, 1896–1902, and the Petersburg Academy of Arts under Repin, 1902–08. After the October Revolution 1917, specialized in paintings glorifying the new leaders, and made a career as the party boss in the arts. Considered to

be a master of socialist realism in painting, became in effect Stalin's court painter. Director of the Leningrad Academy of Arts, 1934. Died in Leningrad.

Bronshtein, Matvei Petrovich
1906–18.2.1938. Scientist.
Professor of physics at Leningrad University. Wrote scientific textbooks for children. Son-in-law of K. Chukovskii. Arrested 6 Aug. 1937 and later shot.
See: *Pamiat* Nr. 3, p. 322.

Bronskii, Moisei (Varshavskii)
1882–1941. Politician, economist.
Born in Lodz (at that time in Russian Poland). Polish social-democrat later Bolshevik. Emigrated to Switzerland in 1907. Became close to Lenin, and took part in the Kienthal conference. After the October Revolution 1917, one of the editors of *Pravda*. Deputy Minister of Trade and Industry of the USSR. Soviet Ambassador to Austria, 1920–22.

Bruevich, Nikolai Grigor'evich
12.11.1896–1972? Lt.-general.
Born in Moscow. Graduated from Moscow University, 1922. Graduated from the Moscow Aviation Institute, 1930. Professor at the Zhukovskii Air Force Academy, 1929. Specialist in kinematic and kinetostatic analysis for machines. Later specialized in computers.

Bruk, Isaak Semenovich
9.11.1902– . Scientist.
Graduated from the Moscow Technical College, 1925. Worked at the Institute of Energetics, 1935. Designed a series of Soviet computers (the M–1,–2, and –3), 1950–55.

Brumel', Valerii Nikolaevich
14.5.1942– . Athlete.
Born in the village of Razvedki, Amur Oblast'. Honoured Master of Sports (track and field athletics), 1961. Graduated from the Moscow Institute of Physical Culture, 1967. Coach. Member of the CPSU, 1964. USSR champion, 1961-63. European champion, 1962. World record holder, 1961-71. Olympic champion, 1964. Silver medal, 1960.

Bruni, Lev Aleksandrovich
1894–1948. Artist.
Landscape and portrait painter. Also graphic artist and book illustrator. Studied at the M. K. Tenisheva Art School, 1904–09, then at the Academy of Arts, Petersburg 1909. Pupil of the famous battle painter, F. A. Rubo. Later studied in the studios of N. S. Samokish and I. F. Tsionglinskii, 1911. Went to Paris and studied at the Academy, 1912. Member of the Mir Iskusstva, 1915. Exhibitions: Modern Russian Painting, Moscow, 1915, Petersburg, 1916; Drawings at the Tsvetkovskaia Gallery, Moscow, 1924; Makovets, 1924–26; the Four Arts, 1925–26. Other exhibitions: Moscow, 1927, 1936, 1945, 1947. Personal exhibitions: together with V. Tatlin, P. Miturich, and N. Kupreianov, 1925. Posthumous exhibitions in Moscow, 1956 and 1958.

Brusilov, Aleksei Alekseevich
31.5.1853–17.3.1926. General.
Born in Tiflis. Son of a general. Educated at the Pages Corps, 1872. Commander of a cavalry division, 1906. During WWI, commander of the 8th army, and later of the South-West front. Commanded the most successful Russian operation during WWI – an offensive against the Austrians, 1916. One of the front commanders, who persuaded Nicholas II to abdicate. Supreme Commander of Russian Forces under the Provisional Government June–Aug. 1917. After the defeat of the July 1917 offensive, replaced by Kornilov. During the Civil War, one of the most prominent military specialists on the side of the Bolshevik government (no direct command posts). During the Soviet-Polish war, signed an appeal to all former Tsarist officers to recognize the Soviet government and serve it for patriotic reasons. Inspector of the Cavalry of the Red Army, 1923-24. Died in Moscow.

Brutskus, Ber Davidovich
1878–1938. Economist.
Graduated from the Novo-Aleksandriiskii Institute of Agriculture and Forestry, 1898. Became widely known for his scientific research on Jewish life and Russian agrarian problems. Defended the agrarian

reforms of Stolypin. After the February Revolution 1917, appointed member of the Supreme Council on agrarian matters. Spoke out against the Bolshevik take-over in October 1917 and continued his anti-Marxist polemics in the press. At the agrarian congress in Moscow 1922, publicly accused the Soviet government of causing millions to starve during the famine in 1921. Arrested and expelled to Germany, 1922. Continued to write in the Russian and international press and organized protests in the west against the collectivization campaign in the USSR. Moved to Palestine, and became Professor of Agrarian Economics at Jerusalem University. Died in Palestine.

Main works: *Professionalnyi Sostav Evreiskogo Naseleniia Rossii*; *Statistika Evreiskogo Naseleniia*; *Agrarnyi Vopros i Agrarnaia Politika*; *Ekonomiia Selskogo Khoziaistva*; *Agrarentwicklung und Agrarrevolution in Russland*.

Bublikov, A. A.
1875–1936? Politician.
Engineer. Member of the 4th Duma. At the time of the February Revolution 1917, appointed commissar of railways by the Duma. On his own initiative used the railway telegraph (the most efficient telecommunications network at the time) for transmitting revolutionary appeals throughout Russia. By preventing the return of the Tsar's train from Military HQ in Mogilev to Tsarskoe Selo, made a decisive contribution to the victory of the February Revolution 1917. After the revolution, appointed commissar of transport. Disappeared from the scene, probably perished in the Gulag.

Bubnov, Andrei Sergeevich (Khimik, Iakov, A. Glotov, S. Iaglov)
4.4.1883–12.1.1940. Revolutionary, politician, educationalist.
Born in Ivanovo-Voznesensk. Son of a textile factory director. Member of the Bolshevik Party, 1903. Elected to the Politburo of the Cen. Cttee. of the Bolshevik Party on the eve of the October Revolution 1917. Commissar of all Petrograd railway stations during the take-over in 1917. Left-wing communist, 1918. During the Civil War, held several high administrative positions in the Ukraine,

1918–19. Took part in the suppression of the Kronstadt sailors revolt, 1921. Head of the Agitprop of the Cen. Cttee., 1922–23. At first a Trotskyite, later supported Stalin. After Trotsky's defeat, appointed head of the political administration of the Red Army, 1924–29, replacing Antonov-Ovseenko. Secretary of the Cen. Cttee. of the Bolshevik Party, 1925. Minister of Education of RSFSR, replacing Lunacharskii, 1929–37, and responsible for the school reforms of the 1930s. Arrested, died in the Gulag camps. Rehabilitated under Khrushchev.

Budennyi, Semen Mikhailovich
25.4.1883–26.10.1973. Marshal.
Born in Koziurin near Rostov. Joined the army in 1903. Served in a Don Cossack regiment (not Cossack by birth) in the Russo-Japanese war, 1904–05. During WWI, became known for his bravery as a Cossack NCO (4 St George's Crosses, the highest military award for valour). In 1917 became a revolutionary activist, and a member of the Bolshevik Party, 1918. Organized a Red Cavalry detachment, later a division fighting against the Whites at Tsaritsyn and Voronezh. Became famous as 1st Cavalry Army Commander during the Civil War, with Voroshilov as his political commissar. A good horseman, poorly educated, and with his enormous moustaches, he became a folklore figure. Inspector of the Cavalry of the Red Army, 1924–37. A willing tool of Stalin during the purges of the Red Army just before WWII. During WWII, proved himself quickly to be completely incapable of understanding modern warfare, and removed from the front to administrative posts at HQ. Commander of the Soviet Cavalry, 1943 and Deputy Minister of Agriculture in charge of horse-breeding. Member of the Cen. Cttee. of the Bolshevik Party, 1939–52. Highly decorated, in his old age he continued his interest in horse-breeding and played the role of a living relic of the heroic age of revolutionary victories in the Civil War. Died in Moscow.

Budker, Gersh Itskovich
1.5.1918–   . Nuclear scientist.
Graduated from Moscow University,

1941. Joined the Institute of Nuclear Energy, 1946. Worked in different areas of nuclear physics and technology. Director of the Institute of Nuclear Physics of the Siberian Branch of the USSR Academy of Sciences.

Budnikov, Petr Petrovich
21.10.1885–6.12.1968. Chemist.
Born in Smolensk. Graduated from the Riga Polytechnical Institute, 1911. Professor at Khar'kov and Moscow Technical Institutes. Highly decorated (3 Stalin Prizes). Specialist in concrete and cement, involved in the Stalinist industrialization drive. Died in Moscow.

Bugaenkov, Ivan Vasil'evich
18.2.1938–   . Athlete.
Born in the Volgograd Oblast'. Honoured Master of Sports (volleyball), 1964. With Riga Daugava. Graduated from the Latvian Institute of Physical Culture, 1959. European champion, 1967. World champion, 1960, 1962. Olympic champion, 1964, 1968.

Bugaev, Boris Pavlovich
1923–   . State official, marshal.
Pilot–instructor at the Aktiubinsk School of Civil Aviation, 1942–43. Pilot, then commander of an aviation department in the Ukrainian Civil Aviation Administration, 1943–46. Member of the CPSU, 1946. Captain, then commander of a pilots' department of the CAA, 1947–66. Graduated from the Senior Flying School of Civil Aviation, 1966. Chief Marshal of the Air Force. Deputy, then 1st Deputy Minister, 1966–70, and Minister of USSR Civil Aviation from 1970. Member of the Cen. Cttee. of the CPSU from 1971. Received a State Prize for participating in the construction of the TU-134, 1972. By the time of the Paris salon in June 1987, replaced by A. Volkov.

Buinakskii, Ullubii Danialovich
8.9.1890–16.8.1919. Revolutionary.
Born in the village of Ullu-Buinak in Daghestan. Studied law at Moscow University. Returned to Daghestan, and after the Bolshevik take-over

became the local Bolshevik leader, 1918. After the defeat of the communists, became head of the underground party organization. Arrested by local anti-Bolshevik authorities, sentenced to death and shot at Shakhmal. The town Temir-Khan-Shura in Daghestan was later renamed Buinaksk after him.

Buiukli, Vsevolod Ivanovich
6.12.1873–1920? Pianist.
Born in Sergievskii Posad, Moscow Gouvt. Pupil of Pavel Pabst. Known for his interpretation of Skriabin. See: *Vsevolod Buiukli,* Moscow, 1904; *Sovetskaia Muzyka,* N.10, 1965.

Bukharin, Nikolai Ivanovich
9.10.1888–13.3.1938. Politician.
Born in Moscow. Son of a teacher. In his childhood showed an interest in literature and collecting birds and butterflies which he kept up throughout his life. Early involvement in revolutionary activity. Joined the Bolsheviks, 1906. Studied economics at Moscow University, 1907–10, but was more involved in organizing student rallies and in revolutionary propaganda work. Became a prominent leader of the Moscow Bolsheviks. Arrested in 1909, but soon released. Re-arrested in the autumn of 1910, imprisoned in Moscow for 6 months, and then exiled to Arkhangelsk region, June 1911. Escaped at the end of Aug. 1911, and went to Germany. Remained a political emigré until 1917. Became a prominent Bolshevik theoretician sometimes entering into polemics with Lenin. In 1913 in Vienna, on Lenin's instructions, helped Stalin to write his first major theoretical article, *Marxism and the National Question.* During WWI, stayed in Lausanne. Moved to Sweden in 1915 to organize links between Russia and the emigré Bolshevik Party leadership. Arrested and deported to Norway, 1916. After strong disagreements with Lenin on important theoretical subjects, went to the USA, Nov. 1916. Settled in New York, and became, with Trotsky, one of the editors of the Russian socialist daily *Novyi Mir,* Jan. 1917. Returned to Russia through Japan and Siberia in May, 1917. Resumed his former position of influence in Moscow Bolshevik circles, mainly through his control of the press. Reported on the Bolshevik take-over in Moscow in Nov. 1917 to the party leadership in Petrograd. Given the task of speaking for the Bolsheviks at the session of the Constituent Assembly before it was dissolved. Entrusted by Lenin with the nationalization of the country's economy, and with formulating the first policy statements of the Bolsheviks as ruling party. Called by Lenin the 'darling of the party' (liubimets partii). At first considered to be the leader of the left-wing communists, opposed to the Brest-Litovsk peace treaty, and demanding immediate world revolution; later became the main defender of the NEP, and leader of the right-wing of the party. After the adoption of a new party program, wrote, together with Evgenii Preobrazhenskii, a popular explanation of the document, called the *ABC of Communism,* March 1919. This and another of his works, *Historical Materialism,* became the standard texts of pre-Stalinist communist propaganda. As editor of *Pravda,* he defended the terror campaign, and sided with Stalin in his struggle for power against Trotsky. In the late 1920s became very popular for his defence of the NEP, advising the peasants to 'enrich themselves'. Took part in Stalin's defeat of Zinov'ev and Kamenev, Dec. 1925. Replaced Zinov'ev as head of the Comintern. As editor of both the party newspaper, *Pravda,* and the theoretical party journal, *Bolshevik,* made a decisive contribution to his own and Stalin's triumph in the party's internal struggles. He was immensely popular among young party intellectuals, and was considered the most liberal and human among the top Bolshevik leadership. Attempted, with Rykov and Tomskii, to oppose Stalin's bid for the leadership with the liquidation of the NEP, forced collectivization, and the industrialization drive, but was unable to organize an effective opposition, as all potential allies among the old Bolshevik leaders had been removed earlier (with his help). Though retaining his popularity in the country at large, he was easily overcome by the Stalinist majority in the Politburo. Vilified by Stalinists as the leader of the right-wing deviationists. Expelled from Politburo, 17 Nov. 1929. After several recantations, was able for a time to remain among the Soviet elite. One of the official speakers at the Inaugural Congress of Soviet Writers, Aug. 1934, where he praised B. Pasternak. Appointed editor of *Izvestia,* 1934–36. According to some sources, responsible for the new Soviet constitution (later known as the Stalin Constitution). In 1936, travelled to Western Europe, where he met some Russian emigrés from former revolutionary circles, whom he had known as comrades before 1917. According to all accounts, he was very frank in his condemnation of Stalin and Stalinism, and was convinced that he himself would soon perish. During the Zinov'ev and Kamenev trial in Aug. 1936, the Stalinist prosecutor Vyshinskii announced the beginning of investigations into Bukharin and others implicated by confessions of the accused. Arrested on 27 Feb. 1937, and tried in Mar. 1938 in the last show trial of the old Bolsheviks. Accused of plotting to kill Lenin during the Brest-Litovsk negotiations, 1918, and condemned to death in an atmosphere of frenzied vilification, outstanding even by Stalinist standards. Sentenced to be shot, with Rykov and others, on 13 Mar. 1938. The execution was confirmed in *Pravda,* 15 Mar. 1938. The memoirs of his widow, A. Larina, were published in late 1987 in the magazine *Ogonek* together with other material concerning him. According to Larina, he was a 'sensitive, emotional man, who was capable of bursting into tears. He lived poorly, donating all the proceeds from the sale of his articles and books to the Party'. The *Moscow News* of 3 Dec. 1987 published his last letter, in which he told of his 'helplessness in the face of a hellish machine seeking his physical destruction'. The letter was addressed to A Future Generation of Soviet Leaders. On the 4 Feb. 1988 the Supreme Court of the USSR rehabilitated him together with 9 others executed as the result of the trial of the so-called Right-Wing Trotskyist Centre (Rykov, Rozengolts, Chernov, Bulanov, Levin Kazakov, Maksimov-Dikovskii, Kriuchkov and Rakovskii). Another 10 of the executed, including Krestinskii and Pletnev, had been rehabilitated earlier.

Sources: Lev Trotsky, *Portrety*, USA, 1984; *The Bukharin Trial*, published by the British and Irish Communist Organisation (no year of publication); *The Times* 4 and 6 Dec. 1987; *La Pensée Russe*, 11 Feb. 1988.

Bukinik, Mikhail Evseevich
10.11.1872–1947. Cellist, music critic.
Born in Dubno. Pupil of Alfred Glen. Taught in Saratov, 1900–1904, and in the People's Conservatory, Moscow, 1907-18. Emigrated. Wrote pieces and studies for cello. Died in the USA.

Bukovskii, Vladimir Konstantinovich
1942– . Dissident, author.
Son of Communist party official. As a student of biology at Moscow University, became involved in the human rights movement. One of the best known activists, wrote samizdat short stories. First arrest in 1963 for photocopying the book *New Class* by M. Djilas. Put into a psychiatric hospital in Leningrad, 1963–65. Arrested again at the end of 1965 for organizing a demonstration in Moscow in defence of the writers Siniavskii and Daniel. Another term in psychiatric hospitals, 1965–66. In Jan. 1967 sentenced to three years in labour camps for taking part in a demonstration in defence of Galanskov. In Jan. 1971 collected and presented materials on the political misuse of psychiatry to the World Congress of Psychiatrists in Mexico. Arrested in Mar. 1971, sentenced in Jan. 1972 to 7 years imprisonment and 5 years exile. In Dec. 1976 exchanged for the Chilean communist leader, Louis Corvalan. Left the USSR for England. Wrote an autobiography, relating his experiences in human rights groups and during his terms of imprisonment. Continues to take part in human rights movements abroad. Lives in England, lectures around the world. President of the Resistance International, 1983.

Bulach, Tatu Omarovna
1901–1979. Revolutionary.
Joined the Bolshevik Party, 1917. The first woman Komsomol and party member in Daghestan. Secretary of the Soviet of the Youth of

the East. Studied at the Plekhanov Institute in the 1920s, and later worked in the Ministry of Foreign Trade and Soviet trade mission in Istanbul.

Bulak-Balakhovich, Stanislav Nikodimovich
22.2.1883–1940. Major general.
Born near Kovno. Son of a peasant. Volunteered for military service during WWI. In Feb. 1918, joined the Red Army, but soon went with his regiment over to the Whites, and became one of the most persistent of White military leaders. Took part in Gen. Iudenich's advance on Petrograd in summer 1919. In Aug. 1919, on military service in Estonia; later moved to Poland. Organized and led large White partisan detachments in Belorussia. Worked closely with B. Savinkov. Invaded Soviet territory from Poland, Nov. 1920, but soon retreated. On good terms with the Polish authorities. During WWII, killed on a Warsaw street, probably by a SMERSH agent.

Bulatov, Erik
1934– . Artist.
Became a famous non-conformist artist in Moscow in the 1970s. A major exhibition of his work took place in Jan. 1988 in Zürich. The exhibition, containing 20 large paintings, was also shown in Frankfurt-am-Main, Bonn, Paris, Amsterdam, Oxford, and the USA. Another major exhibition took place at the Pompidou Centre, Paris, 27 Sept. 1988.

Bulatov, Vladimir
1929–1976. Athlete.
Honoured Master of Sports (track and field athletics). Won 9th place in the pole vault at the XVIth Olympic Games. Many times USSR and European champion.

Bulatov, Vladimir Semenovich
1910– . Politician.
Party and Komsomol activist from 1930. 1st secretary of the party obkom in the Crimea, 1939. During WWII, remained in the Crimea, becoming the head of the local communist partisan movement, 1942–44. After WWII, administrator in the Volga shipping system.

Bulatovich, Aleksandr Ksaver'evich
8.10.1870–1919. Explorer.
Born in Orel. Served as a member of the Russian diplomatic mission in Ethiopia. Explored Ethiopia, 1896–1900. Gathered ethnographic information on some Ethiopian tribes (Sidamo, Galla). Became a monk in the early 1900s. Returned to Ethiopia, 1911–12, to try to organize a Russian Orthodox monastery and school. Wrote religious works. Returned to Russia. Died in Lutsikovka in Belorussia.
Works: *Ot Entoto do Reki Baro*, 1897; *S Voiskami Menelika II*, 1900.

Buldakov, Igor'
26.8.1930–30.4.1979. Athlete.
Honoured Master of Sports (rowing). Silver medallist at the XVIth Olympic Games. Many times USSR and European champion.

Buldakova, Liudmila Stepanovna
25.5.1938– . Athlete.
Born in Leningrad. Honoured Master of Sports (volleyball), 1960. With Moscow Dynamo. Graduated from the Moscow Institute of Physical Culture, 1962. Coach. USSR champion, 1960-73. European champion, 1958, 1967, 1971. Olympic champion, 1968, 1972. Silver medal, 1964. World champion, 1956, 1960, 1970.

Bulgakov, Mikhail Afanas'evich
14.5.1891–10.3.1940. Author.
Born in Kiev. Son of a professor. Graduated from Kiev University in medicine. Worked as a doctor till 1919. Became a well-known writer of grotesque Gogol-like stories in the 1920s. His novel *Belaia Gvardiia* (White Guard) in the stage version *Dni Turbinykh* (Days of the Turbins) found approval from Stalin himself for its attitude towards the revolution as an invincible force. This made it possible for him to work in the Soviet press. But his greatest work, *Master i Margarita*, was written in secret and published only many years after his death, creating a sensation and influencing a whole post-Stalin generation of writers. Died in Moscow. Other major works: *Diavoliada, Rokovye Iaitsa, Sobach'e Serdtse, Poslednie Dni*.

Bulgakov, Sergei Nikolaevich
16.6.1871–13.7.1944. Philosopher, economist, theologian.
Born in Livny, Orel Gouvt. Son of a priest. Graduated from Moscow University, 1894. Embraced atheism and Marxism in his youth. Became a well-known representative of 'legal Marxism'. Professor of political economy at Kiev Polytechnic, 1901. Professor at the Institute of Commerce in Moscow. Member of the 2nd Duma. Became one of the most prominent members of the group of intelligentsia which moved from Marxism towards a religious approach, and warned against the dangers of radicalism and political activism (Vekhi). Ordained priest of the Orthodox church, 11 June 1918. During the Civil War, professor at the Simferopol University in the Crimea, 1918. Dismissed on account of his religious convictions, 1921. Expelled from Russia, 1 Jan. 1923. Worked as a professor in the Russian faculty of law in Prague. Moved to France. Long serving Dean of the St. Sergius Theological Institute in Paris, making the institute a brilliant centre of Orthodox thought, 1925–44. Criticized for some of his dogmatic innovations (sophiology). One of the most active initiators of the world-wide oecumencial movement (often acting as an intermediary between traditionally hostile Protestant and Catholic circles in Western Europe). Works: *The Market in Capitalist Production, Capitalism and Agriculture* 2 vols, *From Marxism to Idealism, The Two Cities, The Philosophy of Economics, Quiet Thoughts, Autobiographical Notes,* a number of monographs on Christian dogmatic subjects.

Bulgakov, Valentin Fedorovich
25.11.1886–1976? Author.
Born in Kuznetsk. Began writing in 1904. Studied at Moscow University, 1906–10. Became the private secretary of Lev Tolstoy in 1910 and an active Tolstoy follower. Published his diary of life at Yasnaia Poliana (Tolstoy's estate) in 1911, then several reworked editions, the last published in Moscow in 1960. Emigrated in 1923, and lived in Prague. Returned to the USSR in 1949. Became a member of the Tolstoy museum staff at Yasnaia Poliana.

Bulganin, Nikolai Aleksandrovich
1895–26.2.1975. Marshal, politician.
Born in Nizhnii Novgorod (now Gorkii). Member of the Bolshevik Party, 1917. During the Civil War a Cheka official, 1918–22, later in the Supreme Council for the National Economy (VSNH), 1922–27. Head of Moscow city administration, 1931–37. Deputy Prime Minister of the USSR, 1938–41. High ranking political officer during WWII. Deputy Defence Minister, 1944. Defence Minister 1947. Deputy Prime Minister of the USSR, 1949. After Stalin's death, gained an international reputation as Prime Minister, under Khrushchev. Travelled with Khrushchev to Britain during the post-Stalin thaw. Member of the Politburo of the Cen. Cttee. of the CPSU, 1948–58. Joined the Stalinist group (Molotov, Kaganovich, Malenkov), 1957. Recanted, but expelled the following year from the Presidium of the Cen. Cttee. and demoted (worked in the State Bank, later in the Stavropol Economic Council). Retired and settled near Moscow, 1960. Died there.

Bulich, Sergei Konstantinovich
8.9.1859–1921. Philologist, music historian.
Born in Petersburg. Professor at Petersburg University and at the Russian Institute of History from 1919. Editor of the music section of the Brockhaus and Efron Encyclopaedia. Author of *Pushkin i Russkaia Muzyka,* Petersburg 1900, and *Neskol'ko Finno-Slavianskikh Muzykal'noetnograficheskikh Parallelei (Zapiski Imperatorskogo Russkogo Geograficheskogo Obshchestva po Otdelu Etnografii)* v. 34, Petersburg, 1909. Died in Finland.

Bulla, Viktor Karlovich
1883–1944. Photographer.
Born in St. Petersburg, son of an established photographer, K. K. Bulla. Studied photography with his elder brother Aleksander under the guidance of his father. Soon became an indefatigable reporter of great ability, taking tens of thousands of pictures, capturing the historic events and personalities of the time. Made his debut as a reporter for the magazine *Niva,* taking pictures of the battle front in the Russo-Japanese

war, 1904–05. On his return to St. Petersburg, turned to cinematography and founded the Apollo Company, which produced historical and documentary films. However, his career was to remain that of a photo-journalist. Photographed the events of the February Revolution – the artillery battle on Gostinyi Dvor and the destruction of the police archive on the Ekaterininskii canal etc. Many of his photographs taken from the roofs of buildings were used in films by Sergei Eisenstein and Chiaureli. After the October Revolution 1917, became head of the Petrograd Soviet Photographic Studio, which had previously belonged to his father. Continued work as a documentary photographer. Photographed Lenin who had come to Petrograd to take part in the Second Comintern Congress. His best-known photos were of Lenin in the Winter Palace, and of Maksim Gorkii. Took part with his brother in the 1928 exhibition, Ten Years of Soviet Photography. Gave the State Archive over 130,000 negatives from the Bulla photographic collection.
See: *Soviet Photography, 1917–40,* London, 1984.

Bulychev, Viacheslav Aleksandrovich
24.9.1872–10.4.1959. Conductor, composer, music critic.
Born in Piatigorsk. Organised and directed the Moskovskaia Simfonicheskaia Kapella, 1901. Emigrated. Lived in Rumania from 1918. Wrote on the Renaissance composer, Orlando Lasso, on the art of singing, and on the style of the MSK. Died in Bucharest.

Buniachenko, Sergei Kuzmich
1904?– 7.1946. Major-general.
Son of a peasant from the Ukraine. Joined the Communist Party, 1919. Rose rapidly in the Soviet Army. In 1939 in command of a division in Vladivostok, later a member of Marshal Timoshenko's staff. Deserted to the Germans at the start of WWII. Promoted by General Vlasov to major-general. Took over command of a volunteer unit, first on the Eastern Front and then in France. Commander of the 1st Division of the ROA organized in 1944–45 at Muensingen. Became a bitter enemy

of both Stalin and National Social-ism. According to those who knew him, he was a short-tempered, strong-willed and powerful personality, and a gifted military commander. After an engagement with the Red Army near Frankfurt/Oder in 1945, led his troops to Czechoslovakia contrary to German orders. Nearing Prague, he received calls for help from the Czechs, who had started an uprising but had been confronted by elite SS forces. Personally made the decision to help the Czechs, and by his resolute action drove the SS units out of Prague (which was the last engage-ment of WWII in Europe). At the end of WWII, handed over with his soldiers to SMERSH by the US Army authorities. Tried at Lubianka prison and hanged with Vlasov and his other co-defendants.

Buniatzade, Dadash Khodzha ogly
8.4.1888–1938. Cheka official, poli-tician.
Born near Baku. Son of an Azer-baidzhani peasant. Became a worker and Bolshevik agitator, 1908. Active in the Caucasus among local Mus-lims. Cheka official in Baku, 1918. One of the organizers of the Bolshe-vik takeover in Azerbaidzhan, 1920. Azerbaidzhani Minister of Educa-tion, Food, Agriculture. One of the main organizers of the complete communist re-organization of the way of life of the local Moslems. Arrested, probably shot.

Bunin, Ivan Alekseevich
22.10.1870–8.11.1953. Author, Nobel Prize winner.
Born at Voronezh. Grew up at Butyrki, Orel Gouvt. Educated at a secondary school in Elets. Worked in provincial newspapers. First volume of poems published in 1891. Pushkin Prize in 1901. Honorary academ-ician, 1909. Travelled abroad. Became an acknowledged master of Russian prose before WWI. Emigrated in 1920 to France. His later master-pieces were published abroad. Res-olute opponent of communist dic-tatorship (Okaiannye Dni). Received the Nobel Prize for Literature in 1933, the first Russian writer to receive it. Lived in the South of France during WWII. Died in Paris. Considered (together with Ivan Tur-

genev) the greatest stylist in the Russian language. A basically tragic world view, later heightened by life in exile, lends a quite special bitter-sweet and non-sentimental atmo-sphere to his novels and short stories. Because of his open anti-communism, he was not published or mentioned in the USSR during his life time. Posthumously recognized as one of the greatest Russian writers of the 20th century. Now published in the USSR in millions of copies.
Main works: *The Life of Arsen'ev, The Well of Days, Collected Works* (in several editions), *Memoirs*, 2 vol, published abroad only.

Burda, Liubov' Viktorovna
11.4.1953–   . Athlete.
Born in Voronezh. Honoured Master of Sports (gymnastics), 1972. With Voronezh Spartak. Studied at the Vladimir Pedagogical Institute. Over-all champion of the USSR, 1969–70. USSR champion, 1968–69. World champion, 1970. Olympic champion, 1968, 1972.

Burdenko, Nikolai Nilovich
3.6.1876–11.11.1946. Military surgeon.
Born in Kamenka near Penza. Gradu-ated from Yuriev (now Tartu) Uni-versity, 1910. Professor at Yuriev University, 1910. Chief medical in-spector of the Russian army, 1917. Professor at Voronezh University, 1918. Professor of Moscow Univer-sity and head of the University Clinic, 1923 till his death. Founder of a neurosurgery clinic, 1929. Chief Surgeon of the Soviet Army, 1937 (and throughout WWII). Fellow of the International Surgeons Society, fellow of the Royal Society. A pioneer and world authority in neurosurgery. Died in Moscow.

Burenin, Viktor Petrovich
19.3.1841–15.8.1926. Journalist.
Born in Moscow. Started as a journa-list by sending reports to Herzen's *Kolokol* in London, 1861, and became known as a radical journalist during the 1860s. From the 1870s, moved to a right-wing position. Became one of the star commentators of the centre-right newspaper *Novoe Vremia*. In-fluential in his time, though attacked

and vilified by the radical intelligent-sia. Died in Leningrad.

Buriatse, Boris
1946–   . Actor.
Born into a gypsy family. Graduated from the Moscow GITIS. Once a singer (tenor). Actor in the Moscow Roman Gypsy Theatre. Famous Moscow playboy. Became an inti-mate friend of Galina Brezhneva. Openly appeared with her in public while she was still married to Iurii Churbanov, 1st Deputy Minister of the Interior. Promoted by Galina into the Bolshoi Theatre. His main occupation became that of a black-market dealer in precious stones. Arrested after a robbery from the flat of the famous animal trainer I. Bugrimova when her collection of diamonds was stolen. His flat on A. Chekhov Street was searched by the KGB (sent by I. Churbanov), and most of the diamonds were recovered. Sentenced to 5 years in jail. Recently released. Has been seen again in public but without Galina. Fired from the Bolshoi Theatre and return-ed to the Romen Gypsy Theatre, 1987.

Burliaev, Nikolai (Kolia) Petrovich
3.8.1946–   . Actor.
At the age of 15, given a part by A. Tarkovskii in his first major film, *Ivanovo Detstvo*. Graduated from the Shchukin Theatre School, 1967, and from the VGIK, 1975. Member of the Mossovet Theatre, 1961–64. In 1971 acted in another Tarkovskii film, *Andrei Rublev*.

Burliuk, David Davidovich
21.7.1882–10.2.1967. Poet, painter, art promoter.
Born at Semirotovshchina, Khar'kov Gouvt. Son of an estate-manager. Nephew of the novelist Vladimir Burliuk. Studied at art schools in Kazan' and Odessa, 1898–99, at the Munich Academy of Art, 1902–03, at the Ecole des Beaux Arts in Paris, 1905, and at the Moscow School of Art, 1910–14. His first modernist works were printed in 1899. Dis-covered and promoted Mayakovsky. Also met and became close to the Russian poets Khlebnikov and Kamenskii. In 1910 Franz Marc and

Kandinskii invited him to exhibit in Der Blaue Reiter exhibition in Munich, in which Paul Klee, Jawlensky, Goncharova, Picasso, Derain and Delaunay also participated. He became one of the pioneers and promoters of modern art in Russia. In the same year he published in St. Petersburg *The Bait Box of Judges*, which created a scandal by challenging established literary taste. In 1911, organized the Jack of Diamonds exhibitions, which included paintings by Tatlin, Falk, Malevich, Kandinskii and others. In 1912, married Marusia Elenevskaia. Conducted futurist tours throughout Russia with Mayakovsky and Kamenskii, 1913–14, lecturing on the new art and scandalizing the establishment. In 1913, with Mayakovsky, published a booklet, *A Slap at Public Taste*, for which they were expelled from the Moscow Art Academy. Emigrated in 1919 through Vladivostok, having left behind him some 1700 paintings. In Japan, Oct. 1920, and in New York, 22. Sept. 1922. Became an American citizen, 1930. Settled at Hampton Bays, Long Island, 1941. Worked in Southern Europe – Capri, Positiano and Arles, 1949–50. In 1956, visited the USSR in connection with the Mayakovsky celebrations. The following year visited Czechoslovakia and Paris. Made a seven month trip around the world in 1962. His first London exhibition was held at the Grosvenor Gallery, 1966. Also exhibited in the USA, Germany, Russia, Milan and Rome. Died in America. One of the most colourful personalities in the modernist art world in the 1920s, when artists considered themselves the allies of the revolution, and the Soviet authorities had not yet imposed the conformism of the later period under Stalin.
See: Herbert Marshall's introduction to the David Burliuk exhibition in London, 15 Mar.–7 Apr. 1966.

Burobin, Nikolai Aleksandrovich
25.5.1937–   . Athlete.
Born in Pushkino, Moscow Oblast'. Honoured Master of Sports (volleyball), 1960. Graduated from the Moscow Oblast' Institute of Physical Culture, 1970. USSR champion, 1958–66. World champion, 1960, 1962. Olympic champion, 1964.

Burtsev, Mikhail Ivanovich
21.6.1956–   . Athlete.
Born in Moscow. International Master of Sports (fencing), 1977. Student at the Moscow Institute of Physical Culture. World champion, 1977, 1979. Olympic champion, 1976.

Burtsev, Vladimir Lvovich
1862–1942. Politician, editor, historian.
Born in Fort Aleksandrovskii. Became a member of Narodnaia Volia (People's Will) in the 1880s. Arrested in 1885, exiled to Siberia. Fled abroad, 1888. Active in the revolutionary Russian press in London, Geneva. Edited the historical magazine *Byloe* from 1900, a very valuable primary source on the history of the Russian revolutionary movement. Joined the SR Party. Later moved closer to the Cadets. Returned to Russia in 1905, and continued editorship of *Byloe* in Petersburg. Emigrated again in 1907. Specialized in unmasking police agents within the revolutionary groups. Gained fame by revealing the police connections of both Azef (head of the BO, the SR terrorist wing) and Malinovskii (leader of the Bolshevik deputies group in the Duma). Edited emigré papers in Paris, 1911–14. Returned to Russia, 1915. Put on trial and sentenced, but soon amnestied. Radical opponent of Bolshevism from Oct. 1917. Edited the first anti-Bolshevik newspaper in Petersburg, *Obshchee Delo*, 1917. Emigrated again, continued to publish his newspaper in Paris, taking a consistent anti-Bolshevik line. During his long revolutionary career, gained the reputation of the revolutionary conscience. In his later years moved from his earlier belief in revolutionary terror to an appreciation of liberal values and the condemnation of revolutionary dictatorship.

Buryshkin, Pavel Afanas'evich
9.2.1887–1959. Businessman, politician.
Born in Moscow into the family of a rich merchant. Representative of the famous dynasties of the Moscow merchant princes, whose generosity financed the cultural flowering of pre-WWI Russia. Created the Museum of Old Moscow. His sister was attracted to anthroposophy and the first Goetheanum in Munich was built by Rudolf Steiner with money from the Buryshkins. Active member of Moscow city administration during WWI and after the February Revolution 1917. Connected with the newspaper *Utro Rossii*. In 1918 left for Khar'kov. Emigrated and settled in France. Wrote a book on the Moscow merchant families, *Moskva Kupecheskaia*, published in the USA in the 1950s. A well-known freemason and historian of the Russian freemason movement.

Buryshkin, Vladimir (Burda, Val Williams)
17.8.1913–18.8.1968. Resistance fighter.
Member of a well-known Moscow merchant family. Emigrated with his parents to France after the 1917 October Revolution. Educated at the Russian High School in Paris. Organized the Russian Basketball Club in Paris. Trained the Rumanian national basketball team before WWII. During the German occupation of France, became a very active fighter in the French resistance. Became a colonel in the British Army under the name Val Williams. Saved the lives of many allied pilots. Received several French, British and American military decorations. Died in Paris.

Burzhuademov, K. (Sokirko, Viktor Vladimirovich)
1939–   . Dissident.
Early involvement in the human rights movement. Expelled from the Komsomol, 1961. Witness at the trial of P. Iakir, 1973. Sentenced to 6 months in the camps for non-cooperation with the authorities. Protested against the Soviet invasion of Afghanistan in a letter to Brezhnev, 1980. Arrested, 1980. Sentenced to 3 years, but released on parole.

Bushuev, Viktor Georgievich
18.5.1933–   . Athlete.
Born in Balakhana, Gorkii Oblast'. Honoured Master of Sports (weight lifter), 1960. Graduated from the Higher School of Trainers. USSR champion, 1958, 1960. World record-holder, 1957–60. European champion, 1958–59. World champion,

1957–59. Olympic champion (heavy weight, 397,5 kg), 1960.

Butaev, Kazbek Savvich
4.12.1893–1937. Politician.
Active in the communist takeover in the North Caucasus, secretary of the Mountaineers Party Committee, commissar of a partisan division. Studied at the Institute of Red Professors, 1925–29. Subsequently in senior planning posts. In 1931–34, professor of the Institute of Red Professors, and editor of the magazine *Problemy ekonomiki*. First secretary of the North Ossetia party obkom, 1934–36. Victim of Stalin's purges, probably shot.

Butovskii, Aleksei Dmitrievich
1833–1917. Sports official, general.
One of the founders of the contemporary Olympic Games. Founder-member of the International Olympic Cttee., and ordinary member, 1894–1900. Lt.-general of the Imperial Russian Army. Educated at the Petrovskii and Konstantinovskii Cadet Corps. In 1888, member of the commission working on the methods of military gymnastics in civil educational institutions. Headed the courses for future officer-tutors of physical training at the cadet corps. Follower of P. Leshaft's ideas about physical education of young people. Works: *Nastavlenie Dlia Proizvodstva Gimnasticheskikh Uprazhnenii v Grazhdanskikh Uchebnykh Zavedeniiakh; Ruchnoi Trud i Telesnoe Razvitie; Polevaia Gimnastika v Gosudarstvakh Zapadnoi Evropy; Zapiski Po Istorii i Metodike Telesnykh Uprazhnenii.*

Bychkov, Viacheslav Pavlovich
1877–1954. Artist.
Landscape and genre painter. Studied at the Moscow School of Painting, Sculpture and Architecture 1896–1903, under N. Kasatkin. Exhibitions: The Union of Russian Artists, 1910–17, 1922–23, AKHRR (8th Exhibition), Moscow, 1926, (11th Exhibition), Moscow, 1929. Personal exhibition, with E. Komzolkin, Moscow, 1950. Died in Moscow.

Bychkova, Anna Nikolaevna
1886–1971? Revolutionary.
Joined the Bolshevik Party, 1906. Communist organizer in the Urals. Sentenced to life exile in Siberia, 1907. Fled abroad, 1911. Returned to Russia in April 1917. Member of the Sverdlovsk obkom.

Bykov, Anatolii Mikhailovich
6.8.1953– . Athlete.
Born in Magadan. Honoured Master of Sports (wrestling), 1975. With Alma-Ata Dynamo. Graduated from the Kazakh Institute of Physical Culture, 1975. USSR champion, 1975. World champion, 1975. Olympic champion, 1976.

Bykov, Roland Anatol'evich
12.11.1929– . Actor, director.
Graduated from the Shchukin Drama School, 1958. Acted at the Moscow Young Spectators' Theatre. Chief Director at the Leningrad Komsomol Theatre, 1958–60. First film at Kiev Film Studios, 1956. Became famous in *The Overcoat* (after N. Gogol's story, directed by Aleksei Batalov in 1960, Lenfilm). Directed and played in *Aibolit–66* (Mosfilm, 1966). First noted drama part in A. Tarkovskii's *Andrei Rublev*, 1970, in the role of the iurodivyi (God's fool). Other films: *Chuchelo* (Scarecrow, 1983, as director), and *Letters of a Dead Man* (Lenfilm, 1986, as actor, directed by K. Lopushanskii).

Bykov, Vasil' (Vasilii) Vladimirovich
19.6.1924– . Writer.
Born in the village of Bychki, Vitebsk Oblast'. Took part in WWII. Became known in the 1960s for his novels about his wartime experiences which gave a much more realistic picture of these tragic events than the usual Stalinist heroic stereotypes.

C

Chabukiani, Eteri Vissarionovna
1.4.1932–6.4.1968. Ballerina.
Born in Tbilisi. Graduated from the Tbilisi Choreographic School, 1955. Dancer, and later soloist at the Paliashvili Theatre. Died in Tbilisi.

Chabukiani, Tamara Mikhailovna
18.8.1907– . Ballerina.
Born in Tbilisi. Sister of Vakhtang Chabukiani. Graduated from the choreographic school attached to the Tbilisi Theatre, 1923. Continued her training at the Leningrad Choreographic School, 1930. From 1921, with the Paliashvili Theatre. Leading dancer there, 1936–61. Choreographer-coach, 1961–64. Taught two generations of young ballet dancers. Lives in Tbilisi.

Chabukiani, Vakhtang Mikhailovich
12.3.1910– . Ballet dancer, choreographer.
Born in Tbilisi. Graduated from the M. Perini Ballet Studio, Tbilisi, 1924. Continued his training at the Leningrad Choreographic School, 1926–29. Debut at the Kirov Theatre, 1929. Until 1941 with the Kirov Theatre. Leading dancer. Returned to Georgia at the beginning of WWII. Leading dancer and chief choreographer at the Paliashvili Theatre, 1941–73. Staged many new productions and taught two generations of young ballet dancers at the Tbilisi Choreographic School, 1950–73. Director of the same school after 1973. Ballet Director at the Rustaveli Theatre School, Tbilisi, 1965–70. Acted as scriptwriter and choreographer in the film *Mastera Gruzinskogo Baleta*, 1955, and *Otello*, 1961. Many state prizes. Made appearances in the USA, Japan, Iran, and Europe.

Chagall, Marc (originally Segal)
7.7.1896–8.3.1985. Artist.
Born in Vitebsk into a large, working class, Hasidic family. In 1907 moved to Petersburg with no money, no job and no residence permit. Became a sign writer for small businesses. Entered Leon Bakst's art school. In 1910 went to Paris where he lived in a community of then unknown artists such as Leger, Soutine and Modigliani. Met and befriended Guillaume Apollinaire and Blaise Cendrars. Influenced by cubism. Returned to Russia in 1914. Married a Jewish girl. After the October Revolution 1917 and the Civil War, appointed Commissar of Fine Arts in his native Vitebsk where he founded an art academy, but he resigned after conflict with the Soviet authorities and

his colleague Malevich. Went to Moscow, and worked as a stage designer. Also ran an art school for a short time. Left the Soviet Union in 1922 for Berlin, and in 1923 went to Paris. Although influenced by many trends such as surrealism, impressionism and cubism, retained his own original and very personal style. In 1941, the Museum of Modern Art in New York invited him to America. In 1946, returned to France and lived there near St. Paul-de-Vence until his death in March 1985. His early work (*Birthday*, 1915, *The Violinist*, 1911, *Visit to the Grandparents*, 1915) reflects his background well. In 1961, completed a series of stained glass windows of the Twelve Tribes of Israel for a synagogue near Jerusalem. Also made mosaics and tapestry for the Knesset in 1966. Produced designs for the Metropolitan Opera in New York, 1966 after the success of his ceiling for the Paris Opera in 1964, his stained glass windows at Tudeley in Kent, 1967, and Chichester Cathedral, 1978. Over 500,000 Soviet art lovers visited his posthumous exhibition in Oct. 1987 at the Pushkin Museum in Moscow. (He had already staged a smaller one in the Soviet Union in 1973). The October exhibition was attended by the artist's widow, Valentina, who had helped to organize it.

Chaianov, Aleksandr Vasil'evich
1888–1939. Politician, economist.
Well-known economist and theoretician on agrarian subjects. Published *Puteshestvie Moego Brata Alekseia v Stranu Krest'ianskoi Utopii* (Journey of My Brother Aleksei to the Peasants' Utopia), 1920. Accused, with 15 other outstanding agrarian specialists, of organizing an anti-Soviet Peasant Labour Party. Arrested in the summer of 1930. Died in the Gulag.

Chaikovskii, Boris Vital'evich
1888–5.11.1924. Film director.
Entered the film industry, 1909. From 1911, a director. Soon became a master of melodrama and adventure films. Worked with leading actors and actresses. Best known for *Miss Mend*, 1918. After October 1917, made some agit-films. Worked with P. Petrov-Bytov on *Na Zhizn' i*

Na Smert', 1925. In 1918, was allowed to set up a private film studio which was later named the Chaikovskii State Film School.

Chaikovskii, Nikolai Vasil'evich
1850–1926. Politician, revolutionary.
Born in Viatka. Son of an official. Graduated from Petersburg University's Physical-Mathematical Faculty. While studying at the Medical-Surgical Academy, organized (with M. Natanson and V. Aleksandrov) the first narodnik revolutionary group, 1869. The group included many people who later became famous (P. Kropotkin, P. Akselrod, Zheliabov and others), and was known as the 'chaikovtsy' in the 1870s. Summoned to appear in court at the 'trial of the 193', but went underground instead. After meeting in Orel the peasant religious preacher Malikov, became his follower. Emigrated, 1874 and settled in the USA, 1875. Together with Malikov and a group of like-minded enthusiasts, created a commune in Kansas, trying to realize principles of absolute justice. The commune fell apart in 1877. Worked at a factory, for one year lived among the sect of shakers. Returned from America to Europe, first to Paris, 1878, then to London, June 1880. Active in the British Labour movement, and in the Red Cross organization of Narodnaia Volia. Organized (with Kravchinskii and others) the Free Russian Press in London, 1891, which became one of the main revolutionary enterprises of its time. Joined the SRs, 1904, and returned to Russia, 1905. Became a moderate socialist, and a member of the Cen. Cttee. of the Trudovik and NS parties. Most of his attention at this time was given to the organization of the agricultural cooperative movement, which proved very successful in Siberia, and elsewhere. Condemned the Bolshevik take-over of Oct. 1917. Organized the anti-Bolshevik Soiuz Vozrozhdenia Rossii, went to Arkhangelsk and became Prime Minister of Arkhangelsk territory. Invited General Miller to take command of the local forces, and cooperated with the British Expeditionary Corps. After the evacuation of the British and the defeat of Miller, emigrated to France. Actively involved in political activity

among Russian political post-revolutionary exiles. Died in London.

Chakhotin, Petr
1943– . Artist.
Born in Paris of Russian emigré parents. Son of an internationally known biologist. In the early 1960s, the family returned to the Soviet Union. Settled in Moscow. Originally trained as an oceanographer. Worked for 10 years in the Far North. Started painting there. In 1978, returned to Paris. Exhibited all over Europe. Lives in Genoa.

Chaliapin, Fedor Ivanovich
1873–1938. Singer (bass), actor.
The most famous bass in the world. Started his career in 1896 in Mamontov's Private Opera Company in Moscow. Most famous parts were Boris, Ivan the Terrible and the miller in *Rusalka* by Dargomyzhskii. In 1901, went to Milan. In America in 1908. Worked for Diaghilev in Paris, 1908–09. In 1913, appeared at Drury Lane during the Russian Season organized by Sir Thomas Beecham. Left Soviet Russia in 1921. Went to America again, 1922–25. Continued to perform, although his health deteriorated. Recognized as a bass of genius and a great operatic actor. Died in Paris and was buried at Batignolles. The Soviet Government made several approaches to his children to allow him to be reburied in the Soviet Union but the requests were declined. After the death of his favourite daughter, Dasia Fedorovna, the request was granted by other relatives. Re-buried with pomp in the exclusive Novodevich'e cemetery in Moscow, 62 years after his departure. Members of the government attended the ceremony.

Chalidze, Valerii Nikolaevich
1938– . Publisher, writer, editor.
Born in Moscow. Graduated in physics from Tbilisi University. Became involved in the human rights movement in the mid-1960s. Editor of *Obshchestvennye Problemy*, 1969–72. Founding member of the Human Rights Committee (together with Andrei Sakharov and A. Tverdokhlebov). Left the USSR for the USA on a lecture tour, 1972 and was stripped

of Soviet citizenship. Settled in Vermont. Founder and editor of *Khronika Press* and *Chalidze Publications*. Editor of *SSSR – Vnutrennie Protivorechiia*.

Books: *Prava Cheloveka i Sovetskii Soiiuz*, 1974, USA; *Ugolovnaia Rossiia*, 1978, USA; *Inostranets v Sovetskom Soiuze*, 1980, USA.

Changa, Evgenii Ianovich
23.10.1920–   . Ballet dancer, choreographer.
Born in Pskov Oblast'. Graduated from the Riga Choreographic School, 1940, then from the Ballet Department of the GITIS, Moscow, 1950. Dancer, and soloist, 1940–60, then choreographer, 1950–61, at the Riga Theatre. State Prize of the Latvian SSR, 1958. Choreographer at the Spendiarov Theatre, 1961–67. Director of the Moscow Ensemble on Ice, Ballet on Ice, 1968–77. From 1977 taught at the GITIS.

Chapaev, Vasilii Ivanovich
1887–1919. Revolutionary commander.
A former labourer, who became the commander of a division, fighting Kolchak's forces during the Civil War. His political commissar, Furmanov, became a well-known writer, by using him as a model to create the image of a down-to-earth, though uneducated and simple, self-made revolutionary commander, who became a sort of folk hero. The book called *Chapaev* (1923), and the classic Stalinist film adaptation (1934), had much more to do with his reputation than with his brief and not very successful military career (he was killed in action during the Civil War, 1919). His glorification was clearly excessive, and Vasilii Ivanovich has much greater significance as the folk hero of innumerable anecdotes and jokes satirizing the official propaganda approach.

Chaplin, Boris Nikolaevich
8.9.1931–   . State official, diplomat.
Born in Moscow. Son of Nikolai Chaplin, Secretary-General of the Cen. Cttee. of the Komsomol during the 1930s. Graduated from the Moscow Mining Institute, 1955. Mining

engineer, 1955–57. Member of the CPSU, 1961. Researcher at the Skachinskii Institute of Mining Works of the Academy of Sciences, 1957–61. Deputy Secretary, later Secretary, of the Party Cttee. of the Mining Institute, 1961–65. Senior party posts in Moscow, 1961–68, including the post of 1st Secretary of the Cheremushki Raikom, Moscow. In 1974 responsible for the so-called Bulldozers Art Exhibition, when the police and KGB smashed artists' works using bulldozers. The case attracted bad international publicity. Fired from his post. USSR Ambassador to Vietnam, 1974–86. Deputy Foreign Minister from May 1986. Candidate member of the Central Committee of the CPSU.

Chaplin, Nikolai Pavlovich
1900?–1937. Party official.
Son of an Orthodox priest. During the 1930s, Secretary-General of the Cen. Cttee. of the Komsomol. Victim of the Gulag. Disappeared in 1937, presumably perished in the camps.

Chaplygin, Nikolai Petrovich
26.11.1905–   . Music editor.
Born in Voronezh. Wrote an opera, symphonic music and songs for films and stage. Chief music editor with the All-Union Radio Moscow.

Chaplygin, Sergei Aleksandrovich
1869–1942. Mathematician, physicist.
Graduated from Moscow University, 1890. Professor of Moscow University, 1903, Director of the Moscow Vysshie Zhenskie Kursy (Higher Women's Courses). Member of the USSR Academy of Sciences from 1929. Director of the Central Aero-Hydrodynamic Institute until the mid-1930s. Pioneered research on dynamics of gases and was involved in the Soviet military industry on work on the profiles of aircraft wings.

Chaplygin, Valerii Andreevich
23.5.1952–   . Athlete.
Born in Kursk. Honoured Master of Sports 1975, (cycling). With Kursk Spartak. Graduated from the Velikie Luki Pedagogical Institute, 1979. Schoolmaster. USSR champion,

1976–77. World champion, 1977. Olympic champion, 1976. Member of the USSR international team which won the Velogonka Mira, 1975.

Chardynin, Petr Ivanovich
1878–1934. Film director.
Graduated from the Musical Drama High School of the Moscow Philharmonic. Worked in provincial theatres. Entered the film industry, 1907. One of the first major directors of the Russian silent cinema. Made melodramas and comedies. His main players were Vera Kholodnaia and Ivan Mozzhukhin. Made over 60 films including *Kreitserova Sonata*, 1911, *Domik v Kolomne*, 1913, and *Natasha Rostova*, 1915. After the death of Kholodnaia and the emigration of Mozzhukhin, he himself emigrated in 1921. In 1923 returned to the USSR.

Chasiunas, Vladislavas Adol'fovich
15.3.1940–   . Athlete.
Born in Lithuania. Honoured Master of Sports, 1972 (rowing). With Vil'nius Dynamo. Graduated from the Vil'nius Railway Technical School, 1970. USSR champion, 1970, 1972–74. World champion, 1973–75. Olympic champion (with Iu. Lobanov), 1972.

Chavdar, Elizaveta Ivanovna
23.2.1925–   . Singer.
Born in Odessa. Pupil of O. Aslanova. Soloist at the Kiev Opera and Ballet Theatre from 1948. 1st prize at the International Competition of Singers-Soloists, Berlin, 1951.

Chazov, Evgenii Ivanovich
1929–   . Cardiologist, medical administrator, politician.
The Soviet Union's leading cardiologist. Graduated from the Kiev Medical Institute in 1953. Cardiologist, Dr of Medical Sciences, 1963. Professor, 1965. Member of the CPSU from 1962. Corresponding member of the USSR Academy of Medical Sciences, 1967. Member of staff at the Clinical Consultation Office in the First Medical Institute, Moscow, 1953–58. Member of staff at the Institute of Cardiology, Moscow, 1958–67. Chief of the Depart-

63

ment of Intensive Care at the Institute of Cardiology, 1967. Deputy USSR Minister of Health, 1968. Deputy to the USSR Supreme Soviet, 1974. Director General of the Cardiological Scientific Centre from 1976. Candidate member of the Cen. Cttee., 1981–82. Full member from 1982. Minister of Health of the USSR, 1987. As chief therapist, has been personal physician to all post-Khrushchev party leaders including Brezhnev, Chernenko and Andropov. One of his functions is to sign medical bulletins and authorize the post-mortem after the death of a Soviet leader.

Chebrikov, Viktor Mikhailovich
27.4.1923– . Security services official, head of the KGB, marshal.
Served in the Soviet Army during WWII. Member of the CPSU, 1944. Graduated from the Dnepropetrovsk Metallurgical Institute, 1950. Party posts, 1951–67. 2nd, then 1st Secretary of Dnepropetrovsk City Cttee. of the Ukrainian CP, 1961–71. Various top party posts in Dnepropetrovsk until 1967. Close to Leonid Brezhnev. Head of Personnel, 1967–68, then Deputy Chairman of the KGB, 1968–82. Chairman Dec. 1982–Oct. 1988. Army General, Nov. 1983. Candidate member of the Cen. Cttee. of the CPSU, 1971–81. Full member, 1981. Politburo member from Apr. 1985. Head of the commission for legal reform of the Cen. Cttee., Oct. 1988.

Chebyshev, Nikolai Nikolaevich
1865–1937. Editor, journalist.
Senator before WWI. During the Civil War in the Crimea under Wrangel, edited the newspaper *Velikaia Rossia*, and after the evacuation in Constantinople, the newspaper *Zarnitsy*, 1920–21. Head of the Russian press office in Constantinople, 1920–21. Moved to Paris, where he contributed to the right-wing newspaper *Vozrozhdenie*.

Chekasin, Vladimir
1947– . Jazz musician.
Born in Sverdlovsk. Started playing the violin at the age of 6, clarinet at 11, and alto saxophone at 18. Gradu-

ated from the Sverdlovsk Conservatory as a clarinetist. From 1967, appeared with several professional jazz bands. Won 1st prize at the 1970 International Competition in Czechoslovakia. Appeared at the 1971 Prague Jazz Festival, which led to him recording a solo album on the Supraphon label. His records are also issued by Leo record company, London.

Chekhonin, Sergei Vasil'evich
2.2.1878–23.2.1936. Artist.
Born in the village of Lykoshino, Novgorod Oblast', son of a railway worker. Grew up in the town of Chudovo. Studied at the art school of the Society for the Encouragement of the Arts and in the Petersburg Free Workshops, 1896–00. Member of the Mir Iskusstva with whom he exhibited. Headed the enamel art school in Rostov, 1913–17. Chief artist at the State Porcelain Factory in Leningrad in the post-revolution years. Famous for his modernist designs. Emigrated in 1928. Many of his miniature portraits of friends are held in the Leningrad Museum of Artistic Culture. Died in Lorrach, Germany.
See: Ivan Bilibin, *Statii, Pisma, Vospominaniia o Khudozhnike*, Leningrad, 1970.

Chekhov, Sergei Mikhailovich
1901–1963. Artist.
Graphic artist and stage designer. studied at the D. Kardovskii Studio of Drawing and Painting, Moscow, 1923–27, and at the same time in the art studios of the Bolshoi Theatre under M. I. Kurilko, 1925–26. Exhibitions: Moscow, 1939, 1943, 1948–57, 1960.

Chekrygin, Aleksandr Ivanovich
7.8.1884–17.5.1942. Ballet dancer, choreographer.
Born in Petersburg. Graduated from the Petersburg Theatre School, 1902. Pupil of P. Karsavin, N. Legat and A. Shiriaev. Dancer at the Mariinskii Theatre until 1923. Choreographer at the Leningrad Malyi Theatre, 1923–29. Taught young dancers from 1904. Together with his brother Ivan Chekrygin, organized a ballet school, 1914. Taught at the Moscow Choreographic School, 1930–41. Evacua-

ted with the school at the beginning of WWII to Tashkent where he died. Author (with N. Tarasov and V. Morits) of *Metodika Klassicheskogo Trenazha*, 1940.

Chekrygin, Ivan Ivanovich
1880–1942. Dancer, composer.
Born in Petersburg. Brother of Aleksandr Chekrygin. Graduated from the Petersburg Theatre School, 1897. Until 1917, dancer with the Mariinskii Theatre. Graduated from the Petersburg Conservatory, 1911. Pupil of A. Liadov. Wrote music for piano and violin. Conductor and concert pianist. Wrote the music for several new ballets such as *Kukly Gospodina Mareshalia*, 1900. Also ballet critic. In 1914, opened a ballet school with his brother. Director of the school until 1925. From 1939, taught at the Leningrad Conservatory (plasticity and dance). Died during the Siege of Leningrad.

Chekrygin, Vasilii Nikolaevich
1897–1922. Artist.
Graphic artist and painter. Studied in the art studio of the Kievo-Pecherskaia Lavra, 1908–10, then at the Moscow School of Painting, Sculpture and Architecture, 1910–14. Exhibitions: Moscow, 1912–14; The Mir Iskusstva 1917; The 5th State Exhibition, Moscow, 1918–19; The Union of Artists and Poets, Moscow, 1922. Personal exhibition: posthumously in Moscow, 1923.

Chelnokov, Nikolai Vasil'evich
1906–1974. Major-general
Joined the Red Army, 1928. Educated at a naval pilot's school, 1931. Took part in the Soviet-Finnish War and WWII. Graduated from the Academy of the General Staff, 1949. Several high command posts in naval aviation in the 1950s and 1960s.

Chelomei, Vladimir Nikolaevich
1914–1984. Space technology designer.
Graduated from the Kiev Aviation Institute, 1937. Designer at the Central Aviation Engine Design Institute, 1941. Professor of the Moscow Technical University, 1952. Involved in the design of sputniks and other

space technology. Highly decorated, 4 state prizes, twice Hero of Socialist Labour. Academician, 1962.

Chelpanov, Georgii Ivanovich
1862–1936. Philosopher, psychologist.
Professor of philosophy and psychology at Kiev University, 1892–1906, and Moscow University, 1907–23. Founded the Institute of Experimental Psychology in Moscow, 1911; director until 1923.
Main works: *Brain and Soul* (1900), *On Contemporary Philosophical Trends* (1902), *Introduction to Philosophy* (1916), *Introduction to Experimental Psychology* (1924).

Chemodurov, Evgenii Grigor'evich
10.2.1914–   . Stage designer.
Born in Shumikha, Kurgan Oblast'. Graduated from the Leningrad Academy of Arts, 1938. Worked in various theatres in Dushanbe and Moscow. Chief stage designer at the Aini Theatre, 1947–51, then at the Cheliabinsk Theatre, 1955–59, and the Minsk Theatre, 1959–76. Worked with leading choreographers, such as A. Messerer. Designed the decor for the Moscow Ballet on Ice.

Cheremisov, Vladimir Andreevich
1885?–after 1945. General.
General during WWI, Commander of the Northern Front. Personal enemy of General Kornilov. After the Bolshevik take-over, joined the Red Army. In charge of Red Army operations against General Iudenich.

Cherepanov, Aleksandr Ivanovich
1895–1984. Lt.-general.
Took part in WW1 as a captain. Joined the Red Guards, 1917, and the Red Army, 1918. Took part in the Civil War. Graduated from the Military Academy of the Red Army 1923. Military adviser in China, 1923–27, and 1938–39. Professor at the Academy of the General Staff, 1939. Army commander during WWII. Deputy Chairman, 1944, and Chairman, 1947, of the Allied Control Commission in Bulgaria. Chief adviser to the Bulgarian Army in the same year. Head of the administration of military higher education

establishments, 1948–55. Retired, 1955.

Cherepnin, Aleksandr Nikolaevich
8.1.1899–   . Pianist, composer.
Born in Petersburg. Son of the composer Nikolai Cherepnin. Emigrated, 1921. Lived in the USA and France. Author of operas, 5 symphonies, 6 concertos, music for violin and cello and cantatas.

Cherepnin, Nikolai Nikolaevich
15.5.1873–27.6.1945. Composer, conductor.
Born in Petersburg. Studied at the Petersburg Conservatory. Pupil of N. Rimskii-Korsakov. Professor of conducting at the Conservatory, 1908–12. S. Prokof'ev was one of his pupils. Operatic conductor at the Petersburg People's House, 1908–14. Conductor with Diaghilev's company in Paris, 1909, 1911, 1912. Taught at the Tiflis Music School, 1918–21. Emigrated. Settled in Paris, 1921. His music is in the classical tradition of the Beliaevskii Kruzhok; also influenced by French impressionism and by the music of R. Strauss. Died near Paris.

Cherepovich, Anatolii
1936–1970. Athlete.
Honoured Master of Sports (cycling). 6th place at the XVIth Olympic Games. Died in a car crash.

Cherevichenko, Iakov Timofeevich
1894–1976. Col.-general.
On active service during WWI. Joined the Red Army, 1918, and the Bolshevik Party, 1919. Took part in the Civil War as commander of a cavalry regiment. Graduated from the Frunze Military Academy, 1935. Several high command posts during WWII. Deputy Commander of the Tauria Military District, 1945–50.

Cherkassov, Nikolai Konstantinovich
1903–9.1966. Film actor.
Distinguished actor of the 1930s. Played leading parts in several Eisenstein films, including *Ivan the Terrible* and *Aleksandr Nevskii*. His first forceful performance was in 1937 as Peter the Great's son, the Tsarevich Aleksei, in the film of the same name.

As an actor under Stalin, had to take on many political roles. One of them was that of Professor Polezhaev in *The Baltic Deputy*, 1937. Also played Maksim Gorkii in *Lenin 1918*, the film made by M. Romm in 1939. Very close to Eisenstein for 15 years.
Memoirs: *Notes of a Soviet Actor*, Moscow, 1958.

Chernaia, Elena Semenovna (b. Berliand)
4.6.1903–   . Musicologist.
Born in Moscow. Wife of the writer and musician, O. Chernyi. Lecturer at the GITIS, Moscow. Authority on Mozart and the music of his time.

Chernenko, Konstantin Ustinovich
24.9.1911–10.3.1985. Politician.
Born in the village of Novoselovo, Krasnoiarskii krai. Son of a peasant. Joined the Communist Party, 1930. Served in Cheka detachments (border guard). Several party posts in Siberia. In the 1950s, moved to Moldavia and became the right-hand man of the local party leader, L. Brezhnev, whose loyal assistant he remained all his life, moving later with him to Moscow. Candidate member of the Cen. Cttee. of the CPSU, 1966, member, 1971, secretary, 1976. Member of the Politburo, 1978. After Brezhnev's death in 1982, was denied succession by Andropov, but after Andropov's death, he was elected party leader on the Brezhnevite backlash, aided by the uncertainty of succession among the younger generation (rivalry between Gorbachev and Romanov). Old and visibly ailing, he was elected to the post of leader as a compromise candidate, to give the younger pretenders time to sort out the question of the real succession. Became the last of the gerontocrats characteristic of the Brezhnevite period of stagnation. Died in Moscow after a long illness, leaving the stage free for his much younger successor Gorbachev and a new epoch in Soviet life.

Chernetskii, Semen Aleksandrovich
1881–1950. Major-general, conductor.
Graduated from the Petersburg Con-

servatory, 1917. Joined the Red Army, 1918. Well known military composer and conductor. Inspector of all military bands in the Soviet Army, 1924–49. Organized the entire music system of the Soviet armed forces. Wrote over 100 military marches and songs.

Cherniaev, Il'ia Il'ich
20.1.1893–1970? Chemist.
Graduated from Petersburg University, 1915. Professor at Leningrad University, 1932. Director of the Institute of Inorganic Chemistry, 1941. Professor at Moscow University, 1945. Specialist in the chemistry of complex compounds.

Cherniakhovskii, Ivan Danilovich
1906–1945. General.
Joined the Red Army, 1924, and the Bolshevik Party, 1928. Graduated from the Mechanization Academy of the Red Army, 1936. During WWII, became widely known as a tank forces commander. Commander of the Western Front, 1944. Mortally wounded in battle during the Soviet offensive in Eastern Prussia. The Prussian town Insterburg was renamed Cherniakhovsk in his honour after WWII. Twice Hero of the Soviet Union.

Cherniavin, Vladimir Nikolaevich
1928–   . Admiral.
Born in Nikolaev, son of a naval officer. Member of the CPSU, 1949. Graduated from the Naval Academy, 1965, and the Academy of the General Staff, 1969. Admiral, 1978. Commander of the Northern Fleet, Jan. 1977. Replaced Admiral Gorshkov as Commander-in-Chief of the Military Naval Fleet, Dec. 1985.

Chernigovskii, Vladimir Nikolaevich
1.3.1907–   . Physiologist.
Graduated from Perm' University, 1930. Professor at the Institute of Experimental Medicine in Leningrad, 1944. Professor at the Naval Academy in Leningrad, 1941–53. Director of the Pavlov Institute of Physiology, 1961. Research on reflex control in the blood system.

Chernomordikov, David Aronovich
17.7.1869–31.1.1947. Composer.
Born in Baku. Participant in the 1905–07 Revolution. One of the first composers of revolutionary songs. Author of *Pervyi Sbornik Revolutsionnykh Pesen*. Died in Moscow.

Chernov, Dmitrii Konstantinovich
1839–1921. Scientist.
Graduated from the Petersburg Technological Institute, 1858. Professor of Metallurgy at the Mikhailovskaia Artillery Academy, 1889. Specialist in artillery and ammunition design.

Chernov, Mikhail Mikhailovich
22.4.1879–1.8.1938. Composer.
Born in Kronstadt. From 1910, taught at the Petersburg Conservatory. Professor there from 1918 until his death. Among his many pupils was E. Mravinskii. Sergei Prokof'ev also came to him to take lessons. Wrote 3 symphonies, choral music, and pieces for piano. Died in Leningrad.

Chernov, Viktor Mikhailovich
1876–1952. Politician.
Leader of the SR Party. Minister of Agriculture in the Provisional Government, 1917. As the leader of the majority party, presided at the first and only session of the Constituent Assembly, which was closed by its revolutionary sailor-guards on Lenin's orders. Tried without success to organize resistance to the Bolsheviks on the Volga. Emigrated, 1920. Wrote memoirs, which were published in the 1930s.

Chernova, Aglaia (Alla) Mikhailovna
1.4.1920–   . Ballerina, teacher.
Born in Petrograd. Graduated from the Leningrad Choreographic School, 1939. Pupil of M. Romanova, E. Shiripina. Graduated from the Pedagogical Dept. of the Leningrad Conservatory. Pupil of A. Vaganova, 1949. Dancer at the Kirov Theatre, 1939–47. From 1949 taught at the Leningrad Choreographic School.

Chernova, Natalia Iur'evna
6.1.1937–   . Ballet critic.
Born in Moscow. Worked at the Moscow Bakhrushin Theatre Museum. Joined *Teatr* magazine. From 1964, worked at the Moscow Research Institute of Art. First articles published, 1960. Author of many monographs on ballet personalities such as G. Ulanova, N. Timofeeva, and V. Vasil'ev.

Chernyi, Sasha (Glikberg; Glueckberg, Aleksandr Mikhailovich)
1880–1932. Poet, humorist.
Widely-known and extremely popular writer of humorous and children's verse before WWI. Emigrated after the Bolshevik take-over. Continued to write and was published all over the world in the Russian emigré press, retaining his popularity, especially with children, to the end. Died in Southern France.

Chernyshev, Vasilii Efimovich
1908–1969. Politician.
Joined the Bolshevik Party, 1928. Graduated from the Briansk Communist University, 1930. Secretary of the Baranovichi obkom, 1941. Organized the communist partisan movement during the German occupation of Belorussia. Secretary of several Belorussian obkoms, and of the Cen. Cttee, of the Belorussian CP after WWII. First secretary of the Kalingrad obkom, 1951–59, and of the Primorskii kraikom (Far East), 1959–69. Member of the Cen. Cttee. of the CPSU, 1952. Deputy Chairman of the Cttee. for Party Control of the Cen. Cttee. of the CPSU, 1969.

Chernysheva, Liubov' Pavlovna
17.9.1890–1.3.1976. Ballerina.
Born in Petersburg. Graduated from the Petersburg Theatre School, 1908. Pupil of M. Fokin. Dancer at the Mariinskii Theatre. Took part in Diaghilev's Russian Seasons in Paris, 1911. In 1912 went to Europe again, and settled in France. With Diaghilev's Ballets Russes until 1929. From 1932, with the Ballet Russe de Monte Carlo, and the Ballet Russe de Colonel de Basil. Worked closely with M. Fokin, L. Miasin, George Balanchine and B. Nijinskaia. Married Diaghilev's right-hand man, and chief stage-director, S.L. Grigor'ev and moved with her husband to England. Co-choreographer with

Grigor'ev of some ballets at La Scala, and Sadlers Wells. Renewed Fokin's ballets at these theatres. From 1938 taught ballet in London, and from 1955 at Sadlers Wells. Died in Richmond, Surrey.

Chernyshov, Evgenii Vasil'evich
22.2.1947– . Athlete.
Born in Moscow Oblast'. Honoured Master of Sports (handball), 1976. With the Moscow Armed Forces team. USSR champion, 1973 and 1976–78. Olympic champion, 1976.

Cherokov, Viktor Sergeevich
1907– . Vice-admiral.
Joined the Red Navy, 1926. Graduated from the Navy Academy, 1939. Took part in the Soviet-Finnish war and WWII. After WWII, Commander of the Riga Naval Base. Graduated from the Academy of the General Staff, 1950. Professor at the Academy of the General Staff, 1957–70.

Chertkova, Anna
1935– . Religious dissident.
Baptist dissident known for her fight for the right to pursue her religion. Longest religious woman prisoner (14 years in various psychiatric hospitals). Released in Dec. 1987 after a long campaign led by the Rev. Richard Rodgers in Birmingham.

Chertok, Semen Markovich
1931– . Journalist, writer.
Born in Moscow. Graduated from the Moscow Institute of Law. Film critic, editor of *Sovetskii Ekran* and other film periodicals. Left the USSR, 1979. Settled in Israel. Author of *Posledniaia Liubov' Maiakovskogo*, USA, 1983. Very active in the Russian emigré press.

Cherviakov, Evgenii Ven'iaminovich
27.12.1899–17.2.1942. Film director.
Graduated from the Studio of Dramatic Art in Ufa, 1918, and from the State Film School, Moscow, 1927. Entered the film industry, 1925 as an actor. Assistant to V.P. Gardin on his films *Zolotoi Zapas* and *Krest i Mauzer*, 1925. Co-scriptwriter and co-director with Gardin in *Poet i Tsar'*, 1927 (an important silent film

about the relationship between A. Pushkin and Tsar Nicolas I in which Cherviakov played the part of Pushkin). In 1928, made his own film, *Devushka s Dalekoi Reki*. Other films include *Moi Syn* and *Zolotoi Kliuv*. Mortally wounded during the Battle for Leningrad. Completely forgotten after his death. Re-discovered in the early 1960s. His films, now at the State Film Archive, are regarded as Soviet classics.

Cheshikhin, Vsevolod Evgrafovich
1865–1934. Music critic.
Born in Riga. Moved to Leningrad. Worked as a poet and author, but was most famous for his articles on music. His main work was *Istoriia Russkoi Opery*, Moscow, 1902. Also wrote on Tchaikovskii. Died in Leningrad.

Chesnokov, Iurii Borisovich
22.1.1933– . Athlete, sports official, colonel.
Born in Moscow. Honoured Master of Sports (volleyball), 1960. Honorary Coach of the USSR, 1976. Chief Coach of the USSR international volleyball team, 1976. Graduated from the Kuibyshev Military Engineering Academy, 1958. Member of the CPSU, 1968. Colonel, 1977. Vice-president of the International Federation of Volleyball from 1976. Captain of the USSR international team, 1954–64. USSR champion, 1954–66. World champion, 1960, 1962. Olympic champion, 1964. Senior coach of various teams, 1970–76.

Chesnokov, Pavel Grigor'evich
24.10.1877–14.3.1944. Choir conductor.
Born near Voskresensk, Moscow Oblast'. Taught at the Choral Academy (Sinodal'noe Uchilishche), 1895–1920. From 1920, professor at the Moscow Conservatory. Chief conductor of the Moscow State Choir, 1917–22. Chief conductor of the Moscow Academic Capella, 1922–28. Wrote choral music. Died in Moscow.

Chiaureli, Sofiko Mikhailovna
21.5.1937– . Actress.
Born into an artistic family.

Daughter of Mikhail Chiaureli, Stalin's favourite film director for his films about the latter's native Georgia, and the famous theatre and film actress Veriko Andzhaparidze. Graduated from the VGIK (Moscow Film School) in 1960. Works at Gruziafilm with all the leading Georgian directors. First film, *Our Courtyard*, directed by Rezo Chkheidze in 1957. Played in her father's films. Played 2 roles in Paradzhanov's *Sayat-Nova*. Other films: *Melodies of the Veri Suburbs*, 1974; *The Khevsur Ballad*, 1967; *Cheer Up!* (Gruziafilm together with Mosfilm) 1969; *The Little Incident*, 1975.

Chibisov, Konstantin Vladimirovich
1.3.1897–1974? Photographer.
Graduated from Moscow University, 1922. Specialized in aerial photography, 1918–30. One of the founders of the Scientific Research Photo-Cinema Institute, 1930. Became an authority on scientific photography.

Chibisov, Nikandr Evlampievich
1892–1959. Col.-general.
On active service during WWI as a captain. Joined the Red Army, 1918. Took part in the Civil War. Graduated from the Frunze Military Academy, 1935. Joined the Bolshevik Party, 1939. Took part in the Soviet-Finnish war, 1939–40. Several high command posts during WWII. Head of the Frunze Academy, 1944. Vice-chairman of DOSAAF, 1949.

Chicherin, Georgii (Iurii) Vasil'evich
1872–1936. Diplomat.
Son of a nobleman. Graduated from Petersburg University. Joined the SD party. Emigrated in 1904, and became leader of the Mensheviks in Berlin. Active for a decade in socialist movements in England, France and Germany. After the October Revolution 1917, joined the Bolsheviks. During his stay in London, imprisoned in Brixton prison as a Bolshevik agent. Released and deported to Russia in exchange for the British ambassador, Sir George Buchanan. Became a high-ranking Soviet diplomat. As Commissar for Foreign Affairs, negotiated and signed the Treaty of Rapallo with Germany in 1922. Ill health forced him to resign in 1930.

Chichibabin, Aleksei Evgen'evich
1871–1945. Chemist.
Graduated from Moscow University. Professor at the Moscow Higher Technical School from 1909. One of the most prominent chemists in Russia. Member of the Chemistry Section of the USSR Academy of Sciences from 1928. Worked in organic chemistry and the results of his research were used in many fields, including the pharmaceutical industry. Did not return to the USSR after one of his scientific trips to Europe. Settled in France. His laboratory at the College de France gained international recognition. His methods have since been called Chichibabin reactions in European laboratories. Published over 250 scientific works. Died in America.

Chichinadze, Aleksei Vissarionovich
26.12.1917– . Ballet dancer, choreographer.
Born in Tbilisi. Graduated from the Moscow Choreographic School, 1941. Pupil of P. Gusev. Graduated from the GITIS, 1955. Pupil of L. Lavrovskii. Joined the Bolshoi Theatre, 1941. From 1944, soloist, and from 1966, choreographer at the Bolshoi Theatre. From 1971, choreographer at the Stanislavskii and Nemirovich Danchenko Theatre. Guest choreographer in Paris and Amsterdam. Choreographer at the Vel'ki Theatre, Poland, 1967–70.

Chikvaidze, Elena Georgievna
17.10.1910.– . Ballerina, choreographer.
Born in Tbilisi. Studied at the M.I. Perini private ballet studio, Tbilisi. Graduated from the Leningrad Choreographic School, 1929. Pupil of A. Vaganova. Dancer, and later soloist with the Kirov Theatre until 1941. Also appeared at the Leningrad Malyi Theatre from 1938. At the beginning of WWII, left Leningrad for Erevan where she joined the Spendiarov Theatre, 1941–43. Returned to Moscow in 1943. Worked in the Bolshoi Theatre until 1957. From 1956, choreographer-coach. Also taught at the Moscow Choreographic School, 1954–56.

Chikviladze, Parnaoz
14.4.1941–14.6.1966. Athlete.
Born in Georgia. Honoured Master of Sports (judo). Bronze medal winner at the XVIIIth Olympic Games. Believed to have died as a result of taking dangerous steroids.

Chimishkian, Rafael' Arkad'evich
23.3.1929– . Athlete.
Born in Tbilisi. Honoured Master of Sports (heavy athletics), 1952. With Tbilisi Dynamo. Graduated from the Tbilisi Technical School of Physical Education, 1957. Member of the CPSU, 1957. USSR champion, 1949, 1951, 1954–55. 1960. European champion, 1950, 1952, 1954–57. World champion, 1954–55. Olympic champion, 1952. World-record holder, 1952–58.

Chinakal, Nikolai Andreevich
19.11.1888–1969? Mining engineer.
Educated at Simferopol' High School. Graduated from the Dnepropetrovsk Mining Institute, 1912. Involved in restoring working conditions after the Civil War in the Donbas, and in developing the Kuzbas in the 1930s. Director of the Institute of Mining of the Siberian Branch of the Academy of Sciences, 1957.

Chinnov, Igor Vladimirovich
1922?– . Poet.
Born in Riga. Son of a judge. Graduated in law from Riga University. During WWII, refugee in Germany. Settled in France after the war. Became known as a poet of the Paris Note, the narrow limits of which he soon transcended. Moved to West Germany, 1953. Worked on the Russian desk of Radio Liberty in Munich, 1955–62. Moved to the USA, 1962. Professor of Russian Literature at the universities of Kansas, Pittsburgh, and Vanderbilt. Retired, 1977, lives in Florida. Has become one of the best Russian emigré poets. His deceptively light, sceptical, modernist and essentially tragic verse has no direct parallel in Russian literature. Though at present he is known only to specialists, his stature seems certain to grow. His verse has been published in small volumes in Paris and New York.

Chirkova, Svetlana Mikhailovna
5.7.1945– . Athlete.
Born in the Chuvashskaia ASSR.
Honoured Master of Sports (fencing), 1972. With the Tallinn Armed Forces team. Graduated from the Tallinn Vil'de Pedagogical Institute, 1970. Schoolmaster. World champion, 1970–71. Olympic champion, 1968.

Chistiakov, Ivan Mikhailovich
1900–1979. Col.-general.
Joined the Red Army, 1918. Took part in the Civil War. Joined the Bolshevik Party, 1926. Graduated from the Vystrel courses, 1930. Commander of several armies during WWII. Graduated from the Academy of the General Staff, 1949. Deputy Commander of the Transcaucasian military district, 1954. General Inspector of the Ministry of Defence, 1957–68.

Chistiakov, Mikhail Nikolaevich
1896–1980. Marshal.
On active service during WWI as a sub-lieutenant. Joined the Red Army, 1918. Took part in the Civil War as an artillery officer. Graduated from the Frunze Military Academy, 1930. Head of military training in the Soviet artillery before WWII. Deputy Commander of Soviet Artillery, 1943. Commander of Soviet Artillery in the Far East, 1945. Again Deputy Commander of Soviet Artillery, 1946. General Inspector of the Ministry of Defence, 1957.

Chistiakov, Pavel Petrovich
1832–1919. Painter.
Professor of the Russian Academy of Arts, 1892. Best known as the teacher of many later famous Russian painters, among them V. Serov, V. Polenov, V. Surikov, V. Vasnetsov and M. Vrubel.

Chistiakova, Valeria Vladimirovna
8.3.1930– . Ballet critic.
Born in Vladivostok. Graduated from the Leningrad Theatre School, 1952, as a theatre critic. Head of the literary department at the Volkov Teatre, Iaroslavl', 1952–55. From 1958 taught at the Leningrad Theatre School (now the Leningrad Institute of Theatre, Music and Film). From 1952, ballet critic. Has written many articles and books about ballet personalities.

Chizhova, Nadezhda Vladimirovna
29.9.1945– . Athlete.
Born in Irkutskaia Oblast'. Honoured Master of Sports (track and field athletics), 1968. With Leningrad Spartak. Graduated from the Leningrad Institute of Physical Culture, 1974. Coach and sports instructor. USSR champion, 1967–74. European champion, 1966–74. World record-holder, 1968–73. Olympic champion, 1972.

Chkalov, Valerii Pavlovich
1904–1938. Pilot.
Joined the Red Army, 1919. Educated at a pilot's school, 1923. Fighter pilot, 1924, and test pilot, 1930. Made several record-breaking flights in the 1930s, which received enormous publicity and made him a folk hero of the Stalin epoch (Moscow–Kamchatka, 1936, Moscow–North Pole–Vancouver, 1937). Died in an aircrash.

Chkalova, Nina Nikolaevna (Chorokhova)
12.11.1918– . Ballet dancer.
Born in Moscow. Studied at the Choreographic School of Variety and Circus Enterprises. Graduated from the Moscow Choreographic School, 1939. Pupil of E. Gerdt. Dancer at the Bolshoi Theatre, 1939–59. From 1960, taught at the Stanislavskii and Nemirovich Danchenko Theatre. With the Ankara Theatre, Turkey, where she choreographed *Don Quixote*, with R. Tsulukidze, 1975. Taught classical dance at the Moscow Choreographic School, 1963–66, then acting, 1971–72.

Chkheidze, N.S.
1864–1926. Politician.
Menshevik leader. Member of the 4th Duma and, along with Kerenskii, one of the main orators of the left. Member of the Workers' Group of the Military-Industrial Cttee. After the February revolution 1917, first chairman of the Petrograd Soviet. Cautiously greeted Lenin on his arrival from Switzerland in Apr. 1917 (Lenin is said to have disregarded him completely). After the Bolshevik take-over, moved to Georgia. When Georgia was incorporated into USSR, emigrated to Western Europe. Settled in Paris where he died (suicide suspected, though not proved).

Chkheidze, Revaz Davidovich
9.12.1926– . Film director.
Georgian. Graduated from the Tbilisi Theatrical Institute in 1946, then from the Moscow VGIK (Film School) as a director. His tutors were Sergei Iutkevich and Mikhail Romm. Up to 1956, made all his films with Tengiz Abuladze – in 1957, *Our Courtyard*. All films made at Gruziafilm and all about Georgia. Films include *Maia From Tskhneti*, 1960, *The Treasure*, 1961, and *A Soldier's Father*, 1969, in which Sergo Zakhariadze gave a forceful performance.

Chkhenkeli, Akakii Ivanovich
1874–1931? Politician.
Menshevik member of the influential Caucasian group in the Duma (3rd and 4th). When the Georgian Mensheviks proclaimed Georgia independent during the Civil War he served as Minister of Foreign Affairs in the government in Tbilisi (1918–21). Emigrated after the Red Army entered Georgia. Settled in France.

Chkhikvadze, Zakharii Ivanovich
5.12.1862–27.4.1930. Folklorist, choir conductor.
Born in Telavi. Founder of the Georgian Philharmonic Society, 1905. Founded and headed several music schools in Signakhi, and Telavi, 1919. From 1925, Keeper of the Museum of Ancient Georgian Art. Published a collection of Georgian folk songs, *Salamuri*, 1906. Organized many concerts of church music in Georgia. Died in Tiflis.

Chochishvili, Shota Samsonovich
10.7.1950– . Athlete.
Born in Georgia. Honoured Master of Sports (judo), 1972. With Gori Burevestnik. Graduated from the Gori Pedagogical Institute, 1976. Schoolmaster. Member of the CPSU, 1972. Olympic champion, 1972.

Chokmorov, Suimenkul
9.11.1939– . Actor.
Leading Kirghiz film actor. Born in the village of Chon-Tash, in the mountains of Kirghizia, into a peasant family. One of eleven children. Entered Frunze Art School in 1953. Studied at the famous Leningrad Academy of Fine Arts in 1960s. Returned to Frunze. Taught painting and composition in the art school where he had himself been a student. Met Bolot Shamshiev, the leading Kirzhiz film director. Acted for the first time in his film, *A Shot on the Karash Pass*, in 1969. Became famous in *The Red Poppies of Issyk-Kul'* directed in 1971 by Bolot Shamshiev. Other films of note: *The Ferocious One* by Tolomush Okeev, 1973, and especially Akira Kurosawa's *Dersu Uzala* in 1975.

Chornovil, Viacheslav Maksimovich
1938– . Journalist, dissident.
Born in Erki, Cherkassy Oblast'. Graduated from Kiev University. Worked as a journalist and editor. Involved in Ukrainian nationalist activity. Arrested 1967, and sentenced to 3 years in the camps. Released in 1969. Became widely known through his samizdat articles. Rearrested, 1972. One of the best known Ukrainian nationalist voices in the Soviet Union in recent years.

Chudinov, Sergei Vasil'evich
24.8.1889–2.8.1977. Ballet dancer.
Born in Moscow. Son of Vasilii Chudinov. Graduated from the Moscow Theatre School, 1907. Pupil of V. Tikhomirov. Dancer, and later soloist, at the Bolshoi Theatre until 1949. Character dancer. Taught character dance at the Lunacharskii Technical School, Moscow, 1923–32. From 1941 choreographer-coach at the Bolshoi Theatre. Died in Moscow.

Chudinov, Vasilii Alekseevich
22.6.1865–12.4.1933. Ballet dancer.
Born in Moscow. Graduated from the Moscow Theatre School, 1881. Pupil of I. Nikitin. Joined the Bolshoi Theatre. Character roles. Taught at the Moscow Theatre School, 1905–25. Also taught in various other schools and colleges. Died in Moscow.

Chufarov, Grigorii Ivanovich
14.11.1900– . Scientist.
Graduated from the Ural Polytechnic Institute, 1928. Dean of the Urals University, 1946–56. Research in the field of metallurgical processes.

Chugaev, Aleksandr Georgievich
27.1.1924– . Composer.
Born in Eisk. Teaches at the Gnesin Music Pedagogical Institute. Author of a ballet, pieces for orchestra, string quartet, piano, and music for films.

Chugaev, Lev Aleksandrovich
1873–1922. Scientist.
Professor of inorganic chemistry at Leningrad University. Founder and director of the Institute for the Study of Platinum of the Academy of Sciences. Also worked at the Bacteriological Institute of Moscow University and published studies of organic chemistry.
See: L. Chugaev. *Sbornik Rechei i Dokladov*, Leningrad, 1924.

Chuguev, Vladimir Tikhonovich (Czugunow)
2.7.1936– . Editor, lexicographer, journalist, linguist.
Born in Bobruisk. Son of a professor of psychology and Russian literature. Lived near Moscow before WWII. With his parents in Nazi labour camps and DP camps in Germany, 1944–48. Educated at a private school in Bernkastel, 1953. With Polish Guards in the US Army in West Germany, Kaiserslautern, 1954–55. Journalist and news editor with Radio Liberty, Munich, 1955–61. Moved to London. Journalist with the BBC External Services, 1961–66. Bibliographer and academic bookseller (Iskander), 1966–75. London correspondent of Radio Liberty, 1975–81. With the BBC Russian Service, 1981. Travelled widely in Europe and America. Met and interviewed many famous personalities (Kerenskii, Akhmatova, Solzhenitsyn, Rostropovich, Medvedev and many religious leaders). Wrote on historical, philosophical and religious subjects. Edited modern Russian writers. Lives in London and Somerset.

Chugunov, Aleksandr Petrovich
21.6.1891–26.2.1964. Conductor, composer.
Born in the village of Zhegalovo, Bogorodskii District, Moscow Gouvt. Professor in the military conducting department of the Moscow Conservatory. Author of military marches, pieces for orchestra, and symphonies. Died in Moscow.

Chuikov, Vasilii Ivanovich
12.2.1900–18.3.1982. Marshal.
Joined the Red Army, 1918. Took part in the quelling of the left-SR revolt in Moscow, 1918. Joined the Bolshevik Party, 1919. Took part in the Civil War as a regimental commander. Soviet military adviser in China, 1927. Took part in the occupation of Western Belorussia (East Poland), 1939. Commander of an army during the Soviet-Finnish war, 1939–40. Military attaché in China, 1940–42. Several high posts during WWII, becoming widely known during the battle of Stalingrad. After WWII, Deputy Commander, and from 1949, Commander of Soviet forces in Germany. Commander of the Kiev military district, 1953. Commander in Chief of Land Forces, and Deputy Minister of Defence, 1960. Non-voting member of the Cen. Cttee. of the CPSU, 1952, and full member, 1961. Head of the civil defence system of the USSR, 1961–72.

Chukanov, Anatolii Alekseevich
10.5.1951– . Athlete.
Born in Rostov Oblast'. Honoured Master of Sports (cycling), 1976. With Voroshilovgrad Spartak. Sports instructor. USSR and Olympic champion, 1976. World champion, 1977.

Chukarin, Viktor Ivanovich
9.11.1921– . Athlete, sports official.
Born in Donetskaia Oblast'. Honoured Master of Sports (gymnastics), 1951. With Lvov Burevestnik. Graduated from the Lvov Institute of Physical Culture, 1950. Lecturer, 1963. Member of the CPSU, 1951. International referee, 1967. Honorary Coach of the Ukraine, 1972. Coach and sports instructor. USSR champion, 1948–56. World champion, 1954. Olympic champion, 1952, 1956.

Chukhanov, Zinovii Fedorovich
21.10.1912– . Engineer.
Graduated from the Moscow Chemical Technological Institute, 1932. Suggested new methods of fuel utilization.

Chukhrai, Grigorii Naumovich
23.5.1921– . Film director.
A participant in the Finnish war and WWII. Wounded five times, returned to Moscow with the rank of 2nd Lieutenant in the Guards. In 1946 entered the director's faculty of the VGIK. Worked as an assistant director in M. Romm's *Admiral Nakhimov*. In 1956, filmed the second screen version of Boris Lavrenev's story *The Forty First* (the first was made in 1927 by Iakov Protazanov). His advisers were Sergei Iutkevich and Mikhail Romm. His treatment of a love story concerning a Red Army soldier girl and a White nobleman officer made a sensation. Second film, *The Ballad of a Soldier* (1959, Mosfilm), brought him immediate international fame and was awarded a prize at the Cannes Film Festival. *A Clear Sky* (1961, Mosfilm) was another sensation in the Soviet Union with its anti-Stalinist subject matter. Other films: *There Lived an Old Woman and an Old Man* (1965, Mosfilm), *Memory* (1971), *Untypical Story* (1977), *They Made Him A Criminal* (1979, made in Italy). From the mid-1970s, turned to administrative work in the film industry. His first three films have become modern Soviet classics.

Chukhrai, Sergei Alekseevich
31.5.1955– . Athlete.
Born in Amurskaia Oblast'. Honoured Master of Sports (rowing), 1976. From 1978, with the Black Sea Navy sports club. Graduated from the Novaia Kakhovka Electromechanical Technical School, 1974. USSR and Olympic champion, 1976. World champion, 1978–79.

Chukhrov, Fedor Vasil'evich
15.7.1908 . Scientist.
Graduated from the Moscow Geological Survey Institute, 1932. Director of the Institute of the Geology of Ore Deposits, 1955. Made studies of ore deposits in Kazakhstan, and the mineralogy of oxidized ozone.

Chukovskaia, Lidia Korneevna
24.3.1907– . Author, editor.
Daughter of Kornei Chukovskii. Lives in the writer's colony, Peredelkino, some 20 miles from Moscow. Author of *Opustelyi Dom* (*Sof'ia*

70

Petrovna) and *Zapiski ob Anne Akhmatovoi* (she was a very close friend of Akhmatova). Expelled from The Union of Soviet Writers in 1974. Unable to publish her work, she still remains one of the most respected literary figures in the USSR.

Chukovskii, Kornei Ivanovich (real name – Korneichukov, Nikolai Vasil'evich)
31.3.1882–28.10.1969. Author.
Born in Petersburg. Lived in his childhood near Odessa with his mother, a Ukrainian peasant woman. Began to write in Odessa newspapers. Correspondent in London, 1903–4. Became a well-known journalist before WWI. Children's writer. His books (*Moidodyr, Tarakanishche, Mukha Tsokotukha, Barmalei, Aibolit*) have remained bestsellers since their publication. Many of his stories became the basis for radio programmes, operas, ballets and TV films. He also wrote books for adults, mostly critical essays. His 6-volume *Complete Works* was published in Moscow, 1965–69. Stood in the centre of Russian literary life for over half a century. Father of the writer Lidia Chukovskaia. Oxford honorary Doctor of Literature, 1962. Died at Kuntsevo and buried at Peredelkino.

Chulaki, Mikhail Ivanovich
19.11.1908– . Composer, state official.
Born in Simferopol'. Graduated from the Leningrad Conservatory, 1931. Director of the same conservatory, 1955–59. Professor, 1962. Director and Artistic Director at the Bolshoi Theatre, 1963–70. Chairman of the Artistic Council of Choreography attached to the Ministry of Culture. Wrote music for ballets based on Russian and foreign classics (Pushkin, Molière). Contributed to musical propaganda (*Kak Zakalialas' Stal'* and similar). His ballets have been produced by nearly all the important Soviet theatres, and also in other Eastern European countries.

Chulkov, Georgii Ivanovich
1879–1939. Poet, literary critic.
Studied at Moscow University. Arrested for revolutionary activities (with I. Tsereteli), 1901, and exiled to Iakutia. In Nizhnii–Novgorod, 1904,

published his first book. Moved to Petersburg, 1904. On the editorial board of the philosophical journal *Novyi Put'*. Became close to A. Blok. Moved to Moscow, 1912. Preached mystical anarchism, a doctrine which has eluded definition for generations. Continued his literary researches in the Soviet period, writing on Russian literature and cultural history.

Churbanov, Iurii Mikhailovich
1936– . State security official.
Graduated from Moscow University in 1964. As a first year student, became a member of the CPSU. After graduating, promoted to Lt.-general holding top positions in the Komsomol, 1957–70. Deputy Chief of the Police Dept. in the USSR Ministry of Internal Affairs 1970–71. Deputy Chief of Police Administration of the Security Police Force (MVD troops), 1971–75. Member of the Central Auditing Cttee. of the CPSU, 1976–81. Candidate member of the Cen. Cttee. of the CPSU, 1981. Deputy Minister of Internal Affairs, 1977–80. First Deputy Chairman of the KGB, 1980. Assigned to Galina Brezhneva as her security guard. Married her (her third husband). Brezhnev quickly promoted him after the marriage. Arrested by KGB officers in 1986 (some believe on Gorbachev's personal order) and tried in 1988 for corruption and accepting bribes totalling hundreds of thousands of roubles.

Churikova, Inna Mikhailovna (m. Panfilova)
5.10.1943– . Film actress.
Discovered by the film director Gleb Panfilov, who later married her. Outstanding modern comedy actress. Graduated from the Shchepkin Drama School, 1965. Worked in the Moscow Young Spectators' Theatre, then in the Moscow Lenin Komsomol Theatre. First film, 1961. Remained in obscurity until she played a leading role in Panfilov's film, *V Ogne Broda Net*. Became a celebrity. Her next film, *Nachalo*, directed by Panfilov, confirmed her reputation as a comedy actress, and was followed by *Proshu slova* (also by Panfilov).

Churilin, Tikhon Vasil'evich
1892–1944. Poet.
Close to the futurist poets. Published several collections of experimental poetry. Also wrote short stories.

Chuvanov, Mikhail Ivanovich
1891–15.4.1988. Bibliographer, book collector, Old Believer leader.
Born in Usady near Moscow into an Old Believer family. Worked in printing shops before WWI. In the 1920s started his collection of books on literature and philosophy, and especially on Old Moscow and the Old Believers. Collected a unique library of some 20,000 volumes. Continued the traditions of such collectors of Old Believer descent as Tretiakov and Shchukin. His library has become a cultural landmark of Moscow. Chairman of the Moscow Old Believers Association. Died in Moscow.

Chuzhikov, Nikolai Fedorovich
5.5.1938– . Athlete.
Born in Belgorodskaia Oblast'. Honoured Master of Sports (rowing), 1964. With Lisichansk Avangard. Graduated from the Voroshilovgrad Pedagogical Institute, 1971. Schoolmaster. Member of the CPSU, 1967. USSR champion, 1962–69. World champion, 1966. Olympic champion, 1964.

Chuzhoi, Anatolii
1894–24.1.1969. Ballet critic.
Born in Riga. Studied law in the universities of Riga, Warsaw and Petrograd. Moved to the USA in the early 1920s. Began writing for the American ballet press. Founder, in 1936, of the American journal *Dance Magazine*. From 1942 till his death, publisher and editor of *Dance News*. Author, translator and editor of numerous dance books, also *Dance Encyclopaedia* (1949, latest ed. 1967), *New York City Ballet*, 1953, and *Fokine, Memoirs of a Ballet Master*, 1961. Died in New York.

Chyzhevskyi, Dmitrii Ivanovich
23.3.1894– . Philosopher, literary scholar.
Born in Aleksandria, Kherson Gouvt. Studied at Kiev and Petersburg

Universities. Lectured at Kiev University. Emigrated in 1921. Lived in Germany, studied philosophy at Heidelberg and Freiburg. Professor at the Ukrainian University in Prague, 1924–29. Professor at Halle, 1932–45. After WWII, moved to the USA. Professor of Slavonic Studies at Harvard University, 1949–55. Returned to Europe. Professor of Slavonic Studies at Heidelberg, 1956. One of the best known names in Slavonic studies, especially in the German-speaking countries. Published over 600 monographs and articles on subjects, concerning Slavonic philosophy, literature and culture, with a special stress on Russian and Ukrainian subjects.

Main works: *Hegel in Russia, Philosophy in the Ukraine, Skovoroda's Philosophy, Outline of Comparative Slavic Literature, Das heilige Russland, History of Old Russian Literature.*

Costakis, George (Georgii Dionisovich)

1913– . Art collector.

Famous Russian art collector of Greek parentage known in 1960s Moscow, as the 'crazy Greek who buys junk'. Saved from destruction more than 2000 masterpieces by pioneers of Russian avant-garde art. Born in Moscow, son of a wealthy Greek tobacco merchant who later lost his tobacco plantations in Uzbekistan. In the 1920s, served as a choirboy at the Orthodox church in Pushkin Square. At an early age, started collecting rare stamps, Russian icons, porcelain, Russian silver and other objets d'art. After the 1917 Revolution, a minor employee at the Greek Embassy in Moscow, then a chauffeur at the Canadian Embassy with only a modest salary but in foreign currency (which increased his buying power enormously). After Stalin's death, started a search for forgotten artists, their widows or other relations. Met the remarkable Vladimir Tatlin, Rodchenko, and Rodchenko's wife, the artist Stepanova. Found some 100 artists, participants in the mighty Russian avant-garde movement from 1910–25. By the mid-1960s, was a major collector. His collection attracted the interest of several Western VIPs including Senator Edward

Kennedy, David Rockefeller and Igor Stravinskii.

The Soviet government suddenly realised the collection's value and started to pay great attention. Backed by powerful members of the Politburo such as Ekaterina Furtseva, the then Minister of Culture. With Khrushchev's fall, things changed at once. Constant conflict with the authorities arose. Watched by the KGB as a speculator who buys and sells (an activity banned by law in the Soviet Union). Forced to leave the Soviet Union in 1978. Left a considerable part of his collection in Moscow (the price of his exit visa). Now lives in a suburb of Athens. His famous and unique collection was displayed in America, Britain and all over Europe.

Source: Interview given to Jeanne Vronskaya in Sept. 1981.

Cui, Cesar Antonovich

18.1.1835–26.3.1918. Composer, music critic, engineer general.

Born in Wil'no. Specialist in military engineering. General. Professor at the Academy of Engineering, Petersburg. Member of the Mighty Handful. One of the most distinguished music critics in the 1860–90s. Author of 10 operas, 4 operas for children, symphonies and vocal symphonies, 4 suites, 3 string quartets, and pieces for piano. Finished the opera *Kamennyi Gost'* by Dargomyzhskii, 1866. Among the composers who put the finishing touches to M. Mussorgskii's opera *Sorochinskaia Iarmarka*.

Literary works: *Russkii Romans*, Petersburg, 1896; *Muzykal'no-kriticheskie Stat'ii*, Petrograd, 1918; *Izbrannye Stat'ii ob Ispolniteliakh*, Moscow, 1957.

Czapski, Jozef

1898– . Author.

Educated at the Corps des Pages, Petersburg, 1917. During the Civil War, joined the Polish corps of Dowbor-Musnicki. Lived in independent Poland between the world wars. At the beginning of WWII, taken prisoner by the Red Army. One of a handful of Polish officers who escaped the NKVD mass murders at Katyn and other places. Left the Soviet Union in the Polish Army of General Anders after the German invasion of the USSR. Wrote one of

the earliest and best accounts of the Gulag, *Terre Inhumaine*, Paris, 1949. Settled in France. One of the founders of the Polish magazine, *Kultura*.

Czugunow, Tikhon Kuz'mich

26.5.1902–28.12.1977. Pedagogue, psychologist, sociologist.

Born at Borodino, near Orel. Son of a Stolypin farmer (khutorianin). Much influenced by L. Tolstoy and the traditional peasant way of life. Educated at Orel High school, 1917. Worked as a teacher in many parts of Russia, 1920–22. Graduated from Moscow University, 1926. Worked at the Moscow Psychological Institute under Blonskii, 1926–29. Assistant professor at the Moscow University, 1932–36. At the start of WWII, near Orel. In Nazi labour camps and DP camps in Germany, 1944–48. Settled in Munich. Works on the Russian and Soviet education system and on collectivization published in Russian and German. Contributor to many Russian publications in Europe and America in the 1950–70s. Died near Munich.

Czugunow-Schmitt, Nikolai Tikhonovich

1943– . Economist.

Born in Bobruisk. With his parents in Nazi labour camps and DP camps in Germany, 1944–48. Educated at Simmern High School, 1964. Married Heidemarie Schmitt, 1968. Graduated from Munich University in economics, 1971, and in law, 1975. Doctor of economics at Munich University, 1988. Worked at the Institut der Finanzwissenschaft and Hochschule für Politik, Munich. Wrote on Soviet economics in the *Handbuch der Finanzwissenschaften*, 1982. Specialist in East-West trade. Lives in Munich.

D

Dakhadaev, Mahomet-Ali (Makhach)

1882–1918. Revolutionary.

Organizer of the local Red Army detachments in Daghestan during the Civil War. Fought against the Whites and the anti-communist local population. Taken prisoner by the Whites and shot.

Dali, Galia (Gala)
1902?–6.1982. Wife of Salvador Dali. Emigrated from Russia after the Civil War. Settled in France. Met Dali in Paris, c. 1932. Became his inspiration and model for many years. In 1936 he constructed a surrealist object with her old slipper and a glass of warm milk. This became Mme. Schiaparelli's famous slipper-hat, which Gala was the first to wear. Lived with Dali in Spain and New York. Died in Port Ligat, Spain.

Dalin, David Iul'evich (Levin)
1889–1962. Politician, sociologist. Member of the RSDRP in 1907. Member of the Cen. Cttee. of the Menshevik Party in 1917. During the Civil War arrested, and later expelled from Russia in 1921. During the 1930–50s became a leading Sovietologist in America.

Damaev, Vasilii Petrovich
19.4.1878–11.10.1931. Singer (tenor). Born in the Cossack village of Otradnaia, in the Northern Caucasus. Pupil of A. Uspenskii. Soloist with Moscow Theatres, 1908–24 (with the Zimin Opera, 1908–17). Took part in the Russkie Sezony (Ballets Russes) and opera performances abroad, 1910. Died in Moscow.

Damaskin (Tsedrik), Bishop of Glukhov
1890?–10.9.1943. Russian Orthodox clergyman.
Arrested many times during the 1930s atheist campaigns of the Soviet government. Inmate of the Solovki concentration camp. Wandered around Russia. One of the organizers of the Catacomb Church. Died in prison either in Kazakhstan or Siberia.

Dan, Fedor Ill'ich (Gurvich)
1871–1947. Revolutionary, politician.
Educated as a doctor. Became involved in revolutionary activity as a teenager. Member of the SDs from 1894. Emigrated to Germany, 1901. Joined the Mensheviks after the split in the SD Party (one of the main opponents of Bolshevism within the SD Party). Editor of the newspaper *Golos Social Demokrata*. Member of the Menshevik Cen. Cttee. After the February Revolution 1917, member of the Cen. Executive Cttee. Supported the Provisional government. After the October Revolution, worked as a doctor. Continued to appear at party congresses as a representative of Menshevism. Expelled from the USSR by Lenin in 1922, stripped of Soviet citizenship, 1923. Took part in the founding of the Socialist International, 1923. Edited the magazine *Novyi Put'*. Died in the USA.

Dan, Lidia Osipovna (Tsederbaum)
1878–1963. Revolutionary.
Member of the Menshevik Party. Sister of Martov. Married F. Dan. Emigrated after the Bolshevik takeover to Berlin, in the 1920s. Later moved to Paris to escape Hitler. Settled in the USA where she contributed to the Menshevik journal *Sotsialisticheskii Vestnik*.

Danelia, Georgii Nikolaevich
25.8.1930– . Film director.
Born in Tbilisi into an artistic family. His mother, M. Andzhaparidze, was a famous actress. Trained originally as an architect, but suddenly dropped his career and enrolled in the Advanced Directors's Course at Mosfilm Studios, 1960. First film effort as a student was a 10-minute film about Vassisualii Lokhankin with the distinguished comedian Evgenii Evstigneev in the leading role. This was based on Ilf and Petrov's *The Twelve Chairs* and *The Golden Calf*. His first feature, *Serezha* (1960, Mosfilm), was scripted by Vera Panova. Gained recognition with *I Walk About Moscow* (1963), an experimental film (scripted by the talented Gennadii Shpalikov, with the remarkable camera work of one of the best Soviet cameramen, Vadim Iusov). *The Thirty-Three* (1965), made again at Mosfilm, is a biting satire on Soviet bureaucrats, and was withdrawn after a few screenings. The film was re-released in summer 1987 when Elem Klimov became head of the film industry. Other films: *Cheer Up!* 1969, *Hopelessly Lost*, the screen version of Huckleberry Finn, which was shown at the 1972 Cannes Film Festival; *Afonia* 1975, *Mimino*, 1977.

Daniel', Iulii Markovich (Arzhak, Nikolai)
1925– . Writer, translator.
Born in Moscow. Took part in WWII. Graduated from the Moscow Oblast' Teachers' Institute. School teacher and translator of poetry. In the late 1950s and early 1960s, his short satirical stories appeared in the West under the pseudonym Nikolai Arzhak. Arrested in 1965 and put on trial with A. Siniavskii. Accused of anti-Soviet propaganda and slander on Soviet life. Sentenced to 5 years in prison camps. The trial became an international literary scandal and focus of protests, and was well documented as the first show trial of writers in post-Stalin USSR. After serving his term, he was not allowed to live in Moscow. Settled in Kaluga. Lives now in Moscow.
Books: *Govorit Moskva*, USA, 1962; *Ruki. Chelovek Iz Minapa*, USA, 1963; *Stikhi Iz Nevoli*, Holland, 1971.

Danielian, Aikanush Bagdasarovna
15.12.1893–19.4.1958. Singer (soprano).
Born in Tiflis. Pupil of N. Iretskaia. Soloist with the Tbilisi Opera from 1924, and the Erevan Opera, 1933–48. Professor at the Erevan Conservatory 1943–51. Died in Erevan.

Danielson, Nikolai Frantsevich
1844–1918. Economist.
Left-wing populist, later Marxist. Translator of *Das Kapital* into Russian. Corresponded with Marx and Engels in London. Lenin was highly critical of his liberal Marxist approach.

Danilin, Nikolai Mikhailovich
3.12.1878–6.2.1945. Conductor.
Born in Moscow. Professor at the Moscow Conservatory. Chief conductor with the Synodal Choir, 1910–18. After the October Revolution 1917, worked as choir conductor at the Bolshoi Theatre. Directed the choir of the Leningrad Academic Band, and the State Choir of the USSR. Died in Moscow.

Danilov, Stepan Nikolaevich
6.1.1889–1972? Chemist.
Graduated from Petersburg University, 1914. Taught at Petersburg University from 1915. Editor of *Zhurnal Obshchei Khimii* from 1946.

73

Danilova, Aleksandra Dionis'evna
20.11.1904–   . Ballerina, ballet teacher.
Born in Petergof. Graduated from the Petrograd Theatre School, 1921. Pupil of E. Gerdt and V. Semenov. Dancer at the Petrograd Theatre of Opera and Ballet, 1921–24. Left the USSR, 1924. Joined Sergei Diaghilev. A star in the Ballets Russes until 1929. From 1929–38, with the ballet companies of de Basil in Monte Carlo and Paris, and starred in L. Miasin's productions. From 1938–52, danced with the Ballet Russe de Monte Carlo (USA), and made guest appearances with Sadler's Wells Ballet, 1949, and the Festival Ballet, 1952 and 1955. Created her own ballet company in 1952. Became very famous as a classical ballerina in the USA. Retired, 1957. Returned several times at the request of the Metropolitan Opera to stage some dances. Taught at the American Ballet School throughout the 1970s.
See: 'A Conversation with Aleksandra Danilova', *Ballet Review*, 1973; A. Fay, 'The Belle of the Ballets Russes: Aleksandra Danilova', *Dance Magazine*, Oct. 1977.

Danilova, Pelageia Aleksandrovna
4.5.1918–   . Athlete.
Born in the village of Boroviki, Pskov Oblast. Honoured Master of Sports (gymnastics), 1952. With Leningrad Burevestnik. Graduated from the Leningrad Institute of Physical Culture, 1953. Coach. USSR champion, 1948–50. World champion, 1954. Olympic champion, 1952. Silver medal, 1952.

Dan'kevich, Konstantin Fedorovich
24.12.1905–   . Composer.
Born in Odessa. Graduated from the Odessa School of Musical Drama, 1929. Taught from 1929. With the Odessa Institute of Musical Drama from 1935. During WWII, artistic director of the Song and Dance Ensemble of the NKVD troops in Transcaucasia. Director of the Odessa Conservatory, 1944–51. Professor from 1948. Professor at Kiev Conservatory from 1953. Followed the classical tradition. Composed operas, musical comedies, cantatas, works for the piano, and choral and orchestral works.

Danzas, Iulia Nikolaevna
1879–1942. Author, nun.
Born in Athens. Daughter of a Russian diplomat. Lady-in-waiting to the last Empress, Aleksandra Fedorovna, before WWI. Became a freemason. Interested in theosophy. Author of *V Poiskakh Bozhestva*. Professor of History of Religion at Petrograd University, 1917. Close to M. Gorkii. Head of the Petrograd Dom Uchenykh (House of Scientists), 1920. Converted to catholicism, 1920. Catholic nun, 1923. Arrested with a group of Catholics in Nov. 1923, and sent to the Solovki concentration camp. Released, thanks to Gorkii, in 1932, and allowed to join her brother in Berlin. Settled in France, organized the Centre of Soviet Studies, Istina, and published the magazine *Russie et Chretienté*, as well as her Solovki memoirs, *Bagne Rouge*, 1935. Wrote a biography of the last Tsarina *L'Imperatrice tragica e il suo tempo*, published in Verona, 1942.

Dar, David (Ryvkin, David Iakovlevich)
1910–1980. Author.
Born in Petersburg. Started to write in the 1920s. Husband of Vera Panova. For many decades an official Soviet writer. In his old age, became a promoter of young, unofficial poets in Leningrad, defending Pasternak, Solzhenitsyn and Brodskii. Emigrated, 1977. Settled in Israel. Died of heart failure.

Dar'in, Gennadii Aleksandrovich
1922–   . Artist.
Born in Iaroslavl'. Studied at the Iaroslavl' Art School, 1938–41, under N. Oparin, I. Druzhinina, V. Kartovich. Studied at the Moscow Repin School of Painting, Sculpture and Architecture, 1945–51, under Boris Ioganson. Member of the Union of Artists, Iaroslavl' branch. Exhibited from 1951 in Moscow and Iaroslavl'. Genre painter.

Daunene, Tamara Viktorovna
22.9.1951–   . Athlete.
Born in Oshkar-Ola, Mari ASSR. Honoured Master of Sports (basketball), 1976. With Moscow Dynamo from 1977. Student at the Latvian Institute of Physical Culture. USSR

champion, 1974–76. European champion, 1974 and 1976. World champion, 1971. Olympic champion, 1976.

Davidenko, Aleksandr Aleksandrovich
13.4.1899–1.5.1934. Composer.
Born in Odessa. Early musical training at the Odessa Conservatory, 1918–19, where he studied under Malishevskii, and at the Khar'kov Music Institute, 1921. Finished his studies at the Moscow Conservatory, 1922–29. Pupil of R. Glier. Postgraduate studies, 1929–32. Also studied at the Choir Academy, 1922–24. Pupil of A. Kastalskii. Directed choral societies from 1924. Organised and directed *Prokoll*. Specialized throughout his career in vocal music. Died in Moscow.

Davidovich, Bella Mikhailovna
16.7.1928–   . Pianist.
Born in Baku. Pupil of Ia. Flier. 1st prize at the International Chopin Piano Competition, Warsaw, 1949. Teacher at the Moscow Conservatory until 1975. Emigrated to Israel (1975) with her violinist son, Vitalii Sitkovskii. Many guest performances in Europe and America.

Davidovskii, Grigorii Mikhailovich
18.1.1866–13.4.1953. Conductor, composer.
Born in the village of Mel'nia, near Konotop. Organizer of several Ukrainian and Russian choirs, (eg the Ukrainian Band, 1908, with which he travelled all over Russia). Head of the Poltava Band. Author of fantasies on Ukrainian themes, 1896. Died in Poltava.

Davitashvili, Evgenia Iuvashevna (Dzuna)
1943–   . Healer, hypnotist.
Of Assyrian origin, born in Krasnodar in the Northern Caucasus. After school, worked as a waitress in a restaurant in Tbilisi. At an early age, discovered her hands' extrasensory curative properties and started treating people's swollen legs, hands, faces and backs. It was such a success that she was besieged by crowds of ill people. Brought to Moscow and allowed to open an exclusive private clinic at her flat on Leningradskii

Prospekt. Awarded the diploma of medical nurse and masseuse. After some initial suspicions, the Soviet scientific establishment took an interest in her miracle hands. They were photographed and researched by several scientific groups and recognized as having special healing qualitites. Eventually she was praised by the Academy of Sciences and adopted by the Kremlin and the Soviet artistic establishment. Patients included Leonid Brezhnev, who before his treatment could hardly walk, Cen. Cttee. Secretary, Ponomarev, GOSPLAN Chairman, Baibakov, Olympic Games Cttee. Chairman, Novikov, comedian Arkadii Raikin, and Iurii Andropov. Even the Health Minister, Boris Petrovskii asked her to treat his back. Later foreign correspondents and foreign communists received her treatment. Dzuna (Georgian for magician) became a living legend in the Soviet Union. The Russian press called her a female Rasputin. Her lifestyle was said to be bohemian. Became a Russian millionairess.

Davydov, Aleksandr Mikhailovich (Levenson)
1872–28.6.1944. Singer (tenor).
Born in the Poltava Gouvt. Pupil of K. Everardi. Soloist with the Mariinskii Theatre, 1900–17. Honorary Artist of the RSFSR, 1924. Died in Moscow.

Davydov, Vitalii Semenovich
1.4.1939–   . Athlete.
Born in Moscow. Honored Master of Sports (ice hockey), 1963. With Moscow Dynamo. Honorary Coach of the USSR, Graduated from the Moscow Oblast' Pedagogical Institute, 1965. Member of the CPSU, 1970. World Champion, 1963–71. European champion, 1963–70. Olympic champion, 1964, 1968 and 1972.

Davydova, Vera Aleksandrovna (m. Mchedlidze)
30.9.1906–   . Singer (mezzo soprano).
Born in Nizhnii-Novgorod. Pupil of E. Devos–Soboleva. Soloist with the Leningrad Theatre of Opera and Ballet, 1929–32, with the Bolshoi Theatre, 1932–56.

Deborin, Abram Moiseevich (Ioffe)
16.6.1881–8.3.1963. Philosopher.
Born in Upino, Lithuania. Member of the SD Party from the late 1890s. After the split of the SDs, joined the Bolsheviks, 1903. Became Menshevik, 1908–17. After 1928, member of the Communist Party. Appointed editor of the Soviet Marxist philosophical magazine *Pod znamenem marksima* (Under the banner of Marxism), 1926–30. Criticized for Menshevik deviation in 1931 (an extremely dangerous accusation during the Stalin years), but survived. Became a classic Soviet official Marxist.

Degtiarev, Aleksandr Vladimirovich
26.3.1955–   . Athlete.
Born in the village of Tolmachevo, Moscow Oblast'. Honoured Master of Sports (rowing), 1976. With Moscow Oblast' Trudovye Rezervy. Graduated from the Moscow Oblast' Institute of Physical Culture, 1979. USSR champion, 1975. Olympic champion (4 x 1,000m.), 1976.

Degtiarev, Georgii Ermolaevich
1893–1973. Col.-general.
Joined the Red Army and Communist Party, 1920. Took part in WWI and the Civil War. Graduated from the Frunze Academy, 1933. During WWII, artillery commander at the Volkhov, Karelian and Far Eastern Fronts.

Degtiarev, Vasilii Alekseevich
1880–1949. Weapon designer.
Head of a design shop in an armaments works, 1918. Head of a design office for automatic weapons, 1931. Designed infantry (PPD) and anti-tank weapons (PTRD). 4 Stalin Prizes.

Deich, Lev G. (Deutsch)
1855–1941. Revolutionary.
Together with Plekhanov founded the first Russian Marxist organization, the Emancipation of Labour Group. One of the leaders of the SD party, and after the split, a Menshevik leader. After the February Revolution 1917, edited Plekhanov's newspaper, *Edinstvo*. After the October Revolution 1917, retired from politics. Editor of Plekhanov's works, and writer on the Russian revolutionary movement.

Deineka, Aleksandr Aleksandrovich
1899–1969. Artist.
Studied at the Khar'kov Art School and Moscow Art and Technical Workshops (Vkhutemas), 1921–25. Member of the Oktiabr' left-wing artists group. Adopted socialist realism and became an establishment artist, although he was occasionally criticized by Stalinists for not being Soviet enough. Many works on sport and war themes.

Delmas, Liubov' Aleksandrovna (Andreeva)
1884–1961? Singer.
Opera singer, mezzo-soprano. Appeared at the Theatre of Musical Drama in Petrograd, 1913–19. Attracted attention in the role of Carmen, and was immortalized by her admirer A. Blok in his famous cycle of poems, *Carmen*.

Delone, Boris Nikolaevich
15.3.1890–1973? Mathematician.
Born in Petersburg. Graduated from Kiev University, 1913. Professor at Leningrad University, 1922–35, and Moscow University, 1935–42. Carried out research connected with the geometry of numbers and the structural analysis of crystals. Famous rock climber.

Delone, Vadim Nikolaevich
1947–1983. Poet, dissident.
Born in Moscow. Expelled from the Moscow Teachers' Institute for his attempt to organize an independent society of writers (with V. Bukovskii and I. Galanskov). In 1967, took part in a demonstration, protesting against Galanskov's arrest. Spent 9 months in prison. Arrested in 1968 for participation in a demonstration on Red Square against the Soviet invasion of Czechoslovakia. Became internationally known as a human rights campaigner. Left the USSR in 1975 and settled in Paris. Died of a heart attack.
Books: *Portrety V Koliuchei Rame*, London, 1984; *Stikhi, 1965–83*, Paris, 1984.

Dement'ev, Petr Vasil'evich
1907–1977. Col.-general, Minister of the Aviation Industry.
Graduated from the Zhukovskii Air Force Academy, 1931. 1st Deputy Minister of the Aviation Industry of the USSR, 1941, involved in the rebuilding of the Soviet air force after its complete destruction at the beginning of WWII. Minister of the Aviation Industry, 1953–57, and from 1965 onwards. Chairman of the State Committee for Aviation Technology, 1957–65. Member of the Cen. Cttee. of the CPSU, 1956–77.

Dement'eva, Elizaveta Grigor'evna
5.3.1928– . Athlete.
Born in Kostroma. Honoured Master of Sports (rowing), 1956. With Kostroma Krasnoe Znamia. Coach. USSR champion, 1956–58, 1960. European champion, 1957, 1959. World champion, 1958. Olympic champion, 1956.
See: Golubev, *Pobeda, Zavoevannaia Za Okeanom*, Kostroma, 1957

**De Meo, Pamela Colombina
(b. Vinyk; m. Synge)**
1927– . Artist, singer, dancer.
Daughter of the doctor and scientist, Boris Vinyk (who left Russia in 1912). Educated at Cheltenham Ladies' College, the Royal Academy of Dramatic Art, St. Martin's School of Art, and the Chelsea School of Art. Studied ballet at the Russian School of Ballet in Cannes, France. Pupil of Marie Karsovska (partner of one of the Legat brothers). Exhibited at the Paris Salon, the Royal Society of British Artists, Chelsea Artists, the Bankside Galleries, the Mall Galleries, and the Great Britain-USSR Association, 1987. Portrait and landscape painter strongly influenced by Cézanne and the Russian artists Serov and Venetsianov. Paints in powerful colours, influenced by Russian folklore. Has travelled widely in South Africa, Brazil, India, China and throughout Europe, and has made many trips to the USSR. Performed with the Balalaika Dance Group as a solo Russian singer, and as a group dancer in Russian folk dances at many theatres and venues, including the Queen Elizabeth Hall, London. Singer with the choir at the Dormition Russian Cathedral in Exile, Emperor's Gate. Married Major Brian Synge, Irish Guards.

Demichev, Petr Nilovich
3.1.1918– . Politician.
Born in the village of Pesochnaia, Kaluga Oblast'. Graduated from the Moscow Mendeleev Institute of Chemical Technology, 1944, and the CPSU Cen. Cttee's Higher Party School, 1953. Began as a party secretary of the Komsomol Cttee., 1937. Joined the CPSU, 1938. Served in the Soviet Army, 1939–44. Assistant Professor at the Mendeleev Institute, 1944–45. Dept. Head, and Secretary of the CP Cttee. in Moscow, Deputy Dept. Head of Moscow City CPSU Cttee., and staff member of the Cen Cttee. of the CPSU, 1945–56. Secretary of Moscow Oblast' CPSU Cttee., 1956–58. Senior posts with the USSR Council of Ministers, 1958–59. Member of the Presidium of the USSR Supreme Soviet, 1962–66. 1st Secretary of Moscow Oblast' Cttee., 1959–60, and Moscow City CPSU Cttee., 1960–62. Member of the Bureau of the Cen. Cttee. of the CPSU for the RSFSR, 1959–61. Secretary, 1961–74. Candidate member of the Politburo from 1964. Chairman of the Bureau for the Chemical and Light Industries of the Cen. Cttee., 1962–64. USSR Minister of Culture from Nov. 1974 until 1986.

Demidov, Georgii Georgievich
1908–19.2.1987. Author, dissident.
Graduated from Khar'kov University, as a physicist, 1933. Arrested after a false denunciation, 1935. Spent 10 years in labour camps. Spent a second term of 10 years for his criticism of Beria. Worked as an electrician in the labour camps where he met the author, Varlam Shalamov. Influenced by Shalamov, he began writing. Settled in Ukhta and worked as the head of a construction bureau. Scientist and inventor. Retired and continued to write about the camps. In 1980, the KGB confiscated his manuscripts despite protests from other writers. Died in Ukhta. One of the longest term Kolyma prisoners who survived the Gulag.

Demidova, Alla Sergeevna
29.9.1936– . Film and theatre actress.
One of the leading film and theatre actresses in the Soviet Union. Initially trained as an economist. A graduate of the economics faculty of Moscow University in 1960. Graduated in 1964 from the Shchukin Drama School. Worked in the famous Taganka Theatre. First film, *The Leningrad Symphony* in 1957. Played Julia von Mekk in *Tchaikovskii*, 1970, which made her famous. Other films of note: Larisa Shepit'ko's *You and I*, Andrei Tarkovskii's *The Mirror*, Iulii Karasik's *The Seagull*.

Demin, Mikhail (Trifonov, Georgii Evgen'evich)
1926–1984. Writer, journalist.
Born in Finland, grew up in Moscow. Cousin of the Soviet writer Iurii Trifonov. Son of a prominent Soviet Army commander who perished in the Gulag in 1937. Became a homeless child. Arrested for theft and spent a few years in the camps as a common criminal. After serving his term, settled in Siberia. In 1954, published his first poems in the local press. Encouraged by his success, he continued to write, and had his stories published in the national press. Became a reporter for a number of Moscow Komsomol newspapers. Published a book of poems, *Pod Nezakatnym Solntsem*, 1958. In 1968, allowed to visit Paris to see his relatives. Did not return to the USSR. Married a distant cousin, and remained in Paris writing for the Russian emigré press and contributing to Radio Liberty programmes. Became an alcoholic and died of a heart attack.
Books: *Blatnoi* (autobiography, 1981, tr. into French), *Taezhnyi Brodiaga*, USA, 1986.

Demirchian, Karen Seropovich
1932– . Party and state official.
Armenian. Born in Erevan. Graduated from the Erevan Polytechnical Institute and the Party Higher School of the Cen. Cttee. of the CPSU, 1961. Chief engineer-designer and division head of a scientific research institute in Leningrad. Senior party posts in Armenia. Member of the Cen. Cttee. of the Armenian CP, 1966–72. 1st Secretary of the Cen. Cttee. of the Armenian CP, 1974. Member of the Cen. Cttee. of the CPSU, 1976. Trade

Minister of the Armenian Republic till Apr. 1986. Replaced as first secretary of Cen. Cttee. of the Armenian CP after the ethnic unrest in Armenia, May 1988.

Demutskii, Daniil Porfir'evich
16.7.1893–7.5.1954. Cameraman.
Son of the composer Porfirii Demutskii. Graduated from Kiev University, 1917. Photographer with *Vestnik Fotografii* and *Solntse Rossii*, two leading photographic magazines. Met A. Dovzhenko in 1925. Cameraman in many of his films, including *Vasia-Reformator*, and *Iagodka Liubvi*, both in 1926, followed by *Arsenal*, 1929, *Zemlia*, 1930, and *Ivan*, 1932. These films are now considered masterpieces of early Russian cinema.

Demutskii, Porfirii Danilovich
10.3.1860–3.6.1927. Folklorist, conductor, composer.
Born in the village of Ianishivtsy in the Kiev Gouvt. Member of the Ukrainian Academy of Sciences Cttee. for Ethnography. Taught at the N. V. Lysenko Institute for Musical Drama, Kiev. One of the first to record Ukrainian folk motives. Author of several works on Ukrainian folk music. Died in Kiev.

Denike, Iurii Petrovich
1887–1964. Revolutionary, politician, journalist.
Bolshevik, 1904–07. Menshevik after Mar. 1917. One of the leaders of the Kazan Soviet, 1917. One of the initiators of the movement of workers' representatives (non-Bolshevik) in Petrograd in 1918. Arrested in July 1918. Member of the Soviet Embassy in Berlin in 1922, soon became an emigré. Joined the German Social Democratic Party. Spent several months in prison in Nazi Germany. Moved to Paris. During WWII, moved to USA. Member of the editorial board of *Sotsialisticheskii Vestnik* (Socialist Herald). Later became a writer and broadcaster with Radio Liberty in Munich.

Denikin, Anton Ivanovich
16.12.1872–8.8.1947. General.
Born near Warsaw. Son of an officer serving in Poland. Graduated from the Kiev military school in 1892, then from the Academy of the General Staff in 1899. During WWI, a divisional commander in the Southern Army, then Lt-general of the 8th Army Corps (Rumanian front) in 1916. Chief-of-staff of the High Command, Apr.-May 1917. Took part in the Kornilov rebellion against the Provisional Government. Arrested, fled with Kornilov from Bykhov prison in Dec. 1917. Went to the Don and became one of the organizers of the White armies. After Kornilov's death (13 Apr. 1918), commander of the Dobrovolcheskaiia army and commander-in-chief of the White forces in southern Russia, recognizing Admiral Kolchak (who was in Siberia) as Supreme Ruler. In summer-autumn 1919 led a march on Moscow, which reached Orel. Defeated there by Red forces in collusion with Makhno (anarchist) partisans who cut his lines of communication in the rear. On 4 Apr. 1920 after the appointment of General Wrangel (the former commander of his Caucasian army with whom he had previously quarrelled), left for Constantinople. Between the wars, lived in France. After WWII, went to the USA. Died in Ann Arbor, Michigan. Politically close to the Cadet party, fought under the slogan 'Russia United and Indivisible'. His 5-vol memoirs, *Ocherki Russkoi Smuty* (Berlin-Paris, 1921–26), is a valuable source on the revolutionary and civil war years. Also *Pokhod na Moskvu* (March on Moscow), Moscow, 1928.

Denisov, Edison Vasil'evich
6.4.1929– . Composer.
Avant-garde composer. Regarded by specialists as an outstanding master of modern music. During the Brezhnev era, often attacked by official critics. His *Requiem*, written for the Nord Deutsche Rundfunk (premiered in Hamburg, 1980), was widely acclaimed.

Denisovskii, Nikolai Fedorovich
1901– . Artist.
Portrait and landscape painter, also political poster artist. Studied at the Moscow Stroganov Central Artistic Industrial School, 1911–17, under D. Shcherbinovskii, P. Pashkov, K. Gorskii. Also at VKHUTEMAS, 1918–21, under G. Iakulov. Exhibited from 1926. Personal exhibition: Moscow, 1956.

Dereviankin, Andrei
1960– . Dissident, lawyer.
Lives and was probably born in the Volga town of Saratov. Graduated in law from Saratov University. One of the 150 founding members of the Democratic Union, an illegal party opposing the CPSU. In early May 1988, briefly detained and severely beaten by a militiaman.

Derevianko, Vladimir Il'ich
15.1.1959– . Ballet dancer.
Born in Omsk, Siberia. Studied at Novosibirsk and Moscow choreographic schools. Joined the Bolshoi Theatre in 1977, and became one of its leading dancers. Married Paola Belli, the Italian ballerina, 1982. Lives with his wife in Rome. Has performed with various ballet companies.
See: Vittoria Ottolenghi, 'Vladimir Derevianko, la storia italiana di un ballerino strano', *Balletto Oggi*, Roma, Nr. 32, 1986.

Deriagin, Boris Vladimirovich
4.8.1902– . Scientist.
Graduated from Moscow University, 1922. Head of the Laboratory of Surface Forces at the Institute of Physical Chemistry. Works on properties of thin layers of liquids, and the electric theory of adhesion.

Deribas, Terentii Dmitrievich
1883–1939. State security official.
Born in the village of Onufrievka near Kremenchug in the Ukraine. Son of a Ukrainian Cossack. Early involvement in revolutionary activity. After the October Revolution 1917, an active Cheka official. Conducted mass executions of 'class enemies' (officers, clergy, merchants) in Siberia (Pavlodar, Troitzk). Moved to Moscow, head of the secret operations department of the Cheka-GPU, later, 1928–1938, local leader of the OGPU-NKVD in the Soviet Far East. Denounced by a colleague (who later defected to Japan). Arrested and shot.

77

Deriugin, Ivan Konstantinovich
5.12.1928–   . Athlete.
Born in Zmiev, now Gotvald, Khar'-kov Oblast'. Honoured Master of Sports (modern pentathlon), 1956. With the Kiev Armed Forces team. Lecturer with the Armed Forces. Graduated from the Kiev Institute of Physical Culture, 1957. Member of the CPSU, 1974. World champion, 1961. Olympic champion, 1956.

Derzhanovskii, Vladimir Vladimirovich
14.4.1881.–19.9.1942. Music critic.
Born in Tiflis. Publisher and editor of the periodical *Muzyka*. Editor of other periodicals, 1923–27, including *Sovremennaia Muzyka*. Died in Moscow.

Derzhinskaia, Ksenia Georgievna
6.2.1889–9.6.1951. Singer (soprano).
Born in Kiev. Pupil of E Terian-Korganova. Soloist with the Bolshoi Theatre, 1915–48. Professor at the Moscow Conservatory, 1947. Died in Moscow.

Deshevov, Vladimir Mikhailovich
11.2.1899–27.10.1955. Composer
Born in Petersburg. Composed mainly for ballet, also an opera, orchestral works, and music for films. Died in Leningrad.

Deterding, Lydia Pavlovna, Lady (Bagratuni, Princess Donskaia)
1895–30.6.1980. Benefactor.
Emigrated from Russia after the Civil War. After her first marriage to Bagratuni, married the oil millionaire, Sir Henry Deterding. Lived in England and France. Well known in France as a benefactor of various famous causes (the restoration of the Palace of Versailles, the Museum of the Legion d'Honneur and others). Freely gave aid to the Russian refugee community, which was used to repair many churches, including the Russian cathedral in Paris, and to found and finance a Russian high school in Paris between WWI and WWII. Died in Paris.

Deviatkov, Nikolai Dmitrievich
11.4.1907–   . Scientist.
Graduated from the Leningrad Poly-technical Institute, 1931. Worked at the Institute of Radio Engineering and Electronics. Specialized in gaseous discharge devices for modulated radiation, and UHF devices.

Diaghilev, Sergei Pavlovich (Diagilev; Serge de Diaghileff)
31.3.1872–19.8.1929. Ballet impresario, stage director, editor.
Born near Novgorod. Son of a landowner. Grew up in Perm'. Graduated in law from Petersburg University, 1896. Studied at the Petersburg Conservatory (pupil of Rimskii-Korsakov). Organized and edited the arts magazine *Mir Iskusstva* (World of Art) with A. Benois, 1898–1904, which signalled the flowering of the arts in Russia at the beginning of the 20th century. Organized exhibitions, which made a great impact (*Old Russian Portraits*, Petersburg, 1905, *Russian Art*, Paris, 1906). By organizing the Russian Seasons in Paris, became a celebrity and drew the attention of the world to Russian art (symphonic concerts with Rimskii-Korsakov, Rachmaninov, Glazunov, Chaliapin, 1907, Russian opera, 1908, opera and ballet seasons, 1909). Though not an artist himself, he had the rare talent of bringing different artists together and inspiring them (musicians, painters, dancers). His Ballets Russes, 1911–29, re-awakened interest in ballet throughout the world. After the October Revolution 1917, Diaghilev stayed in the West and became practically homeless, until offered a base in Monaco. Personal (stormy homosexual involvement with Nijinskii) and financial worries led to frantic efforts to keep up with modern trends in the late 1920s, efforts which were controversial and only partly successful. The bitterness of oncoming old age was to some extent relieved by his faithful last ballet star, Sergei Lifar. His last passion was collecting Russian antiquarian books. In the last year of his life, involved with the young composer Igor Markevich. Died and was buried in Venice (setting another trend, even in his death).

D'iakov, Abram Borisovich
12.1.1905–1943? Pianist.
Born in Sevastopol. Pupil of Konstantin Igumnov. Professor at the Moscow Conservatory until June 1941. Killed at the front.

Didenko, Valerii Antonovich
4.3.1946–   . Athlete.
Born in Kliaz'ma, Moscow Oblast'. Honoured Master of Sports (rowing), 1970. With Moscow Lokomotiv from 1968. USSR champion, 1966–73. European champion, 1967 and 1971. World champion, 1970–71. Olympic champion, 1972. Later became a teacher.

Diebabov, Dmitrii Georgievich
1901–1949. Photographer.
From an early age, worked as a machinist in a metal-working factory. Became a painter. From 1921, attended the drama and film studio of Proletkult where he met Sergei Eisenstein and Grigorii Kozintsev. On Eisenstein's advice, took up photography and studied under him at the VGIK. In 1924, assisted Eisenstein with his film, *Strike*. One of his first successful photographs, *Off to Work*, appeared in the magazine, *Sovetskoe Foto*. Invited after this to take up a job on *Izvestia*, 1926, on which he worked as a photo-reporter all his life, as well as contributing to *Komsomolskaia Pravda*. Travelled to the Arctic and Siberia on expeditions with the icebreakers *Krasin*, *Sedov* and *Stalin*. Together with the author G. El-Registan produced a book, *Trackers in the Far North*. Exhibited in the USA in 1939. One of his photographs, *Polar Night*, was acquired by President Roosevelt, and was hung on the wall of his study until his death. Author of *Taken With His Leica*, an illustrated book about his travels. One of the few photo-reporters who kept a diary. Took pictures of his great contemporaries such as Sergei Eisenstein, Grigorii Aleksandrov, Vsevolod Pudovkin, O. Shmidt, Academician Karpinskii. One of the pioneer photographers in the Arctic.
Source: *Soviet Photography, 1917–40*, London, 1984.

Dikii, Aleksei Denisovich
1889–1.10.1955. Actor, director.
In 1909 studied under S. V. Khaliutina. Entered the film industry in 1919. Leading actor at MKHAT in the 1920s. In 1931, founded and headed the Dikii Studio. Worked in the Vakhtangov, Malyi and Drama Theatres. In 1936 his theatre studio

was closed and he was sent for a short time to the Gulag. Became a rival to Gelovani in his portrayals of Stalin, *Tretii Udar*, 1948, and *Stalingradskaia Bitva*, 1949. Stalin liked both films, and rewarded him accordingly with Stalin Prizes.

Dikushin, Vladimir Ivanovich
26.7.1902– . Engineer.
Graduated from the Moscow Higher Technical School, 1928. Developed automatic metal-cutting systems.

Dimitriadi, Odissei Akhillesovich
7.7.1908– . Conductor.
Born in Batumi. Georgian by nationality. Pupil of I. Musin. Conductor from 1937. Chief conductor with the Tbilisi Theatre of Opera and Ballet from 1952. Chief conductor with the Georgian State Orchestra, 1947–52. Conductor with the Bolshoi Theatre from 1965.

Dinkov, Vasilii Aleksandrovich
1926– . Politician.
USSR 1st Deputy Minister of the Gas Industry, 1979–81, Minister from May 1981. Appointed Minister of the Oil Industry at the end of 1986, replacing Nikolai Mal'tsev.

Diushen, Boris Viacheslavovich
1886–1949. Engineer, journalist.
Member of the Constituent Assembly, during the Civil War with the Whites (Iudenich). Later prominent member of the Smena Vekh (change of landmarks) movement. One of the editors of the pro-Soviet Berlin newspaper *Nakanune*. In 1926, returned to the Soviet Union, lived in Moscow, working in the adult education system.

Dmitrevskii, Georgii Aleksandrovich
21.3.1900–2.12.1953. Conductor.
Born in Moscow. Artistic director and chief conductor with the Glinka Academic Band, Leningrad, 1944–53. Professor at the Moscow Conservatory, and at the Leningrad Conservatory from 1945. Author of a work on choral conducting. Died in Leningrad.

Dmitriev, Anatolii Nikodimovich
28.3.1908– . Musicologist.
Born in Saratov. Teacher at the Leningrad Conservatory. Author of *Muzykal'naia Dramaturgia Orkestra M. I. Glinki*, Leningrad, 1957, and *Polifoniia, Kak Faktor Formoobrazovaniia*, Leningrad, 1962.

Dmitriev, Roman Mikhailovich
7.3.1949– . Athlete.
Born in the village of Zhigansk, Iakut ASSR. Honoured Master of Sports (free-style wrestling), 1972. With the Moscow Military Forces team. USSR champion, 1969, 1971–73, 1976. European champion, 1969. World champion, 1973. Olympic champion, 1972. Silver medal, 1976.

Dneprov, Mitrofan Ivanovich
13.6.1881–11.1.1966. Singer (baritone).
Born in Uman', in the Tambovskaia Gouvt. Appeared in various operettas from 1907. Leading singer with the Moscow Operetta Theatre, 1939–51. Author of *Polveka v operette* (memoirs), Moscow, 1961. Died in Moscow.

Dobrokhotov, Boris Vasil'evich
21.10.1907– . Musicologist, cellist, gamba player.
Born in Baku. Son of the cellist, Vasilii Stepanovich Dobrokhotov (1872–1939). Pupil of S. Kozolupov and M. Iampol'skii. Lecturer at the Gnesin Pedagogical Institute of Music, Moscow. Author of several works on composers and composition, e.g. *J. S. Bach's Brandenburg Concerto*, Moscow, 1962.

Dobrovein, Isai Aleksandrovich (Barabeichik)
27.2.1894–9.12.1953. Pianist, conductor, composer.
Born in Nizhnii-Novgorod. Professor at the Moscow Conservatory, 1917. With the Bolshoi Theatre from 1919. Was praised by V. Lenin, who was among the audience at a private concert given at the house of M. Gorkii's wife, E. Peshkova. Emigrated, 1923. Guest appearances in many countries. Conductor with the Stockholm Opera from 1941. Author of an opera, concerto for piano and orchestra, sonatas for piano and piano and violin. Died in Oslo.

Dobrynin, Anatolii Fedorovich
16.11.1919– . Diplomat.
Born in Krasnaia Gorka near Moscow. Son of a worker. Graduated from the Moscow Aviation Institute in 1942, then from the Higher Diplomatic School of the Ministry of Foreign Affairs. Member of the Communist Party from 1945. Entered the Diplomatic Service in 1946. Assistant Deputy Minister of Foreign Affairs, 1949–52. Embassy Councillor, then Ambassador to the USA, 1952–55. Assistant Deputy Minister of Foreign Affairs, 1955–57. Deputy Secretary-General of the UN, 1957–60. Board member and head of the American Department at the Ministry of Foreign Affairs, 1960–62. Long-serving Ambassador to the USA, 1962–86. Candidate member (1966–71) and full member (1971) of the Cen. Cttee. of the CPSU. Now lives in Moscow. Considered the foremost specialist on the USA in the Soviet Union. Retired, Oct. 1988.

Dobrzhanskii, Feodosii Grigor'evich (Theodosius)
25.1.1900– . Professor of genetics.
Born at Nemirov near Vinnitsa. Graduated from Kiev University, 1921. Took part in the flowering of genetic research in the USSR in the 1920s. Lecturer in genetics at Leningrad University, 1924. Published works on zoology. During a trip abroad in 1927, decided not to return to the USSR. Settled in the USA. Professor of Genetics at the Californian Technological Institute. Professor of Zoology at Columbia University in New York, 1940. Became one of the outstanding American specialists in genetics.

Dobuzhinskii, Mstislav Valer'anovich
14.8.1875–20.11.1957. Painter, stage designer.
Born in Novgorod. Studied art in Petersburg and Munich with Azbe, 1899–1901. In his youth, influenced by the Jugendstil, Benois and Somov. Before WWI, worked on the art journals *Mir Iskusstva, Zolotoe Runo* and *Appolon*. Famous for his stage designs (*A Month in the Country*, 1909, and *Nikolai Stavrogin*, 1913, in the Moscow Arts Theatre, and many Diaghilev stage settings). Professor of the Arts Academy in Petrograd, 1922. Emigrated to Lithuania, 1929. At the beginning of WWII, moved to

England, and later to the USA, working mainly as a stage designer. Died in New York.

Dodin, Lev
1940– . Stage director.
Drama teacher for 20 years, mainly at the Leningrad Theatre Institute. Took over as the director of the Leningrad Malyi Theatre in 1983 after being a guest director there. Staged various foreign and Soviet plays including V. Rasputin's *Live and Remember*. In 1988, brought his production of *Stars in the Morning Sky* by A. Galin to Britain. Received overwhelming acclaim from the British press.

Dokshitser, Timofei Aleksandrovich
13.12.1921– . Trumpet player, conductor.
Born in Nezhin. Pupil of I. Vasilevskii and M. Tabakov. 3rd prize at the All-Union Competition of Musicians (wind instruments), 1941. Soloist with the orchestra of the Bolshoi Theatre, 1945, gained a reputation as a virtuoso trumpet player. Lecturer at the Gnesin Pedagogical Institute of Music.

Dolgikh, Vladimir Ivanovich
5.12.1924– . Politician.
Started as a shift foreman in industry. Member of the CPSU from 1942. Served in the Soviet Army during WWII. In 1949, graduated from the Irkutsk Mining Institute. Worked as a mining engineer at various places in Krasnoiarsk, Siberia until 1958. Chief Engineer, 1958–62, and Director 1962–69 of the Zaveniagin Metallurgical Combine in Norilsk. Various senior party posts in Krasnoiarsk Krai. Member of the Cen. Cttee. of the CPSU from 1971. Moved to Moscow. Secretary of the Cen. Cttee., 1972. Candidate member of the Politburo, 1976. Retired, Oct. 1988.

Dolgoplosk, Boris Aleksandrovich
12.11.1905– . Organic chemist.
Graduated from Moscow University, 1931. Worked in synthetic rubber plants, 1932–46. Carried out research into polymerization processes and their practical application. Developed new methods of synthetic rubber production.

Dolgorukov, Pavel Dmitrievich, Prince
1866–1927. Politician.
A veteran Zemstvo (local self-government) leader. One of the founders of the Cadet Party. After the October Revolution, arrested with other Cadet leaders, 28 Nov. 1917. Emigrated in 1920. Twice illegally crossed the border into Soviet Russia, disguised as a worker. During his last secret trip was betrayed, and arrested by the GPU in Kharkov in 1927. Sent to Moscow prison. After the assassination of the Soviet ambassador Voikov (a participant in the murder of the Imperial family) in Warsaw by a young White emigré (Apr. 1927), was among 20 hostages executed in Moscow by the GPU.
Main Work: *Velikaia Razrukha* (memoirs).

Dolgushin, Aleksandr Ivanovich
7.3.1946– . Athlete.
Born in Moscow. Graduated from the Moscow Institute of Economical Statistics, 1972. Honoured Master of Sports (water polo), 1970. Member of the CPSU, 1978. USSR champion, 1964–78. European champion, 1966, 1970. World champion, 1975. Olympic champion, 1972. Silver medal, 1968.

Dolidze, Viktor Isidorovich
30.7.1890–24.5.1933. Composer.
Born in Ozurgeti, Georgia. Author of the first Georgian comic opera, *Keto and Kote* (first performance in 1919). Composed operas, symphonic works, and a concerto for piano and orchestra. Died in Tiflis.

Dolina, Maria Ivanovna (b. Saiushkina; m. Gorlenko)
13.4.1868–2.12.1919. Singer (contralto).
Born in the Gouvt. of Nizhni-Novgorod. Pupil of E. Grening-Vil'de. With the Mariinskii Theatre, 1886–1904. Organized annual symphonic concerts in Petersburg from 1904. Emigrated. Promoted Russian music in Paris. Died in Paris.
Source: M. Kamenev, *Maria Ivanovna Gorlenko-Dolina*, Petersburg, 1912.

Dollezhal', Nikolai Antonovich
15.10.1899– . Nuclear scientist.
Graduated from Moscow Higher Technical School. Built thermonuclear power stations. Chief designer of the reactor in the first Soviet nuclear power station.

Dolmatovskii, Evgenii Aronovich
1915– . Poet.
Poems set to music by many Russian composers including D. Shostakovich and S. Prokof'ev. Composed the lyrics for songs in many films.

Dolukhanova, Zara (Zarui Agas'evna)
5.3.1918– . Singer (mezzo soprano).
Born in Moscow of Armenian parents. Pupil of V. Beliaeva-Tarasevich. Soloist with the All-Union Radio from 1944. State Prize, 1951. Lenin Prize, 1966.

Dolzhanskii, Aleksandr Naumovich
12.9.1908– . Musicologist.
Born in Rostov-on-Don. Lecturer at the Leningrad Conservatory. Author of *Kratkii Muzykal'nyi Slovar'*, Leningrad, 1952. Works on Shostakovich and Tchaikovskii.

Dombaev, Grigorii Savel'evich
29.6.1905– . Musicologist.
Born in Tsaritsyn, now Volgograd. Lecturer at and Director of the Gorkii Conservatory. Authority on P. Tchaikovskii. Works include *Tvorchestvo Petra Il'icha Chaikovskogo v Materialakh i Dokumentakh*, Moscow, 1958 and *Muzykal'noe Nasledie Chaikovskogo. Spravochnik*, Moscow, 1958.

Dombrovskii, Iurii Osipovich
1909–1978. Writer.
Born in Moscow. Graduated from the Higher Literary Courses, 1932. First novel, *Krushenie Imperii*, 1938. Victim of the Gulag. Gained fame in 1964 during Khrushchev's thaw when the magazine *Novyi Mir* published his anti-Stalinist novel, *Khranitel' Drevnostei*. Other books: *Fakultet Nenuzhnykh Veshchei*, Paris, 1978, and *Khranitel' Drevnostei*, Paris, 1978, which has been translated into English and French. Became a cult figure among dissidents in the 1960–70s.

Donadze, Vladimir Grigor'evich
18.3.1905– . Musicologist.
Born in Ozurgeti, Georgia. Professor

at the Tbilisi Conservatory. Author of *Shalva Mshelidze*, Tbilisi, 1964 (in Georgian) and *Zakharii Paliashvili*, Moscow, 1958.

Donskoi. D. D.
1881–1936. Revolutionary.
Son of a country doctor. During WWI, military doctor in the Caucasus. Member of the Constituent Assembly, 1917. Member of the Cen. Cttee. of the SR Party, 1917. During the Civil War, active in the Caucasus. Head of the military commission of the SR Party, 1918. At the trial of the SR leaders, 1922, alleged to have sanctioned a new post-revolutionary anti-Bolshevik SR terrorist organization, and to be connected with Dora Kaplan, who had made an attempt on Lenin's life. Sentenced to death but not executed. Later became victim of the Gulag.

Donskoi, Lavrentii Dmitrievich
1858 – 5.12.1917. Singer (tenor), theatrical manager.
Born in the Kostromskaia Gouvt. Pupil of V. Samus' and K. Everardi. Soloist with the Bolshoi Theatre, 1883–1903. With private operas, 1904–08. Professor at the School of Musical Drama of the Philharmonic Society, Moscow from 1909. Died in Moscow.

Donskoi, Mark Semenovich
6.3.1901–1981. Film director.
Born in Odessa. Graduated in law from Simferopol University, 1925, but never practised as a lawyer. Published a book of stories, *The Prisoners*, based on his own impressions from the 10 months he had spent in prison during the period when the White Army controlled the Crimea. From 1926, in the film industry first as actor and scriptwriter. First debut as director, *The Fop*, filmed for Sovkino in Leningrad in 1929. Became known for his trilogy based on Gorkii's memoirs: *Gorkii's Childhood, My Apprenticeship* and *My Universities*, 1938–39, which became classics. Other films as director: *Life*, 1927, *In the Big City*, 1927, *The Price of Man*, 1928 *The Song of Happiness*, 1934 (Vostokkino), *How the Steel Was Tempered*, 1942, *Aliet Goes Into the Mountains*, 1949, *Mother*, 1955 *Nadezhda*, 1973.

Dorinskaia, Aleksandra Aleksandrovna (Pasia)
1896–1978. Ballerina.
Partner of Vaclav Nijinskii in Diaghilev's Ballets Russes. In 1914, went from London to Petersburg for a holiday and was trapped there by WWI. Met Mayakovsky and Lili Brik and became their close friend. Also became Lili Brik's private teacher.

Dorliak, Ksenia Nikolaevna (d'Orleac)
11.1.1882–8.3.1945. Singer (soprano).
Born in Petersburg into a rich aristocratic family of French ancestry. Her mother was a lady-in-waiting to the Tsarina Aleksandra, wife of Nicholas II. Mother of the singer Nina Dorliak, and the actor Dmitrii Dorliak. Pupil of S. Gladkaia and N. Iretskaia. Professor at the Petrograd Conservatory, 1918. Professor at the Moscow Conservatory from 1930. Doctor of art history. Among her pupils were N. Dorliak, E. Kruglikova, S. Kromchenko, T. Talakhadze, and T. Ianko. Died in Moscow.

Dorliak, Nina L'vovna
6.8.1908– . Singer (soprano).
Born in Petersburg. Daughter of the singer Ksenia Dorliak. Wife of the pianist S. Richter. Professor at the Moscow Conservatory.

Dorodnitsyn, Anatolii Alekseevich
2.12.1910– . Scientist.
Graduated from the Petroleum Institute in Groznyi in the Caucasus, 1931. Worked at the Mathematical Institute of the Academy of Sciences, 1944–55. Director of the Computer Centre (now the Institute of Cybernetics) of the Academy of Sciences, 1955. Highly decorated (3 Stalin Prizes). Carried out research into dynamic meteorology, aerodynamics and applied mathematics.

Doronin, Ivan Vasil'evich
1903–1953. Pilot.
Joined the Red Navy, 1920. Transferred to Polar Aviation, 1930. Member of the Communist Party, 1934. Graduated from the Zhukovskii Air Force Academy, 1939. Head of test-pilot groups in an aviation construction works, 1939–47.

Doroshevich, Vlas Mikhailovich
17.4.1864–22.2.1922. Writer, journalist, theatre critic.
Famous pre-revolutionary reporter. Covered a variety of subjects from theatre life to criminal trials. Wrote over 30 books, including, *Staryi Palach*, 1900, *P. N. Durnovo* and *Graf Vitte*, both 1906, and *Chernosotentsy*, 1916. His articles about life in the theatre were published in *Staraia Teatral'naia Moskva* in 1923. His 9-vol. *Sobranie Sochinenii* was published in 1905, and *Izbrannye Rasskazy i Ocherki*, in Moscow 1966.

Dosekin, Nikolai Vasil'evich
1863–1935. Artist.
Studied at the E. Shreider Art School, Kharkov, 1878–82. Under A. Kiselev in Moscow, then in Paris, 1886. Landscape and portrait painter, also sculptor. Exhibitions: TPKHV (1888–97, 1899–1900), MOLKH (1889–91, 1893–1900), MTKH (1895, 1899–1901, 1912), All-Russian Exhibition, Nizhnii Novgorod, (1896), the Society of Russian Water-Colour Painters, St. Petersburg, (1896), the Mir Iskusstva (1900–03), the Union of Russian Artists (1903–18, 1922–23), the 8th State Exhibition, Moscow, 1919, AKHRR the 8th Exhibition, Moscow, 1926, and the Society of Realist Artists, Moscow, 1928.

Dostoevskaia, Anna Grigor'evna (b. Snitkina)
1846–1918. Author.
Stenographer, who worked for and later married Fedor Dostoevskii, 1867. Published his works. Kept a diary, which was published after her death as *Dnevnik 1867*, Moscow, 1923.
Memoirs: *Vospominaniia*, 1925.

Dostoevskii, Fedor Fedorovich
1871–1921. Horse breeder.
Son of the writer F. Dostoevskii. Became one of the best-known and most successful horse breeders in Russia.

Dovator, Lev Mikhailovich
1903–1941. Major-general.
Joined the Red Army, 1924. Member of the Communist Party, 1928. Graduated from the Frunze Military Academy, 1939. Cavalry commander at the beginning of WWII, distinguished himself during the battle of Moscow. Fell in action.

Dovlatov, Sergei Donatovich
1941–. . Journalist, dissident.
Began writing in the 1960s. Published abroad in various literary magazines: *Vremia I My, Kontinent, Tret'ia Volna.* Ardis, USA, published *Nevidimaia Kniga* separately after it was published in *Vremia I My* magazine. Emigrated in 1978. Editor-in-chief of *Novyi Amerikanets* (New American, weekly), 1980–82. Lives in New York.
See: P. Vail, A. Genis, *Sovremennaia Russkaia Proza,* U.S.A. 1982.

Dovzhenko, Aleksandr Petrovich
1894–1956. Film director.
Son of a Cossack officer. Born in a Ukrainian village. Graduated in 1914 from the Glukhov Teachers' Institute. Worked briefly as a teacher. At one time was an artist, then a Soviet diplomat in Berlin. In 1926, turned to film-making in Kiev. His first film effort was the script for *Vasia-Reformator*, which he also co-directed. Became internationally known for his three films *Zvenigora,* 1928, *Arsenal,* 1929, and *Zemlia,* 1930. Although *Zemlia* was attacked at the time by Stalinist critics for not being revolutionary enough, it glorified Stalin's collectivisation campaign in the Ukraine. In 1939, made *Shchors,* another propaganda film about the Red Army during the Civil War (Stalin Prize). In 1949, he made *Michurin* in colour (2nd Stalin Prize). Died before being able to complete *Poem of the Sea* (which was finished by his wife, Iulia Solntseva). His war documentaries are less noteworthy. Taught at the Moscow VGIK, 1949, and in 1955, when he was already ill. Died at the Kremlin hospital. After his death the film studio in Kiev was renamed in his honour.

Dowbor-Musnicki, Jozef (Iosif Romanovich)
25.10.1867–28.10.1937. General.
Born in Garbow, then in Russian Poland. Educated at the Konstantinovskoe Military School in 1888. Graduated from the Academy of the General Staff in 1902. Took part in the Russo-Japanese war, 1904–05. On active service in the Russian Army during WWI. Took command of the 1st Polish Legionnaires Corps, organized by the Provisional Government in Aug. 1917. After the Bolshevik take-over, refused to recognize the communist authorities and raised a rebellion in Byelorussia, Jan. 1918. His corps, centred around Bobruisk, fought against the Red forces, commanded by Vatsietis and Pavlunovskii (both Cheka). Occupied Minsk and entered into an agreement with the German army. After Polish independence, joined the Polish army. Became a rival of Pilsudski, and was removed from his command, 1919. Retired soon thereafter. Died in Batorow in Poland.

Dragunskii, David Abramovich
1910– . Col.-general.
Joined the Bolshevik Party, 1931, and the Red Army, 1933. Graduated from the Frunze Military Academy, 1941. During WWII, tank troops commander, distinguished himself at the Vistula and at Berlin. Twice Hero of the Soviet Union, 1944, 1945. Head of the Vystrel Courses, 1969. In the 1980s, became the figure-head of an anti-Zionist movement in the Soviet Union.

Dranishnikov, Vladimir Aleksandrovich
10.6.1893–6.2.1939. Conductor.
Born in Petersburg. With the Mariinskii Theatre (later the S. M. Kirov Theatre of Opera and Ballet) from 1914. Chief conductor there, 1925–36. Artistic director and chief conductor with the Kiev Theatre of Opera and Ballet. Died in Kiev. Author of musical compositions, and several articles.

Dreval', Aleksandr Konstantinovich
17.7.1944– . Athlete.
Born in Moscow. Honoured Master of Sports (water polo), 1972. With Moscow Burevestnik. Graduated in journalism from Moscow University, 1975. USSR champion, 1972–74. European champion, 1970. World champion, 1975. Olympic champion, 1972.

Dronnikov, Nikolai Egorovich
1930– . Painter, publisher.
Born in Tula Oblast'. Son of a peasant (who died of hunger during the collectivization). Grew up in the Moscow suburbs. Graduated from the Surikov Institute in Moscow. Taught painting in Moscow art schools. Started to contribute to samizdat publications in the early 1950s, while still in the army. One of the organizers of the unofficial *Klassika* exhibition at the Surikov Institute. Left the USSR in 1972 to join his French wife. Lives in Paris. Publisher of an interesting series of booklets, *Statistika Rossii 1907–17.* Continues the tradition of art editions, established by Russian painters in Paris in the 1900s. Works shown at many exhibitions in Europe.

Drozd, Valentin Petrovich
1906–1943. Vice-admiral.
Joined the Red Navy, 1925. Graduated from the Frunze Naval School, 1928. Member of the Communist Party, 1930. Sent to help the communists in the Spanish Civil War, 1936–37. Commander of the Northern Fleet, 1938. During WWII, in the Baltic Fleet. Died near Kronstadt.

Drozdov, Aleksandr Mikhailovich
1895–1963. Author.
Before the 1917 Revolution, close to liberal circles. During the Civil War with the Whites, worked in the propaganda department Osvag in Rostov-on-Don. Described this period in his article 'Intelligentsia na Donu', published in the *Archive of the Russian Revolution*, vol. 3. Emigrated to Berlin, wrote novels, and regarded then as one of the brightest hopes of Russian literature. Tried to keep a neutral position between Red and White (with Iashchenko, Stankevich and others). Founded in Berlin the magazine *Spolokhi,* 1921. Returned to the Soviet Union, Dec. 1923. Wrote a novel which sharply condemned Russian emigrés: *Lokhmot'ia,* Khar'kov, 1928. Became a trusted Stalinist editor, working in the 1940–50s on *Molodaia Gvardia,* and from the end of the 1950s on the magazine *Oktiabr'.*

Drozdov, Vladimir Nikolaevich
6.6.1882–10.3.1960. Pianist.
Born in Saratov. Brother of the pianist and composer Anatolii Nikolaevich Drozdov. Pupil of A. Esipova. Taught at the Petersburg Conservatory, 1907–17. Professor from 1914. Gave concerts and taught in the Ukraine from 1918. Emigrated, 1923. Died in New York.

Drozdova, Margarita Sergeevna
7.5.1948– . Ballerina.
Born in Moscow. Graduated from the

Moscow Choreographic School as a dancer, 1967. Starred with the Stanislavskii and Nemirovich Danchenko Theatre, in Moscow. Received the Anna Pavlova Award in Paris, 1968.

Drozdovskii, Mikhail Gordeevich
7.10.1881–1919. General.
Born in Kiev, son of a general. Educated at Polotsk and Pavlovskoe military schools. Volunteered for active service during the Russo-Japanese war in 1904. Graduated from Petersburg Military Academy in 1908. During WWI, commander of a regiment, later a division. After the October Revolution, organized a detachment of volunteers in Bessarabia, some 1000 men (Dec. 1917), and fought his way through the revolutionary chaos in the Ukraine to the Don (spring 1918), where he joined the White armies, thus drastically changing their fortunes at that moment (almost doubling their strength). Badly wounded, Oct. 1918. Died of his wounds in Novocherkassk. His diary of the march from the disintegrating front to Rostov has been published in USA.

Drozhzhin, Spiridon Dmitrievich
1848–1930. Poet.
His poetry deals with the life of peasants and children. His works have been used by composers for choral works, by vocal ensembles, and in ballads and children's songs, some of which form part of the repertoire of F. Chaliapin, N. Plevitskaia, and A. Vial'tseva. Met Rilke during his trip to Russia before WWI.

Druskin, Mikhail Semenovich
14.1.1905– . Musicologist.
Born in Kiev. Professor at the Leningrad Conservatory. Doctor of art history. Author of works on musicology and music history, e.g. *Istoriia Zarubezhnoi Muzyki XIX Veka*, Moscow, 1958 and 1963, and *Istoriia i Sovremennost'* (collection of articles), Leningrad 1960.

Druzhinin, Vsevolod Nikolaevich
1914–1946. Artist.
Born in Iaroslavl'. Portrait and landscape painter. Studied at the Iaroslavl' Art Pedagogical Technical School, 1929–1932 under B. Petrukhin, also at the Moscow School of Painting, Sculpture and Architecture of the Academy of Arts, 1933–40 under S. Abugov, P. Naumov and A. Osmerkin. Taught art in Iaroslavl'. Exhibitions: Iaroslavl' Oblast' Artists (1940–46); RSFSR Artists, Moscow (1940–46); Artists of Gorkii, Ivanovo and Iaroslavl' Oblasts, Moscow, (1945).

Druzhinina, Iuzefa Mikhailovna
1912– . Artist.
Genre painter. Born in Vitebsk. Studied at the Vitebsk Art School, 1928 under V. Shults, also at the Moscow School of Painting, Sculpture and Architecture, 1933–40 under S. Abugov, P. Naumov, A. Osmerkin. Taught at Iaroslavl' Art School in the post-war years. Began exhibiting from 1940 in Iaroslavl', Gork'ii and Moscow.

Druziakina, Sof'ia Ivanovna
29.5.1880–30.10.1953. Singer (soprano).
Born in Kiev. Pupil of A. Santagano–Gorchakova. Soloist with the Zimin Opera, 1910–17, and the Theatre of the Moscow Soviet of Workers' Deputies, 1917–24. Took part in the Russian Seasons in Paris, 1910. Professor at the Moscow Conservatory, 1930–45. Died in Moscow.

Dubianskii, Aleksandr Markovich
13.1.1900–4.1920. Pianist.
Born in Petersburg. Pupil of M. Gelever, A. Esipova and F. Blumenfeld. Graduated from the Petersburg Conservatory at the age of 15 (piano and composition). Gave concerts (works by Skriabin, historical concerts, children's programmes). Commited suicide in Kiev.
Source: *Zhizn' Iskussva*, Nr. 437, 1920.

Dubinda, Pavel Khristoforovich
1914– . Sailor.
Joined the Red Navy, 1936. Wounded and taken prisoner by the Germans, 1942. Escaped and returned to active service in March 1944. Distinguished himself in battle in Poland and East Prussia. Highly decorated. From the end of WWII until 1966, worked in the Soviet whaling fleet.

Dubinin, Iurii Vladimirovich
1930– . Diplomat.
On Diplomatic Service from 1955. Worked at the USSR Ministry of Foreign Affairs (MID), 1960–63 and 1968–78. 1st Secretary, and Councillor at the Soviet Embassy in Paris, 1963–68. In 1978, appointed Ambassador to Spain. After A. Dobrynin's return to Moscow, took over as Soviet Ambassador to the USA. Took part in the negotiations on the removal of intermediate-range nuclear missiles from Europe.

Dubinin, Mikhail Mikhailovich
20.12.1900– . Scientist.
From the 1920s, involved in the study of absorption of gases, vapours and dissolved substances by porous solids. During WWII, worked on chemical defence problems. Academician, 1943.

Dubinin, Nikolai Petrovich
1. 1907– . Biologist.
Professor at the Moscow Zootechnical Institute, 1935. Worked at the Institute of Biophysics, 1955. Works on genetics and the theory of evolution.

Dubovoi, Ivan Naumovich
1896–1938. Revolutionary, military commander.
Joined the Bolsheviks, 1917. One of the communist organizers in the Donbass, 1917. Took part in the Civil War in the Ukraine, commander of the 1st Ukrainian Army. Liquidated by Stalin during the purges of the military forces.

Dubovskoi, Nikolai Nikanorovich
17.12.1859–28.1.1981. Artist.
Born in Novocherkassk. Landscape painter. Studied at the Petersburg Academy of Arts, 1877–81 under M. Klodt. Professor at the same academy from 1911. From 1886 a member of the peredvizhniki. Exhibitions: TPKHV, 1884–1918, 1903, 1913–16. All-Russian Exhibition, Nizhnii Novgorod, 1896, MOLKH, 1911. Personal exhibition (posthumous): Leningrad, 1938. Died in Petrograd.

Dubrovskii, Vladimir Iakovlevich
8.10.1939– . Athlete.
Born in Moscow. Honoured Master of Sports (rowing), 1964. Graduated from the Moscow Pedagogical Institute, 1966. USSR champion, 1963–65. European champion, 1964. Olympic champion, (with O. Tiurin), 1964.

Dudarova, Veronika Borisovna
5.12.1916– . Conductor.
Born in Baku. Ossetin by nationality. Pupil of N. Anosov and Leo Ginsburg. Chief conductor and artistic director with the Moscow State Symphony Orchestra.

Dudinskaia, Natal'ia Mikhailovna
21.8.1912– . Ballet dancer.
Born in Khar'kov. A pupil of Agrippina Vaganova at the Leningrad Choreographic School. Graduated in 1931. Soloist with the Kirov Theatre. Performed leading parts in most important ballet productions for the next 20 years. Taught at the Kirov Theatre from 1951, and at the Leningrad Choreographic School from 1964 until her retirement in 1970.

Dudintsev, Vladimir Dmitrievich
1918– . Author.
Born near Khar'kov. Studied law at Moscow University. Became famous overnight when his novel *Ne Khlebom Edinym* (Not by Bread Alone), about the struggle of an idealist with bureaucracy, was published in 1956 by the magazine *Novyi Mir*. Only Solzhenitsyn's *One Day in the Life of Ivan Denisovich* attracted more publicity and controversy in recent Soviet history. Published a new novel, *Belye Odezhdy*, 1988.

Dudko, Dimitrii Sergeevich
1922– . Russian Orthodox clergyman.
Born near Briansk. As a student at the Moscow Theological Academy, arrested and spent several years in the Gulag camps. Released, 1956. Continued his religious studies. Priest, 1960. Breaking a long established taboo, delivered simple sermons and made direct appeals to believers, followed by discussions. Achieved great popularity, especially among the Soviet intelligentsia interested in religious questions. His sermons circulated in samizdat. Arrested 1979. Under KGB pressure, appeared on TV denouncing his former activity. Released and given a parish in the provinces. Reviled by dissidents as a renegade, he defended his TV appearance as an act of humility.

Duiunova, Vera Illarionovna
14.4.1945– . Athlete.
Born in Krasnodar. Honoured Master of Sports (volleyball), 1968. With Tashkent Spartak. World champion, 1970. Olympic champion, 1968 and 1972. Graduated in journalism from Tashkent University, 1975.

Dukelskii, Vladimir (Duke, Vernon)
10.10.1903– . Composer.
Born in the village of Parfianovka near Pskov. Studied at the Kiev Conservatory under R. Glier. Moved to France, 1920, and to the USA in 1929. Wrote his first music for L. Miasin's ballet *Zefir i Flora* (Diaghilev's Ballets Russes, Monte Carlo, 1925). Strongly influenced by American jazz and music hall. Worked for Leonid Miasin and George Balanchine. Became a very successful composer in the USA.

Dukhonin, Nikolai Nikolaevich
13.12.1876–3.12.1917. General.
Son of a nobleman from Smolensk Gouvt. Educated at the Aleksandrovskoe Military School. Graduated from the Academy of the General Staff in 1902. Commander of a regiment during WWI. June 1917, Head of Staff of the South-Western front. Aug. 1917, at the Western front. Appointed Chief-of-staff of the Supreme Commander (Kerenskii), 23 Sept. 1917. After the October Revolution and Kerenskii's flight, took over the duties of Supreme Commander. Refused to execute the order of the Council of People's Commissars, 20 Nov. 1917, to enter into peace negotiations with the Germans. Arrested, 3 Dec. 1917, and murdered by a revolutionary mob of soldiers at Mogilev railway station.

Dukhov, Nikolai Leonidovich
1904–1964. Tank designer.
Graduated from the Leningrad Polytechnical Institute, 1932. Designer at the Kirov Works, responsible for designing the heavy WWII tanks, KV and IS. Member of the Communist Party, 1941. Chief designer at a research institute 1948–54. Chief of a design bureau in the Ministry of Defence, 1954. Corresponding member of the Academy of Sciences, 1953. Lt.-general, 1954. Highly decorated (5 State Prizes, 3 times Hero of Socialist Labour).

Dulov, Georgii Nikolaevich
16.7.1875–4.9.1940. Violinist.
Born in Moscow. Pupil of I. Grzhimali. Taught from 1901. Professor at the Moscow Conservatory, 1912–24. Died in Moscow. Author of violin and vocal pieces, and collections of exercises, e.g. *Sbornik Polnogo Kursa Skripichnoi Igry* (in 12 parts).

Dulova, Vera Georgievna
27.1.1910– . Harpist.
Born in Moscow. Daughter of the violinist, G. Dulov. Wife of the singer, A. Baturin. Pupil of K. Erdeli. 1st prize at the All-Union Competition of Musicians, Leningrad, 1935. Professor at the Moscow Conservatory.

Dumanskii, Anton Vladimirovich
20.4.1880–14.5.1967. Chemist.
Graduated from the Kiev Polytechnical Institute, 1903. Founded a laboratory of colloidal chemistry at Voronezh, 1913, which later became an institute of the Academy of Sciences. One of the founders of colloidal chemistry in Russia and international authority in this field. Founder and editor of the *Colloidal Journal* from 1935. Died in Kiev.

Dumchev, Konstantin Mikhailovich
1.10.1879–24.11.1948. Violinist.
Born in Novocherkassk. Pupil of Staudzha in Novocherkassk, L. Auer and I. Grzhimali. First appearance at the age of 10. Taught at music schools in Novocherkassk from 1929. Author of 2 concertos and other pieces for violin. Died in Novocherkassk.

Dumenko, Boris Mokeevich
1888–1920. Revolutionary, military commander.
Joined the Red Army, 1918. Member of the Bolshevik Party, 1919. One of the organizers of the Red Cossack detachments on the Don River during the Civil War.

Dunaevskii, Isaak Osipovich
30.1.1900–25.7.1955. Composer.
Born in Poltava Gouvt. Given violin lessons by G. Polianovskii. Entered the Khar'kov Conservatory in 1910. Pupil of I. Akhron and S. Bogatyrev. First compositions date from the time. Studied concurrently at the High School, then at the University (Faculty of Law). On graduating from the Conservatory in 1919,

accepted by the Khar'kov Theatre of Russian Drama as director of the musical department, composer and conductor. Moved to Moscow, 1924, and directed the music departments of several theatres. Moved to Leningrad, 1929–34. Wrote music for many films from 1932. Head of the Leningrad Union of Composers, 1937–41. Entertained troops and war workers during WWII. Lived in Moscow from 1943. Wrote operettas, and music for films and plays. Died in Moscow.

Dundich, Toma (Ivan, Oleko)
13.4.1896–8.7.1920. Revolutionary.
Born in Grabovac, Dalmatia. Son of a Croatian peasant. As a teenager, emigrated to Latin America, and worked as a gaucho in Argentina and Brazil. Returned to Croatia, conscripted into the Austro-Hungarian army, 1914. POW in Russia, 1916. Joined the Serbian Volunteer Corps, fighting on the Russian side in WWI. After the revolution, joined the Red guard detachments in Odessa. Became well known in the Red cavalry for his dashing exploits. Member of an international revolutionary battalion under Voroshilov and Budennyi. Fought against General Wrangel at Tsaritsyn. Killed in action.

Durov, Anatolii Anatol'evich
1894–1928. Circus entertainer.
Representative of a well-known circus dynasty founded by his father, A. L. Durov. Took over the circus business on the death of his father, 1916. Died in a shooting accident during a hunt.

Durova, Elena Robertovna
1873–1967. Circus rider, animal trainer.
Wife of A. Durov. Appeared as a circus rider. Helped to create the best-known group of trained circus animals in Russia.

Dushenov, Konstantin Ivanovich
1895–1940. Revolutionary, naval commander.
Revolutionary sailor during the Bolshevik take-over, 1917. Took part in the storming of the Winter Palace, and fought against Krasnov. During the Civil War, commander of river ports on the Volga. Commander of the Northern Flo-

tilla, 1935. Commander of the Northern Fleet, 1937.

Dushkin, Samuel
13.12.1891–after 1970. Violinist.
Born in Suvalki, Russia. Pupil of Leopold Auer and Fritz Kreisler. Emigrated to the USA. Appeared in guest performances, 1931–37, with Igor Stravinskii, who wrote a violin concerto for him. Died in the USA.

Dutov, Aleksandr Il'ich
17.8.1879–7.3.1921. Lt-general, Cossack commander.
Born in the Cossack village of Orenburgskaia. Graduated, from the Nikolaevskoe Cavalry school, and the Academy of the General Staff in 1908. During WWI, deputy commander of a Cossack regiment. After the February Revolution 1917, elected chairman of the All Russia Union of Cossack Armies, head of the All Russia Cossack Congress in June 1917. Elected Ataman (head) of the Orenburg Cossacks, Sept. 1917. Together with the Czech Legion, fought Bolsheviks in the Urals. Commander of the Orenburg Cossack army under Admiral Kolchak, 1918–19. After the defeat of the Whites, retreated to China in Mar. 1921. Believed to have been assassinated in Suidin, China, by a Cheka agent.

Dvarionas, Balis Dominiko
19.6.1904–23.8.1972. Composer, conductor, pianist.
Born in Libava (now Liepaia), Latvia. His musicial training began at the age of 6. Musician with the local cinema at the age of 10. Directed a voluntary youth orchestra, 1916–18. Studied musical theory from 1918.Pupil of A. Kalnyn'. Received further musical education at the Leipzig Conservatory, 1920. Pupil of R. Teichmüller, S. Krell, Z. Karg-Elert. Pursued piano studies in Berlin under E. Petri, 1925–26. Graduated in conducting from the Leipzig Conservatory as an external student, 1939. Taught at the Kaunas Music School 1926–32, and at the Kaunas Conservatory from 1933. Conductor of the Kaunas Symphony Orchestra, 1936–38. Conductor of the Vilnius State Philharmonic, 1940–41. Professor at the Vilnius Conservatory from 1947, at

the same time chief conductor of the Philharmonic, 1958–61. Made several appearances as a concert pianist in the USSR, Germany, France, and Sweden. His music shows realistic tendencies. Wrote an opera, music for a ballet, music for strings, music for Shakespeare's *Twelfth Night* and *Othello*, etc. Died in Vilnius.

Dybcho, Sergei Afanas'evich
17.7.1894–29.11.1952. Operetta singer.
Born in Odessa. With the Sverdlovsk Theatre of Musical Comedy from 1933. Honoured Artist of the RSFSR, 1944. Died in Sverdlovsk.

Dybenko, Pavel Efimovich
1889–1938. Revolutionary, military commander.
Involved in revolutionary activity, 1907. Sailor with the Baltic fleet, 1911. Played a great role in mobilizing the Baltic sailors, and creating from them the military backbone of the new regime. Chairman of Tsentrobalt, 1917. People's Commissar for the navy, 1918. During the Civil War, used the sailors as the shock troops of the Red Army in the Ukraine and the Crimea. Head of the artillery administration of the Red Army, 1925–26. Held many high military posts in the late 1920s and 1930s. Liquidated by Stalin.

Dymshits, Veniamin Emmanuilovich
1910– . Politician.
Member of the CPSU, 1937. Graduated from Bauman Technical College Moscow, 1945. Head of the Main Board for the Construction of Industrial Enterprises; USSR Deputy Minister for the Construction of Metallurgical and Chemical Industrial Enterprises, 1950–57. Chief engineer at the construction of a metallurgical plant in Bhilai, India, 1957–59. Member and Head of the Capital Construction Dept. of GOSPLAN with the rank of USSR Minister, 1959–61. 1st Deputy Chairman of GOSPLAN, 1961–62. Member of the Cen. Cttee. of the CPSU from 1961. Chairman of the State Cttee. for Material and Technical Supply with the USSR Council of Ministers, 1965–76. Chairman of the State Commission for the Development of the West Siberian Pet-

roleum and Gas Complex from 1981. Retired in Dec. 1985.

Dyrdyra, Vitalii Fedorovich
4.11.1938– . Athlete.
Born in Kiev. Honoured Master of Sports (sailing), 1972. With the armed forces in Kiev. Military lecturer. Graduated from the Kiev Institute of Physical Culture, 1962. USSR champion (Finn class), 1969, and (Tempest class), 1972. Olympic champion (Tempest class), 1972.

Dzeneladze, Roman
1933–1966. Athlete.
Prominent Georgian athlete. Honoured Master of Sports (wrestling). Bronze medallist at the XVIth Olympic Games. Many times USSR and European champion. The cause of his early death, reported in the American and Canadian press, has not been explained by the Soviet authorities.

Dzerzhinskii, Feliks Edmundovich
11.9.1877–20.7.1926. Secret police chief, founder of the Cheka.
Born in Dzerzhinovo near Minsk. Son of a Polish landowner. Educated at a Wilno secondary school, 1896. On leaving school, became a professional revolutionary at first SR, later SD. Active in Kovno, arrested in 1897, exiled, 1898, to Viatka, escaped, 1899. Active in Warsaw underground SD organizations. Arrested in 1900, exiled to Siberia, 1902, but escaped the same year. Participated in the 1905 revolution, organizing demonstrations in Warsaw. Arrested July 1905, amnestied, Oct. 1905, and continued revolutionary activity in Warsaw and Petersburg. Arrested, Dec. 1906, released May 1907, re-arrested Apr. 1909, exiled to Siberia 1909, escaped to Berlin at the end of 1909. Returned to Poland (Cracow, then Austro-Hungary), 1910. Arrested in Russian Poland, Sept. 1912. In Warsaw citadel prison, 1912–14. Transferred to Orel prison, and later to Moscow. Released after the February Revolution 1917, from Butyrki prison. One of the organizers of the October Revolution, 7 Nov. 1917. Soon thereafter, on 20 Dec. 1917, appointed first head of the Cheka becoming thus the founder and organizer of one of the most ruthless terror organizations in the world.

Personified the fanatical, inquisitorial side of communism (in his youth inclined towards Catholic fanaticism, and wanted to become a Jesuit). Knowing the Tsarist system of repression and all its weaknesses, took care not to repeat the mistakes of leniency and moral restrictions. Introduced the system of hostages and class terror on a wide scale. To a large extent personally responsible for shocking the country into obedience during the early years of Bolshevik rule. During the uprising of the left SRs in July 1918, arrested by the rebels, but soon released as a fellow revolutionary. During the Civil War, sent to several crisis points, restoring discipline and imposing obedience by unremitting terror. In command of the rear of the South-West front during the war with Poland, 1920. Appointed member of the Provisional Government of Poland during the Soviet offensive, 1920. Head of the Children's Commission, 1921 (when the problem of homeless children, who were victims of terror and the Civil War, was at its height). Appointed Minister of Transport, 1921. Retained the post of Chairman of the Cheka and Minister of the Interior throughout. Organized an extensive spy network abroad. Chairman of the Supreme Council of the National Economy, Feb. 1924. Died of heart failure after making a speech at a plenary session of the Cen. Cttee. of the party. His life-size statue stands before the infamous Lubianka prison and the KGB HQ on Dzerzhinskii Square in the centre of Moscow. Officially glorified as 'Zheleznyi Feliks' with his 'warm heart, cool head and clean hands' (his own description of a member of the secret police). First criticism of his terror policies appeared in the Soviet press in 1988.

Dzerzhinskii, Ivan Ivanovich
9.4.1909–18.1.1978. Composer.
Born in Tambov. Studied composition at the Leningrad Conservatory, 1932–34. Pupil of P. Riazanov and B. Asaf'ev. In the early years of WWII, in Orenburg, and in Leningrad from 1944. His main work was in opera. Member of the board of the Leningrad Union of Composers, 1936–48. Died in Leningrad.

Dzhalil', Musa Mustafovich
1906–1944. Poet.
Wrote the libretti for Zhiganov's

opera *Altynchech* (The Golden Haired Woman), and *Il'dar*. Gravely wounded, prisoner of war, 1942. Inmate at a Nazi concentration camp. Executed for underground activities. Wrote poems in prison in Moabit, collected into the *Moabitskaia Tetrad'*, which served as the libretto for an opera. Poems set to music by several composers. Made a Hero of the Soviet Union. Lenin Prize (posthumously), 1957.

Dzhamanova, Roza Umbetovna
16.4.1928– . Singer (soprano).
Born in Aktiubinsk. Soloist with the Abai Kazakh Theatre of Opera and Ballet.

Dzhambul Dzhabaev
2.1846–22.6.1945. Folk poet (akyn).
Born in the village of Semirech'e. Pupil of the akyn, Saiumbai. Expert on Kazakh music. Remembered a great number of tunes. Sang accompanied by the dombra at aitysy (Kazakh story-telling competitions) in the tolgau style (a recitative traditional with the akyn.). Stalin Prize, 1941. Died in Alma-Ata. Received enormous publicity in the 1930s for his primitive hymns on Stalin.

Dzhanelidze, Iustin Ivlianovich (Iulianovich)
1883–1950. Surgeon, lt.-general.
Graduated from Moscow University, 1911. Specialized in heart surgery before WWI. During WWII, chief surgeon of the navy. Professor the Military-Medical Academy. After WWII, deputy chief surgeon of the armed forces. Wrote scientific works on heart and wound surgery.

Dzhangildin, Alibi Togzhanovich
1884–1953. Revolutionary, politician.
Joined the Bolsheviks, 1915. One of the leaders of the Kazakh revolt, 1916. Organized Red Kazakh detachments during the Civil War. After the Civil War, held several high government posts in the Kazakh SSR.

Dzhansugurov, Il'ias
1894–1937. Poet.
Kazakh by nationality. Dedicated one of his poems to Music (*Kiushi*, 1935). His best poem remains *Kulager*, 1936. His premature death

the poet-singer. His premature death in 1937 is unexplained in official publications, but probably victim of Stalin's purges.

Dzhavakhishvili, Ivan Aleksandrovich
1876–1940. Historian, academician.
Historian of Georgia. Member of the Academy of Sciences. Also wrote on Georgian music. Author of *Osnovnye Voprosy Istorii Gruzinskoi Muzyki* (in Georgian), Tbilisi, 1938.

Dzhelepov, Boris Sergeevich
12.12.1910– . Scientist.
Graduated from Leningrad University, 1935. Specialized in nuclear physics.

Dzhemilev, Reshat
1931– . Human rights campaigner.
Born in the Crimea. In 1944, deported with all other Crimean Tatars to Soviet Central Asia after they were accused by Stalin of collaborating with the Germans during WWII. Became one of the leaders of the movement which sought the restoration of the Tatars' ancestral homeland, 1956. In 1967, member of the Tatar delegation received by Iurii Andropov. As a dissident, imprisoned 3 times: 1967, 1972 and 1979 in Krasnoiarsk and Norilsk labour camps. For several years, tried unsuccessfully to obtain a visa for medical treatment in the USA. In 1987, one of the leaders of the 800-strong delegation which took part in negotiations with Andrei Gromyko. Works in the construction industry. According to him, there are now one million people of Crimean Tatar origin in the Soviet Union, while up to 125,000 out of the 250,000 who were shipped east in railway trucks by Stalin's NKVD died en route.

Dzhugashvili, Iakov Iosifovich
1922–1943. Joseph Stalin's son, lieutenant.
Eldest son of Stalin by his first marriage to Ekaterina Svanidze, a Georgian woman. In June 1941, volunteered for the front when the German armies invaded the Soviet Union. Taken prisoner by the Germans near Smolensk later the same year. The German High Command offered to exchange him for Field Marshal von Paulus, the defeated German commander at Stalingrad in 1942. Stalin's answer was 'There are no Soviet POWs, only traitors'. According to the SS guard who later shot him, he threw himself deliberately on the barbed wire fence at Sachsenhausen concentration camp. This report by the guard, Conrad Harfich, was found in the archives seized by the Allies, and confirmed by Thomas Cushing, a British POW officer, who was with Dzhugashvili at the camp. Stalin was not informed about the way his son had died by the Allies, who in 1945 did not want to upset him. Dzhugashvili's son, Vissarion, lives now in Gori, Stalin's birth town in Georgia.
Source: Thomas Cushing, *The Sunday Times*, 25.2.1980.

Dzhugeli, Medeia Nikolaevna
1.8.1925– . Athlete.
Born in Kutaissi, Georgia. Honoured Master of Sports (gymnastics), 1952. With Tbilisi Dynamo. Honoured Coach of the Georgian SSR, 1971. Graduated from the Georgian Institute of Physical Culture, 1958. Member of the CPSU, 1962. USSR champion, 1946–55. Olympic champion, 1952. Silver medal, 1952.

Dzigan, Efim Lvovich
14.12.1898–31.12.1981. Film director.
Graduated from the B. Chaikovskii Film School. Started as an assistant director, 1924. Made his first film with M. Chiaureli, *Pervyi Kornet Streshnev*, 1928. Best known for *My Iz Kronshtadta*, 1936 (script by V. Vishnevskii), which received 1st prize at the Paris International Exhibition, 1937. Also received a Stalin Prize for the film in 1941. From 1937, taught at the VGIK. From 1965, professor.

E

Echeistov, Georgii Aleksandrovich
1897–1946. Artist.
Water-colour painter, also worked with engraving, etching and woodcut techniques. Studied at the Moscow VKHUTEMAS, 1927. Pupil of Vladimir Favorskii. Produced a series of industrial designs, portraits and illustrations. First exhibition in Moscow, 1927.

Other exhibitions: Leningrad, 1932, Moscow, 1933, 1939, the All-Union Exhibition, 1945.

Edel'man, Vladimir Adol'fovich (Eidel'man)
6.10.1910– . Conductor.
Born in Nikolaev. Studied at the Gnesin Technical School of Music. From 1929, first violinist, and from 1931, conductor of the Moscow Artistic Ballet under V. Kriuger. Conductor at the Stanislavskii and Nemirovich Danchenko Theatre until 1973. First violinist and conductor of the Moscow Classical Ballet from 1973.

Edeshko, Ivan Ivanovich
25.3.1945– . Athlete.
Born in the village of Stetski near Grodno, Belorussian SSR. Honorary Master of Sports (basketball), 1972. Graduated from the Belorussian Institute of Physical Culture, 1970. With the Moscow armed forces team. Member of the CPSU, 1979. USSR champion, 1971–79. European champion, 1971 and 1979. Olympic champion, 1972. Bronze medal, 1976.

Eduardova, Evgenia Platonovna
1882–10.12.1960. Ballerina, teacher.
Born in Petersburg. Graduated from the Petersburg Theatre School, 1901. Until 1917, dancer and soloist at the Mariinskii Theatre. With Anna Pavlova, 1908–09, in London, Berlin and other cities. Character dancer. Founded and taught at her own ballet school in Berlin, 1920–35. Influenced a generation of dancers in Germany. Left Germany, 1935. Taught in Paris until 1947. Moved to the USA. Died in New York.

Efimov, Aleksandr Nikolaevich
1923– . Marshal.
Joined the Red Army, 1941. Fighter pilot during WWII. Graduated from the Air Force Academy, 1951. Deputy commander of the Soviet Air Force, 1969. Commander of the Soviet Air Force and Deputy Minister of Defence, 1984. Member of the Cen. Cttee. of the CPSU, 1986.

Efimov, Igor Markovich
1937– . Writer.
Published essays in samizdat in the

early 1960s. Wrote under the pseudonym Andrei Moskovit for the magazine *Grani* in 1973 when he lived in Moscow. Emigrated in 1978. Founder and head of Hermitage Publishing House in the USA.

Books: *Arkhivy Strashnogo Suda*, 1982; *Bez Burzhuev*, 1982.

See: P. Vail, A. Genis, *Sovremennaia Russkaia Proza*, USA, 1982.

Efimov, Pavel Ivanovich
1906–1983. Political officer.
Joined the Bolshevik Party, 1925, and the Red Army, 1932. Graduated from the Lenin Military Political Academy, 1938. Took part in the Soviet-Finnish war and WWII. 1st Deputy Head of the Political Department of the Soviet Armed Forces, 1958–74.

Efimova, Ekaterina Matveevna
1910– . Artist.
Landscape painter. Studied at the Leningrad Academy of Arts, 1933, and at the studio of B. Fogel and L. Ovsianikov. Also studied at the Moscow Repin School of Painting, Sculpture and Architecture, 1944–50, under A. Osmerkin and M. Avilov. Exhibited from 1943.

Efrem, schema-hieromonk
1862?–1942. Russian Orthodox clergyman.
Monk at the Valaam monastery on the Ladoga lake. Father confessor of Grand Duke Nikolai Nikolaevich, Commander in Chief of the Russian Army, who continued the Romanov family tradition of pilgrimage to this monastery. After the Civil War, Valaam was on Finnish territory, but during the Soviet-Finnish war the monks were evacuated before the advance of the Red Army, 1940. Settled at New Valaam (Valamo). Died and buried at New Valaam. Revered as a representative of the starets tradition.

Efremov, Boris Ivanovich
1904–1962. Artist.
Portrait and genre painter. Born in Omsk. Studied at the Omsk Art Pedagogical School, 1928–31 under V. Trofimov, and then at the Odessa Art School, 1933–38 under L. Muchnik, D. Krainev and A. Shovkunen-

ko. Taught art in Iaroslavl'. Began exhibiting from 1939. Exhibitions: Moscow, Iaroslavl', Gorkii. Died in Iaroslavl'.

Efremov, Mikhail Grigor'evich
1897–1942. Lt.-general.
Joined the Red Army, 1918, and the Bolshevik Party, 1919. Took part in the Civil War. Regimental and divisional commander. On active service during WWII as commander of the 33rd Army. Fell in action.

Efremov Oleg Nikolaevich
1.10.1927– . Actor, stage director.
Outstanding actor and one of the most talented modern stage directors. Graduated in 1949 from the Moscow Arts Theatre Drama Studio. Actor at the Central Children's Theatre. In 1956, one of the founders, and later head, of the most revolutionary theatre in Moscow, Sovremennik. Artistic director of the Moscow Arts Theatre. Very popular film actor, best in comedies. First film in 1956. Worked with every director of note. His cameo roles were an asset to every film. Played the officer Dolokhov in *War And Peace*. Became famous as Aibolit in Roland Bykov's film of the same title. Gave master classes in Oxford, 1987 and to the Royal Shakespeare Company in Stratford.

Efron, Ariadna Sergeevna
1912–1975. Author.
Born in Moscow. Daughter of Marina Tsvetaeva and Sergei Efron. Grew up in Czechoslovakia and France with her mother. Worked for a communist newspaper in Paris. Returned to the USSR in 1937. Arrested in 1939 and spent 8 years in prison camps. Arrested again in 1949 and exiled to Siberia. Rehabilitated, 1955. Returned to Moscow. Worked as a French translator. Became the guardian and editor of her mother's work, also editing several books and writing many articles on her. Died in Moscow.

See: *Stranitsy Vospominanii*, Paris, 1979, and *Pisma iz Ssylki*, Paris, 1982.

Efron, Sergei
1893–1940. Journalist.
In 1911, met the young poetess, M. Tsvetaeva and married her soon afterwards, while still a cadet in an officers' school. During the Civil War, joined the White Army. Evacuated with the Whites, lived near Prague, where Tsvetaeva joined him in 1922. Contributed to the left-wing (SR) magazine *Volia Rossii*. In 1925, joined Tsvetaeva in Paris. Gradually adopted a pro-Soviet position, and finally became involved in GPU operations abroad. In 1937 after his participation in the murder of the GPU defector, Ignatii Reiss, he had to flee from police investigations. Contacted GPU representatives in Spain and from there returned to the Soviet Union, followed shortly afterwards by Tsvetaeva (their daughter Ariadna had returned earlier). Disappeared in the Gulag, probably executed.

Efros, Anatolii Vasil'evich
3.6.1925–1987. Stage director.
Graduated from the GITIS, 1950. From 1954–63, director at the Central Children's Theatre. From 1963–67, chief director at the Komsomol Theatre, and from 1967–85, at the Theatre on Malaia Bronnaia. When Iu. Liubimov did not return from the West, replaced him as chief director of the Taganka Theatre. Died in Moscow.

Egiazarian, Grigorii Egiazarovich
21.12.1908– . Composer.
Born in the village of Blur, Armenia. In 1918, his family moved to eastern Armenia. Early musical training at the Military Musicians' Boarding School of Erevan. At the Moscow Conservatory (in the wind instrument department), 1927. Accepted into the composition class, 1930. Pupil of N. Miaskovskii. On graduating in 1935, directed a course for amateur composers in the Union of Composers. Returned to Armenia in 1936. Taught at a music school. Concurrently musical director at the Drama Theatre. Taught in Erevan from 1938 and during WWII. Professor of classical composition from 1959. Director of the conservatory, 1954–60. Exponent of the ornamental variety of Armenian music. Wrote ballads, symphonies, music for films, etc.

Eglevskii, Andrei (Eglevsky, André)
21.12.1917–4.12.1977. Ballet dancer.
Born in Moscow. Studied ballet with
L. Egorova, M. Kshesinskaia, and N.
Legat. Emigrated in the 1920s with
his parents. Dancer with the Ballet
Russe du Colonel de Basil, 1931.
With the Wojcikowski company,
1935, the American Ballet Theatre,
1937–38, the Ballet Russe de Monte
Carlo, 1939–41, the Ballet Theatre,
1942–43, 1945, Ballet International,
and then L. Miasin's Original Ballet
Russe, 1946–47. Joined New York
City Ballet, 1951–58. Worked with
M. Fokin and G. Balanchine. Took
part in C. Chaplin's film, *Limelight*,
1952. Retired in 1961. Taught at the
School of American Ballet. Director
at the School of Classical and Charac-
er Dance, Massapequa, New York.
Died in Elmer, New Jersey.
Source: D. Leddick, 'André Eglevsky:
from Moscow to Massapequa', *Dance
Magazine*, Sept. 1959.

Egor'ev, Vladimir Nikolaevich
3.3.1869–20.9.1948. General.
Born in Moscow. Educated at the
Aleksandrovskoe Military School,
1889. Graduated from the Academy
of the General Staff, 1901. Sent as an
army instructor to Montenegro,
1910–13. On active service during
WWI. Lt.-general, 1917. During the
Civil War, military specialist and
commander with the Red Army
against Denikin. Took part as a
military expert in the peace negotiations with Finland and Poland.
Editor of the theoretical military
journal, *Voennaia mysl'*, 1921–26,
and lecturer in military establishments. Retired in 1934. Died in
Moscow.

Egorov, Aleksandr Aleksandrovich
1.5.1887–1959. Choir conductor,
composer.
Born in Petersburg. Professor at the
Leningrad Conservatory. Author of
cantatas. Literary works on the
theory and practice of choral singing
and composing. Died in Leningrad.

Egorov, Aleksandr Il'ich
25.10.1883–23.2.1939. Marshal.
Born in Buzuluk, Samara Gouvt.
Educated at Samara High School.
Volunteered for military service.

Studied at the Kazan' Infantry
School, 1905. At the front during
WWI. Colonel, Nov. 1917. Close to
the left SRs, but changed to the
Bolsheviks in the summer of 1918.
Chairman of the commission which
selected former officers of the
Imperial Army for service in the Red
Army. In 1918, commander of the
10th Army which failed to defend
Tsaritsyn against Wrangel. Commander on the Southern front against
Denikin, 1919. In the early 1920s,
several high commands in the Caucasus, Ukraine and Crimea. Military
attaché in China, 1925–26. Head of
the Red Army General Staff, 1931,
Head of the USSR General Staff,
1935. Deputy Defence Minister,
1937–38. Victim of the Stalin purges,
executed.

Egorov, Egor Egorovich
3.8.1877–15.2.1949. Singer (bass).
Born in Moscow. Pupil of Varvara
Zarudnaia-Ivanova. With Kiev, Moscow, Odessa and Tiflis Operas, 1904–
10. Professor at the Moscow Conservatory, 1924–39. At the Urals Conservatory from 1939. Doctor of art
history. Among his pupils were G.
Bushuev, A. Okaemov, and A. Khali-
leeva. Died in Sverdlovsk.

Egorov, Georgii Mikhailovich
1918–   . Admiral.
Joined the Red Navy, 1936. During
WWII, submarine commander in the
Baltic. After the war, held high
positions in the submarine fleet,
Deputy Commander in charge of
military training, and Commander of
the Northern Fleet, 1972–77. Chief of
the Navy's General Staff and 1st
Deputy Commander of the Soviet
Navy, 1977. Chairman of the Cen.
Cttee. of DOSAAF, 1981. Member
of the Presidium of the Supreme
Soviet of the USSR, 1984.

Egorov, Iurii (Youri)
1955–17.4.1988. Pianist.
Became a successful musician in his
early 20s. Solo performances abroad.
Recorded several records. Died suddenly while on tour in Amsterdam.
The cause of his death is unknown.

Egorov, Mikhail Alekseevich
1923–1975. Sergeant.
During WWII, joined the partisans

in Smolensk Oblast'. Later in the Red
Army. Distinguished himself at the
Vistula and Oder rivers. One of two
Soviet soldiers (with Kantaria) who
planted the Red Flag on the top of the
Reichstag at the end of WWII. Hero
of the Soviet Union, 1946. Joined the
Communist Party, 1950.

**Egorova, Liubov Nikolaevna (Alek-
sandrovna)**
8.8.1880–18.8.1972. Ballet dancer.
Born in Petersburg. Graduated from
the Petersburg Theatre School, 1898.
A pupil of E Cecchetti. Joined the
Mariinskii Theatre, and soon became
one of its leading dancers. In 1917
joined Diaghilev's Ballets Russes. In
1921, made a triumphal appearance
in London in the *The Sleeping
Beauty*. In 1923, organized her own
ballet school, and in 1937 founded
the Ballet de la Jeunesse. Died in
Paris.

Egorova, Liudmila Borisovna
24.2.1931–   . Athlete.
Born in Lomonosov, Leningrad
Oblast'. Honoured Master of Sports
(gymnastics), 1957. Graduated from
the Leningrad Institute of Physical
Culture, 1955. Coach. USSR champion, 1950–53 (acrobatic high jump).
Olympic champion, 1956. Bronze
medal, 1956.

**Eideman, Robert Petrovich (Eide-
manis)**
1895–1937. Military commander.
Educated at the Kiev Military School,
1916. Joined the Bolshevik Party,
1917, and the Red Army, 1918.
Active participant in the Civil War.
Head and Commissar of the Frunze
Military Academy. Editor of the
magazine *Voina i Revoliutsiia*, 1927–
36. Liquidated by Stalin during the
purge of the military leadership.

Eifman, Boris Iakovlevich
22.7.1946–   . Choreographer.
Graduated from the Kishinev Chore-
ographic School, 1964, and from the
Choreographic Department of the
Leningrad Conservatory, 1972.
Choreographer at the Leningrad
Choreographic School, 1970–77.
Author and director of several TV
ballet films. Worked for East Berlin
TV.

Eiges, Iosif Romanovich
28.2.1887–6.1953. Literary and
music critic, pianist.
Born in Briansk. Brother of K. R.
Eiges. Pupil of K. Kipp. Author of
*Muzyka v Zhizni i Tvorchestve Push-
kina*, Moscow, 1937, and *Chekhov i
Muzyka*, Moscow, 1953.

Eiges, Konstantin Romanovich
18.6.1875–2.2.1950. Pianist, composer, musicologist.
Born in the village of Bogodukhovo,
Kharkov Gouvt. Pupil of A. Iaro-
shevskii. Many articles and books on
music, including *Osnovnye Voprosy
Muzykal'noi Estetiki*, Moscow, 1905,
and *Ocherki Po Filosofii Muzyki*,
Moscow, 1921. Died in Moscow.

Eiges, Oleg Konstantinovich
13.5.1905–   . Composer.
Born in Moscow. Son of K. R. Eiges.
Taught at the Sverdlovsk Conservatory from 1939, at the Gorkii Conservatory from 1949, and at the Gnesin
Music School, Moscow from 1959.
Author of 12 symphonies, chamber
music, and pieces for piano.

**Eikhe, Genrikh Khristoforovich
(Eiche, Heinrich)**
1893–1968. Military commander,
politician.
Educated at a military school, 1915.
Took part in WWI as a captain.
Joined the Red Army, 1918. Active
participant in the Civil War. Commander in Chief of the Far Eastern
Republic (Soviet buffer state). Military commander in Minsk, 1921–22,
and in Fergana, 1922–23. Subsequently held high posts in the Ministry of Foreign Trade, 1924. Wrote on
the history of the Civil War.

Eikhenvald, Anton Aleksandrovich
13.5.1875–1952. Composer, conductor.
Born in Moscow. From 1894, conductor at many theatres in various
cities. His ballet *Zhar-Ptitsa*, or *Ivan-
Tsarevich*, was produced in Paris.
Emigrated, 1923. Returned to the
USSR, 1928. Author of operas,
symphonic music, music for violin
and cello, and songs. Died in Leningrad.

**Eikhenvald, Margarita Aleksandrovna
(m. Trezvinskaia)**
2.12.1866–after 1948. Singer.
Born in Moscow. Daughter of the
harpist, Ida Eikhenvald (1842–1917).
Pupil of E. Taliabue. Soloist at the
Bolshoi Theatre, 1889–1901, and at
the Tiflis Opera Theatre, 1901–17.
Emigrated to France where she died.

**Eikhfeld, Iogan Gansovich (Eichfeld,
Johann)**
25.1.1893–1975? Botanist.
Graduated from the Petrograd Agricultural Institute. Head of the Polar
department of the Institute of Plant
Growing, 1923–40, and Director of
the Institute, 1940–51. President of
the Estonian Academy of Sciences,
1950. Specialist on agriculture under
polar conditions. Experimented on
the Kola Peninsula and in Northern
Karelia.

Eisenstein, Sergei Mikhailovich
10.1.1898–11.2.1948. Film director.
Born in Riga, the son of a civil
engineer and architect. Attended the
Petrograd Institute of Civil Engineers, Sept. 1915–spring 1917. In
Feb.–Mar. 1917, became a member
of the city's militia in the Narva
District. In the autumn of the same
year, published his first caricature,
The Militia Introduces Order, in the
St. Petersburg Gazette. Then published a caricature of Kerenskii in the
weekly *Ogonek*. Continued his education at the Institute of Civil Engineers. In 1918, volunteered for the Red
Army as an engineer. First amateur
productions at the Communist Club
of Vozhega, Vologda District, as
director, stage designer, and actor in
1919. In the same year, became a
technician with the 1st Division of
the 18th Army Corps of Engineers. In
1920, designed the scenery and costumes for the production of *The Twin*
by Arkadii Averchenko, performed
later at the Velikie Luki Garrison
Club (he also acted in this production). After demobilization, studied
Japanese at the General Staff Academy. Worked on the production of
The Mexican based on the Jack
London story. Appointed to the post
of Director of the Art Section of the
Proletkult's 1st Workers' Theatre.
Among his students was his future
close collaborator, Grigorii Alek-

sandrov, and actor M. M. Shtraukh.
In 1921, taught art to officers and
soldiers of the Kremlin garrison. At
the same time, studied at the State
Higher Directors' Workshops, under
Vsevolod Meyerhold. In 1922, began
working at Meyerhold's Theatre
Workshops on the production of
Heartbreak House by Bernard Shaw.
Director of Proletkult's 1st Workers'
Theatre. Assistant Director on the
production of *The Death of Tarelkin*
by Sukhovo-Kobylin produced by
Meyerhold. In 1924, one of the re-
editors of *Doctor Mabuse* by Fritz
Lang, distributed in the Soviet Union
under the title *Pozolochennaia Gnil'*.
Broke with Proletkult, and began
working on *Strike*, his first film. In
1925, shot *The Year 1905* in Leningrad, based on the script by N.
Agadzhanova-Shutko, later renamed *The Battleship Potemkin*. It
was first screened on 21 Dec. 1925
at the Bolshoi Theatre. In Mar.
1926, arrived in Berlin with the
cameraman E.K. Tisse to learn the
latest film techniques. In Sept. 1926,
signed by Goskino to make *The
General Line* which he shot in the
Mugansk steppe and in the northern
Caucasus. In 1927, made *October* in
Leningrad with Grigorii Aleksandrov and Eduard Tisse. In Sept. 1929,
visited Switzerland for the Congress
of Independent Filmmakers. Travelled to Berlin where he met Georg
Grosz and Luigi Pirandello. Visited
Belgium, London and Paris; returned
to England and lectured at Cambridge. Continued to tour Europe:
gave a lecture in Amsterdam; met
Albert Einstein in Berlin; lectured at
the Sorbonne; met Abel Gance,
James Joyce and Jean Cocteau. In
Apr. 1930, signed a contract with
Paramount to work in Hollywood.
On 12 May, arrived in New York,
where he met Charlie Chaplin and
Walt Disney. Lectured in Holly-
wood. On 23 Oct., Paramount broke
the contract. Went to Mexico, where
in 1931 he made *Que Viva Mexico!*
Returned to America for a lecture
tour, and then returned to Moscow.
In July 1935, began shooting *Bezhin
Meadow*, but filming was interrup-
ted. From 1937, professor at the
VGIK. At the end of 1938, com-
pleted *Aleksandr Nevskii*. In Aug.–
Oct. 1939, began shooting *The Great
Fergana Canal*, but this too was
interrupted by Goskino. In Dec.

1939, produced *Die Walküre* at the Bolshoi Theatre. Began shooting *Ivan the Terrible*, but on 6 Oct. 1942, was relieved of his post of artistic director. This first part of *Ivan The Terrible* was premiered in Jan. 1945 at the Udarnik cinema. A year later the second part was withdrawn. Suffered a heart attack and was taken to the Kremlin hospital. Died in Moscow and buried in Novodevich'e Cemetery. Became a legend and a classic of early Soviet cinema. During his working life, suffered terrible persecution from nonentities and party bureaucrats. Many of his projects were left unrealised. Recognized worldwide as a genius of remarkable talent. *Bezhin Meadow* (not to be confused with I. Turgenev's short story of the same title) was in fact a glorification of Pavlik Morozov, the boy who during the collectivization campaign reported his own father to the authorities. *The Great Fergana Canal* was one of Stalin's industrialization projects using Gulag prisoners. Proved by his life and art that artistic genius and moral compromise (subservience to dictatorship) are compatible. Married to Pera Atasheva, a Jewish girl who was his childhood friend in Riga and who later became his assistant. By all accounts, the marriage was platonic. In 1933, met an unknown young actor, N. Cherkassov, whom he turned into a major star (Aleksandr Nevskii, Ivan the Terrible). Remained close to Cherkassov until his death.
See: Sergei Eisenstein, *Immoral Memories, An Autobiography,* translated by Herbert Marshall, London, 1983.

Ekk, Nikolai Vladimirovich (real name – Ivakin)
14.6.1902–14.7.1976. Director.
Pupil of V. Meyerhold. Became his assistant director. Graduated from the State Film School, 1927. His major film was *Putevka v Zhizn'*, 1931, which won a prize at the Venice Film Festival in 1932.

Ekster, Aleksandra Aleksandrovna
1884–1949. Artist, stage designer.
Born in Belostok. Studied at the Kiev Art School until 1907, then at l'Academie Grand-Chaumière, Paris. Exhibited from 1908. Exhibitions: the Venok, 1908; the New Society of Artists, 1908–09; the Bubnovyi Valet, 1910–11, 1912–14, 1916; Moscow Salon, 1911–12, the Mir Iskusstva, 1913–14, 1916, also in Petrograd, 1914 (a charity exhibition for old and infirm artists); theatre design art, Moscow, 1918–23. Personal exhibitions: Varst, Vesnin, Popova, Rodchenko, Ekster, Moscow, 1921. From 1921 in France. Settled in Paris, 1924. Professor at the Academie Moderne. Continued to show her work: personal exhibition at the Claridge gallery, London, 1928. One of the pioneers of constructivist theatre decor in Russia. Died at Fontenay-aux-Roses in France.

Ekston, Anna Moiseevna
30.9.1908– . Choreographer.
Born in Tallinn. Graduated from the Tallinn Ballet Studio, 1925. Pupil of E. Litvinova. Later trained by O. Preobrazhenskaia in Paris, and V. Gzovskii in Berlin. Soloist at the Opera Belge, Antwerp, 1925–31. With the V. Gzovskii Company on tour in Europe. Choreographer of the Estonia Theatre, 1940–41 and 1944–51. Founder, artistic director and director of the Tallinn Choreographic School.

Ekzempliarskii, Vasilii Il'ich
1875–7.7.1933. Theologian.
Professor at the Kiev Theological Academy. Dismissed by the Holy Synod for an article comparing L. Tolstoy to John Chrysostomos. Returned to his chair, 1917. Editor of the monthly *Khristianskaia Mysl'*, 1916–18. One of the best representatives of the Kievan theological school. Published many works on theology and religious philosophy.

Elagin, Iurii Borisovich
1910–8.1987. Violinist, author.
Born in Moscow. Grandson of a textile millionaire. Son of an engineer in the textile industry. Studied violin with the first violinist of the Moscow Opera, Ferdinand Grabbe. Violinist with the MKHAT orchestra, the Vakhtangov and other theatres. Arrested with his father in 1929 by the OGPU. Released, but his father was exiled. During WWII, in German concentration camps, then in DP camps after the war. Moved to America. Settled in Houston, Texas. First violinist of the Houston Symphony Orchestra under Leopold Stokowsky. Author of two remarkable books: *Ukroshchenie Iskusstv*, Chekhov Publishing House, N.Y., 1952, and *Temnyi Genii. Vsevolod Meyerhold*, Chekhov Publishing House, N.Y., 1955, foreword by Mikhail Chekhov (considered one of the best biographies of Meyerhold). Died in Washington.

Elanskii, Nikolai Nikolaevich
1894–1964. Surgeon.
Graduated from the Military Medical Academy, 1917. Joined the Red Army, 1921. Professor at the Military Medical Academy. Chief surgeon at different fronts during WWII. Chief Surgeon of the USSR, 1947–55. Scientific works on military surgery.

Elena Vladimirovna (Romanova)
29.1.1882–14.3.1957. Grand Duchess.
Born at Tsarskoe Selo. Daughter of Grand Duke Vladimir, the younger brother of Aleksander III. Married her cousin, Prince Nicholas of Greece (younger brother of King Constantine of the Hellenes and uncle of Prince Philip, the Duke of Edinburgh). Mother of Marina, Duchess of Kent. After her marriage, lived in Greece from 1902. After the Revolution, involved in relief work for Russian exiles. Died in Athens.

Eliasberg, Karl Il'ich
10.6.1907– . Conductor.
Born in Minsk. Artistic Director and chief conductor of the Grand Symphonic Orchestra of the Leningrad Radio Cttee. from 1931.

El'iash, Nikolai Iosifovich
31.10.1916– . Ballet historian, lecturer.
Born in Kerch'. Graduated from the Crimea Pedagogical Institute, 1937, and from the Moscow GITIS, 1950. Prolific author of articles. Lecturer at

the Moscow Choreographic School, 1951–57. Lecturer at the GITIS from 1950, and professor from 1975.

Eliseev, Ivan Dmitrievich
1901–1974. Vice-admiral.
Joined the Red Army, 1920. Took part in the Civil War. Graduated from the Frunze Naval School, 1929. Sent to Spain to fight against Franco, 1937–38. During WWII, Chief of Staff of the Black Sea fleet, after 1944 worked in the Naval General Staff. Professor of the Military Academy of the General Staff, 1948. Editor of *Morskoi Vestnik*. Chairman of the Scientific Technical Cttee, and Deputy Chief of Staff of the Soviet Navy, 1955–66.

Eliutin, Viacheslav Petrovich
1907–   . Politician.
Graduated from the Moscow Steel Institute, 1930. Deputy Minister of Higher Education, 1951–54, and Minister, 1954–59. Minister of Higher and Middle Special Education, 1959. Accompanied Khrushchev during his US tour, 1959. Non-voting member, 1956, and full member, 1961, of the Cen. Cttee. of the CPSU. Deputy Chairman of the Cttee. for Lenin Prizes for Science and Technology. In his early career, published research work on metallurgy.

Elizarov, Aleksandr Matveevich
7.3.1952–   . Athlete.
Born in the village of Viazovka, Penza Oblast'. Honorary Master of Sports (biathlon), 1976. With Moscow Oblast' Trud. Graduated from the Moscow Institute of Physical Culture, 1978. USSR champion, 1973 and 1975. World champion, 1977. Olympic champion, 1976. Bronze medal, 1976.

El'kin, Boris Isaakovich
1887–1972. Politician, lawyer.
Member of the Cadet Party. Editor of the last (posthumous) volume of Miliukov's memoirs. Editor of Adamovich's biography of Maklakov. After the 1917 Revolution, lived in London. Successful lawyer in Britain.

Eller, Kheino Ianovich
7.3.1887–16.6.1970. Composer, violinist.
Born in Yur'ev, now Tartu. Gradua-

ted in 1920 from the Petrograd Conservatory. Pupil of V. Kalafati. Before entering the Conservatory studied law at Petersburg University, 1908–12. Worked as a violinist with theatrical orchestras, 1919–20. With the Petrograd Bolshoi Theatre of Drama, 1919. Taught concurrently at the music school. Taught at and directed the department for the theory of composition at the Music School of Tartu, 1920–40. Professor at the Tallinn Conservatory from 1940. Wrote mainly instrumental music (chamber and symphony). Died in Tallinn.

El'man, Mikhail Saulovich (Elman, Mischa)
20.1.1891–1967. Violinist.
Born in the Ukraine. Pupil of L. Auer. Visited the USA, 1908, on a concert tour. Returned to Russia where he performed solo concerts. Returned to the USA. American citizen, 1923. Maintained the highest international reputation. Wrote *Memoirs of Mischa Elman, Father*, New York, 1933. Died in America.

El'tsin, Boris Nikolaevich
1.2.1931–   . Politician.
Graduated from the Ural Polytechnical Institute, 1955. Worked as a foreman, work superintendent, engineer, and chief of a construction office of the Iuzhgorstroi Trust, 1955–63. Member of the CPSU, 1961. Chief engineer, then chief of the House Construction Combine in Sverdlovsk Oblast' Cttee., 1966–76. Secretary of the Sverdlovsk Obkom, 1968–76, 1st Secretary, Nov. 1974. Met Mikhail Gorbachev who brought him to Moscow. Deputy of the USSR Supreme Soviet, 1974. From 1981, member of the Cen. Cttee. of the CPSU. In 1985, replaced Viktor Grishin as Moscow party leader, and began a ruthless campaign against corruption. Nicknamed the 'no-nonsense Moscow boss'. After a speech attacking opponents of perestroika on 21 Oct. 1987, removed from his post of Moscow party boss, Nov. 1987. During President Reagan's visit to Moscow, June 1988, gave sensational TV interviews to BBC and American TV, demanding the resignation of Ligachev, whom he called an opponent of perestroika.

Maintained also that previous reports of his criticism of Gorbachev and of his recantation were inaccurate.

El'tsin, Sergei Vital'evich
4.5.1897–196? Conductor.
Born in Petersburg. Pupil of L. Nikolaev. Conductor from 1928. Chief conductor with the S. M. Kirov Theatre of Opera and Ballet, Leningrad, 1953–56. Died in Leningrad.

Elvin, Violetta (Prokhorova)
3.11.1925–   . Ballerina.
Born in Moscow. Graduated from the Moscow Choreographic School, 1942. Dancer at the Tashkent Theatre, 1943. Dancer and soloist at the Bolshoi Theatre and the Stanislavskii and Nemirovich-Danchenko Theatre until 1946. Married an Englishman. She was the first Soviet citizen allowed to leave the country during Stalin's life. With Sadler's Wells, 1946–56. Leading role in the first performance of the *Dying Swan* in the UK. Worked with F. Ashton. Made some films. Retired, 1956. Lives in Italy.
See: *Violetta Elvin*, ed. Hugh Fisher, London, 1953.

Emanuel, Nikolai Markovich
1.10.1915–   . Chemist.
Graduated from the Leningrad Polytechnical Institute, 1938. Professor at Moscow University, 1950. Authority on chemical kinetics.

Emel'ianov, Nikolai Aleksandrovich
1871–1958. Worker, revolutionary.
Worker in Petersburg factories. Involved in revolutionary work. Member of the Bolshevik Party, 1904. In the summer of 1917, hid Lenin and Zinoviev in his hut at Razliv near Petersburg, when they were threatened with arrest by the Provisional Government as organizers of an uprising and as suspected German spies. Arrested with all his family in 1935, and spent almost 20 years in the Gulag camps. Released after Stalin's death (1953 or 1954).

Emel'ianov, Vasilii Semenovich
12.2.1902–   . Metallurgist.
Graduated from the Moscow Mining

Academy, 1928. Chairman of the Council on Standards, 1940–46. Head of the Atomic Energy Administration, 1957–60. Represented the USSR at discussions on Atomic Energy at the UN, and at the International Atomic Energy Agency in Vienna. Specialist on developing new grades of steel and armour.

Emel'ianov, Vladimir
25.4.1942–27.5.1977. Athlete.
Honoured Master of Sports (boxing). Bronze medallist at the XVIIIth Olympic Games. Many times USSR and European champion. The cause of his premature death, reported in American press, has not been explained by the Soviet authorities.

Emel'ianova, Nina Petrovna
29.11.1912–   . Pianist.
Born in Kherson Gouvt. Pupil of S. Feinberg. Professor at the Moscow Conservatory.

Emel'ianova, Polina Aleksandrovna
7.1.1907–   . Singer (soprano).
Born in Melitopol'. Appeared in operettas. Soloist with Sverdlovsk Theatre of Musical Comedy from 1933. Honorary Artist of the RSFSR, 1947.

Emliutin, Dmitrii Vasil'evich
1907–1966. Partisan commander, state security officer.
Joined the Communist Party, 1931. Joined the partisan movement, 1941. Commander of the partisan groups in Orel Oblast', 1942. In the central staff of the partisan movement (under the NKVD), 1943. From the end of WWII until 1957, officer in the state security system.

Engel', Iulii Dmitrievich
16.4.1868–11.2.1927. Music critic, editor, composer.
Born in Berdiansk. One of the founders of The People's Conservatory (Narodnaia Konservatoriia) in Moscow, 1906. Editor and translator of the *Music Dictionary* by Hugo Riemann, Moscow, 1901–04. Author of many articles and books including *Ocherki Po Istorii Muzyki*, Moscow, 1911. Emigrated, 1922. Settled in Palestine. Died in Tel-Aviv.

Engelgardt, Vladimir Aleksandrovich
3.12.1894–1971. Biochemist.
Graduated from Moscow University, 1919. Professor at Kazan' University, 1929–33, at Leningrad University, 1934–40, and at Moscow University, 1936. Academician, 1953. Specialist on processes of cellular metabolism.

Engibarian, Vladimir Nikolaevich
24.4.1932–   . Athlete.
Born in Erevan, Armenia. Honoured Master of Sports (boxing), 1957. With Erevan Trudovye Rezervy. Member of the CPSU from 1961. Graduated from the Erevan Institute of Physical Culture, 1958. USSR champion, 1955–56 and 1958. European champion, 1953, 1957, 1959. Olympic champion, 1956.

Enukidze, Avel Safronovich (party name–Avel, Abdul, Zolotaia rybka–Goldfish)
19.5.1877–30.10.1937. Politician.
Born in the Georgian village of Tskhadisi, son of a Georgian peasant. Worked on the railways. Joined the SD Party in 1898. One of the founders of a local RSDRP cell in Baku. Exiled to Turukhansk, Siberia in 1914. Active in party politics after the October Revolution. Occupied various top party posts including secretary of the Central Executive Committee of Soviets. Personally decent and inoffensive, one of the last old Bolsheviks liquidated by Ezhov on Stalin's orders (smeared by accusations of amorality).

Epifanova, Vassa Iosifovna
1870–1942. Artist.
Studied at the Higher Art School of the Academy of Arts, Petersburg, 1899–1904. Pupil of Il'ia Repin. Genre painter. Exhibitions: Spring Exhibitions of the Academy of Arts, Petersburg (1907, 1914–17), the Society of Russian Water-Colour Painters, Petersburg, 1907.

Epishev, Aleksei Alekseevich
1908–1985. General, state security official.
Joined the Red Army, 1930. High posts as political officer before and during WWII. Secretary of the Cen. Cttee. of the Communist Party in the

Ukraine, 1946–50, engaged in the re-Stalinization of the Ukraine. 1st Secretary of the Odessa obkom of the party, 1950–51 and 1953–55. Deputy Minister of State Security of the USSR 1951–53, Soviet Ambassador to Romania and Yugoslavia, 1955–62. Head of the political administration of the armed forces, 1962–85. Member of the Cen. Cttee. of the CPSU, 1964.

Erdeli, Ksenia Aleksandrovna
8.3.1878–after 1970. Harpist.
Born on her parents' estate, Miroliubovka, near Elisavetgrad. Pupil of E. Bal'ter-Kiune. Soloist of the Bolshoi Theatre Orchestra, 1900–07 and 1919–38. Professor at the Moscow Conservatory. Many pupils. Wrote music for the harp.
Memoirs: *Moia Zhizn' v Muzyke*, Moscow, 1962.

Erdman, Nikolai Robertovich
1902–1970. Playwright.
His comedy, *The Mandate*, was staged in 1925 by V. Meyerhold and nearly created a political scandal. From the auditorium, according to foreign newspaper reports, shouts could be heard of 'Down with Stalinist bureaucrats!' Kamenev, Bukharin and Frunze praised the play. His second play, *The Suicide* (Samoubiitsa), 1928, was allowed to be staged thanks to Gorkii's personal request to Stalin. After 6 months of rehearsals, Kaganovich banned it (obviously on Stalin's orders). The author was arrested and sent to Siberia. Later lived in exile in Kalinin. After his release, his script *Volga-Volga* was filmed in 1938 by S. Eisenstein's collaborator, Grigorii Aleksandrov. The lead was played by Aleksandrov's wife, Liubov' Orlova. This film was much praised for its boundless enthusiasm, and for Orlova's singing talent. Received the Stalin Prize in 1951 for his script of *Smelye Liudi*, which was a typical example of Stalinist cinema. In his later years, he hardly wrote anything. *The Suicide* is now permanently in the repertory of Soviet theatres. In 1980, the Lithuanian director, I. Iurashas, staged it on Broadway.

Eremeev, Konstantin Stepanovich
1874–1931. Revolutionary, military commander.
Joined the SD Party, 1896. Very active during the Bolshevik take-over, October 1917. Took part in the storming of the Winter Palace. Fought against Krasnov. Commander of the Petrograd military district, Dec. 1917. Chief of the Kremlin guards during the revolt of the left-wing SRs in July 1918. Directed the mobilization of the Red Army during the Civil War, 1919–22. High military posts in the early 1920s.

Eremenko, Andrei Ivanovich
14.10.1892–19.11.1970. Marshal.
Joined the Red Army and the Communist Party, 1918. Took part in the Civil War as a cavalry regiment commander. Graduated from the Frunze Military Academy, 1935. During WWII, commander at different periods of the Western, Stalingrad, Baltic and Ukrainian fronts. In active service until 1958.

Eremin, Sergei Nikolaevich
22.5.1903–   . Trumpet player.
Born near Riazan. Pupil of M. Adamov and M. Tabakov. 2nd Prize at the All-Union Competition of Musicians, Leningrad, 1935. Soloist with the orchestra of the Bolshoi Theatre, 1928–47, and the Symphony Orchestra of the Moscow Philharmonic, 1928–34. Professor at the Moscow Conservatory.

Erenberg, Vladimir Georgievich
1875–14.9.1923. Composer, conductor.
Musical director and chief conductor of the Krivoe Zerkalo Theatre in Petersburg from 1908. Author of many musicals. Wrote music based on Koz'ma Prutkov's poetry, *Muzykal'nye Illustratsii*. Died in Khar'kov.

Erenburg, Il'ia Grigor'evich (Ehrenburg)
27.1.1891–31.8.1967. Author, journalist.
Born in Kiev. Son of an engineer. Early involvement in revolutionary activity. Arrested, 1908. Emigrated to Paris, Dec. 1908. Published several volumes of verse. Correspondent for Russian papers during WWI, Returned to Russia in July 1917. Denounced the Bolshevik take-over in his volume of verse *Molitva za Rossiiu*, 1918. Emigrated in spring 1921. Lived in Paris, 1921–24. Took an active part in the flowering of emigré Russian literary life in Berlin. Became more and more left-wing politically. Returned to the Soviet Union at the end of the 1920s. Like A. Tolstoy, used as a man of European culture and education at all kinds of international gatherings, serving as a mouthpiece of Stalinism. Correspondent of *Izvestia* during the Spanish Civil War. Regular Soviet spokesman at anti-fascist congresses in Europe in the late 1930s. At the beginning of WWII, wrote the novel, *Padenie Parizha*. During WWII, as a journalist, made several trips to the front. Author of the slogan 'Kill the German' (Ubei nemtsa). After the war, helped to prepare a book called *Chernaia Kniga* (Black Book) on German atrocities against the Jewish population on Soviet territory (the book was banned by Stalin and only published much later in Israel). Continued to serve Stalin loyally, both inside and outside the USSR. After the latter's death, he was the first, as usual, to catch the mood of the moment in his novel *Thaw* (Ottepel'), 1954–56, which gave the name to the whole period. Later published his memoirs, *Liudi, Gody, Zhizn'*, describing his meetings with many famous personalities in the West and in Russia (including his meetings with General Vlasov before his defence of Moscow, one of the first times his name was allowed to be mentioned in the Soviet press). Believed his own survival under Stalin's was due to chance ('a lucky lottery ticket'). Died in Moscow.

Ermachenkov, Vasilii Vasil'evich
1906–1963. Col.-general.
Joined the Communist Party, 1925. Graduated from the Naval Military Academy, 1931. In the Soviet armed forces 1931–47, and from 1949 (1947–49 probably a Gulag inmate). Naval pilot. As commander of the Baltic naval air force, took part in the Soviet-Finnish war, 1939–40. Commander of the naval air force in the Black Sea, 1942. After WWII, deputy commander of the naval air force and naval air defence forces. Head of the Naval Institute, 1956–61.

Ermakov, Arkadii Nikolaevich
1899–1957. Lt.-general.
Joined the Red Army, 1918. Took part in the Civil War, the Soviet-Finnish war and WWII. Senior military advisor with the Chinese Communist Army, 1953–57.

Ermash, Filipp Timofeevich
1923–   . State official.
Member of the CPSU, 1945. Graduated from the Ural State University, 1951. During WWII, served in the Soviet Army. 1st Secretary of Sverdlovsk City Cttee. of the Komsomol, 1951–56. Deputy chief, and chief of a dept. of Sverdlovsk City Oblast' Cttee. of the CPSU, 1952–62. Worked in the apparatus of the Cen. Cttee, 1962–72. Chairman of the USSR Cttee. for Cinematography from Aug. 1972. Candidate member of the Cen. Cttee. of the CPSU from 1981. Replaced as Head of Cinematography by Elem Klimov in May 1985. Remembered as a ruthless and ignorant party bureaucrat. Played an active role in the arrest and imprisonment of one of the most talented Soviet filmmakers, Sergei Paradzhanov. Under his rule hundreds of films were shelved.

Ermilov, Vladimir Vladimirovich
29.10.1904–19.11.1965. Literary critic.
Born in Moscow. Graduated from Moscow University in 1924. Member of the Communist Party from 1927. Editor of *Molodaia Gvardiia* in the late 1920s. One of the leaders of RAPP, 1928. Became known later as a servile and virulent Stalinist, his denunciations leading to the imprisonment and death of many of his former literary colleagues. Chief editor of *Literaturnaia Gazeta*, 1946–50, during the Zhdanovshchina. Lost his influence after Stalin's death.

Ermler, Fridrikh Markovich
13.5.1898–12.7.1967. Film director.
Cheka officer during the Civil War, 1919–21. Studied at the Leningrad Institute of Actors' Art, 1923–24. Worked in the script department of Sevzapkino. In 1924, founded KEM

(Film Experimental Workshops) where he made his first film, *Skarlatina*. With E. Ioganson, made *Kat'ka-Bumazhnyi Ranet*, 1926. Other films include *Dom v Sugrobakh*, 1928, and *Oblomok Imperii*, 1929. From 1929-31, studied at the Film Academy. With S. Iutkevich, made *Vstrechnyi*, 1932. Also made the documentary *Pered Sudom Istorii*, 1965, using rare archive material.

Ermogen (Golubov, Aleksei Stepanovich), Metropolitan of Kaluga
3.3.1896-7.4.1978. Russian Orthodox clergyman.
Born in Kiev. Son of a famous church historian (S. Golubov). Educated at high school in Kiev. Graduated from Moscow Theological Academy, 1919. Monk, 1919. Became abbot of the Kiev Caves Monastery, 1926-31. After WWII, lived in Astrakhan and Samarkand. Bishop of Tashkent, 1953. Bishop of Alma Ata, 1955-58. Archbishop, 1958. Archbishop of Omsk, 1962. Metropolitan of Kaluga, 1963-65. Best known for his forceful opposition to the Khrushchev anti-religious campaign (in marked contrast to most other bishops). Forced to retire. Sent to Zhirovitsy monastery in Belorussia, where he spent his last years.

Ermolenko-Iuzhina, Natal'ia Stepanovna (Plugovskaia)
1881-after 1945. Singer (soprano).
Born in Kiev. Pupil of M. Zotova. Soloist with the Mariinskii Theatre, Petersburg, 1901-04, and the Bolshoi Theatre, Moscow, from 1905. Emigrated. In Paris from 1924. Appeared in the Grand Opéra. Died in Paris.

Ernesaks, Gustav Gustavovich
12.12.1908- . Composer, conductor.
Born in the village of Perila, Estonia. Studied at the Tallinn Conservatory while still at high school. Graduated in 1931. Further studies at the same Conservatory. Pupil of A. Kapp, 1931-34. Taught singing in schools and conducted choirs from 1931. His first compositions date from that time. Taught at the Pedagogical Department of the Tallinn Conservatory, 1937-41. During WWII, directed the Iaroslavl' Ensemble and founded the Estonian Professional Choir Collective. After the war, Director of the Faculty of Choral Conducting at the Tallinn Conservatory. In 1944, founder, chief conductor and artistic director of the male voice choir of the Tallinn Philharmony (now the State Male Voice Choir of the Estonian SSR). Wrote mainly operatic and choral music.

Ernst, Sergei Rostislavovich
1900?-4.8.1980. Art historian.
The last Keeper of the Hermitage Museum in Petersburg before the Revolution 1917. Major authority on Russian art in pre-revolutionary Russia. After Oct. 1917, left for France. Died in Paris.

Erofeev, Venedikt
1939- . Writer.
Author of *Moskva-Petushki*, a novel on alcoholism in Russia, which for a long time circulated in samizdat, and was then published in the West (first in the magazine *AMI*, Nr. 3, 1973, and later as a separate book, by the YMCA Press, 1977). This was followed by *Vasilii Rozanov Glazami Ekstsentrika* (Serebrianyi Vek, USA, 1979) and the novel, *Shostakovich*. Lives in Moscow.
Source: P. Vail, A. Genis, *Sovremennaia Russkaia Proza*, USA, 1982.

Ershov, Ivan Vasil'evich
21.11.1867-21.11.1943. Opera singer, actor, sculptor and artist.
Born at Malyi Nesvetai, now Rostov Oblast'. His mother was originally a serf who was seduced by a local landowner. Started singing at the age of 5. Local rich merchants heard his singing and sent the talented boy to study in Petersburg where Anton Rubenstein took an interest in him. Entered the Petersburg Conservatory. Studied under Stanislav Gabel'. Graduated in 1893. 1893-94 in Italy. In 1894, soloist at the Khar'kov Opera Theatre. From 1895, soloist at the Petersburg Mariinskii Theatre (now the Kirov Opera House). Invited by Cosima Wagner to come to Bayreuth. Taught singing from 1915. Professor, 1916. Worked with many famous composers such as Glazunov, E. Napravnik, E. Mravinskii and D. Shostakovich. Died in Tashkent. Reburied at the Aleksandro-Nevskaia Lavra.

Erté (De Tirtov, Romain)
22.11.1892- . Artist.
Born in Petersburg. After studying art privately there, went to Paris, 1912. Influenced by Beardsley and Bakst. In 1913, became a designer for the fashion house of Poiret. Achieved fame by designing for *Harper's Bazaar*, 1916-37, the music hall, and cinema. Designed costumes for the Folies-Bergère, 1919-30, and other theatres. In the 1920-30s, adapted this style to the conventions of Art Deco. Reached the peak of fashion during the Art Nouveau revival of the 1960s. Later turned to lithographs and sculpture.

Er'zia, Stepan Dmitrievich (Nefedov)
1876-1959. Sculptor.
Studied in an icon painters' studio in Alatyr', now in the Chuvash ASSR. Also studied at the Moscow Stroganov Central Artistic-Industrial School, 1901, and at the Moscow School of Painting, Sculpture and Architecture, 1902-06, first as a painter, then sculptor under N. Kasatkin, A. Arkhipov, S. Ivanov, K. Korovin and V. Serov. From 1906, lived and worked in Italy and France. Returned to Russia in 1914. Emigrated after the October Revolution 1917. Settled in Argentina. Returned to the Soviet Union in 1950. Exhibitions from 1903 until 1954. Died in Moscow.

Esenin, Sergei Aleksandrovich
3.10.1895-27.12.1925. Poet.
Born in the village of Konstantinovo, now Riazan' Oblast'. Son of a peasant. In youth, influenced by the rural way of life and Orthodoxy. Began writing poetry at the age of 9. By 18, had already become a famous poet published by the leading Petersburg magazines. Met Blok, Gorodetskii and Kliuev, a poet of similar peasant background, who became his mentor. Was under the influence of the Scythian ideology of the left SR, Ivanov-Razumnik. Never joined the Communist Party, considering himself further to the left. Attended the Shaniavskii University

in Moscow. Met Anatolii Mariengof, Shershenevich and Ivnev. Joined the Imaginists. In the 1920s, became very fashionable for his bohemian poetry, unconventional life-style and good looks, being blond with blue eyes. In 1917, married Zinaida Raikh, a beautiful but insignificant actress with GPU connections. Divorced her after one year. In 1921, married the ageing American dancer Isadora Duncan, and left with her for Europe and America. The marriage was a disaster: the couple had no common language and he was by then already a hopeless alcoholic. The relationship soon turned into one long drunken party and a succession of private and public scandals. Left Duncan and returned alone to Soviet Russia, where he sank into a state of depression. This mood was not changed by his marriage to S. A. Tolstoy on 18 Sept. 1925, and soon thereafter, in a state of complete despair, he hanged himself in the hotel Angleterre in Leningrad, after writing a farewell poem in his own blood from a cut vein. His suicide reflected a widespread mood of post-revolutionary despair among youth in the Soviet Union and led to a whole wave of suicides, prompting attempts to counteract this (Mayakovsky's poem, articles by Trotsky and others). During his life-time and immediately after his death, disapproved of by the Soviet literary establishment. His poems were either lyrical or bohemian (*Moskva Kabatskaia, Chernyi Chelovek, Pismo k Materi*), and his heroes were anarchists (the 18th-century rebel, Pugachev, the anarchist leader of the Civil war, Makhno (Nomakh), fighting the Cheka agents). Always very popular; many of his poems became folk songs and were sung widely all over the country. Together with Mayakovsky, the most influential poet of the 1920s.

Esenin-Volpin, Aleksandr Sergeevich
1925– . Dissident, mathematician.
Born in Moscow. Son of the poet S. Esenin. Arrested in 1949 for anti-Soviet propaganda, and sent to a psychiatric hospital. In the late 1950s, became one of the leaders of the dissident movement, stressing the legality of their demands, and urging the authorities 'to respect their own

laws'. Several terms in psychiatric hospitals in Leningrad and Moscow. Emigrated to the West, 1972. Settled in the USA and retired from political activity.

Eshinov, Vladimir Nikolaevich
18.2.1949– . Athlete.
Born in Kirshi, Leningrad Oblast'. Honoured Master of Sports (rowing), 1975. Coach with Leningrad Dynamo. USSR champion, 1970–78. European champion, 1973. World champion, 1974–75. Olympic champion, 1976.

Eshpai, Andrei Iakovlevich
15.5.1925– . Composer, pianist.
Born in Kosmodemiansk. Son of the composer and folklorist Ia. Eshpai. Entered the Gnesin Music School for Children. Pupil of V. Listova. Began to compose early. Entered the Chkalov Machine Gun School, 1943. Graduated from the Military Institute of Foreign Languages, 1944. Sent as interpreter to the 1st Belorussian front. In Red Army Military Intelligence in Poland and Germany. After the war, accepted into the Music School of the Moscow Conservatory. Studied piano and composition. Entered the Moscow Conservatory, 1948. Pupil of N. Rakov, N. Miaskovskii, (composition) and V. Sofronitskii (piano). While a student, took part in folkloristic expeditions in the Volga district. Accepted for postgraduate studies at the Moscow Conservatory, 1953. Pupil of A. Khachaturian. Taught composition at the Conservatory, 1965–70. First Secretary of the Union of Composers of the RSFSR, 1973–78.

Eshpai, Iakov Andreevich (real name-Ishpaikin)
29.10.1890–20.2.1963. Composer, folklorist.
Born in the village of Kokshamary, Kazan' Gouvt. Father of the composer A. Eshpai. Collected and researched Mari folk songs. Arranged and recorded over 500 Mari songs. Wrote music for folk orchestra, choral music, and pieces for the piano. Author of the book *Natsional'nye Muzykal'nye Instrumenty Mariitsev*, Ioshkar-Ola, Mari SSR, 1940. Died in Moscow.

Etkind, Efim Grigor'evich
1918– . Literary scholar.
Born in Leningrad. Graduated from Leningrad University, 1941. Participant in WWII. Doctor of Philological Studies, 1965. Editor of a series on modern Russian poets. In 1963, defence witness at the trial of Iosif Brodskii. In 1974, expelled from the Union of Writers and stripped of his academic degrees. Left the USSR, 1974, and settled in Paris. Lecturer at Nanterre University.
Works: *Zapiski Nezagovorshchika*, London, 1977.

Evdokimov, Boris Dmitrievich (Ruslanov, Ivan; Razumnyi, Sergei)
1923–1979. Dissident, historian.
Born in Leningrad. Graduated in history from Leningrad University. In the 1960s, published his articles under pen-names in the emigré magazine *Posev* in Frankfurt. Arrested in 1971, and incarcerated in psychiatric hospitals. Transferred to those hospitals which were used for political prisoners — in Leningrad, 1971, Dnepropetrovsk, 1972 and the notorious Kazan' hospital, 1976. Released shortly before death from cancer.

Evdokimov, Grigorii Eremeevich
1884–1936. Trade unionist, party official.
A Bolshevik from 1903. Chairman of the Petrograd Union of Trade Unions in 1922. Deputy chairman of the Petrograd Soviet, 1923–25. Leader of the new opposition in 1925. Until 1926, secretary, and until 1927, member of the Cen. Cttee. of the Communist Party. Expelled from the party in 1927. Re-instated after an admission of mistakes in 1928. Arrested in 1934. Sentenced to 8 years imprisonment at a show trial of the Moscow centre, 16 Jan. 1935. One of the chief defendants at a second show trial of the Trotskyist-Zinov'evist terrorist centre. Sentenced to death on 24 Aug. 1936 in Moscow. Presumably shot.

Evelson, Evgenia Antolievna
1914– . Lawyer.
Born in Nikolaev in the Ukraine. Graduated from the Moscow Institute of Law. In the late 1940s, victim

of Stalin's antisemitic campaign. Became involved in the Jewish rights movement. Emigrated, 1975. Settled in Israel. Wrote a valuable study on Soviet trials for economic crimes (i.e. dealing in the black market), *Sudebnye Protsessy po Ekonomicheskim Delam v SSSR*, London, 1986.

Evert, Aleksei Ermolaevich (Ewert)
1857–1926. General.
Took part in the Russo-Turkish war, 1877–78. Graduated from the Academy of the General Staff, 1882. Staff officer during the Russo-Japanese war, 1904–05. Chief of the General Staff, 1906–08, later Ataman of the Transbaikal Cossacks. During WWI, Commander of the 4th Army, and Commander in Chief of the Western Front, 1915–17.

Evgenii (Zernov, Semen), Metropolitan of Gorkii
1877–12.11.1935. Russian Orthodox clergyman.
Born in Moscow Gouvt. Son of a deacon. Graduated from Moscow Theological Academy, 1902. Bishop of Kirensk, 1913. Bishop of Blagoveshchensk, 1914. Archbishop, 1923. Arrested and sent to Solovki concentration camp with a group of church leaders, 1924–26. In exile in Komi ASSR until 1929. Metropolitan of Gorkii (formerly Nizhnii-Novgorod), 1934. Re-arrested in 1935. Died in Gorkii.

Evlakov, Orest Aleksandrovich
17.1.1912–   . Composer.
Born in Warsaw. Professor and head of the composition class at the Leningrad Conservatory. Among his pupils were A. Petrov, S. Slonimskii, and B. Tishchenko. Author of ballets, symphonies, a cycle for soloists, choir and orchestra, other instrumental works, songs, romances, and music for plays and films.
Literary works: *Problemy Vospitaniia Kompozitora*, Leningrad, 1963.

Evlogii (Georgievskii, Vasilii Semenovich), Metropolitan of the Russian Orthodox Archdiocese in France
10.4.1868–8.8.1946. Russian Orthodox clergyman.
Born at Somovo, Tula Gouvt. Son of

a village priest. Educated at Tula seminary 1882–88. Graduated from the Moscow Theological Academy, 1892. Professor, later rector of Kholm seminary, 1897. Bishop of Lublin, 1902. Bishop of Kholm, 1905. Member of the Duma, 1907. Archbishop of Kholm, 1912–14, Archbishop of Volhynia, 1914–19. During the Civil War, left Russia (Poland, Rumania Germany, France) 1920. Appointed temporary head of the Russian Orthodox Church in Western Europe in Berlin, 1921–22. Lived in Paris, 1922–46. Refused to recognize the authority of the Russian Church in Exile, and declared himself independent from the Moscow Patriarchate, which (under the pressure of the Soviet government) demanded political loyalty. Legalized the position of his part of the Russian church as an Exarchate of the Oecumenical Patriarchate (Constantinople). Founded in Paris the St. Sergius Theological Institute, which could draw upon the immense cultural achievements of the Russian spiritual elite, which found itself in exile after 1917. The institute became an outstanding centre of Russian and Orthodox learning and scholarship. Died in Paris.
Memoirs: *My Life's Journey*, Paris, 1947.

Evlogii (Smirnov, Iurii Vasil'evich), archimandrite
1937–   . Russian Orthodox clergyman.
Born in Kemerovo. Educated at a local high school. Served in the army, 1960–63. Graduated from Moscow Theological Academy, 1966. Monk, 1966. Teacher and later professor at the Zagorsk Seminary, 1980. Head of the economic administration of the Troitse-Sergieva Lavra and the Theological Academy. Appointed administrative head of the Danilov monastery, one of the oldest Moscow monasteries, founded in 1282 by Daniil, Aleksander Nevskii's son, which in May 1983 became the first monastery to be restored to the church by the Soviet government.

Evseev, Sergei Vasil'evich
25.1.1894–16.3.1956. Composer, music theorist.
Born in Moscow. Professor at the

Moscow Conservatory. Author of symphonies, piano concertos, concertos for clarinet and orchestra, chamber music, and arrangements of folk songs. Died in Moscow. Literary work: a textbook on harmony, Moscow, 1937, a textbook on polyphony, Moscow 1956.

Evstigneev, Evgenii Aleksandrovich
9.10.1926–   . Actor.
Distinguished comedian. Became famous in the early 1960s after graduating from the MKHAT Studio, 1960. Films include *Beregis' Avtomobilia*, 1966, *Zigzag Udachi* and *Zolotoi Telenok*, both 1968, and *Stariki-Razboiniki*, 1972.

Evstigneev, Kirill Alekseevich
1917–   . Major-general.
Joined the Soviet Army, 1938. During WWII, successful fighter pilot (shot down over 50 planes), twice Hero of the Soviet Union, 1944, 1945. After WWII, graduated from the Air Force Academy, 1955, and the Academy of the General Staff, 1960. Held several high command posts in the air force. Retired, 1972.

Evtushenko, Evgenii Aleksandrovich
18.7.1933–   . Poet, author.
Born at Zima, Siberia. Brought up by his mother, a divorced geologist. Both his grandfathers (one Ukrainian and one Latvian) perished in Stalin's purges. Moved to Moscow, 1944. Became widely known in the mid-1950s as the voice of his generation during the post-Stalin thaw, with such poems as *Stantsiia Zima*. Became the idol of mass poetry readings in the early 1960s. His poems, *Babii Iar* and *Nasledniki Stalina*, were published in a central party newspaper in Moscow and created a sensation. Later became known for his cautious establishment line on official trips abroad, and cautiously liberal line inside the USSR, earning in turn praise and criticism both from the establishment and the dissidents. Although his poetic achievements hardly justify his fame, some of his lyrics belong with the best of modern Soviet poetry. Married Bella Akhmadullina, a poet-

ess of his generation who was equally famous at the time. His third wife was English, and he has called himself a 'son-in-law of Great Britain', a country which he has visited many times, invariably with great success. Has written an autobiography with an interesting and sincere description of his life as a youth, marked by his experiences of WWII and Stalinism (published in London). Also published his photographic work and made films. Influential in the Union of Writers during the glasnost period.

Ezhov, Nikolai Ivanovich
1895–1939. Head of secret police. Bolshevik from Apr. 1917. During the Civil War political commissar with the Red Army, later carried out the same work in the provinces. Member of the Cen. Cttee. of the CPSU in 1934. People's Commissar for Internal Affairs (NKVD) in 1936 after Iagoda's fall and arrest. Chairman of the Commission of Party Control and member of the Politburo, 1937. Dismissed from the NKVD, Dec. 1938, and appointed Minister of Water Transport. Arrested and disappeared in Mar. 1939. Probably executed soon after arrest. A complete nonentity, whose name, during his short rule, struck terror into the hearts of the whole country; this period is known as 'ezhovshchina'. Brought in by Stalin with the specific aim of an unprecedented blood bath. Extolled by the Soviet press of the time as 'Zhelezny Narkom' (The Iron Narkom, People's Commissar) he earned the nickname of 'the bloody dwarf' (due to his short stature and sickly appearance). According to those who knew him well, was totally dependent on drugs towards the end of his stay in office. Even compared to his predecessor, Iagoda, who according to rumours, he had shot personally, and his successor Beria (who shot him in turn), he stands out as a bloodthirsty henchman, one of the most sinister figures of the Stalinist era. At the 20th Party Congress in Oct. 1956, Nikita Khrushchev called him a 'criminal' and 'narkoman' (drug addict) who 'deserved what he got'. Ezhov's appalling crimes are now becoming the subject of investigation in the USSR.

Ezhov, Sergei Osipovich (Tsederbaum)
1879–1937. Revolutionary, politician. Member of the SD Party from the 1890s. Brother of Iu. Martov. Exiled several times before 1917. Member of the Cen. Cttee. of the Mensheviks, 1917. Arrested in 1921, re-arrested, 1922. Exiled to Viatka. During the 1920s and 1930s, arrested several times and sent into exile. Again arrested in Feb. 1937. Died in a prison in Moscow after a long hunger strike.

F

Fabergé, Aleksandr Karlovich
1913-1988. Geneticist.
Born in Petersburg. Grandson of the jeweller, Karl Fabergé. After the October Revolution 1917, when the family lost all their shops, emigrated with his parents to Europe. Moved to the USA, where he graduated as a geneticist. In his later years, worked as a research geneticist at Texas University. Died in Texas.

Fabergé, Karl Gustavovich (Carl Peter)
30.5.1846-1920. Jeweller.
Born in Petersburg into a family of Huguenot origin from Picardy, which, during the flight from France changed its name to Fabri, then Fabrier, reverting to the original name only after settling in the Russian Empire (Estonia). Learned his craft at Dresden, Frankfurt-on-Main, Italy and Paris. Took over the family jewellers' business in St. Petersburg, 1870. Won a gold medal for his objects d'art at the Pan-Russian Exhibition in Moscow, 1882. Made the first of the famous Easter eggs ordered by Tsar Alexander III in 1884. His world-wide fame came when his art was shown at the Paris World Exhibition, 1900. Proclaimed Maitre and given the Legion d'Honneur. Became jeweller to the courts of Europe, especially the Romanov court. WWI and the revolution brought an end to the dreamlike world of Faberge's art. When, after October 1917, the communist authorities came to his famous workshop on Morskaia street in Petrograd to take it into state

ownership, he is said to have asked for 10 minutes 'to put on my hat and coat'. Died in exile in Lausanne.

Fabritsius, Ian Fritsevich
1877–1929. Military commander. Involved in revolutionary activity from 1891. Joined the Bolshevik Party, 1903. Took part in WWI. Chairman of the Regiment Soldiers Cttee of the 1st Latvian Infantry Regiment, October 1971. Joined the Red Army, 1918. Active participant in the Civil War, one of the leaders of the Latvian regiments, often used for Cheka duties. Prominent during the crushing of the sailors' revolt in Kronstadt, 1921. Graduated from academic courses of the Red Army, 1925. Head and political commissar of the courses for commanders of the Red Army in the 1920s. Deputy commander of the Red Army in the Caucasus. Died in an aircrash.

Fadeechev, Nikolai Borisovich
27.1.1933–   . Ballet dancer.
Born in Moscow. Graduated from the Moscow Choreographic School, 1952. With the Bolshoi Theatre since then. Soloist. Worked with the leading choreographers, Iu. Grigorovich, V. Chabukiani, and L. Lavrovskii. Partnered G. Ulanova and M. Plisetskaia for 10 years. Many performances abroad.

Fadeev, Aleksandr Aleksandrovich (Bulyga)
1901–1956. Author.
Classic Stalinist author. Became famous in the late 1920s. Praised officially as one of the best representatives of socialist realism. Became very influential as a literary official. General Secretary of the Writers Union, 1946–55. Personally responsible for many denunciations of writers during the Stalin years, leading to imprisonment or death. After the secret speech by Khrushchev denouncing the crimes of Stalin at the XXth Party Congress, committed suicide in a state of fear and depression. His literary reputation is largely based on two propaganda novels, *The Rout,* 1927, about the Civil War, and *The Young Guard,* 1945, which was revised after official criticism in 1951, and which concerns

a group of young communist resistance fighters during the German occupation.

Faier, Iurii Fedorovich
17.1.1890–3.8.1971. Conductor, violinist.
Born in Kiev. Graduated from the Moscow Conservatory, 1909. From 1906, violinist, soloist, and first violinist with various orchestras. First violinist and conductor at the Riga Opera, 1909–10. With the Zimin Private Opera, Moscow, 1914–15. From 1916 first violinist and soloist at the Bolshoi Theatre, and from 1919, conductor at the same theatre. Conducted over 50 ballet productions. Worked closely with all leading choreographers at the Bolshoi Theatre. Several State Prizes. Died in Moscow.

Faif, Gari (Garry)
12.6.1942–   . Artist.
Born in Tbilisi. Graduated from the Moscow Institute of Architecture and the École des Beaux Arts in Paris. Sculptor. Exhibited in Tbilisi and Moscow. Carried out several important architectural projects. Married a Frenchwoman and moved to Paris, 1973. Exhibited in France, Germany, Austria, Italy, Japan, Switzerland, Canada and the USA.

Faiko, Aleksei Mikhailovich
1893–1978. Playwright.
His play, *Bubus* (originally *Uchitel' Bubus*), was staged by V. Meyerhold at his theatre for the first time on 23 Jan. 1925. Other works include: *Dilemma*, 1921; *Kar'era Pirpointa Bleka*, 1922; *Ozero Liul*, 1923; *Evgraf, Iskatel' Prikliuchenii*, 1926; *Chelovek s Portfelem*, 1928. The 1987 edition of the *Literaturnyi Entsiklopedicheskii Slovar'*, published in Moscow, shows a blank period between 1936 and 1946. Arrested and spent this time in the Gulag, according to many theatre researchers and authors. Apparently survived the camps and returned to normal life after Stalin's death. Published many articles, and his memoirs in 1971.

Fainberg, Viktor Isaakovich
1931–   . Dissident
Born in Leningrad. Graduated in English philology from Leningrad University. Arrested in Red Square, 25 Aug 1968 with a small group of dissidents, protesting against the Soviet invasion of Czechoslovakia. Beaten up and certified insane by the Serbskii Institute. In psychiatric establishments from 1968–74. During this time fell in love and married his own psychiatrist, Dr Maria Voikhanskaia (divorced later). Released 1974 and emigrated the same year. Lived at first in Britain, later moved to France.

Fait, Andrei Andreevich
29.8.1903–17.1.1976. Actor.
Graduated from the State Film School, 1927. Entered the film industry, 1922. Always played spies, villains and nasty characters. Made over 70 films.

Falaleev, Fedor Iakovlevich
1899–1955. Marshal.
Joined the Bolshevik Party, 1918, and the Red Army, 1919. Took part in the Civil War. Joined the air force, 1932. Educated at a pilot's school, 1933. Graduated from the Zhukovskii Air Force Academy, 1934. General Inspector of the Air Force, 1941. On active service during WWII. Chief-of-staff and Deputy Commander of the Soviet Air Force, Oct 1942. Head of the Air Force Academy, 1946–50.

Falin, Valentin Mikhailovich
1926–   . Diplomat, journalist.
Born in Leningrad. Graduated from the Moscow Institute of International Relations in 1950. Member of the Communist Party from 1953. Entered the Diplomatic Service. Posts in the Ministry of Foreign Affairs, 1952–70. Councillor, Deputy Chief of the 3rd European Dept. Chief of the 2nd European Dept., member of the Collegium, and Chief of the 3rd European Dept. Elected to the Cen Cttee. of the CPSU, 1976. 1st Deputy of the International Information Dept. of the Cen. Cttee., 1972–82. Political observer for *Izvestia*, 1982. Ambassador to West Germany, 1984–86. Chief of the Novosti Press.

Falk, Robert Rafailovich
1886–1958. Artist.
Genre, portrait, landscape and still-life painter and stage designer. Studied at the K. F. Iuon and I. Mashkov Art School, Moscow, 1903–04, then at the Moscow School of Painting, Sculpture and Architecture, 1904–09 under V. Serov and K. Korovin. First exhibition: Young Artists, 1906. Other exhibitions: the Zolotoe Runo, 1909–10; the Bubnovyi Valet, 1910–16, 1927; the Mir Iskusstva, 1911, 1917, 1921–22; Permanent Exhibition of Modern Art. St. Petersburg, 1913; The Artists of Moscow to the Victims of War, Moscow, 1914–15; Pictures of the Left Movement, Petersburg, 1915; Painting, Moscow, 1915; Ten Years of Russian Drawing, Moscow, 1927; the October Revolution, Ten Years, Moscow, 1928; the Society of Moscow Artists, 1928. Personal exhibitions: Moscow, 1923, 1924, and 1927. For 30 years, was unable to exhibit his work. Died in Moscow almost forgotten. A posthumous exhibition was organized during Khrushchev's thaw in 1958.

Falz-Fein, Fridrikh Eduardovich (Falz-Fein, Friedrich von) Baron
1853–1920. Landowner, natural park director.
Born into a well-known family of German colonists in the Ukraine (Northern Tauria). Educated at Dorpat and Odessa. One of the finest cattle breeders in Russia, regular winner at shows at the world-famous Nizhnii Novgorod trade fair. Created the first and largest open air zoo in the world at Askania Nova, 1875. About 11,000 hectares of untouched steppe have been preserved, with a huge collection of animals from grassland habitats living freely in the wild. Also a scientific breeding station and very large sheep rearing business (over 500,000 sheep). During the Civil War, 1918, arrested by Bolsheviks, but soon released after protests from scientists and the local population. Emigrated with his family to Germany, died at Bad Kissingen and buried in Berlin. The nature park was almost wiped out during the Civil War and again during WWII, but has since recovered and exists to this day as a state enterprise, continuing the tradition of the founder. The Falz-Fein family lives at present in Lichtenstein.

Famar, Mother (Mardzhanova, Tamara Aleksandrovna), Princess
1878?–23.6.1936. Nun.
Born into a princely Georgian family. Appointed abbess of an ancient Georgian convent, devoted to the patron of Georgia, St. Nina, 1902. Close to Ioann Krontadtskii, a priest, known for his sermons before WWI and later proclaimed a saint. Transferred to the Moscow Pokrovskii Convent, 1905. Worked with the older sister of the Tsarina, Grand-Duchess Elizaveta Fedorovna (who, after the murder of her husband, Grand Duke Sergei, became a nun, and was murdered by the Bolsheviks in 1918). Abbess of the Seraphim-Znamenskii convent, 1912, until it was closed by the Bolshevik authorities in 1924. Continued to lead a monastic life with a group of nuns, organized officially as a group of women-workers, sewing bed sheets. Arrested in 1931 and sent to Butyrki prison in Moscow. Exiled for 5 years to a village near Irkutsk. After her release, became widely known and attracted many pilgrims seeking advice and solace.

Farmaniants, Georgii Karapetovich
4.11.1921–   . Ballet dancer, choreographer.
Born in Kalinin Oblast'. Brother of the ballerina, Evgenia Farmaniants. Graduated from the Moscow Choreographic School, 1940. With the Bolshoi Theatre, 1940–62. Many leading parts in various ballets. On tour abroad many times. From 1962, choreographer with the A. Aleksandrov Soviet Army Ensemble.

Fat'ianov, Aleksei Ivanovich
1919–1959. Poet.
His poetry has been used by many Soviet composers of popular songs (Na Krylechke Tvoem, V Gorodskom Sadu, Gde Zhe Vy Druz'ia Odnopolchane, Khvastat' Milaia Ne Stanu).

Federov, Evgenii Konstantinovich
10.4.1910–   . Geophysicist.
Graduated from Leningrad University, 1932. Took part in several polar expeditions in the 1930s. Head of the Soviet Hydrometeorological Service, 1939–47. Academician, 1960.

Fedicheva, Kaleria Ivanovna
20.7.1936–   . Ballet dancer.
Born in Ust'-Izhora. Studied at the Leningrad Choreographic School. From 1955 with the Kirov Ballet Company. Starred in Swan Lake, Hamlet and other ballets. Left the Soviet Union in 1975 to live with her American husband, Martin Fridman. Danced in the USA in the late 1970s.

Fedin, Konstantin Aleksandrovich
24.2.1892–1977. Author.
Born in Saratov. Son of a merchant. Studied in Germany, 1914, interned at the beginning of WWI. Returned to Russia after the October Revolution 1917. Began to write as a member of the literary circle Serapionovy Bratia, 1921. His novel, Goroda i Gody (1924), was one of the first works about the intelligentsia during the years of war and revolution. Visited Berlin in the 1920s. Gradually became a conformist. Academician, 1958. First Secretary of the Union of Writers, 1959–71, a typical figure of the years of stagnation (epokha zastoia).

Fediukin, Anatolii Viktorovich
26.1.1952–   . Athlete.
Born in Voronezh. Honoured Master of Sports (handball), 1976. With the Moscow Armed Forces Club. Student at the Technical School attached to the Likhachev Automobile Works. USSR champion, 1978–79. Olympic champion, 1976.

Fediuninskii, Ivan Ivanovich
1900–1977. General.
Joined the Red Army, 1919. Took part in the Civil War. Joined the Bolshevik Party, 1930. Graduated from the Vystrel Courses, 1931. Took part in WWII (Leningrad, Volkhov, Briansk). After WWII, commander of several military districts. Deputy Commander of Soviet Forces in Germany, 1951–54.

Fed'ko, Ivan Fedorovich
1897–1939. Military commander.
On active service during WWI. Joined the Bolshevik Party, 1917, and the Red Army, 1918. Took part in the Civil War, Commander in Chief of the North Caucasian Army, and of the Crimean Army. Took part in the crushing of the sailors' revolt at Kronstadt and the

peasant revolt in Tambov. Graduated from the Academy of the Red Army, 1922. Commander of several military districts in the 1930s. 1st Deputy Defence Minister, 1938. Liquidated by Stalin.

Fedorchuk, Vitalii Vasil'evich
1918–   . General, KGB official, politician.
Ukrainian. Worked for various local newspapers in Zhitomir and Kiev Oblast', 1934–36. Student at military school, 1936–39. Graduated from the KGB Higher School. Worked in the state security service, 1939–70. Head of the 3rd Directorate, which supervises the armed forces. Has acquired a reputation for toughness. Head of the Ukrainian KGB, 1970–82. Responsible for the crackdown on Ukrainian nationalist dissidents. Candidate member of the Politburo of the Cen. Cttee. of the Ukrainian CP, 1973–76. Full member, 1976–82. Chairman of the USSR Cttee. for State Security (KGB), May–Dec. 1982. Replaced by Viktor Chebrikov. USSR Minister of the Interior, Dec. 1982–86.

Fedorenko, Iakov Nikolaevich
1896–1947. Marshal.
Joined the Bolshevik Party, 1917, and the Red Army, 1918. Took part in the Civil War as a commander of an armoured train. After the Civil War, commander of a regiment of armoured trains. Graduated from the Frunze Military Academy, 1934. Commander of a tank regiment before WWII. Commander of Tank Forces of the Soviet Army, Dec. 1942. Deputy 1942. Deputy Minister of Defence, 20 July 1941–May 1943. After WWII, Commander of Soviet Tank Forces, Apr. 1946.

Fedorov, Aleksei Fedorovich
1901–   . Major-general, politician.
Joined the Bolshevik Party, 1927. Graduated from a technical building institute, 1932. 1st Secretary of the Chernigov Party Obkom, 1938. Went underground during WWII. Communist partisan organizer near Chernigov and in Volhynia. 1st Secretary of the Volhynia (underground) Party Obkom, 1943. Secretary of a number of party obkoms after WWII. Minister of Social Security of the Ukrainian SSR, 1957–79.

Fedorov, Evgenii Petrovich
1911– . Major-general.
Joined the Red Army, 1930. Bomber
pilot, 1933. Took part in the Soviet-
Finnish war, 1939–40. Commander
of bomber detachments during WWII.
Graduated from the Air Force
Academy, 1948. High command
posts in the Soviet Bomber Force
after WWII.

Fedorov, Evgraf Evgrafovich
8.11.1880–1969? Climatologist.
Graduated from the University of
Petersburg, 1910. Worked at the
Pavlovsk Observatory, 1911–34.
Member of the Institute of Geography
of the Academy of Sciences, 1934–51.
Specialist in cloud and solar radia-
tion.

Fedorov, Mikhail Ivanovich
1903– . Vice-admiral.
Joined the Red Navy, 1923, and the
Bolshevik Party, 1926. Graduated
from the Navy Academy, 1939. On
active service during WWII on the
Volga, and in the Northern and
Pacific fleets. Worked in the HQ of
the Navy after WWII, 1949–53.

Fedorov, Mikhail Mikhailovich
1886–1946. Politician, social worker.
Member of the Cadet Party, and of
the Duma. Editor of the newspaper
Slovo, 1907–08. Deputy Minister of
Trade and Industry before 1917.
With the Whites during the Civil
War. Chairman of the National
Centre, 1918. Emigrated after the
Civil War and settled in Paris.
Became widely known as the Head of
the Organization for Aid to Russian
Students Abroad. Together with
Kartashev created a National Com-
mittee in Paris, which tried un-
successfully to unite Russian
monarchists and republicans abroad.
Died in France.

Fedorov, Sergei Filippovich
13.7.1896–1971? Geologist.
Graduated from the Moscow Mining
Academy, 1924. Professor at the
Moscow Oil Institute, 1934–54. Studied mud volcanism and the connection between mud volcanoes and oil
deposits.

Fedorov, Sviatoslav
1930– . Eye surgeon.
Head of the Moscow Research
Institute for Eye Microsurgery. One
of the world leaders in the application
of microsurgery. Invented several
new medical techniques including
radial keratotomy (minute radial
incisions of the eye-retina) for short-
sightedness. Opened an ophthalmic
clinic in Moscow in the 1970s which
charges foreigners £200–300 an operation in order to raise hard currency
to pay for more Western technology.
Appeared in a BBC2 television series,
Comrades, to describe his conveyor-
belt system for processing patients.
Enjoys a lavish lifestyle, with two
homes, a dacha and servants. His
leisure activity is riding. His method
has gained recognition in the USA.
Gave several lectures in London,
Oct. 1988.

Fedorov, Vasilii Fedorovich
1897–1942. Artist.
Landscape and historical artist. Born
in Leningrad. Studied at the VKHU-
TEIN, Leningrad, 1922–26, under G.
Bobrovskii, A. Savinov, A. Rylov
and I. Braz. Exhibitions: Moscow,
1928, 1935, 1939, and Leningrad,
1940. Fell in action during WWII.

Fedorov, Vladimir
5.1.1955–11.8.1979. Footballer.
Kazakh athlete. Honoured Master of
Sports (football). Bronze medallist at
the XXIst Olympic Games. Many
times USSR champion. The cause of
his early death, reported in the
American press, has not been explained by the Soviet authorities.

Fedorov, Vladimir Grigor'evich
1874–1966. Gun designer.
Graduated from the Mikhailovskoe
Artillery School, 1900. Designed
automatic rifles before WWI, and the
first automatic handgun, 1916.
Director of a factory which produced
his guns, 1918–31. Consultant at the
Ministry of Armaments, 1942–46.

Fedorov, Vladimir Mikhailovich
5.8.1901– . Musicologist.
Born in Chernigov. Emigrated, 1922.
Settled in Paris. Librarian at Sorbonne University, 1933–43. Chief
librarian of the Music Department of
the Bibliotheque Nationale from
1946. General Secretary, 1950–55,
and later Vice-President of the
International Association of Music
Libraries. From 1954, editor of
Fontes Artis Musicae. Author of
many articles about music and
musicians. Author of a biography of
Musorgskii, 1935. From 1965, President of the International Music
Union.

Fedorova, Olga Vasil'evna
1882–1942. Ballerina.
Born in Moscow. Graduated from
the Moscow Theatre School, 1900.
Pupil of A. Gorskii. With the Bolshoi
Theatre, 1900–09, and the Mariinskii
Theatre, 1909–28. Died during the
Siege of Leningrad.

Fedorova, Sofia Vasil'evna
28.9.1879–3.1.1963. Ballerina.
Born in Moscow. Graduated from
the Moscow Theatre School, 1899.
Joined the Bolshoi Theatre. Ballerina, then prima ballerina. Took part
in Diaghilev's Ballets Russes in Paris,
1909–13. Emigrated from Russia in
1922, and settled in Paris. With A.
Pavlova's company, 1925–26. In
1928, taught for a short while, then
retired. Died in Neuilly, near Paris.

Fedorova, Viktoria
1945– . Film actress.
Born in Moscow. Daughter of Zoia
Fedorova and an American officer.
Graduated from the VGIK. Became
a successful actress. Appeared in the
leading role in the film *The Two*
(Dvoe), produced at the Riga Studio
by Mikhail Bogin in 1965. Until the
director's emigration to the USA, the
film was considered a modern Soviet
classic. Played in *Crime and Punishment* and many other films. In the
1970s, tracked down her father, and
went to the USA to meet him. During
her visit, met an American pilot,
married him, and remained in the
USA. Wrote a book, *The Admiral's
Daughter*. Since then, among other
things, has appeared on TV advertising cosmetics.

Fedorova, Zoia Alekseevna
21.12.1909–10.12.1981. Film actress.
Graduated from the Moscow Theatre
School, 1934. Became a very popular

film actress in the 1930–40s. Comedienne. At a diplomatic reception in early 1945, met an American officer, fell in love and became involved in an affair with him. Soon after the birth of her daughter, she was arrested, accused of being an American spy and sent to the Gulag for 25 years. Released and rehabilitated after Stalin's death, she set about finding the father of her daughter, and was eventually successful. The matter became of international concern when her daughter Viktoria, and she herself went to visit him in the USA. Continued to pester the Soviet authorities for a visa, and the western press documented her every step. Soon found murdered in her flat. The investigation found no trace of forced entry. Buried at the Vagan'-kovskoe Cemetery, Moscow.

Fedorovich, Sofia (Fedorovitch)
15.2.1893–25.1.1953. Stage designer.
Born in Minsk. Stage designer with various Russian theatres. Emigrated in 1920, and settled in England. Worked with the Ballet Rambert and became one of Britain's leading stage designers. Chief stage designer of several ballet productions in the major British theatres. Died in London.

Fedorovskii, Fedor Fedorovich
26.12.1883–7.10.1955. Stage designer.
Born in Chernigov. Graduated from the Moscow Stroganov Industrial Art School, 1907. Worked with the Zimin Private Opera and the Ballets Russes abroad. With the Bolshoi Theatre, 1927–29, and 1947–53. State (Stalin) Prize, 1941, 1943, 1949, 1950, 1951. Member and Vice-President of the Academy of Arts, 1947–53. Died in Moscow.

Fedoseev, Anatolii Pavlovich
1910–   . Engineer, author.
Born in Petersburg. Graduated from the Leningrad Institute of Electrical Technology, 1936. Began as a research engineer at a scientific research institute. Later held senior positions in several research institutes. In 1971, defected while on an official trip to the Paris Air Exhibition. Books: Zapadnia: Chelovekii Sotsializm, Ger-

many, 1976; O Novoi Rossii, London, 1980. Settled in Britain, Active contributor to the Russian emigré press.

Fedoseeva-Shukshina, Lidia Nikolaevna
25.9.1938–   . Actress.
Graduated from the VGIK, 1964. Pupil of S. Gerasimov. Married Vasilii Shukshin and played in all his films until his death. Her major role was in Shukshin's Kalina Krasnaia, 1974.

Fedotov, Georgii Petrovich (Bogdanov, E.)
1.10.1886–1.9.1951. Philosopher, sociologist, historian.
Born in Saratov. Son of a Tsarist police officer. Member of the SD Party, had to flee abroad due to involvement in revolutionary activity. Studied in Germany 1906–08. Returned to Russia illegally, legalized his position at the beginning of WWI. Graduated from Petersburg University, later taught history in Petersburg and Saratov universities. Emigrated from the Soviet Union. 1925. Moved to France and lectured at the St. Sergius Theological Institute in Paris. Edited the philosophical magazine Novyi Grad, 1931–40. Almost alone of the generation which, starting with radical left-wing views, moved to Orthodoxy, kept a general left-wing approach, which made him popular among like-minded intellectuals. During WWII, after a most adventurous sea voyage, reached the USA with a shipload of refugees from France, 1943. Became professor at the St. Vladimir seminary in New York, 1946. Died in New York.
Main works: St Philipp; Saints of Old Russia; The Russian Religious Mind, 2 vols (in English); The Treasure of Russian Spirituality; Novyi Grad; The Face of Russia.

Fefelov, Valerii Andreevich
1949–   . Disabled worker, human rights campaigner.
Born in Iuriev-Polskii. Became disabled after an accident at work, and was thus closely acquainted with the plight of invalids in the Soviet Union. Became involved in defending the rights of the disabled. Founded a

group with this aim, 1978. After constant harassment by the KGB and confiscation of the documents he had collected, emigrated in 1982. Settled in West Germany where he continues his human rights activity. Wrote a book, published in the West, about the life of invalids in the Soviet Union.

Fefer, Itsik (Isaak Solomonovich)
23.9.1900–1952. Poet.
Born in Shpola in the Ukraine. Son of a teacher. Joined the Communist Party and the Red Army, 1919. Wrote verse in Yiddish, praising the victory of the revolution during the Civil War and in the 1930s. Arrested, 1948, and probably shot. Posthumously rehabilitated.

Feierman, Emanuel' (Feuermann)
22.11.1902–25.5.1942. Cellist.
Born in Kolomyia, Galitsia. Pupil of A. Val'ter, and Iu. Klengel'. Member of a trio whose other members were A. Shnabel' and B. Guberman. Emigrated to the USA and settled in New York. Several tours in the USSR in the 1930s. Died in New York.

Feigin, Leo
1932–   . Music journalist, promoter of Soviet jazz.
Emigrated from the Soviet Union, 1973. Settled in London, 1974. Involved in the jazz programmes broadcast by the BBC Russian Service. In 1980 formed the record company, Leo Records. Issued many records by Soviet jazzmen, including the Ganelin Trio and the pianist, Sergei Kurekhin. Impresario and ardent promoter of Soviet jazz musicians. Also a writer on the subject.

Feigin, Leonid (Lazar') Veni-aminovich
6.3.1923–   . Violinist, composer.
Born in Bobruisk. Moved to Moscow. Graduated from the Moscow Conservatory. Made several tours abroad, and many concert appearances in Moscow and Leningrad. Author of an opera, ballets, suites, and music for films, theatre, and musicals.

Feinberg, Samuil Evgen'evich
26.5.1890–22.10.1962. Composer, pianist.
Born in Odessa. Graduated from the Moscow Conservatory, and later became a professor there. Trained a generation of pianists. Wrote 3 concertos, pieces for piano and organ, and songs. Wrote a book on the art of piano playing, published after his death, *Pianizm Kak Iskusstvo,* Moscow, 1965.

Fel'dman, Grigorii Petrovich
27.2.1910–5.10.1963. Composer.
Born in Kremenchug, in the Ukraine. Author of symphonic suites, chamber music, pieces for piano, and songs based on Jewish folk motives. Died in Moscow.

Fel'dman, Zinovii Petrovich
1893–9.4.1942. Composer.
Born in Berdichev, in the Ukraine. Brother of Grigorii Fel'dman. Composer of military music. Author of the *Jewish March (Evreiskii Marsh).* Received 6 prizes at the Competition of Military Marches in Moscow in 1940. Died in Moscow.

Feldt, Pavel Emil'evich
21.2.1905–1.7.1960. Composer, conductor.
Born in Petersburg. Graduated from the Leningrad Conservatory, 1930. From 1929, first violinist. Conductor at the Leningrad Malyi Theatre, 1934–41. From 1941, conductor with the Kirov Theatre. Wrote the music for several ballets, including *Fadetta,* and *Katerina,* 1936. Died in Leningrad.

Felshtinskii, Iurii Georgievich
1956– . Historian.
Born in Moscow. Studied history at the Moscow Teacher's Institute. Emigrated to the USA, 1978. Continued his historical studies in America. Graduated from Brandeis University. Wrote and published in the West studies on many modern historical subjects, especially on the fate of the socialist parties after the Bolshevik take-over and other early problems of communist rule in Russia. Author of *K Istorii Nashei Zakrytosti,* London, 1988.

Fel'tsman, Oskar Borisovich
18.2.1921– . Composer.
Born in Odessa. Author of 8 operettas. Also wrote music for circus, cinema, plays, and radio and television.

Fenster, Boris Aleksandrovich
30.4.1916–29.12.1960. Choreographer.
Born in Petrograd. Graduated from the Leningrad Choreographic School, 1936, and from the choreographers' courses attached to the school, 1940. Pupil of F. Lopukhov. Dancer from 1936. At the Leningrad Malyi Theatre as Assistant Artistic Director, 1944–45, Artistic Director, 1945–53, and Chief Choreographer, 1953–56. Choreographer with the Kirov Theatre, 1956–59. Taught at the Leningrad Conservatory, 1949–50. State (Stalin) Prize, 1948, 1950. Died in Leningrad.

Feodor, schema-hieromonk
1865?–1942. Russian Orthodox clergyman.
Monk at the most famous monastery in Northern Russia, Valaam, on the Ladoga Lake. Evacuated with the monastery to Finland before the advancing Red Army, 1940. One of the founders of New Valaam in Eastern Finland. Representative of the hesychaste movement. Died and buried at New Valaam.

Feodora (Pilipchuk, Nadezhda Vladimirovna), Hegumenia
27.12.1953– . Russian Orthodox nun.
Born in Belousha, Brest Oblast'. Moved to Moscow, 1976. Settled in Zagorsk, worked in the library of the Moscow Theological Academy. Nun, 1980. Soon thereafter sent with a group of nuns to the Holy Land. Appointed mother superior of the Convent of the Moscow Patriarchate in Jerusalem, from Nov. 1983.

Ferdman, David Lazarevich
7.1.1903– . Biochemist.
Graduated from Khar'kov University, 1925. Worked at the Biochemistry Institute of the Ukrainian Academy of Sciences, 1928. Professor at Kiev University, 1944.

Specialist on the biochemistry of muscles.

Feriabnikova, Nelli Vasil'evna (b. Bil'maier)
14.5.1949– . Athlete.
Born in Vorkuta in the Komi ASSR. Probably of Gulag parents. Honoured Master of Sports (basketball), 1971. With Moscow Oblast' Spartak. European champion, 1970–78. World champion, 1971, 1975. Olympic champion, 1976. Graduated from the Moscow Technological Institute, 1976. USSR champion, 1978.

Fersman, Aleksandr Evgen'evich
1883–1954. Geologist, academician.
Born in Leningrad. Educated at the universities of Odessa, Moscow, Paris and Heidelberg. Member of the USSR Academy of Sciences from 1919. Taught at Moscow and Leningrad universities. His tutor was the academician Vladimir Vernadskii. Worked with Vernadskii in mineralogy and geochemistry. Made a serious contribution to the study of mineral deposits such as apatites in the Kola Peninsula, and radium ores in Fergana in Soviet Central Asia. Wrote the 4-vol. *Geokhimiia,* Moscow, 1933–39. Honorary member of the Mineralogical and Geological Societies of London. Member of the Geological Society of America.

Fesenkov, Vasilii Grigor'evich
13.1.1889–1975? Astrophysicist.
Graduated from Khar'kov University, 1911. Studied the physics of planets, meteors, the sun, the evolution of stars, and the structure of space nebulae.

Fesin, Ivan Ivanovich
1904– . Major-general.
Joined the Red Army, 1926, and the Bolshevik Party, 1929. Graduated from Frunze Military Academy, 1941. Served in NKVD forces from 1930. Took part in WWII. Professor at the Academy of the General Staff, 1950–65.

Figner, Medea Ivanovna (b. Mei)
4.4.1859–8.7.1952. Singer (mezzo-soprano).
Born in Florence of Italian parents.

Wife of Nikolai Figner. Pupil of H. Panofka. Soloist at the Mariinskii Theatre, 1887–1912. Appeared also as a concert singer, later taught. Moved to Paris, 1930, where she died. Memoirs: *Moi Vospominaniia*, St. Petersburg, 1912.

Figner, Nikolai Nikolaevich
21.2.1857–13.12.1918. Singer.
Born in the village of Nikiforovka, Kazan' Gouvt. Brother of Vera Figner. Pupil of I. Prianishnikov. On tour all over Europe, and later in America, 1882–87. Soloist at the Mariinskii Theatre, 1887–07. Director of the Opera Studio of the People's House, Petersburg, 1910–15. Died in Kiev.

Figner, Vera Nikolaevna
1852–1942. Revolutionary.
Born in Kazan, daughter of a wealthy nobleman. Became involved in revolutionary activity after becoming acquainted with revolutionary students while studying at Zurich University. Member of the Cen. Cttee. of Narodnaia Volia, 1879. After the assassination of Aleksander II and the arrest of practically the whole leadership of Narodnaia Volia, almost single-handedly lead the remnants of the organization under most difficult conditions. Arrested, Feb. 1883, sentenced to death, sentence commuted to life imprisonment. Spent 20 years in solitary confinement in Shlusselburg Fortress. Sent into exile in 1904 (Arkhangelsk, Kazan, Nizhnii-Novgorod). Revered as a legendary figure of the revolutionary heroic period. Released after the 1905 Revolution. Travelled around the world, 1906–15, giving lectures, gathering funds and describing the life of political prisoners under Tsarism. Returned to Russia in 1915. After the October Revolution 1917, retired from political activity. Honorary President of the Political Red Cross (headed by E. Peshkova, Gorkii's first wife, helping mostly old revolutionaries in trouble with the Soviet authorities). Wrote memoirs. According to former Soviet journalist M. Popovskii, protested in a letter to Stalin about the falsification of the Narodnik record in Soviet books, and about the abuse of power by communist authorities. The letter was not published and is presumably held in the Lenin Library in the special department inaccessible to the general public. In old age, lived in a special home for old revolutionaries.

Fikhtengolts, Mikhail Izrailevich
1.6.1920– . Violinist.
Born in Odessa. Pupil of P. Stoliarskii, A. Iampol'skii and M. Poliakin. 2nd prize at the All-Union Competition of Musicians-Soloists, 1935, Moscow. 6th prize at the Ysaye International Violinists Competition, Brussels, 1937. Taught at the Gnesin Music-Pedagogical Institute. Writes music for violin and is also author of many music articles. Lives in Moscow.

Filaret (Philaret, Voznessenskii, Georgii Nikolaevich), Metropolitan of New York and Eastern America
1903–1985. Russian Orthodox church leader.
Born in Kursk. Son of a priest. During the Civil War joined his father who was evacuated with the Whites, in Harbin, 1920. Graduated from the Harbin Polytechnical Institute, then from the Harbin Theological Institute, where he later became a lecturer. During the Japanese occupation of Manchuria and later under Chinese communist rule, gained high moral authority among the local Russian population by his fearless defence of the faith. Expelled by the Chinese communist authorities, 1957, and moved to Australia. Orthodox Bishop of Brisbane, 1963. Elected Head of the Russian Church in Exile with the title of Metropolitan of New York and Eastern America, 31 May 1964. Remained head of the Church until his death. The main event of his rule was the canonization of the new Russian martyrs of the 20th century, a move which was considered very bold and controversial, but which found widespread acceptance among Orthodox believers in the Soviet Union itself.

Filatov, Iurii Nikolaevich
30.7.1948– . Athlete.
Born in Khmel'nitskaia Oblast' in the Ukraine. Honoured Master of Sports (rowing), 1970. Graduated from Kiev Institute of Physical Culture, 1972. Member of the CPSU, 1972. USSR champion, 1969–72, 1976. Olympic champion, 1972, 1976. With the Kiev Armed Forces Club from 1974. World champion, 1970–71.

Filatov, Nikolai Mikhailovich
1862–1935. Ballistics expert.
Graduated from the Mikhailovskoe Artillery School, 1887. Head of a military school, 1915. Lt.-general, 1917. Joined the Red Army, 1918. Head of the Vystrel Courses of the Red Army, 1918. Published works on the theory of ballistics.

Filatov, Petr Mikhailovich
1893–1941. Lt.-general.
Joined the Red Army, 1918. Commander of a regiment during the Civil War. Graduated from the Frunze Military Academy, 1935. Army commander at the start of WWII. Fell in action.

Filatov, Sergei Ivanovich
25.9.1926– . Athlete.
Born in Tambovskaia Oblast'. With the Moscow Armed Forces Club. Member of the CPSU, 1946. Graduated from the Higher Cavalry School, 1951. USSR champion, 1954, 1957–63. Olympic bronze-medallist 1960. Honoured Master of Sports (riding), 1960.

Filatov, Vladimir Petrovich
1875–1956. Ophthalmologist, surgeon.
Famous eye specialist. Taught at Odessa and Moscow universities. Pioneered the transplantation of the cornea and tissue therapy. An eye clinic in Moscow bears his name. Created the Soviet school of ophthalmologists.

Filatova, Maria Evgen'evna
19.7.1961– . Athlete.
Born in Kemerovskaia Oblast'. Olympic champion, 1976. Honoured Master of Sports (gymnastics), 1977. With Leninsk-Kuznetskii Burevestnik. Absolute champion of the USSR, 1977. European champion, 1977. World champion, 1978.

Filchenkov, Nikolai Dmitrievich
1907–1941. Political officer.
Joined the Bolshevik Party, 1930. According to official information, in a battle near Sevastopol in Nov. 1941, girded himself with grenades and threw himself under a German tank. Posthumously awarded the title Hero of the Soviet Union, 1942. Used to bolster the prestige of political officers in the Red Army during WWII.

Filipchenko, Anatolii Vasil'evich
1928–   . Cosmonaut.
Joined the Red Army, 1947. Graduated from the Zhukovskii Air Force Academy, 1961. Space flights, 1969 (Soiuz 7), and 1974 (Soiuz 16). After each of the flights, awarded the title Hero of the Soviet Union. Major-general, 1978.

Filippov, Boris Andreevich
1905–   . Author, poet, editor.
Son of an officer of the Imperial Army. Hid his class origins in order to get higher education in the Soviet Union. Studied at Leningrad University. Arrested, 1927, 1929 and 1936. Sentenced to 5 years in the Gulag. After release, lived in Novgorod. Moved to Germany during WWII. In DP camps in West Germany, 1945–50. Moved to the USA, 1950. Taught at several American universities, published volumes of essays, short stories and verse, and many articles in Russian emigré publications. As an editor, with Gleb Struve, and his wife, E. V. Zhiglevich, prepared very valuable first editions of collected works of Russian modern classics, which were unavailable at that time in the Soviet Union (Akhmatova, Zabolotskii, Gumilev, Kliuev, Voloshin, Mandelshtam, Rozanov and others).

Filippovskii, Nikolai Nikolaevich
9.4.1906–   . Ballet dancer.
Born in Petersburg. Graduated from the Leningrad Choreographic School, 1928. Pupil of V. Ponomarev. In 1929, toured with I. F. Kshessinskii around the USSR. With the Tbilisi Theatre, 1930. From 1931, with the Leningrad Malyi Theatre. Soloist. Taught from the late 1930s.

Filonenko, Maksimilian Maksimilianovich
1880?–1947? Lawyer, politician.
Became prominent in the summer of 1917 during the Kerenskii-Kornilov controversy (representing Kerenskii). Emigrated after the fall of the Provisional Government. Became a successful lawyer in Paris. Defended Plevitskaia during her trial after the kidnapping of General Miller, 1938. After WWII, became an active member of the Society of Soviet Patriots. Probably returned to the USSR.

Filonov, Pavel Nikolaevich
1883–1941. Artist.
Born in Moscow. Moved to Petersburg. Educated at the Petersburg Academy of Arts. From 1910, recognized as one of the most original artists of the Russian avant-garde. Throughout the 1920–30s taught and exhibited in Leningrad. Founder of the so-called Collective of Masters of Analytical Art. From 1932, persecuted and ostracized by the Soviet cultural authorities. Died at the beginning of the Siege of Leningrad. In June 1988, his first posthumous exhibition was opened in Leningrad.
Source: Nicoletta Misler and John E. Bowlt, *Pavel Filonov: A Hero and His Fate, Collective Writings on Art and Revolution, 1914–40*, USA 1985.

Filosofov, Dmitrii Vladimirovich
26.3.1872–1940. Literary critic, philosopher, journalist.
Born in Petersburg. Graduated in law from Petersburg University, 1895. Leading literary critic with the journal *Mir Iskusstva*. Close collaborator and personal friend of Merezhkovskii and Gippius. Editor of the philosophical journal *Novyi Put'*, 1904. After the Bolshevik takeover, emigrated with the Merezhkovskiis to Poland. While they moved on to France, he remained in Warsaw, editing anti-Bolshevik Russian newspapers. Died in Otwock near Warsaw.

Finagin, Aleksei Vasil'evich
16.3.1890–4.2.1942. Musicologist.
Born in Petersburg. Worked at the Leningrad State Institute of the History of Arts, and became Scientific Secretary of the same Institute, 1926–29. Author of *Russkaia Narodnaia Pesnia*, 1923. Major contributor to *De Musica*, 1923. Died during the Siege of Leningrad.

Findeizen, Nikolai Fedorovich
23.7.1868–20.9.1928. Musicologist, music editor.
Born in Petersburg. Founder, publisher and editor of *Russkaia Muzykal'naia Gazeta*, 1894–1918, and *Muzykal'naia Starina*, issues 1–6, Petersburg, 1903–11. Author of many books including biographies of Verstovskii, Dargomyzhskii, Grieg, and Glinka. Also wrote *Muzyka v Norvegii*, Petersburg, 1909?, and *Ocherki Po Istorii Muzyki v Rossii*, Moscow, 1928–29. Renowned music scholar. Died in Leningrad.

Finogenov, Pavel Vasil'evich
1919–   . Politican
Engineer at an armaments factory, 1941. Graduated from the Leningrad Military Mechanical Institute (correspondence courses), 1953. Deputy chairman of Vladimir Sovnarkhoz, 1960–63. Deputy Minister of the Armaments Industry, 1965–1979, and Minister, Jan, 1979. Member of the Cen. Cttee. of the CPSU, 1981.

Firsov, Anatolii Vasil'evich
1.2.1941–   . Athlete.
Born in Moscow. Honoured Master of Sports (hockey), 1964. With the Central Sports Club of the Army. USSR champion, 1963–73. European champion, 1964–70. World champion, 1964–71. Olympic champion, 1964, 1968, 1972. Regarded as the best forward at the 1968 Olympic championship, and the 1967 and 1971 world championships. Member of the CPSU, 1968. Graduated from the Moscow Institute of Physical Culture, 1977. Became a legendary athlete. His professional life is well documented in the Soviet press.

Flerov, Georgii Nikolaevich
2.3.1913–   . Physicist, academician.
Graduated from the Leningrad Industrial Institute in 1938. Worked

at the Physico-Technical Institute of the USSR Academy of Sciences, 1938–44. Member of the CPSU from 1955. Worked in various scientific institutes of the Academy of Sciences until 1960. Director of the Laboratory of the United Institute of Nuclear Research from 1960. Member of the USSR Academy of Sciences. Head of the Institute of Nuclear Research in Dubna and the Institute of Crystallography which, together with the Virology Institute, is involved in research to improve a method of trapping and diagnosing the Aids virus, based on a plastic nuclear filter developed by Soviet researchers.

Flerov, Ivan Andreevich
1905–1941. Captain.
Joined the Red Army, 1927. Took part in the Soviet-Finnish war, 1939–40. Studied at the Dzerzhinskii Artillery Academy, 1941. Artillery officer during WWII, first commander of the new rocket artillery battery (Soviet nickname 'Katiusha', German nickname 'Stalinorgel'), which later played a very important role in the Soviet victory. Killed in action near Orsha.

Flier, Iakov Vladimirovich
21.10.1912– . Pianist.
Born in Orekhovo-Zuevo. Pupil of K. Igumnov. Professor at the Moscow Conservatory. 1st prize at the All-Union Competition of Musicians-Soloists, Moscow, 1935, and at the International Competition of Pianists, Vienna, 1936. Many solo concerts in Moscow, Leningrad, and abroad. Trained a generation of pianists, including Bella Davidovich.

Florenskii, Pavel Aleksandrovich
1882–1943. Orthodox priest, theologian, philosopher, scientist.
Son of a railway engineer. Educated at Tiflis High School. Graduated from Moscow University as a mathematician. A pupil of Bugaev, Andrei Belyi's father. Graduated from Moscow Theological Academy, 1908. Orthodox priest, 1911. Became a professor of philosophy at the Theological Academy. His dissertation, 'Stolp i Utverzhdenie Istiny', 1914, gave him the reputation of one of the most interesting religious thinkers of

his time. Known for his 'superhuman erudition', according to N. Losskii, and described by V. Rozanov as the Russian Pascal. Continued his scientific studies with the same energy. One of the main authors of the *Soviet Technical Encyclopaedia* (1927–36). Used to appear in his priest's cassock at specialist conferences of the Institutes of the Soviet Academy of Sciences, scandalizing the new Soviet elite. Arrested in 1928, exiled to Nizhnii-Novgorod (now Gorkii), but soon released. Re-arrested in 1933, and spent the rest of his life in different camps in the Gulag, including the notorious Solovki camp. Died in one of those camps, killed by a falling tree.
Source: N. Zernov, *Russkoe Religioznoe Vozrozhdenie XX Veka,* Paris, 1974.

Florensov, Nikolai Aleksandrovich
1909– . Geologist.
Graduated from Irkutsk University, 1936. Worked in the local geological administration, 1945–47. Professor at Irkutsk University, 1956–59. Specialist in the field of tectonics and neotectonics, especially with regard to Eastern Siberia.

Florovskii, Antonii Vasil'evich
1890–27.3.1968. Historian.
Brother of the famous theologian, Georgii Florovskii. Emigrated after the 1917 Revolution. Settled in Czechoslovakia. Professor of Russian History at Prague University, chairman of the Russian Historical Society in Prague. Among his works are the 2 vol. *Chekhi i Vostochnye Slaviane.* Also carried out research into the time of Peter the Great.

Florovskii, Georgii Vasil'evich
23.8.1893– . Archpriest, church historian, theologian.
Born in Odessa. Graduated from Novorossiisk University in 1916. Emigrated during the Civil War. Lived in Prague. In the early 1920s was close to the Eurasian movement, distancing himself from it later. Professor of patrology at the Paris Theological Institute, 1926–39. Gained a worldwide reputation as a scholar of patristics. Professor, later Dean of the St. Vladimir Theological

seminary in New York, 1939–55. Professor of Harvard and Princeton Universities. Active participant in the oecumenical movement, where he represented the orthodox tradition. Widely respected for his scholarship and erudition.
Main works: *Oriental Fathers of the Church of the IV Century; Byzantine Fathers of the V–VIII Centuries; The Ways of Russian Theology, Christianity and Culture.*

Fogel', Boris Aleksandrovich
1872–1928? Artist.
Landscape painter. Studied at the Petersburg Academy of Arts, 1898–1902, and with the artist P. Kovalevskii. Exhibited from 1894. Exhibitions: MOLKH 1894–95, 1903–04, the New Society of Artists 1904–05, 1910, 1912–13, MTKH 1911, Exhibition of the Peoples of the USSR 1917–27, Moscow.

Fogel', Vladimir Petrovich
1902–8.6.1929. Actor.
Lived a short but very active life as a comedy actor. Graduated from the State Film School. Pupil of Lev Kuleshov. Worked with A. Khokhlova, V. Pudovkin and B. Barnet. Showed a remarkable talent in: *Neobychainye Prikliucheniia Mistera Vesta v Strane Bolshevikov,* 1924; *Luch Smerti,* 1925; *Shakhmatnaia Goriachka,* 1925; *Protsess o Trekh Millionakh,* and *Miss Mend,* both in 1926; *Tret'ia Meshchanskaia,* 1927; *Kukla s Millionami,* 1928. His major work was *Po Zakonu,* 1926. Other films include *Devushka s Korobkoi,* and *Dom Na Trubnoi.*

Fok, Vladimir Aleksandrovich (Fock)
22.12.1898–1979? Scientist.
Graduated from Petrograd University, 1922. Professor at Leningrad University, 1932. Academician, 1939. Research in quantum mechanics, theory of relativity, mathematics and mathematical physics.

Fokin, Mikhail Mikhailovich (Fokine, Michel)
5.5.1880–22.8.1942. Ballet dancer, choreographer.
Born in Petersburg. Graduated from

the Petersburg Theatre School, 1898. Pupil of N. Legat, P. Karsavin and P. Gerdt. Debut, 1898, at the Mariinskii Theatre. First ballet production, 1905 *(Atsis i Galateia)*. Worked closely with A. Benois, L. Bakst, N. Roerikh, A. Golovin, M. Dobuzhinskii, N. Goncharova and I. Stravinskii. He was a daring experimenter, adopting music which had never previously been used for ballet. In 1909–12 and 1914, chief choreographer of Diaghilev's Ballets Russes. Taught at the Petersburg Theatre School, 1901–11. Among his pupils were E. Gerdt, L. Lopukhova and P. Vladimirov. In 1918, went to work in Sweden. From 1921, worked in the USA. With the Paris Opera, 1933–34, and the Ballet Russe de Monte Carlo, 1936–39. Directed a ballet studio in New York from 1923 until his death.
See: C. Beaumont, *Michel Fokine and his Ballets*, London, 1935; I. Ivanov, *M. Fokin*, Petrograd, 1923.

Fokina, Vera Petrovna (Antonova)
3.8.1886–29.7.1958. Ballerina.
Born in Petersburg. Wife of Mikhail Fokin. Graduated from the Petersburg Theatre School, 1904. Pupil of K. Kulichevskaia. With the Mariinskii Theatre until 1918. Soloist. Took part in Russian Seasons abroad, 1909–12, and 1914. Toured Sweden with her husband. From 1921, lived in the USA. From 1923, taught at her husband's ballet studio in New York. Died in New York.

Fomichev, Mikhail Georgievich
1911– . Lt.-general.
Joined the Red Army, 1933, and the Bolshevik Party, 1939. Graduated from the Tank Forces Academy, 1941. Successful tank brigade commander during WWII (capture of Lvov, storming of Berlin, capture of Prague). Twice Hero of the Soviet Union. Graduated from the Academy of the General Staff, 1948. General Inspector of the Ministry of Defence, 1969–72.

Fomin, Nikolai Petrovich
1864–1943. Pianist, composer.
Born in Petersburg. Professor at the Petersburg/Leningrad Conservatory. Specialized in Russian instrumental music. With V. Andreev, perfected folk instruments such as the domra, balalaika and gusli. Wrote music for folk orchestras. Died during the Siege of Leningrad.

Fomin, Nikolai Sergeevich
1895–1980? Colonel-general.
Graduated from an artillery school, 1917. Joined the Red Army, 1919. Artillery officer during the Civil War. Joined the Bolshevik Party, 1937. Graduated from the Frunze Military Academy, 1941. Several artillery commands during WWII. Head of military training in artillery after WWII. Deputy Commander of Soviet Artillery, 1949. Professor at the Academy of the General Staff, 1956–64.

Fominykh, Liubov' Nikolaevna
20.8.1952– . Ballerina.
Born in Kurgan. Graduated from the Perm' Choreographic School, 1970. Joined the Perm' Theatre. First prize at the Moscow All-Union Competition of Ballet Dancers, 1976. Moved to Moscow. With the Bolshoi Theatre. Toured abroad in the late 1970s.

Fondaminskii, Il'ia Isidorovich (Bunakov)
1897–1943. Politician, journalist.
Member of an SR terrorist group. Close friend of Gippius and Merezhkovskii. Well-known member of intellectual circles before WWI. After the February Revolution 1917, Commissar of the Black Sea Navy. Emigrated after the Civil War. One of the editors of the Paris magazine, *Sovremennye Zapiski* in the 1920s and 1930s. After the German occupation of Paris, deported to a Nazi concentration camp, where he died.

Fonvizin, Artur Vladimirovich
1882–1963. Artist.
Portrait, landscape, water-colour painter and book illustrator. Studied at the Moscow School of Painting, Sculpture and Architecture, 1901–04, then at a private academy in Munich, 1904–06. Exhibitions: The Blue Rose, 1907; The Zolotoe Runo, 1908–09; The Mir Iskusstva, 1913; The Makovets, 1922,

1925; Russian Drawing For Ten Years, Moscow, 1927. Other exhibitions: Leningrad, 1932, Moscow, 1934, 1936, 1945, 1947, 1957, 1961. Personal exhibitions: Moscow, 1936, 1955.

Forshteter, Mikhail Adolfovich
1893–21.7.1959. Poet.
Born in Moscow. Graduated from Moscow University, 1917. In the Caucasus during the 1917 Revolution. Emigrated through the Ukraine to Czechoslovakia. Settled in Prague. Later moved to France. As a poet, continued the traditions of I. Annenskii. Also wrote literary criticism. Died in France.

Fotiadi, Epaminond Epaminondovich
23.1.1907– . Geophysicist.
Graduated from Leningrad University, 1933. Specialist in geophysical methods of oil prospecting. Wrote manuals for gravimetric and topogeodesic work.

Frank, Il'ia Mikhailovich
23.10.1908– . Scientist.
Graduated from Moscow University, 1930. Professor at Moscow University, 1944. Research in physical optics and nuclear physics. Nobel prizewinner, 1958.

Frank, Semen Ludvigovich
16.1.1877–10.12.1950. Philosopher.
Born in Moscow in a family with old rabbinical heritage. Studied at Moscow University, expelled for distributing Marxist propaganda in 1899. Continued his education at Berlin University. Returned to Russia and graduated from Kazan University, 1901. Together with P. Struve (a lifelong friend) was one of the initiators of 'Legal Marxism'. Later evolved towards liberalism and spiritual and religious approach to life. One of the main authors of *Vekhi* (Signposts), criticizing the shallow radicalism of the Russian intelligentsia, 1909. Converted to Russian Orthodoxy, 1912. Became widely-known as one of the most profound philosophers in Russia (of the traditional, academic type). According to himself, the main influence on his thought was the late Renaissance German philosopher,

Cardinal Nicholas Cusanus. After the October Revolution 1917, moved to Saratov, becoming Dean of Saratov University, 1917–22. Expelled by the communist authorities (with a large group of intelligentsia) in 1922. Lived in Berlin until 1939, when, in order to escape from Hitler, he moved to France. During WWII, spent several years in hiding in Vichy France. Moved to London, 1945, where he spent the last years of his life. A quiet and contemplative spirit, engrossed in purely philosophical problems, he was again and again confronted with all the evils and difficulties of the 20th century, which gave him very unusual and profound insights.

Main works: *Religion and Science, The Collapse of the Idols, The Basis of Marxism, The Spiritual Foundation of Society, La Connaissance et l'Etre, The Unfathomable, Light and Darkness.*

Frelikh, Oleg Nikolaevich
24.3.1887–1953. Actor, director.
Entered the film industry in the 1920s. Worked as a director but is better known as an actor. Always played the part of an elegant good-looking crook, a sort of cad from an aristocratic background. From 1943–51 worked at the Moscow Komsomol Theatre.

Frenkel, Naftalii Aronovich
1890?–1961? State security official.
Born in Constantinople. Businessman before WWI, and later of the NEP period. Arrested, inmate of the Solovki concentration camp, 1927. Became an adviser of the camp administration and soon one of its most important administrators. Organized the economic side of camp life with the utmost level of exploitation of the prisoners, which was gradually extended to the whole Gulag system. Practically became the economic boss of the Gulag. In his old age, lived as a retired MVD Lt-general in Moscow, refusing to see or talk to anyone. Accorded an official military funeral, cremated in the cemetery of the Donskoi monastery. (See: *Kontinent* Nr. 23, 1980.)

Frenkin, Mikhail Samoilovich
1910–1986. Historian.
Born in Baku. Graduated in history from the Leningrad Teachers' Institute. Arrested in the early 1930s, and spent one year in prison. Re-arrested in 1939. Spent 18 years in the Gulag. Released, 1958. Worked at the Moscow History and Archives Institute. His studies on subjects connected with early Soviet history have been published in the West.

Frents, Rudolf Rudolfovich
1888–1956. Artist.
Battle painter. Pupil of N. S. Samokish. Studied at the Petersburg Academy of Arts, 1912-18. Exhibitions: Academy of Arts, 1917; the Association of Artists of Revolutionary Russia, Moscow, 1924; Artists of the RSFSR, 15 Years, Leningrad, 1932–Moscow, 1933; Moscow, 1933, 1938, 1939, 1947–51. Posthumously: Moscow, 1958. Personal exhibitions: Leningrad, 1925 and 1928.

Fridliand, Semen Osipovich
1905–1964. Photographer.
Born in Kiev, the son of a shoemaker. From the age of 14, had to work in a shoemaker's workshop. His cousin, Mikhail Koltsov, who was appointed editor-in-chief of the first Soviet illustrated magazine, *Ogonek*, in 1923, invited him to Moscow to train as a photographer. Taken on as a laboratory assistant. Began to take photographs in 1925, and a year later took part in a Soviet photographic exhibition, receiving 2 awards, one for dynamic composition and the other for excellent printing. At the 1928 exhibition, *Ten Years of Soviet Photography*, already recognized as one of the 6 best photo-reporters in the USSR, and won the first prize. In 1930, was taken on by the Unionfoto agency (later Soiuzfoto), where he worked as a picture editor, reporter and department head until 1932. At the same time, studied at the State Institute for Cinematography (VGIK). Graduated in 1932 as a cameraman but remained a photojournalist all his life. From 1932 until his death, worked for *Pravda* and for the magazines *USSR in Construction* and *Ogonek* as head of the picture desk. Under his supervision such big names as G. Koposov and Lev

Sherstennikov were trained. Frequently contributed articles to photographic magazines. As department head of *Ogonek*, laid the foundations for planning photographic information in Soviet illustrated periodicals. Died in Moscow.
Source: *Soviet Photography, 1917–40*, London, 1984.

Fried, Oscar
10.8.1871–5.7.1941. Conductor, composer.
Born in Berlin. Visited Russia for the first time in 1905. Guest conductor. First foreign conductor to be asked by the Soviet Government to perform in Soviet Russia, 1921. Moved to the USSR, 1934. Gave up his German nationality and took Soviet citizenship. Author of pieces for orchestra, and songs. His memoirs, *Zametki Dirizhera*, Moscow, 1953, were published in *Sovetskaia Muzyka*.

Frolov, Aleksandr Sergeevich
1902–1952. Vice-admiral.
Joined the Red Army, 1918, the Red Navy, 1922, and the Bolshevik Party, 1929. Commander of submarine forces during WWII. Graduated from the Academy of the General Staff, 1951. Professor at the same academy, 1951–52.

Frolov, Valer'ian Aleksandrovich
1895–1961. Colonel-general.
Took part in WWI. Joined the Red Army, 1918. Graduated from the Frunze Military Academy, 1932. Took part in the Soviet-Finnish war, 1939–40. During WWII, commander in the North at the Karelian front. After WWII, continued his career as commander in the North, 1948–56, in the White Sea and Arkhangelsk military districts.

Frolov, Vasilii
1895–1936?. Worker, politician.
Worker on the Moscow trams. Early involvement in revolutionary activity. Joined the Mensheviks. Remained as one of the last Mensheviks, a member of the Mossoviet (until 1921 or 1922). Arrested, 1923. Sentenced to 3 years in the Solovki concentration camps. Left Solovki in 1925 to spend one year in Tobolsk

prison. In Siberian exile from 1926. Victim of the Gulag, place and time of death unknown.

Froman, Margarita Petrovna
8.11.1890–24.3.1970. Ballerina, teacher.
Born in Moscow. Graduated from the Moscow Theatre School, 1909. With the Bolshoi Theatre until 1921. Emigrated to Yugoslavia. Soloist, then choreographer at the National Theatre, Zagreb, where, with her brother Max Froman, she organized a ballet school. In Belgrade, 1927–31. Returned to Zagreb. Emigrated to the USA in 1950. Taught ballet at various studios. Died in Boston.

Frumkin, Aleksandr Naumovich
24.10.1895–1971? Scientist.
Graduated from Odessa University, 1915. Professor at Odessa University, 1920–22. Researcher at the Physico-Chemical Institute in Moscow, 1922–46. Guest lecturer at Wisconsin University, 1928–29. Professor at Moscow University, 1930. Academician, 1932. Carried out research into electrochemical reactions.

Frunze, Mikhail Vasil'evich (cover names – Trifonych, Arsenii)
2.2.1885–31.10.1925. Revolutionary, military commander.
Born in Pishpek (now Frunze, capital of the Kirghiz Soviet Socialist Republic). Son of a Moldavian assistant army surgeon. Grew up in Vernii (now Alma-Ata). As a student at the Petersburg Polytechnic, joined the Bolsheviks, and was sent to organize workers in the textile industry near Moscow, 1904. Leader of large strikes during the 1905 Revolution (Ivanovo-Voznesensk, Shuia). Imprisoned, 1909–10, and exiled, 1910–16. Escaped, 1916. Party agitator among troops during WWI. After the February Revolution 1917, returned to Ivanovo-Voznesensk. One of the organizers of the Bolshevik take-over in Moscow during the October Revolution 1917. During the Civil War, gained fame as a talented organizer and commander (against Kolchak, 1918). Commanded the Red armies which conquered Central Asia, defeating the Emir of Bukhara. At the end of the Civil War, in charge

of the military campaign against Wrangel in the Crimea. Telegraphed Lenin on 16 Nov. 1920 reporting the victory and the end of the Civil War in the Crimea. Member of the Cen. Cttee. of the Bolshevik Party, 1921. Minister for Military and Naval Affairs and Chairman of the Revolutionary Military Council of the USSR, Jan. 1925. Wrote on military theory and strategy. Head of the Military Academy later renamed after him. Personally popular with the troops, aroused jealousy among party leaders. Died in Moscow under suspicious circumstances on the operating table (persistent rumours blamed this accident on Stalin's machinations). A fictionalized description of his death appeared in *Povest Nepogashennoi Luny* by Pilniak.

Fudel, Sergei Iosifovich (Udel, F.)
1901–1977. Philosopher, theologian. Son of a priest. Connected with many of the Christian philosophers before 1917. Arrested, 1921, inmate of the Gulag camps for many years. Released during the Khrushchev thaw. Lived near Vladimir. His articles on religious, historical and cultural subjects circulated in samizdat. His memoirs were published in Paris in late 1970s.

Furer, Samuil Isakievich
22.3.1909– . Violinist.
Born in Odessa. Pupil of P. Stoliarskii and L. Tseitlin. 3rd prize at the All-Union Competition of Musicians-Soloists, Moscow, 1933.

Furmanov, Dmitrii Andreevich
1891–1926. Author, political officer. On active service during WWI. Became a Bolshevik organizer. During the Civil War, as a political officer in the Red Army on the Eastern front, led the suppression of an anti-communist revolt in Vernii (now Alma-Ata). Later in the South, fought against the Whites at the Kuban' river. Secretary of the Moscow Association of Proletarian Writers, 1924–25. Became known for his novels about the Civil War, such as the classics of Soviet literature, *Chapaev* and *Revolt*. Created the image of Chapaev as a revolutionary

hero of the people (Furmanov was the political controller of Chapaev's detachment).

Furtseva, Ekaterina Alekseevna
1910–10.1974. Politician.
Born in Vyshnii Volochek near Tver'. Daughter of a worker. Started work in a textile factory. Active member of the Komsomol from 1924. Member of the Communist Party, 1930. High administrative posts in the Komsomol, 1930–37. Political work in several technical schools where she studied civil aviation and chemical technology. During WWII, Secretary of the Frunze Party raikom in Moscow. Second Secretary of the Moscow City Cttee. of the CPSU, 1950, 1st Secretary, 1954. Elected member of the Cen. Cttee. of the CPSU, 1956, appointed Secretary of the Cen. Cttee. by Khrushchev, to whom she was close. During Khrushchev's rule, autocratic Minister of Culture of the USSR. Lost importance after his removal.

G

Gabai, Il'ia Iankelevich
1935–1973. Dissident.
Born in Baku. Graduated from the Moscow Teachers' Institute. In the late 1960s and early 1970s, one of the best known activists of the human rights movement. Spent several years in concentration camps. Released, 1972. Committed suicide soon thereafter.

Gabel', Stanislav Ivanovich
7.5.1849–24.1.1924. Singer (bass).
Born on the Dudori estate, Kiev Gouvt. Pupil of K. Everardi. Taught at the Petersburg Conservatory from 1882, professor from 1886. Among his pupils were P. Andreev, A. Bonachich, I. Ershov, O. Kamionskii, and A. Sekar-Rozhanskii. Died in Petrograd. Author of a collection of songs, and textbooks on singing.

Gabovich, Mikhail Markovich
7.12.1905–12.7.1965. Ballet dancer, choreographer.
Born in the village of Velikie Guliaki,

Kiev Oblast'. Graduated from the Moscow Choreographic School. With the Bolshoi Theatre, 1924–52, and one of its leading dancers. From 1952, choreographer, also taught at the Moscow Choreographic School. V. Vasil'ev was among his many pupils. Dominated the ballet school development at the Bolshoi Theatre. Died in Moscow.

Gabriadze, Revaz Levanovich (Rezo)
29.6.1939– . Scriptwriter.
Important Georgian scriptwriter. Worked with every Georgian director of note.Born in Kutaissi,Georgia. Graduated from the Higher Scriptwriters' Courses held in Moscow. Previously correspondent on the *Youth of Georgia* newspaper. Scripts: *An Unusual Exhibition, Cheer Up!, Feola, The Pitcher, Serenade, Love, Dagger and Treason.*

Gabrielian, Avet Karpovich (Ter-Gabrielian)
19.4.1899– . Violinist.
Born in Rostov-on-Don. Pupil of N. Av'erino and L. Tseitlin. Head of the Komitas State Quartet from 1925. Lecturer at the Moscow Conservatory. Stalin Prize, 1946.

Gabrilovich, Osip Solomonovich (Gabrilowitsch)
7.2.1878–14.9.1936. Pianist, conductor.
Born in Petersburg. Pupil of V. Tolstov and T. Leshetitskii. Concerts all over Russia. Lived abroad from 1894, and in the USA from 1914. Directed the Detroit Symphony Orchestra from 1918. Promoted Russian music in America. Married to the singer Clara Clemens, daughter of the writer Mark Twain. Died in Detroit.
Source: C. Clemens, *My Husband, Gabrilowitsch*, NY, 1938.

Gachev, Dmitrii Ivanovich
29.1.1902–17.12.1945. Music and literary critic.
Born in the town of Bratsigovo, Bulgaria. Came to the USSR as a political refugee, 1926. Took Soviet citizenship. Arrested and sent to the Gulag, 1938. Rehabilitated after his death. Author of works on C. W. Glück, R. Wagner, D. Diderot, Stendhal, H. Heine, and R. Rolland. According to Soviet official information, died in Magadan camp, Siberia. His wife was Mirra Bruk, musicologist and lecturer at the Gnesin Pedagogical Institute for Music.

Gadzhibekov, Sultan Ismail ogly
8.5.1919–19.9.1971. Composer, conductor.
Born in Shusha (now Nagorno Karabakhskaia Oblast'). Graduated from the Baku Music School, 1939. Pupil of A. Kolpinskii. Graduated from the Conservatory in 1946. Pupil of B. Zeidman (composition) and N. Chumakov (musical theory). Influenced by his uncle, the Azerbaidzhan composer U. Gadzhibekov. For a year after graduation, guided by D. Shostakovich. While a student at the Conservatory, appeared as conductor of the orchestra of the Teatr Muzykalnoi Komedii, 1938–40. Directed the Azerbaidzhan Ensemble of the Magomaev Philharmonic Society. Artistic director of the Baku Philharmonic Orchestra, 1942–45. Director from 1947. Taught instrumentation at the Conservatory from 1948. Lecturer, 1957. Professor from 1965. Director from 1969. His compositions include songs, ballet music, symphonies, and pieces for strings. Died in Baku.

Gadzhibekov, Uzeir Abdul Gussein ogly
17.9.1885–23.11.1948. Composer, conductor.
Born in Agdzhabedi, now in Azerbaidzhan. Early musical training at the Teachers' Seminary in Gori, 1899–1904. Studied the violin, cello and wind instruments, sang in the choir, and took part in the orchestra. Began collecting folk tunes. In Baku, 1905. Composed operas and musical comedies, 1907–13. Joined the music classes of A. Il'inskii, Moscow, 1911. Pupil of N. Ladukhin and N. Sokolov. Entered Petersburg Conservatory, 1914. Pupil of V. Kalafati. After the establishment of Soviet power in Azerbaidzhan on 28 Apr. 1920 became a member of various Soviet organisations. Founded the first music school (later known as the Technical School for Music) in the Republic. Founder, performer and director of the Azerbaidzhan Conservatory. Directed many musical organisations, including Azerbaidzhan Radio. Member of the Academy of Sciences of Azerbaidzhan. Director of the Institute for the History of Art. Laid the foundations of Azerbaidzhan professional music and opera. Died in Baku.
Works: *Osnovy Azerbaidzhanskoi Narodnoi Muzyki.*

Gagarin, Iurii Alekseevich
9.3.1934–27.3.1968. Cosmonaut.
Born in the village of Klushino, Smolensk Oblast'. Son of a kolkhoz farmer. Educated at a workers' school at Liubertsy near Moscow, 1951, later at the Saratov Polytechnic, 1955. In Saratov, became a member of the local aviation club. Graduated from Chkalov Military Aviation School, 1957. Fighter-plane pilot, 1957–60. Selected for the team of pilots which was trained as cosmonauts, 1960. First cosmonaut in the world, made the first orbit of the earth on 12 Apr. 1961, starting a new chapter in the history of mankind. After his sensational flight, paraded by the Soviet authorities in many countries, being used by Khrushchev for propaganda purposes. Member of the Cen. Cttee. of the Komsomol. Became engaged in the training of new Soviet cosmonauts. Died in a crash during a training flight near the village of Novoselovo, Vladimir Oblast'. According to a report published 20 years later, the cause of the crash was the slipstream from another jet.

Gaidai, Leonid Iovich
30.1.1923– . Film director.
Graduated from the VGIK as a director. Pupil of Grigorii Aleksandrov. One of the best comedy-makers in the Soviet Union. Films: *A Fiancé From the Other World*, 1957–58; *Barbos, the Dog and a Cross-Country Run*, 1961; *Business People*, 1963; *Operation 'Y' and Shurik's Other Adventures*, 1965; *Prisoner of the Caucasus*, 1967; *The Diamond Hand*, 1969; *The Twelve Chairs*, 1971; *Ivan Vasil'evich Changes His Profession*, 1973. Winner of the Vasil'ev Brothers Prize, 1970, People's Artist of the RSFSR, 1974.

Gaidai, Zoia Mikhailovna
2.7.1902–21.4.1965. Singer (soprano).
Born in Tambov. Daughter of the folklorist Mikhail Petrovich Gaidai. Pupil of E. Murav'eva. Soloist with the Opera and Ballet Theatre, Kiev, 1928–55 (except for 1933–34, which she spent in Khar'kov.) 1st prize at the All-Union Competition for Musicians, 1933. Taught at the Kiev Conservatory. Died in Kiev.

Gaidar, Arkadii Petrovich (real name– Golikov)
1904–1941. Writer.
Popular children's writer. Printed in millions of copies. Some of his stories have been made into films, and radio and television plays.
Works: 4-vol. *Sobranie Sochinenii*, 1971–72.

Galaev, Boris Aleksandrovich
22.3.1889–195? Composer, ethnographer.
Born in the village of Chernoiarsk in the Terskaia Oblast', northern Caucasus. Ossetian by nationality. Organizer and artistic director of the South Ossetian State Ensemble for Song and Dance, 1938–51. Author of an opera, works for wind instruments, and adaptations and recordings of Ossetian folk songs.

Galanskov, Iurii Timofeevich
1939–1972. Dissident.
Born in Moscow. One of the first dissidents. Wrote samizdat poetry and edited the samizdat magazine *Feniks*. Several incarcerations in psychiatric hospitals. Arrested, 1967, and sentenced to 7 years imprisonment. Died in a labour camp.

Galich, Aleksandr Arkad'evich (Ginzburg)
19.10.1918–15.12.1977. Poet, playwright, popular ballad singer.
Born in Moscow. Worked at the Stanislavskii Studio in Moscow. During WWII, took part in theatrical shows at the front as an actor. After WWII, started writing plays, film-scripts and songs. Became immensely popular in the USSR in the 1960s, singing his own popular ballads, playing the guitar. Recordings of his songs heralded the beginning of magnitizdat (uncensored popular songs and music, recorded on tape). Severely reprimanded in 1968, expelled from the Union of Soviet Writers and the Union of Film Makers, 1971. Emigrated, 1974. Joined the NTS (an anti-Communist party). Worked with Radio Liberty, at first in Munich, later in Paris. Died in Paris from an accident (electrocuted while fumbling with his stereophonic equipment). Under Gorbachev's glasnost, rehabilitated in the Soviet Union. Posthumously re-instated in the Union of Cinematographers, May 1988.

Galin, Aleksandr
1942– . Playwright.
One of a new wave of playwrights who appeared in the mid-1970s. Factory worker, then actor in a puppet theatre. His first play *The War* was written when he was still a student, but staged only recently in Moscow. Received recognition after his play *Red Pro* opened in a Moscow theatre. His play *Here Fly the Birds* was staged at the Student Theatre of Leningrad University. *Stars in the Morning Sky* was much disliked by the cultural authorities, yet despite strong resistance was shown at several theatres in Moscow, Leningrad and in the provinces. It also received critical acclaim during the Malyi Theatre's tour of Britain in 1988.

Galin, Lev Aleksandrovich
28.9.1912– . Engineer.
Graduated from the Moscow Technological Institute of Light Industry. Specialist in plastics technology. Professor at Moscow University, 1956.

Galler, Lev Mikhailovich
1883–1950. Admiral.
During WWI, naval captain. Joined the Red Navy, 1918. Served thereafter mostly as staff officer in the Baltic fleet. Head of the Naval Academy, 1947–48.

Galperin, Iurii Aleksandrovich
1947– . Writer.
Born in Leningrad. Graduated in history from Leningrad University. First publication, 1967. Left the USSR, 1979. Settled in Switzerland. His book, *Most Cherez Letu*, received the Vladimir Dal' Literary Prize in Paris in 1981.

Gamalei, Iurii Vsevolodovich
23.9.1921– . Conductor.
Born in Leningrad. Graduated from the Leningrad Conservatory, 1950. From 1951, conductor at the Leningrad Malyi Theatre. From 1953, with the Kirov Theatre.

Gamarnik, Ian Borisovich
2.6.1884–31.5.1937. Politician, political officer.
Born in Zhitomir. Involved in revolutionary activity from 1913. Studied law at Kiev University. Member of the Bolshevik Party from 1916. During the Civil War, organizer of the Communist underground in the Ukraine, later a high-ranking political commissar in the Red Army. After the Civil War, had several party posts in the Ukraine and the Far East, 1920–28. Secretary of the Cen. Cttee. of the Bolshevik Party in Belorussia, 1928. Head of the political administration of the Red Army and editor of the military newspaper *Krasnaia Zvezda* from Oct. 1929. Member of the Cen. Cttee. of the CPSU. Deputy Minister of Defence, Deputy Chairman of the Revolutionary Military Council of the USSR, June 1930. Caught up in the Stalinist purge of the Red Army along with Marshal Tukhachevskii and other military leaders. Committed suicide (shot himself) in Moscow while awaiting arrest.

Gamburg, Grigorii (German) Semenovich
22.10.1900– . Composer, conductor, viola player.
Born in Warsaw. Member of the Stradivarius State Quartet, 1924–30. Conductor with the Symphony Orchestra of the Ministry of Cinematography from 1931. Taught at the Moscow Conservatory (chamber ensembles), 1928–41. Professor from 1939. With the Institute of Military Conducting, 1945–54. Professor at the Gnesin Pedagogical Institute of

Music. Author of works for strings orchestra, and viola.

Ganelin, Viacheslav
1944– . Jazz-band leader, composer.
Born in Moscow. Started playing piano at the age of 4. Graduated in composition from the Vilnius Conservatory. Member of the USSR Union of Composers. Has written a number of scores for cinema, television and radio. First appeared with his own jazz band in 1961. Worked with several other jazz bands. Later founded his first trio. His first major success came in Oct. 1970 at the Gorky Jazz Festival, where he played his own work, *Opus a Due,* with the drummer Vladimir Tarasov. The Ganelin Trio was invited to Britain in 1984 by the Arts Council as part of its £200,000 Contemporary Music Network scheme. Records by the Ganelin Trio were issued in London in 1980 on Leo, an independent record label. Attracted the attention of Western musicians, music-lovers and the press. Melodia, the official Soviet record company, issued 3 Ganelin albums. Recently recognized by the Soviet cultural authorities. Goskontsert (the State concert organization) has started to send Ganelin and his musicians abroad regularly.

Ganetskii, Iakov Stanislavovich (Fuerstenberg)
1879–1937. Revolutionary, politician, businessman.
Born in Warsaw. Social Democrat from late 1890s. Member of the Polish and Russian SD parties. In Poland, opposed Rosa Luxemburg. Close to Lenin from 1912. Joined Lenin in Cracow in 1914, and later in Switzerland. Moved to Scandinavia as head of the business firm of Parvus, 1915. Active in Stockholm with Radek as an intermediary between Lenin and his German sources of finance. After the October Revolution 1917, Chief Commissar of banks in Soviet Russia. Diplomatic assignments, 1920–25. After Lenin's death, Minister of Foreign Trade of the USSR. Director of the Museum of Revolution, 1935. Arrested in 1937 during the purges, presumably shot. His wife and son perished with him.
See: A. Solzhenitsyn, *Lenin in Zurich.*

Ganina, Maia Anatol'evna
1932– . Journalist, author.
In Feb. 1988, *Moscow News* ran her remarkable article in which she argued the woman's cause in critical terms unheard of since the expulsion of 3 Leningrad feminists in 1980. Author of the controversial novel *I Hope As Long As I Live*, 1987, in which she complained that, despite lofty words about equality, women in the Soviet Union were prevented at all levels from obtaining senior posts in government.

Ganzen, Aleksei Vasil'evich (Vilgelmovich)
1876–early 1940s. Artist.
Studied under I. Aivazovskii in Feodosia in the Crimea, then under R. Flery and J. Lefeuvre in Paris, under E. Bracht in Leipzig and K. Salsman in Berlin. Painter of seascapes and landscapes. Also watercolour painter.
Exhibitions: Spring Exhibitions of the Academy of Arts, Petersburg, 1904, 1917; the Society of Russian Water-Colour Painters, Petersburg, 1907–09, 1911–16; the Association of Artists, 1911–16, and the Petersburg Society of Artists, 1914–15.

Ganzhenko, Vera Stepanovna (Lantratova)
11.5.1947– . Athlete.
Born in Baku. European champion, 1967. International Master of Sports (volley-ball), 1968. Olympic champion, 1968. World champion, 1970. Graduated from the Azerbaidzhan Polytechnical Institute, 1971. Engineering degree.

Gaposhikin, Vladimir Illarionovich
1907–1961. Artist.
Landscape painter, graphic artist. Born in the Ukraine. Studied at the Zaporozh'e Professional Art School, 1926–27, under A. Kuznetsov. Also at the Moscow VKHUTEIN, 1927–30, under S. Gerasimov, G. Fedorov, I. Rabinovich, P. Konchalovskii and D. Kardovskii. Studied at the Leningrad Institute of Proletarian Art, 1930–31. Exhibitions: Iaroslavl' Artists, 1934; Iaroslavl' Oblast' Art, 1939, the All-Union Young Artists, Moscow, 1939, 1940. Other exhibitions: RSFSR Young Artists, Mos-

cow, 1941, the All-Union Exhibition, 1949; Paintings of Moscow Artists, Moscow, 1954; Paintings and Graphic Art of Moscow Artists, Moscow, 1956. Died in Moscow.

Gapurov, Makhamednazar
1922– . Politician.
Graduated from the Chardzhou Teachers' Training Institute, 1954. Member of the CPSU, 1944. Senior Komsomol and party positions from 1954. 1st Secretary of the Central Cttee. of the Turkmen CP, 1969–1985. In Dec. 1985, replaced by the republic's Prime Minister, S. Niiazov. Retired at the age of 63.

Garin, Erast Pavlovich
10.11.1902–4.9.1980. Actor.
Graduated from the Higher Experimental Theatre Workshops, 1926. In 1922, joined the Meyerhold Theatre. Popular comedian. After the closure of the Meyerhold Theatre and his arrest, moved to Leningrad and joined the Comedy Theatre. His first film role was in *Poruchik Kizhe*, 1934. Became famous for his roles in adaptations of N. Gogol. Made many films, mainly adaptations of Russian classical writers.

Gartman, Foma Aleksandrovich
21.9.1885–26.3.1957. Composer, conductor.
Born on his family's estate of Khoruzhevka, near Khar'kov. Studied music with A.Arenskii and S. Taneev. Lived abroad from 1921. Composer and conductor of many ballet productions. Worked successively with the Mariinskii Theatre, 1907, the Bolshoi Theatre, 1911 with A. Gorskii, and at Nice, 1935. Moved to the USA. Died in Princeton.

Garvy, Petr Abramovich (Iurii)
15.1.1881–28.1.1944. Trade unionist.
Born in Odessa. Joined illegal SD circles, 1899. Participant in the 1905 Revolution. After the split of the SDs, joined the Mensheviks. Active in Petersburg, close to Potresov. One of the leaders of the 'liquidators', refused to work with the Bolsheviks, 1910. Adviser to the SD faction of the Duma. Arrested, 1916, released after the February Revolution 1917. Distri-

butor of revolutionary propaganda among workers, and one of the editors of *Rabochaia Gazeta*, 1917. Organizer of the All-Russian Trade Union Congress, June 1917. After the October Revolution, moved to Odessa. His paper *Iuzhnyi Rabochii* was closed by the Bolsheviks, and he was arrested, 1921. Soon released but re-arrested in 1922 and exiled to Siberia. Received permission to go abroad, and settled in Germany. Moved to France in 1933, and to the USA in 1940. Member of the Menshevik leadership in exile, participated in the activities of the International Socialist Movement. Published valuable memoirs, *Vospominaniia Sotsial-Demokrata*, and a monograph on the pre-Bolshevik trade-union movement in Russia, (which comprised 967 trade unions), based on his unique knowledge of the subject (*Professional'nye Soiuzy Rossii*, NY, 1981). Died in the USA.

Gasparian, Goar Mikaelovna
12.2.1922–   . Singer (soprano).
Born in Cairo. Armenian. Her parents fled from Armenia after the 1915 massacre. Lived in Egypt. Stalin took a personal interest in her remarkable singing talent. She was approached by the Soviet cultural authorities who invited her to live in Armenia or in Moscow. Moved to the USSR in 1948. Soloist with the Erevan Theatre of Opera and Ballet from 1949. Many guest performances at the Bolshoi Theatre.

Gassii, Valerii Dmitrievich
22.4.1949–   . Athlete.
Born in Kolymyia, Ivano-Frankovsk Oblast' in the Ukraine. USSR champion, 1973. Honoured Master of Sports (handball), 1976. Graduated from the Kuban' University. With the Krasnodar Burevestnik. Olympic champion, 1976.

Gastello, Nikolai Frantsevich
6.5.1907–26.6.1941. Pilot.
Born in Moscow. Son of a worker. Captain of the Soviet Air Force. Member of the CPSU, 1927. Took part in the fight against the Japanese at Khalkin-Gol, and in the Soviet-Finnish war, 1939-40. At the start of WWII, given a mission to attack a German military column. After his plane was damaged by gunfire and caught fire, unwilling or unable to bale out, directed his burning aircraft (and 3 crew members) in kamikaze fashion into a column of German military vehicles. This incident was used extensively in war-time propaganda, partly because the Soviet Air Force, built up with enormous effort before WWII, was almost completely destroyed on the ground during a surprise German attack, and was badly in need of heroic examples to boost morale.

Gastev, Aleksei Kapitonovich
1882–1939. Poet.
Modernist proletarian poet of the 1920s and main theorist of the scientific organization of labour. Organized the Central Institute of Labour of which he was director until his sudden arrest and disappearance. Victim of the Gulag.

Gauk, Aleksandr Vasil'evich
15.8.1893–30.3.1963. Conductor, composer.
Born in Odessa. Professor at the Leningrad Conservatory till 1934. Among his pupils were E. Mravinskii, and A. Melik-Pashaev. In Moscow from 1934. Chief conductor with All-Union Radio Bolshoi Symphony Orchestra. Professor at the Moscow Conservatory. Reconstructed Rakhmaninov's first symphony. Died in Moscow.

Gaven, Iurii Petrovich (Dauman, Ian Ernestovich)
1884–1936. Revolutionary.
Joined the Bolsheviks, 1902. A local communist leader in the Crimea during the Civil War. Held a large number of posts, including that of Minister of the Interior. Head of the Government of the Crimean ASSR, 1921-24. After that worked in Gosplan. Disappeared during the Stalinist purges.

Gavro, Lajos
1894–1937. Revolutionary.
Member of the Hungarian SD Party, 1912. During WWI, prisoner of war in Russia. After the October Revolution, joined the Bolsheviks. Commander of a brigade in the Red Army during the Civil War. After the war, commander of Soviet troops in Kiev. Active in the Comintern, 1924–25. Soviet General Consul in China, 1926–28. Graduated from the Military Academy, 1931. Commander of a division, 1931–37. Victim of Stalin's purges.

Gazdanov, Gaito (Georgii) Ivanovich
1903–1971. Author.
Became involved in the Civil War, 1919-20. Evacuated with the White armies. Settled in Paris. Like many of his former comrades, became a Paris taxi driver. Started to write sketches of Parisian night life (*Vecher u Kler*, 1930, and other novels). Was recognized as one of the finest young emigré writers in Paris before WWII. In the 1950-60s, worked at Radio Liberty in Munich and Paris. Died in France. His books are marked by an impeccable literary Russian style only equal to that of V. Nabokov.

Gazenko, Oleg Georgievich
12.12.1918–   . Physiologist, medical official.
Born in Nikolaevka, Stavropol' Krai. Graduated from the Second Medical Institute, Moscow, 1941. Director of the Institute of Medical-Biological Problems attached to the Ministry of Public Health from 1969. Medical controller of cosmonauts' health. Has been involved in cosmonauts' long-term flights. Confident that man can adapt to space but has warned against flights longer than 2 years.

Gazhiu, Valerii
1938–   . Scriptwriter, director.
Important Moldavian scriptwriter turned director. Graduated from the VGIK as a scriptwriter. Works mainly at Moldova Film Studio in Kishinev.
Important scripts: *Man Following the Sun*, 1961 (highly praised experimental film); *When Storks Fly Away*, 1964. As director-scriptwriter: *Bitter Grains*, 1967; *Ten Winters In One Summer*, 1969; *Time Bomb*, 1971.

Gazov, Aleksandr Vasil'evich
17.6.1947–   . Athlete.
Born in Brykovo, Moscow Oblast'.

Honoured Master of Sports, (shooting), 1976. European champion, 1973, 1977-78. USSR champion, 1974, 1976. World champion, 1973-74, 1979. Olympic champion, 1976.

Gedda, Nikolai Mikhailovich
1925– . Opera singer.
Born in Stockholm. Son of a Swedish mother and a Russian father, who was a member of the Don Cossack choir. Educated at the high school, university and conservatory in Stockholm. Served in the Swedish Army. Began to sing at the Stockholm opera, 1952. His first teacher was Martin Eman, a famous Swedish Wagnerian tenor in the 1930s. Recommended by Karajan to La Scala. Moved to the Paris Opera, 1954. Since then has appeared at most great opera houses in the world to great acclaim. Well known for his welfare and cultural work among Russian exiles.

Gedike, Aleksandr Fedorovich
4.3.1877–9.7.1957. Composer, pianist, organist.
Born in Moscow into a family of German origin which gave Russia musicians for generations. Pupil of V. Safonov. Professor at the Moscow Conservatory from 1909. Taught piano, later organ, and chamber ensembles. Author of 4 operas, cantatas, symphonies, pieces for organ and for piano, and transcriptions. Died in Moscow.

Gedris, Marionas Vintsovich
16.3.1933– . Film director.
Lithuanian. Graduated from the Moscow VGIK as a director in 1964. Important film: One episode from *The Living Heroes*, 1960, which won the Grand Prix at the 12th Film Festival at Karlovy Vary; *The Strangers*, 1962; *The Summer of Men*, 1970.

Gedymin-Tiudesheva, Praskov'ia Innokent'evna
1883–1975. Revolutionary.
Involved in revolutionary work from 1902. Several times exiled before WWI. Joined the Bolsheviks during the Civil War, 1920. Cen. Cttee. representative in Irkutsk, 1921, and later at Ulan Ude.

Gegechkori, Evgenii Petrovich
1881–1954. Politician.
Member of the Menshevik Party. Member of the 3rd Duma. After the October Revolution 1917, Prime-Minister of independent Georgia, 1918–1921. Emigrated after the occupation of Georgia by the Red Army.

Geidarov, Arif
1930–4.7.1984. Minister of the Interior of Azerbaidzhan.
A senior officer in the Azerbaidzhan KGB for 25 years. Began his career as a party secretary in the local KGB in Baku. Deputy to the Supreme Soviet. Became an active public figure in the Republic. Shot by Muratov, a young prison official. Died instantly in front of his 2 close assistants who had also been fatally wounded. An obituary in the Azerbaidzhani newspaper *Bakinskii Rabochii*, was signed by N. Shchelokov, the then Minister of the Interior of the USSR, and other senior government figures. No details of the incident were given but it was suggested that he had been involved in the investigation of a case of serious corruption in which Muratov's family was involved.

Geiten, Lidia Nikolaevna
1857–20.2.1920. Dancer.
A leading dancer while still a student at the Moscow Theatre School, 1869. Graduated in 1874. Pupil of G. Legat. Until 1893, with the Bolshoi Theatre. In 1887, appeared in London. Performed with summer theatres in Petersburg, 1890 and 1893. In 1894, toured with a dance company all over Russia. In 1895,

Gekker, Anatolii Il'ich
1888–1938. Military commander.
Graduated from the Academy of the General Staff, 1917. Sent to the front, joined the revolutionary movement. Chairman of a soldiers' cttee., Dec. 1917. During the Civil War, held high command posts at several fronts (Commander of the Donetsk army, Supreme Commander of the Union of the Southern Republics). Chief of Staff of the VOKHR troops (internal security, including camp guards), 1920. Head of the Red Army Military Academy, 1922. Later military attaché in China and Turkey. Member of the General Staff, 1934. Liquidated by Stalin.

organized the Letnii Sad (Summer Theatre), and the Geiten Theatre in Moscow. Starred in her own theatre. Died in Moscow.

Gel'fand, Izrail Moiseevich
20.8.1913– . Mathematician.
Born near Odessa. Graduated from Moscow University, 1940. Research on the theory of normalized rings, which found application in trigonometric series, group theory, and the theory of the functional analysis of equations. Received an international prize in Israel, 1988.

Gel'fond, Aleksandr Osipovich
24.10.1906– . Mathematician.
Born in Petersburg. Graduated from Moscow University, 1927. Professor at the same university, 1931. Introduced new methods of analyzing the transcendence of numbers.

Geller, Mikhail Iakovlevich
1922– . Critic, author, historian.
Born in Mogilev. Graduated in history from Moscow University. High school teacher. Left the USSR for Poland in the mid-1950s. In 1969 moved to France. Books: *Kontsentratsionnyi Mir I Sovetskaia Literatura*, London, 1974; *Andrei Platonov V Poishkakh Shchastia*, Paris, 1981; *Utopia U Vlasti* (with A. Nekrich), London, 1982. Authority on modern Russian literature.

Gelovani, Archil Viktorovich
1915–1978. Marshal.
Graduated from the Kirov Industrial Institute, Georgia, 1936. During WWII, chief engineer in the Black Sea Fleet. After the war, head of the Navy's Construction Department. Deputy Head, 1969–71, of the Construction Department of the Ministry of Defence of the USSR. Head of Department, and Deputy Minister of Defence, 1974-78. Marshal of Engineering Troops, 1977.

Gelovani, Mikhail Georgievich
6.1.1893–21.12.1956. Film and stage actor.
Georgian actor who began his career at the Black Sea resort of Batumi in 1913. Worked in the theatres of Baku, Kutaissi and Tbilisi. Moved to

Moscow. Due to his physical likeness and Georgian accent, became the official choice for the role of Stalin in theatre and cinema. Was the first Stalin in theatre (*Iz Iskry* and *Chelovek s Ruzh'em*) and in cinema (*Velikoe Zarevo*, 1938, *Chelovek s Ruzh'em*, 1938; *Vyborgskaia Storona* and *Lenin in 1918*, 1939; *Oborona Tsaritsina*, 1942; *Kliatva*, 1946; *Padenie Berlina*, 1950). Received several Stalin Prizes for his portrayal and was the leader's favourite actor. Died of a heart attack during the height of Khrushchev's anti-Stalin campaign. It was rumoured that he became over-worried at the possibility of being investigated.

Geltser, Anatolii Fedorovich
2.4.1852–1918. Stage designer.
Graduated from the Moscow Stroganov Art School, 1873. Worked as a stage designer for the Imperial Moscow Theatres. Assistant to K. Valts at the Bolshoi Theatre. Pupil of the artist P. Isakov. Travelled all over Russia and Europe. From 1888, chief stage designer at the Moscow Malyi Theatre. In the 1880–90s, was very much in demand for ballet productions. Experimented with stage lighting. One of his best works was *The Sleeping Beauty*, 1899, for the Bolshoi Theatre.

Geltser, Ekaterina Vasil'evna
4.11.1876–12.12.1962. Ballerina.
Born in Moscow. Daughter of the ballet dancer Vasilii Geltser. Graduated from the Moscow Choreographic School, 1894. Joined the Bolshoi Theatre and soon became a star. With the Mariinskii Theatre from 1896. Worked under Marius Petipa. Returned to the Bolshoi in 1898. In 1910, performed in Brussels and Berlin, and took part in the Ballets Russes seasons in Paris. In 1911, with the Bolshoi in London, and in America with M. Mordkin. Her career lasted nearly until the beginning of WWII. Believed to have been one of Stalin's favourite ballerinas. Performed privately at the Kremlin. Died in Moscow.

Gelvikh, Petr Avgustovich
1873–1958. Major-general.
Graduated from the Artillery Academy, 1903. Specialist in ballistics. Wrote fundamental works in this field. Joined the Red Army, 1918. Professor of the Artillery Academy. Major-general, 1940.

Genshler, Vladimir Ivanovich
28.1.1906– . Clarinet player.
Born in Petersburg. Pupil of V. Brecker and A. Berezin. 1st prize at the All-Union Competition for Musicians, Leningrad, 1935. Professor at the Leningrad Conservatory.

Gerasimenko, Vasilii Filippovich
1900–1961. Lt.-general.
Joined the Red Army, 1918. Took part in the Civil War. Graduated from the Frunze Military Academy, 1931. On active service during WWII. Commander of Khar'kov Military District, 1944. Minister of Defence of the Ukrainian SSR, 1944–45.

Gerasimov, Aleksandr Mikhailovich
1881–1963. Artist.
Portrait, landscape and historical painter, illustrator and stage designer. Born in Kozlov (now Michurinsk). First studied privately with the artist S. Krivolutskii in Kozlov, then at the Moscow School of Painting, Sculpture and Architecture, 1903–10, as a painter then as an architect 1910–15, under Leonid Pasternak, A. Korin and A. Arkhipov. Pupil of Valentin Serov and Konstantin Korovin. Important exhibitions: the Association of Independent Artists, 1909–10, TPKHV, 1913–15, AKHRR, 8th Exhibition, Moscow, 1926. Also: Moscow, 1927–28, Leningrad, 1932, Moscow, 1933 and 1938 and 1938–39, 1942–43. Personal exhibitions: Moscow, 1935–36, Michurinsk, 1950, India-Egypt, Jan.–March 1954 and Moscow 1954 and 1956, Leningrad 1956–57.

Gerasimov, Anton Vladimirovich
1900–1978. Colonel-general.
Joined the Red Army, 1919. Took part in the Civil War. Graduated from the Higher Artillery School, 1923, and from the Frunze Military Academy, 1931. Deputy military-attaché in Nazi Germany. During WWII, held command posts in anti-aircraft defence (incl. Moscow). 1st Deputy Chief of the General Staff, 1964.

Gerasimov, Gennadii
1932– . Politician, journalist, editor.
Editor of several magazines in the 1970s. Head of the Press Department. In the Soviet Ministry of Foreign Affairs under Gorbachev. Introduced Western-style press conferences and briefings for Western journalists in the Soviet Union. One of the main spokesmen of the glasnost and perestroika policy.

Gerasimov, Sergei Apolinar'evich
3.6.1906–11.1985. Film director.
Born in Ekaterinburg (now Sverdlovsk). Graduated from the Leningrad Institute of State Arts, 1928. Began as an actor in the FEKS studio (Slapstick Actors' Workshop), 1924. Acting debut: *The Bears Versus Iudenich*, 1925. His best films (all directed by G. Kozintsev and L. Trauberg): *The Devil's Wheel*, 1926, *The Overcoat*, 1926, and *Buddy*, 1926. Directorial debut: *The Woods*, 1931. Member of the CPSU, 1943. An officially trusted film director under Stalin. Won 3 Stalin Prizes and 2 Orders of Lenin. Active in many of the Soviet government's international public-relations exercises. Married the actress Tamara Makarova. Remembered for his film version of *And Quiet Flows the Don*, 1957. His last film was *Young Peter*, the story of Peter of Great, 1981.

Gerasimov, Sergei Vasil'evich
1885–1964. Artist.
Landscape and water-colour painter, also book illustrator and historical artist. Studied at the Stroganov Central Artistic-Industrial School, 1901–07, in Moscow, then at the School of Painting, Sculpture and Architecture, 1907–12, under K. Korovin, S. Ivanov, A. Arkhipov, L. Pasternak and N. Kasatkin. Began exhibiting from 1906. Exhibitions: the Leonardo da Vinci Society of Water Colour Artists, Moscow, 1906; 3rd State Exhibition Moscow, 1918–; the Mir Iskusstva, 1921; the Makovets, 1922, 1924–26; Russian Drawing, Moscow, 1927; the Society of Moscow Artists, Moscow, 1928–29. Personal exhibitions: Moscow, 1934, 1945, 1956. Died in Moscow.

Gerdt, Elizaveta Pavlovna
29.4.1891–6.11.1975. Ballet dancer.
Born in Petersburg. Daughter of the

115

dancer, Pavel Gerdt, and the ballerina, A. Shaposhnikova. Graduated from the Petersburg Theatre School, 1908. A pupil of Mikhail Fokin. Dancer at the Mariinskii Theatre. Soon became a star. In 1927, gave up dancing to teach at the Leningrad Choreographic School. From 1935–1960, taught at the Moscow Choreographic School. Among her pupils were Maia Plisetskaia, A. Shelest, R. Struchkova, Violetta Bovt and E. Maksimova.

German, Boris Vladimirovich
1861?–after 1930. Author.
Before WWI, an active member of the SR Party. First husband of N. Krupskaia (who later married V. Lenin). Close friend of Dora Kaplan, who made an attempt on Lenin's life. Wrote books criticizing the communist dictatorship in Russia. Lived in Argentina from 1918.

Germaniuk, Uliana Sergeevna
1931–3.7.1987. Religious dissident.
Leading member of the Council of Relatives of Christian Baptist Prisoners of Conscience. Arrested in July 1985, and sent to a labour camp. Released early 1987 when the authorities realised she had cancer of the stomach. Died 3 months later.

Germogen (Dolganov), Bishop of Tobolsk and Siberia
?–26.6.1918. Russian Orthodox clergyman.
During the Civil War, arrested by the Cheka and drowned in the river Tura together with a group of Orthodox priests.

Gershenzon, Mikhail Osipovich
1.7.1869–19.2.1925. Literary scholar, editor, philosopher.
Born in Kishinev. Graduated from Moscow University, 1894. Soon became known as a serious writer on Russian intellectual history, especially of the early 19th century (monographs on Chaadaev, Pecherin, the Moscow of Griboedov, the Slavophiles and Westerners). One of the authors of the *Landmarks*, 1909, criticizing the revolutionary mania of the Russian intelligentsia. Wrote on Pushkin and Turgenev, and edited the Ogarev archives. In 1920, in the remarkable *Correspondence from Two Corners* with V. Ivanov, complained of the burden of erudition and culture, and expressed a yearning for the *tabula rasa* approach ('a naked man on a naked earth'). Died in Moscow.

Gershfeld, David Grigor'evich
28.8.1911–   . Composer.
Born in Bobrinets, Moldavia. Son of the violinist and composer Grigorii Isaakovich Gershfeld (born 1883). Author of the first Moldavian opera, *Grozovan*, other operas, a violin concerto, songs, and music for theatres.

Gershuni, Vladimir Lvovich
1932–   . Dissident.
Relative of G. A. Gershuni, leader of the SR Party and famous terrorist (1870–1908). First arrested in 1949, aged 17, for belonging to an illegal anti-Stalinist youth group, the Union of Young Leninists. Received a 10-year sentence which he served in the Akibastuz camp (well documented by A. Solzhenitsyn in *One Day in the Life of Ivan Denisovich*). Had met Solzhenitsyn earlier in the Butyrki prison in Moscow, and later in Akibastuz. Released in 1955. Various manual jobs. Took part in the human rights campaign. Arrested, 1969. Sentenced to a term in the Orel Special Psychiatric Prison to be treated for schizophrenia. In 1971, managed to send his notes about the hospital out to the West. As a result, Amnesty International protested to the Soviet Government. Released, 1974. Dedicated his time to literary activity. His articles about history and ethnography appeared in the academic press. Arrested again in 1981, and sent to psychiatric hospital in Alma-Ata. Released, 3 Dec. 1987.

Gertovich, Iosif Frantsevich
24.5.1887–12.12.1953. Double-bass player.
Born in Wil'no. Conductor with the orchestra of the Bolshoi Theatre from 1910, also appeared as a soloist. Taught at the Moscow Conversatory from 1922. Professor from 1940. Died in Moscow. Author of exercises, pieces and adaptations for the double-bass.

Gessen, Iosif Vladimirovich (Hessen)
1866–1943. Politician, historian.
One of the founders of the Cadet Party, and member of its Cen. Cttee. Emigrated after the Bolshevik take-over, 1917. Settled in Berlin. Published and edited a valuable multi-volume collection of documents, *Arkhiv Russkoi Revoliutsii*. One of the editors of the Russian newspaper *Rul'* (right of centre) published in Berlin in the 1920s.

Gessen, Vladimir Matveevich (Hessen)
1876?–1920. Politician.
Professor of Petersburg University. Member of the Cen. Cttee. of the Cadet Party. Member of the 2nd and 3rd Duma. Emigrated after the Bolshevik take-over.

Getman, Andrei Lavrent'evich
1903–   . General.
Joined the Red Army, 1924. Graduated from the Red Army Mechanics Academy, 1937. During WWII, tank corps commander. After WWII, held several high posts in tank armies. Chairman of the Cen. Cttee. of DOSAAF, 1964–71.

Geviksman, Vitalii Artem'evich
11.2.1924–   . Composer.
Born in Leningrad. Son of the conductor A. A. Geviksman. Author of orchestral works, and music for theatres and films.

Gibalin, Boris Dmitrievich
24.4.1911–   . Composer.
Born in Niazepetrovsk, Perm' Gouvt. Director of the Ural Conservatory in Sverdlovsk. Author of cantatas, suites for voice and symphony, 2 symphonies, concertos, operas for children, and choral works.

Gikalo, Nikolai Fedorovich (Hykalo)
1897–1938. Politician.
Educated at a school for medical orderlies, 1915. During the Civil War, active leader of Red detachments in the northern Caucasus (Groznyi, Terek, Daghestan), 1918–20. Commander of Red forces in the Terek Oblast', 1920. Secretary of the Moscow Party committee, 1931. 1st Secretary of the Cen. Cttee. of the Bolshevik Party in Belorussia, 1932.

1st Secretary of the Kharkov party obkom, 1937. Liquidated by Stalin.

Gilel's, Elizaveta Grigor'evna
30.9.1919– . Violinist.
Born in Odessa. Pupil of P. Stoliarskii and A. Iampol'skii. Sister of the pianist, Emil Gilel's. Wife of the violinist, Leonid Kogan. 3rd prize at the E. Ysaye International Violin Competition in Brussels, 1937.

Gilel's, Emil' Grigor'evich
19.10.1916–14.10.1985. Pianist.
Born in Odessa. Pupil of B. Rengbal'd, and G. Neigaus. 1st prize at the E. Ysay'e Piano Competition in Brussels, 1938. Professor at the Moscow Conservatory. Among his pupils were I. Zhukov, M. Mdivani. During the post-war years, became an international celebrity.

Giliarovskii, Vladimir Alekseevich (Uncle Giliai)
1853–1935. Writer, journalist.
Famous pre-revolutionary writer. Published his first book, *Trushchobnye Liudi*, in 1887. His articles about Russian life and its people were published in *Moskva Gazetnaia* in 1960. Wrote a remarkable book about theatre personalities: *Liudi Teatra*, 1941.
See: V. Gura, *Zhizn' i Knigi Diadi Giliaia* (Life and Books of Uncle Giliai), Vologda, 1959.

Giliazova, Nailia Faizrakhmanovna
2.1.1953– . Athlete.
Born in Kazan'. World champion, 1974–79. With Kazan' Dynamo. Graduated from the Kazan' Pedagogical Institute, 1975. Honoured Master of Sports (fencing), 1976. Olympic champion, 1976. USSR champion, 1979.

Gintsburg, Il'ia Iakovlevich
1859–1939. Sculptor.
Pupil of the famous Jewish sculptor Mark Antokolskii. Studied at the Petersburg Academy of Arts, 1878–86, under A. R. von Bok. Exhibitions: the Academy of Arts (The Society of Exhibitions of Works of Art, 1882); the Academy of Arts, 1884–98; TPKHV, 1895; the All-Russian Exhibition, Nizhnii-Novgorod, 1896: Spring Exhibitions at the Academy of Arts 1899–1917. Emigrated after the Revolution.

Ginzburg, Aleksandr Il'ich
1936– . Human rights campaigner.
Born in Moscow. Studied journalism at Moscow University. In 1959–60, edited 3 issues of the samizdat magazine, *Sintaksis*. Arrested and sentenced to 2 years in prison camps. In 1966, compiled documents about the trial of A. Siniavskii and I. Daniel (*Belaia Kniga*). Arrested, 1967. Tried and sentenced to 5 years in a strict regime camp. In 1972, together with A. Solzhenitsyn, organized a fund to help political prisoners and their families. In 1974 after Solzhenitsyn's expulsion from USSR, chief distributor of the Solzhenitsyn Fund (royalties from the *Gulag Archipelago*). In 1976, founder-member of the Helsinki Group (Moscow branch). Arrested Feb. 1977 and received a new sentence. In 1979, exchanged with Ed. Kuznetsov and others for 2 Soviet spies. Lives in Paris. Active in political, cultural and literary Russian emigré life.

Ginzburg, Evgenia Semenovna (m. Aksenova)
1906–1977. Writer.
Born in Moscow. Mother of the writer Vasilii Aksenov. Graduated in history from Kazan' University. Professor of history at Kazan' University. Journalist. After the arrest in 1937 of her husband, a senior party worker, she was arrested as the wife of an enemy of the people. Spent 18 years in prisons, camps, and exile. Released and rehabilitated in 1955. Returned to Moscow. Her memoirs, *Krutoi Marshrut*, were published in 1967 by Mondadori, Milan (the second volume appeared in 1979). Both were translated into several languages and received international attention. Died in Moscow.

Ginzburg, Grigorii Romanovich
29.5.1904–5.12.1961. Pianist.
Born in Nizhnii-Novgorod. Pupil of A. Goldenveiser. Professor at the Moscow Conservatory. Among his pupils were G. Aksel'rod, S. Dorenskii, and A. Skavronskii. Author of 'Zametki o Masterstve', *Soviet Music*, No. 12, 1963. Died in Moscow.

Ginzburg, Leo Moritsevich
12.4.1901– . Conductor.
Born in Warsaw. Pupil of K. Saradzhev and G. Sherkhen. Professor at the Moscow Conservatory. Among his pupils were K. Ivanov, and A. Stasevich.

Ginzburg, Lev Solomonovich
23.1.1907– . Music critic, cellist.
Born in Mogilev. Professor at the Moscow Conservatory. Doctor of art history. Author of *Luigi Boccherini*, Moscow, 1978, and of several methodological works on the cello.

Ginzburg, Semen L'vovich
23.5.1901– . Musicologist.
Born in Kiev. Professor at the Leningrad Conservatory. Author of *Istoriia Russkoi Muzyki v Notnykh Primerakh* (3 vols), Moscow, Leningrad, 1940–52.

Ginzburg, Vitalii Lazarevich
4.10.1916– . Physicist, academician.
Born in Moscow. Graduated from Moscow University in physics, 1938. Member of the CPSU, 1944. Member of the Institute of Physics of the USSR Academy of Sciences from 1940, and professor at Gorkii University from 1945. Member of the USSR Academy of Sciences from 1966. A leading theoretical physicist. State Prize, 1953. Lenin Prize, 1966. Leader of a team of Soviet scientists attempting to communicate with extra-terrestrial civilizations, 1987. Lives between Moscow and Gorkii.

Gippius, Evgenii Vladimirovich
7.7.1903– . Musicologist.
Born in Petersburg. Doctor of

musicology. Professor at the Moscow Conservatory. Author of several works on folk music.

Gippius, Zinaida Nikolaevna (Hippius, Merezhkovskaia. Pen-name –Anton Krainii)
8.11.1869–9.9.1945. Poet, author, literary critic.
Born at Belevo, Tula Gouvt. Daughter of an official. Grew up in Tiflis. First poetry published in 1888 in *Severnyi Vestnik*, where the first Russian symbolist poems appeared. Soon thereafter met another early symbolist, Dimitrii Merezhkovskii, and married him. This created one of the most remarkable literary partnerships in Russian literature. Though by all accounts platonic, the relation was remarkably stable; the couple never parted until Merezhkovskii's death over 50 years later. With her husband she became the focal point of Petersburg philosophical and literary circles, movements and intrigues. Wrote verse (which was much better than she was credited for during her life time) demanding the impossible ('Khochu togo, chego net na svete'), and despairing over the vulgarity of the world ('Moia dusha'). Wrote criticism under the male pseudonym Anton Krainii, and in general liked to play the male and domineering role with her husband and her many (platonic) admirers, especially D. Filosofov. Her strange pre-revolutionary diaries, published much later in Paris, reveal perplexing sexual confusion. Considered herself the mentor of both Belyi and Blok. Admired and feared as the leading star of Petersburg literary salons before WWI. Being close to the SRs (Savinkov and Kerenskii), she put high hopes on the February Revolution 1917. The Bolshevik take-over aroused her whole-hearted condemnation as the ultimate victory of vulgarity. Escaped with Merezhkovskii and Filosofov to Poland, and then settled in France. Continued her role as hostess of a literary salon (the Green Lamp in Paris). Wrote in the emigré press. Her memoirs and correspondence reveal a sharp intellect and sardonic and malicious sense of humour. Credited with the classical justification of the political emigration ('my ne v izgnanii, my v

poslanii'). Wrote a biography of Merezhkovskii after his death. A major representative of the Silver Age of Russian poetry. Died in Paris, buried at Ste. Genevieve-des-Bois. Her collected poetic works were published in the 1970s in Munich.

Girei Klych, Sultan, Prince (Ghirei, Sultan Kelech)
1893?–17.1.1947. Major-general.
Born in the Caucasus. During WWI, commander of a division of Caucasian volunteers (the Dikaia diviziia), which was involved in the first attempt to topple the Bolshevik government. Took part in the Civil War as a cavalry commander. Evacuated after the defeat of the Whites. During WWII, joined anti-Stalin Cossack detachments in the German army. After the war, handed over to the Red Army in Austria. Sentenced to death in Moscow and hanged.

Girgolav, Semen Semenovich
1881–1957. Lt.-general, surgeon.
Graduated from the Petersburg Military Medical Academy, 1904. Professor at the same academy, 1919. During WWII, Deputy Chief Surgeon of the Red Army. After the war, taught at the Military Medical Academy. Specialist in wound therapy. Author of scientific works on this subject.

Gittis, Vladimir Mikhailovich
1881–1938. Military commander.
Educated at the Infantry Cadet Corps, 1902. Colonel during WWI. Joined the Red Army, 1918. Military specialist on many fronts during the Civil War. Thereafter Commander of the Petrograd Military District, and later in the supply system of the Red Army.

Gladilin, Anatolii Tikhonovich
1935– . Writer, journalist.
First published in the mid-1950s in the magazine, *Iunost*, Moscow; *Khronika Vremen Viktora Podgurskogo*, 1956; *Brigantina Podnimaet Parusa*, 1959; *Vechnaia Komandirovka*, 1962. Came into conflict with the Soviet authorities and in 1976 emigrated. Wrote and published for *YMCA Press, Posev,* and *Tret'ia Volna.* Chief correspondent for

Radio Liberty's Paris office. Lives in Paris.

Glagolev, Aleksandr
1882?–25.11.1938. Russian Orthodox clergyman.
Priest in the Orthodox church. Professor of the Old Testament at the Kiev Theological Academy. Gave important evidence for the defence at the famous Beilis trial in Kiev in 1913. Well-known theological writer. Arrested, 1930, but soon released. Re-arrested, 1938. Died in prison.

Glazunov, Aleksandr Konstantinovich
10.8.1865–21.3.1936. Composer, conductor.
Born in Petersburg. Studied under N. Rimskii-Korsakov and M. Balakirev. One of the major Russian symphonists. Wrote his first symphony aged 16. Began conducting in 1888. Director of the Petersburg Conservatory, 1905–28. One of the active members of the Beliaevskii Kruzhok. Honorary Doctor of Oxford and Cambridge Universities. Left the Soviet Union in 1928 and settled in Paris. Died in Paris.

Glazunov, Il'ia
1931– . Artist.
One of the most famous and controversial Russian artists on the Soviet art scene today. Born in Leningrad. Orphaned during the siege of 1941. Graduated from the Leningrad Repin Art Institute in 1958. When still a student in 1957, attracted attention with his one-man exhibition at the TSDRI (the Central House of Art Workers) in Moscow. Was then mainly a graphic artist and illustrator of Dostoevskii's books. Second major exhibition in 1963 in Italy. Attracted the attention of the Western press and audiences. Third major personal exhibition in 1964 at the Manezh (the principal art hall in Moscow — to have a one-man exhibition there was and is the supreme accolade in the USSR). His historical and allegorical subjects attracted huge crowds. Exhibited 600 paintings. Became the enfant terrible of the Soviet art world, attacked by both the conservative establishment and the liberal intelligentsia. Was permitted to travel abroad and to sell his work to Western diplomats, a

privilege denied to other artists. Seen by some as a publicity seeker and Kremlin 'court painter'. He painted portraits of top party leaders and their wives, also the Soviet Government's official guests such as Indira Ghandi and Gina Lollobrigida. His portrait of Kurt Waldheim was donated to the United Nations in New York. *The Return of the Prodigal Son*, exhibited at the Manezh in 1978, became the focus of a controversy. One of the few Soviet millionaires, but his lifestyle is said to be very modest.

Glazunov, Vasilii Afanas'evich
1896–1967. Lt.-general.
Joined the Red Army in 1918. On active service during WWI and the Civil War. Airborne Troops Commander, 1941. Decorated for action on the Vistula. After WWII, General Inspector of Airborne Troops.

Glazunova, Olga Nikolaevna (Mother Aleksandra)
1875?–1968. Nun.
Wife of the composer A. K. Glazunov. After the 1917 Revolution, moved with him to France. After his death, devoted herself to charity work. Later moved to Jerusalem, and became a nun at a Greek convent. Died in Jerusalem. Buried at Gethsemane.

Gleb (Smirnov, Ivan Ivanovich), Archbishop of Orel and Briansk
26.8.1913–25.7.1987. Russian Orthodox clergyman.
Born in Orekhovo-Zuevo. Son of a priest. Received a technical education in Moscow in the 1930s. Worked as an engineer in Riazan'. Deacon, 1953. Priest, 1965. Monk, 1976. Bishop of Orel and Briansk, 1976. Archbishop, 1978. Popular among his flock and known for the restoration of many disused churches in the Orel diocese.

Glebov-Avilov, Nikolai Pavlovich
1887–1942. Revolutionary.
Joined the SD Party, 1904. Took part in the October Revolution 1917. Minister of Post and Communications, 1917. Commissar of the Black Sea Fleet, 1918. Supervised the sinking of the fleet before the German advance. Later held several high party administrative posts.

Glebova-Sudeikina, Olga Afanas'evna
1885–1945. Actress.
Made her name as an actress and ballet dancer. Married to the famous painter and stage designer, Sergei Sudeikin. Emigrated in the early 1920s.

Glen, Alfred Edmundovich (Glen, Konstantin von)
18.1.1858–1927. Cellist.
Born in Revel, Estonia. Pupil of K. Davydov (1838–1889). Professor at the Moscow Conservatory, 1890–1921. Among his pupils were E. Belousov, G. Piatigorskii, and I. Press. Emigrated. Died in Berlin.

Glezer, Aleksandr Davydovich
1934–   . Art critic, journalist, arts promoter, publisher.
Born in Baku. Trained as an engineer. First book of poetry, 1965. Translated into Russian 7 books of Georgian poetry. Behind every event featuring unofficial Soviet artists during the 1960s–early 70s. One of the organizers of the so-called Bulldozer Exhibition in Moscow, Sept. 1974. Became a collector of works by unofficial Soviet artists. Emigrated in 1975 and settled in Paris. Organizer of numerous exhibitions all over Europe. In 1976, founded the Museum of Russian Art in Exile in Montgeron, near Paris. In 1980, set up a branch in Jersey City, USA, and at the same time the publishing house Tretia Volna. Founder and editor of the magazine of the same name. Lives between Paris and New York. Has written several books and numerous essays on art. Books include: *Iskusstvo Pod Bulldozerom: Siniia Kniga,* London, 1977: *Chelovek S Dvoinym Dnom,* Paris, 1979; *Russkie Khudozhniki Na Zapade,* Paris, NY, 1986.

Glier, Reingold Moritsevich
11.1.1875–23.6.1956. Composer, conductor.
Born in Kiev. Graduated from the Moscow Conservatory, 1900, under M. Ippolitov-Ivanov. Studied conducting with O. Fried in Germany, 1906–08. Began composing at the age of 13. Conductor and Professor of Composition at the Kiev Conservatory, 1913–20. Professor at the Moscow Conservatory, 1920–41 (class of composition). Wrote the music for the opera *Shakhsenem* 1927, and the ballets *Krasnyi Mak,* 1927, *Mednyi Vsadnik,* 1949, and *Taras Bulba,* 1952. Also taught at the Gnesin Music School. Died in Moscow.

Glukh, Mikhail Aleksandrovich
13.5.1907–   . Composer, musicologist.
Born in Moscow. Author of the Opera *Denis Davydov,* produced in 1957, orchestral and chamber music, romances, songs, and various articles.

Glumov, Aleksandr Nikolaevich
1 9.1901–   . Musicologist, actor, writer.
Born in Moscow. Works: *Muzykal'nyi Mir Pushkina,* Moscow, 1950; *Muzyka v Russkom Dramaticheskom Teatre,* Moscow, 1955; and the novel *Iunye Vol'nodumtsy,* 1959.

Glushchenko, Tatiana Grigor'evna
12.7.1956–   . Athlete.
Born in Kiev. USSR champion, 1974–78. Honoured Master of Sports, (handball), 1976. With Kiev Spartak. Student at the Kiev Institute of Physical Culture. Olympic champion, 1976.

Glushko, Valentin Petrovich
1908–   . Rocket designer.
Graduated from Leningrad University, 1929. Pioneer of Soviet rocket designing in the early 1930s. Later directed the design of liquid-fuel rockets, used in Soviet cosmic research. Academician, 1958. Member of the Cen. Cttee. of the CPSU, 1976.

Glushkov, Viktor Mikhailovich
1923–1982. Mathematician.
Graduated from Rostov University, 1948. Head of the Laboratory of Computer Technology, 1956. Director of the Cybernetics Institute, Vice-President of the Academy of Sciences of the USSR, 1962. Author of scientific works on computers and cybernetics.

Gluzdovskii, Vladimir Alekseevich
1903–1967. Lt.-general.
Joined the Red Army, 1919. Took part in the Civil War. Cheka and GPU official, 1921. Command posts in the border guards before WWII. Graduated from the Frunze Military Academy, 1936. On active service during WWII. Faculty head at Frunze Military Academy after WWII.

Gluzman, Semen Fishelevich
1946– . Psychiatrist.
Graduated from the Kiev Medical Institute. Became known for his professional opposition to the use of psychiatry for political purposes, which became widespread in the years when Iu. Andropov was head of the KGB. Using official data on General Grigorenko, wrote a medical report arguing against the conclusion that Grigorenko was insane. Arrested in 1972 and sentenced to 7 years in prison. Living in the Gulag camps with V. Bukovskii, he compiled the *Short Guide to Psychiatry for Dissidents.*

Gmyria, Boris Romanovich
1903– . Singer (bass).
Studied at the Khar'kov Constructional Engineering Institute. Graduated from the Khar'kov Conservatory, 1939. Worked at the Shevchenko Theatre in Kiev. Became a famous bass singer and one of the best performers of Ukrainian vocal music.

Gnatiuk, Dmitrii Mikhailovich
28.3.1925– . Singer (baritone).
Born in the village of Starosel'e, in Bukovina. Pupil of I. Patorzhinskii. Soloist with the Theatre of Opera and Ballet in Kiev from 1951.

Gnedin, Evgenii Aleksandrovich
1898–1983. Diplomat.
Son of Parvus. Lived with his parents in Western Europe. Brought by his mother to Russia in 1904. Held Soviet diplomatic posts in the 1920s. Also involved in journalistic work. First Secretary of the Soviet Embassy in Berlin, 1935. Head of the Press Section of the Ministry of Foreign Affairs, 1937–39. Arrested, 1939, and sentenced to 10 years in the Gulag camps. In exile in Kazakhstan, 1949. Moved to Moscow, 1955. Some of his historical studies circulated in samizdat.

Gnesin, Mikhail Fabianovich
22.2.1883–5.5.1957. Composer, musicologist.
Born in Rostov-on-Don. Pupil of N. Rimskii-Korsakov and Liadov. Taught in music schools in Ekaterinodar, Rostov-on-Don, and Moscow. Professor at the Moscow Conservatory, 1925–35, at the Leningrad Conservatory, 1935–44, and at the Gnesin Pedagogical Institute for Music, Moscow, 1944–51. A. Khachaturian was one of his many pupils. Used Jewish folk motifs in some of his early works. Travelled in Palestine. Author of operas (such as *The Youth of Abraham* and *The Maccabees*), choral and orchestral works, symphonies, music for strings, voice and piano, and for plays. Died in Moscow.

Gnesina, Elena Fabianovna
30.5.1874–4.6.1967. Pianist.
Born in Rostov-on-Don. Pupil of V. Safonov. Founder and director of the Gnesin Music School, 1895, and the Pedagogical Institute of Music, Moscow, 1944. Her sisters, Eugenia, Maria and Olga, and her brother Mikhail were also famous musicians. Author of *Fortepiannaia Azbuka* and *Malen'kie Etiudy Dlia Nachinaiushchikh.* Her memoirs were published in *Sovetskaia Muzyka,* No. 5, Moscow, 1964. Died in Moscow.

Godunov, Aleksandr
1948– . Ballet dancer.
Ex-Bolshoi ballet star. Born on the island of Sakhalin, north of Japan. Raised in the Latvian capital of Riga. Won a Gold Medal in 1973 at the Moscow International Ballet Competition. A star of the Bolshoi after that. First visited America in the late 1960s. Defected on his second visit in 1979. Lives with the British actress Jacqueline Bisset in Los Angeles. Has performed all over the world. First film, *Witness,* 1985.

Gofman, Rostislav Modestovich (Hoffman, Michel)
28.4.1915– . Musicologist.
Born in Petrograd. Son of the Pushkin specialist and poet, M. L, Gofman. In France from 1923. Member of the society Muzykal'naia Molodezh' Frantsii. Promoter of Russian music in France. Visited the USSR in 1963. Author of *Un Siecle d' Opera Russe,* Paris, 1945, *La Musique en Russie des Origines á nos Jours,* Paris, 1956, and *Histoire Générale de la Musique,* 1959. Works in French on Tchaikovskii, Rimskii-Korsakov, Shostakovich, Prokof'ev, and Musorgskii.

Gofshtein, David Naumovich (Hofstein)
6.8.1889–summer 1952. Poet.
Born in Korostyshev. Educated in Petersburg and Kiev. Appeared in print, 1917. Became one of the pioneers of Jewish communist poetry in Yiddish in the Soviet Union. Arrested after WWII, during the anti-Semitic campaign, with a group of Jewish writers (Kvitko, Bergelson and others). All were shot on Stalin's orders. According to Soviet official sources, died 12 July 1952, but according to close friends living Israel, the whole group was shot on one day, in 12 Aug. 1952. Witnesses have stated that compilers of the *Great Soviet Encyclopaedia* have been officially given instructions to alter the dates of death, so that days of mass executions do not become too conspicuous. Posthumously rehabilitated.

Gogoberidze, Lana Levanovna
13.10.1928– . Film director.
Born in Georgia. Graduated from the VGIK in 1953. Originally educated at Tbilisi University. Studied English and American literature. Pupil of S. Gerasimov. Films: *Guelati,* 1957 (debut); *I See the Sun,* 1965; *When the Almond Trees Blossom,* 1972; *Some Interviews About Personal Problems,* 1977 (which won the Grand Prix at San Remo in 1978, and was shown at the London Film Festival and during the Georgian Film Week at the NFT); *Day Longer Than Night,* 1983, (shown at the 1984 Cannes Film Festival).

Gokieli, Ivan (Vano) Rafailovich
21.10.1899– . Composer.
Born in Tiflis. Georgian. Lecturer at the Tbilisi Conservatory. Author of

120

operas, choreographic poems, a symphony and other instrumental pieces, songs, and music for stage and film.

Goldberg, Anatolii Maksimovich (Anatol)

1910–1982. Journalist.
Born in Petersburg. Emigrated with his parents after the Bolshevik take-over, and settled in Berlin in the 1920s. Studied architecture in Berlin. After the Nazi take-over in Germany, moved to Britain. Joined the BBC as a linguist (specialist in Chinese), 1939. Member of the Russian Service of the BBC from its beginning in 1946. Became widely known and was highly respected for his regular political commentaries in Russian for listeners in the Soviet Union. Wrote a biography of I. Erenburg, published in Britain. Died in London.

Goldenveizer, Aleksandr Borisovich

10.3.1875–26.11.1961. Pianist, composer.
Born in Kishinev. Pupil of A. Ziloti and P. Pabst. Doctor of art history. Professor. Director of the Moscow Conservatory, 1922–24 and 1939–42. Founded one of the most important Soviet piano schools. Among his pupils were G. Ginzburg and D. Bashkirov. Author of 3 operas, a cantata, and piano pieces. Edited piano works of Beethoven, Schumann and others. Died in Moscow.
Source: A Nikolaev, *Mastera Sovetskoi Pianisticheskoi Shkoly,* Moscow, 1954.

Gol'din, Solomon Borisovich (Gold, Sid)

17.5.1887–   . Revolutionary, watchmaker.
Born in Mstislavets, Mogilev Gouvt. Son of an estate manager. Moved to Tula at the age of 10 and became an apprentice watchmaker. At 17 became a Bolshevik and entered a local Marxist cell in Tula. Began reading Marx's *Das Kapital.* In charge of printing equipment for a local Bolshevik group printing proclamations and other Marxist literature. Also in charge of guns (cleaning them and keeping them in a safe place). Took part in the 1905 Revolution. Met

Grigorii Zinoviev at the home of his great uncle, whose daughter Zinoviev married. One of the printers was arrested which in turn led to Gol'din's arrest. Questioned by the police but released because of his young age. Immediately left Tula, and moved to Warsaw where he became a watchmaker. Continued his Bolshevik activity. In 1911, travelled through Germany by train and then by fishing boat to Grimsby. Made bomb timing systems for the British army during WWI. Settled in Twickenham, where he started his own business. Designed a clock for which he received an award from the Royal Observatory in Greenwich in 1938; also designed a special electric clock. Opened up 3 factories employing more than 100 people. In 1961, visited the USSR with his son, Boris. They were among the first Western tourists to visit the Soviet Union after Khrushchev had opened the border.
Source: Interview with Jeanne Vronskaya.

Gol'dina, Maria Solomonvna

11.5.1899–1975? Singer (mezzo soprano)
Born in the village of Pechinsk, in Smolensk Gouvt. Pupil of E. Zbrueva. With the operatic studio of the Bolshoi Theatre from 1923. Later a soloist with the K. S. Stanislavksii and V. I Nemirovich-Danchenko Theatre of Musical Drama, Moscow.

Goldinger, Ekaterina Vasil'evna

1881–196? Artist.
Pupil of K. Savitskii, 1895–98, then at the Moscow Stroganov Central School of Graphic Art, 1897–98. Pupil of Leonid Pasternak, 1899–02. With Witti and Kormon in Paris, 1900, 1906, 1908. Graduated from Moscow University, in history and philology, 1921. Portrait and landscape painter, also interior designer. Art historian and graphic artist. Exhibitions: MOLKH, 1904, 1906; MTKH, 1905–13, 1915, 1924; the New Society of Artists, 1910; 22 Artists, Moscow, 1927. Personal exhibition: 80th Anniversary and 50 Years in the Arts, Moscow, 1961.

Goldmann, Leon Isaakovich

1877–1938/9. Revolutionary, politician, economist.
Member of the social-democratic

movement from 1898. Exiled for revolutionary activity. After the February Revolution 1917, Chairman of Irkutsk Soviet, member of the Cen. Cttee. of the Menshevik Party. Later, member of the Siberian Political Centre. After the Civil War, worked as an economist. In the early 1920s, arrested several times. Re-arrested in 1937. Died in prison.

Goldshtein, Boris Emmanuilovich

6.1.1921–   . Violinist.
Born in Odessa. Pupil of P. Stoliarskii, A. Iampol'skii and L. Tseitlin. 4th prize at the G. Wieniawski International Violin Competition, Warsaw, 1935, and at the E. Ysaye Competition, Brussels, 1937.

Goldshtein, Mikhail Emmanuilovich

1917–   . Violinist, musicologist, author.
Born in Odessa. Brother of Boris. Graduated from the Moscow Conservatory. Became a well-known concert violinist. Sent to East Berlin in 1974. Left for Israel in 1967. Moved to West Germany where he teaches and writes articles on music.
Memoirs: *Zapiski Muzykanta,* Germany, 1970.

Goldshtein, Pavel Iul'evich

1917–1982. Writer, critic.
Born in Essentuki. Wrote a letter to Stalin in defence of Vsevolod Meyerhold, 1938. Was arrested, and spent 17 years in prisons and camps. After his release, worked as a journalist for a short time in Moscow. Became active in the Jewish national movement. Left the USSR, 1971. Settled in Israel. Editor of the magazine *Menora.* Died in Israel.
Works: *Tochka Opory: V Butyrskoi Tiur'me 1938-go Goda,* Jerusalem, 1974; *Tochka Opory: 17 Let V Lageriakh Zhizni I Smerti,* Jerusalem, 1982.

Goleizovskii, Kasian Iaroslavovich

5.3.1892–4.5.1970. Ballet dancer, choreographer.
Born in Moscow. Received private ballet training from N. Domashev. From 1907, studied at the Petersburg Theatre School under Mikhail Fokin. Graduated in 1909. Dancer at the

Mariinskii Theatre. From 1910, with the Bolshoi Theatre. Took part in the ballet experiments of M. Fokin and A. Gorskii. From 1916, choreographer with the Mamontov Theatre of Miniatures and the Letuchaia Mysh Theatre. Left the Bolshoi, 1918. Organized his own studio school, the Children's Ballet. Head of the studio until 1925, when he rejoined the Bolshoi Theatre. From the mid-1930s, with provincial theatres in Khar'kov, Minsk, Lvov and Dushanbe. Died in Moscow, 1964.

Golenkin, Fedor Il'ich
1871–1936. Military engineer, major-general.
Graduated from Nikolaevskaia Military Engineering Academy, 1899. Professor at the same academy, 1901–17. On active service as major-general during WWI. Joined the Red Army, 1918. During the Civil War, built fortifications around Petrograd and in Kronstadt. Head of the Military Engineering Academy, 1918–23. Wrote works on military fortifications.

Golikov, Filipp Ivanovich
29.7.1900–29.7.1980. Marshal.
Joined the Bolshevik Party and the Red Army, 1918. Took part in the Civil War. Thereafter made a career as a political officer. Graduated from the Frunze Military Academy, 1933. Just before the beginning of WWII, head of the intelligence service of the army. Some researchers blame him for the appalling state of Soviet intelligence at the start of WWII, which ensured complete success for the German surprise attack. Held several high command posts until spring 1943. Then returned to political and security work. Deputy Defence Minister, Head of the Personnel Department, April 1943. Head of the Repatriation Commission, in charge of hunting down anti-Stalin refugees after WWII. Commander of the Armed Forces Academy, 1950. Head of the Chief Political Administration of the Armed Forces, 1958–62. Member of the Cen. Cttee. of the CPSU, 1961–66.

Golikov, Ivan Ivanovich
1887–1937. Artist.
Miniature painter. Specialized in papier-mâché, cloth, wood, glass, metal and oil paper. Illustrated *Slovo O Polku Igoreve* (published by Academia, 1934). RSFSR People's Artist. Exhibitions: The Art of Palekh, Moscow, 1932 and 1939; Ivanovo, 1936; Folk Art, Moscow, 1937; Thirty Years of Soviet Palekh (posthumously), Moscow, 1955.

Golikov, Leonid Aleksandrovich (Lenia)
1926–1943. Partisan.
Joined the Komsomol, 1942. Took part in WWII as a partisan scout. Fell in action. Posthumously awarded the title Hero of the Soviet Union, 1944.

Golitsyn, Anatolii (Goleniewski, Michael)
1911?– . KGB defector.
Worked in Moscow in the 1st Chief Directorate of the KGB, also in Poland and East Germany. In 1961, defected to the CIA in Helsinki. Responsible for exposing many Soviet moles including Philby, Blunt, Blake and Vassall. Received by Robert Kennedy. Recognized as an expert on KGB operations. American citizen, 1963. Commanded respect among some senior officers in the counter-intelligence branches of the American CIA and the British MI5 and MI6. In 1984, Bodley Head, London, published his memoirs, *New Lies for Old.*

Golitsyn, Georgii Vladimirovich (Galitzine, Prince George)
3.5.1916– . International company director, lecturer.
Born in Tiflis into one of Russia's oldest and most distinguished families. Second son of Prince Vladimir Emmanuilovich Golitsyn, officer in the Chevalier Guards, Aide-de-camp to the Grand Duke Nicholas (Nikolaevich), and his wife Catherine Carlow, daughter of Duke Georg Aleksander of Mecklenburg-Strelitz. Left Georgia with his parents in the general exodus of the Russian aristocracy after the October Revolution

1917. Grew up in England. Educated at Lancing College and St. Paul's School, and the Sorbonne. Won a scholarship to Oxford, where he obtained an MA Hons. degree in history in 1936. Holder of a medal from the Royal Humane Society (for life-saving), 1939. During WWII, served in the Welsh Guards (Major, General Staff). In the post-war years, had made a study of Russian art and history, and since 1961, has travelled frequently to the Soviet Union — at first on business, later as guest lecturer on cultural tours. Speaks with unique authority from his personal background experience on a variety of aspects of Russian life, art, architecture and history. Has given illustrated talks on the palaces of St. Petersburg, Fabergé, and travels in the Soviet Union (Moscow, Samarkand, Burkhara and the Caucasus). Multilingual. Has lived in Pakistan, India, Paris, and Milan. Occupied managerial positions in the Plessey Group, Rank Xerox, Sperry, and the British Steel Corporation. A leading member of the Russian community in London. Together with his wife, Jean Mary Dawney, divides his time between Belgravia and his country house in Hampshire.
See: N. N. Golitsyn, *Rod Kniazei Golitsinykh* (The Family Tree of the Princes of the House of Golitsyn), St. Petersburg, 1892.

Gollerbakh, Erikh Fedorovich
1895–1942. Art critic, poet, bibliophile.
In 1922, published his correspondence with, and a monograph on, his close friend, V. Rozanov.

Goloded, Nikolai Matveevich
21.5.1894–1937. Politician, state security official.
Born in the village Staryi Krivets near Briansk. Active revolutionary as a soldier during WWI. Head of the troika (tribunal) of the Cheka during the early years of Soviet power in Belorussia, 1921–24. Member of the Cen. Cttee. of the Communist Party of Belorussia, 1924. Secretary of the Cen. Cttee. 1925–27. Head of government of Belorussia, 1927–37. Disappeared during Stalin's purges, probably shot.

Golodnyi, Mikhail Semenovich (Epstein)
24.12.1903–20.1.1949. Poet.
Born in Bakhmut (now Artemovsk). Member of the literary group Molodaia Gvardiia in the 1920s. Became known in the 1930s as a classic stalinist poet ('Partisan Zhelezniak', 'Pesnia o Shchorse'). Member of the CPSU, 1939. During WWII, published a lot of propaganda verse. His death in Moscow (at the age of 45, according to the *Great Soviet Encyclopedia*) is suspicious; probably perished during the post-war wave of new arrests.

Golomshtok, Igor' Naumovich
1929–   . Art critic.
Born in Moscow. Graduated in art history from Moscow University. Senior research consultant at the Moscow Pushkin Museum of Fine Art. Published several books on the history of Western art including a book on Picasso (with A. Siniavskii). Left the USSR in 1972. Translated into Russian Nicholas Bethell's *Posledniia Taina*, London 1974. Writes for the Russian emigré press. Lectures on Russian art in England and the USA.

Goloshchekin, Filipp Isaevich
9.3.1876–18.10.1941. Dentist, revolutionary.
Born in Nevel. Joined the Bolsheviks, 1903. Member of the Cen. Cttee., 1912. Participant in the Bolshevik take-over in Petrograd, 1917. Secretary of the Perm', Ekaterinburg and Ural party obkoms, where the murders of the members of the Romanov dynasty were committed. 1918. During the Civil War, political commissar with the Red Army. Thereafter a number of high administrative posts in different parts of the USSR.

Golosov, Il'ia Aleksandrovich
31.7.1883–29.1.1945. Architect.
Born in Moscow. Educated at the Moscow Arts School, 1907–12, and Petersburg Academy of Arts, 1912–15. Became the foremost modernist Soviet architect, erecting some of the most advanced modernist buildings in Moscow in the 1920s. Veteran teacher at the Moscow Architectural Institute, Vkhutein-Vkhutemas, and other artistic and architectural establishments, 1919–45. In the 1930s, changed to Stalinist architecture. Died in Moscow.

Golovach, Platon Romanovich
1.5.1903–29.10.1937. Author.
Born in the village Pobokovichi, near Bobruisk. Joined the Communist Party, 1924. Active supporter of the collectivization campaign. Became a classic of communist literature in Belorussia. Perished in Stalin's purges.

Golovanov, Aleksandr Evgen'evich
1904–1975. Air force marshal, state security official.
In the Red Army during the Civil War, 1919–20, and from the beginning of WWII. GPU official, 1924. Educated at a pilots' school, 1932. Worked in civil aviation from 1932. Commander of a bomber regiment, 1941. After WWII, commander of the Soviet Strategic Bomber Force.

Golovanov, Nikolai Semenovich
21.1.1891–28.8.1953. Conductor, pianist, composer.
Born in Moscow. Husband of the singer A. Nezhdanova. Conductor, 1919–36. Professor at the Moscow Conservatory, 1925–29. Chief conductor with the Bolshoi Theatre, 1948–53. Concurrently with the All-Union Radio Bolshoi Symphony Orchestra from 1937. Works include 2 operas, and symphonies. Died in Moscow.

Golovanov, Oleg Sergeevich
17.12.1934–   . Athlete.
Born in Leningrad. USSR champion, 1959–63. Olympic champion, 1960 (with V. Boreiko). Honoured Master of Sports (rowing), 1960. Graduated as a coach from the Leningrad Institute of Physical Culture, 1962. Honoured Coach of the USSR, 1979.

Golovanov, Vladimir Semenovich
29.11.1938–   . Athlete.
Born in the village of Batamai, Iakut ASSR. USSR champion, 1964, 1969. World and European champion, 1964. Olympic champion, 1964 (487.5 kg). Honoured Master of Sports (heavy-weight wrestling), 1965. Member of the CPSU, 1966. Graduated from the Khabarovsk Pedagogical Institute, 1971.

Golovatyi, Ferapont Petrovich
1890–1951. Kolkhoz farmer.
Beekeeper in a kolkhoz farm in Saratov Oblast'. Gave up his personal savings for the war effort in 1942. Accepted into the party, 1944, and transformed into a cult figure, symbolizing the devotion and love of the simple people for the Soviet government and Stalin personally. After WWII, Hero of Socialist Labour, 1948, and Deputy of the Supreme Soviet of the USSR.

Golovin, Aleksandr Iakovlevich
1.3.1863–17.4.1930. Artist.
Born in Moscow. Studied at the Moscow School of Painting, Sculpture and Architecture, 1881–84. As a painter under V. Makovskii, V. Polenov, E. Sorokin and I. Prianishnikov. Studied also at the F. Colarossi Academy, 1889, and with Witti, 1892, in Paris. Stage designer, portrait and landscape painter, also worked in the applied arts. Lived in Moscow until 1901. Member of the Mir Iskusstva group. Moved to Petersburg. In the 1890s, belonged to the Abramtsevo Kruzhok specializing in majolica and wood. Influenced by Konstantin Korovin (*Pskovitianka* by Rimskii-Korsakov). Worked for Diaghilev in Paris on *Boris Godunov* by Musorgskii, and *Zhar-Ptitsa* by Stravinskii. From 1910, stage designer at various theatres. From 1889, took part in all exhibitions of note in Moscow and Petersburg. Personal exhibition: his 10th anniversary (posthumous), Leningrad, 1940; Moscow, Leningrad in 1956. Died in Detskoe Selo, now Pushkin, Leningrad Oblast.

Golovin, Fedor Aleksandrovich
2.1.1868–1937? Politician.
Born in Moscow. Prominent zemstvo leader, one of the founders of the Cadet Party, and member of its Cen. Cttee. President of the 2nd Duma, 1907. Active member of Zemgor (union of rural and town local governments), 1914–18. After the Bolshevik take-over, remained in

Russia, working as an office clerk. Probably victim of the purges.

Golovin, Nikolai Nikolaevich
4.12.1875–1944. General, historian.
Son of a general. Born in Moscow. Educated at the Pages Corps, 1894. Graduated from the Academy of the General Staff, 1900. Professor of the Academy of the General Staff, 1908–13. Well-known specialist in military theoretical and historical subjects. During WWI, Chief of Staff of the 7th Army and the Rumanian front. Of liberal convictions, a delegate to the pre-parliament in 1917. With the Whites during the Civil War. Evacuated from the Crimea to Gallipoli. Moved to France, continued to lecture on military subjects. Wrote a history of WWI. During WWII, kept in close touch with the Russian anti-Stalin movement in Germany. Sentenced to death by French communist guerillas.

Golovkina. Sofia Nikolaevna.
1915– . Ballet teacher.
Graduated from the Moscow Choreographic School of the Bolshoi Theatre in 1933. With the Bolshoi from 1933. Teacher in the late 1940s. Director of the Choreographic School from 1960. Former ballet star of that generation of Russian dancers which included Igor Moiseev and Olga Lepeshinskaia. Among her recent pupils is the prima ballerina Galina Stepanenko, who took the London Coliseum by storm in the summer of 1987.

Golovko, Arsenii Grigor'evich
1906–1962. Admiral.
Joined the Red Navy, 1925. Expert on mines. Graduated from the Navy Academy, 1938. Took part in the Spanish Civil War, 1936–38. Commander of the Northern fleet, 1940–46. Chief of Staff of the Navy and Deputy Chief Commander, 1947. 1st Deputy Chief Commander, 1956.

Golovnia, Anatolii Dmitrievich
2.2.1900–25.6.1982. Cameraman.
Prominent cameraman on nearly all of V. Pudovkin's films: *Shashmatnaia Goriachka*, and *Mekhanika Golovnogo Mozga*, both in 1925, followed by *Mat'*, 1926, *Konets Sankt-Peter-*

burga, 1927, and *Potomok Chingiz Khana* — all of which are now regarded as masterpieces of the early Russian cinema. From 1935, taught at the VGIK. Professor from 1939. Wrote several books, including *Svet v Iskusstve Operatora,* 1945, *Fotokompozitsiia*, 1962 (with L. Dyko), and *Masterstvo Kinooperatora*, 1965.

Golstein, Aleksandra Vasil'evna (Holstein, Weber)
1849–1937. Society hostess.
Lived most of her life in Paris. In the late 19th century, hostess of a literary salon frequented by French celebrities. Later became a friend of Russian writers and artists visiting Paris in the early 20th century (Voloshin, Merezhkovskii and Gippius, M. Kovalevskii, Vengerov, Kropotkin, Minskii, and Repin). In the 1920s, became a close companion of Prince Pavel Dolgorukov, who returned to Russia and was executed by the Cheka. Her daughter married Iu. Semenov, editor of the Parisian right-wing Russian daily *Vozrozhdenie.*

Golubev, Evgenii Kirillovich
16.2.1910– . Composer.
Born in Moscow. Professor at the Moscow Conservatory. Pupils include G. Grigorian, T. Nikolaeva, A. Kholminov, G. Shantyr', A. Shnitke, and A. Eshpai. Author of a ballet, oratorios, symphonies, concertos for piano, cello, and viola, sonatas, and choral works.

Golubev, Konstantin Dmitrievich
1896–1956. Lt.-general, SMERSH officer.
On active service during WWI. Joined the Red Army, 1918, and the Communist Party, 1919. Regimental commander during the Civil War. Graduated from the Frunze Academy, 1926, and the Academy of the General Staff, 1938. Taught at the Frunze Academy. Took part in WWII. From 1944, involved in the hunting down of Russian refugees in the West. Later taught at the Academy of the General Staff, 1949–53.

Golubinov, Sergei (Golon)
1903–1973. Author.
Born in Bukhara. Son of a diplomat.

Emigrated with his parents during the Civil War. Settled in France. Educated at a French lycée. Graduated as an engineer. Worked in the Congo, where he met his French wife. Together under the pen-name Golon they started to write a series of romantic historical novels, *Angelica*, set at the time of the Roi Soleil (Louis XIV). The series had phenomenal success: 75 million copies were published and the series was translated into 25 languages. Died in Canada.

Golubnichii, Vladimir Stepanovich
2.6.1938– . Athlete.
Born in Sumy, Ukraine. At 17, became the Ukrainian adult champion in the 10 kilometres walk, beating many veterans of the event. Set many Ukrainian records at various distances. First world record in walking in 1955 (20 kilometres). Repeated his success in 1975. Participant in 5 Olympic Games. Gold medal winner in Rome and Mexico. Silver medal in Munich, bronze medal in Tokyo, and in Montreal 1976. Champion of the USSR, Europe, and Olympic champion.

Goncharova, Natal'ia Sergeevna (Larionova)
3.6.1881–17.10.1962. Painter.
Born at Ladyzhino near Tula. Studied at the Moscow School of Painting, Sculpture and Architecture. From 1909, started to work as a stage designer and gained a great reputation working for Sergei Diaghilev. Met Mikhail Larionov, and became his wife and constant companion (officially married at 74 years of age). Together with Larionov, became one of the originators of the rayonist style of painting. Took part in early 20th century modernist exhibitions (Bubnovyi Valet, Oslinyi Khvost) in Russia. From 1915 till her death, lived in Paris. Spent her latter years in great poverty, largely forgotten. Combined primitivist and modernist tendencies in her art (Lubok, cubism). Her theatrical work shows the influence of Russian folklore with its strong colours and simplified forms. Died in Paris. Regarded now as one of the most important Russian artists of the early avant-garde.

Goncharskaia, Sofia Samoilovna
1889–1973. Revolutionary.
Took part in the 1905 Revolution in Odessa. Emigrated, 1911. Member of the Socialist Party in the USA, where she represented the Bolshevik tendency. Returned to Russia, 1917. Took part in the Bolshevik take-over in Petrograd, October 1917. During the Civil War, political officer with the Red Army in the Urals. Government representative of the Soviet buffer state–the Far Eastern Republic in the RSFSR, 1920. Graduated from the Institute of Red Professors.

Gorbachev, Boris Sergeevich
1892–1937. Military commander, revolutionary.
On active service during WWI. Joined the Communist Party, 1917, and the Red Army, 1918. Active Red Army leader during the Civil War (cavalry regiment and brigade). Highly decorated (3 Orders of the Red Banner). Graduated from the Frunze Academy, 1926. Continued his career in the cavalry. Liquidated during the Stalin purges of the military.

Gorbachev, Georgii Efimovich
26.9.1897–10.10.1942. Literary critic. Graduated from Leningrad University, 1922. Professor at Leningrad University, 1924. Left-wing critic, close to RAPP. Became well-known for his literary polemics in the 1920s. Victim of Stalin's purges, Died in the Gulag.

Gorbachev, Mikhail Sergeevich
2.3.1931–   . Politician.
Born in the village of Privol'noe in the Krasnogvardeiskii District of Stavropol' Krai. Both parents and grandparents were peasants. Lived in an area which was under German occupation from Aug. 1942–Jan. 1943. From the end of WWII until about 1950, worked as a manual worker in a kolkhoz in Stavropol'e Oblast'. During this time, probably continued his education which had been interrupted by the war. As a law student at Moscow University after WWII, was remembered by his fellow students wearing the high award of the Order of the Red Banner of Labour, although then aged only 19. Joined the CP in 1952. Graduated in 1955 and returned to his native Stavropol'e. Active in the Komsomol first, then in local party administration. In 1967, graduated from the Stavropol' Agricultural Institute. In the next year, appointed 1st Secretary of the Stavropol' City CPSU Cttee. Worked closely with Fedor Kulakov, 1st Secretary of the Stavropol' party organization. In 1970, invited to Moscow by Kulakov, who had moved there in 1964 as head of the Agriculture Dept. of the Cen. Cttee. Close to Suslov and Andropov. Both used to go for health reasons to the Northern Caucasus, to that area of Stavropol'e where Gorbachev was the party boss, and were excellently looked after by the local administration. Became a Politburo member in 1980. After Chernenko's stroke in Dec. 1984, approved by 7 out of 10 Politburo members as the new leader, edging aside the only other serious contender, the Leningrad party boss, G. Romanov, who retired soon thereafter. Took up office on 11 March 1985 at the age of 54. Brought to an end the Kremlin gerontocracy and turned towards a course of reforms, at first stressing the continuation of the Andropov line, but later developing a much more comprehensive momentum of reform (perestroika and glasnost). Among immediate measures were the unpopular but necessary anti-drink laws, anti-corruption drive, some economic liberalization and a more liberal approach in the arts and media. The measures were put through in the teeth of bitter conservative resistance from the old guard — Brezhnevites and Stalinists. His newest reforms include the legalization of independent art shows, allowing artists to trade by themselves (paying a 13% tax to the State — a thing which used to earn prison terms before), some easing of censorship in literature, films and the press, and a willingness to fill in major blank pages in Soviet history. As the result of the glasnost policy, hundreds of films and books which had been shelved for decades are now being released. Every day Soviet newspapers publish much more *real* information for their readers. The reforms have met with stiff opposition from party hardliners and bureaucrats who do not wish to lose their privileges, and from the man in the street who doesn't want to lose his vodka. But there is widespread support from all layers of Soviet society. It is the general opinion that Gorbachev is a leader who could win a free election, if there ever was one in the Soviet Union. In Jan. 1987, addressing Soviet journalists, he declared he would resign if unable to carry through his reform programme (Source: *Moscow News*). He is the first Soviet leader since Lenin to do walkabouts, meeting people in the street in person. Banned the hanging of his portrait in government offices. Refused to sit in the grand box at the Bolshoi. After Khrushchev, he is the first Soviet leader who, after the long years of stagnation under Brezhnev and his gerontocracy, has awakened some hopes in the Soviet people. Proposed important structural changes at the party conference in July 1988. Head of State, Oct. 1988.

Gorbachev, Nikolai Stepanovich
15.5.1948–   . Rower.
Born in Rogachev, Gomel' Oblast'. USSR champion, 1968–75. Graduated from the Belorussian Institute of Physical Culture, 1972. Honoured Master of Sports (rowing), 1972. With Rogachev Spartak. Olympic champion, 1972 (with V. Kratasiuk). World and European champion 1974. Member of the CPSU, 1975.

Gorbacheva, Raisa Maksimovna
(Mrs. Gorbachev, b. Titorenko)
1934–   . First lady of the USSR. Both parents were doctors. Holds a degree in philosophy from Moscow University, 1957. Lecturer in philosophy (Marxism) at the same university. Married Gorbachev in early 1960. Her daughter, Irina, is also a doctor. Known as a patron of the arts in the Soviet Union. Since her husband took up office in March 1985, has accompanied him everywhere, the first among the Soviet leaders' wives to do so (with the exception of Nina Petrovna Khrushcheva). Made a favourable impression in the West with her intelligence, taste and looks. Known for her love of music, and knowledge of English and French. Has broken the Soviet leadership tradition of invisible wives,

and takes a high profile in cultural, diplomatic and political life at the side of her husband.

Gorbanevskaia, Natal'ia Evgen'evna
1936– . Poet, journalist, dissident, editor.
Born in Moscow. Graduated in philology from Leningrad University. Her poems circulated in samizdat from the early 1960s. In 1968, became active in the human rights movement. Founding member of *Khronika Tekushchikh Sobytii*. In August 1968, pregnant and with a child in her arms, took part in a small demonstration in Red Square protesting against the Soviet invasion of Czechoslovakia. Arrested, but soon released. Re-arrested in 1969 and sent to a psychiatric hospital in Kazan. Released and left the USSR in 1975. Lives in Paris. Editor of the valuable historical magazine *Pamiat*. Has published several books of poetry. Translator of Polish dissident publications.

Gorbatov, Aleksandr Vasil'evich
1891–12.1973. General.
Joined the Red Army and the Communist Party, 1919. Cavalry brigade commander during the Civil War. Arrested during the army purges in the 1930s (later described part of his Gulag experience in *Novyi Mir* magazine). Released during WWII. Commander of the 3rd Army. Commander of the Baltic military district, 1954–58.

Gorbiatkova, Nelli
25.6.1958–7.8.1981. Hockey player. Honoured Master of Sports (hockey). Bronze medallist at the XXIInd Olympic Games. Her death was reported in the American press.

Gorbunov, Nikolai Petrovich
21.6.1892–7.9.1937. Politician.
Born at Krasnoe Selo, son of an engineer. Joined the Bolshevik Party in 1917. Graduated from Petersburg Technological Institute in 1917. Secretary of the Council of Peoples' Commissars and Lenin's private secretary from Nov. 1917. Intermediary between the Soviet government and the members of the pre-revolutionary Academy of Sciences, who were reluctant to work for the Bolsheviks. Lenin's right hand in matters of science. Occupied many executive positions at various scientific institutions. Academician, 1935. Secretary of the Academy of Sciences of the USSR, 1935. Arrested in 1937 during the purges and disappeared, probably executed.

Gordeli, Otar Mikhailovich
18.11.1928– . Composer.
Born in Tiflis. Author of works for voice and symphony orchestra, orchestral works, concertos, a piano sonata and other instrumental pieces. Also created music for films and variety.

Gordievskii, Oleg
1939– . Security services officer, counter-intelligence agent.
Head of the KGB in London who defected in Sept. 1985 and revealed the names of 25 Soviet agents working in the West. According to his own information, graduated from Moscow training school (presumably the KGB special school) in 1963. Spent much of the next 10 years dealing, both in Moscow and abroad, with Soviet 'illegals', a euphemism for KGB agents planted in foreign countries to operate totally undercover. Until his defection in London, worked as a KGB officer at the 3rd Department inside the 1st Directorate (KGB), which has responsibility for KGB secret operations abroad. His zone was Britain and the Scandinavian countries where he operated under diplomatic cover. Posted to Denmark in 1966 as a press attaché at the Soviet Embassy in Copenhagen. Worked there for 4 years. In 1972, returned to Denmark with the rank of 2nd Secretary of the Soviet Embassy. After 6 years promoted to 1st Secretary, in which role he became economic and political adviser to the Ambassador. In June 1982, arrived in the Soviet Embassy in London as a councillor, ranking number 6 in the embassy hierarchy. His job was to make contact with religious groups, peace organisations and trade unions. Promoted 2 years later after the London KGB chief Arkadii Guk was publicly exposed during the trial of Michael Bettaney. Became controller of the KGB in Britain and possibly all Europe. Married in Moscow. After his defection, the family's fate was unknown. Revealed many KGB secret operations in the West. Probably now lives in the USA.

Gordov, Vasilii Nikolaevich
1896–1951. Col.-general.
Took part in WWI and the Civil War. Joined the Communist Party, and the Red Army, 1918, infantry regiment commander. Graduated from the Frunze Academy, 1932. During WWII, commander of the 21st Army, and the Stalingrad Front. After WWII, commander in the Far East.

Gorelenko, Filipp Danilovich
1888–1956. Lt.-general.
Joined the Red Army, 1918, and the Communist Party, 1928. Regimental and divisional commander during the Civil War. Graduated from the Frunze Academy, 1934. Corps commander in the Soviet-Finnish war, 1939–40. In WWII, commander of the 2nd, and the 32nd Armies.

Gorelov, Gavriil Nikitich
1880–1956? Artist.
Born in Penza. Portrait, genre and historical painter. Studied at the N. Seliverstov Art School, 1898–03, under K. Savitskii, then at the Petersburg Academy of Arts, 1903–11, under P. Chistiakov. Pupil of I. Repin and A. Rubo. Studied at academies in France, Germany and Italy, 1911–12. Exhibitions from 1906. Personal exhibition: Moscow, 1950. Died in Moscow.

Gorelov, Rostislav Gavrilovich
1916– . Artist.
Born in Moscow. Son of the artist Gavriil Gorelov. Studied at the Moscow School of Painting, Sculpture and Architecture, 1936–39, also at the Moscow State Art Institute, 1939–42, under G. Riazhskii, and then, in 1943–44, at the M. Grekov Military Artists Studio. Started exhibiting in 1943.

Goremykin, Ivan Loginovich
8.11.1839–11.12.1917. Statesman.
Born in Novgorod. Graduated from the Law High School. Civil servant in

various government departments. Minister of the Interior 1895–99. Member of State Council from 1899. Appointed Chairman of the Council of Ministers, Apr. 1906. Responsible for the dissolution of the 1st Duma. Replaced by Stolypin in July 1906. Returned to his post in Jan. 1914 and stayed there till Jan. 1916. Remained hostile to the Duma and the Progressive Bloc. Killed by revolutionary soldiers in the Caucasus after the October Revolution.

Gorenstein, Fridrikh Naumovich
1932– . Writer, scriptwriter.
In 1962, published a short story, *Dom s Bashenkoi* in *Iunost'* magazine. Wrote the script for A. Tarkovskii's *Solaris*. Emigrated to West Germany where he has published short stories and plays in various emigré magazines. Has also contributed to the almanac *Metropol'*, Ardis, 1979–.

Gorev, Boris Isaakovich (Goldman)
1874–1937. Politician.
Brother of the Menshevik leader, Liber. Involved in revolutionary activity from 1893. Member of the SD Party, 1898. Was at different times member of both wings of the SD Party (Menshevik and Bolshevik). After the February Revolution 1917, member of the Cen. Cttee. of the Mensheviks. One of the editors of *Rabochaia Gazeta*. Left the Mensheviks, 1920. Attacked for Menshevist sympathies, 1931. Wrote an article vilifying the Menshevik Party and its role in the revolution in *Katorga i Ssylka*, 1932. Continued to write in the official press. Fell silent, 1936, probably arrested. No further details available, probably vanished in the Gulag.

Goriachev, Semen Petrovich
1911– . Artist.
Born in Iaroslavl'. Landscape painter. Member of the Union of Artists. Studied at the Iaroslavl' Pedagogical Technical Art School 1930–33, under S. Shitov, B. Petrukhin and G. Kozyrev. Studied at the Moscow State Art Institute, 1940–43, under S. Gerasimov. Exhibited from 1936, mainly in provincial art exhibitions.

Goricheva, Tatiana Mikhailovna
1947– . Editor, feminist.
Born in Leningrad. Graduated in philosophy (Marxism) from Leningrad University. In 1974, organized religious and political seminars in Leningrad. Co-edited with Viktor Krivulin the samizdat magazine *37*. In 1979, became one of the founders of the Free Women's Movement in Leningrad. Edited the samizdat magazines *Zhenshchina I Rossiia* and *Maria*. In 1980, on the opening day of the Olympic Games in Moscow, deported from the USSR. Lives in Paris. Continues her work with the Russian Free Women's Press. Writes on the position of the Russian church in the Soviet Union.

Gorkii, Maksim (Peshkov, Aleksei Maksimovich)
28.3.1868–18.6.1936. Author.
Born in Nizhnii-Novgorod (now Gorkii). Spent his youth as a vagabond and itinerant workman. First story *Makar Chudra*, published in 1892 in Tiflis. Soon became known as a genuine proletarian, turned writer. Two volumes of stories and sketches, published in 1898, about the colourful and carefree life of tramps and similar characters made him widely popular, and turned him into a best-selling author. The play *Lower Depths* (1902) made him known throughout the world. Wrote and financed revolutionary propaganda during the 1905 Revolution, and joined the Bolshevik Party. Left Russia for America in 1906. Travelled around the USA lecturing, and causing a scandal in the country by travelling in the company of the actress Maria Andreeva without being legally married to her (she became his wife later). Lived on Capri, 1906–13, and organized and financed a Bolshevik Party school. Returned to Russia in 1913. Remained close to the Bolsheviks, condemned WW1. After the October Revolution 1917, sharply criticized the communist dictatorship in his newspaper *Novaia Zhizn'*. During the chaotic revolutionary years, felt that his duty lay in saving as much culture as possible. Organized many cultural initiatives (the publishing house World Literature, and so on), and became the natural focus of requests for help from the intelligentsia. His

relations with Lenin became so strained that he left Russia in autumn 1921 (officially for health reasons). Lived in Sorrento, 1924–31. Became the best-known communist author in the world, living and writing freely in Mussolini's fascist Italy. In the late 1920s his world popularity diminished considerably. Returned to Moscow in 1931. In the last years of his life, he was proclaimed the founding father of socialist realism and was showered with honours. In complete contrast to his courageous stand against Lenin's dictatorship in the early revolutionary years, adopted a servile attitude towards Stalin, praising collectivization (he was always anti-peasant, supporting the tramp against the farmer), glorifying Stalin personally, approving of the activity of the Cheka in general and the show trials in particular (the quotation 'if the enemy does not surrender, he must be annihilated' became virtually the motto of the secret police, and completely erased in the memory of many Soviet prisoners the considerable humanistic work of his previous years). Died in Moscow, allegedly – as officially stated at that time – poisoned by fascist agents in the GPU. According to other versions, this was only a cover for Stalin's personal involvement in his death, after he had shown signs that he was unwilling to approve of further Stalinist crimes. In fact, the exact circumstances of his death are still unknown (apart from anything else, he had a lung illness dating from his youth). Buried at the Kremlin Wall. As with many best-selling authors, his posthumous fame shrank, despite all the official support. The constant stress on him as the father of socialist realism, the hated official literary dogma, has further damaged his reputation. Some of his plays and his autobiography remain popular, while some of his articles dating from 1918–19 condemning the communist dictatorship remain banned in the USSR.
Main works: *Collected Works*, 25 vols, Moscow-Leningrad, 1933–34.

Gorlov, Aleksandr Mikhailovich
1931– . Engineer, author.
Born in Moscow. Graduated from the Moscow Institute of Transport Engineering. Worked as an engineer

and researcher. Published a book and numerous articles on professional subjects in the Soviet press. In Aug. 1971, became a chance witness of the KGB's illegal search of A. Solzhenitsyn's house. Severely beaten up by the KGB. Published his testimonies in the West and became famous. Lost his job in 1974 and was forced to leave the country in 1975.
Works: *Sluchai Na Dache*, Paris, 1977.

Gorodetskii, Sergei Mitrofanovich
18.1.1884–1967. Poet.
Born in Petersburg. Educated at Petersburg and Orel High Schools. Studied at Petersburg University. Constant visitor to all the Petersburg literary salons before the revolution. Scored a great success with his very first volume of poetry, *Iar*, 1906, with its neo-heathen Slavonic stylizations. Joined N. Gumilev in creating the Acmeist group, and the Tsekh Poetov where he acted as a leader (one of two syndics). Through his interest in folklore, became the link between the capital and the emerging peasant poets such as Kliuev and Esenin. During WW1, served as a correspondent at the Caucasian front, writing about the Armenian massacre, and about Persia. During the Civil War remained in Tiflis, and was an active member of the modernist poetic circles. Returned to Moscow, 1921. His life thereafter was one constant negation of all the promise of his youth. Became a model Stalinist poet and careerist, not averse to denouncing his former friends. Wrote libretti for Stalinist operas (*Proryv, Prometei, Dumy pro Opanasa*). Author of the libretto for John Reed's *Ten Days That Shook the World*. Wrote a completely new libretto for Glinka's *A Life for the Tsar*, renamed *Ivan Susanin*. During WWII, evacuated to Tashkent. After the war, returned to Moscow. Remained a member of the official Soviet literary establishment till his death.

Gorodinskii, Viktor Markovich
23.2.1902–9.5.1959. Musicologist, critic.
Born in Petersburg. Author of articles on musical culture, also *Muzyka Dukhovnoi Nishchety*, Mos-cow-Leningrad, 1950, and *Izbrannye Stat'i*, Moscow 1963. Died in Moscow.

Gorodovikov, Oka Ivanovich
1.10.1879–26.2.1960. General.
Born in Mokraia Elmuta near Rostov. Son of a Kalmuck peasant. On military service during WW1. Became a Bolshevik agitator and joined the Red Army in 1918. Member of the Bolshevik Party, 1919. During the Civil War, commanded Red cavalry detachments against Makhno and Wrangel. Graduated from the Frunze Military Academy in 1932. Before WWII, Commander of the Red Cossacks, and Assistant Commander of the Central Asian military district, 1932–38. Inspector of Cavalry, 1938–41. During WWII, in charge of the formation of cavalry units. Deputy Commander of Soviet Cavalry, 1943–47. Also in charge of the deportation of the whole Kalmuck nation and the liquidation of the Kalmuck Autonomous Region (which was later restored). Gained the reputation of being an utterly ruthless Stalinist henchman. Retired, 1947. Died in Moscow.

Gorodtsov, Aleksandr Dmitrievich
11.11.1857–1918. Conductor, operatic singer.
Born in the village of Pozdnoe, in Rianskaia Gouvt. Contributed to the development of choral singing in the Russian provinces. Directed folk singing in Perm' Gouvt. Organised village and factory choirs, concerts and music course. Author of an anthology of choral folk music, *Narodnopevcheskie Khory* 1907–17. Edited Russian operas and transposed them for People's Choirs. Author of *Narodopevcheskoe delo Permskoi Gubernii*, Perm', 1909. Died in Perm'.

Gorokhova, Galina Evgen'evna
31.8.1938– . Athlete.
Born in Moscow. Honoured Master of Sports (fencing), 1960. Graduated from the Moscow Institute of Physical Culture, 1961, and from the Academy of Social Sciences of the Cen. Cttee. of the CPSU, 1973. Member of the CPSU, 1964. With Moscow Dynamo. World champion, 1958–71. USSR champion, 1960–70. Olympic champion, 1960, 1968 and 1972. Silver medal, 1964. Bronze medal, 1972.

Gorokhovskaia, Maria Kondrat'evna
17.10.1921– . Athlete.
Born in Evpatoria, Crimea. Honoured Master of Sports (gymnastics), 1952. USSR champion, 1948–54. Absolute champion of the USSR, 1951–52. World champion, 1954. Olympic champion, 1952. Silver medal, 1952. Graduated from the Kiev Institute of Physical Culture, 1956.

Gorozhanin, Valerii Mikhailovich
1889–1941. Security services agent, author.
Worked in the Ukrainian Cheka, then the GPU. Wrote with Mayakovsky (when the latter was in Yalta) a script entitled *Engineer D'Arcy (Inzhener D'Arsi)*, which Mayakovsky registered in VUFKU, but which was never performed.

Gorshkov, Aleksandr Georgievich
8.10.1946– . Athlete.
Born in Moscow. Honoured Master of Sports (figure skating), 1970. Graduated from the Moscow Institute of Physical Culture, 1970. USSR champion, 1969–75 with L. Pakhomova in pair skating. World and European champion, 1970–76. Olympic champion, 1976.
See: *Zvezdy Ledianoi Areny*, Moscow, 1976.

Gorshkov, Lev Aleksandrovich
26.6.1910– . Violin maker.
Born in Penza. His violins were commended at the 3rd G. Wieniawski International Competition, Poznan, 1957, and at the All-Union Competition of String Instruments, Moscow, 1958 and 1966.

Gorshkov, Sergei Georgievich
26.2.1910–13.5.1988. Admiral.
Born in Kamenets-Podolsk. Son of a teacher. Joined the Red Navy, 1927. Member of the Communist Party, 1942. Graduated from the Frunze Naval School, 1931. From 1932,

commander of military ships and naval units. During WWII, commander in the Azov sea, head of the defence of Novorossiisk, 1942. Danube flotilla commander, 1944. From 1945, in the Black Sea, 1948–51, as Chief of Staff, and later as Commander of the Black Sea Fleet. Deputy Chief Commander of the Navy, 1955. For almost 30 years, Commander in Chief of the Navy, 1956–85 (and Deputy Minister of Defence). Organized the transformation of the USSR into a great naval power. Member of the Cen. Cttee. of the CPSU, 1961. Retired 1985. Has done more for the growth of the Russian Navy than anybody since Peter the Great.

Gorskaia, Rozalia Grigor'evna (b. Fainberg; m. Ekskuzovich)
12.7.1891–? Singer (soprano)
Born in Bratslav, in Podol'skaia Gouvt. Pupil of S. Gladkaia. Soloist with the Narodnyi Dom (People's House) from 1915, and with the Mariinskii Theatre, Petrograd (Kirov Theatre of Opera and Ballet) from 1918. Emigrated, 1920, and died abroad.

Gorskii, Aleksandr Alekseevich
18.8.1871–20.10.1924. Choreographer.
Born in Petersburg. In 1889, graduated from the Petersburg Theatre School. A pupil of P. Karsavin and M. Petipa. Dancer at the Mariinskii Theatre, 1889–1900. From 1901, a choreographer. From 1902 until his death, chief choreographer at the Bolshoi Theatre. Revived the ballets of his tutor, Petipa. Invited talented artists such as K. Korovin to work for the Bolshoi. Created his own original ballets: *Doch' Guduly*, 1902, *Salambo*, 1910, and *Liubov' Bystra*, 1913. Influenced a generation of dancers, including T. Karsavina, A. Messerer, M. Gabovich, A. Abramova and L. Bank. Died in Moscow.

Gorskii, Ivan Ivanovich
12.9.1893–1972? Geologist.
Professor at the Leningrad Mining Institute, 1935. Director of the Geological Institute, 1943–47. Chairman of the Palaeontological Society,

1954. Chief editor of geological maps of several regions of the USSR.

Gorskii, Konstantin (Gorski)
13.6.1859–31.5.1924. Violinist, composer.
Born in Lida. Pupil of Ap. Kontskii and L. Auer. Taught in Penza, Saratov, Tiflis, and Khar'kov. Lived in Poland from 1919. Author of an opera, symphonic works, songs, and works for violin. Died in Poznan.

Gostev, Boris Ivanovich
1927– . Politician.
Graduated from the Moscow Technological Institute of Light Industry, 1951. Joined the Communist Party, 1954. Engineer, then Chief Engineer of Burevestnik Shoe Factory, Moscow, 1951–53. Senior positions in the USSR Ministry of Light Industry, 1953–63. Various senior positions in the Cen. Cttee. of the CPSU, 1963–66. 1st Deputy Head of the Dept. of Trade and Finance of Cen. Cttee., 1966–75. Finance Minister, 1987. Member of the CPSU Cen. Auditing Cttee., 1971–76. Candidate member of the Cen. Cttee., 1976–81. Full member from 1981.

Gotlib, Adolf Davidovich
24.8.1910– . Pianist.
Born in Moscow. Younger brother of Mikhail Gotlib. Professor at the Gnesin Pedagogical Institute for Music. From 1926, performed in a duet with his brother. Author of transcriptions for two pianos.

Gots, Abram Rafailovich
1882–1940. Revolutionary.
Born in Moscow into a rich Russian-Jewish family. Younger brother of M. Gots, who was leader of the SR Party until his death in 1906. Member of the SR terrorist group. After the 1905 Revolution, sentenced to 8 years hard labour, 1907. After the February Revolution 1917, leader of the SR faction in the Petrograd Soviet. Elected chairman of the VTSIK by the 1st Congress of Workers and Soldiers' Deputies in June 1917. Active opponent of the Bolshevik take-over in Nov. 1917. Arrested by the Bolsheviks, 1920. One of a group of SR leaders sentenced to death at

the first show trial of anti-communist socialists in the USSR, 1922. Pardoned and, according to Soviet sources, able to work in Soviet administrative offices. As the place and the exact date of death is not given, this information sounds suspect. According to *Pamiat'*, issue 3, shot in Alma-Ata.
Sources: *Pamiat' Istoricheskii Sbornik*, issue 1 Moscow, 1976, NY, 1978; issue 2, Moscow, 1977, Paris, 1979; issue 3, Moscow, 1978, Paris, 1980.

Gotsinskii, Nazhmutdin, Imam of the Northern Caucasus
1859–1925. Muslim leader.
Born in the aul of Gotso in Daghestan. Son of one of the closest friends and comrades-at-arms of Shamil, the hero of the Caucasian War in the 19th century. After the February Revolution 1917, joined local government as a mufti (spiritual leader). Proclaimed the 4th Imam of the Northern Caucasus highlanders and fought the Red Army, 1917–21. After the defeat of his forces in Daghestan, Mar. 1921, fled to Chechnia and continued the resistance. Taken prisoner by the Reds. Brought to Rostov-on-Don, sentenced to death and shot.

Govorov, Leonid Aleksandrovich
22.2.1897–19.3.1955. Marshal.
Joined the Red Army, 1920. Took part in the Civil War. Graduated from the Frunze Military Academy, 1933, and from the Academy of the General Staff, 1938. Professor at the Artillery Academy before WWII. Took part in the Soviet-Finnish war, 1939–40. During WWII, Commander of the Leningrad Front, 1942. After WWII, Chief Inspector of the Armed Forces and Deputy Minister of Defence.

Gozenpud, Abram Akimovich
23.6.1908– . Literary critic, musicologist.
Born in Kiev. Doctor of art history (Leningrad).
Works: *N. A. Rimskii-Korsakov, Temy i Idei Ego Opernogo Tvorchestva*, Moscow, 1957; *Muzykal'nyi Teatr v Rossii. Ot Istokov do Glinki*, Leningrad, 1959; *Russkii Sovetskii Opernyi Teatr, 1917–41. Ocherki Istorii*, Leningrad, 1963.

Grabar' Andrei Nikolaevich
26.7.1896–1960? Byzantinist.
Born in Kiev. Graduated from Kiev and Petrograd universities. Curator of the Archaeological Museum in Sofia, 1920–21. Lecturer in the history of art at Strasbourg University, 1928–37. Director of Studies in Byzantine Christianity and Christian Archaeology at the École des Hautes Études in Paris, 1937–46.
Main works: *La Peinture Religieuse en Bulgarie, La Decoration Byzantine, L'Empereur Dans I'Art Byzantin, La Peinture Byzantine, L'Iconoclasme Byzantin.*

Grabar', Igor' Emmanuilovich
25.3.1871–16.5.1960. Painter, art historian.
Born in Budapest. Son of a Carpatho-Russian member of the Hungarian Parliament. His father was persecuted by the Austro-Hungarian authorities for his Russophile position, and fled to Russia. Brought up by his mother in Chertezhnoe in Carpathian Russia (then Hungary). In mid-1880s, his mother (the daughter of A. Dobrianskii, a famous Carpatho-Russian scholar) moved with her children to Russia. Educated at Kiev secondary school. Graduated from Kiev University in law. Joined the Petersburg Academy of Art, 1894–96. From 1898, teacher of painting at Azbe's school in Munich. Member of the World of Art group in Petersburg, and of the Union of Russian Painters in Moscow. Editor of the first multi-volume *History of Russian Art*, 6 vol., 1909–16. Director of the Tretiakov Gallery in Moscow, 1913–25. After the October Revolution, organized the central studios for restoring works of art (helped in the rediscovery of icons as works of art.) Edited the 13-vol *History of Russian Art* (published after WWII). Director of the Institute of Art History of the Soviet Academy of Sciences. Director of Moscow Art Institute, 1937–43.

Grabin, Vasilii Gavrilovich
1900–1980. Artillery designer.
Joined the Red Army, 1920, and the Communist Party, 1921. Graduated from the Dzerzhinskii Military Academy, 1930. Chief designer in an artillery works, 1934. Head of the Chief Artillery Design Bureau during WWII, 1942–46. Head of the Scientific Institute of Artillery, 1946–60. Designed the Soviet anti-tank weapons of WWII.

Grachev, Mikhail Oskarovich
28.1.1911–   . Composer.
Born in the village of Fel'shtin, in Kamenets-Podol'skaia Gouvt. Author of works for voice and orchestra, cantatas, a symphony and music for the circus.

Grachev, Panteleimon Vladimirovich
11.7.1889–1955. Musicologist.
Born in Petersburg. Author of works on the composers André Grétry, S. I. Davydov, O. I. Kozlovskii, and on Russian music in general, such as *Ocherki po Istorii Russkoi Muzyki, 1790–1825*, Leningrad, 1956.

Granin, Daniil Aleksandrovich (real name – German)
1919–   . Author.
Born in Volyn', Kursk Oblast'. Son of a forester. Graduated from the Leningrad Polytechnical Institute, 1940. Chief engineer in the Energy Laboratory and Construction Bureau at the Kirov Works, Leningrad, 1940–49. Probably worked in the military industry since there is no trace of his military service during the war. First publications in 1949. Became an established writer in the 1960s. Very often appeared in *Literaturnaia Gazeta* and *Moscow News*. In a brief article in the latter reviewing the 1970s, condemned L. Brezhnev as a medal-lover, who had lost contact with reality and fallen for praise from toadies.
Works: *Iskateli*, 1954; *Idu Na Grozu*, 1962; *Sad Kamnei*, 1972.

Grashchenkov, Nikolai Ivanovich
26.3.1901–   . Neurologist.
Graduated from Moscow University, 1926. Director of the Institute of Experimental Medicine, 1939–44. Deputy Health Minister, 1937–39. On active service during WWII. Director of the Neurological Institute, 1944–48. President of the Academy of Sciences of Belorussia, 1948–51. Assistant Director of the World Health Organization, 1959–61.

Grave, Dmitrii Aleksandrovich
1863–1939. Mathematician.
Professor at Kiev University. Academician, 1929. A pupil of Chebyshev. Worked in the field of higher algebra, theory of numbers, theory of groups and the mathematical aspects of cartography.

Grave, Ivan Platonovich
1874–1960. Major-general.
Graduated from the Mikhailovskaia Artillery Academy, 1900. Rocket inventor, 1916. Took part in the organization of the Red Army Artillery Academy, 1918. Taught at this academy until 1943. Specialist on ballistics. Wrote scientific works on this subject.

Grebenshchikov, Boris
1962–   . Rock singer.
Lead singer of the extremely popular folk-rock group Aquarium. Probably the Soviet Union's biggest pop star today. In 1987, at last acknowledged by the Soviet cultural authorities. Aquarium have made television appearances all over the USSR, and Melodia, the official record company, has at last issued their cassettes. Leads an unconventional lifestyle, and is a millionaire.

Grebenshchikov, Georgii Dmitrievich (Sibiriak)
6.5.1883–11.1.1964. Author.
Born near Tomsk in Siberia. Son of a peasant. Before WWI, gained fame as a writer on Siberian subjects, *V Prostorakh Sibiri*, 2 vol. 1913–15. During the Civil War, emigrated in 1920 to France. Settled in the USA. Wrote a saga about a Siberian peasant family, *Churaevy*, 6 volumes, 1922–36. Renamed his American estate Churaevka. Died in Florida.

Grechaninov, Aleksandr Tikhonovich
25.10.1864–4.1.1956. Composer.
Born in Moscow. Trained at the Moscow and Petersburg conservatories (1881–90 and 1890–93). Pupil of V. Safonov and N. Rimskii-Korsakov. Lived in Moscow, 1896–1922. Professor of the Musical Drama School of the Moscow Philharmonic Society. Emigrated, 1925. Lived in Paris. Moved to the USA in

1939. His art is in the Russian classical tradition, especially of the Mighty Handful. Left over 200 works, among them operas and music for Ostrovskii's play *Snegurochka*. Also composed cantatas, piano music and songs. Died in New York.

Grechkin, Aleksei Aleksandrovich
1893–1964. Lt.-general.
Joined the Red Army, 1918. Took part in the Civil War as an infantry colonel. Graduated from the Vystrel Courses, 1926. Took part in the Soviet-Finnish war, 1939–40. Commander of several armies during WWII. After WWII, Deputy Head of the Vystrel Courses, and Faculty Head at the Military Institute for Foreign Languages (training intelligence officers), until 1954.

Grechko, Andrei Antonovich
17.10.1903–26.4.1976. Marshal, politician.
Joined the Red Army, 1918, and took part in the Civil War. Graduated from the Frunze Academy, 1936, and from the Academy of the General Staff, 1941. Several high posts during WWII. Commander of the Voronezh Front, 1943, Commander of the 1st Guards, 1943–45. After WWII, Commander of the Kiev military district, 1945–53. Commander of the Soviet Occupation Forces in Germany, 1953–57. Commander of Ground Forces and Deputy Minister of Defence, 1957. Supreme Commander of the Warsaw Pact Forces, 1960. Minister of Defence of the USSR, 1967–76. Member of the Cen. Cttee. of the Communist Party, 1961–76, and member of the Politburo, 1973–76.

Grekov, Boris Dmitrievich
1882–1953. Historian.
Pupil of Kliuchevskii. Specialized in the field of medieval Russian history. Just before and during WWII, his nationalist school of history replaced that of the marxist Pokrovskii when Stalin realised that in order to win the war, he had to resurrect the Russian people's national values.
Works: *Kievan Rus,* 1939; *Peasants in Russia from the Earliest Times to the 17th Century,* 1946.

Grekov, Mitrofan Borisovich (Martyshchenko, Mitrofan Pavlovich)
1882–1934. Painter.
Studied at the Petersburg Academy of Art under his real name, Martyshchenko, 1903–11. On active service during WWI. Joined the Red cavalry during the Civil War. Made his career as a painter of war scenes, glorifying the exploits of the Red cavalry (*Tachanka, Trubachi 1-oi Konnoi Armii* and over 300 similar paintings).

Gren, Ivan Ivanovich
1898–1960. Vice-admiral
Joined the Red Navy and the Communist Party, 1918. Graduated from higher naval courses, 1922. Naval artillery expert in the Baltic fleet, 1927–30. Head of the naval artillery defence of Leningrad, 1941–43. Head of the navy's artillery department, 1943–45. Taught at the Naval Academy, 1946–60.

Grendal, Vladimir Davydovich
1884–1940. Col.-general.
Graduated from the Mikhailovskaia Artillery Academy, 1911. On active service during WWI as an artillery colonel. Joined the Red Army, 1918. During the Civil War, artillery inspector on different fronts. Taught at the Frunze Military Academy, and worked in the Central Artillery Administration. High command posts during the Soviet-Finnish war, 1939–40.

Griaznov, Ivan Kensorinovich
1897–1938. Military commander.
Joined the Red Army, 1918. Member of the Communist Party, 1922. Graduated from the Frunze Academy, 1927. Several high commands in the 1930s. Liquidated by Stalin.

Grigorenko, Petr (Petro) Grigor'evich
16.10.1907–21.2.1987. General, human rights campaigner.
Born in the Ukraine. Son of a poor peasant. In his youth, a member of the Komsomol and a soldier in food requisitioning detachments (prodotriady) during the 1920s. Served in the Red Army. Division commander during WWII. After WWII, lecturer at Frunze Military Academy in Moscow. Major-general, 1959. After

a speech at a local party meeting criticizing Stalinism, dismissed from the Academy, stripped of his rank and expelled from the party, 1961. Sent to the Far East, 1963. Imprisoned in a psychiatric hospital, 1964. Became one of the best known dissidents. Paid special attention to the cause of the Crimean Tatars, who were accused by Stalin of pro-German sympathies in 1944 and deported en masse from the Crimea to Central Asia. Joined the campaign for their return to the Crimea, where they had lived for centuries. One of the founders of the Helsinki monitoring group in Moscow. Left the USSR with his wife to visit his son in the USA in 1977. Stripped of Soviet citizenship and spent the rest of his life in the USA, continuing his campaign for human rights in the USSR.

Grigor'ev, Aleksandr Dmitrievich
15.10.1874–4.11.1940. Ethnographer.
Born in Warsaw. Graduated from Moscow University. During expeditions to the shores of the White Sea collected over 400 byliny – religious songs and folk songs from the local peasants – 1899–1901. Discovered the folk singer Krivopolenova. Published several volumes of *Arkhangelskie Byliny,* 1904–10, containing texts of the legends, musical notation and explanations of the local dialects. Emigrated in 1922. Lived in Poland and Czechoslovakia. Published in Prague a further volume of *Arkhangelskie Byliny*. Died in Prague.

Grigor'ev, N.A.
1891?–27.7.1919. Guerilla leader.
Army captain during WWI. Leader of Ukrainian peasant detachments during the Civil War. At first supported the Ukrainian Central Rada, and later Hetman Skoropadski. After his fall, changed over to Petliura in Dec. 1918. In Feb. 1919, accepted with his partisans into the Red Army, keeping his independent position as Ataman of the partisans of Kherson and Tauria. Fought against the White armies at Nikolaev, Kherson and Odessa. In May 1919, staged an uprising against the Reds, gathering some 20,000 volunteers in the Donbass, and, proclaiming his

aim as being 'Soviets without communists', gained a large part of Southern Ukraine (Kherson and Ekaterinoslav). Spoiled the Soviet attempt to send troops to help the Hungarian Soviet Republic, which was consequently defeated by Horthy. After his 'Greens' had been defeated by the Red Army in the summer of 1919, joined up with the forces of N. I. Makhno, who, considering him a rival, had him shot.

Grigor'ev, Oleg Georgievich
25.12.1937– . Athlete.
Born in Moscow. Honoured Master of Sports (boxing), 1960. USSR champion, 1958, 1962–65, 1967. European champion, 1957, 1963, 1965. Olympic champion, 1960. Member of the CPSU, 1965. Graduated from Ivanovskii Pedagogical Institute, 1967.

Grigor'ev, Sergei Leonidovich
17.10.1883–28.6.1968. Ballet dancer, choreographer.
Born in Tikhvin. Graduated from the Petersburg Theatre School, 1900. Dancer at the Mariinskii Theatre until 1912. At the same time studied in the Drama department of the Petersburg Theatre School under V. Davydov and A. Sanin. Toured around Russia and abroad. From 1909, assistant to Mikhail Fokin. From 1909–1929, choreographer, administrator and from time to time dancer with Diaghilev's Ballets Russes. Danced in Leonid Miasin's productions (Shakhriar in *Shekherazada*, 1910, Russian merchant in *Volshebnaia Lavka*, 1919). After Diaghilev's death, choreographer with Les Ballets Russes de Monte Carlo, the Original Ballet Russe, the Ballet Russe de Colonel de Basil, and others. With his wife, the dancer L. Chernyshova, revived Mikhail Fokin's productions for Sadler's Wells and La Scala: *L'Oiseau de Feu, Les Sylphides,* and *Petrushka* in 1954, 1955 and 1957. His book, *The Diaghilev Ballet, 1909–29,* published in 1953, became a classic. Died in London.

Grigorian, Grant Aramovich
10.4.1919–27.1.1962. Composer.
Born in Sukhumi in the Caucasus to Armenian parents. Taught at the Iakutsk Music School from 1953. Author of a concerto on a Iakut subject for violin and orchestra, an oratorio, an opera, and an operetta. Also arranged Iakut folk songs. His residence in Iakutsk, the coldest place in Siberia, in 1953 and his premature death there remain unexplained by official sources. Probably a Gulag inmate in Iakutia where there were many camps at the time.

Grigoriants, Sergei Ivanovich
1947– . Editor.
Spent 9 years in the Gulag. Founded the bulletin, *Glasnost'*, printing information which did not appear in the official press, 1987. Became the main source of information on the ethnic unrest in 1988 in Armenia and Azerbaidzhan. After this the bulletin was closed and he was arrested, but was soon released and has continued his journalistic activities.

Grigorii, Bishop (Grabbe, Count)
1900?– . Russian Orthodox clergyman.
For many years Secretary of the Holy Synod of the Russian Church in Exile. Consistently represented a right-wing view.

Grigorovich, Iurii Nikolaevich
2.1.1927– . Choreographer.
Born in Leningrad. Graduated from the Leningrad Choreographic School, 1946. Star at the Kirov Ballet Theatre until 1964. From 1964, choreographer, and later chief choreographer, of the Bolshoi Theatre. Revived other choreographers' ballets, also created his own productions, eg. *Spartak*, 1968 (awarded the Lenin Prize, 1970). In 1978, staged *Romeo and Juliet* at the Paris Opera House. Staged a new version of this ballet in 3 acts at the Bolshoi Theatre, 1979. Works only with the stage designer, Simon Virsaladze. From 1973, Professor of the Ballet Department of the Leningrad Conservatory.

Grigorovich, Ivan Konstantinovich
7.2.1853–3.3.1930. Admiral, politician.
Educated at the Naval Corps, 1874. Took part in Russo-Japanese war as captain of a warship, later commander of the naval base at Port Arthur. Admiral, 1911. The last tsarist navy minister, 1911–1917. Liberal in outlook, popular with the Duma. Resigned after the February Revolution 1917. Emigrated to France, 1923. Died in Menton.

Grigorovich, Karl Karlovich (Gregorovich)
1868–25.3.1921. Violinist.
Born in Petersburg. Pupil of V. Bezekirskii and J. Ioakhim. Professor at the Musical Drama School of the Philharmonic Society, Moscow, from 1904. From 1910 leader of the first Mecklenburg Quartet, the first Russian chamber ensemble to tour in Europe. Died in Mogilev.

Grikurov, Eduard Petrovich
11.4.1907– . Conductor.
Born in Tiflis. Pupil of A. Gauk. Conductor from 1937. Chief conductor, 1944–56, and from 1964, of the Leningrad Malyi Opera Theatre. Chief conductor at the Kirov Theatre of Opera and Ballet, 1956–60. Teacher at the Leningrad Conservatory. Married to the pianist Sofia Borisovna Vakman.

Grin, Aleksandr Stepanovich (Grinevskii)
23.8.1880–8.7.1932. Author.
Born in Slobodskoi, Viatka Gouvt, Son of an exiled Polish revolutionary. In his youth, wandered about Russia, changing his profession several times. Joined the army, 1902, and the SRs, 1903. Several times arrested for revolutionary activity, several escapes. First story published in 1908. Became widely known for his novels which had a vaguely Western and exotic background, and later became an object of official criticism for the same reason. Could be regarded as the Russian Joseph Conrad. Retains his popularity among readers of romantic fiction. Died in Staryi Krym.
Main works: *Alye parusa*, 1923; *Serdtse pustyni*, 1923; *Begushchaia po volnam*, 1928; *Collected Works*, 6 vols, 1965.

Grinberg, Grigorii Borukhovich
193?-   . Human rights campaigner.
One of the leading human rights campaigners in the 1980s. Long time refusenik. Expert in Soviet law. With a group of 42, courageously put to the test the new emigration regulations introduced under Gorbachev. His letter about violations of the right to emigrate was published in the *The Times* (2 March 1988).

Grinberg, Maria Izrailevna
6.9.1908-   . Pianist.
Born in Odessa. Pupil of F. Blumenfeld and K. Igumnov. Lecturer at the Gnesin Pedagogical Institute of Music.
See: D. Rabinovich, *Portrety Pianistov*, Moscow, 1962.

Grinberg, Moisei Abramovich
19.7.1904-   . Music producer, journalist.
Born in Rostov-on-Don. Head of the All-Union Musical Broadcasts, 1941–49. Artistic director the Moscow Philharmonic from 1953. Author of articles on Soviet music.

Grinevitskii, Vasilii Ignat'evich
1871–1919. Engineer, economist.
Professor and director of the Moscow Bauman School (Higher Technical School), Moscow's elitist technical educational establishment. A prominent representative of the technical intelligentsia in pre-1917 Russia. Condemned the Bolshevik take-over. Left a valuable work, *The Post-War Prospects of Russian Industry*, Kharkov, 1919. The second edition was published in Moscow in 1922. It became the basis of future 5-year plans, and dominated Soviet economic thought for decades. Died in Ekaterinodar.

Grinkrug, Lev Aleksandrovich
1889–1971? Finance director.
Born in Smolensk. Son of Aleksandr Grinkrug, a Jewish banker and doctor, and Anna Germanovna Schmel'kina, daughter of a Moscow banker. Met Mayakovsky and Lili Brik, and became a close friend and member of the family. Graduated in law from Moscow University, 1911.

Worked at his father's bank. From 1919–25, worked as a financial director of ROSTA (later, the TASS Agency). In 1925, spent 6 months in Paris and Juan-les-Pins, in the South of France. Did not return to the USSR.

Grinkrug, Mikhail Aleksandrovich
1887–1959. Bank clerk.
Son of a Jewish banker. Brother of L.A. Grinkrug. Emigrated in 1920. Settled in Berlin. In 1916, Mayakovsky dedicated his poem, *Ei!* to him. Emigrated from Germany, 1933.

Grishin , Anatolii Kuzmich
8.7.1939-   . Athlete.
Born in Moscow. Honoured Master of Sports (canoe), 1964. Olympic champion (4-man canoe), 1964. Member of the CPSU, 1964. World champion, 1966. USSR champion, 1960–67 with various teams. European champion, 1967. Graduated from the Volgograd Institute of Physical Culture, 1969.

Grishin, Evgenii Romanovich
23.3.1931-   . Athlete.
Born in Tula. In the early 1950s, was the USSR's best cycle racer. Honoured Master of Sports (skating), 1952. European champion, 1956. Olympic champion, 1960. Graduated from the Smolensk Institute of Physical Culture, 1965. Member of the CPSU, 1962. USSR champion, 1956–65. World record holder, 1955–68 (500, 1,000 and 1,500 metres race). Silver medal, 1964.

Grishin, Ivan Tikhonovich
1901–1951. Col.-general.
Joined the Red Army, 1920, and the Communist Party, 1927. Graduated from the Frunze Academy, 1936. Took part in WWII. After WWII, head of military and physical training of ground forces.

Grishin, Viktor Vasil'evich
18.9.1914-   . Politician.
Born in Serpukhov. Son of a railway worker. Graduated from the Moscow College of Geodesy, 1932, then, from the Technical College of Railway Engine Economics, 1937.

Graduated from the Higher Party School of the Cen. Cttee. Deputy Head of the Engine Department in Serpukhov, 1937–38, and 1940–41. Member of the CPSU, 1939. During WWII, Secretary of the CPSU Cttee. at Railway Junction in Serpukhov. 2nd, then 1st Secretary of the Serpukhov City CPSU Cttee. until 1950. Moved to Moscow as head of the Department of Machine Building, 1950–52. From 1952, member of the Cen. Cttee. of the CPSU, deputy to the USSR Supreme Soviet. Chairman of Trade Unions, 1956–67. Candidate member, 1961–71, full member of the Politburo of the Cen. Cttee. from 1971. 1st Secretary of the Moscow City CPSU Cttee, from 1967. Member of the Presidium of the USSR Supreme Soviet from 1967. As Moscow party boss, he allowed the capital to sink into deep corruption. A follower of Brezhnev and one of Gorbachev's main rivals, replaced by Boris Eltsin when Gorbachev took over.
See: A. Avtorkhanov, *Ot Andropova k Gorbachevu* (From Andropov to Gorvachev), Paris, 1986.

Grishkevich, Margarita Nikolaevna
5.8.1917-   . Ballet dancer, teacher.
Born in Petrograd. Graduated from the Leningrad Choreographic School, 1937. A. Vaganova's pupil. Dancer with the Kirov Theatre, 1937–47. From 1947–63, dancer with the Paliashvili Theatre, Tbilisi. From 1949 taught in Tbilisi, then Cuba, 1963–64, Egypt, 1966–67, and Columbia, 1970.

Grishko, Mikhail Stepanovich
27.2.1901-   . Singer (baritone).
Born in Mariupol'. Pupil of Iu. Reider. Soloist with the Kiev Theatre of Opera and Ballet from 1936. Appeared in films such as *Shchit Dzhurgaia,* 1950. State Prize, 1950.

Gritsevets, Sergei Ivanovich
1909–1939. Pilot.
Joined the armed forces and the Communist Party, 1931. Educated at a pilots' school, 1932. Sent to fight in the Spanish Civil War, 1936–39. Fought in the Far East at Khalkin-Gol, 1939. Died in an aircrash.

Gromadin, Mikhail Stepanovich
1899–1962. Col.-general.
Joined the Red Army, 1918. Member of the Communist Party, 1925. Graduated from the Frunze Academy, 1933. Specialist in anti-aircraft defence. During WWII, Deputy Defence Minister, responsible for anti-aircraft defence, and commander of the anti-aircraft defence forces. Kept this post after WWII.

Groman, Vladimir Gustavovich
1874–1937. Economist, politician.
Of half-German parentage. Joined the social-democratic movement in the 1890s. Menshevik, 1905. Prominent adviser to the Cen. Cttee. of the Menshevik Party propaganda, 1905–1921. Joined the Cen. Cttee. in 1922. Became disillusioned with Marxism and left the party. Leading member of the Presidium of Gosplan in charge of food supply, 1923–28. Dismissed in 1928. Arrested in 1930. One of the chief defendants at the trial of the Union Bureau of Mensheviks, 1931 where he 'confessed' to subversive activities. Actively cooperated with the authorities. Sentenced to 10 years. Probably died in the camps.
See: *Pamiat'*, Nr 3, Paris.

Gromov, Boris
1944– . General.
Until 15 May 1988, commander of the Soviet armed forces in Afghanistan. In charge of pulling Soviet troops out of the country.

Gromov, Mikhail Mikhailovich
1899–1985. Air force col.-general.
Joined the Red Army, 1918. Educated at a pilots' school, 1918. Took part in the Civil War. Instructor and test pilot in the 1930s. Made a non-stop flight, Moscow — North Pole — St Jacinto, USA, 1937. This flight was well publicized in the Soviet press. Head of an air force research institute, 1940–41. Joined the Communist Party, 1941. Air force commander on different fronts during WWII. Chief of air force training, 1944. Deputy Commander of the Strategic Bomber Force, 1946. High posts in the aviation industry ministry, 1949–55.

Gromova, Liudmila Pavlovna
4.11.1942– . Athlete.
Born in Miass, Cheliabinsk Oblast'. Master of Sports (gymnastics), 1961. Olympic champion, 1964. Graduated from the Moscow Oblast' Pedagogical Institute, 1975. Coach.

Gromyko, Anatolii Andreevich
1932– . Politician, author, professor.
Son of Andrei Gromyko. 1st Secretary at the USSR Embassy in London, 1961–65. Head of a section at the Institute of Africa of the Academy of Sciences, 1966–69. Head of an Academy section studying general trends in US foreign policy (renamed the Institute of the United States and Canada), 1969–76. Director of the Institute of Africa from Dec. 1976. Corresponding member of the USSR Academy of Sciences from 1981. Author of about 200 publications on US and African countries. Lecturer on disarmament matters. In a lecture at the Stockholm International Peace Research Institute in July 1987, said, 'It is vital for us to do away with the arms race before it does away with us.'

Gromyko, Andrei Andreevich
18.7.1909– . Diplomat, politician.
Veteran Soviet Foreign Minister (of 40 years standing), known as Grim Grom for always looking grim and also as Mr Niet. Born in the village of Starye Gromyki, Gomel Oblast' in Belorussia. Son of a peasant. Joined the Communist Party in 1931. Graduated from the Economics Institute, 1932, then from the Minsk Agricultural Technical School, 1936. Doctor of Economic Science. Senior researcher at the Institute of Economics of the USSR Academy of Sciences, 1936–39. Entered the diplomatic service in 1939. Head of the American Department in the USSR People's Commissariat for Foreign Affairs. Staff member at the USSR Embassy in Washington, 1939–43. Soviet Ambassador to the USA, then to Cuba, 1943–46. Present at the founding of the United Nations after WWII, became the Soviet Permanent Representative in the UN, 1946–48. Deputy, 1947–49, then 1st Deputy Soviet Minister of Foreign Affairs, 1949–52. Soviet Ambassador to the

UK, 1952–53. Candidate member, 1952–56, full member of the Cen. Cttee. of the CPSU from 1956. Again 1st Deputy, 1953–57, later Minister of Foreign Affairs from 1957. Member of the Politburo of the Cen. Cttee. from 1973. President of the USSR, 1987. Gorbachev, ending the Kremlin gerontocracy by getting rid of the old guard, made an exception in Gromyko's case, promoting him to the (largely ceremonial) post of Head of State (Chairman of the Presidium of the Supreme Soviet). In 1987 suddenly emerged as a glasnost reformer. According to his own daughter Emilia, 'My father lives in the skies . . . for 25 years he has not set foot in the streets of Moscow'. His unique career in foreign affairs has covered the epochs of Stalin, Khrushchev and Brezhnev at home, and abroad the days of Roosevelt and Churchill, to the times of Reagan and Thatcher. Retired Oct. 1988.

Gross, Evgenii Fedorovich
20.10.1897–1978? Physicist.
Graduated from Leningrad University, 1924. Professor at Leningrad University, 1938. Research on light-scattering and excitons.

Grossman, Leonid Petrovich
24.1.1888–15.12.1965. Literary scholar.
Born in Odessa. Graduated from Odessa University, 1911. Professor at the Moscow Pedagogical Institute. Became known for his excellent studies of classical 19th century Russian literature (Pushkin, Dostoevskii, Sukhovo-Kobylin, Leskov). Died in Moscow.

Grossman, Vasilii Semenovich (Iosif Solomonovich)
12.12.1905–14.9.1964. Author.
Born in Berdichev, Ukraine. Graduated from Moscow University in 1929. His name was associated with Stalinist novels about workers. Joined the Communist Party in the 1930s. During WWII, war correspondent of the army newspaper *Krasnaia Zvezda*. Used the war-time material in his later novels. Considered a conformist during his lifetime, became widely known in the West (and in a completely new light in the

USSR) after the posthumous publication of *Vse Techet*, a novel written in secret, which is a clear condemnation of Stalinism. Also wrote *Stepan Kolchugin, Narod Bessmerten, Gody Voiny,* and the *Chernaia Kniga* (The Black Book), co-edited with Il'ia Erenburg and others, and published in Israel, containing documents on Nazi atrocities against the Jews in the occupied territory of the Soviet Union. Died in Moscow.

Grozdova, Svetlana Khristoforovna
29.1.1959– . Athlete.
Born at Rostov-on-Don. International class Master of Sports (gymnastics), 1975. Student at the Rostov Pedagogical Institute. USSR champion, 1974, 1976. Olympic champion, 1976.

Grundman, Elsa Iakovlevna
16.5.1891–30.3.1931. State security official.
Born in Latvia, Daughter of a peasant. Involved in revolutionary activity, 1905. Joined the Bolsheviks, 1906. Took part in the storming of the Winter Palace, Oct. 1917. Commissar of Cheka detachments on the Eastern front, 1918. Cheka work in Moscow, 1919, and on the West-Southern front and in the Caucasus, 1920–1930. Transferred to high GPU posts in Moscow, 1930. Died in Moscow.

Gruzenberg, Oskar Osipovich
1866–27.12.1940. Lawyer.
Born in Ekaterinoslav (now Dnepropetrovsk). Son of a merchant. Educated at Kiev high school. Graduated in law from Kiev University, 1889. Moved to Petersburg. Became an assistant legal attorney. Widely known as a defence lawyer in trials connected with pogroms, ritual accusations and Zionism, often gaining verdicts in favour of the accused. Defended Trotsky and other leaders of the Petrograd Soviet during the 1905 Revolution at their trial in 1906. Although one of the best-known lawyers in the country, remained officially only an assistant, refusing to abandon the Jewish faith, and became a lawyer only in 1905, when religious requirements for the legal profession were dropped. Defended

Beilis (with Maklakov and others) during the famous ritual murder trial in Kiev, 1913 (the accused was acquitted). During WWI, defended Jews accused of espionage. Appointed senator by Kerenskii, 1917. Member of the Constituent Assembly from Kherson. After the Bolshevik take-over, moved to Tiflis, where his brother was a prominent lawyer. Moved to Kiev and Odessa, emigrated to Germany, and settled in Berlin, 1921. Moved to Riga, 1926, and became chairman of the local Russian Law Society. Published a Russian law journal, *Zakon i Sud*. Settled in Southern France, 1932. Died in Nice.

Gryzunov, Ivan Vasil'evich
22.4.1879–29.10.1919. Singer (baritone).
Born in Moscow. Pupil of K. Krzhizhanovskii. Appeared in operas from 1903. Soloist with the Bolshoi Theatre 1904–15. Died in Moscow.

Grzhebin, Zinovii Isaevich
1869–1929. Publisher, artist.
Partner of Kopelman in the publishing house Shipovnik before the 1917 Revolution. Emigrated during the Civil War. Organized a publishing house in Berlin, 1919–23, which published many outstanding Russian writers who found themselves abroad at that time.

Gubaidullina, Sofia Asgatovna
1931– . Composer.
Born in Chistopol'. Graduated from the Kazan' and Moscow Conservatories. Appeared at the Paris event, *Moscow – Paris*, 1979. Noticed by the French press and invited to perform her violin concerto at La Maison de Radio Offertorium. Avant-garde composer. Her British premiere in 1987, *Symphony in 12 Movements*, attracted much media attention. Also a conductor. Leading Soviet music figures, such as G. Kremer and G. Rozhdestvenskii, praise her talent.

Gubarev, Vladimir Stepanovich
1937?– . Journalist, playwright.
The first journalist to reach the crippled nuclear reactor a few days after the explosion in Chernobyl.

Reported everything he saw and heard. As a result, wrote a play entitled *Sarcophagus*. Although it was his first play, he managed to create a gripping documentary, which was discovered and turned into a work of art by Michael Glenny and Michael Birch. The RSC staged the British première in early 1987 at the Barbican. The play was later shown at the Mermaid Theatre with the same success.

Gubkin, Ivan Mikhailovich
21.9.1871–21.4.1939. Geologist.
Born in the village of Pozdniakovo near Nizhnii-Novgorod (Gorkii). Graduated from the Petersburg Mining Institute, 1910. Spent some time in the USA, 1917–18, studying the US oil industry. From 1918, one of the main organizers of the Soviet oil industry. Chairman of the commission for the study of the Kursk Magnetic Anomaly, 1920–25 (a rich store of iron ore and other minerals). Academician, 1929, vice-president of the USSR Academy of Sciences, 1937. Professor, 1920, and Dean, 1930, of the Moscow Mining Institute. Actively involved in the Soviet industrialization drive. Many works on oil exploration. Died in Moscow.

Guchkov, Aleksandr Ivanovich
26.10.1862–1936. Politician, industrialist.
Born near Moscow. Son of a rich merchant (Old Believer stock). Energetic and widely travelled. Volunteered to fight for the Boers during the Boer War (a popular cause in Russia at the time), wounded in the leg by a British bullet which left him slightly lame for life. Founded the right-of-centre Octobrist party, which after the 1905 Revolution accepted the reforms agreed by the Tsar, and actively collaborated in the Duma with Prime Minister P. Stolypin. Elected representative of trade and industry in the State Council (Upper Chamber), 1907. Member of the 3rd Duma, 1907. President of the Third Duma, 1910–11. Before and during WWI, an extremely bitter personal enemy of the Tsar and especially the Tsarina. Organized the system of commercial and public bodies which were helping to supply the front during WWI. Though

without any official capacity, he persuaded Nicholas II, on his way home from military HQ in Pskov, to abdicate in favour of his brother, Grand Duke Mikhail, thus bringing about the end of the monarchy in Russia. Became Minister of War in the Provisional Government, Mar.-May 1917. Resigned, being unable to restore order in the army, which started to dissolve under the influence of revolutionary propaganda. Took a resolute anti-Bolshevik position after Oct. 1917. Emigrated to Berlin, 1918. Died in Paris.

Gudkov, Viktor Panteleimonovich
16.9.1899–17.1.1942. Composer, folkorist.
Born in Voronezh. Recorded folk songs and folk instrumental music, published in 1941 in collaboration with N. Levi. Founded an orchestra of players of the kantele (a pizzicato musical instrument) now known as the Kantele State Ensemble. Author of choral and instrumental arrangements of folk songs popular in Finnish Karelia. At the beginning of WWII, evacuated to Kirgizia with his musicians. Died in Frunze.

Gudymenko, Petr Emel'ianovich
1898–1953. Lt.-general.
Joined the Red Army, 1918. Member of the Communist Party, 1919. Several artillery command posts in the 1920s. Graduated from the Frunze Academy, 1930. In Transcaucasia during WWII. Command posts in anti-aircraft defence, 1946–49.

Guenther, Johannes von
1886–1973. Poet.
Born in Mitava, of Baltic-German descent. Lived in Petersburg, 1908–1914. Contributed to *Apollon*. Close to the Russian Symbolist poets. Later moved to Germany. Translated modern Russian poets into German. Wrote memoirs on the Silver Age of Russian poetry, published in West Germany.

Gukova, Margarita Georgievna
28.3.1887–1970? Singer (soprano).
Born in Zhitomir. Wife of the singer A. Bogdanovich. Pupil of Umberto

Mazetti. Soloist with the Bolshoi Theatre, 1906–14. Taught singing at the operatic studio of the Bolshoi Theatre, 1906–14, and at the Stanislavskii Opera and Drama Studio in Moscow, from 1935.

Gul, Roman Borisovich
1896–1986. Author, editor.
Born in Perm'. Volunteered for the front during WWI. After the Bolshevik take-over, Nov. 1917, joined the Whites. Close to Kornilov. After Kornilov's death, moved to the Ukraine. Interned by the German occupation authority, deported to Germany. In the 1920s, lived in Berlin. Wrote critical memoirs of his time with the Whites, which were noticed by Lenin himself and published in the Soviet Union. Correspondent of Soviet papers in Berlin until 1927. Worked with Prof. Iashchenko at the office of his bibliographical bulletin. Used the peculiar situation in Berlin in the 1920s to make connections with Russian emigrés and visiting Soviet writers. After the take-over by the Nazis, interned in a concentration camp. After his release, moved to France. Wrote several widely-acclaimed biographies (Bakunin, Dzerzhinskii, Kotovskii, Savinkov). Was an historical film consultant with Sir Alexander Korda in England. After WWII, close to the historian Melgunov in Paris. Moved to the USA, 1950. Secretary, member of the editorial board, and then for many years editor of the magazine *Novyi Zhurnal*. Wrote memoirs, which are an invaluable source on Russian literature abroad (*Ya unes Rossiu*, 2 vols). Died in the USA.

Guliaev, Nikolai Dmitrievich
1918–1985. Col.-general.
Joined the Red Army, 1938. Member of the Communist Party, 1943. During WWII, a very successful fighter pilot (shot down 57 enemy planes), and twice Hero of the Soviet Union, 1943, 1944. After WWII, graduated from the Zhukovsky Air Force Academy, 1950, and the Academy of the General Staff, 1960. High command posts in anti-aircraft defence until 1979.

Guliaev, Vadim Vladimirovich
1.2.1941–   . Athlete.
Born in Moscow. USSR champion,

1964–75. European champion 1966, 1970. Silver medal, 1968. Olympic champion, 1972. Honoured Master of Sports (water polo), 1972.

Gumilev, Lev Nikolaevich
1911–   . Orientalist.
Son of N. Gumilev and A. Akhmatova. Was 9 years old when his father was shot. Arrested after the Kirov murder, 1934, and sent to the Gulag. Second arrest, 1937. During WWII, like many other Gulag inmates, sent to the front until 1945. In 1949, arrested again and sent to the camps. Released during the Khrushchev thaw, 1956. Highly respected specialist on Central Asian nomadic people.

Gumilev, Nikolai Stepanovich
3.4.1886–24.8.1921. Poet
Born in Kronstadt, the son of a naval doctor. Grew up in Tsarskoe Selo and Tiflis. At Tiflis secondary school, fell under the influence of revolutionary Marxism. Returned to Tsarskoe Selo in 1903. First volume of poetry, *Put' Konkvistadorov* published in 1905. Studied French literature at the Sorbonne, 1907–08. First voyage to Africa (from France) in 1907. Married Anna Akhmatova in 1910 and a son, Lev, was born in 1911. Before WWI, became a well-known literary figure (poet, member of the editorial board, and literary critic of the Petersburg magazine *Apollon*). Close to Annenskii, later to Briusov. Leader of the acmeist school (in opposition to the Symbolists). Travelled to Italy in 1912. Second voyage to Africa (Abyssinia) in 1913 on an expedition organised by the Russian Academy of Sciences. In 1914, volunteered for military service, served in cavalry regiments, twice awarded the St. George Cross. Published *Notes of a Cavalryman*. After the February Revolution 1917, went on a military mission through Scandinavia and Britain to France, trying to get to the Eastern front (submitted a report on Ethiopia to the French). Returned in Apr. 1918 through London and Murmansk to Petrograd. Divorced from Akhmatova. Married Anna Engelhardt in 1919 (she and her daughter presumably died of hunger during the Leningrad siege in WWII). During

the revolutionary years, active as lecturer, translator and editor. Elected chairman of the Petrograd Union of Poets (in preference to A. Blok). 1921, continued to promote acmeism (*Tsekh Poetov*). Arrested 3 Aug. 1921, and accused of an anti-Bolshevik, monarchist conspiracy. Shot with 61 others by the Cheka. Although excluded almost completely from all anthologies and reference books, and not republished for 6 decades, remained one of the most loved and influential among the modern Russian poets. The only rival of Blok among the early 20th century Russian poets, and his opposite in style, feeling and mode of expression. The centenary of his birth saw his comeback in the Soviet Union.

Gundartsev, Vladimir Il'ich
13.12.1944–   . Athlete.
Born in Satka, Cheliabinsk Oblast'. Honoured Master of Sports (biathlon), 1968. With Moscow Dynamo. USSR champion, 1966–67. Olympic champion, 1968. Bronze medal, 1968. World champion, 1969. Graduated from the Moscow Institute of Physical Culture, 1974.

Gurdzhiev, Georgii Ivanovich (Gurdjieff)
1873–1943. Occultist, guru.
Born in the Caucasus. Son of Greek settlers. As a dealer in Levantine carpets, travelled widely in the Middle East. Middleton Murry, the husband of Katherine Mansfield, described him as a 'man of violent temper, greedy for money, personally lustful, extravagant and boastful', and T. S. Eliot, in a letter to Ezra Pound, called him 'a maniac'. First known as a guru of small groups, seeking an increased awareness of life in Moscow before WWI. One of the first to notice and use the attractiveness to Western minds of Eastern esoteric teachings and mysticism. Worked out his own eclectic system with elements of Sufism and exercises based on yoga and dervish dancing. Not very well educated, was able to gain influence only after the arrival among his disciples of the highly educated P. Uspenskii, who in his works gave a detailed interpretation of the enigmatic utterings of the

Eastern mystic. Had some success before WWI in Russia in the highly charged atmosphere that led to the emergence of several similar figures (Rasputin, Badmaev). During the Civil War, met Uspenskii again in the Caucasus, emigrated to Turkey, and later followed him to England. In the 1920s, with Uspenskii's help, set up a teaching centre or an early guru commune (The Institute for the Harmonious Development of Man) in Fontainebleau, where for a time they both taught. After breaking with Uspenskii, continued to teach until he became seriously ill after a car accident. Wrote several mystical works, drawing on Indian and Persian esoteric traditions. Wrote an account of his alleged early meetings with wise men of the East.
Works: *All and Everything; Meetings With Remarkable Men* (turned into a film in 1979 by Peter Brook); *Life is Real Only Then When I Am.*
See: J.H. Reyner, *Ouspensky*, London, 1981.

Gureikin, Sergei Aleksandrovich
1900?–26.7.1979. Actor.
As a teenager, took part in the Civil War. With the White Army as a junior officer. Joined a theatre group in Germany, 1920. Pupil of N. Massalitinov. Moved to Paris. Worked as a taxi driver during the day, and acted in the evenings. Appeared in the *Brothers Karamazov, Uncle Vania*, and *Krechinskii's Wedding*. Became a famous emigré actor. Acted also as à compère. Russian Paris knew him well for his appearances at every cultural event. Died in Menton, France.

Gurevich, Boris Mikhailovich
23.2.1937–   . Athlete
Born in Kiev. Honoured Master of Sports (wrestling), 1967. USSR champion, 1957–67. Graduated from the Kiev Institute of Physical Culture, 1969. European champion, 1967, 1970. World champion, 1967, 1969. Olympic champion, 1968. Member of the CPSU, 1976.

Gurevich, Maksim Maksovich
23.3.1931–   . Athlete.
Born in Moscow. Honoured Master of Sports (wrestling), 1952. Olympic

champion, 1952. USSR champion, 1950, 1955. World champion, 1953, 1958.

Gurevich, Mikhail Iosifovich
12.1.1893–1976. Aircraft designer.
Born in Rubanshchina, near Kursk. Educated at the aviation faculty of the Khar'kov Technological Institute, 1925. Just before WWII, designed (with Mikoian) the famous fighter plane, the MIG-1 (Mikoian-Gurevich). The MIG-3 in the same series became a well-known Soviet fighter plane of WWII. The series has been continued and improved ever since, and has become one of the main weapons of the Soviet air force.

Gurii (Egorov, Viacheslav Mikhailovich), Metropolitan of Simferopol and the Crimea
13.7.1891–12.7.1965. Russian Orthodox clergyman.
Born near Novgorod. Educated at the Petersburg Commercial School, 1911. Graduated from the Petersburg Theological Academy, 1917. Monk, 1915. Head of the Aleksandr Nevskii Monastery in Petrograd, 1925. Exiled to Central Asia. Priest in Samarkand and Tashkent during WWII. Head of the Troitse-Sergieva Lavra (Zagorsk Monastery), 1945–46. Bishop of Tashkent and Central Asia, 1946. Archbishop, 1952. Metropolitan of Leningrad, 1959. Member of the Holy Synod. Due to ill-health, transferred to the Crimean diocese, 1961. Author of works on relations between the Orthodox and the Anglican churches.

Gurko, Vasilii Iosifovich (Romeiko-Gurko)
20.5.1864–11.11.1937. General.
Son of a field-marshal. Educated at the Pages Corps, 1885. Graduated from the Academy of the General Staff, 1892. During the Boer War, Russian military agent with the Boers, 1899–1902. Took part in the Russo-Japanese war, 1904–05. Commander of a cavalry division, 1911. Several high posts during WWI. In charge of the HQ of the Russian Army, Oct. 1916–Feb 1917 during Alekseev's illness. After the February Revolution 1917, commander of the Western front. From May 1917, in

difficulties with the Provisional Government for his monarchist views. In July 1917, arrested for corresponding with the deposed Tsar, and expelled from Russia in Aug. 1917 by Kerenskii. Later declined to take part in the Civil War. Settled in Italy. Published his memoirs in the 1920s. Died in Rome.

Gurov, Kuz'ma Akimovich
1901–1943. Lt.-general.
Joined the Red Army, 1919. Member of the Communist Party, 1921. Made a career as a political officer. Graduated from the Military-Political Academy, 1936. Head of the Military-Pedagogical Institute, 1940. Took part in WWII. Killed in action.

Gurov, Leonid Simonovich
3.7.1910– . Composer.
Born in the village of Arkhangel'skoe, Kherson Gouvt. Taught at the Odessa Conservatory. Head of the Department of Theory and Composition at the Kishenev Conservatory from 1945. Director from 1960, professor from 1962. Among his pupils were many Moldavian composers and musicologists. Author of symphonies, choral works, songs, arrangements of folk songs, and works on musicology.

Gurvitch, Georgii Davydovich
2.11.1894–10.12.1965. Sociologist.
Born at Novorossisk. Member of the SDs (Mensheviks). Professor at Tomsk and Petrograd universities, 1915–21. Emigrated, 1921. Lived in France. Professor of sociology at Strasbourg, 1935. During WWII, emigrated to the USA. After WWII, returned to France. Professor at the Sorbonne in Paris, 1948. Founded and edited the *Cahiers internationaux de Sociologies*, 1946. Founder and president of the Sociological Institute in Paris, 1953–56. Died in Paris.
Main works; *La Vocation actuelle de la Sociologie*, 2 vols, 1963; *Traite de Sociologie*, 2 vols, 1963.

Guryshev, Aleksei Mikhailovich
14.3.1925– . Athlete.
Born in Moscow. Honoured Master of Sports (ice hockey), 1954. USSR champion, 1957. European champion, 1954–56, 1958–59. World champion, 1954, 1956. Olympic champion, 1956. With Moscow Krylia Sovetov. Graduated from the Moscow Institute of Physical Culture, 1964.

Gusakova, Maria Ivanovna
6.2.1931– . Athlete.
Born in the village of Simoshkino, Riazan' Oblast'. Honoured Master of Sports (skiing), 1960. Graduated from the Leningrad High School of Physical Culture, 1959. USSR champion, 1960–66. Olympic champion, 1960. World champion, 1962. Silver medal, 1960. Bronze medal, 1964.

Gusakovskii, Iosif Iraklievich
1904– . General
Joined the Red Army, 1928. Tank troop commander in WWII. Graduated from the Academy of the General Staff, 1948. Commander of the Baltic military district, 1959. Head of the Personnel Dept. of the Ministry of Defence of the USSR, 1964–70.

Gusev, Aleksandr Vladimirovich
21.1.1947– . Athlete.
Born in Moscow. Honoured Master of Sports (ice hockey), 1973. USSR champion, 1970–78. World and and European champion, 1973–74. Olympic champion, 1976.

Gusev, Fedor Tarasovich
1905–1987. Diplomat.
Graduated from the Leningrad Institute of Economic Planning in 1931. Until 1935, worked in the Economic Planning Commission of the Leningrad area. In 1935, accepted as a student at the Institute for Diplomatic and Consular Officials, and specialized in British institutions. Graduated in 1937. Spent a year in Ottawa, 1942–43. Transferred to London, 1943, to replace Ivan Maiskii as Soviet Ambassador. Participant at the Tehran, Yalta and Potsdam conferences. Soviet representative, 1943–45, on the European Advisory Commission which drew up the terms for capitulation and occupation of enemy states. Delegate at the United Nations and at the deliberations of the Allied foreign ministers.

During his stay in London as Soviet Ambassador, 1943–46, was often seen at the frequently empty diplomatic gallery in the House of Commons. Recalled to Moscow, Aug. 1946, and appointed Deputy Minister of Foreign Affairs and at the same time Deputy of the Supreme Soviet. Soviet Ambassador to Sweden in 1956–62. Retired in 1975.

Gusev, Nikolai Ivanovich
1897–1962. Col.-general.
Joined the Red Army, 1918, and the Communist Party, 1919. Took part in the Civil War. Graduated from the Academy of the General Staff, 1941. During WWII, Commander of the First Cavalry, and later of several armies. Military attaché in Czechoslovakia, 1950. Worked in the Soviet General Staff, 1954–62, thereafter Deputy Chief of Staff of the Warsaw Pact.

Gusev, Nikolai Nikolaevich
21.3.1882–23.10.1967. Author.
Born in Riazan. Became a follower of Lev Tolstoy and was his personal secretary, 1907–09. Director of the L. Tolstoy Museum in Moscow, 1925–31. Took part in the editing of the definitive collected works of Tolstoy (Jubilee edition) in 90 vols (1928–58). Died in Moscow.

Gusev, Petr Andreevich
29.12.1904– . Choreographer, ballet teacher.
Born in Petersburg. Graduated from the Petrograd Choreographic School, 1922. One of the organizers of the Ballet de la Jeunesse, 1923. Dancer at the Leningrad Opera and Ballet Theatre, 1922–35, and soon one of its leading dancers. Starred with the Bolshoi Theatre, 1935–45. Made guest appearances at the Leningrad Malyi Theatre, 1933–35. Artistic Director of the Kirov Theatre, 1945–50. Choreographer of the Kirov Theatre, 1960–62. From 1958–60, headed a ballet school in China. Organizer of the Ballet Theatre in Peking. Organizer of choreographic schools in Shanghai and Canton. At the same time taught in ballet theatres and schools in Leningrad and Moscow. From 1976, head of the Ballet Department of the Leningrad Conservatory. From 1973, professor.

Author of many monographs about leading ballet personalities such as Mikhail Gabovich.

Gusev, Sergei Ivanovich (Drabkin, Iakov Davidovich)
1874–1933. Revolutionary, politician. Joined the SD Party, 1896. Took part in the 1905 Revolution. During the October Revolution 1917, Secretary of the Petrograd Military-Revolutionary Committee. Very active political commissar during the Civil War. Head of the political administration of the Red Army, 1921. Head of the press department of the Cen. Cttee. of the Bolshevik Party, 1925–26.

Gusev, Viktor Mikhailovich
30.1.1909–23.1.1944. Poet, playwright, scriptwriter.
Born in Moscow. Introduced his songs into all his plays and in films made from his scenarios. The words of his poems have been used as texts and libretti by several composers. An anthology of twelve songs was published based on his poems. Author of the most popular film comedies of the 1930s–40s: *Svinarka i Pastukh*, 1942, and *V Shest' Chasov Vechera Posle Voiny*, 1944. Stalin took a personal interest in his films and awarded him several state prizes. His premature death in Moscow is unexplained in official sources.

Gusev-Orenburgskii, Sergei Ivanovich
5.10.1867–1.6.1963. Author.
Born in Orenburg. Son of a merchant. Village priest, 1893. Left the church in 1898 due to revolutionary inclinations. First literary works published in 1890. Was much influenced by Gorkii and was close to him. Wrote about life in the villages in an anti-Tsarist and anti-clerical light. Emigrated after the October Revolution 1917. Settled in the USA. Died in New York.
Main works: *Collected works*, 16 vols, Petrograd, 1913–18.

Gushchin, Aleksei Petrovich
5.1.1922– . Athlete.
Born in the village of Aleksandrovka, Voronezh Oblast'. Member of the CPSU, 1952. Honoured Master of Sports (shooting), 1960. Coach at the DOSAAF, Moscow. World champion, 1958, 1962. Olympic champion, 1960. USSR champion, 1961.

Gussein-zade Mekhti Hanifa ogly (Hussein-zade)
1918–1944. Partisan.
Took part in WWII as a private. Heavily wounded and taken prisoner by the Germans in the Soviet Union, 1942. Escaped from a POW camp in Yugoslavia, 1944. Joined the Yugoslav partisans and directed several of their actions in Yugoslavia and Italy. Fell in action. Cult figure in Tito's Yugoslavia, and Hero of the Soviet Union (posthumously), 1957.

Gutman, Teodor Davydovich
11.11.1905– . Pianist.
Born in Kiev. Pupil of G. Neigauz. 8th prize at the Chopin International Piano Competition, Warsaw 1932, and 3rd prize at the All-Union Music Competition, Moscow, 1933. Professor at the Gnesin Pedagogical Institute of Music and at the Moscow Conservatory.

Gutnikov, Boris Lvovich
4.7.1931– . Violinist.
Born in Vitebsk. Pupil of Iu. Eidlin. 1st prize at the J. Slaviík and F. Ondricek International Violin Competition, Prague, 1956, at the J. Thibaud Competition, Paris, 1957, and at the P.I. Tchaikovskii Competition, Moscow, 1962. Lecturer at the Leningrad Conservatory. Solo performances in the USSR and abroad.

Gutor, Aleksei Evgen'evich
1868–1938. General.
Graduated from the Academy of the General Staff, 1895. Took part in the Russo-Japanese war, 1904–05. During WWI, lt.-general, commander of a division, a corps, and later the South-Western front. After the October Revolution, joined the Red Army. Taught at the Military Academy of the Red Army, 1922–31.

Guzenko, Igor (Gouzenko)
1919– . Intelligence officer.
Educated at the Moscow Engineering Academy, where as a student he was recruited by the NKVD and became a GRU agent. During WWII, served a year at the front, 1941–42, and was then sent to Ottawa, 1943, as a cipher clerk. Disillusioned with Soviet life, he defected on 7 Sept. 1945 with his wife and child, and revealed the enormous size of the Soviet espionage network in the West, which had a marked effect on public opinion and created a lasting impression. Many of the revelations about Soviet penetration of Western intelligence networks, for example that concerning Philby, Maclean et al., can be traced back to information originally supplied by him. Published an autobiography, *This Was My Choice*, London, 1948, and also a novel about the life of Gorkii, *The Fall of a Titan*, London, 1954. Settled in Canada.

Guzikov, Evgenii Mikhailovich
9.4.1887–1969? Violinist.
Born in Khar'kov. Pupil of I. Grzhimali and L. Kape. Doctor of art history. Professor at the Moscow Conservatory (class of Quartet Specialists), 1923–61. Among his pupils were the Komitas Quartet Players.

Gvozdev, Kuz'ma A.
1883–1923? Politician.
Active member of the Workers Movement before WWI. Member of the Council of the Military Industrial Committee, organized by Guchkov, chairman of the Workers' Group. After the February Revolution 1917, Minister of Labour in the Provisional Government (Sept.–Oct. 1917). Close to the right-wing SR Avksentiev. Denounced by the Bolsheviks as a renegade and an enemy of the working class.

Gzovskaia, Olga Vladimirovna
23.10.1883–2.7.1962. Actress.
Worked at the Malyi Theatre from 1905. At the MKHAT, 1910–17, and 1919–20. Entered the film industry, 1915. Leading actress of the silent cinema. Emigrated, 1920. Made about 6 films in Germany. Returned to the USSR. Worked at the Leningrad Drama Theatre, 1943–56.

H

Hackel, Aleksei Alfredovich
1892–1951. Art and literary critic.
Born in Petersburg into a Russo-German family. Educated at the Reformed Church Gymnasium (Reformatskoe Uchilishche) in Petersburg. Graduated from Petersburg University, 1914. Volunteered for service in the Russian Army, 1915–17, wounded. During the revolutionary years, worked as a teacher in Southern Russia until 1921. Defended Christianity in public debates with atheists. Emigrated to Germany, 1922. Lived in Berlin. Doctor of Heidelberg University, 1931. Received into the Orthodox Church. Lecturer at German and Dutch universities until 1932, specialist on Russian religious art (icons). Invited to teach in the USA by Metropolitan Benjamin, Exarch of the Moscow Patriarchate in North America, but WWII prevented his emigration to America. Moved to France, 1946. Elected professor at the Orthodox Theological Academy of St. Denis. Moved to Holland, 1948. Lecturer in Russian literature and art at Leiden University, 1950. Died in Leiden.
Main works: *Die Trinitaet in der Kunst*, *Ikon–Zeugen ostkirchlicher Kunst*, *Sergij von Radonesch*.

Hackel, Sergei Alekseevich, Archpriest
24.8.1931–   . Russian Orthodox clergyman, literary scholar.
Born in Berlin. Son of A.A. Hackel. Moved with his parents to the Netherlands, 1938, and England, 1940. Graduated from Oxford University, 1952. From 1964, taught Russian language and literature at Sussex University. Became a priest, and established an Orthodox parish in Sussex, 1964. Has remained its rector ever since. Chairman of the council of the diocese of the Moscow patriarchy in Britain. Editor of the Orthodox magazine *Sobornost'*. Took part in ecumenical work in the World Council of Churches. Published works on A. Blok, and a biography of Mother Maria (Skobtsova), which has been translated into many languages. Contributor to many publications and reference works on Russian literature, philosophy, history, and Orthodoxy. Editor of the BBC's Russian religious programmes, 1983.

Halpern, Aleksandr Iakovlevich
1892?–after 1960. Politician.
Born in Khar'kov. During the last period of the Provisional Government, Sept.–Oct. 1917, in charge of the government secretariat. Member of the Menshevik Party. After the Bolshevik take-over emigrated to London. Married to Salomee Andronikova (Mandelstam's Solominka). Died in London.

Heifetz, Jascha (Kheifets, Iosif Robertovich)
2.2.1901–10.12.1987. Violinist.
Born in Wilno. Studied at the Petersburg Conservatory under L. Auer. Became known as a violinist *wunderkind*, giving concerts all over Europe at the age of 12. Emigrated after the Bolshevik take-over, settled in the USA, 1925. Returned for a very successful tour of the Soviet Union, 1934. Appeared in films, married the ex-wife of Hollywood director Vidor. One of the greatest violinists of all time. Died in Los Angeles.

Helfand, Aleksandr Lazarevich (Helphand, Parvus, Israel)
1867–12.12.1924. Revolutionary, businessman.
Born in Berezino near Minsk. Studied at Basel Univesity, 1887, where he met Plekhanov, Zasulich, and Akselrod and became a Marxist. Graduated in philosophy, 1891. Moved to Stuttgart, collaborating with Kautskii and Klara Zetkin. Editor of *Arbeiterzeitung* in Dresden, 1897, collaborated with Marchlewski and Rosa Luxemburg. Moved to Munich where he edited *Iskra* with Lenin. During the 1905 Revolution, moved to Petersburg, and with Trotsky became the real leader of the revolution in Russia. Invented the concept of Soviet power. Arrested, spent several months in the Peter and Paul Fortress in Petersburg, exiled to Siberia, but escaped on the way and went to Germany. Became Gorkii's literary agent, collecting his royalties all over the world. Kept most of the money for himself, accused of embezzlement (Gorkii's money was then one of the main incomes of the Bolshevik Party) condemned by a party court (including Bebel, Kautski and Deutsch), and had to leave Germany in 1907. Went to Vienna, and from there to Turkey. Lived in Constantinople, 1910–15, and became the middleman between the Germans and the Young Turks government, handling very large sums of German money. Became personally very rich in the process and soon turned to an even more profitable business, becoming the main German expert on subversion in Russia through revolutionary channels. Moved to neutral Denmark, making Copenhagen the capital of his growing business empire and founding the Institute for Research into the Causes and Results of the World War. Members of the Institute were, among others, Ganetskii (Fuerstenberg), sent by Lenin (and later Radek), and Uritskii (later head of the Cheka). According to *The Merchant of Revolution*, by Zeman and Scharlau, OUP, 1965, he was instrumental in acquiring German help to transport Lenin and his group to Russia in spring of 1917, and in channeling to the Bolsheviks very large amounts of money from German government sources, which played a crucial role in the Bolshevik victory. Just before the German defeat in 1918, he moved to Switzerland, and then returned to Germany in Nov. 1920. Died of heart failure at his luxury villa at Wannsee.

Herzen, Natalia Aleksandrovna (Tata)
1844–1936. Literary historian.
Eldest daughter of A. Herzen. Lived with her father in the different countries of his exile in Western Europe. After his death, settled in Switzerland. Became the main guardian of the heritage of her father and his circle (Ogarev, Bakunin and others). Welcomed the 1917 Revolution in Russia, but later became bitterly disappointed with the Communist government.

Horowitz, Vladimir Samoilovich
1.10.1904–   . Pianist.
Born in Kiev. Studied at the Kiev Conservatory, 1921. Debut, 1922. Many concert tours in Russia in the 1920s. Emigrated, 1925. Lived in the

USA and Switzerland. Settled in New York, 1928. One of the greatest pianists of his time. Stopped giving concerts in 1950 but continued to make records. Re-appeared as a concert pianist, 1965. Married to Toscanini's daughter, Wanda. In his old age, visited the USSR for a triumphal tour.

Hrushevskii, Mikhail Sergeevich
29.9.1866–25.11.1934. Historian, politician.
Ukrainian. Born in Kholm. Graduated from Kiev University, 1890. Professor at Lvov University, 1894. Chairman of the Shevchenko Scientific Society, 1897. During the 1890s, active member of the Hromada (Ukrainian Liberal Nationalists). One of the founders of the Ukrainian National Democratic Party in Galicia, 1899. Moved to Kiev, 1908, and became close to the Cadets. Was in favour of Ukrainian autonomy. During WWI, took a pro-German stance. Arrested and sent to Simbirsk, 1914. After the February Revolution 1917, SR in the Ukraine, President of the Central Ukrainian Rada. After the fall of the Rada, emigrated, 1919. In Vienna founded the Ukrainian Sociological Institute, which became one of the main centres of Ukrainian nationalism. Broke with his colleagues and returned to the USSR in 1924. Member of the Academy of Sciences of the USSR, 1929. Moved to Moscow, 1930. Died at Kislovodsk in the Northern Caucasus. Author of a Ukrainian history and a history of Ukrainian literature from a nationalist point of view.
Main works: *Istoriia Ukrainy-Rusi*, 10 vols, 1898–1936; *Istoriia Ukrainskoi Literatury*, 5 vols, 1923–27.

Hurok, Sol (Gurok, Solomon)
9.4.1888–5.3.1974. Impresario.
Born in Pogar in the Ukraine. In 1905, emigrated to the USA and became a famous impresario. Managed many famous Russian artists in America. Organizer of the Berezka Ensemble tour in the USA. Died in New York.

I

Iagoda, Genrikh Grigor'evich
1891–1938. Secret police chief.
Active revolutionary from 1904. Exiled in 1911–13. Member of the Bolshevik Party from 1907. For a short time worked as a statistician, later in the medical insurance office of the Putilov Works in Petrograd. On military service in 1915. After the October Revolution, held various military posts, 1917–19. Senior member of the Ministry of Foreign Trade, 1919–22. From 1920, one of the chiefs of the Cheka. Deputy chairman of the GPU in 1924. Commissar for Internal Affairs (NKVD) in 1934–July 36. Financed Soviet spyrings by forged dollars printed in the USSR. Stalin's chief executor during the early part of the party purges. On Stalin's orders, replaced by Ezhov and arrested. One of the chief defendants at the show trial of the Anti-Soviet Bloc of Rightists and Trotskyists in 1937. Executed at Lubianka prison. A huge statue of him at the entrance to the Belomor-Baltiiskii canal, built by slave labour, was dynamited together with the rock on which it stood.

Iagudin, Iulii Grigor'evich
7.1.1907–   . Flute player.
Born in Starodub, Orel Gouvt. Pupil of V. Tsybin. 3rd prize at the All-Union Competition of Musicians-Soloists in Leningrad in 1935. From 1941, soloist with the Symphonic Orchestra of the Moscow Philharmonic. Professor at the Moscow Conservatory.

Iagudin, Shamil' Khairulovich
10.2.1932–   . Ballet dancer.
Born in a village in Penza Oblast'. Graduated from the Moscow Choreographic School, 1952. Soloist at the Bolshoi Theatre from 1952. Teacher at the Bolshoi Theatre from 1974.

Iakir, Iona Emmanuilovich
1896–1937. Military commander.
Joined the Bolshevik Party, 1917, and the Red Army, 1918. Active participant in the Civil War in the Ukraine as a political officer, and later military commander. After the Civil War, held high military posts in the Ukraine. Non-voting member of the Cen. Cttee. of the Bolshevik Party, 1930, and full member, 1934. Head of military educational establishments. Member of the Revolutionary Military Council of the USSR, 1930–34, and of TSIK. Shot on Stalin's orders, shouting 'Long live Stalin!' according to witnesses.

Iakir, Petr Ionovich
1923–1982. Historian, author, dissident.
Born in Kiev. Son of Iona Iakir. After his father's arrest in 1937, was arrested together with his mother. Spent 17 years in camps as a 'son of an enemy of the people'. In 1956, returned to Moscow. Graduated from the Moscow Historical-Archival Institute. In the early 1960s, became involved in the de-Stalinization campaign. Gave numerous lectures on Stalin's crimes all over the Soviet Union. After Khrushchev's fall, became a focus of persecution by the KGB. One of the founders of the human rights movement in Moscow and Leningrad. Instrumental in collecting information on political arrests, camps and psychiatric institutions, also distributed samizdat. Arrested in 1972, together with V. Krasin. Under physical threat, was broken and cooperated with the KGB. Released, 1974. Ostracized by dissident circles. Died in Moscow completely isolated. Wrote memoirs, *Detstvo V Tiur'me*, London, 1972.

Iakobson, Anatolii Aleksandrovich
1935–1978. Editor
Born in Moscow. Literary critic and translator of poetry. In the late 1960s, became active in the human rights movement. One of the editors of *Khronika Tekushchikh Sobytii*, the publication which monitored information on arrests, detentions in psychiatric hospitals, illegal imprisonment and all kinds of harassment. Closely watched by the KGB from whom he received violent threats. Forced to leave the USSR, 1973. Settled in Israel. Commited suicide.

Iakobson, Leonid Veniaminovich
15.1.1904–18.10.1975. Dancer, choreographer.
Born in Petersburg. In 1958, founded the ballet group Choreographic Miniatures. Died in Moscow. In 1983, his wife, the ballet dancer Irina Pevzner, emigrated to Israel, where she staged her late husband's ballets.

Iakovlev, Aleksandr Nikolaevich
2.12.1923– . Politician.
Served in the Soviet Army, 1941–43. Member of the CPSU, 1944. Graduated from the Iaroslavl' Pedagogical Institute, 1946. Party posts in Iaroslavl' Oblast'. Deputy Editor of *Severnyi Rabochii*. Lecturer at Iaroslavl' Oblast' Party School, 1948–50. Member of staff on the Cen. Cttee. of the CPSU, 1953–56, and 1960–65. 1st Deputy Head of the Department of Propaganda of the Cen. Cttee, 1965–73. Member of the Cen. Auditing Cttee. of the CPSU, 1971–76. USSR Ambassador to Canada, 1973–83. Gorbachev's most trusted aide. Elected to the Secretariat of the Cen. Cttee. of the CPSU on 6 Mar. 1986. Responsible for domestic ideological affairs and culture. In 1987, promoted to full membership of the Politburo. Regarded as the man behind many of Gorbachev's international public-relations triumphs. Head of the International Policy Commission of the Cen. Cttee., Oct. 1988.

Iakovlev, Aleksandr Sergeevich
1906– . Aircraft designer.
Joined the Red Army, 1924. Graduated from the Zhukovskii Air Force Academy, 1931. Engineer at an aviation factory, 1931. Designer, 1935. Deputy Minister of the Aviation Industry, 1940–46. Designed many types of Soviet military aircraft (Iak–1,–3,–7, BB–22, Iak–28, and UT–2), civil aircraft (Iak–40, and –42), the helicopter Iak–24, the first Soviet jump jet, and sporting and training aircraft. Highly decorated (7 State Prizes). Academician, 1976.

Iakovlev, Boris Nikolaevich
1890–1960. Artist.
Landscape painter. Studied at the Moscow School of Painting, Sculpture and Architecture, 1916–18,

under N. Kasatkin, A. Vasnetsov, A. Arkhipov and S. Maliutin. Exhibited from 1915. Member of the Mir Iskusstva, 1921. Died in Moscow. Personal exhibitions: Moscow, 1934, 1936, 1944, 1950, 1955, 1956. Mobile exhibitions: Iaroslavl', Rybinsk, Gorkii, 1958, and Kiev, 1959.

Iakovlev, Egor Vladimirovich
1930– . Journalist, editor.
Revolutionary editor-in-chief of the *Moscow News (Moskovskie Novosti)*, 1987. Enthusiastic adherent of Gorbachev's glasnost policy. Has printed debates about Stalin's legacy, a letter from 10 famous defectors and emigrés pouring scorn on Gorbachev's reform plans, and uncensored articles by such strong foreign critics as Zbignew Brzezinski, the former American national security adviser. First to publish articles in defence of religion. Doubled the Russian edition of his paper to 250,000 copies, with 750,000 copies going abroad in English, French, German, Spanish and Arabic. Described himself as working to three principles: firstly there should be no forbidden themes, censorship should only be concerned with keeping military or state secrets; secondly, the paper, with its large foreign circulation, should reflect the opinions of other societies and the views of other leading politicians; and thirdly, the paper should give real information to its Russian readers, with no more nonsense, but rather some real critical material, which is both constructive and important. Regarded as the voice of glasnost and perestroika in the Soviet Union.

Iakovlev, Ivan Kirillovich
1918– . General, state security officer.
Joined the Red Army, 1939. Took part in the Soviet-Finnish war, 1939–40. Junior commander during WWII. Graduated from the Military Academy of the Tank Forces, 1949, and from the Academy of the General Staff, 1958. Chief of Military Training of the Land Forces, and Deputy Commander of the Moscow military district. Commander of the Internal Armed Forces of the Ministry of the Interior, 1968.

Iakovlev, Iurii Vasil'evich
25.4.1928– . Actor.
Graduated from the Shchukin Theatre School, 1952. Joined the Vakhtangov Theatre, Moscow. Gave an unforgettable performance as Prince Myshkin in an adaptation of *The Idiot*, 1958.

Iakovlev, Mikhail Nikolaevich
1880–1942. Artist.
Landscape and still life painter, also stage designer. Studied at the Moscow Stroganov Central School of Graphic Art 1898–1900, then at the N. Silverstov Art School, Penza, 1900–01, under K. Savitskii. Continued his training at the M.K. Tenisheva School-Studio, from 1901, under Il'ia Repin and D. Shcherbinovskii. Exhibitions: the Union of Russian Artists 1910–14, 1915–18, 1922–23, also in Moscow, 1918, 1942. Personal exhibitions: Moscow, 1941, Tbilisi, 1942. Died in Tbilisi, Georgia.

Iakovlev, Nikolai Dmitrievich
1898–1972. Marshal.
Took part in WW1. Joined the Red Army, 1918. Took part in the Civil War. Joined the Bolshevik Party, 1923. Commander of an artillery regiment, 1931–41. On active service during the Finnish-Soviet war, 1939–40. Chief of the Artillery Administration (GAU) during WWII. Deputy Commander of Soviet Artillery, 1946–48. Deputy Defence Minister, 1948. Deputy Commander of the Anti-Aircraft Defence Forces of the USSR, 1953.

Iakovlev, Vasilii Nikolaevich
1893–1953. Artist.
Portrait, landscape and genre painter. Studied at the Moscow School of Painting, Scupture and Architecture, 1914–17. Exhibited from 1915. Member of the Mir Iskusstva, 1921. Member of the Union of Russian Artists, 1922–23. Last exhibition: Moscow, 1952.

Iakovlev, Vladimir Georgievich
22.1.1899– . Make-up artist.
Master of his profession. Chief make-up artist in films about Stalin, Lenin, Sverdlov, and other political figures.

Entrusted with the job of turning actors into Stalin or Lenin, which was quite a dangerous task in the 1930–40s. His job was approved by Stalin when he was invited to a preview of films about himself (*Kliatva, Padenie Berlina, Rasskazy o Lenine, Lenin v Pol'she,* and *Iakov Sverdlov*). Later created make-up for Rasputin in E. Klimov's film *Agonia*.

Iakovlev, Vsevolod Fedorovich
1895–1974. Lt.-general.
Took part in WW1. Joined the Red Army, 1918, and the Bolshevik Party, 1919. Graduated from the Frunze Military Academy, 1934. Several high command posts during WWII. After the war, Commander of Stavropol military district.

Iakovleva, Tat'iana Alekseevna (Countess du Plessix)
1906– . Society lady.
Introduced to Mayakovsky on 25 Oct. 1925 in Paris, either by E. Triolet or I. Erenburg. Acquired the reputation of a femme fatale. According to her letters to her mother, she saw Mayakovsky every day, and became very close to him. By all accounts it was a relationship of mutual interest, and a serious matter on Mayakovsky's part. In Nov. 1928, he dedicated two poems to her – *Pis'mo tovarishchu Kostrovu iz Parizha o Sushchnosti Liubvi,* and *Pis'mo Tatiane Iakovlevoi.* However, when he proposed to her, she declined the offer, and never saw him again. According to some sources, her marriage to Viscount du Plessix was one of several possible reasons for Mayakovsky's suicide. Moved to the USA. Married a director of *Vogue* magazine.

Iakubovich, Mikhail
1891–after 1975. Politician.
Early involvement in revolutionary activity. Bolshevik before WWI. Later became a Menshevik, but after the Bolshevik take-over, in contrast to most members of his party, favoured collaboration with the Bolsheviks. Left the Mensheviks in 1920. Several posts in the Soviet administration. Arrested, 1930, and tried, 1931. In Gulag camps from 1931. Released after Stalin's death,

1953, and rehabilitated, 1956. Wrote about his camp experiences. Became a rare link between the non-communist socialists of the revolutionary period and present-day dissidents.

Iakubovskii, Ivan Ignat'evich
7.1.1912–30.11.1976. Marshal.
Joined the Red Army, 1932. Took part as a tank officer in the Soviet-Finnish war, 1939–40. Commander of tank detachments during WWII. After the war, commander of a tank army. 1st Deputy Commander of Soviet Forces in Germany, 1957–60, and 1961–62, and Commander, 1962–65. Commander of Kiev military district, 1965. 1st Deputy Minister of Defence of the USSR, and Supreme Commander of Warsaw Pact Forces, 1967.

Iakulov, Georgii Bogdanovich
1884–1928. Artist.
Portrait and genre painter and stage designer. Studied at the Moscow School of Painting, Sculpture and Architecture, 1901–03. Exhibitions: the Moscow Association of Artists, 1907, 1911; The Union of Russian Artists, 1909–10; The Moscow Salon, 1910–1911; Mir Iskusstva, 1911–17; Painting, Moscow, 1915; Pictures of New Tendencies, Petrograd, 1915; Stage Design, Moscow, 1918–23; Masters of the Blue Rose, Moscow, 1925.

Iakunin, Gleb Pavlovich
1934– . Russian Orthodox clergyman.
Born in Moscow. Graduated from the Irkutsk Fur Trading Institute, 1959. Studied at the Moscow Seminary. Priest, 1962. Became involved in the struggle for the rights of believers. Together with another Orthodox priest, N. Eshliman, wrote an open letter to Patriarch Aleksii, critizing the conformism of the church hierarchy, 1965. His studies on the situation of the church and religion circulated in samizdat and contributed to the religious revival in the Soviet Union. Founded a committee for the defence of the rights of believers in Moscow, 1976. Arrested, 1979, and spent several years in prisons, camps and exile. Released, 1987. Pleaded for a more active role

for the church under the present conditions in the USSR, 1988.

Iakushev, Aleksandr Sergeevich
2.1.1947– . Athlete.
Born in Balashikha, Moscow Oblast'. Honoured Master of Sports (hockey), 1970. With Moscow Spartak. Graduated from the Moscow Oblast' Pedagogical Institute, 1972. Member of the CPSU, 1974. USSR champion, 1967, 1969, 1976. World and European champion, 1967, 1969–70, 1973–75, 1979. Olympic champion, 1972, 1976.

Iakushev, Viktor Prokhorovich
16.11.1937– . Athlete.
Born in Moscow. Honoured Master of Sports (hockey) 1963. With Moscow Lokomotiv. Factory worker. Bronze medal-winner at the Winter Olympic Games, 1960. European champion, 1959–60, 1963–67. World champion, 1963–67. Olympic champion, 1964.

Iampol'skii, Abram Il'ich
11.10.1890–17.8.1956. Violinist, teacher.
Born in Ekaterinoslav. Pupil of S. Korguev. Professor at the Moscow Conservatory. Involved in the training of many internationally-famous Soviet violinists, such as Igor Bezrodnyi, Leonid Kogan, Boris Gol'dshtein, and V. Zhuk. Died in Moscow.

Iampol'skii, Izrail' Markovich
21.11.1905– . Violinist, musicoloist.
Born in Kiev. Son of the cellist, Mark Iampol'skii. Taught, with intervals, at the Moscow Conservatory, 1935–49. Also taught the history and theory of violin playing. Music editor of the *Bol'shaia Sovetskaia Entsiklopediia*, 1950–59.
Works: *Muzyka Iugoslavii,* Moscow, 1958; *David Oistrakh,* Moscow, 1964.

Iampol'skii, Mark Il'ich
5.2.1879–18.2.1951. Cellist.
Born in Ekaterinoslav. Brother of Abram Iampol'skii. Pupil of F. Mullert, and E. Gerbek. Professor at the Moscow Conservatory. L. Ginz-

burg was one of his many pupils. Author of *Violonchel'naia Tekhnika. Gammy i Arpedzhio*, Moscow, 1939. Died in Moscow.
Source: L. Ginzburg, *Istoriia Violonchel'nogo Iskusstva*, Moscow, 1965.

Iampol'skii, Vladimir Efimovich
1905–2.6.1965. Pianist.
Born in Cherkassy, Kiev Gouvt. Pupil of L. Nikolaev. In the 1920s, appeared together with M. Poliakin, and in the 1940s, with David Oistrakh. Died in Kemerovo.

Iangel', Mikhail Kuz'mich
1911–1971. Rocket designer.
Worked as a designer with Mikoian, Miasishchev and Korolev. Graduated from the Academy of the Aviation Industry, 1950. Director of a research and design institute, 1952–54. Chief designer, 1954. Took part in the construction of the fighter planes I–16, I–17 and others. Later became involved in the design of Soviet space rockets. Academician, 1966. Non-voting member of the Cen. Cttee. of the CPSU, 1966.

Iankelevich, Arsenii Aleksandrovich
1.2.1905– . French-horn player.
Born in Smolensk. Pupil of F. Ekhert. 2nd prize at the All-Union Competition of Musicians-Soloists, Leningrad, 1935. Soloist in the Bolshoi Theatre Orchestra, 1927–31, and in the Moscow Philharmonic from 1928. Taught at the Gnesin Music-Pedagogical Institute. Wrote music for French horn for theatre plays.

Iankelevich, Iurii Isaevich
7.3.1909– . Violinist, teacher.
Born in Basel, Switzerland. Pupil of A. Iampol'skii. Professor at the Moscow Conservatory. Trained a generation of violinists. Among his pupils was Nelli Shkol'nikova.

Ianko, Tamara Fedorovna
7.7.1912– . Singer.
Born in Zhmerinka, Kherson Gouvt. Pupil of Ksenia Dorliak. Soloist at the Stanislavskii and Nemirovich–Danchenko Musical Theatre from 1938.

Iankovich, Leonid Dushanovich
1897–10.10.1975. Agro-chemist.
Born in Kiev. Son of a German language tutor at a Kiev school. During the Civil War, worked as a radio telegraphist in the Black Sea fleet. Continued his education in France. Graduated, 1925, as an agronomist engineer. From 1927, head of La Laboratoire Agrochimique du Service Botanique et Agrochimique in Tunis. Authority in his field. Taught at the Agronomical Institute, Algeria. Spent his last years in Montpellier, France.

Ianov, Aleksandr Lvovich
1934– . Historian.
Born in Odessa. Graduated from Moscow University in history. Established Soviet journalist. Became involved in the Jewish rights movement. Emigrated, 1974. Settled in the USA. Many articles on Russian historical subjects.

Ianovskii, Boris Karlovich
1875–19.1.1933. Composer, conductor.
Born in Moscow. Music critic and conductor in Kiev, Moscow, and Petrograd. From 1918, taught the history of music in Khar'kov. Wrote 10 operas, including *Dva P'ero ili Kolombina*, 1907, *Florentiiskaia Tragediia*, 1913, and *Araviiskaia Noch'*, 1916. Also author of many Ukrainian songs and romances. Died in Khar'kov.

Ianush, Leonid Borisovich
1897–1957. Artist.
Landscape painter. Studied at an art school of the Society for the Encouragement of the Arts, 1914–20, under N. Khimon and A. Rylov. Graduated from the Leningrad Technological Institute. Exhibited from 1918 until 1956, mainly in Leningrad. Died in Leningrad.

Iarkov, Petr Glebovich
27.8.1875–18.12.1945. Singer.
Born in the village of Sel'tso, Moscow Gouvt. Folk singer and major collector and performer of Russian folk songs. In 1919, organized the Peasants Choir, which in 1925 became the major Russian Folk

Choir (later known as the Iarkov Choir) and which, in 1930, won 1st prize at the All-Union Olympic Games. Toured all over the USSR with his choir. Wrote many original songs. Died in Moscow.

Iaron, Grigorii Markovich
25.2.1893–31.12.1963. Operetta comedian, stage director.
Born in Petersburg. Founder of, and comedian at, the Moscow Operetta Theatre from 1927 until his death in Moscow.
Memoirs: *O Liubimom Zhanre*, Moscow 1960.

Iaroslavskii, Emelian Mikhailovich (Gubelman, Minei Izrailevich)
1878–1943. Politician, historian, journalist.
Joined the Social Democratic Labour Party in 1898. Professional revolutionary before 1917. During 1907–17, in exile. One of the chief organizers of the October Revolution 1917. Joined the left-wing Bolsheviks in 1918. Chairman of the Society of Old Political Prisoners, chairman of the Society of Old Bolsheviks in 1931. Member of the Cen. Cttee. of the Bolshevik Party. A firm supporter of Lenin's policies after the latter's death, but later became a militant Stalinist. Led a vicious anti-religious campaign throughout the 1930s as head of the Union of Atheists. Prolific contributor to all important party publications such as *Pravda, Bolshevik* and *Istorik-Marxist*. Was one of the chief falsificators of the history of the Bolshevik Party and the revolution.

Iarovoi, Denis Vladimirovich
4.4.1921– . Viola maker.
Born in Trieste, Italy. Gold medal winner at the International Competition of Viola Makers in Italy, 1959. All major Soviet viola players use his instruments. Lives in Moscow.

Iarullin, Farid Zagidullovich
1.1.1914–9.1943. Composer.
Born in Kazan'. Wrote the music for the first Tatar ballet *Shurale* (produced only in 1945). Killed near Kursk during WWII.

Iarvet, Iuri Evgen'evich
18.6.1919–   . Actor.
Leading Estonian film actor. Graduated from the Tallinn Theatre Institute, 1949. Became internationally known for two parts – King Lear in Grigorii Kozintsev's film of the same title, and the part of Snaut in A. Tarkovskii's *Solaris*. Works mainly at Tallinn Film Studio. First film role, 1961. Continued acting and made dozen of films but remained unknown until *King Lear*. Speaks Russian with a strong Baltic accent, and his choice for the part was the subject of some controversy. Apparently Kozintsev deliberately chose him for his accent and non-Slav looks since the film was for the international market.

Iarygin, Ivan Sergeevich
7.11.1948–   . Athlete.
Born in Kemerovskaia Oblast'. Honoured Master of Sports (wrestling), 1972. With Krasnoiarsk Trud. USSR Champion, 1970, 1973. European champion, 1972, 1975–76. World champion, 1973. Olympic champion, 1972, 1976. Graduated from the Krasnoiarsk Pedagogical Institute, 1978.

Iashchenko, Aleksandr Semenovich (Sandro)
24.2.1877–10.6.1934. Editor, bibliographer.
Born in Stavropol. Graduated from Moscow University in mathematics and law, 1900. Professor in law at Iuriev University, 1909. Professor at Petersburg University, 1913. Published a bibliography of Russian philosophical and religious literature in Iuriev, 1915. Professor at Perm' University, 1917–18. Member of the first Soviet delegation to Berlin as an expert on international law, 1919. Remained in Berlin. Took part in the organization of the YMCA Press (collaborator of P. Anderson) in the early 1920s. Published the bibliographical magazine *Russkaia Kniga*, 1921, later *Vestnik Russkogo Knizhnogo Rynka*, 1921–23, both excellent sources on literary life in the 1920s. Organized the Dom Iskusstv in Berlin, where Russian book publishing and cultural life flourished at that time, and where the representatives of all circles and artistic and political

tendencies could meet each other. Professor of law at Kaunas University, Lithuania, 1923. Published books on law in Lithuanian. Died in Berlin.

Iashin, Aleksandr Iakovlevich (Popov)
27.3.1913–11.7.1968. Author.
Born in Bludovo near Vologda. Graduated from the Gorkii Literary Institute in Moscow, 1941. Political officer in the army during WWII. Wrote one of the first true accounts of kolkhoz life, *Rychagi*, published during the Khrushchev thaw, 1956. Died in Moscow.

Iashin, Lev Ivanovich
22.10.1929–   . International goalkeeper.
Born in Moscow. Honoured Master of Sports (football), 1957. With Moscow Dynamo. Graduated from the Moscow Higher Party School attached to the Central Committee, 1972. Member of the CPSU, 1957. USSR champion, 1954–55, 1957, 1963. Olympic champion, 1956. Member of the European Cup-winning team, 1960. In 1963, named Europe's best player. Recipient of the Golden Ball award.
See: L. Gorianov, *Novelly o Vratare*, Moscow, 1973.

Iashvili, Marina Luarsabovna
2.10.1932–   . Violinist.
Born in Tiflis. Daughter of the violinist, L. Iashvili. Pupil of K. Mostras. At the International Violinists Competition in Prague, 1949, received 4th and 5th prizes. 3rd prize at the International Violinists Competition, Poznan, 1952. Teaches at the Moscow Conservatory.

Iashvili, Paolo (Pavel Dzhibraelovich)
29.6.1895–22.7.1937. Poet, painter.
Born in Georgia. Studied painting in Paris. Founded in Tbilisi a group of Georgian Symbolist poets, the Blue Horns. Victim of Stalin's purges, committed suicide. Posthumously rehabilitated. Considered to be one of the great modern Georgian poets.

Iastrebtsov, Vasilii Vasil'evich (Iastrebtsev)
30.8.1866–25.9.1934. Music writer.
Born in Mogilev. Biographer of, and

leading authority on, Nikolai Rimskii-Korsakov. Wrote several books on him. Died in Leningrad.

Iatsevich, Iurii Mikhailovich
5.11.1901–   . Composer.
Born in Poltava. Author of 6 symphonies, 2 concertos for violin with orchestra, and pieces for piano.

Iaunzem, Irma Petrovna
27.9.1897–   . Folk singer.
Born in Minsk. Pupil of Ksenia Dorliak. Became very famous during the 1920s–30s, attracting huge crowds to her concerts. Sold millions of records in the USSR.

Iavorskii, Boleslav Leopol'dovich
22.6.1877–26.11.1942. Pianist, musicologist.
Born in Khar'kov. One of the organizers of the Narodnaia Konservatoriia (People's Conservatory) in Moscow, 1906. Professor at the Kiev and Moscow conservatories. Major music scholar in the USSR. Died in Saratov after being evacuated from Moscow.
Works: *Stroenie Muzykal'noi Rechi*, Moscow, 1908; *Vospominaniia, Stat'ii, Pis'ma*, Moscow, 1964. Editor of S. Protopopov's *Elementy Stroeniia Muzykal'noi Rechi*, Moscow, 1930.

Iazov, Dmitrii Timofeevich
1923–   . General.
Joined the Red Army, 1941. During WWII, junior commander at the Volkhov and Leningrad fronts. Graduated from the Frunze Military Academy, 1956. In the early 1960s, served in the Leningrad military district. Graduated from the Academy of the General Staff, 1967. Worked in the Personnel Department of the Ministry of Defence, 1974–76. First Deputy Commander of the Far Eastern military district, 1976. Commander of the Central Group of Armies (in Czechoslovakia), 1979–80. Commander of the Central Asian military district, 1980. Non-voting member of the Cen Cttee. of the CPSU, 1981. Commander of the Far Eastern military

district, 1984. After Gorbachev's reorganization of the military leadership, appointed Minister of Defence of the USSR, 1987.

Ibarruri, Ruben
1920–1942. Captain.
Son of Dolores Ibarruri, the leader of the Spanish communists. After the defeat of the Republicans in the Spanish Civil War, evacuated to the Soviet Union. Joined the Komsomol, 1938. During WWII, went to the front, commander of a machine-gun detachment. Killed in action in the Battle of Stalingrad. Posthumously awarded the title of Hero of the Soviet Union, 1956.

Idelshon, Abraham Zebi
13.7.1882–14.8.1938. Musicologist, cantor (baritone).
Born in Latvia. Singer at a Jewish synagogue in Riga where he studied music. Lived in Jerusalem, 1906–21. Founded the Institute of Jewish Music, 1910, and the Jewish School for Music, 1919. Professor at the Hebrew College in Cincinnati, USA, 1924–34. Important works on ancient and modern Jewish music (in Hebrew, German and English). Gave a new insight into early Christian psalmody in *Sokrovishchnitsa Evreisko-Vostochnykh Melodii (Hebraisch-Orientalischer Melodienschatz)*, 1914–32. Author of the musical drama *Ievfai*, 1922. Liturgical and other musical works. Literary works: *Istoriia Evreiskoi Muzyki*, 1924, 1928, (in Hebrew), *Jewish Music in its Historical Development*, New York, 1929 and 1944, 'Musical Characteristics of East European Jewish Folk Songs', *The Musical Quarterly*, NY, 1932, No 3. Died in Johannesburg, South Africa.

Ignat'ev, Aleksei Alekseevich, Count
1877–1954. Lt.-general.
Graduated from the Academy of the General Staff, 1902. Russian Military Attaché in Scandinavia, 1908–12, and France, 1912–17. After the October Revolution, joined the Red Army, and became one of the best-known aristocrats on the side of the communists. Wrote memoirs about his career under the Tsar, Lenin, Trotsky, and finally Stalin (*50 Let v Stroiu*).

Ignat'ev, Semen Denisovich
1903– . State security official
Joined the Communist Party, 1926. Made his career during the 1930s. Took an active part in the purges. First Secretary of the Party Cttees. in Buriat-Mongolia, 1938, Bashkiria, 1944–47 and 1954–57, and Tataria, 1957–60. Replaced Abakumov as Minister of State Security (MGB), 1951–53. Member of the Presidium of the party's Cen. Cttee., 1952–53. Secretary of the Cen. Cttee., 1953. Relieved of his posts for 'political blindness' in connection with the Doctors Plot (the anti-Semitic arrest and trial of a group of doctors, most of them Jewish). During his famous anti-Stalin speech in 1956, Khrushchev said that Ignat'ev had acted on Stalin's personal orders. It was he who gave Stalin the figure of the total Gulag population (12 million according to *Moskovskii Komsomolets*, Feb. 1988).

Ignatovich, Boris Vsevolodovich
1899–1976. Photo journalist.
Born in Lutsk in the Ukraine. Joined the Lugansk newspaper *Severo-Donetskii Kommunist* as an editorial assistant at the age of 19. From 1919, worked on the Khar'kov newspaper *Krasnaia Zvezda*. In 1920, editor of *Krasnaia Bashkiria*. In 1921, editor of *Gorniak*, Moscow. Collaborated with Mayakovsky. From 1922–25, worked in Leningrad as the chief editor of humorous magazines. In 1923, discovered photography and began photographing everything. In 1926, returned to Moscow and became one of the leaders of the Association of Photographic Reporters in the Press House. Worked as a photographer on *Ogonek*, *Prozhektor* and *Krasnaia Niva*. From 1927, picture editor and reporter on the newspaper *Bednota*. Influenced by Rodchenko when he started, but later found his own style. When Rodchenko was expelled from the October group in 1931, Ignatovich took over from him. The group was dissolved a year later. From 1930–32, made several documentary films including the short film *Today*, directed by Esfir Shub, and also made a documentary about the Kukryniksy artists. During the 1930s, head of the illustrated section of *Vecherniaia Moskva*. Headed also the photo agency Soiuz Foto, where he

drew together many talented photographers. The members of the agency did not sign their name but used to put 'Ignatovich Brigade' under the photographs. The first photographer to take pictures from an aeroplane (over Leningrad, 1931) which were published in the magazine *USSR in Construction*. From 1937 until the beginning of the war in Russia, worked on the magazine *Construction of Moscow* for which he took many architectural photographs. During WWII, served as war correspondent for *Boevoe Znamia*, the newspaper of the 30th Army. In 1943, was sent with partisans to take action pictures. In the post-war years, turned to landscape photography. A personal exhibition of this series took place in 1948. Was also a remarkable portrait photographer, working in colour. Other exhibitions were held in Prague in 1947, in Moscow, 1969, and in Vilnius, 1972.

Igumnov, Konstantin Nikolaevich
1.5.1873–24.3.1948. Pianist.
Born in Tambovskaia Gouvt. Pupil of Paul Pabst. Founder of one of the most important Soviet piano schools. Among his pupils were Lev Oborin, M. Grindberg, A. Iokheles, and Iakov Flier. Professor at the Moscow Conservatory, and its director from 1924–29. Stalin Prize, 1946. Died in Moscow.
See: Ia. Mil'shtein, *Mastera Sovetskoi Pianisticheskoi Shkoly*, Moscow, 1954.

Ikonnikov, Aleksei Aleksandrovich
1905– . Musicologist.
Born in Tul'skaia Gouvt. Teacher at the Gnesin Pedagogical Institute of Music, Moscow. Author of articles, and works on N. Miaskovskii.

Il'enko, Iurii Gerasimovich
9.5.1936– . Cameraman, director.
Remarkable Ukrainian cameraman famous for his work on the film *Shadows of Our Forgotten Ancestors*, made in 1964 by the Armenian director, Sergei Paradzhanov. The film collected no fewer than 16 international prizes (most of them for the camera work). Not since Eisenstein's triumphs had Russian cinema

enjoyed such international esteem. Unfortunately, after Paradzhanov's conviction and imprisonment, the film was banned in the Soviet Union for some 10 years, but attracted a lot of attention in the West. Graduated from the VGIK in 1960 as a cameraman. Shot 2 films at Yalta Studios (Crimea). Directed and shot *On the Eve of Ivan Kupala Day*, based on Nikolai Gogol's fantastic stories. Works mainly at Dovzhenko Film Studios in Kiev. Other films include: *A White Bird With a Black Spot*, 1971, and *To Dream and To Live*, 1974.

Ilf, Il'ia Arnoldovich (Fainzilberg)
16.10.1897–13.4.1937. Writer.
Born in Odessa, son of a bank clerk. Graduated from Odessa Technical School. Worked as a designer, telephone operator, technician at an aviation factory, statistician, and editor of the humorous magazine *Sindetikon*. Wrote and published poetry under a female pseudonym. Worked as an accountant. Member of the Presidium of the Poets' Union, Odessa. In 1923, moved to Moscow. Reporter on several newspapers. Contributor to satirical magazines. Met Evgenii Petrov, who had also come to Moscow from Odessa. This meeting turned into a life-long collaboration. In 1927, they published their first novel *Dvenadtsat' Stuliev* (The Twelve Chairs). Both became famous overnight. The sequel, *Zolotoi Telenok* (The Golden Calf), appeared in 1931. Both books became, and remain until today, bestsellers in the Soviet Union. Several films have been made of them both in Russia and abroad. After visiting America as *Pravda* correspondents in the 1930s, they published *Odnoetazhnaia Amerika* (Little Golden America), an unfriendly but humorous description of the country of which both had been admirers. Died in Moscow of TB. *Complete Works*, 5 vols, Moscow, 1961.

Ili'in, Anatolii Mikhailovich
27.6.1931–   . Athlete.
Born in Moscow. Honoured Master of Sports (football), 1956. With Moscow Spartak. USSR champion, 1952–53, 1956 and 1958. Olympic champion, 1956. Graduated from the Moscow Institute of Physical Culture,

1970. Author of *My Byli Pervymi*, Moscow, 1978.

Il'in, Ivan Aleksandrovich
28.3.1883–21.12.1954. Philosopher, religious author, lawyer.
Born in Moscow. Educated at Moscow High School. Graduated from Moscow University in law, 1906. Studied at universities in Germany and France, 1910–12. Lecturer at Moscow University in law, 1912–22. Under communist rule, arrested several times from 1918 till 1920. Expelled with a group of Russian professors in 1922. Lived in Berlin, 1922–38. Professor at the Russian Scientific Institute in Berlin. Published many articles and books, stressing the necessity of resistance by force to evil in all its forms. Dismissed by the Nazi authorities. Moved to Zurich in 1938, where he spent the rest of his life.
Main works: *Resistance to Evil by Force, The Way of Spiritual Renewal, The Foundation of Christian Culture, Wesen und Eigenart der russischen Kultur, Das verschollene Herz, The Way Towards Self-evidence.*

Il'in, Vasilii Petrovich
8.1.1949–   . Athlete.
Born in Leningradskaia Oblast'. Honoured Master of Sports (handball), 1976. With Moscow Burevestnik. Student at the Moscow Oblast' Institute of Physical Culture. USSR champion, 1970–72, 1974–75. Olympic champion, 1976.

Il'in, Vladimir Nikolaevich
16.8.1891–1960? Philosopher, musicologist, theologian.
Born near Kiev. Graduated from Kiev University, 1913. Emigrated, 1919. Stayed at Constantinople, 1920–22. Moved to Berlin, 1922–25. Moved to France. Lecturer at the St. Sergius Theological Institute, 1925–40. Professor of church music at the Russian Musical Academy in Paris. Well-known contributor to Russian emigré literary magazines. Died in Paris.
Main works: *St. Seraphim of Sarov, The Sealed Grave, The Vigil Service, The Enigma of Life, Materialism and Matter, Atheism and the Death of Culture, The Six Days of Creation.*

Il'inskii, Aleksandr Aleksandrovich
24.1.1859–23.2.1920. Composer.
Born in Tsarskoe Selo (now the town of Pushkin). Professor at the Moscow Philharmonic Society and at the Moscow Conservatory. Musical works include an opera, choreographic pictures, a symphony, orchestral suites, choral works, romances, and music for the theatre. Literary works: *Biografii Kompozitorov* and *Kratkoe Rukovodstvo k Prakticheskomu Izucheniiu Instrumentovki*, Moscow, 1917. Died in Moscow.

Il'inskii, Igor Vladimirovich
1901–   . Film and stage actor.
Studied at the Fedor Komissarzhevskii Theatre, 1917. Made his debut at the Vera Komissarzhevskaia Theatre, 1918. Worked with V. Meyerhold at his theatre and remained close to him until his arrest in 1939. Acted in many film comedies. Became extremely popular during the 1960s.
Works: *Sam o Sebe*, Moscow, 1961, and *So Zritelem Naedine*, Moscow, 1964.

Iliukhin, Aleksandr Sergeevich
4.5.1900–   . Balalaika player, conductor.
Born in Moscow. Conductor of the Orchestra of Folk Instruments. Lecturer at the Gnesin Pedagogical Institute of Music. Author of manuals on folk instrument playing.

Iliushin, Sergei Vladimirovich
1894–1977. Aircraft designer.
Joined the Bolshevik Party, 1918. Joined the Red Army, 1919. Graduated from the Zhukovskii Airforce Academy, 1926. Head of an aircraft design bureau, 1931. Became one of the best-known designers of Soviet military and civil aircraft (the Iliushin, or IL series). Academician, 1968. Highly decorated (3 times Hero of Socialist Labour, many state awards).

Illarion (Troitskii, Vladimir Alekseevich), Archibishop of Vereya
1866–15.12.1929. Russian Orthodox clergyman.
Born in Lipitsy, Moscow Gouvt. Graduated from Moscow Theologi-

cal Academy, 1910. Professor there. Sent to the monasteries of Mount Athos in Greece in 1913 to arbitrate on a theological dispute among monks. Member of the Russian Church Council in Moscow, 1917–18, his speech swayed the assembly in favour of the re-instatement of the patriarchate. Gained the reputation of being an outstanding scholar and theologian. Secretary to Patriarch Tikhon. Bishop of Vereya, 1920. Archbishop, 1923. Arrested among a group of church leaders and sent to Solovki concentration camp in a former monastery on an island in the White Sea, Dec, 1923. One of the authors of the *Solovki Letter* from the imprisoned bishops to the authorities, giving a reasoned answer to atheist attacks, 1926. Died of typhoid in prison in Leningrad on the way to exile in Alma-Ata.

Imanov, Amangeldy
1873–18.5.1919. Kazakh guerilla leader.
Born in Turgai, Kazakhstan, the son of a poor peasant. Took part in the unrest during 1905–07. Became head of an uprising in Kazakhstan in 1916. Joined the Bolshevik Party in 1918, and became one of the organizers of the first Red Army detachments in Kazakhstan, fighting the forces of Admiral Kolchak. Taken prisoner by anti-Bolshevik Kazakhs (Alash Orda, the White Horde) and executed in Turgai.

Imshenetskii, Aleksandr Aleksandrovich
8.1.1905– . Microbiologist.
Graduated from the Voronezh University, 1926. Director of the Institute of Microbiology, 1949. Academician, 1962. Carried out research into different groups of bacteria.

Inashvili, Aleksandr (Sandro) Iovich
23.8.1887–4.6.1958. Singer (baritone).
Born in Tiflis. Pupil of E.K. Riadnov and E. Dzhiraldoni. Soloist with the Tbilisi Opera from 1916. Professor at the Tbilisi Conservatory. Died in Tbilisi.

Innokentii (Petrov, Ivan Afanas'evich), Bishop of the Argentine and Paraguay
26.12.1902–23.12.1987. Russian Orthodox clergyman.
Born in Elabuga. Educated at a military school. During the Civil War, served under Kolchak, and took part in many military operations with the White armies. Several times wounded, highly decorated. After the defeat of the Whites, moved to China, and later to Yugoslavia. Graduated as a railway engineer in Belgade, 1925. During WWII, moved to Germany, and lived in DP camps. Emigrated to Argentina, and settled in Buenos Aires. Priest of the Russian Church in Exile, 1962. Bishop, 1983, and Head of the Argentine and Paraguay Diocese of the Russian Church in Exile. Died in Buenos Aires.

Ioann (Alekseev, Ivan Alekseevich), schema-igumen
26.2.1873–5.6.1958. Russian Orthodox clergyman.
Born near Tver'. Son of a peasant. In his early youth entered the Valaam monastery on Lake Ladoga. Left the monastery to serve in the Russian Army. Returned to Valaam, 1900. Monk, 1910. Igumen, 1921. Head of the Pechenga (Petsamo) monastery, 1926. Returned again to Valaam, 1932. During the Finnish-Soviet war, together with other monks, evacuated to Finland. One of the founders of the New Valaam (Valamo) in Finland. Highly revered as a representative of the starets tradition in modern times, known as the Elder of Valaam. Died at Valamo. His spiritual letters have been published in several languages.

Ioann (Maksimovich, Mikhail Borisovich), Archbishop of Shanghai
4.6.1896–2.7.1966. Russian Orthodox clergyman.
Born in Adamovka, Khar'kov Gouvt. Son of a nobleman. Educated at the Poltava Cadet Corps, 1914. Graduated from Khar'kov University in law, 1918. Emigrated during the Civil War. Graduated in theology from Belgrade University, 1925. Monk, 1926. Bishop of Shanghai, 1934. After the communist victory in China, moved to the USA, 1949. Archbishop of Brussels (Russian Orthodox Church in Exile), 1951–63.

Archbishop of San Francisco, 1962–66. Widely revered for his ascetic achievements and saintly life.

Ioann (Shakhovskoi, Dmitrii Alekseevich. Pen-name–Strannik), Prince, Archbishop of San Francisco.
23.8.1902– . Russian Orthodox clergyman, religious author, poet.
Born in Moscow. Educated at the Lyceum in Petersburg, 1915–17. During the Civil War, for a short time fought with the Whites. Emigrated in June 1920. Graduated from Louvain University, Belgium. Organized and edited a literary magazine (*Blagonamerennyi*) in Brussels. After a visit to Mount Athos in the early 1920s, decided to become a monk. Monk deacon, Paris, 1926. Priest in Yugoslavia, 1927. In the 1930s and early 1940s, priest in Berlin. After WWII, moved to the USA, and lived in San Francisco from 1947, becoming Bishop and Archbishop of the local diocese. Became known as a poet (under his pen-name), and gained popularity in the USSR by his religious broadcasts.
Main works: *Thoughts on Pushkin, The Philosophy of Orthodox Pastoral Work, God's Will and Man's Will, The Glory of the Resurrection, A Moscow Discussion of Immortality, Collections of Radio Talks and Poems.*

Ioann (Snychev, Ivan Matveevich), Archbishop of Kuibyshev and Syzran'
9.10.1927– . Russian Orthodox clergyman.
Born in Novomaiachka near Kherson. Son of a peasant. Red Army soldier during WWII. Met at Orenburg (then Chkalov) the local bishop Manuil (Lemeshevskii) and became his spiritual son. Helped to compile the multi-volume *List of Russian Bishops for 60 Years, 1897–1956*, an invaluable source for contemporary church history. Graduated from the Leningrad Theological Academy, 1955. Professor at Minsk Seminary, 1956, and Saratov Seminary, 1957. Archimandrite, 1964. Bishop of Syzran', 1965. Archbishop, 1976.

Ioffe, Abram Fedorovich
29.10.1880–14.10.1960. Physicist.
Born in Romny, Poltava Gouvt. Educated at the Petersburg Technological Institute, 1902. Graduated from Munich University, 1905. Assistant of Roentgen, 1903–06. Professor at Petrograd (now Leningrad) Technological Institute, 1913–48. Founder and director of the Physico-Technical Institute of the Academy of Sciences of the USSR, 1918. Founder and director of the Semiconductors Institute of the Academy of Sciences of the USSR, 1955. Many scientific research works, especially pioneering work on semiconductors. Died in Leningrad.

Ioffe, Adolf Abramovich (Krymskii, Viktor)
22.10.1883–17.11.1927. Politician, diplomat.
Born in Simferopol'. Son of a businessman. Educated as a doctor. Involved in revolutionary activity from the 1890s. Member of the mezhraiontsy group of the SDs, and accepted with them into the Bolshevik Party, 1917. Active participant in the Bolshevik take-over in October 1917. Member of the Constituent Assembly. Head of the Soviet government peace delegation during negotiations with the Germans at Brest-Litovsk, 1918. Defended Trotsky's position of 'neither peace, nor war'. Soviet Ambassador in Berlin, 1918. Head of the Soviet peace delegation to the Baltic countries (Estonia, Latvia, Lithuania) and Poland, 1920. Head of the Turkburo of the Cen. Cttee. of the Bolshevik Party, 1921. Member of the Soviet delegation at the Genoa conference, 1922. Soviet Ambassador to China, 1922. Soviet Ambassador to Austria, 1924. Prominent member of the group of Trotsky supporters in opposition to Stalin. Committed suicide.

Ioffe, Iurii Matveevich
1921– . Poet.
Born in Khar'kov. Teacher of mathematics. Involved in the human rights movement. His poems circulated in samizdat in the 1960s. Emigrated, 1972. Lives in West Germany. Many books of his poetry have been published in the West.

Ioffe, Maria Mikhailovna
1900– . Journalist.
Born in New York into the family of a Russian Jewish political exile. Involved in revolutionary activity in Russia. Worked on Bolshevik newspapers after 1917. Married the Soviet diplomat A. Ioffe, 1918. Arrested for a speech in defence of L. Trotsky, 1929. Spent the next 28 years in the Gulag. Released, 1957. Emigrated, 1975. Settled in Israel. Became a chronicler of her Gulag experience. Published several books of memoirs in the West.

Iokheles, Aleksandr L'vovich
11.3.1912– . Pianist.
Born in Moscow. Pupil of Konstantin Igumnov. 2nd prize at the All-Union Moscow Music Competition, 1933. Professor and head of department at the Gnesin Pedagogical Institute of Music.

Iokhelson, Vladimir Il'ich
26.1.1855–2.11.1937. Ethnographer.
Born in Wilno. Narodnik revolutionary, arrested, 1885, exiled to Kolyma in Iakutia, 1888. Took part in expeditions to Northern Siberia, 1894–96 (studied the Iukagir language), and later in expeditions to research the connections between North-East Asia and North America, 1900–02, and 1908–11. Specialist on the language and culture of North-Siberian and Far Eastern tribes (Iukagirs, Koriaks and Aleutians). Emigrated, 1922, and lived in the USA. Died in New York.

Ionov, Anatolii Semenovich
6.8.1939– . Athlete.
Born in Noginsk, Moscow Oblast'. Honoured Master of Sports (hockey), 1965. With the Central Sports Club of the Army. Coach. Graduated from the RSFSR Central School of Sports Instructors, 1970. USSR champion, 1964–66, 1968, 1970. World and European champion, 1965–66, 1968. Olympic champion, 1968.

Ionov, Il'ia Ionovich (Bernstein)
1887–1942. Revolutionary, censor.
Early involvement in revolutionary activity. Spent several years imprisoned in Schluesselburg fortress.

In the 1920s, a Proletkult poet and head of *Gosizdat*, where he eagerly promoted the party line. Later became a victim of Stalin's purges.

Ionov, Viacheslav Nikolaevich
23.5.1940– . Athlete.
Born in Moscow. Honoured Master of Sports (rowing), 1964. With the Central Sports Club of the Navy. Member of the CPSU, 1965. Graduated from the Volgograd Institute of Physical Culture, 1969. USSR champion, 1961–67. Olympic champion, 1964. World champion, 1966. European champion, 1967. Honoured Coach of the USSR, 1976.

Iordan, Irina Nikolaevna
22.11.1910– . Composer.
Born in Saratov. Wife of the composer G. Kirkor. Author of a symphony, concertos, works for violin with orchestra, and chamber music.

Iordanskii, Mikhail Viacheslavovich
28.12.1901– . Composer.
Born in Vladimirskaia Gouvt. Editor of Muzgiz (State Music Publishing House), 1933–52. Known for his children's compositions (songs, operas, music and plays). Author of choral works, romances, pieces for piano, and songs.

Iordanskii, N.I. (Negorev)
1876–1928. Journalist, politician.
Editor of the magazine *Sovremennyi Mir*, 1909–17. Menshevik, close to Plekhanov, a member of the Edinstvo group. After February 1917, Commissar of the Provisional Government on the South-Western front. After the Bolshevik take-over 1917, emigrated to Finland. Founded the newspaper *Put'*, which took a smenovekhovtsy, pro-Soviet position. Expelled from Finland, 1921, and returned to Moscow. Joined the Bolshevik Party. Worked in high posts in the Foreign Affairs Ministry and in the State Publishing House.

Ioseliani, Otar Davidovich
2.2.1934– . Film director.
Distinguished Georgian director Originally trained as a conductor.

Graduated from the VGIK in 1961 as a director under Aleksandr Dovzhenko and Mikhail Romm. Also graduated from the Tbilisi Conservatory as well as being a painter and graphic artist. For two years studied mechanics and mathematics at Moscow University. Worked for a living as a sailor and miner. Films: *April* (1961, short film, not released until 1987), *Listopad* (When Leaves Fall). This film was completed in 1967 and became a huge success with Russian critics and the public. Was shown during the Directors' Fortnight at the 1972 Cannes Film Festival. Since then every film society in the world has acquired a copy. The film earned its maker the highest reputation. His next film, *There Was a Singing Blackbird*, was a huge success with critics all over the world. Invited to make a film in France. Other films: *Cast Iron* (1964, documentary), *Day After Day* (1970), *The Summer in the Country* (1976), *Pastorale, Euskadi*, and *Les Favoris de la Lune* (made in France in 1984). Also works as a university lecturer. Regarded as one of the leading contemporary directors in Georgia.

Iosif (Petrovykh, Ivan Semenovich), Metropolitan of Leningrad
15.12.1872–1938. Russian Orthodox clergyman.
Born in Ustiuzhin, Novgorod Gouvt. Educated at Novgorod seminary. Graduated from the Moscow Theological Academy, 1899. Monk, 1901. Bishop of Uglich, 1909. In charge of the Novgorod diocese, 1920–25. Metropolitan of Leningrad, Aug. 1926. Became leader of the right wing of the church, opposed to the attempts of Metropolitan Sergii to reach accommodation with the authorities by complete submission. Persecuted by the authorities and expelled from the church, worked as an accountant at a coppermine in Kazakhstan. Became head of the Catacomb Church. Arrested in 1937 for connections with wandering secret priests of the Catacomb Church and probably executed.

Ipat'ev, Vladimir Nikolaevich
21.11.1867–29.11.1952. Chemist.
Born in Moscow. Graduated from the Mikhailovskaia Artillery Acade-my, Petersburg, 1892. Professor of the same academy from 1900. Member of the Academy of Sciences, 1916–26. Went on a business trip abroad in 1927 and stayed in the West. Settled in the USA, 1930. Researcher at Universal Oil Products Co. and professor at the Northwestern University in Chicago. Worked mainly on catalytic reactions. Gained a worldwide reputation in this field. Died in Chicago.

Ippolitov-Ivanov, Mikhail Mikhailovich
19.11.1859–28.1.1935. Composer.
Born in Gatchina. Graduated from the Petersburg Conservatory (pupil of Rimskii-Korsakov), 1882. Moved to Tiflis, 1882–93, and became deeply attracted to Caucasian and Eastern music. Conductor of the private opera of the millionaire Mamontov, 1899–06. Director of the Moscow Conservatory, 1905–1922. Conductor of the Bolshoi Theatre, 1925. Composer of several operas and other musical works, mostly with Caucasian themes. Very influential in the Soviet music world in the 1920s and 1930s. Died in Moscow.

Iretskaia, Natal'ia Aleksandrovna
1845–15.11.1922. Singer (soprano).
Pupil of Genrietta Nissen – Saloman (1819–79). Taught at the Petersburg Conservatory from 1875, professor from 1881. Among her pupils were Elizaveta Petrenko, Nadezhda Zabela, Elena Katul'skaia, and Lidia Lipkovskaia. Died in Petrograd.

Irinei (Bekish, Ivan), Metropolitan of All America and Canada
2.10.1892 – 18.3.1981. Orthodox clergyman.
Born in Western Ukraine. Educated at the theological seminary at Kholm, 1914. Priest, 1916. Deputy Dean of the cathedral in Lublin. After WWI, Orthodox clergyman in Poland. During and after WWII, in refugee camps in Germany. Moved to Belgium, 1947, and to the USA, 1952. Orthodox priest in Pennsylvania. Bishop of Tokyo and Japan from the mid-1950s. Re-opened the Orthodox seminary in Tokyo, 1954. Returned to the USA, 1960. Archbishop of Boston and New England. Elected Archbishop of New York, and Metropolitan of All America and Canada after the death of Metropolitan Leontii on 23 Sept. 1965. In June 1970, under his rule, the (former Russian) American Archdiocese received (from the Moscow Patriarchate) the right of an autocephalous (independent) church. Thus became the first head of the Autocephalous Orthodox Church in America. Retired after the 5th All American Church Council, 1977. Died in New York.

Isaakian, Avetik
1875–1957. Poet.
Armenian by nationality. His poems have been set to music by many composers. Wrote in Russian and Armenian.
See: M. Arutiunian, *Avetik Isaakian i Muzyka*, 1955 (in Armenian).

Isachev, Aleksandr (Sasha)
1955–5.12.1987. Artist.
Avant-garde artist. Workaholic: used to produce up to 250 pictures a year, and thousands of sheets of graphics. Very active in the nonconformist movement in the 1970s. In constant conflict with the cultural authorities. Became an alcoholic and lived the last 10 years of his short life on dangerous drugs. Was once locked up in a psychiatric hospital by the KGB. 21 days before his death there was a major exhibition of his works. Died of heart failure.

Isaev, Aleksei Mikhailovich
24.10.1908–25.6.1971. Space rocket designer.
Born in Petersburg. Graduated from the Moscow Mining Institute, 1932. Joined the aviation industry, 1934. Designed the first Soviet jet engine, 1942. Worked on rocket engines from 1942. Engines designed under his instructions were used on the space ships Vostok, Voskhod, Soiuz, and on the Soviet orbiting space stations. Died in Moscow.

Isaev, Anatolii Konstantinovich
14.7.1932– . Athlete.
Born in Moscow. Honoured Master of Sports (football), 1957. With Moscow Spartak. USSR champion,

1956, 1958. Olympic champion, 1956. Member of the CPSU, 1962. Sports lecturer. Honoured Sports Instructor of the RSFSR, 1969. Graduated from the Moscow Institute of Physical Culture, 1972.

Isaev, Andrei Alekseevich
19.10.1851–1924. Economist, statistician, sociologist.
Taught at Petersburg University and the Demidov Lycée in Iaroslavl', 1879–93. One of the best-known late 19th century, early 20th century statisticians and economists in Russia. Supporter of cooperative socialism. Pioneer of sociology in Russia. Over 20 books on political economy, finance, sociology and statistics. Died in Moscow.
Main works: *Promysly Moskovskoi Gubernii*, 2 vols, *Arteli V Rossii; O Sotsializme Nashikh Dnei; Voprosy Sotsiologii; Nachala Politicheskoi Ekonomii; Mirovoe Khoziaistvo.*

Isakov, Ivan Stepanovich
22.8.1894–11.10.1967. Admiral.
Joined the Red Navy, 1918. Took part in the Civil War. Graduated from the Naval Academy, 1928. Commander of the Baltic Fleet, 1937. Deputy Minister of the Navy, 1938–46. Chief of Staff of the Navy, 1946, Deputy Chief Commander of the Navy, 1947.

Isakov, Petr Ivanovich
17.1.1886–28.4.1958. Guitar player.
Born near Sevastopol. Author of many arrangements for the 7-string guitar. Died in Leningrad.

Isarov, Boris Iur'evich
24.3.1942– . Actor, director.
Born in Kuibyshev. Son of an officer in the General Staff and a Moscow Radio newscaster. At the age of one, taken to Moscow by his mother. Graduated from the Leningrad Theatre Institute in 1963. Joined the Moscow Ostrovskii Drama Theatre, and later worked with S. Obraztsov in his Central Puppet Theatre. Also worked in TV and films. Married the English actress Eileen Benskin. Moved to London, 1973. Made his first stage appearance in London in his one-man show, *Bobok* by Dostoevskii at

the National Theatre, 1977 (later seen at the Lincoln Center, New York). Appeared in, and was Assistant Director to O. Tabakov, in *The Government Inspector*, at the Crucible, Sheffield, 1978, and in Iurii Liubimov's *Crime And Punishment*, London, 1983. Appeared on British TV and worked with directors David Jones, Jack Gold, Alan Gibson, Marvin Chomsky, and Herbert Wise. He played the artist Soutine in Wise's TV film *Skin* by Roald Dahl in *Tales of the Unexpected*, which won an Edgar Award in the USA. Also appeared in British and American films such as: *Reds*, dir. Warren Beatty, *The Human Factor*, dir. Otto Preminger, *Superman 4*, dir. Sydney Furie, *Border*, dir. Mischa Williams, and *American Roulette*, dir. Maurice Hatton. Radio work: *Bobok, Tolstoy in London, The Harshness of Time* and *A Bullet in the Ballet.* Tom Stoppard also directed him in his play *Every Good Boy* at the Riverside Studios, London. Drama translations: *Marriage, Three Girls in Blue, Orpheus,* and *Playing Moliere.* Lives in London.

Ishchenko, Mikhail Alekseevich
19.5.1950– . Athlete.
Born in Morozovsk, Rostov Oblast'. Honoured Master of Sports (handball), 1976. With Zaporozh'e Burevestnik. From 1976, with the Kiev Armed Forces team. Graduated from the Zaporozh'e branch of the Dnepropetrovsk Metallurgical Institute in engineering, 1975. Olympic champion, 1976.

Ishlinskii, Aleksandr Iul'evich
6.8.1913– . Scientist.
Graduated from Moscow University, 1935. Professor at the same university, 1945 and at Kiev University, 1948–55. Academician, 1960. Specialist in gyroscopes.

Ishmukhamedov, Elier Mukhitdinovich
1.5.1942– . Film director.
One of the best-known Uzbek film directors. Born in Tashkent. Child actor. Graduated from the VGIK, Moscow. His diploma film in 1966, *Tenderness*, put him on the same level as his teachers. Other films: *Rendez-vous*, 1967, *In*

Love, 1969, *Meetings and Partings*, 1974, and *The Birds of Our Hopes*, 1977.

Ishutina, Elena
1903–1962. Author.
Lived in Western Belorussia. After the occupation of the region by the Red Army at the beginning of WWII, arrested and sent to the Gulag camps, 1941. Released, 1946. Lived in provincial Russia. Wrote about her experience in the concentration camps for women at Narym during Stalin's time. This work circulated in samizdat and was published in the USA in the mid–1960s, attracting wide attention.
See: 'Narym: Dnevnik Ssylnoi', introduction by Roman Gul, NY, *Novyi Zhurnal*, 1965.

Iskander, Fazil' Abdullovich
1929– . Author.
Born in Sukhumi. Graduated from the Moscow Gorkii Literary Institute. First poems published, 1952. Became known for his novel *Sozvezdie Kozlotura*, published in the magazine *Novyi Mir* in the mid–1960s. Best known for his humorous novel *Sandro iz Chegema*, USA, 1979, a censored version of which has been published in the USSR.

Isupov, Aleksei Vladimirovich
1889–1957. Artist.
Studied at the Moscow School of Painting, Sculpture and Architecture, 1908–13. Pupil of L. Pasternak, K. Korovin, A. Vasnetsov and A. Arkhipov. Landscape, portrait and genre painter. Exhibitions: Moscow School of Painting, Sculpture and Architecture, Moscow, 1908–13; MOLKH, 1910; the Union of Russian Artists, 1910–16; Spring Exhibitions of the Academy of Arts, 1911; TPKHV, 1912–17, 1922; AKHRR, Moscow, 1925; the Association of Realist Artists, Moscow, 1927.

Itskov, Iosif Pavlovich
1905– . Lawyer.
Born in Moscow. Graduated from the Moscow Institute of Economics and from Moscow University in law. Through his ex-wife (who was involved with high Kremlin society in

151

the 1930s), gained knowledge of secret intrigues during the years of the Stalin purges. Maintains that Ordzhonikidze did not die of heart failure (official version) nor committed suicide (usual unofficial version), but was shot on Stalin's orders on the eve of a planned anti-Stalin speech. Arrested for a short time, 1938, released 1939. Re-arrested during Stalin's anti-Semitic campaign, 1949. Released, 1955. Under Khrushchev, worked as a lawyer. Became active in the human rights movement. Emigrated, 1979. Settled in the USA. See: 'Odna iz Pervykh Zhertv Stalina', *Kontinent*, 1983.

Iudenich, Nikolai Nikolaevich
1862–1933. General.
Educated at Aleksandrovskoe Military School in 1887. Graduated from the Academy of the General Staff. Served in the army in Turkestan in 1892. Took part in the Russo-Japanese war, 1905. Chief-of-staff of the Caucasian military district in 1912. Commander-in-chief of the Caucasian Army, 1915. After the February Revolution 1917, commander-in-chief of the Caucasian front. Dismissed by the Provisional Government in Apr. 1917. Went underground in Petrograd during the October Revolution 1917. Moved to Finland in autumn 1918, then to Estonia. Appointed commander of local White detachments by Admiral Kolchak. In Oct. 1919, made a surprising bid to capture Petrograd, drawing upon himself very large reserves of the Red Army. Forced to retreat with his North-Western Army to Estonia, where he was interned. Emigrated to France. Died in Nice.

Iudin, Konstantin Konstantinovich
1896–30.3.1957. Film director.
From 1923–26 worked at Soiuzpechat' (All-Union Press), and later in the all-union photo-film department. First film, 1927. Best remembered for his two films *Devushka s Kharakterom*, 1939, and *Serdtsa Chetyrekh*, 1941. Both films had a huge commercial success.

Iudovin, Solomon Borisovich
1892–1954. Artist.
Genre and landscape painter and

book illustrator. Also a wood and linoleum-cutter. Born in Vitebsk. Studied at the I.M. Pen Studio, then at the art school of the Society for the Encouragement of the Arts, 1910–13. Pupil of M. D. Bernshtein and Mstislav Dobuzhinskii until 1919 in Petrograd. Graduated from the Vitebsk Institute of Practical Art, 1922. Exhibitions: Paintings and Sculptures of Jewish Artists, Moscow, 1917–18, and Ten Years of Russian Xylography, Moscow, 1927. Other exhibitions: Leningrad, 1932, Moscow-Leningrad, 1934, Moscow, 1939, 1942, Kiev, 1934, Iaroslavl', 1943, Minsk, 1945, Leningrad, 1947, and Moscow, 1948. Personal exhibitions: Iaroslavl', 1944 and (posthumously), Leningrad, 1956.

Iukha, Sigmas
13.7.1935–7.10.1980. Athlete.
Born in Lithuania. Honoured Master of Sports (rowing). Silver medal-winner at the XVIIth Olympic Games, 5th place at the XVIIIth Olympic Games, and bronze medal-winner at the XIXth Olympic Games. Believed to have died through steroid misuse.

Iukhov, Ivan Ivanovich
14.10.1871–28.1.1943. Choir conductor.
Born in Moscow. In 1900 founded and headed a choir in Moscow, later known as the Iukhov Choir. This formed the basis for the Respublikanskaia Russkaia Khorovaia Kapella, founded in 1942. Died in Moscow.

Iumashev, Andrei Borisovich
1902– . Major-general.
Joined the Red Army, 1918. Educated at a pilot's school, 1924. Test pilot, 1927. Made a non-stop flight, Moscow – North Pole – USA, 1937. Commander of fighter pilot forces during and after WWII.

Iumashev, Ivan Stepanovich
1895–1972. Admiral.
Joined the Bolshevik Party, 1918, and the Red Navy, 1919. Took part in the Civil War. Graduated from the Naval Academy, 1932. Commander of the Black Sea fleet, 1938, and of

the Pacific fleet, 1939. Took part in operations against Japan in the final stages of WWII. Deputy Minister of Defence, and Commander in Chief of the Soviet Navy, 1947. Non-voting member of the Cen. Cttee. of the Bolshevik Party, 1941–56. Soviet Naval Minister 1950. Head of the Naval Academy, 1951–57.

Iumin, Vladimir Sergeevich
18.12.1952– . Athlete.
Born in Omsk, Siberia. Honoured Master of Sports (wrestling), 1976. With Makhach-Kala Dynamo. USSR champion, 1973–75, 1978. European champion, 1975–77. World champion, 1974, 1977–79. Olympic champion, 1976.

Iuon, Konstantin Fedorovich
1875–1958. Artist.
Landscape, genre and portrait painter. Also stage designer and graphic artist. Studied at the Moscow School of Painting, Sculpture and Architecture, 1894–98, under N. Kasatkin, K. Savitskii, A. Korin, L. Pasternak and others. Pupil of V. Serov, 1899–1900. First exhibition, 1894. Became an official artist, carrying out political propaganda orders. Took part in every official exhibition. Died in Moscow.

Iuon, Pavel Fedorovich (Juon, Paul)
6.3.1872–21.8.1940. Composer.
Born in Moscow. Brother of the artist, K.F. Iuon. Wrote 2 symphonies, 3 concertos, music for string quartet, pieces for piano, violin and cello and songs. Professor at the Higher Music School, Petersburg. Emigrated, 1919. Member of the German Academy of Arts. After 1934, moved to Switzerland. Died in Vevey, Switzerland.

Iurasovskii, Aleksandr Ivanovich
27.6.1890–31.1.1922. Composer, conductor.
Born on his parents' estate in Mtsentsk District, Orel Gouvt. Son of the singer, N. Salina. Author of the opera *Tril'bi* (based on his own libretto, 1919). Also composed symphonic music, concertos, romances, and songs. Presumably killed during the Civil War.

Iurchenko, Vitalii

1935–   . Intelligence and security services officer, general.

Served with the KGB for 25 years. Former 1st Secretary in the Soviet Embassy in Washington, 1975–80. Recalled to Moscow. Rose to head one of the 8 minor departments in the KGB (probably the 7th Directorate, in charge of surveillance, or the 8th, in command of communications intelligence) with the rank of general. In July 1985, disappeared in Rome where he had been sent on a business trip (in fact high-ranking personnel are banned from leaving the Soviet Union). Defected to the USA. Brought to Washington and, according to the press, faced months of aggressive interrogation. His defection came to light only in Oct. 1985. Disappeared from his secure flat the following month, and surfaced in the Soviet Embassy claiming he had been kidnapped, tortured and offered by the CIA $1m plus $180,000 a year if he became a consultant to the CIA. Normally such press-conferences of re-defectors take place in Moscow. This time it was presented to American and other Western journalists on American territory, and only days before the summit meeting between Reagan and Gorbachev in Geneva. President Reagan remarked that he was surprised that 3 Soviet citizens, Iurchenko, Miroslav Medvid and Aleksandr Sukhanov, had asked for political asylum in the USA and had then decided to return to the Soviet Union. Both Medvid and Sukhanov, a soldier in Afghanistan who had tried to desert from the Soviet Army there, were reassured that they would not be punished if they returned. In fact dissident sources indicate that both are now in labour camps. The Iurchenko 'defection' was probably a successful KGB operation, though its real purpose remains unclear.

Iur'enen, Sergei Sergeevich

1948–   . Author, journalist.
Born in Frankfurt an der Oder (East Germany). Son of a Soviet official. Graduated from Minsk University in journalism and from Moscow University in Russian literature. Worked as a journalist. Published some prose in the official press. In 1977, visited his wife's family in France and

remained there. Later moved to West Germany.
Works: *Volnyi Strelok*, Paris, 1984; *Narushitel' Granitsy*, Paris, 1986; *Syn Imperii*, USA, 1986.

Iurenev, Konstantin Konstantinovich (Krotovskii)

1888–1938. Politician.
Joined the Bolshevik Party, 1905. Member of the Mezhraiontsy group, 1913–17. Re-admitted into the Bolshevik Party with the whole group, 1917. Chairman of the Bureau of the HQ of the Red Guards, 1917. One of the organizers of the Red Army, 1918–19. Chairman of the All-Russian Bureau of Military Commissars, 1918. Active participant in the Civil War. Diplomatic work from 1921. Member of TSIK and VTSIK. Victim of Stalin's purges.

Iurenev, Rostislav Nikolaevich

13.4.1912–   . Film critic, author.
Graduated from the VGIK, 1936. Author of *Kratkaia Istoriia Sovetskogo Kino*, 1979. Wrote scripts for the documentary films *Sergei Eisenstein*, 1958, and *Vsevolod Pudovkin*, 1960. Author of many articles. From 1963, professor at the VGIK.

Iur'ev, Boris Nikolaevich

1889–1957. Helicopter designer.
Graduated from the Moscow Higher Technical School, 1919. Deputy Head of the Zhukovskii Air Force Academy, 1942–49. Pioneered the construction of Soviet helicopters in the 1930s and 1940s.

Iur'in, Evgenii Vasil'evich

1898–   . Artist.
Miniature painter. Studied at the Mstera icon art school, 1913. Worked as an icon painter and restorer. Since 1923, has lived and worked in Mstera. RSFSR People's Artist. Exhibitions: Moscow, 1937, Ivanovo, 1940, Vladimir, 1945, 1947–49, Moscow, 1949.

Iurlov, Aleksandr Aleksandrovich

11.8.1927–   . Choir conductor.
Born in Leningrad. Pupil of A. Sveshnikov. Deputy dean of the

choir-conducting department at the Gnesin Music-Pedagogical Institute. From 1958, chief artistic director and chief conductor of the Republic's Russian Choir Capella.

Iurskii, Sergei Iur'evich

16.3.1935–   . Actor.
Popular comedian. Son of the artistic director of the Leningrad Circus. Graduated from the Leningrad Theatrical Institute in 1959. From 1957, actor at the Leningrad Bolshoi Drama Theatre. First film, *Dostigaev and Others*, 1959. Became famous for his part of Ostap Bender in *The Golden Calf* (Mosfilm, 1968). Other films: *A Man From Nowhere*, 1961, *The Shkid Republic*, 1967, *The Deer King*, 1970, *The Broken Horseshoe*, 1973.

Iushkevich, Igor (Youskevitch)

13.3.1912–   . Ballet dancer.
Born in Piriatin, Poltava Gouvt. Emigrated in the 1920s to Belgrade. Pupil, then partner, of the ballerina K. Grunt, 1932. With B. Nizhinskaia, 1934, and L. Vuitsikovskii, 1935. Trained by O. Preobrazhenskaia in Paris. With the Ballet Russe du Colonel de Basil, 1937, and the Ballet Russe de Monte Carlo, 1938–44, and 1956–57. With Leonid Massin, 1946. Soloist with the American Ballet Theatre, 1946–55. Worked with George Balanchine. Acted in some films. Taught at a ballet school in NY. In 1960, visited the USSR on tour with the American Ballet Theatre. Retired, 1962
See: S. Cohen, *Prince Igor, 25 Years of American Dance*, NY, 1954.

Iusov, Vadim Ivanovich

20.4.1929–   . Cameraman.
Master-cameraman of the Soviet cinema. Born in Moscow. Graduated from the Moscow VGIK. Cameraman on nearly all Tarkovskii's films — *The Steam-Roller and the Violin*, a short, which won a prize in New York for the camera-work; *Ivan's Childhood* (the camera-work was called 'a revelation' by international critics, and won the film 15 international awards including the Golden Lion in Venice and the Selznick prize in the USA); *Andrei Rublev* and *Solaris*, both master-

pieces of camera-work. Other films: *I Walk About Moscow* and *Cheer Up!* (both directed by Danelia).

Iutkevich, Sergei Iosifovich

28.12.1904–23.4.1985. Film director and theoretician.
Pupil of V. Meyerhold, 1921–23. Worked as an artist in the N. M. Foregger Theatre Workshops. Staged some theatrical productions with S. Eisenstein. Director and artist of the agit-group, *Siniaia Bluza*. In 1922, with G. Kozintsev, L. Trauberg and G. Kryzhitskii, issued the manifesto *Eccentricity*, which became the basis of FEKS. After his first film in 1924, made over 50 more, including *Vstrechnyi* (with F. Ermler), 1932, and *Rasskazy o Lenine*, 1958. Produced a considerable number of propaganda films during the Stalinist period. Continued his *Leniniana* series with *Lenin v Pol'she*, 1966, and *Lenin v Parizhe*, 1981. Heavily decorated with several Stalin and state prizes.

Iuvenalii (Maslovskii, Evgenii Aleksandrovich), Archbishop of Riazan

15.1.1878–1937. Russian Orthodox clergyman.
Born in Livny, Orel Gouvt. Educated at high school in Orel. Graduated from Kazan Theological Academy. Monk, 1901. Abbot of a monastery near Pskov, 1906. Bishop of Kashira, 1914. Archbishop of Kursk, 1923. Arrested and imprisoned, 1925–28. After his release, Archbishop of Riazan, 1929. Re-arrested in 1936, disappeared, probably executed, 1937. Had a reputation as an excellent liturgical scholar.

Ivanitskii, Aleksandr Vladimirovich

10.12.1937– . Athlete, sports journalist.
Born in the village of Iarovoe, Donetsk Oblast'. Honoured Master of Sports (free-style wrestling), 1963. With the Armed Forces Sports Club, Moscow. Member of the CPSU, 1964. USSR champion, 1964–65. World champion, 1962–63, 1965–66. Olympic champion, 1964. Graduated from the Moscow Institute of Physical Culture, 1966. From 1973, editor-in-chief of the sports programme on state TV and radio. Deputy chairman

of the Federation of Sports Journalists from 1975.
Works: *Shestoe Chuvstvo*, Moscow, 1971.

Ivannikov, Vladimir Sergeevich

19.9.1906– . Composer.
Born in Orsha. Author of the ballet *Chernyi Monakh* (based on a story by Chekhov), an oratorio, pieces for violin, baian, and guitar, choral works, and songs (including songs for children). Also arranged folk songs.

Ivanov, Aleksandr Antipovich

12.9.1907– . Inventor of electrical musical instruments.
Born in Petersburg. Constructor of the 'emiriton' jointly with A.V. Rimskii-Korsakov, V. L. Kreitser and V. P. Dzerzhkovich. First model, 1935. The instrument's name derives from the first letters of 'elektricheskii muzkal'nyi instrument', the initials of two of the constructors, and the suffix 'ton'.

Ivanov, Andrei Alekseevich

13.12.1900– . Singer (baritone).
Born in Liublinskaia Gouvt. With the operas of Kiev, Baku, Odessa and Sverdlovsk from 1925. Soloist with Kiev Opera from 1934, and with the Bolshoi Theatre, 1950–56.

Ivanov, Eduard Georgievich

25.4.1938– . Athlete.
Born in Moscow. Honoured Master of Sports (hockey), 1963. With the Central Sports Club of the Army. Coach. USSR champion, 1963–66. World and European champion, 1963–65, and 1967. Olympic champion, 1964. Graduated from the Moscow Oblast' Institute of Physical Culture, 1977.

Ivanov, Georgii Vladimirovich

10.11.1894–1958. Poet.
Born in Kovno (Kaunas) in Lithuania. Educated at a cadet corps, 1910. First verse published, 1911. Member of the Acmeist *Tsekh Poetov*, close to N. Gumilev. His collection of poetry, the exquisite *Otplytie na Ostrov Citeru* was published in 1912 in Petersburg. Emigrated, 1923. Mar-

ried the poetess Irina Odoevtseva. Lived in Paris. In the 1930s, published a prose work, *Raspad Atoma*, which created a literary scandal with its nihilism and disregard of all conventions. Published memoirs on literary life in pre-WWI Petersburg, *Peterburgskie Zimy*, which, according to many witnesses, cannot be considered reliable. In his old age, matured into an outstanding and very original poet, expressing complete despair in verse of icy beauty (*stal nashim khlebom – tsianistyi kalii, nashei vodoi – sulema*), poignantly capturing the essence of life in exile, and the absurdity of modern life in general. Died in poverty in France.

Ivanov, Ianis Andreevich (Ivanovs)

9.10.1906– . Composer, conductor.
Born in Latgalia, Latvia. Early musical training in Smolensk, 1918–20. Studied in Riga with I. Maevskii, 1922–23. At the Latvian Conservatory from 1924. Pupil of I. Vitol. Finished his postgraduate training under Vitol, 1933. Taught composition at the Riga Musical Institute and at the Vigner Musical Institute, 1931–40. Musical director, concurrently, with Riga Radio. Conducted symphony concerts. Taught at the Latvian Conservatory from 1944. Lecturer from 1946. Professor from 1955. Composed mainly symphonies.

Ivanov, Il'ia Ivanovich

1899–1967. Lt.-general.
Joined the Red Army, 1918. Took part in the Civil War. Graduated from the Dzerzhinskii Military Technical Academy, 1928. Became an outstanding artillery designer, creating several types of heavy guns. Wrote theoretical works on this subject.

Ivanov, Konstantin Konstantinovich

21.5.1907– . Conductor.
Born in Tul'skaia Gouvt. Pupil of Leo Ginsburg. 3rd prize at the All-Union Competition of Conductors, Moscow, 1938. Chief conductor with the State Symphony Orchestra, 1946–65. Stalin Prize 1949.

Ivanov, Leonid Aleksandrovich
24.2.1871–12.4.1962. Scientist.
Graduated from Moscow University, 1895. Veteran professor at the Forestry Institute, 1904–41. Specialist in plant physiology, photosynthesis and plant systematics.

Ivanov, Mikhail Fedorovich
5.1.1889–5.6.1953. Guitarist, composer.
Born in Tverskaia Gouvt. Author of many pieces, arrangements, and a manual for guitar playing, 1948. Died in Pakhra, Moscow Oblast'.
Works: *Russkaia Semistrunnaia Gitara*, Moscow, 1948.

Ivanov, Mikhail Mikhailovich
23.9.1849–20.10.1927. Critic, composer.
Born in Moscow. Head of the music department of the newspaper *Novoe Vremia*, 1876–1917. Opposed to the Soviet regime. Author of operas, such as *Gore ot Uma* (based on the play by Griboedov), the ballet *Vestalka*, works for orchestra and piano, and romances. Author of *Istoriia Muzykal'nogo Razvitiia v Rossii*, 2 vols, Petersburg, 1910–12. Emigrated to Italy after the revolution. Died in Rome.

Ivanov, Modest Vasil'evich
1875–1942. Vice-admiral.
Graduated from the Naval Academy. Took part in the Russo-Japanese war, 1904–05, and WWI. After the October Revolution, joined the Bolsheviks, and played an important part in the organization of the Red Navy and the sea border guards. Moved to the merchant fleet, 1924.

Ivanov, Nikolai Iudovich
1851–1919. General.
Graduated from the Mikhailovskoe Artillery School, 1869. Took part in the Russo-Turkish war, 1877–78, and the Russo-Japanese war. During WWI, commander of the South-Western Front, 1914–16. At the beginning of the February Revolution, 1917, sent by the Tsar from Supreme Headquarters on a mission to restore order in Petrograd. The mission was soon abandoned, ensuring the victory of the revolutionaries.

Ivanov, Nikolai Petrovich
20.8.1949– . Athlete.
Born in Leningrad. Honoured Master of Sports (rowing), 1976. With Leningrad Dynamo. Coach. USSR champion, 1970–75. European champion, 1973. World champion, 1974–75. Olympic champion, 1976. Member of the CPSU, 1978.

Ivanov, Viacheslav Ivanovich
16.2.1866–16.7.1947. Poet, literary critic, classical scholar.
Born in Moscow. Educated at Moscow secondary school. Studied at Moscow University, later in Berlin (pupil of Mommsen), Paris, London and Rome. Lived in Italy, Greece and Switzerland. After 1905, the literary salon The Tower, run by him and his wife Lidia Zinov'eva-Annibal in Petersburg, became the centre of the Symbolist movement. Moved to Moscow in 1913, contributor to all Symbolist publications. Professor of classical philology at Baku University in 1920. Emigrated in 1924. In Rome from 1926, converted to Catholicism. Professor of Russian language at the Vatican Oriental Institute, 1936. Died in Rome. By far the most erudite scholar-poet in an age of erudition, and one of the most colourful personalities of the Russian Silver Age.
Works: *Collected Works*, 4 vol., Bruxelles, 1971–87.

Ivanov, Viacheslav Nikolaevich
30.4.1938– . Athlete.
Born in Moscow. Honoured Master of Sports (rowing), 1956. With the Central Sports Club of the Navy. USSR champion, 1956–66. European champion, 1956, 1959, 1961 and 1964. World champion, 1962. Olympic champion, 1956, 1960, and 1964. Graduated from the Volgograd Institute of Physical Culture, 1969.
Works: *Vetry Olimpiiskikh Ozer*, Moscow, 1972.

Ivanov, Vladimir Dmitrievich
1900–1968. General.
Joined the Red Army, 1918, and the Bolshevik Party, 1919. Graduated from the Frunze Military Academy, 1930. Military administrator and staff officer, working in the General Staff and the Defence Ministry. 1st

Deputy Chief of the General Staff, 1959–65. Head of the Academy of the General Staff, 1965–68.

Ivanov, Vladimir Timofeevich
10.9.1940– . Athlete.
Born in Gomel'. Honoured Master of Sports (volleyball), 1968. Graduated from the Kiev Institute of Physical Culture, 1968. European and USSR champion, 1967. Olympic champion, 1968. Member of the CPSU, 1974.

Ivanov-Barkov, Evgenii Alekseevich
4.3.1892–18.5.1965. Film director.
Graduated from the Stroganov Art Industrial High School, 1915. Director and then executive director of Goskino, 1918–24. In 1919, with V. Gardin, co-produced the State Film School's first film, *Zheleznaia Piata*, based on a Jack London short story. Worked as a stage designer on two films — *Iz Iskry Plamia* and *Krasnyi Tyl*, 1924–25. Made his debut as a director with Iu. Tarich in *Moroka*, 1925, followed by *Mabul*, based on a short story by Sholem-Aleichem, about the events of 1905 Revolution, and *Iad* (script by A Lunacharskii), both 1927. In 1938, moved to Turkmenia and worked at the Ashkhabad Film Studio, now the Turkmenfilm Studio. From 1945, its director. From 1956, worked at the Odessa Film Studio.

Ivanov-Boretskii, Mikhail Vladimirovich
26.6.1874–1.4.1936. Musicologist, composer.
Born in Moscow. Professor at the Moscow Conservatory. Author of operas, a suite, a piano trio, choral works, and romances. Literary works include *Orlando Lasso*, Moscow, 1918, *Palestrina*, Moscow, 1909, *Mendelssohn*, Moscow, 1910, *Schumann*, Moscow, 1910, and *Materialy i Dokumenty po Istorii Muzyki*, 2 vols., Moscow, 1934. Died in Moscow.

Ivanov-Kramskoi, Aleksandr Mikhailovich
2.9.1912– . Guitarist.
Born in Moscow. Pupil of P. Agafoshin. 1st prize at the All-Union Competition for Folk Music Per-

formers, 1939. Author of various pieces and a manual for the 6-string guitar.

Ivanov-Radkevich, Nikolai Pavlovich
10.11.1904–4.2.1962. Composer.
Born in Krasnoiarsk. Professor of Classical Instrumentation at the Moscow Conservatory and at the Institute of Military Conductors. Head of department. Composer of brass band music, symphonies, suites, overtures, tone poems, and music for films. Literary works: *Obshchie Osnovy Instrumentovki Dlia Dukhovogo Orkestra* (with E. Vilkovir), Moscow, 1937, and editor of *Instrumentovedenie*, Moscow, 1951. Stalin Prize, 1943. Died in Moscow.

Ivanov-Razumnik (Ivanov, Razumnik Vasil'evich)
24.12.1878–9.6.1946. Sociologist, literary scholar.
Born in Tiflis. Son of a nobleman. Graduated from the mathematical faculty of Petersburg University. Close to the populists, came under the influence of Lavrov. Involved in revolutionary activity, several arrests. Wrote a history of Russian social thought in 2 volumes, 1907, which became one of the most influential books among the Russian intelligentsia at that time. Wrote on Belinskii, Herzen and others, preaching a Scythian approach of intensity and sincerity, disregarding everything he considered bourgeois. In 1917, close to the left-wing SRs. His main influence was indirect, through poets who were under the spell of his thinking on the revolution (Blok, Esenin). After the Bolshevik takeover, soon became the victim of the revolutionary dictatorship, which brought him nearer to a moderate approach to life. After many years in prison and exile, moved at the beginning of WWII to Pushkin (Tsarskoe Selo), and later to Germany. Among the Displaced Persons in refugee camps in Bavaria. Wrote very valuable memoirs, *Tiurmy i Ssylki*, comparing his practical experience of persecution under Tsarism and Soviet rule. Died in Bavaria.

Ivanov-Vano, Ivan Petrovich
8.2.1900– . Film director.
One of the first animated film

directors of the early Soviet cinema. Graduated from VKHUTEMAS, 1923. Stage designer on the first Soviet animation film, *Kitai v Ogne*, 1925. Made remarkable films, which are now considered classics — *Sen'ka Afrikanets*, 1927, *Pokhozhdeniia Miunkhgauzena*, 1928, *Strekoza i Muravei*, 1935, and *Kotofei Kotofeevich*, 1937. With Iurii Norshtein, made *Vremena Goda* and *Secha Pri Kerzhentse*, 1969–71, and with L. Mil'chin, *Skazka o Tsare Saltane*, 1984. Taught at the VGIK from 1939. Most of his films have been shown abroad, receiving international prizes.

Ivanova, Lidia Gavrilovna (Kalinina)
27.1.1937– . Athlete.
Born in Moscow. Honoured Master of Sports (gymnastics), 1960. With Moscow Burevestnik. USSR champion, 1958. World champion, 1958 and 1962. Olympic champion, 1956 and 1960. Bronze medal, 1956. Graduated from the Moscow Institute of Physical Culture, 1973. International referee from 1970. Honoured Coach of the USSR from 1979.

Ivanovskii, Aleksandr Viktorovich
29.11.1881–12.1.1968. Film director.
Graduated from Kazan' University, 1906. Director of the Zimin Opera Theatre, 1904–17. In 1920–21, director of various music-drama theatres. Entered the film industry, 1918. Assistant to Ia. Protazanov. Specialized in classical adaptations, such as *Punin i Baburin* and *Tri Portreta* (both Turgenev short stories), 1919, *Komediantka* (based on an N. Leskov story), 1923, *Dvorets i Krepost'* (based on an Olga Forsh novel), 1924, and *Iudushka Golovlev* (M. Saltykov-Shchedrin). Published his memoirs, *Vospominaniia Kinorezhissera*, in 1967.

Ivanovskii, Nikolai Pavlovich (Ivanov)
2.8.1893–28.11.1961. Ballet dancer.
Born in Petersburg. Graduated from the Petersburg Theatre School, 1911. Pupil of Mikhail Fokin. With Diaghilev's Ballets Russes, 1912–14. Joined the A. M. Fokin Theatre of Miniatures, Petrograd, 1914. With

the Mariinskii Theatre, 1915–42. One season, 1930–31, with the Tbilisi Theatre. From 1925, with some interruptions, taught at the Leningrad Choreographic School. Dean of the Dance Department at the Leningrad Conservatory, 1954–61. Professor, 1956. Died in Leningrad.

Ivasheva, Valentina Vasil'evna
15.1.1908– . Literary scholar.
Born in Petersburg. Graduated from Leningrad University. Professor at Moscow University, specializing in English literature. Co-editor of the Russian edition of the complete works of Charles Dickens in 30 volumes, published in Moscow, 1957–63.

Ivashov, Vladimir Sergeevich
28.8.1939– . Actor.
Graduated from the VGIK, 1963. Pupil of M. Romm. Became a celebrity overnight following his appearance in *Ballada o Soldate*, by the director G. Chukhrai, in 1959.

Iverni, Violetta (Betaki, Violetta Isaakovna)
1937– . Poetess.
Born in Leningrad. Wrote critical articles about Soviet theatre. Emigrated, 1973, and settled in France where she has published several volumes of verse.

Ivinskaia, Olga Vsevolodovna
1913– . Author.
Born in Tambov. Graduated from the Moscow Editorial Workers' Institute. Editor. Became close to B. Pasternak, who dedicated some of his post-war poetry to her. Described as Lara in *Doctor Zhivago*. Arrested, 1949. Sentenced to 5 years in prison camps. Remained close and supportive to Pasternak during the official persecution campaign against him after his Nobel Prize for Literature award. Arrested again, 1960, this time together with her daughter, Irina, and accused of being Pasternak's link with the Western publishers. Sentenced to 8 years in prison camp. Released, 1964.
Memoirs: *V Plenu Vremeni: Gody s Borisom Pasternakom*, Paris, 1978.

Ivnev, Riurik (real name – Kovalev, Mikhail Aleksandrovich)
1891–1981. Poet.
Talented imaginist poet. Belonged to the circle of S. Esenin, A. Mariengof, A. Kusikov and V. Shershenevich. Appeared in the futurist publications *Glashatai* and *Ocharovannyi Strannik*. Became an ego-futurist, and contributor to its magazine, *Mezonin Poezii*. Appeared in *Ogonek, Zhurnal Dlia Vsekh* and *Vershiny*. His essays about his circle were published in 1921 (*Chetyre Vystrela*). Published his memoirs in 1973. *Izbrannye Stikhotvoreniia i Poemy, 1907–81*, Moscow, 1985.

Izmailov, Nikolai Fedorovich
1891–1971. Sailor, revolutionary.
Active Bolshevik organizer of the Baltic sailors during the October Revolution 1917. Chairman of Tsentrobalt, 1917–18. Political Commissar during the Civil War. Commander of the Black Sea ports, 1921. Later party administrator in Moscow.

Izotov, Nikita Alekseevich
9.2.1902–14.1.1951. Worker.
Born in the village of Malaia Dragunka near Orel. Glorified as a model miner during the Stalin years. According to Soviet newspapers of the period, fulfilled 30 norms in one working day. From 1937, involved in administrative work in the mining industry. Died in Enakievo, Donetsk Oblast'.

Izvitskaia, Izol'da Vasil'evna
21.6.1932–1.3.1971. Film actress.
Graduated from the VGIK, 1955. Became very famous after her film, *Sorok Pervyi* (The Forty First), 1956, made by G. Chukhrai. Never repeated her initial success. Committed suicide.

Izvolskii, Aleksandr Petrovich
18.3.1856–16.8.1919. Diplomat.
Born in Moscow. Russian Ambassador to the Vatican, 1894–97, Belgrade, 1897, Munich, 1897–99, Tokyo, 1899–1903, Copenhagen, 1903–6. Minister of Foreign Affairs, 1906–10. Ambassador to France, 1910–17. Retired, May 1917. After the October Revolution 1917, remained in France as a political emigré. Died in Paris.

K

Kabakov, Il'ia Iosifovich
1933– . Artist.
Born in Dnepropetrovsk. Famous book illustrator. Active in the unofficial art life in Moscow. Took part in numerous unofficial art exhibitions in Russia and in the West. Catalogues and references to his art are well documented in *A – IA* art magazine, Paris, (editor, Igor Shelkovskii). Achieved commercial success in the West.

Kabalevskii, Dmitrii Borisovich
30.12.1904–1986. Composer, musical official, conductor, pianist.
Born in Petersburg. In 1918, moved with his parents to Moscow. Completed N. Miaskovskii's course in composition in 1929, then A. Goldenveizer's course in piano in 1930 at the Moscow Conservatory. From 1922–32, accompanist and teacher at the Moscow Music School. Professor at the Moscow Conservatory from 1939. Prolific composer, best known for his lively suite *The Comedians*, and the overture to his opera *Colas Breugnon*. Won high honours from the Soviet government for his reverential, musically-conservative treatment of patriotic themes in compositions like the grandiloquent cantata *Great Motherland*. Secretary of the Union of Soviet Composers from 1952. From 1969, headed the Council on Aesthetic Education under the Presidium of the Academy of Pedagogical Sciences. Involved in many political public-relations exercises. Died in Moscow.

Kabanov, Aleksandr Sergeevich
14.6.1948– . Athlete.
Born in Moscow. Honoured Master of Sports (water-polo), 1972. USSR champion, 1972–79. Olympic champion, 1972. World champion, 1975. With Moscow Burevestnik. From 1975, with the Central Sports Club of the Navy. Member of the CPSU, 1978.

Kachalov, Vladimir Iakovlevich
1890–1941. Lt.-general.
On active service in WWI. Joined the Red Army, 1918. Graduated from the Frunze Military Academy, 1935. Took part in WWII. Killed in action.

Kacharava, Vazha Solomonovich
2.1.1937– . Athlete.
Born in Tbilisi. Honoured Master of Sports (volleyball), 1965. Olympic champion, 1964. European champion, 1967. Graduated from the Bauman Higher Technical School, Moscow, 1972. Electronics engineer. From 1973, with Moscow Burevestnik. Honorary Coach of the USSR, 1973.

Kachin, Dmitrii Ivanovich
1929– . Diplomat, politician.
Graduated from the Technical Institute of the Fishing Industry, Moscow, 1964, and the Higher Party School, of the Cen. Cttee. of the CPSU. Worked as a sailor on various fishing boats 1945–47. Member of the CPSU, 1953. Trawler foreman and engineer with Kamchatrybprom, 1954–59. Senior party posts in Kamchatka Oblast' until the mid-1970s. Member of the Central Auditing Cttee. of the CPSU, 1971–76. Candidate member of the Cen. Cttee. of the CPSU, 1976–81. Member, 1981. USSR Ambassador to Vietnam from Aug. 1986, replacing B. Chaplin.

Kaganovich, Lazar' Moiseevich (Kogan)
22.11.1893– . Revolutionary, politician.
Born in the village of Kabany, Kiev Gouvt., into a poor working-class Jewish family. Worked in shoe factories. Joined the Bolshevik Party in 1911. Conscripted into the army during WWI. Became a Bolshevik agitator. After the October Revolution 1917, proclaimed communist power in Gomel (Belorussia), elected Bolshevik member of the Constituent Assembly. Came to Petrograd and stayed there. During the Civil War, political commissar in the Red Army (fought against Denikin, later sent to Turkestan, 1920). Stalin recalled him, making him head of the

157

organizational department of the Cen. Cttee. in 1922, shortly after becoming General Secretary. From then on, remained one of Stalin's closest assistants and advisers, and throughout the 1930s was the second most powerful man in the USSR. Secretary of the Cen. Cttee. of the Communist Party, 1924. General Secretary of the Cen. Cttee. of the Ukrainian Communist Party, 1925. Active in the purges of the Ukrainian communist leaders, accusing them of nationalist tendencies and sending them to the Gulag. Recalled to Moscow during the power struggle between Stalin and the Old Bolsheviks. Again Secretary of the Cen. Cttee., 1928. Used by Stalin to publicly attack Krupskaia, Lenin's widow, 1930. During the collectivization campaign, repeatedly sent by Stalin on ruthless missions, wherever difficulties arose (Ukraine, Voronezh, Western Siberia, Northern Caucasus), conducting an unprecedented terror campaign against the rural population, leading to the death and exile of millions of peasants and their families. Appointed Moscow party chief and member of the Politburo, 1930–35 (succeeded by Khrushchev). Behind the modernization of Moscow, including the building of the metro, and the ruthless destruction of many historically or religiously significant old buildings, including the Cathedral of Christ the Saviour (built by general subscription among the people as a monument to the Russian victory over Napoleon). During the purges in the late 1930s, personally conducted many terror campaigns, demanding arrests, executions and deportations of victims of the purges. Extended his callousness to his own family — his older brother Mikhail, who had persuaded him to become a Bolshevik, and who was Minister of the Aviation Industry, shot himself when he heard of Beria's decision to arrest and execute him. Jews complained about his anti-Semitism, while for the rural population at large, and in the Ukraine especially, he remains the most hated symbol of Stalinist oppression. In the late 1930s, appointed to many government posts – Minister of Transport, 1935, Minister of Heavy Industry, 1937, Minister of the Fuel Industry, 1939, Minister of the Oil Industry, 1940, and Deputy Prime Minister. In all these capacities, tried to increase productivity by relentless and extreme exploitation and by terror. During WWII, sent to the front to organize the work of the Draconian military prosecution system, again resulting in countless executions. Minister of the Building Materials Industry, 1944. After the war, sent again to the Ukraine, 1947, as party boss. After Stalin's death, one of the most prominent heirs to the throne. Apparently agreed to Beria's execution, but later joined forces with Molotov, Malenkov and Shepilov in order to halt the de-Stalinization campaign. Was outmanoeuvred by Khrushchev, and expelled from the Cen. Cttee. (antiparty group). Sent as a factory director to Solikamsk in the Urals. Worked there until 1961. At the 22nd Party Congress, Oct. 1961, Khrushchev raised the question of his role during the purges. He was dismissed, returned to Moscow, and expelled by his local party organization (Krasnopresnenskii Raikom in Moscow). After Khrushchev's fall, re-applied for party membership, but was refused. His name does not figure in the 3rd edition of the *Great Soviet Encyclopaedia*. Lived in Moscow on a state pension. Often seen by people but shunned by most. No official information on his death has been given, still alive in the early 1980s (R. Medvedev, *Oni Okruzhali Stalina*, USA, 1984).

Kaganskaia, Maia Lazarevna (Brusilovskaia)
1939–   . Journalist.
Born in Kiev. Graduated from Kiev University. Successful Soviet literary critic. Became involved with the Jewish rights movement. Emigrated, 1976. Lives in Israel. Many articles published in the West.

Kaidanovskii, Aleksandr Leonidovich
23.6.1946–   . Actor.
Entered the film industry, 1967. Graduated from the Moscow Shchukin Theatre School, 1971. Joined the Vakhtangov Theatre as an actor. Moved to MKHAT, 1971. Best known for his part in A. Tarkovskii's *Stalker*, 1980.

Kakabadze, David
1900?–1951. Artist.
Georgian artist, who emigrated with his parents after the October Revolution. Lived in Paris. Many exhibitions in France and the USA. After WWII, returned to the USSR. Member of the Georgian Union of Artists. During the *zhdanovshchina*, was attacked by the press for modernism and expelled from the Georgian Academy of Art. After his death, rediscovered in Georgia. Several exhibitions were held in Tbilisi, and a small private museum was set up there by his widow.

Kakhovskaia, Irina Konstantinovna
1888–1960. Revolutionary.
Member of the SR Maximalists Party, 1906. Members of the left SRs, 1917. In exile for revolutionary activity, 1908–17. Leader of a partisan group fighting the German army in the Ukraine, 1918. Together with B. Donskoi, assassinated the commander of the German army in the Ukraine, Field-Marshal Eichhorn, 30 July 1918. Arrested and sentenced but managed to escape (Donskoi was hanged). Under Stalin, one of the longest-serving Gulag prisoners, 1921–55. Released only after Stalin's death. In old age, lived near Moscow.

Kakurin, Nikolai Evgen'evich
16.9.1883–29.7.1936. General, military historian.
Born in Orel. Son of an officer. Educated at the Mikhailovskoe Artillery School, 1904. Graduated from the Academy of the General Staff, 1910. Colonel, WWI. During the Civil War, in the Ukrainian detachments which joined Petliura, 1919, and the Red Army, 1920. Soviet military specialist during the Polish campaign, 1920. Participated in the suppression of the Antonov uprising in Tambov, 1921. Fought against anti-communist partisans (basmachi) in Central Asia, 1922. Thereafter, lecturer at the Military Academy. One of the main authors of a 2 vol. history of the Civil War, 1928–30. Many other military historical works. Victim of Stalin's purges, probably shot.

Kalachikhin, Valerii Alekseevich
20.5.1939–   . Athlete.
Born in a sovkhoz in the Krasnodarskii Krai. Graduated from the Rostov Financial Economical Institute, 1961. Olympic champion, 1964. Honoured Master of Sports (volleyball), 1967. With the Rostov-on-Don Armed Forces Sports Club. Works as an economist.

Kalafati, Vasilii Pavlovich
10.2.1869–3.1942. Composer.
Born in Evpatoria. Professor at the Leningrad Conservatory (taught from 1907–29). Among his pupils were Igor Stravinskii and L. Collingwood (b.1887). Edited a dictionary, *Sputnik muzykanta*, 1911. Author of an opera, orchestral works, a symphony, and a piece in honour of Franz Schubert. Awarded 1st prize at the International Schubert Competition, 1928. Composed pieces for wind instruments and chamber ensembles, and choral works. Died during the Siege of Leningrad.

Kalamatiano, Ksenofont Dmitrievich (de Blumenthal)
5.1882–19.11.1923. Intelligence agent.
Born in Vienna. Son of a Greek merchant and a Russian aristocrat. Educated at private schools in Switzerland. Moved with his mother and his stepfather de Blumenthal to the USA, 1895. Taught Latin and Greek at American schools. Graduated from Culver Military Academy in Indiana, 1899, and from the Chicago University, 1903. Taught Russian at Chicago University, 1903–07. Returned to Russia as a businessman selling American agricultural machinery and soon became very prosperous. Became an American intelligence agent in Russia. Reported to the US government on the chaotic situation in Russia after the 1917 Revolution. Arrested by the Cheka, sentenced to death, 1918. Twice taken out to execution, but not shot. Remained a prisoner at Lubianka, death sentence commuted in May 1920. Released (with other American prisoners) due to a categorical demand by Hoover, head of ARA, the American relief agency. Transported to Narva, Estonia, 10 Aug. 1921. Returned to the USA, and resumed teaching Russian and other modern languages at Chicago University and Culver Academy. Died from blood poisoning, resulting from a hunting accident.

Kalandarishvili, Nestor Aleksandrovich
1874–1922. Revolutionary.
Joined the revolutionary movement, 1903. During the Civil War, organized Red partisan groups near Irkutsk in Siberia. Commander of Red forces in the Iakutsk region, 1921. Fell in action.

Kalantarova, Olga Kalantarovna
8.4.1877–6.11.1952. Pianist.
Born in Tiflis. Pupil of E. Esipova. Taught at the Leningrad Conservatory, 1903–50. Professor from 1912. Died in Leningrad.

Kalashnikov, Mikhail Timofeevich
10.11.1919–   . Gun designer.
Born in the village of Kuria, Altai region. After WWII, the most successful Soviet gun designer (automatics and machine guns). His *avtomat Kalashnikova* (AK) has become the standard battle equipment of the Soviet army, known throughout the world, due to massive Soviet arms sales to revolutionary governments and groups. Also designed machine guns (PK, PKS) and tank machine guns (PKT).

Kalatozishvili, Georgii Mikhailovich (Kalatozov Jr.)
1937–   . Cameraman, director.
Son of the celebrated film director Mikhail Kalatozov. Born in Georgia. Graduated from the VGIK as a cameraman in 1958. Went to the North Pole where he shot *Two Captains* in very harsh conditions for the Lenfilm Studio. Thereafter worked for Gruzia Films, in charge of the lighting on *I, Grandma, Iliko and Ilarion, The White Caravan* and *I See the Sun*. Turned to directing in 1971 with *Death of a Philatelist*, a thriller which was a great commercial success.

Kalatozov, Mikhail Konstantinovich (real name – Kalatozishvili)
28.12.1903–26.3.1973. Film director.
Born in Georgia. Entered the film industry in Georgia in 1923. Worked as an editor, laboratory technician, assistant cameraman, and then cameraman. Worked as an assistant to N. Shengelaia and I. Perestiani on a number of feature films. Director's debut in 1928 with *Ikh Tsarstvo*. His best-known early film is *Sol' Svanetii*, 1930, followed by *Gvozd' v Sapoge*, 1932. Studied at the Leningrad Academy of Arts (Akademiia Iskusstvoznaniia). Took over as head of the Tbilisi Film Studio in 1936. In the late 1930s–early 40s, made dull official films. During WWII, sent to the USA as a representative of the Cttee. of Cinematography. Returned to Moscow. Head of the Chief Directorate of the Production of Feature Films until 1948. After his remarkable success with *The Cranes Are Flying* (Letiat Zhuravli), which received the main prize at the 1957 Cannes Film Festival, made a much-discussed film, *The Letter That Was Never Sent*, 1960. Commercially it was a flop, a cult film which was hardly understood by the mass audience. In 1964, with his cameraman of previous films, Sergei Urusevskii, made *I Am Cuba* (Ia-Kuba) starring the poet, Evtushenko. His last, moderately successful, film was the Soviet-Italian co-production, *Krasnaia Palatka* (The Red Tent), 1970.

Kaledin, Aleksei Maksimovich
1861–1918. Cossack commander.
Don Cossack. Graduated from the Academy of the General Staff, 1889. Cossack commander during WWI. Cavalry general, 1917. Elected Ataman of the Don Cossacks, 1917. Began the opposition to communist rule on the Don. Committed suicide when it became clear that his initiative was not receiving enough support. His death became the signal for the widespread involvement of the Don Cossacks in the anti-communist struggle during the Civil War.

Kalesnik, Stanislav Vikent'evich
23.1.1901–   . Glaciologist, geographer.
Born in Petersburg. Graduated from Leningrad University, 1929. Profes-

sor of physical geography at Leningrad University, 1950. Director of the Institute for Lake Studies of the Academy of Sciences of the USSR, 1955. President of the USSR Geographical Society, 1964. Vice-president of the International Geographical Union, 1968–72. Regarded as one of the most outstanding modern glaciologists.

Kaliagin, Aleksandr Aleksandrovich
25.5.1941–   . Actor.
Graduated from the Moscow Shchukin Theatre School, 1965. Played in several Moscow theatres. Entered the film industry, 1967. From 1971 at MKHAT. Best known for his part in N. Mikhalkov's film *Neokonchennaia P'esa Dlia Mekhanicheskogo Pianino*, 1977.

Kalin, Ivan Petrovich
1935–   . Politician.
Moldavian. Son of a collective farmer. Member of the CPSU, 1955. Graduated from the Frunze Agricultural Institute, Kishinev, and the CPSU Cen. Cttee. Higher Party School. Senior party posts in the Moldavian Republic. Chairman of the Presidium of the Moldavian Supreme Soviet, Apr. 1980. Replaced I. Ustiian as chairman of the Council of Ministers of the Moldavian SSR in Dec. 1985. Candidate member of the Cen. Cttee. of the CPSU from 1981.

Kalina, Aleksandr
1933–   . Engineer, inventor.
Son of a Jewish soldier (killed during WWII). Graduated from the Odessa Institute of Refrigeration Engineering. According to his professors, a mathematical genius. In 1966, Candidate of Technical Sciences. Engineer at the Moscow Institute of Gas Industry from the late 1960s. Inventor and consultant at GOSPLAN and the Soviet of Ministers on the gas industry. Doctor of Technical Sciences. Emigrated to America in the early 1970s. Produced 20 inventions for the oil and gas industry in America. Inventor of the most important development in power station design for 100 years. Early in 1987, the Stone and Webster Corp. of Boston gave the go-ahead to his idea to use, instead of water, a mixture of 70% ammonia gas and 30% water. The temperature rises steadily as the volatile ammonia vaporizes first, and the boiler mixture gets richer in water. This method has world-wide implications in that it produces very cheap electricity. Lives in Houston, Texas.

Kalinchuk, Ekaterina Illarionovna
2.12.1922–   . Athlete.
Born in the village of Zhitovo, Tula Oblast'. Honoured Master of Sports (gymnastics), 1952. Graduated from the Moscow Oblast' Pedagogical Institute, 1952. Sports instructor. With Moscow Stroitel'. USSR champion, 1952. Olympic champion, 1952.

Kalinin, Mikhail Ivanovich
19.11.1875–3.6.1946. Revolutionary, politician.
Born in Verkhniaia Troitsa, Tver Gouvt. Son of a peasant, became a worker, involved in revolutionary activity in several towns (Petersburg, Tiflis, Revel). Member of the SD Party from 1898. An organizer of revolutionary workers during the 1905 Revolution. Participated in the October Revolution. Was elected revolutionary mayor of Petrograd. Member of the Cen. Cttee. of the Bolshevik Party, 1919. After Sverdlov's death, elected Chairman of the Central Executive Committee (de facto head of state), 1919. From 1922 (the formal founding of the USSR) until Mar. 1945, Head of State (1922–37, Chairman of the Central Executive Committee of the USSR, 1938–45 Chairman of the Presidium of the Supreme Soviet). Member of the Politburo from 1925. Without any real political strength, successfully played the role of symbol of the power of the people in a jovial manner, (officially nicknamed 'Vsesoiuznyi starosta', the All-Union village elder) while presiding over one of the darkest periods of Russian history. For some, a beacon of hope (received innumerable requests for help against the terror measures of the secret police), disliked by others (especially the peasant victims of collectivization, who saw him as a traitor to their class). Died after a long illness in Moscow. Two historical towns with a proud tradition were renamed after him (without much enthusiasm from the local inhabitants) – Tver, at one time a rival to Moscow, is now Kalinin, and Koenigsberg, the former German capital of East Prussia (since 1945 part of the Soviet Union) became Kaliningrad after WWII.

Kalinin, Petr Zakharovich
1902–1966. Politician.
Member of the Communist Party, 1928. 2nd secretary of the Cen. Cttee. of the Bolshevik Party in Belorussia, 1941. During WWII, remained at the rear of the German armies, organizing partisan detachments. Major-general, 1943. Chief of Staff of the partisan movement in Belorussia. After WWII, Prime-Minister of Belorussia, 1948. Responsible for the re-Stalinization of Belorussia.

Kalinina, Maria (Masha) Fedorovna
1971–   . Model.
On 12 June 1988, won the Miss Moscow Beauty Contest in the first event of its kind in the USSR. The 12 judges chose her from 6 finalists in the bathing-suit contest.

Kalishevskii, Iakov Stepanovich
21.10.1856–9.11.1923. Conductor.
Born in Kiev Gouvt. Director of a workers' choir from 1879. Conductor with the operas of Kiev and Khar'kov. Conductor of the choir of the Sofiiskii Cathedral, Kiev, 1883–1920. Author of songs and choral arrangements. Died in Kiev.

Kalita, Ivan Aleksandrovich
14.1.1927–   . Athlete.
Born in the village of Bolshaia Alekseevka, Tambov Oblast'. Honoured Master of Sports (riding), 1970. With the Moscow Armed Forces Club. Sports instructor. Member of the CPSU, 1952. USSR champion, 1959–75. Graduated from the Frunze Military Academy, 1961. Silver medal, 1968. World champion, 1970. Olympic champion, 1972.

Kallistrat (Tsintsadze, Kallistrat Mikhailovich), Patriarch-Catholicos
25.4.1866–3.2.1952. Georgian Orthodox church leader.
Born in Tobanieri in Western

Georgia. Son of a priest. Educated at the seminary at Kutaisi, 1882, and at the Tiflis seminary, 1888. Graduated from the Kiev Theological Academy, 1892. Thereafter, a priest at Tiflis. Took part in the Council of the Georgian Church, Mar. 1917, which decided to restore the independence of the Georgian Church (abolished in 1811, when Georgia joined the Russian Empire). Bishop, 1925. Elected Patriarch-Catholicos (Head of the Georgian Church), Jan. 1932. Died in Tbilisi (Tiflis).

Kalmanovich, Shabtai
1945– . Businessman.
Arrived in Israel in 1971 as an immigrant from the USSR. Set up several firms dealing with properties and commodities operating in sub-Saharan Africa. Soon achieved great success in the black homeland of Bophuthatswana in South Africa. Set up his HQ in the capital, Mmabatho. His firm, Liat Construction, obtained multi-million dollar contracts for some extraordinary projects. Became a millionaire and befriended President Mangope. Appointed by Mangope to represent his 'state' in Israel. Shortly afterwards, opened an office in Tel Aviv opposite the British Embassy. Travelled to London where he stayed in the Sheraton Hotel, Knightsbridge. In July 1987, the police stormed his room and arrested him. He was held in Pentonville prison. The US government approached the British government in order to extradite him on charges involving cheque frauds worth $2 million. Eventually deported to Israel whose security services, Shin Bet, arrested him on arrival (23 Dec. (1987). Put on trial, Sept. 1988. Shin Bet has been quoted as saying that he is 'one of the highest-paid KGB moles to operate in Israel'.
Source: *The Times*, 12 Jan. and 6 Sept. 1988.

Kalmykov, Ivan Leonidovich
1866–1925? Artist.
Studied at the Moscow School of Painting, Sculpture and Architecture, 1884–89, under V. Makovskii, V. Polenov, E. Sorokin, and I. Prianishnikov. Landscape painter. Exhibitions: MOLKH, 1890, 1893–99, 1901, 1906–07, MTKH, 1894,

1897, 1899–1901, 1904, Academy of Arts, Petersburg, 1898, Spring Exhibitions, 1898, 1901–02, TPKHV, 1904–07, St. Petersburg Society of Artists, 1909. Personal exhibitions: Moscow, 1904–05, 2nd Exhibition, Moscow, 1908 — both with A. Chirkhov.

Kalnyn', Alfred Ianovich (Kalnius)
23.8.1879–23.12.1951. Composer, organist.
Born in Latvia. Professor at the Riga Conservatory, director of the same, 1945–48. Author of the first Latvian opera. Wrote operas, a ballet, cantatas, pieces for piano, organ and other instruments, over 300 romances, and music for plays and films. Died in Riga.

Kalnyn', Teodor Petrovich (Kalnins, Theodore)
23.11.1890–17.10.1962. Choir conductor.
Born in Latvia. Choir conductor from 1921. Chief choir conductor with the Latvian Theatre of Opera and Ballet from 1934. Taught at the Riga Conservatory. Died in Riga.

Kamanin, Nikolai Petrovich
1908–1982. Col.-general.
Joined the Red Army, 1927. Graduated from the Zhukovskii Air Force Academy, 1938. Became widely known as one of the pilots involved in the rescue of the Cheliuskin expedition, 1934. On active service in the Soviet-Finnish war and WWII. Directed the training of the Soviet cosmonauts, 1966–71.

Kamenetskii, Boris Evseevich
1922– . Lawyer.
Born in the Ukraine. Grew up in Tashkent. Graduated from Tashkent University in law. As a deputy prosecutor of the Uzbek SSR, was accused of excessive leniency towards dissidents, and of Zionism. Emigrated, 1978. Settled in Israel.

Kamenev Lev Borisovich (Rosenfeld)
1883–1936. Politician.
Educated in Tiflis, Georgia. Became

involved in revolutionary activity while reading law at Moscow University. Expelled from the university. Joined the Social Democratic Party in 1901. Emigrated in 1903, became a Bolshevik. Returned to Russia several times. Arrested several times. While abroad ran the Bolshevik Party with Lenin and Zinov'ev. Arrested at a secret meeting with Bolshevik Duma members in 1914. Given a lenient sentence in 1915 for denouncing Lenin's anti-war propaganda. Sent to Siberia, freed after February 1917. Led the Bolsheviks in Petrograd until Lenin's return from Switzerland. Edited *Pravda*. With Zinov'ev, objected to Lenin's plans to seize power in Oct. 1917, and advocated a coalition of all Socialist parties. After the October Revolution, chairman of the 2nd Congress of Soviets, chairman of the Central Executive Committee, deputy chairman of the Council of People's Commissars. Participated in the Brest-Litovsk peace negotiations. Among the leaders standing in for Lenin during his sickness (from 1922). Member of the Politburo, 1919–25. Supported Zinov'ev and Stalin against Trotsky, later supported Trotsky against Stalin, then an ally of Zinov'ev in opposition to Stalin. Ambassador to Italy, 1926–27. Expelled several times from the party and then re-admitted. Arrested in 1935, tried in 1936. Sentenced to death and executed. Rehabilitated, 13 June 1988.

Kamenev, Sergei Sergeevich
16.4.1881–25.8.1936. General.
Born in Kiev. Son of a military engineer. Educated at the Aleksandrovskoe Military School in 1900. Graduated from the Academy of the General Staff in 1907. Took part in WWI. Joined the Red Army in 1918, led the Red forces against Admiral Kolchak in the Civil War, 1918–19. Supreme Commander of the Army of the Soviet Republic, 1919–24. Military specialist' (officer of the Imany senior positions in the Red Army and awarded many decorations. Died in Moscow and buried at the Kremlin wall with other famous revolutionary figures. A typical 'military specialist' (officer of the Imperial Army, who under Trotsky

insured highly qualified military leadership of the new Red Army). Memoirs: *Zapiski o Grazhdanskoi Voine i Voennom Stroitelstve* (Notes on the Civil War and military reconstruction), 2 vol., Moscow, 1963.

Kameneva, Olga Davydovna (b. Bronstein)
1881?–1936. Cultural functionary.
Sister of L. Trotsky and wife of L. Kamenev. Became prominent after the Bolshevik take-over 1917, as head of the theatre department (TEO) of the People's Commissariat for Education, and as an organizer of a revolutionary salon, where the hungry writers and poets of the time could find hospitality and some semblance of former literary gatherings. Described by her guests as 'conceited and dull but without malice'. Arrested after the execution of her husband, and perished in the Gulag.

Kamenskaia, Maria Danilovna
1854–1925. Singer (mezzo soprano).
Born in Petersburg. Pupil of the Swedish singer Genrietta Nissen-Saloman. Soloist with the Mariinskii Theatre, Petersburg, 1874–86, and from 1891. Died in Leningrad.

Kamenskii, Aleksandr Danilovich
12.12.1900–7.11.1952. Pianist.
Born in Geneva. Pupil of L. Nikolaev. Professor at the Leningrad Conservatory. Author of concertos, and arrangements for piano. Died in Leningrad.

Kamenskii, Vasilii Vasil'evich
17.4.1884–11.11.1961. Futurist poet, pilot.
Born near Perm'. Son of a gold mine inspector. First works published in 1904. Became a star of Futurism. In his youth close to Mayakovsky. One of the first Russian pilots, 1910–11. Participant in many Futurist provincial tours in the 1920s. After the clamp-down on revolutionary art, wrote safe poems on the Russian historical rebels Razin, Bolotnikov and Pugachov. Famous as an organizer of Futurist events and author of absurdist verse. Died in Moscow.

Kamera, Ivan Pavlovich
1897–1952. Col.-general.
Joined the Red Army and the Bolshevik Party, 1918. Took part in the Civil War. Commander of Artillery on the Western Front, 1941–44.

Kaminskaia, Dina Isaakovna
1920– . Lawyer.
Born in Dnepropetrovsk. Graduated in law from Moscow University. Member of the Moscow Bar Association. In the 1970s, became famous for her defence of human rights activists, including Aleksandr Ginzburg and Vladimir Bukovskii. In 1977, received threats from the KGB. Left the USSR. Lives in the USA. Memoirs: *Zapiski Advokata*, USA, 1978.

Kaminskii, Bronislav (Mieczyslaw)
1900?–1944. General.
Of Polish descent. Trained as an engineer. During WWII, among the organizers of a self-defence group of peasants against NKVD partisans near Briansk (RONA-Russkaia Osvoboditelnaia Narodnaia Armia). After the death in action of Voskoboinikov, took over command of about 5,000 men. Appointed brigadier-general by the German general Schmidt. Worked out an agreement with the German Army for a self-governing Russian region, the Lokot' Republic, in return for keeping the area free of partisans. At the approach of the Red Army, successfully evacuated his people with their families (30,000) to Silesia. Opposed the merger with General Vlasov. Agreed to have the command of his brigade transferred to the SS, and have it renamed the 29th Division of the Waffen-SS. Himmler awarded him the Iron Cross, 1st Class, and appointed him an SS colonel. Ordered to take part in the suppression of the Warsaw uprising. Resisted at first, but eventually, under pressure from Himmler, sent 1,700 of his men under the command of Major Frolov to Warsaw, where they acted ruthlessly and commited many atrocities. Kaminskii himself spent 10 days in Warsaw and attempted to reward his men with stolen goods, especially jewellery. His troops were withdrawn from combat. After a heated verbal exchange, arrested in Lodz by SS

General Bach-Zelewski, in charge of the suppression of the Warsaw uprising. Brought before an SS court-martial, quickly sentenced and shot in secret without his brigade being informed. After his disappearance, his troops joined the Vlasov Army (ROA), forming the bulk of its field forces, and later liberated Prague from the SS during the uprising in 1945.
See: G. Deschner, *Warsaw Rising*, London 1972; Ausky, *Predatelstvo i Izmena*, USA; J. Hoffmann, *Die Geschichte der Wlassow-Armee*, Freiburg, 1984.

Kaminskii, Dmitrii Romanovich
17.8.1907– . Composer.
Born in Ekaterinoslav. Chairman of the Belorussian Union of Composers. Author of orchestral works, concertos for cymbals and orchestra, a concerto for cymbals, a fantasy for violin, chamber music, and music for films.

Kaminskii, Vladimir Vladimirovich
18.4.1950– . Athlete.
Born in Minsk. Graduated from the Minsk Electrotechnical School of Communications, 1969. Honoured Master of Sports (cycling), 1976. With Minsk Spartak. USSR champion, 1976–78. World champion, 1977. Olympic champion, 1976. Works as an electrical engineer.

Kamionskii, Oskar Isaevich
1869–15.8.1917. Singer (baritone).
Born in Kiev. Pupil of S. Gabel'. Debut in Italy, 1892. With Russian operas from 1893. With the Zimin Opera in Moscow, 1905–08. Moved to the south of Russia after the February Revolution. Died in Yalta.
See: S. Levik, *Zapiski Opernogo Pevtsa*, Moscow, 1962, p.26–33.

Kamkov, Boris Davidovich (Katz)
3.6.1885–29.8.1938. Politician.
Born in the village of Kobylnia, Bessarabia. Son of a country doctor. Educated in Kishinev. Arrested for revolutionary activity in Nikolaev in 1904, exiled to Turukhansk, Siberia in 1905. Fled abroad in 1907. Graduated from Heidelberg University in law in 1911. Took part in

the Zimmerwald conference during WWI. Returned to Russia in 1917. Member of Petrograd Soviet. Supported the Bolsheviks in Oct. 1917. After the expulsion of the left wing from the SR Party (for collusion with the Bolsheviks), became leader of the left SRs. Joined the coalition government with the Bolsheviks, Dec. 1917. After the ratification of the peace treaties of Brest-Litovsk by the 4th Congress of Soviets, Mar. 1918, the left-wing SRs left the coalition. Became a radical critic of Lenin, took part in the 3rd Congress of the left SRs, June 28–July 1, 1918. Trotsky demanded his execution (together with his group) as saboteurs of the Brest-Litovsk treaties. After the assassination of the German Ambassador Mirbach, became leader of the left SRs' uprising in Moscow, July 1918, suppressed by the Latvian Cheka detachments of Vatsietis. Went underground, but continued to lead the left SRs. Arrested in Jan. 1920 in Moscow. Released for cooperating with the government by writing a series of articles, urging support for the Bolsheviks in the war with Poland. Re-arrested in Feb. 1921 with all the other left SR leaders. In prison, 1921–23, and arrested and imprisoned on several subsequent occasions. All the left SRs were arrested again, 6 Feb. 1937. Prosecution witness at the Bukharin trial, yet sentenced to death and executed.

Kamkov, Fedor Vasil'evich
1898–1951. Lt.-general.
Joined the Red Army and the Bolshevik Party, 1918. Cavalry commander in the Civil War. Graduated from the Cavalry School, 1924. Took part in the Soviet-Finnish war and WWII. Continued his career in the cavalry until his death.

Kamo (Ter-Petrosian, Simon Arshakovich)
27.5.1882–14.7.1922. Revolutionary.
Born in Gori, Georgia, Son of a wealthy trader. Expelled from school for his atheist views. Joined the revolutionary movement. Under the influence of his older comrade from the same town, Dzhugashvili (Koba, later Stalin) took part in several 'expropriations' (robberies) in order to supply the Bolshevik Party with

funds, including the famous Tiflis robbery of state funds, masterminded by Stalin in June 1907. Wounded and arrested, but escaped. Arrested in Germany with a suitcase full of explosives, autumn 1907. Feigned madness, but was extradited to Russia at the end of 1909. Escaped from the prison hospital of Metekhskii Castle, Aug. 1911. On Lenin's orders, acted as an underground courier (arms and ammunition), re-arrested on his return to Russia, 1912. Court-martialled and sentenced to death, commuted to 20 years' imprisonment. Released after the February Revolution 1917. During the Civil War, active as a Cheka official in Baku, and as organizer of the Red partisans in the rear of the White armies. Later, official in the Ministry of Foreign Trade, 1921, and the Ministry of Finance in Georgia, 1922. Run over by a car in Tbilisi.

Kamov, Nikolai Il'ich
1902–1973. Helicopter designer.
Graduated from the Tomsk Technological Institute, 1923. Chief designer of Soviet helicopters from 1940 (the Ka-series).

Kandel, Feliks Solomonovich (Kamov)
1932– . Scriptwriter.
Born in Moscow. Educated as an aviation engineer. Became famous as the scriptwriter of a very popular animated cartoon series *Nu,pogodi*. Involved in the Jewish rights movement. Refusenik, 1973–77. Emigrated to Israel, 1977.

Kandelaki, Gela Iraklievich
2.5.1940– . Actor, director.
Born in Georgia. Graduated from the VGIK, 1965. Returned from Moscow to Tbilisi. Joined the Georgia Film Studio. Made several documentary films for Georgian television, including *Futbol Bez Miacha*. His first feature film was *Proishestvie*, 1980. Best-known for his title role in O. Ioseliani's film, *Zhil Pevchii Drozd*, 1971.

Kandelaki, Vladimir Arkad'evich
29.3.1908– . Singer (bass baritone), stage director.
Born in Tiflis. Pupil of Evgenii

Vronskii (1883–1942). Soloist with the V. Nemirovich-Danchenko Theatre of Musical Drama from 1929, the K. Stanislavskii and Nemirovich-Danchenko Theatre after 1941. Stage director from 1943. Chief stage director with the Moscow Operetta Theatre, 1954–64. Many concerts and records.

Kandinskaia, Nina (Mme. Nina Kandinsky; b. Andreevskaia)
1899–2.9.1980. Wife of Vasilii Kandinskii.
Daughter of a general. Met Vasilii Kandinskii at the age of 17 (he was then 50). Married him on the day of the October Revolution 1917. In 1921, left the USSR for Weimar, where they were received and taken care of by Gropius. Moved to Paris on the day Hitler took power in 1933. After Kandinskii's death in 1944, became his sole heiress. For tax reasons, moved to Gstaadt. Became obsessed with diamonds and other precious stones, and used to wear diamonds even when shopping. Was found strangled in her bathroom. It was assumed she had let her murderer in herself since there were no signs of a forced entry.

Kandinskii Vasilii Vasil'evich
16.12.1866–13.12.1944. Painter, art theoretician.
Pioneer of abstract painting and one of the founders of modern art. Born in Moscow. Graduated from Moscow University in law and economics. Gave up his academic career to study painting. Studied with Azbe in Munich, 1897–98, and at the Munich Academy of Art with F. Stuck in 1900. Lived in Berlin and Munich, and founded the artist group Der Blaue Reiter (with F. Marc and others). His first abstract paintings were in the expressionist manner. Later introduced into his work geometrical elements similar to those of Malevich. Returned to Russia in 1914. One of the organizers of the Museum of Painting in Petrograd and INHUK in Moscow. Emigrated to Germany in 1921. Professor at the Bauhaus (Weimar) from 1922. During this period influenced by Paul Klee. After Hitler came to power, moved to France, 1933. Died at Neuilly-sur-Seine.

Works: *Über das Geitstige in der Kunst*, Munich, 1912.

Kankarovich, Anatolii Isaakovich
20.10.1885–17.8.1956. Conductor, composer, music critic.
Born in Petersburg. Stage director with the Zimin Opera, Moscow, the Mariinskii Theatre, Petrograd, and elsewhere. Conducted symphony concerts. Author of an opera, a ballet, choral works, romances, and music for theatrical performances. Literary works: *Putevoditel' po Operam*, 2 vol., Leningrad, 1926–27; *Novyi Put' Pevtsa*, Moscow, 1931. Died in Moscow.

Kanegisser, Leonid Akimovich
1898–1918. Student, poet.
Son of a wealthy Jewish engineer and public figure. At his parents' salon, met politicians, literati and artists. Published a book of poems. In Italy when WWI broke out. Returned to Petrograd. Totally apolitical and did not belong to any party until the spring of 1918. Then the arrest and execution of a long-time friend turned him into a terrorist. Entered the reception-hall of the Ministry of Foreign Affairs in Petrograd, and shot the Chairman of the Petrograd Cheka, Moisei Uritskii, 30 Aug. 1918. Tried to escape by bicycle. Seized near the English Club. Executed by the successor of Uritskii, G. Bokii, with some 500 hostages arrested at random on Petrograd streets.
Sources: Mark Aldanov, *Sovremenniki*, Berlin, 1932; Grigorii Zinov'ev, 'Ot Chrezvychainoi Komissii' (announcement of Kanegisser's execution), *Severnaia Kommuna*, Nr. 133, 31 Aug. 1919; I. Antipov, *Ocherki iz Deiatel'nosti Petrogradskoi Komissii, Petrogradskaia Pravda*.

Kantaria, Meliton Varlamovich
1920– . Sergeant.
Born in Georgia. Drafted into the army at the beginning of WWII. Infantry soldier, and later sergeant. With his Russian colleague, Egorov, on 30 Apr. 1945, planted the Red flag on the Reichstag building in Berlin, signifying victory and the end of the war. Hero of the Soviet Union, 1946. Accepted into the Communist Party, 1947.

Kantorovich, Leonid Vital'evich
19.1.1912– . Mathematician, economist.
Born in Petersburg. Graduated from Leningrad University, 1930. Professor there from 1934. Academician, 1964. Member of the Siberian branch of the Academy of Sciences, 1958–71. Member of the Institute of Economic Planning of the State Cttee. on Science and Technology of the USSR Council of Ministers from 1971. Honorary doctor's degrees from various Western universities. Honorary member of the Budapest and Boston academies.

Kapitonov, Viktor Arsen'evich
25.10.1933– . Athlete.
Born in Kalinin. Honoured Master of Sports (cycling), 1959. With the Moscow Armed Forces Club. Member of the CPSU, 1967. Graduated from the Leningrad Institute of Physical Culture, 1968. Honoured Sports Instructor of the USSR, 1970. USSR champion, 1956–64. Olympic champion, 1960. Bronze medal, 1960. Author of several sports books, such as *Radi Etogo Stoit Zhit'*, Moscow, 1978.

Kapitsa, Andrei Petrovich
9.7.1931– . Geographer, geomorphologist.
Born in Cambridge. Son of the physicist, P. Kapitsa. Graduated in geography from Moscow University, 1953. Member of the CPSU, 1962. Corresponding member of the Academy of Sciences, 1970. Worked in the Geographical Dept. of Moscow University until 1970. Participated in four Soviet Antarctic expeditions. Lives in Moscow.

Kapitsa, Petr Leonidovich
1894–8.4.1984. Physicist, academician.
Born in Kronstadt. Son of a military engineer. Academician, 1939. Fellow of the Royal Society. Educated at the Petrograd Polytechnic Institute. Pupil of Ioffe. Worked in England under Rutherford, 1921. From 1924, deputy head of the Cavendish Magnetic Research Laboratory at Cambridge. When he visited Moscow in 1934, was not allowed to return to England on Stalin's personal orders. After a serious conflict with the

Soviet government which threatened his life, his laboratory was bought and moved to Moscow. It later became the Institute of Physical Problems. He was director there until 1946, when he was arrested and sent to the Gulag for refusing to work for the military who wanted him to carry out research into the use of nuclear energy. After Stalin's death, he was released immediately and brought back to Moscow, where he again headed his institute. Member of numerous international colleges and universities.

Kaplan, Emmanuil Iosifovich
28.1.1895–14.12.1961. Singer (tenor), stage director.
Born in Riga. Soloist with the Petrograd Malyi Opera, 1920–25. Stage director with the Kirov Theatre of Opera and Ballet, 1929–58. Stage manager with the operatic studio, 1927–52, organizer, and later head of the department of operatic stage management of the Leningrad Conservatory. Professor from 1939. Died in Leningrad.

Kaplan, Fanny (Dora)
1893–5.9.1918. Revolutionary.
Member of the SR Party. On 30 Aug. 1918, made an attempt on Lenin's life after a meeting at the Mikhelson factory in Moscow, and seriously wounded him. Arrested and soon thereafter executed by Pavel Mal'kov, the Kremlin's security commandant.
See: Pavel Mal'kov, *Zapiski Komendanta Moskovskogo Kremlia*, Moscow, 1959.

Kaplan, Isaak Mikhailovich
12.12.1924– . Stage designer.
Graduated from the VGIK, 1950. From 1953 worked with the Lenfilm Studio. His films include *The Lady With the Little Dog*, *The Coat* (Shinel'), and *The Three Fat Men*.

Kapler, Aleksei Iakovlevich
11.10.1904–1979. Scriptwriter.
Born in Kiev. In 1920, one of the founders (together with Sergei Iutkevich and Grigorii Kozintsev) of the Arlekin Theatre in Kiev. Entered the film industry in 1926. Acted in

several films including *The Great-coat*. In 1929–30, director-script-writer of many art documentaries. Wrote scripts for many official films between 1935–43 which are now regarded as Stalinist propaganda, such as *Shakhtery, Tri Tovarishcha, Kotovskii, Ona Zashchishchaet Rodinu* and others. Won the Stalin Prize, 1941. Was involved emotionally with Svetlana Allilueva, Stalin's daughter, then aged 16. Arrested, and accused of being a British spy. Spent 10 years in prisons and camps and then in exile. Returned to Moscow after Stalin's death. Rehabilitated. First script filmed in 1957. Continued working in the film industry until the mid-1970s. Taught at the VGIK.

Kapp, Artur Iosifovich (Kapp, Arthur)
28.2.1878–14.1.1952. Composer.
Born in the Lifliandskaia Gouvt, Estonia. Son of the organist and choir conductor, Ioosep Kapp. Studied under N. Rimskii-Korsakov. Director of and teacher at the Astrakhan' Music School, 1904–20. Professor at the Tallinn Conservatory, 1925–43. After the war, retired from pedagogical work and devoted himself to full-time composing. Mainly known for his choral works. Also author of an opera, cantatas, a vocal symphony, compositions for wind instruments, pieces for piano, and music for theatrical performances. Died at his place of birth.

Kapp, Eugen Arturovich
26.5.1908– . Composer.
Born in Astrakhan'. Son and pupil of the Estonian composer Artur Kapp. Graduated from the Tallinn Conservatory, 1933. Gave music lessons till 1935. Taught at the conservatory from 1935. Composed for the theatre. Conductor and composer with the Estonian Singing Ensemble in Iaroslavl' during WWII. Chairman of the Board of the Union of Estonian Composers, 1944. Professor of composition from 1947. Director of the Tallinn Conservatory, 1952–65. Wrote operas, cantatas, sonatas and other genres, also music for the plays of Shakespeare, Schiller, Goldoni and others.

Kapp, Villem Khansovich
7.9.1913–24.3.1964. Composer.
Born in the Lifliandskaia Gouvt,

Estonia. Son of the choir conductor, Hans Kapp, and nephew of the composer, Artur Kapp. Lecturer at the Tallinn Conservatory. Mainly known for his choral works. Also author of an opera, cantatas, a vocal symphony, composition for wind instruments, pieces for piano, and music for theatrical performances. Died in Tallinn.

Kappel', Vladimir Oskarovich
28.4.1883–25.1.1920. General.
Born in the village of Nizhneozernaia. Educated at the Nikolaevskoe Cavalry School in 1903. Graduated from the Academy of the General Staff in 1913. Took part in WWI. During the Civil War, a commander of the detachments of the Komuch (Committee of the Constituent Assembly on the Volga). Took Simbirsk and Kazan from the Red Army in 1918. His army included the Izhevsk and Votkin regiments of Ural workers, who in Aug. 1918 rebelled against the Bolsheviks. A legendary commander of the Kolchak Army. His men called themselves 'kappelevtsy'. From 11 Dec. 1919, Commander-in-Chief. During the retreat of the Whites in Siberia, commanded the rear-guard. Severely affected by frost-bite, lost the use of both legs. Died of pneumonia in Nizhneudinsk.

Kapralov, Georgii Aleksandrovich
8.10.1921– . Film critic, journalist.
Graduated from the Leningrad Theatre Institute, 1948. First appeared in print in 1944. Staff film critic on *Pravda* from 1950. Doyen of the Russian press corps at the Cannes Film Festival from 1960, as deputy-editor of the literature and art page of *Pravda*. Author of many books. Lives in Moscow.

Kapustin, Sergei Alekseevich
13.2.1953– . Athlete.
Born in Ukhta, Komi ASSR. Honoured Master of Sports (hockey), 1975. From 1977 with the Central Sports Club of the Army. Studied at the Moscow Oblast' Institute of Physical Culture. USSR champion, 1974, 1978–79. World and European champion, 1974–75, 1978–79. Olympic champion, 1976.

Karaev, Kara Abul'faz ogly
5.2.1918–13.5.1982. Composer.
Born in Baku. Early training in piano at the Workers' Faculty of the Azerbaidzhan Conservatory, where he also studied composition. Pupil of L. Rudolf. Entered the Moscow Conservatory in 1938. Pupil of An. Aleksandrov and S. Vasilenko. Training interrupted by WWII and resumed in 1943. Pupil of D. Shostakovich. Graduated from the Moscow Conservatory, 1946. Artistic director of the Azerbaidzhan Philharmonic, 1941. Taught composition at the Azerbaidzhan Conservatory from 1946. Professor from 1959. Director from 1949–53. Director of the Music Department of the Institute of Arts of the Academy of Sciences of the AzSSR. Died in Moscow.

Karalli, Vera Alekseevna (Koralli)
27.7.1889–16.11.1972. Ballet dancer.
Graduated from the Moscow Choreographic School, 1906. Pupil of A. Gorskii. Joined the Bolshoi Theatre and soon became one of its stars. In 1909, with Diaghilev's Ballets Russes. Partner of Vaclav Nijinskii. From 1914, starred in many silent Russian films. Went abroad in 1918. In 1919–20, with S. Diaghilev again. Appeared with other ballet companies. Toured in Europe and the USA. In 1928, founded the Lithuanian National Ballet. Taught there. From 1930–35, choreographer with the Rumanian Opera. Choreographer of the Bukharest Dance Studio. From 1941, lived in Vienna. Died in Baden, Austria.

Karasev, Nikolai Aleksandrovich
1909– . Artist.
Studied at an enamel art school. Pupil of A.A. Nazarov. Has worked in Rostov art shops from 1935. Enamel painter. Exhibitions: International Exhibition, New York 1939.

Karaseva, Olga Dmitrievna
24.7.1949– . Athlete.
Born in Moscow. Honoured Master of Sports (gymnastics), 1970. With the Central Sports Club of the Army. Graduated from the Moscow Oblast' Pedagogical Institute, 1973. Inter-

national referee from 1976. Sports instructor. Olympic champion, 1968. USSR champion, 1969–71. European champion, 1969. World champion, 1970.

Karasik, Iulii Iur'evich
24.8.1923– . Film director.
Graduated from the VGIK, 1951. Pupil of S. Gerasimov and T. Makarova. Worked at the Sverdlovsk Film Studio, later moved to Mosfilm.
Films: *Dikaia Sobaka Dingo*, 1962, (huge commercial success); *Shestoe Iulia* (The 6th of July), 1968; *The Seagull*, 1972.

Karatsiupa, Nikita Fedorovich
25.4.1910–1988. Security services officer, dog handler.
Born in Alekseevka near Dnepropetrovsk in the Ukraine. Son of a peasant. Served from the early 1930s in border-guard detachments under the control of the NKVD-KGB. Member of the CPSU, 1939. Specialized in the training of dogs (Alsatians for tracking and concentration camp duties). Until his retirement in 1961, managed to catch about 500 people trying to cross the Soviet border. One of the most qualified dog handlers in the Soviet state security system. Hero of the Soviet Union, 1965. Awarded the Order of Lenin and other high awards.

Karatygin, Viacheslav Gavrilovich
17.9.1875–23.10.1925. Music critic, composer.
Born in Pavlovsk. One of the organizers of the circle Vechera Sovremennoi Muzyki. Author of *Mussorgskii, Chaliapin,* Petrograd, 1922, *Izbrannye Stat'ii i Materialy*, Leningrad, 1927, and *Izbrannye Stat'ii*, Moscow-Leningrad, 1965. Died in Leningrad.

Karavaev, Oleg Nikolaevich
20.5.1936–23.8.1978. Athlete.
Born in Minsk. Honoured Master of Sports (wrestling), 1960. With Minsk Burevestnik. Graduated from the Belorussian Institute of Physical Culture, 1966. USSR champion, 1956–60, 1962. World champion, 1958, 1961. Olympic champion, 1960.

Karbyshev, Dmitrii Mikhailovich
1880–1945. Lt.-general.
Graduated from the Nikolaevskaia Military Engineering Academy, 1911. Joined the Red Army, 1918. Took part in the Civil War. In the 1920–30s, professor at the Frunze Academy and the Academy of the General Staff. During WWII, seriously wounded and taken prisoner. Died in Mauthausen concentration camp in Germany. Wrote many scientific works on military engineering.

Kardovskii, Dmitrii Nikolaevich
5.9.1866–9.2.1942. Artist.
Born in the village of Osurovo, now Pereiaslavl'-Zalesskii, Iaroslavl' Oblast'. Studied at the architect A. Gunst's Classes of Fine Arts, Moscow, under N. Klodt, then at the Higher Art School of the Petersburg Academy of Arts, 1892–96. Under P. Chistiakov and Il'ia Repin, and at the Azbe School in Munich, 1896–1900. Graduated in law from Moscow University, 1891. Illustrator, stage designer, genre painter specialising in historical subjects. Also graphic artist. Exhibitions: the New Society of Artists, 1904–15, MTKH, 1909–18 with some interruptions, AKHRR 4th exhibition, Moscow, 1923, Zhar-Tsvet Society, 1925, 10 Years of the Malyi Theatre, Moscow, 1927, Russian Drawing, 10th Anniversary of the October Revolution, Moscow, 1927. Personal exhibitions: Jubilee (with O. Della-Vos-Kardovskaia), Moscow, 1938, and Moscow, 1953 (posthumously). Died in Pereiaslavl'-Zalesskii.

Karelin, Vladimir Aleksandrovich
1891–1938. Revolutionary, politician.
Involved in revolutionary activity before the 1917 Revolution. Member of the SR Party. After 1917, one of the organizers of the left-wing SRs who joined in a coalition government with the Bolsheviks (and were expelled from the SR Party). Member of the Cen. Cttee. of the left-wing SRs. Minister of State Property in the first Soviet government, Dec 1917. Member of the Soviet delegation at the Brest-Litovsk negotiations. Resigned in protest over the peace treaty. One of the organizers of the left SRs' revolt in Moscow in July

1918. Arrested in Feb. 1919, but soon released. Fled abroad, and continued his anti-Bolshevik activity in emigration.

Karetnikov, Nikolai Nikolaevich
28.6.1930– . Composer.
Born in Moscow. Author of ballets, an oratorio, 4 symphonies, a dramatic poem, a concerto for wind instruments, pieces for piano, choral works, romances, and music for plays, films, and radio.

Kargareteli, Ia (Il'ia) Georgievich
1867–31.3.1939.
Composer, folklorist, conductor, singer.
Soloist, 1896–1905, then stage director with the Tiflis Opera. One of the earliest composers of Georgian romances. Literary works: *O Gruzinskoi Muzyke*, Moscow, 1893, and *Ocherk Gruzinskoi Narodnoi Muzyki*, Tiflis, 1901. Died in Tbilisi.

Kargin, Valentin Alekseevich
23.1.1907– . Chemist.
Graduated from Moscow University, 1930. Worked at the Physico-Chemical Institute in Moscow. Specialist in colloidal chemistry and polymers.

Kari-Iakubov, Mukhitdin
1896–1957. Singer (baritone), impresario.
Organized a variety ensemble, 1926, later called the Uzbek Musical Theatre. Artistic director of the same. Artistic director of the Uzbek Philharmonic. Soloist with the Uzbek Theatre of Opera and Ballet in Tashkent, from 1936.

Kariagdy, Dzhabbar
1861–28.4.1944. Folk singer.
Born in Shusha, Azerbaidzhan. Took part in the first musical production in Shusha of the classical Azerbaidzhanian poems *Leili i Medzhnun* and *Farkhad i Shirin*. Organized a trio with K. Primov (tar) and A. Oganezashvili (kemancha) in Baku in the 1900s. Many of his folk songs were recorded by S. Rustamov and published (*50 Azerbaidzhanskikh Pesen*, Baku, 1938).
Source: *Sovetskaia Muzyka*, 1940, Nr 2.

Karindi, Alfred Eduardovich
30.5.1901–   . Composer, organist, choir conductor.
Born in Estlandskaia Gouvt. Professor at the Tallinn Conservatory. Author of cantatas, works for orchestra, suites, chamber music, 4 sonatas for organ, 2 sonatas for piano, choral works, and romances.

Kariofilli, Georgii Spiridonovich
1901–1971. Col.-general.
Joined the Red Army, 1918. Took part in the Civil War. Graduated from the Frunze Military Academy, 1935. During WWII, artillery commander of several armies. Chief of Staff of artillery and rocket ground forces, 1956–68.

Karlova, Larisa Aleksandrovna
7.8.1958–   . Athlete.
Born in Kiev. Honoured Master of Sports (handball), 1976. With Kiev Spartak. Studied at the Kiev Institute of People's Management. USSR champion, 1976–79. Olympic champion, 1976.

Karmaliuk, Pavel Petrovich
24.12.1907–   . Singer (baritone).
Born in Zhitomirskaia Gouvt. Ukrainian by nationality. Pupil of D. Evtushenko. Soloist with the L'vov Theatre of Opera and Ballet from 1944. People's Artist of the USSR, 1960.

Karmanov, Vasilii
1927–1967. Athlete.
Honoured Master of Sports (swimming). 10th place at the XVth Olympic Games. Many times USSR champion.

Karmen, Roman Lazarevich
16.11.1906–28.4.1978. Documentary film-maker.
Graduated from the GIK (VGIK), 1932. Sent with others to cover the Spanish Civil War. Made compilation films in 1939, *K Sobytiiam Ispanii* and *Ispaniia*, using his own material and old footage to provide the line required by the Soviet government. In 1967, returned to this subject, changing the political line according to the new times. In 1945,

chief cameraman-director of the Soviet film group covering the Nuremberg Trials. Made a film about China, 1941, using the same method of compilation of new and archive material. Film correspondent during WWII. His material was used in several films, such as *Leningrad v Bor'be* and *Berlin*. In 1947 made a propaganda film, *Sud Narodov*, which was awarded a Stalin Prize. After Stalin's death, became a documentary film-maker on industrial sites all over the USSR. Went with Genrikh Borovik to Cuba to make *Pylaiushchii Ostrov* and *Gost's Ostrova Svobody*. In 1960, headed the cameraman's department in the VGIK, Moscow. Wrote several books about his travels and filming activities all over the world.

Karnitskaia, Nina Andreevna
5.5.1906–   . Composer.
Born in Kiev. Author of a symphony, concertos (e.g. concerto for violin and piano), orchestral works for folk instruments, works for chamber ensembles, some on Ossetian themes, pieces for piano, romances, and music for the stage. Moved to Baku, and then in 1948 to Ordzhonikidze, Northern Ossetia.

Karotamm, Nikolai Georgievich
1901–1969. Revolutionary, politician.
Joined the Bolshevik Party, 1928. In 1928–29, on underground communist work in his native Estonia. Moved to the USSR, 1929–40. After the annexation of Estonia, 2nd secretary of the Cen. Cttee. of the Estonian Communist Party, 1940. Directed the communist underground movement in Estonia, from 1942. First Secretary of the Cen. Cttee. of the Estonian Communist Party, 1944–50. Responsible for the re-Stalinization of Estonia, including the deportation of many Estonians to Siberia. Worked at the Economics Institute of the Soviet Academy of Sciences, 1951.

Karpinskii, Aleksandr Petrovich
7.1.1847–15.7.1936. Geologist.
Born in Tur'inskie Rudniki (now Krasnotur'insk) near Ekaterinburg (now Sverdlovsk) in the Urals. Son of

a mining engineer. Graduated from the Petersburg Mining Institute, 1866. Mining engineer in the Urals, 1866–9. Professor of geology at the Petersburg Mining Institute, 1869–97. Organizer and head of the Geological Committee, 1885–1903. Academician, 1886. President of the Russian, later Soviet, Academy of Sciences, 1916–36. Specialist on the geological structure of the Ural mountains. Produced the first geological map of European Russia, 1892. Discovered rock salt, coal and oil deposits in Russia. Member of many foreign scientific societies and academies. Buried at the Kremlin wall.
Main works: *Collected works*, Moscow-Leningrad, 1939–49, 4 vols.

Karpov, Anatolii Evgen'evich
23.5.1951–   . Chess player, grandmaster.
Born in Zlatoust in the Urals. Graduated from Moscow University as an economist. World youth champion, 1969. World champion, 1975. Retained his title after 2 famous contests, 1978 and 1981, with the one-time Soviet grandmaster, V. Korchnoi, but lost it in 1985 to G. Kasparov. Member of the CPSU and fully promoted by the Soviet government.

Karpov, Viktor
1929–   . Politician.
Member of the CPSU from the early 1960s. Later attached to the Soviet Embassy in Washington. Took part in the Strategic Arms Limitations Talks (Salt One and Two), and was chief negotiator at Salt Two from 1978. Head of the Soviet delegation at the Strategic Arms Reduction Talks (Start) in Geneva, 1982–83. An accomplished negotiator, admired for his grasp of detail. Married with one daughter.

Karpovich, Mikhail Mikhailovich
1887–1959. Historian.
Member of the SR Party since his schooldays in Tiflis. Studied history at Petersburg University. After graduation, lecturer in history there, 1914. Under the Provisional Government, sent to the Russian Embassy in the USA, 1917. Remained there after the

October Revolution, 1917, becoming a political refugee, and later an American citizen. Lecturer in Russian history at Harvard, from 1927, professor until 1957. Head of the Slavonic department at Harvard, 1949–54. Editor of one of the best Russian emigré magazines after WWII, *Novyi Zhurnal*, New York, 1943–59.

Main works: *A History of Russia*, Yale, 3 vols (with G. Vernadskii).

Karpovich, Petr Vladimirovich
15.10.1874–13.4.1917.
Revolutionary.
Studied at Moscow and Iur'ev universities, 1895–99. Expelled for revolutionary activity. Went to study at Berlin University, 1899. Joined a terrorist group of the SR Party. Returned to Russia, and shot the education minister Bogolepov, 1901. Condemned to 20 years imprisonment in Schluesselburg, transferred to Siberia, 1906. Escaped 1907. Abroad became one of the collaborators of Azef in his SR terrorist activities. Made an unsuccessful attempt on the life of Nicholas II, 1908. After Azef was unmasked as a police spy, he left the SR Party. Drowned on his return to Russia after the February Revolution 1917, when his ship was sunk in the North Sea by a German mine.

Karsavin, Lev Platonovich
13.12.1882–12.7.1952. Philosopher, historian, theologian, linguist.
Son of a ballet master, brother of prima ballerina Tamara Karsavina. Studied history at Petersburg University, 1901–06. Studied abroad (France and Italy), 1910–12. Graduated from Petersburg University in 1913. Professor of medieval history at Petersburg University, 1913–22. Lecturer at Petrograd Theological Academy, 1920. Arrested and expelled (with a group of professors) in 1922. After a short stay in Berlin, moved to Lithuania. Professor of history at Kaunas University (learned Lithuanian and taught in that language), 1928. Professor at Wilno University, 1940. Dismissed when Wilno was occupied by Soviet troops in 1940. After the re-occupation of the Baltic countries by Soviet troops towards the end of WWII, arrested and sent to the Gulag camps, 1947. Died in a

labour-camp hospital near Abez in Komi ASSR. Attained a reputation as an outstanding scholar of the Middle Ages, as a religious philosopher and (before WWII) as an active member of the Eurasian movement. Main works: *Noctes Petropolitanae*, *Giordano Bruno*, *The Philosophy of History*, *Dialogues*, *The Church, Personality and the State*, *Catholicism*, *Istorijos Teorija* (in Lithuanian), *Saligia*.

Karsavin, Platon Konstantinovich
29.11.1854–1922. Ballet dancer.
Born in Petersburg. Father of Tamara Karsavina. Graduated from the Petersburg Theatrical School, 1875. Pupil of Marius Petipa. One of the leading dancers at the Mariinskii Theatre. From 1891–1896, taught at the Petersburg Theatrical School.

Karsavina, Tamara Platonovna
9.3.1885–25.4.1978. Ballerina.
Born in Petersburg. Daughter of Platon Karsavin. Graduated from the Petersburg Theatrical School, 1902. Was trained by P. Gerdt and Enrico Cecchetti. Member of the Ballet of the Mariinskii Theatre from 1902. Prima-ballerina of the Mariinskii Theatre, 1912–18. Partner of Mikhail Fokin and star of his ballet productions. Star of the Diaghilev Ballet, 1909–29. Left the Soviet Union, 1918. Became an internationally known dancer in Europe. Partner of Vaclav Nijinskii. Created the female leading roles in Fokin's *L'Oiseau de Feu* and *Petrushka* by Stravinskii, and *Sheherezade* with music by Rimskii-Korsakov. From 1930, with the Ballet Rambert. Taught from 1931. Acted as a consultant and choreographer mainly on Fokin's ballets. Vice-president of the Royal Academy of Dance in London, 1930–55. Died in London. One of the legendary stars of the Russian ballet of the first half of the 20th century. Wrote *Theatre Street*, London, 1930, and *Ballet Technique*, NY, 1968.

Karskii, Efimii Fedorovich
1861–1931. Philologist.
Educated at the Institute of History and Philology in Nezhin, Ukraine. Professor at Warsaw University from

1884. Member of the Academy of Sciences from 1916. Founder of Belorussian linguistics and philology. Wrote a monumental work, *Belorussy*, 3 vols, on which he worked nearly all his professional life, 1903–22.

Kartashev, Anton Vladimirovich
11.7.1875–10.9.1960. Procurator of the Holy Synod, historian.
Born in Kishtim (Urals). Son of a civil servant, former miner. Educated at Perm' seminary, 1894. Graduated from Petersburg Theological Academy in 1899. Taught the history of religion at the University College for Women in Petersburg, 1906–18. Chairman of the Religious-Philosophical Society in Petersburg, a meeting place for the intelligentsia and the clergy, 1909. Appointed Procurator of the Holy Synod by the Provisional Government and after the abolition of this office, Minister for Religious Affairs, 1917. Arrested in 1918 after the October Revolution. Emigrated 1919. Lived in Paris from 1920. Professor at the St. Sergius Theological Institute in Paris, 1925–60. Died in Paris. An outstanding representative of the new religious intelligentsia of the 20th century. Historian of the church and religious thought.
Works: *Reform, Reformation and the Fulfilment of the Church*, *The Restoration of Holy Russia*, 2 vols, *History of the Russian Church*.

Kartoziia, Givi Aleksandrovich
29.3.1929– . Athlete.
Born in a Georgian village. Honoured Master of Sports (wrestling), 1953. From 1955, with Tbilisi Burevestnik. Graduated from the Georgian Institute of Physical Culture, 1957, and from Tbilisi University, 1963, in economics. Works as an economist and sports instructor. Member of the CPSU, 1964. USSR champion, 1952–55. World champion, 1953, 1955, 1958. Olympic champion, 1956. Bronze medal, 1960.

Kasatkin, Nikolai Alekseevich
25.12.1859–17.12.1930. Artist.
Born in Moscow. Studied at the Moscow School of Painting, Sculpture and Architecture, 1873–83,

under V. Perov. Genre and portrait painter. Taught at the same school, 1894–1917. Member of the peredvizhniki from 1891. Exhibitions: MOLKH, 1890–94, 1908–11, All-Russian Exhibition, Nizhnii Novgorod, 1896, AKHRR, 3rd Exhibition, Moscow, 1922, the Association of Realist Artists, Moscow, 1927–28. Personal exhibitions: Jubilee, Moscow, 1929 and 1953 (posthumously). Died in Moscow.

Kasatonov, Vladimir Afanas'evich
1910– . Admiral.
Joined the Red Navy, 1927. Graduated from the Navy Academy, 1941. Took part in WWII as a staff officer. 1st Deputy Commander of the Soviet Navy, 1964–74.

Kashcheeva, Vera Sergeevna
1922–1975. Red Cross nurse.
Became famous as a Red Cross lieutenant at the Battle of Stalingrad, where she saved over 200 wounded from the battlefield. Awarded a medal of the International Red Cross. Hero of the Soviet Union, 1944.

Kashevarova, Olga Afanas'evna
4.6.1905– . Singer (soprano).
Born in Kazan'. Pupil of E. Devos-Soboleva and S. Merovich. Soloist with the Kirov Theatre of Opera and Ballet, Leningrad, from 1931.

Kashirin, Nikolai Dmitrievich
1888–1938. Military commander.
Joined the Red Army and the Communist Party, 1918. Active participant in the Civil War. One of the main organizers of Red partisans in the Urals. Graduated from courses at the Red Army Military Academy, 1924. Head of the army military training system, 1937. Victim of Stalin's purges.

Kashkarov, Iurii Danilovich (Skalon, D.)
1940– . Historian, editor.
Born in Ordzhonikidze (Vladikavkaz). Graduated from Moscow University. Worked as an editor of Soviet magazines. Emigrated, 1976. Settled in the USA, 1977. After the death of

R. Gul, became editor of the Russian literary magazine *Novyi Zhurnal*.

Kashkin, Nikolai Dmitrievich
9.12.1839–15.3.1920. Music critic.
Born in Voronezh. Studied music with A. Diubiuk. Taught at the Moscow Conservatory, 1866–1906. Professor, 1875. Music critic of *Moskovskie Vedomosti* and *Artist* from 1862. Also wrote for *Russkaia Muzykalnaia Gazeta* and *Muzykalnyi Sovremennik*. Promoted Mikhail Glinka's music and the composers of Moguchaia Kuchka. Died in Kazan'.

Kas'ianov, Aleksandr Aleksandrovich
29.8.1891–12.2.1982. Composer.
Born in a village in the Simbirsk Gouvt. Graduated from high school and the Music School of Nizhnii Novgorod. Entered Petersburg University. Studied at the Petersburg Conservatory, 1911–17. Pupil of S. Liapunov and M. Balakirev. Also influenced by A. Glazunov. Lecturer and pianist in Novgorod from 1918. Wrote songs for the People's Conservatory, and later for the Glinka Conservatory in Gorkii. Professor from 1957. Conductor with Nizhnii Novgorod Symphony Orchestra, 1919. Director of the Technical School for Music, 1921–23. Worked for radio, 1922. Musical director of theatre productions. Composer for radio till 1936. Followed the traditions of Mussorgskii, Borodin, and Rimskii-Korsakov, and was influenced by Skriabin in his instrumental music. Wrote operas and composed in various other genres. Died in Gorkii.

Kasparov, Gari Kimovich (Vainshtein)
13.4.1963– . Chess player, grandmaster, world champion.
Born in Baku. Known by his father's name, Vainshtein, until the age of 13. When 4 years old, became interested in mathematics. At the age of 18, chess grandmaster in the Soviet Union. Champion in the youth category in 1981 (Dortmund, Germany). Gold medals in Malta, 1980, and Lucerne, 1982. World champion, 1985. Chess player of brilliant style. Popular with the Western press and the public for his spontaneity, good looks and command of the English language.

Kassil', Lev Abramovich
1905–1970. Writer.
His two books, *Konduit*, 1930, and *Shvambraniia*, 1933, became permanent bestsellers. Wrote for teenagers. Published in millions of copies. Works: *Sobranie Sochinenii*, Moscow, 1965–66 (5 vols).

Kastal'skii, Aleksandr Dmitrievich
28.11.1856–17.12.1926. Composer, music folklorist.
Born in Moscow. Taught at the Moscow Synodal School from 1887, director from 1910. With the People's Choral Academy from 1918. Director until 1923. Professor at the Moscow Conservatory from 1923. Composed mainly church music. Author of the first revolutionary songs. Wrote a special song for Lenin's funeral. Author of an opera, various choral and orchestral works, piano pieces. Literary works: *Osobennosti Narodno-Russkoi Muzykal'noi Sistemy*, Moscow-Petrograd, 1923, 2nd edition, Moscow 1961, and *Osnovy Narodnogo Mnogogolosiia*, edited by V. Beliaev, Moscow, 1941. Died in Moscow.
Source: B. Asaf'ev, 'O Kastal'skom', *Sovetskaia Muzyka*, 1956, Nr.12.

Kastorskii, Vladimir Ivanovich
14.3.1871–2.7.1948. Singer (bass).
Born in Kostromoskaia Gouvt. Soloist with the Mariinskii Theatre from 1898. Appeared in concerts. Died in Leningrad.

Kataev, Valentin Petrovich
29.1.1897–1986. Author.
Born in Odessa. Son of a schoolmaster. Elder brother of the famous satirical writer, Evgenii Petrov. His grandfather was dean of a cathedral, while his maternal grandfather was a major-general. Educated at the Odessa 5th Gymnasium. Began writing poetry at the age of 9. Volunteered for the Russian Army during WWI, but joined the Bolsheviks during the Civil War. By 1930, had become an established writer. His *Vremia Vpered*, 1932, is a typical socialist-realist novel. Gained fame with a popular novel for youth, *Beleet Parus Odinokii*, 1936. The novel was a long-time bestseller, published in millions of copies and

also filmed. His play, *Kvadratura Kruga*, 1928, although famous at the time, was later forgotten. His early books (e.g. *Rastratchiki*, 1926) remain his best. His later works are conformist. In 1956, appointed Editor-in-Chief of the leading literary youth magazine, *Iunost'*. Published many young talented writers (A. Kuznetsov, Aksenov, Gladilin and others), but took part in the official condemnation of Boris Pasternak and later A. Solzhenitsyn. Died in Moscow.

Katanian, Vasilii Abgarovich
1902–1980. Author.
In 1927, with his wife, Galina Dmitrievna, moved from Tiflis to Moscow. Later wrote valuable memoirs on Mayakovsky.

Kats, Arnold
1931–   . Conductor.
Founder and leading conductor of the State Philharmonic Orchestra of Novosibirsk. Made a 9-city tour of the UK with his orchestra in Apr. 1988. Conducted Tchaikovskii's 'Pathétique' with great success at the Royal Festival Hall, London.

Kats, Sigizmund Abramovich
4.4.1908–   . Composer.
Born in Vienna. Author of songs, an opera, *Kapitanskaia Doch'*, several operettas, a cantata, a symphonic suite, orchestral and choral works, works for wind instruments, and music for films, theatre and radio.

Katsman, Evgenii Aleksandrovich
1890–1955? Artist.
Portrait painter. Studied at the Saratov Bogoliubov Art School, 1903–05, under V. Konovalov. Studied under Nikolai Roerich and A. Shchusev at the art school of the Society for the Encouragement of the Arts, then at I. Goldblatt's studio, 1907, and later at the School of Painting, Sculpture and Architecture, 1909–16, under L. Pasternak, A. Arkhipov, A. Vasnetsov and K. Korovin. Exhibitions from 1910: all in Moscow. Personal exhibitions: Kazan', 1929, Moscow, 1934–35, 1950. Died in Moscow.

Katsman, Klara Abramovna
31.5.1916–   . Composer.
Born in Surazh. Author of operas, operettas, cantatas, symphonies, choral works, songs, and music for children, including music for plays.

Katukov, Mikhail Efimovich
1900–1976. Marshal.
Took part in the Civil War. Graduated from courses at the Military Academy of the Red Army, 1935. During WWII, commander of tank forces. Commander of Soviet tank forces in East Germany, 1948.

Katul'skaia, Elena Kliment'evna
2.6.1888–195 ? Singer (soprano).
Born in Odessa. Pupil of N. Iretskaia. Professor at the Moscow Conservatory. Soloist with the Mariinskii Theatre, Petersburg, 1909–11. With the Bolshoi Theatre in Moscow, 1913–45. Stalin Prize, 1950. T. Milashkina was one of her pupils.

Katushev, Konstantin Fedorovich
1.10.1927–   . Party official, diplomat.
Born in the village of Boldino, Gorkii Oblast'. Graduated from Gorkii Polytechnical Institute in 1951. Worked as a designer. Joined the Communist Party in 1952. Party Secretary of Gorkii Automobile Plant, 1951–59. Various party posts in Gorkii Oblast'. In 1966, a member of the Cen. Cttee. of the CPSU. Various party posts in Moscow including Secretary of the Cen. Cttee. of the CPSU from 1968–77. Deputy Chairman of the USSR Council of Ministers, 1977–82. USSR Ambassador to Cuba from 1982.

Kaufman, Leonid Sergeevich
14.10.1907–   . Musicologist, composer.
Born in Kiev. Author of a ballet for children. Music for Ukrainian dances, choral works, and music for plays and films.

Kaufman, Mikhail Abramovich
4.9.1897–11.3.1980. Documentary film-maker, cameraman.
Brother of Dziga Vertov and the American cameraman, Boris Kaufman (1906–80). One of the first cameramen and documentary makers of the early Soviet propaganda cinema. From 1922, leading cameraman in Vertov's film group, producing such films as *Kinopravda* and *Shestaia Chast' Mira*, 1926, *Odinnadtsatyi*, 1928, and *Chelovek s Kinoapparatom*, 1929. His own films include *Moskva* and *Den' v Iasliakh*, 1927, *Vesnoi*, 1929, and *Nebyvalyi Pokhod*, 1931. From 1941 worked with the Popular Science Film Studio, Moscow.

Kauzov, Sergei
1941–   . Shipping agent.
Worked in several European countries as a representative of a Soviet shipping agency. In 1976 met Christina Onassis and soon became her third husband. Lived with her in Moscow and various countries in Europe. Their marriage did not last long, however.

Kavaleridze, Ivan Petrovich
14.4.1887–3.12.1978. Sculptor, film director, dramatist.
Studied at an art school in Kiev, then at the Petersburg Academy of Arts. Studied under the sculptor N. Aronson in his Paris studio, 1907–11. Returned to Russia. From 1911–15, sculptor and stage designer in the film industry. Worked closely with the directors, Ia. Protazanov and V. Gardin on *Kak Khoroshi Kak Svezhi Byli Rozy*, *Ukhod Velikogo Startsa* (about the death of L. Tolstoy), *Kliuchi Shchast'ia*, *Kreitserova Sonata*, and *Voina i Mir*. Started making his own films using his own scripts: *Liven'*, 1929, *Perekop*, 1930, *Shturmovye Nochi*, 1931, *Koliivshchina*, 1933, and *Prometei*, 1935. *Guliashchaia*, 1961, was his last film.

Kaverin, Veniamin Aleksandrovich (Zilber)
19.4.1902–   . Author.
Born in Pskov. Graduated from Leningrad University in 1924. In the 1920s, a member of the writer's group, the Serapion Brothers. During WWII, war correspondent of TASS and *Izvestia*. In later years, enjoyed great prestige as a survivor of the 20s. Immensely popular as a children's writer in the USSR.

Main works; *Konetz Khazy, Baron Brambeus, Dva Kapitana* (also screen version), *Sem' Par Nechistykh.*

Kaviatskas, Konradas Vlado (Kaveckas)
3.11.1905–   . Composer, conductor.
Born in the Mazheiskii region, Lithuania. Conductor with the choir of Kaunas University, 1933–40. One of the organizers of the music school in Vil'nius, 1940, director 1946–49, and head of the conducting department from 1945. Professor at the Vil'nius Conservatory. Chief conductor of the Lithuanian SSR State Choir, 1944–62. Author of an oratorio, a cantata, a tone poem for soloist, choir and orchestra. Also arranged folk songs.

Kazachenko, Grigorii Alekseevich
3.5.1858–18.5.1938. Composer, conductor.
Born in Petersburg. Choir conductor with the Mariinskii Theatre from 1889. Professor at the Leningrad Conservatory from 1924. Author of operas (e.g. *Kniaz Serebrianyi* based on a novel by A.K. Tolstoi), cantatas, works for choir, romances and duets. Died in Leningrad.

Kazakov, Iurii Ivanovich
24.12.1924–   . Baian player.
Born in Arkhangel'sk. Pupil of N. Chaikin. 1st prize at the International Festival of Youth and Students, Warsaw, 1955.

Kazakov, Konstantin Petrovich
1902–   . Marshal
Joined the Soviet Army, 1921. Graduated from the Frunze Military Academy, 1936. Commander of the Artillery against Germany and Japan in WWII. Commander of Soviet Rocket Forces, 1963–69.

Kazakov, Mikhail Il'ich
1901–1979. General.
Joined the Bolshevik Party, 1919. In the Red Army from 1920. Took part in the Civil War. Graduated from the Frunze Academy, 1931, and from the Academy of the General Staff, 1937. During WWII, held several high staff positions. Chief of Staff of the Warsaw Pact, 1965.

Kazakov, Rustem Abdullaevich
2.1.1947–   . Athlete.
Born in Tashkent. Honoured Master of Sports (wrestling), 1969. With the Sports Club of the Armed Forces in Tashkent, and from 1975 in Moscow. Graduated from the Uzbek Institute of Physical Culture, 1972. Member of the CPSU, 1975. USSR champion, 1971. World champion, 1969, 1971. Olympic champion, 1972.

Kazakov, Vasilii Ivanovich
1898–1968. Marshal.
Joined the Red Army, 1918. Graduated from a military artillery school, 1925. Member of the Bolshevik Party, 1932. Graduated from the Frunze Military Academy, 1934. During WWII, artillery commander on many fronts. Commander of Soviet Artillery Forces in the Soviet occupation zone in Germany, 1945–50. Commander of Anti-aircraft Forces, 1958.

Kazankina, Tatiana Vasil'evna
17.12.1951–   . Athlete.
Born in Petrovsk, Saratov Oblast'. Honoured Master of Sports (track and field athletics), 1976. With Leningrad Burevestnik. Graduated in economics from Leningrad University, 1975. USSR champion, 1975–77. Olympic champion, 1976 (800m and 1,500m). World record holder for 1500 and 3000 metres. Suspended for refusing a drug test in Paris.
See: R. Orlov, *Dva Tatianinykh Dnia*, from the collection *Tvoi Chempiony*, Moscow, 1977.

Kazanskii, Boris Aleksandrovich
13.4.1891–1973? Chemist.
Born in Odessa. Graduated from Moscow University, 1918. Professor at Moscow University, 1935. Academician, 1946. Director of the Zelinskii Institute of Organic Chemistry, 1954. Specialized in conversion of hydrocarbons.

Kazanskii, Evgenii Sergeevich
1896–1937. Military commander.
Joined the Bolshevik Party, 1912, and the Red Army 1918. During the Civil War, organized Bolshevik groups in the rear of the White forces in Baku and near the Black Sea. Participated in the suppression of the Kronstadt sailors' revolt, 1921. Graduated from military academy courses, 1925. Disappeared during Stalin's purges of the military, probably shot.

Kazantsev, Aleksandr Stepanovich
1908–1963. Journalist.
Born in Cheliabinsk. During the Civil War, evacuated with a cadet corps to Vladivostok, and then Shanghai. Later moved to Yugoslavia, 1924. Studied law at Belgrade University. Became a member of the group of political activists, NTS, which united young Russians abroad with the aim of struggling against communist dictatorship. Editor in clandestine NTS printing shops in Berlin, later Rumania, financed by the Japanese. During WWII, joined the Vlasov movement in Germany, becoming a close associate of General Vlasov himself. Edited the newspaper of the movement, *Volia Naroda*, but left in protest against interference by the German authorities. One of the signatories of the Prague Manifesto. After WWII, was in DP camps in West Germany. In the 1950s worked at Radio Liberty, Munich. Memoirs: *Tret'ia Sila*, 1974, Germany.

Kazantseva, Nadezhda Apollinar'evna
28.3.1911–   . Singer (soprano).
Born in Irkutsk. Pupil of G. Gorodetskaia and L. Shor-Plotnikova. Appeared in many concerts in Moscow from 1934. Stalin liked her voice and she performed many times at the Kremlin. Stalin Prize, 1949.

Kazarnovskii, Isaak Abramovich
29.9.1890–1975? Chemist.
Born in Nikolaev. Graduated from Zurich University, 1914. Worked at the Karpov Physico-Chemical Institute in Moscow from 1922. Academician, 1939. Specialist in metal chlorides and peroxides.

171

Kazei, Marat Ivanovich
1929–1944. Partisan.
As a teenager, took part in partisan operations against the German occupation forces in Belorussia near Minsk. Active as a scout, secretly visiting the German garrisons. He was spotted by the Germans, and in order to escape capture, killed himself with his own grenade.

Kazem-Bek, A.L.
1890?–after 1970. Politician.
Emigrated after the Civil War. In the 1920s and 1930s, created the right-wing Mladorossy Party. Became its leader (glava), 1923, receiving Fascist-like adulation at public meetings. Very popular for a short time, but later lost his influence. Returned to the Soviet Union. Worked in the administration of the Moscow patriarchy, and contributed to its magazine, *Zhurnal Moskovskoi Patriarkhii*.

Kazhlaev, Murad Magomedovich
15.1.1931– . Composer.
Born in Baku. Teacher at the music school in Makhachkala. Chairman of the Daghestan section of the Union of Composers. Author of orchestral works, pieces for string orchestra and harp, piano pieces, a string quartet, pieces for the variety stage, and music for films.

Kaz'min, Petr Mikhailovich
17.10.1892–30.6.1964. Folklorist.
Born in Voronezhskaia Gouvt. Artistic director of the M.E. Piatnitskii State Russian Folk Choir. Author of *Stranitsy iz Zhizni M.E. Piatnitskogo*, Moscow, 1961. Died in Moscow.

Kedrov, Mikhail Sergeevich
1878–1941. Revolutionary, state security official.
Joined the SD Party, 1901. Took part in the 1905 Revolution. On active service during WWI. After the October Revolution 1917, chairman of the local Soviet at Omsk. Deputy Minister of Defence, 1917. During the Civil War, commander of the Red forces in the North. Chairman of the Special Department of the Cheka, Jan. 1919, and other positions in the state security system. Known for his cruelty. In the 1920s, became an economics administrator. Liquidated by Beria after prolonged torture (his written appeals for mercy were quoted by Khrushchev in his secret speech).

Keldysh, Iurii Vsevolodovich
29.8.1907– . Musicologist.
Born in Petersburg. Son of V. Keldysh. Graduated from the Moscow Conservatory, 1930. Member of staff, then professor at the conservatory from 1948. Head of the Music Section at the Institute for the History of the Arts, Moscow, 1961. Wrote the 3-volume *History of Russian Music*. Member of the CPSU, 1947. Author of many articles on music and musicians.

Keldysh, Leonid Veniaminovich
7.4.1931– . Physicist.
Born in Moscow. Graduated from Moscow University, 1954. Worked at the Moscow Physics Institute from 1954. Professor, 1969. Corresponding member of the Academy of Sciences from 1968.

Keldysh, Mstislav Vsevolodovich
10.2.1911– . Scientist, academician.
Younger brother of the musicologist, Iurii Keldysh, and son of V. Keldysh. Born in Riga. Mathematician. Graduated from Moscow University, 1931. Professor, 1937. Worked at the Moscow TSAGI (Central Aerodynamics Institute). Academician, 1943. Director of the Institute of Applied Mathematics from 1953. Member of the Presidium of the Academy of Sciences from 1953. Vice-president, 1960–61, and President of the Academy of Sciences, 1961–75. Involved in space research. Member of various foreign academies. Member of the Cen. Cttee. of the CPSU, 1961. Works in the field of hydro-dynamics.

Keldysh, Vsevolod Mikhailovich
25.6.1878–19.11.1965. Scientist, major-general.
Born in Vladikavkaz, now Ordzhonikidze. Graduated from the Riga Polytechnical Institute, 1902. Professor, 1918. At several institutes and the Kuibyshev Academy of Military Engineering, 1932. Major-general in the military technical service. Was behind many important state projects such as the Moscow Canal, the Moscow metro, the Dnepropetrovsk Aluminium Plant and similar. Died in Moscow.

Kell', Nikolai Georgievich
20.1.1883–22.12.1965. Geodesist, cartographer.
Graduated from the Petrograd Mining Institute, 1915. Topographer with the Kamchatka expedition of the Russian Geographical Society, 1908–11. Professor of geodesy at the Petrograd Mining Institute, 1921. Chairman of the Committee on Aerial Survey. Works on geodesy, aerial photogrammetric methods and cartography. Died in Leningrad.

Kemarskaia, Nadezhda Fedorovna
28.9.1899– . Singer (soprano).
Born in Starobel'sk. Pupil of A. Sekar-Rozhanskii, A. Labinskii and V. Zarudnaia. Entered the Music School of the Moscow Art Theatre, 1922. Soloist with the Nemirovich-Danchenko Musical Drama Theatre from 1926. Stage director from 1950. Stalin Prize, 1952.

Keneman, Fedor Fedorovich
20.4.1873–29.3.1937. Pianist, conductor, composer.
Born in Moscow. Pupil of N. Zverev and V. Safonov. Professor at the Moscow Conservatory in the Department of Harmony and Instrumentation from 1899, and in the Piano Department from 1912. Appeared as a soloist. Accompanist of Fedor Chaliapin. Arranged songs, including *Ei ukhnem!*, for Chaliapin. Author of a cantata, a prelude, pieces for piano, romances, choral works, and marches for orchestra and wind instruments. Died in Moscow.

Keosaian, Edmond Gareginovich
9.10.1936– . Film director.
Graduated from the VGIK, 1965. Pupil of E. Dzigan. In 1967 his film *Neulovimye Mstiteli* was a huge box-office success with teenagers. A continuation of this film, *Novye Prikliucheniia Neulovimykh*, appeared in 1968 with the same success. In

1971, a third part, *Korona Rossiiskoi Imperii ili Snova Neulovimye*, was released. From 1972–76, with the Armenfilm Studio, Erevan.

Kepinov, Grigorii Ivanovich
1886–1963. Sculptor.
Graduated from Petersburg University in physics and mathematics, 1909. Went to Paris to study at the R. Julien Academy, 1910–13. Exhibions: The Union of Armenian Artists, Tiflis, 1917; The Zhar-Tsvet Society, 1925; The Association of Artists of Revolutionary Russia, Moscow,1926; ORS, 1927, 1931; Moscow, 1928–60. Personal exhibition with V. Mukhina, I. Slonim, V. Favorskii and I. Frikh-Khara, Moscow, 1935.

Kerenskii, Aleksandr Fedorovich
4.5.1881–1.6.1970. Politician, lawyer.
Born in Simbirsk (now Ulianovsk). Son of a headmaster (of a secondary school at which Lenin was a pupil). Moved with his parents to Tashkent, 1889. Studied law at Petersburg University, practised in Saratov, and gained fame as a defence lawyer in political cases (Armenian nationalists, Dashnaks, protests against the Beiliss trial in Kiev, 1912 etc). Member for Saratov at the 4th Duma, 1912, leader of Trudovik (Labour) group. Joined the SRs (officially) in Mar. 1917. Secret member of the Masonic lodge Malaia Medveditsa. After the February Revolution 1917, became deputy head of the Provisional Cttee. of the Duma (precursor of the Provisional Government), and deputy chairman of the Petrograd Soviet, thus establishing a personal link between both rival centres of power. The only socialist in the Provisional Government. Minister of Justice, Mar.–May 1917, Minister of Defence, May–Sept. 1917. Prime Minister of the Provisional Government from 21 July 1917, and commander-in-chief (after the Kornilov affair), Aug. 1917. Insisted that Russia remain in WWI, keeping faith with her allies. Organized an offensive, June 1917 (failed a month later). Crushed the Bolshevik revolt of July 1917, forcing Lenin to go underground. Quarrelled with commander-in-chief Kornilov,

Aug. 1917. Lost the army's support after the defeat of Kornilov's march on Petrograd. Increasingly isolated from left- and right-wing circles, left the Winter Palace in a car flying the US flag to get reinforcements, Oct. 1917. Mission to get help from the army in Pskov and Ataman Krasnov's Cossacks ended in failure. Went underground in Russia until the end of 1917, then in Finland. Returned secretly to Petrograd in Jan. 1918. Moved to Moscow. Emigrated with the help of Bruce Lockhart in May 1918 (left by train, disguised as a member of the Serbian mission to Arkhangelsk, and from there by ship to Great Britain). Edited the SR newspaper *Dni* (Days) in Berlin and later in Paris, 1922–32. Moved to the USA in 1940. Taught at American universities, wrote memoirs. Immensely popular for a short time in 1917, judged very harshly from opposite directions — by the Bolsheviks as a 'lackey of the bourgeoisie', and by right-wing circles as the man who made the Bolshevik victory possible. Died in New York.

Kerer, Rudolf Richardovich
10.7.1923– . Pianist.
Born in Tiflis. Pupil of Z. Tamarkina. 1st prize in the All-Union Competition of Musicians – Performers, Moscow, 1961. Teacher at the Moscow Conservatory.

Kereselidze, Archil Pavlovich
24.12.1912– . Composer.
Born in Daghestan. Georgian by nationality. Author of operas, musical comedies, a symphony, 2 concertos for piano and orchestra, songs for the variety stage, and music for films and stage. People's Artist of the Georgian SSR, 1961.

Kerzhentsev, Platon Mikhailovich (Lebedev)
1881–1940. Party official.
Born in Moscow. Son of a doctor. Studied at Moscow University's Historico-Philological Department. Participant in the 1905 Revolution. Party worker in Moscow, Petersburg, Novgorod and Kiev. Journalist with the newspaper *Zvezda* and the maga-

zine *Prosveshchenie*. From 1912, worked for *Pravda*. Emigrated the same year. Lived in London, New York and Paris. Returned to Russia after October 1917. Deputy editor of *Izvestia*, 1918. Headed ROSTA, 1919–21. Ambassador to Sweden, 1921–23. Member of staff at *Pravda*, 1923–24. Ambassador to Italy, 1925–26. Deputy head of the Propaganda Department of the Cen. Cttee. of the CPSU, 1928–30. Deputy chairman of the Presidium of the Communist Academy, Moscow, 1930. Director of its Institute of Literature, Art and Language. Chairman of the Soviet of People's Commissars, 1931–33. Chairman of the Cttee. of Arts, 1936–38. The boss of Soviet cinema, and one of the people responsible for the persecution of major Soviet filmmakers such as Eisenstein and Pudovkin. Died in Moscow.

Keskula, Aleksandr Eduard
1882–1963. Revolutionary.
Born in Tartu, Estonia. Participated in the 1905 Revolution. Arrested, amnestied, emigrated to Switzerland. During WWI, became the linkman between the German Ambassador Baron Romberg and various Russian revolutionary leaders, including Lenin. Tried to enlist German help for Estonian independence. Ensured the link between Switzerland, Scandinavia and Russia for Russian revolutionary emigrés during WWI.

Kevorkov, Boris Sarkisovich
1932– . Party official.
Armenian. Member of the CPSU, 1954. Graduated from Azerbaidzhan University. Komsomol and party posts after graduating. 1st Secretary of the Azerbaidzhan CP in the Nagorno-Karabakh Autonomous Oblast' from 1973. Dismissed, Feb. 1988, after mass demonstrations by Armenians demanding reunification with the Oblast', which is populated by Armenians, and which had been incorporated into Azerbaidzhan in the 1920s. Expelled from the Communist Party.

Khabalov, Sergei Semenovich
1858–1924. Lt.-general.
Graduated from the Academy of the General Staff, 1886. Ataman of the

Ural Cossacks, 1914. Commander of the Petrograd military district, Feb. 1917. Provincial general, rather over-awed by the events and personalities in the Imperial capital, especially by the Duma leaders, during the February Revolution 1917. In the absence of the monarch (who was at his HQ in Mogilev), let the power slide out of his hands. Emigrated, 1919.

Khachaturian, Aram Il'ich
6.6.1903–1.5.1978. Composer, conductor.
Born in Kodzhory, near Tbilisi. Studied at the Gnesin Technical School of Music, 1922–29. Pupil of M. Gnesin. At the Moscow Conservatory, 1929–34. Pupil of N. Miaskovskii and S. Vasilenko. Graduated with distinction. Accepted for postgraduate study under N. Miaskovskii. Graduated, 1936. Began his career as a conductor in 1950. Conducted his own works in the USSR and abroad. Professor of composition at the Moscow Conservatory and at the Gnesin Pedagogical Institute of Music from 1952. Honorary member of the Italian Musical Academy, Santa Cecilia, 1960. Wrote music for ballets and plays, including Shakespeare productions. Died in Moscow.

Khadeev, Aleksandr Aleksandrovich
1894–1957. Lt.-general.
On active service during WWI as a captain. Joined the Red Army, 1918. Took part in the Civil War. Graduated from the Vystrel Courses, 1929. Joined the Bolshevik Party, 1938. Took part in the Soviet-Finnish war and WWII as an army commander. Retired, 1945.

Khaikin, Boris Emmanuilovich
26.10.1904– . Conductor.
Born in Minsk. Pupil of N. Mal'ko, and K. Saradzhev. Artistic director and chief conductor of Leningrad Malyi Opera and Ballet Theatre, 1936–41. Artistic director and chief conductor of the Kirov Opera and Ballet Theatre, 1944–53. Conductor at the Bolshoi Theatre, from 1954 onwards. Highly decorated.

Khakhanian, Grigorii Davidovich
1896–1939. Military commander.
Joined the Bolshevik Party, 1917,

and the Red Army, 1918. Graduated from courses at the Military Academy of the Red Army, 1924. Took part in the Civil War. Head of the political administration of the Ukrainian military district, 1929, and of the political administration of the Far Eastern Army, 1936. Liquidated by Stalin.

Khalepskii, Innokentii Andreevich
1893–1938. Military commander.
Joined the Red Army and the Bolshevik Party, 1918. Communications commissar of all fronts, 1918. Minister of Post and Communications of the Ukraine, Mar. 1919. Head of the Red Army's communications network, 1920, its Military Technical Administration 1924–29, its Motorization and Mechanization Administration, 1929, and its Tank Administration, 1934. Member of the Revolutionary Military Council of the USSR, 1932–34. Minister of Communications of the USSR, 1937–38. Liquidated by Stalin.

Khalip, Iakov N.
1908–1980. Photo-journalist.
Born into a theatrical family in Petersburg. From 1921 lived in Moscow. Studied at the VGIK. While a student, worked in the film showroom of the State Academy of the Arts. At this stage began taking photographs. Received training from such masters as Rodchenko, Shaikhet, Fridliand and Alpert. Graduated from the VGIK as a cameraman in 1929. Worked as an assistant cameraman and photographer in film studios until 1931. At the same time did freelance work for *Pravda* and *Izvestia*, and the magazines *Krasnaia Niva* and *USSR in Construction*. Also worked for Soiuzfoto. After 1931, devoted himself entirely to photography. In 1938, took part in an expedition to the North Pole as a photographer, to take pictures of North Pole I, a research station led by Ivan Papanin, which was drifting on an ice-flow. Produced an impressive series of pictures, which were praised in the press, and for which he was awarded a medal. Worked for *USSR in Construction*, 1938–41. Travelled throughout the Soviet Union, reporting on the life of the people. During

WWII, war correspondent for *Krasnaia Zvezda*, 1944–46, then worked for the Soviet Information Office. His photographs of this period were a significant contribution to Soviet press photography. After WWII, worked for the magazines *Ogonek* and *Smena*, and from 1954 for *Sovetskii Soiuz*. Exhibited in Moscow in 1967 and 1968, in Czechoslovakia in 1963, 1965 and 1967, in Helsinki in 1975 and in London in 1960.
Source: *Soviet Photography, 1917–40*, London, 1984.

Khamzin, Adol' Sagmanovich
7.2.1934– . Ballet dancer, choreographer.
Born in Ufa. Graduated from the Leningrad Choreographic School, 1953. Until 1975, with the Leningrad Malyi Theatre. Soloist. From 1975, artistic director of the Leningrad Ballet on Ice.

Khanamirian, Vanush Gerasimovich
5.9.1927– . Ballet dancer, choreographer.
Born in Erevan. Graduated from the Erevan Choreographic School, 1944. Until 1971, dancer and soloist at the Spendiarov Theatre. From 1968, artistic director and chief choreographer with the Armenian State Ensemble of Dance.

Khanzhonkov, Aleksandr Alekseevich
8.8.1877–26.9.1945. Film producer.
First major producer of Russian films. Founded a film studio in 1907, later named the Aktsionernoe Obshchestvo Khanzhonkov. Produced feature, animation and documentary films. Employed the best directors, actors and artists. With director V.M. Goncharov, made the first full-length feature film, *Oborona Sevastopolia*. After the October Revolution 1917, when all his staff emigrated, he remained, hoping to continue to make films. Worked as a film consultant for Goskino, and later as executive producer at the Proletkino. See: *Pervye Gody Russkoi Kinematografii*, Moscow-Leningrad, 1937.

Kharchenko, Viktor Kondrat'evich
1911–1975. Marshal.
Joined the Red Army 1932. Gradua-

ted from the Military Electrotechnical Academy, 1938. During WWII, engineering officer on several fronts. Graduated from the Academy of the General Staff, 1948. Head of research and development at the Institute of Engineering Forces, 1951, Head of the Technical Cttee. of Engineering Forces, 1953–61. Deputy Commander, 1961, and Commander, 1965 of the Engineering Forces of the Soviet Army. Died in an accident.

Kharchev, Konstantin Mikhailovich
1935–   . Diplomat, politician.
Lost his parents in his childhood and grew up in an orphanage in Gorkii. Originally trained as an engineer. Doctor of Economical Sciences. Senior party position in Vladivostok. In 1978, sent on a special course for diplomats. From Mar. 1981, USSR Ambassador to Guyana. Connections with the KGB from the early 1970s. In Jan. 1985, appointed chairman of the Council for Religious Affairs (a body closely connected with the KGB, which supervises religious life in the USSR). Recently put in charge of the new liberal policy towards the church, and has mentioned 'mistakes made in the past'.

Kharin, Pavel Petrovich
12.11.1927–   . Athlete.
Born in Leningrad. Honoured Master of Sports (rowing), 1957. With Leningrad Pishchevik. Coach. USSR champion, 1956, 1958–60. Olympic silver medallist, 1956. European champion, 1957.

Khariton, schema-igumen
1868?–1947. Russian Orthodox clergyman.
Monk at the Valaam Monastery. Evacuated to Finland during the Soviet-Finnish war, 1940. One of the founders of New Valaam (Valamo) in Eastern Finland. Compiled an anthology of the Jesus prayer.

Khariton, Boris Osipovich
1875–after 1942. Journalist.
One of the organizers of the Dom Literatorov in Petrograd, 1918–21, where many writers tried to survive the hunger and poverty of the

revolutionary years. Emigrated in the early 1920s. Settled in Latvia. Editor of the evening paper *Segodnia Vecherom* in Riga. After the occupation of Riga by Soviet troops, 1940, arrested by the NKVD and deported to the Gulag.

Khariton, Iulii Borisovich
27.2.1904–   . Nuclear scientist.
Graduated from the Leningrad Polytechnic Institute, 1925. Studied in England under E. Rutherford, 1927–28. Worked with the academician Ia. Zeldovich on Soviet nuclear weapons after WWII. Academician, 1953.

Kharitonov, Fedor Mikhailovich
1899–1943. Lt.-general.
Joined the Bolshevik Party, 1918, and the Red Army, 1919. Took part in the Civil War. Graduated from the Vystrel Courses, 1931. Took part in WWII as an army commander.

Kharitonov, Nikolai Vasil'evich
1880–1921? Artist.
Genre, portrait and landscape painter. Studied under L. Dmitriev-Kavkazskii at the school of the Society for the Encouragement of the Arts, then at the Academy of Arts, Petersburg, 1901–09, under Il'ia Repin and P. Chistiakov. Exhibited from 1907. Exhibitions: Spring exhibitions at the Academy of Arts, Petersburg, 1907, 1911–17, Petersburg Society of Artists, 1912, the Association of Artists, 1914–15, A. Kuindzhi Society, 1917, First State Free Exhibition of Arts, Petrograd, 1919. The last picture by this artist is recorded by the Tutaev Museum as 1921.

Kharitonov, Petr Timofeevich
1916–   . Colonel.
Joined the Red Army, 1938. Fighter pilot during WWII. Known for his daring involvement in dog fights. One of the first Heroes of the Soviet Union during WWII. Seriously wounded, but later returned to active service. Graduated from the Air Force Academy, 1953.

Kharlamov, Aleksei Alekseevich
1842–1922? Artist.
Genre and portrait painter. Studied

at the Petersburg Academy of Arts, 1852–68 under A. Markov. Also studied at the Paris Academy of Arts from 1869. Trained in Paris by L. Bonne. Exhibitions from 1868: the Academy of Arts, Petersburg, 1868–74, TPKHV, 1879–1917, MOLKH 1881–82, All-Russian Exhibition, Moscow, 1882, the Society of Russian Water-Colour Artists, Petersburg, 1885, the Society of Artists of Historical Painting, Moscow, 1896, St. Petersburg Society of Artists, 1910. His last picture is recorded by the Tutaev Museum as 1921.

Kharlamov, Valerii Borisovich
14.1.1948–27.8.1981. Athlete.
Born in Moscow. Honoured Master of Sports (hockey), 1969. With the Central Sports Club of the Army. Studied at the Moscow Oblast' Pedagogical Institute. USSR champion, 1968–79. European champion, 1969–79. World champion, 1969–71, 1973–75, and 1978–79. Olympic champion, 1972, 1976. Died in a drinking and driving accident.

Kharms, Daniil Ivanovich (Iuvashev)
1905–1942. Author, poet, playwright.
Born in Petersburg. Prominent member of the OBERIU literary group in the 1920s. Wrote only works for children in the 1930s. Arrested in Aug. 1941. Died of hunger in a Leningrad prison. Interest in his modernist works revived in the 1960s. Now officially recognized in the USSR. His *Sobranie Sochinenii* was published in Germany, 1978–80. A full-length feature film on his fate by the Yugoslav director Pesic was shown at the Cannes Film Festival, 1988.

Kharzhevskii, Vladimir Grigor'evich
1899?–4.6.1981. Major-general.
On active service during WWI. Took part in the Civil War as commander of the Drozdovskii regiment, an elite regiment of the Whites. After the defeat of the Whites, evacuated to Gallipoli. Chairman of White Veterans of the Civil War abroad (ROVS). Moved to the USA. Died in Lakewood.

Khartov, Aleksandr
1945–   . Dissident.
One of the leaders of the Democratic

175

Union Party which seeks to be an opposition party in the Soviet Union as a challenge to Communist Party rule. Its first attempt to seek legality failed—47 members of the party were detained on 8 May 1988 in Moscow. 25 were released within hours, having proved their Moscow residence, but 22 were deported from Moscow.

Khatisov, Aleksandr Ivanovich
1874–1945. Politician.
Mayor of Tiflis. Armenian, married to a Russian. Personal friend of Grand Duke Nikolai Nikolaevich (commander-in-chief at the Caucasian front). Emigrated after the Civil War. Settled in Paris. Chairman of the Armenian Refugee Cttee. at the League of Nations.

Khazin, Evgenii Iakovlevich
1893–1974. Writer, literary historian.
Brother of Nadezhda Mandelshtam. Published some work in the Soviet press.
See: *Vse Pozvoleno: Razmyshlenia O Tvorchestve Dostoevskogo*, Paris, 1972.

Kheifits, Iosif Efimovich
17.12.1905– . Film director.
Celebrated director of *The Lady with a Little Dog* (1960, based on the Chekhov story), and *Asia* (1977, based on a Turgenev story). Graduated from the Leningrad Technical School of Film Art, 1927, then from the Institute of Art History, 1928. Worked together with Aleksandr Zarkhi until the early 1950s, making 15 films, among them *The Baltic Deputy* and *Member of the Government*, classic examples of Stalinist cinema. First solo film in 1951, *Soviet Mordovia*. *The Rumiantsev Case* (1955) was one of the fresh new films which appeared after Stalin's death. Collaborated on the screenplay of *My Dear Man* (1958). Enormous national and international success with *The Lady with a Little Dog*, partly due to the forceful performances from leading actors Iia Savina and Aleksei Batalov. A veteran director. Made about 100 films, including *Shurochka*, 1982, starring Liudmila Gurchenko.

Khenkin, Kirill Viktorovich
1916– . Journalist.
Born in Petrograd. Left the USSR in 1923 with his parents. Graduated from the Sorbonne. Became attracted to communism and went to Spain in 1937 as a member of the international brigades. Involved with NKVD officers. 1939–40, lived in America. Returned to the USSR in 1941. Served in the NKVD Special Motor Rifle Brigade. From the end of the war until 1965, journalist with the French Section of Moscow Radio, and later with the Prague-based *Problemy Mira i Sotsializma*. Became completely disillusioned with communism. Re-emigrated, 1973. Lives in Munich. Wrote valuable memoirs *Okhotnik Vverkh Nogami* (Germany, 1980), in which he brilliantly describes his friendship with the Soviet Union's top spy Colonel Rudolph Abel.

Khessin, Aleksandr Borisovich
19.10.1869–3.4.1955. Conductor.
Born in Petersburg. Pupil of A. Nikish, and F. Motl'. From 1910, artistic director and chief conductor of Count A.D. Sheremet'ev's Music-Historical Society in Petersburg. Taught in Moscow from 1924. Chief conductor of the Opera Studio of the Moscow Conservatory. From 1943 musical director and consultant of the Ensemble of Soviet Opera, attached to the VTO (All-Union Theatre Society). Wrote memoirs: *Iz Moikh Vospominanii*, Moscow, 1959.

Khetagurov, Georgii Ivanovich
1903–1975. General.
Joined the Red Army, 1920. Took part in the Civil War. Joined the Bolshevik Party, 1924. Took part in WWII. Graduated from the Academy of the General Staff, 1949. Commander of the Baltic military district, 1963–71.

Khimich, Andrei Ivanovich
14.12.1937– . Athlete.
Born in Chernigovskaia Oblast'. Honoured Master of Sports (rowing), 1964. With Cherkassy Avangard. Graduated from the Cherkasskii Pedagogical Institute, 1959. Schoolmaster. Member of the CPSU, 1960. USSR champion, 1961–66.

European champion, 1961, 1965. Olympic champion, 1964.

Khisamutdinov, Shamil' Shamshatdinovich
20.9.1950– . Athlete.
Born in Tul'skaia Oblast'. Honoured Master of Sports (wrestling), 1972. With the Moscow Oblast' Spartak. Member of the CPSU, 1976. Honorary Coach of the USSR, 1978. Graduated from the Omsk Institute of Physical Culture. USSR champion, 1971–74. Olympic champion, 1972. European champion, 1973–74. World champion, 1973, 1975.

Khitrin, Lev Nikolaevich
20.2.1907– . Scientist.
Graduated from Moscow University, 1930. Professor at Moscow University, 1953. Specialist in carbon-burning processes and furnace design.

Khitruk, Fedor Savel'evich
1.5.1917– . Film director.
From 1937–41, and again from 1947, worked at the Soyuzmultfilm Studio. Made over 200 animated films. From 1961, cartoonist. Many of his films have received prizes at the Cannes and Venice film festivals. Teaches at Higher Directors' Courses in the animation department. From 1981, secretary of the Board of the Union of Film-makers.

Khitrun, Leonid Ivanovich
1930– . Party official.
Began as a tractor-driver in Lida, Grodno Oblast', 1946–48. Graduated from the Belorussian Agricultural Academy, 1953. Joined the Communist Party in 1955. Chief engineer of a machine and tractor station, 1953–60. Chairman of Grodno Oblast' Selkhoztekhnika, 1961–62. Chairman of the Belorussian Association for Agricultural Technology, Belselkhoztekhnika, 1961–71. Deputy chairman of the Council of Ministers of the Belorussian SSR, 1971–72 and 1976–79. 1st Deputy USSR Minister of Agriculture, 1972–76. Member of the Cen. Cttee. of the Belorussian CP, 1966–72. Chairman of the USSR State Cttee. for the Supply of Production Equipment for

Agriculture, 1980. Member of the Cen. Auditing Cttee. of the CPSU, 1981. USSR Minister for Livestock Farming and Fodder Machinery from 1982 to July 1987, when he was removed from his post.

Khlebnikov, Nikolai Mikhailovich
1895–1981. Col.-general.
On active service during WWI as a sub-lieutenant. Joined the Red Army, 1918, and the Bolshevik Party, 1919. Artillery officer during the Civil War. Commander of artillery detachments during WWII. Graduated from the Academy of the General Staff, 1952, later professor at the same academy. Senior military adviser in communist China, 1956–60.

Khlebnikov, Velimir (Viktor Vladimirovich)
9.11.1885–28.6.1922. Poet.
Born in Tundutovo (or Malye Derbety) near Astrakhan'. Son of a scientist. Studied at Kazan' University, 1903, and Petersburg University, 1908–11. First poems published, 1908. Soon became one of the leading spirits of futurism in Russia (characteristically coined for the futurists the Russian term 'budetliane'). His brilliant verbal experiments were highly regarded by most of his contemporaries, from Gumilev to Mayakovsky. Took part in many futurist happenings in different parts of Russia. Differed from his colleagues in the complete absence in him of any element of publicity-snatching or self-promotion, exhibiting instead a sort of serious naiveté even in his utopian projects of global and cosmic reforms (Truba marsian, Lebedia budushchego), which survived even his attempts to call himself President of the Globe ('president zemnogo shara'). Apart from grammatical experimenting, he introduced primitivist, archaic and exotic elements into his poetry (Lesnaia Deva, Shaman i Venera, Truba Gul-Mully, 1921, Zangezi, 1922). Identified himself with revolution, but not in any political sense. In practical terms, became a homeless vagrant, showing complete disregard not only to any career possibilities, but to any settled, and thus restricted, form of life. Much too esoteric to become truly and widely popular, he is regarded by

some as by far the greatest futurist poet in Russia. According to available information, he died of hunger and neglect in the village of Santalovo, near Novgorod. His 5-volume collected works were published posthumously in Leningrad, 1928–33. Lately has become the subject of great interest both in Russia and abroad.

Khliustin, Ivan Nikolaevich
18.8.1862–21.11.1941. Ballet dancer, choreographer.
Born in Moscow. Graduated from the Moscow Theatre School, 1882. Pupil of G. Legat. From 1878, with the Bolshoi Theatre. From 1886, first soloist at the Bolshoi. From 1893, choreographer. Taught at the Moscow Theatre School, 1898–1902. Moved to Paris, 1903, where he opened a ballet school. Choreographer and teacher at the Paris Opera, 1911–14. Promoted Russian composers and Russian ballet productions. From 1914–31, with the Anna Pavlova company as a choreographer and teacher. Retired after Pavlova's death. Died in Nice.

Khlystov, Nikolai Pavlovich
10.11.1932– . Athlete.
Born in Riazanskaia Oblast'. Honoured Master of Sports (hockey), 1952. With Moscow Kryl'ia Sovetov. Factory worker. World champion, 1954, and 1956. Olympic champion, 1956. USSR champion, 1957. European champion, 1954–56, and 1958.

Khodasevich, Valentina Mikhailovna
25.3.1894–5.5.1970. Stage designer.
Born in Moscow. Studied at the Moscow Rerberg private art school, then in Munich and later in Paris. In the 1920s worked in the state workshops responsible for art propaganda. Began working on ballet productions in Leningrad theatres (Shostakovich's Zolotoi Vek, 1930). Chief stage designer at the Kirov Theatre, 1932–36. Personally responsible for the decor of many famous productions, such as Spartak, 1956. Died in Leningrad.

Khodasevich, Vladislav Felitsianovich (Chodasiewicz, Władysław)
28.5.1886–14.6.1939. Poet.
Born in Moscow. Son of a painter.

His family was of Polish origin. Studied at Moscow University. First collection of poems published in Moscow in 1908 (Molodost'). Emigrated, 1922. Lived in Germany, Czechoslovakia, Italy, and England. Settled in Paris. Often visited Gorkii on Capri. Editor of the poetry section of Vozrozhdenie, Paris, and as such became a respected judge and mentor of young emigré poets. His 3rd volume of poetry under the title Evropeiskaia Noch', which included Putem Zerna and Tiazhelaia Lira, was published in Paris in 1927. Wrote an excellent biography of Derzhavin (1931, Paris), and a collection of articles on his contemporaries, Nekropol', 1939. Died of cancer in Paris a few months later. His blend of classicism and modernism was unique at a time when experiments were very much in vogue. His literary criticism belongs to the best in Russian 20th-century writing. Considered by Nabokov as the greatest modern Russian poet.
Works: Molodost', Moscow, 1908; Sshchastlivyi Domik, Petersburg, 1914; Putem Zerna, Moscow, 1920 (2nd ed., Petersburg, 1921); Iz Evreiskikh Poetov, Petersburg, 1921 (2nd ed., Berlin, 1923); Stat'ii o Russkoi Poezii, Petersburg, 1922; Zagadki, Petersburg, 1922; Tiazhelaia Lira, Berlin, 1923; Sobranie Stikhov, Paris, 1927.

Khodorovich, Tatiana Sergeevna
1921– . Human rights campaigner.
Born in Moscow. Graduated from the Moscow Teachers' Institute. Researcher at the Russian Language Institute of the USSR Academy of Sciences. Published some articles in the professional Soviet press. In the mid-1960s, became involved in the human rights movement. Lost her job in 1971. Member of the Initiative Group for the Defence of Human Rights. After continuous harassment from the KGB, forced to leave the country, 1977. Lives in Paris. Author of many human rights publications.

Khodskii, Leonid Vladimirovich
1854–1919. Economist.
Professor at Petersburg University.

Editor of *Narodnoe Khoziaistvo*, 1900–05. Editor of the daily *Nasha Zhisn'*, 1904–06 (later called *Tovarishch*). Editor of *Stolichnaia Pochta* and *Nasha Gazeta*. Member of the Labour group of the Duma and one of the Russian followers of Bernstein (with Kuskova, Prokopovich and others).

Khokhlov, Ivan Sergeevich
1895–1973. Politician.
Joined the Bolshevik Party, 1918. Took part in the Civil War. Graduated from the Financial Academy, 1931. Chairman of the Moscow oblispolkom, 1937. Chairman of Tsentrosoiuz USSR, 1938–40. RSFSR Prime Minister, 1940–41. Political officer on different fronts during WWII. Lt.-general. After the war, head of Tsentrosoiuz.

Khokhlov, Nikolai
1919–   . SMERSH agent, defector.
One of the most skilful SMERSH agents of his time. As Oberleutnant Wittgenstein, operated during WWII behind German lines in Minsk, Eastern Poland and Lithuania. In 1953, assigned to kill Igor' Okolovich, an active member of the NTS (the Russian anti-Soviet emigré organization) whom SMERSH regarded as the brain behind the anti-Soviet propaganda campaign. But under the influence of his Polish wife, Ianina Timashkewicz, refused to carry out the assassination. On 18 Feb. 1954, told his intended victim about his assignment. After defecting, wrote his memoirs. The KGB tried to poison him in Vietnam, but were unsuccessful. Lives in America under an assumed name. His wife and son, however, perished at the hands of SMERSH.
See: N. Khokhlov, *Pravo na Sovest'*, Frankfurt/Main.

Khokhlova, Aleksandra Sergeevna
4.11.1897–22.8.1985. Film actress.
Entered the film industry, 1916. Appeared in small parts. Studied at the State Film School, 1919–20. Met the director Lev Kuleshov. Married him. Became his pupil, 1920–23. Appeared in Kuleshov's adventure film *Na Krasnom Fronte*. Best known in the West for Kuleshov's comedy *Neobychainye Prikliucheniia Mistera*

Vesta v Strane Bol'shevikov, 1924. She appeared in nearly all Kuleshov's (as well as in other directors') films: *Luch Smerti, Vasha Znakomaia, Sasha, and Igrushki*. Contributed to her husband's book *Stat'ii Materialy*, 1979. Taught at the VGIK. Died in Moscow. Considered a great actress of the early period of the Soviet cinema.

Khokhlova, Olga (m. Mme Picasso)
1897–after 1950. Ballerina.
Ballet dancer with Diaghilev. Daughter of an officer. Met Picasso in Rome, 1917. Married him at the Russian Cathedral in Paris (60 Diaghilev dancers and many French poets and painters were present). Gave birth to a son, Paolo, 1921. Picasso divorced her in Dec. 1940.

Kholodnaia, Vera Vasil'evna
1893–17.2.1919. Film actress.
Leading actress in the Russian silent cinema. First film, 1914. Mainly worked with the director, P.I. Chardynin. Soon became the queen of Russian melodrama. Of striking appearance. Died in Odessa during the Civil War. Crowds came to her funeral. Her death at the age of 26 was as mysterious as was her life. Many articles and books were dedicated to her.
See: A. Kapler, *Zagadka Korolevy Ekrana*, Moscow, 1979.

Kholostiakov, Georgii Nikitich
1902–1983. Vice-admiral.
Joined the Bolshevik Party, 1920, and the Red Navy, 1921. Took part in the Civil War. Submarine officer in the 1930s and during WWII. Commander of the Novorossiisk naval base and the Danube fleet, 1944, and of the Caspian fleet, 1950. Graduated from the Academy of the General Staff, 1950. Deputy Head of Military Training in the navy, 1953–69. Later worked in the Ministry of Defence.

Khomenko, Vasilii Afanas'evich
1899–1943. Lt.-general.
Joined the Red Army, 1918, and the Bolshevik Party, 1919. Took part in the Civil War. Graduated from the Frunze Military Academy, 1928. Served in the border guards (NKVD),

1935–41. Commander of border guards in Moldavia and the Ukraine. Army commander during WWII. Fell in action.

Khomutov, Petr Ivanovich
29.8.1927–   . Ballet dancer.
Born in Tula Oblast'. Graduated from the Moscow Choreographic School, 1947. Until 1968, with the Bolshoi Theatre. Soloist. From 1968, senior superviser, and from 1970, ballet manager at the Bolshoi Theatre.

Khorun, Iosif Ivanovich
1884–1962. Major-general.
Joined the Red Army and the Bolshevik Party, 1918. Cavalry regiment commander during the Civil War in Turkestan. Graduated from the Frunze Military Academy, 1935. Corps commander during WWII. After WWII, Military Commander of Chemnitz (now Karl Marx Stadt) in East Germany, 1945–47.

Khoruzhaia, Vera Zakharovna
1903–1942. Partisan.
Joined the Bolshevik Party, 1921. Secretary of the illegal Cen. Cttee. of the Komsomol, and member of the Cen. Cttee. of the Communist Party in Western Belorussia (then Poland). Moved to the USSR. Party functionary, 1932. During WWII, partisan leader in Belorussia near Pinsk and Vitebsk. Arrested by the Germans and shot.

Khorvat, Dmitrii Leonidovich
1858–1937. Lt.-general, railway expert.
Graduated from the Nikolaevskii Engineering Institute. Served in the Life Guards, 1878. Railway administrator in the Far East. Director of the East China Railway, 1902–18. Head of Kharbin government in 1918. From Nov. 1918, recognized the authority of Admiral Kolchak. His administration at Kharbin ended in Mar. 1920. Remained in China. Became expert on the East China Railway. From 1924, local chairman of the ROVS (the Russian Military Union, White veterans of the Civil War).

Khozin, Mikhail Semenovich
1896–1979. Col.-general.
Sub-lieutenant during WWI. Joined the Bolshevik Party and the Red Army, 1918. Took part in the Civil War. Graduated from the Frunze Military Academy, 1925. Head of the Academy, 1939. During WWII, held high posts on the Leningrad and Baltic fronts. Head of Higher Military Educational Establishments, 1946–56. Professor at the Academy of the General Staff, 1956–63.

Khrennikov, Tikhon Nikolaevich
10.6.1913–   . Composer, state official.
Born in Elets in Orel Gouvt. Attended the Gnesin Technical School of Music, 1929–32. At the Conservatory from 1932. Graduated, 1936. In charge of the Central Soviet Army Theatre, 1941–54. From 1948, General Secretary of the Union of Composers of the USSR. Administrative boss of Soviet musical life for 40 years. Candidate member of the Cen. Cttee. at the 25th Party Congress. Taught at the Gnesin Pedagogical Institute of Music in the post-war years and at the Conservatory from 1962. Three Stalin Prizes, 1942. During Stalin's last years, responsible for the persecution of D. Shostakovich and the general obscurantist situation in Soviet music. Severely criticized in the Soviet press for his role in musical life, 1988. Defended himself by stating that he did not send members of his union to the Gulag, as the leaders of the Union of Writers did.

Khrenov, Arkadii Fedorovich
1900–   . Col.-general.
Joined the Red Army, 1918. Took part in the Civil War. Professor at military engineering educational establishments. Joined the Bolshevik Party, 1931. On active service in engineering forces during the Soviet-Finnish war and WWII. After the war, General Inspector of the Engineering Forces of the Soviet Army, 1949–1960.

Khrenov, Konstantin Konstantinovich
25.2.1894–1978? Scientist.
Graduated from the Petrograd Electrotechnical Institute, 1918. Developed methods of underwater welding used in bridge and ship repairs.

Khristianovich, Sergei Alekseevich
27.10.1908–   . Scientist.
Graduated from Leningrad University, 1930. Worked at the Hydrological Institute in Leningrad. Academician, 1946. Highly decorated (3 Stalin Prizes). Specialist in the mechanics of liquids and gases. Vice-President of the Siberian Development of the Academy of Sciences, 1961.

Khriukin, Timofei Timofeevich
1910–1953. Col.-general.
Joined the Bolshevik Party 1929, and the Red Army, 1932. Educated at a pilots' school, 1933. Graduated from the Academy of the General Staff, 1939. Bomber pilot. Fought in Spain during the Spanish Civil War, and against the Japanese in the late 1930s in China. Took part in the Soviet-Finnish war and WWII. Several high commands in the air force after WWII.

Khrulev, Andrei Vasilievich
1892–1962. General.
Joined the Red Army and the Bolshevik Party, 1918. Political officer during the Civil War. Graduated from the Higher Political Courses of the Red Army, 1925. Head of the Financial Administration of the Red Army, and of the Military Building Administration (Glavvoenstroi). Head of Supply of the Red Army, July 1940. During WWII, Deputy Minister of Defence, Head of the Rear Administration of the Red Army, and Minister of Railways, 1942–43. Head of the Rear Administration of the Soviet Armed Forces, 1946. Deputy minister in several ministries, 1951–58.

Khrushchev, Grigorii K.
3.3.1897–22.12.1962. Biologist.
Graduated from Moscow University, 1919. Professor at the Moscow Veterinary Institute, 1933–45. Specialist in leucocytes.

Khrushchev, Nikita Sergeevich
5.4.1894–11.9.1971. Politician.
Born in the village of Kalinovka near Kursk. Son of a miner. Started work as a local cowherd. Joined the Communist Party, 1918. During the Civil War, minor political officer with Budennyi's 1st Cavalry Army. In the 1920s, engaged in administrative work in the Ukraine. Student at the Industrial Academy in Moscow, 1929, co-student of Stalin's wife, N. Allilueva, who brought him to the attention of her husband. Started work in the Moscow political administration, 1931. 1st Secretary of the Moscow City Party Cttee, 1935. 1st Secretary of the Cen. Cttee. of the Communist Party in the Ukraine, 1938. Throughout the 1930s, one of the most active Stalinists. During WWII, political commissar at the front (including Stalingrad) officially Lt.-gen. After WWII, head of the local government in the Ukraine, 1944–47, presiding over the re-Stalinization after the German retreat. Member of the Politburo, 1939–52. 1st Secretary of the Cen. Cttee. of the CP in the Ukraine, 1947–49. Again 1st Secretary of Moscow City Party Cttee., 1949. Member of the Presidium of the Cen. Cttee. of the CPSU, 1952. At the moment of Stalin's death, Mar. 1953, member of the ruling group, but undoubtedly the least-likely successor. Surprised everybody by showing uncommon shrewdness, first uniting all rivals by a well-timed attack on the hated secret-police chief, Beria, 1953, then removing Malenkov from his position as head of government, and finally playing the anti-Stalinist card (his secret report at the 20th Party Congress, 1956). Broke with Soviet tradition by visiting foreign countries – Yugoslavia, Britain, and the USA. Took the initiative in limiting the overgrown Gulag empire, and promoted the rehabilitation of many of Stalin's victims. Other reforms were much less successful – for example the administrative restructuring, and the ecological disaster of the Virgin Lands. In 1956, ruthlessly suppressed the Hungarian Revolution, which was developing his own ideas of de-Stalinization much too far. In 1957, had a successful showdown with his increasingly isolated Stalinist colleagues. A majority of the Politburo (at that time the Presidium of the Cen. Cttee.) voted to remove him, but in an unprecedented move, with the help of

Zhukov and the KGB, he demanded and got a plenary session of the Cen. Cttee. (flying in members by special planes from all over the Soviet Union), which overturned the Politburo decision. His rivals were branded as the 'anti-party group' (Malenkov, Kaganovich, Molotov and Shepilov) and were demoted or expelled from the party. In a similar surprise move, later in the same year, got rid of his too-powerful ally, Marshal Zhukov, removing him from his post as Defence Minister during his visit to Yugoslavia. In 1958, demoted Bulganin, who had previously vacillated between him and his rivals, from the post of Prime Minister, and became both head of the party and head of the government (1958–64). In foreign policy, healed the rift with Yugoslavia by stopping the anti-Tito propaganda of the Stalin years and visiting Tito personally. At the same time, became anathema to Mao Tse-tung, who remained faithful to Stalinism. In US-Soviet relations, came close to war in 1962 by sending Soviet rockets to Cuba, but at the last moment agreed to withdraw them. With his colourful personality, coarse humour and unconventional behaviour (for example, banging his shoe on a table at the UN in New York), he aroused amusement and sympathy, more so in the West than in the Soviet Union itself, where people were much more aware of his former Stalinist record, his very low cultural level, his rudeness and the obviously harmful character of some of his pet campaigns: for example the vicious persecution of religion, comparable only with the early Soviet years and the 1930s, his attempts to grow maize on a US scale in a clearly unsuitable climate, and generally his incompetent directions in agriculture (where he retained Lysenko as his adviser) or even in literature and painting. On 14 Oct. 1964, removed from his position by his colleagues in the Politburo (the move was proposed while he was on holiday in the Crimea) for 'subjectivism and voluntarism', and replaced by the grey but safe bureaucrat Breznhev. Alleged to have dictated his memoirs (which were published abroad) during his retirement. They seem to have a genuine Khrushchev touch and certainly contain some characteristically unconventional passages. Died and buried in Moscow. A monument (ordered by relatives) was made on his grave by the well-known dissident sculptor Ernest Neizvestnyi, who had previously been viciously attacked by him during his reign. Was not mentioned under Brezhnev, but attempts at objective judgement were made in the Soviet press under Gorbachev in the late 1980s. Inside information on his last years was given by his son in *Ogonek* in 1988.

Khrustalev-Nosar', Grigorii Stepanovich
1877–1918. Lawyer, politician.
Became the nominal leader of the 1905 Revolution as the chairman of the Petersburg Workers' Soviet (the real leaders were Trotsky and Parvus). After the defeat of the revolution, went abroad. Returned just before the February Revolution 1917, but was unable to play a part in it. Shot during the Civil War in the Ukraine.

Khrykov, Nikolai Mikhailovich
1912–   . Artist.
Enamel painter. Pupil of A. A. Nazarov. Studied at an enamel art school. From 1925, worked in enamel art shops in Rostov. Participant in the New York International Exhibition, 1939. Also exhibited in Moscow, 1952. Maker of many objets d'art in enamel.

Khubov, Georgii Nikitich
9.5.1902–   . Music scholar, editor.
Born in Kars (now Turkey). Editor of the magazine *Sovetskaia Muzyka*, 1952–57. Author of many books, including *A.P. Borodin*, Moscow, 1933, *Zhizn A. N. Serova*, Moscow-Leningrad, 1950, and *Aram Khachaturian*, Moscow, 1962.

Khudaiberdyev, Narmankhonmadi Dzhuraevich
1928–   . State and party official. Uzbek. Graduated from the Uzbek Agricultural Institute, Tashkent, 1949. Member of the CPSU, 1948. Lecturer and associate professor at the Samarkand Agricultural Institute, 1953–54. Senior posts in the Uzbek CP from 1954 until Jan. 1985. His last post was as chairman of the Uzbek Council of Ministers. According to *Pravda Vostoka*, the Uzbek CP newspaper, expelled from the CPSU, July 27, 1986.

Khudekov, Sergei Nikolaevich
1837–20.2.1927. Journalist, ballet critic, playwright, author.
Graduated in law from Moscow University. Theatre and ballet critic from the mid-1860s under the pseudonym 'Zhalo'. From 1871, editor-proprietor of the *Petersburg Gazette*. Active in many theatre commissions and helped run the Narodnyi Teatr. Author of many ballet scenarios. Collected an immense amount of material (15,000 items) on 17-19th century choreography. Wrote *Istoriia Tantsev Vsekh Vremen i Narodov*, Petersburg, 1913–17. Author of many plays staged at the Aleksandrinskii and other theatres.

Khudenko, Ivan
1930?–1975. Collective farm chairman.
Manager of a collective farm in Kazakhstan. Under Brezhnev, carried out an experiment reducing his workforce to a minimum and paying the workers a maximum salary. Achieved the highest quality products. For his independent initiative, was arrested and put on trial. Quickly sentenced to a prison term. Died in prison. Rediscovered by Moscow legal journalists under Gorbachev. His methods are now widely discussed. Attempts are being made to prosecute those who jailed him.

Khudiakov, Sergei Aleksandrovich (Khanferiants, Armenak Artemovich)
1902–1950. Marshal.
Joined the Red Army, 1918. Took part in the Civil War as a cavalry officer. Graduated from the Zhukovskii Air Force Academy, 1936. Took part in WWII. Commander of the air force of the Western front, 1942. Chief-of-Staff and Deputy Commander of the Soviet air force, 1943.

Khutsiev, Marlen Martynovich
4.10.1925–   . Film director.
Born in Tbilisi of Georgian parents but grew up in Moscow. Returned to Tbilisi to attend school. Worked at

the Tbilisi Film Studios as a photographic assistant for one year. Returned to Moscow and entered the Directors' Faculty of the VGIK. Graduated in 1955. First film, *Spring on Zarechnaia Street*, produced by Odessa Film Studios in 1956, a fresh treatment of a modern theme about young people. Became famous with *I Am Twenty* (Mosfilm, 1965) and *July Rain* (Mosfilm, 1967). Both films are still discussed on the pages of the film press. Other films: *Two Fedors* (Odessa Film Studios, 1958, based on Anatolii Kuznetsov's story), *In the Month of May* (Mosfilm, 1970), and *The Scarlet Sail of Paris* (Ekran TV Studios, 1973).

Khvesin, Tikhon Serafimovich
1894–1938. Military commander.
Joined the Bolshevik Party, 1911, and the Red Army, 1918. Took part in the Civil War on the Don, in Turkestan, and on the Western Front. In the mid 1920s, chairman of GOSPLAN. Liquidated by Stalin.

Khvostenko, Aleksei Lvovich
1940– . Poet, singer.
Born in Sverdlovsk. Studied at the Leningrad Art School. Wrote verse, which circulated in samizdat. Sang his own verse. Emigrated, 1977. Settled in France.

Khvylovyi, Mikola
1893–1933. Author.
Ukrainian nationalist. Became the outstanding figure in Ukrainian literature of the 1920s, considered to be the Golden Age of modern Ukrainian culture. Victim of Stalin's purges. Committed suicide.

Kiaksht, Georgii Georgievich
7.2.1873–22.3.1936. Ballet dancer.
Son of a peasant from Kovno, now Kaunas, Lithuania. Graduated from the Petersburg Theatre School, 1891, in the class of N. Volkov and P. Gerdt. Dancer and later leading dancer at the Mariinskii Theatre until 1910. With the A. Shiriaev company on tour in Monte Carlo, 1902. From 1909–11, with the Ballets Russes in Paris. From 1903–04, he and his sister, the ballerina Lidia Kiaksht, performed with the Bolshoi Theatre.

In 1910, left Russia. In 1920, choreographer of the Vienna State Theatre, also director of the company and ballet school there. Moved to Buenos Aires where he worked as a choreographer. One of the founders of the Argentinian National Ballet. Returned to his birthplace and from 1930 worked as a dancer, choreographer and teacher with the Kaunas Theatre.

Kiaksht, Lidia Georgievna (Lydia)
25.3.1885–11.1.1959. Ballerina.
Born in Kovno, now Kaunas. Daughter of a Lithuanian peasant. Sister of Georgii Kiaksht. Graduated from the Petersburg Theatre School, 1902, in the class of P. Gerdt. Leading dancer with the Mariinskii Theatre, 1902–08. From 1903–04, performed with her brother at the Bolshoi Theatre. Appeared in London at the Empire Theatre, the Coliseum and the Alhambra, 1908–12. Toured in Russia during the 1911 and 1916–17 seasons. Later toured the USA and Italy. In 1933, retired. Organized the Touring Ballet of English Youth, 1939–46, which was later re-named the Lydia Kiaksht Russian Ballet. Taught at Sadler's Wells. From 1953–59, taught at the Nikolaeva-Legat Ballet School. Died in London. Memoirs: *Romantic Recollections*, London, 1929.

Kibkalo, Evgenii Gavrilovich
12.11.1932– . Singer (baritone).
Pupil of V. M. Politkovskii. Soloist with the Bolshoi Theatre from 1956. Honorary Artist of the RSFSR, 1959.

Kidiaev, Iurii Konstantinovich
29.2.1955– . Athlete.
Born in Moscow. Honoured Master of Sports (handball), 1976. With the Moscow Sports Club of the Armed Forces. USSR champion, 1976–78. Olympic champion, 1976.

Kidiashvili, David Samsonovich
1862–1931. Author.
Classical Georgian writer. His subject was always Georgia and the Georgian people. Many of his books were made into films by the Georgia Film Studio.
Works: *Machekha Samanishvili*, 1897;

Nevzgody Sem'i Kamushadze, 1900; *Memuary*, 1925; *Sobranie Sochinenii*, 2-vol. 1980–81 (in Georgian).

Kiizbaeva, Saira
7.11.1919– . Singer (soprano)
Born in Kirghizia. Soloist with the Kirghiz Musical Drama Theatre from 1936. Teacher at the Kurenkeev Music School, and at the studio of the Opera and Ballet Theatre, Frunze, from 1956.

Kikabidze, Vakhtang Konstantinovich
20.3.1938– . Actor.
Born in Georgia. Soloist and conductor of the vocal-instrumental ensemble Orero from 1966. Entered the film industry, 1967. Comedian. Best-known for his major role in *Ne Goriui* (Cheer Up!) Other films: *Sovsem Propashchii Melodii Veriiskogo Kvartala* and *Mimino*.

Kiknadze, Anzor
26.3.1934–17.11.1977. Athlete.
Georgian. Honoured Master of Sports (judo). Bronze medallist at the XVIIIth Olympic Games. Many times USSR champion.

Kikvidze, Vasilii Isidorovich
1895–1919. Military commander.
Took part in WWI. Active in revolutionary work. Commander of the South-Western Front, 1918. During the Civil War, commander of Red detachments in the Ukraine. Fell in action.

Kiladze, Grigorii Varfolomeevich
25.10.1902–3.4.1962. Composer.
Born in Batumi. Georgian by nationality. Professor at the Tbilisi Conservatory, director from 1945. Author of operas, a ballet, 2 symphonies, choral works, and music for films. Stalin Prize, 1941 and 1948. Died in Tbilisi.

Kim, Iulii
1937– . Poet, ballad singer.
Graduated from the Moscow Teachers' Institute, 1960. For a short time taught in Kamchatka. In 1968 returned to Moscow. His poems became known in samizdat. Became

a poet-singer. Belongs to the generation of ballad singers which includes Okudzhava, Vysotskii, Galich and Matveeva, whose songs were distributed through magnitizdat (self-made tapes). Now officially recognized, some of his songs have been recorded by Melodia, the USSR's official record company.

Kim, Nelli Vladimirovna
29.7.1957– . Athlete.
Born in Shurab, Tadzhik SSR. Honoured Master of Sports (gymnastics), 1976. With Chimkent Spartak. USSR champion, 1973–76. Olympic champion, 1976. European champion, 1975 and 1977. World champion, 1974, 1978–79. Graduated from the Kazakhskii Institute of Physical Culture, 1978.
See: S. Tokarev, *Talant i Smelost', Olimp-76*, Moscow, 1976.

Kim, Roman Nikolaevich
1899–1967. Author.
Specialized in spy thrillers. Printed in millions of copies. Also translator and specialist in Japanese literature. Works: *Agent Osobogo Naznacheniia*, 1959; *Kobra Pod Podushkoi*, 1960; *Po Prochtenii Szhech*, 1962.

Kin, Viktor Pavlovich (Surovikin)
1903–1937. Author.
Born in Borisoglebsk. Son of a railway worker. Joined the Bolshevik Party, 1920. Before that, already active as one of the first members of the Komsomol. Fought against the peasant uprising in Tambov. Political commissar during the Soviet-Polish war. Communist underground agent in the Far East. At the end of the Civil War, started to write, and became a well-known journalist with *Komsomolskaia Pravda*. At the end of the 1920s, began to write novels. In the 1930s, Soviet correspondent in Italy and France. His novels, glorifying the young communists' exploits during the Civil War, were popular, and were made into films and plays. Arrested and perished in the purges. See: *Vsegda po etu Storonu. Vospominaniia o Kine*, Moscow, 1966.

Kipen, Grigorii Abramovich
1881–1937? Economist.
During the 1917 Revolution, one of the Menshevik leaders in Moscow. Vice-chairman of the Moscow Soviet, 1917. Secretary of the Moscow SD Cttee. (from the Mensheviks). In the 1920s, taught in institutes of higher education in Moscow. Arrested, 1930. Imprisoned in the Urals until 1933, after that in exile in Tomsk. The place and circumstances of his death are not known.

Kiporenko-Damanskii, Iurii Stepanovich
24.3.1888–6.8.1955. Singer (tenor).
Born in Kiev. Pupil of A. Labinskii and G. Tanar. Appeared with the operas of Moscow, Saratov, Khar'kov and other cities from 1913–38. Soloist with the Kiev Theatre of Opera and Ballet from 1938. Taught at the Kiev Conservatory. Died in Khar'kov.

Kireev, Grigorii Petrovich
1890–1938. Naval commander.
Revolutionary sailor in 1917. Brought ships of the Baltic fleet from Helsingfors (Helsinki) to join the Red Navy, 1918. In the 1920s, political commissar in the Red Navy. Commander of the Pacific fleet, 1937. Arrested, presumably shot, during Stalin's purges.

Kireiko, Vitalii Dmitrievich
23.12.1926– . Composer.
Born in Dnepropetrovsk district. Ukrainian by nationality. Lecturer at the Kiev Conservatory. Author of an opera, the ballet *Teni Zabytykh Predkov* (later turned into a film by S. Paradzhanov), symphonies, overtures, a concerto for cello and orchestra, a string quartet, choral works, and romances. Also arranged folk songs, and music for stage productions.

Kirichenko, Aleksei Illarionovich
1908– . Politician.
Son of a Ukrainian soldier. Secretary of the party organization in Odessa during the 1940s. Promoted by N. Khrushchev in the mid-1950s. Previously secretary of the party organization in the Ukraine. Became Khrushchev's associate, and was promoted by him to become a member of the Presidium of the CPSU. Secretary of the Cen. Cttee. of the CPSU, 1957. In the early 1960s, lost his position and was sent to Rostov Oblast' as 1st secretary of the party organization. After Khrushchev's fall, disappeared from the political scene.

Kirienko, Zinaida Mikhailovna
9.7.1933– . Film actress.
Graduated from the VGIK, 1958. Joined the Film Actors' Theatre Studio, 1961. Best known for her parts in *And Quiet Flows the Don*, 1957–58, and *Sud'ba Cheloveka*, 1959.

Kirill (Gundiaev), Archbishop of Smolensk and Viaz'ma
1937– . Russian Orthodox clergyman.
Dean of the Leningrad Theological Academy. Archbishop of Vyborg, 1976. Active theologian and church leader. Head of the church commission, which worked out the new constitution of the Russian Orthodox Church, which removed some of the worst features of the rules imposed by Khrushchev, restoring the priest to his rightful place in the parish from his previous position of hired employee, and introducing several other changes. The constitution was approved at the Council of the Church, June 1988, convened in connection with the Millennium of Russian Christianity in the new liberal atmosphere under Gorbachev.

Kirill Vladimirovich (Romanov), Grand Duke
1876–1938. Naval officer.
Grandson of Alexander II. Married Victoria, daughter of Alfred, Duke of Edinburgh (son of Queen Victoria). Joined the Guards Equipage of the Russian navy. In 1917, welcomed the February Revolution, but in the autumn of the same year, after sailors' disturbances, forced to flee with his family by sea to Finland. Settled in France. Proclaimed by some Russian monarchist organizations to be head of the Romanov dynasty and pretender to the Romanov throne (some preferred Nikolai Nikolaevich, the Tsar's uncle and one-time commander of the

Russian armies during WWI). Died and buried in France.

Kirkor, Georgii Vasil'evich
12.10.1910– . Composer.
Born in Moscow. Husband of the composer I. Iordan. Author of 4 symphonies, concerto fantasies for alto and piano, concertos, and chamber music.

Kirov, Sergei Mironovich (Kostrikov)
27.3.1886–1.12.1934. Revolutionary, politician.
Born in Urzhum near Viatka. Brought up in an orphanage. Educated at the Kazan' Technical School, 1904. Member of the Bolshevik Party, 1904. Worked as a draughtsman in Tomsk Town Hall. Organized a railway strike in Siberia during the 1905 Revolution. Several arrests after 1905. Moved to Vladikavkaz, 1909, where he worked for the newspaper *Terek*. One of the most capable Bolshevik organizers before and during WWI. After the February Revolution 1917, member of the Vladikavkaz Soviet. As a delegate to the 2nd Congress of Soviets in Petrograd, took part in the October Revolution 1917. Returning to Vladikavkaz, became one of the organizers of Soviet rule in the North Caucasus, 1918. Organized the defence of Astrakhan' against the Whites during the Civil War, 1919. In the early 1920s (with Ordzhonikidze and Mikoian), led the struggle for communist power in the Caucasus and Azerbaidzhan, nationalizing the Baku oilfields. During the power struggle among Lenin's heirs, joined Stalin against the Old Bolsheviks and became his closest collaborator. After the removal of Zinoviev, appointed party boss in Leningrad and North-West Russia, Feb. 1926. Member of the Politburo, 1930, Secretary of the Cen. Cttee. and member of the Orgburo, 1934. Effective orator, gained wide popularity, overshadowing Stalin and arousing his jealousy. Assassinated in Dec. 1934 by a minor party functionary under very suspicious circumstances. His death, which still remains a mystery, was officially blamed on Fascists and their allies in the Communist Party and signalled the beginning of Stalin's worst purges. According to some historians, this was the purpose of the murder, which had been engineered personally by Stalin. An official investigation of the murder, promised by Khrushchev in the 1950s, never materialized, but was promised again in the late 1980s. Extremely intricate shifts in the Leningrad NKVD at the time of the murder and thereafter seem to confirm suspicions.
See: A. Avtorkhanov, *Proiskhozhdenie Partokratii*, Frankfurt, 1973, *Tekhnologiia Vlasti*, Frankfurt, 1976, and *Memuary*, 1983; V.A. Antonov-Ovseenko, *Portret Tirana*, USA, 1983.

Kirponos, Mikhail Petrovich
1892–1941. Col.-general.
Took part in WWI and the Civil War. Joined the Red Army and the Bolshevik Party, 1918. Graduated from the Frunze Military Academy, 1927. On active service during the Soviet-Finnish war, 1939–40. Commander of the South-Western front at the beginning of WWII. Committed suicide.

Kirsanov, Petr Semenovich
1919– . Marshal.
Joined the Red Army, 1936. During WWII, fighter pilot and air force instructor. After WWII, held several high positions in the air force.

Kirsanov, Semen Isaakovich
18.9.1906–10.12.1972. Poet.
Born in Odessa. Son of a Jewish tailor. Graduated from the Odessa Institute of People's Education, 1925. First publication, 1922. Close to V. Mayakovsky. Member of the communist futurist *Left Front*. Played an active part in poetry propaganda during Stalin's time. During WWII, war correspondent for many newspapers and for the TASS news agency. Some of the poetry he wrote during this period was sincere. Found himself popular during the Khrushchev thaw. Died in Moscow.

Kirsanova, Nina
1900?– . Ballerina.
Granddaughter of Wilhelm Vanner, soloist at the Bolshoi Theatre. Trained at ballet schools under Nelidova and Sobeshchanskaia. Graduated from the Music and Ballet School of Aleksandr Shor. Debut at the Zimin Opera, Moscow. Worked with V.I. Nemirovich-Danchenko, N. Legat and A. Gorskii. During the Civil War, lived in Kiev, then Belgrade. Prima ballerina at the Belgrade Opera, 1923. With Anna Pavlova on tour, 1926–31. Worked as a consultant with Valerii Panov in Belgrade.

Kirshon, Vladimir Mikhailovich
6.8.1902–28.7.1938. Author, playwright.
Born in Nalchik, in the Northern Caucasus. During the Civil War, fought with the Reds, 1918–20. Graduated from Sverdlov University, Moscow. One of most vocal exponents of radical communist views in the late 1920s–early1930s. Leader of RAPP (Russian Association of Proletarian Writers). In his plays, praised the Stalinist type of ruthless political leader and glorified the collectivization campaign. Became a victim of false accusations, and perished during the Stalin purges. Officially rehabilitated under Khrushchev, 1956.

Kirzhinov, Mukharbii Nurbievich
1.1.1949– . Athlete.
Born in the village of Koshekhabl', Adygeiskaia Autonomous Oblast'. Honoured Master of Sports (heavy athletics), 1972. With the Moscow Sports Club of the Armed Forces. USSR champion, 1971–75. European champion, 1973–74. World champion, 1972–73. Olympic champion, 1972.
See: V. Volkov, *M. Kirzhinov, Syn Ekateriny Izmailovny, Polevoda, Tvoi Chempiony*, Moscow, 1973.

Kiselev, Grigorii Leonidovich
19.4.1901–10.4.1952. Musicologist.
Born in the Ukraine. Lecturer. Taught at the Sverdlov and Kiev conservatories. Author of works on M. Balakirev, S. Gulak-Artemovskii, and L. Revutskii. In collaboration with L. Kulakovskii, wrote the textbook *Muzykal'naia Gramota* (in Ukrainian) 1932, (in Russian) 1934, 1936. Died in Kiev.

Kiselev, Vasilii Aleksandrovich
14.6.1902– . Musicologist.
Born in the Kaluzhskaia Gouvt.
Author of several works on Russian operatic composers.

Kistiakovskii, Andrei Andreevich
1936–30.6.1987. Translator, dissident.
Born in Moscow. Graduated from Moscow University, 1974. Translator of English literature. Translated Arthur Koestler's *Darkness At Noon* into Russian. Also, Faulkner, Snow, O'Connor, Pound, and Tolkien. Became involved in dissident activity in the late 1970s. Involved with the Russian Public Fund of Help to Political Prisoners' Families, financed by A. Solzhenitsyn. Under KGB surveillance, much troubled by the authorities. Died of cancer in Moscow.

Kizevetter, Aleksandr Aleksandrovich (Kizewetter)
1881–1933. Historian.
Professor of history at Moscow University. Emigrated after the October Revolution 1917. Professor at the Russian law faculty in Prague, 1918–33. Contributed articles to many Russian emigré publications. Died in Prague.

Kizhevatov, Andrei Mitrofanovich
1907–1941. Lieutenant, security officer.
Joined the borderguards (GPU), 1929. With the security service until his death. During the first week of the German advance into the Soviet Union, took part in the defence of Brest. Killed in action.

Kizimov, Ivan Mikhailovich
28.6.1928– . Athlete.
Born in a village in Rostov Oblast'. Honoured Master of Sports (riding), 1968. With Leningrad Trud. Sports instructor. Graduated from the Jockey School, 1947. USSR champion, 1967–73. Olympic champion, 1968 and 1972. World champion, 1970. Bronze medal, 1964. Silver medal, 1968.

Klado, Nikolai Lavrent'evich
1862–1919. Major-general.
Graduated from the Naval Academy,

1886. Professor at the Academy, 1895. Staff officer during the Russo-Japanese war, 1904–05. Again professor at the Naval Academy, 1910. Head of the Academy, 1917–19.

Klebanov, Dmitrii L'vovich
25.6.1907– . Composer, conductor.
Born in Khar'kov. Professor at the Khar'kov Institute of Arts. Among his pupils were B. Iarovinskii, I. Pol'skii and V. Gubarenko. Author of operas, ballets, a Ukrainian concertino, a Ukrainian suite, concertos for orchestra, 2 pieces for violin, music for dombra, a chamber ensemble, works for choir, romances, and music for stage and film.

Kleiman, Liudmila Borisovna
1936– . Critic, literary historian.
Born in Tambov. Graduated in philology from Moscow University. Left the USSR, 1961 and settled in Israel. Ph.D in Russian literature from Jerusalem University.
Works: *Ranniia Proza Fedora Sologuba*, USA, 1983.

Klembovskii, Vladislav Napoleonovich
1860–1921. General.
Graduated from the Nikolaevskaia Military Academy, 1885. Took part in the Russo-Japanese war and WWI. Deputy chief-of-staff at Supreme HQ, and commander of the Northern front, 1917. After the October Revolution 1917, worked in the Soviet administration.

Klenitskis, Abel Ruvimovich (Klenickis)
14.7.1904– . Composer, violinist, conductor.
Born in Lithuania. Teacher at the Vil'nius Conservatory. Author of an opera, an oratorio, a cantata, a symphonietta, a piece for violin and orchestra, a concerto, 3 string quartets, and suites for choir and orchestra.

Klepikov, Aleksandr Grigor'evich
23.5.1950– . Athlete.
Born in Leningrad. Honoured Master of Sports (rowing), 1976. With

Leningrad Trud. Graduated from the Leningrad Industrial Pedagogical High School, 1977. World champion, 1975. Olympic champion, 1976. USSR champion, 1977–78.

Klepikov, Iurii Nikolaevich
24.8.1935– . Scriptwriter.
Graduated from Moscow University, 1960, and from Scriptwriters' Courses, 1964. Best known for his script *Voskhozhdenie*, filmed by L. Shepit'ko.

Klepikova, Elena Konstantinovna
1942– . Journalist.
Born in Kostroma. Graduated from Leningrad University. Member of the Union of Journalists. In 1977, together with her husband, V. Soloviev, set up an independent press agency with the aim of providing Western journalists with information about the Soviet Union. Received international publicity. Threatened by the KGB, left the USSR in 1977, and settled with her husband in the USA. Works: *Bor'ba V Kremle: Ot Andropova Do Gorbacheva*, NY-Jerusalem-Paris, 1986.

Kleshchev, Aleksei Efimovich
1905–1968. Major-general, politician.
Joined the Bolshevik Party, 1928. During WWII, one of the organizers of partisan detachments in Belorussia near Pinsk. 1st Secretary of Pinsk obkom, 1944, and of Polotsk obkom, 1946. Prime Minister of Belorussia, 1948–53. 1st Secretary of Kokchetav obkom, 1955–60.

Kliachkin, Rafail
1905–28.5.1987. Actor.
Born in the Ukraine. At the age of 7, went with his parents to Palestine. On finishing school there, went back to Russia. Returned to Tel-Aviv in 1921. Worked there as a labourer and a baker's apprentice. In 1924, entered the Teatron Eretz Iisrael (Palestine Theatre) working closely with its founder Menahem Gessin. In 1928, made his debut with the Habimah which had been originally formed in Moscow in 1917 for the production of plays in Hebrew. Minor part in the 1928 revival of the Evgenii Vakhtangov Theatre production of *The*

Dybbuk in Moscow. Went on the company's international tours. The group visited Britain 3 times and appeared in the first BBC TV transmission of *The Dybbuk* from Alexandra Palace in 1937. Appeared in Sir Peter Daubeny's World Theatre Season, 1965. Died in Israel.

Klim, Romuald Iosifovich
3.5.1933–   . Athlete.
Born in the village of Khvoevo, Minsk Oblast'. Honoured Master of Sports (track and field athletics), 1964. With Vitebsk Krasnoe Znamia, 1964, then with the Minsk Sports Club of the Armed Forces. Graduated from the Belorussian Institute of Physical Culture, 1956. USSR champion, 1966–68, and 1971. Olympic champion, 1964. European champion, 1966. World record holder, 1969. Silver medal, 1968.
See: V. Veltner, *Belorusskie Olimpiitsy*, Minsk, 1978.

Klimenko, Iurii Viktorovich
24.3.1944–   . Cameraman.
Graduated from the VGIK, 1976. His film, *Chelovek Ukhodit Za Ptitsami*, 1976, won a prize at the Venice Film Festival.

Klimenko, Viktor Iakovlevich
25.2.1949–   . Athlete.
Born in Moscow. Honoured Master of Sports (gymnastics), 1971. With the Central Sports Club of the Army. Member of the CPSU, 1976. Graduated from the Moscow Oblast' Pedagogical Institute, 1972. USSR champion, 1967–72. European champion, 1969, 1971 and 1973. Olympic champion, 1972. Overall USSR champion, 1974. Bronze medal, 1968. Silver medal, 1972.

Klimentova, Maria Nikolaevna (m. Muromtseva)
1857–1946. Singer (soprano).
Born in the Kurskaia Gouvt. Pupil of Giacomo Galvani. Soloist with the Bolshoi Theatre, Moscow, 1880–89. Later taught singing. Emigrated about 1920. Died in Paris.

Klimov, Aleksandr Ignat'evich
12.9.1898–   . Conductor.
Born in Kustanai, Kazakhstan. Pupil of V. Berdiaev. Conductor from 1929. Chief conductor with the Kiev Theatre of Opera and Ballet, 1954–61. Chief conductor with the Kirov Theatre of Opera and Ballet, Leningrad, from 1961.

Klimov, Elem Germanovich
9.7.1933–   . Film director, head of the Film-makers Union.
Came to the film industry from science. Originally graduated as an aviation engineer. Later graduated from the VGIK. Acquired a reputation for his satirical short films when he was a film student — *Careful Banality, Look, The Sky*, etc. His children's film (for adults) *Welcome*, 1964, became a classic. His second full-length film, *Adventures of a Dentist*, 1967, confirmed his reputation as a master of satire. Neither film was widely distributed because they annoyed the authorities with their criticism of Soviet bureaucracy (both are transparent allegories on the way of life in the USSR). His next film, *Agoniia* (Agony), about Rasputin and the last years before the revolution, took him nearly 20 years to make. The film was ready in 1975 but was released only in 1985, having been distributed abroad the previous year to test reaction. It made a sensation both abroad and in the USSR with its subject-matter, which had previously been regarded as taboo, and with its sympathetic treatment of Nicholas II. *Agoniia* was a major box office hit in 1985–87. His film *Farewell to Matera* is based on V. Rasputin's story, and was started by his wife Larissa Shepitko, who died (together with her 7 crew) in a car crash during the shooting. Supplemented the film with short sequel, *Larissa*, in her memory. He was unanimously elected General Secretary of the Film-makers Union (practically the head of the Soviet film industry) and released all the films which had been shelved in the previous 30 years (literally hundreds, including all his own films). This had been made possible thanks to the historic Congress of the Film-makers' Union in May 1986, which had shifted the decision-making role from the bureaucrats and censors to the film-makers.
See: Jeanne Vronskaya, *Young Soviet Film-makers*, London, 1972, and 'Down the Drain: Anatoly Kuznetsov's Struggle with the Soviet Censors', 'Sergei Paradzhanov', and '51 Suppressed Films', *Index on Censorship*, Vol. 10, No. 4, Aug. 1981.

Klimov, Iurii Mikhailovich
22.7.1940–   . Athlete.
Born in Ukhta, Komi ASSR. Graduated from Leningrad Polytechnical Institute, 1965. Honoured Master of Sports (handball), 1973. With Moscow Burevestnik. Works as an engineer. USSR champion, 1965–75. Olympic champion, 1976. Member of the CPSU, 1976.

Klimov, Mikhail Georgievich
21.10.1881–20.2.1937. Choir conductor.
Born in the Moscow Gouvt. Assistant conductor, 1902, chief conductor of the Leningrad Academic Choir (formerly the Court Choir), 1913–37. Taught at the Petersburg Conservatory. Professor from 1916. Died in Leningrad.

Klimov, Valerii Aleksandrovich
16.10.1931–   . Violinist.
Born in Kiev. Son of A. I. Klimov. Pupil of David Oistrakh. 1st prize at the I. Slavik and F. Ondříček International Competition, Prague, 1956, and at the P. Tchaikovskii Competition, Moscow, 1958.

Klimov, Vladimir Iakovlevich
1892–1962. Aircraft engine designer.
Graduated from the Moscow Higher Technical School, 1918. Chief designer of aircraft engines, 1935. After WWII, designed jet engines for Soviet planes. Academician, 1953. Many state awards.

Klimova, Natal'ia Genrikhovna (Nazemblo)
31.5.1951–   . Athlete.
Born in Zhdanov, Donetsk Oblast'. Honoured Master of Sports (basketball), 1975. With Kiev Dynamo. European champion, 1972–76. World champion, 1971 and 1975. Olympic champion, 1976. Graduated from the Kiev Institute of Physical Culture, 1977. Sports instructor.

Kliuchnikov, Iurii Veniaminovich
1886–1938. Lawyer, politician.
Before 1917, lecturer in law at Moscow University. Articles printed in the newspaper *Russkoe Slovo*. After the Bolshevik take-over in October 1917, participated in the Iaroslavl' anti-Bolshevik uprising, and after its suppression, fled to Siberia. Minister of Foreign Affairs in Admiral Kolchak's government. Emigrated. In Paris, joined the Cadet Party, 1919. Soon changed his position and became a leader of smenovekhovtsy, preaching a positive re-appraisal of Bolshevik power. Edited the Paris weekly *Smena vekh*, 1921–22. Moved to Berlin, founded the pro-Soviet newspaper *Nakanune*, 1921. On Lenin's suggestion, was included as an expert on international law in the Soviet delegation to the Genoa conference. Made a trip to the USSR, 1922, and was offered the chair of international law at Moscow University. With other smenovekhovtsy, like Aleksei Tolstoi, returned to the Soviet Union in Aug. 1923. Appointed head of the department of international politics of the Communist Academy, 1923. Arrested and perished in the Gulag during Stalin's purges. Circumstances of his death are unknown.

Kliuev, Leonid Lavrovich
1880–1943. Lt.-general.
Graduated from the Academy of the General Staff, 1914. On active service during WWI as a lt.-colonel. During the Civil War, in the Red Army. Chief-of-staff of the Southern front, 1918–19, and of the 1st Cavalry, 1920–21. Thereafter, professor at military educational establishments. Professor at the Military Academy, 1933.

Kliuev, Nikolai Alekseevich
1884–1937. Poet.
Born in the village of Koshtug, Olonetskaia Gouvt. Son of a peasant. His mother was a talented folk singer. Moved with his parents to Vytegra, 1896. Studied at the Petrozavodsk Medical School, but after 1 year gave up his studies due to ill health. Grew up among Old Believers, guardians of old Russian traditions. Became involved in revolutionary propaganda work. First poems prin-
ted in 1904, but gained wider fame after the publication of his first collections in 1911–12. Became the voice of rural Northern Russia with his very original poetry full of traditional folk motifs. All his life during visits to cities, he would play the simple peasant, though in fact he was very well informed in modern culture and knew several foreign languages. In 1915, discovered another poet from a similar background, Esenin, and became his tutor. Welcomed the revolution of 1917 as a realization of the traditional peasant dream of universal justice. Joined the Communist Party, 1918, and started to write revolutionary verse, but soon became disillusioned. His first disagreements with the new rulers in the early 1920s were connected with the religious character of his poetry. Later, during the collectivization, he was accused of being 'the bard of the kulak' and was arrested. Died as a Gulag inmate, building rail-roads in Siberia. For decades his name was banned in Soviet literature, but in recent years he has found his rightful place as one of the genuinely original representatives of the Silver Age of Russian poetry.

Kliuzner, Boris Lazarevich
1.6.1909– . Composer.
Born in Astrakhan'. Moved to Leningrad. From 1961 in Moscow. Author of 2 symphonies, 3 overtures, concertos for orchestra and piano, and for violin, concerto for violin and cello, sonatas, romances, and music for films.

Klochkov-Diev, Vasilii Georgievich
1911–1941. Political commissar.
Joined the Bolshevik Party, 1939. Drafted into the army, 1941. According to his official biography, wounded during the battle for Moscow, 1941, and lay down with his grenades under an advancing German tank. To him are attributed the words (which were later extensively used as a slogan): 'Russia is large, but there is nowhere to retreat—Moscow is behind us'.

Klodt, Nikolai Aleksandrovich
1865–1918. Artist.
Born in St. Petersburg into an artistic
family of painters and sculptors. Studied at the Moscow School of Painting, Sculpture and Architecture, 1880–86, under E. Sorokin, V. Makovskii, I. Prianishnikov and V. Polenov. Landscape painter, also stage designer. Main exhibitions: 1889, 1892–95, 1897, MTKH, 1893–96, 1899, 1901, TPKHV, 1894, the 36 Artists, 1901–02, 1902–03, the Union of Russian Artists, 1903–18, 2nd State Exhibition, Moscow, 1918–19. Personal exhibitions: Moscow, Leningrad, 1940.

Klova, Vitautas Iuliono
31.1.1926– . Composer.
Born in Lithuania. Worked in Vil'nius. Wrote operas, 2 symphonic poems, concertos for violin, for piano, and for cello, works for piano, and for violin and piano, choral works, and music for the stage.

Klubov, Aleksandr Fedorovich
1918–1944. Fighter pilot.
Joined the Red Army, 1939. Graduated from the Chuguev Pilots' School, 1940. Distinguished himself during WWII. Died in an air crash. Twice Hero of the Soviet Union.

Klychkov, Sergei Antonovich (Leshenkov)
13.7.1889–21.1.1940. Author, poet.
Born in the village of Dubrovki near Tver'. Son of a shoemaker. Before WWI, became known as one of the talented peasant poets, along with Kliuev and Esenin. In the 1920s, became a well-known prose writer. Used folklore (fairy tale) stylistic methods and created a highly original fantastic world connected with rural Russia. Arrested, 1937, victim of the Gulag.

Kmit, Leonid Aleksandrovich (Aleksei)
9.3.1908–11.3.1982. Actor.
Entered the film industry, 1929. Graduated from the Leningrad Institute of Stage Art, 1931. Best known for his part in the film *Chapaev*, 1934, now a Soviet classic.

Kniagnitskii, Pavel Efimovich
1884–1938. Military commander.
Took part in WWI. Joined the Red

Army during the Civil War. Commander of an armoured train. Commander of a division and a corps in the 1930s. Victim of Stalin's purges of the military.

Kniazev, Boris (Kniaseff)
1.7.1900–7.10.1975. Ballet dancer.
Born in Petersburg. Graduated from the Petersburg Theatre School. Pupil of K. Goleizovskii and M. Mordkin. In 1917, emigrated to Bulgaria. Taught in Sofia. Moved to Paris, 1924. From 1921–29 with Diaghilev, then de Basil, and Rene Blum in the Ballets Russes. Partner of Olga Spesivtseva. Taught at the Paris Opera Theatre, 1932–34. In 1937, opened his own ballet school. In 1953, taught at his own ballet school in Lausanne. Head of the International Academy of Choreography in Geneva. Taught in Rome and Athens. See: *Decor and Costume Designs: the Collection of Boris Kniaseff*, London, 1969.

Kniazeva, Ol'ga Nikolaevna
9.8.1954– . Athlete.
Born in Kazan'. Honoured Master of Sports (fencing), 1976. With Kazan' Dynamo. Studied at the Kazan' Financial Economical Institute. World champion, 1974–75, 1977–78. Olympic champion, 1976.

Kniazhinskii, Aleksandr Leonidovich
24.1.1936– . Cameraman.
Graduated from the VGIK, 1960. Shot A. Tarkovskii's film *Stalker*, 1980. His other films include *Ia Rodom Iz Detstva*, 1966, *Ty i Ia*, 1972, *Osen'*, 1975, and *Podranki*, 1977.

Knipper, Lev Konstantinovich
1898–1978? Composer, conductor.
Born in Tbilisi. Private pupil of E. F. Gnesina. Also studied under P. Glier. From 1923, member of the Association of Contemporary Music. Head of the Red Army Orchestra. From 1932, musical instructor at the Osobaia Far East Army (security services). Author of several operas, ballets and symphonies. One of his songs, *Poliushko*, became internationally known (said to be a reworking of a White Army song).

Knushevitskii, Sviatoslav Nikolaevich
6.1.1908–19.2.1963. Cellist.
Born in Saratov Gouvt. Brother of the composer and conductor, Viktor Knushevitskii. Pupil of S. Kozolupov. Professor at the Moscow Conservatory. Member of a trio (with Lev Oborin and David Oistrakh). Stalin Prize, 1950. Among his pupils was M. Khomitser. Died in Moscow.

Kobakhidze, Mikhail Germanovich
5.4.1939– . Director.
One of the greatest talents of Georgian cinema. A descendant of one of the greatest Georgian classical writers, Ilia Chavchavadze. Graduated from the Moscow VGIK as a director in 1958. Specializes in aesthetic featurettes of up to 30 minutes. His short films are delicate in form and symbolic in character. First short film, *The Wedding*, 1965, won the Grand Prix at Oberhausen Film Festival in Germany. *The Umbrella*, 1967, a comical pantomime won the Grand Prix at the Cracow Short Film Festival. The 15-minute *Musicians*, 1970, is a mini-masterpiece. Other films: *The Merry-Go-Round*, 1962, *Mikha*, and *The Wide Green Valley*, 1967.

Kobzarev, Iurii Borisovich
1905– . Scientist.
Graduated from the Khar'kov Pedagogical Institute, 1926. Later specialized in radar research at institutes in Leningrad and Moscow. Author of scientific works on this subject.

Kochergina, Tatiana Ivanovna (Makarets)
26.3.1956– . Athlete.
Born in Odessa Oblast'. Honoured Master of Sports (handball), 1976. With Kiev Spartak. Studied at the Kiev Institute of Physical Culture. USSR champion, 1972–79. Olympic champion, 1976.

Kocheshkov, Ksenofont Aleksandrovich
12.12.1894–1974? Chemist.
Graduated from Moscow University, 1922. Professor at the university, 1935. Specialist in metallo-organic compounds.

Kochetov, Nikolai Razumnikovich
8.7.1864–3.1.1925. Music critic, composer, conductor.
Born in Oranienbaum. Son of the singer Aleksandra Aleksandrova-Kochetova. Father of the composer Vadim Kochetov. Taught at the Moscow People's Conservatory. Wrote an opera, 2 symphonies, an Arabian suite, concertos for piano and orchestra, pieces for the piano, and for violin and piano, choral works, and a cycle of romances. Died in Moscow.

Kochetov, Vadim Nikolaevich
22.11.1898–31.7.1951. Composer.
Born in Moscow. Son of the composer, critic and conductor, Nikolai Razumnikovich Kochetov. Author of the music for the internationally famous communist song *No Pasarán* (the hymn of the 11th International Brigade in the Spanish Civil War). Also wrote 2 operas for children, orchestral works (e.g. 2 suites of the ballet *Til Eulenspiegel*), chamber ensembles, pieces for piano, choral works, music for the theatre, and for puppet shows, films and radio. Died in Moscow.

Kochina, Pelageia Iakovlevna (Polubarinova-Kochina)
1.5.1899– . Scientist.
Graduated from Petrograd University, 1921. Professor at Leningrad University, 1935. Specialist in ground waters and filtration. Wrote a biography of the 19th century mathematician S. Kovalevskaia.

Kochubei, Ivan Antonovich
1893–1919. Revolutionary.
Took part in WWI on the Caucasian front. After the October Revolution, organized Red Army detachments in the Northern Caucasus. Taken prisoner and shot by the Whites.

Kochurov, Iurii Vladimirovich
25.6.1907–22.5.1952. Composer.
Born in Saratov. Taught at the Leningrad Conservatory. Author of the *Macbeth Symphony*, the prelude *Pamiati Pushkina* for voice and organ, *Sonet Petrarki*, and romances. Finished the restored score of Tchaikovskii's *Voevoda*, the exercises

for voice and piano by Glinka, and the suite *Gore ot Uma* based on the play by Griboedov. Stalin Prize, 1952. Died in Leningrad.

Kogan, Grigorii Mikhailovich
4.7.1901–   . Musicologist, pianist.
Born in Mogilev. Pupil of V. Pukhal'skii. Taught at the Moscow Conservatory, 1926–43 (with interruptions). Professor from 1932. Head of the Department of History and Theory of Piano Playing from 1936. Works: *U Vrat Masterstva*, Moscow, 1958; *O Fortep'iannoi Fakture*, Moscow, 1961; *Rabota Pianista*, Moscow, 1964.

Kogan, Leonid Borisovich
14.11.1924–   . Violinist.
Born in Ekaterinoslav. Husband of the violinist Elizaveta Gilel's. Professor at the Moscow Conservatory. 1st prize at the Queen Elizabeth International Competition, Brussels, 1951.

Kogan, Lev Lazarevich
6.3.1927–   . Composer.
Born in Baku. Composer of ballets, including the first Moldavian ballet, *Sestry* (produced 1959), an opera for children, a sinfonietta, concertos, and arrangements of Jewish songs.

Koka, Evgenii Konstantinovich
15.4.1893–9.1.1954. Composer.
Born in Bessarabia. Author of the children's opera *Fire Bird*, a ballet, 2 symphonies, symphonic poems, fantasies for violin and orchestra, works for string instruments, 2 string quartets, choral works without accompaniment, songs, romances, and music for stage and screen. Died in Kishinev.

Kokha, Iaan Oskarovich (Koha)
17.12.1929–   . Composer.
Born in Estonia. Wrote a ballet, cantatas, orchestral works, a symphony, a symphonic story, symphonic preludes, concerto for piano and orchestra, works for wind instruments, quartet for wind instruments, pieces for piano, violin and piano, choral works, romances, music for children, and music for theatre and radio.

Kokhno, Boris (Kochno)
3.1.1904–   . Ballet impresario.
Educated at the Moscow Lycée. Emigrated, 1920. In 1921, as a young poet, became Diaghilev's secretary. Involved in the management of the Ballets Russes, combining administrative and artistic duties. Became Diaghilev's right-hand man and was in charge of the planning of repertoires for forthcoming seasons. Also wrote libretti for several ballets which were then produced by B. Nizhinskaia and L. Miasin. After Diaghilev's death, became one of the impresarios of Les Ballets Russes de Monte Carlo, 1932–37, with one break in 1933. Wrote several ballets staged by L. Miasin and Balanchine. In 1933, together with Balanchine and V. Dmitriev, founded the company Ballet 33. In 1945, wrote the libretto for *Brodiachie Muzykanty* for Les Ballets des Champs Elysees (disbanded in 1949).
Works: *Le Ballet – Le Ballet en France du XV Siècle à nos Jours*, Paris, 1954; *Diaghilev et les Ballets Russes*, Paris, 1973.

Kokochashvili, Merab Archilovich
21.3.1935–   . Film director, actor.
Joined the Georgia Film Studio. Graduated from the VGIK, 1960. Films include *Mikha*, *Kanikuly*, and *Stranitsy Proshlogo*. As an actor, best remembered for his part in *Ne Goriui* (Cheer Up!), 1969.

Kokoshkin, Fedor Fedorovich
1871–1918. Politician, lawyer.
Born in Kholm, Lublin Gouvt., now Poland. One of the founders and leaders of the Cadet Party. Member of the Cen. Cttee. of the Cadets. Member of the 1st Duma. From July–Aug. 1917, State Controller in the Provisional Government. Arrested, 11 Dec. 1917 by the Bolshevik government, sent to Peter and Paul fortress in Petrograd, transferred to a hospital, 20 Jan. 1918. Murdered in the Petrograd hospital by revolutionary sailors.

Kokovtsov, Vladimir Nikolaevich, Count
1853–1943. Politician, statesman, economist, banker.
Born in Novgorod. Son of a wealthy

landowner. Educated at Aleksandrovskii Lycée, 1872. Served as a civil servant in several ministries including the Ministry of Justice, the Ministry of Internal Affairs and the State Chancellery. During 1904–14 (with one short break), Minister of Finance (under Witte, Goremykin and Stolypin). Prime Minister after Stolypin's assassination, Sept. 1911–Jan. 1914 (retaining the Ministry of Finance). Saw his main aim as maintaining a deficit-free budget. Resigned in Jan. 1914. Held several high posts in banking during WWI. After the October Revolution, emigrated, 1918. Lived in France. Died in Paris. Memoirs: *Iz Moego Proshlogo*. 2 vol, Paris, 1953.

Kol'bin, Gennadii Vasil'evich
1927–   . Politician.
Started as a technical designer, promoted to chief of a technical office, shop superintendent, deputy chief engineer in a plant in Nizhnii Tagil, 1947–59. Graduated from the Ural Polytechnical Institute, 1955. Top party positions, 1959–62. 2nd Secretary of Nizhnii Tagil City Cttee., 1962–64. 1st Secretary, then Secretary, of Sverdlovsk Oblast' Cttee., 1964–71. 2nd Secretary of the Cen. Cttee. and member of the Bureau of the Cen. Cttee. of the Georgian CP, 1975. Candidate member of the Cen. Cttee. of the CPSU, 1975–81. Full member from 1981. Replaced Kunaev as party boss in Kazakhstan SSR, Dec. 1986, in the anti-corruption drive by M. Gorbachev. His appointment was met with demonstrations by Kazakhs in Alma-Ata, protesting against the appointment of a non-Kazakh to the local party leadership.

Kolchak, Aleksandr Vasil'evich
16.11.1874–7.2.1920. Admiral, arctic explorer, Supreme Ruler.
Born in Petersburg, Crimean Tatar. Son of a naval artillery officer. Graduated from the Navy Cadet Corps in 1894. Took part in many long sea voyages, and published scientific reports on them. Participated in Polar expeditions: 1900–02, to the Northern coast of Siberia (Taimyr, Kotelnii, Kolchak island, now Rastorguev), 1903 expedition searching for E. Toll, the leader of a

previous expedition. On active service at Port Arthur during the Russo-Japanese war, as a captain, and later as a fortress battery commander. Wounded, taken prisoner in hospital, returned to Russia from Japan via the USA in 1905. Leader of a group of young naval officers, who helped to reform the Russian navy after the defeat in the Russo-Japanese war. Took part in a new polar expedition in 1909–10 (Bering Straits). After 1914, on active service in the Baltic, specialist in mine barriers. Commander of the fleet in Riga, 1915. Later Commander of the Black Sea fleet. Cleared the Black Sea of Turkish and German vessels, closing the Bosphorus by use of mines. Resigned in June 1917 after disturbances among the sailors and refused to hand over his personal arms. Left the Crimea with the US mission of Admiral Glennon (who was impressed by his expertise on mines and submarines). Left Petrograd through Scandinavia and England to the USA to lecture on his specialist subjects. Returned through Japan, India and China to Manchuria and Siberia. Minister of War of the right-wing socialist Directoria in Omsk from 4 Nov. 1918. After a coup d'etat by right-wing officers and the abolition of the Directoria on 18 Nov. 1918, proclaimed Supreme Ruler of Russia. Recognized by General Denikin as such on 30 May 1919. From Mar–Apr. 1919, reached the summit of his success with his conscripted anti-Bolshevik army, making a quick military offensive, and seizing large gold reserves (the State reserves, taken 7 Aug. 1918 in Kazan by the Komuch and Czechs, and later kept in trust by the Directoria and Kolchak). By autumn 1919, after a strong counter-attack by the Red Army, suffered a complete military collapse. By order of the Allied Mission head, the French general, Janin, handed over by the Czechs to the SRs and Mensheviks in Irkutsk on 15 Jan. 1920. Transferred to the Bolsheviks, sentenced to death and shot on 7 Feb. 1920.
Main source: published texts of the Kolchak interrogation by his captors.

Kolchin, Pavel Konstantinovich
9.1.1929–   . Athlete.
Born in Iaroslavl'. Honoured Master of Sports (skiing), 1956. Member of the CPSU, 1962. With Moscow Dynamo. Graduated from the Moscow Institute of Physical Culture, 1968. Honorary coach of the USSR, 1970. USSR champion, 1953–64. Olympic champion (15 and 30 km race), 1956. Author of *O Lyzhakh i o Sebe*, Moscow, 1978 (co-author, A. Kolchina).

Kolchina, Alevtina Pavlovna
11.11.1930–   . Athlete.
Born in Pavlovsk, Perm' Oblast'. Graduated from the Moscow Institute of Physical Culture, 1956. Honoured Master of Sports (skiing), 1958. With Moscow Dynamo. Member of the CPSU, 1962. USSR champion, 1956–67. World champion, 1958–66. Olympic champion, 1964. Silver medal, 1956. Bronze medal, 1964 and 1968. Wife of Pavel Kolchin and co-author of their book, *O Lyzhakh i o Sebe*, Moscow, 1978.

Kol'chinskii, Aleksandr Leonidovich
20.2.1955–   . Athlete.
Born in Kiev. Honoured Master of Sports (wrestling), 1976. With the Kiev Armed Forces Club. Graduated from the Kiev Institute of Physical Culture, 1978. USSR champion, 1974, 1976–78. Olympic champion, 1976 (heavy-weight). World champion, 1978.

Koldunov, Aleksandr Ivanovich
1923–   . Marshal of aviation, military commander.
Served at the front, 1943–45. Joined the Communist Party in 1944. Commander of a fighter aviation regiment, then of a fighter aviation division. Deputy Commander, later Commander of Aviation of Baku Air Defence District, 1st Deputy Commander of Baku Air Defence District, 1952–70. Commander of Moscow Air Defence District, 1970–75. Candidate member of the Cen. Cttee., 1971–76. Full member, 1981. 1st Deputy Commander-in-chief of the USSR Air Defence Forces, 1975–78. Commander-in-chief, 1978. Deputy USSR Minister of Defence, 1978. Head of USSR Air Defences. Fired in June 1987 as a result of the affair of Mathias Rust, a 19-year-old West German pilot who landed his light plane, a Cessna, near the Kremlin in broad daylight. When woken by an aide and told of the event Koldunov replied, 'Next you will be telling me that there are German tanks patrolling on Red Square. You are drunk and I'm going back to bed'.

Kolegaev, Andrei
1887–1937. Revolutionary, politician. Leader of the left-wing SRs. Commissar of Agriculture in the Bolshevik-left SR coalition government, 1917–18. Broke with his party after the left SR revolt in July 1918 and joined the Bolsheviks. Active participant in the Civil War. Liquidated by Stalin.

Kolesnikov, Nikolai Alekseevich
15.3.1952–   . Athlete.
Born in a village in the Tatarskaia ASSR. Honoured Master of Sports (heavy athletics), 1976. With Rostov-na-Donu Trud. From 1977, with Bugul'ma Trud. Graduated from the Moscow Institute of Physical Culture, 1977. USSR champion, 1975, 1977–79. European champion, 1976–79. World champion, 1976–78. Olympic champion, 1976.

Kolesov, Anatolii Ivanovich
18.1.1938–   Athlete, sports official.
Born in the Karaganda Oblast', Kazakh SSR. Graduated from the Kazakh Institute of Physical Culture, 1958. Honoured Master of Sports, (wrestling) 1963. Member of the CPSU, 1964. USSR member of the Presidium of the Olympic Committee from 1969. Deputy chairman of the USSR Sports Committee from 1969. Honoured Sports Instructor of the USSR, 1972. USSR champion, 1959 and 1964. World champion (wrestling), 1962–63, and 1965. Olympic champion, 1964. Chief coach of the USSR international wrestling team. See: D. Ivanov, *Anatolii Kolesov. Eto I Est' Bor'ba*, Moscow, 1975.

Kolessa, Filaret Mikhailovich
17.7.1871–3.3.1947. Musicologist, folklorist, composer, literary critic. Born in L'vov Oblast'. Father of the composer Nikolai Kolessa. Member of the Academy of Sciences of the

Ukrainian SSR, 1929. Professor at the I. Franko University, L'vov. Director of the L'vov branch of the Institute of History of Art, Folklore and Ethnography attached to the Academy of Sciences of the Ukrainian SSR. Author of works on Ukrainian and Slav folklore, and choral works with words by T. Shevchenko. Several works in Ukrainian on Ukrainian folk music. Died in L'vov.

Kolessa, Nikolai Filaretovich
1.1.1904– . Composer, conductor.
Born in Sambor, Galicia. Son of the musicologist and composer Filaret Kolessa. Professor at and director of the L'vov Conservatory. Among his pupils were S. Turchak and Iu. Lutsiv. Wrote orchestral works, 2 symphonies, a suite, a piano quartet, pieces for piano, choral works, and music for the stage.

Koliada, Nikolai Terent'evich
4.4.1907–30.7.1935. Composer.
Born in Poltava Gouvt. Wrote a poem for voices and symphony, a suite, a piano quintet, works for piano, violin and piano, romances, songs for children, arrangement of folk songs and music for films. Died while climbing in the Caucasus.

Kollontai, Aleksandra Mikhailovna (b. Domontovich)
31.3.1872–9.3.1952. Revolutionary, feminist, diplomat.
Born in Petersburg. Daughter of a general. Married to escape parental discipline. Joined the revolutionary movement in the 1890s. Bolshevik, 1904–05, later Menshevik until 1915, and again Bolshevik. Lived abroad, 1908–17, taking an active part in the social-democratic movement in Europe. Member of the International Bureau of Women Socialists. Returned to Russia after the February Revolution in 1917. During WWI, close to Lenin, helping him to set up an international Bolshevik branch. After her return, became a great success as an orator, addressing revolutionary soldiers, sailors and crowds, preaching political radicalism and free love. In July 1917, arrested with other Bolsheviks after an un-

successful attempt to seize power. After the October Revolution 1917, Commissar for Social Security in the first Soviet government. Resigned after Brest-Litovsk, disapproving of the peace treaties. Leader of the left-wing Bolsheviks in 1918, later returned to the general line of the party. In charge of the womens' department of the Cen. Cttee. in 1920. Head of the International Womens' Secretariat of the Comintern, 1921–22. From 1923, embarked on a diplomatic career. Soviet Ambassador in Norway, 1923–26 and 1927–30, Mexico, 1926–27 and Sweden, 1930–45. Died in Moscow.

Kolmanovskii, Eduard Savel'evich
9.1.1923– . Composer.
Born in Mogilev. Author of a musical comedy, suites for voices and symphony orchestra (based on music for Shakespeare's *Twelfth Night*), a concerto for alto with orchestra, choral works, romances, and music for stage and screen.

Kolmogorov, Andrei Nikolaevich
25.4.1903–20.10.1987. Mathematician.
Born in Tambov. Graduated from Moscow University, 1925. Professor, 1931. Held the chair of theory of probability from 1937 at Moscow University. His book *Foundations of the Calculus of Probabilities* was published in 1933 in German. Simultaneously with, and independently from, Norbert Wiener, developed the theory of the smoothing and prediction of stationary time-theories. Academician, 1939. During WWII, worked in many branches of science, such as the birth and death processes of plants, and genetic processes. The results brought him into serious conflict with Lysenko, who dominated in this area. Made a very important contribution to research into turbulence. This work was published in English in 1941 by the Academy of Sciences of the USSR and delivered to English libraries during the war. His greatest contribution came in 1954 when he demonstrated that a large set of nested toroidal (ring-shaped or tori) surfaces survived perturbation. This led to a breakthrough in the study of general Hamiltonian systems in which the

K.A.M. tori (named after Kolmogorov and his two pupils, V. Arnold and J. Moser) played a pivotal role. Was known as a generous Russian host who wined and dined the international set of mathematicians at his magnificent country house not far from Moscow. One of the greatest mathematicians of the 20th century. Wrote on the theory of probability, theory of functions, mathematical logic, functional analyses and other subjects. Died in Moscow.
See: *The Times*, 22 Oct. 1987.

Kolodub, Lev Nikolaevich
1.5.1930– . Composer.
Born in Kiev. Author of symphonies, a Ukrainian-Carpathian rhapsody, and works for choir and orchestra.

Kolomiitsev, Viktor Pavlovich
7.12.1868–26.6.1936. Music critic, translator.
Born in Petersburg. Translated into Russian, in identical rhythms, the operas and musical dramas of Wagner, the operas of Glück, Boieldieu, Gounod, and Bizet and the texts of several romances by foreign composers. Died in Leningrad.

Kolotilova, Antonina Iakovlevna
4.4.1890–6.7.1962. Singer of Russian folk songs.
Born in Velikii Ustiug in Vologda Gouvt. Organizer and artistic director of the Russian State Choir of Northern Songs. Author of the collection *Severnye Russkie Narodnye Pesni*, 1936. Stalin Prize, 1949. Died in Arkhangelsk.

Kolpakchi, Vladimir Iakovlevich
1899–1961. General.
Joined the Red Army and the Communist Party, 1918. Took part in the Civil War. Graduated from the Frunze Military Academy, 1928. During the Spanish Civil War, sent to help the communists, 1936–38. During WWII, held several high staff positions. Worked in the Ministry of Defence, 1956. Head of ground forces training. Died in an air crash.

Kolpakova, Irina Aleksandrovna
22.5.1933– . Ballerina.
Born in Leningrad. Graduated from

the Leningrad Choreographic School, 1951. Pupil of A. Vaganova. Leading dancer with the Kirov Theatre. Two documentary films have been made about her, and she has also appeared in several TV films. Prize at the 3rd International Festival of Dance in Paris, 1965.

Kol'tsov, Mikhail Efimovich (Fridliand)
13.6.1898–4.3.1942 (or 4.4.1942). Journalist, party and state official.
The best known and most influential Soviet journalist and editor of the 1930s. Brother of the Stalinist press caricaturist, Boris Efimov. Born in Kiev, the son of a Jewish artisan. First publications in 1916. Member of the CPSU from 1918. Active participant in both the February and October Revolutions. Joined *Pravda* as a reporter. Became a satirical writer, but soon realised the danger of this profession in Stalin's Soviet Union. Sent as *Pravda* correspondent to the Spanish Civil War, 1936–37, but had in fact more important functions, including direct connections with the security services. Founder and one of the most powerful editors of the mass illustrated weekly *Ogonek*, the satirical magazine *Krokodil, Chudak* and a chain of other minor publications. Had close links with the fearful security chiefs, Genrikh Iagoda and Nikolai Ezhov. Took part in GPU/NKVD provocations. For some time a favourite of Stalin himself, but later recalled from Spain and sent to the Gulag. Exact circumstances of his death are still unknown.

Komar, Vitalii Anatol'evich
1943– . Artist.
Born in Moscow. Graduated from the Stroganov Art School. Became active in unofficial art circles. Left the USSR in 1977 for Israel. Later settled in the USA. Has worked with Aleksandr Melamid in the field of political collage, and has staged a number of exhibitions which have attracted a lot of attention from the Western press. Published his theoretical views on political art in *A-IA*, the magazine of unofficial Russian art, published in Paris, (editor I. Shelkovskii). Lives in New York.

Komarov, Vladimir Mikhailovich
1927–1967. Cosmonaut.
Born in Moscow. Joined the Soviet army, 1945. Graduated from the Zhukovskii Air Force Academy, 1959. First Soviet cosmonaut to make a second space flight. Cosmic flights on Voskhod, 1964, and Soyuz-1, Apr. 1967. On its return to earth, Soyuz-1 burnt up in the Earth's atmosphere, killing the crew. Twice Hero of the Soviet Union.

Komarovskii, Aleksandr Nikolaevich
1906–1973. General, state security official.
Graduated from the Moscow Institute of Transport Engineering, 1928. In the 1930s, directed the construction of the Moscow-Volga canal. Deputy Minister of the Merchant Navy, and later Deputy Minister of Construction. Chief of the Construction Department of the NKVD. During WWII, in charge of military construction resources in the Ministry of Defence. Head of Glavpromstroi (industrial construction), 1944, and other organizations which freely used slave labour during the Stalin years. Hero of Socialist Labour, 1949.

Komissarzhevskii, Fedor Fedorovich (Komissarjevsky, Theodore)
1882–1954. Stage director.
Brother of V. Komissarzhevskaia. Became prominent as a stage director and theoretician of the theatre. Emigrated, 1919, and settled in the USA. Opened an actors' school. Author of various works on the theatre, including *The Theatre and a Changing Civilisation*, London, 1935.

Komitas (real name – Sogomonian, Sogomon Gevorkovich)
8.10.1869–22.10.1935. Composer, musicologist, conductor, singer, impresario.
Born in Turkey. Armenian by nationality. Founder of classical Armenian polyphony and scientific Armenian musical ethnography. Known for his choral arrangements of folk songs. Recorded over 3000 songs, about 500 of which have been preserved. Main activity near Erevan. Head of music classes and the choir at the Theological Academy. Moved to Constantinople following conflict with the church, 1910. Suffered from a psychiatric illness for the last 20 years of his life. Died in Paris. He influenced several generations of Armenian composers.

Komnatov, Gennadii Viktorovich
18.9 1949–31.3.1979. Athlete.
Born in the village of Zhelannoe, Odessa Raion, Omsk Oblast'. Honoured Master of Sports (cycling), 1972. With Omsk Burevestnik. Graduated from the Omsk Institute of Physical Culture, 1973. USSR champion, 1970–74. Olympic champion, 1972. Died in Omsk. The reason for his premature death remains unexplained.

Kompaneets, Zinovii Lvovich
22.6.1902– . Composer.
Born in Rostov-on-Don. Prolific song writer. Brother of the composer David Lvov-Kompaneets. In Moscow from the 1930s. Wrote symphonic compositions, works for string instruments, concertos for violin and cello, a string trio, pieces for piano and for violin, choral works, songs, and music for the variety stage.

Kon, Igor
1938– . Professor of sexology.
Published in Moscow in 1988 the first study of sex in the Soviet Union, which includes subjects such as homosexuality which were previously taboo. The book was ready for publication 10 years earlier but was not allowed to be printed. It is available only to medical workers and the like. Compares the attitudes to sex in the USSR with that in Victorian England.
Source: *Introduction to Sexology*, Moscow, 1988.

Konchalovskii, Mikhail Petrovich
1906– . Artist.
Portrait, landscape and still-life painter. Born in Moscow. Son of the artist Petr Konchalovskii. Studied under his father, also at the Moscow VKHUTEIN, 1923–30. Pupil of I. I. Mashkov. Exhibited from 1939 only in Moscow.

Konchalovskii, Petr Petrovich
1876–1956. Artist.
Born in Slaviansk (now Don Oblast').

191

Portrait, landscape, still-life painter, stage designer. Studied at the M. Raevskaia-Ivanova Art School, Kharkov, then at the Stroganov Central School of Graphic Art, Moscow, under V. Sukhov. Also studied at the R. Julien Academy, Paris, 1896–98, under J.-P. Lorain and J. Benjamin-Constant, then at the Petersburg Academy of Arts, 1898–1905, under I. Tvorozhikov, V. Savitskii and G. Zaleman. Pupil of P. Kovalevskii. Graduated in 1907. One of the founders of the Bubnovyi Valet Society. Taught at Moscow, 1918–21, then at the VKHUTEIN, 1926–29. Exhibitions: from 1903, including the Zolotoe Runo, 1909–10, the Mir Iskusstva, 1911–22, the Bubnovyi Valet, 1912–14. Academician, 1947. Personal exhibitions: from 1922, all in Moscow.

Kondakov, Nikodim Pavlovich
1844–1925. Art scholar, authority on icons.
Professor at Novorossiisk University, 1870–1919. Emigrated after the October Revolution 1917. Professor at Sofia University, 1920–23, and at Prague University, 1923–25. Considered the foremost authority on icons in the world.
Main works: *Reminiscences and Thoughts*; *Russian Icon*; *History of Medieval Art and Culture*, 2 vol.

Kondrashin, Kirill Petrovich
6.3.1914–7.3.1981. Conductor.
Born in Moscow. Pupil of B. Khaikin. Conducted operas in Moscow and Leningrad from 1934. With the Bolshoi Theatre from 1943. Conducted symphonic works only from 1956. Head of the symphony orchestra of the Moscow Philharmonic from 1960. In 1978, during a tour abroad, asked for political asylum in Holland. Died in Amsterdam from heart failure.

Kondrat'ev Nikolai Dmitrievich
1892–1936? Economist.
Member of the SR Party, 1917–19. Deputy Minister of Food in the Provisional Government, 1917. Professor at the Moscow Agricultural Academy. Founder and first director of the Moscow Kon'iunkturnyi Insti-

tute, 1920–28. One of the authors of the first five year plan for agriculture 1923–24. Defended private agriculture and criticized the government's economic planning. Accused of 'right deviation', and arrested in late 1930. Witness at the Menshevik trial, 1931. One of the first senior economists to perish in the Gulag. Known for his work on economic cycles: formulated his general thesis in *The World Economy and Economic Fluctuations in the War and Post-War Periods*, 1922, and *Major Economic Cycles*, 1928, both in Russian, the latter translated into English as *The Long Wave Cycle*. Identified 3 long cycles of economic expansion and contraction occuring roughly from 1790 to 1844–51, 1844–51 to 1890–96, and 1890–96 onwards (average duration about 50 years). His theory was greeted in the USSR as 'wrong and reactionary' while Joseph Schumpeter, Arthur F. Burns and Wesley C. Mitchell gave it serious consideration. It is occasionally cited as applicable to present conditions.
Sources: Vincent J. Tarascio, *Encyclopedia Americana, Who's Who in Economics*. See also: N. Jasny, *Soviet Economists of the 1920s: Names to be Remembered*.

Kondrat'ev, Sergei Aleksandrovich
8.4.1896–1969? Composer, musicologist, folklorist.
Born in Petersburg. Author of an opera, a ballet, cantatas, a quintet for string instruments and clarinet, a string quartet, choral works, vocal ensembles, romances, archaic songs, and music for stage and radio.

Kondrat'ev, Viktor Nikolaevich
1.2.1902–   . Chemist.
Graduated from the Leningrad Polytechnical Institute, 1924. Academician 1953. Worked on chemical kinetics, molecular spectroscopy and photochemistry. Prominent member of the International Union of Pure and Applied Chemistry.

Kondratov, Iurii Grigor'evich
6.2.1921–14.7.1967. Ballet dancer.
Born in Moscow. Graduated from the Moscow Choreographic School, 1940. Leading dancer with the Bolshoi Theatre. Partner of Galina

Ulanova, Olga Lepeshinskaia and Maia Plisetskaia. Ballet teacher from 1942. Artistic director of the Moscow Choreographic School, 1959–64. From 1964, artistic director of the Ballet on Ice Ensemble. Performed all over the Soviet Union and abroad. Died in Moscow.

Konenkov, Sergei Timofeevich
10.7.1874–9.10.1971. Sculptor.
Born in the village of Karakovichi, Smolensk Oblast'. Son of a rich peasant. From 1892–96, studied at the Moscow School of Painting, Sculpture and Architecture under S. Ivanov and S. Volnukhin. From 1899–1902, studied at the Petersburg Academy of Arts (corresponding member, 1916). Member of the Mir Iskusstva group and of the Union of Russian Artists. His first sculpture was *Kamneboets*, 1898, one copy of which was bought by the Moscow Sokolnicheskii Museum, the other in bronze was bought privately. After the October Revolution 1917, contributed to the 'monumental propaganda' ordered by the Soviet government. In 1924, emigrated and lived until 1945 in the USA. After WWII, returned to the Soviet Union. Honorary member of the USSR Academy of Arts, 1954. People's Artist, 1958. Was proclaimed a father figure of socialist realism in sculpture. Died in Moscow.

Konev, Anatolii
1921–9.11.1965. Athlete
Many times USSR basketball champion. Honoured Master of Sports. Silver medal-winner at the XVth Olympic Games.

Konev, Ivan Stepanovich
28.12.1897–21.5.1973. Marshal.
Joined the Red Army and the Communist Party, 1918. Took part in the Civil War, commander of an armoured train, infantry brigade, and later division. In the 1930s, held several high military and political army appointments. During WWII, one of the more successful Soviet commanders. At the end of WWII, directed the Soviet thrust into Hungary and Czechoslovakia. Commander of Soviet ground forces, 1946–50 and 1955–56, and First Deputy

Minister of Defence. Commander of the Warsaw Pact forces, 1956. Commander of Soviet forces in East Germany, 1961–62. Long-serving member of the Cen. Cttee. of the CPSU, 1952–73. Twice Hero of the Soviet Union. Represented the Soviet Union at the funeral of W. Churchill in London.

Koni, Anatolii Fedorovich
9.2.1844–17.9.1927. Lawyer, judge, author.
Born in Petersburg. Son of the dramatist Fedor Koni. Graduated from Moscow University in law, 1865. Judge, later senator of the criminal cassation department of the Senate. Appointed member of the State Council, 1906. Was the presiding judge at the trial of the revolutionary Vera Zasulich. After this case, in 1872, became an instant celebrity with the liberal intelligentsia. His pleas and summing-ups made him one of the best-known judges in Russia. After the October Revolution 1917, professor of law at Petrograd University, 1918–22. In his old age turned to writing. His memoirs, *Na Zhiznennom Puti*, 5 vol., give a panorama of the cultural scene in Russia during the 60 years of his activity. Knew many celebrated figures in literature and the arts. Died in Leningrad.

Konius, Georgii Eduardovich
13.10.1862–28.8.1933. Music scholar, composer.
Born in Moscow. Brother of the violinist and composer Iulii Konius (1869–1942). Professor at the Moscow Conservatory. Among his pupils were S. Vasilenko, A. Gedike, R. Glier, A. Goldenveizer, N. Metner, and A. Skriabin. Author of a ballet, a choral symphony, a suite for orchestra and choir, pieces for piano and violin, and romances. Died in Moscow.

Konius, Natal'ia Georgievna
2.7.1914–   . Ballet dancer.
Born in Moscow. Daughter of G. Konius. Graduated from the Moscow Choreographic School, 1931. Joined I. Rubenstein's company and the Ballets Russes de Monte Carlo, 1931–32. Returned from France to the USSR. Leading ballerina with the

Bolshoi Theatre until 1943. With the Stanislavskii and Nemirovich Danchenko Theatre from 1943–60. From 1960, choreographer and teacher. From 1964, taught at the GITIS, Moscow.

Konobeevskii, Sergei Tikhonovich
26.4.1890–26.11.1970. Physicist.
Born in Petersburg. Graduated from Moscow University, 1913. Professor at the University, 1935. Specialist in the aging of alloys, decomposition of solid solutions and the effect of radiation on materials. Died in Moscow.

Kononov, Ivan Nikitich
1907?–1946. Major-general.
A Don Cossack. Member of the Communist Party, 1927. Graduated from the Military Academy, 1930. Took part in the Soviet-Finnish war, decorated for bravery (Order of the Red Banner). Took part in WWII as a major. On 22 Aug. 1941, volunteered to join the Germans in order to fight Stalin with his whole regiment. Later organized a Cossack corps on the side of the Germans, and became the commander of Cossack detachments of the ROA (Vlasov's army). In 1945, handed over to SMERSH, tried and executed. A 2-vol. biography was published in Australia in 1963 by his adjutant K. Cherkassov.

Konovalenko, Viktor Sergeevich
11.3.1938–   . Athlete.
Born in Gorkii. Honoured Master of Sports (hockey), 1963. With Gorkii Torpedo. Coach. Graduated from the Leningrad Institute of Physical Culture, 1969. Goal-keeper with the USSR International team, 1961–71. European champion, 1963–68, and 1970. World champion, 1963–68, 1970–71. Olympic champion, 1964 and 1968.
See: M. Marin, *Konovalenko Bez Maski. Eto Khokkei*, Moscow, 1971.

Konovalets, Evgenii
1891–23.5.1938. Ukrainian nationalist leader.
Born near Lvov (then Austro-Hungary). During WWI, conscripted into the Austrian army as a lieutenant. POW in Russia, 1915. During the

Civil War, organized the core of Ukrainian nationalist forces from former POWs in Russia (Sich riflemen), supporter of Petliura. After the Civil War, interned with his corps in Poland. Organized the Ukrainian underground partisan movement, 1921–23, which was most active in Western Ukraine (at that time Poland). After Petliura's death, became the leading Ukrainian leader. Killed in Rotterdam by a parcel bomb delivered by a GPU secret agent pretending to be an underground courier from the Ukraine.

Konovalov, Aleksandr Ivanovich
1875–1948. Businessman, politician.
Born into the family of a rich textile factory owner. Educated in England. One of the founders of the Russian Union of Trade and Industry. Prominent member of the military industrial committees, close to Guchkov. Member of the 4th Duma, representing the progressivist faction (to the left of the Cadets). His factories were known for their excellent working conditions (own hospitals, and so on). Minister of Trade and Industry in the Provisional Government and Deputy Prime Minister to Kerenskii. Joined the Cadets, Aug. 1917. Financed the newspaper *Utro Rossii*. During the October Revolution, in Kerenskii's absence, head of the group of ministers of the Provisional Government. Arrested by the Bolsheviks after the storming of the Winter Palace, 7 Nov. 1917. Released soon thereafter. Emigrated to France. Business manager of Miliukov's newspaper *Poslednie Novosti* in Paris. Chairman of *Zemgor*. Spent his last years in absolute poverty. Died in France.

Konstantin (Zaitsev, Kiril), Archimandrite
1886–   . Russian Orthodox clergyman.
Educated as an economist and lawyer. Left Russia during the Civil War. Well-known publicist in the Russian refugee press. Became a lecturer at the Russian law faculty in Prague. Moved to the Far East. Dean of the Russian Pedagogical Institute at Harbin (a city with a Russian majority in China). Became a monk.

Moved to the USA. Lived at the Jordanville monastery of the Russian Church in Exile, whose active spokesman he became. Died in Jordanville Main works: *Das Recht Sowjetrusslands, Ethics*, 2 vols, *The Orthodox Church in Soviet Russia, The Mystery of the Last Tsar.*

Konstantinov, Anatolii Ustinovich
1923–   . Marshal.
Joined the Soviet Army in 1940. Pilot, squadron commander, 1941–45. In 1943, joined the Communist Party. Regiment commander, 1952–56. Graduated from the Moscow Military Academy of the General Staff in 1964. Col.-general of the air force. Marshal. Commanding posts, 1956–73. Commander of the Air Defence Districts (PVO) of Baku, then Moscow, 1980. Removed from his post together with 4 others as a result of the landing of a private plane in Red Square on 28 May 1987 by the West German teenager, Mathias Rust.

Konstantinov, Dimitrii
21.3.1908–   . Russian Orthodox clergyman.
Born in Petersburg. Graduated from the Pedagogical Institute in Leningrad, 1927, and the Publishing Institute, Leningrad, 1930. Involved in religious work, openly until 1930, clandestinely later, when he worked officially as a Soviet journalist. During WWII, on active service. POW in Germany. After the war in DP camps. Active in the Russian emigré press in Germany. Priest, 1945. Moved to Argentina, 1949–60. Archpriest, 1955. From 1960, has lived in the USA. Has written a number of books and many articles on the situation of the Russian Orthodox Church and believers in general under communist rule in the USSR.

Konstantinov, Vitalii Viktorovich
28.3.1949–   . Athlete.
Born in Ulianovskaia Oblast'. Honoured Master of Sports (wrestling), 1975. With Ulianovsk Dynamo. Graduated from the Volgogradskii Institute of Physical Culture, 1978. World champion, 1975. Olympic champion, 1976 (feather-weight). USSR champion, 1976–77.

Kopelev, Lev Zinov'evich
1912–   . Author.
Born in Kiev. Fanatical communist in his youth, active participant in the collectivization campaign. Graduated from the Moscow Foreign Languages Institute. Specialist in Soviet propaganda in German. Arrested in 1945 for protesting against the barbaric behaviour of the Soviet Army in conquered Germany. Sentenced to 10 years in prison camps. Met A. Solzhenitsyn in a sharashka (KGB-controlled scientific research institute which employs imprisoned scientists from the Gulag). Became the prototype for Rubin, one of the characters in Solzhenitsyn's *The First Circle*. Released in 1954. Through his communist connections, became responsible for Solzhenitsyn's literary fate: it was he who took the manuscript of *Ivan Denisovich* to the editor-in-chief of *Novyi Mir*, A. Tvardovskii. In his own right published books, articles and translations of German writers. From 1966, very active in the human rights movement. Expelled from the Communist Party, then in 1977, from the Union of Writers. Fired from all his jobs, and was unable to publish anything. In Nov. 1980, left the USSR for West Germany with his wife, Raisa Orlova. In 1981, both were stripped of Soviet citizenship.
Works: *Khranit Vechno*, USA, 1976, *I Sotvori Sebe Kumira*, USA, 1978, *Utoli Moia Pechali*, USA, 1981, *O Pravde i Terpimosti*, USA, 1982, *Sviatoi Doktor Fedor Petrovich*, London, 1985.

Koptiaev, Aleksandr Petrovich
12.10.1868–17.1.1941. Music critic, composer.
Born in Petersburg. Author of symphonies, pieces for piano, romances. Literary works: *C. Cui Kak Fortep'iannyi Kompozitor*, Petersburg, 1895, *Putevoditel' K Operam i Muzykal'nym Dramam Vagnera*, Petersburg, 1898, *K Muzykal'nomu Idealu*, Petrograd, 1916, and *Skriabin*, Petrograd, 1916. Died in Leningrad.

Korbut, Olga Valentinovna
16.5.1955–   . Athlete.
Born in Grodno. Honoured Master of Sports (gymnastics), 1972. With the Grodno Armed Forces team.

From 1978, with the Minsk Armed Forces team. Graduated from the Grodno Pedagogical Institute, 1977. USSR champion, 1970, 1974 and 1976. World champion, 1974. Overall USSR champion, 1975. Olympic champion, 1972, and with her team in 1972 and 1976. Silver medals, 1972 and 1976. Became an internationally-known athlete, with a film being made about her in the USSR, and several books being written about her life and career.

Korchmarev, Klimentii Arkad'evich
3.7.1899–7.4.1958. Composer.
Born in Verkhnedneprovsk. One of the first composers to use the Soviet revolution as a theme. Composer of the first national ballets, e.g. *Veselyi Obmanshchik* (produced 1942). Author of 4 operas, 5 ballets, 2 operettas, 3 vocal symphonies, a cantata, works for the variety stage, instrumental pieces, and music for stage and screen. Stalin Prize, 1951. Died in Moscow.

Korchnoi, Viktor Lvovich
1931–   . Chess player.
Born in Leningrad. Became one of the Soviet Union's leading chess players. Defected in 1976 in Holland. Settled in Switzerland. Has been playing since independently. His matches against the official Soviet champion A. Karpov became world famous as duels of political, psychological and physical effort. Fought for many years to bring his family to the West and eventually won. Wrote memoirs: *Antishakhmaty* (introduction by V. Bukovskii), London, 1981.

Koren', Sergei Gavrilovich
6.9.1907–1969. Ballet dancer, choreographer.
Born in Petersburg. Graduated from the Leningrad Choreographic School, 1927. Dancer with the Leningrad Malyi Theatre. Leading dancer with the Leningrad Opera and Ballet Theatre, 1930–42. Leading dancer with the Bolshoi Theatre, 1942–60. Artistic director of several armed forces ensembles, 1950–54. Choreographer with the Bolshoi Theatre, 1960–69. Died in Moscow.

Koreshchenko, Arsenii Nikolaevich
18.12.1870–3.1.1921. Composer, pianist, conductor, music critic.
Born in Moscow. Author of three operas, one of which was *Ledianoi Dom* (produced 1900), a ballet, a lyrical symphony, an Armenian rhapsody, and pieces for piano. Also arranged Armenian and Georgian songs for choir and orchestra. Died in Khar'kov.

Korev, Iurii Semenovich
27.7.1928– . Musicologist, editor.
Born in Moscow. Son of the musicologist Simon Korev. Husband of the musicologist Ekaterina Dobrynina. Deputy editor of the periodical *Sovetskaia Muzyka*. Author of many articles on Soviet musical composition.

Korganov, Vasilii Davidovich
3.2.1865–6.6.1934. Musicologist.
Born in Tiflis. Armenian by nationality. Wrote *Verdi, Biograficheskii Ocherk*, Moscow, 1897, *A. S. Pushkin V Muzyke*, Tiflis, 1899, *Kavkazskaia Muzyka*, Tiflis, 1902, and *Chaikovskii Na Kavkaze*, Erevan, 1940. Died in Erevan.

Koriagin, Anatolii
1939– . Psychiatrist.
Psychiatric doctor who in the mid-1970s worked in a small provincial psychiatric hospital in Poimo-Tinsk, south of Krasnoiarsk in Siberia. Attracted his colleagues' attention by his erudition. In the summer of 1977, deputy chief psychiatrist at Kyzyl Psychiatric Hospital. Refused an order of the KGB to recognize as a 'mental case' an army major who had come into conflict with his superiors. The major was however detained by other less scrupulous doctors, while Koriagin was put onto the KGB black-list. At the end of 1979, became psychiatric adviser to the Moscow branch of the International Association Against the Use of Psychiatry as a Political Weapon (APUP). Moved to Khar'kov in the Ukraine, where he met David Satter, the Moscow correspondent of the *Financial Times*. Became involved in the case of Aleksei Nikitin's arrest. The case was well covered by Satter and others. Pressure was put on the World Psychiatric Association to expel the Soviet Union who pre-empted the decision by resigning in Jan. 1983. Koriagin spent 6 years in very harsh conditions in the camps, often in solitary confinement. His case became a cause for concern for every member country of the WPA. While in detention, his family, including his 75-year-old mother-in-law and 3 sons, were beaten up in the streets and at school. Released in Feb. 1987 from the Perm' labour camp. Arrived in Zurich, Switzerland. 3 times — 1985, 1986 and 1987 — a candidate for the Nobel Peace Prize as a world humanitarian. His book was published early in 1987 in Holland. An annual prize 'for contributions to medical ethics' was named after him.

Koridze, Avtandil Georgievich
15.4.1935–11.4.1966. Athlete.
Born in Tbilisi. Honoured Master of Sports (wrestling), 1960. With Tbilisi Burevestnik. Graduated from the Georgian Polytechnical Institute, 1965. Olympic champion, 1960. World champion, 1961. Died in Tbilisi. Official sources do not give the reason for his premature death.

Korin, Aleksei Mikhailovich
1865–1923. Artist.
Studied at the Moscow School of Painting, Sculpture and Architecture, 1884–89, under V. Makovskii, V. Polenov, E. Sorokin and I. Prianishnikov. Genre painter. Main exhibitions: MOLKH, 1890–94, 1908, 1910, TPKHV, 1891–1900, 1902–10, 1912–14, 1916–18, 1922–23, MTKH, 1893, 1895, All-Russian Exhibition, Nizhnii Novgorod, 1896, 2nd State Exhibition, Moscow, 1918–19. Personal exhibition: (posthumously) Moscow, 1936. Died in Moscow.

Korin, Pavel Dmitrievich
7.7.1892–22.11.1967. Painter.
Born in Palekh. Son of an icon painter. Studied at the Moscow Arts School, 1912–16 (with K. Korovin and S. Maliutin). Friend of M. Nesterov. In the 1920s, worked on a monumental group picture, *Rus' Ukhodiashchaia*. Head of the very active restoration department of the Pushkin Museum in Moscow, 1932–59. In the 1930s, created a series of portraits of famous contemporaries. During WWII, worked on historical and patriotic subjects (Aleksandr Nevskii and others). After the war, with his brother A. Korin, involved in restoration work on paintings from the Dresden Arts Gallery which were removed to the USSR from Germany but later returned. In the 1950s, involved in designing mosaics for the Moscow metro. Died in Moscow.

Kork, Avgust Ivanovich
3.8.1887–11.6.1937. Military commander.
Born in Kazepia, Estonia. Son of a peasant. Educated at Chuguev Infantry School in 1908. Graduated from the Academy of the General Staff in 1914. Lt-colonel during WWI. In June 1918, volunteered for the Red Army. Commander of the 9th Army from Dec. 1918. Consultant to the People's Commissar of the Estonia Workers' Commune. Deputy commander of the 7th Army, Feb. 1919. June 1919–Oct. 1920, commander of the 15th Army defending Petrograd against General Iudenich. Commander of the 6th Army against General Baron Wrangel. 1921–1935 occupied senior army positions in the Ukraine, Crimea, Turkestan, the Caucasus, Belorussia, Leningrad and Moscow districts. Member of the CPSU from 1927. Director of the Frunze Military Academy, 1935–37. Arrested in 1937, tried in secret and shot with Marshal Mikhail Tukhachevskii and 7 other senior officers. Rehabilitated under Khrushchev.

Korkiia, Mikhail Shotaevich
10.9.1948– . Athlete.
Born in Kutaissi. Honoured Master of Sports (basketball), 1972. With Tbilisi Dynamo. Studied at the Tbilisi Polytechnical Institute. USSR champion, 1968. Olympic champion, 1972. Bronze medal, 1976. Member of the CPSU, 1978.

Kormer, Vladimir Fedorovich
1939–1986. Physicist, author.
Born near Novosibirsk. Graduated from the Moscow Physics Engineering Institute. Worked as a computer engineer. Switched to journalism. Editor of *Voprosy Filosofii*. Published many articles in the Soviet press. In

Feb. 1979, emerged as a writer. Received the Vladimir Dal' Literary Prize in Paris for his novel *Krot Istorii*.

Kornblit, Evgenii Mikhailovich
19.9.1908–15.10.1969. Conductor.
Graduated from the Leningrad Conservatory as a conductor, 1936. Conductor with the Leningrad Theatre of Comedy, 1936–41. Chief conductor at the Orenburg Theatre of Musical Comedy, 1941–43. From 1944, conductor at the Leningrad Malyi Theatre. Wrote the music for ballets such as *Korsar* and *Goluboi Dunai*. Died in Leningrad.

Korneichuk, Aleksandr Evdokimovich
25.5.1905–14.5.1972. Playwright.
Born in Khristinovka in the Ukraine. Son of a worker. Made his name by sycophantic panegyrics to the communist leaders. First story devoted to Lenin under the characteristic title *He Was Great*, 1925. Active propagandist of collectivization. Propaganda plays during WWII, including *Front*, much acclaimed at the time. Chairman of the Ukrainian Union of Writers, 1938–41, and 1946–53. Member of the Cen. Cttee. of the CPSU, 1952, Chairman of the Supreme Soviet of the Ukrainian SSR. Remembered as a particularly odious Stalinist figure, his literary achievements are referred to mostly in jokes about Stalinism. Died in Kiev.

Kornienko, Georgii Markovich
1925– . Diplomat, politician.
Member of the CPSU, 1947. Graduated from the Moscow Law Institute, 1953. Began his diplomatic career while still a student in 1949. Chief of a department in the USSR Ministry of Foreign Affairs, 1959–60. Councillor in the USSR Embassy in the USA, 1960–63. Embassy Councillor-Envoy, 1963–65. Chief of the American Department in the Ministry of Foreign Affairs, 1965–78. Deputy USSR Minister from 1977. Deputy to the USSR Supreme Soviet from 1979. Member of the Cen. Cttee. of the CPSU from 1981.

Korniets, Leonid Romanovich
1901–1969. Politician.
Joined the Bolshevik Party, 1926.

Chairman of the Presidium of the Supreme Soviet of the Ukraine (nominal head of state), 1938–39, Prime Minister of the Ukrainian SSR (nominal), 1939–44. During WWII, lt.-general, involved in directing the partisan operations in the German-occupied Ukraine. Minister for Bread Supply of the USSR, 1953. Member of the Cen. Cttee. of the CPSU, 1939.

Kornilov, Aleksandr Aleksandrovich
30.11.1862–1925. Historian, politician.
Born in Petersburg. Graduated from Petersburg University. Civil servant in Russian Poland, later in Irkutsk Gouvt. Went to Paris and worked on the liberal newspaper *Osvobozhdenie*, edited by P. Struve, 1904. Returned to Russia, and took part in the founding of the Cadet Party. Secretary of the Cen. Cttee. of the Cadet Party, 1905–08. Professor at the Petersburg Technical Institute, teaching history, 1909. Wrote *Kurs Istorii Rossii 19-go veka*, 3 vols, 1912–14. Wrote several monographs on the political and social problems of 19th century Russia.

Kornilov, Boris Petrovich
16.7.1907–21.11.1938. Poet.
Born at Pokrovskoe near Nizhnii Novgorod (Gorkii). Wrote talented verse, full of revolutionary enthusiasm and exuberance. Considered one of the main hopes of Soviet poetry in the 1930s. Arrested, disappeared in the Gulag. Posthumously rehabilitated.

Kornilov, Lavr Georgievich
30.8.1870–13.4.1918. General.
Born at Ustkamnegorsk (now Karkaralinsk), near Karaganda. Son of an officer in the Siberian Cossack army. Educated at Mikhailovskoe Artillery School, 1982. Graduated from the Academy of the General Staff, 1898. Served in Central Asia. On active service during the Russo-Japanese war in 1904–05. Military attaché in China in 1907–11. During WWI, commanded a brigade, later the 48th Division (Steel Division). Wounded and taken prisoner by the Austrians in 1915, escaped in 1916.

After the February Revolution 1917, commander of Petrograd military district. On Kerenskii's orders, put the Imperial family under guard in Tsarskoe Selo. Commander of the South-Western front in summer 1917. After negotiations with Kerenskii, which are still unclear, tried to take Petrograd (maintained that Kerenskii had asked for military help. Kerenskii took it as an attempted coup d'etat). The attempt failed due to the lack of reliable troops: detachments which were sent (the Wild Caucasian Division) disintegrated under the influence of revolutionary propaganda. Kornilov was sacked and imprisoned for high treason in Bykhov on Kerenskii's orders (with General Denikin and other officers). Escaped in Dec. 1917 to Novocherkassk, and became one of the organizers of the Dobrovolcheskaia (Volunteer) Army together with General Alekseev. Commander-in-chief (after Alekseev), led the retreat from Rostov-on-Don to Kuban. Killed trying to take Ekaterinodar (now Krasnodar). His grave was found by the advancing Red Army, and his body was dug up and burned. See: General Baron Petr Wrangel, *Vospominaniia* (Memoirs), Frankfurt, 1963. Also, *Vozhdi Belogo Dvizhenia* (Leaders of the White Movement), Frankfurt, 1985.

Korol' Petr Kondrat'evich
2.1.1941– . Athlete.
Born in Cheliabinskaia Oblast'. Honoured Master of Sports (heavy athletics), 1974. With Lvov Dynamo. In the military forces. USSR champion, 1972. European champion, 1975. World champion, 1974–76. Olympic champion, 1976 (featherweight).

Korolenko, Vladimir Galaktionovich
27.7.1853–25.12.1921. Author.
Born in Zhitomir. Son of a Ukrainian judge and a Polish gentlewoman. Educated at Rovno High School. Studied at the Petersburg Technical Institute, 1871, and the Petrovskaia Agricultural Academy in Moscow, 1874. Expelled for organizing a student protest. Lived in Petersburg, and took up journalistic and revolutionary activity. Exiled to Northern Russia, the Urals and Iakutia, 1879–81. From 1885, lived in exile in

Nizhnii Novgorod. Became famous for his short stories about people he met in exile. His populist tendencies and high moral integrity made him known and influential among the intelligentsia. His journey to the USA to the World Exhibition in 1893 gave him material for the description of the first mass emigration from Russia to America at the end of the 19th century. Defended the Udmurt peasants accused of ritual murder in Northern Russia (the Multan trial), 1895–96. Resigned, with Chekhov, from the Russian Academy after Gorkii's election to the Academy was annulled by the Tsar. Investigated the circumstances of the Kishinev pogrom in 1903. Editor of the influential, populist, SR magazine, *Russkoe Bogatstvo*, 1904–18 (with intervals). From 1902, lived mainly at Poltava in his native Ukraine. Played a very active part in the defence of Beilis, who was accused of ritual murder, but was acquitted by the jury. Became known as an energetic defender of any victim of injustice. Wrote a monumental 3-vol. work, *Istoriia Moego Sovremennika*, describing his own life and development, 1905–21. After the October Revolution and during the Civil War, protested vigorously against acts of injustice and terror committed by all participants. Completely rejected communist claims of speaking in the name of the whole people, and was sharply rebuked by Lenin. His diary of the revolutionary years, giving a devastating and completely honest picture of the Ukraine in the grip of the Civil War under the different regimes including the communist one, has never been published in the Soviet Union. Died of hunger and deprivation in Poltava.
Works: *Collected Works*, 10 vols, 1953–56.

Korolev, Sergei Pavlovich
12.1.1907–14.1.1966. Space rocket designer.
Born in Zhitomir in the Ukraine. Graduated from the Odessa technical designers' school, 1924. From 1927, worked in the aviation industry. Graduated from the Moscow Higher Technical School and the Moscow School of Aviators. From July 1930, a senior engineer at TSAGI (Central Air-Dynamics Institute). Designer of

a series of planes. Worked closely with K. Tsiolkovskii, father of rocketry and the theory of cosmic travel in the USSR. In 1931, together with F. Tsander, organized the Group for the Study of Cosmic Travel (GIRD), which he headed from May 1932. Became a leading figure in the development of the Soviet ballistic missile programme. Arrested in June 1938 by the NKVD, accused of selling blueprints to a German airplane manufacturing firm. Returned from the Gulag to work for the Soviet defence industry following Germany's attack on the Soviet Union in June 1941. *Litera-turnaia Gazeta* for the first time described his arrest and the search of his apartment in an article published in June 1987. Designed many rockets including Vostok, Voskhod, Elektron, Molniia 1, Kosmos, etc. Became corresponding member of the Academy of Sciences, 1953. Member of the CPSU, 1953. Academician, 1958. Was rehabilitated after Stalin's death. Because of his prison record, for a long time he was referred to in the Soviet press only anonymously as 'The Designer' in articles about space exploration. Died of cancer. Buried at the Kremlin wall on Red Square.

Korol'kov, Evgenii Viktorovich
9.10.1930–   . Athlete.
Born in Moscow. Honoured Master of Sports (gymnastics), 1952. With Moscow Dynamo. Graduated from the Moscow Oblast' Pedagogical Institute, 1957. Member of the CPSU, 1961. Honoured coach of the USSR, 1968. Olympic champion, 1952. Silver medal, 1952. World champion, 1954.

Korotchenko, Demian Sergeevich
29.11.1894–7.4.1969. Politician.
Born in the village of Pogrebki (now Korotchenkovo) in the Ukraine. Son of a peasant. Joined the Communist Party, 1918. Railway worker, conscripted during WWI. Communist guerrilla in the Ukraine during the German occupation, 1918. During the Civil War, political commissar in the Red Army, 1919–20. Held several high party administrative posts. Secretary of Moscow obkom, 1936–37, Head of the Soviet of People's Commissars of the Ukraine, 1938–

39. Member of the Cen. Cttee. of the Bolshevik Party, 1939. During WWII, secretary of the Cen. Cttee. of the Ukrainian Communist Party, 1939–47. Organizer of the partisan movement in the Ukraine. After WWII, again head of the Ukrainian government until Stalin's death, 1947–54. Member of the Presidium of the Cen. Cttee. of the Bolshevik Party, 1952–53. Chairman of the Presidium of the Supreme Soviet of the Ukraine (head of state) and deputy chairman of the Presidium of the Supreme Soviet of the USSR, 1957. Non-voting member of the Politburo, 1957–61.

Korotich, Vitalii Alekseevich
26.5.1936–   . Editor, journalist, poet, author.
Ukrainian. Born in Kiev. Graduated from the Kiev Medical Institute. Physician, 1959–66. Edited a number of Ukrainian journals and papers in the 1960s. Secretary of the Ukrainian Union of Writers, 1966–69. Member of the CPSU, 1967. Translator of English-speaking poets and writers and Russian writers into Ukrainian. Also writes his own poetry. Editor-in-chief of the magazine *Ogonek*, the flagship of glasnost. Turned *Ogonek*, previously known mainly for its socialist-realist art reproductions, and with a circulation of little more than 300,000, into a very much sought-after leading political and cultural magazine with a 1,113,000 readership, despite its relatively expensive price of 40 kopecks. Published many sensational historical revelations about Stalin's period throughout 1988. With Egor Iakovlev, editor of the weekly *Moscow News*, has become an outstanding editor and journalist backed by a large section of the Soviet population.

Korovin, Konstantin Alekseevich
5.12.1861–11.9.1939. Painter.
Born in Moscow. Graduated from the Moscow School of Painting, Sculpture and Architecture (under Savrasov and Polenov), 1875–86, and

197

from the Petersburg Academy of Fine Arts, 1882. Reformer of stage design, making it an art in its own right. Member of the Mir Iskusstva group. Designed sets for the private opera of Mamontov, 1885–91 and 1896–98. Stage designer of the Bolshoi Theatre 1903–10. Chief stage designer and arts consultant of the Imperial theatres in Moscow, from 1910. Designer at the All-Russian Exhibition in Nizhnii Novgorod, 1896, and the World Exhibition in Paris, 1900. Worked in an impressionist style. Professor at Moscow Arts School, 1901–18. After the Revolution, emigrated, 1923. Lived in France, continuing to paint and to work in stage design. Died in Paris. Left interesting memoirs describing the arts world in Russia at the beginning of the 20th century.

Korshikov, Gennadii Egorovich
19.2.1949–   . Athlete.
Born in Leningrad. Honoured Master of Sports (rowing), 1972. With Leningrad Dynamo. From 1973 with Moscow Dynamo. Coach. USSR champion, 1971–77. Olympic champion, 1972. Member of the CPSU, 1978.

Koshel', Antonina Vladimirovna
20.11.1954–   . Athlete.
Born in Smolevich, Minsk Oblast'. Honoured Master of Sports (gymnastics), 1973. With Minsk Trudovye Rezervy. Sports instructor. Graduated from the Belorussian Institute of Physical Culture, 1977. Olympic champion, 1972.

Korsov, Bogomir Bogomirovich (real name – Gering, Gotfrid)
1845–1920. Singer (baritone).
Born in Petersburg. Husband of the singer Aleksandra Krutikova. Pupil of G. Korsi. Soloist with the Mariinskii Theatre, Petersburg. With the Bolshoi Theatre, Moscow, 1882–1904. Died in Tiflis.

Korsun, Nikolai Georgievich
8.1.1877–14.11.1958. General.
Educated at the Konstantinovskoe Artillery School, 1897. Graduated from the Academy of the General Staff, 1905. During WWI, at the

Supreme HQ, 1915–16, commander of a Cossack regiment, 1916–17. Transferred to the General Staff in Petersburg as Major-general. From 1918, a military specialist with the Red Army. Professor at the Frunze Military Academy, 1922–54. Retired, 1954. Died in Moscow.

Korzh, Vasilii Zakharovich (Komarov)
13.1.1899–5.5.1967. Secret police official.
Born in Khorostovo, near Brest. Took part in the pro-communist partisan movement in Poland, 1921–25. Moved to the USSR, 1925. Member of the Communist Party from the time of the collectivization campaign, 1929. One of the activists in the collectivization of Belorussia, 1929–31. Official of the NKVD in Belorussia, 1931–36. NKVD official in Spain during the Civil War, 1936–39. During WWII, one of the organizers and controllers of partisan detachments in Belorussia. Major-general, 1943. Hero of the Soviet Union, 1944. After WWII, retired but later during the last Stalin years, Deputy Minister of the Forestry Industry of Belorussia, 1949–53. Chairman of the Kolkhoz Partizanskii Krai in Brest Oblast', 1953–63. Died in Minsk.

Korzhavin, Naum Moiseevich (Mandel)
1925–   . Poet.
Born in Kiev. His first work was published in 1941. Graduated from the Moscow Literary Institute. First book of poems, *Gody*, 1961. Became an established Soviet poet, but came into conflict with the Soviet literary establishment and left the USSR in 1973. Lives in the USA.
Works: *Vremena: Stikhi*, Germany, 1976; *Spletenia: Stikhi*, Germany 1981; *Izbrannye Stikhotvorenia*, USA, 1983.

Korzhenevich, Feodosii Konstantinovich
1899–1972. Lt.-general.
Joined the Red Army, 1918. Took part in the Civil War as a cavalry commander. Graduated from the Frunze Military Academy, 1931. Cavalry officer and professor at military educational establishments

in the 1930s. During WWII, staff officer on several fronts. Continued his staff and education work after WWII. Member of the General Staff, 1957–60.

Korzhinskii, Dmitrii Sergeevich
13.9.1899–   . Geologist, geographer.
Born in Petersburg. Son of the famous botanist, S. Korzhinskii. Graduated from the Leningrad Mining Institute, 1926. Worked at the Institute of Geology. Academician, 1953. Geological studies of Siberia and Central Asia. Winner of the Vernadskii Gold Medal, 1972.

Korzun, Pavel Petrovich
1892–1943. Lt.-general.
Took part in WWI and the Civil War. Joined the Red Army, 1918, cavalry regiment commander. Graduated from the Frunze Military Academy, 1936. Fell in action during WWII.

Kos-Anatol'skii, Anatolii Iosifovich (real name – Kos)
1.12.1909–   . Composer.
Born in Galicia. Lecturer at the L'vov Conservatory. Chairman of the Union of Composers. Author of an opera, an operetta, ballets, a vocal symphony, a cantata, an overture, concertos for piano and orchestra, pieces for piano, violin and piano, choral works, romances, and music for the theatre and variety stage. Stalin Prize, 1951.

Kosarev, Vasilii Vasil'evich
1896–1958. Lt.-general.
Joined the Red Army, 1918. Member of the Bolshevik Party, 1919. Took part in the Civil War. Graduated from the Military-Technical Academy, 1929. Commander of military engineers during and after WWII.

Kosenko, Viktor Stepanovich
23.11.1896–3.10.1938. Composer, pianist.
Born in Petersburg. One of the foremost representatives of Ukrainian music. Professor at the Institute for Musical Drama, Kiev, and at the Kiev Conservatory. Author of works for symphony orchestra, a trio for

piano, violin and cello, 3 sonatas, exercises, preludes, 24 pieces for children, romances, songs, and music for stage and screen. Died in Kiev.

Koshelev, Nikolai Andreevich
1840–1918. Artist.
Studied at the Petersburg Academy of Arts, 1861–65. Genre painter. Main exhibitions: the Academy of Arts, 1862–93 (with interruptions), MOLKH, 1881–82, 1887, 1913, All-Russian Exhibition, Moscow, 1882, the Society for the Encouragement of the Arts, the 1st December Exhibition, 1889, St. Petersburg Society of Artists, 1894–96, 1902, 1904, 1905–07, 1909, 1913–15, 1st Exhibition of Artists of Historical Painting, Moscow, 1895, All-Russian Exhibition, Nizhnii Novgorod, 1896.

Koshevaia, Marina Vladimirovna
1.4.1960–   . Athlete.
Born in Moscow. Honoured Master of Sports (swimming), 1976. With the Iunost team. From 1976, with Moscow Burevestnik. Studied at the Moscow Institute of Physical Culture. USSR champion, 1976. World record-holder, 1976–78. Olympic champion, 1976 (100m).
See: V. Kaliadin, *Olimpiiskaia Chempionka s Olimpiiskim Spokoistviem*, Moscow, 1977.

Koshevoi, Oleg Vasil'evich
8.6.1926–9.2.1943. Partisan.
Born in Priliki, Chernigov Oblast'. Educated in Krasnodon, Voroshilovgrad Oblast'. During WWII, organized an underground resistance group of teenagers, July 1942–Jan. 1943, becoming the commissar of the group. Arrested trying to cross the front line at the railway station at Kortushino. Tortured and shot by the Germans. His 'Molodaia Gvardiia' group became cult figures in the Stalinist propaganda-machine, described in many literary, journalistic, artistic and cinematic works. Since Stalin's death, the factual details of such works have been called into question.

Koshevoi, Petr Kirillovich
21.12.1904–30.8.1976. Marshal.
Joined the Red Army, 1920. Took part in the Civil War. Graduated from the Frunze Military Academy, 1939. On active service during WWII. After WWII, held several high posts including deputy and commander of Soviet forces in Germany.

Koshevskii, Aleksandr Dmitrievich (Krichevskii)
1.4.1873–26.7.1931. Actor.
Born in Akkerman. Appeared in the provinces from 1895, in Petersburg from 1902, and Moscow from 1915. Author of the operetta *Vozvrashchenie Sabinianok*. Died in Moscow.

Koshits, Nina Pavlovna
30.12.1894–1967? Singer (soprano).
Born in Kiev. Daughter of the singer P. Koshits (1863–1904). Pupil of Umberto Masetti. Appeared in opera and chamber ensembles (with S. Rakhmaninov in one ensemble) from 1913. Emigrated. Singing teacher in Hollywood from 1941.

Koshkin, Mikhail Il'ich
1898–1940. Tank designer.
Joined the Communist Party, 1919. Took part in the Civil War. Graduated from the Leningrad Polytechnic, 1934. Became a leading tank designer. Designed the best known Soviet tank of WWII, the T-34.

Kosichkin, Viktor Ivanovich
25.2.1938–   . Athlete.
Born in the village of Moshki, Rybnovskii Raion, Riazan' Oblast'. Honoured Master of Sports (skating), 1960. With Moscow Dynamo. Graduated from the MVD Higher School, 1969. Trained as an intelligence officer. USSR champion, 1960–65, at various distances. Olympic champion, 1960 (5,000 metres). European champion, 1961. World champion, 1962. Silver medal, 1960 (10,000 metres). Member of the CPSU from 1966.

Kosior, Stanislav Vikent'evich
1889–1939. Politician.
Joined the Bolshevik Party, 1907. Took part in the October Revolution 1917 in Petrograd. During the Civil War, Bolshevik forces organizer in the Ukraine. Secretary of the Cen. Cttee. of the Bolshevik Party of the Ukraine, 1920. Head of the Siberian bureau of the Cen. Cttee. of the Bolshevik Party, 1922. Member of the Cen. Cttee. of the Party, 1924, and Secretary, 1926. General secretary of the Ukrainian Cen. Cttee, 1928. Member of the Politburo, 1930, Deputy Prime Minister of USSR, 1938. Liquidated by Stalin.

Kosminskii, Evgenii Alekseevich
2.11.1886–24.7.1959. Historian.
Graduated from Moscow University in 1910. Head of the Department of Medieval History at Moscow University, 1934–49, and at the Institute of History of the Soviet Academy of Sciences, 1936–52. Best known as an authority on British medieval agrarian history, and as an author of Soviet high-school textbooks. Died in Moscow.

Kosmodemianskaia, Zoia Anatol'evna (Tania)
13.9.1923–29.11.1941. Partisan.
Born in the village of Osinovye Gai, Tambov Oblast'. Educated at a Moscow secondary school. Member of the Komsomol, 1938. Volunteered for partisan service during WWII. Sent to the rear of the German forces near Moscow in autumn 1941. Almost immediately seized by the Germans and executed (hanged), allegedly making a heroic defiant speech under the gallows. Despite her very short military career and the relatively minor importance of her mission (to set fire to some German cavalry stables), turned into a cult figure of almost Joan of Arc proportions. Died at the village of Petrishchevo near Vereia, now reburied in the Novodevich'e Cemetery in Moscow.

Kostelovskaia, Maria Mikhailovna
19.3.1878–29.1.1964. Politician.
Born in Ufa. Studied at the Women's Higher Courses in Petersburg. Took part in the 1905 Revolution in the Crimea. Joined the Bolshevik Party, 1903. On party underground work in many provincial towns. In Oct. 1917, one of the military leaders of the Bolsheviks in Moscow. In 1918, chairwoman of the Military Food

Procurement Bureau in charge of requisitions, commander of the pro-dotriady (military detachments for requisitioning food from peasants). During the collectivization campaign, head of the political department of the MTS (the agrotechnical side of the kolkhoz system). Retired in 1946. Died in Moscow.

Kostenko, Fedor Iakovlevich
1896–1942. Lt.-general.
Joined the Red Army, 1918. Took part in the Civil War. Member of the Bolshevik Party, 1921. Graduated at the Academy of the General Staff, 1940. Fell in action during WWII.

Kostenko, Mikhail Polievktovich
16.12.1889–1975? Engineer.
In his youth, involved in revolutionary activity, for which he was exiled to Siberia. Graduated from the Petersburg Polytechnic Institute. Designer at the Elektrosila plant in the 1930s. Designed generators for many hydroelectric stations built during the Stalinist industrialization programme. Academician, 1953. Highly decorated (2 Stalin Prizes, 1 Lenin Prize).

Kostiaev, Fedor Vasil'evich
1878–1925. Major-general.
Graduated from the Academy of the General Staff, 1905. Corps commander during WWI. Drafted into the Red Army, staff officer at different fronts. Professor at the Military Academy of the Red Army, 1919. Wrote on military geography and the history of the Civil War.

Kostrichkin, Andrei Aleksandrovich
24.8.1901–28.2.1973. Actor.
Studied at the FEKS studio. Pupil of G. Kozintsev and L. Trauberg. Graduated from the Leningrad Institute of Stage Art, 1926. Worked at the Leningrad Theatre of the Young Spectator (TIUZ), 1938–41, and at the Kommissarzhevskaia Drama Theatre, 1942–70. Entered the film industry in 1925. Best remembered for his parts in *Shinel'*, *S.V.D.*, *Novyi Babilon*, by G. Kozintsev and L. Trauberg, and *Poruchik Kizhe*.

Kosygin, Aleksei Nikolaevich
21.2.1904–18.12.1980. Politician.
Born in Petersburg. Son of a worker. Soldier in the Red Army during the Civil War, 1919–21. In the 1920s, worked in the cooperative system in Siberia. Studied at the Leningrad Textile Institute, 1930–35. Thereafter, director of textile factories, later Minister of the Textile Industry, 1939. During WWII, Deputy Prime Minister of the USSR, 1940–46. In charge of the evacuation of industrial enterprises to the East during the German offensive. After the war, continued to work as Deputy Prime Minister until Stalin's death. Also Minister of Finance, 1948, Minister of the Light and Food Industries, 1949–53. Under Khrushchev, again Deputy Prime Minister and in 1959–60, head of GOSPLAN. In Oct. 1964, became Prime Minister of the USSR and member of the ruling troika (with Brezhnev and Podgornyi). Considered a technocrat, and the most intelligent of the troika, but with only limited power. Member of the Politburo of the Cen. Cttee. of the CPSU from 1948. Retired, 23 Oct. 1980. Died in Moscow. Buried at the Kremlin wall.

Kosygin, Iurii Aleksandrovich
22.1.1911– . Geologist.
Graduated from the Moscow Oil Institute, 1931. Authority on the oil deposits in many parts of the Soviet Union.

Kosykh, Grigorii Georgievich
9.2.1934– . Athlete.
Born in Uralsk. Honoured Master of Sports (shooting), 1968. With Moscow Oblast' Dynamo. From 1973, with Moscow Dynamo. Graduated from the Moscow Pedagogical Institute, 1969, then from the MVD (KGB) Academy of the USSR, 1975. European and USSR champion, 1962–76. World record-holder, 1969–76. Olympic champion, 1968. Author of 'Borot'sia Do Poslednego Mgnoven'ia' in the almanac *Pobeda Liubit Geroev*, Moscow, 1972.

Kotelnikov, Gleb Evgen'evich
1872–1944. Aviation specialist.
Educated at the Kiev Military School,

1894. Invented the first folding parachute, 1911. Designed many types of parachutes used by the Soviet Army.

Kotelnikov, Valentin Sergeevich
1911–1935. Border guard.
During an engagement against the Japanese in the Far East, sacrificed himself in order to save his brother. Posthumously used by the Stalinist propaganda machine for a campaign called 'Brother for brother' (Brat na smenu bratu).

Kotelnikov, Vladimir Aleksandrovich
1908– . State official.
Radio and electronics engineer by profession. Graduated from the Moscow Molotov Institute of Power Engineering, 1931. Professor and dean of the Department of Radio Engineering at the same institute, 1931–37, and in 1947 professor and head of the Department of Radio Engineering Principles. Member of the CPSU, 1948. Member of the USSR Academy of Sciences, 1953. Director of the Institute of Radio Engineering and Electronics, 1954. Vice-president of the USSR Academy of Sciences, 1970. Many decorations: Stalin Prize, Lenin Prizes and medals. Academician and chairman of Intercosmos, the Soviet International Space Office throughout the 1980s. Acts as a link between the Soviet government and scientists in the USSR.

Kotin, Zhozef (Joseph) Iakovlevich
1908–1979. Tank designer.
Graduated from the Dzerzhinskii Military Technical Academy, 1932. Became the most important tank designer in the Soviet Union during WWII, making an enormous contribution to Soviet success in the war. Designer of the heavy tanks KV, KV–1c, KV–85, IS–1, and IS–2 (Iosif Stalin–1 & 2). Designed an amphibious tank and the heavy tractors KT–12 and K–700. Many state awards.

Kotkas, Iokhannes Iokhannesovich
3.2.1915– . Athlete.
Born near Tartu, Estonia. Honoured Master of Sports (wrestling), 1943.

With Tallinn Dynamo. Coach. Member of the CPSU, 1945. USSR champion, 1943 (hammer-throwing), and 1947 (wrestling). European champion, 1938–39, 1947. USSR champion, 1940–56 (4 times, 1940–45, over-all champion). Olympic champion, 1952 (heavy-weight).
See: V. Pashinin, *Kotkas – Eto Sokol*, Moscow, 1970.

Kotliar, Leontii Zakharovich
1901–1954. Col.-general.
Joined the Red Army, 1920. Graduated from the Dzerzhinskii Military Technical Academy, 1930. During WWII, head of the military engineering administration. Head of the Kuibyshev Military Technical Academy, 1945–51.

Kotliarevskii, Sergei Andreevich
1873–1940/41? Lawyer.
Professor of law. One of the leaders of the Cadet Party. Assistant Procurator of the Holy Synod, later Assistant Minister for Religious Affairs in the Provisional Government, 1917. Arrested, Feb. 1920, in connection with the National Centre, and sentenced to 5 years in prison, Aug. 1920. Professor of Moscow University, worked in the Ministry of Justice in the 1920s. Published an article on the new constitution, 1936. Lived in Moscow. Arrested, 1940. Died in the Gulag; the place, date and exact circumstances are unknown.

Koton, Mikhail Mikhailovich
1908– . Chemist.
Graduated from Leningrad University, 1935. Professor at the Leningrad Pediatric Institute, 1946. Director of the Institute of Higher Molecular Weight Compounds, 1960. Authority on the chemistry of organic, metallo-organic and high molecular weight compounds.

Kotov, Petr Ivanovich
8.7.1889–4.7.1953. Artist.
Born in the village of Vladimirovka (now Astrakhan Oblast'). Portrait and battle painter. Studied at the Kazan Art School, 1903–09, under N. Feshin, then at the Petersburg Academy of Arts, 1909–16, under I. Tsionglinskii. Pupil of N. Samokish

and F. Rubo. From 1923, lived in Moscow. Member of AKHRR (1923). Taught at the Moscow VGIK, 1944–48, then at the Moscow Art Institute, 1948–51. Died in Moscow.

Kotovskii, Grigorii Ivanovich
24.6.1881–6.8.1925. Military commander.
Born in Gancheshty (now Kotovsk) in Moldavia. Son of a worker. Became an estate manager. Arrested for revolutionary activity, 1902. Participated in the 1905 Revolution leading gangs of rebellious peasants in Moldavia. Sentenced to 12 years in exile in 1907. Escaped from Nerchinsk, 1913. Again became leader of a guerrilla group in Bessarabia, 1913. In 1917, close to the left-wing SRs, revolutionary activist in the army. During the Civil War, famous cavalry commander in the Red Army, but joined the Communist Party only in 1920. Fought against Makhno, Antonov and Petliura. Died and buried at Birzula (also renamed Kotovsk) near Odessa.

Kotsiubinskii, Iurii Mikhailovich
7.12.1896–1937. Politician.
Born in Vinnitsa. Son of a well-known Ukrainian writer. Joined the Communist Party in 1913. During WWI, in the army, revolutionary activist, participated in the taking of the Winter Palace in Oct 1917. Commanded detachments sent to defend Petrograd against Krasnov, 1918. Supreme commander of Soviet troops in the Ukraine during the Civil War, toppled the Ukrainian Central Rada at Kiev. From 1925, on Soviet diplomatic work abroad (Austria, Poland). Victim of Stalin's purges of the local leadership in the Ukraine. Probably shot.

Kotukhin, Aleksandr Vasil'evich
1886–1957. Artist.
Miniature painter, icon artist, graphic artist-illustrator, porcelain master. Studied at the Safonovs' Icon Studios in Palekh, then in private icon studios in Moscow from 1909. Pupil of A.P. Bolshakov and F. I. Rerberg. One of the organizers and the 1st chairman of the Studio of Ancient Painting in Palekh. Worked in papier-mâché and lacquer materials. Exhibitions: The

Art of Palekh, Moscow, 1932 and 1939, Ivanovo, 1936, 1940, 1947, Folk Art, Moscow, 1937, Works of Applied Art, Moscow, 1952, 30 Years of Soviet Palekh, Moscow, 1955, Palekh Art, Ulianovsk, 1956.

Kotukhin, Vladimir Vasil'evich
1897–1957. Artist.
Miniature painter. Studied at an icon studio in Palekh. Exhibitions: Russian Artistic Lacquers, Moscow, 1933, Folk Art, Moscow, 1937, The Art of Palekh, Moscow, 1939, Ivanovo, 1947, Works of Applied Art, Moscow, 1952, 30 Years of Soviet Palekh, Moscow, 1955.

Kouts, Albert (Coates)
23.4.1882–11.12.1953. Conductor, composer.
Born in Petersburg. Descended from a line of English settlers in Petersburg. Conductor with the Mariinskii Theatre, Petersburg, 1910–19. Left Russia after the revolution. Worked in England, the USA, and other countries. Conductor with the Symphony Orchestra of Johannesburg. Guest appearance in the USSR, 1927. Author of operas and other compositions. Died in Cape Town, South Africa.

Koval', Marian Viktorovich (real name – Kovalev)
17.8.1907– . Composer.
Born in Olonetskaia Gouvt. Author of operas, including the opera for children *Volk i Semero Kozliat*, an oratorio, cantatas, choral works, vocal solos and piano cycles.

Koval'-Samborskii, Ivan Ivanovich
16.9.1893–10.1.1962. Actor.
In 1922–23, at the Meyerhold Theatre. In films from 1924. Best known for his part in *Miss Mend*, 1926. Played leading parts in *The Forty First* (first adaptation of *Sorok Pervyi*), *Chelovek Iz Restorana*, and *Devushka s Korobkoi*, all in 1927.

Kovalenko, Sergei Ivanovich
11.8.1947– . Athlete.
Born in Port Arthur. Honoured Master of Sports (basketball), 1972. With Tbilisi Burevestnik. From 1969,

with Kiev Stroitel'. From 1976, with the Central Sports Club of the Army. Sports instructor. USSR champion, 1976–79. European champion, 1969. Olympic champion, 1972. Bronze medal, 1968.

Kovalenko, Vitalii Aleksandrovich
17.6.1934–   . Athlete.
Born in Moscow. Honoured Master of Sports (volleyball), 1961. With the Central Sports Club of the Army. Graduated from the Moscow Building Engineering Institute, 1956. USSR champion, 1955–66. World champion, 1960 and 1962. Olympic champion, 1964. Member of the CPSU, 1965. Works as an engineer.

Kovalenkov, Valentin Ivanovich
25.3.1884–14.7.1960. Inventor.
Graduated from the Petersburg Electrotechnical Institute, 1909. Graduated from Petersburg University, 1911. Inventor in the field of telephony and sound movie technology. Died in Moscow.

Kovalenok, Vladimir Vasil'evich
1942–   . Cosmonaut.
Joined the Soviet Army, 1959. Graduated from the Air Force Academy, 1976. Several flights into space (in 1978 spent 140 days on Salyut-6). Deputy head of the Cosmonauts Training Centre, 1984.

Kovalev, Anatolii Gavrilovich
18.5.1923–   . Politician.
Born in Rostov Oblast'. Graduated from the Moscow MGIMO (Institute of International Relations), 1948. Member of the CPSU, 1945. Entered the Diplomatic Service, 1948. Worked in the apparatus of the political adviser in the Soviet Control Commission in Germany, 1949–53, attached to the Soviet Embassy in the GDR. 1st secretary and councillor in the 3rd European Department of the MID (Ministry of Foreign Affairs), 1955–58. Deputy head, later head of the Councillors' Group at the MID, 1958–59, and 1959–65. Head of the 1st European Department of the MID (Belgium, Spain, Italy, Luxemburg, The Netherlands, Portugal, France and Switzerland), 1965–71. Deputy Foreign Minister of the USSR, 1971–86. 1st Deputy Foreign Minister of the USSR from May 1986.

Kovalev, Nikolai Nikolaevich
22.2.1908–   . Turbine designer.
Graduated from the Leningrad Technological Institute, 1933. Worked at the Leningrad Metal Plant, 1933–59. Designed hydroturbines for many Soviet power plants both before and after WWII.

Kovalevskii, Evgraf Petrovich
30.12.1865–1941. Educationalist.
Born in Petersburg. Graduated from Moscow University in law in 1887. Worked at the Ministry of Education, tried to introduce a European education system in Russian schools. Prepared reports on education for the Duma, 1907–17. Prepared a law of universal primary education by 1922, sanctioned by the Duma. Member of the Russian Church Council, 1917–18. Emigrated to France in 1919. Organized the teaching of Russian in French schools.

Kovalevskii, Petr Evgrafovich
16.12.1901–   . Historian.
Born in Petersburg. Emigrated during the Civil War, 1920. Settled in Paris. Graduated from the Sorbonne in 1922. Lecturer in Russian at the Sorbonne, 1930. Professor at the St. Sergius Theological Institute, 1925–50. Active in Russian Orthodox Church affairs and in the oecumenical movement. Published works on the Russian emigré community after 1917.
Main works: *Leskov, The Historical Ways of Russia, La dispersion Russe, Our Achievements* (Russian emigrés in the West), *Zarubezhnaia Rossiia*.

Koval'skii, Aleksandr Alekseevich
10.9.1906–   . Nuclear scientist.
Graduated from the Leningrad Polytechnic Institute, 1930. Specialist on kinetics and chemical reactions. Worked on the problems of high energy particles in nuclear physics.

Koverda, Boris Sofronovich
21.8.1907–18.2.1987. Engineer.
Born near Wilno. During WWI,
evacuated to Samara, educated at Samara High School. After the revolution, returned to Wilno (then Lithuania, later Poland). Worked on the newspaper *Belorusskoe Slovo*. On 7 June 1927, shot in Warsaw railway station the Soviet Ambassador P. Voikov, a participant in the murder of the Tsar's family. Sentenced to life imprisonment, but released on 15 June 1937. Lived in Yugoslavia and Poland before WWII. After WWII, moved through Lichtenstein to the USA, 1956. Worked for Russian newspapers in the USA. Died in Adelphi, USA.

Kovner, Iosif Naumovich
29.12.1895–4.1.1959. Composer.
Born in Wilno. Director of the music department and chief conductor with the State Central Theatre for Juveniles, Moscow. Many of his own pieces performed there. Author of the operetta *Akulina*, 1948, operettas, a symphonic poem, a suite for children, songs, and music for stage and screen. Died in Moscow.

Kovpak, Sidor Artem'evich
26.5.1887–11.12.1967. General, partisan commander.
Born in the village of Kotelva near Poltava. Son of a peasant. During the Civil War, joined communist partisans fighting the Germans, and later the Whites, in the Ukraine, against Kolchak in the East and Wrangel in the Crimea. In the 1920s, in the Red Army in the Ukraine. During WWII, organized partisan detachments. Made an extremely long, celebrated raid over 10,000km, which was in fact a constant retreat from his pursuers, from the Briansk forests in central Russia through the whole of German-occupied Ukraine to the Carpathian mountains, 1942–43. Promoted to Major-general, 1943. Member of the Presidium of the Supreme Soviet of the Ukraine, 1947. Member of the Presidium of the Supreme Soviet of the USSR, 1967. Died in Kiev.

Kovtiukh, Epifan Ionovich
9.5.1890–28.7.1938. General.
Born in Baturino near Kherson. Son of a peasant. Captain, 1917. During

the Civil War, joined the Reds. Commander of the Taman' Army, glorified as the epitome of the revolutionary commander in Serafimovich's *The Iron Flood*. Commanded the Red forces during the attempted return of the White Cossacks under General Ulagai to the Kuban River in 1920. Deputy military commander in Belorussia, 1936. Victim of Stalin's purge of the Red Army, probably shot.

Kozak, Evgen Teodorovich
22.4.1907– . Composer.
Born in L'vov. Lecturer at the L'vov Conservatory. Author of choral works. Arranged folk songs.

Kozhevnikov, Boris Tikhonovich
13.12.1906– . Composer.
Born in Novgorod. Lecturer in classical instrumentation at the military faculty of the Moscow Conservatory. Rank of colonel. Author of music for wind orchestra, 3 symphonies, suites, overtures, a concerto for trumpet and orchestra, pieces for solo wind instruments, and vocal compositions.

Kozintsev, Grigorii Mikhailovich
22.3.1905–11.5.1973. Film director.
Studied at the A. Ekster Art School, Kiev. Worked as an assistant stage designer at the Solovtsov Theatre, Kiev. In 1920, moved to Petrograd. Studied at the Academy of Arts. In 1921, with L. Trauberg, founded FEKS (Fabrika Ekstsentricheskogo Aktera). In 1924, with actors, joined Sevzapkino, now Lenfilm. First film: *Pokhozhdeniia Oktiabriny*, 1924. Until 1945, all his films were made with L. Trauberg: *Mishki Protiv Iudenicha*, 1925, *Chertovo Koleso*, 1926, *Bratishka*, 1927, and *Novyi Vavilon*, 1929. His first sound film was *Odna*, 1931. From the mid-1930s, forced to make films under the strictest party control: *Iunost' Maksima*, *Vozvrashchenie Maksima*, and *Vyborgskaia Storona*. His last film with L. Trauberg was *Prostye Liudi*, 1945, which was shelved until 1956. He is best-remembered for his Shakespearian adaptations: *Hamlet*, 1964 (prize-winner at the Venice Film Festival) and *King Lear*, 1971. Wrote a book about Shakespeare. Taught at

the FEKS, 1922–26, at the Leningrad Institute of Stage Art, 1926–32; and at the VGIK, 1941–64. Professor there. Head of a workshop at the Lenfilm Studio, 1965–71. Trained a generation of film-makers.

Kozitskii, Filipp Emel'ianovich
23.10.1893–27.4.1960. Composer.
Born in Kiev Gouvt. Professor and head of the Department of the History of Music at the Kiev Conservatory. Author of operas, works for symphony orchestra, choral works, instrumental pieces, romances, arrangements of folk songs, and music for films. Died in Kiev.

Kozlov, Fedor Mikhailovich
3.2.1882–21.11.1956. Ballet dancer.
Graduated from the Moscow Choreographic School, 1900. Dancer with the Bolshoi Theatre, 1900 and 1904–10, and with the Mariinskii Theatre, 1901–04. In 1909, with the Ballets Russes in Paris. Organized his own company in 1910. Performed in England and the USA. Organized his own ballet schools in San Francisco, Dallas, and Hollywood, and thus had some influence on American ballet. Among his many talented students was De Mille. Died in Hollywood. See: S. Hurok, *The World of Ballet*, London, 1955.

Kozlov, Frol Romanovich
18.8.1908–30.1.1965. Politician.
Born in the village of Loshchinino, Riazan' Oblast'. Son of a peasant. Worker in the textile industry. Graduated from the Leningrad Polytechnical Institute. Engineer, 1936. Various senior party posts from the late 1930s. Member of the Cen. Cttee., 1952. 1st Secretary of Leningrad obkom, 1953. Member of the Presidium of the Cen. Cttee, 1957, and chairman of the RSFSR Council of Ministers, 1958. 1st deputy chairman of the USSR Council of Ministers, 1958. Secretary of the Cen. Cttee. under Khrushchev, and at one time considered a possible successor to him. Had a stroke in 1963, and retired in 1964. Died in Moscow. Buried at the Kremlin wall.

Kozlov, Leonid
1947– . Ballet dancer.
Born in Moscow. Graduated from the Moscow Choreographic School, 1965. Dancer with the Bolshoi Theatre. In 1979, while on tour in Los Angeles, defected with his wife, also a ballerina with the Bolshoi. Both became leading dancers in the Australian Ballet, and from 1983, in the New York City Ballet.

Kozlovskii, Aleksei Fedorovich
15.10.1905– . Composer, conductor.
Born in Kiev. In Tashkent from 1936. Artistic director and chief conductor of the symphony orchestra of the Uzbek Philharmonic. Professor of composition and conducting at the Tashkent Conservatory. Among his pupils were D. Zakirov, G. Zubatov, and D. Saatkulov. Author of an opera, 2 musical dramas, a comedy, a ballet, cantatas, a vocal symphonic poem, 2 symphonies, 5 suites, 4 tone poems, a tone poem for gidzhak and alto with piano, romances, and music for stage and screen.

Kozlovskii, Ivan Semenovich
24.3.1900– . Singer (tenor).
Born in Kiev Gouvt. Pupil of E. Murav'eva. Soloist with the Bolshoi Theatre, Moscow, 1926–54, Organized and directed an operatic ensemble, 1938–41. Stalin Prize, 1941, 1944.

Kozlovskii, Mechislav Iul'evich (Kozlowski, Mieczislaw)
13.1.1876–3.3.1927. Soviet lawmaker, politician.
Born in Wilno. Graduated from Moscow University in law. Involved in revolutionary activity in Lithuania from 1896. Close to his countryman Dzerzhinskii. Emigrated in 1906. Member of the Bolshevik Party. Trade-union activist in Petersburg in 1909. In 1917, ensured the Petrograd link between Lenin and Helphand through Ganetskii in Stockholm. Member of the Executive Cttee. of the Petrograd Soviet in 1917. Arrested in July 1917. Released after the Kornilov affair, Aug. 1917. After the October Revolution, worked in the People's Commissariat of Justice, 1917–20. Soviet consul in Austria,

1922–23. After 1923, legal expert in the Ministry of Transport. Regarded as the Bolshevik's top legal expert in 1917. Author of many Soviet decrees. Died in Moscow.

Kozlovskii, Nikolai Feofanovich
1887–1.5.1939. Cameraman.
In 1908, shot (with A. Drankov) the first Russian feature film, *Ponizovaia Mel'nitsa* (or *Sten'ka Razin*). Shot over 60 films before Oct 1917, including *Obryv* and *Prestuplenie i Nakazanie*, 1913, and *Brat'ia Karamazovy*, 1915. Filmed Lenin in 1921–22. Shot over 20 feature films including *Chudotvorets*, 1922, *Gospoda Skotininy*, 1927 (with D. Shliugleit), and *Sumka Dipkur'era*, 1928.

Kozlovskii, Sergei Vasil'evich
3.4.1885–19.11.1962. Stage designer.
Studied at the Odessa Art School. In the Ukrainian theatre from 1903. Entered the film industry, 1913. Among his best silent films are: *Polikushka*, *Aelita*, *Papirosnitsa Ot Mossel'proma*, *Mat'*, *Sorok Pervyi*, *Potselui Meri Pikford*, *Konets Sankt Peterburga*, *Potomok Chingiz Khana* and *Prazdnik Sviatogo Iorgena*. Worked closely with V. Pudovkin. His sound films include: *Dezertir*, *Okraina*, and *Marionetki*. Taught at the VGIK from 1924. Regarded as a major stage designer of the Russian silent cinema.

Kozolupov, Semen Matveevich
22.4.1884–18.4.1961. Cellist.
Born in Orenburg Gouvt. Father of the cellist Galina Kozolupova, and the violinist Marina Kozolupova. Pupil of I. Zeifert and A. Verzhbilovich. Professor at the Moscow Conservatory. Among his pupils were S. Knushevitskii, M. Rostropovich, and V. Feigin. Died in Moscow.

Kozolupova, Galina Semenovna
26.8.1912– . Cellist.
Born in Moscow. Daughter and pupil of the cellist Semen Kozolupov. Professor at the Moscow Conservatory. Among her pupils were E. Al'tman, and N. Gutman.

Kozolupova, Marina Semenovna
25.4.1918– . Violinist.
Born in Moscow. Daughter of the cellist Semen Kozolupov. Pupil of K. Mostras and M. Poliakin. 5th prize at the E. Ysaye International Competition, Brussels, 1937. Lecturer at the Moscow Conservatory.

Krainiukov, Konstantin Vasil'evich
1902–1975. Political commissar.
Joined the Red Army, 1919, and the Bolshevik Party, 1920. Took part in the Civil War. Graduated from the Military Political Academy, 1934, professor of the Academy, 1934. During WWII, political assignments with several armies. Head of the Lenin Military Political Academy (preparation of political commissars for the armed forces). Deputy, and later head of the Political Administration of the Soviet Armed Forces, 1949. Deputy chief of the General Staff for Political Affairs, 1960–69.

Krakhmalnikova, Zoia Aleksandrovna
1929– . Literary critic, editor.
Born in Khar'kov. Wife of Feliks Svetov. Graduated from the Moscow Literary Institute, 1954. Published numerous books, articles and translations in the Soviet press. In 1971, became involved in religious rights campaigns, distributing samizdat religious literature. Fired from her job at the Moscow Sociological Research Institute. Editor of the religious samizdat magazine *Nadezhda*. Arrested in Aug. 1982, accused of 'anti-Soviet propaganda' and sentenced to 1 year in prison and 5 years in exile. Under Gorbachev, returned to Moscow from her exile in Altai, 1987. Author of *Blagovest* (intro. by T. Goricheva), Switzerland, 1983.

Kramarov, Savelii
1939– . Comedian
Very often compared with Norman Wisdom for his parts of funny little working-class fellows in slapstick comedies, adventure films and thrillers. Made 42 feature films during his 15-year career in the Soviet Union. Always a huge box-office success. Applied to emigrate and lost his job. In 1974, a Moscow film source explained: 'we can't afford to let him go because that would mean putting all 42 films on the shelf'. Emigrated eventually and settled in the USA. In

the USSR, became a non-person. The *Kino-entsiklopedicheskii Slovar'* published in Moscow in 1986 does not contain an entry for him.

Kramskaia-Iunker, Sofia Ivanovna
1866–1936. Artist.
Born in Petersburg. Pupil of her father, Ivan Nikolaevich Kramskoi (1837–87). Studied at the Academy of Arts, Petersburg, 1886–88. Exhibitions: at the same academy, 1888–92, 1894, 1897–99, the Society of Water-Colour Painters, 1895–96, 1900, All-Russian Exhibition, Nizhnii Novgorod, 1896, St. Petersburg Society Artists, 1907–10, 1912–13.

Krapivianskii, Nikolai Grigor'evich
1889–1948. State security official.
Educated at the Chuguev Military School, 1913. On active service during WWI as a Lt.-colonel. Joined the Bolsheviks, 1917. Took part in the Civil War in the Ukraine. After the Civil War, commander of the Cheka forces in the Ukraine and the Crimea. High state-security and border-guard posts after 1928.

Krasev, Mikhail Ivanovich
16.3.1897–24.1.1954, Composer.
Born in Moscow. Author of an opera for juveniles, 4 operas for children and for the professional theatre (among them *Mukha-Tsokotukha*, 1942, and *Morozko*, 1949), operettas, choral works, romances, songs, musical games and musical stage productions for children of or below school age, music for the theatre and for puppet plays, pieces for piano, and for the balalaika. Died in Moscow.

Krasil'nikov, Sergei Nikolaevich
1893–1971. Lt.-general.
On active service during WWI as a captain. Joined the Red Army, 1918, and the Bolshevik Party, 1920. Took part in the Civil War. Professor at the Frunze Military Academy. Worked in the General Staff. During WWII, in charge of the reserve forces and forces in training. After WWII, professor at the Academy of the General Staff, 1948–68. Wrote works on military theory.

Krasin, Leonid Borisovich
15.7.1870–24.11.1926. Engineer, revolutionary, diplomat.
Born in Kurgan, Tobolsk Gouvt. Grew up with exiled revolutionaries and soon took part in revolutionary activity himself. Studied at Petersburg and Khar'kov Technological institutes. Graduated from Khar'kov Technoglical Institute in 1900. Arrested several times for revolutionary activity. Successful engineer, working on the construction of the trans-Siberian railway and the electrification of the Baku oil fields, and revolutionary organizer, setting up illegal printing shops and disseminating revolutionary literature. Member of the Cen. Cttee. of the Bolshevik Party in 1903. Worked at the Morozov textile plants at Orekhovo-Zuevo in 1904, head of the electricity board of Petrograd. Persuaded the millionaire Savva Morozov to make regular large donations to the Bolsheviks. One of the organizers of the first legal Bolshevik newspaper, *Novaia Zhizn'* (New Life). Specialist in party finance and technology. Member of the Petrograd Soviet, 1905–07. Emigrated in 1908. Removed from leading positions in the party, and retired from politics. Head of Siemens and Schuckert, Moscow, 1912, and Petersburg and all Russia, 1913. After the October Revolution, returned to political activity. Took part in the Brest-Litovsk negotiations. During the Civil War, in charge of supplying the Red forces. People's Commissar of Trade and Industry and Minister of Railways in 1919. Conducted peace negotiations with Estonia, Dec. 1919. Ambassador to England in 1920, signed the Anglo-Soviet trade agreement in 1921. Participant of the Genoa and Hague conferences in 1922. Ambassador to France in 1924. Again Ambassador to Great Britain in 1925. Died in London.

Krasin, Viktor Aleksandrovich
1929– . Dissident.
Born in Kiev. His father was arrested during the purges, 1937 and died in the Kolyma camps. Arrested, 1947, sentenced to 8 years in the Gulag camps. Released after Stalin's death, 1954. Resumed his studies at Moscow University, graduating in economics in 1966. During the late 1960s, one of the best known Soviet dissidents. Arrested, 1969. Returned to Moscow, 1971. Re-arrested, 1972. Under threat, agreed to cooperate with the KGB, according to his own subsequent confession. Emigrated, 1975. Settled in the USA.

Krasnogliadova, Vera Vladimirovna
27.2.1902– . Composer.
Born in Poltava Gouvt. Author of cantatas, *Liricheskaia Uvertiura* for orchestra, pieces for piano, romances, and songs and choral works for children.

Krasnopevtsev, Semen Aleksandrovich
1896–1954. Col.-general.
Joined the Red Army, 1918. Took part in the Civil War. Graduated from the Frunze Military Academy, 1931. Artillery commander during the Soviet-Finnish war and WWII.

Krasnoschchekov, Aleksandr Mikhailovich
1880–26.11.1937. Economist, lawyer, politician.
Born in Chernobyl, Kiev Gouvt. Son of a Jewish manager. Member of the SD Party from 1896. Several short arrests, imprisonments and exiles. In Nov. 1902, escaped a new arrest and left for Berlin. Moved to the USA. Worked as a tailor and interior decorator. Member of the American Social Democratic Party. Graduated in law from Chicago University, 1912. In July 1917, arrived in Vladivostok. Chairman and Minister of Foreign Affairs of the Soviet Far East Republic, Dec. 1917–Sept 1918. After the republic's crash, escaped to Siberia. Arrested near Samara, but released by Irkutsk Bolsheviks. In 1920, member of the Soviet delegation at the 2nd Congress of the Komintern. Various senior party positions in Moscow, 1921–23. Chairman of the Prombank (Industrial Bank). Arrested, 19 Sept. 1923. Released in Nov. 1924. Wrote a book, *The Modern American Bank* (Sovremennyi Amerikanskii Bank), which was to be published in 1926, but was delayed because of his arrest. (It was eventually published in 1927.) The story of his arrest was turned into a play by B. S. Romashov: *Vozdushnyi Pirog* (premiere, Feb. 1925). In the summer of 1922, with his daughter Llewella, lived in Pushkino, where he met Mayakovsky and helped him overcome the delays in the publication of his works. In 1937, arrested, tried as an American spy, and executed.

Krasnov, Nikolai Nikolaevich
1918–1959. Lieutenant.
Born in Moscow. Grandson of the Cossack general P. Krasnov. Emigrated with his parents after the defeat of the Whites in the Civil War. Educated in Yugoslavia. During WWII, junior officer in the Cossack corps with his father and grandfather. Handed over to SMERSH in 1945 in Lienz. Spent over 10 years in the Gulag, 1945–56. Released, and left for Sweden. Settled in Argentina. Wrote one of the most harrowing eye-witness accounts of the handover of the Cossacks to SMERSH by the British military authorities, of the pre-trial life of his relatives and colleagues at arms in Lubianka prison in Moscow, 1945–46, and of life in the Gulag camps. His book, *Nezabyvaemoe*, was published in 1957. Died of heart failure (suspected by some of having been poisoned by KGB agents).

Krasnov, Petr Nikolaevich
22.9.1869–17.1.1947. Cossack General, author.
Born in Petersburg, son of a Cossack General. Educated at the Pavlovskoe Military School, 1888. Served in the Life Guard Cossack regiment, 1910–13, on the Chinese border. During WWI, commander of a Cossack brigade and division. After the October Revolution 1917, the first to try — without success — to fight the Red forces (with Kerenskii, who joined him in Gatchina). Elected Don Cossack Ataman, on 18 May 1918, cleared the Don region of Bolsheviks. Acted independently in representing a pro-German orientation, in contrast to the Dobrovolcheskaia Army (General Denikin), which upheld the war-time alliance with England and France. Acknowledged the overall control of Denikin in Jan. 1919, but resigned on 19 Feb 1919. Took part in the operations of General Iudenich against the Bolsheviks (near Petrograd). After the Civil

War, emigrated and settled in Germany. Became a writer of popular historical novels. During WWII, organized anti-Bolshevik Cossack forces financed by the Third Reich. Opposed the joining of forces between the Cossacks and General Vlasov's ROA (Russian Liberation Army), considering Vlasov an upstart and former communist. Interned in Austria by British forces and in May 1945 handed over (with his family, officers and soldiers) to SMERSH, on whose wanted list he had been since the Civil War. Tried in Moscow for treason with a group of former White generals and hanged. See: N. Tolstoy, *Victims of Yalta*.

Krasnov-Levitin, Anatolii Emmanuilovich
21.9.1915–   . Journalist, church historian.
Born in Baku. Moved with his parents to Leningrad, 1920. Educated at secondary school in Leningrad. Graduated from the Herzen Pedagogical Institute. As a young man, was an active member of the Living Church (a radical group, encouraged by the authorities to undermine Patriarch Tikhon), close to A. Vvedenskii. Taught literature at secondary schools. During WWII, ordained deacon by Vvedenskii. Left the Living Church and joined the official Orthodox Church in 1944. After WWII, lived in Moscow. Arrested, 1946. Released during the Khrushchev thaw in 1956. Writing on church and religious subjects, became a well-known samizdat author from the late 1950s. Many young Soviet dissidents became interested in religion through his writings or personal contact with him. Emigrated in 1977. Lives in Switzerland, continuing to campaign for human rights and religious freedom. Author of many articles on the situation of believers in the USSR, several volumes of memoirs (valuable source on the Living Church, its initial successes and subsequent total failure).

Krasnovskii, Aleksandr Abramovich
1913–   . Biochemist.
Born in Odessa. Studied at the Mendeleev Chemical Institute in Moscow. Works on chlorophyll chemistry and photosynthesis.

Krasovskii, Stepan Akimovich
1897–1983. Marshal.
Joined the Red Army and the Communist Party, 1918. Pilot during the Civil War. Graduated from the Zhukovskii Air Force Academy, 1936. Took part in WWII as an aviation commander. Head of the Air Force Academy, 1956.

Kratasiuk, Viktor Ivanovich
30.1.1949–   . Athlete.
Born in Poti, Georgia. Honoured Master of Sports (rowing), 1972. With the Armed Forces team in Poti. USSR champion, 1971–72. Olympic champion, 1972 (with N. Gorbachev, in the 1000 metres race). Graduated from the Georgian Institute of Physical Culture, 1978.

Kravchenko, Aleksandr Diomidovich
1881–1923. Partisan.
Commissar of a Red partisan group in Siberia, 1918. Organized a partisan army which fought against Kolchak, 1919. Divisional commander in the regular Red Army, 1920. Later worked in the Ministry of Agriculture.

Kravchenko, Andrei Grigor'evich
1899–1963. Col.-general.
Joined the Red Army, 1918. Took part in the Civil War. Graduated from the Frunze Military Academy, 1928. On active service during the Soviet-Finnish war, 1939–40. Tankforce commander during WWII.

Kravchenko, Grigorii Panteleevich
1912–1943. Lt.-general.
Joined the Red Army and the Communist Party, 1931. Educated at a pilots' school, 1932. Flight instructor and test pilot. Fought against the Japanese at Khalkin Gol. Also fought in the Soviet-Finnish war. Fell in action during WWII.

Kravchenko, Mikhail Stephanovich
1858–22.4.1917. Musician.
Born in Poltava Gouvt. Ukrainian. Pupil of S. Iashnyi and F. Kholodnyi. Played the kobza (a stringed folk instrument). Appeared in Petersburg, Moscow, in many towns in the Ukraine, and in Kuban'. Many of his songs were recorded by F. Kolessa.

Kravchenko, Valerii Ivanovich
2.2.1939–   . Athlete.
Born in Tadzhikistan. Honoured Master of Sports (volleyball), 1968. With Alma-Ata Burevestnik. From 1973, with Alma-Ata Dorozhnik. Olympic champion, 1968. USSR champion, 1969. European champion, 1967, 1971. Bronze medal, 1972.

Kravchenko, Viktor Andreevich
10.1905–2.1966. Engineer, author.
Born in Ekaterinoslav (now Dnepropetrovsk). Son of a revolutionary. Worked as a miner in Donbass. Joined the Communist Party, 1929. Throughout the 1930s, industrial manager, working in metallurgy. During WWII, as an army captain, appointed to the Soviet Purchasing Commission in Washington. In Apr. 1944, defected and denounced the policies of Stalin. Wrote a book, *I Chose Freedom*, about his life in the Soviet Union, which appeared in 1947 and became an international bestseller. The book gives a truthful picture of the situation in the USSR soon after collectivization and under Beria's regime of terror. Because Stalin was a recent wartime ally, the revelations were met with scepticism in the West. Denounced by the Stalinist propaganda machine, and by a French communist publication as a 'fascist and liar'. Brought a libel case against *Lettres Françaises* in Paris, 1948–49, and won, with the help of witnesses from refugee camps. Later, put great hopes on the Khrushchev reforms, but was disappointed by the slow internal developments in the Soviet Union. Lived in the USA. Found dead with gun-shot wounds in his flat in unclear circumstances (officially pronounced a suicide case).
See: Viktor Kravchenko, *I Chose Freedom*, England, 1947. 'Trial of Viktor Kravchenko', *La Pensée Russe*, Paris, 1949.

Kravtsov, Vladimir Nikolaevich
19.10.1949–   . Athlete.
Born in Lithuania. Honoured master of Sports (handball), 1976. Studied at the Moscow Aviation Institute. USSR champion, 1974–75. Olympic champion, 1976. Works in the military industry.

Krein, Aleksandr Abramovich
20.10.1883–21.4.1951. Composer.
Born in Nizhnii Novgorod. Brother of the composer Grigorii Krein. Author of an opera, ballets, 2 symphonies, symphonic suites and poems, instrumental ensembles, romances, music for the theatre (e.g. for *The Dancing Master* by Lope de Vega), and for films. Died in Staraia Ruza near Moscow.

Krein, David Sergeevich
1869–26.8.1926. Violinist.
Born in Kurlandia. Brother of the composers Aleksandr and Grigorii Krein. Pupil of I. Grzhimali. First violin and soloist with the ballet orchestra of the Bolshoi Theatre, 1900–26. Professor at the Moscow Conservatory, 1918–26. Member of the Moskovskoe Trio (with D. Short the founder, M. Al'tshuler, and later R. Erlikh). Author of pieces for violin. Died in Moscow.

Krein, Grigorii Abramovich
16.3.1879–6.1.1955. Composer.
Born in Nizhnii Novgorod. Brother of the composer Aleksandr Krein. Author of orchestral works, a symphony, 2 poems, a ballad, concerto for violin and orchestra, chamber music (e.g. *Evreiskaia Rapsodiia*) pieces for string quartet, piano and clarinet, sonatas, pieces for piano, and for violin and piano. Died near Leningrad.

Krein, Iulian Grigor'evich
5.3.1913–   . Composer, writer on music.
Born in Moscow. Son of the composer Grigorii Krein. Husband of the musicologist Nina Rogozhina. Author of a ballet, a work for orchestra, voices and narrator (*Rembrandt*), musical poems, ballads, suites, a chamber ensemble, pieces for piano and other instruments, and romances.

Kreitner, Georgii Gustavovich
30.12.1903–14.7.1958. Composer.
Born in Libava (Liepaia). Author of operas, operettas, cantatas, symphonic works, works for wind instruments, pieces for the variety stage, a chamber ensemble, romances, and music for animated films. Died in Moscow.

Kreitser, Leonid Davidovich
1884–30.10.1959. Pianist.
Born in Petersburg. Pupil of A. Esipova. Professor at the School for Higher Studies, Berlin, 1921–33. At the Tokyo Music Academy from 1938. Literary works: *Das normale Klavierpedal*, Leipzig, 1915, and *Das Wesen der Klaviertechnik*, Berlin, 1923. Died in Tokyo.

Kreizer, Iakov Grigor'evich
1905–1969. General.
Joined the Red Army, 1921. Graduated from the Military Academy of the General Staff, 1942. Took part in WWII. Head of the Vystrel Courses, 1963–69.

Kremlev, Iulii Anatol'evich
19.6.1908–   . Musicologist, composer.
Born in Esentuki. Doctor of History. (Leningrad). Author of a symphony, sonatas, and romances.
Literary works: *Leningradskaia Gosudarstvennaia Konservatoria, 1862–1937*, Moscow, 1938; *Frederik Shopen*, Leningrad–Moscow 1949; *Fortep'iannye Sonaty Betkhovena*, Moscow, 1953; *Russkaia Mysl' o Muzyke*, 3 vol, Leningrad, 1954–60; *Simfonii P. I. Chaikovskogo*, Moscow, 1955; *Ocherki po Voprosam Muzykal'noi Estetiki*, Moscow, 1957; *Edvard Grig*, Moscow, 1958; *Vyrazitel'noe i Izobrazitel'noe v Muzyke*, Moscow, 1962.

Kremshevskaia, Galina Dmitrievna
27.4.1913–   . Ballet critic.
Born in Petersburg. Graduated from the Leningrad Choreographic School, 1931. Pupil of A. Vaganova. Graduated from the Pedagogical Department, 1938, then in stage production with the Moscow GITIS, 1954. Dancer with the Leningrad Malyi Theatre, 1931–34, the Paliashvili Theatre, Tbilisi, 1934–35, the Opera Studio of the Leningrad Conservatory, 1935–37, and the Kirov Theatre, 1937–53. From 1954, ballet critic. Author of numerous books and articles.

Krepkina, Vera Samoilovna (Kalashnikova)
16.4.1933–   . Athlete.
Born in Kotelnich, Kirov Oblast'.

With Vologda Lokomotiv, 1950–53, and Kiev Lokomotiv, 1954–65. Member of the CPSU, 1955. Honoured Master of Sports (track and field athletics), 1960. Sports instructor. Graduated from the Kiev Institute of Physical Culture, 1961. USSR champion, 1952–65. World record-holder, 1958–61 (100 metres). European champion, 1954 and 1958. Olympic champion, 1960.

Kreps, Evgenii Mikhailovich
30.4.1899–   . Physiologist.
Born in Petersburg. Graduated from the Military Medical Academy, 1923. Pupil of Ivan Pavlov. Professor at the Military Medical Academy, 1924–31. Involved in naval rescue work, 1931–51. Works on the regulation of enzyme activity by the central nervous system, and on the medical problems connected with the work of divers.

Kriger, Viktorina Vladimirovna
9.4.1893–23.12.1978. Ballerina.
Born in Petersburg. Born into a famous artistic family (both parents were actors). Graduated from the Moscow Theatre School, 1910. Leading dancer with the Bolshoi Theatre, 1910–48. In 1929, with I. M. Shlugleit organized the Truppa Moskovskogo Khudozhestvennogo Baleta which in 1933 formed the basis for the ballet of the Nemirovich-Danchenko Music Theatre. Became its artistic director and leading dancer. From 1920–23, with the Ballets Russes. From 1926, permanent contributor to ballet magazines. Wrote *Moi Zapiski*, Moscow, 1930. Head of the Bolshoi Theatre Museum, 1955–63. One of Stalin's favourite ballerinas during the 1930–40s. Died in Moscow.

Kriss, Grigorii Iakovlevich
24.12.1940–   . Athlete.
Born in Kiev. Honoured Master of Sports (fencing), 1964. With the Kiev Armed Forces team. USSR champion, 1964–70. Olympic champion, 1964. World champion, 1967–71. Graduated from the Kiev Institute of Physical Culture, 1972.

Kriuchkov, Nikolai Afanas'evich
6.1.1911–   . Film actor.
Popular film actor. Born into a working class family. As a young worker came to the Moscow Young Worker's Theatre after some experience in amateur theatre groups. Studied under the guidance of Il'ia Sudakov, Nikolai Khmelev and Igor Savchenko. Discovered by film director, Boris Barnet, who in 1933 gave him a small part in *Outside the City* produced by Mezhrabpomfilm in Moscow. Worked with other famous directors: Leonid Trauberg, Grigorii Kozintsev, Sergei Iutkevich, Sergei Gerasimov. Made over 150 films. Best in comedies. Films include: *Right By the Blue Sea* (1936, Barnet), *Maksim's Return* (1937, Kozintsev and Trauberg), *The Man With the Rifle* (1938, Iutkevich), *The Tractor Drivers* (1939, Ivan Pyriev), *Kotovskii* (1943, Faintsimer), *Three Encounters* (1950, Iutkevich, Pudovkin, Ptushko), *Sadko* (1953, Ptushko), *The Rumiantsev Case* (1956, Kheifits), *The Hussar Ballad* (1962, Riazanov), *The Marriage of Balzaminov* (1965, Voinov), *There Lived an Old Man and Old Woman* (1965, Chukhrai).

Kriuger, Emmanuil Eduardovich
30.4.1865–25.4.1938. Violinist.
Born in Tver. Pupil of L. Auer. Soloist with the Mariinskii Theatre (now the Kirov Theatre of Opera and Ballet, Leningrad) from 1895. Taught at the Petersburg Conservatory, 1900–29. Professor from 1906. Died in Leningrad.

Kriukov, Vladimir Nikolaevich
22.7.1902–14.6.1960. Composer.
Born in Moscow. Brother of the composer, Nikolai Kruikov. Head of the Composition Department at the Gnesin Pedagogical Institute of Music, 1957–59. Author of operas, a rhapsody, sinfoniettas, tone poems, orchestral works, concertos, sonatas and other instrumental pieces, romances, and music for stage, film and radio. Died in Staraia Ruza near Moscow.

Kriukova, Agrafena Matveevna (b. Kozhina)
10.7.1855–27.4.1921. Story teller, folk singer.
Born on the Tersk side of the White Sea. Teller of ancient tales, and singer of traditional songs. Died in Verkniaia Zolotitsa, on the Zimnii side of the White Sea.

Kriukova, Marfa Semenovna
1876–7.1.1954. Story teller, folk singer.
Born in Arkhangelsk Oblast'. Daughter of Agrafena Kriukova. Teller of ancient tales of the north. Adapted her craft to modern demands and politicized her songs. Author of *Kamenna Moskva Vsia Proplakana*, dedicated to Lenin.

Krivchenia, Aleksei Filippovich
12.8.1910–   . Singer (bass).
Born in Odessa. Pupil of V. Seliavin. Appeared in operas in Voroshylovgrad, Dnepropetrovsk, and Novosibirsk from 1938. Soloist with the Bolshoi Theatre, 1949–62. Stalin Prize, 1950.

Krivda, Fedot Filippovich
1923–   . General.
Drafted into the army, 1941. Took part in WWII. Graduated from the Frunze Military Academy, 1954, and the Academy of the General Staff, 1966. Head of the Vystrel Courses, 1985.

Krivitskii, Walter (Ginsberg, Samuil)
1899?–11.2.1941. Intelligence agent.
Head of Soviet espionage network in Vienna, later in Holland. To escape Stalin's purges, defected in France. Moved to the USA. Wrote articles on NKVD work which were published in many newspapers in the West. Found dead of gun-shot wounds 2 days before he was due to testify before a commission of the US Senate. A revolver and a farewell note were at his side. Officially considered a victim of suicide, probably murdered by the NKVD.

Krivonosov, Vladimir Mikhailovich
6.12.1904–4.10.1941. Composer, folklorist.
Born in Moscow. Researcher into Churvash folk songs. Wrote many articles. Author of a musical comedy, orchestral works, dance music, a string quartet, a suite for violin and piano, and music for the theatre. Killed in action near the river Sozh.

Krivopolenova, Maria Dmitrievna
31.3.1843–2.2.1924. Folk singer.
Born in the village of Ust'- Ezhuga, Northern Russia. Discovered (by A. Grigoriev in 1900) as a talented singer of old folk tales (byliny) and historical folk songs. Retained in her memory a whole treasury of folklore, based on the traditional oral recitals of Northern Russia (although the byliny cycle revolves around the old Southern capital of Kiev and the figure of Vladimir Krasnoe Solnyshko, in whom St. Vladimir and Vladimir Monomakh merge in a semi-mythical figure of Arthurian proportions). Died in the village of Veegora near her birth place.

Krivoshein, Aleksandr Vasil'evich
31.7.1857–28.10.1921. Statesman.
Born in Warsaw. Served in the Ministry of Agriculture, involved in the programme of voluntary resettlement of Russian peasants in Siberia and Turkestan. Became widely known as the right-hand man of Prime Minister Stolypin in the execution of his land reforms. In 1896–1905, head of the gentry and peasant banks (founded to facilitate the peaceful transfer of land from landowners to the peasantry). Tried to organize the Government of Trust during WWI. The attempt was rejected by the Tsar, and led to his retirement in Oct. 1915. After the October Revolution, one of the organizers of the Right Centre in Moscow. During the Civil War, Prime Minister under General Wrangel in the Crimea, where he worked out and for a short time put into practice his ideas of land reform, which proved popular but came too late. Emigrated after the defeat of the Whites, lived in France. Died in Berlin.

Krivoshein, Igor Aleksandrovich
1899–   . Engineer.
Son of the pre-WWI minister A. Krivoshein. Emigrated with his parents during the Civil War, after Wrangel's defeat in the Crimea. Lived in France. Electrical engineer.

After WWII, became a Soviet patriot and returned to the Soviet Union, 1948. Arrested, and sent to the Gulag. Was allowed to return to Paris after Stalin's death.

Krivoshlykov, Mikhail Vasil'evich
3.12.1894–11.5.1918. Guerilla leader.
Born in Ushakov (now Krivoshly-kov) near Rostov-on-Don. Son of a blacksmith. During WWI, became one of the best-known communist organizers among the Cossacks at the front. During the Civil War, became head of the Don Cossack Revolutionary Committee, 1918. Took part in the suppression of an anti-communist Cossack uprising in the North of Don Oblast'. Taken prisoner by White Cossack detachments and executed (hanged) at khutor Ponomarev.

Kromiadi, Konstantin Grigor'evich (WWII pseudonym – Sanin)
1900? – 1987. Colonel.
Took part in the Civil War in the Caucasus fighting with L. Bicherakhov against the Red Army. Emigrated after the defeat of the Whites. Settled in Germany. During WWII, organized one of the first Russian anti-Stalin military groups on the German side. Later joined General Vlasov as head of his office. Tried (unsuccessfully) to explain the situation of the anti-Stalin Russians in Germany to General Eisenhower, 1946. In the 1950s and 1960s, worked for Radio Liberty in Munich. Wrote memoirs, *Za Zemliu, Za Voliu*, published in the USA, 1980. Died in Munich.

Kropivnitskaia, Valentina Evgen'evna
1924– . Artist.
Both her father, Evgenii Leonidovich Kropivnitskii, and her mother, Olga Anan'evna Potapova, were artists. Married the artist Oscar Rabin. Expelled, together with her husband, and stripped of Soviet citizenship, 23 June, 1978. Participant in many exhibitions of Russian artists in Europe. A major exhibition of her work took place in London in 1978, organized by the Parkway Focus Gallery. Lives in Paris.

Kropivnitskii, Evgenii Leonidovich
1893–1979. Artist.
Graduated from the Stroganov Art School in Moscow, 1917. Taught at various art schools. In 1963, Khrushchev criticized his work, and he was expelled from the Union of Artists. Regarded as one of the major modern Soviet artists. Influenced a generation of young unofficial Russian artists. Died in a village near Moscow.

Kropotkin, Petr Alekseevich, Prince
9.12.1842–8.2.1921. Revolutionary, philosopher, geographer.
Born in Moscow. Educated at the exclusive aristocratic Pages Corps, 1862. Volunteered to go to the Far East with the Amur Cossacks, later served with the Governor-General of East Siberia. Visited completely unexplored parts of Manchuria and Eastern Siberia, 1864–66. Under the influence of Herzen, became interested in revolutionary activity. Resigned from the service, 1867. During a trip to Switzerland in 1872, joined the Bakunists in the 1st International. Returning to Russia, joined the revolutionary circle of N. Chaikovskii. Arrested, 1874, escaped abroad, 1876. Spent over 40 years abroad as a political emigré. Became famous for his geographical research and his philosophical and politicial works on anarchism (especially influential in Western Europe). Expelled from Switzerland, 1881. Sentenced in Lyon to 5 years in prison, 1883. Released from French jail, 1886. Moved to Britain, where he lived until 1917. From the very start of his revolutionary career, a resolute opponent of Marxism for moral reasons. In contrast to the Darwinist struggle for survival and the Marxist theory of the class struggle, stressed the principle of solidarity and cooperation as the basis of all life in the world (animal, as well as human), and certainly all social life. During WWI, supported the war effort, and was attacked by Lenin. Returned to Russia after the February Revolution in June, 1917. Opposed the Bolshevik take-over in Oct. 1917. In an open letter, condemned as barbaric the Soviet government's policy of declaring whole groups of the population to be class enemies, and especially the practice of taking (and executing)

hostages as a means of reprisal. From 1918, lived in Dmitrov. Died of hunger.

Kroshner, Mikhail Efimovich
1900–1942. Composer.
Born in Kiev. Author of the first Belorussian ballet, *Solovei* (produced in 1939), cantatas, (e.g. *Utoplennik* based on a story by Pushkin), romances, and arrangements of Belorussian and Jewish songs. Killed in action in Minsk.

Krotkii, Emil (real name – German, Emmanuil Iakovlevich)
1892–1963. Poet.
Satirist poet. Appeared in *Novyi Satirikon*, *Letopis'*, *Novaia Zhizn'* and *Vecherniaia Zvezda*.

Krotkov, Iurii Vasil'evich
1917–1982. Author.
Born in Kutaissi. Studied at the Moscow Literary Institute. Scriptwriter and author of propaganda plays. Connected with the KGB. Used by the KGB to set up a sex trap for the French Ambassador in Moscow, M. Dejean. Sent by the KGB to befriend Boris Pasternak and report on him (in the guise of a family friend). In 1963, as a member of the Soviet delegation in London, asked for political asylum. In 1969, moved to the USA. Confessed to his long cooperation with the KGB in detailed articles in the Russian emigré press. Regular contributor to *Novyi Zhurnal*, NY. One of his plays about Stalin has been shown on British TV. Died in the USA.
See: 'Pasternaki', *Grani*, 1965–67; 'Konets Marshala Beriia', *Novyi Zhurnal*, 1978; 'Arest', *Novyi Zhurnal*, 1982.

Krovopuskov, Viktor Alekseevich
29.9.1948– . Athlete.
Born in Moscow. Honoured Master of Sports (fencing), 1976. With the Moscow Armed Forces team. USSR champion, 1976. Olympic champion, 1976. World champion, 1974–75, 1978. In 1979, the International Fencing Federation called him the world's best fencer.

Kruchenykh, Aleksei Eliseevich
1886–1968. Poet, author.
Pioneer of modernist and absurdist literature in Russia. His poetry includes *Igra v Adu, Mirskontsa* (both in 1912 with V. Khlebnikov), and *Vzorval'*, 1913. Opera libretto: *Pobeda Nad Solntsem*, 1913. Novels in verse: *Razboinik Van'ka-Kain i Son'ka-Manikiurshchitsa*, 1925; *Zhivoi Mayakovsky. Razgovory s Mayakovskim*, 2 vol., 1930.

Kruchinin, Nikolai Nikolaevich (real name – Khlebnikov)
29.10.1885–1.1.1962. Guitarist, ethnographer.
Born in Moscow. Collected gypsy folklore. Directed the Ethnographic Ensemble of Old Gypsy Song, 1925–29 (founded by him as a studio in 1920). Edited a collection of *Old Russian Songs Preserved in the Gypsy Musical Tradition*, 1929. Died in Moscow.

Krug, Grigorii I.
12.1907–6.1969. Icon painter.
Born in Petersburg into a family of Swedish origin. Protestant by religion. In 1921, emigrated with his parents to Estonia. Finished high school at Narva. Moved to Revel where he was praised for his talent as a painter. Moved to Paris, 1931. Became attracted to Orthodoxy. Orthodox monk, 1948. One of the best known and most prolific 20th century icon painters. Died in France.

Kruglikova, Elena Dmitrievna
16.6.1907–   . Singer (soprano).
Born in Podol'sk, in Moscow Gouvt. Pupil of K. Dorliak. Soloist with the Bolshoi Theatre, Moscow, 1932–56. Teacher at the Moscow Conservatory.

Kruglov, Nikolai Konstantinovich
31.1.1950–   . Athlete.
Born in Krasnyi Mys, Gorkii Oblast'. Honoured Master of Sports (biathlon), 1975. With the Gorkii Armed Forces team. USSR champion, 1973–75. World champion, 1974–75, 1977. Olympic champion, 1976. Graduated from the Leningrad Institute of Physical Culture, 1976. See: M. Marin, *Trudnoe Delo Nikolaia Kruglova*, Moscow, 1977.

Kruglov, Sergei Nikiforovich
1892?–1957. General, chief of state security.
Head of the NKVD (MVD), July 1945 – Mar. 1953 and KGB, June 1953 – Mar. 1954. After the war, awarded many of the highest Western awards for his contribution to victory in WWII. After Beria's fall, practically the only member of the old secret-police leadership who survived and helped to adapt the security system to the new party leadership. Replaced by Serov.

Krupskaia, Nadezhda Konstantinovna (m. Ulianova)
26.2.1869–27.2.1939. Revolutionary, politician, educationalist.
Born in Petersburg. Daughter of an army officer. Member of the SD Party, 1898. A student at the Higher Courses for Women. Started to frequent marxist student circles, 1890s. Became involved in marxist propaganda work among the workers. Met Lenin in these circles, 1894. Arrested, Aug. 1896. In 1898, condemned to 3 years exile to Ufa Gouvt. On her own wish, was allowed to change her place of exile to Shushenskoe in Siberia, where Lenin was in exile. Married Lenin there (her 2nd husband: the first, a member of the SR Party, emigrated after the October Revolution and died in Argentina). In 1900, ended her term of exile in Ufa. After her release, went abroad in 1901 to join Lenin in Munich, and from then on became his constant companion and assistant in his journalistic and party work. Returned with him to Russia in Nov. 1905. Worked as a secretary of the Cen. Cttee. of the party in Petersburg, later Kuokkala in Finland. At the end of 1907, emigrated with Lenin again, lived in Switzerland, and later taught at the party school at Longjumeau near Paris, 1911. In 1912, moved with Lenin to Cracow (then Austro-Hungary). At the beginning of WWI, moved to Switzerland. Returned with Lenin through Germany in 1917. After the October Revolution 1917, started to organize the new communist educational system. Personally responsible for the complete removal of all noncommunist books from Russian libraries. After Lenin fell ill, received appalling treatment from Stalin. Was the main cause of Lenin's friction with Stalin. After Lenin's death, was obliged to write abject statements distancing herself from any opposition to Stalin, after his unmistakeable threats. (Stalin once remarked 'We can make somebody else Lenin's widow'.) In her later years, as the Deputy Minister of Education of the RSFSR, 1929, became almost a symbol of the better Leninist times and a magnet for many people seeking help and advice. Protested against the placing of Lenin's mummified body in the Mausoleum. Became completely isolated and helpless in the Stalinist party when the Old Bolsheviks were vilified, persecuted, and perished in the purges during the 1930s. Died in Moscow, falling suddenly ill on her birthday. According to some unconfirmed versions, she intended to use her birthday celebrations for a public anti-Stalin statement, and was poisoned on Stalin's orders.
Main works: *Vospominaniia o Lenine*, Moscow, 1957; *Pedagogical Works*, II vols, Moscow, 1957–63.

Krushel'nitskaia, Solomeia Amvros'evna
23.9.1873–16.11.1952. Singer (soprano).
Born in Ternopol' Gouvt. Pupil of V. Vysotskii and F. Krespi. Appeared with the L'vov, Odessa and Petersburg operas. Guest performances in Italy, France, South America, and Canada from 1893. Professor at the L'vov Conservatory from 1946. Died in L'vov.

Krutikova, Aleksandra Pavlovna
1851–1919. Singer (mezzo soprano).
Born in Chernigovskaia Gouvt. Wife of the singer B. Korsov. Pupil of P. Vartel' and G. Nissen-Saloman. Soloist with the Mariinskii Theatre, Petersburg, 1872–76, and with the Bolshoi, Moscow, 1880–91. Died in Moscow.

Krylenko, Nikolai Vasil'evich
14.5.1885–29.7.1938. Revolutionary, politician, lawyer.
Born in the village of Bekhteevo, near

Smolensk. Son of an exiled revolutionary. Joined the Bolshevik Party, 1904. Graduated in history from Petersburg University, 1909, and in law from Khar'kov University, 1914. Took part in the 1905 Revolution. Emigrated at the beginning of WWI, 1914. Returned, 1915, and sent to the front, 1916. Very active revolutionary propagandist during the February Revolution 1917. After the Bolshevik take-over Oct. 1917, appointed Supreme Commander of the Russian Army (his military rank then was a warrant officer). From Mar. 1918, worked in the Soviet judicial and security system. Until 1931, the Chief Public Prosecutor at political trials, gaining the fearful reputation of Stalin's henchman. From 1931, Minister of Justice of the RSFSR. In 1936, Minister of Justice of the USSR. Remained Public Prosecutor at the early Stalinist trials, but fell from favour and was himself arrested and executed on Stalin's orders.

Krylov, Aleksei Nikolaevich
1863–1945. Scientist, ship designer.
Graduated from the Naval Academy, 1890. Professor at higher educational establishments for over half a century. Became very influential in Soviet ship design. Head of the Naval Academy, 1919–20. Head of the Physical-Mathematical Institute of the Academy of Sciences, 1927. Author of works on ship design and mathematics.

Krylov, Iurii Nikolaevich
11.3.1930–4.11.1979. Athlete.
Born in Moscow Oblast'. Honoured Master of Sports (hockey), 1954. With Moscow Dynamo. USSR Champion, 1954. European champion, 1954-56, 1958-59. World champion, 1954, 1956. Olympic champion, 1956. Graduated from the Moscow School of Sports Instructors at the Institute of Physical Culture, 1964.

Krylov, Nikolai Ivanovich
29.4.1903–9.2.1972. Marshal.
Joined the Red Army, 1919. Took part in the Civil War. Member of the Bolshevik Party, 1972. Graduated from the Vystrel Courses, 1928.

Commander of several armies during WWII (the attack on Berezina, the occupation of East Prussia, and action against Japan in the Far East). Commander of Strategic Rocket Forces and Deputy Defence Minister, 1963–72. Member of the Cen. Cttee. of the CPSU, 1961–72.

Krylov, Porfirii Nikitich (Kukryniksy)
2.8.1902– . Artist.
Born in the village of Shchekunovo (now Tula Oblast'). Studied at the Proletkult art studio in Tula, 1918–21, under G. Shegal', then at the Moscow VKHUTEIN, 1921–28, under A. Osmerkin and A. Shevchenko. Became one of the three graphic artists working under the pseudonym Kukryniksy (Kupriianov, Krylov and Sokolov) in 1924. Worked also as an illustrator, caricaturist, stage designer, portrait and landscape painter. From 1925, worked for *Pravda* and *Krokodil*. Apart from illustrating M. Saltykov-Shchedrin, Ilf and Petrov, and A. Chekhov's short stories, the Kukryniksy mainly worked as propaganda artists whose satires were directed first of all against foreign and internal state enemies. During WWII and the postwar years, they contributed to almost every official political magazine and newspaper. Exhibited from 1931 at every political exhibition. Personal exhibitions as the Kukryniksy also took place from 1932 onwards.

Krylov, Vladimir Pimenovich
1878–1968. Businessman, publisher.
Successful businessman in Petersburg. Published the magazine *Stolitsa i Usad'ba* with descriptions of the luxury residences of the Russian nobility in the cities and in the country. Immediately after the February Revolution 1917, transferred all his capital abroad and went on a world tour. Settled in Berlin. Became active in East-West trade. After Hitler came to power, moved to Paris. Died a millionaire in France.

Krym, Solomon Samoilovich
1868–1938. Politician.
Member of the Cadet Party. Member of the State Council and the Duma. Chairman of local government in the Crimea, and during the Civil War, under German protection, rose to become head of local government. Emigrated, lived in France.

Krymov, A.M.
1880–1917. General, politician.
Close to Guchkov. Before the February Revolution. 1917, planned a coup against the Tsar. At the front during WWI. Involved in the Kornilov–Kerenskii confrontation in summer 1917. After the defeat of the Kornilov revolt and a stormy meeting with Kerenskii in Petrograd, shot himself.

Krymov, Nikolai Petrovich
2.5.1884–6.5.1958. Artist.
Born in Moscow. Pupil of his father, P. A. Krymov. Studied at the Moscow School of Painting, Sculpture and Architecture, first as an architect, 1904–07, then as a painter, 1907–11, under A. Arkhipov, N. Kasatkin, S. Miloradovich, L. Pasternak and V. Serov. Landscape painter, stage designer. Exhibitions: the Blue Rose, 1907, the 5th Iaroslavl' Art Society, 1914, 2nd and 4th State Exhibitions, Moscow, 1918–19, the Mir Iskusstva group, 1921–22, Artists of the RSFSR: 15 Years, Leningrad, 1932, Industria Sotsializma, Moscow, 1939. Personal exhibition: Moscow, 1954. Died in Moscow.

Krymskii, Agafangel Efimovich
15.1.1871–25.1.1942. Author, orientalist, academician.
Born in Vladimir-Volynskii in the Ukraine. Graduated from the Moscow Lazarevskii Institute of Eastern Languages, 1892. Graduated in history and philology from Moscow University, 1896. Taught at the Moscow Institute of Eastern Languages, 1898–1918, Professor from 1900. Taught at Kiev University, 1918–41, on Iran and Turkey. Member of the Ukrainian Academy of Sciences from 1918 until the early 1930s. Published many works, including the *History of the Arabs and Arab Literature* and the *History of Turkey and its Literature*. Wrote also on Ukrainian history. Wrote 3 books of poetry, *Palmovye Vetki*, 1901–22, and the novel *Andrei Logovskii*, 1905. Was a close friend of Ivan Franko, Mikhail Kotsiubinskii and Lesia Ukrainka. Died in Kustanai in Kazakhstan during the evacuation.

Kryzhanovskii, Ivan Ivanovich
8.3.1867–9.12.1924. Medical scientist, composer, musicologist.
Born in Kiev. Doctor of medicine. At the Petersburg Medical Institute. Worked in Ivan Pavlov's laboratory. Pupil of N. Rimskii-Korsakov at the Petersburg Conservatory (the cantata presented at his final examination was *Rai i Peri*, 1900). Author of symphonies and chamber music, a piano concerto, pieces for violin, and romances. Member of the Beliaev Circle. One of the founders of the circle Vechera Sovremennoi Muzyki. Wrote newspaper articles on music criticism. Gave a course on the physiology of piano-playing at the Petrograd Conservatory, and also on the biological bases of musical evolution at the State Institute for the History of Art. The composer N. Miaskovskii came to him as a private pupil. Author of *Fiziologicheskie Osnovy Fortepiannoi Tekhniki*, Petersburg, 1922. Died in Leningrad.

Ksenia Aleksandrovna (Romanova)
1875–1960. Grand Duchess.
Sister of Tsar Nicholas II. Married a close relative, the Grand Duke Aleksander Mikhailovich. Her daughter Irina, considered a great beauty, married Prince Feliks Yusupov, the future assassin of Rasputin. During the revolution, rescued in the Crimea by the British Navy. Moved to Britain. Lived out her last 25 years in Wilderness House, a grace-and-favour mansion provided by the British Royal family.

Ksenofontov, Ivan Ksenofontovich
29.8.1884–23.3.1926. Secret police official.
Born in Moscow. Son of a worker. Member of the Bolshevik Party, 1903. Before WWI, active in revolutionary circles in many provincial towns. During WWI, conscripted, revolutionary activist in the army, and organizer of Bolshevik committees among the soldiers. Took part in the Bolshevik take-over in Oct. 1917 in Petrograd. One of the founders and organizers of the Cheka, and chairman of the special revolutionary tribunal, 1917–21. Took part in the suppression of the Kronstadt revolt of sailors against the Soviet government, 1921. Later worked in the Cen. Cttee. of the Bolshevik Party, 1922–25. Deputy Minister of Social Security. Died in Moscow.

Kshesinskaia, Matil'da Feliksovna (Kschessinska, Mathilde)
31.8.1872–6.12.1971. Prima ballerina.
Born in Ligovo near Petersburg. Daughter of the ballet dancer Feliks Kschessinski. Graduated from the Petersburg Theatre School, 1890. Trained by Enrico Cecchetti. From 1890–1917, prima ballerina at the Mariinskii Theatre. Mistress of Tsarevich Nikolai Aleksandrovich (the future Tsar Nicholas II) before his marriage. Performed in Vienna, 1903, Paris, 1908–09, Ballets Russes seasons, Warsaw, 1909. With Diaghilev, 1911–12. During 1917, when her mansion in Petersburg was occupied by the Bolshevik Party, Lenin used to make speeches to the crowds from the balcony of the house. From 1920, lived in Paris. Wife of Grand Duke André. In 1929, set up her own ballet school. Among her famous pupils were T. Riabushinskaia, B. Kniazev, I. Chauviré and M. Fonteyn. Died in Paris. Memoirs: *Souvenirs de la Kschessinska*, London, 1960.

Kshesinskii, Iosif Feliksovich
5.2.1868–1942. Dancer, choreographer.
Born in Petersburg. Brother of Mathilde Kschessinska. Graduated from the Petersburg Theatre School, 1886. Dancer at the Mariinskii Theatre, 1914–28, with some intervals. Taught at the Petersburg Theatre School, 1896–1905, and at the Leningrad Choreographic School, 1918–27. Left memoirs which remain unpublished (the manuscript is in the Bakhrushin Theatre Museum, Moscow). Died during the Siege of Leningrad.

Ktorov, Anatolii Petrovich
24.4.1898–30.9.1980. Actor.
Graduated from the F. F. Komissarzhevskii Studio, 1919. On the stage from 1917. From 1920–22, at the Korsh Theatre, Moscow. Entered the film industry, 1925. Joined MKHAT, 1933. His best parts were in Ia. Protazanov's films: *Protsess O Trekh Millionakh*, 1926, and *Prazdnik Sviatogo Iorgena*, 1930. Played Prince Bolkonskii's father in *War and Peace*.

Ktorova, Alla (Kochurova-Shandor, Viktoria Ivanovna)
1931–   . Author.
Graduated from the Moscow Foreign Languages Institute, 1955. Worked as a stewardess with Aeroflot. Later an English language school teacher. Married an American citizen, 1958. One of the first Soviet women who, after Stalin's death, received permission to join her husband in the USA. Began writing in America under the pen name of Alla Ktorova. Her most famous novel is *Litso Zhar-Ptitsy. Obryvki neokonchennogo antiromana*, USA, 1969. Other books include *Eksponat molchashchii*, Germany, 1964. Writes mainly short stories using subculture slang. Lives in the USA.

Kubalov Aleksandr Zakhar'evich
9.10.1871–1937. Poet, lawyer.
Born in the village of Staryi Batakoiurt in Northern Ossetia. Graduated in law from Kiev University, 1899. Practised as a lawyer. At the turn of the century, published in Russian his versions of the epic folklore of the Caucasian peoples. Translated Russian poetry into his native Ossetian language. Victim of Stalin's purges, probably shot.

Kubatskii, Viktor L'vovich
18.3.1891–1975? Cellist.
Born in Moscow. Pupil of A. Brandukov. Soloist with the orchestra of the Bolshoi Theatre, 1914–21. Founder of the State Collection of Unique Musical Instruments, 1919. Organizer and member of the Stradivarius State Quartet, 1920–30. Professor at the Gnesin Pedagogical Institute of Music. Author of arrangements for cello. Published the first version of Tchaikovskii's *Variatsii Na Temu Rokoko*.

Kubikov, Ivan Nikolaevich (Dement'ev)
1877–1944. Literary critic, politician.
Member of the SD Party, 1902. Worked as a printer, 1890–1905. After the 1905 Revolution, twice exiled. Active Menshevik in 1917–18. After the Bolshevik take-over, suffered several short arrests. After the Civil War, ceased his political activity, and became known as a professor of literature and literary critic.

Kublanovskii, Iurii Mikhailovich
1947– . Poet, journalist.
Born in Rybinsk (now Andropov). Graduated from Moscow University in art history. His verse achieved popularity in samizdat. Emigrated, 1982. Settled in France. Several volumes of his poetry have been published in the West.

Kuchevskii, Alfred Iosifovich
17.5.1931– . Athlete.
Born in Moscow. Honoured Master of Sports (hockey), 1954. With Moscow Kryl'ia Sovetov. Works as a civil servant. World champion, 1954 and 1956. Olympic champion, 1956. USSR champion, 1957. European champion, 1954–56, 1958 and 1960. Bronze medal, 1960.

Kuchinskaia, Natal'ia Aleksandrovna
8.3.1949– . Athlete.
Born in Leningrad. Honoured Master of Sports (gymnastics), 1966. With Leningrad Trud. Overall USSR champion, 1965–68. World champion, 1966. Olympic champion, 1968. Bronze medal, 1968.

Kudreva, Natalia Alekseevna
8.6.1942– . Athlete.
Born in Krasnodar. Honoured Master of Sports (volleyball), 1972. With Leningrad Burevestnik. Olympic champion, 1972. Graduated from the Leningrad Institute of Physical Culture, 1974. Sports instructor.

Kudriavtsev, Aleksandr Ivanovich
1873–1942. Artist.
Pupil of Il'ia Repin. Worked as an artist-restorer for the Archaeological Commission of the Academy of Material Culture and the Russian Museum in Leningrad. Studied at the Petersburg Academy of Arts, 1907. Exhibitions: the Academy of Arts Spring Exhibition 1902–03, 1910, 1914–16, the AKHRR, Moscow, 1924, RSFSR Artists for 15 Years, Leningrad, 1932, Moscow, 1933 (twice), and Moscow 1939. Died during the Siege of Leningrad.

Kudriavtsev, Nikolai Nikolaevich
2.10.1893–1970? Domra player.
Born in Moscow. Member of the domra quartet organized by G. Liubimov, 1914–41. Director of the same from 1934. Taught in workers'

clubs and children's institutions. Author of *Shkola Igry na 4-kh Strunnykh Domrakh*, in collaboration with S. Tesh, Moscow, 1927. Literary works: *Massovye Muzykal'nye Instrumenty dlia Kruzhkovoi Samodeiatel'nosti*, Moscow, 1931, and *Novye Formy Massovoi Raboty*, Moscow, 1931.

Kudriavtsev, Petr Pavlovich
1868–7.1937. Philosopher.
Professor of the history of philosophy at the Kiev Theological Academy. Member of the Russian Church Council, 1917–18. Published works on religion and philosophy before WWI. Arrested at the beginning of the 1930s. Inmate of the Gulag. Died of heart failure.

Kugel', Aleksandr Rafailovich (pen-name – Homo Novus)
26.8.1864–5.10.1928. Drama critic.
Born in Mozyr, Belorussia. Graduated in law from Petersburg University, 1886. The most influential theatre critic in Russia at the beginning of the 20th century. Editor of the magazine *Teatr i Iskusstvo*, 1897–1918. In 1908, founded the famous satirical theatre Krivoe Zerkalo. Remained its director to the end of his life. Died in Leningrad.

Kugul'tinov, David Nikitich
13.3.1922– . Poet.
Born in the village of Gakhan-Avnagara in the Kalmuck ASSR. First poems published in 1936. On active service during WWII. After the war, together with the whole Kalmuck nation, sent to the Gulag (like the Crimean Tatars, the Chechen and Ingushi, the Kalmucks were deported en masse allegedly for high treason). Released after Stalin's death. Graduated from Gorkii Literary Institute, 1960. Became a conformist poet, mentioning neither the fate of his own people nor his own Gulag experience during the Stalin years. Broke his silence on the subject in *Ogonek* in 1988.

Kugushev, Viacheslav Aleksandrovich, Prince
3.2.1863–30.8.1944. Politician, revolutionary, banker.
Born in Ufa. Graduated from the

Petersburg Forestry Institute. From the 1880s, actively involved in revolutionary activity. In the 1900s, gave substantial financial support to the SD Party. Several times arrested and exiled, several stays abroad as a political emigré. Being a Bolshevik sympathizer, joined the Cadet Party, 1906. Elected member of the State Council (upper chamber) before the revolution. Banker in the important Don Agricultural Bank, 1906–17, continuing at the same time his secret revolutionary activity. During the Civil War, carried out several important missions for Lenin. Member of the Committee of Aid to the Hungry 1919–23. Inspector of the All-Russia Cooperative Bank, 1923–30. Died in Moscow.

Kuibyshev, Nikolai Vladimirovich
25.12.1893–1.8.1938. Military commander.
Born in Kokchetav in Kazakhstan. Son of an officer. Brother of V. Kuibyshev. During WWI, commander of a battalion. After the October Revolution 1917, elected commander of a regiment. During the Civil War, commander of Red detachments at various fronts. After the suppression of the Kronstadt rebellion, commander and commissar of Kronstadt, 1922–23. Director of the Higher Military Courses, Vystrel, 1923–25. Commander of the Siberian military region, 1928–36. Commander of the Transcaucasian military region, 1937. Arrested, disappeared, probably shot.

Kuibyshev, Valerian Vladimirovich
6.6.1888–25.1.1935. Politician.
Born in Omsk. Son of an officer. Educated at the Omsk Cadet Corps. Joined the Bolshevik Party, 1904. Studying at the Military Medical School in Petersburg, took part in the 1905 Revolution. Expelled from the school, 1906. Continued his revolutionary activity underground, mainly in Siberia. After the February Revolution 1917, came to Samara and during the October Revolution 1917, seized power there for the Bolsheviks. Left-wing communist in 1918. Political commissar in the Red Army during the Civil War. Member and secretary of the Cen. Cttee. of the

Bolshevik Party, 1922. Deputy Prime Minister, 1923. Chairman of the Supreme Council of the National Economy, 1926. Chairman of Gosplan, 1930. Ally of Stalin during his power struggle with his rivals. Died in Moscow, probably from natural causes, although at the time his death was blamed on Trotskyite conspirators (later this accusation was quietly dropped). Because of his untimely death, allegedly as a victim of villains, a great number of towns were re-named after him (including the historic city of Samara on the Volga, to which during WWII the Soviet government was evacuated, when the German armies were approaching Moscow).

Kukel, Vladimir Andreevich
1885–1940. Naval officer.
Graduated from the Naval Corps, 1902. Took part in WWI as a captain. Joined the Red Navy, 1918, in the Caspian fleet. Chief-of-staff of the Baltic fleet, 1930. Commander of the naval border guards in the Far East, 1935. Joined the Bolshevik Party, 1932.

Kukharskii, Vasilii Fedos'evich
7.1.1917– . Musicologist.
Born in Belaia Tserkov, in Kiev Gouvt. Author of articles on Soviet musical culture, and a book on Khrennikov (1957).

Kukobaka, Mikhail Ignat'evich
1939– . Worker.
Born in Bobruisk. One of the few workers to become prominent in the human rights movement. Put into a psychiatric clinic, 1970. Released, 1976, hospitalized again, 1976–77. Publicly rejected Soviet citizenship, 1977. Re-arrested, 1978, and sentenced to 3 years in the camps, but before his release, re-arrested in prison for anti-Soviet slander, 1981, and given 3 additional years. Before the end of his term, re-arrested, 1984, and sentenced to 7 more years of camps and 5 years of exile. Under Gorbachev, released, Feb. 1987.

Kulaev, Sozyryko Aleksandrovich (Siko)
1.1900–4.1938. Author.
Born in the village of Zgubiri in Southern Ossetia. Joined the Bolshevik Party in 1919. During the Civil War, Red partisan in the North Caucasus. Graduated from the Moscow Timiriazev Agricultural Academy, 1928. Minister of Education of Southern Ossetia, 1935–38. Published many short stories describing the first years of Soviet rule in the Caucasus in the 1920s–30s. Victim of Stalin's purges, probably executed.

Kulagin, Nikolai Mikhailovich
19.1.1860–1.3.1940. Entomologist, zoologist.
Born in the village of Shilovichi, near Smolensk. Graduated from Moscow University in 1884. Worked at the University until 1911. Academician, 1913. Professor at Moscow University 1919, where he founded the entomological laboratory which he headed until his death. World authority on apiary and on agricultural pests. Published several zoological monographs (on elks and European bison).

Kulakov, Nikolai Mikhailovich
1908–1976. Vice-admiral, political officer.
Joined the Bolshevik Party, 1927. Joined the Red Navy, 1928. Graduated from the Military Political Academy, 1936. Head of the Higher Military Political Courses of the Navy, 1944–46. Deputy Commander of the Navy for Political Affairs, 1946. Head of the Kronstadt fortress political department, of the Navy's Leningrad political department, and of naval educational establishments in Leningrad.

Kulakova, Galina Alekseevna
29.4.1942– . Athlete.
Born in the village of Logachi, Udmurt ASSR. Honoured Master of Sports (skiing), 1972. With the Izhevsk Trud. Graduated from the Izhevsk Pedagogical High School, 1962. World and USSR champion, 1969. Olympic champion, 1972 and 1976. Silver medal, 1968. Bronze medal, 1976. Author of *Komu Pokoriaetsia Lyzhnia*, Moscow, 1974.

Kulakovskii, Lev Vladimirovich
12.11.1897–1969? Musicologist.
Born in Volynskaia Gouvt. Works:

Stroenie Kupletnoi Pesni, Moscow, 1939, *O Russkom Narodnom Mnogogolosii*, Moscow, 1951, *Kak Nauchit'sia Sobirat' i Zapisyvat' Narodnye Pesni*, Moscow, 1926, *Pesnia, ee Iazyk, Struktura, Sud'by,* Moscow, 1962.

Kulebakin, Viktor Sergeevich
1891–1970. Scientist.
Educated at the Moscow Higher Technical School, 1914. Professor at the Zhukovskii Air Force Academy in the 1920s. Participated in the preparation of the Soviet electrification plan (GOELRO). Founder and first director of the Institute of Automation and Telemechanics of the Academy of Sciences, 1939–41. Academician, 1939. Major-general, 1942. Outstanding authority on problems of automatic systems and equipment.

Kuleshov, Lev Vladimirovich
13.1.1899–29.3.1970. Film director.
Born in Tambov. Started as a stage designer in the film industry in 1916. One of the pioneers of Russian cinema. Experimented in the fields of editing and special effects. First documentary maker during the Civil War, 1918–21. Played an active part in film propaganda during the 1920s. His first film, *Na Krasnom Fronte*, 1920, was one of the first agit-films. In 1919, founded the State Film School. Among his pupils were Vsevolod Pudovkin, Boris Barnet, A. Khokhlova (later his wife), and S. Komarov. His films include *Neobychainye Prikliuchenia Mistera Vesta v Strane Bolshevikov*, 1924, *Po Zakonu*, 1926, after a Jack London story, and *Velikii Uteshitel'*, 1933, after O. Henry. Attacked for formalism in the Soviet film press when he applied his theory that an actor should lose his identity and become an instrument of the director. Taught at the VGIK from 1944. His film, *The Siberians*, 1940, portrayed Stalin. After WWII, completely exhausted himself. In 1945, applied for party membership when it was already too late, since his career was over by then. Died in Moscow.
See: M. Levidov, *Lev Kuleshov*, Moscow, 1927; V. Pudovkin, 'Masterskaia Kuleshova', *Iskusstvo Kino*, 1940, Nr 1–2.

Kuleshov, Pavel Nikolaevich
1908– . Marshal.
Joined the Red Army, 1926. Graduated from the Dzerzhinskii Artillery Academy, 1938, and from the Academy of the General Staff, 1941. During WWII, held several high positions in the artillery, including Deputy Chief-of-staff of Soviet Artillery. After WWII, Deputy Head of the Dzerzhinskii Artillery Academy, and Deputy Commander of Anti-aircraft Forces.

Kulichevskaia, Klavdia Mikhailovna
6.11.1861–1923. Ballerina.
Graduated from the Petersburg Theatre School, 1880. Leading dancer with the Mariinskii Theatre until 1918. From 1901–17, taught at her former ballet school. A legendary ballerina and dedicated teacher. Among her famous pupils were Olga Spesivtseva, G. Bolshakova and E. Biber. Staged some ballets at her ballet school, reviving, especially for Spesivtseva, *Skazka Beloi Nochi*, 1913. Left the USSR, 1918. Died in Tokyo.

Kuliev, Tofik Alekper ogly
7.11.1917– . Composer.
Born in Baku. Azerbaidzhanian by nationality. Author of musical comedies, symphonic works, pieces for piano, and violin and piano, choral works, romances, songs, notation and arrangements of folk songs, and music for stage and screen.

Kulik, Grigorii Ivanovich
9.11.1890–24.8.1950. Marshal.
Took part in WWI. Joined the Red Army, 1918. During the Civil War, active as an artillery commander. In the 1920s and 1930s, twice Commander of Soviet Artillery. Graduated from the Frunze Military Academy, 1932. At the beginning of WWII, Deputy Minister of Defence, demoted to Major-general, 1942. At the end of WWII, in charge of Soviet Army recruitment. Posthumously promoted again to the rank of Marshal, 1957.

Kulikov, Artem Vladimirovich
1937– . Nuclear scientist.
Graduated in physics from Leningrad University. Senior high-energy physicist at the Leningrad Nuclear Physics Institute. Defected while in Chicago on a business tour with a group of Soviet physicists, 1988. Granted political asylum in the USA.

Kulikov, Evgenii Nikolaevich
25.5.1950– . Athlete.
Born in Bogdanovich, Sverdlovsk Oblast'. Honoured Master of Sports (skating), 1976. With Leningrad Burevestnik. Studied at the Leningrad Institute of Physical Culture. USSR champion, 1975–76. World record-holder (500 metres), 1975. Olympic champion (500 metres), 1976.

Kulikov, Ivan Semenovich
1875–1941. Artist.
Studied at an art school of the Society for the Encouragement of the Arts, 1893, under E. Lipgart, then a correspondence student at the Higher Art School of the Academy of Arts, Petersburg, 1896 and 1897–02. Pupil of Il'ia Repin. Studied art in Germany, France and Italy, 1903–05. Genre and portrait painter, also water-colour painter. Exhibitions: MOLKH 1900, 1908–10, Spring Exhibitions, the Academy of Arts, 1901–02, 1904–17, the Society of Russian Water-colour Painters, Petersburg, 1907–08, 1912–14, I. Repin Society of Artists, Moscow 1927–29. Personal exhibitions: Murom (posthumously), 1942, Gorkii, 1959.

Kulikov, Viktor Georgievich
1921– . Marshal.
Son of a peasant. Member of the CPSU from 1942. In the Soviet Army from 1939. Chief-of-staff of a tank brigade during WWII. After the war, commander of a regiment, then a division, and finally an army. Graduated from the Frunze Military Academy in 1953 and from the Voroshilov General Staff Academy in 1959. Deputy Commander-in-chief, 1962–69. Commander-in-chief of the Soviet Forces Group in Germany, 1969–71. Chief of the General Staff of the Soviet Army and Navy, 1971–77. USSR 1st Deputy Minister of Defence from 1971. Marshal, 1977. Commander-in-chief of the Warsaw Pact Forces from Jan. 1977.

Kulishova, Anna Moiseevna (Rosenstein; Kuliscioff; m. Makarevich)
9.1.1854–29.12.1925. Politician, revolutionary.
Born in Simferopol'. Daughter of a merchant. In the 1870s, studied at Zurich University and became close to the Bakunist narodniks. Active in Russia in the revolutionary movement, 1873–77, under her married name Makarevich. Fled to Paris, 1877. Expelled for organizing a local section of the Marxist International. Moved to Italy, where she spent the rest of her life. Became one of the founders of the Italian Socialist Party, 1892, and later one of its leaders on the right wing of the party.

Kulybin, Mikhail Mikhailovich
1910– . Artist.
Born in Rostov. Enamel painter. Studied at an enamel art school. Pupil of A. A. Nazarov. From 1927, worked in art studios in Rostov. Exhibition: 1938–39, Moscow and Rostov.

Kun, Bela
20.2.1886–30.11.1939. Revolutionary, secret police official.
Born in Transylvania (then in the Austro-Hungarian Empire). Son of a minor official. Educated at a secondary school in Cluj (now Rumania). Joined the Hungarian Social Democratic Party in 1902. Mobilized in 1914 into the Austro-Hungarian Army and sent to the Russian front. POW in Russia in 1916, sent to Tomsk, came into contact with Russian revolutionaries. Joined the Bolsheviks in 1917. In Jan. 1918, went to Petrograd, later to Moscow. Bolshevik propagandist among former POWs. Edited many party publications. Commanded the International Red Brigades during the Civil War. Took part in quelling the left SR rebellion in Moscow in July 1918. Returned secretly to Hungary in Nov. 1918. One of the founders of the Hungarian Bolshevik Party. Arrested in Feb. 1919, and released on the proclamation of the Hungarian Soviet Republic, 21 Mar. 1919. People's Commissar of Foreign Affairs of Hungary, later Commissar for Military Affairs. Responsible for the Red Terror during the Hungarian Civil War. After the defeat of the Red

forces in Hungary, fled to Austria. Returned to the Soviet Union in 1920. Chairman of the Crimean Revolutionary Cttee., responsible for an appalling blood-bath in the Crimea after the end of the Civil War and the evacuation of General Wrangel's forces. Sent to Germany to organize revolution in 1921 (unsuccessful). Held high party posts in the Urals, 1921–23. Active in the Comintern. At the same time, a Soviet agent in Hungary. In Apr. 1928, arrested in Vienna as a Soviet agent but soon released and returned to the USSR. Head of the underground Hungarian Communist Party. Arrested in 1938. Died in the camps.

Kunaev, Dinmukhamed Akhmedovich
12.1.1912–   . Party official.
Kazakh. Son of a clerk. Graduated from the Moscow Institute of Non-Ferrous and Fine Metallurgy, 1936. Member of the CPSU, 1939. Worked as a foreman. Deputy head and chief engineer at the Balkash Copper Refinery. Deputy chief engineer at the Altaipolimetal Combine. Director of Leninogorsk Ore Board, 1936–42. Deputy chairman of the council of Ministers of the Kazakh SSR. President of the Kazakh Academy of Sciences, 1942–55. Member of the Cen. Cttee. of the Kazakh CP from 1949. Deputy to the USSR Supreme Soviet from 1950. Chairman of the Council of Ministers of the Kazakh SSR, 1955–60. Member of the Cen. Cttee. of the CPSU from 1956. Member of the Presidium of the USSR Supreme Soviet from 1962. 1st secretary of the Cen. Cttee. of the Kazakh CP from 1964. Candidate member, 1966–71, and full member of the Politburo of the Cen. Cttee. of the CPSU from 1971. Holder of 8 Orders of Lenin and many other awards. Close associate of Leonid Brezhnev. When, in Dec. 1986, he was fired from all his posts by Mikhail Gorbachev after 22 years of autocratic rule and replaced by the Russian-born Gennadii Kolbin, one of Gorbachev's men, the Soviet Republic of Kazakhstan saw fierce riots organized by his supporters, in which several people were killed and some 200 injured.

Kunin, Iosif Filippovich
28.4.1904–   . Musicologist.
Born in Moscow. Author of books on Tchaikovskii (1958) and Rimskii-Korsakov (1964) in the series *Zhizn' Zamechatel'nykh Liudei.*

Kupala, Ianka (Lutsevich, Ivan Dominikovich)
7.7.1882–28.6.1942. Poet.
Born at Viazynka near Minsk. Belorussian. First poem published in 1905, first collection of poems published in 1908 (*Zhaleika*). Lived in Petersburg, 1909–13. Edited a Belorussian newspaper, *Nasha Niva*, 1914–15. Close to M. Gorkii. After the October Revolution, became the official bard of Soviet Belorussian poetry (Stalin Prize, 1941), and a well-known establishment figure (member of the Supreme Soviet of the Belorussian Republic). Died during WWII in Moscow. In 1945 a museum was set up in his memory in Minsk.
Works: *Collected works* (in Belorussian), 6 vols, Minsk, 1961–3.

Kupchenko, Irina Petrovna
1.3.1948–   . Actress.
Graduated from the Shchukin Theatre School, 1970. Best known for her two films *Dvorianskoe Gnezdo*, 1969, and *Diadia Vania*, 1971.

Kuper, Emil Albertovich
13.12.1877–16.11.1960. Conductor.
Born in Kherson. Studied at the Odessa Music School, then in Berlin and Vienna. From 1897, conductor at theatres in Kiev and Rostov-on-Don, from 1907–09 at the S. Zimin Opera Theatre, Moscow, and from 1910–19 at the Bolshoi Theatre. Conductor for Diaghilev's Ballets Russes seasons in Paris, conducting the ballets *Pir* and *Petrushka*. From 1919–24, member of the board and conductor at the Petrograd Theatre of Opera and Ballet. In late 1920, left the USSR. Conductor at the Paris Opera and La Scala, 1932–36, at the Metropolitan Opera, 1944–50, and at the Montreal Opera Theatre, 1950–60. Died in New York.

Kuprevich, Vasilii Feofilovich
24.1.1897–17.3.1969. Botanist.
Born in Minsk Oblast'. Worked at the Botanical Institute of the Academy of Sciences. President of the Academy of Sciences of the Belorussian SSR, 1952. Specialist in the physiology and biochemistry of diseased plants and the classification of mushrooms. Died in Moscow. Buried in Minsk.

Kupriianov, Mikhail Vasil'evich (Kukryniksy)
21.10.1903–   . Artist.
Born in Tetiushi (now Tatar ASSR). One of the Kukryniksy (the graphic artists Kupriianov, Krylov and Sokolov). Studied at the Tashkent Art School, 1920–21, then at the graphic faculty of the Moscow VKHUTEIN, 1921–29, under P. Miturich and N. Kupreianov. Member of the Kukryniksy from 1924. Worked as a designer of political posters and press propaganda cartoons. Separately worked as a landscape painter and stage designer. Exhibited from 1932 at every political official exhibition (with the Kukryniksy and separately).

Kupriianov, Petr Andreevich
1897–1973. Surgeon.
Graduated from the Military Medical Academy, 1912, professor of the Academy, 1930. During WWII, chief surgeon on several fronts. World authority on heart surgery.

Kuprin, Aleksandr Ivanovich
26.8.1870–25.8.1938. Author.
Born in Narovchat near Penza. Educated in military schools, later rising to the rank of officer in provincial infantry regiments, serving in Podolia. Retired from military service, 1894, and became a full-time writer. Travelled all over Russia. Settled in Petersburg, 1901. Encouraged by Chekhov and Gorkii. Before the 1917 Revolution, became one of the most popular writers in the country with his short stories and novels, criticizing the evils of capitalism and prostitution, and depicting the boredom of provincial life. During the Civil War, emigrated, 1919. Settled in France, continued to write, living in isolation and poverty.

Shortly before his death, sick and almost completely blind, he was brought back to Russia by his wife. Died in Leningrad. Several editions of his collected works are available. He is still widely read and admired for his colourful, but unpretentious, and thoroughly human approach.

Kuprin, Aleksandr Vasil'evich
22.3.1880–18.3.1960. Artist.
Born in Borisoglebsk, now Voronezh Oblast'. First studied at private studios in Petersburg, 1902–04, then in Moscow 1904–06, and also in Voronezh, 1899–1901. Studied under L. Solov'ev, M. Ponomarev (Voronezh), L. Dmitriev-Kavkazskii (Petersburg), and K. Iuon and I. Dudin (Moscow). Continued his education at the Moscow School of Painting, Sculpture and Architecture, 1906–09, under N. Kasatkin, A. Arkhipov and Konstantin Korovin. Landscape painter. One of the founders of the association Bubnovyi Valet, 1910. Member of the Moskovskie Zhivopistsy from 1925. Taught at the VKHUTEMAS-VKHUTEIN, 1918–52. Until the mid-1920s, worked in the style of cubism. Main exhibitions: the Bubnovyi Valet, 1912–14, 1916, 1927, the Mir Iskusstva, 1917, 1921, 1st State Peredvizhniki Moscow, 1925, Industry of Socialism, Moscow, 1939. Personal exhibitions: Moscow, 1923, 1934, 1948. Died in Moscow.

Kurasov, Vladimir Vasil'evich
1897–1973. General.
On active service during WWI. Joined the Red Army, 1918. Took part in the Civil War. Graduated from the Frunze Military Academy, 1932, and from the Academy of the General Staff, 1938. Taught at the Academy of the General Staff. Several high staff positions during WWII, thereafter Chief-of-Staff of the Soviet military administration in East Germany. Head of the Academy of the General Staff, 1949–56, and 1961–63. Deputy Chief of General Staff and Head of the Military Scientific Committee, 1956–61. Promoted to the Warsaw Pact Supreme Command HQ, 1963.

Kurbas, Les'
25.2.1887–1938. Stage director.
One of the leading theatrical figures in the Ukraine in the 1920–30s. Born in the Galician city of Sambir, Western Ukraine. Studied philosophy at the University of Vienna, then theatre art with the Austrian actor, Joseph Kainz. In 1912, returned to Galicia and toured with the theatre group until the outbreak of WWI. When the Russian Army occupied Galicia in 1914, moved East, settling in Kiev in 1915. Became an actor in the Ukrainian Ethnographic Theatre, Berezil. Staged productions reflecting the influence of expressionism. During the 1920–30s, became an educator and the reformer of theatrical life in the Ukraine. Organiser of theatrical groups all over the Ukraine. Also acted and directed. Lectured on music and drama in Kiev and Khar'kov. Edited the magazine *Barricades of the Theatre*. In 1933, was stripped of the title People's Artist of the Ukraine, and banned from working in theatres in the Ukraine. Accepted an invitation from the distinguished Jewish stage director-producer Mikhoels to work in Moscow. Staged *King Lear* at the Moscow Jewish State Theatre. Arrested and accused of nationalism, formalism and Ukrainian counter-revolution and deviation from Soviet reality. Sent to the concentration camp on the Solovetskii Islands. Shot there in 1938. Until 1961, his name was purged from all Soviet publications. In Feb. 1987, rehabilitated. The centennial of his birth was commemorated both in the Ukraine and in other parts of the USSR.
See: *Smoloskyp*, Nr. 33, vol. 8. 1987.

Kurchatov, Igor Vasilievich
12.1.1903–7.2.1960. Nuclear physicist.
Born in Sim near Cheliabinsk. Graduated from the Crimea University in Simferopol', 1923. Taught physics and mathematics at technical institutes in Baku and Leningrad. Founded in Leningrad the Institute of Nuclear Energy, 1943. Member of the Academy of Sciences of the USSR, 1943. From 1943 till his death, directed nuclear research for peaceful and defence purposes — first cyclotron, 1944, first atomic reactor, 1946, first Soviet atomic bomb, 1949, first thermo-nuclear bomb, 1953. The 104th element of the periodical table is called 'kurchatovium' after him. Died in Moscow.

Kurekhin, Sergei
1954– . Jazz pianist.
Born in Murmansk. At the age of 2, moved with his parents to Moscow. Started playing piano when he was 4. Studied at a music school. In 1971, moved with his parents to Leningrad. Appeared with a number of rock groups. His first record was issued by the London-based Leo record company, 1981. Recognized by the music press as a brilliant performer and a representative of a new generation of Soviet jazz musicians.

Kurentsov, Viktor Grigor'evich
5.4.1941– . Athlete.
Born in the village of Tukhinka, Vitebsk Oblast'. Honoured Master of Sports (heavy athletics), 1966. With the Khabarovsk Armed Forces Club, 1962–65. From 1966, with the Moscow Oblast' Armed Forces Club. Member of the CPSU, 1969. Graduated from the Moscow Institute of Physical Culture, 1977. USSR champion, 1964–70, 1972 and 1974. European champion, 1964–71. World champion, 1965–70. Olympic champion, 1968. Silver medal, 1964.
See: D. Ivanov, *Ave, Viktor! Rekordy, Sobytiia, Liudi* (almanac), Moscow, 1970.

Kurgapkina, Ninel Aleksandrovna
13.2.1929– . Ballerina.
Born in Leningrad. Graduated from the Leningrad Choreographic School, 1949, in the class of A. Vaganova. One of the leading ballet dancers of the Kirov Theatre until 1969. Afterwards, taught at the Choreographic School.

Kurilko, Mikhail Ivanovich
12.6.1880–1.3.1969. Stage designer, architect.
Born in Kamenets-Podolsk. Graduated from the Petersburg Academy of Arts, 1913, and the Petersburg Archaeological Institute, 1914. Stage designer for theatres in Moscow, Leningrad, Kiev and elsewhere. From 1924–28, chief stage designer of the Bolshoi Theatre. One of the architects of the Novosibirsk Theatre of Opera and Ballet. Professor, 1940. Died in Malakhovka near Moscow.

Kurkin, Aleksandr Mikhailovich
1916–   . Artist.
Miniature painter, stage designer and mural artist. Studied at the A. Gorkii Art School in Palekh, 1935–40. Exhibitions: Ivanovo, 1947, 1952, RSFSR Artists, Moscow, 1949–57, Moscow, 1952, 1955, Ivanovo Artists, Moscow, 1956, Applied and Decorative Folk Art, Moscow, 1956–57, Applied Arts, Moscow, 1957.

Kurkotkin, Semen Konstantinovich
13.2.1917–   . Marshal.
Joined the Red Army, 1937. Member of the Communist Party, 1940. Tank officer during WWII. Graduated from the Tank Forces Academy, 1951, and from the Academy of the General Staff, 1958. Commander of Soviet Forces in Germany, 1971–72. Deputy Defence Minister, 1972. Member of the Cen. Cttee. of the CPSU, 1976.

Kurochkin, Pavel Alekseevich
1900–   . General.
Took part in the storming of the Winter Palace, Nov. 1917. Active in the Civil War as a cavalry commander. Graduated from the Frunze Military Academy, 1932, and the Academy of the General Staff, 1940. On active service during the Soviet-Finnish war and WWII. Commander of several fronts. Several senior posts after WWII, including head of the Frunze Academy, and high posts in the Supreme Command of the Warsaw Pact Forces.

Kuropatkin, Aleksei Nikolaevich
29.3.1848–16.1.1925. General.
Born near Pskov. Son of an officer. Educated at the Pavlovskoe Military School, 1866. Graduated from the Academy of the General Staff, 1874. Took part in the conquering of Turkestan in the 1860s–80s. Chief-of-staff to Skobelev in the Russo-Turkish war, 1877–78. Minister of War, 1898–1904. Commander-in-chief during the Russo-Japanese war, 1904–05. Dismissed after the defeat at Mukden. During WWI, Commander of the Northern front, 1916. Transferred to the post of Governor-General of Turkestan, directed the suppression of the rebellion in Turkestan, 1916–17. From May 1917, lived in retirement on his former estate near Pskov, taught at local schools. Did not take part in the Civil War. Died at Sheshurino near Tver.

Kursanov, Andrei Lvovich
8.11.1902–   . Biochemist.
Graduated from Moscow University, 1926. Professor at the Timiriazev Agricultural Academy, 1929–38. Professor at Moscow University, 1944. Director of the Institute of Plant Physiology, 1952. Academician, 1953. Worked on plant metabolism.

Kurskii, Dmitrii Ivanovich
1874–1932. Revolutionary, state security official, diplomat.
Graduated in law from Moscow University, 1900. Took part in the 1905–07 Revolution as a Bolshevik organizer. During the October Revolution, active in Odessa. Took part in the Civil War. Minister of Justice, 1918, 1st Soviet State Prosecutor General. At the same time, high-ranking political commissar in the armed forces, 1919–20. Soviet Ambassador to Italy, 1928.

Kurviakova, Raisa Vasil'evna
15.9.1945–   . Athlete.
Born in eastern Kazakhstan. Honoured Master of Sports (basketball), 1976. With Dnepropetrovsk Avangard. Sports instructor. European champion, 1972–76. World champion, 1971 and 1975. Olympic champion, 1976.

Kurynov, Aleksandr Pavlovich
8.7.1934–30.11.1973. Athlete.
Born in Gus'-Khrustalnyi, Vladimir Oblast'. Honoured Master of Sports (heavy athletics), 1960. With Kazan' Burevestnik. USSR champion, 1960. Olympic champion, 1960. European champion, 1960–63. World champion, 1961–63. Gold medal winner, XVIIth Olympic Games. World recorder-holder (light-heavy weight), 1958–65. Graduated from the Kazan' Aviation Institute, 1963. Plane designer in the military industry. Member of the CPSU, 1967.

Kuryshko, Ekaterina Sergeevna (Nagirnaia)
12.4.1949–   . Athlete.
Born in Poltava Oblast'. Honoured Master of Sports (rowing), 1972. With Kiev Dynamo. Studied at the Kiev Institute of Physical Culture. USSR champion, 1970–72. World and European champion, 1971. Olympic champion (with L. Pinaeva), 1972.

Kusevitskii, Sergei Aleksandrovich (Kussevitsky)
26.7.1874–4.6.1951. Conductor, double-bass player, musical authority.
Born in Vyshnii Volochek. Graduated from the Music and Drama School of the Moscow Philharmonic Society, 1894, in the double-bass class. Taught there from 1901. Virtuoso double-bass player who gave concerts all over Russia and abroad. From 1905, lived in Berlin. Studied conducting under K. Muk and F. Weingartner. In 1909, founded in Berlin the Rossiiskoe Muzykal'noe Izdatel'stvo (the Russian Music Publishing House), in order to promote Russian composers and Russian music. In 1909, founded the Moscow Symphony Orchestra, with which he toured all over Russia. Chief conductor of the State Symphony Orchestra (formerly the Imperial Symphony Orchestra), Petrograd, 1917–20. In 1920, emigrated. Settled in the USA. Conductor of the Boston Symphony Orchestra, 1924–49. Promoted and performed Russian music such as the 4th Symphony by Prokof'ev, the *Symphony of Psalms* by Stravinskii, etc. First performer in the USA of Shostakovich's 9th Symphony, and Prokof'ev's 5th. Mentor of the young Leonard Bernstein and other talented musicians. Died in Boston.

Kushner, Boris Anisimovich
1888–1937. Poet.
Member of the Left Bloc, 1917. Author of a brochure, *Demokratizatsiia Iskusstva*, 1917. Published his futurist prose *Miting Dvortsov*, 1918. Collaborated with Mayakovsky and O. Brik in *IZO, Narkompros*, and with Mayakovsky in *LEF* and *Novyi LEF*. Disappeared in the Gulag.

Kushniriuk, Sergei Georgievich
15.3.1956– . Athlete.
Born in Chernovitskaia Oblast'. Honoured Master of Sports (handball), 1976. With Zaporozh'e Burevestnik. Studied at the Zaporozhskii Industrial Institute. Olympic champion, 1976.

Kuskova, Ekaterina Dmitrievna
1869–22.12.1958. Politician, sociologist, journalist.
Daughter of an official. Member of a Populist group in Saratov, 1892. Joined the SD Party, 1897. With her husband, Prokopovich (later a minister of the Provisional Government), formed a partnership reminiscent of that of S. and B. Webb in England. Together they wrote sociological, economic and statistical works. On the initiative of Plekhanov, expelled from the SD Party, 1898. Criticized by Lenin for 'economism'. Became a leading light in Russian freemason circles. Elected to the Cen. Cttee. of the Cadets (but refused to join them), 1905. Disapproved of the Bolshevik take-over, 1917. Involved in the founding of Pomgol (Help to the Hungry Cttee). Expelled from the USSR in 1922. Settled (with her husband) first in Prague, later in Geneva. Prolific writer in emigré publications. After WWII, put her hopes on the possibility of reforms by Stalin. Actively involved in the forcible repatriation of refugees from Soviet Russia. Influential in left-wing Russian emigré circles until the end of her life. Died in Geneva.

Kustodiev, Boris Mikhailovich
7.3.1878–26.5.1927. Artist.
Born in Astrakhan'. First studied privately at P. Vlasov's studio in Astrakhan', 1894–96, then at an art school of the Academy of Arts in Petersburg, 1896–1903. Pupil of Il'ia Repin. Member of the Union of Russian Artists from 1907. Member of the Mir Iskusstva group from 1911. Worked for the Satirical magazines, *Zhupel*, *Adskaia Pochta*, and *Iskry*, 1905–07. Genre and portrait painter, book illustrator, stage designer. Also worked in historical painting and in sculpture. Studied at academies in France and Spain, 1904–05. Painter of Russian merchants. Died in Leningrad.

Exhibitions: MOLKH, 1900–01, Spring Exhibitions at the Academy of Arts, 1900–03, the Mir Iskusstva, 1910–13, 1915–18, 1922, 1924. Personal exhibitions: Petrograd, 1920, posthumously in Leningrad, 1928, Moscow, 1929, Leningrad, 1959, then in Moscow and Kiev, 1960.

Kutakhov, Pavel Stepanovich
1914–3.12.1984. Marshal.
Born in the village of Malokirsanovka, now Rostov Oblast'. Served in the Soviet Army from 1935. Military commander throughout WWII. Member of the CPSU, 1942. Command posts in the Soviet Air Force, 1945–67. Graduated from the Academy of the General Staff, 1957. 1st Deputy Commander-in-chief of the USSR Air Force, 1967–69, and Commander-in-chief from 1969. USSR Deputy Minister of Defence, 1969. Member of the Central Committee of the CPSU, 1971. Marshal, 1972.

Kutepov, Aleksandr Pavlovich
28.9.1882–1930. General.
Born in Cherepovets, Novgorod Gouvt. Educated at the Petersburg Infantry School, 1904. Took part in the Russo-Japanese war, 1904–05. Colonel of the Preobrazhenskii regiment, 1917. Being accidentally in Petrograd during the February Revolution 1917, was practically alone in organizing resistance with detachments which he put together on the spot. After the Bolshevik take-over 1917, joined the Whites. Governor of Novorossiisk, Aug. 1918. Commander of the 1st Army under Wrangel in the Crimea. After evacuation to Turkey, 1920, commander of the interned White forces in the camp on Gallipoli. Stern disciplinarian, able to maintain order during this time of defeat and despair. Moved to Bulgaria, later to France. Succeeded Wrangel, 1928, as head of ROVS (Union of White Veterans). Continued the struggle with the Bolsheviks by sending his agents on underground missions to the USSR with some limited success (e.g. the bombing of GPU buildings in Moscow). The GPU created a trap, masquerading as a monarchist organization, Trust, to fight his agents.

On 26 Apr. 1930, kidnapped on a Paris street (with the help of a former comrade-in-arms, Skoblin, turned GPU agent) and disappeared. It was thought that he was killed soon thereafter in France, but in the *Gulag Handbook* by Jacques Rossi, published 1987, he is mentioned as a Lubianka inmate. Details of his death remain unknown.

Kutiakov, Ivan Semenovich
1897–1938. Military commander.
Joined the Communist Party, 1917, and the Red Army, 1918. Graduated from the Red Army Military Academy, 1923. Commander of the Soviet forces in Khorezm in Central Asia, 1924. Author of works on the history of the Civil War. Liquidated by Stalin.

Kuts, Vladimir Petrovich
7.2.1927–16.8.1975. Athlete.
Born in the village of Aleksino, Sumy Oblast'. Member of the CPSU, 1955. Graduated from the Leningrad Institute of Physical Culture. European champion, 1954. Many times USSR champion during the 1950–60s. Olympic champion, 1956. Became an internationally famous long-distance runner. His premature death has been blamed on a physiological reaction to a sudden halt in his training. Wrote memoirs: *Povest' o Bege*, Moscow, 1964.

Kutuzov-Tolstoi, Mikhail Pavlovich, Count
3.11.1896–9.1980. Linguist, historian.
Born in Tsarskoe Selo. Grew up in Paris. Educated at high school in Baden-Baden. Moved to Darmstadt where his step-father, the Baltic baron Knorring, was Russian Ambassador at the court of the Grand Duchy of Hesse (the local Grand Duke was the brother of the Tsar's wife). Graduated from the Imperatorskii Aleksandrovskii Lyceum, 1915. Married Princess Marie Volkonskii. Remained through the Revolution 1917 on the Volkonskii estate near Tambov. Saved by local peasants from execution at the hands of a Cheka squad. Witnessed the murder of the German Ambassador Mirbach in Moscow, and the Uritskii

219

terror in Petrograd. Managed to flee to Finland to a former army comrade of his father, Mannerheim. Settled in Brussels, where his wife died after an operation, 1928. Moved to Latvia, and married the Belgian Countess de Villers in Riga, 1939. Just before the Soviet occupation of the Baltic states, moved to Yugoslavia, and later Transylvania, where he managed the estates of Hungarian aristocrats. At the end of WWII, in Budapest, organized an international hospital for wounded soldiers, under the protection of the Swedish Red Cross. Arrested by SMERSH, 1944, but soon released. In 1951, expelled with his wife from communist Hungary. Moved to Ireland. Founded an international school of languages at Delgany, County Wicklow, and taught Russian history at Trinity College, Dublin. His valuable memoirs – *The Story of My Life*, 1986 – depicting the changes in Russia and Europe from pre-WWI to post-WWII society were published in Germany. Died in Ireland.

Kuuzik, Tiit (Kuusik, Ditrikh Ianovich)
11.9.1911–   . Singer (baritone).
Born in Estonia. Pupil of A. Arder. 1st prize at the International Singing Competition, Vienna, 1938. Soloist with the Estonian Theatre of Opera and Ballet from 1944. Professor at the Tallinn Conservatory, where Georg Ots was one of his pupils. Stalin Prize, 1950, 1952.

Kuvykin, Ivan Mikhailovich
22.6.1893–14.6.1950. Choir conductor.
Born in Nizhnii Novgorod Gouvt. Chief conductor of choir collectives of the All-Union Radio Committee, Moscow from 1935 until his death. Died in Moscow.

Kuzin, Aleksandr Mikhailovich
1.7.1906–   . Radiobiologist, biochemist, professor.
Born in Moscow. Graduated from Moscow University, 1929. Worked at the 1st Medical Institute, Moscow, 1930–38. Professor there, 1938–51. Director, then head of the Department of Radiobiology at the Institute of Biophysics, 1952–57. Correspon-

ding member of the Academy of Sciences 1960. Editor-in-chief of the magazines *Biofizika* until 1961, and *Radiobiologiia* from 1961. Founder of the structure-metabolic hypothesis in radiobiology. Won the 1987 State Prize for a study revealing how radiation sickness develops, and specifically, how the body's protective white blood cells are destroyed by radiation. Began this research immediately after the first atom bomb was dropped on Hiroshima in 1945. Senior radiobiologist in the Soviet Union.

Kuzin, Valentin Egorovich
23.9.1926–   . Athlete.
Born in Moscow. Honoured Master of Sports (hockey), 1954. With Moscow Dynamo. Works as a plumber. USSR champion, 1954. European champion, 1954–56. World champion, 1954 and 1956. Olympic champion, 1956.

Kuzin, Vladimir Semenovich
15.7.1930–   . Athlete.
Born in the village of Lampozhnia, Arkhangelskaia Oblast'. Honoured Master of Sports (skiing), 1954. With Leningrad Burevestnik. Honorary coach of the USSR, 1970. Graduated from the Leningrad Institute of Physical Culture, 1957. Member of the CPSU, 1975. Candidate of Biological Sciences, 1972. Reader, 1976. USSR champion, 1953 and 1958. World champion, 1954 (30 and 50 km race). Olympic champion, 1956.
See: E. Simonov, *Korol' Lyzh iz Lampozhni*, Moscow, 1970.

Kuz'kin, Viktor Grigor'evich
6.7.1940–   . Athlete.
Born in Moscow. Member of the CPSU, 1966. Honoured Master of Sports (hockey), 1967. With the Central Sports Club of the Armed Forces. Graduated from the Moscow Oblast' Pedagogical Institute, 1969. USSR champion, 1959–75. European champion, 1963–69. Olympic champion, 1964, 1968 and 1972. World champion, 1963–69, 1971. In 1966 and 1972, captain of the USSR international team.

Kuz'menko, Galina Andreevna
1899?–   . Guerrilla leader.
Common-law wife of the anarchist leader, N. Makhno, during the Civil War. Head of the commission of Anti-Makhno Affairs (security service) in charge of terror actions. After the defeat of Makhno, fled with him to Rumania, and then to Poland, where they were imprisoned. Gave birth to Makhno's daughter in a Warsaw prison. Later released, and moved to Paris. During WWII, in labour camps in Germany. Handed over to SMERSH in 1945. Sent to the Gulag. Released under Khrushchev. In the 1960s, visited Gulai Pole, the former HQ of the Makhno cavalry.

Kuz'min, Mikhail Alekseevich
23.9.1875–3.3.1936. Poet.
Born in Iaroslavl', into a rich family. First appeared in print in 1905. Became almost a symbol of aesthetic circles before WWI: delicate, dandified and homosexual, nevertheless had a craftsman's grip on verse and prose, becoming the counterpart in literature of the Mir Iskusstva painters. Universally liked for his polished behaviour and wide knowledge of world culture and art. Produced excellent translations of Boccaccio and Shakespeare. During WWI, his 9-volume collected works was published in Petrograd, 1914–18. Died completely forgotten, but since then has re-gained his rightful position as an important representative of the Silver Age of Russian poetry.

Kuz'min Nikolai Nikolaevich
1883–1939. Revolutionary, state security official.
Member of the Bolshevik Party, 1903. Commissar of the staff of the South Western Front, Nov. 1917. In the Red Army from 1918. Commissar of the Baltic fleet, 1920. Took part in the Civil War as a commander of revolutionary sailors. After the Civil War, Commissar of the Baltic fleet. In the mid-1920s, military commander in Turkestan, later Military Prosecutor in the Military Collegium of the Supreme Court of the USSR. From 1932, held posts in party and state administration.

Kuz'min-Karavaev, Dmitrii Vladimirovich
1890?–after 1970. Cardinal.
Son of the general, V. D. Kuz'min-Karavaev. Member of the intelligentsia before WWI. Emigrated after the Revolution 1917. Lived in France. Married E. Pilenko (who, after their divorce, became the nun Mother Maria). Converted to Catholicism. Became a cardinal in Rome.

Kuzmin-Karavaev, Vladimir Dmitrievich
1859–1927. General.
Professor of the Military Academy of Petersburg University. Right-wing Cadet. Member of the editorial board of *Vestnik Evropy*. Member of the 1st and 2nd Duma. Close to the mathematician M. Kovalevskii, and the philosopher V. Soloviev. During the Civil War, member of the anti-communist government in Arkhangelsk, 1919. Emigrated, lived in France.

Kuz'mina, Elena Aleksandrovna
17.2.1909–15.10.1979. Film actress.
Studied at the FEKS workshops, and later at the Leningrad Institute of Stage Art, 1930. Best known for her part in *Novyi Babilon*, 1929. Other films include: *Odna*, 1931, *Mechta*, 1943, and *Chelovek Nr. 217*, 1945 (Stalin Prize, 1946).

Kuzminskaia, Tatiana Andreevna (Bers)
29.10.1846–8.1.1925. Author.
Sister of L. Tolstoy's wife, and the prototype of Natasha Rostova in *War and Peace*. Close to Tolstoy during his life-time, herself started writing in the 1880s, encouraged by her famous brother-in-law. After the revolution, settled in Yasnaia Poliana, 1919, and became the guardian of the Tolstoy family traditions. Her memoirs *Moia Zhizn' doma i v Yasnoi Poliane* are one of the best sources of the life of L. Tolstoy and his household in the 1860s.

Kuznetsov, Aleksandr Vasil'evich
1847–1918 (or 1919?) Cellist, composer.
Born in Petersburg. Pupil of K. Davydov. With the orchestra of the Mariinskii Theatre, 1861–94. Member of the Russkii Kvartet, Petersburg, 1871–83. Author of the opera *Iskuplenie* (produced in 1910), cantatas, a string quartet, 3 suites for 4 cellos, and romances.

Kuznetsov, Aleksei Aleksandrovich
20.2.1905–1.10.1950. Politician.
Born in Borovichi. Son of a worker. Komsomol leader in Novgorod and Leningrad, 1924–32. 2nd secretary of the Leningrad Communist Party obkom, 1937–38. Secretary of the Leningrad Communist Party city cttee. (gorkom), 1938–45. One of the organizers of defence during the WWII Siege of Leningrad. Lt-general, 1943. 1st secretary of Leningrad gorkom and obkom, 1945–46. Secretary of the Central Cttee. of the CPSU, 1946–49. One of the main victims of the Leningrad Affair, a post-WWII Stalin-Beria purge involving several thousands of party workers. Victim of the Gulag, probably shot.

Kuznetsov, Anatolii Vasil'evich
18.8.1929–13.6.1979. Author.
Born in Kiev. During WWII, lived through the German occupation of the Ukraine. Received a national prize for a short story in *Pionerskaia Pravda*, 1946. Worked on construction sites of hydroelectric stations (Kakhovka, 1952, Irkutsk,1956). The sincere description of the life of young workers in *Prodolzhenie Legendy*, 1956, brought him fame in the USSR and abroad. Accepted into the elite Gorkii Literary Institute in Moscow, from which he graduated in 1960. Trusted by the authorities. Ordered to go to court in France over an unauthorized French edition of his book (he won the case to his own great displeasure, as he confessed later), 1960. Considered one of the brightest hopes of the young generation of Soviet writers at that time. Wrote a sensational novel about the Nazi mass murders of the Jewish population of Kiev, *Babii Yar*, giving Evtushenko the theme for his famous poem on the same subject. The novel was heavily censored, which hardened his resolve to leave the Soviet Union. During a trip to London, July 1969, ostensibly to gather material on Lenin's life in Britain, asked for political asylum, although still at the height of his fame and popularity among young people in the Soviet Union. Published an uncensored version of *Babii Yar* in the West which has since been translated into many languages, and denounced his own previous conformist position and compromises in the Soviet Union. Did not repeat his literary success in the West, but gained a wide audience in the USSR through his Radio Liberty broadcasts from London, which were marked by style, wit and sincerity. Died in London of heart failure, leaving a 30-day-old daughter.

Kuznetsov, Boris Dmitrievich
14.7.1928– . Athlete.
Born in Moscow. Honoured Master of Sports (football), 1957. With Moscow Dynamo. Member of the CPSU, 1963. Graduated from the Moscow Institute of Physical Culture, 1964. USSR champion, 1954–55, 1957 and 1959. Olympic champion, 1956.

Kuznetsov, Boris Georgievich
23.2.1947– . Athlete.
Born in Astrakhan'. Honoured Master of Sports (boxing), 1972. With Astrakhan' Trudovye Rezervy team. USSR champion, 1972 and 1974. Olympic champion, 1972 (light-heavy weight).
See: A. Korshunov, *Vse Zvezdy Polulegkogo Vesa, Tvoi Chempiony* (almanac), Moscow, 1973.

Kuznetsov, Eduard Samuilovich
1939– . Dissident, editor.
Born in Moscow. As a student studying philosophy-marxism at Moscow University, arrested for participation in the samizdat magazine *Feniks* with V. Osipov, 1961. Sentenced to 7 years in a strict regime prison camp. Released, 1968. Settled in Riga. Became active in the Jewish national movement. 15 June 1970, arrested with a group of others attempting to hijack a Soviet plane in order to flee to the West. Sentenced to death. The Leningrad *Delo Samoletchikov* received world-wide publicity, and as a result the death sentence was commuted to 15 years in prison camps. In 1979, exchanged for Soviet spies. Went to Israel, then

moved to West Germany. News editor at Radio Liberty, Munich. Chairman of the Resistance International, 1983.

Memoirs: *Dnevniki*, France, 1973; *Mordovskii Marafon*, Israel, 1979; *Russkii Roman*, Israel, 1982.

Kuznetsov, Fedor Fedotovich

1904–1979. Col.-general.
Made his career as a political officer. Graduated from a rabfak (rabochii fakultet), 1931. Secretary of a party raikom, 1937. Joined the army and the political administration of the armed forces, 1938. Deputy head of the propaganda department of the armed forces. Head of the political administration of the armed forces, 1949. Head of personnel in the Ministry of Defence, in control of all important army appointments, 1953. Head of the Lenin Military Political Academy, 1957.

Kuznetsov, Fedor Isidorovich

1898–1961. Col.-general.
Took part in WWI. Joined the Red Army, 1918. Active in the Civil War. Graduated from the Frunze Military Academy, 1926, went on to become a professor at the academy. On active service during the Soviet-Finnish war and WWII. Head of the Academy of the General Staff, 1942–43.

Kuznetsov, Konstantin Alekseevich

21.9.1883–25.5.1953. Musicologist.
Born in Novocherkassk. Professor at the Moscow Conservatory. Author of works on the history of music. Editor of the 4-vol. collection, *Istoriia Russkoi Muzyki v Issledovaniiakh i Materialakh*, Moscow, 1923–27. Other works include *Etiudy o Muzyke*, Odessa, 1919, *Glinka i Ego Sovremenniki*, Moscow, 1926, and *Muzykal'no-Istoricheskie Portrety*, Moscow-Leningrad, 1937. Died in Moscow.

Kuznetsov, Konstantin Andreevich

23.10.1899–11.1.1982. Cameraman, photographer.
Entered the film industry in 1914. Pupil of the cameraman, A. A. Levitskii. Photographer-reporter. Photographed and filmed Lenin on many occasions. Filmed many events

in Petrograd, Kazan' Baku, and Erevan. From 1923, cameraman on such feature films as: *Abrek Zaur,* and *Po Zakonu*, 1926; *Vasha Znakomaia, Baby Riazanskie*, and *Moskva v Oktiabre*, 1927; *Kukla s Millionami*, 1928; and *Velikii Uteshitel'*, 1933. In 1946, joined the Popular Science Film Studio.

Kuznetsov, Mikhail Nikolaevich

4.6.1952–　　. Athlete.
Born in Moscow. Honoured Master of Sports (rowing), 1976. With the Central Sports Club of the Navy. Member of the CPSU, 1978. USSR champion, 1974 and 1977. Olympic champion, 1976.

Kuznetsov, Nikolai Aleksandrovich

1896–1965. Lt.-general.
Joined the Red Army, 1918. Took part in the Civil War. Graduated from the Frunze Military Academy, 1930. Professor at the Military Economic Academy. During the Soviet-Finnish war and WWII, served in the rear supply system. After WWII head of the administrative and economic departments of the Ministry of Defence. Professor at the Academy of the General Staff, 1946–62.

Kuznetsov, Nikolai Dmitrievich

1911–　　. Aircraft engine designer.
Joined the Red Army, 1933. Graduated from the Zhukovskii Air Force Academy, 1938. Member of the Bolshevik Party, 1939. During and after WWII, prominent designer of aircraft engines (for the An-22, Il-62, Il-86, Tu-114, Tu-144, and Tu-154). Also designed engines for sea and inland shipping. Academician, 1974.

Kuznetsov, Nikolai Gerasimovich

24.7.1902–12.1974. Admiral.
Born in the village of Medvedki near Vologda. Son of a peasant. Joined the Red Navy in 1919. Took part in the Civil War. Educated at a naval school, 1926. Graduated from the Naval Academy, 1932. Naval captain, 1934–36. Soviet naval attaché in charge of personnel sent to Spain during the Civil War, 1936–7. Deputy commander, and later commander of the Pacific fleet, 1937–9. Minister of the Navy, 1939–46. Supreme Com-

mander of the Soviet Navy during WWII. In 1945 Stalin ordered his trial for handing over Soviet sea maps to Allied navies during WWII. Demoted and sent to the Pacific, 1950. Found not guilty, appointed Navy Minister, 1951. Supreme Commander of the Soviet Navy after Stalin's death, Mar. 1953, 1st Deputy Defence Minister. Retired, Feb. 1956. Member of the Cen. Cttee of the CPSU, 1939–55.

Kuznetsov, Nikolai Ivanovich
partisan name – Grachev; German cover name – Oberleutnant Paul Siebert)
27.7.1911–9.3.1944. Intelligence officer, partisan.
Born in the village of Zyrianka near Sverdlovsk. Son of a peasant. Before WWII, worked as an engineer in Sverdlovsk and Moscow. Intelligence officer during WWII. In Aug. 1942, sent to the rear of the Germans to the partisan detachments of Medvedev in the Ukraine. Active in the Rovno district. Speaking German well, made contact with the occupation forces in the guise of a German officer, Siebert. Killed the chief German judge in the Ukraine, Funk, the functionaries of the Reichskommissariat, Hall and Winter, the vice-governor of Galicia, Bauer, kidnapped General Ilgen. Was killed near the village of Boratin, L'vov Oblast', by Ukrainian nationalists who considered him a dangerous and very effective agent of the NKVD and SMERSH.

Kuznetsov, Pavel Varfolomeevich

17.11.1878–21.1.1968. Artist.
Landscape and still-life painter. Born in Saratov. Studied at the Saratov Society for the Encouragement of the Arts, 1892–96, under V. Konovalov and S. Barakki, then at the Moscow School of Painting, Sculpture and Architecture, 1897–1904, under Konstantin Korovin and Valentin Serov. One of the organizers of the Golubaia Roza (Blue Rose) exhibition, 1907. Member of the Mir Iskusstva, and the Chetyre Iskusstva groups. Taught art, 1917–37 and 1945–48 at the VKHUTEMAS-VKHUTEIN. Influenced in the 1900s by the V. Borisov-Musatov style. At that time, travelled widely in Russia, especially

in Central Asia (Kirghizia). Exhibitions from 1899 with the Mir Iskusstva, the Blue Rose and the Four Arts. Personal exhibitions, with Elena Bebutova, in Moscow, 1923, 1929, 1956–57. Died in Moscow.

Kuznetsov, Valerii Alekseevich
12.4.1906–   . Geologist.
Graduated from the Tomsk Geological Survey Institute, 1932. Specialist in the geology of Siberia, in particular, its mercury deposits. Also carried out research into geotectonics and magnetism in Siberia and Central Asia.

Kuznetsova, Galina Nikolaevna
1900–1976. Author.
Emigrated after the Civil War. A pupil of I. Bunin at whose villa she lived, 1927–38. Left reminiscences on Bunin and Russian literary life in France before WWII.

Kuznetsova, Maria Nikolaevna
1880–1966. Singer.
Born in Odessa. Daughter of the artist Nikolai Kuznetsov. She was backed by N. Rimskii-Korsakov who valued her talent. Pupil of Ioakhim Tartakov. Debut at the Mariinskii Theatre, 1905. The *Daily Mail* praised her during the Russian season at Covent Garden, Feb. 1911. In the same year, appeared with tremendous success at the Grand Opera in Paris. Partnered F. Chaliapin. Her last performance at the Mariinskii Theatre was in 1917. Emigrated. Settled in Paris. Continued her career appearing in various European theatres. Died in Paris.

Kuznetsova-Budanova, Anna Konstantinovna
20.9.1898–13.4.1974. Doctor.
Born at Bezhitsa near Orel. Daughter of a worker in Briansk. Studied at Petersburg and Khar'kov universities. Paediatrician. In German camps during WWII, and in DP camps after the war. Settled in Munich where she was an active welfare worker in the Russian refugee community. Died in Munich. Her interesting memoirs, *I U Menia Byl Krai Rodnoi*, were published posthumously in Germany.

Kvachadze, Emmanuil Iakovlevich
3.1.1913–2.8.1987. Professor, scientist, journalist.
Born in Tiflis. Son of Ia. Kvachadze, a professor of Tiflis University. Graduated from the Odessa Medical Institute, 1936. Worked at the Leningrad Medical Academy. Military doctor during WWII. Lecturer in the Military Surgery Department of the Crimea Medical Institute, Simferopol', 1945–49. Head of the Surgery Department of the Kremlin Hospital, 1949–52. Professor, and dean of Vilnius State University, 1969. Became involved in the human rights movement, defending Lithuanian catholics harassed by the KGB, and thus attracted the attention of the KGB. Emigrated to Austria, 1979. Active in Vienna helping Soviet immigrants with their everyday needs. Died in Vienna.

Kvasha, Igor' Vladimirovich
4.2.1933–   . Actor.
Graduated from the MKHAT Studio School, 1955. From 1957 with the Sovremennik Theatre, Moscow. Played the part of Karl Marx in G. Rosha's film *God Kak Zhizn'*, 1966.

Kvernadze, Aleksandr Aleksandrovich (Bidzina)
29.7.1928–   . Composer.
Born in Georgia. Author of a ballet (*Choreographic Novellas*), a cantata, orchestral works, a symphony, concertos (with orchestra), 2 pieces for piano, pieces for violin, miniatures for piano and other instruments, choral works, works for the variety stage, and music for plays and films. Stalin Prize, 1950.

Kvitka, Kliment Vasil'evich
4.2.1880–19.9.1953. Folklorist, musicologist.
Born in Kiev. Husband of the poetess Lesia Ukrainka. Worked in Kiev, later in Moscow. Author of articles on Ukrainian folklore. Published the collection *Narodni Melodii z Golosy Lesi Ukrainki*, 1917–18, and *Ukrainski Narodni Melodii*, 1922 (both in Ukrainian). Died in Moscow.

Kvitko, Lev Moiseevich (Leib)
15.10.1890–12.8.1952. Poet.
Born in Goloskovo, Ukraine. Or-

phan, began independent life at the age of 10. His poem *Red Storm*, 1918, was the first Jewish poem on the October Revolution. Began writing children's poems in Yiddish, 1919. Victim of Stalin's purges after WWII. Arrested in 1949 and shot (with a group of Jewish cultural figures). See: *Chernaia Kniga* (The Black Book), compiled by V. Grossman, I. Ehrenburg and others, Jerusalem, 1980.

Kvitsinskii, Iulii
1938–   . Diplomat.
In the diplomatic service from the mid-1960s. Served in both East and West Germany. Headed the Soviet delegation at the Intermediate-range Nuclear Force talks (INF) in Geneva in 1981–83, and discussed the informal compromise known as the 'walk in the woods' formula. Dealt with space matters at the 1987 Geneva talks. Member of the CPSU from the early 1960s. Married with two children. Appointed Soviet Ambassador to West Germany, 1987.

Kyrvits, Kharri Augustovich (Körvits)
16.10.1915–   . Musicologist.
Born in Estonia. Author of articles on Estonian music, and a book on E. Kapp, 1959.

L

Labinskii, Andrei Markovich
1871–8.8.1941. Singer (tenor).
Born in Khar'kov. Pupil of S. Gabel' and V. Samus'. Soloist with the Mariinskii Theatre, Petersburg, 1897–1911, and the Bolshoi Theatre, Moscow, 1912–24. Died in Moscow.

Labourbe, Jeanne Marie
1877–1919. Revolutionary.
Member of the Bolshevik Party, 1918. Took part in the Civil War. Organized a French communist cell in the Soviet Union. Underground communist organizer and propagandist among French soldiers in Odessa, 1919. Arrested and shot by French army authorities in Odessa.

Ladinskii, Antonin Petrovich
19.1.1896–4.6.1961. Poet, author.
Born in the village of Obshchee Pole

near Pskov. Emigrated after the October Revolution 1917. Settled in France. Became known as a poet between WWI and WWII. Took Soviet citizenship in 1946. Returned to the Soviet Union, late 1940s. Wrote and published a series of historical novels which gained wide popularity. They deal mostly with the period of Kievan Rus (*Kogda pal Khersones*, *Anna Iaroslavna*, *Vladimir Monomakh*), and are based on solid historical research. His books opened for the young Soviet generation pages of neglected periods of the Russian past. Died in Moscow.

Ladukhin, Nikolai Mikhailovich
3.10.1860–19.9.1918. Music theorist, composer.
Born in Petersburg. Professor at the Moscow Conservatory. Author of textbooks on elementary musical theory and harmony. Composed orchestral works, pieces for violin and piano, songs and choral works. Died in Moscow.

Ladyzhenskii, Vladimir Nikolaevich
8.3.1859–19.1.1932. Author.
Born into a land-owning family. Lived in Penza Gouvt., locally well-known as an educationalist. Began to appear in print in the 1890s. Edited a newspaper at Penza, 1906. Translated the *Marseillaise* into Russian. Close to Chekhov. Wrote a popular history of Russian literature. After the October Revolution, emigrated to France, 1919. Died at Nice.

Ladyzhnikov, Ivan Pavlovich
13.1.1874–20.10.1945. Editor, publisher.
Born in Peskovskoe near Perm'. At the end of the 19th century, became a close friend and collaborator of Gorkii. Founded first at Geneva (1905), then at Berlin, a publishing house in his name, which printed Gorkii's works in Russian. Sold the publishing house, 1913 (after the revolution, under new management, it brought out many of the works of post-revolutionary emigré writers in the 1920s). Member of the editorial board of *Vsemirnaia Literatura* (founded by Gorkii), 1918–21. One of the directors of the Soviet book-

trade organizations Kniga and Mezhdunarodnaia Kniga, 1921–30. In his old age, consultant at the Gorkii archive, 1937–43. Died in Moscow.

Lagidze, Revaz Il'ich
10.7.1921– . Composer.
Born in Bagdadi, now Maiakovskii, Georgia. Lecturer. Head of the Music Department at the Tbilisi Pedagogical Institute. Author of a musical comedy, an operetta, a cantata, a symphonic poem, works for cello with piano and orchestra, romances, and music for stage and screen.

Lagutin, Boris Nikolaevich
24.6.1938– . Athlete.
Born in Moscow. Honoured Master of Sports (boxing), 1963. With Moscow Trud. From 1963, with Moscow Spartak. Graduated from the Moscow Institute of Physical Culture, 1965, and from Moscow University, 1971. Member of the CPSU, 1966. USSR champion, 1959–68. European champion, 1961 and 1963. Olympic champion, 1964 and 1968. Bronze medal, 1960. From 1977, Chairman of the Boxing Federation of the USSR.
See: V. Kommunarov, *Proba Na Muzhestvo*, from the collection *Zolotye Imena*, Moscow, 1975.

Lagutin, Iurii Vasil'evich
15.2.1949–2.5.1978. Athlete.
Born in Zaporozh'e. Honoured Master of Sports (handball), 1976. With Zaporozh'e Burevestnik. From 1976, with the Kiev Armed Forces Club. Graduated from the Dnepropetrovsk Metallurgical Institute as an engineer, 1975. Olympic champion, 1976. Died in Zaporozh'e. His premature death remains unexplained.

Laidoner, Iokhan (Ivan Iakovlevich)
31.1.1884–13.3.1953. General.
Born in Estonia. Son of a peasant. Joined the Russian Army, 1901. Graduated from the Academy of the General Staff, 1912. On active service during WWI, Lt.-colonel, 1918. Commander of an Estonian division in Soviet Russia, 1917–18. In Dec. 1918, returned to Estonia, appointed head

of the Estonian Army. Ally of Iudenich (White Army), 1919. Quelled a communist revolt in Estonia, 1924–5. After the Soviet occupation of Estonia, as a result of the Stalin-Hitler pact, arrested, July 1940. Sent to the Gulag. Died in a concentration camp.

Laiok, Vladimir Makarovich
1904–1966. Political officer.
Served in the Red Navy, 1923–27. Joined the Bolshevik Party, 1926. Secretary of Poltava obkom, 1941. Political officer during WWII. Worked in the Ministry of Defence in the same capacity, 1949–65.

Lamanov, Ivan Ivanovich
1898–13.9.1931. State security official.
Born near Khar'kov. Son of a peasant. Joined the Bolshevik Party in 1917. Fought against Denikin during the Civil War, 1918–20. Joined the border guards and Cheka detachments in 1922. Graduated from the Frunze Military Academy in 1928. Deputy head of the GPU forces in Central Asia, fighting against local anti-communist partisans (basmachi). Killed in action near Chagyl in the Karakum desert. Awarded the medal Pochetnyi Chekist (Honorary Cheka Man).

Lamanova, Nadezhda Petrovna
1861–1941. Clothes designer.
Famous clothes designer after the October Revolution 1917. Worked at IZO Narkompros as a clothes design instructor. Lili Brik and Elsa Triolet were among those to be seen in her dresses and hats.

Lambin, Petr Borisovich
15.5.1862–11.1.1923. Stage designer.
Graduated from the Petersburg Academy of Arts, 1885. From 1893, stage designer for the Imperial Theatres (Mariinskii, Aleksandrinskii and Bolshoi). Worked in Petipa and Fokin productions with K. Korovin and A. Golovin.

Lamm, Pavel Aleksandrovich
27.7.1882–5.5.1951. Musicologist, critic, pianist.
Born in Moscow. Artistic director of

the Rossiiskoe Muzykal'noe Izdatel'-stvo, 1912. Professor at the Moscow Conservatory. Restored Mussorgskii's opera *Boris Godunov* to its original form, 1928. Editor of Mussorgskii's *Collected Works*. Restored, in collaboration with S. Popov, Tchaikovskii's opera *Voevoda*. Died in Nikolina Gora, near Moscow.

Landau, Lev Davydovich
22.1.1908–1.4.1968. Physicist, academician.
Born in Baku. Son of an oil engineer. Graduated from Leningrad University, 1927. Sent to Niels Bohr, the Danish physicist, then to England and Switzerland. On his return, headed the Theoretical Department of the Ukrainian Institute of Physics and Chemistry. Pioneered the mathematical theory of magnetic domains. Worked with Petr Kapitsa on superfluid helium, and explained its properties in terms of quantum theory. For this work on superfluidity, he received the Nobel Prize, 1962. Member of academies in Europe and America. His *Sobranie Trudov*, 2 vols., was published in 1969 in Moscow. Died in Moscow.

Langemak, Georgii Erikhovich
1898–1938. Weaponry designer.
Joined the Red Army, 1919. Military engineer, worked in naval artillery in Kronstadt, and in the Black Sea ports. Graduated from the Military Technical Academy, 1928. Deputy Director and Chief Engineer of the Rocket Research Institute. Created the basis for a wide application of rocket systems in field artillery – the Katiusha, which made a significant contribution to Soviet victory. Victim of Stalin's purges.

Lapauri, Aleksandr Aleksandrovich
15.6.1926–6.8.1975. Ballet dancer, choreographer.
Born in Moscow. Graduated from the Moscow Choreographic School, 1944, and GITIS as a choreographer, 1958. A leading dancer at the Bolshoi Theatre, 1944–67. Taught at the Moscow Choreographic School, 1945 –61. From 1952, taught at the GITIS. Professor, 1972.

Lapchinskii, Aleksandr Nikolaevich
1882–2.5.1938. Air force officer.
Born near Tver. Educated at Alekseevskoe Military School, studied at Moscow and Munich universities before WWI. Pilot, air force lieutenant during WWI. Joined the Red Army, 1918. Chief of Staff of the Red Air Force. After 1925, taught at the Frunze Military Academy and the Zhukovsky Air Force Academy. Stressed the necessity of air superiority in modern warfare. Theoretician of mass bombing. Victim of Stalin's purge of the Red Army, probably shot in Lubianka prison in Moscow.

Lapikov, Ivan Gerasimovich
7.7.1922– . Film actor.
Studied at the Khar'kov Theatre School. Worked at a theatre in Volgograd. Entered the film industry, 1954. Best known for his two films *Predsedatel'*, 1964, and *Andrei Rublev*, 1969. Remarkable dramatic actor.

Lapin, Albert Ianovich (Lapinsh)
27.5.1899–5.1937. General.
Born in Riga. Was among the Latvians who joined the Bolsheviks after October 1917. Participant in the Bolshevik take-over in Moscow. During the Civil War, political commissar with the Red Army, and intelligence officer (Cheka), 1918–20. Commander of the Army of the Far Eastern Republic (Soviet satellite state), 1921. Graduated from the Military Academy, 1927. Various military posts in the Far East, 1932–37. Victim of Stalin's purges, probably shot.

Lapinskii, Evgenii Valentinovich
23.3.1942– . Athlete.
Born in Voronezh Oblast'. Honoured Master of Sports (volleyball), 1968. With Odessa Burevestnik. Graduated from the Odessa Pedagogical Institute, 1965. Sports instructor. USSR champion, 1967 and 1971. Olympic champion, 1968. Bronze medal, 1972.

Lapitskii, Iosif Mikhailovich
28.1.1876–5.11.1944. Operatic director.
Born in Minsk. Stage director with the Solodovnikov Opera, 1903–06,

and the Bolshoi Theatre, Moscow, 1906–08. Organized the Musical Drama Theatre in Petersburg, 1912. Artistic and general director of the same till 1919. Later with the Bolshoi Theatre, and in Kiev, Khar'kov and elsewhere. Died in Moscow.

Lappo, Ivan Ivanovich
1869–23.12.1944. Historian.
Graduated from Petersburg University in history, 1892. Professor of Russian history at Tartu University, 1905–1916. After the October Revolution 1917, went abroad. Lived in Prague, 1921–33. Professor of Kaunas (Kovno) University in Lithuania, 1933–40. Specialist on the history of Western Russia (Belorussia, Grand Duchy of Lithuania). At the end of WWII, among the Russian refugees in Germany. Died in Dresden.

Lappo-Danilevskii, Aleksandr Sergeevich
27.1.1863–7.2.1919. Historian, philosopher.
Born in the village of Udachnoe near Dnepropetrovsk (then Ekaterinoslav). Graduated from Petersburg University in history, 1886. Taught at the University from 1890. Member of the Academy of Sciences, 1899. Close to the Cadets (liberals), criticized the Marxist view of history. Contributed to the philosophical symposium *Problems of Idealism*, 1902. Original contribution to historical methodology, especially treatment of sources (insisted on including psychological considerations). Died of hunger and cold during the revolution in Petrograd.
Main works: *Metodologiia Istorii*, 2 vols, 1910–13.

Lapshin, Ivan Ivanovich
1870–1952. Philosopher, musicologist.
Professor of philosophy at Petersburg University. Emigrated. Professor at Prague University from 1923. Author of *N. A. Rimskii-Korsakov. Dva Ocherka*, Petersburg, 1922, *Zavetnye Dumy Skriabina*, Petersburg, 1922, and *Khudozhestvennoe Tvorchestvo*, 1922. Other works in Czech. Died in Prague.

225

Laptev, Konstantin Antonovich
3.11.1904– . Singer (baritone).
Born in Kiev. Pupil of M. Engel'kron.
With the theatres of Odessa, 1930–41,
and Kiev, 1941–52. Soloist with the
Kirov Theatre of Opera and Ballet,
Leningrad, 1952.

**Larin, Iurii (Lur'e, Mikhail
Zal'manovich; also Aleksandrovich)**
29.6.1882–14.1.1932. Revolutionary,
politician, economist, author.
Born in Simferopol' into a middle-
class Jewish family. In 1900, active in
revolutionary circles in Odessa. In
1901–02, head of the SD Party in
Simferopol'. One of the organizers of
the Crimea Union of the RSDRP.
Several short arrests. Exiled to
Yakutia, 1902. Escaped abroad.
With the Mensheviks in Geneva,
1904. Returned to Russia in 1905. SD
Party worker in Kiev, 1906–07.
Delegate at the 4th (1906), and 5th
(1907), RSDRP Congresses. Secre-
tary of the Union of Oil Industry
Workers, 1907–09. Wrote on econo-
mic and party subjects, 1909–12.
Joined the so-called 'Liquidators'.
During WWI, abroad. Returned to
Russia after the February Revolution
1917. Chief writer and head of the
journal *International*. Member of the
Executive Cttee. of the Petrograd
Soviet. Became a member of the
Bolshevik Party, Aug. 1917. After the
October Revolution 1917, worked in
the VSNKH (All-Union Soviet of
People's Management), dealing with
financial matters, trade, and the
setting up of the sovkhoz system
(state farms). Candidate member of
the Cen. Executive Cttee. Author of
many brochures and books on
economic and financial matters as
well as political issues. Died in
Moscow. Buried at the Kremlin wall.

**Larina, Anna Mikhailovna (b. Lur'e;
m. Bukharina)**
1914?– . Wife of Nikolai Bukharin.
Daughter of the Bolshevik Mikhail
Lur'e (Iurii Larin). Married Nikolai
Bukharin (his second wife) in 1934.
According to some sources, threats
to the life of his young wife forced
Bukharin to confess to fantastic
crimes at his trial. After his execution
in 1938, arrested as the wife of an
enemy of the people. Spent nearly 20
years in prisons and Gulag camps.
Approached Khrushchev in 1962 in
an attempt to rehabilitate her husband. Thereafter continued her fight
for many years until she received the
full support of Soviet intellectuals
and later the party leadership. In
Dec. 1987, interviewed by the editor
of *Ogonek*, Vitalii Korotich, and
published in the *Moscow News* (3
Dec. 1987) her husband's last letter to
'A Future Generation of Soviet
Leaders'. Lives in Moscow. Her aim
is to publish all Bukharin's archives
and explain his views. Finally saw the
complete success of her life-long
campaign with the complete rehabi-
tation of N. Bukharin in 1988.

Larionov, A. N.
1919?–1960. Politician.
1st secretary of the Riazan' party
obkom. When Khrushchev proclaimed his aim to overtake the USA
in meat and milk production in Jan.
1959, Larionov promised to double
meat production during the next
year. This pledge was highly publicized as an example to others. An
extraordinary scene ensued — practically every animal in the Riazan'
oblast' was confiscated and slaugh-
tered. Buyers were sent all over the
country to buy up meat, and workers
had to use their wages to purchase
meat for the state since taxes were
taken only in that commodity. At the
end of the year, it was announced
that meat production in Riazan'
oblast' had quadrupled. An immense
propaganda campaign followed. He
was awarded the Order of Lenin and
the title Hero of Socialist Labour. The
next year, agriculture in Riazan'
oblast' suffered a complete collapse.
On the eve of a plenary session of the
Riazan' party obkom at the end of
1960, he shot himself in his office.
The story earned the name of 'the
great Riazan' fiasco'.

Larionov, Mikhail Fedorovich
22.5.1881–10.5.1964. Painter.
Born in Tiraspol', Bessarabia. Studied at the Moscow School of
Painting, Sculpture and Architecture
at the end of the 19th century. Met
Natalia Goncharova with whom he
formed a life-long association. In
1915, joined Diaghilev in Switzerland. Under the influence of Diaghilev, became a pioneer of the avant-
garde in Russian painting, and took
part in futurist happenings. Became
one of the early abstractionists,
calling his method 'Luchism' (Rayon-
nism). From 1915, lived in Paris.
Died at Fontenay-aux-Roses.

Lashchenko, Petr Nikolaevich
1910– . General.
Joined the Red Army, 1930. Member
of the Bolshevik Party, 1931. Graduated from the Frunze Military Academy, 1940. On active service during
WWII. Graduated from the Academy of the General Staff, 1951. 1st
Deputy Commander of Land Forces,
1968–76.

Lashchilin, Lev Aleksandrovich
29.11.1888–10.11.1955. Ballet dancer.
Born in Moscow. Graduated from
the Moscow Theatre School, 1906.
Dancer, and soon leading dancer
with the Bolshoi Theatre all his
professional life until 1949. With
Diaghilev's Ballets Russes, 1909–11,
and with Anna Pavlova on tour in
Paris, London, Berlin, Rome and
Brussels. Died in Moscow.

Lashevich, Mikhail Mikhailovich
1884–1928. Revolutionary, military
commander.
Joined the SD Party, 1901. Active
participant in the Bolshevik take-
over, 1917. High command posts
during the Civil War. Deputy Army
and Navy Minister, 1925. Member of
the Cen. Cttee. of the Bolshevik
Party, 1918–19 and 1923–24.

Latri, Mikhail Pelopidovich
1875–1935. Artist.
First studied privately at the I.
Aivazovskii Studio in Feodosia in the
Crimea, then at the Higher Art
School of the Academy of Arts in
Petersburg (1896–02) under A. Kuindzhi and A. Kiselev. Landscape and
sea painter. Exhibitions: Spring
exhibitions at the Academy of Arts,
1900–02, 1904–05, the New Society
of Artists, 1905–06, 1914–15, MTKH,
1908, 1912, the Mir Iskusstva, 1912–
13, the Zhivopis exhibition, Moscow,
1915. Personal exhibition in Feodosia, 1929.

Latse, Renate
1943–1967. Athlete.
Prominent Lithuanian athlete. Honoured Master of Sports (track and field athletics). 4th place at the XVIIIth Olympic Games. Many times USSR champion. The cause of her death, reported in the American press, has not been explained in the Soviet media.

Latsis, Martyn Ivanovich (Sudrabs, Ian Fridrikhovich)
1888–1938. State security official.
Took part in the 1905–07 Revolution in Latvia as a Bolshevik organizer. Active participant in the Bolshevik take-over in Petrograd in Nov. 1917. One of the organizers of the Red Guard and the Latvian detachments, which were the Praetorian Guard of the Bolshevik government in its early days. One of the most active organizers of the Cheka (Secret Police), 1918–21. Quelled the left SR revolt in Moscow in July 1918. Director of the Plekhanov Economic Institute, 1932. Liquidated by Stalin.

Latynina, Larisa Semenovna
27.12.1934– . Athlete.
Born in Kherson in the Ukraine. Honoured Master of Sports (gymnastics), 1956. Graduated from the Kiev Institute of Physical Culture, 1959. Sports instructor. Honorary coach of the USSR, 1972. Member of the CPSU, 1963. International referee from 1968. USSR champion, 1956–64. European champion, 1957 and 1971. World champion, 1959 and 1962, and, with her team, in 1954, 1958 and 1962. Olympic champion (free exercises), 1956, 1960 and 1964, and with her team, in 1956, 1960 and 1964. Silver medal, 1964. Bronze medal 1956. Overall world champion, 1958 and 1962. Overall European champion, 1957 and 1961. USSR overall champion, 1961–62. From 1966–77 coach of the USSR international women's team. From 1977 member of the Organisational Cttee, Olimpiada 80. Author of two books: *Ravnovesie*, Moscow, 1975; *Gimnastika Skvoz' Gody*, Moscow, 1977.

Laurushas, Vitautas Antano (Laurusas)
8.5.1930– . Composer.
Born in Lithuania. Director of the Academic Theatre of Opera and Ballet of the Lithuanian SSR (Vil'nius). Author of a ballad, a symphonic poem, a sonata for cello and piano, instrumental pieces, and a vocal cycle.

Lavochkin, Semen Alekseevich
1900–1960. Aircraft designer.
Educated at the Moscow Higher Technical School, 1927. Worked in aircraft design offices from 1929. Since the mid-1930s, chief designer. Designed the La- series of Soviet fighter planes.

Lavr, Archbishop of Holy Trinity and Syracuse
1922?– . Russian Orthodox clergyman.
Carpatho-Russian in origin. Secretary of the Holy Synod of the Russian Orthodox Church in Exile. Head of the St. Trinity monastery in Jordanville, USA, the main centre of the Russian Church in Exile, comprising, apart from the monastery, a seminary, a publishing house of religious literature, an icon painting shop, and a museum with some valuable collections of the Russian emigration including the archive of the pre-revolutionary lawyers' society, and archives and museums of some regiments of the Russian Imperial Army.

Lavrenko, Evgenii Mikhailovich
24.2.1900– . Geobotanist.
Worked in the Khar'kov Botanical Gardens, 1921–28. Professor at the Khar'kov Agricultural Institute, 1929–34. Researcher in the Botanical Institute of the Academy of Sciences, 1934. Developed a new classification for steppe vegetation. Compiled vegetation maps, and wrote on the history of flora and vegetation. Suggested the concept of the phytogeosphere.

Lavrent'ev, Mikhail Alekseevich
19.11.1900– . Mathematician.
Born in Kazan'. Graduated from Moscow University, 1922. Professor at the University, 1931. Vice-president of the Academy of Sciences of the USSR, and chairman of the Siberian branch, 1957. Highly decorated (two Stalin Prizes, Order of Lenin). Member of the Cen. Cttee. of the CPSU, 1961.

Lavrov, Kiril Iur'evich
15.9.1925– . Film and stage actor.
Born in Kiev into an artistic family. Entered the Naval School. After WWII, worked in a factory. Joined the army, studied in the Air Force School and served on the Kuril Islands. Went back to Kiev and decided to work in the theatre. Was accepted into an auxiliary company. In 1955, was invited to work in Leningrad as a film actor. His first film was *The Honeymoon* (Lenfilm, 1956). Other films: *Andreika* (Lenfilm, 1958), *The Girl I Knew* (Lenfilm, 1962), *The Bridegrooms and the Knives* (Lenfilm TV Studio, 1964), *The Living and the Dead* (Mosfilm, 1964), *The Brothers Karamazov* (Mosfilm, 1969, dir. Ivan Pyriev; Lavrov played Ivan Karamazov), *Chaikovskii* (Mosfilm, 1970), *White Queen To Move* (Lenfilm, 1972), *The Story of a Heart* (Mosfilm, 1975). Also worked in theatre, first in the Kiev Lesia Ukrainka Drama Theatre. From 1955, acted in the Leningrad Bolshoi Drama Theatre. Moved to Leningrad Gorkii Theatre. With the Leningrad Gorkii Theatre company which came to the 1987 Edinburgh Festival, playing Doctor Astrov in *Uncle Vanya*.

Lavrov, Nikolai Stepanovich
5.2.1861–7.12.1927. Pianist.
Born in Pskov Gouvt. Nephew of the populist, P. Lavrov. Pupil of K. Zike. Member of the Beliaev Circle. Taught from 1881. Professor from 1899. Inspector and vice-director of the Petersburg Conservatory, 1915–21. Died in Leningrad.

Lavrova, Tat'iana Nikolaevna
30.12.1911– . Singer (soprano).
Born in Samara. Pupil of S. Akimova. Soloist with the Leningrad Malyi Opera Theatre from 1944.

Lavrovskaia, Elizaveta Andreevna (m. Tserteleva)
13.10.1845–4.2.1919. Singer (contralto).
Born in Tver' Gouvt. Pupil of G.

Nissen-Saloman. Soloist with the Mariinskii Theatre, Petersburg, 1868–72, and 1879–80. Gave Tchaikovskii the idea for his opera *Evgenii Onegin.* Professor at the Moscow Conservatory from 1888. Among her pupils were E. Zbrueva and E. Tsvetkova. Died in Moscow.

Lavrovskii, Leonid Mikhailovich (Ivanov)
18.6.1905–27.11.1967. Ballet dancer, choreographer.
Born in Petersburg. Graduated from the Leningrad Choreographic School, 1922. Dancer, and soon leading dancer, with the Leningrad Theatre of Opera and Ballet (Kirov Theatre) until 1935. Artistic director of ballet at the Leningrad Malyi Theatre, 1935-38. Artistic director of the Kirov Theatre, 1938–44. In 1942–43, with the Spendiarov Theatre in Erevan as its artistic director. From 1944–64, with some intervals, chief choreographer of the Bolshoi Theatre. Took part in the filming of his production of *Romeo and Juliet*, with director Lev Arnshtam. A TV film of this production was made in London in 1973. Died in Paris.

Lavrovskii, Mikhail Leonidovich
29.9.1941–   . Ballet dancer.
Born in Tbilisi. Son of Leonid Lavrovskii and E. Chikvaidze. Graduated from the Moscow Choreographic School, 1961. Dancer, and soon leading dancer, at the Bolshoi Theatre. Appeared in several TV ballet films (*Romeo i Dzhul'etta, Fedra, Belye Nochi, Zhizel'*). Awarded the Vaclav Nijinsky Award, Paris, 1972. In 1979, graduated from the GITIS, Moscow. Directed and appeared in the film *Mtsyri* (after Lermontov's poem), 1977.

Lavut, Pavel Il'ich
1898–1979. Arts promoter.
Organized Mayakovsky's lectures all over the Soviet Union, 1926–30. Mentioned by Mayakovsky in his poem *Khorosho.* In 1963 in Moscow, published his book, *Mayakovsky Edet Po Soiuzu.*

Lazakovich, Tamara Vasil'evna
11.3.1954–   . Athlete.
Born in Kaliningradskaia Oblast'.

Honoured Master of Sports (gymnastics), 1972. With Vitebsk Dynamo. Graduated from the Vitebsk High School of Physical Culture, 1974. World champion, 1970. USSR champion, 1970–71. European champion, 1971. Over-all champion of the USSR and Europe, 1971. Olympic champion, 1972. Silver medal, 1972.

Lazareva, Regina Fedorovna
13.12.1899–1979? Singer (soprano).
Born in Odessa. Appeared in operetta from 1917. With the Moscow Operetta Theatre, 1928–57.

Lazarevich, Vladimir Salamanovich
1882–1938. Military commander.
Graduated from the Academy of the General Staff, 1912. Took part in WWI as a Lt.-colonel. Joined the Red Army, 1918. Several high staff positions on the Eastern and Western Fronts, and in Turkestan. Thereafter, active in military training. Head of the Air Force Academy. Liquidated by Stalin.

Lazimir, Pavel Evgen'evich
21.1.1891–20.5.1920. Revolutionary.
Medical orderly in a Petersburg military hospital. Before 1917, left-wing SR. Involved in revolutionary propaganda among soldiers. Active participant in the October Revolution 1917, worked out the statute of the Military Revolutionary Commission. 1st chairman of the Military Revolutionary Commission (Revolutionary General Staff). In Nov. 1917, worked in the Ministry of the Interior. During the Civil War, head of supply for the Red Army in the Ukraine. Died of typhoid at Kremenchug.

Lazo, Sergei Georgievich
23.2.1894–5.1920. Revolutionary.
Born in Piatry (now Lazo) in Moldavia. Studied at Petersburg Technical Institute and Moscow University. During WWI, attended the Alekseevskoe Military School, and appointed officer of a Siberian reserve regiment in Krasnoiarsk. Left-wing SR, involved in revolutionary propaganda among soldiers. After the October Revolution 1917,

Revolutionary Commander of Irkutsk. Joined the Communist Party, 1918, appointed commander of the Transbaikal front, fought against ataman Semenov. Organized an underground communist committee in Vladivostok, 1918. Commander of Red partisan detachments in the Far East, 1919. In Jan. 1920, after a successful coup, took power in Vladivostok. In Apr. 1920, Vladivostok was occupied by the Japanese, and he was executed, (burned alive in a locomotive, according to Soviet sources).

Lebedenko, Aleksandr Geras'evich
1892–1975. Author, journalist.
Member of the Bolshevik Party, 1919. Wrote children's stories about polar explorers. After Kirov's death, arrested, 1935. Spent 20 years as an inmate of the Gulag camps. Released, 1955. Returned to Leningrad, 1956, and resumed his literary activity. Member of the management committee of the Leningrad division of the Union of Writers. Wrote extensively about his Gulag experiences in the 1950–60s. Some of this material was published in the almanac *20 Vek,* 1977, vol. 2.

Lebedev, Pavel Pavlovich
3.5.1872–2.7.1933. General.
Born in Cheboksary. Son of a landowner. Educated at the Aleksandrovskoe Military School, 1892. Graduated from the Academy of the General Staff, 1900. Major-general, 1914–18. Volunteered for the Red Army during the Civil War. Head of the mobilization commission of the Soviet government, 1918–19. Fought against Kolchak, 1919, planned operations against Denikin and Iudenich. Head of the Military Academy, 1922–24. Died in Khar'kov.

Lebedev, Vladimir Vasil'evich
1891–1964? Artist.
Illustrator of children's books, genre and portrait painter. Also a graphic artist. Studied at the M. D. Bernstein Studio in Petersburg, then at the Academy of Arts, 1912–16. First exhibition in 1909. Other exhibitions: Moscow, 1927–28, Leningrad, 1932, Moscow, 1934, 35, 36, 39, Leningrad,

1940, Moscow, 1943, 1954. Personal exhibitions: Moscow, 1925, and Leningrad, 1928.

Lebedev-Kumach, Vasilii Ivanovich (real name – Lebedev)
5.8.1898–20.2.1949. Poet.
Born in Moscow. Son of a shoemaker. During the Civil War, active in communist propaganda with his revolutionary slogans in verse. In the 1920–30s, a famous song writer, who often wrote songs for films, especially comedies. Author of the popular *Marsh Veselykh Rebiat*. During WWII, wrote the official song *Sviashchennaia Voina*. Died in Moscow.

Lebedev-Polianskii, Pavel Ivanovich (Polianskii, Valerian)
2.1.1882–4.4.1948. Literary critic.
Born in Melenki, near Vladimir. Involved in revolutionary activity. Lived abroad (Geneva), 1908–1917. After the October Revolution, appointed commissar of the publishing department of the Ministry of Education (Narkompros), 1917–19. First Soviet editions of Russian classics published under his supervision. Chairman of Proletcult, 1918–20. Head of Glavlit (censorship commission), 1921–30. One of the editors of the first edition of the *Bolshaia Sovetskaia Entsiklopediia* and editor of *Literaturnaia Entsiklopediia*, 1934–39. Died in Moscow.

Lebedeva, Anastasia Rodionovna
1888–after 1969. Singer.
Born in Voronezh Gouvt. Organized a folk choir in her village, 1926, and appeared with it in Moscow, 1928. One of the organizers of the Voronezh Russian Folk Choir, 1943. 20 songs by this choir (recorded by S. Popov) were published as the anthology *Russkie Narodnye Pesni Voronezhskoi Oblasti*, 1939.

Lebedeva, Evdokia Iakovlevna
25.2.1903– . Singer (soprano).
Born in Tula Gouvt. Pupil of L. Shor-Plotnikova. With the Moscow Operetta, 1929–64.

Lebedinskii, Lev Nikolaevich
5.11.1904– . Musicologist, folklorist.
Born in Miusskii Zavod in the Urals.

Author of *Bashkirskie Narodnye Pesni*, Moscow, 1962, *Khorovye Poemy Shostakovicha*, Moscow, 1957, and *Sed'maia i Odinnadtsataia Simfoniia D. D. Shostakovicha*, Moscow, 1960.

Leblan, Mikhail Varfolomeevich
1875–1940. Artist.
Landscape and portrait painter. Also still-life painter and stage designer. Born in Orel. Studied at P. Sychev's private art school (1892–93), then at the Moscow School of Painting, Sculpture and Architecture (1893–07) under S. Korovin, L. Pasternak, A. Arkhipov, A. Stepanov, A. Vasnetsov, V. Serov and K. Korovin. Pupil of Il'ia Repin at the Petersburg Academy of Arts. In 1910–12, worked in Paris. Studied at the Grand-Chaumiere Academie Libre, also under H. Matisse. Exhibitions (from 1894): The Union of Russian Artists, the Mir Iskusstva, the Bubnovyi Valet, the Moscow Association of Artists, the Zhar-Tsvet. Posthumous exhibition of his work: Moscow, 1941.

Ledenev, Roman Semenovich
4.12.1930– . Composer.
Born in Moscow. Author of oratorios (e.g. *Slovo o Polku Igoreve)*, a cantata, a suite for children, concertos for violin and viola, a nocturne, concerto for flute and orchestra, a piano sonata, choral works, songs, and music for stage and screen.

Lednev, Pavel Serafimovich
25.3.1943– . Athlete.
Born in Gorkii. Honoured Master of Sports (pentathlon), 1972. With the L'vov Armed Forces Club. Graduated from the L'vov Institute of Physical Culture, 1966. Member of the CPSU, 1975. USSR champion, 1968 and 1973. Olympic champion, 1972. World champion, 1973–75 and 1978. Silver medal, 1968 and 1976.

Legasov, Valerii
1936–27.4.1988. Scientist.
First scientist to visit Chernobyl hours after the explosion and fire which devastated one of the reactors.

Held a senior position at the Kurchatov Atomic Institute. Professor and leading member of the Academy of Sciences. Gave an honest report of the Chernobyl situation to enquiries from foreign nuclear scientists. Soviet scientific circles believe that his premature death was caused by his exposure to dangerous levels of radiation but this is not admitted officially.

Legat, Nikolai Gustavovich
27.12.1869–24.1.1937. Ballet dancer, choreographer.
Born in Moscow. Son of Gustav Legat, the Swedish ballet dancer and choreographer. Elder brother of the dancer Sergei Legat. Graduated from Petersburg Theatre School, 1888. Trained first by his father, then by N. Volkov and P. Gerdt. Partner of Anna Pavlova, Mathilde Kschessinska, Tamara Karsavina, and Olga Preobrazhenskaia. Became famous for his brilliant technique. His only rival was V. Nijinsky. Performed with the Ballets Russes all over Europe. Choreographer, 1902. From 1910 chief choreographer of the Mariinskii Theatre *(Feia Kukol*, 1903, with his brother; *Kot v Sapogakh*, 1906; *Alen'kii Tsvetochek*, 1907). Famous tutor, 1896–1914, at the Petersburg Theatre School. Among his distinguished pupils were A. Pavlova, M. Fokin, T. Karsavina, L. Kiaksht, Bronislava and Vaclav Nijinsky, A. Vaganova, F. Lopukhov. His contract was not renewed by the Mariinskii in 1914. Gave private lessons and taught at A. Volynskii's ballet school. Went abroad, 1922. Taught at Diaghilev's Ballets Russes, 1925–26. In 1923, set up his own ballet school in London, which was run in 1926 by his wife N. Nikolaeva-Legat. Among his pupils were N. de Valois, A. Markova, M. Fonteyn, and F. Ashton. In 1932, published his memoirs, *Story of the Russian School*. He and his brother published the album *Russkii Balet v Karikaturakh*, Petersburg, 1903. Died in London.

Léger, Nadia
1905?– . Wife of Fernand Léger.
Born in Gorno, a small village near Vitebsk. Studied art in a Moscow art school and was once a pupil of

229

Malevich. Probably met Fernand Léger in Moscow. Came to France in 1925 as an art student. Became a teacher. Eventually married Léger. After his death in 1955, dedicated her time and energies to his heritage. Donated some 300 of his paintings to France. These are now housed in a small museum in Biot, just north of Antibes. To celebrate his centenary, opened a new museum, La Maison de Fernand Léger, filled with his books, tapestries, mosaics and stained-glass windows. Tireless organizer of lectures and exhibitions on Léger. Always maintained close relations with the Soviet authorities and is thought to have her own flat in Moscow. Entertains Soviet ambassadors, writers and artists in her house near Paris. Soviet diplomats in Paris call her 'Svoi Paren' v Parizhe' (Our Fellow in Paris).

Legostaev, Filipp Mikhailovich
1905?– . Military commander, physiotherapist.
Took part in WWII. Taken prisoner by the Germans. Joined the ROA. After WWII, lived in DP camps in West Germany. Emigrated to Venezuela. Became the founder of the Institute of Physiotherapy in Carácas. Took part in the work of Russian political organizations abroad (S-BONR – Vlasov Veterans). Active in medical-personnel education in Venezuela.

Leliushenko, Dmitrii Danilovich
1902–1987. Marshal.
A participant in the Civil War, commander of armoured forces during WWII. Commanded the 1st and 3rd Guards Armies in offensive operations against the Wehrmacht in 1943. Led the 4th Tank Army in the Ukrainian campaign. Held many high military posts in the army in the post-war years. Died in Moscow.

Leman, Albert Semenovich
7.12.1915– . Composer.
Born in Saratov Gouvt. Professor at the Kazan' Conservatory. Author of a symphony, suites, an overture, a rhapsody, piano and violin concertos, a string quartet, pieces for piano, romances, and music for the stage. Stalin Prize, 1952, State Prize, 1957.

Lemba, Artur Gustavovich
24.9.1885–21.11.1963. Composer.
Born in Revel (Tallinn). Taught at the Petersburg Conservatory, 1908–20. Professor in Helsinki from 1915, and in Tallinn from 1922. Author of operas, 2 symphonies, overtures, 4 concertos for piano with orchestra, a chamber ensemble, sonatas, choral works, and romances. Died in Tallinn.

Lemberg, Aleksandr Grigor'evich
22.10.1898–9.6.1974. Cameraman.
Entered the film industry, 1914. From 1916, cameraman on feature films. Worked under his father, Grigorii Lemberg. In 1917, war cameraman. Filmed Lenin on many occasions from 1918–22. Member of the team which filmed Lenin's funeral, Jan. 1924. Cameraman during the Civil War. Member of the Kinoki (Kino-Eye) group. Worked with D. Vertov on *Shestaia Chast' Mira*, 1926. From 1938–41, and from 1946, staff cameraman at the VDNKH (Permanent Exhibition of People's Achievements).

Lemberg, Grigorii Moiseevich
1873–30.7.1945. Cameraman.
Started as a photographer. From 1911–17, made some 30 films as a cameraman. Filmed the events of the February and October Revolutions. In 1920, head of the so-called 'agit-trains' and 'agit-boats'. From 1923, with Goskino (Kultkino). Later with the Popular Science Film Studio.

Lemeshev, Sergei Iakovlevich
10.7.1902– . Singer.
Born in the village of Staroe Kniazevo near Tver'. Graduated from the Moscow Conservatory, 1925. First appearance on stage in the Sverdlovsk Opera in 1926. Soloist (tenor) of the Bolshoi Theatre in Moscow, 1931–65. Very popular opera performer and singer of folk songs. Idol of generations of music lovers in Russia.

Lemeshev, Viacheslav Ivanovich
3.4.1952– . Athlete.
Born in Moscow. Honoured Master of Sports (boxing), 1972. With the Moscow Armed Forces Club. Olympic champion, 1972. USSR champion, 1974. European champion, 1973 and 1975.

Lemke, Mikhail Konstantinovich
12.11.1872–18.8.1923. Literary scholar.
Born in Demiansk, Novgorod Gouvt. Educated at Konstantinovskoe Military School in Petersburg in 1893. Began work as a journalist in 1894. Editor of the newspapers *Orlovskii Vestnik*, 1898–1901, *Pridneprovskii Krai*, 1901–06. Editor of the magazine *Kniga*, 1906. Member of the SR Party. During WWI, military censor at the headquarters of the Russian Army, 1915–16. Author of the classic study of censorship in Russia *Nikolaevskie Zhandarmy i Literatura*. Editor of the best edition of Herzen's works (22 vol.). Published a detailed diary of his life at army HQ during WWI, *250 Dnei v Tsarskoi Stavke* (250 Days at the Tsar's HQ). Joined the Bolshevik Party shortly before his death. Died in Petrograd.

Lenin, Vladimir Il'ich (Ul'ianov)
22.4.1870–21.1.1924. Politician, revolutionary, statesman.
Born in Simbirsk (now Ulianovsk). Son of a school-inspector of devout Orthodox beliefs and Russian-Kalmuck descent, and Maria Blank, the daughter of a doctor of German-Jewish extraction. Educated at Simbirsk High School, 1879–87. His elder brother, Aleksandr, was involved, with other narodnik terrorists, in the attempted assassination of Alexander III, was sentenced to death and, after refusing to plead for mercy, hanged in 1887. After this event (and his father's death in 1886), Lenin became very interested in revolutionary activity and atheism (reading first Chernyshevskii and later Marx). Entered Kazan' University, but was expelled in 1887. Graduated in law as an external student of Petersburg University in 1891, already deeply involved in Marxist underground activity in Kazan' and Samara. From 1891–93, active as a lawyer in Samara, this being the only time in his adult life when he was not fully occupied by revolutionary activity. Moved to Petersburg in 1893 and became prominent in local Marxist circles,

engaging in polemics with populists and legal Marxists (P. Struve and others). In 1895, after a trip abroad to see Plekhanov and other social-democrats, together with Martov, the future Menshevik leader, founded the Union for the Struggle for the Liberation of the Working Class, a precursor of the SD Party. Arrested in 1895, spent 2 years in Petersburg Prison (continuing to write research and propaganda works). Exiled to Siberia for 3 years in 1897. Lived there with his wife N. Krupskaia. In exile, wrote about 30 revolutionary works, and in 1899, started polemics with his opponents within the party which did not cease until his death. At the 1903 Congress (Brussels-London) split the party into the democratic (Menshevik, minority) faction, and the totalitarian (Bolshevik, majority) faction. His astute propaganda sense was demonstrated by this labelling, because the Menshevik faction was in reality the larger. From 1900-05, lived in Munich, London and Geneva, always fighting for complete control of the party newspaper *Iskra*, the party Cen. Cttee., and the party funds, with variable success. Had no qualms in accepting funds for the party from robberies (Stalin's expropriations), capitalist donations (from the millionaire Savva Morozov and others), fictitious marriages of his party members, and later, during WWI, from German official circles. In Nov. 1905, returned to Russia, but was able to play only a negligible role in the revolution (in contrast to Trotsky and Helphand, who created and led the Petrograd Soviet). In summer 1906, moved to Finland (Kuokkala), which was part of the Russian Empire but, due to Finnish autonomy, was largely inaccessible to the Tsarist police. In Dec. 1907, again went abroad, first to Switzerland, then to France, resuming the life of a political emigré, and leader of bickering, minuscule Marxist groups. In 1909, published his main philosophical work *Materialism and Empiriocriticism*, which was much more a work of aggressive invective against all his opponents (from the followers of idealist philosophy and religion to liberal Marxists) than of any real philosophical value. Founded the party school in Longjumeau near Paris in 1911. Though a convinced

internationalist and participant in the Stuttgart (1907) and Copenhagen (1910) International Socialist Congresses, was regarded by West European socialists as a fringe fanatic. Largely isolated, he organized a conference of his own group in Prague (then in Austro-Hungary) in Jan. 1912, expelling Mensheviks and all other opponents from the party (and electing Stalin in absentia onto the Cen. Cttee.). Moved in June 1912 to Cracow (also in Austro-Hungary). At the beginning of WWI, was arrested by the local police as a Russian subject, but soon, with the help of Austrian social-democrats, was allowed to move to neutral Switzerland. Stayed in Bern until 1916, and Zurich until Apr. 1917. One of the main participants of the anti-war socialist conferences at Zimmerwald, 1915, and Kienthal, 1916. At the time of the fall of Tsarism in Russia, he was in complete despair, both financial and political. Unsuccessfully tried to split the Swiss and Swedish social-democratic parties and to start revolutions in these 2 countries, finally acknowledging, practically on the eve of the February Revolution 1917, that 'we shall not see the revolution, but future generations will'. Immediately after the February Revolution, arranged, through intermediaries, official German help for his return to Russia in a special train (the Germans being keen to see him spread his defeatist propaganda inside Russia). The extent of German financial help is a matter of controversy, but it seems to have been considerable. Having arrived in Apr. 1917 by train at Petrograd (through Germany, Denmark, Sweden and Finland), he at once launched a virulent campaign against the Provisional Government, and in July 1917, started a revolt, which proved unsuccessful. After that, went into hiding to avoid arrest, but in Nov. 1917 (October old style), the successful Bolshevik take-over was staged, facilitated by the preceding quarrel between the Prime Minister, Kerenskii, and the Commander-in-Chief, Kornilov. The practical leadership of the takeover was executed brilliantly by L. Trotsky. Lenin proclaimed Soviet power, and thus became the founder and first head of the Soviet state. The Constituent Assembly, once it became clear

that the Bolsheviks were in the minority, was forcibly dissolved after its first session, 5 Jan. 1918, by its Bolshevik sailor-guards on Lenin's orders. Lenin drew support from the masses, promising them immediate peace and land confiscated from the land-owners. (Both promises were an illusion, as peace returned to Russia only in 1922, and the additional land did not noticeably enrich the peasants). Managed to split the largest Russian party, the SRs, by offering a coalition to their leftwing (the coalition broke down half a year later). In Aug. 1918, he was seriously wounded by the SR, Dora Kaplan. Against opposition from all sides (including some of his party colleagues), insisted on the acceptance of the humiliating German peace terms of Brest-Litovsk, 1918, arguing that this was necessary to gain time (in this he was proved right). During the ensuing Civil War (it had long been his intention to 'turn the imperialist war into civil war'), he made systematic use of efficient shock troops – revolutionary sailors, Latvian cheka detachments, and former POWs – to fight at the front and keep the population subdued by terror (Cheka was established on 20 Dec. 1917). He thought of Russia as a base for world revolution, pinning his hopes on a Marxist take-over in the highly-developed European countries, especially Germany. In 1919, founded the Communist International (Comintern), which pretended to be, and to a great extent became, the headquarters of the world communist movement, under the leadership of his closest collaborator, Zinoviev. In 1921, after the shock caused by the rebellion of the Kronstadt sailors, who had previously been the mainstay of the revolution, he proclaimed the New Economic Policy (NEP), partly restoring private ownership, and replacing requisitions by taxing the peasants. This quickly restored the standard of living almost to pre-WWI levels. But the following year, he was incapacitated by strokes, and 2 years later finally succumbed to progressive paralysis of the brain. The exact cause of this fatal illness is still a matter of controversy. His last years were embittered by physical suffering and the complete disregard shown towards him (and especially his wife) by the party's General

Secretary, Stalin. After his death, he was practically deified, his body being embalmed and placed in the Mausoleum on Red Square (despite protests from his widow). The former imperial capital, Petersburg (Petrograd), was renamed Leningrad (a change bitterly resented by many Russians then as now). His eventual successor, and the tormentor of his last days, Stalin, for his own reasons, created an image of Lenin as an immensely kind, benevolent and modest father-figure, which is in glaring contradiction to the historical figure, who was above all a supreme tactician of political power. His name is still quoted incessantly in the Soviet Union, and in connection with the most contradictory policies. His collected works have been published many times, most recently in 55 volumes, 1958–65. For a different angle, the memoirs of those who knew Lenin well before his deification should be consulted: N. Valentinov, *Vstrechi S Leninym* and *Maloznakomyi Lenin*; G. Solomon, *Lenin I Ego Sem'ia*; D. Shub, *Lenin*; R. Abramovich, *The Russian Revolution*. Also, Marietta Shaginian, 'Predki Lenina', *Novyi Mir*, Moscow, Nr. 11, 1937.

Lenskii, Aleksandr Stepanovich
25.3.1910– . Composer.
Born in Penza Gouvt. Teacher at the Music School, and the Studio for Composers, in Dushanbe. Artistic director of the local Folk Instrument Orchestra. Chairman of the Union of Composers of Tadzhikistan. Author of operas, cantatas, a quartet, pieces for piano, choral works, romances, songs, arrangements of folk melodies, and music for stage and screen.

Lentulov, Aristarkh Vasil'evich
16.1.1882–15.4.1943. Painter, stage designer.
Born at Nizhnee Lomovo near Penza. Studied at Penza and Kiev art schools, 1897–1907. Worked as a painter in Petersburg and Paris. One of the organizers of the arts group Knight of Diamonds (Bubnovyi Valet), 1910. Professor of the VKHUTEMAS-VKHUTEIN, 1919. Member of AKHRR, 1926. Influenced by Cubism, futurism and ortism. Landscape and portrait painter. A leading turn-of-the-century modernist, reduced in the 1930s to painting socialist-realist industrial landscapes (*Kreking Nefteperegonnogo Zavoda*, 1931). Died in Moscow. Posthumous exhibition: Moscow, 1956.

Leonida (Romanova, b. Princess Bagration-Mukhranskii)
1914– . Grand-Duchess.
Wife of Grand-Duke Vladimir Kirillovich, the head of the Romanov family in exile and claimant to the throne of Russia. Descendant of the Bagrations, a Georgian princely family, previously the Georgian royal family, one of the oldest Christian dynasties in the world, claiming descent from King David of the Old Testament. Lives with her husband in St-Briac-sur-Mer, Brittany.

Leonkin, Dmitrii Maksimovich
16.12.1928– . Athlete.
Born in the village of Mys Dobroi Nadezhdy, Riazan' Oblast'. Honoured Master of Sports (gymnastics), 1949. With the L'vov Armed Forces team. Coach. Graduated from the Sports Instructors' School attached to the Military Institute of Physical Culture (which prepares agents for dangerous military missions), 1951. USSR champion, 1951 and 1954. Olympic champion, 1952. Bronze medal, 1952.

Leonov, Aleksei Arkhipovich
1934– . Cosmonaut.
Joined the Red Army, 1953. Graduated from the Zhukovskii Air Force Academy, 1968. During his first space flight, was the first man to step outside his craft into space, Mar. 1965. Deputy head of the Cosmonaut Training Centre, 1972.

Leonov, Aleksei Ivanovich
1902–1972. Marshal.
Joined the Red Army, 1918. Took part in the Civil War, Graduated from the Military Electro-Technical Academy, 1938. Communications specialist. On active service in WWII. Commander of Communications Forces, 1958–1970.

Leonov, Dmitrii Sergeevich
1899–1981. Lt.-general, state security official.
Joined the Bolshevik Party, 1918. Joined the Red Army, 1922. Political Commissar. Graduated from the Lenin Military Political Academy, 1941. Deputy Chief of the General Staff for Political Affairs, 1944. After WWII, continued his political career in the armed forces. Held high posts in the secret police (MVD and KGB), 1953–59.

Leonov, Evgenii Pavlovich
2.9.1926– . Actor.
Popular comedian. Graduated from the Moscow Drama Studio in 1947. From 1948, worked in the Moscow Stanislavskii Drama Theatre, then in the Moscow Lenin Komsomol Theatre. His tutor was Mikhail Ianshin. First film, *Lucky Flight*, in 1949. Became famous in comedies directed by Riazanov and Danelia. Other films: *The Rumiantsev Case* (1956), *Unforgettable Spring* (1957), *A Serf-Actress* (1963), *A Tale of the Don* (1964), *The Snow-Queen* (1967), *Zigzag of Success* (1969), *Cheer Up!* (1969), *Shine Bright, My Star* (1970), *Tchaikovskii* (1970), *The Gentlemen of Fortune* (1972), *Afonia* (1975).

Leonov, Leonid Maksimovich
31.5.1899– . Author.
Born in Moscow. Grew up with his grandfather, who was a small-scale merchant. Son of the poet, M. Leonov. Reporter on local newspapers in Arkhangel'sk, to where his father had been exiled, 1915. Joined the Red Army, 1920. Soldier, and later war correspondent for various army newspapers. First publication, 1922 (*Buryga*, fairy-tale). Became famous for his novel *Barsuki*, 1924, and for two other very successful books, *Vor*, 1927, and *Sot'*, 1930. Praised by M. Gorkii and A. Lunacharskii. Re-wrote *Vor* in 1963, and published it along with *Evgeniia Ivanovna*, which he had written in 1938 but had been unable to publish.

Leont'ev, Leonid Sergeevich
9.4.1885–6.6.1942. Ballet dancer, choreographer.
Born in Petersburg. Graduated from the Petersburg Theatre School, 1903,

(class of N. Legat). Dancer with the Mariinskii Theatre, and its manager, 1920 and 1922–25. With the Ballets Russes, 1908–10. A leading virtuoso dancer. Worked as a choreographer, reviving previous ballet productions. Taught, 1911–16 and 1918–41, at the Leningrad Theatre School. Among his students were G. Balanchine and A. Viltzak. Died in Perm'.

Leont'eva, Galina Aleksandrovna (El'nitskaia)
6.11.1941–   . Athlete.
Born in the village of Lykushino, Iaroslavl' Oblast'. Honoured Master of Sports (volleyball), 1968. With Leningrad Spartak. Works as a sports instructor. European champion, 1967 and 1971. World champion, 1970. Olympic champion, 1968 and 1972.

Leontii (Turkevich, Leonid) Metropolitan of All America and Canada
1898?–14.5.1965. Russian Orthodox clergyman.
Graduated from the Kiev Theological Academy. An active aide to Tikhon (the future patriarch) when he was in charge of the Orthodox diocese in America. Created the basis for an autocephalous (independent) Orthodox church in America. Active in promoting the Orthodox faith and Orthodox learning in the United States. On his initiative, the St. Vladimir Theological Academy was founded in New York in 1938. It later became a centre of learning with a high international reputation. Died in the USA.

Leontovich, Mikhail Aleksandrovich
7.3.1903–2.4.1981. Physicist, academician.
Born in Moscow. Son of the scientist A. V. Leontovich. Graduated from Moscow University, 1923. Member of the Research Commission of the Kursk Magnet Anomaly. Worked at Moscow University from 1929 until 1945. From 1955, professor. At the Physics Institute of the Academy of Sciences, 1946–52. From 1951, at the Institute of Atomic Energy. Leading scientist in the atomic industry. Lecturer and author of many scientific works. Founded a school of radiophysics and plasma physics. Together with A. Sakharov, signed many petitions protesting against the conviction of writers and artists. Protested against Stalin's rehabilitation in the Soviet media during the 1960–70s. Died in Moscow.

Leontovich, Nikolai Dmitrievich
13.12.1877–23.1.1921. Composer, collector of folk music.
Born in Podol'sk Gouvt. Worked in Kiev. Created classical examples of Ukrainian choral music, and arrangements of Russian folk songs. Some original choral works. Died in the Podl'sk district during the Civil War.

Lepeshinskaia, Olga Vasil'evna
28.9.1916–   . Ballerina.
Born in Kiev. Graduated from the Moscow Choreographic School, 1933. Leading dancer with the Bolshoi Theatre for the next 30 years. During WWII, entertained the Red Army troops in order to boost morale. Made several ballet-films, such as *Graf Nulin* and *Kniaz Igor*. After 1963, taught in Moscow and in foreign ballet schools.

Lepin, Anatolii Iakovlevich (Leipins)
17.12.1907–   . Composer.
Born in Moscow. Author of an opera, ballets, operettas, a suite, songs, music for the variety stage, and for stage and screen.

Lepnurm, Khugo Liudvigovich
31.10.1914–   . Organist, composer.
Born in Estonia. Pupil of A. Topman and A. Kapp. Professor at the Tallinn Conservatory. Author of cantatas, symphonic works, works for organ, piano and choir, and solo pieces.

Lerner, Aleksandr
1914–   . Scientist, professor.
One of the first Jewish refuseniks. Fought for 16 years for a Soviet exit visa for Israel. Denied permission to leave under the state-secret clause. Left the USSR, Dec. 1987. Resumed his scientific work in the Weitzman Institute in Israel.

Lert, Raisa Borisovna
1905–1985. Author, critic.
Born in Kiev. Lost her job in 1949 during Stalin's anti-Semitic campaign. In the post-war years, especially under Khrushchev, contributed to the samizdat magazines *XX-yi Vek* and *Poiski*. Expelled from the Communist Party, 1979, for her involvement in the human rights movement and samizdat. Author of many articles. Died in Moscow.

Leshchenko, Petr Konstantinovich
3.7.1898–16.7.1954. Cabaret singer.
Born in Kishinev, Bessarabia (then Russia, later Rumania). Moved to Paris to study ballet, 1923. Became instead a famous cabaret singer of Russian gypsy songs in the 1920–30s. Gained immense popularity among Russians abroad (who knew him by his personal appearances all over the world and by his records), as well as inside the Soviet Union (where his records were highly priced on the black market). His only rival in popularity between the wars was Aleksandr Vertinskii. From 1935, lived in Bucharest, where he had his own restaurant and cabaret. After WWII, toured Rumania. Very popular with Red Army soldiers, but treated with the utmost suspicion by SMERSH. In 1951, arrested on stage in the middle of a concert in Brasov. Disappeared in the Rumanian Gulag. According to some sources was seen among convicts digging a Danube canal. Died in a prison hospital from illness and exhaustion.

Leskov, Andrei Nikolaevich
1871?–after 1950. Colonel.
Son of the writer N. Leskov. Took part in WWI as a colonel. Joined the Red Army and served in the Cheka border-guard detachments. Wrote a biography of his father.

Lesman, Iosif Antonovich
14.3.1885–29.3.1955. Violinist, methodologist.
Born in Warsaw (then in Russian Poland). Pupil of L. Auer. Taught at the Alma-Ata Conservatory, 1935–51, and the Gorkii Conservatory, 1951–1955. Author of *Skripichnaia Tekhnika i ee Razvitie v Shkole Professora L.S. Auera*, Petersburg,

1909, *O Postanovke Igry na Skripke*, Petersburg, 1911, *Ob Igre na Skripke*, Petersburg, 1914, *Shkola Igry na Skripke*, Leningrad, 1924, and *Ocherki po Metodike Obucheniia Igry na Skripke*, Moscow, 1964. Died in Gorkii.

Lesnoi, Sergei (Paramonov, S.Ia.)
1910?– . Historian.
During WWII, moved to Germany. After 1945, in DP camps. Settled in Australia. Amateur historian with a sceptical approach to official Russian historiography. Collected a large amount of very interesting material. Published research on several historical subjects (*Slovo o Polku Igoreve*, 4 parts, 1950–54, and *Istoria Russov v Neizvrashchennom Vide*, 10 parts, 1953–60). Opponent of the Norman theory of the founding of Russia. Recently, his views have found some adherents among Soviet historians.

Levandovskii, Mikhail Karlovich
1890–1937. Military commander.
Educated at the Vladimirskoe Military School. Took part in WWI as a captain. Joined the Red Army, 1918. During the Civil War, Minister of War of the Terek Soviet Republic (Caucasus). Commander of Red forces in the Caucasus, and later in Turkestan. Liquidated by Stalin.

Levanevskii, Sigizmund Aleksandrovich
1902–1937. Pilot.
Joined the Red Army, 1918. Educated at the Naval Pilots' School, 1925. Took part in the rescue of the Cheluskin expedition, 1934. Made a long-distance flight from Moscow to Los Angeles, 1936. Died in an air crash.

Levashev, Vladimir Aleksandrovich
16.1.1923– . Ballet dancer.
Born in Moscow. Graduated from the Moscow Choreographic School, 1941. Until 1978, at the Bolshoi Theatre. Dancer, and soon leading dancer. Appeared in the TV ballet film *Fedra*. From 1978, taught at the Bolshoi Theatre.

Levasheva, Olga Evgen'evna
30.3.1912– . Musicologist.
Born in Blagoveshchensk on the Amur River. Professor at the Moscow Conservatory.
Works: *Edward Grieg*, Moscow, 1962; *Muzyka v Kruzhke Del'viga, Voprosy Muzykoznaniia*, Moscow, 1955; *Russko-Pol'skie Muzykal'nye Sviazi*, Moscow, 1963.

Levashov, Valentin Sergeevich
6.8.1915– . Composer, choir conductor.
Born in Moscow. Artistic director of the Song and Dance Ensemble of the Krasnoznamennaia Amurskaia Flotiliia, 1946–49, and of the Siberian Folk Choir, 1962. From 1962, conductor of the Piatnitskii Russian Folk Choir. Author of choral works, arrangements of folk songs, an operetta, symphonic suites, pieces for folk instrument orchestras, and romances.

Levchenko, Gordei Ivanovich
1897–1981. Admiral.
On active service during WWI. Bolshevik organizer among sailors of the Baltic fleet. Took part in the storming of the Winter Palace, 1917. Joined the Red Navy, 1918. During WWII, commander of the Leningrad and Kronstadt naval bases, 1942–44. Deputy Minister of the Navy, 1944. After WWII, deputy commander of the Soviet Navy.

Levchenko, Stanislav
1943?– . KGB defector.
High-ranking officer in the KGB in the 1970s. Defected in 1979. Lives in the USA. Published his memoirs *On the Wrong Side: My Life in the KGB*, London, 1988. Describes in the book how he had been trained in Moscow to perform a suicide mission in Liverpool, should a third world war begin. Maintains that a hit-man is employed full-time by the Soviet embassy in Washington to track him down and kill him. Lives with his wife, Alexandra Costos.

Levental', Valerii Iakovlevich
17.8.1938– . Stage designer.
Born in Moscow. Graduated from the VGIK, Moscow, 1962. Class of Iu. Pimenov and M. Kurilko. From 1963, worked for various theatres. From 1965, with the Bolshoi Theatre. Stage and costume designer for the ballet film *Anna Karenina*, 1975, with Maia Plisetskaia, and for the TV films *Romeo i Dzhulieta*, 1968, and *Fedra*, 1972.

Levi, Natalia Nikolaevna (real name – Smyslova)
10.9.1901– . Composer.
Born in Petersburg. Author of pieces for children, music for theatrical performances and radio, suites for soloists, choir and folk instrument orchestra, romances, and songs. Arranged Karelian folk songs, taking part in expeditions to collect them. Also wrote the music for 18 popular science films.

Levich, Veniamin Grigor'evich
30.3.1917– . Physicist.
Graduated from Khar'kov University, 1937. Worked at the Institute of Physical Chemistry of the Academy of Sciences, 1940–58. Specialist in physico-chemical hydrodynamics. In the 1970s, involved in the Jewish rights movement. After an international campaign, allowed to emigrate to Israel. Taught in Israel and the USA.

Levidov, Mikhail Iul'evich
1891–1942. Journalist, author.
In 1917–18, journalist on the magazine *Letopis'* and with the newspapers *Novaia Zhizn'* and *Vecherniaia Zvezda*. Worked at the Press Bureau of the Soviet delegation in London. Member of LEF. Disappeared in the Gulag.

Levik, Boris Veniaminovich
5.11.1898– . Musicologist.
Born in Kiev. Nephew of the singer Sergei Levik. Lecturer at the Gnesin Pedagogical Institute of Music, Moscow. Author of *Istoriia Zarubezhnoi Muzyki Vtoraia Polovina XVIII veka*, Moscow, 1961.

Levik, Sergei Iur'evich
28.11.1883–after 1969. Singer (baritone), translator, writer on music.
Born in Belaia Tserkov', Kiev Gouvt. Uncle of the musicologist Boris Levik. Soloist with the Theatre of

Musical Drama, Petersburg, 1912–19. Author of many translations of operatic librettos, texts of romances and oratorios, and articles on singing. Author of *Zapiski Opernogo Pevtsa*, Moscow, 1955.

Levin, Fedor Arkad'evich
11.2.1878–10.4.1944. Flautist.
Born in Moscow. Brother of the pianist I. Levin. Pupil of V. Krechman. With the orchestras of the Bolshoi Theatre, and the Kusevitskii Symphony Orchestra, then Persimfans (Pervyi Simfornicheskii Ansambl' Mossoveta), 1927. With the State Symphony Orchestra from 1936. Member of the Wind Instrument Quartet of the All-Union Radio, 1928–38. Died in Moscow.

Levin, Iosif Arkad'evich
13.12.1874–1.12.1944. Pianist.
Born in Orel. Brother of the flautist F. Levin. Married to the pianist Rosina Bessi-Levina. Pupil of V. Safonov. Professor at the Moscow Conservatory, 1902–05. Concert tours in Europe and the USA, 1906–14. Emigrated. In New York from 1919. Taught at the Juilliard Music School. V. Cliburn was one of his pupils. Died in New York.

Levina, Zara Aleksandrovna
5.2.1906–   . Composer.
Born in Simferopol'. Wife of the composer Chemberdzhi. Author of vocal-symphonic works, including a triptych for choir, soloist, orchestra, organ and piano, a concerto for piano and orchestra, sonatas and pieces for piano, violin, and cello, romances, and songs, including about 200 songs for children. Also arranged folk songs.

Levinson, Andrei Iakovlevich
1.1.1887–3.12.1933. Ballet critic and historian.
Born in Petersburg. Graduated from Petersburg University. Ballet critic for *Annual of the Imperial Theatres*, *Apollon*, *Iskusstvo*, *Propilei*, and also for numerous Russian and European newspapers. Much respected in the world of ballet. From 1919, lived in Lithuania. Moved to Germany, then Paris. Editor of the theatre section of

Comoedia, Paris. Multi-lingual. Ballet critic with *Candide* and *Les Nouvelles Literaires*. Wrote numerous essays and books. Died in Paris.

Levitin, Iurii Abramovich
28.12.1912–   . Composer.
Born in Poltava. Author of an opera, oratorios, cantatas, a symphony for chamber orchestra and mezzo soprano, a sinfonietta, orchestral suites, concertos for piano and oboe with string orchestra, pieces for symphonic and variety stage orchestras, 7 string quartets, chamber ensembles, 24 preludes and other piano pieces, romances, songs, and music for stage, screen and radio.

Levitskii, Aleksandr Andreevich
23.11.1885–4.7.1965. Cameraman.
One of the first cameramen in the Russian silent cinema. Started as an artistic photographer. Joined the film industry, 1910. Films: *1812 God* (one of the first historical films, made in 1912); *Anna Karenina*, *Dvorianskoe Gnezdo*, and *Kreitserova Sonata*, all 3 in 1914; *Voina i Mir, Otsy i Deti*, and *Portret Doriana Greia*, all 1915. During the February and October Revolutions, filmed Lenin on many occasions. His films *Neobychainye Prikliucheniia Mistera Vesta v Strane Bol'shevikov*, 1924, and *Luch Smerti*, 1925, marked the beginning of the Soviet experimental cinema of the 1920s. During WWII, war cameraman. Taught at the GIK (later known as the VGIK) from 1924. Professor, 1939. His many pupils include A. Golovnia, L. Kosmatov and V. Monakhov.

Levitskii, Sergei Aleksandrovich
1910–   . Philosopher.
Born in Libau (Latvia). Educated at high school in Tallinn (Estonia). Graduated from Prague University in 1939. After WWII, in refugee camps in Germany. Settled in the USA. Pupil and follower of Nikolai Losskii.
Works: *Osnovy Organicheskogo Mirovozzreniia*, *Tragediia Svobody*, *Ocherki po Istorii Russkoi Filofsofskoi i Obshchestvennoi Mysli*, 2 vols.

Liadova, Liudmila Alekseevna
29.3.1925–   . Composer.
Born in Sverdlovsk. Prize-winner at

the Competition for Variety Artists, 1946, (vocal duet). Author of operettas, a concerto for piano and orchestra, and songs for the variety stage.

Liagachev, Oleg
1939–   . Artist.
Born in Leningrad. Graduated from the Leningrad Repin Academy of Arts, 1966. Became a famous non-conformist artist in Leningrad. Has lived in Paris since 1975. Exhibits all over Europe and the USA.

Liakhovich, Konstantin Ivanovich
1885–1921. Politician.
Participant in the 1905 Revolution. Joined the Mensheviks. Arrested, 1909, exiled, but escaped and went abroad. Married V. Korolenko's daughter. Returned to Russia, 1917. Leader of the Mensheviks in Poltava, 1917–21. Arrested, 1921. Fell ill with typhoid, and was released a few days before his death. Died in Poltava.

Liapkin, Iurii Evgen'evich
21.1.1945–   . Athlete.
Born in Balashikha, Moscow Oblast'. Graduated from the Kolomenskii Pedagogical Institute, 1972. Honoured Master of Sports (hockey), 1973. With Voskresensk Khimik, 1972–76. From 1978, with Moscow Spartak. Coach. Member of the CPSU, 1976. European champion, 1973–75. World champion, 1971, 1973–75. Olympic champion, 1976. USSR champion, 1976.

Liapunov, Aleksandr Mikhailovich
6.6.1857–3.11.1918. Mathematician.
Born in Iaroslavl'. Pupil of P. Chebyshev. Graduated from Petersburg University, 1880. Professor at Khar'kov University from 1892. Academician of the Petersburg Academy of Sciences, 1901. Worked on the problem of stability of movement, the theory of potential, and the theory of probabilities. Became internationally known. Died in Odessa.

Liapunov, Aleksei Andreevich
8.10.1911–23.6.1973. Mathematician.
Born in Moscow. Member of the

CPSU, 1944. Worked at the Siberian branch of the Academy of Sciences in the field of cybernetics. Professor at Moscow University, 1952–62. Died in Moscow.

Liapunov, Boris Mikhailovich
6.8.1862–22.2.1943. Linguist, academician.
Born in the village of Bolobonovo, Gorkii Oblast'. Graduated from Petersburg University, 1885. Pupil of I. Iagich. Professor at Odessa University, 1903–23, and at Leningrad University, 1924–29. Follower of F. Fortunatov. Worked in the field of the grammar of Slavonic languages. Academician, 1923. Member of many European academies. Died in Borovoe, Akmolinsk Oblast'.

Liapunov, Sergei Mikhailovich
30.11.1859–1924. Composer.
Born in Iaroslavl'. Studied at the Moscow Conservatory, 1878–83. Pupil of K. Klindvort and S. Taneev. Studied in Petersburg under Balakirev, 1885. Commissioned by the Russian Geographical Society to go on an expedition for the collection of folk songs, 1893. Vice-director of the Court Chantry, 1894. Taught at the Bezplatnaia Muzykalnaia Shkola, 1908–11. Professor at the Petersburg Conservatory. Compositions in the tradition of the Moguchaia Kuchka (the Mighty Handful). Went abroad on a tour, 1923, and did not return. Died in Paris.

Liapunova, Anastasia Sergeevna
9.4.1903– . Musicologist.
Born in Petersburg. Daughter of the composer Sergei Liapunov. Author of articles and publications on Balakirev, S. Liapunov and Glinka.

Liashchenko, Nikolai Grigor'evich
1910– . General.
Joined the Red Army, 1929. Graduated from the Frunze Military Academy, 1941. Took part in the Spanish Civil War and WWII. Member of the Cen. Cttee. of the CPSU, 1971–81.

Liashko, Aleksandr Pavlovich
1915– . Politician.
Ukrainian. Son of a worker. Member of the CPSU, 1942. Served in the army during WWII. After the war, graduated from the Donetsk Industrial Institute as an engineer. Worked as an engineer, head of a department, later director of Novokramatorsk Machine Construction Plant until 1952. Senior party posts in the Ukraine included 1st secretary of Kramatorsk City Cttee., and 1st secretary of Donetsk Oblast' City Cttee. Chairman of Communications for Industry, Transport, Post and Telecommunications in the USSR Supreme Soviet, 1966–69. Member of the Cen. Cttee. of the Ukrainian CP, 1960. Member of the Presidium and Politburo, 1963. Secretary, 1963–66, then 2nd secretary of the Cen. Cttee. of the Ukrainian CP, 1966–69. Chairman of the Bureau for Industry in the Cen. Cttee. of the Ukrainian CP, 1963–64. Chairman of the Presidium of the Supreme Soviet of the Ukraine and deputy chairman of the Presidium of the USSR Supreme Soviet, 1969–72. Removed from these posts in July 1987.

Liatoshinskii, Boris Nikolaevich
3.1.1895– . Composer.
Born in Zhitomir. Professor at the Kiev Conservatory. Among his pupils were G. Taranov and L. Grabovskii. Author of operas, 2 cantatas, 4 symphonies, symphonic poems, orchestral works, instrumental ensembles, 4 string quartets, pieces for piano, choral works, romances, music for stage and screen, arrangements of folk songs, and instrumentation for the opera, *Taras Bulba*. Stalin Prize, 1952.

Liatskii, Evgenii Aleksandrovich
1868–1942. Ethnographer.
Made his name as a specialist in Russian folklore. Emigrated after the Bolshevik take-over, 1917. Settled in Prague. Founded the publishing house Plamia, and was its editor-in-chief.

Liber, Mikhail Isaakovich (Goldmann)
5.6.1880–4.10.1937. Politician.
Born in Wilno. Member of the Social Democratic Party from 1898. One of the founders and leaders of the Bund (Jewish Social Democrats) and the Mensheviks. Member of the Cen. Cttee. of the RSDRP from the Bund in 1907. Leader of the Bund delegation at the 2nd Congress of the RSDRP (SD). Joined the Mensheviks after the split of the SDs. Sharp critic of Lenin. During WWI, took a patriotic stance. After the February Revolution, member of the Executive Committee of the Petrograd Soviet. Condemned the October Revolution, 1917. Member of the Bureau of the Cen. Cttee. of the RSDRP, 1922–23. Arrested in autumn 1923, exiled to Semipalatinsk, Kazakhstan. Held minor economic posts. Re-arrested in 1937 and disappeared. Presumably shot at Alma-Ata.
See: *Pamyat*, 3, Paris.

Lido, Serge (Lidov, Sergei Pavlovich)
28.1.1906–6.3.1984. Ballet photographer.
Born in Moscow. Left the USSR in the 1920s. Became a distinguished ballet photographer in Paris. Author of many photographic books, e.g. *Dance*, 1947, and *Les Etoiles de la Dance dans le Monde*, Paris, 1975. Photographer for many ballet magazines. Married to Irene Lido (Irina Sergeevna Kaminskaia, also Moscow-born), reporter for many ballet magazines and one of the organizers of the Soirées de Dance at the Sarah Bernhardt Theatre, 1944, which was the forerunner of Les Ballets des Champs Elysées. Died in Paris.

Liepa, Maris-Rudolf Eduardovich
27.7.1936– . Ballet dancer.
Born in Riga. First trained at the Riga Choreographic School. Graduated from the Moscow Choreographic School, 1955. With the Stanislavskii and Nemirovich Danchenko Theatre, Moscow from 1956. From 1960, leading dancer with the Bolshoi Theatre. His triumph was his leading part in *Spartak* (choreography by Iu. Grigorovich, 1968). Choreographer from 1979 (*Don Quichotte*). Directed some ballet-films. Wrote articles for the ballet press on productions and personalities. Awarded the V. Nijinskii Award, Paris, 1971, and the M. Petipa Award, Paris, 1977.

Lieven, Aleksandr Pavlovich, Prince
13.9.1919–31.3.1988. Controller of the European Service of the BBC. Born in Rostock, Germany (now GDR). Son of Prince Pavel Pavlovich Lieven and younger brother of Leonid Lieven. Graduated from the Lycée Français Brussels, Lille, and Trinity College, Dublin. Took part in WWII. Captain in the British Army. Expert on Russian affairs at the Foreign Office. In the 1960s, head of the Russian and Eastern European Service of the BBC. Retired, 1979. Died in Pebmarsh, Essex.

Lieven, Anatolii Pavlovich, Prince
29.11.1872–1937. Pioneer of mechanized farms, military commander. Born in Petersburg. Son of Prince Pavel Ivanovich Lieven, High Lord Chamberlain to Emperor Alexander II, and Head of Nobility of the Province of Livonia. Graduated from Petersburg University, 1895. One of the first to mechanize his farms in the Baltic Provinces of Russia with the latest equipment. Took part in WWI as an officer of the Chevalier Guarde (Horse Guards). Awarded the British Military Cross for outstanding bravery in the East Prussian campaign. Founder and 1st commander of a Russian Free Corps in the former Baltic Provinces of Russia. Participated in the capture of Riga in May 1919. Severely wounded and retired from further military activity. Died in Latvia, and received a state funeral from the Latvian government for his participation in the liberation of Latvia.

Lieven, Dina Maksimilianovna, Princess (Anrep, von Dina)
4.11.1903– . Arts expert. Born in Homeln, Northern Livonia. Daughter of Maksimilian von Anrep, deputy of a Livonian district to the Council of the Livonian Nobility. Educated in Yuriev (now Tartu, Estonia), and Berlin. Worked as a secretary to Bodo Ebhardt, the famous architect and restorer of German medieval castles, and then as an estate secretary in East Prussia. Married her distant Russian cousin, Professor Gleb von Anrep. Lived in Egypt and Germany. Divorced, and married Prince Leonid Lieven. In London, worked as head of the

overseas office of Christie's auction house for over 20 years. Retired, 1979.

Lieven, Dominik Aleksandrovich, Prince (Lieven, Dominic)
19.1.1952– . Lecturer, author. Born in Singapore. Son of Prince Aleksandr Lieven. Graduated in history from Cambridge University with 1st Class Honours with distinction, 1975. Postgraduate studies at Moscow University. PhD. Kennedy Scholarship at Harvard University. Senior lecturer in Russian government and history at the London School of Economics. Works include *Russia and the Origins of WWI*, London, 1983, and *Russia's Rulers under the Old Regime*, London and Newhaven, 1988. Lives in London.

Lieven, Leonid Pavlovich, Prince
24.5.1909– . Barrister, translator, lt.-colonel. Born in Smiltene, former province of Livonia. Son of Prince Pavel Pavlovich Lieven. Educated first privately in Livonia, then in Germany and England. Left Russia with his family in Sept. 1917. Returned to the former Russian Baltic provinces in 1918, then re-emigrated to Germany, 1919. Moved to England, 1923. Graduated in law from Oxford University, 1931. Called to the Bar, 1932. Sub-editor with the BBC World Service during WWII. Served in the British Army as a lt.-colonel. Retired. Awarded the MBE. In the 1980s, concentrated on literary translations.

Lieven, Pavel Pavlovich, Prince
24.4.1875 – 11.5.1963. Land-owner, railway engineer, Red Cross worker. Born in Petersburg. Son of Prince Pavel Ivanovich Lieven and younger brother of Prince Anatolii Lieven. Graduated from the Institute of Railways and Roads, Petersburg, 1899. Took part in the construction of the Trans-Caspian railways, and later of a Northern Russian link with the Trans-Siberian railway joining the latter at Ekaterinburg (now Sverdlovsk). Worked with Leonid Krasin on this project. On his own estate in the small town of Smiltene (now in Latvia), built a railway linking this town to the Baltic Sea for

the export of timber. Electrified Smiltene and built a hospital which offered free treatment to the poor. Took part in WWI as a Red Cross representative at the front. At great risk, rescued retreating Russian troops in a goods train during the 2nd battle of the Mazurian Lakes in early 1915. Captured by the Germans. Shared his captivity with the future Soviet marshal, M. Tukhachevskii. Set free thanks to the personal intervention of the German Prince, Max of Baden, but on condition that he would bring to the attention of the Empress Maria Fedorovna the appalling conditions of Austro-Hungarian and German POWs in Russia. This resulted in an international conference of the warring powers being called in 1915 in Stockholm, concerning the registration of POWs held by the Russians. In 1917, travelled in Siberia, from the Arctic to Mongolia, as a Red Cross representative accompanying representatives of the Central Powers, checking on the conditions of POWs. Left Russia for Sweden in Dec. 1917, with the help of L. Krasin. Returned to his estate on the Baltic in 1918, but soon left again for Germany. Lived in Belgium and Ireland. Died in London.

Lifar, Sergei Mikhailovich (Lifar, Serge)
2.4.1905–16.12.1986. Ballet dancer, choreographer. Born in Kiev into a wealthy land-owning family. Studied dancing under Bronislava Nijinska (Vaclav's sister) at the age of 16. Joined Diaghilev'_ Ballet Russe in Monte Carlo, Jan. 1923. Diaghilev was impressed by his exotic looks, youth and fitness rather than by his dancing, and started to promote his career, arranging lessons with the great Cecchetti. Was given solo parts in *La Pastorale* opposite Tamara Karsavina, *Zephire et Flore*, *La Chatte*, etc. Danced the leading parts in Balanchine's *Apollo*, 1928, and *The Prodigal Son*, 1929. Also starred in L. Massine's *Le Pas d'Acier* and *Ode*. Encouraged by Diaghilev, developed an interest in choreography. After Diaghilev's death in 1929, became a leading dancer, director and choreographer at the Paris Opera Theatre. Tried to turn the whole ballet into a

one-man show, and made many enemies. During the German occupation of Paris was director of L'Opera de Paris and, according to himself, the 'king of the artistic world'. Received 3 times by Hitler in Berlin. Met with senior Nazis in Paris. After the Liberation, was put on trial. Found not guilty, but was forced to leave the theatre. Appeared in Monte Carlo's Nouveaux Ballets 3 years later. Returned to the Paris Opera as a choreographer in 1958, dancing occasionally. Regarded himself as the heir to Diaghilev's heritage. Took Nijinskii's body from England to France for reburial. Every year in August, he used to invite international high-society figures to Venice to mark the anniversary of Diaghilev's death. Arranged a place for himself next to the great Vestris in the exclusive Père Lachaise cemetery.

See: A. Gold and R. Fizdale, *Misia,* London, 1980; Jeanne Vronskaya, 'Diaghilev's Last Great Dancer'. *The Sunday Times,* 15 Aug. 1982.

Lifshitsaite, Nekhama
7.10.1927–   . Singer (soprano).
Born in Wil'no. Singer of Jewish folk songs from 1956. Prize-winner at the All-Union Competition for Variety Singers, 1958. Her concerts in Moscow and Leningrad attracted crowds of Soviet Jews.

Ligachev, Egor Kuzmich
29.11.1920–   . Politician.
Joined the Communist Party in 1944. Graduated from the Moscow Aviation Institute in 1943, then from the Moscow Higher Party School in 1951. Engineer, head of a plant group. Secretary and then 1st secretary of Novosibirsk Oblast' Komsomol Cttee., 1943–49. Party lecturer at Novosibirsk City Cttee. Deputy head of Novosibirsk Oblast' Cttee. Deputy chairman of Novosibirsk Oblast' Soviet, 1949–61. Deputy head of the Department of Propaganda and Agitation. Deputy head of the Department of Party Organs for Industry of the Cen. Cttee. of the CPSU for the RSFSR, 1961–65. 1st secretary of Tomsk Oblast' Cttee., 1965. Candidate member of the Cen. Cttee. of the CPSU, 1966–76, full member, 1976. Member of the Cttee. for Industry, Transport, Post and

Telecommunications, 1966–68. Member of the Youth Affairs Cttee., 1968–74. Member of the Planning and Budget Cttee. ot the USSR Supreme Soviet, 1974. Worked with Gorbachev from 1980. Regarded as number two in Gorbachev's party leadership, but considered to be the representative of conservative forces in the Politburo. Head of the Agricultural Commission of the Cen. Cttee., Oct. 1988.

Likhachev, Dmitrii Sergeevich
28.11.1906–   . Historian, academician.
Born in Petersburg. Graduated from Leningrad University in 1928. Arrested, Oct. 1928. Solovki concentration camp, 1928–31. Released, 4 Aug. 1932. Worked at the Institute of Russian Literature (Pushkinskii Dom) from 1938. Head of section and specialist in ancient Russian literature from 1954. Professor at Leningrad University, 1946–53. Member of the USSR Academy of Sciences from 1970. One of the initiators of the movement for the protection of ancient monuments. In 1987, appointed chairman of the board of the newly established Soviet Cultural Fund, of which Raisa Gorbachev is a member. Called for the return of artefacts and archives which were taken out of Russia during and after the 1917 Revolution. During the 1970s, experienced difficulty in pursuing his work as a historian and took no part in public life. Became M. Gorbachev's adviser on cultural and historical heritage matters in early 1985. Appeared again in official publications. Member of the editorial board of *Nashe Nasledie.* Dr. of many foreign universities, including Oxford and Cambridge. Instrumental in the rehabilitation of N. Gumilev and the general cultural revival in the late 1980s.

Likhachev, Ivan Alekseevich
15.6.1896–24.6.1956. Politician, industrial manager.
Born in Ozertsy near Tula. Son of a peasant. Worked at the Putilov plant in Petersburg, 1908. During WWI, sailor in the Baltic fleet, 1914–18. Joined the Communist Party, 1917. During the Civil War, member of the Red Guard, Cheka official, 1917–21. After the Civil War, received a

technical education at a mining and electrotechnical institute. Became famous as an energetic manager of the Moscow car works, 1926–39 and 1940–50. In 1939, Minister of Machine Building. From 1953, Minister of Road Transport of the USSR. In 1956, the Moscow car works ZIS (Zavod Imeni Stalina) was re-named after him ZIL (Zavod Imeni Likhacheva). This factory manufactures special black limousines for the Soviet elite. Died in Moscow, buried at the Kremlin wall.

Likhachev, Nikolai Petrovich
24.4.1862–14.4.1936. Art historian.
Born in Chistopol' into a middle-class family. Graduated from Kazan' University, 1884. Professor of the Petersburg Archaeological Institute, 1902. Editor of many Russian historical documents. Specialist in palaeography, author of a basic reference work on water marks. Wrote on Italo-Greek and Russian ancient art, Rublev, and Byzantine archaeology. Set up a unique Museum of Palaeography (starting with Egyptian, Mesopotamian and Coptic texts, and including unique Arabic, Greek and Latin works and medieval incunabula), which in 1925 was handed over to the Soviet Academy of Sciences.

Likhachev, Valerii Nikolaevich
5.12.1947–   . Athlete.
Born in Novosheshminsk, Tatar ASSR. Honoured Master of Sports (cycling), 1970. With Gorkii Trud. Studied at the Gorkii Agricultural Institute. USSR champion, 1969–72. World champion, 1970. Olympic champion, 1972.

Likhtenshtadt, Vladimir Osipovich (Lichtenstadt)
16.12.1882–15.10.1919. Revolutionary.
Son of a high-ranking official. Studied at Petersburg and Leipzig universities. Involved with SR terrorist groups, 1905–07. Took part in the assassination attempt against Prime Minister Stolypin. Sentenced to death, commuted to life imprisonment. Inmate of Petropavlovskaia and Shlusselburg fortress prisons, 1906–17. Released after the revolu-

tion, 1917. Joined the Bolsheviks, 1919. Head of the Comintern Publishing Department. Volunteered for the Red Army during the Civil War, and appointed Political Commissar. Taken prisoner by the Whites and shot. Buried at Leningrad.

Lilina, Maria Petrovna (Perevoshchikova)
3.7.1866–24.8.1943. Actress.
Born in Moscow. Married K. S. Stanislavskii in 1889. One of the leading actresses of the Moscow Arts Theatre from the moment of its creation in 1898. Best known for her roles in plays by Chekhov. Taught acting in the Stanislavskii studio. Died in Moscow.

Lilov, Boris
1923–1969. Athlete.
Honoured Master of Sports (equestrian sports). Many times USSR champion. Member of the USSR team at the XVth and XVIth Olympic Games.

Limonov, Eduard (Savenko, Eduard Ven'iaminovich)
1943– . Author.
Born in Dzerzhinsk. Moved with his family to Khar'kov. Member of an unofficial group of artists and writers. His works circulated in samizdat. Left the USSR with his wife, the model Elena Shchapova, in 1974 (she later divorced him). Moved to the USA in 1975, and then to France. Became famous for his novel, *Eto Ia, Edichka* (NY, 1979), also for his unconventional views. Provoked several literary scandals in the Russian emigré press. Other books: *Dnevnik Neudachnika*, NY, 1982, and *Podrostok Savenko*, France, 1983.

Lineva, Evgenia Eduardovna (b. Paprits)
9.11.1854–24.1.1919. Singer (contralto), choir conductor, folklorist.
Born in Brest-Litovsk. Undertook several folkloristic expeditions, recording Russian and Ukrainian folk songs, 1897–1914. Transcribed Slovene and Croat songs in Austro-Hungary. Author of *Velikorusskie Pesni v Narodnoi Garmonizatsii*, Moscow, 1904–09, and *Opyt Zapisi*

Fonografom Ukrainskikh Narodnykh Pesen, Moscow, 1905. Died in Moscow.

Lipaev, Ivan Vasil'evich
29.5.1865–25.9.1942. French horn player, music critic.
Born in Saratov Gouvt. Founded the Orchestral Players' Mutual Aid Society, 1903. Editor-in-chief of the periodicals *Muzykal'nyi Truzhenik* and *Orkestr*. Taught at the Saratov Conservatory, 1912–21, professor from 1917. Wrote essays on Rakhmaninov, Skriabin and Taneev. Author of *Ocherki Byta Orkestrovykh Muzykantov*, Moscow, 1891, *Finskaia Muzyka*, Petersburg, 1906, and *Muzykal'naia Literatura (Bibliograficheskii Ukazatel')*. Moscow, 1908. Died in Tashkent.

Lipkin, Semen Izrailevich
1911– . Poet, translator.
Born in Odessa. Graduated from Moscow Institute of Engineering and Economics. One of the best translators of Georgian and other national minority poets. Some critics thought that he himself created, rather than translated, this folklore. Very few original works published in the Soviet press. Contributed to the unofficial almanac *Metropol*. Resigned from the Union of Writers in protest against the crackdown on *Metropol* in 1979. Well-known literary figure at home and abroad.

Lipkovskaia, Lidia Iakovlevna (Marshner)
6.6.1882–22.3.1958. Singer (soprano).
Born in Bessarabia. Pupil of N. Iretskaia. Soloist with the Mariinskii Theatre, 1906–08 and 1911–13. Soloist with the Theatre of Musical Drama, Petrograd, 1914–15. Emigrated after the 1917 Revolution. Lived abroad from 1919. Appeared in the USSR, 1928–29. Died in Beirut.

Lipshits, Iakov Abramovich (Lipschitz, Chaim Jacob; Lipchitz, Jacques)
22.8.1891–26.5.1973. Sculptor.
Born in Druskieniki, Lithuania. Son of a businessman. Educated in

Bialystok and Wil'no, 1902–9. Moved to Paris to study art, 1909, lived in Montparnasse. Became a prominent member of the modernist arts movement before WWI. His sculpture *Man with a Guitar* created a sensation, 1916. In the 1920s and 1930s, became one of the most famous modernist sculptors in the world. Spent the WWII years in the USA. Returned to France, 1946–47. From 1948, permanently settled in the USA. Died on Capri. Buried in Jerusalem.

Lisenko, Natal'ia Andrianovna
1884/6?–after 1950. Film actress.
Played opposite Ivan Mozzhukhin. Later married him. Graduated from the MKHAT Studio, 1904. Played in provincial theatres, then at the Korsh Theatre, Moscow. Entered the film industry, 1915. Appeared in all her films with her husband. Emigrated, 1920. Lived and died in Paris.

Lisitsian, Pavel Gerasimovich
6.11.1911– . Singer (baritone).
Born in Vladikavkaz. Soloist with the Erevan opera, 1937–40. With the Bolshoi Theatre from 1940.

Lisitsian, Srbui Stepanovna
27.6.1893–1979. Ballet historian.
Born in Tbilisi. Graduated from the Ger'e Higher Women's Courses and the Studio of the Expressive Word in the class of O. Ozarovskaia, 1917. In 1917, founded the Studio of Declamation, Rhythm and Plastic. Worked in the field of folk dance and carried out research into ethnographic aspects of the dance. Founder and director of the Erevan Choreographic School, 1930–37. Author of several valuable books, including *Zapis' Dvizhenia*, Moscow, 1940, and *Starinnye Pliaskii i Teatralnye Predstavleniia Armianskogo Naroda*, 2 vols, Erevan, 1958–72. The latter was the result of her life's research into Armenian folk-dance history. Also choreographer, stage director and teacher.

Lisitsin, Mikhail Aleksandrovich
1871–1918. Composer, writer.
Composed liturgical music. Literary works: *Obzor Dukhovno-Muzykal'noi Literatury* (110 authors, about 1500

works), Petersburg, 1901, *O Novom Napravlenii v Russkoi Tserkovnoi Muzyke*, Moscow, 1909, and *O Drevnikh i Novykh Pesnotvortsakh*, Petersburg, 1910.

Lisitskii, Lazar' Markovich (El Lissitzky)
22.11.1890–30.12.1941. Painter, architect.
Born in the village of Pochinok, near Smolensk. Studied architecture at the Darmstadt Higher Technical School, 1909–14. During the revolution, taught at the Vitebsk Art School, 1919–20, VKHUTEMAS, 1921, VKHUTEIN, from 1926. Lived in Germany and Switzerland, 1921–25. Member of the Dutch arts group de Stijl. Leading exponent of Suprematism. One of the most talented representatives of world modernist art in the 1920s and 1930s (paintings, posters, design of polygraphic, photographic, stage, architectural art). Produced designs for Soviet pavilions at international exhibitions, 1925–34. Died in Moscow.

Lisnianskaia, Inna Lvovna
1928–   . Poetess.
Born in Baku. First poems published, 1949. First book of poetry *Eto Bylo So Mnoiu*, 1957. Several books published by official Soviet publishing houses. Became famous in the Soviet Union. Contributed to the unofficial almanac *Metropol*. Resigned from the Union of Writers in protest against the crackdown on *Metropol*, 1979. Some poems circulated in samizdat, while some books of her poetry were published abroad.

Lisovskii, Nikolai Mikhailovich
13.1.1854–19.9.1920. Bibliographer.
Edited the magazine *Bibliograf*, 1884–94. Compiled a full bibliography of 18th–19th century Russian periodicals (*Russkaia Periodicheskaia Pechat' 1703–1900*), also bibliographical lists on many specialized subjects. Lectured on bibliography at Petrograd University, 1913–17, and Moscow University, 1916–19. Died in Moscow.

Lissim, Semen Mikhailovich (Lissim, Simon)
24.10.1900–   . Artist.
Born in Kiev. Left for Paris in the 1920s. Studied art at the École National des Arts Décoratifs in Paris. Stage designer, influenced by Leon Bakst, also by Ukrainian folklore, leaning towards the grotesque. Renowned for his designs for the Sevres porcelain factory. Moved to the USA. Taught stage design at the City College in New York.

Listopadov, Aleksandr Mikhailovich
18.9.1873–14.2.1949. Musician, folklorist.
Born in the Cossack village of Ekaterininskaia-na-Donets. Collector of, and researcher into, songs of the Don Cossacks. Also transcribed Russian songs from the central regions, and Ukrainian and Tadzhik songs. Author of the 5-volume *Pesni Donskikh Kazakov*, Moscow-Leningrad, 1949–54. Died in Rostov-on-Don.

Listov, Konstantin Iakovlevich
2.10.1900–   . Composer, conductor.
Born in Odessa. Variety stage and operetta conductor, 1920–30. Author of songs for the masses, operas, operettas, orchestral pieces, pieces for violin and piano, romances, over 400 songs, and music for stage and radio.

Litinskii, Genrikh Il'ich
17.3.1901–   . Composer.
Born in the Ukraine. Husband of the composer Roza Romm. Professor at the Gnesin Institute, and concurrently at the Kazan' Conservatory from 1949. Taught at the Moscow Conservatory, 1923–43. Among his pupils were A. Babadzhanian and T. Khrennikov. Author of operas, in collaboration with M. Zhirkov, ballets, a symphony, suites, concertos for solo instruments with orchestra, a string octet, 12 string quartets, vocal works, and arrangements of folk songs.

Litoshenko, Maria Petrovna
24.9.1949–   . Athlete.
Born in Kiev. Honoured Master of Sports (handball), 1976. With Kiev Spartak. Graduated from the Kame-nets-Podolskii Pedagogical Institute, 1972. Schoolmaster. USSR champion, 1969–79. Olympic champion, 1976.

Litvak, Anatol (Anatolii)
5.5.1902–15.12.1974. Film director.
Born in Kiev. Studied philosophy at Petrograd University. Actor and director with E. Vakhtangov. Worked with V. Meyerhold. Emigrated, 1923. From 1925, worked in theatres in Paris. His debut as a film director was in Germany, 1930. Also made films in England and France. In 1936, moved to the USA. Became a prominent American director.

Litvin, Felia Vasil'evna (b. Schutz, Françoise Jeanne; m. Litvinova)
1861–12.10.1936. Singer (dramatic soprano).
Born in Petersburg. Pupil of Pauline Viardot-Garcia. Debut in the Italian Opera, Paris, 1885. Returned to Russia. Appeared on the stage from the 1890s. Guest performances in Europe and the USA. Especially famous for her Wagner roles. One of the most famous singers in the world at the turn of the century. Emigrated after the October 1917 Revolution. Author of *Moia Zhizn' i Moe Iskusstvo*, 1933 (translated from the French). Died in Paris.

Litvin-Sedoi, Zinovii Iakovlevich (Zvulon Iankelev; cover names – Villonen, Igolkin, Bystrov)
16.3.1879–15.10.1947. Revolutionary, politician.
Born in Kolomna. Son of a worker. Member of the SD Party, 1897. Became a revolutionary organizer among metal workers. One of the organizers and chief-of-staff of the Presnia uprising in Moscow during the 1905 Revolution. Secretary of the military organization of Bolsheviks in Finland, 1906. Participated in the sailor's rebellion at Sveaborg. Emigrated, lived in France, Canada and the USA. Returned after the February Revolution, 1917. During the Civil War, political commissar with Red detachments. Thereafter, director of a technical school in Moscow. Died in Moscow.

Litvinenko, Vasilii Konstantinovich
2.2.1899 – 1968. Ballet dancer, choreographer, opera singer.
Born in the village of Savel'evka, Kuibyshev Oblast'. From 1915, worked at the Saratov Opera House. Graduated from the Saratov Ballet School, in the class of A. Aleksiuto-vich, 1918. From 1921–24, and 1935–48, dancer and choreographer at various theatres all over Russia. Trained by M. Mordkin at his Tbilisi studio, 1921–22. Graduated from the Tbilisi Conservatory as a singer, 1924. Died in Moscow.

Litvinenko-Vol'gemut, Maria Ivanovna
6.2.1895–4.4.1966. Singer (soprano).
Born in Kiev. Pupil of M. Alekseeva-Iunevich and M. Ivanitskii. Soloist with the Khar'kov Opera, 1923–35, and the Kiev Theatre of Opera and Ballet, 1935–51. Professor at the Kiev Conservatory. Stalin Prize, 1946. Died in Kiev.

Litvinov, Maksim Maksimovich (Wallakh, Meer Genokh Moiseevich)
17.7.1876–31.12.1951. Revolutionary, politician, diplomat.
Born in Belostok (then Russian Poland). Son of a merchant. Educated at Belostok Secondary School. Joined the army, 1893–98, served in Baku. Worked as a clerk in Kiev. Joined the SD Party, 1898. Arrested in 1901, escaped 1902, went to Switzerland, then moved to London and joined Lenin. Returned to Russia (Riga) and organized (with Krasin) the smuggling of Bolshevik propaganda into Russia. Organized the smuggling of arms for revolutionaries during the 1905 Revolution. Organized the first legal Bolshevik newspaper *Novaia Zhizn'* (with Krasin, financed by Gorkii) in Petersburg. Again emigrated, organized gun-running expeditions (with Kamo), represented the Bolsheviks at the 12th International Socialist Congress at Stuttgart, Aug. 1907. Arrested in Jan. 1908 in Paris trying to launder rouble notes from the great robbery in Tiflis (by Kamo and Stalin). After release from jail, went to England, were he worked as a clerk of the name of Harrison in the publishing firm of Williams & Norgate, and married Ivy Low, daughter of a journalist. After the October Revolution 1917, ap-pointed Soviet representative in Britain, 1918, but the British authorities arrested him. Exchanged for the British diplomat Bruce Lockhart, who was arrested by the Cheka. Ambassador to Estonia, 1920. Deputy Foreign Affairs Minister, 1921. Deputy head of the Soviet delegation (under Chicherin) at the Genoa conference, 1922. Head of the delegation at the Hague conference, chairman of the Moscow Disarmament Conference, 1922. Head of the Soviet delegation at the Geneva disarmament conference, 1927–30. Minister of Foreign Affairs, 1930–39, brought the USSR into the League of Nations (Soviet representative, 1934–38), established diplomatic relations between the USSR and the USA. Very effective in covering up Stalin's horrors inside the USSR during the 1930s by his constant exploitation of two popular themes — disarmament and anti-fascism. Replaced by Molotov at the moment when Stalin reached an understanding with Hitler (the Molotov-Ribbentrop pact). Remained Deputy Foreign Affairs Minister, 1941–43, at the same time becoming Ambassador to the USA, when it was necessary to stress common aims in the struggle with Nazi Germany during WWII. Member of the Cen. Cttee. of the Bolshevik Party. Unusual among the Kremlin elite for having a foreign wife (who retained her British citizenship and personal independence). Died in Moscow.

Litvinov, Pavel Mikhailovich
1940– . Dissident.
Born in Moscow. Grandson of Stalin's Foreign Minister. Graduated in physics from Moscow University. Active in the human rights movement, 1967. Lost his job. Arrested, 1968, for participating in the demonstration on Red Square against the Soviet invasion of Czechoslovakia. Exiled to Siberia. Released, 1972, and resumed dissident activity. Threatened by the KGB, he left the USSR in 1974. Lives in the USA.
See: *Pravosudie Ili Rasprava?*, England, 1968; *Protsess Chetyrekh*, Holland, 1971.

Liuban, Isaak Isaakovich
23.3.1906– . Composer.
Born in Mogilev Gouvt. In Moscow from 1945. Author of cantatas, songs, arrangements of Belorussian folk songs, and music for stages and screen.

Liubarskii, Kronid Arkad'evich
1934– . Human rights campaigner.
Born in Pskov. Graduated from Moscow University in astrophysics. Numerous articles in the Soviet press. Became involved in human rights activity. One of the editors of the samizdat publication *Khronika Tekushchikh Sobytii*. Arrested, 1972. Sentenced to 5 years of strict regime camps. Transferred to the Vladimir jail. After release, left the USSR, 1977. Settled in West Germany. Editor of *Vesti Iz SSSR*, an important news bulletin about arrests, prisons and psychiatric institutions. Publishes an annual list of political prisoners in the USSR. Co-editor (with B. Khazanov and S. Maksudov) of *Strana i Mir*.

Liubimov, Grigorii Pavlovich (Karaulov, Modest Nikolaevich)
25.1.1881–17.7.1934. Musician, conductor, ethnographer.
Born in Petersburg. Son of the populist N. Karaulov. Studied music at the Music Drama School of the Moscow Philharmonic Society. Noticed by Sergei Kusevitskii, and became his pupil. Attracted to the balalaika, domra and other folk instruments. Became a domra virtuoso and learned how to make the instruments. Involved in revolutionary activity. Several arrests and exile in Siberia. Created with S. Burov the 4-string domra. In 1913, organized the Domra Quartet. In 1919, head of the 1st State Orchestra of Ancient Folk Instruments. Died in Moscow.

Liubimov, Isidor Evstigneevich
1882–1937. Politician.
Member of the SD Party, 1902. Took part in the Civil War, organizing supplies for the Red Army. Thereafter, held party posts in Turkestan and the Ukraine. Chairman of Tsentrosoiuz, 1926–30. Minister of Light Industry of the USSR, 1932. Member of the Cen. Cttee. of the Bolshevik Party, 1972. Victim of Stalin's purges.

Liubimov, Iurii Petrovich
30.9.1917–   . Stage director, actor.
Born in Iaroslavl'. Graduated from the Moscow Shchukin Theatre School at the Vakhtangov Theatre, 1939. Served in the Soviet Army, 1940–46. From 1946, an actor at the Evgenii Vakhtangov Theatre, Moscow. Joined the Communist Party, 1952. Principal Director of the Taganka Drama and Comedy Theatre, Moscow from 1964. Harassed by Ministry of Culture bureaucrats, but protected by Iurii Andropov, whose daughter Irina had married one of the actors in the Liubimov circle. Won Andropov's respect by turning down his two children who had wanted to join the Taganka. His production of *Boris Godunov* was banned under Brezhnev for its political overtones. During his visit to Britain in 1983, decided to stay in protest against harassment from the Ministry of Culture. Immediately fired from the Taganka Theatre, and stripped of Soviet citizenship in 1984. Became artistic director of the Bobigny, a suburban Paris Arts Centre. Worked for 6 weeks at the Lyric Theatre, London. Staged Dostoevskii's *Crime and Punishment*. Has been staging his avant-garde productions around the world since. Settled in Israel. In 1988, visited Moscow and was present at a performance of his own show in memory of V. Vysotskii at the Taganka Theatre.

Liuboshits, Anna Saulovna
25.7.1887–1969? Cellist.
Born in Odessa. Sister of the American violinist Lia Liuboshits (1885–1965). Pupil of A. Glen. Honorary Artist of the RSFSR, 1933.

Liudkevich, Stanislav Filippovich
24.12.1879–1969. Composer, musicologist.
Born in Iaroslav, Galicia (now in Poland). Doctor of musicology. Collector of folk songs. Author of operas, cantatas, orchestral works, symphonic poems, concertos, instrumental pieces, arrangements of folk melodies, and an anthology of Ukrainian folk songs. Shevchenko Prize, 1964, for his symphonic works *Kavkaz* and *Zaveshchanie*.

Liudmilin, Anatolii Alekseevich
26.6.1903–   . Conductor.
Born in Kiev. Chief conductor of the operas in Perm', 1944–55, and Sverdlovsk, 1955–60. With the Musical Theatre in Voronezh from 1962. Stalin Prize, 1947, 1951.

Liudnikov, Ivan Il'ich
1902–1976. Col.-general.
Joined the Red Army, 1918. Took part in the Civil War. Member of the Bolshevik Party, 1925. Graduated from the Frunze Military Academy, 1938. Several high posts during WWII. After WWII, deputy commander of Soviet forces in Germany. Later head of the Vystrel Courses, and professor at the Academy of the General Staff.

Liugailo, Stanislav Antonovich
1.1.1938–   . Athlete.
Born in Sukhumi, Abkhazia. Honoured Master of Sports (volley-ball), 1964. Olympic champion, 1964. With Riga Daugava. Coach. Graduated from the Latvian Institute of Physical Culture, 1970.

Liukom, Elena Mikhailovna
5.5.1891–27.2.1968. Ballerina.
Born in Petersburg. Graduated from the Mariinskii Theatre School, Petersburg, 1909. Pupil of M. Fokin. Appeared in Diaghilev's Ballets Russes in 1910. Showed a dramatic and expressive element in her mature work. Leading roles in Fokin's productions. Returned to Russia. Left the stage in 1941. Taught 1953–65. Died in Leningrad.
See: *Moia Rabota v Balete*, Leningrad, 1940.

Liul'ka, Arkhip Mikhailovich
1908–1984. Aircraft engine designer.
Educated at Kiev Polytechnic, 1931. Designer at the Kirov Aviation Works, 1939. Inventor and designer of Soviet turbojet engines. Member of the Bolshevik Party, 1947. Academician, 1968.

Liushkov, Genrikh Samuilovich
1900?–1945. State security officer.
Protegé of Ezhov. Took the place of Deribas as head of the Secret Operations Department of the NKVD. In order to escape the purges, which threatened him personally, defected to Japan, 1939, taking with him many sensitive secrets. Kept under close supervision by Japanese security police and shot by them just before the Japanese defeat, 1945.

Livanov, Vasilii Borisovich
19.7.1935–   . Actor, director.
Son of the actor, Boris Livanov. Graduated from the Shchukin Theatre School, 1958, and from the Higher Directors' Courses, 1966. As an actor, best known for his film *Neotpravlennoe Pis'mo*, 1960, and his TV film series as Sherlock Holmes, *Prikliucheniia Sherloka Kholmsa and Doktora Votsona*, 1979–83. Directed such films as *Samyi Samyi*, 1966, and *Siniaia Ptitsa*, 1970.

**Livanova, Tamara Nikolaevna
(m. Ferman)**
18.4.1909–   . Musicologist.
Born in Kishenev. Professor at the Moscow Conservatory, 1939–46 and 1948–54.
Works: *Ocherki i Materialy po Istorii Russkoi Muzykal'noi Kul'tury*, Moscow, 1938; *Istoriia Zapadno–Evropeiskoi Muzyki do 1789 goda*, Moscow-Leningrad, 1940; *Russkaia Muzykal'naia Kul'tura v ee Sviaziakh s Literaturoi, Teatrom i Bytom* 2 vol., Moscow, 1952–53; *Muzykal'naia Bibliografia Russkoi Periodicheskoi Pechati XIX veka*, Moscow, 1960–66.

Livshits, Benedikt Konstantinovich
1887–1939. Poet, writer.
Well-known modernist poet before WWI. The only one (apart from N. Gumilev) of the prominent intelligentsia who volunteered to go to the front in WWI. Served in the army until the 1917 Revolution. In the 1920s, became an activist of avant-garde art. Memoirs: *Polutoraglazyi Strelets*, 1933. Victim of Stalin's purges, perished in the Gulag.

Livshuts, Aleksandr
1886–1951? Historian, diplomat.
Born in Petersburg. Educated in Germany. Russian vice-consul in Spain, 1912. After the October Revolution 1917, remained in Spain, where he became the Greek consul in

Madrid. Published historical works, and also created an important collection of antique coins. Took part in welfare work amongst Russian emigrés. Member of the Spanish Academy of History.

Lizichev, Aleksei Dmitrievich
1928– . General.
Joined the Red Army, 1946. Member of the Communist Party, 1949. Graduated from the Lenin Military Political Academy, 1957. Political and Komsomol officer in the armed forces. Head of the Political Administration of the Army and Navy, 1985.

Lobachev, Grigorii Grigor'evich
8.7.1888–18.6.1953. Composer.
Born in Moscow. Composed Soviet propaganda songs for school children. Took part in an ethnographic expedition. Many arrangements of folk melodies of the peoples of the USSR and elsewhere. Author of works for voice and violin, choral pieces, symphonies, and 4-string domra quartets. Used folk motives in his music for stage and screen. Died in Moscow.

Lobanov, Iurii Terent'evich
29.9.1952. Athlete.
Born in Dushanbe, Tadzhikistan. Honoured Master of Sports (rowing), 1972. With Dushanbe Tadzhikistan. USSR champion, 1972–77. World champion, 1973–79. Olympic canoeing champion, 1972 (with V. Chesiunas). Graduated from the Tadzhik Institute of Physical Culture, 1977. Works as a sports instructor.

Lobanov-Rostovskii, Nikita Dmitrievich, Prince
1.1.1935– . Art collector, banker.
Born in Sofia. Son of Prince Dimitrii Ivanovich Lobanov-Rostovskii, whose family goes back to Vsevolod the 'Big Nest', a Grand Prince of Russia in the 13th century. His mother was Princess Irina Vyrubova, a relative of Anna, the Tsarina's lady-in-waiting. In Jan. 1949, with his parents, tried to escape from communist Bulgaria. Crossed the border to Greece without realising that the area was controlled by communist forces who were fighting the Monarchists in the

Civil War. Caught, arrested and brought back. Put into the military prison in Sofia, where he was immediately separated from his parents. Befriended by a young thief with whom he stole food and clothes. With the help of his uncle, Nikolay Vyrubov, who was an officer with De Gaulle, he was let out of prison and later out of the country. Left Sofia for Paris on the Orient Express. Arrived in Paris on New Year's Eve, 1953. In Jan. 1954, arrived penniless to study at Christ Church, Oxford. Sponsored by a Refugees from Eastern Europe grant set up by an anonymous Russian millionaire. Graduated from Oxford, 1958. Moved to New York to continue his education at Columbia University. Graduated in geology, 1960, and left the USA for Patagonia, Argentina. Soon returned to New York and entered a business school. Started his banking career as a junior clerk. Became a naturalized American. Returned to England, 1969. Works in an American bank in London. His 1,000-strong collection of the works of some 150 Russian artists who created stage designs for Diaghilev was shown in Moscow and several cities in the US. Promotes his collection on both sides of the Atlantic.
Source: Interview with J. Vronskaya, Jan. 1986.

Lobkovskii, Abram Mikhailovich
28.12.1912– . Composer.
Born in Vitebsk. Author of violin concertos, orchestral works, and works for the variety stage.

Lobov, Semen
1888–1937. Politician, security officer.
Joined the Bolshevik Party, 1913. Left-communist at the time of the Brest-Litovsk peace treaty. Leading Cheka officer, 1918–20. Later held several administrative posts. Liquidated by Stalin.

Lobov, Semen Mikhailovich
1913–1977. Admiral.
Joined the Red Navy, 1932. Educated at a naval school, 1937. Member of the Bolshevik Party, 1940. Took part in WWII. Deputy commander of the Northern fleet, 1961, and comman-

der, 1964–72. Deputy chief of the General Staff of the Navy, 1972.

Lobova, Nina Romanovna
20.7.1957– . Athlete.
Born in Georgia. International Class Master of Sports (handball), 1976. With Beregovo Kolos (Zakarpatskaia Oblast'). Olympic champion, 1976. Works as a civil servant in the Ukraine.

Lodii, Zoia Petrovna
30.6.1886–24.12.1957. Singer (soprano).
Born in Tiflis. Daughter of the tenor, P. Lodii (1855–1920). Professor at the Leningrad Conservatory. Died in Leningrad.

Loginov, Evgenii Fedorovich
1907–1970. Marshal.
Joined the Red Army, 1926. Educated at a pilots' school, 1928. During WWII, commander of bomber groups. After WWII, deputy head of the Air Force Academy. Later deputy commander of the Soviet Air Force. Head of Civil Aviation, 1959–64. Minister of Civil Aviation, 1964. Member of the Cen. Cttee. of the CPSU, 1967.

Loginov, Vadim Petrovich
19.6.1927– . Diplomat, state official.
2nd secretary of Leningrad Oblast' Komsomol Cttee., 1956. Secretary of the Cen. Cttee. of the USSR Komsomol, 1958–61. 1st secretary of Vyborg City Cttee., 1963. 1st secretary and councillor in the USSR Embassy to the USA (under Dobrynin), 1968–71. Councillor in the USSR Embassy to Poland, 1971–74. Head of the 4th European Department (Poland and Czechoslovakia) in the MID (Ministry of Foreign Affairs), 1974–78. USSR Ambassador to Angola, 1978–83. Head of the 5th European Department in the MID (Albania, Bulgaria, Hungary, Greece, Rumania and Yugoslavia). Deputy Foreign Minister of the USSR from Dec. 1985. Candidate member of the Cen. Cttee. of the CPSU.

Lokshin, Aleksandr Lazarevich
19.9.1920– . Composer.
Born in the Altai region. Worked in

243

Moscow. Author of an oratorio, 2 choral symphonies, a suite for a film, a symphonic poem for violin and orchestra, a Hungarian fantasy, a quintet for clarinet and string instruments, a sonata for violin and piano, and piano variations.

Lokshin, Daniil L'vovich
28.11.1907–20.5.1966. Musicologist.
Born in Starodub. Doctor of musicology. Lecturer in music at the Gnesin Pedagogical Institute, Moscow. Author of *Vydaiushchiesia Russkie Khory i Ikh Dirizhery*, Moscow, 1953, *Khorovoe Penie v Russkoi Dorevoliutsionnoi i Sovetshoi Shkole*, Moscow, 1957, and *Rukovodstvo Smeshannym Khorom Starshykh Shkol'nikov*, Moscow, 1960. Died in Moscow.

Loktev, Konstantin Borisovich
16.6.1933–   . Athlete.
Born in Moscow. Honoured Master of Sports (hockey), 1964. Honoured coach of the USSR, 1976. With the Central Sports Club of the Armed Forces. Graduated from the Moscow Oblast' Pedagogical Institute, 1969. USSR champion, 1955–66. European champion, 1958–66. Bronze medal, 1960. World champion, 1964–66. Olympic champion, 1964.

Loktionov Aleksandr Dmitrievich
1893–1941. Col.-general.
Joined the Red Army, 1918. Regimental commander during the Civil War. Commander of the Soviet Air Force, 1937–39. Deputy Minister of Defence and commander of the Soviet occupying forces in the annexed Baltic states, 1939–40.

Lomakin, Trofim Fedorovich
2.8.1924–13.6.1973. Athlete.
Born in the village of Baranch in the Altai Krai. Honoured Master of Sports (weight-lifting), 1952. With the Moscow Armed Forces Club. Graduated from the Leningrad Institute of Physical Culture, 1950. Olympic champion, 1952 (middle-weight, 417. 5kg). USSR champion, 1952–60. European champion, 1952–58. World record-holder, 1953–60. World champion, 1957–58. Author of *Put' Shtangista*, Moscow, 1953. Died in Moscow.

Lomeiko, Vladimir
1929–   . Politician.
Emerged on the political scene during the last years of Konstantin Chernenko's leadership. Promoted in 1984 to head of the Foreign Ministry Press Department, replacing Leonid Zamiatin. His dry, professional manner at press conferences with the Western press has made him well-known. Belongs to the Andrei Gromyko circle. Married to his daughter, and has written a book (together with Anatolii Gromyko, Andrei's son) on international affairs and USSR foreign policy. Has a perfect command of English, but insists on conducting his briefings in Russian only, sometimes with translation into English. Conducted Svetlana Allilueva's press conference when she suddenly returned to Moscow after 18 years in the West.

Lomonosov, Iurii Vladimirovich
1876–1936? Engineer.
Railway engineer. Major-general. Deputy head of the administration of Russian railways, 1912. During the February Revolution 1917, close collaborator of Bublikov, Minister of Transport in the Provisional Government. Emigrated to the USA, 1918–19. Returned to the Soviet Union. Close collaborator of Krasin in the rebuilding of the transport system after the chaos of the revolution and civil war. Disappeared from the scene, probably perished in the Gulag.

Lomov-Opokov, Georgii Ippolitovich (Lomov, A.; Afanasii, George)
5.2.1888–30.12.1938. Politician.
Born in Saratov. Son of a nobleman. Joined the Bolsheviks, 1903. Before WWI, on party underground work in Moscow and Petersburg. Exiled to Arkhangel'sk, 1910. Released, graduated in law from Petersburg University, 1913. Exiled to Siberia, 1916. After the Bolshevik take-over, 1st Peoples Commissar (minister) of Justice, 1918. Later joined the left-wing communists. During the Civil War, active in Siberia and the Urals. Member of the Politburo of the Cen. Cttee. of the Ukrainian Communist Party, 1926–29. Victim of Stalin's purges.

Lopatin, Aleksei Vasil'evich
1915–1941. Lieutenant, state security officer.
Joined the border guards (NKVD), 1937. At the start of WWII, his border-guard detachment fought to the death for 11 days against the advancing German Army. Posthumously awarded the title Hero of the Soviet Union, 1957. The extremely long delay in acknowledging this heroic feat has never been explained.

Lopatin, Anton Ivanovich
1897–1965. Lt.-general.
Joined the Red Army, 1918. Member of the Bolshevik Party, 1919. Took part in the Civil War. Commander of several armies during WWII. Hero of the Soviet Union, 1945. Graduated from the Academy of the General Staff, 1947. Staff officer after WWII.

Lopatin, Lev Mikhailovich
1.6.1855–21.3.1920. Philosopher.
Born in Moscow. Graduated from Moscow University, 1879. Professor at Moscow University until his death. Editor of *Voprosy Filosofii i Psikhologii*. Chairman of the Moscow Psychological Society from 1899 until 1917 when it was closed. Friend of Vladimir Solov'ev. Follower of Leibnitz. His ideas of creative causality were similar to those developed later by Henri Bergson. Died from hunger and deprivation during the Civil War.
Works: *Istoriia Drevnei Filosofii*, 1901; *Psikhologiia*, 1902; *Polozhitelnye Zadachi Filosofii*, 2 parts, Moscow, 1911; *Lektsii Po Istorii Novoi Filosofii*, Part 1, Moscow, 1914.

Lopukhin, Aleksei Aleksandrovich
1864–1927/28. Secret police official.
Graduated from Moscow University in law in 1886. Son of a nobleman. Childhood friend of Stolypin. Worked as a legal official in various provincial towns. In May 1902, appointed director of the Police Department. Dismissed after the assassination of Grand-Duke Sergei and appointed governor of Estland (Estonia). At the end of 1905, retired after disturbances in Reval. Exposed Azef's collaboration with the police in 1908 during a chance 6-hour talk

on a train to Berlin with Vladimir Burtsev. Later confirmed his information at a meeting with members of the Cen. Cttee. of the SR Party — Chernov, Argunov and Savinkov. After his return from abroad in Jan. 1909, arrested and tried for divulging state secrets. Defended himself by claiming that he wanted to prevent further terrorist actions by Azef. Sentenced to 5 years hard labour in May 1909. After his release, worked in banking. Emigrated after the October Revolution 1917. Wrote memoirs on his work as head of the secret police and the life and activities of the revolutionaries.
See: Mark Aldanov, *Azef*, Paris, 1931.

Lopukhov, Andrei Vasil'evich
20.8.1898–23.5.1947. Ballet dancer.
Born in Petersburg. Brother of Fedor Lopukhov. Graduated from the Petrograd Theatre School, 1916. Until 1945, a leading dancer at the Kirov Theatre. From 1927, combined dancing with teaching at the Leningrad Choreographic School. One of the first tutors of folk dance methodics. One of the authors of *Osnovy Kharakternogo Tantsa*, 1939. Left an unpublished memoir, *Dvadtsat Let Kharakternogo Tantsovshchika* (the manuscript is kept at the VTO, Leningrad branch). Among his many pupils was Iurii Grigorovich. Died in Leningrad.

Lopukhov, Fedor Vasil'evich
20.10.1886–28.1.1973. Ballet dancer, choreographer.
Born in Petersburg. Graduated from the Petersburg Theatre School, 1905. Trained by N. Legat. From 1905, dancer, then soloist at the Mariinskii Theatre. With the Bolshoi Theatre, 1909–10. Took part in a US tour, 1910–11. From 1918, combined his dancing career with choreography. From 1922–1945, with some intervals, artistic director of the Bolshoi Theatre. Artistic director of the Leningrad Choreographic School, 1936–41. Revived some classical ballets. Founded a department at the Leningrad Choreographic School, 1937, and headed it until 1941. From 1962, headed the choreographic department of the Leningrad Conservatory. Pro-

fessor, 1965. Immensely respected figure in Soviet ballet. Trained and influenced a generation of ballet dancers. Died in Leningrad.

Lopukhova, Evgenia Vasil'evna
7.12.1884–21.8.1943. Ballet dancer.
Born in Petersburg. Sister of Fedor Lopukhov. Graduated from the Petersburg Theatre School, 1902. Trained by N. Legat and others. Until 1924, ballerina with the Mariinskii Theatre. During the seasons 1909–11, with the Ballets Russes in Europe. Died during the WWII Siege of Leningrad. Left memoirs, *Dvadtsat Let Stsenicheskoi Deiatelnosti*, Petrograd, 1923.

Lopukhova, Lidia Vasil'evna (Lopokova, Lydia; Mrs Maynard Keynes)
21.10.1891–1981. Prima ballerina.
Born in Petersburg. Graduated from the Petersburg Theatre School, 1909. Pupil of Mikhail Fokin. Joined the Mariinskii Theatre in 1909. In 1910, appeared with Diaghilev's Ballets Russes. Became a prima ballerina and a dramatic actress. With Diaghilev, performed mostly in the productions of her tutor, Fokin (*L'Oiseau de Feu*). With the Ballets Russes toured the USA, Italy and Latin America, 1911–15. Performed with M. Mordkin, L. Miasin, and her brother, F. Lopukhov. In 1916, married Diaghilev's businessmanager, Randolfo Barocchi. Left him 3 years later. Returned to Diaghilev in 1921. Lived in Bloomsbury. Met Maynard Keynes in 1926, and married him shortly afterwards. After 1927, appeared from time to time with British ballet companies, and danced with L. Miasin in F. Ashton's productions. After her husband's death in 1946, lived as a virtual recluse on their Sussex estate until her death.
See: *Lydia Lopokova* (edited by Milo Keynes), London, 1986.

Lopushanskii, Konstantin
1947?– . Film director.
Graduated from the VGIK. In 1986, made *Letters From a Dead Man*, an anti-nuclear film set in a town devastated by a nuclear accident similar to that at Chernobyl. Shot in sepia-tinted monochrome to under-

line the gloomy mood of a dying place. The film was shown on British TV in 1988.

Losev, Aleksei Fedorovich
22.9.1893–5.1988. Philosopher, classical scholar.
Born in Novocherkassk. Graduated from Moscow University, 1915. Taught aesthetics at the Moscow Conservatory, 1921–31, and Greek language and literature at Moscow University in the 1920s. Professor at the Moscow Pedagogical Institute from 1931. Well-known authority on logic, psychology, classical philology, history of philosophy and aesthetics. The last survivor of the blossoming of philosophy in Russia in the early 20th century, who managed to survive inside the Soviet Union despite a short time in the Gulag in the 1930s. Became popular among the young intelligentsia in the 1970s. Translated Aristotle, Plotinus, Cusanus and others into Russian.

Losik, Oleg Aleksandrovich
1915– . Marshal.
Joined the Red Army, 1935. Educated at a school for armoured troops officers, 1938. Took part in the Soviet-Finnish war and WWII as a tank officer. Graduated from the Academy of the General Staff, 1950, later professor at the Academy. Head of the Academy of Armoured Forces, 1969.

Losskii, Nikolai Onufrievich
6.12.1870–24.1.1965. Philosopher.
Born in Kreslavka, Vitebsk Gouvt. After youthful adventures, including the distribution of atheist propaganda, and a short spell in the Foreign Legion, settled down to a distinguished academic career. Graduated from Petersburg University in 1903. Doctor of philosophy, 1907. Professor of philosophy at Petersburg University, 1916. Friend of Askoldov and under the influence of his father, the philosopher Kozlov, became attracted to the Leibniz tradition (monads) and transformed it on the basis of intuitivism and personalism. Considered to be the foremost Russian philosopher of the 20th century (rivalled only by S. Frank). Unable to adapt to the new

conditions under communist rule, dismissed from his teaching posts. In 1922, expelled from Russia (with a large group of professors). Lived in Czechoslovakia until WWII. Professor of philosophy in Bratislava, 1942–45. After WWII, moved to Paris, then to the USA, 1946. Professor of philosophy at the St. Vladimir Seminary NY, 1947–50. Died and buried in Paris.
Main works: *Logics, Matter and Life, The Basis of Intuition, Freedom of Will, The World as an Organic Whole, Les Conditions de la Morale absolue, History of Russian Philosophy* (English ed.), *Memoirs*.

Losskii, Vladimir Appollonovich
30.6.1874–6.7.1946. Singer (bass), theatrical director.
Born in Kiev. Pupil of K. Everardi. Soloist from 1906. Director of the Bolshoi Theatre, 1934–36 and 1943–46. Also directed the operas of Sverdlovsk, Tbilisi, Leningrad, and elsewhere. Died in Moscow.

Lotianu, Emil Vladimirovich
6.11.1936–   . Film director.
Born and grew up in a small mountain village in the Bukovina. Studied in the actors' faculty of the Studio School of the Moscow Art Theatre. For 2 years, played character roles in the Studio's student productions. Entered the director's faculty of the Moscow Film School (VGIK). Studied under Mikhail Romm. His first feature film, *Wait For Us at Dawn*, made in 1963 at Moldova Film Studio in Kishinev, was the first film to deal with the revolution in Moldavia. Won international fame with *Lautary*, 1972, while his next film, *Red Meadows*, was assigned the category of 'poetic cinema'. Both films draw on popular folklore and national traditions. The biographical film *Anna Pavlova*, starring his wife, the former ballerina, Galina Beliaeva, made him known in the West. Secretary of the Union of Soviet Film Makers, 1981.

Louis, Viktor (Levin, Vitalii Evgen'evich)
1928–   . Journalist.
Born in Moscow. Moscow correspondent for many Western publications. A Soviet citizen, non-party,

and a millionaire whose articles have appeared under his own name in the *London Evening News, Washington Post, New York Times, Time* magazine, *France-Soir* etc. Specializes in scoops. Was the first to announce Khrushchev's retirement. Obvious source of inspired Soviet leaks to the world press. Known also for other operations, e.g. passed on Svetlana Allilueva's pirated copy of *Twenty Letters to a Friend* to a publisher in the West in order to dampen the sensation from the book a few months before the official publication date. Arrested as a student, 1947, spent 9 years in Gulag camps. The KGB defector Major Iurii Nosenko alleged in 1964 that Louis had been recruited in the camps by the KGB. On his return to Moscow in 1956, got small jobs in the diplomatic sphere (tightly controlled by the KGB), first with the New Zealand Embassy, later at the Embassy of Brazil. Met his future British wife, Jenifer, at that time a nanny to a British diplomat. They were soon given a 3-room apartment on the exclusive Leninskii Prospekt, an unusual gesture from the authorities, since they were a young childless couple and he was not in employment anywhere officially. This was followed in 1965 by the purchase of a magnificent country house on a large estate in Peredelkino. Lives there now with his wife and three sons. Travels around the world on special missions, e.g. to Taiwan, Israel and South Africa.
Sources: A. Lee, 'The Luxurious Life of a Kremlin Mouthpiece', *Observer Magazine*, Oct. 1980; 'Tainstvennaia Anglichanka v Moskve' (The Mysterious Englishwoman in Moscow), *La Pensée Russe*, 2.1.1975.

Lubentsov, Vasilii Nikitich
25.4.1886–1972? Singer (bass).
Pupil of M. Polli. Soloist with the Russian Opera in Kiev, 1913–23, and the Bolshoi Theatre, 1923–51.

Lufer, Abram Mikhailovich
25.8.1905–13.7.1948. Pianist.
Born in Kiev. Pupil of G. Beklemishev. 1st prize at the All-Ukrainian Competition for Pianists, 1930, and 4th prize at the International Chopin Piano Competition, Warsaw, 1932. Taught at the Lysenko Institute of

Higher Musical Studies from 1934. Professor from 1934. Director of the Kiev Conservatory. Died in Kiev.

Luganskii, Sergei Danilovich
1918–1977. Major-general.
Joined the Red Army, 1936. Took part in the Soviet-Finnish war and WWII as a fighter pilot. Graduated from the Air Force Academy, 1949. Several high posts in the Soviet Air Force. Retired 1964.

Luka (Voino-Iasenetskii, Valentin Feliksovich), Archbishop of Crimea and Simferopol'
27.4.1877–11.6.1961. Russian Orthodox clergyman, surgeon, author.
Born in Kerch, Crimea. Educated at high school in Kiev. Studied painting in Munich. Graduated from Kiev University in medicine, 1903. During the Russo-Japanese war, served as a military doctor, 1904–05. Worked as a surgeon in the provinces. Director of Tashkent Hospital, 1917. Professor of Central Asia State University. Priest, 1921 (without giving up his medical profession). Monk, 1923. Bishop, 1923. Arrested in 1923. Exiled to Siberia and Turkestan, 1924–6. Simultaneously Bishop of Turkestan, 1926–30. Exiled to Arkhangel'sk, 1930–33. Surgeon in Tadzhikistan, 1934–7. In prison and exile, 1937–41. At the beginning of WWII, appointed chief surgeon in Krasnoiarsk Hospital, operating on heavily wounded soldiers, evacuated to Siberia. Archbishop of Krasnoiarsk, 1943. Member of the Holy Synod, 1943. Archbishop of Tambov, Feb. 1944. Stalin Prize for scientific works on surgery, 1944. Took part in Soviet propaganda efforts during WWII. Archbishop of Crimea, 1946. In old age, became completely blind (glaucoma), 1955. During his last years of life, actively opposed the Khrushchev anti-religious campaign. Died in Simferopol', retaining a high reputation both as a religious thinker, and as a medical scientist (surgeon and ophthalmologist).
Main works: *Septic Surgery* (the standard manual on this subject in the USSR), 55 other medical works, 10 vols. of sermons, memoirs. Biography by M. Popovskii published in the USA.

Lukach (Mate Zalka; real name-Bela Frankl)
1896–1937. Revolutionary, state security official.
Born in Hungary. During WWI, prisoner of war in Russia, 1916. Became one of the revolutionary organizers among the Austro-Hungarian prisoners of war in Russia after the October Revolution 1917. Joined the Bolshevik Party, 1920. During the Civil War, in Cheka and GPU detachments, 1921–23. Worked in the Cen. Cttee. of the Bolshevik Party from 1928. During the Spanish Civil War, sent to help the Spanish communists. Commander of the 12th International Brigade, 1936. Fell in action.

Lukas, Dmitrii Aleksandrovich
16.6.1911– . Composer.
Born in the Volhynia, Ukraine, Author of operas, romances, songs, and music for stage and screen.

Lukashevskii, Il'ia Avseevich
20.9.1892–1970? Violinist.
Born in Kiev. Pupil of I. Nalbandian. Professor at the Leningrad Conservatory. In 1919, organized and headed the Glazunov string quartet, the earliest Soviet string quartet.

Lukashova, Iraida Petrovna
14.1.1938– . Ballerina.
Born in Sverdlovsk. Studied ballet at the Odessa School of Choreography, 1946–53. Dancer with the Odessa Theatre, 1954, and with the Shevchenko Theatre from 1955. Taught ballet at the Shevchenko Theatre from 1976. Anna Pavlova Award, Paris, 1964.

Luk'ianov, Aleksandr Viktorovich
19.8.1949– . Athlete.
Born in Moscow. Honoured Master of Sports (rowing), 1976. In the military forces. USSR champion, 1970–77 World champion, 1974. Olympic champion, 1976.

Luk'ianov, Anatolii Ivanovich
7.5.1930– . Politician.
Labourer in the Arsenal plant, 1943. Graduated from Moscow University, 1953. Member of the CPSU, 1955. Senior Consultant of the Legal Cttee. of the USSR Council of Ministers, 1956–6l. Deputy chief of a department of the Presidium of the USSR Supreme Soviet, 1969–76. Posts in the Cen. Cttee. apparatus, CPSU. 1976–77. Responsible for administration and Politburo staff work. Doctor of Juridical Sciences, 1980. Chief of the General Department of the Cen. Cttee. of the CPSU since 1985. Member of the Cen. Cttee. since 1986. Elected to the Secretariat of the Cen. Cttee. on Jan. 28, 1987.

Lukin, Filipp Mironovich
3.7.1913– . Composer, choir conductor.
Born in Kazan' Gouvt. Chuvash by nationality. Chairman of the Chuvash branch of the Union of Composers of the RSFSR. Taught at the Cheboksary Music School. Stalin Prize, 1952, for a series of songs. Author of over 60 songs for children, choral works, arrangements of folk songs, instrumental pieces, and music for the stage.

Lukin, Mikhail Fedorovich
1892–1970. Lt.-general.
Took part in WWI as a lieutenant. Joined the Red Army, 1918. Active in the Civil War. Member of the Bolshevik Party, 1919–41 and from 1955. Graduated from the Frunze Military Academy, 1926. Commandant of Moscow, 1935–37. Distinguished service in the early stages of WWII. In Oct. 1941, heavily wounded, became a prisoner of war in Germany. The German authorities intended him to take over the leadership of the anti-Stalinist Russian detachments, an offer which, according to his memoirs written after the war, he rejected as despicable, using this occasion to condemn Vlasov, who accepted this role later, as a traitor and turncoat. The real story of the war-time negotiations and of Lukin's fate after WWII (in the Gulag, 1945–55), seems to have been more complicated than his officially inspired memoirs admit.

Lunacharskii, Anatolii Vasil'evich
23.11.1875–26.12.1933. Politician.
Born in Poltava. Son of an official. Became a marxist as a high school student in Kiev, 1892. Joined the SD Party, 1895, studied in Switzerland and France, 1895–98. Underground revolutionary work in Moscow, 1898. Arrested, 1899. In exile in Kaluga and Vologda, 1900–04. Wrote on marxism and aesthetics, attracted to the theories of Avenarius. After the split of the SD Party, joined the Bolsheviks, 1903. Political exile, 1904–17, in Western Europe. Worked with Lenin, but was criticized by him for his philosophical deviations (bogostroitelstvo and similar marxist heresies). After the February Revolution 1917, returned to Russia, May 1917. Joined the mezhraiontsy group and was accepted with them into the Bolshevik Party under Lenin. Considered the main cultural specialist in the communist leadership. Identified with the first, rather liberal period of Soviet cultural life, taking a tolerant attitude to modernism in all spheres of the arts. Minister of Education, 1917–29. Prolific writer of theoretical and historical articles. Wrote plays of no literary significance. During the difficult first revolutionary years, recognized by the intelligentsia as one of their own among the new ruling elite, and to a certain extent looked upon as a patron and protector. With the advance of Stalinism, lost his former importance and was forced to abandon his modernist convictions. From 1927, assistant head of the Soviet delegation at the League of Nations disarmament conference. Academician, 1930. Wrote *On Socialist Realism*, 1933. Appointed Soviet Ambassador to Spain, 1933. Died on a train at Mentone, France.

Lundberg, Evgenii Germanovich
1887–1956. Author, philosopher, editor.
In the 1900s, member of the intelligentsia in Moscow, interested in religion and philosophy (with Belyi, Florenskii, Bulgakov, and Shestov). In the 1910s, wrote in Russian liberal newspapers. During the revolutionary years, prominent member of the left SR circle Skify (with Ivanov-Razumnik), 1917–18. Emigrated to Berlin, 1920, receiving references from I. Hessen, the well-known Cadet editor. Founded in Berlin the publishing house Skify, 1920 (probably with secret Soviet funds). In the mid-1920s returned to the USSR, and became an establishment writer, publishing works on Lenin. During the years of terror, arrested, 1938, but

released after only 3 months. Remained a trusted Soviet official writer until his death.

Lunts, Lev Natanovich
2.5.1901–9.5.1924. Author.
Born in Petersburg. Educated at high school until 1918, and graduated from Petersburg University in 1922. Lectured at the university on West European literature. Became known as a writer while still a student. One of the main members of the literary circle Serapionovy Brat'ia, which stressed the unity of world culture, and protested against the isolation of Russia after the revolution. Left the USSR in June 1923 for medical reasons. Died near Hamburg in a sanatorium. For many years, his name was not mentioned in the Soviet Union but interest in him revived in the 1960s. Collection of works published in Israel, 1981.

Lur'e, Artur Sergeevich (Lurie, Arthur)
1892–1966. Composer.
Avant-garde composer. In 1918 wrote music for Mayakovsky's poem *Nash Marsh*. After October 1917, head of MUSO Narkompros. Emigrated, 1922.

Lushev, Petr Georgievich
1923– . General.
Joined the Red Army, 1941. Took part in the Siege of Leningrad. Joined the Bolshevik Party, 1951. Graduated from the Tank Forces Academy 1954, and from the Academy of the General Staff, 1966. Deputy commander of Soviet forces in Germany, 1973–75. Commander of Soviet forces in Germany, 1985. 1st Deputy Minister of Defence, 1986. Member of the Cen. Cttee. of the CPSU, 1981.

Lusis, Ianis Voldemarovich
19.5.1939– . Athlete.
Born in Elgava, Latvia. Graduated from the Latvian Institute of Physical Culture, 1961. Honoured Master of Sports (track and field athletics), 1965. With the Riga Armed Forces Club. Member of the CPSU, 1975. World record-holder, 1968–69 and 1972–73. USSR champion, 1962–66, 1968–73, and 1976. European champion, 1962, 1966, 1969 and 1971. Olympic champion, 1968 (javelin).
See: V. Viktorov, *Vsled Za Kop'em*, Moscow, 1972.

Luspekaev, Pavel Borisovich
20.4.1927–17.4.1970. Film actor.
Graduated from the Shchepkin Theatre School, 1950. Started as an actor in theatres in Tbilisi and Kiev. Entered the film industry, 1955. Best known for his powerful performance in *Respublika SHKID*, 1966, and *Beloe Solntse Pustyni*, 1970.

Lutchenko Vladimir Iakovlevich
2.1.1949– . Athlete.
Born in Ramenskoe, Moscow Oblast'. Honoured Master of Sports, (hockey), 1970. With the Central Sports Club of the Army. USSR champion, 1968–79. European champion, 1969–79. World champion, 1969–71, 1973–75, 1978–79. Olympic champion, 1972 and 1976. Member of the CPSU, 1976.

Lvov, Arkadii L'vovich
1927– . Author.
Born in Odessa. Graduated from Odessa University, 1949. Published several books and numerous short stories and articles in the Soviet press. In 1970, accused of contacts with International Zionism, and found it impossible to publish his work. Left the USSR, 1976. Settled in the USA. Published several books abroad.
See: *Bolshoe Solntse Odessy*, Germany, 1981; *Biznesmen Iz Odessy*, Germany, 1981, *Dvor* (memoirs), Germany, 1982.

Lvov, Georgii Evgen'evich, Prince
2.11.1861–7.3.1925. Politician.
Lawyer, land-owner. Served in the Ministry of Internal Affairs, 1886–93. Well-known representative of the Zemstvo. Member of the 1st Duma. Close to the Cadet Party. During WWI, chairman of the All-Zemstvo Union and Zemgor. The first Prime Minister of the Provisional Government until July 1917 (succeeded by Kerenskii). After the October Revolution 1917, emigrated to France. During the Civil War, head of the Russian Political Conference in Paris, 1918–20. Died in Paris.

Lvov, Lollii Ivanovich
1888–1970. Journalist.
Emigrated after the Civil War. Settled in France. Well-known journalist in the Russian press in Paris between the wars. One of the editors of the magazine *Illiustrirovannaia Rossia*. In the late 1950s and early 1960s, lived in Munich. Worked at the Russian desk of Radio Liberty.

Lvov-Anokhin, Boris Aleksandrovich
9.10.1926– . Choreographer, ballet director.
Born in Moscow. Graduated from the Leningrad Theatre Institute, 1950. Director of the Theatre of the Red Army and the Stanislavskii Drama Theatre. Author of more than 200 books and articles on ballet, including numerous works on ballet personalities such as M. Plisetskaia, E. Maksimova, V. Chabukiani, and N. Bessmertnova. TV ballet presenter. Also scripted the ballet films *Anna Karenina* and *Galina Ulanova*.

Lysenko, Liudmila Ivanovna (Shevtsova)
26.11.1934– . Athlete.
Born in Taman', Krasnodar Krai. Honoured Master of Sports (track and field athletics), 1960. With Dnepropetrovsk Avangard. Coach. Graduated from the Kiev Institute of Physical Culture, 1960. World recordholder, 1960–61. USSR champion, 1955–64 (various distances). Olympic champion, 1960 (800 metres).

Lysenko, Trofim Denisovich
29.9.1898–20.11.1976. Agronomist, biologist, party official.
Born in the village of Karlovka, near Poltava. Graduated from the Kiev Agricultural Institute, 1925. Followed Michurin in practical plant breeding. Rejected the chromosome theory of heredity generally accepted by modern genetics. Believed that heritable changes could be brought about in plants by environmental influences, such as subjecting wheat to extremes of temperature, and by grafting. Claiming that his theory corresponded to Marxism, succeeded in enlisting official party support and was appointed president of the

Academy of Agricultural Sciences in 1938. Started a witch hunt against those of his colleagues who disagreed with his theories, especially vilifying the founder of the Academy, Vavilov (who was dismissed and died in the Gulag). Became the virtual dictator in biological sciences in the USSR under Stalin, to whose personality cult he contributed assiduously. Practically Stalin's henchman in science (a role played by Zhdanov in culture, Voroshilov in the Army, and Beria in the country at large), personally responsible for the exile, torture and death of many talented scientists and the general repressive atmosphere and backwardness of Soviet science. After WWII, during the heyday of Stalinism, precipitated an international scandal in the world of science, claiming the authority of the Cen. Cttee. of the CPSU for his scientific views. After Stalin's death, personally criticized by Khrushchev in Mar. 1953. Dismissed from the post of President of the Academy of Agricultural Sciences in 1954, after 16 years of terror. Retained, however, the position of personal adviser to Khrushchev on agriculture. In subsequent years, Soviet scientists proved that he had often falsified the results of his experiments in order to justify his theories.

Lysenko, Vladil' Kirillovich
1926– . Captain.
Born in Vladivostok. Captain of a Soviet fishing trawler. In 1941, joined the Soviet merchant fleet. Docked at various foreign ports, including some in the USA. In 1945, arrested and accused of espionage, but managed to prove his innocence, and received a sentence of only 3 years on probation. In 1952, after an accident at Kherson Dry Docks, accused of sabotage, but acquitted after an 8-month investigation. Continued to captain fishing trawlers. In 1975, defected in Sweden. His memoirs, *Poslednii Reis*, were published in West Germany in 1982. Has written studies of the ecologically disastrous working methods of the Soviet industrial fishing fleets.

M

Maasik, El'za Paulevna
23.7.1908– . Singer (soprano).
Born in Estonia. Pupil of A. Arder. Soloist in the Estonian theatre from 1942. Honoured Artist of the Estonian SSR, 1952.

Machavariani, Aleksei Davidovich
6.10.1913– . Composer.
Born in Gori. Studied at the Tbilisi Conservatory, 1931–36. Pupil of S. Barkhudarian. Postgraduate course, 1937–39. Pupil of P. Riazanov. Taught at the Tbilisi Conservatory from 1939. Assistant of A. Balanchivadze, 1942. Lecturer from 1952. Professor of Composition from 1963. Director of the Teatr Muzykalnoi Komedii from 1934. Concurrently worked as composer with the Baku Experimental Theatre. Artistic director of the State Symphony Orchestra of Georgia, 1956–58. Took part in an expedition to collect Georgian musical folklore. From 1956, secretary, and from 1962, chairman of the Board of the Union of Georgian Composers.

Madelung, Aage
1872–1949. Author.
Born in Denmark. Commercial representative of a Danish firm in Vologda, where he became a close friend of Russian writers and philosophers exiled for revolutionary activity. Started to write and to publish his works in Russian. Later returned to Denmark, and became a well-known writer in his own language.

Madison, Tiit
1950– . Dissident.
Born in Tallinn, Estonia. Human rights campaigner. In 1981, sentenced to 5 years in labour camps for anti-Soviet activities. In Aug. 1987, involved in demonstrations in the Baltic Republics of Estonia, Lithuania and Latvia urging the Soviet government to disclose full details of the 1939 Molotov-Ribbentrop Pact which led to the annexation of the Baltic states. Deported by the KGB to Sweden in Sep. 1987.

Maevskii, Vikentii Anitsetovich (Gutovskii)
1875–22.12.1918. Politician, journalist.
Joined the SD Party in the 1890s. One of the organizers of the social-democrats in Siberia. Editor of the newspaper *Vlast' Truda* in Cheliabinsk. After the take-over by the Whites under Kolchak, arrested and shot in Omsk.

Magdalina (Magdalene), Mother (Grabbe, Nina Pavlovna, Countess)
1896?–3.9.1987. Nun.
Born into the family of a personal friend of Nicholas II. Evacuated from Russia with the Whites after the Civil War to Lemnos. Settled in Volhynia, where her family had estates. Emigrated before the Soviet invasion of Poland, 1939. Settled in Yugoslavia. Nun at the Lesnenskii Convent. After the convent was destroyed by Tito's partisans in 1943, the nuns moved to Belgrade. After WWII, the convent moved to France. For 10 years, head of the Lesnenskii Convent in Normandy. Died in France.

Magidenko, Mikhail Iakovlevich
15.3.1915– . Composer.
Born in the Ukraine. Author of operas, a symphony, a concerto, variations for piano and orchestra, a tone poem for violin and orchestra, suites for folk instrument orchestras, violin duets, romances, songs, an anthology of songs for children, and music for the stage.

Magomaev, Muslim Magometovich
18.9.1885–28.7.1937. Composer, conductor.
Born in Groznyi. Azerbaidzhanian by nationality. One of the organizers of the Azerbaidzhanian Musical Theatre. Author of operas, orchestral and vocal works. Also recorded folk melodies. Died in Nal'chik.

Maiboroda, Georgii Illarionovich
1.12.1913– . Composer.
Born in the Poltava Gouvt. Graduated from the Kiev Music School, 1936. Graduated from the Kiev Conservatory, 1941. Pupil of L. Revutskii. Composer from 1938.

Taught musical theory at the Kiev Conservatory, 1952–58. Influenced by the musical folklore of the Ukraine.

Maiboroda, Platon Illarionovich
1.12.1918–   . Composer.
Born in Poltava Gouvt. Author of popular songs, and music for stage and screen. Stalin Prize for songs on socialist themes, 1950.

Maikapar, Samuil Moiseevich
18.12.1867–8.5.1938. Composer, pianist, music critic.
Born in Kherson. Began to study music at the age of 6. Pupil of G. Moll. At the Petersburg Conservatory from 1885. Pupil of I. Veis and N. Solov'ev. Graduated in law from Petersburg University, 1890. Perfected his piano-playing under T. Leshetitskii. Appeared in concerts with other performers including L. Auer, 1898–1901. Founded a music school in Tver' (now Kalinin), 1901. Director there until 1903. Lived in Moscow. Gave concerts and appeared regularly in Germany. Participated, under S. Taneev, in the Moscow Society for Musical Research, 1903–10. Taught and appeared in concerts in Petersburg, 1910–30. Author of piano pieces for juveniles. Author of *Musykal'nyi Slukh* (editions: 1890 and 1915), *Znachenie Tvorchestva Bethovena dlia Nashei Sovremennosti* (with a foreword by A. Lunacharskii), 1927, *Gody Ucheniia i Muzykalnoi Deiatelnosti*, and *Kniga o Muzyke dlia Starshykh Shkolnikov*, 1938. Died in Leningrad.

Mailian, Anton Sergeevich (Sarkisovich)
28.3.1880–20.4.1942. Composer.
Born in Tiflis. Father of the composer and conductor, El'za Mailian. Armenian by nationality. Worked with children's choirs in Baku. Edited the periodical *Teatr i Muzyka* (in Armenian), 1910–17. Author of an opera, songs and operas for children, musical dramas and comedies, a cantata, symphonic works, romances, arrangements of folk songs, and music for the theatre. Also wrote a novel and short stories. Died in Baku.

Maiorov, Boris Aleksandrovich
11.2.1938–   . Athlete.
Born in Moscow. Honoured Master of Sports (hockey), 1963. With Moscow Spartak. Coach. Graduated from the Moscow Aviation Technological Institute, 1961. Member of the CPSU, 1967. From 1979, head of the Directorate of Hockey on the USSR Sports Committee. USSR champion, 1962, 1967 and 1969. World and European champion, 1963–68. Olympic champion, 1964 and 1968. Captain of the USSR international team, 1962–65 and 1967–68. Author of *Ia Smotriu Khokkei*, Moscow, 1970.

Maiorov, Evgenii Aleksandrovich
11.2.1938–   . Athlete, TV sports commentator.
Born in Moscow. Twin brother of Boris Maiorov. Honoured Master of Sports (hockey), 1963. With Moscow Spartak. Coach. Graduated from the Moscow Aviation Technological Institute, 1963. USSR champion, 1962 and 1967. World and European champion, 1963–64. Olympic champion, 1964. Famous TV sports commentator from the mid-1960s. Member of the CPSU, 1969.

Maiskii, Ivan Mikhailovich (Liakhovitskii)
19.1.1884–9.1975. Diplomat, politician.
Born in Kirillov, Vologda Gouvt. Joined the social democratic movement in the 1900s. Expelled in 1902 from Petersburg University and exiled to Omsk, Siberia. Menshevik, 1903. Emigrated, lived in Switzerland in 1908. Graduated from Munich University in 1912. Lived in England until 1917, studied the trade union movement. Returned to Russia in 1917, left the Menshevik Party in 1920. Member of the Bolshevik Party from 1921. Diplomat from 1922. Ambassador to Finland, 1929–32, Ambassador to Britain, 1932–43. Was very popular during WWII (nicknamed 'pussy face' Maiskii) Deputy Foreign Minister and head of the Allied reparations commission, 1943–46. Took part in the Yalta and Potsdam conferences in 1945. Academician, 1946.
Books: *Pered Burei* (memoir on pre-revolutionary period); *Memoirs of a Soviet Diplomat*.

Maizel', Boris Sergeevich
17.6.1907–   . Composer.
Born in Petersburg. Author of ballets, a choreographic poem, 5 symphonies, orchestral suites, including *Pis'ma s Mel'nitsy* (based on stories by Alphonse Daudet), symphonic poems, concertos, chamber ensembles, and romances.

Makarenko, Anton Semenovich
13.3.1888 – 1.4.1939. Schoolmaster, author.
Educated on teachers' courses in Kremenchug, Ukraine, 1905. Provincial teacher before the revolution. Graduated from the Poltava Teachers Institute, 1917. Became widely known in connection with one of the most persistent social problems of the 1920s–30s — the great masses of children orphaned by the chaotic conditions of the revolution and Civil War. (Left to fight for themselves or die, these 'besprizornye' reverted to an almost savage level of existence: they were gathered into colonies, which were sometimes little more than camps for juvenile delinquents.) Appointed director of one such colony near Poltava, and later one near Khar'kov. Tried to base his relations with his charges on a humane approach, stressing the necessity of trust and mutual respect, and also of collective work. This was adorned by Stalinist collectivist slogans, which made him especially popular with the authorities. His genuine success in dealing with the young victims of revolutionary chaos was later blown out of all proportion into the Stalinist myth of the creation of a new man. Treated as a superhuman figure, who had allegedly changed the whole education system of mankind. Wrote several books about his work and experiences, and articles on educational problems.
Main works: *Pedagogicheskaia Poema, Kommunisticheskoe Vospitanie i Povedenie, Collected Works* in 7 vols, Moscow 1959–60.

Makarenko, Mikhail Ianovich (Khershkovich)
1931–   . Art promoter.
Born in Rumania. In 1941, ran away to the front and was accepted by a Soviet infantry unit. Wounded and decorated. Became a child hero.

After WWII, worked in various manual jobs. Received no education. Tried to track down his parents in Rumania and was harassed by the KGB. Travelled all over the Soviet Union. Settled in Leningrad. Became an art collector. Moved to Novosibirsk and set up a picture gallery, trying to promote Chagall and other famous artists both Russian and foreign. The gallery became a focus of attention for the KGB and was eventually closed down. Since it was attached to the Novosibirsk branch of the Academy of Sciences, and was backed by some powerful academics, the case attracted the attention of the world's press. Returned to Leningrad. Arrested by the KGB, who accused him of anti-Soviet activity. Vilified in the official press without the right to reply. Sentenced to 8 years in a prison camp. Released in 1977. Left the USSR in 1978. Settled in West Germany and later moved to the USA. Published his story *Iz Moei Zhizni* in Germany in 1984.

Makarenko, Sergei Lavrent'evich
11.9.1937–   . Athlete.
Born in Krivoi Rog. Honoured Master of Sports (rowing), 1960. With Brest Spartak. Member of the CPSU, 1965. Graduated from the Belorussian Institute of Physical Culture, 1969. USSR champion, 1959–63. Olympic champion, 1960 (with L. Geishtor in the 1,000m race). European champion, 1961 and 1963. World champion, 1963.
See: V. Nikolaev, 'Pervoe zoloto', *Belorussian Olympians*, Minsk, 1978.

Makarii, Bishop of Viazma
1880?–1918. Russian Orthodox clergyman.
Arrested shortly after the Bolshevik take-over, 1917. According to a later confession by his Cheka executioner, Makarii blessed him shortly before being shot. Died near Smolensk.

Makarov, Evgenii Petrovich
19.11.1912–   . Composer.
Born in Penza. Lecturer. Head of the Department of Instrumentation at the Moscow Conservatory. Author of a ballet, an orchestral symphony, overtures, a passacaglia and fugue, a string quartet, sonatas, pieces for wind instruments, romances, and music for the cinema.

Makarov, Valentin Alekseevich
23.8.1908–26.9.1952. Composer.
Born in Kazan' Gouvt. Author of a song cycle for soloists, choir and folk instrument orchestra, and a suite. Stalin Prize, 1950 and 1951. Died in Moscow.

Makarov, Vasilii Emel'ianovich
1903–1975. Lt.-general, state security official.
Before WWII, party official. During WWII, political officer in the armed forces. After WWII, political officer in the Soviet forces in Germany. Deputy head of the Political Administration of the Armed Forces, 1948–50. Worked in the Cen. Cttee. of the CPSU. Deputy Minister of State Security, and further posts in the Political Administration of the Armed Forces, 1951–62.

Makarov-Rakitin, Konstantin Dmitrievich
2.6.1912–3.9.1941. Composer.
Born in Shakhty. Husband of the established poetess Margarita Aliger. Graduated from the Moscow Conservatory, and went on to teach there. Author of an opera, a symphony, a concerto for piano and orchestra, a piano quintet, a string quartet, 2 piano sonatas, songs for voice and orchestra, romances, and music for stage and screen. Killed in action near Iartsev.

Makarova, Natal'ia
1940–   . Prima ballerina.
One of the Kirov Ballet's most celebrated stars. Defected to the West in 1970. Internationally acclaimed for her brilliant technique. At the 1987 London Festival Ballet, danced the role created for M. Fonteyn by Frederick Ashton in *Apparitions*, opposite the ballet's artistic director Peter Schaufuss. Appeared as Tatiana in *Evgenii Onegin* with Ivan Liska from the Hamburg Ballet, July 1987. Lives in the USA. Married to the American businessman Edward Karkar. Gave birth to a son, Andriusha, in 1978. Has written memoirs and made appearances on TV teaching ballet. Gorbachev's government approached her with the request that she perform occasionally in the USSR. Appeared with the Kirov Ballet in *Swan Lake* at the Business Design Centre in Islington, Aug. 1988.

Makarova, Nina Vladimirovna
12.8.1908–   . Composer.
Born in Nizhnii Novgorod Gouvt. Wife of the composer A. Khachaturian. Author of operas, a symphony for orchestra, a suite, pieces for piano, violin, cello, oboe and harp, romances, songs, and music for stage, screen and radio.

Makarova-Shevchenko, Vera Vasil'evna (real name – Shevchenko)
25.8.1892–6.12.1965. Singer (mezzo soprano).
Born in Moscow. Pupil of V. Zarudnaia. Soloist with the Bolshoi Theatre, 1918–41. Died in Moscow.

Makeev, Nikolai Vasil'evich
1889–1975. Politician.
Born in Ivanovo. Member of the NS (Narodnye Sotsialisty). Journalist and artist. Deputy of the Constituent Assembly. Emigrated after the Bolshevik take-over. Secretary of Prince G. Lvov (ex-Prime Minister). Active in Zemgor (zemstvo and cities union). Died in France.

Makhaiskii, V.K. (Volskii, A.)
1867–1926. Economist, politician.
Member of the Polish socialist movement. Exiled for revolutionary activity to Siberia. Wrote in the 1890s, in Iakutia, a theoretical work, *Umstvennyi Rabochii* (published in Geneva in 1904–5 in 3 parts), in which he described scientific socialism as a gigantic swindle perpetrated against the working class by a new parasitic class – the intelligentsia – which monopolized knowledge. This train of thought (makhaievshchina) was treated by the Bolsheviks as an especially dangerous heresy, was denounced before the revolution (it found some sympathy among workers in the 1900s), and ruthlessly suppressed after the Bolsheviks came to power.

Makhlis, Isaak Petrovich
13.3.1893–6.9.1958. Artist.
Graduated from a Khar'kov art school. Continued his education at art schools in Paris. From 1914, stage designer at various theatres. Met A. Khanzhonkov in 1917 and started working in his films, including *Po Zakonu, Glush Povolzhskaia, Gospoda Skotininy, Ego Prevoskhoditel'stvo* and *Kain i Artem.*

Makhno, Nestor Ivanovich
29.10.1889–6.7.1934. Anarchist leader.
Born in Guliai Pole, now Zaporozh'e Oblast'. Son of a Ukrainian peasant. Involved in terrorist activity from the age of 16. Murdered a policeman, convicted and sentenced to death, commuted to 10 years imprisonment (because of his age) in 1909. Freed after the February Revolution in 1917. Encountered anarchists during imprisonment in Moscow Butyrki prison. During the Civil War, organized the largest anarchist movement in the Ukraine, which fought both Whites and Reds, and gained a reputation for ruthlessness and anti-Semitism. During the march of General Denikin on Moscow, played an important part in his defeat by cutting the communication and supply lines of the Whites in the rear. Several times concluded alliances with the Red Army, which did not last. Declared a gang leader, bandit and robber by the Soviet authorities in 1921. Defeated and fled to Rumania, moved to Poland in 1922. Later emigrated to France and worked as a shoe-maker. Wrote 2 vols. of memoirs. Idealized by the poet Sergei Esenin (under the name of Nomakh) as a true peasant revolutionary leader. Died in Paris.

Maklakov, Vasilii Alekseevich
22.5.1869–15.7.1957. Lawyer, politician.
Son of a professor. Graduated in law from Moscow University, 1896. Pupil of the famous lawyer F. Plevako. Became a very influential liberal politician (his brother was a right-wing Minister of the Interior). Famous lawyer. Conducted (with Gruzenberg and others) the defence of Beilis, 1913 (anti-Semitic accusation of ritual murder, rejected by the jury). Member of the Cen. Cttee. of the Cadet Party, member of the 2nd, 3rd, and 4th Dumas. Agreed to take part in the murder of Rasputin by providing poison (according to N. Berberova, in his old age he confessed that he gave aspirin tablets instead). Active freemason all his life. In 1917, thought that the preservation of the monarchy was essential (transfer of crown prerogatives to Grand Duke Mikhail). After the February Revolution, given the task of reorganizing the Ministry of Justice. Representative of the Duma Cttee. (precursor of the Provisional Government) in the Ministry of Justice. Arrived in Paris as Russian Ambassador on 7 Nov. 1917, too late to be accredited. Remained in the Russian Embassy. Was present (as a silent observer) at the Versailles peace conference. Chairman of the Council of Russian Ambassadors abroad. After the recognition of the USSR by France, 1924, resigned and handed the Embassy over to Krasin. Thereafter until his death, head of the Office for Russian Refugees with the League of Nations in Paris. During the German occupation of France, short arrest (as a freemason, wrote in prison a memorandum on this subject). After the liberation of Paris, 12 Feb. 1945, visited the Soviet Ambassador, Bogomolov, to drink Stalin's health, an action that estranged him from many of his former friends. Approved of the forcible repatriation of refugees from Soviet Russia to the USSR. Bachelor all his life, his household was kept by his unmarried sister. His memoirs, *Iz Vospominanii*, were published in the USA. Died in Zurich. Biography written by Adamovich.

Makletsova, Ksenia Petrovna
17.11.1890–194? Ballerina.
Born in Moscow. Graduated from the Moscow Theatre School. Pupil of V. Tikhomirov. Dancer with the Bolshoi Theatre, 1908, with the Mariinskii Theatre, 1915–19. Guest appearances abroad, 1919–23. Dancer with Diaghilev's Ballets Russes. Emigrated. Dancer in Japan, Singapore and the USA from 1925 (with Mordkin's company, 1926–27), and afterwards in Brazil.

Makovskii, Sergei Konstantinovich
1877–1962. Art critic, poet, editor.
Son of K. E. Makovskii (court painter to Alexander II). Organized art exhibitions, and wrote many articles on art. Founded, financed and edited the art magazine *Apollon* (one of the best of its time), 1909–17, in Petersburg. Emigrated after the October Revolution 1917, and settled in Paris. Married to society beauty Maria Ryndina. Died in France.
Main works: *Siluety Russkikh Khudozhnikov, Narodnoe Iskusstvo Prikarpatskoi Rusi, Portrety Sovremennikov, Na Parnase Serebriannogo Veka,* also several volumes of poetry.

Makovskii, Vladimir Egorovich
7.2.1846–21.2.1920. Artist.
Born in Moscow. Son of E. I. Makovskii, the famous patron of the arts. Studied at the Moscow School of Painting, Sculpture and Architecture (1861–66) under E. Sorokin and S. Zarianko. Taught there from 1882–94, and at the Petersburg Academy of Arts, 1894–1918. From 1895, rector of the Academy of Arts' School of Arts. From 1872, a member of the Peredvizhniki. All his works from this period are held in the Tretiakov Gallery in Moscow. Exhibitions: from 1862–1905, at the Academy of Arts, TPKHV, MOLKH, All-Russian, Moscow, the Society of Water-Colour Painters, All-Russian, Nizhnii Novgorod, and the Russian Portraits, Tavricheskii Palace. Personal exhibitions: Petersburg, 1902, and Moscow, 1947. Died in Petrograd.

Maksakov, Maksimilian Karlovich (Schwarz, Max)
1869–26.3.1936. Singer (baritone), theatrical director.
Pupil of E. Riadnov. Husband of the singer Maria Maksakova. Appeared mainly in provincial theatres. Opera impresario. Died in Moscow.

Maksakova, Maria Petrovna (Sidorova)
8.4.1902–   . Singer (mezzo-soprano).
Born in Astrakhan'. Pupil and wife of the singer Maksimilian Maksakov. Soloist with the Bolshoi Theatre, 1923–53. With the Leningrad Academic Theatre of Opera and Ballet, 1924–27. Stalin valued her as a singer. Stalin Prize, 1946, 1949, 1951.

Maksimov, Andrei Semenovich
1866–1951. Vice-admiral.
Graduated from the Naval Corps, 1887. Took part in the Russo-Japanese war and WWI. After the February Revolution 1917, elected commander of the Baltic fleet. Inspector in the People's Commissariat for the Navy, 1918. Retired, 1927.

Maksimov, Iurii Pavlovich
1924– . General.
Joined the Red Army, 1942. Commander of a machine-gun detachment. Joined the Bolshevik Party, 1943. Graduated from the Frunze Military Academy, 1950, and from the Academy of the General Staff, 1965. Deputy Minister of Defence, and Commander of Strategic Rocket Forces, July 1985. Member of the Cen. Cttee. of the CPSU.

Maksimov, Stepan Maksimovich
12.11.1892–26.8.1951. Composer, violinist, conductor.
Born in Kazan' Gouvt. Chuvash by nationality. Collected over 2000 Chuvash folk songs and instrumental melodies, partly published in anthologies. Arranged folk songs and instrumental music. Many Chuvash pupils. Died in Cheboksary.

Maksimov, Vladimir Emel'ianovich
1930– . Writer, editor.
First published in the early 1960s. His books *Sem' Dnei Tvorenia* and *Karantin* at first circulated in samizdat, later published in the West. Worked for the magazine *Oktiabr*. Emigrated in 1974. Editor-in-chief of the emigré literary magazine *Kontinent*. Other books include: *Proshchanie iz Niotkuda*, 1976, *Kovcheg dlia Nezvannykh*, 1979, *Sago o Nosorogakh*, 1979, *Compete Works*, 5 volumes, Posev, Germany. His books have been translated into several foreign languages. Well-known for his human rights activities and his acrimonious polemics with Western left-wing intellectuals. Lives in Paris. Executive director of International Resistance, 1983.

Maksimov, Vladimir Salmanovich
14.10.1945– . Athlete.
Born in the Kirghiz SSR. Honoured Master of Sports (handball), 1973. With Moscow Burevestnik. Graduated from Kuban' University, 1970. Lecturer. Member of the CPSU, 1972. USSR champion, 1972, 1974–75. Olympic champion, 1976.

Maksimov, Vladimir Vasil'evich
27.7.1880–22.3.1937. Actor.
Entered the film industry, 1911. Soon became king of the Russian silent cinema. Played lovers only. Combined his film work with stage work. Played in the Malyi Theatre, Moscow, 1906–18, and at the Gorkii Bolshoi Drama Theatre, 1919–24 (one of its founders). His best roles were Fedor Protasov in *Zhivoi Trup*, 1918, and Tsar Alexander I in *Dekabristy*, 1927.

Maksimova, Ekaterina Sergeevna
1.2.1939– . Prima ballerina.
Born in Moscow. Graduated from the Moscow Choreographic School, 1958. Pupil of E.P. Gerdt. Debut in 1957 while a student. Married V.T. Vasil'ev, her permanent partner. Soon became a leading ballerina and international star. Performed all over the world. One of the best-known Soviet ballerinas. Anna Pavlova Award, Paris, 1969.

Malakhovskaia, Natal'ia Lvovna
1947– . Dissident.
Founder member of the feminist group Maria and one of its three leaders who were exiled in July 1980 for protesting against the Soviet invasion of Afghanistan. On 1 Mar. 1980, called on Russian mothers and wives to encourage their sons and husbands to avoid military service in Afghanistan, pointing out that the Soviet Union was not officially at war with Afghanistan, and thus their men by law would not face execution, but only 3 years in prison. Began producing a journal called *Maria*. A graduate in Russian philology, lost her first job in a library. Arrested by the KGB and given the choice of a prison term or exile. Chose exile. Lives in Paris and is engaged in feminist publishing activities.

Malandin, German Kapitonovich
1894–1961. General.
Took part in WWI. Joined the Red Army, 1918. Active in the Civil War as a commander of a regiment. Graduated from the Frunze Military Academy, 1926, and from the Academy of the General Staff, 1938. Staff officer at different fronts during WWII. After the war, Commander of Land Forces, and Deputy Chief of the General Staff. Head of the Academy of the General Staff, 1958–61.

Maldybaev, Abdylas
9.7.1906–1.6.1978. Composer, singer.
Born in Karabulak. Studied at the Pedagogical Technical School in the town of Frunze, 1923–29. Leading actor and singer at the Kirghiz Opera and Ballet Theatre, 1929–62. Composer from 1922. Further musical training at the Moscow Conservatory, 1940–41, 1947–50. Pupil of G. Litinskii and V. Fere. Director of the Technical School for Music and Choreography in Frunze, 1953–54. Compositions influenced by Kirghiz folk music and folklore. Died in Frunze.

Malenkov, Georgii Maksimil'ianovich
8.1.1902–23.1.1988. Politician.
Born in Orenburg. Commissar in the Red Army in Turkestan, 1919. Member of the Bolshevik Party, 1920. Graduated from the Higher Technical Institute, Moscow, 1925. Party worker from the mid-1920s. Worked under Kaganovich throughout the 1930s. In charge of party cadres. In this capacity, probably personally responsible for the disappearance of many leading Old Bolsheviks. Took an active part in Stalin's purges. Candidate member of the Cen. Cttee. of the Politburo, 1941. Member of the State Defence Cttee., 1941–45. Chairman of the Cttee. for Rehabilitation of Formerly Occupied Territories, 1944. Secretary of the Cen. Cttee. and Deputy Prime Minister, 1946. During the last years of Stalin's life, in charge of party organization, and the most influential leader after Stalin himself. Prime Minister and the most prominent member of the 'kollektivnoe rukovodstvo' after Stalin's death, Mar. 1953–Feb. 1955. Approved of Beria's

liquidation. A shrewd political manipulator throughout his career, he immediately took a more liberal line (peaceful coexistence). Lost the power struggle to Khrushchev. In Feb. 1955, forced to recognize his mistakes and lost his post. In 1957, expelled from the Cen. Cttee. as a member of the 'anti-partiinaia gruppa' (the anti-Khrushchev conspiracy of old Stalinists). Sent to East Kazakhstan as a manager of the Ust' Kamenogorsk hydroelectric station. Soon returned to Moscow, but completely disappeared from the political scene and lived quietly in retirement. Allegedly became a church-goer in old age. The news about his death was kept secret for some time at the request of relatives. No details of his burial appeared in the Soviet media. Buried at Kuntsevo.

Malevskii-Malevich, Sviatoslav Sviatoslavovich
1906– . Diplomat.
Born in Petersburg. Studied at Tenishev High School. Emigrated with his parents during the Civil War. Studied at Belgrade and Paris universities. Married the writer Zinaida Shakhovskoy, 1926. Participated in the Eurasian movement. Organized the only Eurasian Congress in Brussels, 1931. Worked in the Belgian Congo before WWII. During the war, moved through Dunkirk to Britain, and joined the Free Belgian Army. After WWII, Belgian diplomat in Bern, and later in Israel. Secretary of the Belgian Embassy in Moscow, 1956. Wrote a book, *SSSR Segodnia i Zavtra*, based on his experiences in the 1950s.

Maliantovich, Pavel Nikolaevich
1870–1939. Politician, lawyer.
Before the October Revolution 1917, a well-known defence lawyer in political trials. Social democrat. The last Minister of Justice in the Provisional Government (from 25 Sept. 1917). Remained with his colleagues in the Winter Palace during the siege by the Bolsheviks. Arrested (25 Oct. 1917) and brought to the Peter and Paul Fortress at Petrograd. Soon released, campaigned for the re-opening of the Constituent Assembly. From the beginning of the 1920s, member of the Moscow City College of Lawyers.

Maliavin, Filipp Andreevich
22.10.1869–23.12.1940. Artist.
Born in the village of Kazanka, now Orenburg Oblast'. Genre and portrait painter. Son of a peasant. Studied in the icon studio of a monastery on the Aion-Oros in Greece, 1895–91, then at the Petersburg Academy of Arts, 1892–99. A pupil of Il'ia Repin. In 1900, visited France. In 1924, emigrated. Lived mainly in Paris. His pictures are now in museums in Paris, London, Riga and Brussels. Exhibitions: from 1895 until 1923 in Russia at the Academy of Arts, Petersburg, the Mir Iskusstva, the 36 Artists, the Spring Exhibitions, and the Union of Russian Artists. Died in Brussels.

Malin, Vladimir Nikiforovich
1906–1982. Party and state security official.
Joined the Bolshevik Party, 1926. Party functionary, 1933. 1st secretary of Mogilev obkom, 1938. Secretary of the Cen. Cttee. of the Belorussian Communist Party, 1939. During WWII, party-political controller of the partisan movement in Belorussia. After WWII, worked in the Cen. Cttee. of the CPSU. Dean of the Academy of Social Sciences attached to the Cen. Cttee, training leading communist cadres.

Malinin, Boris Mikhailovich
1889–1949. Submarine designer.
Graduated from the Ship Design Faculty of the Petersburg Polytechnical Institute, 1914. Chief Engineer for Submarine Construction, 1925. Worked at the Krylov Ship Research Institute, 1939. Professor of the Leningrad Ship Design Institute, 1948. Designed several types of Soviet submarine.

Malinin, Evgenii Vasil'evich
5.11.1930– . Pianist.
Born in Moscow. Pupil of G. Neigauz. 7th prize at the International Chopin Competition, Warsaw, 1949. 2nd prize at the M. Long International Piano Competition, Paris, 1953. Teacher at the Moscow Conservatory.

Malinin, Mikhail Sergeevich
1899–1960. General.
Joined the Red Army, 1919. Took part in the Civil War. Member of the Bolshevik Party, 1931. Graduated from the Frunze Military Academy, 1931. On active service during the Soviet-Finnish war and WWII as a staff officer. Held senior posts in the Soviet forces in Germany and in the Soviet General Staff.

Malinovskaia, Vera Stepanovna
1900– . Film actress.
First film, 1924. Became famous after her film *Kollezhskii Registrator*, 1925. Other films include: *Medvezh'ia Svad'ba*, 1926; *Chelovek Iz Restorana*, 1927; *Ledianoi Dom*, 1928; *Khromoi Barin*, 1928. From 1929, lived in Germany, then Italy and France. In 1929, appeared in the German film *Waterloo*.

Malinovskii, Rodion Iakovlevich
23.11.1898–31.3.1967. Marshal.
Took part in WWI. As a soldier in the Russian Expeditionary Corps in France, acted as a Bolshevik organizer. Joined the Red Army, 1919. Active in the Civil War. Graduated from the Frunze Military Academy, 1930. Took part in the Spanish Civil War, later taught at the Frunze Academy. Commander of several southern fronts during WWII. Khrushchev's choice for Minister of Defence after Zhukov's dismissal, a post he held from 1957–1967. Member of the Cen. Cttee. of the CPSU, 1956–67.

Maliutin, Sergei Vasil'evich
4.10.1859–6.12.1937. Artist.
Born in Moscow. Son of a wealthy merchant. Studied at the Moscow School of Painting, Sculpture and Architecture, 1883–86, under E. Sorokin, I. Prianishnikov, V. Makovskii. Taught at the same school, 1903–17, then at the VKHUTEMAS, 1918–23. Member of the Union of Russian Artists from 1903. Member of the Peredvizhniki from 1915. Portrait and genre painter, book illustrator, stage designer. Illustrated Russian fairy-tales (*Tsar Saltan*, etc). Exhibitions: 1887–1934 at MOLKH, TPKHV, AKHRR, the Mir Iskusstva, the 36 Artists, and the Union of Russian Artists. Personal exhibition: Moscow, 1934. Died in Moscow.

Maliutina, Olga Sergeevna
1894–1962? Artist.
Still-life, portrait and landscape painter and illustrator. Daughter of the artist Sergei Maliutin. Exhibited from 1917 with the Union of Russian Artists, the Mir Iskusstva, TPKHV (Petrograd, Riazan', Moscow, Vladivostok, Kislovodsk, Sochi). Personal exhibitions: Moscow, 1944 (with M. Obolenskii and M. Kharlamov), Moscow, 1957.

Mal'ko, Nikolai Andreevich
4.4.1883–23.6.1961. Conductor.
Born in Rumania. Graduated from the Petersburg Conservatory in 1906. Pupil of N. A. Rimskii-Korsakov and N. N. Cherepnin. Studied in Munich with F. Motl. Conducted ballet productions at the Mariinskii Theatre, 1909–18. Emigrated, 1928. Conductor of the Prague National Opera in the 1930s. Died in Sydney, Australia.

Mal'kov, Nikolai Petrovich
25.4.1882–20.3.1942. Music critic.
Born in Petersburg. Author of many pamphlets on classical opera and Russian symphonic music, articles, and critical reviews. Died during the Siege of Leningrad.

Mal'kov Pavel Dmitrievich
17.11.1887–22.11.1965. State security official.
Born in Kukarka (now Sovetsk) near Perm'. Son of a peasant. Became a worker. Member of the SD Party from 1904. Participated in the 1905 Revolution. Sailor in the Baltic Navy, 1910. Bolshevik agitator, one of the leaders of the sailors' detachments which were the main force behind the Bolsheviks in 1917. Took part in the taking of the Winter Palace during the October coup, 1917. 1st commander of the guard in the Smolnyi (Bolshevik Party HQ, formerly a school for girls from aristocratic families). After the move of the Bolshevik government to Moscow, 1918, 1st commander of the guard in the Kremlin. In his memoirs, published in the late 1950s in Moscow, told how on 5 Sept. 1918 he personally shot Dora Kaplan, the SR who made an attempt on Lenin's life, thus ending some long-standing

doubts about her fate. During the Civil War, fought with Red detachments. From 1923, held different high economic posts. Retired, 1954. Died in Moscow.

Mal'tsev, Aleksandr Nikolaevich
20.4.1949– . Athlete.
Born in the village of Setkovskaia, Kirov Oblast'. Honoured Master of Sports (hockey), 1969. With Moscow Dynamo. In the military forces. European champion, 1969–70, 1973–75 and 1978. World champion, 1969–71, 1973–75 and 1978. Olympic champion, 1972 and 1976.

Mal'tsev, Evdokim Egorovich
1910–1981. General.
Joined the Bolshevik Party, 1931, and the Red Army, 1933. Graduated from a school for political commissars in the armed forces, 1935. Head of political departments at various levels during WWII, and after the war, head of the Political Administration of the Soviet forces in Germany. Head of the Lenin Military Political Academy, 1971–81.

Mal'tsev, Iurii Vladimirovich
1932– . Critic, translator.
Born in Rostov-on-Don. Graduated in philosophy (Marxism) from Leningrad University. Taught at Moscow University. Became an authority on Italian literature. Translator of Italian writers. Human rights activist, mid-1960s. Member of the Initiative Group for the Defence of Human Rights. Lost his job and was put into a special psychiatric institution by the KGB. Became the focus of international protest. Released and allowed to leave the USSR, 1974. Lives in Milan. Published a literary survey, *Vol'naia Russkaia Literatura, 1955–75*, Germany, 1976.

Mal'tsev, Nikolai Alekseevich
1928– . Engineer, politician.
Graduated from the Groznyi Petroleum Institute, 1951. Joined the Communist Party, 1953. Chief engineer with the Almentevneft Trust, and then the Tatneft Association. Senior administrative positions in the oil industry, 1951–61. 1st Deputy USSR Minister of the Petroleum

Industry, 1972–77. Minister from Apr. 1977. Candidate member of the Cen. Cttee. of the CPSU from 1981. Removed from the post of minister due to problems in the oil industry and decline in output. Replaced by Vasilii Dinkov.

Mal'tsev, Viktor Ivanovich
25.4.1895–8.1946. General.
Born near Vladimir. Son of a peasant. Joined the Red Army and the Communist Party, 1918. Took part in the Civil War. In the 1920s, trained as a pilot. High commands in the Red Air Force in Siberia, Central Asia and Transcaucasia, 1930–37. Head of civil aviation in Central Asia and Transcaucasia, 1937. Arrested during Stalin's purges of the military in 1938, tortured and sent to the Gulag. Released, Sep. 1939, appointed director of the sanatorium Aeroflot in the Crimea. After the arrival of the Germans in Yalta, 1941, joined the Russian anti-Stalin movement. Head of the city administration of Yalta under German occupation, organized detachments for defence against NKVD partisans. Wrote a book on his Gulag experiences, *Konveier GPU*, 1942. Applied to join Vlasov, but instead received an invitation to create air force groups from among Red Army prisoners under the control of the Luftwaffe. Created an air force regiment, which in Feb. 1945 he put under Vlasov's command in Czechoslovakia. Proposed to evacuate Vlasov to Spain, but the latter refused to leave his soldiers. Surrendered to the US Army, and was taken to France. After demands from SMERSH, handed over to the NKVD in Paris. Tried to commit suicide (cut his throat), but was rescued and brought by plane to Moscow's Lubianka prison. Tried and hanged with his former colleagues-at-arms. A description of the circumstances of the creation of the ROA air force was given by his adjutant Pliushchov (published in the USA, 1982).

Malygin, Aleksandr Ivanovich
1890–1942. Artist.
Born in Iaroslavl'. Stage designer. Studied at the Iaroslavl' City Art Classes, 1907–11, and Penza Art School. First exhibition in Iaroslavl', 1913. Killed during WWII.

Malyshev, Iurii Aleksandrovich
1.2.1947– . Athlete.
Born in Khimki, Moscow Oblast'. Honoured Master of Sports, (rowing), 1972. With the Moscow Oblast' Vodnik. Coach. USSR champion, 1971–74. Olympic champion, 1972.

Malyshev, Ivan Mikhailovich
1889–1918. Partisan commander.
Joined the Bolshevik Party, 1905. Chairman of the Ural party obkom, 1918. Organized Bolshevik detachments to fight the Czech legions and the White Cossacks during the Civil War. Captured by the Whites and shot.

Malyshev, Viacheslav Aleksandrovich
1902–1957. Col.-general.
Graduated as an engineer from the Moscow Bauman Technical School, 1934. Worked as a technical designer and works manager. Minister of Heavy Industry, 1939. During WWII, Minister of Tank Construction, 1941 –45. Minister of Transport Machine Construction, and of Shipbuilding after WWII. Member of the Cen. Cttee. of the Communist Party, 1939, and of the Presidium of the Cen. Cttee, 1952–53. Vice-Premier of the USSR, 1954–56.

Malyshkin, Vasilii Fedorovich
1890–8.1946. General.
Born in Novocherkassk. Son of a bookkeeper. Took part in WWI as a lieutenant. Took part in the Civil War in the Red Army. Met and became a close friend of Esenin, who once said that Malyshkin could recite his poems better than he could himself. Graduated from the Red Army Academy. Chief-of-staff in the Siberian military district, 1937. Arrested during the purge of the Red Army. Interrogated, tortured, brought back to his cell unconscious several times. Sent to the Gulag. Because of his iron will, survived and never signed the 'confession'. Together with other officers, released at the beginning of WWII and sent to the front. Chief-of-staff of the 19th Army. Taken prisoner by the Germans near Viaz'ma, 1942. Joined General Vlasov and became one of his closest aides. After WWII, handed over by the Americans to

SMERSH, 1945. Brought to the Lubianka, tried and hanged.

Mamatov, Viktor Fedorovich
21.7.1937– . Athlete.
Born in Belovo, Kemerovo Oblast'. Honoured Master of Sports (biathlon), 1967. With Novosibirsk Lokomotiv. Member of the CPSU, 1965. Graduated from the Novosibirsk Institute of Railway Engineers, 1964, and from the Omsk Institute of Physical Culture, 1974. Lecturer. USSR champion, 1968. World champion, 1967 and 1969–71 (20km race). Olympic champion, 1968 and 1972.

Mamedbekov, Rashid
1927–1971. Wrestler.
Azerbaidzhani athlete. Honoured Master of Sports (wrestling). Many times USSR and Azerbaidzhan champion. Silver medal-winner at the XVth Olympic Games.

Mamedov, Maksud Davud ogly
30.5.1929– . Ballet dancer, choreographer.
Born in Kirovabad. Graduated from the Moscow Choreographic School, 1950. Pupil of N. I. Tarasov. Dancer, and soon leading dancer, with the Akhundov Theatre, from 1951. In Algiers as choreographer and teacher, 1972–73.

Mamedova, Shevket Gasan kyzy
18.4.1897–1978? Singer (soprano).
Born in Tiflis. Azerbaidzhanian by nationality. Pupil of A. Shperling. Soloist with the Baku Opera, 1921– 48. Teacher at the Azerbaidzhanian Conservatory from 1945. Professor from 1949. 1st Azerbaidzhanian woman to appear on the stage before the revolution. Author of *Puti Razvitiia Azerbaidzhanskogo Muzykal'nogo Teatra*, Moscow, 1931.

Mamleev, Iurii Vital'evich
1931– . Writer.
Born in Moscow. Educated at the Moscow Forestry Institute. Well-known in samizdat in the late 1950s. Wrote some 100 short stories, 2 novels and essays. Emigrated in 1974. Author of *Shatuny* and *Golos Iz Nichto*. Contributed to the almanac

Apollon, which published uncensored work by the Soviet and emigré writers. Also appeared in the monthly *Novyi Zhurnal*, USA, and *Tretia Volna*.
See: P. Vail, A. Genis, *Sovremennaia Russkaia Proza*, USA, 1982.

Mamonov, Stepan Kirillovich
1901–1974. Lt.-general.
Joined the Red Army, 1919. Member of the Bolshevik Party, 1921. Fought in WWII, first against Germany, and later against Japan. Graduated from the Academy of the General Staff, 1947.

Mamonova, Tatiana Arsen'evna
10.12.1943– . Dissident, chemist, painter and poet.
One of the leading women dissidents protesting against the Soviet invasion of Afghanistan, and calling on Russian women – mothers, wives and sisters – to encourage their men not to go to Afghanistan. For that and for her typewritten work *Women and Russia* (the Soviet Union's first feminist samizdat), taken to the KGB HQ in Leningrad for questioning. Put on a plane for Vienna days before the Moscow Olympics were due to start. Allowed to take her husband and son with her to the West. Lives in Paris. According to herself, a socialist (though not a Marxist). One of the editors of an almanac which is published in Paris.

Mamontov, Efim Mefod'evich
1888–1922. Revolutionary.
Bolshevik organizer at the front during WWI. During the Civil War, Red partisan leader in the Altai Mountains and in Siberia. Transferred to the Southern front, 1920. Killed by peasants.

Mamontov, Konstantin Konstantinovich (Mamantov)
1869–1920. Lt.-general.
Graduated from the Nikolaevskoe Cavalry School, 1890. Cavalry commander during WWI. During the Civil War, an outstanding White Cossack commander. Best known for a long-distance raid behind enemy lines in summer/autumn, 1919. Later defeated by Budennyi.

Mamontov, Savva Ivanovich

15.10.1841–6.4.1918. Arts patron, millionaire, music lover.
Born in Ialutorovsk in Tobolsk Gouvt. Came from a famous merchant family of patrons of the arts. Founded and financed the Moskovskaia Chastnaia Russkaia Opera (the Private Russian Opera) in 1885. Employed the best Russian talents. Acted as stage director for a time. Author of libretti for the operas *Alaia Roza*, *V 1812 Godu*, and *Prizraki Ellady*. His memoirs *Vospominaniia o Russkikh Khudozhnikakh*, were published in Moscow in 1951. Died in Moscow.

Mamoulian, Ruben

8.10.1898?– . Film director.
Armenian. Born in Tbilisi. Studied at Moscow University. Pupil of Evgenii Vakhtangov. Staged several productions in Tbilisi theatres. Emigrated, 1919. Became a prominent American film director.

Managadze, Nodar Shotaevich

19.3.1943– . Film director.
Born in Georgia. Son of the director Shota Managadze. Graduated from the Rustaveli Theatre Institute, Tbilisi, 1965. Made his first films with his father: *Ozhidanie*, 1970, and *Teplo Tvoikh Ruk*, 1972. His own films include: *Obshchaia Stena*, 1973 (for Georgian TV), *Plotina v Gorakh*, 1980, and *Vesna Prokhodit*, 1984. One of his better works, *Ozhivshie Legendy* (Living Legends), was made in 1977 but banned for 10 years. Shown with great success at the 1988 Cannes Directors' Fortnight, it is a remarkable documentary about Georgia's life in the past. Released in the Soviet Union as a result of glasnost at the end of 1987.

Managadze, Shota Il'ich

19.3.1901–21.6.1977. Film director.
Graduated from the VGIK, 1938. Returned to his native Georgia. Film debut in 1945 with *Stroptivye Sosedi*. His film *Poslednii Iz Sabudara*, 1958, received a prize at the Venice Film Festival. Other films include *Khevsurskaia Ballada*, 1966, *Teplo Tvoikh Ruk*, 1972, which also received a prize at the Venice Film Festival, and his last film *Kamen' Chistoi Vody*, 1977. Died in Tbilisi.

Mandelstam, Nadezhda Iakovlevna (Khazina)

31.10.1899–24.12.1980. Author.
Born in Saratov. Grew up in Kiev. Studied painting with A. Ekster. Met the poet O. Mandelstam, 1919, and married him soon after. Shared the life of her husband in Moscow and in exile. During the Stalin years, had to move to different cities (Tashkent, Tarusa, Ulianovsk) as the 'wife of an enemy of the people'. Earned her living by teaching English. During all these decades, kept the literary heritage of her husband, and thus saved from total oblivion the name of one of the finest 20th century poets. Received permission to return to Moscow, 1958. Wrote 2 volumes of memoirs (published abroad), which made her world famous as one of the best chroniclers of the Stalin epoch: *Vospominaniia*, NY, 1970, and *Vtoraia Kniga*, Paris, 1972. Died in Moscow.

Mandelstam, Osip Emil'evich

3.1.1891–27.12.1938. Poet.
Born in Warsaw. Son of a merchant. Educated at the Tenishevskoe School in Petersburg, 1907. Studied French literature at Petersburg University. First poems appeared in the magazine *Apollon*, 1910. Joined the acmeists, 1912. Later acquired an individual poetic voice of exceptional clarity and an almost classic character. During the Civil War and the communist take-over, stressed the continuity and world-wide unity of human culture, and the absolute importance of human dignity. Paradoxically, the son of a provincial Jewish merchant became the outstanding mourning voice of the death of imperial Petersburg, and this rather shy poet was later the only one to dare openly to challenge Stalin, the 'Kremlin highlander and muzhik-fighter', and his 'half-human gang' in an epigram of amazing audacity. Arrested and exiled, 1934, re-arrested, 1938, sent to the Gulag camps, where he died in transit to the Magadan Arctic concentration camps, burial place unknown. He has since been recognized as one of the best Russian poets of the 20th century.

Mandryka, Petr Vasil'evich

1884–1943. Surgeon.
Graduated in medicine from Khar'-kov University, 1910. In the army during WWI. Drafted into the Red Army, 1918. Member of the Bolshevik Party, 1923. Director and Chief Surgeon of the Central Hospital of the Ministry of Defence, 1923–43 (later renamed, in his honour, the P. V. Mandryka Military Hospital). Major-general, 1943.

Manevich, Aleksandr Mendelevich

7.1.1908– . Composer.
Born in Chernigov Gouvt. Author of an opera, a musical comedy, orchestral works, a concerto, romances, and music for the theatre.

Manevich, Berta Semenovna

14.11.1922– . Artist, stage designer.
Graduated from the VGIK, 1949. Joined the Lenfilm Studio, 1949. Her best films are classic adaptations of Dostoevskii, Gogol' and Chekhov: *Krotkaia*, *Delo Rumiantsevykh*, *Shinel'*, *Dama s Sobachkoi*, *V Gorode S.*, and *Tri Tolstiaka*.

Manevich, Lev Efimovich (cover name – Etien)

20.8.1898–11.5.1945. Intelligence officer.
One of the Soviet Union's top spies. Born in the small town of Chausy near Mogilev, Belorussia, into a poor Jewish family. In 1916, received a grant from some rich Jewish patrons of the arts and went to Geneva to study. In 1918, joined L. Trotsky. Graduated in 1921 from the Red Army Military School, then in 1924 from the Red Army Academy. In 1929, graduated from the Zhukovskii Air Force Academy. Entered the intelligence service. A multilingual and very efficient agent. Worked mainly abroad on dangerous assignments, liquidating enemies of the Soviet government. Worked at Narkomindel (Narkomat of Foreign Affairs) under Chicherin. Also on assignments all over Europe kidnapping foreigners and anti-communist former Soviet citizens living abroad. Dealer in stolen diamonds, pictures, tapestries and cocaine. Arrested in Vienna but escaped prosecution. NKVD colonel, 1935. During WWII, taken prisoner by the

Germans. POW under the name of Colonel Starostin in the German concentration camps Mauthausen, Melk and Ebensee. Died in Linz, Austria, from tuberculosis. A film about his exploits was made in the 1960s.

Manikovskii, Aleksei Alekseevich
25.3.1865–1.1920. General.
Educated at the Mikhailovskoe Artillery School, 1886. Graduated from the Mikhailovskaia Artillery Academy, 1891. Head of the artillery administration, 1915–1917. General, 1916. Close to General Alekseev. After the assassination of General Dukhonin, took over at the Russian HQ. When the Minister of War, Verkhovskii, resigned on 21 Oct. 1917, appointed by Kerenskii Deputy Minister. Arrested by the Bolsheviks after the storming of the Winter Palace, Oct. 1917. Joined the Red Army, head of artillery administration, 1918–19, and later head of the Red Army's supply administration. Published a 3-volume report on the supply system of the Russian Army during WWI. Died in a train crash.

Manina, Tamara Ivanovna
16.9.1934–   . Athlete, international referee.
Born in Petrozavodsk. Honoured Master of Sports (gymnastics), 1957. With Leningrad Burevestnik. Graduated from the Leningrad Institute of Precision Mechanics and Optics as an engineer, 1965. MA, 1972. Reader, 1977. Member of the CPSU, 1977. USSR champion, 1953–63. World champion, 1954 and 1958. Absolute champion of the USSR, 1956. World champion with her team, 1954, 1958 and 1962. Olympic champion, 1956 and 1964. Silver medal, 1956, 1964. Bronze team medal, 1956. International referee from 1971.

Manizer, Matvei Genrikhovich
17.3.1891–20.12.1966. Sculptor.
Born in Petersburg. Brother of Genrikh Manizer, the famous ethnographer and linguist. Graduated in mathematics from Petersburg University, 1914. Studied at Shtiglits Central School of Technical Drawing, 1908–09, under V. Savitskii, then at the Academy of Arts, 1911–16,

under G. Zaleman and V. Beklemishev. Participant in projects of monumental propaganda, 1920–21 (Petrovskii Passage, Moscow). Member of the Association of Artists of Revolutionary Russia from 1926. Taught at the Leningrad Academy of Arts, 1921–29, 1935–41, 1945–47. Vice-president of the Academy of Arts from 1947. Member of the Communist Party from 1941. Sculptor of many busts of the leaders (Lenin, Chapaev, Kuibyshev, Zoia Kosmodem'ianskaia). Decorated the Revolution Square and Izmailovskii Park tube stations in Moscow. Died in Moscow.

Mankin, Valentin Grigor'evich
19.8.1938–   . Athlete.
Born in the village of Belokorovichi, Zhitomir Oblast'. Graduated from the Kiev Institute of Building Engineers, 1962. Member of the CPSU, 1967. Honoured Master of Sports (sailing), 1968. From 1968, with the Kiev Armed Forces Club. USSR champion, 1959–77. Olympic champion, 1968 (Finn class), and 1972 (Tempest class) with V. Dyrdyra. World and European champion, 1973 (Tempest class). European champion, 1979 (Zvezdnyi class). Author of *Belyi Treugol'nik*, Moscow, 1976.
See: V. Kukushkin, *Valentin Mankin*, Moscow, 1978.

Mannerheim, Karl Gustav Emil, Baron
1867–1951. Field marshal.
Finnish leader of Swedish extraction. When Finland was part of the Russian Empire, served in the Russian Army, 1889–1917, rising to the rank of lt.-general. During the Civil War, as head of the Finnish Army, defeated the Red Army in Finland. During the Soviet-Finnish war, 1939–40, as commander-in-chief of the Finnish forces, managed to stem the Soviet advance. Ally of Germany, 1941–44. President of Finland, 1944–46.

Mansurov, Sergei P.
?–15.3.1929. Historian, philosopher, priest, theologian.
Member of the religious intelligentsia in Moscow at the beginning of the

20th century. During WWI, worked on a history of the Christian church (fragments of which were published by the Moscow Patriarchate in 1971 in *Bogoslovskie Trudy*). Member of the Commission for the Protection of the Troitse-Sergieva Lavra (Zagorsk monastery), 1918. Member of the Institute of People's Education, 1920. Became sick with tuberculosis, 1924. Priest, 1926. Served at the Dubrovskii Convent near Vereia. Buried at Vereia.

Manuil (Lemeshevskii, Viktor Viktorovich), Metropolitan of Kuibyshev and Syzran'
1888–12.8.1968. Russian Orthodox clergyman.
Born in Luga, Petersburg Gouvt. Educated at high school in Libava. Studied at Petersburg University. Monk, 1911. Member of a church mission in Kirghizia, 1912–16. Studied at Petrograd Theological Academy, 1916. Archimandrite, 1923. Bishop of Luga, 1923. In the 1920s, actively defended Patriarch Tikhon against the Living Church (a group of radicals used by the authorities to split the church). Bishop of Serpukhov, 1928. Archbishop, 1946 (Orenburg, Cheboksary, Kuibyshev). Compiled a multi-volume *List of Russian Hierarchs of the Last 60 Years (1897–1957)*, which is the main source of reference on probably the most turbulent period of the history of the Russian Orthodox Church (partly published in West Germany). Imprisoned, 1924–28, 1930–44, 1948–55. Archbishop of Kuibyshev and Syzran', 1960. Metropolitan, 1962. Retired, 1965.

Manuilov, Aleksandr Appolonovich
28.2.1861–20.7.1929. Economist.
Graduated in law from Odessa University, 1883. Professor of Moscow University, 1901. Rector of Moscow University, 1908–11. As a young scientist, interested in Marxism (translated Marx), then liberal populism, and later joined the Cadet Party. Opponent of Stolypin's agrarian policies. In the spring of 1917, Minister of Education in the Provisional Government. After the October Revolution 1917, emigrated, but soon returned. Taught Marxism in various Russian universities.

Manuilskii, Dmitrii Zakharovich
3.10.1883–22.2.1959. Politician.
Born in the village of Sviatets (now Manuilskoe) in the Ukraine. Son of a peasant. Studied at Petersburg University, 1903. Joined the Bolsheviks, 1903. Organizer of the sailors' revolts in Kronstadt and Sveaborg during the 1905 Revolution. Arrested and exiled, but escaped on the way. Emigrated to France, 1907–12. Graduated from the Sorbonne, 1911. On party underground work in Moscow and Petersburg, 1912–13. Again went to France. Returned to Russia in May 1917. Joined the Mezhraiontsy, later changed to the Bolsheviks. Took part in the Bolshevik take-over in Oct. 1917. Soviet Minister of Agriculture in the Ukraine, 1918. Worked in the Comintern from 1922. Secretary of the Comintern Executive Cttee., 1928–43. From 1944, occupied the post of Foreign Affairs Minister of the Ukraine, representing the Ukraine in the UN. Many works on communist international strategy published. Retired after Stalin's death, 1953. Died in Kiev.

Maramzin, Vladimir Rafailovich
1934–   . Writer, translator.
Trained as an engineer. Author of childrens' books. Harassed and arrested for having published in samizdat Iosif Brodskii's 5-volume *Collected Works*. Emigrated in 1975. Worked for the magazine *Kontinent*. Contributed to *Vremia i My*, Israel-USA. Founder and editor of *Ekho* magazine together with V. Khvostenko from 1978. Lives in Paris. Works: *Blondin Oboego Tsveta*, 1977, *Tianitolkai*, 1981.

Marchenko, Anatolii Tikhonovich
23.1.1938–1987. Author.
Born in Barabinsk, Western Siberia. Son of a railway worker. Employed as a construction worker on a Siberian hydroelectrical project. His arrest after a brawl in a workers' hostel led to his first stay at a camp in Karaganda in Kazakhstan in 1957. Tried to escape to Iran via the Turkmen Soviet Republic. Arrested near the border in Ashkhabad and sentenced for high treason in 1960. This led to a succession of imprisonments and exiles. Wrote extremely forceful accounts of his experiences in the prisons and camps. Unusual

among the dissidents, being genuinely working class. Solely by his own efforts, made himself into an important writer and one of the most respected figures in dissident circles. In Mordovian camps and the notorious Vladimir prison from 1960–66, also worked as a labourer in Aleksandrov near Moscow. His book, *My Testimony*, which circulated in samizdat, was smuggled abroad, published in Russian, and in 1969, translated into English (and later into other major languages). Wrote an *Open Letter* in 1968 trying to warn the population of Czechoslovakia about the possibilty of an invasion. *The Letter* was broadcast by the BBC to Eastern Europe. Again arrested in 1968. Sentenced to a year in a labour camp in the Northern Urals. In 1971, released. Married Larisa Bogoraz, former wife of Iulii Daniel. Allowed to live in a writers' colony in Tarusa in Kaluga Oblast'. Again in camps and prisons in 1975, charged with having broken the terms of his parole. Sent to Chuna, this time for 4 years. Wrote the book *From Tarusa to Chuna*. In 1981, again arrested for anti-Soviet agitation, given a 10-year sentence to be followed by 5 years internal exile. Permanent suffering and continuous hunger strikes ruined his health. Became almost deaf as a result of meningitis. Not allowed to see his wife and son, a measure clearly intended to break his spirit. Due to international pressure, given permission to emigrate, but only to Israel with his Jewish wife. Refused, stating that this would deflect the whole point of his long struggle. After a long illness, died at Chistopol' prison in the Tatar Republic. Became a symbol of courage among the intelligentsia.

Marchevskii, Anatolii
1963?–   . Clown.
Widely regarded as heir-apparent to Oleg Popov. Graduated from the Moscow Circus School. Known as a perfectionist in his profession. His performance became the focus of attention when he arrived in Britain on tour with the Moscow State Circus, 1988.

Marchlewski, Iulian Iuzefovich (Karski, Kujawski)
17.5.1866–22.3.1925. Politician.
Born in Wloclawek, Poland. Gradu-

ated from Zurich University, 1896. Became a well-known activist in social democratic movements in Poland and Germany. During the 1905 Revolution, active in Warsaw. During WWI, one of the founders of the Spartakus communist movement in Germany. Arrested, 1916, by the German authorities. In 1918, released at the request of Lenin and sent to Russia. Member of the VTSIK, 1918. One of the founders of the Comintern. Leader of the Polish communists in the USSR, 1919–20. Dean of the communist University of the National Minorities of Western Countries in Moscow, 1922. Instrumental in the creation of MOPR (International Organization of Aid to Revolutionary Fighters). Died near Nervi in Italy, buried in Berlin. Reburied in Warsaw in 1950.

Mardzhanov, Konstantin Aleksandrovich (Mardzhanishvili, Kote)
9.6.1872–17.4.1933. Stage director.
Born in Georgia. With MKHAT (Moscow Art Theatre), 1910–13. Influenced by Stanislavskii and Nemirovich-Danchenko. Founded his own Svobodnyi Theatre in Moscow, 1913, which specialized in mime. Returned to Georgia. With the Rustaveli Theatre in Tbilisi, 1922. Founded the State Theatre of Georgia, now the Mardzhanishvili Theatre, 1928. Worked also in comic opera, operetta and show business. Regarded as one of the founders of the Soviet Georgian theatre. Guest director at various Moscow theatres. Died in Moscow.

Marenich, Anatolii Grigor'evich
30.1.1905–   . Operetta singer, theatrical director.
With the Sverdlovsk Theatre of Musical Comedy from 1933. People's Artist of the RSFSR, 1960.

Mares'ev, Aleksei Petrovich
1916–   . Colonel.
Joined the Red Army, 1937. Fighter pilot during WWII. Shot down over enemy territory, Mar. 1942. Heavily wounded, crawled for 18 days back to the front-lines. Both legs were amputated, but he returned to service

259

with artificial legs, and continued to serve as a fighter pilot. Graduated from the Higher Party Political School of the Cen. Cttee. of the CPSU, 1952. Secretary of the Soviet War Veterans Association, 1956, and Vice-chairman, 1983. Became a cult figure in the post-war years. B. Polevoi's biography of him, *Povest' o Nastoiashchem Cheloveke*, Moscow, 1946, was later turned into a film.

Maretskaia, Vera Petrovna
31.7.1906–17.8.1978. Film actress.
Graduated from the E. Vakhtangov Theatre School, 1924. Joined the Vakhtangov Theatre under Iu. Zavadskii. From 1936–40, worked in a theatre in Rostov-on-Don. Joined the Mossovet Theatre, Moscow, 1940. First film: *Zakroishchik Iz Torzhka* by Ia. Protazanov, 1925. Best known for her part in B. Barnet's film *Dom Na Trubnoi*, 1928. In 1956, played the leading role in a new version of *Mother* by M. Donskoi. A film was made about her career in 1976.

Margelov, Vasilii Filippovich
1908–   . General.
Joined the Red Army, 1928. Member of the Bolshevik Party, 1929. Took part in the Soviet-Finnish war and WWII. Graduated from the Academy of the General Staff, 1948. Commander of Airborne Troops, 1954–59 and 1961–79.

Margolin, Iulii Borisovich
1900–1985. Author.
Son of a doctor. Grew up in Ekaterinoslav and Pinsk. Graduated from Berlin University. After WWI, lived in Lodz in Poland, wrote in Polish, Russian and Hebrew. Emigrated to Palestine, 1936. Returned to Poland just before WWII. Moved from Lodz to Pinsk (in East Poland) in order to escape the German occupation. Remained there under the Soviet occupation. Arrested, June 1940, during mass arrests of refugees from West Poland by the NKVD, and sentenced to 5 years in the concentration camps for living on Soviet territory without a Soviet passport. Excluded from the amnesty for Polish citizens during WWII after the German attack on the Soviet

Union. Having served fully his sentence, exiled to Altai, June 1945. Later repatriated to Poland, and emigrated to Israel. Settled in Tel Aviv. Wrote a celebrated book about his experiences in the Soviet camps (*Puteshestvie v Stranu Ze-Ka*), one of the best pre-Solzhenitsyn accounts of the Gulag. Died in Israel.

Margulian, Arnold Evad'evich
13.4.1879–15.7.1950. Conductor.
Born in Kiev. Conductor with opera companies in various towns in Russia from 1902. With the Petrograd Theatre of Musical Drama, and then in the Ukraine, 1917–19. Chief conductor and artistic director with the Theatre of Opera and Drama in Sverdlovsk from 1937. Professor at the Ural Conservatory from 1942. Stalin Prize, 1946. Died in Sverdlovsk.

Margulies, Manuil Sergeevich
1869–1939. Lawyer.
Member of the Cadet Party. Friend of professor M. Kovalevskii, the founder of modern Russian freemasonry. Close to French masonic circles. Worked with Guchkov in the Industrial-Military Committees during WWI. During the Civil War, Minister of Trade with General Iudenich. Emigrated to France, continued his freemasonry career. Came into conflict with the French freemasons, when the emigré Russian freemasons tried to solicit help for the starving in Russia (this was condemned by the French as a political initiative). Died in France.

Maria Fedorovna (Romanova; b. Princess Dagmar of Denmark)
1847–1928. Empress of Russia.
Daughter of the King of Denmark. Sister of Queen Alexandra of England (wife of Edward VII). Married the Tsarevich Alexander, later Alexander III. Mother of Nicholas II. Retained influence on her son when he inherited the throne. On bad terms with the wife of Nicholas II, Alexandra, which added to the difficulties that the last Tsar had to contend with. During the revolution, in the Crimea. Saved by British warships. Refused to believe in the execution of her son and his

family until her death. Returned to Denmark to her relatives. Died in Denmark.

Maria, Mother (b. Pilenko, Elizaveta Iur'evna; m. Kuzmina-Karavaeva; m. Skobtsova)
8.12.1891–31.3.1945. Poetess, social worker, nun.
Born in Riga. In youth, combined interests in literature (mentioned by Blok in his poems), revolution (member of the SR Party) and religion (the first woman to graduate from Petersburg Theological Academy). In 1917, during the revolution, elected mayor of the town of Anapa, Crimea. Arrested by the Bolsheviks, but escaped in 1920 to Constantinople. Settled in Paris. Became involved in social and charity work. Nun from 1932. Defended her own position of active Christianity, organized hostels for destitute and mentally-handicapped Russian refugees. During WWII, hid Jews during the German occupation of France. Betrayed, arrested by the Gestapo (along with her son Y. Skobtsov and Rev. Klepinin, who were helping her in this work), 9 Feb. 1943. Sent to Ravensbrück concentration camp where she died in the gas chambers a few months before the Liberation volunteering to take the place of another prisoner. In the 1960s, discovered by Soviet journalists and immediately adopted by the authorities as a Soviet patriot and partisan. Articles and books about her were published and a film was made about her in the Soviet Union, which gave a very slanted version of her life story.
Works: *The Harvest of Souls*, 2 vol. Monographs on Khomiakov, Solov'ev and Dostoevskii, and a collection of poetry. See: S. Hackel, *One of Great Price. The Life of Mother Maria Skobtsova*, London, 1965.

Mariakhin, Sergei Stepanovich
1911–1972. General.
Joined the Red Army and the Communist Party, 1931. Graduated from the Frunze Military Academy, 1941. Officer of armoured troops during WWII. Deputy Minister of Defence, and Commander of the Rear Administration of the Soviet

Armed Forces, 1968–72. Member of the Cen. Cttee. of the CPSU, 1971–72.

Markevich, Igor Borisovich (Markevitch, Igor)

27.7.1912–1985. Conductor, composer, pianist.

Born in Kiev. Grandson of the ethnographer and historian N. A. Markevich. Emigrated to France. Pupil of A. Cortot, N. Boulanger and H. Scherchen. At the age of 16, discovered by S. Diaghilev, who took him to Munich a few months before his death. Early in 1936, married Kira Nijinsky in the Coronation Church in Budapest. Author of the ballets *Rebus*, 1931, and *Polet Ikara*, 1933, an oratorio, a cantata, a sinfonietta, a concerto grosso, and a concerto for piano and orchestra. Held conducting posts in Paris and in Moscow (guest conductor, 1960). Divorced Kira, because according to him she was 'mad like her father'. Conductor with the Orchestra of the Santa Cecilia Academy, Rome. Died in Switzerland from exhaustion following his tour of the USSR with his second wife and children. His memoirs (Etre et Avoir Eté) have been published in French and translated into English.

Other works: *Introduction à la Musique*, Lausanne, 1940.

See: B. Gavoty, *Igor Markevitch*, Geneva, 1954.

Markin, Nikolai Grigor'evich

1893–1918. Revolutionary.

Joined the Bolshevik Party, 1916. Member of Tsentrobalt, the Bolshevik sailors' organization, 1917. Secretary of the People's Commissariat of Foreign Affairs, 1917–18. On Lenin's orders, published all the secret documents of the Tsarist Ministry of Foreign Affairs. Naval commissar for Special Affairs, June 1918. Deputy commander of the Volga fleet during the Civil War. Died in action.

Markish, Ester Efimovna

1912–   . Author.

Born in Ekaterinoslav (now Dnepropetrovsk). Graduated from the Moscow Institute of Philosophy, Literature and History. Married Perets Markish. As a 'wife of an enemy of the people', she was deported to Kazakhstan with her two sons. Returned to Moscow after Stalin's death, 1954. Published many literary translations. Left the USSR, 1972. Settled in Israel. Wrote about the execution of Jewish writers after WWII in *Kak Ikh Ubivali*, Israel, 1982.

Markish, Perets Davidovich

1895–1951. Poet.

Born in the village of Polonnoe, near Rovno. Manual worker at the age of 8. Self-taught, later attended the Shaniavskii People's University. First publication, 1917. Emigrated, 1921. First to describe a Jewish pogrom in verse (*Kucha*), 1922. Returned to the USSR, 1926. Joined the CPSU, 1942. In his poems and novels, described the life of the Jewish people. Arrested during Stalin's anti-Semitic campaign and executed. Rehabilitated in 1954. The latest edition of the *Bol'shaia Sovetskaia Entsiklopediia* (vol. 15, 1974), and the *Literaturnyi Entsikopedicheskii Slovar'* (Moscow, 1987) do not mention the circumstances of his death. Both publications give the year of his death as 1952, while the former gives the day of his death as 12 Aug., both of which are disputed by his family and many Soviet Jewish scholars.

Markish, Simon (Shimon) Peretsovich

1931–   . Author, translator.

Born in Baku. Son of Perets Markish. Graduated in classical philology from Moscow University. As the 'son of an enemy of the people', exiled to Kazakhstan with his mother. Returned to Moscow in 1954. Published several books and translations in the official Soviet press. Left the USSR in 1970 for Hungary, later moved to Switzerland where he is a professor of Russian literature. Translated Georges Nivat's *Solzhenitsyn* from French into Russian (London, 1984).

Markov, Moisei Aleksandrovich

13.5.1908–   . Nuclear physicist.

Graduated from Moscow University, 1930. Worked at the Physics Institute of the Academy of Sciences, 1934, and later at the Dubna Nuclear Research Institute.

Markov, Nikolai Evgen'evich (Markov 2-oi)

1866–1927? Politician.

Land-owner from Kursk Gouvt. Received a technical education. Member of the 3rd and 4th Dumas from Kursk. Was called Markov Vtoroi in the Duma. Represented right-wing opinions. Active member of the Union of the Gentry, and other right-wing organizations, such as the Union of Russian People, and the Union of the Archangel Michael. During the Civil War, with the army of Iudenich, 1918–20. Emigrated, 1920.

Markov, Sergei Leonidovich

12.7.1878–12.6.1918. General.

Son of a military officer. Educated at the Moscow Cadets Corps. Graduated from the Konstantinovskoe Artillery School and the Academy of the General Staff in 1904. At the front during the Russo-Japanese war, 1904–05. Worked in the General Staff, taught in the Academy of the General Staff, 1911. During WWI, on active service as a staff officer. Connected with General Denikin in 1917, arrested for taking part in the Kornilov revolt, escaped and fled to the Don in Nov. 1917. Took part in the founding of the White armies (commander of a regiment, brigade, and later division). Renowned for his dashing exploits. Killed in action in Stanitsa Shablievka, Rostov Gouvt.

Markus, Stanislas Adol'fovich

26.4.1894–1971? Musicologist.

Born in Lodz', then Russian Poland. Moved to Moscow where he worked for musical publications. Wrote many articles and books, including *Istoriia Muzykal'noi Estetiki*, Moscow, 1959.

Marshak, Samuil Iakovlevich

3.11.1887–4.7.1964. Poet.

Born in Voronezh. Lived with Gorkii's family in Yalta, 1904–06. Studied at London University, 1912–14. Published translations of English poetry, 1915–17. Settled at Ekaterinodar (now Krasnodar), 1920, and organized a theatre for children, writing plays and verse which were performed there. Started to publish

261

children's verse, 1923. Soon became a classic in the genre. During the Stalin years, some of his works, such as *Mr Twister*, 1933, had a propagandizing flavour. During WWII, wrote slogans for war posters. Also known as an excellent translator of Shakespeare, Burns, Blake, Wordsworth, Keats, Kipling and Milne.

Martens, Ludvig Karlovich

1.1.1875–19.10.1948. Engineer, editor.
Born in Bakhmut (now Artem'evsk). Studied at the Petersburg Technological Institute in the 1890s, and was involved in Marxist revolutionary activity. Arrested, 1896. After 3 years in prison, expelled to Germany, 1899. Became an active member of the German Social-Democrats. Moved to England, 1906, then to the USA, 1916. After the October Revolution 1917, appointed 1st Soviet representative in America, 1919. Not recognized by the US government. Involved in the build-up of a Soviet spy network in the USA. Returned to the USSR. Chairman of the Inventions Cttee. of the VSNKH, 1924–26. Specialist in diesel engines. Editor of the monumental *Soviet Technical Encyclopaedia*, 1927–41. Died in Moscow.

Martino, Boris Borisovich

5.6.1917–1966? Scoutmaster.
Born in Kronstadt. Son of a naval officer. During the Civil War, evacuated with his parents to the Crimea, and from there to Turkey. Settled in Yugoslavia. Graduated from Belgrade University, and from an infantry officers school. During WWII, became underground leader of the Russian scouts organizations in Europe. Went to Warsaw, trying to get to the German-occupied Russian territories, but was prevented by serious illness. Became an invalid, but remained a very active scout organizer and leader. Deputy chief of the youth department in the Vlasov movement in Germany, 1944. After WWII, as chief Russian scoutmaster in West Germany, tried to recreate the Russian scout movement, which had been shattered by the war. In the 1960s, worked with Radio Liberty in Munich.

Martinson, Sergei Aleksandrovich

6.2.1899–2.9.1984. Film actor.
Prominent Soviet comedian. Graduated from the Leningrad Institute of Stage Art, 1923. In 1924, joined the Meyerhold Theatre and Moscow Theatre of Revolution. Pupil of FEKS under G. Kozintsev and L. Trauberg. Films: *Pokhozhdeniia Oktiabriny, Chertovo Koleso*, 1924–26; *Marionetki*, 1934; *Anton Ivanovich Serditsia*, 1941; *Diadiushkin Son*,1967; *Goroda i Gody* 1974; and *Iaroslavna-Koroleva Frantsii*, 1979.

Martov, L. (Tsederbaum, Iulii Osipovich)

24.12.1865–5.6.1935. Politician.
Born in Constantinople. Son of a merchant. As a student, involved in Marxist circles, close personal friend of Lenin. Exiled to Turukhansk, 1896. Emigrated, 1901. Co-editor of *Iskra* with Lenin. Opposed Lenin's plans of introducing dictatorial methods into party work, and after the inter-party split, 1903, became the most prominent Menshevik leader. In 1917, proposed a coalition government of all socialist parties. After the October Revolution 1917, protested against the dictatorship of the Bolsheviks. Emigrated, Sep. 1920. Prominent figure of international socialism, edited the Menshevik *Sotsialisticheskii Vestnik* abroad. Wrote a number of works criticizing the Bolsheviks and Lenin personally. Died in Berlin.

Martynov, Aleksandr Samoilovich (Pikker)

24.12.1865–5.6.1935. Politician.
Born in Pinsk. Son of a merchant. Member of Narodnaya Volya from 1884. Exiled to Siberia for 10 years, 1886. Joined the SD Party in the 1890s. Prominent Menshevik. Member of the Cen. Cttee. of the Mensheviks, 1917. Broke with the party in 1922, and joined the Bolsheviks in 1923. Worked at the Marx-Engels Institute, Moscow. From 1924, member of the editoral board at the periodical *Kommunisticheskii Internatsional*. Travelled around the country giving lectures denouncing Menshevism. Died in Moscow.

Martynov, Evgenii Ivanovich

1864–1932. Lt.-general.
Graduated from the Academy of the General Staff, 1889. Took part in the Russo-Japanese war and WWI. Joined the Red Army, 1918. Professor at the Academy of the General Staff. Wrote military historical works.

Martynov, Georgii Romanovich

28.8.1925– . Ballet dancer, choreographer.
Born in Ivanovo. Graduated from the Belorussian Choreographic School, 1954. Debut in 1948 while a student. With the Ivanovo Theatre of Musical Comedy from 1954, and the Minsk Theatre, 1952–63. Leading dancer and choreographer with the State Dance Ensemble of Belorussia, 1963–67. Leading dancer with the Belorussian State Philharmonic, 1967–74.

Martynov, Ivan Ivanovich

1908– . Musicologist.
Born in Karachev. Moved to Moscow. Works: *D.D. Shostakovich*, Moscow, 1946; *Muzyka Novogo Mira*, Moscow, 1955; *Bela Bartok*, Moscow, 1956; *Stevan Mokran'iants i Serbskaia Muzyka*, Moscow, 1958; *Berdzhikh Smetana*, Moscow, 1963; *Claude Debussy*, Moscow, 1964.

Martynova, Olga Mikhailovna

15.6.1903– . Theatre, ballet historian.
Born in Moscow. Graduated from the Moscow Choreographic School, 1918. Also studied at the GITIS, 1918. Pupil of Boris Alpers. Dancer with the Bolshoi Theatre, 1919–48. Many articles in the theatre and ballet press.

Masherov, Petr Mironovich

1918–1980. Politician.
Graduated from the Vitebsk Pedagogical Institute, 1939. During WWII, partisan commander in Belorussia. After WWII, 1st secretary of the Cen. Cttee. of the Belorussian Komsomol, 1947–54. Secretary of the Cen. Cttee. of the CPSU in Belorussia, 1959–65, and 1st secretary, 1965. Member of the Cen. Cttee. of the CPSU, 1964, and non-voting

Politburo member, 1966. Member of the Presidium of the Supreme Soviet of the USSR, 1966–80.

Mashkov, Il'ia Ivanovich
29.7.1881–20.3.1944. Artist.
Born in the stanitsa of Mikhailovskaia, now Volgograd Oblast'. Still life and landscape painter. Studied at the Moscow School of Painting, Sculpture and Architecture, 1900–09 under Leonid Pasternak, Konstantin Korovin, and V. Serov. Member of the Bubnovyi Valet from 1910. Member of the Mir Iskusstva from 1916. Influenced by Cezanne and cubism. Taught at his own studio (1902–17) and at the VKHUTEMAS-VKHUTEIN (1918–30). Exhibitions from 1902: the New Society of Artists, the Zolotoe Runo, MTKH, the Mir Iskusstva, the Bubnovyi Valet, Moscow Artists, etc. Personal exhibition: Moscow, 1956. Died in Moscow.

Maslenkin, Anatolii Evstigneevich
29.6.1930–   . Athlete.
Born in Moscow. Honoured Master of Sports (football), 1957. With Moscow Spartak. Graduated from the School of Coaches of the Moscow Institute of Physical Culture, 1968. USSR champion, 1956, 1958 and 1962. Olympic champion, 1956.

Maslennikov, Igor' Fedorovich
26.10.1931–   . Film director.
Graduated from Leningrad University, 1954, and from the Higher Directors Courses, 1967. Pupil of G. Kozintsev. Joined Lenfilm. Best known for his film *Iaroslavna-Koroleva Frantsii*, 1979, and a 6-part TV film, *Sherlock Holmes and Doctor Watson*. Directed *Pikovaia Dama* in 1982.

Maslennikov, Ivan Ivanovich
16.9.1900–16.4.1954. State security official.
Born in the village of Chalykla near Saratov. Joined the Red Army, 1918, commander of a cavalry regiment. From 1928, high ranking GPU and NKVD official. Various high positions during WWII. After the war, in Baku and Transcaucasia, commander of the military region. From

1948, again a high ranking official in the Ministry of the Interior (MVD) under Beria and Abakumov. Many decorations, including 4 Orders of Lenin.

Maslennikova, Irina Ivanovna
3.6.1918–   . Singer (soprano).
Born in Kiev. One of the leading soloists of the Bolshoi Theatre, 1943–60. Teacher at the GITIS from 1956.

Maslennikova, Leokadia Ignat'evna
8.3.1918–   . Singer (soprano).
Born in Saratov. Pupil of D. Evtushenko. Soloist with the Bolshoi Theatre from 1946. People's Artist of the RSFSR, 1961.

Masliukov, Iurii Dmitrievich
1937–   . Politician.
Graduated from the Leningrad Mechanical Institute as an engineer, 1962. Deputy director of a scientific research institute in the late 1960s. Deputy Minister of Defence Equipment in the early 1980s. 1st Deputy Chairman of GOSPLAN, Dec. 1982. Deputy Prime Minister of the USSR, Nov. 1985. Member of the Cen. Cttee. of the CPSU, 1986.

Maslov, Fedor Ivanovich
8.1.1911–   . Composer.
Born in Simbirskaia Gouvt. Artistic director of the Voronezh Russian Folk Choir from 1964. Author of songs and choral suites.

Maslov, Sergei Iur'evich
1940–1982. Essayist, mathematician.
Born in Leningrad. Graduated from Leningrad University in physics and mathematics. Doctor's degree. Many articles in the scientific press. Involved in the human rights movement. One of the contributors to, and editors of, the bibliographical magazine *Sigma*, which was widely circulated in samizdat. Died in a car crash but it was suspected that the crash had been arranged by the KGB, which had been harassing him for a number of years previously.

Maslovskaia, Sofia Dmitrievna
21.6.1885–19.5.1953. Operatic director.
Born in Petersburg. Director of the

Theatre of Musical Drama, 1912–19. Taught at the Leningrad Conservatory, 1914–29, and 1941–51. Professor from 1926. Also worked in Moscow, Sverdlovsk and Khar'kov. Died in Leningrad.

Massalitinov, Konstantin Iraklievich
3.6.1905–24.1.1979. Composer, conductor.
Born in Voronezh. Graduated from the Voronezh School of Music, 1929. Directed amateur choirs in worker's clubs. Founder and artistic director of the Voronezh People's Choir, 1942–64. Collector of folk music. Died in Voronezh.

Massalitinova, Varvara Osipovna
29.7.1878–20.10.1945. Actress.
Graduated from drama courses at the Moscow Theatre School, 1901. Joined the Malyi Theatre. Great dramatic actress. Entered the film industry, 1918. Best remembered for her films *Gospada Skotininy*, 1927, *Groza*, 1934, *Detstvo*, 1938, and *V Liudiakh*, 1939.

Matova, Aleksandra Konstantinovna
16.5.1888–1973? Singer (soprano).
Born in Smolensk. Soloist with the Bolshoi Theatre, Moscow, 1916–41. Honoured Artist of the RSFSR, 1937.

Matrosov, Aleksandr Matveevich
1924–23.2.1943. Soldier, war hero.
Born in Dnepropetrovsk. Orphaned, one of the 'besprizornye' – those children who were victims of the chaotic revolutionary years, educated in children's colonies under quasi-military discipline and constant ideological indoctrination. The successful survivors of this system often became janissaries of Stalinist life-style and values. Conscripted and sent to the front, 1942. In Feb. 1943, during a battle with the Germans in Pskov Oblast', covered the embrasure of an enemy pillbox with his body, silencing the machine-gun and ensuring victory for his detachments. Became a Stalinist cult figure after his death.

Matrosov, Vadim Aleksandrovich
1917–   . General, state security officer.
Joined the border guards (NKVD), 1938. During WWII, on active service in the army, probably with SMERSH. After WWII, returned to the state security system (border guards). Graduated from the Academy of the General Staff, 1959. Chief-of-staff of border guard troops, 1967–72, and commander of the same, 1972. Deputy chairman of the KGB, 1984.

Matsiutin, Konstantin Eremeevich
14.9.1910–   . Composer.
Born in Novorossiisk. Moved to Moscow. Author of a symphonic poem based on *Skazki iz Italii* by Maksim Gorkii, choral works, and arrangements of folk songs.

Matushevas, Vasilius Leont'evich
18.10.1945–   . Athlete.
Born in Lithuania. International Class Honoured Master of Sports, (volley-ball), 1968. Olympic champion, 1968. With Khar'kov Burevestnik. From 1974, with Vilnius Zhalgiris. Graduated from the Khar'kov Pedagogical Institute, 1974. Coach.

Matveev, Aleksandr Pavlovich
1905–1946. State security officer.
Joined the Bolshevik Party, 1925. Komsomol and party functionary, 1926. 1st secretary of Minsk obkom and Minister of the Interior (NKVD) of Belorussia, 1937–41. Probably connected with the mass murder of POW Polish officers at the NKVD rest house in the Katyn forest near Smolensk. In the summer of 1941, fled from the German advance. Appointed 1st secretary of Orel obkom, Jan. 1942. Chief-of-staff of the Briansk partisan detachments, based in the Briansk forests, July 1942. After the advance of the Soviet Army, appointed 1st secretary of Briansk obkom, 1944.

Matveev, Boris
1929–1968. Athlete.
Honoured Master of Sports (track and field athletics). 10th place in the discus at the XVth, and 9th place at the XVIth Olympic Games. Many times USSR champion.

Matveev, Ivan Ivanovich
1890–8.10.1918. Revolutionary.
Born in Alioshki (now Tsiuriupinsk) near Kherson. Son of a sailor. Joined the merchant fleet. During WWI, with the Russian Navy in the Black Sea, involved in revolutionary propaganda. During the Civil War, head of a Red detachment fighting Ukrainian nationalists in Odessa, and the Germans and White Cossacks on the Taman Peninsula. Elected commander of the Red Taman Army, led the legendary march of this army along the Black Sea, 1918. Shot by order of the commander of the Red Army of the North Caucasus, I. Sorokin, who was himself later shot as a traitor to the Red cause.

Mavlikhanov, Umiar Abdullovich
24.9.1937–   . Athlete.
Born in Moscow. Honoured Master of Sports, (fencing), 1964. With the Moscow Oblast' Armed Forces Club. Honoured Coach of the RSFSR, 1975. Member of the CPSU, 1971. Graduated from the Moscow Technological Institute of Light Textile Industry, 1975. USSR champion, 1963 and 1967–68. Olympic champion, 1964 and 1968. World champion, 1965, 1967 and 1969. Bronze medal, 1964.

Mayakovsky, Vladimir Vladimirovich
19.7.1893–14.4.1930. Poet, cartoonist.
Born in Bagdadi (now Mayakovsky) in Georgia. Son of a forester. Educated at Kutaissi and Moscow high schools. After the death of his father, the family moved to Moscow in 1906. Involved in revolutionary activity, arrested on 3 occasions. Student at the Moscow Arts School, 1911. Became acquainted with the futurist group Burliuk, and was expelled from the Arts School for taking part in futurist 'happenings', which scandalized society. During WWI, gained fame with his modernist, intensely personal, anti-war poetry. Enthusiastically welcomed the October Revolution 1917, thinking that the political revolution equalled a revolution in the arts. During the Civil War, worked in a propaganda department (ROSTA), creating cartoon strips with memorable captions in verse, becoming in effect the best

ad-man of the revolution. After the Civil War, became involved in the power struggle of the different groups, speaking in the name of the new elite in arts (LEF, New LEF). Acknowledged as a satirist, but condemned as a poet by Lenin. Extremely gifted master of versification, but failed in his attempts at epic revolutionary poetry (*Vladimir Il'ich Lenin, Good, 150,000,000*). Though preaching complete freedom from morals and bourgeois restrictions, he himself became hopelessly entangled in a quite banal menage à trois with Osip and Lili Brik, and remained under her influence, despite all difficulties and temptations. With the growing bureaucratization of Soviet society, became more and more alienated. Committed suicide in Moscow (shot himself). After his death, was proclaimed by Stalin to be the most talented poet of the Soviet epoch and, in the words of Pasternak, 'was planted everywhere like potatoes'. Despite this, his artistic reputation remained largely intact. His correspondence with L. Brik, published in 1982 in Sweden, shows a man very different from his public image—hypersensitive, almost neurotic and very much interested in success and worldly goods.

Mazel', Lev Abramovich
26.5.1907–   . Musicologist.
Born in Koenigsberg, now Kaliningrad. Professor at the Moscow Conservatory. Doctor of art history. Author of:*Ocherki po Istorii Teoreticheskogo Muzykoznaniia*, Moscow, 1934; *Fantaziia f-moll Shopena. Opyt Analiza*, Moscow, 1937; *F. Chopin*, Moscow, 1947; *O Melodii*, Moscow, 1952; *Simfonii D. D. Shostakovicha*, Moscow, 1960; *Stroenie Muzykal'nykh Proizvedenii*, Moscow, 1960.

Medved', Aleksandr Vasil'evich
16.9.1937–   . Athlete.
Born in Belaia Tserkov', Kiev Oblast'. Honoured Master of Sports (wrestling), 1963. With Minsk Burevestnik. Graduated from the Belorussian Institute of Physical Culture, 1962. Member of the CPSU, 1965. USSR champion, 1961–63, 1966–70. World champion, 1962–63, 1966–67, and 1969–71. Olympic champion, 1964. European champion, 1966,

1968 and 1972.
See: V. Golubev, *Aleksandr Medved'*, Moscow, 1978.

Medvedev, Armen Nikolaevich

28.5.1938– . Film critic, editor. Graduated from the VGIK, 1960. Editor-in-chief of the magazine *Sovetskii Film*, and later of *Iskusstvo Kino* until 1984. Taught at the VGIK from 1980. From 1984, editor-in-chief of the collegium of script-editing of Goskino. Author of many articles and books.

Medvedev, Mikhail Efimovich (Bernstein)

20.7.1852–8.8.1925. Singer (tenor). Born in Belaia Tserkov, Kiev Gouvt. Appeared mainly in provincial operas. Concert tour in the USA, 1898–1900. Taught at the Musical Drama School of the Moscow Philharmonic Society from 1901, at the Kiev Conservatory from 1905, and at the Saratov Conservatory from 1912. Among his pupils were A. Mozzhukhin, F. Mukhtarova, and G. Pirogov. Died in Saratov.
See: S. Levik, *Zapiski Opernogo Pevtsa*, Moscow, 1962.

Medvedev, Roi Aleksandrovich

1925– . Historian, author. Born in Tbilisi. Twin brother of Zhores Medvedev. Graduated in philosophy (Marxism) from Leningrad University. Researcher in various scientific institutes attached to the USSR Academy of Sciences. Published several books and numerous articles in the Soviet press. Edited the samizdat magazine *Politicheskii Dnevnik*. In May 1970, instrumental in organizing an international protest in order to save his brother from forcible psychiatric detention. Edited the samizdat almanac *XX-yi Vek*. Harassed by the KGB, but well-connected in Moscow, backed by powerful Soviet academics and probably by some high-ranking politicians. Highly regarded by Western academics. Lives in Moscow, but keeps in touch with his brother, who lives in London. His main works are published abroad and translated into the major languages. Author of numerous articles published in the international press. Has given inter-views to the BBC defending Gorbachev's policies on perestroika and East-West relations. Works: *Kto Sumasshedshii?* (with Zh. Medvedev), London, 1971; *Kniga O Sotsialisticheskoi Demokratii*, Amsterdam, 1972; *K Sudu Istorii: Genezis I Posledstviia Stalinizma*, NY, 1974; *N. Khrushchev: Gody U Vlasti* (with Zh. Medvedev), NY, 1975; *Oni Okruzhali Stalina* USA, 1984; *Khrushchev: Politicheskaia Biografiia*, USA, 1986.

Medvedev, Vadim Andreevich

29.3.1929– . Politician. Graduated from Leningrad State University, 1951. Worked there, 1951–56. Member of the CPSU, 1952. Assistant professor at the Leningrad Engineering Institute of Rail Transport, 1956–61. Dean of the Leningrad Technological Institute, 1961–68. Professor at Leningrad University, 1968. Deputy Chief of the Propaganda Department of the Cen. Cttee. of the CPSU, 1970–78. Responsible for relations with socialist countries and Comecon. Chief of the Department for Liaison with Communist and Workers' Parties of the Socialist Countries in the Cen. Cttee. since Mar. 1986. Member of the Commission on Science and Technology of the USSR Supreme Soviet since 11 Apr. 1984. Corresponding member of the USSR Academy of Sciences (Economics Department) since 1984. Elected to the Secretariat of the Cen. Cttee. on 6 Mar. 1986. Full member of the Politburo, Oct. 1988.

Medvedev, Zhores Aleksandrovich

1925– . Biologist, author. Born in Tbilisi. Son of a communist official. Twin brother of the historian, Roi Medvedev. Graduated from the Moscow Agricultural Academy. Became known as a biologist and gerontologist whose samizdat works criticized the Lysenko regime in Soviet science under Stalin. Wrote a remarkable samizdat study on Soviet censorship of mail (later published in the West). Arrested, 1970, and put into a psychiatric hospital in Kaluga. Following protests from the international scientific community, released after 2 weeks. Emigrated to Britain, 1973, but kept in touch with his brother and others in the USSR. Has written a number of books interpreting recent events and personalities in the USSR, including Gorbachev. Lives and works in London.
Works: *Mezhdunarodnoe Sotrudnichestvo Uchenykh i Natsional'nye Granitsy. Taina Perepiski Okhraniaetsia Zakonom*, Macmillan, 1971; *Kto Sumasshedshii?* (with Roi Medvedev), Macmillan, 1971; *Desiat' Let Posle Odnogo Dnia Ivana Denisovicha*, Macmillan, 1973; *Khrushchev: Gody u Vlasti* (with Roi Medvedev), NY, 1975.

Medvedkin, Aleksandr Ivanovich

8.3.1900– . Film director. Born in Penza. Began as a scriptwriter at Gosvoenkino (State Military Cinema), 1927. Assistant director at Sovkino, 1929. First film as a director, 1930. Specialized in satires in the form of fairy-tales, which were in fact political propaganda. First full-length film and his most important was *Happiness*, 1934, which was criticized by the Soviet press and not released until 1963. Two other important films, *Miracle-Girl*, 1936, and *The New Moscow*, 1938, were both attacked, and Medvedkin accused of formalism. They remained shelved until the 1960s when they became classics. During the late 1930s and WWII worked on propaganda documentaries. Produced nothing of significance. Disappeared from the scene. Regarded as a major Soviet director of the 1930s abroad, rather than in the Soviet Union.

Medunov, Sergei Fedorovich

1915– . Politician. Graduated from the Party High School of the Cen. Cttee. of the CPSU. Teacher, 1931–39. Served in the Soviet Army, 1939–47. Member of the CPSU, 1942. After the war, held senior party posts in the Ukraine and Crimea. 1st secretary of Sochi City CPSU Cen. Cttee., 1959–69. Chairman of the Krasnodar Krai Executive Cttee. of Workers Deputies, 1969–73. Brezhnev's protegé until his death. His last post was as Deputy Minister of the Fruit and Vegetable Industry. Member of the Cen. Cttee. of the CPSU from 1976. In early 1983, fired by Andropov from the Cen. Cttee., accused of bribe-taking and corruption.

Medyn', Iakov Georgievich (Medinš)
22.3.1885–1974? Composer.
Born in Riga. Brother of Iazep and
Ianis Medyn'. Director of the People's
Conservatory in Elgava, 1921–40.
Taught at the Riga Conservatory
from 1944 (choral conducting). Professor from 1946. Author of choral
and vocal symphonies, orchestral
suites, concertos, romances, and
arrangements of folk songs. Literary
work: *Kora Zinatnu Pamati*, Riga,
1956.

Medyn', Ianis Georgievich (Medinš)
9.10.1890–1975? Composer, conductor.
Born in Riga. Brother of Iazep and
Iakov Medyn'. Emigrated, 1944. In
Stockholm from 1948. Author of 4
operas, a ballet, and symphonic
works.

Medyn', Iazep Georgievich (Medinš)
13.2.1887–12.6.1947. Composer.
Born in Kovno (Kaunas). Brother of
Iakov and Ianis Medyn'. Piano
professor at the Riga Conservatory
from 1945. Author of operas, a
cantata, 3 symphonies, symphonic
poems, orchestral works, concertos
for violin, cello and orchestra,
instrumental pieces, choral works,
romances, and songs. Died in Riga.

**Meerson-Aksenov, Mikhail
Grigor'evich**
1944– . Orthodox clergyman.
Born in Moscow. Graduated in
history from Moscow University.
Became a well-known samizdat author, specializing in historical and
religious subjects. Emigrated in 1972
to France. Moved to the USA.
Graduated from the St. Vladimir
Theological Seminary in New York.
Priest in the American Autocephalous Orthodox Church.

Mei, Varvara Pavlovna
18.1.1912– . Ballerina.
Born in Petersburg. Graduated from
the Leningrad Choreographic School,
1929. Pupil of A. Vaganova. Graduated from the pedagogical department of the same school, 1941, and
the Leningrad Conservatory, 1951.
Taught at the Leningrad Choreographic School from 1938. Taught

ballet in Cairo, 1971–72. Author of
The ABC of Ballet (*Azbuku Klassicheskogo Tantsa*) with N. Bazarova,
1964.

Meichik, Mark Naumovich
28.2.1880–1950. Pianist, music publisher, editor, translator.
Born in Moscow. Pupil of V.
Safonov. Head of the concert division of the musical department of
Narkompros from 1918. Director of
the Institute of Musical Drama,
1919–21. Director and chief editor of
the publishing house Muztorg
(MONO). Translated into Russian
and adapted certain works dealing
with techniques of musical performance (R. Breithaupt, F. Stein-
hausen). Author of pamphlets on
Paganini, Schumann and Skriabin.
Died in Moscow.

Meitus, Iulii Sergeevich
28.1.1903– . Composer.
Born in Elizavetgrad (now Kirovograd). Author of 2 Ukrainian and 2
Turkmenian operas, 5 symphonic
suites, instrumental and choral
works, a vocal cycle, and music for
stage and screen.

Mekhlis, Lev Zakharovich
1889–1953. Politician.
Joined the Bolshevik Party, 1918.
Took part in the Civil War. Graduated from the Institute of Red
Professors, 1930. Head of the Political Administration of the Armed
Forces, 1937–40, Minister of State
Control, 1940 and 1946–50. Member
of the Orgburo of the CPSU,
1938–52. One of the Stalin's most
trusted allies. Member of the Cen.
Cttee. of the CPSU, 1939.

Mekk, Nikolai Karlovich (von Mekk)
1863–1929. Engineer.
Son of Nadezhda von Mekk, the
friend of Petr Il'ich Tchaikovskii.
Received a technical education,
worked as an engineer. During
Stalin's purges, one of the accused at
the so-called Prompartiia trial. Sentenced to death and shot.

Mekokishvili, Arsen Spiridonovich
12.4.1912–5.3.1972. Athlete.
Born in Georgia. Honoured Master

of Sports (wrestling), 1951. With
Tbilisi Dynamo. From 1945 with
Moscow Dynamo. USSR champion,
1945–56. Olympic champion, 1952.
World champion, 1954. Author of *V
Stroiu Bogatyrei*, Moscow, 1959.
Died in Moscow.

Mekshilo, Evdokia Panteleevna
23.3.1931– . Athlete.
Born in Gorno-Altaisk. Honoured
Master of Sports (skiing), 1964.
Graduated from the Leningrad Technical School of Physical Culture,
1954. USSR champion, 1954–66.
Olympic champion, 1964 Silver
medal, 1964.

Melamid, Aleksandr Danilovich
1945– . Artist.
Born in Moscow. Graduated from
the Moscow Stroganov Art School.
Played an active part in unofficial
artistic events. Left the USSR, 1977.
Lives in the USA. Works with the
artist Vitalii Komar in the field of
political collage (posters, book illustrations, cards). Has written articles
for the Russian art magazine *A-IA*,
published in France. Has exhibited
all over the USA, and attracted the
attention of American art critics.

Melan'in, Vladimir Mikhailovich
1.12.1933– . Athlete.
Born in the village of Balyki, Kirov
Oblast'. Honoured Master of Sports
(biathlon), 1962. With the Kirov
Armed Forces Club. World champion, 1959 and 1962–63. USSR
champion, 1959 and 1966. Olympic
champion, 1964 (20km race). Member of the CPSU, 1965. Graduated
from the Kirov Pedagogical Institute,
1974.

Mel'gunov, Sergei Petrovich
6.1.1880–1956. Historian, editor,
politician.
Son of a historian. Graduated from
Moscow University, 1904. Journalist
with the newspaper *Russkie Vedomosti*. One of the founders and
prominent members of the Popular
Socialists (narodnye sotsialisty) from
1907. Founder of the publishing
house Zadruga, 1911–22. Founder of
the historical magazine *Golos Minu-*

vshego, 1913. After the October Revolution 1917, in Moscow illegally. Arrested in 1920 in connection with the Tactical Centre, released 1921. Allowed to emigrate, 1922, but stripped of Soviet citizenship, 1923. Moved to Paris, where he spent the rest of his life, writing historical works and editing emigré publications (*Vozrozhdenie* and others). One of the most scrupulous modern historians. Originally a specialist on Russian sects and the early 19th century (Alexander I), later wrote many monographs on the revolutionary years and personalities (*Red Terror, Fate of the Romanovs, The German Golden Key to Bolshevik Revolution, Fate of Admiral Kolchak*). Actively involved in political activity among Russian expatriates.

Melik-Pashaev, Aleksandr Shamil'evich
23.10.1905–18.6.1964. Conductor.
Born in Tiflis. Armenian. Pupil of A. Gauk. Conductor from 1931. Chief conductor with the Bolshoi Theatre, 1953–62. Guest appearances all over the world. Stalin Prize, 1942, 1943. Died in Moscow.

Melikian, Romanos Ovakimovich
1.10.1883–30.3.1935. Composer, musicologist.
Born in Kizliar, Northern Caucasus. Armenian. One of the originators of the Armenian romance. Founded a music studio in Erevan (later known as the Conservatory), 1921. Artistic director of opera and ballet. Author of romances, songs, pieces for piano, and an anthology of folk-song arrangements. Died in Erevan.

Melikian, Spiridon Avetisovich
1.12.1881–4.5.1933. Musicologist, composer, conductor.
Born in Echmiadzin. Armenian. Founded, in Tiflis, the Armenian Musical Society, 1912, and the Armenian Choral Society, 1916. Transcribed over 1,000 Armenian folk songs. Author of an opera for children, a work for choir and symphony orchestra, romances, and an anthology of Shiraksk and Vansk folk songs.
Literary works: (in Armenian) *Voprosy Razvitiia Nashei Muzyki*, Tiflis,

1909; *Uchebnik po Peniiu*, Tiflis, 1912; *Gammy Armianskoi Narodnoi Muzyki*, Erevan, 1930 (Russian translation, 1932); *Ocherk Istorii Armianskoi Muzyki*, Erevan, 1935. Died in Erevan.

Melngailis, Emil Iakovlevich
15.2.1874–20.12.1954. Composer, folklorist.
Born in Latvia. Professor at the Riga Conservatory. Master of Choral Music. Transcribed over 4500 folk melodies. Author of choral works, arrangements of Latvian folk songs for choir, voice and piano, arrangements of folk songs and dance tunes for instrumental and vocal and instrumental ensembles, and romances. Literary works: *Materialy Latyshskogo Muzykal'nogo Folklora* (3 vol.), Riga, 1951–53. Died in Riga.

Melnikaite, Marite Iuozovna (Mialnikaite)
1923–1943. Partisan.
Lithuanian Komsomol leader. During WWII, organized partisan detachments in Lithuania. Captured by the Germans and executed. Made into a cult figure, 1945–53, with a film being made about her.

Mel'nikov, Boris Borisovich
16.5.1938–   . Athlete.
Born in Leningrad. Graduated from the Leningrad Institute of Physical Culture, 1961. From 1963, with the Leningrad Armed Forces. Honoured Master of Sports (fencing), 1964. With Leningrad Burevestnik. USSR champion, 1964–65. Olympic champion, 1964. World champion, 1965 and 1967. Member of the CPSU, 1973.

Mel'nikov, Nikolai Andreevich
24.1.1948–   . Athlete.
Born in Moscow. Honoured Master of Sports (water polo), 1975. With Moscow Burevestnik. From 1976, with the Central Sports Club of the Navy. USSR champion, 1969–78. Olympic champion, 1972. World champion, 1978.

Mel'nikov, Oleg Aleksandrovich
1912–   . Astronomer.
Graduated from Khar'kov University,

1933. Worked at the Pulkovo Observatory. Professor of astrophysics at Leningrad University, 1946.

Men', Aleksandr Volfovich (Bogoliubov, Andrei; Svetlov, Emmanuil)
1935–   . Russian Orthodox clergyman.
Born in Moscow. Studied at the Irkutsk Fur Trade Institute. Became interested in religion and entered the Orthodox Seminary in Leningrad. Graduated from the Moscow Theological Academy. Priest, 1958. Became known as a religious writer. His popular history of comparative religion has been published in several volumes by the Catholic Russian publishing house Zhizn' s Bogom in Brussels.

Mendele, Moikher-Sphorim (Broide; Abramovich, Sholom Iakov)
2.1.1836–8.12.1917. Author.
Born at Kopyl' near Minsk into a poor Jewish family. After several years of wandering, settled in Kamenets-Podolsk, later in Berdichev. Started to write poems and short stories at first in Hebrew. Became the first classic writer of modern Jewish literature in Yiddish. From the 1880s, lived in Odessa. His collected works in 20 volumes were published in Warsaw, 1911–23.

Mendeleev, Vasilii Dmitrievich
1886–1922. Inventor.
Son of the world-famous chemist D. Mendeleev. Designer at a shipbuilding works, 1908–1916. Worked on early submarine and tank projects.

Men'shagin, Boris Georgievich
9.5.1902–after 1980. Lawyer.
Son of a lawyer. Joined the Red Army, July 1919. Served until May 1927. Graduated in law from Moscow University, 1928. Worked as a lawyer in provincial towns. Returned to Moscow, 1931. In the legal department of various organizations. From 1937, in Smolensk. Remained there when the Germans occupied the city. Appointed mayor of the city of Smolensk. When the Germans retreated in Sept. 1943, he took up

the same position in Bobruisk. At the end of WWII, in Karlovy Vary, Czechoslovakia. Interned by the Americans for a short time. On 25 May 1945, went to the Soviet HQ to find out about his family's whereabouts. Arrested and brought to Lubianka prison in Moscow where he shared a cell with Beria's deputy, Mamulov. Later, the head of Soviet counter-espionage, Shteinberg, was put into his cell. Received a 25-year sentence in prisons and camps. Released in May 1970. Lived in exile in Kniazhaia Guba on the White Sea. Died in an old people's home near the town of Apatity. Left his memoirs which were published in Russian in 1988 in Paris, and which told how he had witnessed the murder of thousands of Polish officers at Katyn. Apparently the Soviet authorities had tried to get him to change his views to support the Soviet version, and when that failed, he had received his prison sentence.

Men'shoi, Adolf Grigor'evich (Gai)
1892?–1937. Journalist.
Secretary at one time to the Deputy Foreign Minister. Worked with Mayakovsky in ROSTA, 1919–20. Disappeared in the Gulag.

Men'shov, Dmitrii Evgen'evich
18.4.1892–1971? Mathematician.
Born in Moscow. Graduated from Moscow University, 1916. Professor at the same University, 1928. Works on orthogonal functions and trigonometric series.

Men'shov, Vladimir Valentinovich
17.9.1939– . Film director.
Graduated from the MKHAT Studio, 1965. Studied at the VGIK. His film *Moskva Slezam Ne Verit* (Moscow Doesn't Believe in Tears) had a huge commercial success all over the world. State Prize, 1980, Oscar, 1981.

Menzbir, Mikhail Aleksandrovich
23.10.1855–10.10.1935. Ornithologist.
Born in Tula. Graduated from Moscow University, 1878. Professor of Moscow University, 1886. Left the university, protesting against the policy of the right-wing education

minister Kasso, 1911. Professor at the Higher Courses for Women, 1911–17. After the revolution, dean of Moscow University, 1917–19. His classic work on birds of Russia and the Caucasus was published at the turn of the century. Popularized Darwinism, in his old age edited the complete works of Darwin in translation. President of the Moscow Natural Research Society, 1915–35. Academician, 1929. One of the best-known Russian zoologists. Died in Moscow.

Menzhinskii, Viacheslav Rudolfovich
19.8.1874–10.5.1934. State security chief.
Born in Petersburg. Son of a teacher at the Pages Corps, personally favoured by the Tsar. Graduated in law from Petersburg University, 1898. Early involvement in revolutionary activity. Edited the propaganda sheet for soldiers, *Kazarma*, during the 1905 Revolution. Arrested, 1906, escaped. Political emigré in Western Europe and America, returned to Russia in the summer of 1917. Bolshevik commissar at the State Bank, after the October Revolution 1917, the 1st Bolshevik Minister of Finance. Soviet General Consul in Berlin, 1918–19. From the end of 1919, one of the heads of the Cheka, assistant head of OGPU, 1923. Chairman of the GPU (Secret Police), July 1926, till his death. During his last years in office, presented the extraordinary picture of a semi-paralyzed aesthete bound to his couch, performing the job of chief henchman. Died in Moscow.

Meretskov, Kirill Afanas'evich
26.5.1897–30.12.1968. Marshal.
Born at Nazar'evo near Moscow. Son of a peasant. Joined the Bolsheviks and the Red Army, 1917. Political commissar during the Civil War. Graduated from the Military Academy, 1921. Several high military posts in the 1920s. During the Spanish Civil War, sent to Spain, 1936–37. Took part in Soviet-Finnish war, commander of the 7th army, which broke the Mannerheim line near Vyborg. Deputy Defence Minister of the USSR, 1941. Commander of the Volkhov front, 1941–44, Karelian front, 1944, Primorskii

group, 1945. In Aug. 1945, commander of the Far East Army occupying Manchuria and North Korea. Died in Moscow, buried at the Kremlin wall.

Merezhkovskii, Dmitrii Sergeevich
2.8.1866–9.12.1941. Author.
Born in Petersburg. Son of a Palace official. Graduated from Petersburg University. In the 1890s, one of the first to embrace Symbolism in Russian literature. With his wife, Z. Gippius, soon became, and remained until the Revolution 1917, one of the main literary figures in Russia during the spiritual revival of the early 20th century. Instrumental in removing the narrow-minded provincial and utilitarian populist influence from Russian literature. By organizing meetings of the Religious-Philosophical Society in Petersburg, he enabled serious dialogue to take place between the Church and the intelligentsia. Had great reformist plans for Russian religious life, preaching a vague Third Testament which would replace the Old and the New, and reconcile the Spirit with the Flesh. Warned against the 'coming kingdom of vulgarity' (Griadushchii Kham). Wrote valuable literary criticisms and historical novels (the trilogy *Christ and Antichrist*). In 1917, close to the SRs, condemned the Bolshevik take-over, fled with Gippius to Poland, 1920, and then settled in Paris, where he was responsible for creating a high-level emigré literary salon, the Green Lamp. In the 1930s, considered a rival to Bunin, but since then his literary reputation has drastically diminished. Remained a convinced anti-communist to his death. As a writer, almost forgotten, but his main achievement, the liberation of Russian spiritual life from populist and revolutionary dogmatism at the beginning of the 20th century, is indisputable. Died in Paris. Complete collection of works (up to WWI), 24 vols, Moscow, 1914.

Merezhkovskii, Konstantin Sergeevich
23.7.1855–10.1.1921. Scientist, biologist.
Born in Petersburg. Brother of the writer D. Merezhkovskii. Graduated from Petersburg University, 1880.

Professor at Kazan' University, 1902–14. Specialist on lichen and aquatic flora, infusoria and bacteria. One of the authors of the symbiogenesis theory in biology. Emigrated after the 1917 Revolution, settled in Switzerland. Died in Geneva.

Merkulov, Sergei Dmitrievich
1881–1952. Sculptor.
Began studying sculpture in Zurich at the studio of A. Meyer, then at the Academy of Arts in Munich, 1902–05, under V. Riuman. Exhibited in Moscow from 1916–52. Died in Moscow.

Merkulov, Vsevolod Nikolaevich
1900–23.12.1953. State security chief. Head of NKGB, later MGB (Ministry of State Security), 1943–50. One of the most ruthless among Stalin's henchmen. Arrested together with Beria in summer 1953. According to Soviet sources tried and executed with Dekanozov and other Beria aides by firing squad.

Meshkov, Vasilii Nikitich
6.1.1868–26.11.1946. Artist.
Portrait painter and graphic artist. Born in Elets. Studied at the Moscow School of Painting, Sculpture and Architecture (1882–89) under V. Polenov, P. Desiatov, E. Sorokin and I. Prianishnikov. Studied at the Petersburg Academy of Arts (1889–90) under P. Chistiakov. Taught at his own art school in Moscow, 1892–1917. Exhibitions from 1891. His last exhibition was in Moscow, 1943. Died in Moscow.

Meshkov, Vasilii Vasil'evich
1893–1963. Artist.
Landscape painter. Studied under his father, V. N. Meshkov, then at the Moscow School of Painting, Sculpture and Architecture, 1909–17, under A. Korin, S. Maliutin, A. Arkhipov, S. Ivanov, N. Kasatkin and K. Korovin. Exhibitions from 1909. Personal exhibitions: Moscow, 1944, 1953. Died in Moscow.

Meskhiev, Dmitrii Davydovich
25.8.1925–16.4.1983. Cameraman.
Graduated from the VGIK, 1951.

Joined the Lenfilm Studio. His most remarkable works are *The Lady With the Little Dog* and *The Gentle One* (Krotkaya — based on Dostoevskii's short story). Other films include *Zvezda Plenitel'nogo Shchast'ia*, *Sentimental'nyi Roman* and *Drama Iz Starinnoi Zhizni*.

Messerer, Asaf Mikhailovich
19.11.1903–   . Ballet dancer, choreographer.
Born in Vilnius. Graduated from the Moscow Choreographic School, 1921. Pupil of A. Gorskii. Joined the Bolshoi Theatre. Leading dancer till 1954. Choreographer from 1925. Taught from 1946. Appeared in Brussels, 1972. In Kiev, 1973. Author of *Uroki Klassicheskogo Tantsa*, 1967, and *Tanets, Mysl', Vremia*, 1979.

Messerer, Boris Asafovich
15.3.1933–   . Stage designer.
Born in Moscow. Son of Asaf Messerer. Graduated from the Moscow Institute of Architecture, 1956. Designed for drama and opera productions from 1959, in Moscow, Leningrad and elsewhere. Designed costumes for folk-dance ensembles. Work characterised by strict structural lines. Tendency towards the grotesque. Designed for many ballets from 1962–78.

Messerer, Sulamif' Mikhailovna
1909–   . Prima-ballerina, ballet teacher.
Prima-ballerina with the Bolshoi Theatre for 25 years, and for 35 years teacher of ballet. Born in the capital of Lithuania, Vilnius. Sister of the dancer and choreographer, Asaf Messerer. The prima-ballerina Maia Plisetskaia is her niece. Trained at the Moscow Choreographic School under Vasilii Tikhomirov. In 1926, became a principal dancer. In 1933, first Soviet ballerina allowed to go on tour in the West (with her brother Asaf as a partner). Performed in Paris, Berlin and Scandinavia. Defected in Tokyo in Feb. 1980, with her son Mikhail, who was a principal with the Bolshoi. Holds classes for the Royal Ballet Company, the Royal Ballet School, Sadlers Wells and Ballet Rambert. Also runs her own school in London, Dancework.

Metner, Nikolai Karlovich
5.1.1880–13.11.1951. Composer, pianist.
Born in Moscow. Studied at the Moscow Conservatory. Pupil of V. Safonov, A. Arenskii and S. Taneev. Professor of the Moscow Conservatory, 1909–10, 1915–21. Emigrated. In Berlin, 1921. Lived mainly in France, 1924–35. Concerts in the USA, England and France, 1928–30. Visited the USSR, 1927. Concerts in Moscow. Lived in London from 1936. Adherent of the classical tradition. Opposed to modernism. Composed mainly chamber music. Author of *Muza i Moda*, 1935. Died in London.

Meyendorff, Ivan Feofilovich, Baron (Meyendorff, John)
2.2.1926–   . Russian Orthodox clergyman, historian, theologian.
Born at Neuilly-sur-Seine. Son of a Russian emigré. Graduated from the Sorbonne and St. Sergius Theological Institute, Paris, in 1949. Lecturer on patristic studies at the Theological Institute, 1950–59. Priest, 1958. Professor of Patrology at St. Vladimir Seminary, NY, since 1959. Later became dean of the Seminary. Widely known as a scholar and representative of Orthodox theology in the West.
Works: *L'Eglise Orthodoxe hier et aujourd'hui*, *Orthodoxie et Catholicité*, *A Study of Gregory Palamas*, *Christ in Eastern Christian Thought*, *Orthodoxy in Life*.

Meyerhold, Vsevolod Emil'evich
1874–1941/2. Actor, stage director.
Born on his parents' estate in Penza. The eighth child of a wealthy German-Jewish family. At his birth, given the names Karl Theodor Casimir. His private tutor, the populist Kaverin, was responsible for his first revolutionary ideas. At the age of 21, joined the Russian Orthodox Church, and at his baptism given the Christian name Vsevolod, in honour of his favourite writer Vsevolod Garshin. Pupil of K. Stanislavskii and V. Nemirovich-Danchenko. Actor at the Moscow Arts Theatre, 1898–1902. Later worked in Moscow, Petersburg, and in various provincial theatres. In 1918, became a member of the Bolshevik Party. Appointed by

A. Lunacharskii to be in charge of all Moscow theatres. Head of the Petrograd branch of TEO, a theatrical section of Narkompros (The People's Commissariat for Educational Affairs). Met the actress Zinaida Raikh, at the time the wife of the poet Sergei Esenin. After their divorce, married her and made her a leading actress in his theatre. On 8 Nov. 1920, given his own theatre in Moscow — RSFSR Teatr-I, at 20 Sadovaia Street. His production of Emile Verhaeren's poems, *Dawn*, elicited a letter to *Pravda* from Lenin's wife, N. Krupskaia, who said that it was an 'insult to listen to this pompous jabbering', and called his theatre a 'mad house'. Other Soviet newspapers reacted in more or less the same way. After Krupskaia's article, the Party Cen. Cttee. closed the theatre. Meyerhold started to teach at the State Directors' Workshops. In Apr. 1922, produced, at the Sohn Operetta Theatre, *Le Cocu Magnifique*, a farce by the Belgian, F. Crommelynck. The play was accompanied by a strange orchestra of unknown instruments of all shapes and sizes (the first jazz-orchestra in the Soviet Union). In the lead was Igor Il'inskii, who produced a kind of Charlie Chaplin performance. The audiences were delirious and the play had a huge commercial success. The newspapers at first bubbled over with enthusiasm until there appeared an article by A. Lunacharskii in *Izvestia*, which called the play pornography. Immediately, other newspapers started to call Meyerhold a 'sadist', a 'mad kangaroo who has escaped from the zoo', and, more kindly, a 'dark genius'. His next play, *The Death of Tarelkin*, based on the work of the playwright A. V. Sukhovo-Kobylin, was his first serious confrontation with the cultural authorities and with the press, which was already party-controlled. In 1923, he was given another theatre, Teatr Revoliutsii, later TIM (Teatr Imeni Meyerkholda). His production there of V. Mayakovsky's play *Mystery Bouffe* pleased the authorities and marked the beginning of Soviet propaganda theatre. His prestige rocketed. Proclaimed his conception of 'Theatrical October'. Became intoxicated with his power and turned into a militant. Accused the great stage director A. Tairov of counter-revolution on the theatrical front, and of bourgeois aesthetism, charges which could have led to Tairov's arrest, and even threatened him with theatre purges. Fulminated against MKHAT but did not dare mention the name of the theatre's founder — K. Stanislavskii. Turned the classical play by A. Ostrovskii, *Forest,* into a kind of American music-hall romp. His production in early 1925 of *The Mandate* by N. Erdman was an indirect satire on Stalin and his entourage, and according to foreign press reports, nearly caused a political demonstration at its premiere. Received much praise from Kamenev and Bukharin, which was later turned against him when he was arrested. Erdman's second play, *The Suicide* (Samoubiitsa), received permission to be staged from Stalin himself after the intervention of M. Gorkii, but after 6 months of rehearsal, it was stopped by Kaganovich (obviously on Stalin's orders). From this moment on, relations between Meyerhold and Stalin became tense. Staged Mayakovsky's fairy-tale, *Klop* (The Bedbug), a witty satire. A hostile reception greeted his next play, *Khochu Rebenka* (I Want a Child), by S. M. Tretiakov, which dealt with family relationships in Soviet society. By 1928, his revolutionary enthusiasm had vanished completely. In 1930, the first performance of Mayakovsky's second play, *Bania* (The Bath), was attacked by the press, which accused him of slandering Soviet reality. In 1932, went on tour to Paris and Berlin, and according to the actor M. Chekhov, the writer's nephew, was fully aware of what his fate would be if he returned to the Soviet Union, but nevertheless refused to stay in France. This was his last trip abroad. In his theatre, he was besieged by foreigners wanting to see him. Retained a most unproletarian life-style, wearing Savile Row suites and expensive leather gloves. It was during this period that he introduced a pompous ceremonial on the lines of a royal household. Whenever he appeared at rehearsals, his deputy would call out 'Be Upstanding! the Master is Coming!' He moved about the theatre always accompanied by a massive entourage consisting of assistants, advisers, beautiful secretaries, stenographers writing down every word he said, and a young girl interpreter from Intourist for the benefit of foreigners. Had a special man (I. Varpakhovskii) to record all his productions for posterity. In the black years of his life, 1936–38, attacked by every newspaper and magazine in the country, endlessly accused and pressurized. Continued to reject official plays. Found some spiritual calm in his work *Boris Godunov.* His theatre was closed on 8 Jan. 1937, as a 'theatre alien to Soviet art', and he was literally thrown onto the street. Nobody, even his ardent admirers, could help. Only Stanislavskii, the father-figure of the Soviet theatre, extended a helping hand to his rebellious pupil. Accepted Stanislavskii's invitation to teach at his studio, and for several months was left in peace by the press. Unfortunately, Stanislavskii died soon thereafter on 6 Aug. 1938. Invited to the All-Union Directors' Conference in June 1939, and on the third day of the conference, asked to speak. The applause was continuous as he appeared on the stage. In a strong and brave speech, he condemned the persecution of the Russian theatre by the Soviet regime. Allowed to finish his speech, but 2 days later, on the night of the 17 June 1939, arrested. The last time for many years his name was mentioned in the press was on that day when I. Altman, editor-in-chief of the magazine *Teatr*, attacked Meyerhold for his speech. In Jan 1940, his biographer and friend N. D. Volkov received a post-card written in pencil and signed by Meyerhold. This was the last authenticated piece of news from him, and the stamp on the card indicated that it had been sent from one of the many Siberian camps. To this day, the exact circumstances and place of his death remain unknown.

See: Iu. Elagin, *Ukroshchenie Iskusstv* NY, 1952; Iu. Elagin, *Temnyi Genii (Vsevolod Meyerhold)*, NY, 1955.

Mezentseva, Galina Sergeevna
8.11.1952–   . Ballerina.
Born in Stavropol, now Toliatti. Graduated from the Leningrad Choreographic School, 1970. Pupil of N. V. Belikov. Afterwards with the Kirov Theatre. Soon became a leading dancer. Has appeared all over the world. 1st prize, Osaka, Japan, 1980.

Mezheninov, Sergei Aleksandrovich
1890–1937. Military commander.
Graduated from the Academy of the General Staff, 1914. Took part in WWI. Joined the Red Army, 1918. Active in the Civil War. High posts in the Soviet Air Force in the 1920s. Deputy chief-of-staff of the Red Army, 1933. Perished in Stalin's purges.

Mezheraup, Petr Khristoforovich
1895–1931. Air force officer.
On active service in WWI. Took part in the Bolshevik take-over in Moscow, 1917. Pilot in the Red Air Force in the Civil War. Commander of the air force at the Turkestan front, 1923–26. Died in an air crash.

Mezrina, Anna Afanas'evna
1853–21.8.1938. Toy artist.
Born in Dymkovo near Viatka. Became famous as the maker of colourful painted clay folklore figures of people and animals, known as the Dymkovo toys. Lived all her life and died in Dymkovo (now part of Kirov).

Miakotin, Venedikt Aleksandrovich
1867–1937. Historian, sociologist.
Born at Gatchina. Graduated from Petersburg University. Taught at the Aleksandrovskii Lyceé, 1891–1901. Editor of the magazine *Russkoe Bogatstvo*, 1904. One of the leaders of the People's Socialist Party (narodnye sotsialisty). Active participant in the February Revolution 1917, but condemned the Bolshevik take-over, October 1917. Member of the anticommunist Soiuz Vozrozhdeniia Rossii, 1918. Emigrated, 1918, lived in Czechoslovakia. Continued to write in Russian emigré publications. Died in Prague.

Miasishchev, Vladimir Mikhailovich
1902–1978. Aircraft designer.
Graduated from the Moscow Higher Technical Institute, 1926. Worked with Tupolev, 1936. Chief designer in an aircraft works during WWII. Head of TSAGI, 1960–67. Designed many of the Soviet Union's long-distance bombers.

Miaskovskii, Nikolai Iakovlevich
20.4.1881–8.8.1950. Composer.
Born near Warsaw. Grew up in Orenburg, Kazan' and Novgorod. Graduated from the School of Military Engineering, 1902. First compositions, 1896–98. Graduated from the Petersburg Conservatory, 1911. Pupil of N. Rimskii-Korsakov and A. Liadov. In the army, 1914–18. Professor at the Moscow Conservatory from 1926 to the end of his life. Composed many symphonies and works for chamber music ensembles. Died in Moscow.

Miasnikov, Aleksandr Fedorovich (Miasnikian)
1886–1925. Politician.
Joined the Bolshevik Party, 1906. Graduated from Moscow University in law, 1911. During the October Revolution, Bolshevik organizer in the army, 1917. Commander of the armies of the Western front, Nov. 1917. Commander of the Volga front against the Czech legions, 1919. Chairman of the Executive Cttee. of Belorussia, and of the Central Bureau of the Belorussian Communist Party, 1919. Secretary of the Moscow Party Cttee., and head of the Political Administration of the Western Front, 1919–20. Head of the Revolutionary Committee, later Council of People's Commissars of Armenia, 1921. Deputy head of the government of the Transcaucasian Federation, 1921. 1st secretary of the Transcaucasian Bolshevik Kraikom. Died in an air crash.

Miasnikov, G.I.
1889–1946. Politician.
Member of the Bolshevik Party from 1906. Member of the Workers Opposition, 1921–22. Expelled from the party for publishing, without official approval, a brochure demanding democratization. One of the founders and leaders of the Workers Group (which included communists and non-communists). In the Manifesto to the Workers Group (1923), demanded the abolition of NEP (Lenin's New Economic Policy), because it favoured peasants against workers. In summer 1923, tried to organize strikes. Arrested, 1923, and exiled to Baku, later emigrated. After WWII, returned to USSR, arrested and perished in the Gulag.

Miasnikov, Gennadii Alekseevich
12.9.1919– . Stage designer.
Graduated from the Perm' Art School, 1938, and from the VGIK, 1943. With M. Bogdanov, worked in several films, including *War and Peace*, their major work which took 5 years. From 1943, taught at the VGIK. Professor from 1976.

Miasnikova, Lidia Vladimirovna
21.9.1911– . Singer (mezzo soprano).
Born in Tomsk. Pupil of M. Brian. Leading singer with the Theatre of Opera and Ballet in Novosibirsk from 1944.

Michurin, Gennadii Mikhailovich
3.9.1897–12.10.1970. Actor.
Actor at the Leningrad Bolshoi Drama Theatre until 1945. Entered the film industry, 1924. Became famous for his portrayal of Dmitrii Karakozov, the terrorist, in *Dvorets i Krepost'*. Made some 40 films including *Moi Syn*, 1928, *Zolotoi Kliuv*, 1929, *Goroda i Gody*, 1930, and *Zakliuchennye*, 1936 (all directed by E. V. Cherviakov). Other films include *Poet i Tsar* and *Dekabristy*, both 1927.

Michurin, Ivan Vladimirovich
27.10.1855–7.6.1935. Plant breeder.
Born in Vershina (now Michurino), near Riazan'. Son of a land-owner. Amateur plant breeder who, through skilful crossing, created a number of varieties of fruit trees suitable to the climate of Central Russia. Started his experiments in 1875. Basing his approach on theories of inheriting acquired characteristics, totally ignored modern genetics. His approach was adopted later by Lysenko and developed into a complete progressive Michurinist biology, which in the Stalin decades become the official line in biology, an excuse for terror against scientists, causing Soviet backwardness in this field. In his old age, and posthumously, became a Stalinist cult figure. Many books and films were devoted to him. The town of Kozlov (founded 1636), where he had lived and died, was re-named Michurinsk, 1932.
Main works: *Collected works*, 4 vols, Moscow, 1948.

271

Middleton, Sybil, Lady (b. Lady Sybil Grey)

1882–6.1966. Social and Red Cross worker.

Born in Northumberland. The eldest daughter of the 4th Earl Grey, once Governor-general of Canada. With no professional qualifications, aged 33, accepted an invitation from Sir George Buchanan, the English Ambassador in St. Petersburg to go there and organize an Anglo-Russian hospital and 2 or 3 field hospitals to treat wounded Russian soldiers, and to be in charge of English doctors, nurses and other medical staff. Took charge of the Anglo-Russian Hospital in Nov. 1915, and worked through a very harsh winter. Suppressed a near mutiny of the medical and nursing staff, and sacked the hospital commandant. Severely wounded in the face at Voropaevo by a fragment of shrapnel. Went back to England for medical treatment, but returned to Russia 3 months later. Her hospital received a blessing from the Tsarina, and her photograph with the Grand Duchess Marie Pavlovna appeared in the *London Sketch*. She accepted both the Reds and the Whites to her hospital which was housed in a palace lent by the Grand Duke Dimitrii Pavlovich. On the night of Rasputin's murder the Grand Duke gave Sybil the key to a door which led from the hospital to his private flat, where Prince Yusupov was hiding from the police. Watched the February Revolution 1917 from the hospital windows. Became a close friend of both the Tsar and the Tsarina until the family's arrest, 1917. At the end of July 1917, returned to England. Her work and life in Russia has been described in full detail in *The Forgotten Hospital* by Michael Harmer, London, 1982. Died in the New Forest, Hampshire.

Midler, Mark Petrovich

24.9.1931– . Athlete.

Born in Moscow. Honoured Master of Sports (fencing), 1958. With the Moscow Central Sports Club of the Army. Graduated from the Moscow Institute of Physical Culture, 1953. Honorary coach of the USSR. USSR champion, 1954–65. World champion with his team 1959, 1961–63 and 1965–66. Olympic champion, 1960 and 1964. Member of the CPSU, 1968.

Mikeshin, Boris Mikhailovich

1873–1937. Sculptor.

Son of the sculptor and painter M.O. Mikeshin. Created several monuments (*Mikhail Lermontov* in Petersburg, *Fallen Soldiers* in Karsk). Exhibitions: Spring Exhibition at the Academy of Arts (1909–11, 1913–14, 1916), 125th Anniversary of Mikhail Lermontov, Leningrad, 1941.

Mikhail (Chub, Mikhail Andreevich), Archbishop of Tambov and Michurinsk

18.2.1912–25.4.1985. Russian Orthodox clergyman.

Born at Tsarskoe Selo (now Pushkin). Son of a deacon. Graduated at the Institute of Foreign Languages, 1940. Taught foreign languages at military schools during WWII. Graduated from the Leningrad Theological Academy, 1950. Priest, June 1950. Professor of the Leningrad Theological Academy, 1950–53. Bishop of Luga, 1953. Closely connected with the New Valaam monastery in Finland. Bishop of Smolensk, 1955. Bishop of Izhevsk, 1959, of Tambov, 1962. Archbishop, 1965, served in Krasnodar, Voronezh and Vologda. Archbishop of Tambov, 1974–85. Highly regarded as a theologian and church historian. Wrote on the Qumran manuscripts and on Russian saints. Buried at Tambov.

Mikhail (Ermakov), Metropolitan of Kiev

1876?–1929. Russian Orthodox clergyman, theologian.

Professor at the Volhynia Seminary and the Petersburg Theological Academy. Bishop of Omsk. Archbishop of Grodno. Member of the Holy Synod. Exarch of the Patriarch of Moscow in the Ukraine, 1921. Actively resisted the various schisms of the 1920s. Arrested, 1922, and exiled, 1923. Released but re-arrested in 1925, and exiled to the Caucasus. Returned to Khar'kov, 1927. Later moved to Kiev where he died.

Mikhail Aleksandrovich (Romanov)

4.12.1878–13.7.1918. Grand Duke.

Younger brother of Tsar Nicholas II. Official heir to the throne before the birth of Tsarevich Aleksei, 1904. After his morganatic marriage to Countess Brasova, lost his succession

rights and was practically exiled (lived in England). Returned to Russia, 1914, in order to serve in the Russian Army during WWI (inspector of cavalry). On his abdication, Feb. 1917, Nicholas II renounced his rights and the rights of his son in favour of his brother (without prior consultation with him). At a meeting with prominent members of the Duma, advised by all except Miliukov, the Cadet leader, not to accept the succession. Decided not to accept the throne without a formal confirmation of the succession by the people's representatives. After the February Revolution 1917, withdrew from state affairs. Arrested in Gatchina, brought to Perm', and shot by Bolsheviks.

Mikhailichenko, Irina Gavrilovna

6.12.1921–1977. Ballerina.

Born in Baku. Graduated from the Baku Choreographic School, 1939. Dancer at the Abai Theatre from 1940. Leading ballerina at the same theatre from 1953. Taught at the Odessa Theatre from 1965. Coached at the Velki Theatre, and taught choreography at the Warsaw School, 1967–69. Died in Baku.

Mikhailov, Aleksandr Aleksandrovich

26.4.1888–1969? Astronomer.

Graduated from Moscow University, 1911. Professor at the University, 1918–48. Director of Pulkovo Observatory, 1947. Vice-president of the International Astronomical Union, 1946–48. Specialist on solar eclipses. Edited stellar atlases.

Mikhailov, Boris Petrovich

6.10.1944– . Athlete.

Born in Moscow. Honoured Master of Sports (hockey), 1969. With the Moscow Central Sports Club of the Army. Member of the CPSU, 1971. USSR champion, 1968–79. European champion, 1969–79. World champion, 1969–79. Olympic champion, 1972 and 1976. From 1973, captain of the USSR international team. Graduated from the Moscow Oblast' Institute of Physical Culture, 1979.

Mikhailov, Iurii Matveevich

25.7.1930– . Athlete.

Born in Kalinin. Honoured Master of

Sports (skating), 1956. USSR champion, 1956. World record-holder, 1956. Olympic champion, 1956 (1,500m race). From 1957, with Kalinin Lokomotiv.

Mikhailov, Konstantin Nikolaevich
29.12.1882–3.4.1961. Pianist.
Born in Chernigov Gouvt. Pupil of V. Pukhal'skii. Professor from 1917. Principal of the Kiev Conservatory, 1922–26, vice-principal 1926–53. His pupils included V. Vronskaia, P. Vidkup, L. Vaintraub, M. Polliak and V. Sechkin. Died in Kiev.

Mikhailov, Maksim Dormidontovich
25.8.1893–after 1956. Singer (bass).
Born in Kazan' Gouvt. Pupil of F. Oshustovich and V. Osipov. Soloist with the All-Union Radio Committee, 1930–32. Leading singer with the Bolshoi Theatre from 1932. State Prize of the USSR, 1941, 1942.

Mikhailov, Mikhail Ermilovich
1884–1959. Lt.-general.
Joined the Red Army and the Communist Party, 1918. Commander of a regiment in Central Asia fighting against local anti-communists in the 1920s. Graduated from the Frunze Military Academy, 1935. During WWII, deputy commander of the Karelian front, 1941–44. Commander of the rear of the strategic air force, 1946–47.

Mikhailov, Mikhail Mikhailovich
18.8.1903–2.2.1979. Ballet dancer.
Born in Petersburg. Graduated from the Petrograd Choreographic School, 1921. Pupil of A. I. Chekrygin and A. V. Shiriaev. With the Kirov Theatre, 1921–59. Graduated from the Academy of Dramatic Art, 1931. Member of the Petrograd Young Ballet. Taught at the Leningrad Choreographic School, 1947–62. Appeared in character parts in show-business. Memoirs: *Zhizn' v Balete*, 1966. Died in Leningrad.

Mikhailov, Nikolai Nikolaevich
9.8.1902–   . Musicologist.
Born in Odessa. Reader at the Kiev Conservatory. Author of many articles and pamphlets on Ukrainian composers.

Mikhailov, Vasilii Mikhailovich
1894–26.9.1937. Revolutionary, politician.
Born in Moscow. Son of a printer. Worked at the Sytin Publishing House. Joined the Bolshevik Party, 1915. Head of the Moscow Cheka, 1917. During the Civil War, political officer in the Red Army. Secretary of the Cen. Cttee. of the Bolsheviks, 1921–22, and of the Moscow Cttee. of the Party, 1922–23 and 1925–29. Deputy head of the construction of Dneproges (built by slave-labour), 1929. Appointed chief of the construction of the Palace of Soviets (planned for the site of the demolished Christ the Saviour Cathedral, the largest church in Moscow), which was never built. Arrested, 1936, and died in the Gulag.

Mikhailovskaia, Liudmila Nikolaevna (Makarova)
21.11.1937–   . Athlete.
Born in Leningrad. Honoured Master of Sports (volley-ball), 1967. With Leningrad Burevestnik. Graduated from the School of Sports Instructors, 1967. USSR champion, 1959. World champion, 1960 and 1970. European champion, 1963 and 1971. Olympic champion, 1968.

Mikhal'chenko, Alla Anatol'evna
2.7.1957–   . Ballerina.
Born in Moscow. Graduated from the Moscow Choreographic School, 1976. Pupil of S. N. Golovkina. Dancer with the Bolshoi Theatre on graduating. Appeared abroad. Laureate, 1st prize at the All-Soviet Competition for Choreographers and Ballet Dancers, 1976. Distinction, 1st class, at the International Competitions of Ballet Dancers in Varna, Bulgaria, 1976, and 1st prize in Mowcow, 1977.

Mikhal'chuk, Viktor Il'ich
5.2.1946–   . Athlete.
Born in Bernau. Honoured Master of Sports (volley-ball), 1968. With Odessa Burevestnik. Graduated from the Odessa Polytechnical Institute, 1971, and from the Odessa Pedagogical Institute, 1976. European and USSR champion, 1967. Olympic champion, 1968.

Mikhalkov, Nikita Sergeevich
21.10.1945–   . Film director, actor.
Born in Moscow. Son of the poet S. Mikhalkov and brother of Andron Mikhalkov-Konchalovskii. Graduated from the VGIK, 1971. Pupil of M. Romm. Started as an actor in *Ia Shagaiu po Moskve*, 1963, and *Krasnaia Palatka*, 1970. Turned to directing while still acting. Directorial debut, 1971. In 1980, filmed *Neskol'ko Dnei iz Zhizni Oblomova*, with Oleg Tabakov in the leading role. The film was shown all over the world with great success. Made a superb adaptation of A. Chekhov's short stories *Chernye Glaza* (Dark Eyes), which was shown at the 1987 Cannes Film Festival. Attracted enormous attention from the international press. Marcello Mastroianni, who played the leading part, received the Best Actor award.

Mikhalkov, Sergei Vasil'evich
13.3.1913–   . Poet, journalist.
Born in Moscow. Studied at the Gorkii Literary Institute, 1935–37. During WWII, correspondent at the front. Member of the CPSU, 1950. Became known for his children's verse and satires. Also known for his complete conformism and cynicism. Author of the Soviet national anthem. Has held many high administrative posts in the Union of Writers.

Mikhalkov-Konchalovskii, Andron Sergeevich
20.8.1937–   . Film-maker.
Son of the poet S. Mikhalkov and the author N. Konchalovskaia. Graduated from the VGIK, 1965. Pupil of M. Romm. A. Tarkovskii's co-scriptwriter on his first two films — *The Steamroller and the Violin*, 1961, and *Andrei Rublev*. His first full-length feature film, *The First Teacher*, 1965, was shown all over the world. Now regarded as a modern classic. His second film, *Asya's Happiness*, was banned shortly after its release in 1966. Later, under Gorbachev, it was re-released. Specialises in adaptations of the Russian classics. *A Nest of*

Gentlefolk (after I. Turgenev) received national acclaim, as did his adaptation of *Uncle Vanya* in 1970. His leading actress on *The First Teacher*, Natalia Arinbasarova, later became his wife. Divorced her for a Frenchwoman who was employed in the French Embassy. Lived between Paris and Moscow. Later moved to Hollywood, keeping his Soviet film-maker's status. Made *Maria's Lovers*, with Natassia Kinski in the leading role. Also filmed *Duet For One*, with Julie Andrews. Now lives between Los Angeles, Paris and Moscow.

Mikhnevich, Nikolai Petrovich
1849–1927. General.
On active service during the Russo-Turkish war, 1877–78. Graduated from the Academy of the General Staff, 1882. Professor of the Academy, 1892. Director of the Academy of the General Staff, 1904–07. Staff officer, 1911–17. Joined the Red Army, 1918. Known as a writer on military theory and history. Professor at the Artillery Academy of the Red Army, 1918–25.

Mikhoels, Solomon Mikhailovich (real name – Vovsi)
16.3.1890–13.1.1948. Actor, director.
Born in Dvinsk. Founded the Jewish Theatre in Moscow, 1925. Worked as a stage producer and actor, appearing in many classical Jewish plays. As an actor, his best performance was in the 1935 production of *King Lear*. From the mid–1930s, taught at the school of the Moscow Jewish Theatre, professor, 1941. Killed in Minsk on Stalin's orders by secret police agents, with the murder being reported as an accident.
See: *Korol' Lir v Moskovskom Gosudarstvennom Evreiskom Teatre*, Moscow, 1935; *Mikhoels*, Moscow, 1948; N. Mikhoels-Vovsi, *Moi Otets Solomon Mikhoels*, Israel, 1984.

Mikhoels-Vovsi, Natal'ia Solomonovna
1921–   . Translator, author.
Born in Moscow. Daughter of Solomon Mikhoels. Graduated from the Moscow Foreign Languages Institute. Published some translations in the Soviet press. Left the USSR, 1972. Settled in Israel. Wrote her

memoirs disclosing the details of her father's murder.
Works: *Moi Otets Solomon Mikhoels: Vospominaniia O Zhizni i Gibeli*, Israel, 1984; *Ubiistvo Mikhoelsa, Vremia i My*, Israel-NY, 1976.

Miklashevskii, Konstantin Mikhailovich
1886–1944. Playwright.
Master of commedia dell'arte. In 1917, published *Teatr Ital'ianskikh Komediantov*, reviewed by Osip Brik in *Novaia Zhizn'*. Member of the historico-theatrical section of the TEO Narkompros, 1918. Emigrated, 1922.

Mikoian, Anastas Ivanovich
25.11.1895–21.10.1978. Politician.
Born in the village of Sanain in Armenia. Joined the Bolshevik Party, 1915. Educated at the Armenian seminary in Tbilisi, and at the Echmiadzin Theological Academy. After the February Revolution 1917, full-time Bolshevik organizer in the Caucasus (Echmiadzin, Tbilisi, Baku). During the Civil War, leader of underground communist organizations in Baku, arrested together with 26 Baku commissars who were shot, but Mikoian escaped unharmed. From this moment until his death, earned a reputation as the most durable survivor in the communist leadership, surviving the Stalin purges, and remaining among the top leadership with Khrushchev and later Brezhnev. In the 1920s, party functionary in Nizhnii Novgorod (Gorkii), Rostov-on-Don, and the Northern Caucasus. Member of the Cen. Cttee. of the Bolshevik Party from 1923. Minister of Trade of the USSR, 1926–30, Minister of Supplies, 1930–34, Minister of the Food Industry, 1934–38. Member of the Politburo from 1935. Deputy Prime Minister of the USSR, 1937–55, and Minister of Foreign Trade, 1938–49. During WWII, chairman of the Cttee. of Supplies for the Red Army. 1st Deputy Prime Minister 1955–64. Minister of Trade, 1953–55. Close ally of Khrushchev, but it was he who rang Khrushchev at his Crimean holiday dacha, summoning him to come to Moscow to be dismissed.

Promoted to head of state, 1964–65. Highly decorated (5 Orders of Lenin). Wrote several volumes of memoirs on his career, stretching from Lenin to Brezhnev. In 1988, his son Sergo was the first among the children of the Old Bolsheviks to acknowledge the guilt of their parents in the tragic events of Russian history in the 20th century.

Mikoian, Artem Ivanovich
5.8.1905–9.12.1970. Aircraft designer.
Born at Sanain, Armenia. Brother of Anastas Mikoian. Metal worker in Rostov-on-Don. Graduated from the Zhukovskii Air Force Academy, 1936. Together with M. Gurevich, developed the MIG (Mikoian-Gurevich) fighter aircraft series, which became the main Soviet fighter plane (MIG–1, 1940, to MIG–21). Highly decorated (6 state awards). Academician, 1968.

Mikulin, Aleksandr Aleksandrovich
2.2.1895–1985. Aviation designer, academician.
Born in Vladimir. Started to design car engines, 1923. Aircraft engine designer, 1929. His engines were installed in the aircraft in which Chkalov flew over the North Pole to the USA in 1937. His engine, the AM–35A, was installed in MIG fighter planes, 1939. After WWII, designer of some of the most important Soviet jet engines (for the TU–104 and other planes). Died in Moscow.

Mil', Mikhail Leont'evich
1909–1970. Helicopter designer.
Graduated from the Novocherkassk Aviation Institute, 1931. From the mid–1930s till his death, involved in the construction of helicopters (Mi-series and others). The foremost Soviet authority in his field.

Miliukov, Pavel Nikolaevich
27.1.1859–31.3.1943. Politician, historian, editor.
Born in Moscow. Son of an architect. Graduated from Moscow University in 1882. Exiled to Riazan' for revolutionary activity, 1894–97. Taught and lectured abroad (Bulgaria, USA) from 1897. Returned to

Russia in 1905. One of the founders and leaders of the Cadet Party. Editor of the party newspaper *Rech'* (Speech), 1907. Prominent member of the 3rd and 4th Dumas. Leader of the Progressive Bloc, the main architect of centre-left wing unity in the Duma. By his own admission, started the revolutionary process, 1916, by his Duma speech ('treason or stupidity') obliquely attacking the Empress and her circle (quoting Western newspaper reports of alleged separate peace negotiations between Russia and Germany, which were false and actually inspired by Radek). The speech was censored in the official Duma report, but gained universal unofficial distribution, creating a sensation. After the abdication of Nicholas II, was the only statesman to urge Grand Duke Mikhail to accept the throne (according to the abdication document), warning of approaching chaos. Minister of Foreign Affairs in the Provisional Government, resigned after Bolshevik-inspired demonstrations. Emigrated, 1920, settled in France. Edited the influential left-wing daily *Poslednie Novosti*. Considered the leader of the left-of-centre Russian émigrés. During WWII, took a pro-Soviet position. Extremely prolific historical and political writer in the liberal positivist mould. His *Ocherki po Istorii Russkoi Kul'tury*, 1898 (and further editions) was the handbook of the Russian intelligentsia. A dynamic participant in, and historian of, early 20th century Russian political life. Died in Aix-le-Bel, Savoie, France.

Miliutin, Georgii (Iurii) Sergeevich
18.4.1903–9.6.1968. Composer, pianist.
Born in Moscow. Studied with Professor Kossovskii, 1917. Further training at the Technical School for Music, Moscow Oblast', 1929–30. Pupil of Vasilenko and A. Aleksandrov. Actor at the Drama Theatre, 1919–23. Pianist and composer with the variety collective, Siniaia Bluza, 1924–25. Worked for many Moscow theatres, and in films from 1935. In later years, composed mainly operettas. Died in Moscow.

Miliutin, Vladimir
1884–1937. Politician.
Member of the SD Party. After the split, joined the Mensheviks. Changed over to the Bolsheviks, 1910. Commissar of Agriculture in the first Soviet government, 1918. Worked in the Comintern, 1922–24, and held several important posts in the 1920s and 1930s. Liquidated by Stalin.

Miller, Evgenii Karlovich
7.10.1867–1937? General.
Born in Dvinsk. Educated at the Nikolaevskii Cadet Corps, 1884, and at the Cavalry School, 1886. Served in the Life Guard Hussars. Graduated from the Nikolaevskoe Military Academy in 1892. Military attaché in Belgium, Holland and Italy, 1898–1907. Head of the Nikolaevskoe Cavalry School, 1910–12. Chief-of-staff of the Moscow military district in 1912. Lt.-general, took part in WWI. During the February Revolution 1917, wounded by revolutionary soldiers. Representative of the Russian High Command with the Italian Army, autumn 1917. Invited by the local anti-Bolshevik government of Arkhangelsk under Nikolai Chaikovskii, the veteran revolutionary, to command the local forces allied to the British Expeditionary Corps (sent to guard British war supplies delivered to Russia). Appointed head of the Northern front forces by Admiral Kolchak in 1919. After the British left Arkhangelsk, tried to continue the fight against the Reds alone. Defeated, he evacuated the rest of his forces in Feb. 1920. In France, appointed by General Wrangel as his chief-of-staff. Later became the deputy of General Kutepov in the leadership of the White Civil War Veterans (ROVS). Head of ROVS after Kutepov's kidnapping in Paris by Soviet agents in 1930. Disappeared himself the same way 7 years later in Paris, 22 Sept. 1937. Presumably killed by his kidnappers soon thereafter.

Miller, Mikhail Aleksandrovich
1881?–1968. Historian.
Specialized in the ancient history of the Don and Azov region. Conducted archaeological expeditions, with his brother A. Miller, in the 1920s. Several of his monographs were published in Rostov, and by the Soviet Academy of Sciences. During and after WWII, in German and DP camps in West Germany. In the late 1950s and early 1960s, published his main work, *Don i Priazov'e v Drevnosti*, 3 vol., Munich. Died in Munich.

Mil'man, Mark Vladimirovich
3.5.1910– . Composer, pianist.
Born in Moscow. Professor at the Moscow Conservatory. Author of a symphony, sonatas, and music for stage and radio.

Mil'ner, Mikhail Arnol'dovich
29.12.1886–25.10.1953. Composer, conductor.
Born in Kiev Gouvt. Musical director of the Jewish Theatre in Moscow, 1924–25. In Khar'kov, 1929–31. Artistic director of the Jewish Vocal Ensemble in Leningrad, 1931–41. Author of operas, sonatas, and music for the stage. Died in Leningrad.

Miloradovich, Sergei Dmitrievich
1852–1942. Artist.
Studied water-colour techniques at the Stroganov School of Graphical Arts under F. Iasnovskii, Moscow, 1874. Then at the Moscow School of Painting, Sculpture and Architecture (1874–78) under V. Perov, I. Prianishnikov, P. Desiatov, and P. Sorokin. Historical and genre painter. Exhibitions: from 1880 at the Moscow School of Painting, Sculpture and Architecture, TPKHV (1885, 1889, 1891, 1894, 1896–1907, 1907–14, 1916–18, 1922–23), MOLKH (1887, 1889–90, 1908, 1911), the Academy of Arts (1890), the All-Russian Exhibition, Nizhnii Novgorod, 1896. Taught at the Moscow School of Painting, Sculpture and Architecture. Emigrated to France after the October Revolution 1917.

Milorava, Shota Ermolaevich
22.1.1925– . Composer.
Born in Tiflis. Author of comic operas, choral music, romances, and music for the theatre and variety stage.

Mil'shtein, Iakov Isaakovich
4.2.1911– . Pianist, musicologist.
Born in Voronezh, Pupil of K.

Igumnov. Professor at the Moscow Conservatory. His pupils include E. Leonskaia, and M. Mdivani. Author of *F. Liszt*, 2 vol., Moscow, 1956.

Mil'shtein, Natan Mironovich (Milstein, Nathan)
31.12.1904– . Violinist.
Born in Odessa. Pupil of P. Stoliarskii, L. Auer, and E. Ysaye. Appeared as a concert violinist, 1920–25. Emigrated 1925. In the USA from 1928. Author of *Paganiniana* and other arrangements for violin.

Minaev, Evgenii Gavrilovich
21.5.1933– . Athlete.
Born in Klin, Moscow Oblast'. Honoured Master of Sports (heavy athletics), 1957. With the Moscow Armed Forces Club. USSR champion, 1957–66. World record-holder, 1956–61. World champion, 1957 and 1962. European champion, 1958, 1960–62. Olympic champion, 1960 at feather weight (372.5kg). Graduated from the Higher School of Sports Instructors of the Moscow Institute of Physical Culture, 1962.

Minaicheva, Galina Iakovlevna (Sharabidze)
29.12.1929– . Athlete.
Born in Moscow of a Georgian father. Honoured Master of Sports (gymnastics), 1952. With Moscow Dynamo. Graduated from the Georgian Institute of Physical Culture, 1957. Worked as a sports instructor. USSR champion, 1952. Olympic champion, 1952. World champion, 1954. Silver and bronze medals, 1952.

Minakov, Petr Andreevich
7.12.1865–5.10.1931. Medical expert.
Born in the village of Deriugino near Kursk. Graduated in medicine from Moscow University, 1891. Worked as a medical expert in the courts from 1900. Vice-dean of Moscow University, 1909. Resigned in protest against the policies of the education minister, Kasso, 1911. Again professor at Moscow University, 1917–31. Specialist on the mummification of bodies, involved in the mummification of V. Lenin's corpse for exhibition in the Mausoleum in Moscow.

Min'iar – Beloruchev, Konstantin Aleksandrovich (real name – Zheltobriukhov)
10.10.1874–10.1.1944. Cellist.
Born in Warsaw Gouvt. Pupil of A. Glen. Professor at the Tbilisi Conservatory. His pupils include A. Aivazian, G. Barnabishvili, R. Garbuzova and G. Tsomyk. Author of instrumental music, and pieces for cello. Died in Tbilisi.

Minkh, Nikolai Grigor'evich
15.3.1912– . Composer, conductor.
Born in Saratov. Worked in Moscow. Author of comic operas, and music for the theatre and variety stage.

Minorskii, Vladimir Fedorovich
5.2.1877–25.3.1966. Orientalist.
Born at Korchev on the Volga. Graduated in law from Moscow University, 1900, and from the Lazarevskii Institute of Oriental Languages, 1903. Diplomat in Iran and Turkey from 1903. Remained abroad as an emigré after 1917. Lived in Iran, 1917–19, and France, 1919–32. Moved to Britain, 1932. Professor at London University, 1937. Died at Cambridge.

Minskii, Nikolai Maksimovich (Vilenkin)
27.1.1855–2.7.1937. Author, poet.
Born in Glubokoe near Vitebsk. Graduated in law from Petersburg University, 1879. Published the first decadent declaration in Russian literature, 1884. Involved with the Bolsheviks at the beginning of the 20th century, but was later criticized by Lenin. After the October Revolution 1917, emigrated. Lived in Berlin, London and Paris. Died in Paris.

Mints, Aleksandr L'vovich
1895–1974. Nuclear scientist.
Graduated from Don University, 1918. Took part in the Civil War. Specialized in radio-communication. Professor at the Leningrad Communications Engineers' Institute, 1934. Director of the Radiotechnical Institute of the Academy of Sciences, 1957–70. In the 1960–70s, in charge of several important nuclear research programmes, including the building of the nuclear research station at Serpukhov.

Mints, Isaak Izrailevich
1896–1976. Political officer, historian.
Joined the Communist Party, 1917. Took part in the Civil War as a political commissar. Graduated from the Institute of Red Professors, 1926. After that, taught Marxism and history at the Higher Party School of the Cen. Cttee. of the Bolshevik Party (theoretical training for high party cadres), and at other educational establishments. Academician, 1946. Actively involved in the Stalinist distortions of history (now acknowledged as such in the Soviet Union). Chairman of the Scientific Council of the Academy of Sciences for historical research on the October Revolution 1917. Highly decorated (3 State Prizes).

Mintslov, Sergei Rudolfovich
13.1.1870–18.12.1933. Bibliographer, author.
Born in Riazan'. Graduated from the Archaeological Institute in Nizhnii Novgorod. Published a number of bibliographical works, including the monumental bibliography of Russian memoirs before 1900 (about 5,000 titles, 5 volumes, published in Novgorod, 1911–12). After the February Revolution 1917, moved to Finland. Died in Riga, Latvia.

Mironov, Filipp Kuz'mich
26.10.1872–2.4.1921. Revolutionary.
Born at Ust' Medveditskaia. Graduated from a Cossack military school, 1898. On active service during WWI as a deputy regimental commander. Elected commander of a Don Cossack regiment, 1917. Joined the Red Army, 1918, one of the organizers of Red Cossack forces. Commander of the 2nd Cavalry Army during the Civil War. Protested against the communist terror campaign in the Don region. Arrested by Trotsky. Shot in Butyrki prison in Moscow as a rebel against Soviet rule. For a long time, unmentionable in the Soviet Union. Rehabilitated. Recently used as the hero of a novel by Iu. Trifonov.

Mironov, Nikolai Nazarovich
22.9.1870–6.7.1952. Musician, ethnographer, composer.
Born in Samarkand Gouvt. His

works include 2 musical dramas. Also wrote literary works, 1929–32, on the music of Eastern peoples. Died in Moscow.

Mironova, Zoia Sergeevna
10.5.1913–   . Surgeon, athlete, sports official.
Born in Moscow. During the 1930s, many times skating champion of Moscow and the USSR. Honoured Master of Sports (skating), 1934. Graduated from the 1st Moscow Medical Institute, specialising in sports injuries, 1940. Surgeon, 1940–1952, and from 1953 head of the Sports and Ballet Injuries Department of the Central Institute of Traumatism and Orthopedy. Chief traumatologist with the Soviet team at the Olympic Games, 1952–76. Author of many medical articles on this subject. Member of the CPSU, 1961. Professor of Sports Medicine from 1967. Member of the USSR Olympic Cttee. from 1974. Member of the Executive Cttee. of the International Association of Olympic Medical Workers from 1974. Author of *Profilaktika i Lechenie Sportivnykh Travm*, 1965, *Sportivnaia Travmatologiia*, 1976, *Vozvrashchenie Chempiona*, 1976 (memoirs), and *Vmesto Vybyvshego Iz Igry*, Moscow, 1970. Awarded the Philipp Noel-Baker Prize by the International Union of Physical Education and Sport, 1975.

Miroshnichenko, Evgenia Semenovna
12.6.1931–   . Singer.
Born in Khar'kov Oblast'. Pupil of M. Donets-Tesseir. 2nd prize at the International Competition in Toulouse, 1958. Leading singer at the Kiev Theatre of Opera and Ballet from 1957.

Mirtskhulava, Didim Lavrent'evich
2.8.1912–   . Conductor.
Born in Georgia. Graduated from the Tbilisi Conservatory in 1937, and joined the Paliashvili Theatre. Taught at the Tbilisi Conservatory from 1951. Professorship in 1970.

Mirzoian, Edvard Mikhailovich
12.5.1921–   . Composer.
Born in Gori. Son of the composer

M. Mirzoian (1888–1958). Graduated from the Erevan Conservatory, 1941. Pupil of S. Barkhudarian and V. Tal'ian. In the army, Mar.–Nov. 1942. Studied at the musical studio of the House of Armenian Culture, 1946. Pupil of G. Litinskii, V. Tsukerman, N. Peiko and N. Rakov. Returned to Erevan, 1948. Taught composition at the Erevan Conservatory from 1949. Professor from 1965. Influenced by Armenian folk music.

Mishakov, Evgenii Dmitrievich
22.2.1941–   . Athlete.
Born in the village of Nikitkino, Moscow Oblast'. Honoured Master of Sports (hockey), 1968. Member of the CPSU, 1970. With the Central Sports Club of the Army. Graduated from the Moscow Oblast' Institute of Physical Culture, 1976. Coach. USSR champion, 1965–73. European champion, 1968–70. World champion, 1968–71. Olympic champion, 1968 and 1972.

Mishuga, Aleksandr Filippovich (pseudonym – Filippi-Mishuga)
19.6.1853–9.3.1922. Singer (tenor)
Born near L'vov. Appeared in opera in Western Europe and Russia from 1883. Taught at the N. Lysenko Drama School, Kiev, and later in Warsaw and Stockholm. His pupils include M. Mikisha, S. Mirovich, A. Kil'chevskaia and L. Ulukhanova. Emigrated, 1921. Died in Freiburg.

Mitaisvili, Liliana Iraklievna
13.9.1937–   . Ballerina.
Born in Gori, Georgia. Graduated from the Tbilisi Choreographic School, 1954. A pupil of V.M. Chabukiani. With the Paliashvili Theatre since 1955.

Mitiunov, Iurii
1950?–   . Dissident.
An official spokesman and one of the founding members of the Democratic Union, a new dissident opposition party. Told Western journalists in early May 1988 that the party's platform called for a new Soviet constitution that would allow for a multi-party system and parliamentary democracy. Stressed that the DU would campaign for the complete

withdrawal of Soviet troops from Eastern Europe. Acknowledged the difficulties of this far-from-new attempt to challenge the authority of the Communist Party, but hoped that this time it would work, under Gorbachev's policy of democratization.

Mitrofan (Krasnopolskii, Dimitrii), Archbishop of Astrakhan
22.10.1869–23.6.1919. Russian Orthodox clergyman.
Born in Voronezh Gouvt. Educated at Voronezh seminary. Graduated from the Kiev Theological Academy, 1897. Bishop of Gomel, 1907. Member of the 3rd Duma. Bishop of Astrakhan, 1916. Well-known orator, resolute opponent of revolutionary ideas. Active participant in the Russian Church Council, 1917. Archbishop, 1918. Murdered during revolutionary disturbances.

Mitta, Aleksandr Naumovich
28.3.1933–   . Film director.
Graduated from the Building Construction Institute. Worked as a cartoonist for the satirical magazine *Krokodil*. Graduated from the VGIK in 1961 as a director. Best known for his comedies. Films: *My Friend, Kolka* (Mosfilm, 1961 together with A. Saltykov); *Without Fear and Reproach* (Mosfilm, 1963); *Someone's Buzzing, Open the Door* (Mosfilm, 1965); *Shine Bright, My Star* (Mosfilm, 1969); *Moscow, My Love* (Soviet-Japanese co-production, 1974); *The Tale of How Tsar Peter Married Off His Moor* (Mosfilm, 1976, shown at the Cannes Film Festival).

Mkrtychan, Grigorii Mkrtychevich
3.1.1925–   . Athlete.
Born in Krasnodar. Honoured Master of Sports (hockey), 1951. With the Central Sports Club of the Army. Member of the CPSU, 1960. Graduated from the Moscow Institute of Physical Culture, 1963. USSR champion, 1948–58. European champion, 1954–56. World champion, 1954, 1956. Olympic champion, 1956.

Mlodek, Rita Veniaminovna
27.2.1906–   . Singer (soprano).
Leading singer at the Minsk Opera and Ballet Theatre, 1932–66.

Mlynarskii, Emil' (Mlynarski)
18.8.1870–5.4.1935. Violinist, conductor, composer.
Born near Suvalok. Pupil of L. Auer. Taught at the music school of the Russkoe Muzykal'noe Obshchestvo in Odessa, 1894–98. Chief conductor at the Warsaw Opera, 1899–1910 and 1919–22. Director and professor at the Warsaw Conservatory, 1904–09, 1919–22. Guest conductor with many European theatres. Author of an opera, a symphony, and 2 concertos. Died in Warsaw.

Mnatsakanian, El'vira Gurgenovna
17.8.1944–   . Ballerina.
Born in Erevan. Joined the Spendiarov Theatre on graduating from the Erevan Choreographic School, 1961. Pupil of A. Bogan'kov. First Armenian Juliet (1970, choreography by O. Vinogradov).

Mochulskii, Konstantin Vasil'evich
28.1.1892–1948. Literary scholar.
Born in Odessa. Graduated from Petersburg University in 1914. Lecturer at the same university, 1916–20. Emigrated in 1920. Taught at Sofia University, 1920–22, then at the Sorbonne, 1924–44, and at the St. Sergius Theological Institute, Paris, 1937–47. Died in France. Wrote classical studies of Vladimir Solov'ev, Fedor Dostoevskii, Aleksandr Blok, Andrei Belyi and Valerii Briusov.

Modorov, Fedor Aleksandrovich
1890–1962? Artist.
Portrait and genre painter. Studied in Mstera, his native town, from 1900–05, then at the Kazan' Art School, 1910–14, under N. Feshin. Pupil of V. Makovskii at the Petersburg Academy of Arts, 1914–18. Exhibitions from 1916, all in Moscow. Personal exhibition: Moscow, 1934.

Mogilat, Elena Tikhonovna
1897–16.12.1980. Linguist, social worker.
Emigrated from Russia during the Civil War, 1921. Settled in the USA. Taught Russian in the Slavonic Languages Department of Columbia University. One of the founders of the Society of Aid to Russian Children Abroad, 1926. Longest-serving member of staff at Columbia University (44 years), retired 1965. Remembered as a distinguished pioneer of Slavistics and a tireless social worker among the Russian community in the USA. Died at the hospital of the Tolstoy Foundation in the USA.

Mogilevskii, Aleksandr Iakovlevich
20.1.1885–1955. Violinist.
Born in Uman'. Pupil of I. Grzhimali. Professor at the Moscow Conservatory. Emigrated 1922. In Japan from the 1930s. Professor at the Tokyo Conservatory. Influenced many Japanese violinists. Author of transcriptions for violin. Died in Tokyo.

Moiseev, Igor Aleksandrovich
21.1.1906–   . Choreographer.
Born in Kiev. Graduated from the Moscow Choreographic School, 1924. Pupil of A. A. Gorskii. After graduating, danced with the Bolshoi Theatre, 1924–39. Co-director with L. A. Lashchilin of *The Football Player* at the Bolshoi Theatre, 1930. Co-director with A. M. Messerer of *Vain Precaution* at the Experimental Theatre. Independent productions in 1932, 1935, 1958. Founded the Choreographic Concert Ensemble of the USSR (later known as the Young Ballet, now the Moscow Classical Ballet). Aimed at unbroken dramatic sequences and realism, using classical and folk-dance techniques. Founded the Ensemble for Folk-Dancing, 1937. Innovator in folk-dance themes. Lenin Prize, 1967. State Prize of the USSR, 1942, 47, 52. Honorary member of the Paris Dance Academy, 1955.

Moiseev, Iurii Ivanovich
15.7.1940–   . Athlete.
Born in Penza. Honoured Master of Sports (hockey), 1968. Member of the CPSU, 1968. With the Central Sports Club of the Army. Graduated from the Moscow Oblast' Pedagogical Institute, 1971. Coach, teacher. USSR champion 1963–72. World and European champion, 1968. Olympic champion, 1968.

Moiseev, Mikhail Fedorovich
24.1.1882–29.6.1955. Ballet dancer and choreographer.
Studied at the Moscow Choreographic School, 1892–99. Pupil of N. P. Domashev and V. D. Tikhomirov. With Zimin's Opera, 1903–10. Appeared in the USA with Anna Pavlova's company, 1910. Began his career as a choreographer in Voronezh, 1918. Later with theatres in Khar'kov, Odessa, Sverdlovsk, and Novosibirsk. State Prize of the USSR, 1948. Directed and taught at ballet classes connected with theatres and choreographic schools.

Moiseeva, Olga Nikolaevna
25.12.1928–   . Ballerina.
Born in Leningrad. Graduated from the Leningrad Choreographic School, 1947. Pupil of A. Vaganova. On graduating, danced with the Kirov Theatre, 1947–73. Coached at the theatre from 1972. Significant achievements in grotesque dance. A TV film was made about her entitled *Tantsuet Olga Moiseeva.*

Mokeev, Al'bert Andreevich
4.1.1936–27.2.1969. Athlete.
Born in Vladimir. Honoured Master of Sports (pentathlon), 1964. With the Moscow Armed Forces Club. Graduated from the Gorkii Pedagogical Institute, 1957. Olympic champion, 1964, and bronze medallist, 1965. USSR champion, 1965. Died in Moscow. Official sports sources do not give the cause of his premature death.

Mokrousov, Boris Andreevich
27.2.1909–   . Composer.
Born in Nizhnii Novgorod. Author of an opera, a comic opera, chamber music, songs, and music for stage and screen. State Prize of the USSR, 1948.

Molchanov, Kirill Vladimirovich
7.9.1922–   . Composer.
Born in Moscow. Graduated from the Composition Class of the Moscow Conservatory, 1949. Pupil of A. N. Aleksandrov. Director of the Bolshoi Theatre, 1973–75. Author of 7 operas, songs, music for films, and for the ballet *Macbeth*, which was performed at the Kirgizskii and Bolshoi Theatres, 1980.
See: *Kirill Molchanov*, Moscow, 1971.

Moldobasanov, Kalyi

28.9.1929– . Composer, conductor.
Born in a village in the Narynskii district. Appeared with the Kirghiz Philharmonic Orchestra at the age of 12. Studied at the Kirghiz Music School in Frunze. Graduated from the Faculty of Symphonic Conducting at the Moscow Conservatory, 1954. Pupil of L. Ginzburg. Conductor with the Kirghiz Theatre of Opera and Ballet. Chief conductor from 1966. As a composer, concentrated on theatrical genres.

Mollo, Victor

17.9.1909–24.9.1987. International bridge player, journalist.
Born in Petersburg into a rich family. After the October Revolution 1917, emigrated with his parents. Later described in his memoirs how his mother had bought a train for the family to escape. Received a private education in Paris. Graduated from the London School of Economics. Freelance journalist in the 1930s. Proof-reader of French and Russian texts for publishers. In 1940, sub-editor, then editor with the BBC's European Service. Bridge correspondent for the *Evening Standard* in the 1970s, and for the *Mail on Sunday* from 1982. Prolific writer on bridge (25 books). Became an internationally known bridge player.

Molodtsov, Vladimir Aleksandrovich

18.6.1911–2.1942. State security official.
Born at Sasovo, near Riazan'. Joined the Communist Party, 1931. Joined the secret police (NKVD), 1934. During WWII, sent to organize partisan groups in Odessa. Arrested by the Germans and shot.

Molodyi, Konon Trofimovich (Lonov, Georgii; Lonsdale, Gordon Arnold)

1923–14.10.1970. Intelligence officer.
Grew up in the USA with the family of his aunt. Returned to the USSR, 1938. Pupil of star spy Rudolf Abel during WWII. Sent to Britain to organize a spy network, 1955. Settled in Britain under the name of Gordon Lonsdale, selling bubble-gum machines and other mechanical devices. Produced a car burglar alarm and received a gold medal for the best British entry at the Brussels Trade Fair, 1960. Together with Peter and Helen Kroger (Morris and Lorna Cohen), organized a sophisticated intelligence-gathering and transmitting centre, spying on NATO bases. Arrested, Jan. 1961, sentenced to 25 years in prison. Exchanged for Greville Wynne, the British contact man for Oleg Pen'kovskii, 1964. While his memoirs, glorifying Soviet espionage work abroad, were being published in *Komsomolskaia Pravda*, suddenly died, allegedly while picking mushrooms in a forest near Moscow.

Molokov, Vasilii Sergeevich

1895–1982. Major-general.
Joined the Red Army, 1918. Graduated from a naval pilots' school, 1921. Joined the Communist Party, 1925. As a pilot, took part in the rescue of the Chel'iuskin expedition, 1934, and the flight to the North Pole 1937. Head of the Civil Aviation Administration, 1938. On active service in the air force during WWII. Head of the Meteorological Service, 1946–47.

Molotov, Viacheslav Mikhailovich (Skriabin)

9.3.1890–11.1986. Revolutionary, politician, statesman, diplomat.
Born in Kukarka, Viatka Gouvt. Educated at the Kazan' High School (real'noe uchilishche.). Joined Marxist student circles. Very close to Tikhomirnov, the son of a rich merchant, who financed the Bolsheviks. Member of the SD Party (Bolshevik) in 1906. Arrested and exiled to Vologda in 1907. After his release, studied at Petersburg Polytechnic. Joined *Pravda*, which Tikhomirnov had organized and financed. Member of the Russian Bureau of the Cen. Cttee. of the SD Party under Shliapnikov in 1915. During the February Revolution 1917, due to the absence of party leaders of real calibre (who were either abroad or in exile), amassed many nominal positions — member of the Cen. Cttee., one of the editors of *Pravda*, member of the Executive Cttee. of the Petrograd Soviet. After the October Revolution 1917, had several party posts in the provinces. During Lenin's differences with Trotsky, recalled by Lenin and appointed secretary of the Cen. Cttee. in 1921, but in 1922, already replaced by Stalin (on the suggestion of Zinoviev and Kamenev). Appreciated by Stalin (who called him 'stone backside') for his ability to sit for hours during interminable party committee meetings. Became Stalin's most trusted and faithful aide. Led the chorus of approval during the purges in the 1930s, signing death warrants for his old friends and comrades. Did not protest even against the imprisonment of his own wife, Polina Zhemchuzhina (she was Jewish). Secretary of the Cen. Cttee., 1921–30. Prime Minister of the USSR, 1930–41. Foreign Minister (replacing Litvinov) from 1939. Signed the pact with Nazi Germany in Berlin, 23 Aug. 1939 (with Ribbentrop). Deputy head of government, 1941–57. Minister of Foreign Affairs, 1941–49 and again 1953–57. Accompanied Stalin to the Teheran, Yalta and Potsdam conferences. At the beginning of the Cold War, became known as Comrade Niet. During the Khrushchev thaw, criticized (initially in connection with his Stalinist line on Yugoslavia), and after the 20th Party Congress in Oct. 1956, dismissed from his post of Foreign Minister, just before Tito's visit to the Soviet Union. In June 1957, with Kaganovich and Malenkov, made a bid for power, gaining a majority in the Politburo, but Khrushchev managed to convene a plenary session of the Cen. Cttee. (bringing members to Moscow by special planes), which voted down the Stalinist group (Molotov, Kaganovich, Malenkov and Shepilov). Practically sent into exile as Ambassador to Mongolia, 1957–60, later appointed Soviet representative at the International Atomic Agency in Vienna, 1960–62. In 1962, however, dismissed from all his posts and expelled from the party. From the early 1960s, lived in retirement in Moscow with his wife, who returned from the camps. Wrote memoirs (which remained unpublished). Under Chernenko, re-admitted into the party, July 1984. Died in Moscow.

Monakhov, Nikolai Fedorovich

30.3.1875–5.7.1936. Singer (baritone), actor.
Born in Petersburg. Appeared in

comic opera from 1904. Turned to acting, 1919. Continued to appear in comic opera until 1927. Died in Leningrad.

Mondzolevskii, Georgii Grigor'evich
26.1.1934– . Athlete.
Born in Orsha, Vitebsk Oblast'. Honoured Master of Sports (volleyball), 1963. With the Central Sports Club of the Army. Graduated from the Odessa Pedagogical Institute, 1956. Member of the CPSU, 1965. Lecturer at the Kuibyshev Military Engineering Academy, 1969. USSR champion, 1956–66. World champion, 1960 and 1962. Olympic champion, 1964 and 1968. European champion, 1967.

Moor, Dmitrii Stakhievich (Orlov)
3.11.1883–24.10.1946. Painter.
Born in Novocherkassk. Became known as a cartoonist in the satirical magazine *Budilnik*, 1908–17. During the Civil War, 1918–20, became one of the originators of the Soviet political poster. Taught at the VKHUTEMAS-VKHUTEIN, 1922, and other Moscow art schools. Died in Moscow.

Mordkin, Mikhail Mikhailovich
21.12.1880–15.7.1944. Ballet dancer, choreographer.
Born in Moscow. Graduated from the Moscow Theatre School, 1900. Pupil of V. D. Tikhomirov. After graduating, danced with the Bolshoi Theatre, 1900–10, and 1912–18. While still a student, appeared as a leading dancer, 1898–99. Appeared in the first season abroad of the Ballets Russes with M. Fokin as choreographer, 1909. Appeared with Anna Pavlova and with his own company in the USA and Britain. Changed to mime, 1914. Taught at the Bolshoi Theatre from 1904, assistant choreographer from 1905. Emigrated, lived in the USA from 1924. There founded and taught at a school of his own. Founded a company, 1926 (known as the Mordkin Ballet from 1937). Appeared again as a dancer, 1937. The company, Ballet Theatre, based on Mordkin's company, though without

his participation, was founded in 1939. Died in Millbrook, New Jersey.

Morfessi, Iurii Spiridonovich
1882–1957. Singer.
Born in Odessa. Became one of the most famous popular romance and gypsy singers in Russia before WWI. Emigrated after the October Revolution in 1917. Settled in Paris. Continued his performances in the 1920s and 1930s, remaining the idol of 2 generations of Russian music lovers. Influenced such famous performers as Vertinskii and Leshchenko. Highly praised by Rachmaninov, Stravinskii and other giants of 20th-century Russian music. After WWII, due to his age and ill-health, gave up his career. Died and buried in Paris.

Morkovina, Liudmila Pavlovna
26.5.1935– . Ballerina.
Born in Leningrad. Graduated from the Leningrad Choreographic School, 1953. Pupil of E. V. Shiripina. After graduating, danced with the Malyi Theatre, Leningrad, 1953–74. Taught in Cairo, 1963–64, and in Panama, 1972–74. Returned to the USSR. Taught the specialized class at the Malyi Theatre, Leningrad, from 1970. Taught at the Leningrad Choreographic School from 1974.

Moroz, Valentin Iakovlevich
1936– . Ukrainian nationalist politician.
Born in Western Ukraine. Graduated in history from L'vov University. Komsomol member. Worked as a teacher. Protested against the destruction of folk culture in Western Ukraine. Arrested, 1965. Sentenced to 4 years in the Gulag. Released, 1969. Wrote verse and articles, which circulated in samizdat. Re-arrested, 1970. After his release, emigrated to the West. Active in Ukrainian nationalist organizations abroad. His memoirs of his life in the camps, *Reportazh iz Zapovednika Imeni Beria* is the most sucessful of his works.

Morozov, Georgii Alekseevich
14.4.1896–1967? Violin maker.
Born in Orel Gouvt. Pupil of D.

Tomashov. Winner of several 1st prizes in All-Union competitions.

Morozov, Igor' Vladimirovich
19.5.1913–24.11.1970. Composer.
Born in Lugansk. Graduated from the Moscow Conservatory, 1936. Composed in various genres, especially for children. State Prize of the USSR, 1948. Director in many theatres in the USSR and other socialist countries. Died in Moscow.

Morozov, Ivan Nikolaevich
1884–1953. Artist.
Icon painter, miniature artist and stage designer. Studied under the Mstera icon painters. Pupil of the icon master, A. I. Tsepkov. From 1926, worked in Mstera. Exhibitions: Ivanovo, 1936, Vladimir, 1947–49, Moscow, 1949. Maker of many miniature objects d'art.

Morozov, Ivan Vasil'evich
1919–5.11.1978. Publisher, editor.
Born in Estonia. Joined the Russian Christian Student Movement. Came to Paris as a student, 1939. Forced to remain in France by the start of WWII. Settled in Paris, at first as a worker, later as a student at the Theological Institute. Graduated, 1944. Editor of *Vestnik RSHD*, 1946. For many years, secretary of the RSHD (Russian Christian Student Movement). Director of the YMCA Press in Paris. Lectured on the history of the Russian Church at the Theological Institute. At the beginning of 1978, was dismissed from the editorial board of *Vestnik* and from the YMCA Press. Committed suicide by hanging himself in Paris.

Morozov, Nikolai Aleksandrovich
7.7.1854–30.7.1946. Revolutionary, scientist.
Born in the village of Borok near Iaroslavl'. Son of a land-owner and peasant woman. Involved in revolutionary activity from the middle 1870s. Member of N. Chaikovskii's circle, later of Narodnaia Volia. Edited the revolutionary newspaper *Rabotnik* in Geneva, and *Zemlia I Volia* in Russia. Went abroad in 1880 and met Karl Marx. Returned in Jan. 1881, arrested at the border, senten-

ced to life imprisonment. Remained in solitary confinement in Schlüsselburg prison until 1905 (almost a quarter of a century). During this time, actively studied many subjects and became famous for his many books (on chemistry, physics, astronomy, history, religion, also poems). During WWI, lectured at the front. From 1918 until his death, director of the Leshaft Institute of Natural Sciences. Popular with the peasants of his village for preserving the traditional way of life, as established by his father, in contrast to the new neighbouring kolkhozes. Died in Borok aged 92, the last survivor of the first generation of Russian narodnik revolutionaries.

Morozov, Pavlik
14.11.1918–3.9.1932. Stalinist cult figure.
Born in the village of Gerasimovka, Sverdlovsk Oblast'. Member of the Pioneers organization. During the collectivization campaign, denounced his father who had tried to help other peasants avoid the grain requisition by the authorities, thus sending him to the Gulag. Allegedly his grandfather took him to a wood and killed him with an axe. Became an official cult figure but widely considered among the population as a symbol of treachery. His cult was recently criticized in the Soviet press, which also expressed grave doubts about the official version of his death.
See: Iu. Druzhnikov, *Voznesenie Pavlika Morozova*, London, 1988.

Morozov, Vladimir Ivanovich
4.3.1940–   . Athlete.
Born in Krasnovodsk. Honoured Master of Sports (rowing), 1964. With the Armed Forces Club, Krasnovodsk. From 1966, with the Kiev Armed Forces Club. Graduated from the Kiev Institute of Physical Culture, 1971. Member of the CPSU, 1974. USSR champion, 1962–72. Olympic champion, 1964 and 1972. European champion, 1967 and 1969. World champion, 1966 and 1970–71.

Morozov, Vladimir Ivanovich
19.7.1952–   . Athlete.
Born in the village of N. Dmitrovka, Moscow Oblast'. Honoured Master of Sports, 1976 (rowing). With the

Central Sports Club of the Navy. USSR champion, 1973–78. World champion, 1977–78. Olympic champion, 1976 (4x1,000m).

Moshkov, Boris Prokop'evich
22.1.1903–3.4.1968. Composer.
Born in Gorkii. Graduated from the Moscow Conservatory, 1930. Conducted and supervised the musical departments of various theatres. Composed several ballets, including *Bela* (after M. Lermontov), 1955, and *Grushen'ka* (after N. Leskov), 1957. Died in Moscow.

Mosiagin, Petr Vasil'evich
1880–1960. Artist.
Born in Iaroslavl'. Studied at the City Art School, Iaroslavl', then at the Moscow School of Painting, Sculpture and Architecture. Landscape and genre painter. Exhibitions: Iaroslavl' Art Society, 1912–15. Emigrated, 1923. His collection is held mainly in Iaroslavl' Museum.

Moskalenko, Kirill Semenovich
11.5.1902–17.6.1985. Marshal.
Born in the village of Grishino, now Donetsk Oblast'. Joined the Soviet Army, 1920. Fought against Makhno's forces during the Civil War, 1920–22. Studied at a military school, 1920. An artillery commander, 1922. Member of the CPSU, 1926. Graduated from the F. Dzerzhinskii Military Academy, 1939. During WWII, became a notable military figure. Deputy Commander of the 6th Army, and later Commander of the 38th Army. His chief was Khrushchev, and A. Epishev was his political commissar. Headed the anti-aircraft forces of the Moscow district, 1948–53. Played an important role in disposing of Lavrentii Beria. Commander of the Moscow military district, 11 Mar. 1955. Marshal of the Soviet Union. From Oct. 1960, Commander-in-chief of Strategic Rocket Forces. Deputy Minister of Defence. Chief Inspector in the Ministry of Defence from 1962. Member of the Cen. Cttee. of the CPSU from 1956.

Moskvin, Andrei Nikolaevich
14.2.1901–18.2.1961. Cameraman.
Worked closely with G. Kozintsev

and L. Trauberg. Influenced by the methods of FEKS. His best films include *Shinel'*, 1926, *S.V.D.*, 1927, *Novyi Vavilon*, 1929, and *Odna*, 1931. With the cameraman E. Tisse, shot both parts of S. Eisenstein's *Ivan the Terrible*, 1945–46.

Moskvin, Ivan Mikhailovich
18.6.1874–16.2.1946. Actor.
Prominent actor in the silent cinema. His major success was the part of Polikushka in the film of the same title in 1922. At his best in Chekhov adaptations — *Chiny i Liudi*, *Smert' Chinovnika*, *Khameleon* and *Kollezhskii Registrator*.

Mosolova, Vera Il'inichna
19.4.1875–29.1.1949. Ballerina.
Born in Moscow. Graduated from the Moscow Choreographic School, 1893–96. Dancer at the Mariinskii Theatre, 1896–1903. Dancer at the Bolshoi Theatre, 1903–18. Taught at the Moscow Choreographic School, 1922–35, and later at the V. Meyerhold Theatre School. Died in Moscow.

Mostras, Konstantin Georgievich
16.4.1886–6.9.1965. Violinist.
Born in Tambovsk Gouvt. Professor at the Moscow Conservatory. His pupils include M. Kozolupova, B. Kuznetsov, M. Terian, and M. Iashvili. Author of adaptations for violin and works on violin-playing. Died in Moscow.

Motovilov, Georgii Ivanovich
1894–1963. Sculptor.
Pupil of Sergei Konenkov. Studied at the Moscow VKHUTEMAS, 1918–21. First exhibition in Moscow. Other exhibitions: Moscow, 1928–29, 1933 (2 exhibitions), 1939–40, 1942–43, 1945, 1947, 1949, 1954, 1957, 1961. Personal exhibitions: Moscow, 1934 and 1957 (with A. Kuprin). Died in Moscow.

Moutafian, Helena, Princess (b. Gagarina, Elena Alekseevna)
2.5.1930–   . Charity worker, painter.
Daughter of Prince Aleksei Ivano-

vich Gagarin, a descendant of Rurik, founder of the Russian monarchy, c. 879. Has devoted her last 30 years to the needs of other people, working tirelessly for some 30 charities: Deputy President of the St. John Ambulance Brigade, London; Honorary Vice President of the Women's Council; patron of the Kingston and District Charity; life patron of the NSPCC: President of Friends of the Unicorn Theatre for Children; patron of the National Association for Health, and the British Council for Peace. Involved in projects for uniting world religions. Vice President of the Sound Press for the Blind, and President of Help the Aged. Received an MBE in 1976 for 25 years service to the community in London. Has also been honoured in France, receiving the Grande Medaille de Vermeil de la Ville de Paris in June 1977. Also received the Étoile Civique, and the Croix de Chevalier. Holds a literary salon at her Hampstead home. Hostess to many interesting international figures and events. Dedicated painter. Silver medal winner (Grollo d'Ore) for her paintings in Venice. Journalist, specializing in society and charity matters. Regular contributor to the annual Debrett magazine *Cities of the World.* Married a city commodity broker, Artin Moutafian, himself an Armenian with strong Russian connections.

Movshenson, Aleksandr Grigor'evich
19.12.1895–27.4.1965. Theatre and arts historian.
Born in Petersburg. Taught at the Repin Institute of the USSR Academy of Art, lecturing on theatrical costume. From 1920, published articles on the opera, circus and other related subjects. Made valuable contributions to scenography, theatrical bibliography and scenic iconography. Contributed comments and publications to Glushkovskii's *Vospominaniia Balletmeistera,* 1940, and to *Iz Arkhiva Balletmeistera* by Val'berkh, 1948. *Agrippina Iakovlevna Vaganova,* 1958. Translated *Pis'ma o Tantse i Baletakh* by J. Noverre.

Mozhaev, Pavel
1928– . Politician.
Secretary of the Leningrad Oblast'

Party Cttee, 1972, with special responsibility for Light Industry. USSR Ambassador to Afghanistan from Aug. 1986.

Mozzhukhin Aleksandr Il'ich
1879–1945. Singer (bass).
Born in Saratov Gouvt. Brother of the film actor Ivan Mozzhukhin. Pupil of M. Medvedev. Leading singer at the Petrograd Theatre of Musical Drama, 1912–15. Appeared mainly in concerts from 1920. Emigrated after 1925. Performed in various European theatres. Died in Paris.

Mozzhukhin, Ivan Ill'ich
26.9.1889–18.1.1939. Film actor.
Studied at Moscow University. Actor in various provincial theatres, also worked at the Vvedenskii Peoples' House. Entered the film industry, 1908. In 1911, appeared in *Kreitserova Sonata,* which made him famous. Played in every important pre-revolutionary film, and is regarded as a major actor of the Russian silent cinema. Appeared in *Domik v Kolomne,* 1913, *Nikolai Stravrogin,* 1915, and *Pikovaia Dama,* 1916. In 1918, experienced his biggest success playing in *Father Sergius.* Emigrated in 1920. Still remained in demand in Berlin and Paris, but after the arrival of the 'talkies', experienced serious difficulties in adapting to new demands. His final success was the 1926 film *Michel Strogov.* After that, found himself out of work and became very depressed. His death in Paris was seen as a great loss by the Russian emigré community. The Parisian magazine *Illiustrirovannaia Rossiia* dedicated a whole issue to him.

Mravinskii, Evgenii Aleksandrovich
4.6.1903–1.1988. Conductor.
Born in Petersburg. Graduated from the Leningrad Conservatory, 1931. Pupil of A. Gauk and N. Mal'ko. From 1921, conductor at the Leningrad Choreographic School. While still a student, was in charge of the School's musical department. Conductor at the Kirov Theatre, 1932–38. Conductor, later chief conductor with the Leningrad Philharmonic Symphony Orchestra from 1938 until

his death, (turning it into one of the world's great orchestras). Illness during his last years limited his appearances with the orchestra. Made several trips to London, where he performed at the Festival Hall. His last appearance with the orchestra in Britain was at the 1961 Edinburgh Festival. State Prize of the USSR, 1946. Lenin Prize, 1961. Professorship, 1963.

Mshvelidze, Shalva Mikahilovich
28.5.1904– . Composer.
Born in Tiflis. Professor at the Tiflis Conservatory. Author of operas, an oratorio, symphonic poems, and music for stage and screen.

Muizhel, Viktor Vasil'evich
1880–1924. Author.
Populist writer influenced by Korolenko and Gorkii. At the turn of the century, often mentioned as an example of the immensely boring and moralizing style of the previous generation.

Mukashev, Salamat
1927– . Party official.
Kazakh. Chairman of the Supreme Soviet in the Central Asian Republic of Kazakhstan. According to *Pravda,* removed from his post, Feb. 1988.

Mukhacheva, Liubov' Alekseevna
23.7.1947– . Athlete.
Born in Staraia Russa, Novgorod Oblast'. Honoured Master of Sports (skiing), 1972. From 1973, with Leningrad Trud. Graduated from the Leningrad Institute of Physical Culture, 1978. USSR champion, 1970–72 and 1975–76. Olympic champion, 1972.

Mukhatov, Veli (Velimukhamed)
5.5.1916– . Composer.
Born in Turkmenia. Early training at the Ashkhabad Music School, 1935–36. Graduated from the Turkmenian National Studio of the Moscow Conservatory, 1941. Pupil of E. Strakhov and G. Litinskii. At the front during WWII. Resumed studies in composition at the Moscow Conservatory, 1946. Pupil of S. Vasilenko. Graduated, 1951. In later years, worked mainly as a composer.

Mukhin, Lev
1936–25.4.1977. Boxer.
Honoured Master of Sports (boxing). Silver medal-winner at the XVIth Olympic Games. Many times USSR champion. Death reported in the American press.

Mukhina, Vera Ignat'evna
19.6.1889–6.10.1953. Sculptor.
Born in Riga. Studied with Iuon and Mashkov, 1909–12, and in Paris with Bourdelle, 1912–14. Taught at the Moscow School of Industrial Design, 1926–27 and at the VKHUTEIN, 1926–30. In her youth, influenced by cubism, later became the main exponent of socialist realism in sculpture. After the October Revolution 1917, became involved in Lenin's monumental propaganda and kept to this direction all her life, becoming the foremost Stalinist sculptor. Arrested, 1930, imprisoned at Lubianka, released after Gorkii's intervention. Her best known achievement is the 24 metre-high stainless steel group *Worker and Kolkhoz Woman* complete with hammer and sickle, made for the Soviet Pavilion at the World Exhibition in Paris, 1937, and now at the entrance to the VDNKH in Moscow.

Mukhtarova, Fat'ma Sattarovna
26.3.1893–1970? Singer (mezzo soprano).
Born in Iran. Azerbaidzhani by nationality. Pupil of M. Medvedev. Leading singer with the Zimin Private Opera, Moscow, 1914–17. Appeared in Leningrad, and in various provincial towns, 1921–37. Leading singer with the Baku Theatre of Opera and Ballet, 1938–53. Her memoirs appeared in the journal *Teatr*, 1936, No. 2.

Muklevich, Romuald Adamovich
1890–1938. Revolutionary, politician.
Joined the Bolshevik Party, 1906, and the Red Army, 1918. Political Commissar. Commander of the Red naval forces, 1926–31. Head of the ship-building industry, 1934. Deputy Minister of the Military Industry, 1936. Liquidated by Stalin.

Muller, Konstantin Aleksandrovich
5.7.1905– . Ballet dancer, choreographer.
Born in Petersburg. Studied at the School of Russian Ballet. Pupil of A. L. Volynskii. Graduated from the Leningrad Choreographic School, 1926. Pupil of V. A. Semenov. Dancer with theatres in Khar'kov, Kiev, Tashkent and Tbilisi, 1926–31. Leading dancer at the Bolshoi Theatre, 1931–37. Choreographer and leading dancer at the Minsk Theatre, 1937–60. Choreographer at the Voronezh Theatre, 1963–71.

Mullova, Viktoria
1960– . Violinist.
Born in a suburb of Moscow. Daughter of an engineer and a teacher of English. Studied at the Central Music School in Moscow, then at the Moscow Conservatory. Pupil of Leonid Kogan. 1st prize in the Wieniawski Competition in Warsaw in 1974. Winner of the 1981 Sibelius Competition in Finland. Winner of the 1982 Moscow Tchaikovskii Competition. Defected to the West in 1983 together with Vakhtang Zhordania, the conductor, through Finland and Sweden. Has performed all over the world since.

Mungalova, Olga Petrovna
11.12.1905–26.8.1942. Ballerina.
Born in Perm'. Graduated from the Petrograd Theatre School, 1923. Pupil of Olga Preobrazhenskaia and A. I. Vaganova. Debut in the same year at the Theatre of Opera and Ballet, later known as the Kirov Theatre. Appeared until 1942. Besides classical ballet, interested in acrobatic dancing (invented training exercises). Her memoirs remain unpublished, and are held in the Leningrad Library, section VTO. Died during the Siege of Leningrad.

Muradeli, Vano Il'ich
6.4.1908–14.8.1970. Composer.
Born in Gori, Georgia. Early musical training at the Tbilisi Technical School, 1925–26. At the Tbilisi Conservatory, 1926–31. Pupil of S. Barkhudarian, V. Shcherbachev and M. Bagrinovskii. Theatrical conductor and composer in Georgia, 1931–34. Studied at the Moscow Conser-

vatory, 1934–38. Pupil of B. Shekhter and N. Miaskovskii. During the war, musical director of the Central Naval Ensemble. Composed mainly vocal music. Also wrote music for films.

Muradian, Matevos Oganesovich
5.5.1911– . Musicologist.
Born in Turkey. Armenian by nationality. Co-author of *Ocherk Istorii Armianskoi Muzyki*, Erevan, 1963. Wrote several more works in Armenian.

Muradian, Zare Muradovich
20.11.1913– . Ballet dancer, choreographer.
Born in Turkey. Graduated from the Moscow Choreographic School, 1935. Pupil of V.A. Semenov. After graduating, danced with the Bolshoi Theatre, and with the Spendiarov Theatre from 1938. Debut as choreographer, 1940. Directed ballets, including *Don Quixote*, 1954–60.

Murakhovskii, Vsevolod Serafimovich
1926– . Politician.
Served in the Soviet Army, 1944–50. Member of the CPSU, 1946. Graduated from the Stavropol Pedagogical Institute, 1954. 1st secretary of Stavropol City Cttee. of the USSR Komsomol, 1954–56. Senior party posts in the same area, 1956–70. 1st secretary of Stavropol City Cttee. of Stavropol Krai, 1970–75. In 1956, replaced as Komsomol boss by the then unknown graduate from Moscow University, Mikhail Gorbachev. Second most powerful man in Stavropol Krai in 1975. Promoted by Gorbachev to 1st deputy chairman of the USSR Council of Ministers, Nov. 1985.

Muratov, Pavel Pavlovich
1881–1951. Author, arts scholar.
Became known as one of the best writers on Italy in the Russian language. As an art expert, wrote on icons. Emigrated, 1922, and lived in Italy and France.

Muratov, Valentin Ivanovich
30.7.1928– . Athlete.
Born in the village of Kostiukovo, Moscow Oblast'. Honoured Master

of Sports (gymnastics), 1952. With Moscow Burevestnik. Graduated from the Moscow Oblast' Pedagogical Institute, 1953. Member of the CPSU, 1958. USSR champion, 1950–56. Olympic champion, 1952 and 1956. World champion, 1954, 1958. Silver medallist, 1956. From 1963, international referee.
See: L. Kuleshov, 'Diplomat v Belom' in *Kavalery Ordena Lenina*, Moscow, 1974.

Muratova, Sofia Ivanovna
13.7.1929– . Athlete.
Born in Leningrad. Honoured Master of Sports (gymnastics), 1955. With Moscow Dynamo. Absolute USSR champion, 1954–55, 1957, 1960 and 1963. Olympic champion, 1956, 1964. World champion, 1958 and 1962. Bronze medallist, 1956. Silver medallist, 1960.

Murauskas, Romualdas
1934–23.5.1979. Boxer.
Prominent Lithuanian athlete. Honoured Master of Sports (boxing). Many times USSR and Lithuanian champion. Bronze medal-winner at the XVIth Olympic Games. Death reported in the Lithuanian and American press.

Murav'ev, Mikhail Artem'evich
25.9.1880–11.7.1918. Military commander.
Born at Burdukovo, near Nizhnii Novgorod. Son of a peasant. Educated at a seminary. Graduated from the Military Infantry School in Kazan' in 1899. Close to the SRs. Participated in the Russo-Japanese war, 1904–05. After the October Revolution 1917, offered his services to the Soviet government. Nov. 1917, in charge of the defence of Petrograd against General Krasnov. Later fought against the Ukrainians and Rumanians. Appointed commander-in-chief of the Eastern front, June 1918. After the left-wing SR revolt in Moscow, staged an uprising in Simbirsk (now Ulianovsk). Shot resisting arrest by the Bolsheviks.

Murav'ev, Nikolai Konstantinovich
1870–1936. Lawyer.
Before the February Revolution

1917, a well-known defence lawyer in political trials. Appointed by the Provisional Government head of the special commission for the investigation of illegal acts of Tsarist officials. After the October Revolution, 1917, again defence lawyer in political trials (the paper *Utro Rossii*, 1918, the Bruce Lockhart trial, 1918, the Tactical Centre, 1920, and the Cen. Cttee. of the SR Party in 1922). From the mid 1920s, member of the Moscow City Collegium of Lawyers. Disappeared during the purges, presumably a victim of the Gulag. (The secretary of the Murav'ev Commission in 1917 was the poet Aleksandr Blok, who described the proceedings in his diaries and in *Poslednie Dni Imperatorskoi Vlasti* (Last Days of Tsarist Rule), 1921.) Author of the Stenographical Report of the Special Commission. *Padenie Tsarskogo Rezhima*, 7 vols., Moscow-Leningrad 1926–27.

Murav'ev, Valer'ian Nikolaevich
28.2.1885–1931. Philosopher.
Son of a minister. Spent his childhood in Britain. Educated at the Aleksandrovskii Lycée. Graduated in law from Petersburg University. In the diplomatic service in Belgrade before WWI. Close to the Cadets before 1917. Continued working in the Foreign Affairs Ministry after the communist take-over, October 1917. Arrested, 1920. After his release, worked as a librarian at the VSNKH. Became a follower of the philosopher, N. Fedorov. During the Stalin purges, arrested as a Trotskyite, 1929. Sent to the Gulag camps, where he died of typhoid.

Murav'eva, Elena Aleksandrovna
3.6.1867–11.3.1939. Singer.
Born in Moscow. Pupil of A. Aleksandrova-Kochetova. Professor at the Kiev Conservatory. Her pupils included I. Kozlovskii, Z. Gaidai, and L. Rudenko. Died in Kiev.

Murav'eva-Loginova, Tatiana (Loguine, Tatiana)
1902?– . Artist, author.
Left the Crimea with her parents in 1920 in the last exodus of Russians, together with General Wrangel's

army. Settled in Paris. Graduated from the Paris Chemical Institute. Studied art, first at the Paris Russian Art Academy, then became a pupil of both N. Goncharova and M. Larionov. Exhibited at the Paris Salon, and other galleries, signing her work as Loguine. Met the Bunins in 1935. Became very close to I. Bunin and remained a great friend of Vera Bunina until her death. Published a book about her teachers, *Gontcharova et Larionov. Cinquante Ans à Saint Germain-des-Pré*, Paris, 1971, which is full of rare personal photographs of the couple. Published her second book in Russian, *Pis'ma Buninykh (1936–61) k Murav'evoi-Loginovoi*, Paris, 1982.

Muravlev, Aleksei Alekseevich
2.5.1924– . Composer.
Born in Tiflis. Brother of the pianist, Iurii Muravlev (b. 1927). Author of piano pieces, and music for stage and screen.

Murzhenko, Aleksei Grigor'evich
1942– . Human rights campaigner.
Born at Lozovaia in the Ukraine. Arrested in Moscow, 1962, for membership of an unofficial students' circle. Sentenced to 6 years in the Gulag camps. Took part in the Leningrad hijacking attempt with E. Kuznetsov and others, 1970. Sentenced to 14 years in the camps. Released, 1984. Re-arrested, 1985, and sentenced to another 2 years. His letters from the camps have been published in samizdat and later abroad.

Mushel', Georgii Aleksandrovich
29.7.1909– . Composer.
Born in Tambov. Taught at the Tashkent Conservatory. Author of musical dramas, orchestral works, and works for violin and organ.

Musin, Il'ia Aleksandrovich
6.1.1904– . Conductor.
Born in Kostroma. Pupil of N. Mal'ko and A. Gauk. Professor at the Leningrad Conservatory.
Works: *Tekhnika dirizhirovaniia*, Leningrad, 1966.

Muskhelishvili, Nikolai Ivanovich
16.2.1891–1973? Mathematician.
Graduated from Petersburg University, 1914. Professor at Tbilisi University, 1922. Organized the Tbilisi Mathematics Institute, 1935. President of the Georgian Academy of Sciences, 1941.

Muzalevskii, Vladimir Il'ich (real name – Bunimovich)
6.4.1894–30.4.1964. Musicologist.
Born in Simferopol'. Professor at the Leningrad and Latvian conservatories. Died in Leningrad.
Works: *Russkaia Muzyka. Ocherki i Materialy po Istorii Russkoi Fortepiannoi Kul'tury 18-Pervoi Poloviny 19 Stoletiia*, Leningrad-Moscow, 1949; *Sovremennaia Tema v Russkom Sovremennom Romanse*, Leningrad, 1964.

Mzhavanadze, Vasilii Pavlovich
20.9.1902–5.9.1988. Politician.
Born at Kutaissi. Son of a worker. Graduated from the Lenin Military Political Academy, 1937. Political officer in the Red Army during WWII. 1st secretary of the Cen. Cttee. of the Communist Party in Georgia, 1953–72. Non-voting member of the Presidium of the Cen. Cttee. of the CPSU, 1957–66, and of the Politburo, 1966–72. Accused of corruption. Retired, 1972. Replaced by Shevardnadze.

N

Nabiev, Rakhman Nabievich
1930–   . Politician.
Graduated from Tashkent Institute of Irrigation and Mechanized Agriculture, 1954. Chief engineer in a machine and tractor station, 1954–58. Director of a maintenance engineering station, 1959–60. Senior party posts in the Tadzhik Republic. 1st secretary of the Cen. Cttee. of the Tadzhik CP from Apr. 1982 until Dec. 14, 1985. Replaced by K. Makhkamov. Official reason given was retirement on grounds of ill health.

Nabokov, Konstantin Dmitrievich
1875–after 1950. Diplomat.
Younger brother of the Cadet leader V. Nabokov, and uncle of the writer V. V. Nabokov. Secretary at the Russian Embassy in London. In charge of the embassy after the death of the Ambassador, Count Benckendorff, 1 Jan. 1917, until the arrival in 1920 of S. Sazonov (the former Minister of Foreign Affairs), who dismissed him. Settled in Norway.

Nabokov, Nikolai Dmitrievich
17.4.1903–6.4.1978. Composer.
Born in Liubcha near Grodno. Cousin of Vladimir Nabokov. Studied in Moscow, then in Berlin. Lived in Paris until 1933. Moved to the USA. General secretary of the Congress for the Freedom of Culture, 1952–63. Artistic director of the Berlin Festival, 1963–68. Wrote music for several ballets (*Oda*, 1934, choreography, L. Miasin; *Poslednii Tsvetok*, 1958, choreography, T. Gzovskii; *Don Quichotte*, choreography, George Balanchine). Published two autobiographies, in which he described his famous friends and collaborators Stravinskii, Diaghilev, Prokof'ev, and Balanchine.
See: *Old Friends and New Music*, 1951; *Memoirs of a Russian Composer*, 1975.

Nabokov, Vladimir Dmitrievich
1869–28.3.1922. Lawyer, politician.
Born in Tsarskoe Selo. Son of the Minister of the Interior during the reign of Alexander II. Father of the writer, Vladimir Nabokov. Graduated in law from Petersburg University, 1890. Professor of criminal law at the exclusive Law School, 1896–1904. Editor of law journals and liberal newspapers. One of the founders and leaders of the Cadet Party, deputy chairman of the Cen. Cttee. of the party. After the October Revolution, a warrant for his arrest was issued by the Bolsheviks. Fled to the Crimea. Minister of Justice of the Crimean government, 1919. Emigrated, 1920. Co-editor with I. Hessen of the rightwing Russian newspaper *Rul'* in Berlin. During an assassination attempt on his party leader Miliukov, at a meeting in Berlin, he shielded the latter with his body and was killed.

Nabokov, Vladimir Vladimirovich (pen name – Sirin)
24.4.1899–2.7.1977. Author.
Born in Petersburg. Son of the famous lawyer and politician, V. D. Nabokov. Educated at the Tenishevskoe School. Emigrated to England, 1919. Graduated from Trinity College, Cambridge, 1922. Lived in Berlin, 1922–37. Became known as a talented young poet and prose writer. Moved to France, 1937–40. From 1940, lived in the USA. Taught Russian literature at American universities. Started to write in English, a language familiar to him since childhood. Became world-famous with his English-language novel *Lolita*, 1955. Moved to Switzerland and embarked on a unique double language career, translating all his previous Russian works into English and publishing them to invariable critical acclaim (although in the 1920s and 1930s, he had managed to publish only one translation of his works, *Camera Oscura*, which went unnoticed) and writing new novels in English and translating them subsequently into Russian. Acknowledged as one of the greatest American writers of the 20th century. In the Soviet Union, attracted great interest among dissenting groups, at first because of his Western success. In the late 1980s, was published officially. Said that his own favourite novel was *Dar (The Gift)*, a witty satire on Chernyshevskii. Relaxed by studying lepidoptera. Fine translator of Russian classics into English (*The Lay of Igor*, Pushkin's *Eugene Onegin* with commentaries) and literary scholar (with controversial views, e.g. his highly critical approach to Dostoevskii, Pasternak etc). Died at Montreux, Switzerland.

Nadezhdin, Boris Borisovich
4.5.1905–7.3.1961. Composer.
Born in Smolensk. Professor at the Tashkent Conservatory. Co-author of musical dramas, and of choral and symphonic music. Died in Tashkent.

Nadezhdina, Nadezhda Sergeevna
3.6.1908–11.10.1979. Ballerina, choreographer.
Born in Vilnius. Graduated from the 2nd State School of Ballet in Petrograd, 1925. Pupil of N. Legat and A. Vaganova. Leading dancer with the Bolshoi Theatre, 1925–28.

Appeared in show business from 1931. Choreographer from 1941 (in ensembles of the Siberian military district and the Karelian front). Choreographer for the Moscow Variety Stage (Mosestrada) from 1943. Artistic director of the ballet department there, 1945–48, and concurrently of the Russian People's Choir of the Kalinin Philharmonic Society, 1945–48. Artistic director and producer of all programmes of the Academic Choreographic Ensemble, Berezka, 1948. Creator of a new choreographic style based on folk and classical dancing. Author of *Russkie Tantsy*, 1951. Gold medallist, the Joliot-Curie Prize, 1959. Died in Moscow.

Nadezhnyi, Dmitrii Nikolaevich
1873–1945. Lt.-general.
Graduated from the Academy of the General Staff, 1901. Took part in the Russo-Japanese war and WWI. Joined the Red Army, 1918. During the Civil War, commander of the Northern and Western fronts. Thereafter, lecturer at higher military educational establishments, 1926–1941.

Nadirov, Ivan Nikitich
1907–12.1941. Composer.
Born in Elisavetpol' (now Kirovabad). Author of the opera *Teren-Kul'*, produced in Alma-Ata, 1939, and the ballet, *Vesna*, 1940. Died in action during WWII near Smolensk.

Nadyrova, Tatiana Pavlovna (Zakharova)
29.1.1951–   . Athlete.
Born in Khristinovka, Cherkasskaia Oblast' in the Ukraine. Honoured Master of Sports (basketball), 1976. With the Moscow Oblast' Spartak. Graduated from the Moscow Technological Institute, 1976, as an economist-engineer. World champion, 1975. Olympic champion, 1976. USSR champion, 1978.

Nafanail (Lvov, Vasilii), Archbishop of Vienna and Austria
30.8.1906–8.11.1986. Russian
Orthodox clergyman, theologian.
Born in Moscow. After the communist take-over 1917, fled with his parents to Kharbin. Monk, 1929. Studied at the Kharbin St. Vladimir Theological Institute. Lived as a missionary in India and Ceylon, 1935–36. Returned to China. Appointed by the Synod of the Russian Orthodox Church in Exile assistant head of the Hiob of Pochaev Monastery at Ladomirovo in Czechoslovakia, 1939. Became a widely-known theological writer. At the end of WWII, evacuated to Germany. After the war, chairman of the Russian Orthodox Cttee. in the British zone, actively saving thousands of Russian refugees from NKVD agents and forced repatriation. Bishop of Brussels and Western Europe, 1946. Moved to Britain, and later Northern Africa with resettled displaced persons, 1951. Returned to West Germany, 1954. Abbot of St. Hiob Monastery in Munich, 1966. Bishop of Vienna and Austria, 1976. Archbishop, 1981. Died at the St. Hiob Monastery in Munich, and buried in the Russian cemetery at Wiesbaden.

Nagornyi, Klimentii
1887?–1918. Sailor.
Served in the Russian Navy. Taken as a servant and male nurse for Tsarevich Aleksei, keeping constant watch against any mishap which could subject the haemophiliac boy to internal bleeding. Often had to carry his charge in his arms during attacks of the illness. Refused to leave the royal family after the revolution 1917, and followed them to Ekaterinburg. Separated from them by force, taken to prison and shot by the Bolshevik guards.

Nagornyi, Nikolai Nikiforovich
1901–1985. Lt.-general.
Joined the Red Army, 1920, and the Bolshevik Party, 1927. Graduated from the Frunze Military Academy, 1933. Served in the anti-aircraft defence system and in the General Staff. During the Spanish Civil War, sent to Spain, 1936–39. During WWII, chief-of-staff of Anti-Aircraft Defence Forces. Continued to serve in the anti-aircraft system after WWII.

Nagornyi, Sergei Viktorovich
8.12.1956–   . Athlete.
Born in Khmel'nitskii in the Ukraine.
Honoured Master of Sports (rowing), 1976. With Khmel'nitskii Dynamo. Studied at the Khmel'nitskii Pedagogical Institute. USSR champion, 1976–77. Olympic champion, 1976 (1,000m race, with V. Romanovskii), and silver medallist, 1976 (500m race).

Nagrodskaia, Evdokia Appolonovna
1866–1930. Author.
Daughter of Avdot'ia Panaeva, the common-law wife of N. Nekrasov. Close friend of the poet M. Kuzmin. Works include the erotic novel *Gnev Dionisa*, 6th ed., St. Petersburg, 1911, and the trilogy, *Reka Vremen*, Berlin, 1924–26.

Naiashkov, Ivan Semenovich
1924–   . State official.
Graduated from the Moscow Energetics Institute, 1949. Member of the CPSU, 1961. Head of a department at the Electrotechnical Institute, 1956–64. Director, 1964–73. Deputy chairman, and later 1st deputy chairman of the USSR State Cttee. for Inventions and Discoveries, 1973–79. Chairman from Jan. 1979. Member of the Central Auditing Cttee. of the CPSU, 1981. As chairman of the State Cttee. for Inventions and Discoveries, called for better utilization of inventions in the fields of technology, materials and production.

Nakhimson, Semen Mikhailovich
25.11.1885–6.7.1918. Revolutionary.
Born in Liepaia. As a high school student, joined the Bund and the Social-Democratic Party, 1902. Active in the 1905 Revolution. Went abroad, 1907. Returned and joined the Bolsheviks, 1912. During WWI, in the army, distributed revolutionary propaganda. In 1917, political commissar of the Latvian detachments which became the main military force of the Bolsheviks. Commander of Bolshevik forces in Iaroslavl', 1918, at the time of the officers' revolt. Shot by the Whites during the uprising. Buried at the Marsovo Pole in Leningrad.

Nalbandian, Ioannes Romanovich
27.9.1871–23.2.1942. Violinist.
Born in Simferopol'. Armenian by

nationality. Pupil of L. Auer. Taught at the Petersburg/Leningrad Conservatory, 1895–1942. Assistant to Auer before 1903. Professor from 1908. I. Lukashevskii was one of his pupils. Died in Tashkent.

Nalbandian, Suren Rubenovich
3.6.1956–   . Athlete.
Born in Gegard, Armenia. Honoured Master of Sports (wrestling), 1976. With the Astrakhan' Armed Forces Club. USSR champion, 1976–77. Olympic champion, 1976.

Nalivkin, Dmitrii Vasil'evich
25.8.1889–1971? Geologist.
Graduated from the Petrograd Mining Institute, 1915. Professor at the Institute, 1920. Worked at the Geological Institute, 1917–49. Chief editor of a geological survey map of the USSR, 1937.

Nappel'baum, Moisei Solomonovich
1869–1958. Portrait photographer.
Born in Minsk. An apprentice at the Boretti Photographic Studio, 1884. Three years later, moved first to Smolensk, then Moscow, Odessa, Warsaw, Vilnius, Evpatoria, and eventually to the USA. In 1895, returned to Minsk and opened a studio of portrait photography. His portrait work appeared for the first time in 1910 in one of the best illustrated magazines of the time, *Solntse Rossii*, published in Petersburg. Became a renowned photographer and technician whose lighting and backgrounds in particular were much admired. Photographed a series of political leaders, writers and artists, among them Dzerzhinskii, Vorovskii and Lunacharskii. In 1919, with Sverdlov's support, set up the first State Photographic Studio of the Central Executive Cttee. Exhibitions were held in Petrograd, 1918, and in Moscow, 1935, 1946 and 1955. His monograph *From Craft to Art* was published in 1958. His photographs of Aleksandr Blok, the young Anna Akhmatova, Vsevolod Meyerhold, Mikhail Kuzmin, Sergei Esenin, Aleksandr Glazunov, and Vladimir Tatlin are among the best examples of Russian photography.
See: *Soviet Photography, 1917–40*, London, 1984.

Narbut, Egor (Georgii) Ivanovich
1886–1920. Graphic artist.
Close to the Mir Iskusstva group. Became known as a master of book design and illustration at the period of the flowering of this art in Russia.

Narbut, Vladimir Ivanovich
1888–1944. Poet.
A minor acmeist poet. After the October Revolution 1917, Communist Party member. Organized the publishing house Zemlia i Fabrika. Victim of Stalin's purges, died in the Gulag.

Nardov, Vladimir Leonardovich (real name – Knipper)
22.6.1876–12.11.1942. Stage director, singer (tenor).
Born in Moscow. Brother of the actress O. L. Knipper-Chekhova (Chekhov's wife). Leading singer at the Zimin Private Opera, 1914–18. Stage director from 1918. With the Bolshoi Theatre, 1920–36. Professor at the Moscow Conservatory from 1940. Died in Moscow.

Naritsa, Mikhail Aleksandrovich
1909–   . Author, teacher.
An older generation dissident, providing a link between the inmates of Stalin's camps of the 1930s and the dissidents of the 1960–70s, suffering from the misuse of psychiatry. First arrested in 1935, and sentenced to 5 years in the labour camps. Sentenced to life exile in Karaganda, 1949. After Stalin's death, rehabilitated, 1957. In 1961, arrested for sending a manuscript abroad for publication. Inmate of the Leningrad psychiatric hospital, 1961–64. A decade later, was again arrested and put into a psychiatric hospital. Released in 1976.

Nasimovich-Chuzhak, Nikolai Fedorovich
1876–1937. Journalist.
Old Bolshevik. Lived in Vladivostok and Chita. At the centre of a circle which included, among others, D. Burliuk, N. Aseev and S. Tretiakov. In 1920, leader of the Tvorchestvo group, which published a magazine of the same name until 1921. Published *K Dialektike Iskusstva* and *Cherez Golovy Kritikov*. Aggressive propagandist of futurism as the art of the proletariat. Fighter against Soviet bureaucracy in Gosizdat. His article, *Opasnost' Arakcheevshchiny* (The Danger of the Arakcheev Approach), became the central point of a talk by Mayakovsky later published in *Tvorchestvo*, 1921, Nr. 7. Published some of Mayakovsky's poems.
Source: *Vladimir Mayakovsky and Lili Brik. Correspondence 1915–30*, ed. by Bengt Jangfeldt, Uppsala, 1982.

Nasonov, Vladimir Trifonovich
1860?–3.1917. Music impresario.
Member of V.V. Andreev's orchestra from 1888. On tour with the orchestra in Russia and Europe. Organized orchestras of folk instruments in military establishments. Author of a textbook on balalaika-playing, a collection of songs, and arrangements for the folk orchestra. Died in Petrograd.

Nasyrova, Khalima
1913–   . Singer (soprano).
Born in Uzbekistan. Singer at the Uzbek Musical Drama Theatre from 1929. Leading singer with the Uzbek Opera from 1939. State Prize of the USSR, 1942, 1951. Author of memoirs, Moscow, 1962.

Natanson, Mark Abramovich
1850–1919. Revolutionary.
Member of the populist movement from its beginnings in the 1860s. Later joined the SR Party. Became a commissar in the Bolshevik-left-SR coalition government in 1917–18.

Natanson, Vladimir Aleksandrovich
1.3.1909–   . Pianist, musicologist.
Born in Ekaterinoslav Gouvt. Pupil of F. Keneman and S. Feinberg. Reader at the Moscow Conservatory. Author of works on method. Literary works include *Proshloe Russkogo Pianizma*, Moscow, 1960.

Nauialis, Iuozas (Naujalis)
22.4.1869–9.9.1934. Composer, organist, conductor.
Born in Kovno (Kaunas). Organized a secular choir in Kaunas, 1898, the first Lithuanian bookshop and a

music shop, 1905, and the first Lithuanian musical journal, *Vargonininkas* (The Organist), 1909. Professor at the Lithuanian Conservatory. Author of mainly choral works. Died in Kaunas.

Naumenko, Nikolai Fedorovich
1901–1967. Col.-general.
Joined the Red Army, 1918. Took part in the Civil War. Graduated from air-force courses at the Red Army Academy, 1934. On active service in the Air Force during the Soviet-Finnish war, 1939–40. Commander of the Air Force at the Western Front during WWII. High air force command posts from 1945 until Stalin's death.

Naumenko, Viacheslav G.
10.3.1880?–1978. General, historian.
Cossack officer during WWI. During the Civil War, elected Ataman of the Kuban Cossacks. After the defeat of the Whites, evacuated to Turkey. Settled in Western Europe. During WWII, joined the anti-communist Cossacks in Austria, 1945. One of the very few to escape being handed over to SMERSH at the end of WWII. Moved to the USA. Published a valuable multi-volume collection of historical documents on the events of this period, *Sbornik Materialov o Vydache Kazakov v Lientse i v Drugikh Mestakh*, USA, 1953–56, which later became the basis of his major work, *Velikoe Predatel'stvo*, NY, 1962. In his old age, worked as a labourer on a chicken farm. Died in the USA.

Naumov, Aleksandr Nikolaevich
1868–1950. Politician.
Landowner. Liberal public figure. Minister of Agriculture before WWI. Popular among the liberal members of the Duma. Regarded as well-meaning, but ineffective. Emigrated after the Bolshevik take-over. 2 volumes of memoirs published in America, where he died.

Naumov, Mikhail Ivanovich
16.10.1908–1974. State security officer, general.
Born in Bolshaia Sosnovka near Perm'. Member of the Communist Party, 1928. Served in GPU and NKVD detachments from 1930 (during the collectivization). Became an officer of the border guards (under the NKVD), 1938. Appointed commander of partisan detachments in the Ukraine, 1942. Made 3 long treks through German occupied territory. Major-general and Hero of the Soviet Union, 1943. After WWII, graduated from the Military Academy of the General Staff. Continued to serve in the MVD system. High commands in the special troops of the MVD (later re-named KGB). Retired 1960. Glorified in the Soviet Union as one of the heroes of the partisan movement, the 'people's avengers'.

Naumov, Pavel Semenovich
1884–1942. Artist.
Landscape, still life and genre painter. Studied at the Petersburg Academy of Arts, 1904–11. Began exhibiting from 1909 with the Zolotoe Runo group. Other exhibitions: the Zolotoe Runo, 1910; the New Society of Artists, 1910, 1912–13; the Union of Russian Artists, 1910, 1915–16; Moscow Association of Artists, 1911; the Mir Iskusstva, 1912–13, 1915; St. Petersburg Contemporary Art, 1913; Sketches, Petrograd, 1917; First State Free Exhibition of Works of Art, Petrograd, 1919; Petrograd Artists of All Directions, Petrograd, 1921; Society of Artists, 1921–22, 1925; Pictures of Russian Artists, Sebastopol, 1925; 10 years of Russian Xylography, Leningrad, 1927; Jubilee Exhibition of Fine Art, Leningrad, 1927.

Navashin, Dmitrii Sergeevich
1889–25.1.1935. Politician, banker, poet.
Son of an academician. Studied law at Kiev University. Before WWI, in Moscow, became known as a young Symbolist poet. In the mid 1920s, came to Paris as a deputy director of the Soviet Foreign Trade Bank. Joined French masonic circles, and printed articles in the French press. Allegedly received an order to return to the USSR and disregarded it. Stabbed to death by an unknown young man, while walking his 2 dogs in the early morning in the Bois de Boulogne. Officially no details of his murder have been released, but it is suspected that the assassin was an NKVD agent. Given a masonic funeral by the French freemasons in Paris.

Nazarov, Nikolai Mikhailovich
9.5.1908– . Military conductor, French horn player.
Born in the Don military district. Pupil of A. Chugunov and F. Ekkert. Major-general. With the Military Orchestra of the Ministry of Defence of the USSR. Chief military conductor.

Nazarov, Nikolai Vladimirovich
6.11.1885–4.2.1942. Oboist.
Born in Vladimir-on-Kliazma. With Persimfans (the 1st Moscow Symphonic Ensemble) from 1923, later with the USSR State Orchestra and the All-Union Radio Quartet. Author of arrangements for oboe. Died in Moscow.

Nazlymov, Vladimir Aliverovich
1.11.1945– . Athlete.
Born in Makhachkala. Honoured Master of Sports (fencing), 1968. With the Moscow Oblast' Armed Forces Club. Graduated from the Daghestan Pedagogical Institute, 1969. Member of the CPSU, 1975. Olympic champion, 1968 and 1976. USSR champion, 1971–77. World champion, 1967–79. Bronze medallist, 1972. Silver medallist, 1976. In 1975 and 1977, the International Fencing Federation recognized him as the world's best fencer.

Nazvanov, Mikhail Mikhailovich
12.2.1914–13.6.1964. Actor.
Studied at a music school attached to the Moscow Conservatory, 1928–31. Actor at MKHAT and later at Mossovet theatres. His major film role was as Prince Kurbskii in *Ivan the Terrible*, 1945–46. Played Claudius in G. Kozintsev's *Hamlet*, 1964.

Nebol'sin, Vasilii Vasil'evich
11.6.1898–29.11.1958. Conductor.
Born in Khar'kov. Professor at the Moscow Conservatory. Choirmaster with the Bolshoi Theatre from 1920,

conductor there from 1922. Author of symphonies and chamber music. Died in Moscow.

Nechaev, Vasilii Vasil'evich
28.9.1895–5.6.1956. Pianist, composer.
Born in Moscow. Professor at the Moscow Conservatory. Author of operas, sonatas, and suites for violin and cello. Died in Moscow.

Necheporenko, Pavel Ivanovich
31.8.1916–   . Balalaika player.
Born in Kiev Gouvt. Pupil of V. Dombrovskii and S. Troianovskii. Reader at the Gnesin Music Pedagogical Institute. Author of arrangements for balalaika. State Prize of the USSR, 1952.

Nedelin, Mitrofan Ivanovich
1902–1960. Marshal.
Joined the Red Army, 1920, and the Bolshevik Party, 1924. Took part in the Civil War, and later in the Spanish Civil War. Graduated from the Dzerzhinskii Artillery Academy, 1941. Artillery officer during WWII at different fronts. Chief-of-staff of Artillery Forces, 1946. Head of the Artillery Administration, 1948. Commander-in-chief of Soviet Artillery, 1950. Deputy Defence Minister. Commander-in-chief of Soviet Strategic Rocket Forces, 1959. Died during an unspecified accident, probably connected with rocket-launching.

Nedel'skaia, Elena Nikolaevna
1906?–31.8.1980. Poetess.
Left Russia during the Civil War with her parents. Grew up in Harbin (Kharbin), which was, in the 1920s–40s, a unique free Russian city on Chinese soil. Became a well-known poetess, publishing her poems in local Russian newspapers. After the Communist take-over in China, moved with other Russian exiles to Australia. Continued to write poetry, and became the 'Poetess of the Russian Harbin'. Died in Stratfield near Sydney.

Negretov, Pavel Ivanovich
1923–   . Literary historian.
Born in Kirovograd. During WWII,

lived under German occupation. At the end of WWII, in Poland and Czechoslovakia. Repatriated, 1945, sentenced to 10 years of Gulag camps (Vorkuta). Released from the camps, 1955. Remained in Vorkuta. Graduated from Leningrad University (by correspondence), 1966. Compiled an excellent documentary biography of Korolenko during the revolutionary years (published in the USA).

Neigauz, Genrikh Gustavovich
12.4.1888–10.10.1964. Pianist, musicologist.
Born in Elisavetgrad. Son of the pianist G.V. Neigauz (1847–1938), nephew of the composer, pianist, conductor F.M. Blumenfel'd. Pupil of L. Godovskii. Professor at the Kiev Conservatory from 1919, and at the Moscow Conservatory from 1922. Taught a generation of internationally-known musicians, such as E. Gilel's, S. Rikhter, Ia. Zak and E. Malinin. Author of a book on piano-playing, Moscow, 1958. Died in Moscow.

Neigauz, Stanislav Genrikhovich
21.3.1927–   . Pianist.
Born in Moscow. Son and pupil of G. G. Neigauz. Reader at the Moscow Conservatory. Gave concerts all over Europe, in the USA, and in the USSR.

Neimark, Iosif Gustavovich
23.4.1903–   . Composer.
Born in Belostok. Author of an oratorio (Dvenadtsat', 1962), cantatas and symphonies.

Neizvestnyi, Ernest Iosifovich
1926–   . Sculptor.
Born in Sverdlovsk. Wounded during WWII. Studied at Moscow University (Philosophy – Marxism). Graduated from the Surikov Art Institute, Moscow. Became a fashionably famous sculptor. Came into conflict with Khrushchev during the latter's visit to his exhibition in the Manezh Hall in 1962. Expelled from the Union of Artists. Despite this, managed to retain his reputation and was showered with private and official orders. At the centre of

Moscow artistic life until his final departure from the USSR in 1976. His last commission was from Khrushchev's family for a memorial on Khrushchev's grave in Novodevich'e Cemetery. Settled in Switzerland, later moved to the USA. Active in Russian artistic life in exile.

Nekrasov, Andrei
1958–   . Film-maker.
Born in Leningrad. Son of a physicist. Studied at the Leningrad Theatre Institute (in the acting, and then the directing department). Emigrated in the 1970s. Studied at Columbia University, NY. Graduated from the Bristol Film School. His first documentary film, A Russia of One's Own, was shown on Channel 4 Television.

Nekrasov, Boris Vladimirovich
18.9.1899–1969? Chemist.
Graduated from the Plekhanov Institute of Economics, 1924. Later worked at the Moscow Textile Institute. Author of a standard textbook on general chemistry (12 editions, translated into many languages).

Nekrasov, Nikolai Vissarionovich
1879–1940. Politician, engineer.
Railway engineer. Left-wing cadet. Member of the 3rd and 4th Dumas. Prominent member of the Progressive Bloc. Minister of Transport in the Provisional Government, 1917. In Aug. 1917, member of the ruling triumvirate, with Kerenskii and Tereshchenko. Deputy Prime Minister, Minister of Finance, Governor-general of Finland, 1917. After the Bolshevik take-over, worked in Tsentrosoiuz, 1921. Arrested, worked as a Gulag inmate on the building of Stalin's pet project, the Belomor-Baltiiskii canal. According to visiting Soviet writers (Gorkii and others), praised the educational and moral value of labour, and its reforming character. Probably went insane. Died in the Gulag.

Nekrasov, Viktor Platonovich
17.6.1911–3.9.1987. Author.
Born in Kiev. His mother was a medical student at Lausanne University. As a boy, lived in Switzerland

and in Paris, where his parents had met. Returned to Kiev after WWI. His father died in 1917. Studied railway engineering, switched to architecture at the Construction Institute, Kiev. Did not graduate. Became attracted to the theatre. Toured for 4 years as an actor, assistant director and stage designer. WWII ended this career. Fought throughout the battle of Stalingrad, which provided him with the material for his famous book, *V Okopakh Stalingrada* (1946, Stalin Prize, 1947). This was an idealized but sincere description of his Stalingrad experiences. After extensive travels to Europe and America in 1957, 1960 and 1962, wrote *Both Sides of the Ocean*, the tone of which displeased Soviet literary ideologists and Khrushchev personally. Tried to get a memorial to the victims of Babii Yar erected in Kiev. Eventually expelled from the party and from the Union of Writers. Became unpublishable. Involved himself in dissident activity. Emigrated in 1974. For some time, editor-in-chief of the emigré magazine *Kontinent*. Settled in a council flat in a Paris suburb. Published several new books: *Zapiski Zevaki*, *Malen'kaia Pechalnaia Povest'*, *Saperlipopet*. Stripped of his Soviet citizenship for his involvement with *Kontinent*. Continued to travel around the world. Left his former actress wife and son who had been allowed to join him in exile. Died in Paris.

Nekrich, Aleksandr Moiseevich
1920– . Historian, editor.
Born in Baku. Took part in WWII. Graduated in history from Moscow University. Published numerous articles and books on Soviet modern history. His book, *1941, 22-e Iulia*, about the first days of the German Army's invasion of the USSR and the handling of the military situation by Stalin's government, became sensational in the USSR. The book was attacked by official Soviet historians, but supported by public opinion. In 1967, expelled from the Party. The book was withdrawn from all Soviet libraries, and a part of the imprint was destroyed. After that, he found it impossible to publish his work. Left the country, 1976. Settled in the USA. Editor of *Obozrenie*, the historico-political supplement of

Russkaia Mysl'. Author of *Nakazannye Narody*, USA, 1978, *Otrekis' Ot Strakha: Vospominaniia Istorika*, London, 1979, and *Utopiia U Vlasti*, London, 1982. Wrote numerous articles in the Russian emigré press.

Nelepp, Georgii Mikhailovich
20.4.1904–18.6.1957. Singer (tenor).
Born in Chernigov Gouvt. Pupil of I. Tomars. Leading singer with the Kirov Theatre of Opera and Ballet, Leningrad, 1929–44. With the Bolshoi Theatre from 1944. State Prize of USSR 1942, 1949 and 1950. Died in Moscow.

Nelidova, Lidia Richardovna (Barto)
1863–1929. Ballerina.
Graduated from the Moscow Theatre School, 1884. Joined the Bolshoi Theatre. At the Mariinskii Theatre, 1896–97. Founded a ballet school in Moscow, 1908, which still existed in the 1920s. Author of *Pis'ma o Ballete*, Moscow, 1894 and *Isskustvo Dvizhenii i Balletnaia Gimnastika*, Moscow, 1908. Probably emigrated. Place of death unknown.

Nemchinova, Vera Nikolaevna (m. Obukhova)
26.8.1899– . Ballerina.
Born in Moscow. Wife of the dancer A. N. Obukhov. Graduated from the private ballet school of L. R. Nelidova in Moscow. Lived abroad from 1915. With Diaghilev's Ballets Russes, 1916–26. Appeared in ballets choreographed by L. Massine and B. Nijinskaia. Founded, with A. Dolin and A. N. Obukhov, the Nemchinova-Dolin Ballet, 1927. Made guest appearances in Great Britain, then in the USA in M. Mordkin's company. Appeared in the Kaunas Opera, 1931–35, then in the Ballets Russes de Monte-Carlo. Gave guest performances in the USA and Australia. Taught at the Ballet School in New York from 1947, then at her own school of classical ballet from 1962.

Nemirovich-Danchenko, Vasilii Ivanovich
5.1.1849–18.9.1936. Author, journalist.
Born in Tiflis. Educated at the Cadet Corps. War correspondent during

the Russo-Turkish war 1877–78, the Russo-Japanese war 1904–5, and WWI. Prolific writer of novels, travel books and memoirs. 50 vol. collected works published in Petrograd, 1916. Emigrated, 1921. Settled in Prague. Died in Czechoslovakia.

Nemirovich-Danchenko, Vladimir Ivanovich
23.12.1859–25.4.1943. Stage director.
Born in Ozurgeti, Georgia. Amateur actor and critic from the 1870s. Studied at Moscow University, 1876–79. Started to write novels and plays under the influence of A. Chekhov. With K. Stanislavskii, founded and directed the Moscow Arts Theatre (MKHAT), 1898. Reformer of the art of acting. Made an important contribution to Soviet drama by producing Russian classical works and works by Soviet playwrights. Organized an operatic school within MKHAT, which was later renamed the Nemirovich-Danchenko Musical Drama Theatre. His aim was to train artists to be both singers and actors. In the comic operas which he produced between 1920–32, his goal was to subordinate the dance to the character of the production and make it an organic part of the action. Directors of dance and music with whom he worked included V. Burmeister, V. Lopukhov and N. Glan. Took part in a production of *Swan Lake* at the Bolshoi Theatre, 1920. Helped the choreographer A. Gorskii to achieve a logical sequence in choreographic action. The Ballet Collective of the Moscow Art Ballet was amalgamated with the Nemirovich-Danchenko Musical Drama Theatre in 1939. Remained until his death closely connected with MKHAT. Starting as a theatre reformer, towards the end of his life he became a conservative influence during the years of Stalinist control of the arts. Many official honours. Died in Moscow.

Nemitz, Aleksandr Vasil'evich
1879–1967. Vice-admiral.
Graduated from the Naval Academy, 1912. During WWI, commander of the Black Sea fleet, Aug. 1917. Joined the Red Navy, 1919. Commander of the Naval Forces of the Soviet Republic, 1920–21. Lecturer at higher naval educational establishments, 1924–47.

Nemtsev, Iosif Vasil'evich
1885–14.6.1939. Conductor.
Born in Samara Gouvt. Chief conductor at the Olympiad of Artistic Initiative, Leningrad, (1st Olympiad, 1927). Taught at the Leningrad Conservatory, 1925–39 (Reader from 1929). Died in Leningrad.

Nenenene, Aldona Iuozovna (Chesaitite)
13.10.1949–   . Athlete.
Born in the village of Daugirdai, Lithuania. Graduated from the Kaunas Institute of Physical Culture, 1972. Honoured Master of Sports (handball), 1976. With Kaunas Zhal'giris. Sports instructor. Olympic champion, 1976.

Nepenin, Andrian (Adrian) Ivanovich
1871–4.3.1917. Vice-admiral.
Educated at the Navy Cadet Corps, 1892. Took part in the Russo-Japanese war, 1904–05. During WWI, head of naval communications in the Baltic, 1914, organized a naval air force. Commander of the Baltic fleet in Sep. 1916. After the February Revolution 1917, deposed by revolutionary sailors. Arrested on the ship *Krechet*. Shot on his way to prison in Sveaborg.

Neradovskii, Petr Ivanovich
1875–1962. Artist.
Born in Moscow. Studied at the Moscow School of Painting, Sculpture and Architecture, 1896, under Konstantin Korovin and Leonid Pasternak. Then at the Petersburg Academy of Arts, 1896–1903. Pupil of Il'ia Repin. Portrait painter, also water-colour and graphic artist. Exhibitions from 1894: the New Society of Artists, the Mir Iskusstva, the Zhar-Tsvet, the Russian Graphic, 10 Years of Revolution, Artists of the RSFSR, 15 Years. Personal exhibition of his graphic work to mark his 80th birthday, Moscow, 1955. Died in Moscow.

Neris, Salomeia (Bachinskaite-Buchene)
17.11.1904–7.7.1945. Poetess.
Born in Kirshiai, near Vilkavishky, Lithuania. Graduated from Kaunas (Kovno) University in 1928. Worked as a teacher. First poems published in 1923. After the Soviet occupation of Lithuania, became deputy of the Supreme Soviet of the USSR, 1941. During WWII, evacuated to Eastern USSR. Died in Moscow. Main work: *Poetry*, 2 vol.

Nesmeianov, Aleksandr Nikolaevich
9.9.1899–1972? Chemist.
Graduated from Moscow University, 1922. Professor at the University, 1935, and President, 1948–51. Prepared the move of the University to the new building complex on the Lenin hills. President of the Academy of Sciences of the USSR, 1951. Specialist in metallo-organic compounds. Active in the Stalinist peace campaigns in the 1940s and 1950s.

Nesterov, Arkadii Aleksandrovich
14.12.1918–   . Composer.
Born in Gzhatsk. Reader at the Gorkii Conservatory. Author of a ballet, symphonies, and choral works.

Nesterov, Mikhail Vasil'evich
31.5.1862–18.10.1942. Painter.
Born in Ufa. Son of a merchant. Educated at Ufa and Moscow high schools, 1880. Studied at the Academy of Arts in Petersburg, 1883. In the late 1880s, while living at Sergiev Posad (now Zagorsk), attracted attention with his paintings on religious subjects. Member of the artists' group in Abramtsevo. Painted frescoes in the St. Vladimir Cathedral in Kiev, 1891–95. Participated in the Mir Iskusstva art exhibitions. Close to Leo Tolstoy, 1906. First personal exhibitions in Petersburg and Moscow, 1907. Invariably tried to capture in his work the spirit of Holy Russia. Prominent figure among the Russian intelligentsia. His painting *Filosofy* (Bulgakov and Florenskii), 1917, is almost a symbol of the Russian religious renaissance of the early 20th century. During the Civil War, 1919–20, in Armavir. Returned to Moscow, 1920. Refused to become a professor of the socialist realist Academy of Arts under I. Brodskii, 1934. In old age, painted some memorable portraits of his contemporaries from the pre-revolutionary intelligentsia, such as Chertkov and Prof. Ivan Pavlov. Died in Moscow.

Nesterova, Klara Ivanovna (Guseva)
8.3.1937–   . Athlete.
Born in the village of Pichersk, Tambov Oblast'. Graduated from the Moscow Institute of Physical Culture, 1959. Honoured Master of Sports (skating), 1960. With Riazan' Spartak. USSR and world champion, 1960 (1,000 metres). Olympic champion, 1960 (1,000 metres).

Nest'ev, Izrail' Vladimirovich
17.4.1911–   . Musicologist.
Born in Kerch'. Reader at the Moscow Conservatory. Author of *S. Prokof'ev*, Moscow, 1957, *Hans Eisler i ego Pesennoe Tvorchestvo*, Moscow, 1962, and *G. Puccini*, Moscow, 1963.

Netto, Igor' Aleksandrovich
9.1.1930–   . Athlete.
Born in Moscow. Honoured Master of Sports (football), 1954. Member of the CPSU, 1966. Graduated from the Moscow Institute of Physical Culture, 1976. USSR champion, 1952–53, 1956, 1958, 1962. Olympic champion, 1956. USSR international team captain, 1954–62. Author of *Eto Futbol*, Moscow, 1974.

Nevezhin, Fedor Ivanovich
1902–1964. Artist.
Genre, landscape and historical painter. Studied at the VKHUTEIN (Higher Artistic-Technical Institute), Moscow, under K. Istomin. Pupil of Pavel Kuznetsov and V. Favorskii. Graduated in 1930. Exhibited from 1929 with: the Association of Artists of Revolutionary Russia, Moscow, 1929; Artists of the RSFSR, 15 Years, Leningrad, 1932; Moscow, 1938–39, 1945, 1947, 1949, 1950–52, 1954, 1957–58, 1960. Died in Moscow.

Nevskii, Georgii Georgievich
1891–1961. Lt.-general.
Joined the Red Army, 1918. Graduated from the Military Engineers' Academy, 1918. Took part in the Civil War. Joined the Communist Party, 1943. On active service during WWII as Commander of Engineering Military Forces in Karelia. Lecturer at the Frunze Military Academy, 1947–54.

Nevskii, Vladimir Ivanovich (Krivobokov, Feodosii Ivanovich)
1876–1937. Revolutionary, politician.
Joined the SD Party, 1897. Graduated from Khar'kov University, 1911. Active participant in the 1905 and 1917 revolutions. One of the leaders of the military organization of the Petersburg Bolshevik Cttee., later the Cen. Cttee. of the Bolshevik Party, 1917. During the Civil War, Minister of Communications, Member of the Presidium, and deputy chairman of VTSIK, 1919–20, simultaneously head of the department of the Cen. Cttee. in charge of rural affairs. Dean of the Communist University, 1921. Deputy head of the commission for the party history of the Cen. Cttee., 1922. Director of the Lenin Library, 1924. Wrote on the history of the revolutionary movement in Russia, and on the history of the Bolshevik Party. Liquidated by Stalin.

Nevzorov, Vladimir Mikhailovich
5.10.1952– . Athlete.
Born in Maikop, Krasnodar Krai. Honoured Master of Sports (judo), 1975. With Maikop Urozhai. Graduated from the Adygeiskii Pedagogical Institute, 1976. Member of the CPSU, 1977. USSR champion, 1975–76. European champion, 1975 and 1977. World champion, 1975. Olympic champion, 1976.

Nezhdanova, Antonina Vasil'evna
29.7.1873–26.6.1950. Singer.
Born near Odessa. Joined the Bolshoi Theatre, 1902. With the Grand Opera, Paris, 1912. Became very famous in the 1920–40s. Taught from 1936. Professor at the Moscow Conservatory from 1943. State Prize of USSR, 1943. Author of *Stranitsy Zhisni*, Moscow, 1960. Died in Moscow.

Neznamov, Aleksandr Aleksandrovich
1872–1928. Major-general.
Graduated from the Academy of the General Staff, 1900. Took part in the Russo-Japanese war and WWI. Joined the Red Army, 1918. Professor at the Military Engineering Academy of the Red Army, 1918–25. Wrote on military engineering and military history.

Neznanskii, Fridrikh Evseevich
1932– . Lawyer, author.
Born near Gomel'. Graduated from the Moscow Law Institute. Worked in the Soviet judicial system for 25 years. Member of the Moscow Bar Association. Published some articles and prose in the Soviet press. Left the USSR, 1977, and settled in the USA. Emerged as a crime writer working with E. Topol. Stories and books appeared in both the Russian and American press.
Books: *Zhurnalist Dlia Brezhneva Ili Smertel'nye Igry* (with E. Topol), Germany, 1981; *Iarmarka V Sokolnikakh*, Germany, 1984; *Operatsiia Faust*, Germany, 1986; *Million Dlia Chempionki* (with E. Topol), 1980.

Nichkov, Vladislav Vlassovich
14.5.1947– . Diplomat, intelligence officer.
Born in New York. For 6 months in 1969, post-graduate in Paris, attached to the Soviet Trade Delegation. Returned to France at least 10 times during the Franco-Soviet Co-operation programme as a technical, scientific and commercial specialist. From 30 Nov. 1979, 1st secretary of the Soviet Embassy in Paris in charge of the Scientific and Technical Exchange Section. Caught by the French counter-espionage service trying to steal technological secrets. Exposed by *Express* magazine as a KGB resident in France and expelled in Feb. 1985.
See: *Express*, 7 Feb. 1985.

Niiazi (Tagi-zade Gadzhibekov Niiazi Zulfugarovich)
20.8.1912– . Composer, conductor.
Born in Tiflis. Son and nephew of the composers Zulfugar and Uzeir Gadzhibekov. Studied composition under M. Gnesin, A. Stepanov and G. Popov, 1921–31. Studied at the Gnesin Music School, Moscow, 1926–31, and at the Baku Conservatory, 1933–34. Pupil of L. Rudolf. Worked in Baku from 1933. Musical director of Azerbaidzhan Radio, 1935–37. Worked concurrently for the Baku Film Studio and in theatre. Artistic director and conductor with the Azerbaidzhan Akhundov Theatre of Opera and Ballet, 1937–51. Conductor and artistic director of the

Gadzhibekov State Symphony Orchestra from 1938 (with intervals). Guest performances abroad. Influenced by Azerbaidzhan folk music. Author of operas, symphonies, vocal and instrumental compositions, music for stage and film as well as for the ballet *Chitra*, based on music composed for R. Tagore's play, 1960, at the Kuibyshev Theatre. His music captures the mood of Indian folk melodies.

Nikanchikov, Aleksei
30.7.1940–28.1.1972. Athlete.
Belorussian athlete. Honoured Master of Sports (fencing). 5th place at the XVIIIth, and silver medal winner at the XIXth Olympic Games. The cause of his premature death, reported in the American press, was not explained in the Soviet media.

Nikiforov, Valentin Mikhailovich
1934– . Politician.
1st secretary of Vyborg CP Raikom in Leningrad before 1977. Head of the Leningrad Obkom CPSU, 1977. Secretary, and then 2nd secretary of Leningrad Gorkom, 1977–78. Moved to Moscow. Deputy head of the department of Organizational Party Work of the Cen. Cttee. of the CPSU, 1979–85. Deputy Foreign Minister from Dec. 1985 dealing with cadres. Candidate member of the Cen. Cttee. of the CPSU.

Nikiforov, Viktor Vasil'evich
4.12.1931– . Athlete.
Born in Moscow. Master of Sports (hockey), 1956. With Moscow Dynamo. World and European champion, 1956. Olympic champion, 1956. Works as a sports instructor.

Nikiforova, Maria (Marus'ka)
1892?–1922. Guerrilla leader.
Close associate of the anarchist leader N. Makhno during the Civil War. With her cavalry gangs, attacked the German occupation forces in the Ukraine, and also the Red and White armies during the Civil War. Sent as an underground guerrilla leader to the Crimea. Captured by the Whites and shot.

Nikitin, Fedor Mikhailovich

3.5.1900– . Actor.
From 1917, worked in theatres in Moscow, Leningrad and Odessa. In 1925, entered the film industry. Prominent actor of the Russian silent cinema. His best films include *Kat'ka-Bumazhnyi Ranet*, 1926, *Dom v Sugrobakh*, 1928, *Parizhskii Sapozhnik*, 1928, and *Oblomok Imperii*, 1929.

Nikitina, E.F.

1880?–after 1960. Author.
Married A. M. Nikitin, the lawyer who was with A. Kerenskii at the Lena goldfields, when he was investigating the shooting of prisoners by Tsarist prison guards. Hostess of the Nikitinskie Subbotniki, 1914–31 (a literary society and publishing house). In 1919, lived in Rostov-on-Don, and created there a literary salon under the Whites at the time of General Denikin.

Nikitina, Tamara Petrovna

28.2.1904– . Ballerina.
Born in Moscow. Graduated from the Moscow Choreographic School. Pupil of V. D. Tikhomirov and N. G. Legat. Dancer with the Bolshoi Theatre, 1920–46. Choreographer and coach at the Bolshoi Theatre, 1946–78. Directed, with A. I. Radunskii, the dances for the opera *Rusalka*, 1937. Took part in the renewal of the ballet *Konek Gorbunok*, 1948.

Nikitina, Varvara Aleksandrovna (Ivanovna)

1857–1920. Ballerina.
Place of birth unknown. Studied at the Petersburg Theatre School. With the Mariinskii Theatre, 1873–93. Created the part of Svanilda in Petipa's *Coppelia (La Fille aux Yeux d'Émail)*, 1884. One of the outstanding Russian classical ballerinas of the 1880s and 90s.

Nikodim (Rotov, Boris), Metropolitan of Leningrad and Novgorod

15.10.1929–5.9.1978. Russian Orthodox clergyman.
Born in Frolovo, Riazan' Oblast'. Son of a communist party official.

Educated at secondary school in Riazan'. Graduated from the Riazan' Pedagogical Institute. Monk, 1947. Member of the clergy of Iaroslavl' Cathedral 1949–55. Graduated from Leningrad Theological Academy in 1955. Member of the Russian Church Mission (Moscow Patriarchate) in Jerusalem, 1956. Head of the mission, 1957. Head of the secretariat of the Moscow Patriarchate, 1959. Bishop, 1960. Head of the foreign relations department of the Patriarchate, 1960–72. Extremely active in international affairs, promoting Soviet official aims (especially peace initiatives) and broadening the international connections of the Moscow Patriarchate. Member of the Cen. Cttee. of the World Council of Churches, 1961. Archbishop, 1961. Exarch of the Moscow Patriarchate in Western Europe, 1974–78. Elected president of the WCC, Nairobi, 1975. Died of a heart attack during an audience in the Vatican with the newly elected Pope John Paul I.

Nikolaev, Aleksandr Aleksandrovich

4.9.1903– . Pianist, musicologist.
Born in Khar'kov. Father of the composer Aleksei Nikolaev. Professor and head of the Department of History and Theory of Piano at the Moscow Conservatory. Author of *Fortepiannoe Nasledie Chaikovskogo*, Moscow-Leningrad, 1949.

Nikolaev, Aleksandr Andreevich

1905–1949. Vice-admiral.
Joined the Bolshevik Party and the Red Navy, 1927. Graduated from a submarine school, 1929. Graduated from Lenin Military Political Academy, 1938. Political Commissar in the Navy, 1938, and during WWII. Deputy head of the Political Administration of the Armed Forces, 1947.

Nikolaev, Aleksei Aleksandrovich

24.41931– . Composer.
Born in Moscow. Son of the pianist A. Nikolaev. Taught at the Moscow Conservatory. Author of operas, symphonies, and music for stage and screen.

Nikolaev, Andriian Grigor'evich

5.9.1929– . Cosmonaut.
Born in the village of Shorshely,

Chuvash ASSR. Educated at a forestry school, 1947. Worked in forestry in Karelia, 1950. Graduated from a military aviation school, 1954. Fighter pilot, selected for the cosmonaut team, 1960. In 1962 and 1970, made long flights into space. Major-general, 1970. Married Valentina Tereshkova (their daughter was the first child of a marriage between cosmonauts). Deputy commander of the cosmonauts training centre.

Nikolaev, Leonid Vladimirovich

13.8.1878–11.10.1942. Pianist, composer.
Born in Kiev. Pupil of V. Pukhal'skii and V. Safonov. Taught at the Petersburg/Leningrad Conservatory from 1909, professor from 1912. D. Shostakovich was one of his pupils. Author of works for piano, violin, and cello. Died in Tashkent.

Nikolaev, Valentin Vladimirovich

6.4.1924– . Athlete.
Born in the village of Donino-Kamenka, Kirovograd Oblast'. Graduated from the Rostov Institute of Railway Engineers, 1948. From 1954, with the Rostov-on-Don Armed Forces Club. Honoured Master of Sports (wrestling), 1955. Energetics engineer. Member of the CPSU, 1955. USSR champion, 1952 and 1954. World champion, 1955. Olympic champion 1956.

Nikolaeva, Margarita Nikolaevna

23.9.1935– . Athlete.
Born in Ivanovo. Honoured Master of Sports (gymnastics), 1960. With the Odessa Armed Forces Club. Graduated from the Odessa Technological Institute of Food and the Freezing Industry, 1962, and from the Odessa Pedagogical Institute, 1966. Olympic champion, 1960.

Nikolaeva, Tat'iana Petrovna (m. Tarasevich)

4.5.1924– . Pianist, composer.
Born in Bezhitsa. Pupil of A. Goldenveizer. 1st prize for Bach interpretation at the International Competition in Leipzig, 1950. Reader at the Moscow Conservatory. Author of a symphony and works for piano. State Prize of the USSR, 1951.

**Nikolai (Iarushevich, Boris
Dorofeevich), Metropolitan of
Kolomna and Krutitsy**
13.1.1892–13.12.1961. Russian
Orthodox clergyman.
Studied physics and mathematics at
Petersburg University. Monk, 1914.
Chaplain in the Russian Army, 1915.
Graduated from the Petrograd Theo-
logical Academy in 1917. Archiman-
drite in charge of the Aleksandr
Nevskii Lavra in Petrograd, 1919.
Bishop of Peterhof, 1922. As an
opponent of the Living Church,
arrested and imprisoned, 1922–24.
After his release, worked with Aleksii
(Simanskii) in the Leningrad archdiocese. Archbishop of Novgorod
and Pskov, 1936–40. During the
period 1936–38, remained as one of
only 4 bishops of the Russian
Orthodox Church (all others having
been liquidated or imprisoned). After
the partition of Poland between
Hitler and Stalin, appointed exarch
of Western Ukraine and Belorussia,
1939. Metropolitan, Mar. 1941. During WWII, took an active part in the
war effort and propaganda campaigns. Member of the commission
on German crimes in the occupied
territories. Testified to the alleged
responsibility of the Germans in the
massacre of Polish POW officers at
Katyn (who, according to the testimonies of others, including witnesses
and participants of the exhumation,
were shot by the NKVD on Stalin's
orders before the German invasion of
the USSR). Took part (with the
future patriarchs Sergii and Aleksii)
in the meeting with Stalin, 4 Sep.
1943, in Moscow where a de facto
concordat was reached (Stalin agreed
to reinstate a patriarch in exchange
for loyalty and patriotic help from
the church). After WWII, as head of
the Foreign Department of the
Moscow Patriarchate, continued to
take part in many propaganda
exercises, especially the Peace
Campaigns, trying to initiate disarmament in the West, while remaining silent about Soviet armaments. Re-imposed Soviet control
of the church in Western areas
of the USSR, which were under
German control during WWII (especially Western Ukraine). Tried
unsuccessfully to impose Soviet control on Russian Orthodox churches in
the Western Countries. After Stalin's
death, took a much more indepen-

dent line. Was instrumental in the
decision to excommunicate the ex-
priest Osipov, who had become a tool
of virulent atheist propaganda.
Opposed Khrushchev's vicious anti-
religious campaign in the late 1950s.
In June 1960, was suddenly removed
from his post of chairman of the
Department of External Church
Relations. In Sep. 1960, released
from his duties as Metropolitan of
Krutitsy (2nd ranking hierarch of the
Russian church). Died suddenly.
There are suspicions that his death
was hastened by the KGB. Buried at
Zagorsk.

**Nikolai II (Nicholas II; Romanov,
Nikolai Aleksandrovich), Tsar**
18.5.1868–17.7.1918. Last Emperor
of the Romanov dynasty.
Born at Tsarskoe Selo. Son of
Aleksandr III and the Danish princess, Dagmar (Maria Fedorovna),
sister of Queen Mary (wife of Edward
VII). Received private education
from tutors, including the right-wing
lawyer and statesman Pobedonost-
sev. Amiable, charming and intelligent, but not diligent, in his youth he
was overawed by his autocratic
father and was little involved in state
affairs. Succeeded to the throne on 1
Nov. 1894, and was crowned in
Moscow on 26 May 1896. Essentially
a timid and private man, preferring
tolerance and compromise, he could
nevertheless show great tenacity and
stubborness, for example insisting on
his marriage to Alice of Hesse,
despite the opposition of his parents
(he married her almost immediately
after his father's death). The life-long
mutual devotion of Nicholas and
Aleksandra was counter-balanced by
a host of personal problems: bad
relations between his wife and his
mother; the estrangement of the
monarch and his family from high
society; 4 daughters and no heir, and
when at last a boy was born, he
turned out to be a haemophiliac. In
affairs of state, he was at his best
when he could find somebody who
was able to govern on his own
initiative (Witte and the economic
boom; Stolypin and his reforms), but
could never be relied upon to give
firm enough support in difficult
times. In retrospect, he must be
judged as presiding over a remarkably colourful historical period,

with rapid economic and political
progress accompanied by the inevi-
table social turmoil, the flowering of
culture and the arts, and the gradual
transition from autocracy to a
parliamentary system. Against his
better judgement, he let himself be
drawn into 2 disastrous wars: with
Japan, 1904–05, leading to the first
unsuccessful revolution; and WWI,
which led directly to his abdication
Feb. 1917. Following the February
Revolution 1917, he was put under
house-arrest with his family at
Tsarskoe Selo by the Provisional
Government, and later sent by
Kerenskii to the Urals. After the
October Revolution, he was shot
with his whole family by Bolshevik
guards, on the orders of Lenin and
Sverdlov in Ekaterinburg (now
Sverdlovsk), the bodies being afterwards hacked to pieces, burned, and
thrown into disused mine shafts in
the nearby forest. The execution of
the Tsar was announced by the Soviet
government immediately, but attributed to the decision of local
authorities. The murder of his family
was acknowledged only much later.

**Nikolai Mikhailovich (Romanov),
Grand Duke**
26.4.1859–28.1.1919. Historian.
On military service, 1884–1903. Became known as a historian, specializing in the early 19th century (2 vol.
biography of Aleksander I, biography of Count Stroganov, 3 vol.
biography of Empress Elizabeth,
wife of Aleksander I). President of
the Russian Historical Society, 1909–
17. Shot in the Peter and Paul
Fortress in Petrograd by the Cheka.

**Nikolai Nikolaevich (Romanov),
Grand Duke**
18.11.1856–5.1.1929. Commander-in-
chief.
Born in Petersburg. Grandson of
Nicholas I. Received a military
education at the Nikolaevskoe Military Engineering School, 1873. Graduated from the Academy of the
General Staff, 1876. During the
Russo-Turkish war 1877–78, in the
staff of his father, who was commander-in-chief of the Russian Army.
Later commander of the Guards
Hussar Regiment. General inspector
of cavalry, 1895–1905. Chairman of

the National Defence Council, 1905–08. Commander of guards regiments and the Petersburg military district, 1905–1914. Through his wife and her sister, Rasputin gained entrance into court circles, but Nikolai later became a fierce enemy of Rasputin, which made him unpopular with Empress Aleksandra. Commander-in-chief during WWI, 2 Aug. 1914–5. Sep. 1915. Succeeded by Nicholas II on the insistence of Aleksandra. Sep. 1915–2 Mar. 1917, Commander-in-chief of the Caucasian front (against Turkey). One of the commanders-in-chief who advised Nicholas II to abdicate. On abdication the tsar again appointed him commander-in-chief of the Russian armies, but he was not able to take up this appointment because of the hostile attitude of the Soviets and the Provisional Government. Emigrated from the Crimea in Mar. 1919 to Italy. Settled in France. Regarded by some Russian emigrés as the heir apparent to the Romanov throne. Died at Antibes in France.

Nikol'skii, Iurii Sergeevich
3.12.1895–1962. Composer, conductor.
Born in Moscow. Author of a cantata, symphonies, music for children's films and for radio productions. Died in Moscow.

Nikonov, Viktor Petrovich
28.2.1929– . Politician.
Son of a peasant. Graduated from the Azovo-Chernomorskii Agricultural Institute in 1950. Member of the CPSU from 1954. Worked as chief agronomist of a machine and tractor station (MTS). Deputy director of an agricultural school. Director of an MTS, 1950–58. Deputy head, then head of the Agricultural Department of Krasnoiarsk Krai CPSU Cttee., 1958–61. 2nd secretary of Tatar ASSR Oblast' CPSU Cttee., 1961–67. 1st secretary of Mari ASSR Oblast' CPSU Cttee., 1967–79. Candidate member, 1971–76, and full member of the Cen. Cttee., 1976. USSR Deputy Minister of Agriculture. Chairman of the All-Union Production-Scientific Association for Agrochemical Services of Agriculture from 1979. A reform-minded technocrat. Promoted by Gorbachev to full voting membership of the Politburo.

Nikonova, Valentina Gennad'evna
5.3.1952– . Athlete.
Born in Kazan'. Honoured Master of Sports (fencing), 1973. With Kazan' Dynamo. Graduated from the Kazan' Pedagogical Institute, 1975. Member of the CPSU, 1978. World champion, 1973, 1974 and 1977. USSR champion, 1974. Olympic champion, 1976.

Nilus, Petr Aleksandrovich
1869–1943. Artist.
Born in Odessa. Studied at the Odessa School of Graphic Art and the Society of Fine Arts, 1887–90, under K. Kostandi, L. Iorini, A. Krasovskii. Continued his education at the Petersburg Academy of Arts, 1890–92. Genre and landscape painter. Exhibitions: from 1891 at the TPKHV, the MOLKH, the Association of Southern Russian Artists in Odessa, All-Russian Exhibition, Nizhnii Novgorod, 1st State Free Exhibition. Petrograd, Kostandi Society, Odessa, 1925. Emigrated in 1926.

Niman, Fedor Avgustovich (pseudonym – Fedorov)
11.9.1860–5.9.1936. Oboist, conductor, composer.
Born in Nuremberg. In Russia from 1880. Naturalized, 1890. Joined the orchestra of the Mariinskii Theatre, 1890. Conductor with the Great Russian Orchestra from 1918. Professor at the Leningrad Conservatory from 1921. Composed for folk instruments. Died in Leningrad.

Nirod, Fedor Fedorovich
13.4.1907– . Stage designer.
Born in Petersburg. Graduated from the Kiev Institute of Art, 1930. Worked with theatres in the Kuban Oblast' and in L'vov. Worked with the Franko Theatre where he created the costumes and scenery for 2 ballets, 1949 and 1955. Worked with the Shevchenko Theatre from 1960. Responsible for the artistic side of several ballets, 1965 and 1972. Worked for the Odessa Theatre, 1974.

Nisnevich, Anatolii Gennad'evich
5.6.1937– . Ballet dancer.
Born in Leningrad Oblast'. Graduated from the Leningrad Choreographic School. Pupil of F. U. Balabina. Dancer with the Kirov Theatre, 1956–76. Appeared in ballets and concerts of the Chamber Ballet, directed by G. D. Aleksidze. Taught at the Leningrad Choreographic School from 1963. Taught and coached at the Leningrad Malyi Theatre, from 1978.

Nisskii, Georgii Grigor'evich
1903– . Artist.
Landscape painter and graphic artist. Born in the Ukraine. Studied at the Gomel' Gubpolitprosvet Art Studio, then at the VKHUTEMAS for one year, 1922. Entered the VKHUTEIN, Moscow, in 1923. Graduated in 1930. Pupil of Robert Falk. Exhibited from 1932. Personal exhibitions: Moscow, 1950, 1960.

Nizhankovskii, Ostap Iosifovich
1862/63–22.5.1919. Composer, choir conductor.
Born in Stryi. Father of the composer, Nestor Nizhankovskii (1894–1940). Author of choral works, and piano pieces. He was a very well-known public figure in Galicia.

Nizhinskaia, Bronislava Fominichna (Nijinska, Bronislava)
8.1.1891–22.2.1972. Ballerina, choreographer.
Born in Minsk. Sister of Vaclav Nijinsky. Graduated from the Petersburg Ballet School, 1908, and was accepted into the Mariinskii Theatre. Left in 1911 in protest at her brother's dismissal. Appeared abroad in the Ballets Russes, 1910–13. Created various parts in M. Fokin's ballets. Danced in London with her brother's company, 1914. Appeared and taught in Kiev, 1915–21. Emigrated. Ballerina, choreographer and producer with Diaghilev's Ballets Russes, 1922–24. Choreographer with the Paris Opera, the Colon Theatre in Buenos Aires, Ida Rubinstein's company and many other theatres all over the world. Also had her own company, 1932–35. Produced mainly one-act ballets. Died in Los Angeles.

295

Nizhinskaia, Kira Vatslavovna (Nijinsky, Kira; m. Markevitch)
1913– . Daughter of Vaclav Nijinsky.
Born in Vienna. Elder daughter of Vaclav Nijinsky and the Hungarian Countess, Romola de Pulszky. Studied ballet, and at one time danced herself. Married Diaghilev's intimate friend, the composer, Igor Markevich. After her divorce, moved to the USA. A film about her life, *She Dances Alone*, was shown at the 1982 Cannes Film Festival.

Nizhinskii, Vatslav Fomich (Nijinsky, Vaclav)
17.12.1889 (according to others 12.3.1890)–8.4.1950. Ballet dancer, choreographer.
Born in Kiev. His Polish mother, Eleonora Bereda-Nijinska, was a dancer at the Warsaw Opera. His father, Thomas Nijinsky, was a dancer and choreographer who toured in Russia with his own company. Nijinsky entered the Petersburg Ballet School in 1898. Graduated in 1907 and joined the Mariinski Theatre. Because of his unique talent as dancer and actor, immediately given the foremost place. Partner of the ballerinas Matilda Kshessinskaia, Olga Preobrazhenskaia, Anna Pavlova and Tamara Karsavina. Created the leading parts in various new ballets, 1907–09. Dismissed from the Mariinskii Theatre in 1911 for wearing, on his own authority, in the ballet *Giselle*, a new costume designed by A. Benois. Leading dancer in Diaghilev's Ballets Russes abroad. Appeared as principal dancer in Mikhail Fokin's ballets, 1909–13. Produced for Diaghilev *L'Après-Midi d'un Faune* and *Le Sacré du Printemps* (music by I. Stravinskii). His productions met with contradictory criticism as they went against the accepted rules of academic repertory, breaking with the picturesqueness of Fokin's productions. Anticipated the ballet of the mid-1920s in his search for new ways. Founded his own company in 1914, and appeared in London. Once more joined Diaghilev's company in 1916. Produced the ballet *Till Ullenspiegel* (music by R. Strauss) for the company's guest performance in America. Renovated male dancing, combining technical virtuosity with plasticity and mime. As a choreo-

grapher, ahead of his time, giving the ballet a wider expressive range. Married Romola de Pulszky, a Hungarian aristocrat and admirer. Close to Diaghilev professionally and intimately until his marriage to Romola. Mental disease, probably inherited, struck him as a result of his marriage and break with Diaghilev. It led to his leaving the stage early. Thanks to his wife's wealth and love, was taken care of and spent long periods at expensive private mental clinics. During the war stayed in Budapest. Died in London. Wrote *Dnevnik Nizhinskogo* in 1919 (published in Paris in 1953). M. Bejart composed a ballet on the subject of Nijinsky: *Nizhinskii, Kloun Bozhii* (Nijinsky, Clown de Dieu) in 1971. A Soviet documentary film, *Vospominaniia o Nizhinskom* (by Iu. Al'dokhin), was released in 1980.
Source: Iu. Grigorovich, *Balet Entsiklopediia*, Moscow, 1981; R. Buckle, *Nijinsky*, London, 1971.

Nizhnikova, Tamara Nikolaevna
9.3.1925– . Singer (coloratura).
Born in Samara. Pupil of M. Vladimirova. Leading singer at the Minsk Theatre of Opera and Ballet from 1951. Taught at the Minsk Conservatory from 1964.

Nogin, Viktor
1879–1924. Politician.
Prominent Bolshevik. Chairman of the Moscow Soviet in 1917. Commissar of Commerce and Industry in the first Soviet government. Later in charge of the USSR textile industry.

Normet, Leo (Leopol'd Tarmovich)
17.9.1922– . Composer.
Born in Estonia. Taught at the Tallinn Conservatory. Author of operas, instrumental works, and music for the stage.

Norshtein, Iurii Borisovich
15.9.1941– . Film director.
Studied at the Soiuzmultfilm Studio. From 1961, staff artist-animator. Made over 40 animated films. Film debut, 1968. In 1971 with I. Ivanov-Vano, directed *Secha Pri Kerzhentse*, which was internationally recognized as a masterpiece. Many of his works have received prizes at the Venice and Moscow Film Festivals.

Nortsov, Panteleimon Markovich
28.3.1900– . Singer (baritone).
Born in Poltava Gouvt. Pupil of V. Tsvetkov. Leading singer at the Bolshoi Theatre, 1925–53. Taught at the Moscow Conservatory from 1951. Reader from 1962.

Nosov, Georgii Nikiforovich
15.4.1911– . Composer.
Born in Orenburg Gouvt. Author of over 200 songs, and music for films.

Novak, Grigorii
5.3.1919–1980. Athlete.
Worked in the circus. Many times USSR and Ukrainian champion. Honoured Master of Sports (weightlifting). Silver medal-winner at the XVth Olympic Games.

Novgorodtsev, Pavel Ivanovich
16.2.1866–1924. Philosopher, lawyer, politician.
Born in Bakhmut (now Artemovsk), Ekaterinoslav Gouvt. Graduated from Moscow University in law, 1888. Studied at Berlin and Paris. Doctor of law, 1903, professor at Moscow University, 1904. Rector of Moscow Commercial Institute, 1906. Member of the Cen. Cttee. of the Cadet Party, member of the 1st Duma, 1906. Signed the Vyborg proclamation. Professor at Moscow University until 1911. During the Civil War, with the Whites, 1918. Evacuated from the Crimea in 1920. Lived in Berlin, 1922–24. Dean of the Russian faculty of law in Prague. Author of *Political Ideas of the Ancient and Modern World* and *The Social Ideal*.

Novgorodtseva, Klavdia Timofeevna
22.3.1876–23.3.1960. Politician.
Born in Ekaterinburg (now Sverdlovsk). Daughter of a merchant. Teacher in the Urals, 1894–97. Studied in Petersburg, 1897–99. Returned to the Urals as a revolutionary activist. Member of the Bolshevik Party, 1904. Became the wife of Ia. Sverdlov. Exiled with her husband to Turukhansk, 1915–17. Head of the Secretariat of the Cen. Cttee. of the Bolshevik Party, 1918–20. Director of organizations concerning children in the Soviet Union, 1920–5. As head of the department of school books in

state publishing, supervised the sovietization of school books in Russia, 1925–31. Worked as a censor in Glavlit, 1931–44. Retired, 1946. Died in Moscow.

Novikov, Aleksandr Aleksandrovich
1900–1976. Marshal of the air force. Joined the Red Army, 1919, and the Bolshevik Party, 1920. Took part in the Civil War. Graduated from the Frunze Military Academy, 1930. Took part in the Soviet-Finnish war, as chief-of-staff of the air force at the Northwestern front. During WWII Commander of the Air Force at the Leningrad front. Deputy Minister of Defence for the Air Force. Arrested 1946, together with the aviation minister, Shakhurin, after Stalin's son, Vasilii, complained at Potsdam to his father that American planes were better than Soviet planes. Beria tried to use his confessions, obtained by torture, against Zhukov. Released from the Gulag after Stalin's death, and resumed his air-force career. Commander of Strategic Aviation, 1953–56.

Novikov, Anatolii Grigor'evich
30.10.1896–1983? Composer, conductor.
Born in Skopin, in the Riazan' Gouvt. Early musical training at the Riazan' Teachers' Seminary, 1912–16, and at the Moscow People's Conservatory, 1916–17. Pupil of V. Paskhalov and A. Krein. Began his career as a composer in Skopin, 1918–21. Continued his studies at the Moscow Conservatory, 1921–27. Pupil of R. Glier. Composer, choir master, and instructor at the Tsentralnyi Dom Krasnoi Armii, 1928–38, and at the club of the Frunze Military Academy, the RKKA, the Moscow Artillery Course, and the Political Administration of Moscow Military District. Artistic director of the Song and Dance Ensemble, 1939–43. Artistic director of the All-Union Radio Song Ensemble, 1948–51. Edited a 3-volume collection of Russian folk songs, 1936–38.

Novikov, Andrei Porfir'evich
30.10.1909–   . Composer.
Born in Barnaul. President of the Siberian branch of the Union of Composers, 1944–65. Author of an opera, symphonic works, and songs.

Novikov, Ignatii Trofimovich
20.12.1906–   . Politician.
Born in the village of Kamenskoe, now Dneprodzerzhinsk. Worker in the 1920s. Member of the CPSU, 1926. Graduated from the Dneprodzerzhinsk Metallurgical Institute, 1932. During the 1930s, held senior party posts. Deputy head during the construction of the Gorkii GES (hydroelectric station), 1950–54. Head of the Administration of the Kremenchug GES, 1954–58. Minister of the GES Building Industry, 1958–62. Member of the Cen. Cttee. of the CPSU from 1961. Deputy chairman of the Council of Ministers of the USSR, and chairman of the GOSSTROI of the USSR from 1962. Chairman of the Organizing Cttee. of Olimpiada-80 (1980 Olympic Games, Moscow).

Novikov, Igor Aleksandrovich
19.10.1929–   . Athlete, sports official.
Born in Drezna, Orekhovo-Zuevo district, Moscow Oblast'. Honoured Master of Sports, 1957. USSR champion (in the Erevan Dynamo team), 1953–64. Olympic champion, 1956, 1964 (pentathlon). 2 silver medals, 1960. World champion, 1957–62. Member of the CPSU, 1958. Honoured Coach of the USSR, 1968. Deputy chairman of the Sports Cttee. of the Armenian SSR from 1969. Vice-president of the International Modern Pentathlon and Biathlon Union from 1972. Author of *Piat' Dnei i Vsia Zhizn'*, Moscow, 1974.

Novikov, Lavrentii Lavrent'evich
24.7.1888–18.7.1956. Ballet dancer.
Born in Moscow. Graduated from the Moscow Choreographic School, 1906. Dancer with the Bolshoi Theatre. Appeared in Diaghilev's Ballets Russes, 1909. Left the Bolshoi Theatre in 1912 and appeared as the partner of Anna Pavlova in London and the USA. Returned to the Bolshoi Theatre in 1914. After the October Revolution 1917, worked as a choreographer. Produced, and appeared as leading dancer in, *Nartsis* by Cherepnin at the Akva-

rium Theatre, 1918. Emigrated. With Diaghilev's Ballets Russes, 1919–21. Dancer and choreographer with Pavlova's company, 1921–28, and with the Chicago Ballet Company, 1929–41. Choreographer at the Metropolitan Opera, 1941–45. Retired from the stage, 1945. Founded a ballet school in New Buffalo where he taught till his death.

Novikov, Mikhail Mikhailovich
1876–1953? Scientist, biologist.
Born in Moscow. Graduated from Heidelberg University, 1904. Lecturer at Moscow University from 1904, professor, 1916. Specialist on education in the Moscow City Duma, 1908–18. Member of the State Duma, 1912. Twice elected dean of Moscow University. End of 1920, resigned, protesting against communist interference in university work. Chairman of the scientific commission of the VSNKH. Expelled, 1922. Settled in Czechoslovakia. Dean of the Russian People's University in Prague, 1922–38. After WWII, in DP camps in Germany. Professor of Munich University. Moved to the USA, 1949, Chairman of the Russian Academics Group. Died in the USA.

Novikov, Nikolai Aleksandrovich
1900–1970. Col.-general.
Joined the Red Army and the Bolshevik Party, 1919. Took part in the Civil War. Graduated from the Frunze Military Academy, 1933. Tank forces commander on several fronts during WWII. Continued his career as tank forces commander after WWII in the Far East and East Germany. Chief inspector of the Ministry of Defence, 1957–61.

Novikov, Sergei Petrovich
15.12.1949–   . Athlete.
Born in Moscow. Honoured Master of Sports (judo), 1974. With Moscow Dynamo. Graduated from the Kiev Institute of Physical Culture, 1972. European champion, 1973–74. USSR champion, 1974–78. Olympic champion, 1976. Member of the CPSU, 1977.

Novikov, Vladimir
25.6.1937–1980. Athlete.
Honoured Master of Sports (water

polo). Many times USSR champion. Silver medal-winner at the XVIIth Olympic Games. His premature death was reported in the American press.

Novikova, Klavdia Mikhailovna
21.3.1898–1969? Singer (mezzo soprano).
Born in Odessa. Pupil of E. Mochalova and E. Zbrueva. With the Moscow Operetta Theatre, 1926–58.

Novitskaia, Maria Georgievna (b. Shavelskaia; m. Khmelevskaia)
1897?–1981. Social worker.
Born in Petersburg. Daughter of G. Shavelskii, the last protopresbyter of the Russian Army and Navy. Educated at the Empress Marie Institute in Petersburg, 1913. Volunteered as a nurse at the beginning of WWI. 2 awards for bravery. Married the engineer Khmelevskii, 1917. Lived with him in Turkestan until 1921. Emigrated to Bulgaria, 1922, and soon afterwards moved to the USA. After her divorce, married G. Novitskii, a founder of the Society of Aid to Russian Children Abroad, and for almost 40 years devoted her life to helping countless refugee children throughout the world, especially during and after WWII. Died in the USA.

Novitskii, Fedor Fedorovich
1870–1944. Lt.-general.
Graduated from the Academy of the General Staff, 1895. On active service during WWI. Joined the Red Army, 1918. Took part in the Civil War. Chief of Staff of the Air Force, 1921. Professor at the Zhukovskii Air Force Academy, 1923.

Novitskii, Petr Karlovich
26.4.1885–7.9.1942. Cameraman.
Graduated from an art school in Kiev, 1909. Entered the film industry, 1910, as a cameraman. During WWI, war cameraman. Filmed the events of the February and October Revolutions, and later his material appeared in the film *Oktiabr'skii Perevorot*. Shot several important documentary films, such as *Ukrainskoe Dvizhenie*, 1917, and *Rospusk Uchreditel'nogo*

Sobraniia, 1918. In Apr. 1918, made the first full-length Soviet documentary film, *Razoruzhenie Anarkhistov*. Cameraman during the Civil War, worked from the agit-train called the October Revolution. The film, *The History of the Civil War*, 1921, contains a lot of this material. Worked closely with Dziga Vertov. Filmed Lenin on many occasions.

Novitskii, Vasilii Fedorovich
1869–1929. Lt.-general.
Graduated from the Academy of the General Staff, 1895. Took part in the Russo-Japanese war, 1904–05. During WWI, commander-in-chief of the Northern front. Joined the Red Army, 1918. Military inspector during the Civil War. Professor of the Military Academy of the Red Army, 1919–29. Wrote on military geography, history and administration.

Nudel, Ida
1931–   . Dissident.
Called the symbol of Russia's refusenik movement, and the most famous prisoner of Zion. Imprisoned for 16 years after her attempt to emigrate. Became a cause célèbre. In Oct. 1987, at last arrived in Israel aboard the private jet of the US billionaire industrialist, Dr. Armand Hammer. Landed at Tel Aviv airport and was welcomed by the actress Jane Fonda, Mr Yitzhak Shamir, the Prime Minister, and Mr Shimon Peres, the Foreign Minister. She arrived with the only companion of her lonely years in exile, her collie dog.

Nureev, Rudolf Gametovich
17.3.1938–   . Ballet dancer, choreographer.
Born on a train between Baikal and Irkutsk. Tatar by nationality. Started to dance in the Bashkir theatre in Ufa. Joined the Leningrad ballet school very late for a dancer (17 years of age), 1955. Due to his exceptional abilities and help from his teacher, A. Pushkin, finished the 8-year course in 3 years. Sensational appearances in the Kirov ballet, and in Vienna at the International Youth Festival, 1959. Triumph in Paris (as the prince in *Sleeping Beauty*), but was suddenly recalled to Moscow, instead of going with the

group to London. Receiving this order in Le Bourget airport, he at once approached the French police and asked for political asylum, 17 June 1961. Became the first of a number of Soviet ballet stars to make this decision and thus achieve spectacular success in the West. His early successes were in London where he formed a permanent partnership with Margot Fonteyn. Later toured all over the world, first as a ballet star, and then as choreographer. Artistic director of the Paris Opera, 1983. Took Austrian citizenship. Productions include *Les Biches*, *Le Spectre de la Rose*, *L'Apres-midi d'un Faune* and *Petrouchka*. Visited the USSR and his elderly mother, Nov. 1987.

O

Oblakov, Andrei Aleksandrovich
8.12.1874–1946? Ballet dancer.
Born in Petersburg. Graduated from the Petersburg Theatre School. With the Mariinskii Theatre, 1892–1907. Taught ballroom dancing at the Corps of Cadets and other educational establishments from 1907. Director of the Petrograd Choreographic School from 1919. Engaged A. Vaganova to improve teaching standards. Staged *La Sylphide* at the school, 1922. Disappeared from the ballet scene, probably emigrated.

Obnorskii, Sergei Petrovich
26.6.1888–13.11.1962. Linguistic scholar.
Born in Petersburg. Graduated from Petersburg University, 1910. Professor of Perm' University, 1916–22, and Leningrad University from 1922. Specialist in studies of the Russian language. Editor of the *Academic Dictionary of the Russian Language*, 1912–37. Academician, 1939. Member of the editorial board of the 17-volume *Dictionary of the Russian Language*, 1950–65. Founder and first director of the Institute of Russian Language of the USSR Academy of Sciences, 1944–50. Died in Moscow.

Obolenskaia, Iuliia Leonidovna, Princess
1889–1945. Artist.
Portrait and genre painter, and

illustrator. Studied at the private art school of E. Zvantseva. Pupil of L. Bakst and M. Dobuzhinskii, 1907–10. Also studied under K. Petrov-Vodkin, 1910–13, in Petersburg. Exhibitions: the Mir Iskusstva, 1912–13, 1915–17, Petrograd, 1914, Moscow, 1915, 1918–19; the Zhar-Tsvet Society, 1924–26, 1928–29; the Association of Graphic Artists, 1926–27; 10 Years of Russian Drawing, Moscow, 1927 and 1928. Died in Moscow.

Obolenskii, Dmitrii Dmitrievich, Sir
1.4.1918–   . Historian, literary scholar.
Born in Petrograd. Descendant of the Princes Obolenskii and Counts Schouvaloff. Educated in Paris (Lycée Pasteur) and Cambridge (Trinity College). Professor at Cambridge, and visiting professor at several American universities. Specialist on Byzantine history and Russian literature. Editor of several anthologies. Lives in Oxford.

Obolenskii, Leonid Leonidovich
21.1.1902–   . Actor, director, sound engineer.
Son of Prince Leonid Obolenskii. Studied under Lev Kuleshov at the 1st State Film School, 1919. Appeared in his tutor's first films — *Neobychainye Prikliucheniia Mistera Vesta v Strane Bolshevikov*, and *Na Krasnom Fronte*, 1924. From 1925–41, taught at the VGIK. As a director at the Mezhrabpom-Rus' Studio, 1925–28 (later Mezhrabpomfilm), made *Kirpichiki*, 1925, and *Ekh Iablochko*, 1926 (both with M. Doller), *Al'bidum*, 1928, and *Torgovtsy Slavoi*, 1929. Turned to sound engineering, and worked on *Okraina* and *Velikii Uteshitel'*, both 1933. In the 1950s, worked at the Sverdlovsk Film Studio. In the 1970–80s, appeared as an actor in several films.

Obolenskii, Mikhail Vasil'evich, Prince
1896–   . Artist.
Portrait and landscape painter and stage designer. Studied privately with the artist P. Izoev, then at the Vtorye Vysshie Svobodnye Gosudarstvennye Khudozhestvennye Masterskie, 1918–19, under S. Maliutin and V. Iakovlev. Main exhibitions: Bytie,

Moscow, 1924–25; Moscow and Local Artists in Riazan', 1925; the Association of Realist Artists, Moscow, 1927–28; the 1st Mobile Exhibition of Paintings and Graphic Art, Moscow, 1929. Others: Moscow, 1931–35, Kislovodsk, 1938, Moscow, 1935–37, Kislovodsk-Sochi, 1938, Moscow, 1939–40, 1952, Moscow, 1942, 1946, Vladivostok, 1946. Personal exhibitions: Moscow, 1944, 1957.

Obolenskii, Sergei Sergeevich, Prince
1908–1980. Author, editor, historian.
Born in Tiflis. Son of the governor of Stavropol'. Emigrated with his parents, 1920. Lived in Hungary and Germany. Moved to France, became a well-known historian, journalist and author. Took part in the Mladorossy movement in the 1930s. Editor of the magazine *Vozrozhdenie* in Paris, 1962–80. Among his books are *Ukraina – Zemlia Russkaia*, and one of the most complete studies of the life of Joan of Arc in any language, *Zhanna – Bozhia Deva*. Died at Etang-la-Ville.

Obolenskii, Vladimir Andreevich, Prince
1869–1938. Politician.
Member of the Cen. Cttee. of the Cadet Party. During the Civil War, with the White armies. Emigrated to France. Lived in Paris.

Obolenskii, Vladimir Nikolaevich
27.7.1877–1942. Meteorologist.
Son of Prince N. Obolenskii. Graduated from Moscow University, 1901. Professor of the Forestry Institute in Leningrad, 1915–38. Director of the Physical Observatory, 1921–23. Founder and director of the Institute of Experimental Meteorology in Leningrad, 1932–40. Professor of meteorology and climatology at Leningrad University, 1938–42. Studied methods of artificial rain-making. Died in Leningrad during the WWII siege.

Oborin, Lev Nikolaevich
11.9.1907–   . Pianist.
Born in Moscow. Pupil of K. Igumnov. 1st prize at the International Chopin Competition, Warsaw,

1927. Professor at the Moscow Conservatory. His pupils include V. Ashkenazi. State Prize of the USSR 1943.

Obukhov, Anatolii Nikolaevich
1896–25.2.1962. Ballet dancer.
Born in Petersburg. Graduated from the Petersburg Theatre School. Pupil of M. K. Obukhov and N. G. Legat. With the Mariinskii Theatre, 1913–20. Partner of A. Pavlova in 1914 during her guest appearance in Russia. Emigrated, 1920. Worked in Berlin with the Russkii Romanticheskii Ballet of B. G. Romanov, then in South America. With the Lithuanian Opera in Kaunas, 1931–35. With the Ballets Russes de Monte-Carlo, and the Original Ballets Russes, 1935–39. Taught at the New York City Ballet School, 1940–62. Died in New York.

Obukhov, Nikolai (Nicholas Illuminé)
22.4.1892–13.6.1954. Composer.
Born in Moscow. Studied at the Petersburg Conservatory, 1911. Emigrated, 1919. Main composition: an oratorio, *Kniga Zhizni*, performed partly in 1926 in Paris. Conceived the idea for an electric instrument, the 'croix sonore'. Often signed his compositions 'Nicolas l'Illuminé.' Died in Paris. After his death, the Obukhov Prize was set up for an innovative composer.

Obukhova, Evgenia Konstantinovna
22.4.1874–28.3.1948. Ballerina.
Born in Petersburg. Graduated from the Petersburg Theatre School. With the Mariinskii Theatre, 1892–1910. Taught at the Russian Ballet School under A. L. Volynskii in Leningrad, 1917–24, at the School of Choreographic Art, at the Tamara Khanum Ballet School, Usbek Republic, 1935–41, and at the ballet school of the Navoi Theatre, 1944–48. Taught and coached at the Sverdlov Theatre in Tashkent till 1944, and at the Navoi Theatre, 1944–48. Died in Tashkent.

Obukhova, Nadezhda Andreevna
6.3.1886–15.8.1961. Singer (mezzo-soprano).
Born in Moscow. Pupil of U. Masetti.

Appeared in concerts from 1912. Leading singer with the Bolshoi Theatre, 1916–48. State Prize, 1943. Author of memoirs and autobiographical notes. Died in Feodosia.

Odinets, Dmitrii Mikhailovich
1882–1951? Historian.
Born in the Ukraine. Professor of history at Kiev University. NS Party member (narodnyi sotsialist). Under the Ukrainian Rada, Minister for Great Russians in the Ukraine, 1918. Emigrated after the Civil War. Settled in Paris. Contributor to Miliukov's paper *Poslednie Novosti*. After WWII, visited the Soviet Ambassador to France, Bogomolov (with Maklakov and others), 1945. Became editor of the pro-Soviet newspapers in Paris *Sovetskii Patriot* and *Russkie Novosti*. Returned to the Soviet Union. According to some information, died in Kazan'.

Odinokova, Liubov' Ivanovna (Berezhnaia)
24.7.1955– . Athlete.
Born in Otradnyi, Kuibyshev Oblast'. Honoured Master of Sports (handball), 1976. With Rostov-on-Don Trud. Olympic champion, 1976. USSR champion, 1978–79. From 1978, with Kiev Spartak.

Odintsov, Georgii Fedotovich
1900–1972. Marshal.
Joined the Red Army and the Bolshevik Party, 1920. Took part in the Civil War. Graduated from the Dzerzhinskii Artillery Academy, 1934. Artillery commander during WWII in Leningrad. Artillery commander in the Far East, 1947. Head of the Dzerzhinskii Artillery Academy, 1953–59.

Odintsov, Mikhail Petrovich
18.11.1921– . Lt.-general.
Born in the village of Polozovo, Perm' Oblast'. Son of a peasant. Joined the Soviet Army in 1938. Graduated from the Perm' School of Pilots, 1939. Served in WWII as a flight and squadron commander, and deputy commander and navigator of the 155th Guards Assault Aviation Regiment. Made over 200 combat flights. Member of the CPSU from

1943. Twice Hero of the Soviet Union (Feb. 1944 and Jan. 1955). After WWII, held high positions in the air force. Graduated from the Lenin Military Political Academy, 1952, and from the Military Academy of the General Staff, 1959. Promoted commander of aviation of a military district, Nov. 1967. Lt.-general of aviation, 1968. From 1976, inspector general of the air force attached to the Chief Inspectorate of the USSR Ministry of Defence.

Odintsov, Sergei Ivanovich
1874–1920. Major-general.
Graduated from the Academy of the General Staff, 1902. On active service during WWI. Joined the Red Army, 1918. Red Army commander in Petrograd, 1919–20.

Odoevtseva, Irina Vladimirovna (Genike)
1901– . Poetess.
Started to write poetry as a pupil of N. Gumilev in the group Tsekh Poetov in Petrograd. Emigrated during the Civil War, and settled in Paris. Continued to write and publish verse. Wife of the poet Georgii Ivanov. Wrote memoirs of her life in literary circles in Petrograd and Paris (*Na Beregakh Nevy, Na Beregakh Seny*). In her old age, alone and in poverty, returned to Leningrad, 1987, where she was welcomed and treated as a VIP.

Ogadzhanian, Sarkis
1964–26.12.1987. Religious dissident.
Born in Erevan, Armenia. One of the leading members of the society of Soznanie Krishny (The Conscience of Krishna) in Armenia. Arrested, 1985, and convicted in 1986 in Erevan according to Article 244, part 2 of the Criminal Code of the Armenian SSR, for the distribution of Krishna's ideas, which were allegedly incompatible with the socialist system. He was detained at the Sol'-Iletsk labour camp for criminals where he continued (in accordance with his religion) to eat only vegetarian food. Died of TB in the camp hospital a month before he was due for release. The authorities turned down his parents' request to bring his body back to Erevan.

Oganesian, Edgar Sergeevich
14.1.1930– . Composer.
Born in Erevan. Graduated from the Erevan Conservatory, 1953. Pupil of G. E. Egiazarian. Postgraduate training under A. I. Khachaturian, 1957. Author of operas, cantatas, compositions for symphony orchestra and choir, and ballets. Director of the Spendiarov Theatre, 1962–68. Artistic director of the Ensemble of Armenian Folk Song and Dance, 1970–74. Director of Armkontsert (Armenian Concert Ensemble) from 1976.

Ogarkov, Nikolai Vasil'evich
30.10.1917– . Marshal.
Born in Molkov, Kalinin Oblast'. Son of a peasant. Graduated from the Energy Work Faculty, 1937, then the Kuibyshev Military Engineering Academy, 1941, and the Operations Engineering Faculty of the same academy, 1947. Member of the Soviet Army from 1938. Served in an engineers' regiment on the Western front. Senior engineer at the Karelian front, regiment engineer in the 289th Rifles, brigade engineer in the 61st Marine Rifles, assistant chief-of-staff of the Engineers of the 32nd Army, assistant chief of the Operations Department of Engineer Troop Forces, division engineer with the 122nd Rifles at the Karelian front and 2nd and 3rd Ukrainian fronts, 1941–45. Member of the CPSU, 1945. Senior positions in the Carpathian military district, and the Primor'e military district, 1945–48. Commander-in-chief of Far Eastern troops, 1948–53, and its deputy chief-of-staff, 1955–59. Graduated from the Military Academy of the General Staff, 1959. Commander of the Motorized Rifle Division of Soviet Troops in Germany, 1959–61. Chief-of-staff, deputy commander of troops of Belorussian military district, 1963. Candidate member of the Cen. Cttee. of the CPSU, 1966–71, full member from 1971. Commander of troops of Volga military district, 1965–68. 1st deputy chief of the General Staff of the USSR Armed Forces, 1968–77, chief, 1977, Deputy Minister of Defence, 1974–77. 1st Deputy Minister of Defence from 1977. Marshal, 1977. Soviet chief-of-staff until Sep. 1984. Dismissed from both posts at the time of the power struggle,

possibly on the orders of K. Chernenko. Vigorously demanded that the army's need for expensive high-technology conventional weapons be satisfied. His dismissal was accompanied by editorials in *Pravda* and *Red Star*, the Soviet Army newspaper, saying that social programmes could not be sacrificed to meet defence needs.

Ognivtsev, Aleksandr Pavlovich
27.8.1920– . Singer (bass).
Pupil of V. Dolev. Leading singer with the Bolshoi Theatre from 1949. Appeared in films. State Prize, 1951.

Ogolevets, Aleksei Stepanovich
29.5.1891–1971? Musicologist.
Born in Poltava. Author of works on harmony, 1941 and 1946, and of *Slovo i Muzyka v Vokal'no-Dramaticheskikh Zhanrakh*, Moscow, 1960.

Ogonbaev, Atai
1904–12.1949. Singer, komuz player, composer.
Born in Kirghizia. Pupil of Toktogul Satylganov. Soloist with the Kirghiz Philharmonic from 1936. Organized a komuz ensemble, 1939 (the komuz is a Kirghiz string instrument played by plucking). Composer of songs.

Ogon'kov, Mikhail Pavlovich
24.6.1932–14.8.1979. Athlete.
Born in Moscow. Football player with Moscow Spartak. USSR champion and Olympic champion, 1956. Graduated from the Higher School of Trainers at the Institute of Physical Culture, Moscow, 1965. Member of the CPSU, 1967. Died in Moscow.

Ogurtsov, Igor Viacheslavovich
1937– . Human rights campaigner.
Graduated from Leningrad University. Worked as a translator in a shipbuilding institute in Leningrad. In the early 1960s, organized a youth group (VSKHSON), which set as its aim resistance to communist dictatorship from socialist Christian posi-

tions. The group was unusual among dissident groups with its well-thought-out programme and organization. Arrested on 15 Feb. 1967 with other members of his group, and sentenced to 7 years in prison, 8 years in camps and 5 years in exile for high treason. After spending 7 years in the Vladimir prison, was transferred to a psychiatric hospital in Mordovia. Released 1987 and emigrated soon thereafter.

Oistrakh, David Fedorovich
30.9.1908–24.10.1974. Violinist.
Born in Odessa. Pupil of P. Stoliarskii. 1st prize at the International E. Ysaye Competition, Brussels, 1937. Professor at the Moscow Conservatory. One of the best-known Soviet musicians in the West. Died during a concert tour in Amsterdam. Buried in Moscow.

Oistrakh, Igor' Davidovich
27.4.1931– . Violinist.
Born in Odessa. Son and pupil of David Oistrakh. 1st prize at the International G. Wieniawski Competition, Poznan, 1952. Taught at the Moscow Conservatory. Became an internationally renowned musician.

Okaemov, Aleksandr Ivanovich
1903–21.2.1943. Singer (bass).
Born in Riazhsk. Pupil of E. Egorov. Singer of Soviet political songs. Shot by the Germans in Krichev during WWII.

Okeev, Tolomush
11.9.1935– . Film director.
The first Kirghiz film director. Graduated from the Leningrad Cinema Engineers Institute, worked as a sound recordist at the Kirghiz Film Studios. In 1964, joined the Directors Course at the Mosfilm Studio. Worked in 1964 on Shepitko's *Heat*, which is now considered a classic. His first feature film *The Sky of Our Childhood* shot in Kirghizia, 1967, won a prize at the Frankfurt Film Festival. *The Ferocious One*, scripted in collaboration with Andron Mikhalkov-Konchalovskii in 1973, became internationally known. Other films: *Horses* (Kirghizfilm, 1965, direction, soundwork), *The Inheri-*

tance (Kirghizfilm, 1970), *Pay Tribute to the Fire* (Kirghizfilm, 1972), *The Red Apple* (Kirghizfilm, 1975), *Uhlan* (Kirghizfilm, 1977). Winner of the Toktogul Prize in 1973.

Okhlopkov, Nikolai Pavlovich
15.5.1900–8.1.1967. Stage producer.
Born in Irkutsk. Appeared as an actor, 1918. Produced some plays in Irkutsk, 1921–22. Actor with the Meyerhold Theatre from 1923. Head of the Realisticheskii Teatr, 1930–37. Producer and actor with the Vakhtangov Theatre, 1938–43. Director, actor at the Drama Theatre in Moscow, 1943–66. Worked as actor and producer in films in the 1920s. Taught at GITIS. Died in Moscow.

Okolovich, Nikolai Andreevich
1876–1928. Artist.
Born in Odessa. Studied at Odessa Art School of the Society of Fine Arts, then at the Petersburg Academy of Arts, 1897–1901, under A. Kiselev. Landscape painter. Exhibitions: the Academy of Arts, 1898, Spring exhibitions, the Academy of Arts, 1898–03, the Mir Iskusstva, 1901. Emigrated in the early 1920s.

Oktiabr'skaia, Maria Vasil'evna
1905–1944. Sergeant.
According to war-time propaganda, offered her personal savings for a tank which she herself commanded and called Boevaia Podruga (Fighting girlfriend). Died heroically in action near Vitebsk. Hero of the Soviet Union.

Oktiabr'skii, Filipp Sergeevich (until 1924, Ivanov)
1899–1969. Admiral.
Joined the Red Navy, 1918, and the Bolshevik Party, 1919. Took part in the Civil War. Graduated from the Frunze Military Academy, 1928. Commander of the Black Sea fleet during WWII. Deputy commander-in-chief of the Soviet Navy, 1948–1952.

Okudzhava, Bulat Shalvovich
9.5.1924– . Poet, singer, author.
Born in Moscow. Son of a party official from Georgia. Volunteered

for service at the front in 1941. Soldier till the end of WWII. Educated in Georgia. Graduated from Tbilisi University in 1950. Worked as a school teacher, later in publishing houses. First volume of poetry published in 1953. Joined the CPSU in 1955. In the 1960s, became immensely popular for his verse, which he sang accompanying himself on guitar. The first quasi pop-idol of the post-Stalin youth generation. Tapes of his songs circulated on the black market all over the country, thus attracting the attention of the KGB. Prevented from publishing his work for a long time. A decision at the very top was made to allow him to address the public, as there was nothing anti-Soviet in his songs. The official record company Melodia then offered him a recording contract. Now receives newspaper coverage, and his books are being published. His lyrics have an intrinsic poetic value. Wrote autobiographical prose about his war-time experiences as a teenager. Books: *Lirika*, 1956, *Veselyi Barabanshchik* (The Merry Drummer), 1964, *Bednyi Avrosimov* (Poor Avrosimov), 1969.

Olbrei, Rakhel Ianovna
13.8.1898–late 1950s? Choreographer.
Born in Tallinn. Graduated from the ballet school of E. Litvinova, Tallinn, 1922. Studied at the school of M. Vigman, under E. Jacques-Dalcroze and R. Laban. With the Estonian Theatre from 1918. Choreographer, 1925–44. Took part in forming and training the first ballet company of the Estonian Theatre. In her productions, combined classical expression with rhythmic and folkloristic effects. Emigrated, 1944.

Oldenburg, Sergei Fedorovich
26.9.1863–28.2.1934. Orientalist, academician.
Born in the village of Biankino, near Nerchinsk. Graduated from Petersburg University, 1885. Lecturer at Petersburg University, 1889, professor, 1894. Academician, 1900. Secretary of the Russian Academy of Sciences, 1904–29. Minister of Education in the Provisional Government, July-Aug. 1917. Member of the Cadet Party. Specialist in Buddhism

and Hinduism. Became the link between the pre-revolutionary Academy of Sciences and the communist establishment.

Oleinikov, Nikolai Makarovich
1898–1942. Author.
Born in the village Kamenskaia-on-Don. Worked as a journalist in the provinces. Moved to Leningrad, 1925. Member of the OBERIU group in the 1920s. Became known as an author of books for children. Edited magazines for children. Together with other Leningrad childrens' writers, arrested, 1937, after Kirov's murder. Died in prison, circumstances unknown. His unpublished poetry circulated in samizdat posthumously in the 1950–60s Some of it was published in the West.

Olekhnovich, Frantsisk
?–1944. Playwright.
Imprisoned for revolutionary activity before the revolution, 1917. After the Civil War lived in Poland. Suffering persecution for his Belorussian nationalism, left for the USSR, 1926. Appointed director of the theatre in Vitebsk, but one month later, arrested by the GPU and sentenced to 10 years' imprisonment. Exchanged, as a Polish citizen, for the Belorussian nationalist leader (head of Belorusskaia hromada), Tarashkevich, who was in a Polish prison, 1933. Published in Poland a book on his experiences in the Solovki concentration camp (1926–32) in 1937. During WWII, killed in Wilno by a Soviet agent.

Olenicheva, Agrafena Maksimovna
1911–28.3.1960. Teller of folk tales. Composer of over 100 songs. Her melodies were much used by Soviet composers. Her collected songs were published in 1956 and 1960. Died in Omsk.

Olenin, Aleksandr Alekseevich
13.4.1865–15.2.1944. Composer.
Born in Riazan' Gouvt. Brother of the singer Maria Olenina d'Algheim. Composer of the opera *Kudeiar*, 1915, orchestral works, and chamber music. Died in Moscow.

Olenin, Petr Sergeevich
1874–28.1.1922. Singer (baritone), stage director.
Born in Riazan' Gouvt. With the Bolshoi Theatre, 1900–03. Stage director with the Zimin Opera, 1904–15. With the Bolshoi Theatre, 1915–18, and the Petrograd Opera and Ballet Theatre from 1918. Opera director, 1921. Died in Petrograd.

Olenina d'Algheim, Maria Alekseevna (b. Olenina)
1.10.1869–1960. Singer (mezzo-soprano).
Born in Riazan' Gouvt. Pupil of Iu. Platonova and A. Molas. Married the French writer, P. d'Algheim (1862–1922). Founded the Dom Pesni in Moscow, 1896. Emigrated. Settled in Paris, 1918. According to official Soviet sources, returned to the USSR at the age of 90. Died in Moscow. Author of a work on Mussorgskii, Paris, 1908.

Olga Aleksandrovna (Romanova)
1882–11.1960. Grand Duchess.
Youngest sister of Nicholas II. During the revolution, in the Crimea with her mother. Rescued by British warships. Lived with her mother's family in Denmark until 1948. Moved to a farm near Toronto, where she lived until 1960. Became too ill to live alone and went to live with a Russian emigré couple in an apartment over a barber's shop in a poor section of East Toronto. Died in complete obscurity in Canada the same year that her sister Ksenia died in England.

Olga Nikolaevna (Romanova)
3.11.1895–17.7.1918. Grand Duchess.
The eldest daughter of Nicholas II. Educated by private tutors. During WWI, involved in charity work, organized by her mother, as a nurse in military hospitals. During the time of the arrest of the Tsar's family, taught English to her sisters and brother. Wrote poetry. Disappeared together with the whole royal family in Ekaterinburg (now Sverdlovsk). According to the latest edition of the Soviet Encyclopaedia and recent Soviet publications, all members of the family were shot.

Olitskaia, Ekaterina Lvovna

1898– . Revolutionary, politician, author.

In the 1920s, became a member of the underground cells of the SR Party. Arrested in 1924 and sent to the notorious Solovki labour camp, 1924–25. Till 1927, in Urals camps. From 1927–30, in exile in Central Asia. Released, lived in Riazan'. Illegally moved near Moscow and printed SR leaflets in 1932. Re-arrested the same year. Until 1937, in Suzdal and Iaroslavl' prisons. Sent to Kolyma camps in 1937. Exiled to Krasnoiarsk in 1947. Released after Stalin's death. Her memoirs, which became widely known through samizdat in the late 1960s, give valuable information on the fate of socialists (especially SRs) in the 1920–30s.

Oliunina, Alevtina Sergeevna (Smirnova)

15.8.1942– . Athlete.
Born in the village of Pchelkino, Kostroma Oblast'. Honoured Master of Sports (skiing), 1970. With Gorkii Trud. Graduated from the Moscow Institute of Physical Culture, 1969. USSR champion, 1967–74. World champion, 1970 (10km. race). Olympic champion, 1972. Silver medallist, 1972.

Ol'khova, Nadezhda Aleksandrovna (Shuvaeva)

9.9.1952– . Athlete.
Born in Barnaul, Altai Krai. Honoured Master of Sports (basketball), 1976. With Alma-Ata Burevestnik. European champion, 1974, 1976 and 1978. World champion, 1975. Olympic champion, 1976.

Onnore, Irina Ivanovna (b. Pilsudska, Honoré)

17.1.1838–1917? Singer (contralto).
Wife of the pianist Léon Honoré. Soloist at the Bolshoi Theatre, 1862–73. Taught singing in Petersburg from the 1880s. Died in Petrograd.

Opekushin, Aleksandr Mikhailovich

1840–1923. Sculptor, academician.
Pupil of the academician D. Iensen. Studied at the Petersburg Academy of Arts. In 1862, awarded the Academy's silver medal. In 1870, received the title of Class Artist. In 1872, academician. Exhibitions: the Academy of Arts, 1862, 1869, 1870, 1884; All-Russian Exhibition, Moscow, 1882. Took part in the competition for the Aleksandr Pushkin memorial project, 1875.

Opperput, Aleksandr (Upelints, Staunits, Kasatkin)

1895–1941. State security officer.
Very successful field operative of the Trest cover organization of the GPU. Infiltrated anti-communist groups in the West in the 1920s. Joined the groups which were sent by Kutepov into the USSR and handed them over to the GPU. Called the 'Soviet Azef'. During WWII, arrested in Kiev by the Gestapo and shot.

Oranskii, Viktor Aleksandrovich (real name – Gershov)

4.5.1899–27.9.1953. Composer.
Born in Feodosia. Musical director at the Ermolova Theatre, Moscow, 1947–50. Author of ballets, instrumental pieces, and music for the stage and screen. Died in Moscow.

Oras, Pavel Iur'evich

1897–1936. State security and intelligence officer.
Born in Reval (now Tallinn). Sailor in the Baltic fleet. Active participant in the Bolshevik take-over, 1917. Joined the Cheka. Organized Soviet espionage in Turkey, Sweden, Norway and Greece in the 1920–30s, declared persona non grata in all of those countries. Appointed 1st Soviet naval attaché in Washington, 1934, built up a Soviet espionage net in the USA. Recalled to the Soviet Union, liquidated on Stalin's orders.

Orbelian, Konstantin Agaparonovich

29.7.1928– . Composer.
Born in Armavir. Artistic director of the Armenian State Variety Theatre from 1956. Graduated from the Erevan Conservatory, 1961. Known for his instrumental chamber music. His songs for the variety stage combine Armenian folk motives with jazz.

Ordzhonikidze, Givi Shioevich

9.4.1917– . Musicologist.
Born in Tiflis. Author of *Fortepiannye Sonaty Prokof'eva*, Moscow, 1962. Biographer of many Georgian composers.

Ordzhonikidze, Sergo (Grigorii Konstantinovich)

24.10.1886–18.2.1937. Revolutionary, politician.
Born in Goresha, Kutaissi Gouvt. in Georgia. Son of a nobleman. Member of the SDs, 1903. Studied medicine in Tiflis, 1901–05. Took part in the 1905 Revolution. Emigrated to Germany. Party worker in Baku, 1907. Arrested, sent to Siberia, escaped, 1909. Went to Paris, 1910. Studied at the Longjumeau party school, met Lenin. Member of the Cen. Cttee. of the Bolshevik Party (elected, 1912, by the Prague Conference). Arrested in Petersburg, 1912, in Schlüsselburg prison, 1912–15, sent to Iakutia. Released after the February Revolution 1917, returned to Petrograd. Took part in the October Revolution 1917. During the Civil War, political commissar in the Red Army at different fronts, 1918–20. In the early 1920s, active in the Caucasus. In the late 1920s, an ally of Stalin in his struggle for power. Member of the Cen. Cttee. of the Bolshevik Party, 1921, member of the Politburo, 1930. Minister for Heavy Industry, 1930. Led the industrialization drive initiated by Stalin. Died suddenly in Moscow. According to the official version, died of a heart attack. According to other versions, either committed suicide or was murdered on Stalin's orders, after he had spoken of his decision to denounce Stalin and his terror campaigns publicly.

Orekhov, Vasilii Vasil'evich

1895– . Editor, journalist.
Born near Orel. As a student, volunteered for military service, 1914. After the Bolshevik take-over, joined the Whites, 1918, took part in the Civil War. After the defeat of Wrangel, evacuated from the Crimea to Gallipoli. Published the newspaper *Gallipoliets*, 1925. Editor and publisher of *Chasovoi*, the magazine of exiled White Army officers, for over half a century from 1929.

Published initially in Paris, and from 1936, in Brussels, it is a mine of information on the history and personalities connected with the White armies during the Civil War.

Orfenov, Anatolii Ivanovich
30.10.1907–   . Singer (tenor).
Born in Riazan' Gouvt. Pupil of A. Pogorel'skii. Leading singer with the K. S. Stanislavskii Musical Theatre from 1934, and the Bolshoi Theatre, 1942–55. Reader at the Gnesin Institute. Author of *Tvorcheskii put' Sobinova*, Moscow, 1965.

Orlanskii – Titarenko, Iakov Fedorovich
21.8.1877–28.12.1941. Bayan player and maker.
Born in Petersburg. Gave concerts in many Russian towns, 1900–1910. Invented several kinds of bayan. Author of many arrangements. Died during the Siege of Leningrad.

Orlikovskii, Vaclav
8.11.1921–   . Ballet-master, dancer.
Born in Khar'kov. Came to Western Europe with the ballet of A. Tumkovskaia. Founded the Russian Classical Ballet Group in Munich, 1950. Ballet-master in Basel, 1955–57, and with the Vienna State Opera, 1966–71. Lives in Austria.

Orlov, Aleksandr (real name – Felbin, Lev Lazarevich; cover name – Shved)
1896–7.4.1973. Intelligence and state security officer.
Head of GPU operations in Western Europe in the 1930s. Sent as GPU chief to Spain during the Civil War. In 1938, ordered by Stalin to return to the USSR. Defected to Paris, and moved to the USA. Lived with his family in seclusion in Cleveland until the moment of Stalin's death, when he published in the American press some information on Stalin's crimes, while not giving away much about his own contributions to GPU operations abroad. According to authorities in this field, his knowledge of GPU and NKVD operations throughout the world was extraordinary. Died in Cleveland.

Orlov, Aleksandr Aleksandrovich
25.10.1889–23.10.1974. Ballet dancer.
Born in Rostov-on-Don. Graduated from the Petersburg Theatre School. Pupil of M. K. Obukhov, M. M. Fokin and A. V. Shiriaev. With the Mariinskii (now Kirov) Theatre, 1908–24. Appeared in the Ballets Russes performances abroad, 1909–11. With the Leningrad Malyi Theatre, 1934–41. With the Leningrad Theatre of Musical Comedy, 1941–59. In his dancing, stressed realism, and combined lyricism with the grotesque. Created with E. V. Lopukhova a comic duet for music hall. Performer of folk dances. Died in Leningrad.

Orlov, Aleksandr Ivanovich
30.8.1873–10.10.1948. Conductor.
Born in Petersburg. Conductor of the S. Kusevitskii Orchestra in Moscow, 1912–17. Chief conductor with the Kiev Opera, 1925–29. His pupils include N. Rakhlin. Conductor of the All-Union Radio Great Symphony Orchestra from 1930. Died in Moscow.

Orlov, Iurii Fedorovich
1924–   . Scientist, dissident.
Before WWII, worked in a factory. During WWII, on active service. Afterwards studied at Moscow University in the physics faculty, 1946–52. Research worker at the Institute of Theoretical and Experimental Physics of the Academy of Sciences of the USSR, 1952–56. During the Khrushchev thaw in 1956, at a party meeting at his institute, openly demanded reforms. Dismissed from his job and expelled from the party. Lived in Armenia. Elected corresponding member of the Armenian Academy of Sciences, 1968. Returned to Moscow and his former job, but was again dismissed after writing a letter to Brezhnev defending academician Sakharov. A prominent member of the dissident movement, one of the founders of the Helsinki Monitoring Group in Moscow. Arrested and exiled for his human rights work. Allowed to go abroad, after the Daniloff affair, and in connection with the Reykjavik summit meeting in 1986. Settled in the USA.

Orlov, Nikolai Andreevich
26.2.1892–31.5.1964. Pianist.
Born in Orel Gouvt. Pupil of K. Kipp and K. Igumnov. Professor at the Moscow Conservatory, 1916–21. Emigrated, 1922. Lived in Paris. Moved to England, 1950. Died in Scotland.

Orlov, Vladimir Mitrofanovich
1895–27.7.1938. Navy commander, political officer.
Joined the Red Navy and the Bolshevik Party, 1918. Political commissar in the Baltic fleet during the Civil War. Naval commissar in the 1920s. Commander of the naval forces in the Black Sea, 1926. Commander-in-chief of the Soviet naval forces, 1931–37. Deputy Minister of Defence, 1937. Victim of Stalin's purges, probably shot.

Orlova, Aleksandra Anatol'evna
2.2.1911–   . Musicologist.
Born in Ekaterinoslav. Wife of the musicologist Georgii Pavlovich Orlov (1900–40). Author of articles and publications on M. Glinka, M. Musorgskii and P. Tchaikovskii.

Orlova, Elena Mikhailovna
18.3.1908–   . Musicologist.
Born in Kostroma. Reader at the Leningrad Conservatory. Author of *Romansy Chaikovskogo*, Moscow – Leningrad, 1948, and *B. V. Asaf'ev: Put' Issledovatelia i Publitsista*, Moscow, 1964.

Orlova, Liubov' Petrovna
11.2.1902–26.1.1975. Film actress.
Studied at the Moscow Conservatory, 1919–22. Singer-actress at the Nemirovich-Danchenko Musical Theatre, 1926–33. Entered the film industry, 1934. Married S. Eisenstein's close collaborator, Grigorii Aleksandrov. Best remembered for her brilliant performances in *Veselye Rebiata*, 1934, *Tsirk*, 1936, and *Volga-Volga*, 1938. Her striking appearance, remarkable singing voice, and comedy talent attracted crowds to her films. Died in Moscow.

Orlova, Raisa Davydovna (Kopeleva)
1918–   . Literary critic, translator, author.
Born in Moscow. Graduated from the Moscow Institute of Philosophy, Literature and History. Specialized in American literature. Published numerous articles and some books in the USSR. Wife of Lev Kopelev. Became involved in the human rights movement in the mid-1960s. In 1980, expelled from the party. Protested publicly against Dr. A. Sakharov's exile to Gorkii. In Nov. 1980, left the USSR with her husband. In Jan. 1981, both were stripped of Soviet citizenship for their interviews and articles in the Western press. Lives in Cologne.
Books: *Vospominaniia O Neproshedshem Vremeni*, USA, 1983; *Dveri Otkryvaiutsia Medlenno*, USA, 1984; *Hemingway V Rossii*, USA, 1986.

Orlovskaia, Natalia Nikolaevna
20.4.1922–   . Ballerina.
Graduated from the Moscow Choreographic School, 1937. With the Bolshoi Theatre, 1938–60. Concert appearances. Taught and coached abroad, at the Cairo Ballet School, the Dutch National Ballet, and elsewhere. Taught choreography at the GITIS from 1963.

Orlovskii, Kirill Prokof'evich
30.1.1895–13.1.1968. State security official.
Born in the village of Myshkovichi, Mogilev Gouvt. Son of a peasant. During WWI, conscripted, became a Bolshevik agitator. Member of the Bolshevik Party, 1918. Cheka official in Bobruisk, 1918–19. Leader of communist partisans in Western Belorussia (Poland), 1920–25. Moved to the USSR. Official of GPU–NKVD in Belorussia, later supervised Gulag prisoners working on the construction of the Moskva-Volga canal, 1925–37. Sent as an NKVD official to Spain during the Civil War, 1937–38. Returned to the USSR and continued to work in the secret police during the Stalin purges. During WWII, sent to control partisans in Belorussia, near Baranovichi, 1942–43, wounded in action. NKVD-SMERSH official, 1943–44. After WWII, given the task of restoring the kolkhoz system (chairman of the kolkhoz Rassvet) in

Mogilev Oblast'. Died in his native village. Non-voting member of the Cen. Cttee. of the CPSU.

Orvid, Georgii Antonovich
8.12.1904–   . Trumpet player.
Born in Nikolaev Gouvt. Pupil of M. Tabakov. Professor at the Moscow Conservatory. 3rd prize at the All-Union Competition, Moscow, 1941. Author of a textbook on trumpet playing, 1933, and of transcriptions.

Oshanin, Lev Vasil'evich
7.3.1884–9.1.1962. Anthropologist.
Born in Tashkent. Son of the entomologist V. F. Oshanin. Professor in the Faculty of Anthropology at the University of Tashkent. Founder of research into the anthropology and ethnic origins of the peoples of Soviet Central Asia. Died in Tashkent.

Oshchepkov, Stepan Mikhailovich
9.1.1934–   . Athlete.
Born in Vladivostok. Honoured Master of Sports (rowing), 1962. With Vladivostok Trud. Graduated from the Moscow Oblast' Institute of Physical Culture, 1963. USSR champion, 1955–58, 1962 and 1964. World champion, 1958 (10,000 metres). European champion, 1959 (10,000 metres), 1965 (1,000 metres). Olympic champion, 1964 (1,000 metres, with A. Khimich).

Osinskii, N. (Obolenskii, Valerian)
1887–1938. Politician.
Son of Prince V. Obolenskii. Joined the Bolsheviks, 1907. Active in party work before WWI. Co-author of the platform of the left-communists, spring 1918. Belonged to the Democratic Centralist, and later Trotskyite opposition to Stalin. Defendant at a show trial, 1938. Convicted and executed.

Osipenko, Alla Evgen'evna
16.6.1932–   . Ballerina.
Born in Leningrad. Graduated from the Leningrad Choreographic School. Pupil of A.I. Vaganova. With the Kirov Theatre, 1950–71. Leading dancer with the Choreographicheskie Miniatiury company, 1971–73, and

with Lenkontsert from 1973. Classical parts, but especially famous for her innovations. Leading dancer with the Leningrad Ballet Ensemble, from 1977.

Osipov, Leonid Mikhailovich
6.2.1943–   . Athlete.
Born in Moscow. Honoured Master of Sports (water polo), 1964. With Moscow State University Burevestnik. Graduated from the Moscow Institute of Physical Culture, 1964, and from Moscow University, 1970. From 1971, with the Moscow Armed Forces. Member of the CPSU, 1971. European champion, 1966 and 1970. USSR champion, 1967 and 1971. Olympic champion, 1972. Bronze medallist, 1964, and silver medallist, 1968.

Osipov, Nikolai Ivanovich
1889–1960s? Historian, journalist.
Born in Riga. Graduated from Petersburg University, 1912. Active in the cooperative movement before and immediately after the Revolution 1917 (Moscow, Khar'kov, Kuban'). Later, taught at different universities. Moved to Germany, 1944. After WWII, in DP camps in West Germany, active in the Russian emigré press. Wrote on Russian history, philosophy and literature. Because of his erudition the other camp inmates gave him the nick-name 'ded-vseved' (the grandfather who knows everything).

Osipov, Nikolai Petrovich
28.1.1896–9.5.1945. Balalaika player.
Born in Petersburg. Brother of the pianist and conductor D. Osipov. Artistic director and conductor of the Russian State Folk Orchestra from 1940. Virtuoso balalaika player. Author of transcriptions for balalaika. Died in Moscow.

Osipov, Vladimir Nikolaevich
1939–   . Editor, journalist, human rights campaigner.
Born in Moscow. Studied at Moscow University, expelled 1959. Became involved in the human rights movement. Edited the samizdat magazine *Bumerang*, 1960. Co-edited the samizdat magazine *Feniks*, 1961.

Arrested, 1961, sentenced to 7 years in the Gulag camps. After his release, started the Russian nationalist samizdat magazines *Veche* and *Zemlia*. Re-arrested, 1974. Sentenced to 8 years in the camps. The best-known voice of the Russian opposition to communism among Soviet dissidents during the Brezhnev–Andropov years.

Osorgin, Mikhail Andreevich (Il'in)
7.10.1878–27.11.1942. Author, journalist.
Born in Perm'. Educated at Perm' High School. Graduated from Moscow University in law. Became involved in revolutionary activity, joined the SR Party, wrote pamphlets against the Marxists (SD). Took part in the 1905 Revolution in Moscow, arrested, but soon released. Emigrated to Italy. Became a correspondent for Russian newspapers in Italy and a well-known author. Returned, 1916. Edited several newspapers. Chairman of the Union of Journalists. Arrested several times under the communist government, expelled, 1922, to Germany. Settled in France. During WWII, moved from Paris to the unoccupied zone of France. Died at Chabry.
Main works: *Ocherki Sovremennoi Italii, Sivtsev Vrazhek, Veshchi Cheloveka, Svidetel' Istorii, Kniga o Kontsakh, V Tikhom Mestechke Frantsii, Pis'ma o Neznachitel'nom.*

Ossovskii, Aleksandr Viacheslavovich
31.3.1871–31.7.1957. Musicologist.
Born in Kishinev. Professor at the Petersburg Conservatory. Author of articles of music criticism and of works on classical Russian music in *Russkaia Muzykal'naia Gazeta*. Died in Leningrad.

Ostriakov, Nikolai Alekseevich
1911–1942. Major-general.
Graduated as a civil aviation pilot, 1932. Joined the Red Navy as a pilot, 1934. Instructor of NKVD airborne commandos, 1934. Sent to Spain during the Spanish Civil War, 1936–39. During WWII, commander of the air force of the Red Navy in the Black Sea. Fell in action.

Ostroukhov, Il'ia Semenovich
1.8.1858–8.7.1929. Artist.
Landscape painter. Born in Moscow. Studied with A. Kiselev, 1880, Il'ia Repin, 1881, and V. Polenov in the 1880s. Also with P. Chistiakov, 1882. Founded the Museum of Painting and Icon-Painting, Moscow. Peredvizhnik from 1891. Member of the Union of Russian Artists from 1903. Influenced by his friend I. Levitan. Also a close friend and art adviser to P. Tretiakov. A member of the Board of Directors, then head of the Tretiakov Gallery, 1898–1903. Trustee of the same gallery from 1905–13. Major collector of Russian icons (after 1918 his collection was nationalized by the Soviet government). Appointed keeper of his own collection, which became a part of the Tretiakov Gallery after his death. Died in Moscow. Personal exhibition: Jubilee, Moscow, 1925.

Ostrovskii, Aleksandr S.
25.9.1893–20.11.1987. Mathematician.
Born in Kiev. At the age of 25, wrote his now celebrated paper, *Acta Mathematica*. Emigrated after the October Revolution 1917. His first work, on the Galois theory of algebraic equations, was published when he was 19 years old. Taught at Hamburg University. Professor at Basel, 1923. Taught there until his retirement in 1961. Author of works on different areas of mathematics, including algebra, geometry and calculus. His 3 textbooks, written in 1940, are still widely used to train mathematicians and other scientists. Died in Switzerland.

Ostrovskii, Arkadii Il'ich
25.2.1914–18.9.1967. Composer, pianist.
Born in Syzran'. Improviser from childhood. Studied at the Central Technical School of Music, Leningrad, 1930–34. Pianist with the State Variety Orchestra, Leningrad and Moscow, 1940–47. Career as a composer during the war years. Lived and worked in Moscow from 1943. Pianist with the Leonid Utesov Jazz Band.

Ostrovskii, Nikolai Alekseevich
29.9.1904–22.12.1936. Author.
Born in the village of Vilia near Rovno (Western Ukraine). Son of a worker. As a teenager, volunteered to fight for the Reds during the Civil War, 1919. A year later, severely wounded while serving in the Red cavalry under Kotovskii. Komsomol official in the Ukraine, 1923–24. From 1927, bedridden. Became paralyzed and blind, 1928. In this state, wrote his autobiographical novel *Kak Zakalialas' Stal'* (How Steel Was Tempered), 1932–34, about the participation of youth in the class struggle and the Civil War. This novel was proclaimed one of the greatest achievements of socialist realism, and its hero, Pavka Korchagin, became the main Stalinist hero to be emulated by Soviet youth. Much praise was heaped upon the author and his work which, without ever having gained genuine popularity, was obligatory study material in Soviet schools until 1987.

Osyka, Leonid Mikhailovich
8.3.1940–   . Film director.
Graduated from the Odessa Theatre Institute, and the VGIK. First film, 1965. Made two important films — *Kamennyi Krest*, 1968, and *Zakhar Berkut*, 1972, which received a prize at the Venice Film Festival.

Ots, Georg Karlovich
21.3.1920–   . Singer (baritone).
Born in Petrograd. Son of the singer K. Kh. Ots. Choral singer from 1942. Graduated from the Tallinn Conservatory, 1951. Pupil of T. Kuuzik. Soloist with the Estonian Opera and Ballet Theatre. Performed in opera, operetta, and chamber music ensembles. Appeared in many films. Guest performances abroad.

Otsup, Nikolai Avdeevich
1894–1958. Poet.
Born in Petersburg. Became known as a poet before WWI. Close to Nikolai Gumilev. Emigrated after the Bolshevik take-over 1917. Settled in Paris. Editor of the magazine *Chisla*, 1930–34. Died in Paris.

Otsup, Petr Adol'fovich
1883–1963. News and portrait photographer.
Born in Petersburg. Son of a clerk. At the age of 9, apprenticed to a portrait photographer. From 1900–17, worked for the magazines *Niva*, *Rodina*, *Iskra*, *Ogonek*, *Solntse Rossii* and others. In 1901, became famous for his pictures of Leon Tolstoy, Anton Chekhov and Maksim Gorkii in Yalta, published in *Niva*. During both the Russo-Japanese war, 1904–05 and WWI, worked as a front-line news photographer. Took pictures during the February Revolution. Was the only photographer at the Smolnyi Institute during the October coup, recording the preparations for the armed revolt and the storming of the Winter Palace. During the Civil War, photographed the attacks of the 1st Cavalry, the suppression of the Kronstadt revolt and the defeat of the Basmachi fighters by the Red Army in Central Asia. His photoportrait of Lenin in Oct. 1918 was published and distributed all over the world in millions of copies, and used by film companies and television. Left a collection of some 40,000 negatives. Exhibited widely, both at home and abroad, and received many diplomas and citations for his work. See: *Soviet Photography, 1917–40*, London, 1984.

Ott, Dmitrii Oskarovich
23.2.1855–17.6.1929. Gynaecologist.
Born in the village of Plokhino, now in the Ul'ianovo, Kaluzhskaia Oblast'. Graduated from the Petersburg Medical-Surgical Academy, 1879. Director of the Petersburg Maternity Institute from 1893. Innovator in the treatment and surgery of maternity, and general gynaecological cases. Constructed new medical instruments. Honorary member of many foreign medical societies. Died in Leningrad.

Otto, Aleksandr Fedorovich (Onegin)
1844–1925. Pushkin specialist.
Lived in France. Collected a great amount of material concerning A. Pushkin. Founded a Pushkin Museum in Paris.

Ovanisian, Nar Mikhailovich
12.4.1913– . Singer (bass).
Born in Tbilisi. Son of the poet Nar-

Dos (M. Ovanisian). Pupil of E. Vronskii. Leading singer with the Theatre of Opera and Ballet, Tbilisi, 1945–51. In Erevan from 1951.

Ovchinnikov, Vladimir
1958– . Pianist.
Graduated from the Moscow Conservatory. Won 1st prize at the Leeds International Competition 1987, performing Brahms' Sonata No. 1 and Rachmaninov's 2nd Concerto.

Ovechkin, Valentin Vladimirovich
1904–1968. Author.
Born in Moscow. Communist Party member. Was one of the editors of the magazine *Novyi Mir*. In the early 1960s, criticised Khrushchev's cult of personality. At the end of 1962, wrote a letter to the Cen. Cttee. of the CPSU demanding agricultural reforms on the Yugoslav model (abolishment of the kolkhozes). Put into a psychiatric hospital, but soon released.

Ovechkina, Nina
1937–3.1988. Hero mother.
Held the honoured title of Hero Mother for having given birth to 10 children whom she then brought up alone in the Siberian city of Irkutsk. 7 of her children became famous as the Seven Simeons Jazz Ensemble. She was shot by her sons during an unsuccessful and dramatic attempt by the Seven Simeons to hijack a Tu-154 to the West. Died instantly with 4 members of the family (2 shot themselves and 2 were shot by security guards).

Ovechkina, Tatiana Nikolaevna
19.3.1950– . Athlete.
Born in Moscow. Honoured Master of Sports (basketball), 1975. With Moscow Dynamo. Graduated from the Moscow Institute of Physical Culture, 1978. European champion, 1970–78. World champion, 1975. Olympic champion, 1976.

Ozerov, Iurii Nikolaevich
26.1.1921– . Film director.
Born in Moscow. Son of the opera singer Nikolai Ozerov. Graduated

from the Frunze Military Academy in 1944 and from the VGIK (Moscow Film School) as a director in 1951. With Mosfilm Studios from 1952. Known in the West for his 5-part serial *Liberation* (documentary on WWII), 1968–71. Other films: *Kochubei*, 1958; *Fortuna* (Soviet-Albanian co-production, 1959); *The Big Road* (Soviet-Czechoslovak co-production, 1963); *The Soldiers of Freedom* (Mosfilm, 1976).

Ozerov, Nikolai Nikolaevich
15.4.1887–4.12.1953. Singer (tenor).
Born in Riazan' Gouvt. Pupil of A. Uspenskii. Appeared on the stage from 1912. Leading singer with the Bolshoi Theatre, 1920–46. Author of *Opery i Pevtsy*, Moscow, 1964. Died in Moscow.

Ozolin', Arvid Karlovich (Ozolin'sh)
22.11.1908– . Ballet dancer, choreographer.
Born in Riga. Studied at the ballet schools of M. Kaulin', 1927, and A. Fedorova, 1928–32. Final training in Paris under L. N. Egorova and O. I. Preobrazhenskaia. Dancer with the company of L. Miasin (Massine) and M. M. Fokin in Paris and other West European cities, 1936–39. With the Latvian National Opera, 1928–36, and from 1939. With the Riga Theatre, 1944–63. New productions of various ballets, 1944–45. Taught theatre ballet classes, 1944–48. Taught at the Tallinn Choreographic School, 1965–77, and at the Riga Choreographic School from 1978.

Ozolina, El'vira Anatol'evna
24.8.1939– . Athlete.
Born in Leningrad. Honoured Master of Sports (track and field athletics), 1960. Graduated from the Leningrad Institute of Physical Culture, 1963. From 1969, with the Riga Armed Forces Club. USSR champion, 1961–73. European champion, 1962. Olympic javelin champion, 1960.

P

Paatashvili, Levan Georgievich
12.3.1926– . Cameraman.
Born in Georgia. Graduated from

the VGIK, 1954. Important films: *Beg*, 1971 (shown at the Cannes Film Festival), *Romans o Vliublennykh*, 1974, and *Sibiriada*, the official Soviet entry at the 1980 Cannes Film Festival. Taught at the VGIK from 1978, and at the Rustaveli Theatre Institute from 1981.

Pakhman, Vladimir (Pachmann, Vladimir de)

27.7.1848–7.1.1933. Pianist.
Born in Odessa. Pupil of J. Dakhs. Appeared in concerts from 1869. Known chiefly for his interpretation of Chopin. After 1917, performed only abroad. Acquired the reputation of being an eccentric virtuoso, interrupting his performances to talk to the audience about the meaning of the piece. Spent the last years of his life in Italy. Died in Rome.

Pakhmutova, Aleksandra Nikolaevna

9.11.1929–   . Composer.
Born near Volgograd. Graduated from the Moscow Conservatory (composition class of V. I. Shebalin), 1953. Finished postgraduate training there, 1956. Became an established composer of Soviet songs (written with the poet N. N. Dobronravov), vocal and symphonic works. Wrote music for a ballet produced at the Bolshoi Theatre, 1973.

Pakhomov, Aleksei Fedorovich

2.10.1900–14.4.1973. Artist.
Born in the village of Varlamovo, now in the Vologodskaia Oblast'. Trained at the Stiglits School in Leningrad. Pupil of V. V. Lebedev and N. A. Tyrsa. Taught at the Repin School of Fine Arts and Architecture, Leningrad, from 1948. Illustrator of children's books. Died in Leningrad.

Pakhomova, Liudmila Alekseevna

31.12.1946–1985. Athlete, coach.
National ice-dancing champion 9 times between 1964–75. Graduated from the Lunacharskii State Institute of Theatrical Arts in 1970. Honoured Master of Sports, 1970. Coached by E. Chaikovskaia. With her husband Aleksandr Gorshkov, dominated ice-dancing in the 1970s winning 6 world championships for the Soviet Union. First Olympic gold medal in Innsbruck in 1976. After their Olympic triumph, she retired, but remained in the sport as a coach, making a big impact with her artistic ideas. In charge of young talents such as Natalia Annenko and Genrikh Sretenskii. Died in Moscow from leukaemia.

Pakul', El'frida Ianovna

2.6.1912–   . Singer (coloratura).
Born in Riga. Pupil of P. Saks and N. Raiskii. Leading singer with the Riga Opera, 1940–41, and 1944–56. Soloist with the Latvian State Philharmonic Orchestra from 1956. State Prize, 1946.

Palantai, Ivan Stepanovich (real name – Kliuchnikov)

11.4.1886–11.7.1926. Composer. folklorist.
Born in Cheboksary Oblast'. Author of choral works. Organized choir singing in the Mari ASSR, 1923. Died in Moscow.

Pal'chinskii, Petr Akimovich

1875–1929. Politician.
Mining engineer. After the February Revolution 1917, member of the Executive Cttee. of the Petrograd Soviet. Chairman of the Council for Defence. In October 1917, Military Governor of Petrograd under the Provisional Government. In charge of the defence of the Winter Palace and the Provisional Government on the day of the October Revolution, 7 Nov. 1917. Arrested by the Bolsheviks after the storming of the Palace. For a time, inmate of the Peter and Paul Fortress. According to Solzhenitsyn in *Gulag Archipelago* shot in a Gulag camp.

Palei, Vladimir Pavlovich, Prince

1897–17.7.1918. Poet.
Son of Grand Duke Pavel Aleksandrovich and Princess Palei. Spent his childhood in France with his parents. Educated at the Pages Corps, Petersburg, 1914. Joined a hussar regiment at the front during WWI. Close to the sons of Konstantin Romanov, translated into French Romanov's *Tsar' Iudeiskii*. Published 2 collections of poems, 1915 and 1918. Arrested with the other Romanovs and their relatives by M. Uritskii, Mar. 1918. Sent to the Urals with Grand-Duke Sergei Mikhailovich and the 3 sons of Konstantin Romanov, Ioann, Konstantin and Igor. In Apr., the prisoners were brought to Ekaterinburg, where the Tsar's family was imprisoned, but kept separately. Transferred with the group of prisoners to Alapaevsk, 18 May 1918. Executed at a disused mine in a nearby forest.

Paleologue, Maurice

1859–1944. French diplomat.
Descendant of a dynasty of Emperors of Byzantium. In his youth in France, close to Turgenev and Viardot, with whose daughter he fell in love. Entered the French Foreign Affairs Ministry, 1880. Served as a French diplomat in Morocco, Italy and China. French Ambassador to Russia, Jan. 1914–summer 1917. Held senior posts in the French Foreign Affairs Ministry, 1917–20. Supported the Allied intervention in Russia during the Civil War. Published the 3-volume history *La Russie des Tsars pendant la Grande Guerre*, and left valuable memoirs of the fall of the monarchy in Russia. Member of the Academie Française, 1928.

Paliashvili, Ivan Petrovich (Russian stage-name – Paliev)

13.10.1868–7.3.1934. Conductor.
Born in Kutaissi. Brother of Z. P. Paliashvili. One of the first Georgian conductors. Studied in Petersburg, 1888–89. Pupil of N. A. Rimskii-Korsakov (composition) and V. I. Suk (conducting). Conductor with operatic companies in various Russian towns. Director of the Georgian Theatre of Opera and Ballet from 1922. Excelled in works by Georgian composers. Taught at the opera class of the Tbilisi Conservatory, 1922–25. Died in Tbilisi.

Paliashvili, Zakharii Petrovich

16.8.1871–6.10.1933. Composer, conductor.
Born in Kutaissi. Church choirboy at the age of 8. Chorister, 1887–89. Organist at the Catholic Church, 1889–1900. Studied at the Tiflis Music School, 1895–99. Pupil of P. Klenovskii, himself a pupil of P. Tchaikovskii. At the Moscow Conservatory, 1900–03. Pupil of S.

Taneev. Taught theory and choral singing at the Music School in Tiflis, 1903–17, and at the Conservatory from 1919. Professor in 1919. Director in 1920, 1923, and 1929–32. One of the founders of the Georgian Philharmonic Society, 1905. Collected folk music from various parts of Georgia.

Palibin, Ivan Vladimirovich
9.4.1872–30.9.1949. Botanist.
Born in Tiflis. Studied at Geneva University. Worked in the Petersburg Botanical Garden (later the Botanical Institute of the AN SSSR) from 1895. Organised the paleobotany section, 1932. Director of the Batumi Botanical Garden, 1916–23. Expeditions to the Far East and to Eastern parts of the USSR. Died in Leningrad.

Palitsyn, Ivan Osipovich (real name –Palitse)
17.11.1865–3.6.1931. Conductor.
Born near Prague. Conductor with operatic companies in Kazan', Saratov, Odessa, Kiev, and Tbilisi. Conductor with the Zimin Opera, Moscow, from 1906, and in Sverdlovsk, 1924–30. Died in Sverdlovsk.

Palladin, Aleksandr Vladimirovich
10.9.1885–6.12.1972. Biochemist.
Born in Moscow. Son of V. I. Palladin. Graduated from Petersburg University, 1908. Professor at the Institute of Forestry at Khar'kov, from 1916. Professor at the Khar'kov Medical Institute from 1921. Director and founder of the Ukrainian Biochemical Institute from 1925 (the Biochemical Institute of the Academy of Sciences of the Ukrainian SSR from 1931). Professor at the University of Kiev, 1934–54. Author of several works on biochemistry. Died in Kiev.

Palladin, Vladimir Ivanovich
23.7.1859–3.2.1922. Botanist, biochemist.
Born in Moscow. Graduated from Moscow University, 1883. Pupil of K. A. Timiriazev and I. N. Gorozhankin. Professor at Khar'kov University, 1889, Warsaw University, 1897, and Petersburg University, 1901–14. One of the initiators of the theory of the breathing of plants. Author of several works on biochemistry. Died in Petrograd.

Panchuk, Liudmila Mikhailovna
18.1.1956– . Athlete.
Born in the village of Tokarovka, Kiev Oblast'. Honoured Master of Sports (handball), 1976. With Kiev Spartak. Studied at the Kiev Institute of Physical Culture . USSR champion, 1974–76. Olympic champion, 1976.

Panfilov, Gleb Anatol'evich
21.12.1934– . Film director.
Initially trained as a chemical engineer in Sverdlovsk. Graduated from the Advanced Directors' Courses at Mosfilm Studio. Became known after his first feature film *No Ford in the Fire*, 1968. *The Debut*, 1970, confirmed his reputation. *I Wish to Speak*, 1975, was attacked by the critics, and was shelved for some time but re-released in 1987. *The Theme* was completed in 1980 but banned for 7 years. Works mainly at Lenfilm Studio in Leningrad. Married to the talented character actress Inna Churikova, who plays leading roles in many of his films.

Panfilov, Ivan Vasil'evich
1.1.1893–19.11.1941. Military commander.
Participant in the Civil War, 1918. Member of the CPSU from 1920. Graduated from Kiev Military School in 1923. In 1938, chief-of-staff of the Central Asian military region. During WWII, participated in the defence of Moscow. Killed in action, Nov. 1941.

Panin, Dimitrii Mikhailovich
1911–18.11.1987. Engineer, physicist, author.
Born in Moscow. Graduated from the Moscow Chemical Engineering Institute. Worked as an engineer. Arrested in 1940, and spent 13 years in prisons and camps. In 1953, exiled for life. Met A. Solzhenitsyn in the camps. Prototype of Sologdin in A. Solzhenitsyn's *V Kruge Pervom*. Rehabilitated in 1956. Convert to Catholicism. Left the USSR, 1972. Settled in Paris. Author of numerous articles and books. Author of *Zapiski Sologdina*, Frankfurt, 1973, *Solzhenitsyn I Deistvitelnost'*, Paris, 1975, *Vselennaia Glazami Sovremennogo Cheloveka*, Belgium, 1976 and *Sozidateli I Razrushiteli*, Paris, 1983. Died in Paris.

Panin-Kolomenkin, Nikolai Aleksandrovich (real name – Kolomenkin)
8.1.1872–19.1.1956. Sportsman.
Born in the village of Khrenovoe, now Bobrovskii district, in the Voronezh Oblast'. Only Russian gold medallist at the 1908 Olympic Games. 1st prize at the World Championship, 1903, and European Championship, 1904, 1908, in figure skating. Repeatedly Russian champion in pistol-shooting, 1906–17. Taught figure-skating in Leningrad from the 1930s. Author of works on figure skating: *Iskusstvo Katania na Kon'kakh*, Moscow-Leningrad, 1938, *Stranitsy iz Proshlogo*, Moscow, 1951, and *Iskusstvo Figurista*, Moscow, 1956. Taught at the Leningrad Institute of Physical Culture. Died in Leningrad.

Panina, Sofia Vladimirovna, Countess (Polovtseva)
1871–1957. Politician.
Member of the Cadet Party. One of the few Russian women politicians in pre-revolutionary Russia. Deputy Minister of Social Security in the Provisional Government in Aug. 1917. Arrested with other Cadet leaders on 29 Nov. 1917 on Lenin's orders, and sent to the Peter and Paul Fortress. Married to P. Polovtsev. Later, the common law wife of N. Astrov. Emigrated, and settled in Paris.

Panov, Valerii Matveevich (Shulman)
12.3.1938– . Ballet dancer, choreographer.
Born in Vitebsk. In 1957, graduated from the Leningrad Choreographic School. A dancer at the Malyi Theatre. A soloist dancer at the Leningrad Kirov Ballet Theatre, 1963–72. Star in many productions including *Petrushka*, *Baryshnia i Khuligan* and *Hamlet*. Lost his job, as did his ballet-dancer wife Galina, after they had applied for exit visas to Israel in 1972, Placed under house

arrest. His hunger strike and other actions attracted world attention to his case. Eventually, in 1974, was allowed to emigrate. Citizen of Israel. Has danced all over the world. Choreographer in Berlin and Holland and with other ballet companies. In collaboration with G. Feifer, wrote his memoirs, *To Dance*, 1978. In 1985, took over the Royal Ballet of Flanders in Antwerp. Ballet productions based on Russian literary sources: *The Idiot*, *War and Peace* and *Three Sisters*. Re-staged *Le Sacré du Printemps* using a score first found in the Deutsche Oper.

Panova, Galina (Ragozhina)
17.3.1949– . Ballet dancer.
Born in Arkhangelsk. Graduated from the Perm' Choreographic School in 1967, became a solo dancer at the Perm' Opera and Dance Theatre. Moved to Leningrad, where she became a star with the Kirov Ballet. Married Valerii Panov. Applied for an exit visa to Israel. Both lost their jobs. Due to international pressure, allowed to emigrate eventually. From 1974, in Israel. Since then, has danced with Panov all over the world. Big success on Broadway in 1983. Starred in the London production *On Your Toes*.

Panova, Vera Fedorovna (Veltman, Vakhtina, Dar)
1905–1973. Author.
Born in Rostov-on-Don. In the 1920–30s, wrote for Rostov newspapers. After the arrest of her husband Vakhtin, moved to Leningrad, 1935. Became a well-known official writer (2 Stalin Prizes). Later wrote novels characteristic of the Khrushchev thaw period (*Vremena Goda, Sentimentalnyi Roman*). Keeping in favour with the authorities, helped her second husband, Dar, and her son B. Vakhtin, who were involved in the human rights movement.

Panso, Vol'demar Khansovich
30.11.1920– . Actor, producer.
Born in Tallinn. Graduated from the Tallinn Theatre School, 1941, and from the GITIS Faculty of Theatrical Production, 1955. Worked in Tallinn at the Kingisepp Estonian Theatre, 1941–50. Founder and chief director of the Estonian Youth Theatre in Tallinn, 1965–76. Has appeared in films. Teacher in the Acting Faculty of the Tallinn Conservatory from 1957. Author of *Maailm Arlekiini Kuues*, Tallinn, 1973, a Russian version of *Trud i Talant v Tvorchestve Aktera*, 1972, and *Udivitel'nyi Chelovek*, Moscow, 1972.

Panteleev, Iurii Aleksandrovich
1901–1983. Admiral.
Joined the Red Navy, 1918. Graduated from the Naval Academy, 1933. Submarine commander before WWII. Commander of the Leningrad Naval Base at the beginning of WWII. Commander of the Volga fleet, 1943, and the White Sea fleet, 1944. Head of the Naval Academy, 1948–51 and 1960–67. Commander of the Pacific fleet, 1951–56. Head of the Shipbuilding Academy, 1956–1960.

Panteleev, Leonid (Real name – Eremeev, Aleksei Ivanovich)
22.8.1908– . Writer.
Born in Petersburg. Orphaned in 1921. His experiences at the F.M. Dostoevskii Home for Homeless Children served as the basis for his first book *Republic Shkid* (co-author with G. Belykh), 1927. Film of the same name, 1967. Wrote books for juveniles and an autobiographical novel, *Len'ka Panteleev*, 1939 (revised version, 1952).

Pantiukhov, Iurii Borisovich
15.3.1931– . Athlete.
Born in Kolomna, Moscow Oblast'. Honoured Master of Sports (hockey), 1956. With the Central Sports Club of the Army. Member of the CPSU, 1961. Graduated from the Military Department of the Leningrad Institute of Physical Culture, 1967. Probably worked in intelligence after graduating. USSR champion, 1952–61. European champion, 1956 and 1958–59. World champion, 1956. Olympic champion, 1956.

Pantiukhov, Oleg Ivanovich
1882–1973. Chief scout.
Son of the well-known anthropologist I. Pantiukhov. Grew up in the Caucasus, where he became interest-ed in mountaineering and hiking. Educated in Tbilisi at a cadet school. Served as an officer in the Russian Army. Met Baden-Powell during his visit to Petersburg, and became the founder of scouting in Russia, which became very popular on the eve of WWI. Scouting was prohibited by the Bolshevik government, which used some of its elements, transformed and politicized, for their own youth movement, the Pionery. Took part in the Civil War on the side of the Whites. Scouting continued to exist, survived the evacuation of the Whites from the Crimea, and was re-created in many countries among Russian emigré communities. From the 1920s, lived in the USA, continued to be active in his role as chief of the Russian Scouts, and in the International Scout Movement. His extremely interesting memoirs, with rare illustrations, have been published in the USA.

Pantofel'–Nechetskaia, Debora Iakovlevna (b. Pantofel')
12.1.1905– . Singer (coloratura).
Born in Omsk. Pupil of E. Bronskaia. Very popular singer from the 1930s to the early 1950s. State Prize, 1946.

Pantserzhanskii, Eduard Samuilovich
1887–1937. Naval commander.
Graduated from the Naval Cadet Corps, 1910. Took part in WWI. Joined the Red Navy, 1918, active on many fronts during the Civil War. Commander of the Soviet Navy, 1921–25, and of the Black Sea fleet, 1925–26. Navy staff worker, 1926. Liquidated by Stalin.

Papaleksi, Nikolai Dmitrievich
2.12.1880–3.2.1947. Physicist.
Born in Simferopol'. Graduated from Strasbourg University, 1904. Studied under K. F. Braun. Worked mainly in radio research from 1914, often in collaboration with L. I. Mandelstam. One of the founders of the Odessa Polytechnical Institute, 1920. Professorship from 1922. From 1955, at the Moscow Physics and Energetics Institute. Died in Moscow. A collection of his works appeared in Moscow, 1948.

Papanin, Ivan Dmitrievich
26.11.1894–30.1.1986. Polar explorer, vice-admiral.
Joined the Bolshevik Party, 1919. Took part in the Civil War. In 1937–38, the fate of his polar expedition on drifting ice (SP-1, Severnyi Polus I) provided a well-publicized drama, presented as a great Soviet achievement. From 1939–46, head of Glavsevmorput', which played an important role in supplying the enormous Gulag empire in the Arctic. Vice-admiral, 1943. Deputy director of the Oceanology Institute of the Academy of Sciences, 1948. Head of the Marine Expeditions Department 1951, and of the Institute of the Biology of Inland Waters of the Academy of Sciences, 1951–1972.

Papanov, Anatolii Dmitrievich
31.10.1922– . Actor.
Born in Viazma. Graduated from the GITIS Faculty of Acting, 1946. With the Moscow Satira Theatre from 1946. Mainly grotesque parts. Appeared in many films during the 1950–70s.

Papazian, Vagram Kamerovich
18.1.1888–5.6.1968. Actor.
Born in Istanbul. Trained in Italy. Acted with E. Duze, E. Novelli and E. Zacconi, G. Grasso and others. With the Armenian Theatre in Istanbul, 1907–22 (with intervals). In the USSR from 1922. Acted with Russian and Armenian companies in Erevan, Tbilisi, Baku and Leningrad. Guest appearances abroad. With the Armenian Sundukian Theatre in Erevan from 1954. Appeared in many Shakespearean parts. Died in Leningrad. Author of *Po Teatram Mira* (Leningrad, Moscow, 1937), and *Zhizn' Artista* (Moscow, Leningrad, 1965).

Papazian, Vartanes Mesropovich
25.4.1866–26.4.1920. Author.
Born in Van, Turkey. Graduated from the Echmiadzin Seminary, later from Geneva University, 1894. Published works from 1883. His tales and novellas are based on life in Western Armenia and in the Turkey of the Sultans. Died in Erevan.

Papko, Iurii Viktorovich
25.2.1940– . Ballet dancer, choreographer.
Born in Moscow. Graduated from the Moscow Choreographic School, 1958. Pupil of Mikhail Gabovich. Graduated from the Choreographic Department of the GITIS, 1973. With the Bolshoi Theatre from 1958. Mainly a character dancer. Produced several ballets, dances for operas, plays and films.

Papkovich, Petr Fedorovich
1887–1946. Ship designer.
Graduated from the ship design faculty of the Petersburg Polytechnic, 1911. Joined the Red Navy, 1918. Head of the Artillery Bureau of the Navy, 1918–22. Pioneer of submarine design in the Soviet Union, 1922. Professor at the Leningrad Shipbuilding Institute, and the Naval Academy, 1934.

Paradzhanov, Sergei Iosifovich (Sarkis)
9.1.1924– . Film director.
Major Soviet Armenian director. Born in Tbilisi. Graduated from the VGIK in Moscow as a director. Pupil of Igor' Savchenko. Made a dozen folklore films but became famous with his *Teni Zabytykh Predkov* (Shadows of Our Forgotten Ancestors) in 1964, which received 16 international prizes for its dazzling camera-work (by Iurii Il'enko), combined with remarkable directing and acting. The film used West Ukrainian folklore from the Carpathian mountains and was produced by the Dovzhenko Film Studio in Kiev, which previously specialized in propaganda and sentimental productions. Another major film was *Sayat Nova* (The Colour of Pomegranates). Like *Shadows*, this was much criticized and not put on general public release. Arrested in the autumn of 1972 and charged with currency dealing (the charge was later dropped) and homosexuality, convicted and imprisoned. In fact, the conviction was for signing a couple of letters demanding the release of Ukrainian intellectuals who had been harassed for years by the Ukrainian KGB. The Paradzhanov Affair became a focus of international attention. Pressure was brought to bear on the Soviet

authorities, and he was released in Jan. 1978. His film *Kiev's Frescoes* was destroyed. This film was set on the eve of the German occupation of the city during WWII, and dealt with the destruction by the NKVD of the Ukrainian capital, including national treasures dating back to the 12th century. After his release from prison, lived in Tbilisi in his mother's home. Was not given permission to work. Tried to emigrate to France but was not allowed to. Disappeared from the film scene for several years. In 1986, visited the Rotterdam film festival. Under Gorbachev, all his films were released and his reputation restored.
See: Jeanne Vronskaya, 'The Paradzhanov Affair', *The Times*, 20 June, 1974.

Paramonov, Boris Mikhailovich
1937– . Philosopher, historian.
Born in Leningrad. Graduated in history from Leningrad University. Emigrated, 1977. Settled in the USA, later moved to West Germany. Published many articles on Russian history and literature in the West.

Paraskeva (Prokop, Iuliania Ivanovna
30.4.1894–4.4.1967. Russian Orthodox nun.
Born in the village of Isa near Khust (then Austro-Hungary). Daughter of a peasant. Several arrests by Hungarian authorities before WWI. Nun at an Orthodox convent at Bessarabia (Rumania), 1923. Head of a convent in Lipcha in the Carpathian region, which she built with her nuns, 1925–47. Head of the St Nicholas Orthodox Convent in Mukachev, 1947–67. Died at Mukachev.

Parenago, Pavel Petrovich
20.3.1906–5.1.1960. Astronomer.
Born in Ekaterinodar. Graduated from Moscow University, 1929. Professorship, from 1938. Academician, 1953. Author of several works on astronomy. Died in Moscow.

Parfenov, Anatolii Ivanovich
17.11.1924– . Athlete.
Born in the village of Dvornikovo, Moscow Oblast'. USSR champion,

311

1954 and 1957. With Moscow Dynamo. Olympic champion (heavyweight), 1956. Honoured Master of Sports (wrestling), 1956. Member of the CPSU, 1965. Graduated from the Moscow Institute of Physical Culture, 1967. Honorary Coach of the USSR, 1975.

Parfenov, Nikolai Gavrilovich
22.10.1893–1942. Harpist.
Born in Kursk. Pupil of A. Slepushkin. Taught at the Moscow Conservatory. Author of *Tekhnika Igry Na Arfe. Metod Professora A. I. Slepushkina*, Moscow, 1927, and *Shkola Igry Na Arfe*, Moscow, 1960.

Parilov, Mikhail Ivanovich
1889–1963. Artist.
Miniature painter and icon artist. Studied at an icon art school of the Committee of Preservation of Icons in Palekh. Specialized in papier-mâché jewellery and objets d'art. Lived and worked in Palekh. Made many miniature objets d'art, especially Palekh boxes.

Parin, Vasilii Vasil'evich
18.3.1903–15.6.1971. Physiologist.
Born in Kazan'. Graduated from the Medical Faculty of the University of Perm', 1925. Worked at the same university. Pupil of A.F. Samoilov. Director of the Sverdlov Medical Institute, 1932–41. Professor at the 1st Moscow Medical Institute, 1941–43. One of the founders of the Academy of Medical Sciences (AMNSSSR) and its 1st academician-secretary. Vice-president, 1963–66. Director of the Institute of Normal and Pathological Physiology of the AMNSSSR, 1965–69. Carried out research in many medico-physiological fields including that of astronautics. Member of the International Academy for Astronautics, 1964. Died in Moscow.

Parkhomenko, Aleksandr Iakovlevich
1886–1921. Revolutionary.
Joined the Bolshevik Party, 1904. Took part in the 1905 Revolution. Active in establishing Bolshevik rule in the Donbass industrial area after Nov. 1917. Joined the Red Army, 1918. Active participant in the Civil War. Military commissar of the Khar'kov Gouvt., Jan. 1919. Defeated the anti-Bolshevik revolutionary partisans of ataman Grigor'ev. Divisional commander in the 1st Cavalry Army, Apr, 1920. Killed in action against Makhno.

Parnas, Iakov Oskarovich
28.1.1884–29.1.1949. Biochemist.
Born in the village of Mokriany, now in the Drogobychskii district of L'vovskaia Oblast'. Graduated from the College of Technology of Berlin-Charlottenburg, 1904. Further courses in Strasbourg, 1905, and in Zurich, 1906–07. Lecturer in Strasbourg, 1913. Head of Warsaw University's Faculty of Physiological Chemistry from 1916. Founder and director of the Laboratory for Biochemistry of the ANSSSR, 1943–49. Among several works, wrote on muscular contraction, and gave an analysis of glycolysis, 1935. Member of the German Leopoldina Academy. Honorary doctor of the Sorbonne, and of Athens University. Died in Moscow.

Parnok, Sof'ia Iakovlevna (pen name – Polianin, Andrei)
1885–1933. Poet.
Born in Taganrog. Published poetry before WWI. Published critical essays under a male pseudonym. Translated French poetry into Russian. Many of her poems written after 1917 circulated in samizdat.

Parsegov, Valerii Vladimirovich
23.3.1936– . Ballet dancer.
Born in Kiev. Graduated from the Kiev Choreographic School, 1955. Pupil of K. V. Tikhomirov. Debut at the Shevchenko Theatre, 1956. Taught at the Kiev Choreographic School, from 1965. V. Nijinsky Prize, Paris, 1964.

Parshin, Georgii Mikhailovich
1916–1956. Major.
Joined the Red Army, 1941, and the Communist Party, 1942. During WWII, fighter pilot. Civil aviation pilot, 1946, and later test pilot. Died in an accident.

Parskii, Dmitrii Pavlovich
1866–1921. Lt.-general.
Graduated from the Academy of the General Staff, 1893. Took part in the Russo-Japanese war, 1904–05. Army commander during WWI. Joined the Red Army, 1918. Commander of the Northern front. Editor of the historical-military commission on WWI. Involved in the preparation of basic military regulations for the Red Army, 1920. Wrote works on the history of WWI.

Partskhaladze, Aleksei Alekseevich
24.4.1897–1969? Composer.
Born in Georgia. Father of the composer Merab Partskhaladze. Taught at the Batumi Music School. From 1936, director of the School. Published *Sbornik Pesen i Pliasok Adzharii*, 1936. Author of orchestral and vocal works and music for the stage.

Parusnikov, Mikhail Pavlovich
11.11.1893–1.2.1968. Architect.
Born in Moscow. Trained at the Moscow School of Art and Architecture and at the VKHUTEMAS, 1913–24. Pupil of S. V. Novakovskii and I. V. Zholtovskii. Taught at the Moscow Institute of Architecture, 1934–41, and from 1948. Professor from 1949. One of the planners of the Lenin Prospect. Died in Moscow.

Pashchenko, Andrei Filippovich
15.8.1885–1971? Composer.
Born in Rostov-on-Don. Author of operas, vocal and symphonic works, and music for stage and screen.

Pashennaia, Vera Nikolaevna
19.9.1887–28.10.1962. Actress.
Born in Moscow, into the theatrical family, Roshchin-Insarov. Entered the Moscow Theatre School, 1904. Pupil of A. P. Lenskii. With the Malyi Theatre from 1907. Classical actress. Took part in guest performances of MKHAT abroad, 1922–23. Taught from 1914. Died in Moscow. Author of *Stupeni Tvorchestva*, Moscow, 1964.
See: C. Durylin, *Vera Nikolaevna Pashennaia*, Moscow-Leningrad, 1946.

Pashkov, Aleksandr Konstantinovich
28.8.1944– . Athlete.
Born in Moscow. Honoured Master of Sports (hockey), 1978. With Moscow Dynamo, and later Voskresensk Khimik. Sports trainer. Graduated from the Moscow Oblast' Institute of Physical Culture, 1972. Olympic champion, 1972. World and European champion, 1978.

Paskhalov, Viacheslav Viktorovich
14.5.1873–26.12.1951. Musicologist.
Born in Moscow. Son of the composer and pianist Viktor Paskhalov. His works on composers include *Chopin i Pol'skaia Narodnaia Pesnia*, Moscow, 1941. Died in Leningrad.

Paskutskii, Nikolai Antonovich
1894–1945. Revolutionary, politician.
Joined the Red Army, 1918, and the Bolshevik Party, 1919. Helped establish Bolshevik rule in Central Asia. Chairman of the Central Asian Economic Council, 1920–25. Deputy Prime Minister, and chairman of GOSPLAN in Turkmenia, 1925. Deputy Minister of Agriculture of the USSR, 1928.

Pasternak, Aleksandr Leonidovich
1893– . Architect.
Born in Moscow. Son of the artist Leonid Pasternak and younger brother of the poet Boris Pasternak. Graduated from the Moscow School of Painting and Sculpture. One of the architects of Lenin's Mausoleum. Wrote interesting memoirs about life before WWI, *Vospominaniia*, Munich, 1983.

Pasternak, Boris Leonidovich
10.2.1890–30.5.1960. Poet, author, translator, Nobel Prize laureate.
Born in Moscow into an artistic Jewish family. Son of painter L. Pasternak, friend of Tolstoy. Educated at a Moscow secondary school. Studied law at Moscow University, changed to the philosophy faculty. Graduated in 1913. Studied music with Skriabin. Studied philosophy at Marburg University in 1912 (with Herman Cohen). First poems published in 1912, first volume of poetry (*A Twin in the Clouds*), 1914. Member of the modernist group Tsentrifuga. Gained a reputation as a master of the poetic art in the 1920s. In the 1930s, became increasingly alienated from Stalinist society, becoming an internal emigré, and turned to translation (Goethe's *Faust*, Shakespeare, Georgian poetry). During the post-Stalin thaw, the publication of his novel *Dr Zhivago*, about life during the revolutionary years (originally published in Italy by Feltrinelli), created a sensation by its implicit criticism of all political narrow-mindedness. Became instantly famous in the West (*Zhivago* was filmed in 1965 by David Lean) and was awarded the Nobel Prize for Literature in 1958. Condemned in a vicious public campaign in the USSR, forced to renounce the Nobel Prize and expelled from the Writers Union. Died in Peredelkino, the writers village near Moscow, where he had lived for many years. Posthumously recognized as one of the great Russian authors of the 20th century, and widely revered as a keeper of the best traditions of Russian literature. *Dr Zhivago* has since been published in the Soviet Union under Gorbachev (poems from the novel had appeared in Soviet publications much earlier). Main works: *Sestra Moia Zhizn'* (My Sister Life), *Lt. Schmidt*, *God 1905* (The year 1905), *Dr Zhivago*.

Pasternak, Leonid Osipovich
4.4.1862–31.5.1945. Artist.
Born in Odessa. Father of Boris Pasternak. Painter and book illustrator. Studied at the Odessa School of Art and at the Academy of Fine Arts in Munich. Close to Leo Tolstoy, illustrated his novel *Resurrection*. From 1894 to 1918, taught at the Moscow School of Painting, Sculpture and Architecture. Exhibited with the Peredvizhniki, the Union of Russian Painters, and the Mir Iskusstva group. From 1921, lived abroad, at first in Berlin and later in Oxford. Died in Oxford.

Pasternak, Petr Leont'evich
20.1.1885–21.9.1963. Engineer.
Born in Odessa. Graduated from the Technical College in Zurich, 1910. Engineer in Geneva, 1912–14. Engineer in Petersburg, 1914–20. Emigrated after the October Revolution 1917. Lecturer at the Zurich Technical College, 1920–29. Returned to the USSR. Research work in construction, 1929–32. Taught structural engineering in Moscow from 1932. Professor, 1934. Responsible for many official buildings in the USSR. Died in Moscow.
Works: *Kompleksnye Konstruktsii*, Moscow, 1948 (from the German edition, Zurich 1927); *Zhelezobetonnye Konstruktsii*, Moscow, 1961.

Paton, Boris Evgen'evich
27.11.1918– . Metallurgist.
Graduated from the Kiev Polytechnical Institute, 1941. Member of the Cen. Cttee. of the CPSU, 1961. President of the Ukrainian Academy of Sciences, 1962. Specialist in welding.

Patorzhinskii, Ivan Sergeevich
3.3.1896–22.2.1960. Singer (bass).
Born in Ekaterinoslav Gouvt. Leading singer with opera companies in Khar'kov, 1925–35, and Kiev from 1935. Professor at the Kiev Conservatory from 1946. State Prize of the USSR, 1942. Died in Kiev.

Paulauskas, Modestas Feliksovich
19.3.1945– . Athlete.
Born in Klaipeda. Honoured Master of Sports (basketball), 1967. With Kaunas Zhal'giris. Graduated from the Kaunas Institute of Physical Culture, 1971. European champion, 1965–71. World champion, 1967, 1974. Olympic champion, 1972. Bronze medal, 1968.

Paverman, Mark Izrailevich
8.6.1907– . Conductor.
Born in Odessa. Pupil of K. Saradzhev. Chief conductor with the Philharmonic Orchestra and professor at the Sverdlovsk Conservatory.

Pavlenko, Petr Andreevich
11.7.1899–16.6.1951. Author.
Born in Petersburg. Son of a clerk. Studied at the Baku Technical School, 1919–20. Joined the Communist Party in 1920. From 1920, on party work in the Red Army in the Caucasus. Sent to Turkey to work at the Soviet Trade Delegation, 1924–27. First publication, 1928. Used

oriental themes in his early writing. During the 1930s, worked in the film industry. With S. Eisenstein, wrote the script for *Aleksandr Nevskii*, 1938 (Stalin Prize, 1941). War correspondent, 1939–40, in Finland, and 1941–45. Wrote the scripts for *Kliatva* and *Padenie Berlina* (1946 and 1947), which were both recognized in the 1960s as classic examples of Stalinist cinema. Author of many propaganda articles and books. Many official decorations. Died in Moscow.

Pavlichenko, Liudmila Mikhailovna
1916–1974. Major.
Drafted into the Soviet Army, 1941. Graduated from the Vystrel Courses, 1943. Made her name as a very successful sniper during WWII. Joined the Bolshevik Party, 1945. Researcher at the HQ of the Red Navy, 1945–53.

Pavlin (Kroshechkin, Petr Kuzmich), Archbishop of Mogilev
19.12.1879–1940. Russian Orthodox clergyman.
Born near Mokshansk, Penza Gouvt. Son of a peasant. Joined the Sarov Pustyn monastery, 1895–8, moved to Novospasskii monastery in Moscow, 1904. Graduated from Moscow Theological Academy. Bishop of Rylsk, 1921. Bishop of Perm', 1928. Archbishop of Mogilev, 1933. Arrested Jan. 1936 and sent to the Gulag camps, where he died.

Pavlinov, Pavel Iakovlevich
24.4.1881–2.2.1966. Artist.
Born in Petersburg. Studied at the Petersburg Academy of Arts, 1903–06, under D. N. Kardovskii. Member of the Moscow Artists Association and the Four Arts, 1914–18. Taught at the VKHUTEMAS-VKHUTEIN, 1921–30. Dean of the Graphic Arts Faculty, 1921–24, also of the Arts' Institutes of Moscow, 1930–50. Worked mainly in xylography from 1916. Died in Moscow.

Pavlov, Aleksandr Vasil'evich
22.12.1880–14.8.1937. General.
Born in Odessa. On active service during WWI. After the October Revolution 1917, joined the Red Army as a lieutenant. Fought against the Ukrainian Rada, and against Admiral Kolchak (division commander). Commander of the 10th Army against General Denikin, 1919. Took part in the suppression of the Antonov peasant uprising in Tambov Gouvt. After the Civil War, inspector of infantry in the Ukraine and Crimea. Deputy head of the Frunze Military Academy, 1930. A victim of Stalin's purge of the army, probably shot.

Pavlov, Aleksei Petrovich
1.12.1854–9.9.1929. Geologist.
Born in Moscow. Graduated from Moscow University. Professor of Moscow University, 1886. Many works on palaeontology and glaciology. Became a worldwide authority on these subjects. Member of the Royal Geographical Society and many foreign scientific bodies. Member of the Russian, later Soviet, Academy of Sciences. Wrote many popular books on natural history. Died in Bad Toelz in Germany, buried in Moscow.

Pavlov, Dmitrii Grigor'evich
1897–1941. General.
Joined the Red Army and the Bolshevik Party, 1919. Took part in the Soviet-Finnish war, 1939–40. Commander of the Belorussian military district, 1940. Commander of the Western front at the time of the surprise German attack and the complete defeat of Soviet forces in the summer of 1941. Blamed by Stalin for the collapse of the Western front. Summoned to Moscow, court-martialled and shot on Stalin's orders. His relatives have conducted a long campaign for his rehabilitation.

Pavlov, Fedor Pavlovich
13.9.1892–2.6.1931. Composer, conductor, folklorist, dramatist.
Born in Kazan' Gouvt. Director of the Chuvash State Choir (founded 1924). Author of songs and plays. Died in Sochi.

Pavlov, Iakov Fedorovich
1917–1981. Lieutenant.
Joined the Red Army, 1938. During WWII, became famous as the sergeant whose small group occupied a building in the centre of the city during street fighting in Stalingrad and held it until the end of the battle. After WWII, worked as an economic administrator.

Pavlov, Igor' Mikhailovich
23.6.1900– . Metallurgist.
Born in the town of Sulin, now Krasnyi Sulin, Rostov Oblast'. Son of the metallurgist and academician M. A. Pavlov. Graduated from the Petrograd Polytechnic Institute, 1923. Worked in factories as a metallurgist. Taught at the Leningrad Polytechnic Institute from 1926. Professor, 1939. In the Moscow Steel Institute from 1943. Corresponding member of the Academy of Sciences from 1946. Head of the Department for Plastic Deformation of Metals, from 1953. Author of many works on metallurgy.

Pavlov, Ivan Nikolaevich
17.3.1872–30.8.1951. Engraver.
Born in Popovka, now in Tula Oblast'. Trained at the Central Technical School. Pupil of Shtiglits. Also at V. V. Mate's studio in Petersburg, 1891–92. Taught at the Stroganov School of Art, 1907–14. At art school attached to the printers of I. D. Sytin from 1915, and at art studios in Moscow (VKHUTEMAS, 1917–22). Started mainly with reproductions, later original work in coloured xylography and linography. Died in Moscow. Author of *Zhizn' Russkogo Gravera*, Moscow, 1963.

Pavlov, Ivan Petrovich
26.9.1849–27.2.1936. Scientist, physiologist.
Born in Riazan'. Educated at Riazan' seminary, 1864. Graduated from Petersburg University, 1875. Specialized in animal physiology. Studied at the Military Medical Academy, 1875–9. Studied in Breslau and Leipzig, 1884–6. Professor of pharmacology. at the Military Medical Academy, 1890, professor of physiology at the Academy, 1896–1924. At the same time, head of the physiological laboratory at the Institute of Experimental Medicine, 1890. Head of the Institute of Physiology of the Academy of Sciences, 1925–35. Worked out

the scientific basis for the study of higher nervous activity. Famous for his discovery of Pavlovian reflexes (conditioned reflexes), working with chimpanzees and dogs. Had an enormous influence on the development of therapy, surgery, psychiatry and neuropathology. Was lionized in the USSR, because his theories were considered a confirmation of the materialistic view of man, although he personally remained a traditional Orthodox believer (and publicly honoured the memory of his son, who had fought with the White Army during the Civil War).
Main works: *Collected Works*, 6 vols, Moscow, 1951–52.

Pavlov, Mikhail Aleksandrovich
21.1.1863–10.1.1958. Metallurgist.
Born in Bozhii Promysel (now in the Lenkoran' district). Graduated from the Petersburg Institute of Mine Engineering, 1885. First publication in the professional press, 1894. Pioneering work on high furnaces. Taught at the Ekaterinoslav (now Dnepropetrovsk) Institute of Mining Engineering, 1906. Professor at the Petersburg Polytechnical Institute, 1904–41. Professor at the Moscow Mining Academy, 1921–41. At the Moscow Steel Institute, 1930–41. Died in Moscow.

Pavlov, Pavel Andreevich
1892–1924. Military commander.
On active service during WWI. Joined the Red Army and the Bolshevik Party, 1919. Took part in the Civil War in the Ukraine and Bukhara. Chief Soviet military adviser in China, 1924. Drowned during a river-crossing in China.

Pavlov, Sergei Pavlovich
19.1.1929–   . Politician.
Born in Rzhev. Graduated from the Moscow Institute of Physical Culture in the early 1950s. From 1952, involved in Komsomol work. Member of the CPSU, 1954. 1st secretary of the Moscow City Cttee. of the VLKSM, 1957–58. Secretary, 1958–59, and 1st secretary of the Cen. Cttee. of the VLKSM, 1959–68. Chairman of the Cttee. of Physical Culture and Sports of the Soviet of Ministers of the USSR from 1968.

Chairman of the USSR Olympic Cttee. from 1975. Author of *Fizicheskaia Kultura i Sport v SSSR*, Moscow, 1979.

Pavlov, Timofei Pavlovich
24.6.1860–23.6.1932. Dermatologist.
Born in Petersburg. Graduated from the Military Medical Academy. Worked under S.P. Botkin and I.P. Pavlov. Professor in the Department of Skin and Venereal Diseases, 1898–1924. Chairman of the Russian Society of Dermatologists, 1900. Specialist on inherited syphilis. At the Leningrad Institute for Medical Specialization, 1924–29. Left several works on dermatology. Corresponding member of the Dermatological Society of France. Died in Leningrad.

Pavlov, Vladimir Nikolaevich
1936–7.6.1979. Professor of Russian history.
Son of an officer in Kolchak's army. Born in Shanghai. After the communist take-over in China, emigrated to Canada with his parents. Chemical engineer. Graduated from a Canadian university. Continued his education at Berkeley University in the USA. Sent to Moscow University on a cultural exchange programme, 1968–69. Deported by the KGB and attacked in *Izvestia*. Stripped of the archive he had collected there for publication. Later deported from Bulgaria, apparently for having distributed dissident material there. In Yugoslavia, arrested for the same offence, and held in prison for 10 days. Lecturer at the Portsmouth Polytechnic. Collaborated with Posev and Grani. Died in London from a heart attack.

Pavlov, Vsevolod Vladimirovich
1.2.1898–16.2.1972. Egyptologist, art historian.
Born in Putivl'. Graduated from Moscow University, 1929. Taught there, 1931–71. Worked at the Pushkin Museum of Fine Arts, 1929–62. Authority on Egypt. Died in Moscow.

Pavlov-Arbenin, Aleksandr Vasil'evich
1871–22.6.1941. Conductor.
Born in Petersburg. Appeared in

symphony concerts and private opera. With the Theatre of Musical Drama in Petersburg, 1913–18, and the Saratov Theatre from 1934. Died in Leningrad.

Pavlova, Anna Pavlovna
12.2.1881–23.1.1931. Prima ballerina.
Born in Petersburg. Daughter of a soldier and a washerwoman. Pupil of P. Gerdt at the Imperial Theatrical School in Petersburg. Made her debut at the Mariinskii Theatre in 1899. Prima ballerina in 1906. Many international tours from 1908, widely acclaimed for her artistic accomplishments. Joined the Diaghilev Ballets Russes in 1909 in Paris in *Les Sylphides*. Left Diaghilev in 1911 and created her own small ballet company. Returned to Russia for the last time in connection with her husband Victor Dandre's complicated financial affairs. Settled in London. Constant tours around the world. Became the best-known and most admired star of Russian ballet at the time of its highest glory. Remained the 'prima ballerina assoluta par excellence'. Died suddenly at the age of 50 in the Hague.
See: Victor Dandre, *Anna Pavlova* (biography), Berlin, 1933; H. Algeranoff, *My Years with Pavlova*, London, 1957.

Pavlova, Maria Vasil'evna
27.6.1854–23.12.1938. Palaeontologist.
Born in Kozelsk, now in the Kaluzhskaia Oblast'. Specialised in palaeontology in Paris under A. Godri. Professor at Moscow University, 1919–30. Together with her husband A. P. Pavlov, founded the Geological Museum at Moscow University. Worked there from 1885. The museum is now called the Pavlovs Geological Institute. Left several works on prehistoric animal remains. Died in Moscow.

Pavlovskaia, Emilia Pavlovna (b. Berman)
9.8.1853–23.3.1935. Singer (soprano).
Born in Petersburg. Graduated from Petersburg Conservatory, 1873. Pupil of K. Everardi. Debut in Italy. Sang with the Malta Opera. Appeared in

theatres in Kiev, Odessa, Tiflis and Khar'kov from 1876. Soloist with the Bolshoi Theatre, 1883–84 and 1888–89. With the Mariinskii Theatre, 1884–88. Taught at the Bolshoi Theatre Opera Class from 1895. Died in Moscow.

Pavlovskii, Aleksandr
14.7.1936–1977. Athlete.
Belorussian athlete. Honoured Master of Sports (fencing). Many times USSR champion. Bronze medal-winner at the XVIIth Olympic Games.

Pavlovskii, Evgenii Nikanorovich
5.3.1884–27.5.1965. Zoologist, lt.-general of the Medical Service.
Born in Biriuch, now Krasnogvardeisk, in Voronezh Oblast'. Graduated from the Petersburg Military Academy of Medicine, 1908. Professor at the same institute from 1921. Worked with the All-Union Institute of Experimental Medicine, 1933–34. Director of the Zoological Institute of the USSR Academy of Sciences, 1942–62. Head of the Department of Parasitology and Medical Zoology from 1946. President of the Geographical Society of the USSR, 1952–64. Leader of several expeditions to the Eastern and Southern parts of USSR. Author of textbooks on parasitology. Died in Leningrad.

Pavlovskii, Evgenii Vladimirovich
22.4.1901– . Geologist.
Born in Moscow. Graduated from the Moscow Military Academy, 1928. Pupil of V. A. Obruchev. Worked in the Geological Institute of the USSR Academy of Sciences, 1932–41 and from 1956. With various geological institutes in Siberia from 1941. Professor at Irkutsk University, 1946–56. Author of works on geotectonics and on the early geological development of the planet.

Pavlovskii, Ivan Grigor'evich
1909– . General.
Joined the Red Army, 1931, and the Bolshevik Party, 1939. On active service during WWII as a divisional commander. Graduated from the Academy of the General Staff, 1948. Deputy Minister of Defence, Apr.

1967. From Nov. 1967, also commander of Soviet land forces. Member of the Cen. Cttee. of the CPSU, 1971–81.

Pavlunovskii, Ivan Petrovich
16.8.1888–10.2.1940. State security official.
Born in Rzhava near Kursk. Joined the Bolshevik Party in 1905. After the 1905 Revolution, exiled to Vologda, 1907. Involved in revolutionary activity in Petersburg 1911–14. Military service during WWI (sub-lieutenant) in Petrograd and Tsarskoe Selo. Bolshevik agitator during the February Revolution 1917. Member of the Petrograd Soviet. Joined the Cheka in Oct. 1917. Worked as a Cheka official in Moscow, 1917–18 and during the Civil War at the Eastern front (Kazan', Ufa). Assigned by the Cheka in Siberia as a special representative and chairman of the revolutionary tribunal at the trial of Admiral Kolchak and his officers and civil servants in Omsk, May 1920. Quelled the uprising in Western Siberia in 1921. Masterminded the kidnapping of Baron Ungern Sternberg in Aug. 1921. Head of the commission for the requisition of food in Siberia in 1922. Operated in Siberia until 1926. Moved to Transcaucasia, 1926–28. Close to Sergo Ordzhonikidze (1st deputy to Ordzhonikidze at the Ministry of Heavy Industry). Responsible for armaments. Non-voting member of the Cen. Cttee. of the CPSU, 1934. Arrested in 1937. Died in prison or camps. Exact circumstances of death unknown.

Pavlushkov, Sergei Nikolaevich
1864–13.2.1942. Veterinary surgeon.
Graduated from the Kazan' Veterinary Institute, 1888. In charge of the Bacteriological Laboratory of the Ministry of the Interior, 1911–17. 1st director of the Laboratory when it became the Institute of Experimental Veterinary Science, 1917–21. Author and translator of several works on veterinary subjects. Died in Moscow.

Pazovskii, Arii Moiseivich
2.2.1887–6.1.1953. Conductor, violinist.
Born in Perm'. Pupil of L. Auer. First

appeared as a violinist. Conductor in Baku, Sverdlovsk, Khar'kov and Kiev, 1929–36. Artistic director at the Kirov Theatre of Opera and Ballet, Leningrad, 1936–43. With the Bolshoi Theatre, 1923–28. Died in Moscow.

Pechkovskii, Nikolai Konstantinovich
13.1.1896–197? Singer.
Began as an actor in 1913 at the Sergievskii People's House in Moscow. From 1918, appeared as an opera singer at the same theatre. Singer at the Opera Studio attached to the Bolshoi Theatre, 1921–23. Soloist at the same Theatre, 1923, and at the Kirov Opera and Ballet Theatre, Leningrad, 1924–41.

Pechnikov, Aleksandr Abramovich
8.2.1873–3.11.1949. Violinist.
Born in Elets. Pupil of I. Grzhimali. Concert tours from 1895, mainly abroad. Lived in Berlin until 1936, when he moved to Buenos Aires, where he gave violin lessons.

Peiko, Nikolai Ivanovich
25.3.1916– . Composer.
Born in Moscow. Professor at the Gnesin Music Pedagogical Institute. Author of an opera, ballets, orchestral works, works for piano and for violin. State Prize of the USSR, 1946, 1947, 1951, 1957, and 1965.

Peisin, Abram Iakovlevich
4.3.1894–24.1.1954. Composer, conductor, stage director.
Born in Tver' Gouvt. Author of an opera, ballets, comic operas, orchestral works, and music for screen and stage. Died in Leningrad.

Peive, Aleksandr Voldemarovich
9.2.1909– . Geologist.
Graduated from the Moscow Geological Survey Institute, 1930. Director of the Geological Institute of the Academy of Sciences, 1961. Carried out research into faults in the earth's crust. Worked on a tectonic map of the USSR.

Peive, Ian Voldemarovich
3.8.1906– . Chemist.
Graduated from the Timiriazev Agricultural Academy in Moscow, 1929.

President of the Latvian Agricultural Academy, 1944–50, and of the Latvian Academy of Sciences, 1951. Chairman of the Council of Nationalities of the Supreme Soviet of the USSR, 1958. Non-voting member of the Cen. Cttee. of the CPSU, 1961. Specialist in soil biochemistry.

Pekarskii, Eduard Karlovich
25.10.1858–29.6.1934. Linguist, ethnologist, folklorist.
Born in the Igumenskii district, now the Chervenskii region of Minsk Oblast'. Studied at the Khar'kov Veterinary Institute, 1877–78. Joined the populists. Published the *Dictionary of the Iakut Language* while exiled in Iakutia, 1881, for his populist activity. Joined the expedition to East Siberia, 1894–96, and the Aiano-Nel'kanskaia expedition, 1903. With the help of the Academy of Sciences, returned to Petersburg, 1905. Editor of the periodical *Zhivaia Starina*, 1914–17. In his last years, worked at the Institute of Oriental Studies. Published works on ethnography in Russian and Polish. Edited *Obraztsy Narodnoi Literatury Iakutov*. Died in Leningrad.
See: *Eduard Karlovich Pekarskii (K Stoletiiu so Dnia Rozhdeniia)*, Iakutsk, 1958.

Pekelis, Mikhail Samoilovich
10.8.1899– . Musicologist.
Born in Kiev. Professor at the Moscow Conservatory, 1925–43. Taught at the Gnesin Music Pedagogical Institute from 1948. Author of several works on Russian music.

Pekker, Ian Borisovich
4.10.1906– . Musicologist.
Born in Astrakhan'. Reader at the Tashkent Conservatory. Author of works on Uzbek music.

Pelikh, Tikhon Tikhonovich, Archpriest
26.8.1895–17.7.1983. Russian Orthodox clergyman.
Born in the village of Lutitsy, Khar'kov Gouvt. Son of a peasant. Orphaned at 6 and brought up by foster parents. Graduated from Moscow University, 1942. Worked as a teacher at Sergiev Posad (now Zagorsk), and formed close ties with the monastery there. Priest, 1947. Served in Moscow churches. Close to the priest Vsevolod Shpiller, who served at the same church. Appointed father confessor of the students of the Moscow Theological Academy, 1979. Universally liked by his flock. Revered as a traditional starets of our time. Married since 1937 to Tatiana Melnikova. On the day of her death in 1983, fell ill and never recovered, dying 2 weeks later. The last 3 years of his life were spent at the Church of the Protecting Veil in the village of Akulovo, where he died.

Pelshe, Arvid Ianovich
7.2.1899–1983. Politician.
Latvian Bolshevik. Born at Mazaia Farm, Bauska District, Kurland, now Latvia. At the age of 16, joined the Bolshevik Party, involved in revolutionary activity. Fled abroad. Met Lenin in Switzerland in 1916. Returned to Russia in 1917, on Lenin's request, as an agitator. Member of the Workers' and Soldiers' Soviet in Petrograd. Worked for Cheka, 1918. Sent to Latvia by Lenin and Trotsky where he initiated a 4-month Red Terror campaign. Was defeated with the help of the British Navy. Security instructor in various Red Army training schools. Graduated from the Institute of the Red Professors in 1931. One of the leading participants in Stalin's collectivization campaign in the 1930s which resulted in the uprooting and death of millions of peasants. In 1940, after the Hitler-Stalin pact, established Soviet rule in Latvia, which was incorporated in the USSR after a so-called referendum in which the Letts allegedly voted to join the USSR. The annexation was not recognized by the West. 1st secretary of the Latvian Communist Party, 1959–66. Moved to Moscow and appointed chairman of the Party Control Commission. Member of the Politburo, 1966. Became one of the last survivors of the Brezhnev 'gerontocracy'.

Peltser, Nina Vasil'evna (Chumakova)
14.3.1908– . Ballerina.
Born in Khar'kov. Trained at the ballet school of N. Dudinskaya-Tal'ori, then at the Leningrad Choreographic School, 1930–33. Pupil of A. I. Vaganova and A. V. Lopukhova. With the Khar'kov Theatre from 1926. Dancer at the Leningrad Theatre of Musical Comedy, 1929–56. Taught and coached there, 1941–76. Character dancer. Produced some ballets.

Pel'tser, Tatiana Ivanovna
6.6.1904– . Actress.
Born in Moscow. Trained by her father, the actor I. R. Pel'tser. Debut, 1920. With the MGSPS Theatre (now Moscow Mossovet Theatre), 1925–40, the Moscow Miniature Theatre, 1940–47 and the Satira Theatre from 1947. Mainly a comedy actress. Appeared in many films.

Pen'kovskii, Oleg
1912?–Spring 1963. Intelligence officer, colonel.
Nephew of a high-ranking Soviet general. Worked in military intelligence (GRU), collecting information on NATO rockets. Became an agent of Western intelligence agencies. Arrested, Oct. 1962, tried, and according to Soviet official sources, shot for high treason. Allegedly he had been for a number of years the most effective Western agent in the higher circles of Soviet intelligence. His diaries were published in the West.

Pen'kovskii, Valentin Antonovich
1904–1969. General.
Joined the Red Army, 1920, and the Bolshevik Party, 1926. Took part in WWII as a commander of anti-aircraft detachments. Commander of several military districts after WWII. Deputy Minister of Defence in charge of military training, 1964. Non-voting member of the Cen. Cttee. of the CPSU, 1961–1969. Uncle of Oleg Pen'kovskii who was executed as an American and British spy.

Pepeliaev, Anatolii Nikolaevich
15.8.1891–14.1.1938. Lt.-general.
Born in Tomsk, brother of V. Pepeliaev. Commander of a Siberian regiment in Omsk, 1918. In May 1918, with Czech troops, rebelled against the Bolsheviks. Commander

317

of the 1st Siberian Army (White). In Dec. 1918, took Perm'. Tried to call a Zemskii Sobor in Siberia. After Admiral Kolchak's defeat, tried to replace him by his own brother. Retreated to the Amur River, later Kharbin. Became close to the SRs, approved of the Soviet war with Poland. In Sep. 1922, illegally crossed the Russian border with a 700-strong detachment to aid the Yakut anti-communist rebellion. Taken prisoner on 17 June 1923 by S. Vostretsov's troops. Sentenced to death, commuted to 10 years imprisonment. A victim of the Gulag.

Pepeliaev, Viktor Nikolaevich
1884–7.2.1920. Politician.
Graduated from Tomsk University in law. Member of the 4th Duma. Member of the Cen. Cttee. of the Cadet Party, 1917. After the February Revolution 1917, became a commissar of the Provisional Government in Kronstadt. Arrested by revolutionary sailors. Chairman of the Eastern department of the Cen. Cttee. of the Cadet Party until Dec. 1918, when he left the party. In spring 1919, Minister of the Interior with Admiral Kolchak. From 22 Nov. 1919, Prime Minister of the Kolchak government. Handed over in Irkutsk to the Revkom (revolutionary committee) and shot together with Admiral Kolchak.

Peredel'skii, Georgii Efimovich
1913–   . Marshal.
Joined the Red Army, 1934, and the Bolshevik Party, 1939. Took part in the Soviet-Finnish war and WWII as an artillery officer. In the 1950s and 1960s, one of the most high-ranking artillery and rocket forces officers. Commander of Soviet rocket and artillery forces, 1962–65. Deputy commander of rocket land forces, 1965, and commander, 1969–83.

Pereiaslavets, Valentina
1907–   . Ballet dancer, teacher.
Born in the Ukraine. Studied at the Moscow Choreographic School. Graduated in 1926. Ballet-dancer in the Khar'kov and Sverdlovsk theatres. Starred in Iakobson's *Utrachennye Illiuzii*, a ballet staged in 1936. Pupil of Vaganova, later her

assistant in Leningrad. In 1940, danced in occupied L'vov. Deported by the Germans as an Ostarbeiter to a factory in Leipzig. After the war, set up a ballet school in Ingolstadt. In 1949, moved to America. Taught at T. Semenova's Ballet Studio in Philadelphia. Moved to New York, where she taught at the American Ballet Theater. From autumn 1982, a teacher at the M. Heiden Ballet School. Travelled all over the world, employed as a ballet teacher by various ballet companies.

Perel'man, Natan Efimovich
1.8.1906–   . Pianist.
Born in Zhitomir. Pupil of G. Neigauz and L. Nikolaev. Professor at the Leningrad Conservatory. Author of transcriptions for piano.

Perel'man, Viktor Borisovich
1929–   . Journalist, editor.
Born in Moscow. Graduated from the Moscow Law Institute. Graduated in journalism from the Poly-graphic Institute. Worked as a staff writer on *Literaturnaia Gazeta*. His articles appeared in leading Soviet periodicals. Left the USSR, 1973, and settled in Israel. Founded the monthly *Vremia I My*. Moved to the USA. Continued to edit *Vremia I My*. Founded a publishing house attached to the magazine. Memoirs: *Pokinutaia Rossiia*, 2 vols, Vremia I My, 1976.

Perepletchikov, Vasilii Vasil'evich
1863–1918. Artist.
Landscape painter. Pupil of A. Kiselev. Studied at the Moscow School of Painting, Sculpture and Architecture. Studied under I. Shishkin. Exhibitions: MOLKH, 1884–1908; MTKH, 1893–99; TPKHV, 1893–1901; the Society of Water-Colour Painters, St. Petersburg, 1894–97; All-Russian Exhibition, Nizhnii Novgorod, 1896; the Mir Iskusstva, 1899–1903; the 36 Artists, 1901–03; Union of Russian Artists, 1903–18. Died in Moscow.

Perestiani, Ivan Nikolaevich
13.4.1870–14.5.1959. Film director, actor.
Theatre actor from 1886. Appeared

in his first film, 1916. Acted in a further 20 films until Oct. 1917. Took part in agit-films during the Civil War. Made the first Georgian revolutionary film, *Arsen Dzhordzhiashvili*, 1921 (also known as *Ubiistvo Generala Griaznova*). His major film was *Krasnye D'iavoliata*, 1923, now a Soviet classic. Worked at the Odessa Film Studio, Armenkino, and Tbilisi Film Studio. As an actor, appeared in *Arsen*, 1937, and *Georgii Saakadze*, 1942–43.

Peresypkin, Ivan Terent'evich
1904–1978. Marshal.
Joined the Red Army, 1919. Took part in the Civil War. Joined the Bolshevik Party, 1925. Graduated from the Electrotechnical Academy of the Red Army, 1937. Deputy head of the communications administration of the Red Army, 1939. Minister of Communications, 1939–44, and Deputy Minister of Defence. After WWII, commander of the communications of the land armed forces. Wrote on the history of Soviet military communications systems.

Pereverzev, Pavel Nikolaevich
1871–1944. Politician.
Member of the Trudovik Party. Minister of Justice in the Provisional Government. In July 1917, with G. Aleksinskii in Burtsev's paper *Obshchee Delo*, published documents about the connections between Lenin and the German General Staff, which had financed Bolshevik defeatist propaganda in Russia. Forced to resign by Kerenskii. Emigrated after the Bolshevik take-over. Settled in France. Died in Paris.

Pereverzev, Valerian Fedorovich
18.10.1882–5.5.1968. Literary historian.
Born in Bobrov, now in Voronezh Oblast'. Studied at the Physico-Mathematical Department of Khar'-kov University, 1901–05. Exiled to Narym for revolutionary activity. Returned to Moscow, 1911. Lecturer, also engaged in literary work. One of the editors of the *Literaturnaia Entsiklopedia*, 1920–30. Professor at Moscow University from 1921. Worked mainly on N. Gogol', F. Dostoevskii and I. Goncharov. Col-

lected works appeared 1929–30. Created *Pereverzevskaia Shkola*, using a Marxist approach to classical Russian literature. His views and writings were influenced by G. Plekhanov. In 1931, accused by the Stalinist press of not being Marxist enough in his aesthetics and methodology. (See: 'Pereverzevshchina i Tvorcheskie Puti Proletarskoi Revolutsii', *Literaturnye Diskussii*, Moscow, 1931). Died in Moscow.

Perkhorovich, Franz Iosifovich
1894–1961. Lt.-general.
On active service in WWI as a lieutenant. Joined the Red Army, 1918. Took part in the Civil War. Joined the Bolshevik Party, 1926. Graduated from the Vystrel Courses, 1941. On active service during WWII. After WWII, worked in the HQ of the land forces of the Soviet Army.

Perl'man, Mikhail Romanovich
21.3.1923–   . Athlete.
Born in Moscow. Master of Sports (gymnastics), 1949. With the Moscow Armed Forces Club. Graduated from the Military Institute of Physical Culture, 1954. Trainer-instructor. Olympic champion 1952.

Permiak, Evgenii Andreevich
31.10.1902–   . Author.
Born in Perm'. Graduated from the Pedagogical Faculty of Perm' University, 1930. Published works from 1924. Playwright from the 1930s. Author of many books for children. Works: *Kem Byt'*, 1946; *Dedushkina Kopilka*, 1957; *Skazka o Serom Volke*, 1960.

Persianinov, Leonid Semenovich
18.8.1908–   . Gynaecologist, academician.
Born in the village of Staroe Selo, now in Smolensk Oblast'. Graduated from the 2nd Medical Institute of Leningrad, 1931. Head of the Department of Gynaecology at the Minsk Institute from 1967. Concurrently director of the All-Union Institute for Gynaecology. Main works on ante-natal care. Vice-president of the International Federation of Gynaecology and Midwifery, 1967–70. Honorary member of several medical bodies.

Pertsov, Viktor Osipovich
1898–1980. Author.
Close to the LEF poets. Later wrote the 3-volume official version of the life and work of V. Mayakovsky, which was reprinted several times.

Pervushin, Nikolai Vsevolodovich
1899–   . Lecturer, historian, editor, translator.
Born in Kazan'. Graduated from Kazan' University, 1923. Lecturer there. In 1923, sent as a researcher to Germany to learn about German industries. He published his work in 1927 in Moscow's *Promizdat*. Worked as an economic consultant in Europe for Soviet organizations. Broke with the USSR, 1930. Lived in Paris as a political emigré. Lecturer on Russian history, language and economics. Moved to the USA, 1946. For the next 16 years, worked at the United Nations. Taught Russian to American diplomats. Senior interpreter at UNESCO. From 1960, head of the Russian School, Norwich, Vermont. Lecturer there on Russian culture and history. Moved to Montreal, 1962. Professor at McGill University. Lecturer at Ottawa University. Well-known public figure in the Russian community in Canada.

Peshekhonov, Aleksei Vasil'evich
2.2.1867–3.4.1933. Politician, statistician, author.
A liberal populist (narodnik) in the 1890s, authority on statistics. One of the founders and leaders of the Popular Socialist Party (narodnye sotsialisty, NS). After the February Revolution 1917, member of the Executive Committee of the Petrograd Soviet. Minister of Food Supply in the Provisional Government, May–Aug. 1917. After the October Revolution, and during the Civil War, took an anti-Bolshevik stance. Member of the Soiuz Vozrozhdeniia Rossii (Union of the Renaissance of Russia), and its representative in the Dobrovolcheskaia armiia (Whites). Expelled from the Soviet Union in 1922. Lived in Riga, Prague and Berlin. Asked several times (unsuccessfully) for permission to return to the USSR. In old age, worked for the Soviet Trade Delegation in the Baltic countries. Author of many works on agricultural problems in connection with the peasants' movement. Died in Riga.

Peshkov, Zinovii Mikhailovich (Sverdlov)
1884–11.1966. General.
Born in Nizhnii Novgorod (now Gorkii). Brother of Iakov Sverdlov. Involved in revolutionary activity. In 1900 became close to Maksim Gorkii (Peshkov), who adopted him. Lived with Gorkii in Kuokkala (Finland), and went abroad with him. Stayed with him at Capri. Left to serve in the French Foreign Legion. Fought in WWI, and lost an arm during the battle of Verdun. During the Russian Civil War, member of the French mission of General Janin in Siberia, 1919–20. Returned to France and to the Foreign Legion. As a former revolutionary, had under his command many former tsarist officers, who, after defeat in the Civil War, fled to the West and joined the Legion. During WWII, escaped to Britain just before the French collapse and became a prominent member of De Gaulle's staff. Appointed representative of the Free French with Chiang Kai-shek's government in China, 1944. After the capitulation of Japan, became the French representative at the Allied Military Control Committee in Japan under General McArthur. Soon thereafter, retired with the rank of General of the French Army. Died in France. Buried at Ste. Genevieve de Bois.

Peshkova, Ekaterina Pavlovna (b. Volzhina)
1876–1965. Politician, social worker.
Born in the Ukraine. Educated at secondary school in Samara, 1895. First wife of Maksim Gorkii (1896–1904), and his life-long friend. In the 1900s, worked in the Red Cross in Nizhnii Novgorod, and helped revolutionary sailors in the Crimea. Lived in Paris, 1907–14, studied at the Sorbonne. Became an SR. Helped political prisoners in Russia when she returned after the start of WWI (from Italy to Odessa). During WWI, head of the Commission for Aid to Children, 1914–18. After the February Revolution 1917, worked at the Moscow office for the help of

released political prisoners. Member of the Cen. Cttee of the SR Party, 1917. After the October Revolution, head of the Moscow Committee for Aid to Political Prisoners (Political Cross-Pompolit, closed by Ezhov in summer 1937). Close to Dzerzhinskii, head of the Cheka. During WWII, in charge of aid to evacuated children. In old age, consultant on Gorkii in literary institutions. The only person in the USSR allowed to continue the old tradition of helping political prisoners, but under the close supervision of state security agents.

Peters, Iakov Khristoforovich
1886–1938. State security officer.
Born in Courland into a Latvian peasant family. A Bolshevik from 1904. Party agitator in rural areas in Latvia, 1905–07. From 1909, in exile in London, worker in the East End. Active member of the London group of the Latvian Bolshevik Party. Joined the British Labour Party. Married an English woman. Leader of the group involved in the Sydney Street siege in London's East End, 1910. Arrested, but released due to identification problems. Returned to Russia after the February Revolution 1917. Held senior positions in the Latvian Bolshevik Party. Head of the Cheka, July–Aug. 1917. Deputy chairman of the Cheka, 1917–1919, and chairman of the Revolutionary Tribunal set up by Feliks Dzerzhinskii. Senior member of the prosecution at the Bruce Lockhart and Sydney Reilly trials. Suppressed the left-SR revolt in Moscow in 1918. Virtual dictator of Petrograd, 1919. Chief prosecutor at the secret Fanny Kaplan trial (the SR revolutionary terrorist who made an attempt on Lenin's life in 1918). Commander of the Kiev and Petrograd military districts in 1919. During the 1920–30s, an important member of the OGPU (secret police). Chief of GPU Eastern Department, 1922–28. Personally responsible for mass executions, hostage-taking, torture and confiscations during the aftermath of the Bolshevik take-over. Commander of the Kremlin guards, 1937. Arrested and shot on Stalin's orders. Posthumously rehabilitated and glorified as a model Chekist.

Peters, Olga
1971–   . Stalin's granddaughter.
Born in the USA. Daughter of the US architect William Wesley Peters, and Svetlana Allilueva. In Aug. 1984, went with her mother to Russia, at that time not speaking a word of Russian. Given Soviet citizenship. Lived for a short time in Moscow, then moved to Gori, her grandfather's birthplace. In Nov. 1986, returned to school in Surrey, England.

Peterson, Karl Andreevich
1877–1926. Revolutionary.
Joined the SD Party, 1898. Took part in the 1905 Revolution. Active participant in the Bolshevik takeover in Petrograd, Nov. 1917. In the Civil War, Political Commissar of the Latvian regiments, which were the mainstay of Bolshevik power at that time. Appointed Defence Minister of the unsuccessful Latvian Communist Government, 1919. In the 1920s, held high administrative posts in the Soviet Union.

Petin, Nikolai Nikolaevich
1876–1937. Military commander.
Took part in the Russo-Japanese war, 1904–05. Graduated from the Academy of the General Staff, 1907. During WWI, on active service as a colonel. Joined the Red Army, 1918. During the Civil War, chief-of-staff of the Western, Southern and South-Western fronts, 1919–20. In the 1920s, held high administrative positions in the Red Army. Commander of Engineers of the Red Army, 1930. Victim of Stalin's purge of the military.

Petipa, Maria Mariusovna
29.10.1857–1940. Ballerina.
Born in Petersburg. Daughter of Marius Ivanovich Petipa, by whom she was trained. Debut as a leading dancer at the Mariinskii Theatre, 1875. Appeared in ballets produced by her father. Was a leading character dancer. Retired from regular stage work in 1907. Appeared sporadically at the Mariinskii and private theatres till 1912. Guest performances in Paris 1897, 1903, 1904, and in Budapest 1899, 1901. Emigrated after October 1917. Died in Paris.

Petliakov, Vladimir Mikhailovich
1891–1942. Aircraft designer.
Graduated from the Moscow Higher Technical School, 1922. Chief designer at an aviation plant, 1936. Helped design several types of Soviet heavy bombers. Died in an aircrash.

Petliura, Simon Vasil'evich (Semen)
17.5.1879–26.5.1926. Ukrainian nationalist leader.
Born in Poltava. Son of a coachman. Started his education in a seminary in the 1890s. Expelled for nationalist activity, emigrated to L'vov (then Austro-Hungary). On his return, worked as an accountant at Kuban and Kiev. Lived in Petersburg in 1907. Editor of the newspaper *Ukrainskaia Zhizn'* (Ukrainian Life), 1912. During WWI, worked in Zemstvo organizations. After the February Revolution 1917, organized the Ukrainian Military Committee. Minister of Defence in the Ukrainian government (Central Rada), 1918. Under the German occupation, Apr. 1918, and Hetman Skoropadski, was chairman of the All Ukrainian Zemstvo Union. From Nov. 1918, after the fall of Skoropadski, member of the Ukrainian Directoria and ataman (commander of the Ukrainian army). Chairman of the Directoria, Feb. 1919. Fought against the Red Army and the White Army of General Denikin in alliance with Poland under Pilsudskii. Defeated at the end of 1919. Reached Kiev again with the Poles in the spring of 1920. Emigrated to Poland after the Polish retreat, and then to France. Assassinated in Paris by the Cheka agent, Shwarzbard.

Petr (Polianskii, Petr Fedorovich), Metropolitan of Krutitsy
1863–11.9.1936. Russian Orthodox clergyman.
Born in Voronezh Gouvt. Graduated from Moscow Theological Academy in 1892. For many years, member of the Educational Commission of the Holy Synod. Private secretary of Grand Duchess Elizaveta Fedorovna (sister of the Tsarina, widow of Grand-Duke Sergei). Bishop of Podolsk, 1920. Archbishop, 1923. Metropolitan of Krutitsy, 1924. Appointed by Patriarch Tikhon as his locum tenens, confirmed by 37

hierarchs after the death of Tikhon, Apr. 1925. As his strong leadership was unacceptable to the authorities, he was at once arrested, Dec. 1925. Exiled to Tobolsk, later kept in complete isolation on the Far Eastern island of Khe, where he died.

Petr (Zverev, Vasilii), Archbishop of Voronezh
18.2.1878–1928. Russian Orthodox clergyman.
Born in Moscow. Son of a priest. Graduated from Kazan' Theological Academy. Bishop of Balakhninsk, 1919. Arrested and exiled to Central Asia, 1922–24. Archbishop of Voronezh, 1925. Actively opposed the Living Church (pro-government schism). Arrested and sent to Solovki concentration camp, 1926, where he died.

Petrauskas, Kipras Ionovich
22.11.1885–1971? Singer (tenor), impresario.
Born in Lithuania. Brother of M. Petrauskas. Pupil of S. Gabel'. Soloist at the Mariinskii Theatre, Petersburg, 1912–20. One of the founders of the Lithuanian National Opera, Kaunas. Professor at the Lithuanian Conservatory. State Prize of the USSR, 1951.

Petrauskas, Mikas Ionovich
19.10.1873–23.3.1937. Composer, conductor, impresario.
Born in Lithuania. Lived in Petersburg and Wil'no. Emigrated in 1906. Lived in Switzerland and the USA. Returned to Lithuania, 1920. Originator of Lithuanian opera. Also composed comic operas and songs. Died in Kaunas. Works include *Iz Oblasti Muzyki*, Chicago, 1909, and *Malyi Muzykal'nyi Slovar'*, Boston, 1916.

Petrazhitskii, Lev Iosifovich
13.4.1867–15.5.1931. Lawyer, politician.
Born in Kollontaevo near Wil'no. Graduated in law from Kiev University. Studied law in Berlin. Professor of the philosophy of law at Petersburg University, 1898–1918. Member of the 1st Duma, member of the Cadet Party. Very influential law

theoretician in his time. After the Bolshevik take-over, emigrated to Poland, 1918. Professor of the sociology of law at Warsaw University, 1918–31. Committed suicide in Warsaw.

Petrenko, Aleksei Vasil'evich
26.3.1938– . Actor.
Graduated from the Khar'kov Theatre Institute, 1961. Worked in various provincial theatres. Became internationally known for his portrayal of Grigorii Rasputin in E. Klimov's film *Agonia*, 1981. Other films include *King Lear*, 1971, *Zhenit'ba*, 1978, and *Zhestokii Romans*, 1984. Powerful dramatic actor.

Petrenko, Elizaveta Fedorovna
5.12.1880–26.10.1951. Singer (mezzo- soprano).
Born in Akhtyrka, in Khar'kov Gouvt. Pupil of N. Iretskaia. Soloist at the Mariinskii Theatre, 1905–15. Appeared in Russian Seasons in Paris, 1908–14. Winner of the Silver Palm Award, 1908. With Diaghilev in Rome and London. Professor at the Moscow Conservatory. Died in Moscow.

Petrenko, Sergei Vladimirovich
8.12.1956– . Athlete
Born in Khmelnitskaia Oblast' in the Ukraine. Honoured Master of Sports (rowing), 1976. With Odessa Lokomotiv. Studied at the Odessa Pedagogical Institute. World champion, 1974–75. USSR champion, 1976–77. Olympic champion, 1976 with A. Vinogradov (500 and 1,000 metres).

Petrik, Larisa Leonidovna
28.8.1949– . Athlete, sports journalist.
Born in Dolinsk, on South Sakhalin Island. Honoured Master of Sports (gymnastics), 1968. With Vitebsk Dynamo. Graduated from the Moscow Institute of Physical Culture, 1974. Coach and sports journalist. USSR champion, 1964 and 1966. Olympic champion, 1968. Bronze medallist, 1968.

Petritskii, Anatolii Anatol'evich
14.12.1931– . Cameraman.
Son of the artist, A. Petritskii.

Graduated from the VGIK, 1955. His best work was on *War and Peace*, 1966–67. Other important films include *Mimino*, and *Moi Laskovyi Nezhnyi Zver'*, both in 1978.

Petritskii, Anatolii Galaktionovich
12.2.1895–6.3.1964. Stage-designer.
Born in Kiev. Graduated from the Kiev School of Art, 1918, then from the VKHUTEMAS, Moscow, 1924. Began his career with the theatre in 1914. His work in connection with ballet began in the 1920s with the Moscow Chamber Ballet, and in the company directed by M. M. Mordkin. His stylised art was later characterized by monumental traits and richness of colour in sets and costumes, using Ukrainian folk motives. Worked for ballets, 1925–60. Principal stage-designer at the Shevchenko Theatre, 1953–60. Died in Kiev.

Petrosian, Tigran Vartanovich
17.6.1929–14.8.1984. Chess player, grandmaster.
Born in Tbilisi. Armenian. Chess world champion, 1963–68. One of the greatest chess players in the Soviet Union.

Petrosiants, Ashot Ivanovich
10.5.1910– . Conductor.
Born in Merv. Reconstructed Uzbek folk instruments (and applied to them the European music score system.) Organizer and conductor of the Uzbek Folk Orchestra, 1938–58. Taught at the Tashkent Conservatory.

Petriosants, Andronik Melkonovich
1906– . Politician.
Joined the Communist Party in 1932. Graduated from the Ural Institute of Mechanical Engineering in 1933. Top position at the Ordzhonikidze Machine Building Plant in the Urals, 1933–39. Deputy People's Commissar for Heavy Machine Building and member of the Collegium of the Ministry of Heavy Machine Building, then USSR 1st Deputy People's Commissar for Machine Tool Building, 1939–41. Deputy People's Commissar for the USSR Armoured Vehicles Industry and member of

staff of the USSR Ministry of Medium Machine Building, 1955–62. Chairman of the State Committee for the Use of Atomic Energy with the USSR Council of Ministers. Head of the investigating team into the nuclear disaster at Chernobyl nuclear power station in Apr. 1986.

Petrov, Aleksandr
1925–1972. Athlete.
Honoured Master of Sports (football). Many times USSR champion. Member of the USSR team at the XVth Olympic Games.

Petrov, Andrei Pavlovich
2.9.1930– . Composer.
Born in Leningrad. Graduated from the Leningrad Conservatory, 1954. Pupil of O. Evlakhov. Taught at a music school. Edited *Muzyka*. His compositions stressed modernity, though he borrowed themes from legends and classical sagas. Composed operas, and music for ballets and many films, such as *I Walk About Moscow*, *Chelovek-Amfibiia*, and *Beregis' Avtomobilia*.

Petrov, Evgenii (Kataev, Evgenii Petrovich)
30.12.1903–2.7.1942. Author, journalist.
Born in Odessa. Son of a schoolmaster. Younger brother of the author V. Kataev. After finishing at the local lycée, worked as a reporter for the Ukrainian Telegraph Agency. Worked for 3 years as a police criminal investigator. This experience sparked in him the desire to write criminal stories. Published short stories in humour magazines. In 1923, went to Moscow, and met Il'ia Ilf. Travelled with Ilf throughout America as a *Pravda* correspondent, and collaborated with him until his death from tuberculosis in 1937. The result of their journey was the book *Odnoetazhnaia Amerika*, a rather biased account but full of humour. For their 2 works, *Dvenadtsat' Stul'ev* (The Twelve Chairs), and *Zolotoi Telenok* (The Golden Calf), Ilf and Petrov have earned the reputation of being 2 of the Soviet Union's most gifted satirists. After Ilf's death, did not produce anything significant. From 1937 until 1941, worked with

Pravda and some satirical magazines. War correspondent during WWII. On his return to Moscow from Simferopol', died in a plane shot down by the Germans.

Petrov, Evgenii Aleksandrovich
16.10.1938– . Athlete.
Born in Moscow. Graduated from the Moscow Polygraphic Institute, 1967. Honoured Master of Sports (shooting), 1968. With the Moscow Armed Forces Club. Member of the CPSU, 1974. USSR champion, 1962–72. World champion, 1970; with his team in 1967, 1969–71 and 1973. World record-holder, 1970. Olympic champion, 1968. Silver medallist, 1972.

Petrov, Fedor Fedorovich
1902–1978. Gun designer.
Graduated from the Military Mechanical Faculty of the Leningrad Polytechnical Institute, 1931. Chief designer at an artillery plant, 1938. Joined the Bolshevik Party, 1942. Joined the Red Army, 1944. Designed many types of artillery and anti-tank guns. Highly decorated (4 State Prizes, Hero of Socialist Labour).

Petrov, Ivan Efimovich
1896–1958. General.
Joined the Red Army and the Bolshevik Party, 1918. Took part in the Civil War. On active service during WWII. Commander of the North Caucasian front, 1943. 1st Deputy Commander of Land Forces, 1955. Chief Inspector of the Ministry of Defence, 1956. Chief scientific consultant of the Deputy Minister of Defence, 1957.

Petrov, Ivan Ivanovich (real name – Krause)
29.2.1920– . Singer (bass).
Born in Irkutsk. Trained at the Glazunov Music School, 1938–41. Pupil of A. K. Mineev. While a student, appeared in concerts with Moscow Philharmonic and with operatic ensembles directed by I. S. Kozlovskii. Soloist with the Bolshoi Theatre, 1945–70. Honorary member of the Paris Grand Opéra. Guest appearances abroad.

Petrov, Nikolai Makarovich
1892–1959. Photographer.
Son of a peasant from the village of Korsakovo, now Kostroma Oblast'. Took up photography at the age of 20. Trainee at the Scherrer and Nabholtz Photographic Studio in Moscow. After finishing his training, worked as a laboratory technician. Served in the army during WWI, was a soldier in the Red Army after the Revolution 1917, and subsequently instructor in the agitation platoons of the Central Executive Committee. Studied news photography under 2 well-known reporters of the old school, A. Saveliev and K. Kuznetsov. In 1924, became a photographer on *Izvestia*, remaining with the paper for the rest of his working life. Took part in the 1926, 1927 and 1928 exhibitions, 10 Years of Soviet Photography. During WWII was a front-line photo reporter for *Izvestia*. Produced many illustrated books in colour, also many propaganda stories, such as *The V. I. Lenin Volga-Don Canal* (a Gulag enterprise). Died in Moscow.
See: *Soviet Photography, 1917–40*, London 1984.

Petrov, Nikolai Nikolaevich
14.12.1876–2.3.1964. Oncologist, surgeon.
Born in Petersburg. Graduated from the Military Medical Academy, 1899. Professor of surgery at Warsaw University, 1912–13. Director of the Institute for Medical Specialisation, 1921–25. Head of the Department of Surgery at the 1st Leningrad Medical Institute. Organizer and director of the Leningrad Oncological Institute, 1926 (renamed the Petrov Oncological Institute of Leningrad in 1966). Author of the first work in Russian on oncology, 1910. Author of several works on transplants and de-oncology. Honorary member of the International Society of Surgeons, 1957. Died in Leningrad.

Petrov, Nikolai Pavlovich
25.5.1836–15.1.1920. Engineer, scientist.
Born in Trubchevsk, Orel Gouvt. Graduated from the Petersburg Engineering Academy, 1858. Taught mathematics there. First research in mechanics under I. A. Vyshnegrad-

skii. Professor at the Petersburg Institute of Applied Technology, where he carried out original research. Director of Russian State Railways, 1888–92. Representative of the Council of Engineers with the Ministry of Transport from 1892. Assistant to the Minister for several years. Participated in the construction of the Trans-Siberian Railway. Founded the Engineering School attached to the Ministry of Transport. Died in Tuapse, a port on the Black Sea coast in the Krasnodar region.

Petrov, Pavel Nikolaevich
1881?–1938. Choreographer.
Graduated from the Petersburg Theatre School, 1900. Joined the Mariinskii Theatre. Various productions at the Petrograd Miniatures Theatre, 1918–20. Directed dances for operas and plays. Ballet production for the Petrograd State Theatre of Opera and Ballet, 1922. Emigrated. Lived in Lithuania from 1925, where he worked as a producer and was regarded as the founder of professional Lithuanian ballet. Worked in France in the 1930s. Died in France.

Petrov, Vasilii Ivanovich
15.1.1917–   . Marshal.
Joined the Red Army, 1939. Took part in WWII. Joined the Bolshevik Party, 1944. Graduated from the Frunze Military Academy, 1948. Member of the Cen. Cttee. of the CPSU, 1976. Deputy Commander of Land Forces, 1976. Deputy Minister of Defence, and Commander of Land Forces, 1980. 1st Deputy Minister of Defence, 1985.

Petrov, Vasilii Rodionovich
12.3.1875–4.5.1937. Singer (bass).
Born in the village of Alekseevka, now Khar'kov Oblast'. Graduated from the Moscow Conservatory, 1902. Pupil of A. I. Bartsal. Soloist with the Bolshoi Theatre, 1902–7. Appeared in concerts. Guest appearances abroad. Director of vocal training with the Stanislavskii Opera, 1925–29, and with the Operatic Studio of the Bolshoi Theatre, 1935–37. Towards the end of his life, taught at the Glazunov Technical School of Music. Died in Moscow.

Petrov, Vladimir Vladimirovich
30.6.1947–   . Athlete.
Born in Krasnogorsk, Moscow Oblast'. Honoured Master of Sports (hockey), 1969. With the Central Sports Club of the Army. Member of the CPSU, 1971. Graduated from the Moscow Oblast' Institute of Physical Culture, 1976. USSR champion, 1968–79. European champion, 1969–79. World champion, 1969–79. Olympic champion, 1972 and 1976.

Petrov-Bytov, Pavel Petrovich (real name – Petrov)
23.2.1895–26.10.1960. Film director.
Born in the village of Bogorodskoe (now Bogorodsk) in Gorkii Oblast'. Graduated from the Petrozavodsk Theatrical Studio, 1921. Attended lectures at the Communist Academy of Literature, Art and Language, 1931–33. Worked at Sevzapkino (now Lenfilm Studio) from 1924. First film, 1924. Other films: *Kain i Artem* (after M. Gorkii), *Chudo*, 1934, and *Pugachev*, 1937. In the post-war years, was completely forgotten as a film-maker. Worked for the Leningrad Studio of Popular Scientific Films. Rediscovered during the late 1960s. Died in Leningrad.

Petrov-Vodkin, Kuz'ma Sergeevich
5.11.1878–15.2.1939. Artist.
Genre, portrait and still-life painter, graphic artist, stage designer. Born in Khvalynsk, Saratov Oblast'. Studied at the Samara Art Classes, 1893–95, under F. Burov, then at the Petersburg Shtiglits Central School of Graphic Art, 1896–98, and at the Moscow School of Painting, Sculpture and Architecture, 1898–1903, under L. Pasternak, I. Levitan and V. Serov. At the Azbe school, Munich, 1904. In Paris at a private art academy, 1905–08. Visited Italy, 1905, and North Africa, 1907. Member of the Mir Iskusstva from 1911, and the Chetyre Iskusstva from 1924. At one time, influenced by symbolism and modernism, also by V. Borisov-Musatov. Taught in Leningrad, 1918–33. Exhibitions: the Zolotoe Runo, 1909–10, the Mir Iskusstva, 1910–24, Zhar-Tsvet Society 1924, the Chetyre Iskusstva, 1925–29. Personal exhibitions: St. Petersburg, 1909, Petrograd, 1920, Leningrad, 1936–37. Died in Leningrad.

Petrova, Galina Petrovna
3.8.1913–   . Ballerina.
Born in Kerch'. Graduated from the Moscow Choreographic School. Pupil of A. I. Chekrygin. With the Bolshoi Theatre, 1933–53. Taught at the Moscow Choreographic School, 1938–41 and 1943–48, and at the Bolshoi Theatre from 1953.

Petrova, Ninel' Aleksandrovna
15.3.1924–   . Ballerina.
Born in Leningrad. Graduated from the Leningrad Choreographic School. Pupil of A. Vaganova. Dancer with the Kirov Theatre, 1944–69. Taught at the Leningrad Choreographic School 1969–71. In charge of the Izuchenie Spektaklei Klassicheskogo Naslediia course in the Choreographic Department of the Leningrad Conservatory from 1971. Taught and coached with the Leningrad Choreographicheskie Miniatiury from 1976. Lecturer from 1977.

Petrova-Zvantseva, Vera Nikolaevna (b. Petrova)
12.9.1876–11.2.1944. Singer (mezzo-soprano).
Born in Saratov. Graduated from the Moscow Conservatory, 1897. Pupil of V. M. Zarudnaia. With the provincial theatre in the same year, a private Moscow opera, 1900–1904, and the Zimin Theatre, 1905–18 (with intervals). Professor at the Moscow Conservatory, 1916–31. Died in Moscow.

Petrovichev, Petr Ivanovich
18.12.1874–4.1.1947. Artist.
Landscape and still-life painter, also interior designer. Born in the village of Vysokovo, now Iaroslavl' Oblast'. Studied at the Moscow School of Painting, Sculpture and Architecture, 1892–1903, under N. Kasatkin, Leonid Pasternak and A. Arkhipov. Pupil of I. Levitan and V. Serov. Member of the peredvizhniki, 1906–12. Member of the Union of Russian Artists from 1911. Exhibited from 1905. Paintings held mainly in the Russian Museum, Leningrad, and the Tretiakov Gallery, Moscow. Exhibitions: MOLKH, the Mir Iskusstva, the Union of Russian Artists, 2nd State Exhibition, Moscow, the Great Patriotic War (WWII), Moscow, 1942.

Personal exhibitions: 1917, 1946, 1959 — all in Moscow. Died in Moscow.

Petrovskaia, Nina Ivanovna

1884–1928. Poetess, bohemian.
At the beginning of the 20th century, a prominent member of symbolist circles. Wife of the symbolist publisher Sokolov-Krechetov. Tried to live out her symbolist fantasies, which brought her emotional misery and ended in drug addiction. Called the 'Russian Carmen' in her youth. Became the focus of an incredibly convoluted love drama with Briusov and Belyi. Briusov's novel *Ognennyi Angel* is about her. Emigrated, 1911. Lived in Rome in absolute poverty. Moved to Berlin, 1921. Died destitute and forgotten by all her former readers and admirers.

Petrovskii, Evgenii Maksimovich

1873–1918. Music critic.
Born in Petersburg. Senior editor of *Russkaia Muzykal'naia Gazeta*, 1892–1912. Wrote the libretto of *Kashchei Bessmertnyi* (music by N. Rimskii-Korsakov).
See: *Sovetskaia Muzyka*, 1952, Nr. 12 (Letters of N. Rimskii-Korsakov to Petrovskii).

Petrovskii Grigorii Ivanovich

4.2.1878–9.1.1958. Politician.
Born in Khar'kov. As a young worker, joined the SD Party, 1897. Underground revolutionary work mainly in Ekaterinoslav (renamed later Dnepropetrovsk in his honour). Revolutionary leader in Ekaterinoslav during the 1905 Revolution. Emigrated to Germany, 1906. Elected member of the 4th Duma for Ekaterinoslav, 1912. As leader of the Bolshevik faction of the Duma, made many anti-government speeches. Kept in touch with Lenin, who was abroad. Publisher of *Pravda*, 1913. In Nov. 1914, arrested with other Bolshevik members of the Duma. Sent to Turukhansk, Feb. 1915. After the October Revolution 1917, became commissar of Iakutia. Returned to Petrograd, June 1917. Took part in the Bolshevik take-over, Nov. 1917. Minister of the Interior in the 1st Soviet government, Nov. 1917–Mar. 1919. Signed the peace agreement with Germany at Brest-Litovsk, 1918. One of the few old Bolsheviks who remained in favour during the Stalin years. Deputy director of the Museum of Revolution from 1940. Candidate member of the Politburo, 1926–39. Died in Moscow, buried at the Kremlin wall.

Petrovskii, Ivan Georgievich

18.1.1901–   . Mathematician.
Graduated from Moscow University, 1927. Professor there, 1933, and rector, 1951. Took part in the Stalinist peace initiatives.

Petrovskii, Vladimir Fedorovich

29.4.1933–   . Diplomat.
Born in Volgograd. Graduated from the Moscow MGIMO (Institute of International Relations), 1957. Member of the CPSU, 1963. Doctor of historical sciences. Professor. Began as a lecturer, translator, and attaché with the Soviet Delegation to the UN, 1957–61. 3rd Secretary in the MID (Ministry of Foreign Affairs), 1961. 2nd Secretary in the Secretariat of A. Gromyko, 1961–64. With the Cttee. for Political Problems and Security of the Secretariat at the UN, 1964–71. Senior adviser, chief adviser, and head of the USA Department of the MID, 1971–79. Head of the Department of International Organizations of the MID, 1979–86. Deputy Foreign Minister of the USSR from May 1986.

Petrunkevich, Ivan Il'ich

1842–1928. Politician.
Born in Pliske, Chernigov Gouvt. Graduated in law from Petersburg University, 1866. Well-known local government (zemstvo) figure. Liberal politician, organizer and chairman of the Union of Liberation (Soiuz Osvobozhdeniia), 1904. One of the founders and leaders, and later the father figure, of the Cadet Party. Chairman of the Cen. Cttee. of the Cadet Party, 1909–15. Editor of the Cadet newspaper *Rech'*. Deputy of the 1st Duma. Signed the Vyborg manifesto. After the Bolshevik take-over 1917, escaped arrest by moving to the Crimea (Gaspra). Emigrated, 1919. Settled in Czechoslovakia. Published memoirs: *Iz Zapisok Obshchestvennogo Deiatelia*. Died in Prague.

Petrusenko, Oksana Andreevna

17.2.1900–15.7.1940. Singer.
Prominent Ukrainian singer. Born in Balakleia, now Khar'kov Oblast'. Pupil of P. Saksaganskii. Soloist at opera theatres in Kazan', Samara and Sverdlovsk, 1927–33, and at the Shevchenko Opera and Ballet Theatre in Kiev from 1934 until her premature death.

Petrusov, Georgii Grigor'evich

1903–1971. Photo-journalist.
Born in Rostov-on-Don. Son of a civil servant. Worked as a bookkeeper in a bank, 1920. Became interested in photography but remained an amateur until he moved to Moscow, 1924. Became a full-time photo-reporter in 1924, first of all for the union magazine *Metallist*. From 1926, worked for *Pravda*. From 1928, head of the information department on the building site of the Magnitogorsk steelworks. Produced a photographic chronicle of this huge project. Worked for the magazine *USSR in Construction*, 1930–41. During WWII, war correspondent for *Izvestia*. Was assigned to the team photographing the fall of Berlin and the German capitulation. In the post-war years, worked on many illustrated publications. From 1957 until his death, with the magazine *Soviet Life*, published in the USA by the Novosti press agency. An exhibition of his photographs was shown in Berlin in 1967. Published a book of photographs of Berlin.
Source: *Soviet Photography, 1917–40*, London, 1984.

Petukhov, Stanislav Afanas'evich

19.8.1937–   . Athlete.
Born in Moscow. Honoured Master of Sports (hockey), 1963. With Moscow Dynamo. Coach. Graduated from the Moscow Oblast' Pedagogical Institute, 1965. Member of the CPSU, 1965. European champion, 1960 and 1963–64. World champion, 1963–64. Olympic champion, 1964.

Petushkova, Elena Vladimirovna

17.11.1940–   . Athlete, biologist.
Born in Moscow. Honoured Master of Sports (horse-riding), 1970. With the Moscow Oblast' Urozhai. Gradu-

ated from Moscow University as a biologist, 1963. Member of the CPSU, 1971. Works as a biologist. World champion, 1970. Olympic champion, 1972.

See: S. Volodina, *Koroleva Amazonok, Rekordy, Sobytiia, Liudi*, Moscow, 1971.

Pevtsov, Illarion Nikolaevich
7.12.1879–25.10.1934. Actor.
Born in Anatol', now Brestskaia Oblast'. Graduated from the Theatre School of the Moscow Philharmonic Society, 1902. Acted with the Tovarishchestvo Novoi Dramy, 1902–05, under the direction of V. E. Meyerhold. In the Studio Theatre, 1905, then in various provincial theatres. Entered the studio of the MKHAT, 1922. With the Pushkin Theatre in Leningrad, 1925. Classical repertoire, but in the 1920s and 30s, appeared mainly in Soviet plays. Died in Leningrad. Author of Stranitsy Avtobiografii' in the collection *I. N. Pevtsov*, Leningrad, 1935.

Pfitsner, Hans Erich (Pfitzner)
5.5.1869–22.5.1949. Composer, conductor.
Born in Moscow of German parentage. Worked in Moscow and Petersburg theatres as a conductor. Moved to Germany where he taught in the Koblenz, Berlin and Strasburg conservatories until 1918. Professor of composition at the Academy of Arts, Berlin, 1920–29. Professor at the Music Academy, Munich, 1930–34. Author of the opera *Palestrina*, together with other operas, a piano concerto, chamber music and songs. According to Soviet sources, his music was little performed outside Germany. Cooperated with the Nazi music authorities during the 1930s. He detested modernism and modernists in music. Died in Salzburg.

Philby, Kim (Harold Adrian Russell)
1.1.1912–11.5.1988. Intelligence officer.
Born in Ambala in India. Son of a British civil service officer and famous Arabist, who later converted to Islam. Educated at Westminster School. Graduated from Cambridge University, where in the 1930s he was recruited as a Soviet intelligence agent. Though married to a communist, cleverly built up the reputation of being right-wing. During the Spanish Civil War, *Times* correspondent with Franco. Joined British intelligence, 1940, and became the most successful Soviet spy ever inside Western intelligence circles. As head of the Iberian desk of the Secret Intelligence Service during WWII, head of the anti-Soviet section in 1944, and especially as linkman between the SIS and CIA in 1949, he was able to render immense service to Stalin's spy network, being party to the most guarded and valuable secrets of Western intelligence. Made a great contribution to communist successes in the post-WWII period. Came under suspicion when his co-spies Maclean and Burgess fled to Moscow, 1951. Worked as a journalist for the *Observer* and the *Economist* in Beirut from 1956. Threatened by further investigations, left Beirut on board a Soviet ship, 23 Jan. 1963. 6 months later, it became known that he had arrived in Moscow, where he worked as a KGB consultant till his death. Highly decorated, given a high rank in the KGB, and buried with military honours (by KGB border guards) at Kuntsevo. Published memoirs, *My Silent War*, 1979, which doubtless contain only a partial description of his life and career.

Philby, Rufa (Mrs Kim Philby)
1933–
Daughter of a Polish Jewish father and Russian mother. Grew up and educated in Moscow. Introduced to Kim Philby in Moscow in late 1969 by George Blake's Soviet wife. Married Philby shortly afterwards (1970), becoming his 5th wife. Could not speak English for at least the first year of their marriage. Lives between her Moscow flat and her country dacha near Kuntsevo.

Piart, Arvo Avgustovich (Pärt)
11.9.1935– . Composer.
Born in Estonia. Wrote music for puppet theatres, films and plays. Works for Estonian TV and radio.

Piast, Vladimir Alekseevich (Pestovskii))
1886–1940. Poet.
Minor symbolist poet. Personal friend of A. Blok. Member of the intelligentsia in Petersburg. Committed suicide after long years of material hardship and persecution.

Piatakov, Grigorii Leonidovich
1890–1937. Politician.
Joined the Bolshevik Party in 1910. While abroad, supported Bukharin against Lenin on several issues. Chairman of the Kiev Soviet in 1917, led the left Bolshevik faction there. Member of the Presidium of the Supreme Council of the National Economy. Head of the tribunal at the trial of the SR leaders in Moscow, 1922. Joined Trotsky in opposition to Stalin after Lenin's death in Jan. 1924. Deputy Minister (Deputy People's Commissar) for heavy industry under Ordzhonikidze in 1930. Demanded the death sentence for Zinoviev and Kamenev. Was later accused himself of being the head of a Trotskyist centre. Chief defendant at a show trial, 1937. Condemned to death, executed. Posthumously rehabilitated.

Piatigorskii, Grigorii Pavlovich (Piatigorsky, Gregor)
17.4.1903–1976. Cellist.
Born in Ekaterinoslav. Pupil of A. Glen and Iu. Klengel. Soloist in the Orchestra of the Bolshoi Theatre, 1919–21. Emigrated, 1921, and lived in Europe. Moved to the USA, 1930. Soloist with the Berlin Philharmonic Orchestra, 1925–29. Internationally acclaimed cellist and cello teacher. Composed and arranged works for the cello. Taught at the Curtis Institute, Philadelphia. From 1957, at Boston University. Visited the USSR, 1962. Wrote his memoirs, 1965. Died in the USA.

Piatkas, Karla
1937–1969. Athlete.
Lithuanian athlete. Honoured Master of Sports (canoeing). 5th place at the XVIIIth Olympic Games. The cause of her premature death was not explained in the Soviet media.

Piatnitsin, Aleksandr Alekseevich
1897–14.4.1969. Cossack officer.
Born in Petersburg. Son of a

trumpeter in the Don Cossack Guards. Educated at the Irkutsk Officers' School, 1916. Took part in WWI. During the Civil War, organized White partisan detachments on the Don. Took part in all operations of the White armies in the South. Left Russia during the evacuation of the Crimea. Through Constantinople, Lemnos and Bulgaria, came to Paris in 1923. Worked in a factory, later became a director. Well-known figure in White Cossack circles in Paris. Buried at Ste. Genevieve des Bois.

Piatnitskii, Iosif Aronovich (Tarshis)
29.1.1882–29.7.1938. Politician
Born in Vilkomir (now Ukmerge) in Lithuania. Worked as a tailor in Kaunas and Vilnius. Joined the SD Party. Arrested, 1902. Escaped from prison in Kiev, and went to Germany. During and after the 1905 Revolution, in charge of a revolutionary underground press. In 1912, appointed head of the transport department of the Cen. Cttee. of the Bolsheviks (smuggling revolutionary literature from abroad into Russia). Banished to Siberia, 1914. Returned to Moscow, 1917. During the Bolshevik take-over 1917, one of the party leaders in Moscow. Head of the Railway Trade Union, 1919–20. From 1921, held high posts in the Comintern. Shortly before his death, member of the Cen. Cttee. of the Bolshevik Party. Victim of a Stalinist show trial, executed.

Piatnitskii, Mitrofan Efimovich
3.7.1864–21.1.1927. Choirmaster.
Born in the village of Aleksandrovka near Voronezh. Son of a deacon. Educated at a seminary. Worked as a clerk in a hospital in Moscow, 1899–1923. Became famous first as a singer of folk songs, later as a collector of folk songs, instruments and costumes. Recorded on a phonograph over 400 folk songs, mainly from around Voronezh. Founded a famous choir of Russian folk music, 1910. This choir, the Piatnitskii State Folk Song Choir, is still one of the main exponents of Russian folk music. Died in Moscow.

Piats, Rikho Eduardovich (Päts)
26.6.1899– . Composer, pianist, conductor.
Born in Yur'ev (Tartu). Professor of

the Tallinn Pedagogical Institute. First appeared as a pianist, then concentrated on choral conducting and composing choral music. Author of operas, cantatas and pieces for children's choirs.

Pigrov, Konstantin Konstantinovich
12.10.1876–22.12.1962. Conductor.
Born in Malaia Dzhalga in Stavropol' Gouvt. Prominent Ukrainian choir conductor. Professor at the Odessa Conservatory. Author of *Upravlenie Khorom*, Kiev, 1956. Died in Odessa.

Pikaizen, Viktor Aleksandrovich
15.2.1933– . Violinist.
Pupil of D. Oistrakh. 2nd prize at the J. Kubelik International Violinists' Competition in Prague, 1949, and at the J. Thibaud Competition in Paris, 1957. 1st prize at the Paganini Competition in Genoa, 1965.

Pikkuus, Aavo Nikolaevich
23.11.1954– . Athlete.
Born in the village of Kapera, near Tartu, Estonia. Honoured Master of Sports (cycling), 1975. With Tartu Dynamo. USSR champion, 1973–79. Olympic champion, 1976. World champion, 1977. Winner of the Velogonka Mira, 1977, and, with his team, in 1975 and 1977–79.

Pikok, Vladimir Robertovich
24.2.1875–1.3.1943. Singer.
Pupil of I. Prianishnikov. Soloist with the Zimin Opera, 1906–16, and the Bolshoi Theatre, 1916–28.

Piliugin, Nikolai Alekseevich
1908–1982. Space equipment designer.
Graduated from the Moscow Higher Technical Institute, 1935. In the late 1930s, worked as an aircraft designer. Academician, 1966. Professor of the Radio Technology, Electronics and Automatics Institute, Moscow, 1969. Chief designer of the control systems of Soviet space rockets and laboratories. Twice Hero of Socialist Labour.

Pil'niak, Boris Andreevich (Wogau)
1894–1937. Author.
Of Volga German descent. One of the creators of Soviet modernist prose (stylistically under the influence of Remizov and Belyi). Together with Babel', left some of the most memorable descriptions of the revolutionary period in his novels. In a later novel, *Povest Nepogashennoi Luny (Smert Komandarma)*, described the death on the operating table of a famous revolutionary military leader by party order, widely understood as a veiled description of the death of Frunze on the orders of Stalin. Arrested, charged with spying for Japan, and shot.

Pil'niak, junior
1926?– .
Born in Moscow. Son of the writer Boris Pil'niak. After his father's arrest and execution also arrested with the other members of his family, and sent to the Gulag. During WWII, sent to the convicts' battalions at the front. In 1945, defected to the American zone in Germany, and lived in DP camps under an assumed name. Later told the story of his father's death.

Pil'skii, Petr Moiseevich (Khrushchev, A.)
1876–1942. Journalist, critic.
Worked as a journalist and literary critic for the paper *Birzhevye Vedomosti*. Under his pen-name, well-known writer of crime fiction. Emigrated after the October Revolution 1917. Settled in Latvia, and worked for the Riga Russian daily *Segodnia*.

Pimen (Izvekov, Sergei Mikhailovich), Patriarch of Moscow
25.7.1910– . Russian Orthodox clergyman.
Born in Bogorodsk, near Moscow. Monk, 1927. Arrested, 1937, inmate of Gulag camps in Central Asia. During WWII, at the front, 1941–43. Re-arrested, inmate of Vorkuta Gulag camps, 1944–45. Released, priest in Murom, 1946. Monk at a monastery in Odessa, 1947. Secretary to the Bishop of Rostov, 1947–49. Abbot of the Pskov Cave monastery, 1949–53. Head of Zagorsk monastery, 1953–57. Archbishop of Tula, 1961–62.

Metropolitan of Leningrad, 1963. Patriarch of Moscow, 1971. Reacted passively to pressure from authorities and to exhortations of an increasingly active religious public opinion (statements by Iakunin, Eshliman, Dudko, Lent letter by Solzhenitsyn). In 1988, with members of the Holy Synod, met Gorbachev, receiving official approval for the celebrations of the Millenium of Christianity in Russia. In summer 1988, presided at the Church Council which approved a new church statute with provisions for a radical reform of parish life and church activity.

Pimenov, Iurii Ivanovich
1903– . Artist.
Painter and graphic artist. Also genre and landscape painter, and stage designer. Studied at the VKHU-TEMAS, Moscow, 1920–24, under V. Favorskii, S. Maliutin, D. Kardovskii and V. Falileev. Exhibited from 1925. Travelled widely around Russia and abroad as an artist correspondent for press and publishers. Personal exhibitions: Moscow-Riga, 1947, Iurii Pimenov's Stage Design Exhibition, Moscow, 1955 and 1961.

Pinaeva, Liudmila Iosifovna (Khvedosiuk)
14.1.1936– . Athlete.
Born in Krasnoe Selo, Leningrad Oblast'. Honoured Master of Sports (rowing), 1964. With Leningrad Trud. Graduated from the Leningrad School of Trainers of the Institute of Physical Culture, 1963. Coach. USSR champion, 1960–73. European champion, 1961–71. Olympic champion, 1964 and 1968, and in 1972 with E. Kuryshko. World champion, 1966–73.

Pinegin, Timir Alekseevich
12.6.1927– . Athlete.
Born in Moscow. Honoured Master of Sports (sailing), 1960. With the Central Sports Club of the Navy. Coach. Graduated from the Moscow Institute of Physical Culture, 1964. USSR champion, 1956–73. Olympic champion, 1960 (with F. Shutkov). Champion of Europe and Northern Africa, 1964.

Pinigin, Pavel Pavlovich
12.3.1953– . Athlete.
Born in Iakutia. Honoured Master of Sports (wrestling), 1976. With the Kiev Armed Forces Club. Graduated from the Kiev Institute of Physical Culture, 1976. Lecturer. USSR champion, 1975–76. European champion, 1975. World champion, 1975, 1977–78. Olympic champion, 1976.

Pipinashvili, Konstantin Konstantinovich
2.10.1912–15.4.1969. Actor.
Born in Kutaissi. Graduated from the Producers' Course of the State Cinematographic Institute (VGIK), 1936. Finished the 2-year directors' course at the VGIK, 1939. Pupil of S. Eisenstein. Worked with the Georgian Theatre. Directed the dubbing into Georgian of films in other languages of the Soviet Union, 1948–54. Died in Tbilisi. Films: *Kadzhana*, 1941, *Most*, 1942, and *Taina Dvukh Okeanov*, 1957.

Pirogov, Aleksandr Stepanovich
4.7.1899–26.6.1964. Singer (bass).
Born in Riazan' into a family of singers. Studied at the Historico-Philological Faculty of Moscow University, 1917–18, and concurrently at the music department attached to the Moscow Philharmonic Society. Pupil of V.S. Tiutiunnik. With the chorus of the Peredvizhnoi Theatre, 1919–22. Soloist with the Moscow Svobodnaia Opera (formerly the Zimin Opera), 1922–24. With the Bolshoi Theatre, 1924–54. Made guest appearances abroad. Died in Medvezhia Golova, an island on the River Oka. Buried in Moscow.

Pirogov, Grigorii Stepanovich
24.1.1885–20.2.1931. Singer (bass).
Born in the village of Novosel', now in Riazan' Oblast'. Elder brother of Aleksandr Pirogov. Graduated from the Music and Drama School of the Moscow Philharmonic Society, 1908. Pupil of M. E. Medvedev and L. D. Donskoi. In the same year, appeared with a private company in Rostov-on-Don, and with the Mariinskii Theatre in Petersburg, 1909. Soloist with the Bolshoi Theatre, 1910–20. Afterwards appeared in many towns in the USSR and abroad. Popular as

a concert singer. Died in Leningrad.

Pirosmani, Niko (Pirosmanishvili, Nikolai Aslanovich)
1862?–5.5.1918. Artist.
Georgian artist-primitivist. Born in the village of Mirzaani, Georgia. Moved to Tbilisi where, in a state of near destitution, he began painting signs for restaurants in exchange for meals. Self-taught romantic artist whose subjects were the peasants, animals and landscapes of his native Georgia. Received recognition much later in his own country and in Russia. A film was made about his life and work by Georgii Shengelaia in 1960, which was internationally acclaimed. 2 major exhibitions took place in Paris (1979) and in Moscow (1981). Several books with reproductions of the artist's work in colour have been published in the Soviet Union, as well as many articles. Died in Tbilisi.
See: *Literaturnaia Gruzia*, Nr. 3, 1984.

Pirozhkova, Vera
1920?– . Scholar, editor, journalist.
During and after WWII in labour camps and DP camps in Germany, 1943–48. Professor at Munich University. Editor of the Russian language magazine *Golos Zarubezhia*. Wrote on Russian history, philosophy, literature and politics in many emigré publications. Published a book on A. Herzen.

Pirozhnaia, Galina Nikolaevna
23.5.1929– . Ballerina.
Born in Leningrad. Graduated from the Leningrad Choreographic School. Pupil of A. I. Vaganova. Dancer with the Leningrad Malyi Theatre. Taught and coached the Leningrad Ballet on Ice from 1969.

Pisarev, Aleksei Afanas'evich
20.8.1909–18.9.1960. Ballet dancer.
Born in Petersburg. Graduated from the Leningrad Choreographic School. Pupil of V. I. Ponomarev. Dancer with the Kirov Theatre, 1928–50. Taught at the Leningrad Choreographic School, 1944–60. Wrote (with V. Kostrovitskaia) *Shkola*

327

Klassicheskogo Tantsa, published 1968. Died in Leningrad.

Pisarevskii, Dmitrii Sergeevich

29.7.1912– . Film critic, editor. Graduated from the Krupskaia Academy of Communist Education, 1934. Editor-in-chief of *Sovetskii Ekran*, 1961–75. Editor of, and contributor to, *Iskusstvo Millionov*, 1958. Also contributed to *Ocherki Istorii Sovetskogo Kino*, 1959–61.

Platon (Kulbush Kzelbut, Pavel Petrovich), Bishop of Revel

13.7.1869–14.1.1919. Head of the Estonian Orthodox Church. Graduated from the Petersburg Theological Academy, 1894. Priest of the Estonian Orthodox Church in St. Petersburg for 23 years. Bishop, 1918. During the occupation of Estonia by the Red Army, arrested (2 Jan. 1919) in Tartu (Yuriev). Shot, together with other hostages, at the moment of the approach of Estonian forces to the town. Buried at the Tallinn Orthodox Cathedral.

Platonov, Andrei (Klimentov, Andrei Platonovich)

1.9.1899–5.1.1951. Author, journalist, poet. Born in Voronezh. Graduated from the Voronezh Polytechnical Institute. Worked as a journalist. Became known for his essays and verse in the 1920s–30s. Moved to Moscow, 1927. Warned against the danger of bureaucratization of the revolution in his works *Chevengur*, *Kotlovan* and others. Heavily criticized in the 1930s. War correspondent during WWII. His post-war work was described as slander by the Stalinist critic Ermilov, 1947. Practically fell silent until his death. Very popular in the 1960s, first in samizdat. Many of his works were re-issued officially later. Became a literary cult figure.

Platonov, Nikolai Ivanovich

19.3.1894–1969? Flute player, composer. Born in Novyi Oskol, Kursk Gouvt. Pupil of V. Tsybin. Professor at the Moscow Conservatory. Author of a concerto and other pieces for flute.

Wrote the opera *Lieutenant Schmidt*, 1938.

Platonov, Sergei Fedorovich

16.6.1860–10.1.1933. Historian. Born at Chernigov. Graduated from Petersburg University, 1882. Academician, 1920. Wrote many historical works, especially on the times of Ivan the Terrible and the Time of Troubles. Refused to take part in the communist distortions of history. Arrested, 1930. Died in exile in Samara.

Plekhanov, Georgii Valentinovich (Beltov, N.)

11.12.1856–30.5.1918. Philosopher, politician. Born in the village of Gudalovka, near Lipetsk. Son of a land-owner. Educated at the Petersburg Mining Institute, expelled for revolutionary activity, 1876 (made a speech at the famous students meeting at the Kazanskii Cathedral in Petersburg, 1876). Member of populist (narodnik) organizations, 'went to the people' in the 1870s (distributing revolutionary propaganda in rural areas). After the split in the Zemlia I Volia group, 1879, became leader of the Black Repartition group (non-terrorist wing of the populists). Lived as a political emigré, 1880–1917, in Western Europe. Became the first important follower of Karl Marx in Russia. As a father figure of Russian Marxists, organized in Geneva in 1883 the Emancipation of Labour Group, the first Russian Marxist organization. Became the idol of the young Lenin. Later personal acquaintance with Lenin in exile resulted in intense mutual dislike. Criticized Lenin's thinking, methods and personal conduct long before the Bolshevik take-over, making the remark, 'of such stuff Robespierres are made'. Rejected the Kienthal and Zimmerwald socialist anti-war conferences. Returned to Russia after the February Revolution 1917. Became one of the most bitter critics of Bolshevism. Died of tuberculosis in a sanatorium in Terioki (then in Finland). After his death, glorified as an outstanding Marxist thinker and founder of the Russian Marxist movement, while his Menshevik mistakes, his quarrels with Lenin, and his condemnation of the Bol-

shevik coup of 1917 were glossed over.
Main works: *Works*, 24 vols, Moscow-Leningrad, 1923–27, *Selected Philosophical Works*, 5 vols, Moscow, 1956–58.

Pleshcheev, Aleksandr Alekseevich

19.10.1858–5.12.1944. Writer, theatre critic. Born in Petersburg. Son of the poet A.N. Plescheev. Published from 1876. Wrote for Petersburg and Moscow periodicals. Published the earliest outlines of the history of the Petersburg ballet in the 18–19th centuries. Emigrated in 1919. Died in Paris.

Plevitskaia, Nadezhda Vasil'evna (b. Vinnikova, Dezhka; Levitskaia; Skoblina)

17.1.1884–5.10.1940. Singer, intelligence agent. Born in the village of Vinnikovo, Kursk Gouvt. 12th child in a peasant family. By 1906, had already become a famous singer (mezzo-soprano). Entertained members of the imperial family and ministers of the government. Married the ballet soloist Edmund Plevitskii. Her second husband was a young officer, Iurii Levitskii, whom she soon left. In 1921, married again, this time to a hero of the Civil War, a major-general in the White Army, Nikolai Skoblin, 11 years her junior. Emigrated with him and settled in Paris. Attracted crowds at Russian restaurants and was surrounded by admirers. Became an idol of the Russian emigrés. One of her songs, *Zamelo Tebia Snegom Rossiia*, became almost an anthem for White Russians. Toured Europe with the same enormous success. Under unknown circumstances, adopted by the OGPU-NKVD, who at the time were very interested in penetrating Russian emigré circles. Influenced Skoblin, whom she always dominated. Eventually took part in the kidnapping (and murder) of General Miller in Paris, 1937. Probably a participant in the kidnapping of General Kutepov, also in Paris 7 years previously, though this was not proven. While Skoblin disappeared, never to be heard of again (probably executed in France or the USSR by the NKVD), she was arrested by the French police. Found guilty after a sensational trial which lasted for months, sentenced to 15 years in prison. Died soon thereafter in the central prison in Rennes. The Soviet press often reported on her singing career, without mentioning her intelligence activities. Her singing is available on records. The true story of her extraordinary life has never been fully established.

Plisetskaia, Maia Mikhailovna
20.11.1925– . Prima ballerina. Born in Moscow. Graduated from the Moscow Choreographic School. Pupil of E. P. Gerdt and M. M. Leont'eva. Joined the Bolshoi Theatre, 1943. Has since become an international star. Her characteristics are a wide step, high easy leap, expressive hands, great musicality, and a harmony between dynamism, tragic power and plasticity. Among her most distinguished roles are *The Dying Swan* (Saint-Saens), and *Anna Karenina* (composed by her husband, Shchedrin). Has appeared in films and in guest performances abroad. Anna Pavlova Prize, 1962.
See: N. Roslavleva, *Maia Plisetskaia*, Moscow, 1968.

Plisetskii, Azarii Mikhailovich
13.7.1937– . Ballet dancer. Born in Moscow. Graduated from the Moscow Choreographic School, 1956. Pupil of N.I. Tarasov. With the Bolshoi Theatre from 1957. Theatre historian on graduation from the GITIS, 1969. Leading dancer with the Cuba National Ballet, 1963–73. Produced several ballets in Cuba, and also worked with the company of Roland Petit in Marseilles. Choreographer and coach with the same company, 1974, 1976, 1977. Choreographer and coach with the XX Century Ballet, Brussels. 1st prize as best partner at the international competitions for ballet dancers in Varna, 1965, 1966, and in Moscow 1969.

Pliukfelder, Rudolf Vladimirovich
6.9.1928– . Athlete. Born in Donetskaia Oblast', of German parents. Honoured Master of Sports (heavy athletics), 1962.

With the Rostovskaia Oblast' Trud. Honorary Coach of the USSR, 1965. Member of the CPSU, 1966. Graduated from the Moscow Institute of Physical Culture, 1969. USSR champion, 1958–63. European champion, 1959–61. World champion, 1959, 1961 and 1964. Olympic champion, 1964. Author of *Metall i Liudi*, Moscow, 1966.

Pliushch, Leonid Ivanovich
1939– . Mathematician, dissident.
Born in Kiev. In his youth, an active Komsomol member. Mathematician. Became involved in the human rights struggle in the Ukraine. Held in a psychiatric hospital, 1972–76. After a long and active protest campaign in the West, released and allowed to emigrate. Represents a left-wing Ukrainian nationalist point of view and continues his human rights activity in the West. Lives in Paris.

Plotnichenko, Grigorii Maksimovich
18.8.1918– . Composer.
Born in Taganrog. Head of the Music Faculty at the Krasnodar Pedagogical Institute. Director of several Kuban' Cossack song and dance ensembles. Published many anthologies of his own Kuban' Cossack songs.

Podbelskii, Vadim Nikolaevich
1887–1920. Revolutionary.
Joined the Bolshevik Party, 1905. Active participant in the October Revolution 1917. People's Commissar for Post and Communications, 1918. During the Civil War, representative of the Cen. Cttee. of the Bolshevik Party in Tambov.

Podgoretskii, Boris Vladimirovich
1873–1919. Composer, folklorist. Author of 2 operas. Moved to Moscow in his last years. Took part in several folklore expeditions. Also worked as a music critic. His opera *Kupal'naia Iskra* was staged successfully in 1901. Author of over 100 Ukrainian romances and other songs. Died in Moscow.

Podgornyi, Nikolai Viktorovich
18.2.1903–12.1.1983. Politician.
Born at Karlovka in the Ukraine.

Educated at a Kiev technical college, 1931. Engineer in the sugar industry. Made a party career. Secretary of the Khar'kov obkom, later secretary of the Cen. Cttee. of the CPSU, 1963–65. After Khrushchev's fall, member of the ruling troika (with Brezhnev and Kosygin), chairman of the Presidium of the Supreme Soviet, 1965–77. Dismissed when Brezhnev himself assumed the title of Head of State, May 1977. Died in Moscow.

Podgornyi, Timofei Filippovich
5.3.1873–20.6.1958. Violin-maker. Born in Stratilatovka, Khar'kov Gouvt. Made over 1,000 violins, cellos, double-basses and similar. Author of *Iz Zapisok Mastera*, Moscow, 1960. Died in Moscow.

Podgornyi, Vasilii Timofeevich
1894–1919. Cellist.
Son of Timofei Podgornyi. Pupil of A. Glen. From 1916, soloist at the Bolshoi Theatre, and from 1918, professor of the Moscow Conservatory. Died in an accident during the Civil War.

Pod'iapol'skii, Grigorii Sergeevich
1926–1976. Geophysicist, dissident. Born in Tashkent. Educated at the Moscow Petroleum Institute. Worked as a geophysicist. Became one of the scientists who were very active in the human rights movement in the 1960s and 1970s. Close to Dr. A. Sakharov. Deprived of his job, 1970, and consistently harassed by the KGB. Died of a heart attack.

Podkovyrov, Aleksei Fedorovich
1899–1957. Artist.
Portrait, landscape and genre painter. Born in Tashkent. Studied at the studio of N. V. Rozanov, Tashkent, 1925–28, and at the N. Seliverstov Art School, Penza, 1928–29, under I. S. Goriushin-Sorokopudov and N. F. Petrov. Exhibited regularly from 1934 in Tashkent and Moscow. Posthumous exhibition of his work held in Alma-Ata, 1959.

Podlas, Kuz'ma Petrovich
1893–1942. Lt.-general.
Took part in WWI as a sergeant.

Joined the Red Army and the Bolshevik Party, 1918. Regimental commander during the Civil War. On active service during WWII. Fell in action.

Podrabinek, Aleksandr Pinkhosovich
1953–   . Medical worker, author, human rights campaigner.
Born in the town of Elektrostal', Moscow Oblast'. Graduated from a medical school. Worked in the Emergency Ambulance Service as a doctor's assistant. In 1977, one of the founders of the Working Commission on the Investigation of Political Abuse of Psychiatry. There followed 10 years of harassment from the KGB, and several arrests. His book on the use of detention in psychiatric asylums for dissidents, *Karatel'naia Meditsina* (Punitive Medicine), resulted in him being sentenced, on 15 Aug. 1978, to 5 years exile to Siberia. His case was taken up by Amnesty International. In 1987, under Gorbachev, wrote an *Open Letter* demanding the publication of Solzhenitsyn's works in the USSR under the new policy of glasnost. Continues his human rights activities.

Podtelkov, Fedor Grigor'evich
1886–1918. Revolutionary.
Don Cossack. On active service during WWI. Became a Bolshevik organizer among the Don Cossacks. Chairman of the Military Revolutionary Cttee. on the Don. Chairman of the Council of People's Commissars of the Don Soviet Republic during the first attempt by the Bolsheviks to take over the Don province. Captured by anti-Bolshevik Cossacks and shot. Later glorified by M. Sholokhov in his works.

Podvoiskii, Nikolai Il'ich
1880–1948. Revolutionary, politician.
Joined the SD Party, 1901. Took part in the 1905 Revolution. One of the leaders of the Military Revolutionary Cttee. in Petrograd during the October Revolution 1917. As chairman of the Cttee. during the Bolshevik takeover, directed the storming of the Winter Palace. Minister for Military Affairs, Nov. 1917–Mar. 1918. During the Civil War, one of the organizers of the Red Army, also

Minister of Military and Naval Affairs of the Ukraine. Head of Vsevobuch (the compulsory military training scheme) and of some Cheka forces. Later held several high party positions.

Pogozheva, Liudmila Pavlovna
29.9.1913–   . Journalist, film critic.
Graduated from the Moscow Pedagogical Institute, 1935. Appeared in the press in 1938. Taught at the VGIK, 1943–58, and at Moscow University from 1964. Editor-in-chief of the monthly magazine, *Iskusstvo Kino*, 1956–69. Acted as a film controller, rigidly following the party line. Lost her position in 1969.

Poiarkov, Iurii Mikhailovich
10.2.1937–   . Athlete.
Born in Khar'kov. With the Khar'kov Burevestnik. Graduated from the Khar'kov Pedagogical Institute, 1963. Member of the CPSU, 1965. Honoured Master of Sports (volleyball), 1968. World champion, 1960 and 1962. Olympic champion, 1964 and 1968. USSR champion, 1967. European champion, 1967 and 1971.

Pokhitonov, Daniil Il'ich
8.4.1878–31.12.1957. Conductor.
Born in Raivola, Vyborg Gouvt. From 1909, conductor at the Mariinskii Theatre, later the Kirov Theatre. Professor at the Leningrad Conservatory. Author of *Iz Proshlogo Russkoi Opery*, Leningrad, 1949. Died in Leningrad.

Pokhitonov, Ivan Pavlovich
8.2.1850–12.12.1923. Painter.
Born in Matrenovka (now Kirovograd Oblast'), Ukraine. Lived in France from 1876. Follower of the Barbizone School. Settled in Belorussia, 1903–5. In the Ukraine, 1913. Emigrated, 1919. Became famous for his miniature landscapes with startling lighting effects. Died in Liège in Belgium.

Pokrass, Daniil Iakovlevich
30.11.1904–16.4.1954. Composer.
Brother of the composers Dimitrii

and Samuil Pokrass. Author of music for films. Died in Moscow.

Pokrass, Dimitrii Iakovlevich
7.11.1899–20.12.1978. Composer.
Born in Kiev. Studied at the Petrograd Conservatory, 1913–17. Appeared in concerts. Joined the Red Cavalry, 1919. Wrote the music for *Marsh Budennogo*, 1920. Conductor and musical director with various Moscow theatres, 1923–26. Directed the Variety Stage Orchestra at the Railway Centre of Culture, 1936–72. Produced most of his songs between 1930–50 in collaboration with his brother Daniil Pokrass. Died in Moscow.

Pokrass, Samuil Iakovlevich
1897–1939. Composer.
Appeared on the variety stage as a pianist. Composed a song which became a Soviet classic: *Krasnaia Armiia Vsekh Sil'nei*, 1920. Emigrated to the USA. Wrote music for *The Three Musketeers*. Died in New York.

Pokrovskii, Aleksandr Petrovich
1898–1979. Col.-general.
Joined the Red Army, 1919. Regimental commander during the Civil War. Graduated from the Frunze Military Academy, 1926. During WWII, held several high positions as a staff officer. After WWII, head of the Scientific Research Department of the General Staff, 1946–61.

Pokrovskii, Boris Aleksandrovich
21.1.1912–   . Opera director.
Born in Moscow. Stage director, 1943–63, and chief director, from 1952, at the Bolshoi Theatre. From 1954, taught at the Moscow Theatre Art Institute.

Pokrovskii, Mikhail Nikolaevich
29.8.1868–10.4.1932. Historian.
Born in Moscow. Joined the Bolshevik Party, 1905. Emigrated and lived abroad, 1908–1917. Returned after the 1917 Revolution. After the Bolshevik take-over, became the virtual dictator of historical science in the Soviet Union, his approach to history becoming the official party view. Coined the phrase 'Istoria —

eto politika oprokinutaia v proshloe'. Academician, 1929. During the 1930s, when Stalin suddenly discovered the use of patriotism in politics, the political approach to history turned against Pokrovskii and his school. Denounced and arrested, his works branded as slander on the Russian past. Died in Moscow. Posthumously rehabilitated and retains his reputation among die-hard Marxists.

Pokryshev, Petr Afanas'evich
1914–1967. Major-general.
Joined the Red Army, 1934. Educated at a pilot's school, 1935. Took part in the Soviet-Finnish war, 1939–40. Fighter pilot during WWII, twice Hero of the Soviet Union. After WWII, in the anti-aircraft defence forces. Retired, 1961.

Pokryshkin, Aleksandr Ivanovich
1913–1985. Marshal.
Joined the Red Army, 1932. Educated at a pilot's school, 1939. Commander of a fighter-pilot division during WWII, highly decorated (3 times Hero of the Soviet Union). Graduated from the Frunze Military Academy, 1948, and from the Academy of the General Staff, 1957. Deputy commander-in-chief of anti-aircraft forces, 1968–71. Chairman of DOSAAF, 1972–81. Non-voting member of the Cen. Cttee. of the CPSU, 1976. Member of the Presidium of the Supreme Soviet of the USSR, 1979–84.

Polbin, Ivan Semenovich
1905–1945. Major-general.
Joined the Red Army and the Bolshevik Party, 1927. Educated at a pilot's school, 1931. Commander of a bomber regiment. Took part in fighting at Khalkin-Gol against the Japanese, and in WWII. Specialist in dive-bombing. Died in an air crash.

Polenov, Vasilii Dmitrievich
1.6.1844–18.7.1927. Artist.
Landscape and genre painter. Worked also in historical painting and stage design. Born in Petersburg. Son of Dimitrii Polenov, the historian. At Petersburg University, 1868–72, graduating in law. Studied at the private studios of P. Chistiakov

and I. Kramskoi, and also at art academies in Germany and Italy, 1872–76. War artist-correspondent during the Balkan War, 1876, and the Russo-Turkish War, 1877–78. From 1878, peredvizhnik. Worked for S. Mamontov's private opera. One of the organizers of the People's Theatre, 1910–18. Taught at the Moscow School of Painting, Sculpture and Architecture, 1882–95. Among his pupils were I. Levitan, K. Korovin and A. Arkhipov. Exhibited with every exhibition of note from 1869. Personal exhibitions: Jubilee, Moscow, 1924, Moscow, 1950, Erevan, Armenia, 1952. Died on his own estate of Borok near Tula, which in 1931 became the Polenov Museum, and in 1939, the State Polenov House-Museum.

Polenov, Vitalii Sergeevich
1901–1968. Lt.-general, state security officer.
Joined the Red Army, 1918. Took part in the Civil War. Thereafter, served in the border guards (GPU-NKVD), 1923–41. Joined the Bolshevik Party, 1929. Graduated from the Frunze Military Academy, 1938. Took part in WWII. Retired, 1958.

Poletaev, Fedor Andrianovich
1909–1945. Soldier, partisan.
On active service during WWII. Taken prisoner by the Germans, 1942. Escaped from a POW camp in Italy near Genoa, 1944. Joined the Italian communist partisans and became an active participant in their campaigns. Fell in action. Posthumously awarded high Soviet and Italian awards.

Poliakin, Miron Borisovich
12.2.1895–21.5.1941. Violinist.
Pupil of L. Auer. Emigrated, and gave performances all over Europe and the USA, 1917–26. Returned to the Soviet Union. Professor at the Leningrad Conservatory from 1926, and at the Moscow Conservatory from 1937. Died on a train journey, probably from a heart attack.

Poliakov, Sergei (Poliakoff, Serge)
1900–1969. Artist, guitarist.
Born in Moscow into a middle-class

family. Emigrated, 1923. Settled in Paris. Earned his living at night clubs as a guitarist. Acted in films as a musician. Studied art at art schools and academies in Paris. Worked at art schools in London (Chelsea and the Slade School), 1935–37. First exhibition in Paris, 1931. Returned to Paris, 1937. Met Kandinskii and Delaunay, 1938. Abstract painter, later influenced by Malevich. Worked in colour lithography. Praised by critics for his remarkable use of colour. Kandinskii Award, 1947. Exhibitions in Brussels, New York, Venice. Major posthumous exhibition in Paris, 1969.

Polikanov, Sergei Mikhailovich
1926– . Nuclear physicist.
Born in Moscow. Graduated from the Moscow Institute of Physical Engineering, 1950. Worked at Moscow Nuclear Power Research Institute, 1950–57. Member of the CPSU, 1955. Lenin Prize, 1967. Corresponding member of the USSR Academy of Sciences, 1974. Worked in Dubna. Had several confrontations with the authorities, who prevented him from meeting his Western colleagues, 1975. Became active in the human rights movement. In 1978, joined the Moscow Helsinki Group. Left the USSR, 1978. Settled in Switzerland, later moved to West Germany. Published his memoirs, *Razryv: Zapiski Atomnogo Fizika*, Frankfurt, 1983.

Polikarpov, Nikolai Nikolaevich
1892–1944. Aircraft designer.
Graduated from the Petrograd Polytechnical Institute, 1916. Worked in the administration of the Red Air Force, 1918. Professor at the Moscow Aviation Institute, 1943. Designed a number of Soviet specialized planes (fighters, training and reconnaissance planes).

Politkovskii, Igor' Vladimirovich
3.4.1930– . Violinist.
Son of Vladimir Politkovskii. Pupil of D. Oistrakh. Winner of international competitions in Brussels, 1955, and in Paris, 1957.

331

Politkovskii, Vladimir Mikhailovich
6.4.1892–1970s. Singer.
Born in Mamatovka, Saratov Gouvt.
Pupil of U. Mazetti. Soloist at the
Bolshoi Theatre, 1920–48. Taught at
the Moscow Gnesin Music School,
1948–54, and at the Moscow Conservatory, 1951–56.

Polivanov, Aleksei Andreevich
16.3.1855–25.9.1920. General, politician.
Graduated from the Nikolaevskoe
Engineering Academy, 1880, and the
Academy of the General Staff, 1888.
Worked in the General Staff, 1899–
1904. Edited military newspapers
(*Russkii Invalid*). Chief of the General
Staff, 1905–06, Deputy War Minister,
1906–12. Close to the liberals in the
Duma, dismissed by the Minister of
War, Sukhomlinov, 1912. Member of
the State Council (Upper Chamber),
1912–15. Minister of War, 1915–16.
Retired soon after. During the Civil
War, military expert with the Red
Army, 1918–20. Military expert in
Riga at the Soviet-Polish peace talks,
1920. Died in Riga.

Polivanova, Maria Semenovna
1922–1942. Soldier.
Drafted into the Soviet Army during
WWII. Became a successful sniper.
According to the official version,
being surrounded by Germans, she
killed herself and them with her last
grenade. Hero of the Soviet Union.

Polivoda, Anatolii Ivanovich
29.5.1947– . Athlete.
Born in Enakievo, Donetsk Oblast'.
Honoured Master of Sports (basketball), 1971. With Kiev Avangard.
Graduated from the Kiev Institute of
Physical Culture, 1975. Sports instructor. USSR champion, 1967.
European champion, 1967, 1969 and
1971. World champion, 1967. Olympic champion, 1972.

Polkovnikov, Georgii Petrovich
1883–1918. Colonel.
Took part in WWI. After the
February Revolution 1917, appointed commander of the Petrograd
military district by Kerenskii. Hanged by the Bolsheviks after the takeover.

Poloka, Gennadii Ivanovich
15.7.1930– . Film director.
Graduated from the Shchepkin Theatre School, 1951, and then from the
VGIK, 1957. Pupil of L. Kuleshov
and A. Khokhlova. Specializes in
adventure films which are highly
commercial, such as *Kapronovye
Seti*, 1963, *Respublika SHKID*, 1968
(prize-winner at the Venice Film
Festival), *Odinozhdy Odin*, 1975, and
his TV film, *Nashe Prizvanie*, 1981.
His major work, *The Invasion*, 1968,
was banned for 17 years. First
distributed in 1985, when E. Klimov
took over as head of the Filmmakers' Union.

Polonskaia, Veronika Vitol'dovna
1908– . Actress.
Daughter of the actor Vitold Polonskii. Leading actress of the Academic
Art Theatre (MKHAT). Wife of
Mikhail Ianshin, an actor at the same
theatre. Mistress of Mayakovsky in
his last years.

Polonskii, Vitold Al'fonsovich
1879–5.1.1919. Actor.
Celebrated actor of the Russian silent
cinema. Combined theatre and film
work. In his films, played aristocratic
lovers. Films include *Brat'ia Boris i
Gleb*, *Irina Kirsanova*, *Posle Smerti*,
and *Zhizn' Za Zhizn'*.

Polovtsev, Petr Aleksandrovich
1874–1930s. Major-general.
In 1905, deputy military attaché in
London. Major-general, May 1917.
Replaced Kornilov as commander of
the Petrograd military district, 1917.
Conducted the search for Lenin and
Zinov'ev after the communist rebellion in July 1917. Later worked in the
Ministry of Foreign Affairs of the
Provisional Government. Emigrated
after the Bolshevik take-over. Settled
in Monaco.

Polozov, Iakov Sergeevich
1890?–22.12.1923. Monk.
Personal servant of Patriarch Tikhon
during his house-arrest. Shot accidentally and killed during a Cheka
attempt on the Patriarch's life.

Pol'skii, Mikhail, Archpriest
6.11.1891–21.5.1960. Russian
Orthodox clergyman.
Born in stanitsa Novotroitskaia,
Kuban' Oblast'. Educated at a
seminary, 1914. Priest, Aug. 1920.
Studied at Moscow Theological Academy from 1921. Could not graduate,
as the Academy was closed by Soviet
authorities. Arrested, July 1923.
Spent 3 years at Solovki concentration
camp, sent into exile to the Urals.
Went underground, 1929, and crossed the border into Iran, 1930. Priest
in the Near East (Jerusalem, later
Beirut). Moved to London, 1938.
After WWII, moved to the USA,
1948. Priest at the Russian Orthodox
Church in San Francisco until his
death. Compiled the first collection
of biographies of persecuted Russian
Orthodox clergymen in the USSR
(*Novye mucheniki*, 2 vols), published
in the USA. Wrote on the situation of
the church in the atheist state.

Poluboiarov, Pavel Pavlovich
1901–1984. Marshal.
Joined the Red Army, 1919, and the
Bolshevik Party, 1920. Took part in
the Civil War. Graduated from the
Mechanization Academy of the Red
Army, 1938. Tank corps commander
during WWII. Deputy commander
of Soviet tank forces, 1953, and
commander, 1954–69.

Poluian, Ian Vasil'evich
1891–1937. Revolutionary, military
commander.
Joined the Bolshevik Party, 1912.
During the Civil War, one of the
most active Bolshevik organizers in
the Northern Caucasus and Kuban'
region, 1918–20. After the Civil War,
held several high administrative
posts. Liquidated by Stalin.

Polunin, Vladimir Iakovlevich
22.4.1880–2.1.1957. Artist.
Born in Kiev. Studied art in Munich
from 1904–07 and later in Russia
under Boris Anisfeld. In 1910, left
Russia and went to live in England.
Most of his theatrical designs were
created for Diaghilev, Sir Thomas
Beecham's company and the Sadler's
Wells Ballet. From 1929 to 1948,
taught stage design at the Slade
School in London. Died in Godalming, Surrey.

Polupanov, Andrei Vasil'evich
1888–1956. Revolutionary, military commander.
Joined the Bolshevik Party, 1912. Bolshevik organizer among sailors. Joined the Red Army, 1918. Active participant in the Civil War as the head of a revolutionary sailors' detachment. Took Kiev from the Rada (Ukrainian nationalist) forces. 1st Bolshevik commandant of Kiev, 1918. Fought on the Dnepr and Volga against the Whites, 1919. Commander of armoured trains, 1920. Several party posts after the Civil War.

Polupanov, Viktor Andreevich
1.1.1946–   . Athlete.
Born in Moscow. Hockey player with the Central Sports Club of the Armed Forces. USSR champion, 1966, 1968 and 1970. European champion, 1966–68 and 1970. World champion, 1966–68 and 1970. Olympic champion, 1968.

Polynin, Fedor Petrovich
1906–1981. Col.-general.
Joined the Red Army, 1928, and the Bolshevik Party, 1929. Studied at a pilot's school, 1931. Sent to China to fight against the Japanese, 1937–38. Took part in the Soviet-Finnish war, 1939–40. Commanded air force armies during WWII. Appointed commander of the Polish Air Force (organized in the USSR from former Polish POWs), 1944. Remained commander of the Air Force in communist Poland until 1947, when he returned to positions in the Soviet Air Force. Commander of the Rear Administration of the Soviet Air Force, 1959–71.

Pomerants, Grigorii Solomonovich
1918–   . Philosopher, journalist.
Born in Wil'no. Studied in Moscow. During WWII, at the front. Expelled from the Communist Party, 1947. Arrested, inmate of the Gulag camps. Rehabilitated, 1958. Became known for his historical and philosophical articles in samizdat.

Ponomarenko, Panteleimon Kondrat'evich
1902–1.1984. Politician, state security officer (SMERSH).
Born in Krasnodar Krai. Took part in the Civil War. Cheka officer. Member of the Bolshevik Party, 1925. Studied at the Moscow Institute of Railway Transport in the early 1930s. Served in the Soviet Army. Worked in the apparatus of the Cen. Cttee. under Malenkov from 1938. 1st secretary of the Cen. Cttee. of the Belorussian CP, 1938. Member of the Cen. Cttee. of the Bolshevik Party, 1939–61. Head of NKVD control of Partisan Operations as head of the Central HQ of the partisan movement, 1942–44. In 1945, appointed by Stalin chairman of the Council of Ministers of Belorussia. Responsible for re-Stalinization of the republic. In 1948, moved to Moscow. Secretary of the Cen. Cttee. of the CPSU. Minister of Supplies of the USSR, 1950. After Stalin's death, for a short time Minister of Culture, 1953, but lost his seat on the Presidium of the Cen. Cttee. In 1954 lost his position and sent to Kazakhstan as secretary of the Cen. Cttee of the CP in Kazakhstan. Soviet Ambassador to Poland, 1956. USSR Ambassador to India, 1957. USSR Ambassador to the Netherlands, 1959. In 1961, declared persona non grata in the Netherlands for his involvement in the attempted kidnapping of a Soviet woman defector in an Amsterdam street. Took part in a fight with the Dutch police. USSR representative at the International Agency of Atomic Energy, Vienna, 1962–64. Pensioned, and became a lecturer at the Academy of Social Sciences. Died in Moscow.

Ponomarev, Boris Nikolaevich
17.1.1905–   . Politician.
Born in Zaraisk near Moscow. Took part in the Civil War. Komsomol leader in Riazan', 1920–22. Graduated from Moscow University, 1926. Deputy director of the Institute of Red Professors, 1932–36. Senior posts in the Comintern, 1936–43. Director of the Marx-Engels-Lenin Institute, 1943–44. Non-voting member of the Politburo, 1972. Editor of a history of the CPSU. For a long time, involved in the work of communist parties outside the Soviet Union.

Ponomarev, Vladimir Ivanovich
22.7.1892–21.3.1951. Ballet dancer, choreographer.
Born in Petersburg. Graduated from the Petersburg Theatre School. With the Mariinskii Theatre from 1910. With Diaghilev's Ballets Russes, 1911–12. Brilliant exponent of the academic style of dancing. Went over to mime from the 1930s. Choreographer from 1922. Produced several ballets independently and as co-producer with F. V. Lopukhova, A. Vaganova and others. Coach with the Theatre Ballet Company, 1939–41 and 1944–45. Taught at the Petersburg Theatre School (later known as the Leningrad Choreographic School) from 1913 till his death. In charge of advanced classes for dancers at the Hungarian Opera, Budapest. Creator of an original method for the teaching of male dancing. Died in Budapest.

Ponomareva, Nina Apollonovna (Romashkova)
27.4.1929–   . Athlete.
Born in Sverdlovsk. Honoured Master of Sports (track and field athletics), 1952. With the Moscow Armed Forces Club. Graduated from the Moscow Oblast' Pedagogical Institute, 1955. Teacher. USSR champion, 1951–56 and 1958–59. World record-holder, 1952 (discus). Olympic champion, 1952 and 1960. European champion, 1954. 1st Soviet woman to win an Olympic gold medal. Autobiography: *Moi Sportivnyi Put'*, Moscow, 1963.

Pontecorvo, Bruno Maksimovich
22.8.1913–   . Nuclear scientist, spy.
Born in Italy. Graduated from Rome University, 1933. Professor at the university, 1933–36. Lived in France, 1936–40. Emigrated to the USA, where he worked in nuclear research, 1940–48. Worked at the Harwell Laboratories in England, 1948–50. Actively involved in the communist movement, became a very successful Soviet spy in nuclear scientific establishments. Fled to East Germany and on to the Soviet Union in 1950. Continued his nuclear research in Soviet nuclear establishments.

Pontriagin, Lev Semenovich
3.9.1908–   . Mathematician.
Born in Moscow. Went blind after an

accident at the age of 14. Graduated from Moscow University, 1929, professor at the university, 1935. Academician, 1958. Specialist on algebra and the theory of continuous groups.

Popenchenko, Valerii Vladimirovich
26.8.1937–1980. Boxer.
Born in Kuntsevo, a suburb of Moscow, into a working-class family. Joined the CPSU, 1960. 6 times USSR champion. Champion of Europe in 1963 and 1965. Champion at the Tokyo Olympic Games in 1964. Dean of the Physical Culture Department at the Bauman Institute of Physics, 1970–75. Developed a serious drink problem, gave up sport and became terribly depressed. Committed suicide by jumping from his fourth floor flat.

Popkov, Vitalii Ivanovich
1922– . Lt.-general.
Joined the Red Army, 1940. Highly decorated fighter pilot during WWII (twice Hero of the Soviet Union). Graduated from the Air Force Academy, 1951, and from the Academy of the General Staff, 1964. Professor at the Zhukovskii Air Force Academy, 1980.

Poplavskii, Boris Iulianovich
7.6.1903–9.10.1935. Poet.
Born in Moscow. Son of a businessman. Educated at secondary school in Moscow. After the October Revolution 1917, left for Yalta in the Crimea in 1918. Travelled to Istanbul in 1919. Returned to Novorossiisk. Emigrated in 1920 from Rostov to Istanbul. Moved to Paris in 1921. Studied painting in Berlin in 1922. First poems appeared in 1928. Became known for his poetry and his bohemian life-style. Died, in Paris, of poison given by a friend in a suicide pact. Became famous as the *poète maudit* of the Russian emigré literary scene in Paris between the world wars. 3-vol. collection of works published in the USA.

Poplavskii, Stanislav Giliarovich
1902–1973. General.
Joined the Red Army, 1923, and the Bolshevik Party, 1928. Graduated from the Frunze Military Academy, 1938, afterwards professor there. On active service during WWII. Commander in the Polish Army (created during WWII from Polish POWs in the USSR), 1944. After WWII, sent by Stalin to Poland as Deputy Minister of Defence of Poland. 1st Deputy Chief Inspector of the Soviet Ministry of Defence, 1956.

Popov, Dmitrii Mikhailovich
1900–1952. Politician.
Served in the Red Army during the Civil War, 1919–22. Joined the Bolshevik Party, 1921. Secretary of the Krasnodar kraikom, 1939. 1st secretary of the Smolensk obkom and gorkom of the Communist Party during and after WWII, 1940–48, in charge of organizing the communist underground during the German occupation, and the re-Stalinization of the region after WWII. Functionary of the Cen. Cttee. of the CPSU, 1949.

Popov, Markian Mikhailovich
1902–1969. General.
Joined the Red Army, 1920, and the Bolshevik Party, 1921. Took part in the Civil War. Graduated from the Frunze Military Academy, 1936. Commander of the Leningrad military district, 1941. Commander of the Leningrad, Stalingrad, Briansk and Baltic fronts. After WWII, head of the Military Training Administration. 1st Deputy Commander-in-chief of Soviet Land Forces, 1956.

Popov, Oleg Konstantinovich
31.7.1930– . Circus artist, clown.
One of the world's most famous clowns. Born at Vyrubovo near Moscow. At the age of 14, joined the circus as a juggler and slackwire artist. At 20, became a clown specializing in the art of mime. Graduated from the School of Circus Art in Moscow in 1950. Extremely popular artist throughout the Soviet Union. A huge box-office success. Has performed abroad with equal success. Created the Popov school of clowns and also teaches young performers. Memoirs: *Moi Geroi*, Moscow, 1961.

Popov, Sergei Maksimovich
12.4.1862–14.6.1934. Musicologist.
Author of musicians' and composers' biographies. Works include *Zhizn' i Tvorchestvo P.I. Chaikovskogo*, Moscow, 1927, and *Muzykal'naia Moskva i Bethoven, 1860–70s*, Moscow, 1927.

Popov, Sergei Sergeevich
14.12.1887–5.3.1942. Musicologist.
Born in Moscow. Son of Sergei M. Popov. Author of works on P. Tchaikovskii and S. Taneev. Restored P. Tchaikovskii's opera *Voevoda* with P. Lamm.

Popova, Tatiana Vasil'evna
5.10.1907– . Musicologist.
Born in St. Petersburg. Author of many works on composers, such as Borodin, Haydn, Mussorgskii and Mozart.

Popovskii, Mark Aleksandrovich
1922– . Journalist, author.
Born in Odessa. Took part in WWII. Graduated in philology from Moscow University. Science journalist. Published many popular science books and hundreds of articles in the Soviet press from 1957–73. Became involved in dissident activity. Came into conflict with the authorities. In 1977, calling himself the Mark Popovskii Press, provided information to Western press correspondents. Harassed by the KGB, left the USSR, 1977, and settled in the USA. Published several valuable books about scientists, including the academician Vavilov. Contributor to many Russian emigré periodicals. Works: *Upravliaemaia Nauka*, London, 1978; *Zhizn' I Zhitie Voino-Iasenetskogo, Arkhiepiskopa I Khirurga*, Paris, 1979; *Delo Akademika Vavilova*, USA, 1983; *Russkie Muzhiki Rasskazyvaiut: Posledovateli L. Tolstogo V Sovetskom Soiuze, 1918–77*, London, 1983.

Popudrenko, Nikolai Nikitovich
1906–1943. Politician, partisan.
Joined the Bolshevik Party, 1929. Party functionary in the Ukraine, 1929–39. Secretary of the Chernigov obkom, 1940. During WWII, head of the underground party and partisan organizations in Chernigov Oblast' in Northern Ukraine. Fell in action.

Poradnik, Liudmila Konstantinovna (Bobrus')
11.1.1946– . Athlete.
Born in Kiev. Honoured Master of Sports (handball), 1972. With Kiev Spartak. Graduated from the Kamenets-Podolskii Pedagogical Institute, 1972. Teacher. USSR champion, 1969–78. Olympic champion, 1976.

Porai-Koshits, Aleksei
1941– . Stage designer.
Studied physics at Leningrad University for 3 years. Became stage designer for a Leningrad theatre. Studied set design under N. Akimov. His first design was for *The Master*, a production of the Leningrad Children's Theatre, which won several awards. Graduated from Leningrad University and developed an interest in stage technology. This and his experiments in the technology brought him to work as a technical director in a number of theatres, including the famous Taganka Theatre in Moscow. Technical director of the Leningrad Malyi Drama Theatre from 1984. Won 1st prize for his stage designs in the All-Russia Theatre Festival in 1987. Involved in the Malyi Theatre's production of *Stars in the Morning Sky*, which toured Britain successfully in 1988.

Porik, Vasilii Vasil'evich
1920–1944. Lieutenant.
Joined the Red Army, 1939, and the Bolshevik Party, 1941. At the beginning of WWII, wounded and captured by the Germans. Escaped from a POW camp in France, 1943, and joined the French Resistance in Southern France. Captured and shot by the Germans.

Portnova, Zina (Zinaida Mikhailovna)
20.2.1926–1.1944. Partisan.
Born in Leningrad. Daughter of a worker. On holiday when WWII started, joined the partisans near Vitebsk. Member of the Young Avengers (Iunye Mstiteli). Took part in intelligence operations. Arrested by the Germans, Dec. 1943. According to Soviet sources, during interrogation she killed her interrogator with his own weapon, and was beaten to death. Posthumously proclaimed a Hero of the Soviet Union (July 1958).

Posern, Boris Pavlovich
1882–1939. Political officer.
Joined the SD Party, 1902. Took part in the 1905 Revolution. During the Bolshevik take-over, Nov. 1917, party organizer in Pskov, thereafter commissar for the Northern Front. During the Civil War, commissar of the Petrograd military district, and the Baltic fleet, 1918. After the Civil War, secretary of the Northwestern Bureau of the Cen. Cttee. of the Bolshevik Party, and of the Southeastern Kraikom. Secretary of the Leningrad obkom of the party, 1923–30. Non-voting member of the Cen. Cttee. of the Bolshevik Party, 1930.

Posmitnyi, Makar Anisimovich
31.1.1895–3.4.1973. Kolkhoz chairman.
Born in Dzhugastrovo near Odessa. Founded an agricultural cooperative, 1924. After the collectivization, became chairman of a famous show kolkhoz. Member of the Cen. Cttee. of the Ukrainian CP. Died in the village of Rassvet near Odessa.

Posnikov, Aleksandr Sergeevich
26.12.1846–1921. Economist.
Born in Viaz'ma. Graduated in law from Moscow University, 1869. Worked abroad, 1873–76. Professor at Odessa University, 1876–82. Wrote on the Russian agricultural commune (*Obshchinnoe Zemlevladenie*), 1875–78. Editor of *Russkie Vedomosti*, 1886–96. A well-known populist publicist. Opponent of Stolypin's agricultural reforms. Member of the Duma, 1912. After the February Revolution 1917, chairman of the Main Land Commission of the Provisional Government. After the October Revolution 1917, taught at the Petrograd Polytechnical Institute. A liberal narodnik, who saw the way forward in agriculture in the obshchina as against the individual farm. Theorist of the cooperative movement.

Pospekhin, Lev Aleksandrovich
23.3.1903– . Ballet dancer. choreographer.
Born in Moscow. Graduated from the Moscow Choreographic School. Dancer with the Bolshoi Theatre, 1926–49. Character dancer. Co-producer of several ballets at the Bolshoi Theatre, 1937, 1939, 1942. Directed performances abroad. Choreographer and coach at the Bolshoi from 1949. Retired in the early 1960s.

Pospelovskii, Dmitrii
1935– . Historian, author.
Born in Rovno in the Ukraine. During and after WWII, in refugee camps in West Germany. Graduated from the London School of Economics. Worked for the BBC, and later for Radio Liberty in Munich. University professor in Canada. Contributed to many publications in Russian and English. Wrote a 2-volume history of the Russian Orthodox Church during the Soviet period, published in the USA.

Postnikov, Sergei Porfir'evich
1883–after 1950. Politician, editor.
One of the leaders of the SR Party. Member of the editorial board of the journal *Zavety*. Emigrated after Oct. 1917. Settled in Czechoslovakia. Founder and first director of the Russian archive in Prague, a unique collection of books and documents which, after WWII, was handed over by the Czech authorities to Stalin and taken to the Soviet Union, where it forms part of the secret state archives.

Postyshev, Pavel Petrovich
1887–1939. Politician.
Joined the SD Party, 1904. Took part in the 1905 Revolution. During the Civil War, active Bolshevik organizer in Siberia, member of Irkutsk Military Revolutionary Cttee, 1917. Organizer of the Red Guards, member of Tsentrosibir'. Secretary of the Cen. Cttee. of the Ukrainian CP, 1926. Member of the Cen. Cttee. of the VKP, 1927. Secretary of the Cen. Cttee. of VKP, 1930. Member of the Orgburo, and non-voting member of the Politburo, 1934. Secretary of the Cen. Cttee., and member of the Politburo and Orgburo of the Cen. Cttee. of the Ukrainian CP, 1933–37. Demoted to secretary of Kuibyshev obkom, 1937. Victim of Stalin's purges.

Potanin, Grigorii Nikolaevich
4.10.1835–30.6.1920. Explorer.
Born at Iamyshevskii near Pavlodar. Educated at the Omsk Cadet Corps, 1852. Studied at Petersburg University, 1859–62. After participating in student demonstrations, exiled to Siberia, 1861. As a member of a group demanding Siberian independence, arrested, imprisoned and exiled, 1865–74. During his exile, took part in an expedition to the Central Asian mountains, 1863–64. In the 1870–90s, explored completely unknown parts of Central Asia, Mongolia, Tibet and China. Later expeditions were undertaken with his wife, who took part in his research, and published reports. (She later died on one of the expeditions.) Collected geographical, botanical, zoological and ethnographical material. Wrote on the history and folklore of the people of the region. Founded the Society for the Study of Siberia in Tomsk. One of the Tianshan' mountain ranges and a large glacier on the Altai have been named after him. Died in Tomsk.

Potapenko, Ignatii Nikolaevich
12.1856–17.5.1929. Author.
Born in Fedorovka near Kherson. Son of a priest. Studied at Odessa University. Graduated from the Petersburg Conservatory as a singer. In the late 19th century, friend (and at that time considered a rival) of A. Chekhov. His naturalistic stories and plays are largely forgotten now. Died in Leningrad.

Potemkin, Vladimir Petrovich
19.10.1874–23.3.1946. Diplomat, educationalist.
Born in Tver' (now Kalinin). Son of a doctor. Graduated from Moscow University, 1898. Teacher at Moscow and Ekaterinoslav, 1900–1917. Joined the Bolsheviks, 1919. Political commissar during the Civil War. Soviet Ambassador to Greece, 1929–32, Italy, 1932–34, and France, 1934–37. Deputy Minister of Foreign Affairs of the USSR, 1937–40. Member of the Cen. Cttee of the CPSU, 1939. Minister of Education of the RSFSR, 1940–46. Editor-in-chief of a 3 vol. *History of Diplomacy*, 1941–45. Died in Moscow, buried at the Kremlin wall.

Potolovskii, Nikolai Sergeevich
8.4.1878–7.1.1927. Composer.
Born in Moscow. Professor at the Moscow Philharmonic Music Drama School. Became its director after it was renamed the Music Drama Institute. Author of the opera *Vasilisa Melent'eva*. Also wrote pieces for violin and cello. Died in Moscow.

Potresov, Aleksandr Nikolaevich
1869–1934. Politician.
Born in Moscow. Son of a general. Active in the social-democratic movement from 1890. Graduated from Petersburg University, 1893. Arrested in 1896, and exiled to Viatka in 1898. One of the founders and editors (with Lenin) of *Iskra*, 1900. Menshevik, 1903, leader of right-wing Menshevism. Left the Mensheviks, 1918. Radically opposed to Bolshevism after the October Revolution 1917. Arrested in 1919, but soon released. Left Russia in Feb. 1925. Lived in Paris, editor of the magazine *Zapiski Sotsial Demokrata* (Notes of a Social Democrat), 1931. Contributor to Kerenskii's *Dni* (Days). One of the best known socialist opponents of the Bolshevik mentality and methods. Published his memoirs *V Plenu U Illiuzii*.

Povolotskii, Iakov
1881–1928. Publisher.
From 1915, Russian publisher and bookseller in Paris. Published many of the early emigré writers. Went bankrupt in the 1920s. Died in Paris.

Pozdeev, Konstantin Rostislavovich
1888–2.1.1981. Major-general.
Took part in WWI as a Cossack officer. Last commander of the Cossack Life Guards before the October Revolution 1917. During the Civil War, fought on the side of the Whites. Evacuated from the Crimea with Wrangel. Settled in France, lived in Paris. Guardian of the Cossack Museum in exile. Died in France. Buried at Ste. Genevieve-de-Bois.

Pozdniakov, Vladimir V.
1920?–21.12.1973. Colonel, author.
Took part in WWII. Taken prisoner by the Germans. Became the adjutant of General Vlasov. Escaped SMERSH, 1945–47. After the war settled in the USA. In Buenos Aires, published 2 large monographs on the history of the Vlasov army, the ROA: *Rozhdenie ROA*, 1972, and *A. A. Vlasov*, 1973. The books contain many rare documents and photographs. Died in the USA.

Pozhedaev, Georgii Anatol'evich
13.1.1899– . Artist.
Born in Kursk. Started work as a stage designer in 1918 in Petrograd, but his main work has been as a book illustrator. Left for France after the 1917 Revolution. Lived in Paris.

Pozner, Solomon Vladimirovich
1880–1946. Journalist.
Emigrated after Oct. 1917. Settled in Paris. Wrote a history of modern Russian literature in French. Secretary of the Union of Russian Journalists in Paris.

Pozniak, Dan Ivanovich
19.10.1939– . Athlete.
Born in the village of Tolchak in the Western Ukraine. Honoured Master of Sports (boxing), 1965. With the Vilnius Trudovye Rezervy team. Sports instructor. Member of the CPSU, 1961. USSR champion, 1962–68. European champion, 1965, 1967 and 1969. Olympic champion, 1968 (light-heavy weight).

Pravdin, Nikolai Aleksandrovich
1893–1959. Artist.
Portrait miniaturist. RSFSR People's Artist. Studied at one of the icon art schools of the Committee for the Preservation of Icons in Palekh. Exhibitions: The Art of Palekh, 1932, 1939; Ivanovo Artists, 1936, 1947; Folk Art, Moscow, 1937; Works of Applied Art and Art Industry, Moscow, 1952; RSFSR Artists, Moscow, 1955; 30 Years of Soviet Palekh, Moscow, 1955; Palekh Art, Ulianovsk, 1955.

Pravdukhin, Valerian Pavlovich
2.2.1892–15.7.1939. Author.
Born in a Cossack village near Orenburg. Educated at Shaniavskii University, 1914–17. Married the

writer L. Seifullina. In 1921, one of the organizers of the Novosibirsk magazine *Sibirskie Ogni*, which became known in the 1920s for its independent stance. Wrote the play *Virineia* with Seifullina. In the late 1920s, wrote stories about hunting and Siberian nature. Perished in the Gulag. Posthumously rehabilitated.

Preobrazhenskaia, Olga Iosifovna
2.2.1871–27.12.1962. Ballerina.
Born in Petersburg. Graduated from the Petersburg Theatre School. Pupil of L. I. Ivanov, M. I. Petipa and Kh. P. Ioganson. Dancer with the Mariinskii Theatre from 1889. Became the leading dancer of the company. A lyrico-comic talent and exponent of classical ballet. Danced under the direction of Petipa, Legat and Fokin. Distinguished as an improvisor. Brought new interpretations and variations into her parts. Guest appearances in Italy, France, England, Germany and South America from 1895. Appearances abroad and at the Mariinskii Theatre from 1909. Directed the movement class at the Mariinskii Opera, and taught classical dance at the Petrograd Choreographic School and at A. L. Volynskii's School of Russian Ballet, 1917–21. Teacher and predecessor of A. I. Vaganova. Emigrated 1921. Founded a ballet school in Paris. Died in Paris.

Preobrazhenskaia, Olga Ivanovna
24.7.1881 or 1884–31.10.1971.
Actress, director.
Entered the film industry, 1913. Played leading parts in over 20 silent films. Taught at the 1st State Film School. Her first film as director was *Kashtanka*, 1927. From then until 1941, made films with her husband, the director I. K. Pravov, including *Baby Riazanskie*, 1927 and *Tikhii Don*, 1931.

Preobrazhenskaia, Sofia Petrovna
27.9.1904–   . Singer (mezzo-soprano).
Born in St. Petersburg. Pupil of N. Zaitseva and I. Ershov. Soloist with the Kirov Opera from 1928. Professor at the Leningrad Conservatory, 1949–53. Highly decorated (Stalin Prize, 1946 and 1951).

Preobrazhenskii, Antonii Viktorovich
28.2.1870–17.2.1929. Musicologist.
Born in Syzran'. Professor at the Leningrad Conservatory. Specialist in Russian church music. Died in Leningrad.
Works: *Slovar' Russkogo Tserkovnogo Peniia*, Moscow, 1896; *Vopros o Edinoglasnom Penii v Russkoi Tserkvi 17-go Veka*, Petersburg, 1904; *Ocherk Istorii Tserkovnogo Peniia v Rossii*, Petersburg, 1910; *Kul'tovaia Muzyka v Rossii*, Leningrad, 1924.

Preobrazhenskii, Evgenii A.
1886–1937. Economist.
The leading Soviet economist of the 1920–30s. Masterminded the Soviet industrialization plan at the expense of rural Russia. In 1927, accused of Trotskyism, fired from the party and sent into exile in Uralsk. Made the statement that 'we have used the printing press as a machine-gun to attack bourgeois society in the rear through the monetary system'. In 1929, recognized his mistakes. Returned to Moscow. Arrested, 1937, and shot.

Preobrazhenskii, Evgenii Nikolaevich
1909–1963. Col.-general.
Joined the Red Navy, 1927. Educated as a navy pilot, 1930. On active service during WWII. As a commander of a bomber regiment, bombed Berlin. Towards the end of the war, served at the Northern front. Deputy commander of the Pacific Navy Air Force, 1945, and commander, 1946. Commander of the Naval Air Force, 1950–62.

Preobrazhenskii, Vladimir Alekseevich
21.1.1921–24.2.1981. Ballet dancer, choreographer.
Born in Petersburg. Graduated from the Leningrad Choreographic School. Pupil of V. I. Ponomarev. Dancer with the Kirov Theatre, 1935–39. Taught ballet at the Sverdlovsk Theatre, 1935–39, at the Moscow Choreographic School, and at the GITIS, 1944–45. With the Shevchenko Theatre, 1939–41, and the Bolshoi Theatre, 1942–58. Directed the Bolshoi company 1960–62. Artistic director of the Moscow People's Ballet at the Palace of Culture of the

factory Serp i Molot, 1963–65. Director of the Moscow Concert Ballet Collective from 1965. Combined emotional romanticism with classical clarity of expression. Remarkable for his plasticity. Partner of G. Ulanova and others. Guest appearances abroad. Produced *Swan Lake* at the L'vov Theatre, 1969. Appeared in several concert performances. Died in Moscow.

Presman, Matvei Leont'evich
22.10.1870–12.11.1941. Pianist.
Born in Rostov-on-Don. Pupil of V. Safonov. From 1911, professor at the Saratov and Azerbaidzhan conservatories. In 1933, moved to the Moscow Conservatory. Author of 'Ugolok Muzykal'noi Moskvy 1880s' (in: *Vospominaniia o Rakhmaninove*, vol. 1, Moscow, 1961). Died in Moscow.

Presniakov, Valentin Ivanovich
27.10.1877–27.3.1956. Ballet dancer, choreographer.
Graduated from the Petersburg Theatre School. Dancer with the Mariinskii Theatre, 1895–1909. Character dancer. Follower of M. M. Fokin. Taught plasticity and stage movement at the Petersburg Conservatory, 1904. Professorship from 1914. Important contribution to musical and choreographic training after 1917. Founded the People's Conservatory of Vitebsk, and courses in rhythmic dance following the system of Jacques-Dalcroze, 1919. Taught at the Institute for Music and Drama in Odessa, 1924–32. Choreographer and teacher at the Erevan Opera, and founder of its ballet company, 1933–38. Artistic director and teacher in the Choreography Department of the Voronezh Music School, 1938–42. Died in Pskov.

Press, Iosif Isakovich
15.1.1881–4.10.1924. Cellist.
Born in Wilno. Brother of Mikhail Press. Pupil of A. Glen. Professor at the Petrograd Conservatory, 1915–18. Member of the Russkoe Trio. Emigrated to France. Concert performer in Europe and the USA. Moved to the USA, 1922. Died in Rochester, USA.

Press, Irina Natanovna
10.3.1939– . Athlete.
Born in Khar'kov. Younger sister of Tamara Press. Honoured Master of Sports (track and field athletics), 1960. With Leningrad Dynamo, and from 1964, with Moscow Dynamo. Graduated from the Leningrad Institute of Railway Engineers, 1962. Member of the CPSU, 1964. USSR champion, 1959–66 (in various fields including the pentathlon). World and European record-holder, 1959–65. Olympic champion, 1960 and 1964. With her sister Tamara, became a legendary athlete in the Soviet Union.

Press, Mikhail Isakovich
22.9.1871–22.12.1938. Violinist.
Born in Wilno. Pupil of I. Grzhimali and E. Ysaye. Professor at the Moscow Conservatory, 1915–18. In 1906, organized the Russkoe Trio. Gave concert tours abroad. Emigrated, 1918. Performed in Germany and Sweden. Moved to the USA, 1922. Appeared as a conductor. Taught in Philadelphia. Wrote pieces for the violin. Died in Michigan.

Press, Tamara Natanovna
10.5.1937– . Athlete.
Born in Khar'kov. Honoured Master of Sports (track and field athletics), 1960. With Leningrad Trud. Graduated from the Leningrad Institute of Building Engineers, 1961. Member of the CPSU, 1962. Also graduated from the Higher Party School of the Cen. Cttee., 1967. USSR champion, 1958–66. European champion, 1958 and 1962. World record-holder, 1960–67 (discus), and 1959–68 (shot-put). Olympic champion, 1960 and 1964 (shot-put), and in 1964 (discus). Author of *Tsena Pobedy*, Moscow, 1977.

Prianishnikov, Ippolit Petrovich
26.8.1847–11.11.1921. Singer.
Born in Kerch'. Soloist with the Mariinskii Theatre, 1878–86. Founder of the first Opernoe Tovarishchestvo in Russia, and its first director. His many pupils include G. Baklanov, E. Mravina and V. Pikok. Author of *Sovety Obuchaiushchimsia Peniiu*, St. Petersburg, 1899. Died in Moscow.

Pribik, Iosif Viacheslavovich
11.3.1855–20.10.1937. Conductor, composer.
Born in Sviataia Gora, Czechoslovakia of Czech parents. Moved to Russia, 1879. Opera conductor with theatres in Khar'kov, Kiev, Tiflis and Moscow. From 1919, professor at the Odessa Conservatory. Conductor at the Odessa Opera Theatre from 1894 until his death.

Pribytkin, Edmund Vladimirovich
24.1.1930–13.4.1986. Mathematician.
Born in Khar'kov. During and after WWII, in labour camps, and later in DP camps in Germany, 1944–47. Moved with his parents to Brazil, 1952. Graduated from a Brazilian university. Emigrated to the USA, 1963, and started work at New York University. Professor of mathematics at Millersville University in Pennsylvania, 1969–86. Chairman of the Congress of Russian Americans, 1979–86. Died in Lancaster, Pennsylvania.

Prigozhin, Lutsian Abramovich
15.8.1926– . Composer.
Born in Tashkent. Author of the ballet *Krug Ada* (produced, 1964), the radio-opera *Doktor Aibolit*, 1965, the cantata *Slovo o Polku Igoreve*, 1966, 2 symphonies, and music for films.

Primakov, Evgenii Maksimovich
29.10.1928– . Economist, historian, politician.
Born in Kiev. Graduated from the Moscow Institute of Oriental Studies in 1953. Worked for the State Radio and Television Cttee., 1953–62. Joined the Communist Party in 1959. Reporter and editor at the Asian and African Desk of *Pravda*, 1962–70. From 1970, deputy director of the Institute of World Economy and International Relations in Moscow. In 1974, corresponding member of the USSR Academy of Sciences. Authority on Arab countries. From 1972, member of the editorial staff of *Mezhdunarodnye Konflikty*, and from 1975, of *Energeticheskii Krizis v Kapitalisticheskom Mire*. Director of the Institute from 1985. Senior foreign policy adviser of Gorbachev (Arab and Asian countries). His theory that the export of world revolution has become outdated and too costly to the Soviet economy and people, and that one should end excessive military expenditure in order to concentrate on reducing the wide economic gap with the USA, was accepted by Gorbachev's government.

Primakov, Vitalii Markovich
30.12.1897–11.6.1937. Military commander.
Born in Semenovka near Chernigov. Son of a teacher. Joined the Bolshevik Party, 1914. As a high school student, sent to Siberia for revolutionary propaganda, 1915. Returned after the February Revolution 1917. Bolshevik activist. At the end of 1917, joined a Red detachment. Took part in the storming of the Winter Palace. Organized a regiment of Red Cossacks, 1918. Became famous during the Civil War as the commander of the Red Cossacks Corps. Director of the Cavalry School in Leningrad, 1924–25. Sent to China, 1925–26. Military attaché in Afghanistan and Japan, 1927–30. Deputy commander of the Leningrad military district, 1935. Victim of Stalin's purge of the Red Army. Executed.

Primov, Kurban
1880–29.8.1965. Folk musician.
Born in Liulably, Azerbaidzhan. Pupil of the famous musician, Sadykhdzhan. Became a well-known tara musician (the tara is a balalaika type of instrument popular in Armenia, Azerbaidzhan and Georgia), and the first tara musician to perform solo at variety concerts. Composed and performed his own music. Died in Baku.

Prishvin, Mikhail Mikhailovich
4.2.1873–16.1.1954. Author.
Born in Khrushchevo near Elets. Son of a merchant. Educated at Elets High School, where one of his teachers was V. Rozanov. Studied at Riga Polytechnicum, 1893–97. Arrested for taking part in Marxist student circles. Graduated from Leipzig University as an agronomist. Became known before WWI for his stories

about his trips to the wilderness of Northern Russia (*V Kraiu Nepugannykh Ptits*, 1907, and *Za Volshebnym Kolobkom*, 1908). During WWI, front correspondent. In the 1920s, worked as a teacher. Continued his literary career. Achieved the reputation of being the best writer on nature in Russia, and became immensely popular. Remained totally outside of politics (and thus socialist realism), apart from once taking part in a collective writers' trip to the Belomor Canal concentration camps (led by Gorkii). Wrote a long autobiographical novel *Kashcheeva Tsep'*, which he began in the 1920s, published 1960. Collected works, in 6 volumes, 1956–57. Died in Moscow.

Pritsker, David Abramovich
24.6.1900–   . Composer.
Born in Kiev. Moved to Leningrad, where he studied music. Wrote mainly for films; also wrote over 200 popular songs, including songs for children.

Privalov, Nikolai Ivanovich
1868–26.9.1928. Musicologist, conductor, composer.
Born in Nizhnii Tagil. Author of the opera *Na Volge*. Wrote music for plays, such as *Il'ia Muromets* and *Skomorokhova Zhena*. Author of a manual for the balalaika, gusli and other similar folk instruments. Appeared in the music press. Died in Leningrad.

Prokhorov, Aleksandr Mikhailovich
11.7.1916–   . Physicist.
Born in Atherton in Australia. Son of a Russian revolutionary. Graduated from Leningrad University, 1939. Professor of Moscow University, 1959. Nobel Prize in physics, 1964. Editor-in-chief of the *Great Soviet Encyclopaedia*, 1969. Specialist in laser theory and technology.

Prokhorov, Sergei Aleksandrovich
20.6.1909–   . Conductor.
Born in Petersburg. Graduated from the Tallinn Conservatory. Conducted the operatic and symphonic orchestras of Tallinn and Leningrad, 1934–39. Worked with the Leningrad Malyi Theatre, 1959–62, where he

contributed to the production of various ballets.

Prokof'ev, Aleksandr Andreevich
1900–1971. Poet.
His rather simple poetry has been set to music by several Leningrad composers. A collection of these popular songs was published in 1950. Took care never to deviate from the party line, and was rewarded by large editions of his works.

Prokof'ev, Grigorii Petrovich
9.1.1884–3.12.1962. Pianist, music critic.
Born in Kozlov. Pupil of K. Igumnov. Taught at the Moscow Conservatory, 1911–24. From 1919, professor at the Conservatory. Founder and 1st director of the Music-Pedagogical Laboratory, 1931–41. Author of *Igra Na Fortepiano*, Moscow, 1928, and *Formirovanie Muzykanta-Ispolnitelia*, Moscow, 1956. Died in Moscow.

Prokof'ev, Oleg Sergeevich
12.1928–   . Artist.
Born in Paris. Returned to Moscow with his father, Sergei Prokof'ev in June 1936. Studied at the Moscow Art School, 1944–47. Pupil of Robert Falk, the Russian post-impressionist, 1949–52. From 1953–55, worked on his thesis on art in India. Worked at the Institute of History of the Arts, Moscow. Wrote *Indian Art*, 1964, and *The Art of South-East Asia*, 1967, but was never allowed to visit the countries of his research. Exhibited from 1958, including the Young Artists, Moscow, 1964. Left the Soviet Union for England. Married Camilla Gray, a researcher and writer on Russian art of the period from 1870–1930. Received the Gregory Fellowship in Painting at Leeds University, 1971–72. Lived in Paris, 1977–78. His wife died on a research trip to Soviet Georgia. Visited the USA, 1977, and turned to working on wood and metal sculptures. Exhibitions in the West: Gallery Coard, Paris, 1975, Surrey University, Guildford, the London Sadler's Wells Theatre, Northern Artists Gallery, Harrogate, 1977. Lives in Greenwich, London.

Prokof'ev, Sergei Sergeevich
23.4.1891–5.3.1953. Pianist, composer, conductor.
Born in Sontsovka, near Ekaterinoslav. Began composing music at the age of 5, and at 9 wrote his first opera. Graduated from the Petersburg Conservatory in composition, 1909. Pupil of A. Liadov and N. Rimskii-Korsakov. Graduated also in piano and conducting. Won the Anton Rubinstein Prize in 1914, playing his first piano concerto. Achieved fame as a pianist. From 1918 to 1933, lived abroad, in London, the USA and Paris. Returned to Moscow in 1934. Composed operas such as *The Love of Three Oranges*, 1919, *War and Peace*, 1941, revised, 1952, several ballets for Diaghilev (*Stal'noi Skok*, L. Massin, 1927), symphonies including the *Classical Symphony*, the *Scythian Suite*, music for films such as *Lieutenant Kizhe*, 1934, and *Aleksandr Nevskii* (dir. S. Eisenstein, 1938), piano concertos, songs and cantatas (e.g. that for the 29th anniversary of the October Revolution, 1946), *Peter and the Wolf*, 1936, a fairy tale, etc. In Stalin's USSR, was forced to contribute to the musical propaganda of the time: the oratorio *Na Strazhe Mira* etc. In 1948, Zhdanov attacked him for formalism and other 'bourgeois sins'. His works were marked by joie de vivre, embodied primitive folk motives, and showed the influence of futurism, structuralism and urbanism. He chose for his subjects Slavonic myths arranged for the stage, expressing the barbarism of primitive Russia. The harsh harmonies of his music were brought into relief by the roughness of the rhythms (themes from the *Russian Tales* of A. Afanas'ev, 1920, arranged for the stage by Prokof'ev and Sergei Diaghilev). Relied on the grotesque for effects of folk comedy (*Stal'noi Skok* etc). Besides having recourse to the grotesque and satirical, introduced an element of mystery and fantasy (*The Stone Flower*, 1949). He blended the realistic and fantastic elements while stressing Russian folk motives. Added to the traditions of classical ballet music the influence of modern symphonic music. This became apparent in the new production of *The Stone Flower*, 1953, staged in 1954, where the ballet came close to

pure drama. His music influenced a generation of musicians all over the world and also the art of Russian dancers such as Galina Ulanova and V. Preobrazhenskii. In 1945, appeared as conductor in Moscow for the last time. He was already ill, and retired to the village of Nikolina Gora near Zvenigorod. Died in Moscow.

Prokopiuk, Nikolai Arkhipovich
7.6.1902–11.6.1975.   State security official.
Born in the village of Samchiki in the Ukraine. In the Red Army during the Civil War, 1918–20, then joined the Cheka. Sent as an NKVD official to Spain during the Civil War. During WWII, head of the special Cheka group Okhotniki on a terror mission in German-occupied Ukraine, 1942–44. Sent as an NKVD official to help Mao Tse-tung in China, 1944–46. Retired, 1950. Died in Moscow.

Prokopovich, Sergei Nikolaevich
1871–1955. Economist, politician.
Born in Tsarskoe Selo. Graduated from Brussels University, 1899. Joined the SD Party abroad. Close to the Mensheviks, joined the Cadets for a short time 1904–5 (member of the Cen. Cttee.). Married E. Kuskova. Minister of Trade and Industry, later Minister of Food Supplies in the Provisional Government, 1917. Arrested by the Bolsheviks, but soon released. In 1921, with Kuskova, member of the Pomgol Cttee. (Pomoshch golodaiushchim). Expelled by Lenin, who said of him in 1922, 'He is more Bernsteinian than Bernstein himself'. Settled in Prague, later in Switzerland. Continued to write on Russian economic problems. Died in Geneva.

Promyslov, Vladimir Fedorovich
15.7.1908–   . Politician.
Fitter at Moscow Construction Trust. Joined the Communist Party in 1928. Trade union posts, 1930–33. Promoted director of a construction project, then deputy head with the Main Board for Planning the Construction of Hydroelectric Plants, 1933–38. Worked for Moscow City Party Cttee., 1938–39. High positions

with the USSR People's Commissariat for Heavy Machine Construction, worked for the USSR Ministry of the Tank Industry and Main Munitions Industry Construction Board, 1939–46. Deputy chairman of Moscow City Executive Cttee., 1949–51 and 1953–54. Graduated from Moscow Institute of Construction Engineers, 1956. Head of the Main Board for Housing Construction and Civil Engineering with Moscow City Soviet. 1st Deputy Chairman of Moscow City Soviet, 1955–59. Chairman of Moscow City Soviet from 1959. Chairman of the State Construction Cttee. of the RSFSR Council of Ministers, 1959–63. Member of the Central Auditing Cttee., 1961–66. Deputy, then member of the Foreign Affairs Cttee. of the USSR Supreme Soviet from 1962. Member of the Cen. Cttee. of the CPSU from 1966. Fired by Gorbachev for failing to submit annual accounts for the 30 years he was in charge of the city of Moscow administration (MOSSOVET).

Proshian, Prosh Perchevich
1883–16.12.1918. Politician.
Born in Ashtarak in Armenia. Son of an Armenian writer. As a student in Odessa, joined the SR Party. After the 1905 Revolution, exiled to Siberia. Escaped from East Siberia. In 1913, arrested and sent back to Siberia. Escaped abroad. Returned to Russia after the February Revolution 1917. Left-wing SR, main proponent of a coalition with the Bolsheviks, twice expelled from the SR Party. Member of the Cen. Cttee. of the left SRs. In the first Soviet (coalition government), Minister for Mail and Telegraph. In Mar. 1918, together with other left SRs, left the coalition in protest against the Brest peace treaty. One of the leaders of the left SR revolt in Moscow in the summer of 1918. After their defeat, went underground. Died of typhoid in Moscow.

Proshliakov, Aleksei Ivanovich
1901–1973. Marshal.
Joined the Red Army, 1920, and the Bolshevik Party, 1921. Military engineering commands before WWII, and during the war, at different fronts. Deputy Commander of Soviet Forces in Germany, 1945–49. Gra-

duated from the Academy of the General Staff, 1951. Commander of Military Engineers of the Soviet Army, 1952–65.

Protazanov, Iakov Aleksandrovich
4.2.1881–8.8.1945. Film director.
One of the first Russian film-makers. Graduated from a Commercial School. Came in to the film industry, 1907. His debut was *Bakhchisaraiskii Fontan*, 1909. Specialized in adaptations of Russian classics. Made about 80 films, including *Voina i Mir*, *Pikovaia Dama*, *Nikolai Stavrogin* and *Besy*. *Pikovaia Dama*, 1916, and *Otets Sergii*, 1918, became his best-known films. Emigrated in 1920, and worked at various film studios in Berlin and Paris. Experienced many difficulties in his professional life while in emigration, and returned to the USSR, 1923. Made *Aelita*, 1924 (an adaptation of an A. Tolstoy story). Employed by the Mezhrabpom-Rus' Film Studio, made many films, including *Zakroishchik iz Torzhka*, 1925, *Protsess o Trekh Mil'onakh*, 1926 and *Prazdnik Sviatogo Iorgena*, 1930. All his films have become Russian silent classics. His last film was the comedy *Nasreddin v Bukhare*, 1943. His heritage has been carefully researched and preserved.

Protopopov, Aleksandr Dmitrievich
30.12.1866–1.1.1918. Politician.
Member of the Oktiabrist Party. Member of the 3rd and 4th Dumas. Prominent member of the Progressive Bloc. Deputy chairman of the Duma, 1914. In Sept. 1916, unexpectedly agreed to join the government as Minister of the Interior. Denounced by his former colleagues in the Duma as the worst of traitors. Had the confidence of the Tsar and especially the Empress. On good terms with Rasputin. According to his political enemies, had shown signs of mental instability. Completely lost his nerve at the moment of the February Revolution, 1917, came himself to the Duma to be arrested, and was taken into custody by Kerenskii. Imprisoned in the Peter and Paul Fortress. Immediately after the Bolshevik take-over, shot by order of the Cheka.

Protopopov, Vladimir Vasil'evich
13.12.1908– . Musicologist.
Professor at the Moscow Conservatory. Author of *Ivan Susanin Glinki, Muzykal'no-Teoreticheskoe Issledovanie*, Moscow, 1961, and *Istoriia Polifonii v ee Vazhneishikh Iavleniiakh*, Moscow, 1962.

Prozumenshchikova, Galina Nikolaevna (Stepanova)
26.11.1948– . Athlete.
Born in Sebastopol'. Honoured Master of Sports (swimming), 1964. With the Central Sports Club of the Army. Graduated in journalism from Moscow University, 1976. USSR champion, 1963–72. Olympic champion, 1964. European champion, 1966 and 1970.

Prudskova, Valentina Aleksandrovna
27.12.1938– . Athlete.
Born in Ershov, Saratov Oblast'. Honoured Master of Sports (fencing), 1960. With Saratov Burevestnik. Graduated from the Saratov Polytechnical Institute, 1962. Engineer. World champion, 1958, 1961 and 1965. Olympic champion, 1960.

Pshennikov, Petr Stepanovich
1895–1941. Lt.-general.
Joined the Red Guards (workers' revolutionary armed detachments), 1917, and the Red Army, 1918. Took part in the Civil War as a brigade commander. Graduated from courses for senior officers of the Red Army, 1925. Fell in action.

Pstygo, Ivan Ivanovich
1918– . Marshal.
Joined the Red Army, 1936, and the Bolshevik Party, 1941. Fighter pilot during WWII. Graduated from the Academy of the General Staff, 1957. Deputy Commander of the Soviet Air Force, 1967. High posts in the Ministry of Defence, 1977–83.

Psurtsev, Nikolai Demianovich
1900–1980. Col.-general.
Joined the Red Army, 1918. Joined the Bolshevik Party, 1919. Took part in the Civil War as a communications specialist. Graduated from the Military Electro-technical Academy of the Red Army, 1934. Commander of the military communications system at the Northwestern front during the Soviet-Finnish war. Deputy head of the military communications system in 1940 and during WWII. Minister of Communications of the USSR, 1948–75. Non-voting member of the Cen. Cttee. of the CPSU, 1961–76.

Ptushko, Aleksandr Lukich
19.4.1900–6.3.1973. Film director.
Prominent puppet-cinema director. Worked as a journalist, actor and interior designer. Entered the film industry, 1927. Made over 70 puppet films. His major work was *Novyi Gulliver*, 1935, in which he used some 1,500 puppets he had made himself. Specialized in adaptations of Russian fairy-tales and stories by foreign writers. His film *Kamennyi Tsvetok* received a prize at the 1946 Cannes Film Festival, while *Sadko*, 1953, was a prize-winner at the Venice Film Festival. Adopted nearly all of Pushkin's stories for the puppet cinema. Trained a generation of puppeteers.

Pubin, Vladimir Il'ich
5.8.1924– . Composer.
Born in Moscow. Author of the opera *Tri Tolstiaka* (produced in 1957). Writes children's songs, and pieces for film, theatre, and television.

Puchkov, Nikolai Georgievich
30.1.1930– . Athlete.
Born in Moscow. Honoured Master of Sports (hockey), 1954. Goalkeeper with the USSR international team, 1952–62. Member of the CPSU, 1954. From 1963, with the Leningrad Armed Forces Club. Honorary Coach of the USSR, 1971. USSR champion, 1951–61. European champion, 1954–60. World champion, 1954 and 1956. Olympic champion, 1956.

Pudovkin, Vsevolod Illarionovich
28.2.1893–30.6.1953. Film director.
One of the classics of the Soviet cinema. Was studying mathematics at Moscow University when WWI broke out. In 1915, became a soldier and soon afterwards, a POW in Germany. Returned to Russia, 1919. In 1920, entered the State Film School (VGIK). First under V. Gardin, later under Lev Kuleshov. While a student, worked on various films as a scriptwriter, stage designer and actor. After graduation in 1925, joined the Mezhrabpom-Rus' Film Studio. His first major work was an adaptation of M. Gorkii's *Mother*, 1926, which later became an internationally-known classic of the early period of Soviet cinema. 2 films followed — *Konets Sankt Peterburga*, 1927, and *Potomok Chingiz Khana*. Both films became internationally recognized as masterpieces. Made *Dezertir*, 1933. In the late 30s and 40s, forced to make academic biographical films with strong nationalistic overtones — *Minin i Pozharskii*, 1939, and *Suvorov*, 1941, which Stalin himself had ordered when war broke out. His last film was *Vozvrashchenie Vasiliia Bortnikova*, 1953, based on G. Nikolaeva's socialist-realist novel *Zhatva*.

Pugachev, Semen Andreevich
1889–1943. Military commander.
Graduated from the Academy of the General Staff, 1914. On active service during WWI as a captain. Joined the Red Army, 1918. Staff officer during the Civil War. Commander of the Turkestan front, 1923–24, thereafter commander of the Caucasian Army. Deputy chief-of-staff of the Red Army, 1925. Head of the Military Transport Academy of the Red Army, 1932. Joined the Bolshevik Party, 1934.

Pugacheva, Alla
1940?– . Variety singer.
Pop idol and queen of the variety stage. Has made millions of records which Melodia, the official Soviet record company, sells with great success. In 1983, the composer A. Shnitke invited her to sing his new oratorio *The History of Doctor Faust*, with Gennadii Rozhdestvenskii conducting. The Moscow Tchaikovskii Concert Hall sold all their tickets immediately, but at the last moment the oratorio was banned. According to Soviet musical sources, the cultural authorities did not think that her pop style was suitable for the performance of a classical work. Lives in Moscow, and by all accounts is one of the few

Soviet millionairesses. Visited Israel in the late 1980s and gave successful performances there.

Pugo, Boris Karlovich
1937– . Politician, state security official.
Probably born in Russia, son of the Latvian communist Karlis Pugo, at a time when the Latvian Communist Party was still illegal. His father was one of the leaders responsible for the establishment of Soviet rule in Latvia (died in Riga in 1955). Boris's career began in the Komsomol in Latvia. Graduated from the Riga Polytechnical Institute, 1960. Several senior posts including 1st secretary and member of the Bureau of the Cen. Cttee. of the Latvian Komsomol, 1969–70. Senior party posts throughout the 1970s. Deputy chairman of the Committee of State Security of the Latvian SSR, 1977–80. In Apr. 1977, fired from his post as candidate member of the Bureau of the Cen. Cttee. of the Latvian CP. Regained his position in Nov. 1980. Chairman of the Latvian KGB, Nov. 1980. Major-general of the KGB, 1981. 1st secretary of the Latvian CP from Apr. 1984.

Pukhal'skii, Vladimir Viacheslavovich
2.4.1848–23.2.1933. Pianist, composer.
Born in Minsk. Pupil of T. Leshetitskii. Moved to Kiev in 1876. Director of a music school in Kiev. Director and professor at the Kiev Conservatory. Educated a generation of musicians, among them Vladimir Horovits, G. Kogan, A. Brailovskii and B. Iavorskii. Author of an opera and many other pieces. Died in Kiev.

Pukst, Grigorii Konstantinovich
27.11.1900–12.11.1960. Composer.
Born in Gomel'. Taught at the Minsk Conservatory. Author of 3 operas, a cantata, and 6 symphonies. Specialized in music for children's theatre. Died in Minsk.

Pul'ver, Lev Mikhailovich
18.12.1883–1949. Viola player, conductor, composer.
Born in Verkhnedneprovsk. Member of the orchestra of the Bolshoi Theatre, first as a violinist, and later as viola soloist, 1909–23. Conductor and music director at the Moscow Jewish Theatre, 1922–49. Wrote music using Jewish folk motives and Jewish classical writers' works. Also wrote music for films, and songs. Disappeared from the musical scene after 1949 at the time of the anti-Semitic campaign. Regarded by critics as a classic of Jewish music.

Puni, Ivan Albertovich
1894–1956. Painter.
Modernist painter, lived in Paris before WW1, and returned there after the October Revolution 1917. Well-known figure in the Paris art world.

Punin, Nikolai Nikolaevich
1888–1953. Art historian.
Husband of A. Akhmatova. Arrested, 1935. Victim of Stalin's purges, died in Gulag exile.

Punkin, Iakov Grigor'evich
8.12.1921– . Athlete.
Born in Zaporozh'e. Graduated from the Kiev School of Trainers, 1940. Honoured Master of Sports (wrestling), 1952. From 1954, with Zaporozh'e Metallurg. USSR champion, 1959–51 and 1954–54.

Purkaev, Maksim Alekseevich
1894–1953. General.
Joined the Red Army, 1918, and the Bolshevik Party, 1919. Took part in the Civil War. Graduated from the Frunze Military Academy, 1936. Took part in operations against the Germans early in WWII, and from 1943, in the Far East. After WWII, held high commands in the Far East. Head of Administration of the Higher Educational Establishments of the Ministry of Defence, 1952.

Pushkarev, Sergei Germanovich
8.8.1888–1973? Historian.
Born near Kursk. Graduated from Khar'kov University, studied at Heidelberg and Leipzig universities. During the Civil War, with the White Army, later with the Black Sea Navy. Evacuated with the White forces, 1921. Settled in Prague, and taught at the Prague Russian University. Published historical research in Russian and Czech. At the end of WWII, in DP camps in West Germany. Taught in schools for Russian refugees. Moved to the USA, 1949. Professor of Russian history at Yale, Fordham and Columbia universities. Worked in Yale Library, preparing 3 volumes of Russian historical sources, 1957–72. Published several books on historical subjects in Russian and English and many articles in historical magazines.

Pushkin, Aleksandr Ivanovich
7.9.1907–20.3.1970. Ballet dancer.
Born in Mikulino, Tver' Oblast'. Trained at the private school of N. G. Legat. Graduated from the Leningrad Choreographic School, 1925. Pupil of V. I. Ponomarev. With the Kirov Theatre, 1925–53. Taught at the Leningrad Choreographic School from 1932. In charge of the Specialized Class at the Kirov Theatre from 1953. Trained several generations of outstanding dancers. Iurii Grigorovich and R. Nureev were among his pupils.

Pushkov, Venedikt Venediktovich
31.10.1896–1970? Composer.
Born in Saratov. Taught at music schools in Leningrad, and then at the Conservatory. Author of an opera and many songs. Worked for the film industry (over 50 films) and in the theatre.

Putna, Vitovt Kazimirovich
1893–1937. Military commander.
On active service during WWI as a captain. Joined the Bolshevik Party, 1917, and the Red Army, 1918. Took part in the Civil War as a divisional commander. High commands in the Far East, 1931–34. Military attaché in Britain, 1934–36. Recalled and liquidated by Stalin.

Puzanov, Nikolai Vasil'evich
7.4.1938– . Athlete.
Born in Kyshtym, Cheliabinskaia Oblast'. Honoured Master of Sports (biathlon), 1968. Graduated from the Leningrad Institute of Physical Culture, 1970. Member of the CPSU, 1978. With the Leningrad Armed

Forces Club. USSR champion, 1963, 1967 and 1969. Olympic champion, 1968.

Puzyrevskii, Aleksei Il'ich
29.7.1855–5.1917. Musicologist.
Born in St. Petersburg. Taught at the Petersburg Conservatory, 1893–1917. From 1907, professor. Author of many theoretical manuals. Also wrote articles on the RMO (Russian Music Society), 1909. Author of a book about the Petersburg Conservatory, published in 1912 (revised with L. Saketti in 1914). Died in Petersburg.

Pyshnov, Vladimir Sergeevich
1901–1984. Aviation scientist.
Joined the Red Army, 1920. Graduated from the Zhukovskii Air Force Academy, 1925. Professor of the Zhukovskii Academy, 1926. Specialist in aerodynamics, wrote on the flight characteristics of aeroplanes. Lt.-general, 1946. Chairman of the Aircraft Section of the Scientific Cttee. of the Soviet Armed Forces, 1949–68.

R

Raab, Vil'gel'mina Ivanovna (b. Bilik)
1848–23.11.1917. Singer.
Born in Austerlitz. Pupil of A. Bukhholts-Falconi and G. Nissen-Saloman. Soloist at the Mariinskii Theatre, 1871–85. Teacher from 1884. From 1901, professor at the Petersburg Conservatory. Died in Petrograd.

Raaben, Lev Nikolaevich
1.1.1913–   . Musicologist.
Born in Groznyi. Lecturer at the Leningrad Conservatory. Works: *Skripichnye i Violonchel'nye Proizvedeniia P. I. Chaikovskogo*, Moscow, 1961; *Sovetskaia Kamerno-Instrumetal'naia Muzyka*, Leningrad, 1963.

Rabin, Oskar Iakovlevich
1928–   . Artist.
Born in Moscow. Studied at the Riga Academy of Arts, then at the Moscow Surikov Art Institute. Expelled for his non-conformist views. Worked as a manual labourer. In the mid-1960s, became one of the USSR's leading unofficial artists. Was showered with private orders from the foreign press and diplomatic corps, and also from private Russian collectors. One of the organizers of the so-called Bulldozer Exhibition in Moscow in Sep. 1974, which received world-wide publicity. Threatened physically by the KGB. Forced to emigrate. Left the USSR with his artist wife Valentina Kropivnitskaia. Lives in Paris. Stripped of Soviet citizenship. Memoirs: *Tri Zhizni: Kniga Vospominanii*, NY, 1986.

Rabinovich, Boris
1938–30.3.1988. Artist.
Born in Leningrad. Painted biblical images of Jewish life. Emigrated and settled in Vienna, 1978. Many exhibitions in European galleries. Under Gorbachev's glasnost, went to Leningrad on a short visit. The day after his arrival, died from a heart attack (brought on, according to some, by an excess of emotion).

Rabinovich, David Abramovich
7.8.1900–   . Musicologist.
Born in Khar'kov. Moved to Moscow. Author of many music articles. Works include *Dimitrii Shostakovich. Kompozitor*, Moscow, 1959 and *Portrety Pianistov*, Moscow, 1962.

Rabinovich, Isaak Moiseevich
11.3.1894–4.10.1961. Stage-designer.
Born in Kiev. Studied at the Kiev School of Art, 1906–12. Worked for stage productions in the Moscow, Leningrad and Kiev theatres. Painted the scenery for various ballets, including *The Sleeping Beauty* (choreographers A.M. Messerer and A. I. Chekrygin) at the Bolshoi Theatre, 1936. Died in Moscow.

Rabinovich, Nikolai Semenovich
7.10.1908–   . Conductor.
Born in St. Petersburg. Brother of the musicologist Aleksandr Rabinovich. Pupil of N. Mal'ko and A. Gauk. Conductor of the Leningrad Philharmonic, and professor at the Leningrad Conservatory.

Radek, Karl Bernhardovich (Sobelsohn),
1885–1939. Politician, journalist.
Born in Galicia (then in the Austro-Hungarian Empire). Member of the Polish and German SD Parties. During the 1905 Revolution, moved to Warsaw (then in the Russian Empire), then to Berlin. After a quarrel with Rosa Luxemburg, expelled from the German SD Party. At the beginning of WWI, went to Switzerland, became close to Lenin and took part in the Zimmerwald and Kienthal conferences. Articles concocted by him about alleged Russo-German peace negotiations were used by Miliukov in the Duma to attack the Tsarina and set in motion the revolutionary process in 1917. Left Switzerland through Germany in Lenin's sealed train. Member of the Bolshevik Party from 1917. Remained in Stockholm with Ganetskii as a Bolshevik agent. After the October Revolution, participated in important missions. Took part in the Brest-Litovsk peace negotiations. Attempted to organize a communist uprising in Germany in 1918. Arrested, but released soon thereafter. Leader of the left wing of the Bolsheviks in 1918. Made several secret trips to Germany in early 1920s, again tried to organize a revolution there in 1923. Member of the Cen. Cttee. of the Bolshevik Party. Member of the Executive Cttee. of the Comintern. Active in the international communist movement, rector of Sun Yat-sen communist university in Moscow for Chinese and other Far Eastern students. Chief foreign affairs commentator in the Soviet press, regarded as the best communist journalist in the world. Leading member of the Trotskyist opposition in 1923. Expelled from the party and exiled to the Urals in 1927. Acknowledged his mistakes, reinstated in 1929. Arrested in 1936. At the trial, gave evidence against other defendants. This gained him 10 years imprisonment, instead of a death penalty. Died in the camps According to *Moscow News*, 1988, was killed by a criminal Gulag inmate. Rehabilitated 13 June 1988.

Radimov, Pavel Aleksandrovich
1887–1962? Artist.
Landscape and genre painter and

poet. Studied art with the artist N. Feshin in his native town, Kazan'. Graduated from the Historico-Philological Faculty of Kazan' University in 1911. Exhibited from 1912: Spring Exhibition of the Petersburg Academy of Arts, 1912–14, TPKHV, 1911–18, 1922–23, MOLKH, 1913, the Association of Artists of Revolutionary Russia, Moscow, 1922–23. Other exhibitions: all in Moscow until 1960. Personal exhibitions: Moscow, 1927 (Radimov, 15 Years in Literature and Art), Abramtsevo, 1933, Moscow, 1934, Ashkhabad, 1935, Zagorsk, 1938, Kalinin, 1939, Cheboksary, 1942, Moscow, 1943, 1950, Ashkhabad, 1951, Noginsk, 1954, Abramtsevo, 1957, Zagorsk, 1958.

Radina, Liubov' Petrovna
1838–3.1917. Ballerina.
Sister of Sofia Radina (1830–70), character dancer. Graduated from the Petersburg Theatre School, 1855. With the Mariinskii Theatre, 1855–85. Died in Petrograd.

Radlov, Ernest Leopoldovich
20.11.1854–28.12.1928. Philosopher.
Born in Petersburg. Graduated from Petersburg University, studied at Berlin and Leipzig. Personal friend and follower of Vladimir Solov'ev. Director of the Petersburg Public Library, 1917–24. Translated Aristotle and Hegel into Russian. Died in Leningrad.

Radunskii, Aleksandr Ivanovich
3.8.1912–   . Ballet dancer, choreographer.
Born in Moscow. Graduated from the Moscow Choreographic School, 1930. With the Bolshoi Theatre, 1930–62. Distinguished for his comic talent and gift for miming and impersonation. Choreographer, from 1937. Choreographer and coach at the Bolshoi Theatre, 1949–62. Choreographer with the Aleksandrov Soviet Army Ensemble of Song and Dance.

Radzhabi, Iunus (Radzhabov)
17.1.1896–1972? Musician, composer.
Born in Tashkent. Artistic director of the Uzbek Folk Orchestra, 1937–53. Major musical figure in Uzbekistan. Wrote pieces for his orchestra, and for radio. Many recordings have been made of his arrangements of Uzbek folk songs.

Radzievskii, Aleksei Ivanovich
13.8.1911–1979. General.
Born in Uman'. Graduated from a cavalry school, 1931. Member of the CPSU, 1931. Graduated from the Frunze Military Academy, 1938, and the General Staff Academy, 1941. Senior command posts at the front, 1941–45. Commander of the Northern Forces Group, 1950–52. Commander of Turkmen military district, 1952–53. Commander of Armoured and Mechanized Troops, 1953–54. Commander of Odessa military district, 1954–59. 1st deputy head of the General Staff Academy, 1959–68. Head of Central Administration of Military Educational Institutions of the USSR Ministry of Defence, 1968–69. Head of Frunze Military Academy, 1968–78.

Rafalskii, Sergei Mil'evich (pen name – Skii)
1895–1981. Journalist.
Born in the Ukraine. Studied at Petrograd University. Emigrated during the Civil War. Continued his studies in Prague, also wrote poetry. Later moved to Paris. After WWII, tried to return to the Soviet Union, but was refused entry. In the 1960s and 1970s, leading writer with the Russian newspaper *Russkaia Mysl'* (La Pensée Russe). Became a mentor of Soviet dissidents arriving in the West in the 1970s. Died in Paris.

Ragulin, Aleksandr Pavlovich
5.5.1941–   . Athlete.
Born in Moscow. Honoured Master of Sports (hockey), 1963. With the Central Sports Club of the Army. Graduated from the Moscow Oblast' Pedagogical Institute, 1966. Member of the CPSU, 1969. USSR champion, 1963–73. European champion, 1963–70 and 1973. World champion, 1963–71 and 1973. Olympic champion, 1964, 1968 and 1972.

Rahr, Lev Aleksandrovich
1910?–8.11.1980. Journalist, publisher.
An active member of the emigré political party, NTS. Head of the publishing house Posev in Frankfurt-on-Main. Died in a car crash in Cologne.

Rahya, Eino
1885–1936. Revolutionary.
Finnish revolutionary, who served as Lenin's bodyguard in 1917. Helped Lenin to safety after the failed coup attempt by the Bolsheviks, July 1917. Was the linkman between Lenin and the Cen. Cttee. of the Party in Petrograd, Aug.–Nov. 1917, while the Bolsheviks were preparing to take power. Took part in the Civil War, served in the Red Army. Retired, 1932.

Raikh, Zinaida Nikolaevna
1902–7.1939. Actress.
Daughter of Nikolai Andreevich Raikh, a railway worker from Silesia, and Anna Ivanovna Viktorova, an impoverished gentlewoman. Worked as secretary of the SR newspaper *Delo Naroda*, where she met her first husband, Sergei Esenin. They had 2 children, but soon afterwards separated. (According to Kostia, their son, she was disliked by Esenin's circle for her infidelities. Esenin even doubted whether Kostia was his son). Soon married V. Meyerhold, who spent a considerable amount of time turning her into his leading actress. Their 4-room apartment on Briusovskii Pereulok became an international salon. Among her guests were Erwin Piscator, Guillaume Apollinaire, John Mason Brown and the head of the Moscow bureau of Associated Press, William Reswick. Russian celebrities included Chekhov's widow, Olga Leonardovna Knipper-Chekhova, V. Mayakovsky, Ivan Moskvin, Il'ia Sel'vinskii, K. Stanislavskii and A. Lunacharskii. But there were always other guests: senior GPU officers such as Iagoda, Agranov and Prokof'ev. W. Reswick, in his book *I Dreamed Revolution*, mentioned that on one occasion a guest, apparently a member of the secret police, tried to involve him in a spy-ring. Among party figures were Enukidze, Trotsky, Bukharin,

Kamenev and Zinov'ev. (All these connections were later used against Meyerhold.) She was an extremely attractive woman and cleverly used her husband's passion for her to obtain what she wanted, such as trips to Baden-Baden, Karlsbad, Venice, and Paris. Served as a decoy for the GPU to attract important foreign visitors. Always surrounded by male admirers, which drove Meyerhold to utter despair. A few weeks after his arrest and disappearance, she was found dead in their flat. Her eyes were gouged out, and there were 42 stab wounds in her body. By all accounts she was silenced because she knew and talked too much.

Raikin, Arkadii Isaakovich
24.10.1911–12.1987. Variety entertainer, popular comedian.
Enormously popular entertainer. Born in Riga, Latvia. Graduated from the Leningrad Theatrical School in 1935. Actor at the Leningrad TRAM and Lenin Komsomol Theatre. In 1939, won the All-Union Estrada Competition in Moscow. Actor, later artistic director of the Leningrad Theatre of Variety and Miniature. The highest point of his career was during the 1960s when television made him a household name. Travelled all over the Soviet Union. Shows in Moscow and Leningrad drew huge crowds. His satirical criticism of Soviet bureaucracy became folklore.

Raiskii, Nazarii Grigor'evich
26.10.1875–4.10.1958. Singer.
Born in Liublin. Pupil of J. Nuvelli. From 1900, concert singer. From 1902, opera singer. With the Zimin Opera, 1904–08. Professor at the Moscow Conservatory, 1919–29 and 1939–53. Sergei Lemeshev was one of his many pupils. Died in Moscow.

Rait, Rita Iakovlevna (Wright, Rita)
1898–after 1981? Translator.
Close friend of Mayakovsky and the Briks. Translated into German Mayakovsky's *Misteria-Bouffe* for the 3rd Congress of the Komintern in the summer of 1921.

Raizman, Iulii Iakovlevich
15.12.1903–   . Film director.
Veteran director, assistant to Protazanov, one of the founders of silent Russian cinema. In 1924, graduated from Moscow University Department of Literature and Art. His directorial debut was *The Ring*, 1927, a story about a trial, which made a great impact during the NEP period. Became known for his comedies *The Pilots*, 1935, and *Mashenka*, 1942. Other films: *Forced Labour* (Gosvoenkino, 1928), *The Earth Thirsts* (Vostokkino, 1930), *The Last Night* (Mosfilm, 1936), *Virgin Soil Upturned* (Mosfilm, 1939), *Moscow Sky* (Mosfilm, 1944), *Berlin* (documentary, Central Documentary Film Studios, 1945), *The Communist* (Mosfilm, 1957), *What If It Is Love?* (Mosfilm, 1961), *Your Contemporary* (Mosfilm, 1968), *A Strange Woman* (Mosfilm, 1977).

Rakhals, Vasilii Aleksandrovich
1890–15.6.1942. Stage designer.
Entered the film industry, 1915. Worked as a scenic artist on S. Eisenstein's *Stachka* and *The Battleship Potemkin*. Other films include *Bukhta Smerti*, *Staroe i Novoe* and *Predatel'*.

Rakhlin, Natan Grigor'evich
10.1.1906–   . Conductor.
Born in Snovsk, Chernigov Gouvt. Pupil of V. Berdiaev and I. Orlov. Conductor of the State Symphony Orchestra of the Ukrainian SSR, 1941–45, and of the State Symphony Orchestra of the USSR from 1952.

Rakhmadiev, Erkegali Rakhmadievich
1.8.1932–   . Composer.
Born in the Semipalatinskaia Oblast'. Son of the well-known folk singer R. Zhabykbaev. Studied at the Tchaikovskii Music School in Alma-Ata in the department of folk instruments and theory of historic music. Entered the Alma-Ata Conservatory, 1952. Pupil of E. Bursilovskii. Graduated, 1957. Followed the specialized course of G. Litinskii in Moscow, 1957–58. Artistic director of the Kazakh Philharmonic Orchestra from 1959. Chief administrator of the Arts Department of the Ministry of Culture of the Kazakh SSR, 1961–65.

Director of the Kazakh Opera and Ballet, 1966, of the Folklore Office from 1958, and of the Alma-Ata Conservatory, 1967–75. Lecturer from 1968, and professor from 1979. Composed mainly operas.

Rakhmaninov, Sergei Vasil'evich
1.4.1873–28.3.1943. Composer, pianist, conductor.
Born on his own estate, Oneg, in the Novgorod Gouvt. Taught music by his mother from the age of 4. Entered the Petersburg Conservatory, 1882. Pupil of V. Demianskii. Studied for 4 years in Moscow from 1885 under N. Zverev. Further study at the Moscow Conservatory. Pupil of A. Ziloti, S. Taneev and A. Arenskii. Graduated in piano playing, 1891, and in composition, 1892. Began his concert career in 1892. Teacher, and later Inspector of Music, at the Mariinskii School and at the Ekaterininskii and Elizavetinskii institutes from 1893. Conductor of the Moscow Private Orchestra of S. Mamontov, 1897–98. Conductor with the Bolshoi Theatre, 1904–06. From 1906–09, lived in Dresden in winter, and in Russia in summer. Appeared as pianist and conductor in various European cities. Made his first appearance in the USA in 1909. Inspector of Russian Music with the Chief Administration of the Russkoe Muzykal'noe Obshchestvo, 1909–12. Guest appearance in Sweden, autumn 1917. Remained abroad as an emigré. Lived in Paris, then in Switzerland and New York. Settled in America, 1935. Collaborated with M. Fokin for the scenario of the ballet *Paganini*. His ballet *Zimniaia Noch'* was performed by the Ballet Rambert in London, 1948. Gained the reputation of being the greatest pianist in the world. Followed the tradition of classical Russian music. Opponent of formalism. Musical heir of Tchaikovskii. Died in Beverley Hills, California.

Rakhmankulova, Mar'iam Mannapovna
20.11.1901–   . Singer, composer.
Born in Kazan'. Mezzo-soprano Tatar singer. Pupil of E. Petrenko. Soloist at the Kazan' Tatar Opera and Ballet Theatre, 1938–59. Author of orchestral music and folk songs.

Rakita, Mark Semenovich
22.7.1938– . Athlete.
Born in Moscow. Honoured Master of Sports (fencing), 1964. With the Moscow Oblast' Armed Forces Club. Graduated from the Daghestan Pedagogical Institute, 1969. Member of the CPSU, 1975. Honorary Coach of the USSR, 1979. USSR champion, 1962 and 1969–70. Olympic champion, 1964 and 1968. World champion, 1965–71.

Rakov, Nikolai Petrovich
14.3.1908– . Composer.
Born in Kaluga. Professor at the Moscow Conservatory. Wrote several symphonies, concertos for piano and violin, romances and other pieces.

Rakov, Vasilii Ivanovich
1909– . Major-general.
Joined the Red Army, 1928, and the Bolshevik Party, 1932. Graduated from the Naval Academy, 1942. During WWII, navy bomber commander. Graduated from the Academy of the General Staff, 1946. Professor at the Naval Academy, 1948–71.

Raksha, Iurii Mikhailovich
2.12.1937–1.9.1980. Stage designer.
Graduated from the VGIK, 1963. Chief designer of A. Kurosawa's *Dersu Uzala*, a Soviet-Japanese co-production, and of L. Shepit'ko's *Voskhozhdenie*.

Rakutin, Konstantin Ivanovich
1901–1941. Major-general, state security officer.
Joined the Bolshevik Party, 1922. In the 1920s and 1930s, held high command posts in state security military detachments (NKVD). Army commander at the beginning of WWII. Fell in action.

Rall, Iurii Fedorovich
1890–1948. Vice-admiral.
Graduated from the Naval Corps, 1912. Joined the Red Navy, 1918. Took part in the Civil War. Head of training of the Soviet Navy, 1935–41. Chief-of-staff of the Baltic fleet, 1941. Joined the CPSU, 1942. Naval commander of Kronstadt, 1943. After WWII, professor at the Naval Academy.

Ramishvili, Nini Shalvovna
19.1.1910– . Ballerina, choreographer.
Born in Baku. Studied at the ballet school in Tbilisi under M. I. Perini, 1922–27. Leading dancer at the Paliashvili Theatre, 1927–36. Appeared as a leading dancer in operas, and in the Georgian Philharmonic Society's Folk Dance Ensemble, 1936–39. Leading dancer in the NKVD USSR Ensemble of Song and Dance, 1939–41. With the Georgian Philharmonic Society, 1942–45. Organizer (with I. I. Sukhishvili), leading dancer and artistic director of the Georgian Folk Dance Ensemble, 1945.

Ramm, Valentina Iosifovna
22.10.1888–1969? Singer, composer.
Born in Khar'kov. Moved to Moscow where she studied singing and composition at the Moscow Conservatory. Author of ballets, including *Skazka o Mertvoi Tsarevne i Semi Bogatyriakh*, 1954. Also wrote children's choral pieces and romances.

Ramonova, Tamara Evgen'evna
26.3.1921– . Choreographer, producer.
Born in Moscow. Graduated from the Moscow Choreographic School, 1940. Pupil of M. A. Kozhukhov. With the Bolshoi Theatre, 1941, and the Paliashvili Theatre in Tbilisi, 1942–43. Graduated from the GITIS Choreographic Department, 1950. Pupil of R. V. Zakharov. Choreographer and producer with the Stanislavskii and Nemirovich-Danchenko Theatre, 1950. Worked in the theatres of Novosibirsk, 1950–51, and Tallinn, 1951–53. Lecturer, 1953. Worked in Perm', 1953–59, and in Voronezh 1961–62. Directed dances for opera and concert programmes. Taught choreography at the Gnesin Music School from 1962.

Randpere, Valdo
4.2.1958– . Lawyer, Komsomol official.
Estonian. Born in Tallinn. Graduated in law from Tartu University in 1982. Legal adviser to 1st Deputy Minister of Justice of the Estonian Soviet Republic. From Oct. 1983, the instructor of Cen. Cttee. of the Komsomol of Estonia in the Department of Propaganda and Culture. Defected to Sweden in Aug. 1984 with his wife, the singer Leila Miller.

Rapgof, Evgenii Pavlovich
25.8.1859–17.3.1919. Pianist, teacher.
Born in St. Petersburg. Pupil of V. Pukhal'skii, K. Fan-Ark and T. Leshetitskii. Founder of the Music Drama Courses in Petersburg, 1882. Concert pianist. Later taught at the Petersburg Conservatory. Died in Petrograd.

Raskol'nikov, Fedor Fedorovich (real name – Il'in)
1892–9.1939. Revolutionary, politician.
Leader of the Bolshevik sailors, and head of the Kronstadt Party Cttee. in 1917. Took part in the Bolshevik take-over in Oct. 1917. Secretary of *Pravda*. Appointed head of the Red Navy. Later given several important diplomatic assignments, including one as Ambassador to Afghanistan (the first country to establish diplomatic relations with Lenin's government). In the 1930s, published *Rasskazy Michmana Il'ina*. Married his fellow-Bolshevik, the beautiful Larisa Reisner, who later left him. Threatened by Stalin's purges, sought political asylum in France in 1939. His defection became a cause célèbre when he wrote an open letter denouncing Stalin and his methods. Died a few months later under suspicious circumstances (fell, or was pushed, from a window), probably murdered by NKVD agents.

Raskova, Marina Mikhailovna
1912–1943. Major.
Educated as a pilot, 1935. In the 1930s, took part in highly-publicized long-distance flights (Sevastopol' to Arkhangelsk, and Moscow to the Far East). Joined the Red Army, 1938. During WWII, organized women's regiments. Commander of a bomber regiment, 1942. Died in an air crash.

Raspletin, Aleksandr Andreevich
1908–1967. Electronics engineer.
Graduated from the Leningrad Electrotechnical Institute, 1936. Created radar and electronics control systems for aircraft. Joined the CPSU, 1945. Academician, 1964.

Rasputin, Valentin Grigor'evich
15.3.1937–   . Writer.
Born in Ust-Uda, Irkutsk Oblast'. Graduated from Irkutsk University, 1959. One of the leaders of the so-called Derevenskaia Proza, together with Shukshin. Conscientious and thoughtful writer, whose concern is the contrast between city pragmatism, its glibness and cynicism, and the frankness of the peasants' moral values. Author of *Chelovek s Etogo Sveta*, 1965, *Prodaetsia Medvezh'ia Shkura*, *Zhivi I Pomni*, and *Proshchanie S Materoi* (filmed by Elem Klimov). A writer who is respected by both the establishment and the general public.

Rassadin, Konstantin Aleksandrovich
27.10.1937–   . Ballet dancer, choreographer.
Born in Leningrad. Graduated from the Leningrad Choreographic School, 1956. Pupil of I. D. Belskii. With the Kirov Theatre Ballet Company from 1956. Character and grotesque dancer. Teacher of choreography at the Leningrad Conservatory from 1977. Graduated as a choreographer from the Leningrad Conservatory, 1979.

Rassadin, Stanislav Borisovich
4.3.1935–   . Film critic.
Graduated from Moscow University, 1958. Leading film critic from the 1960s with the magazine *Iskusstvo Kino*.

Rastvorova, Valentina Ksenofontovna
17.6.1933–   . Athlete.
Born in Odessa. Honoured Master of Sports (fencing), 1956. With Moscow Dynamo. Graduated from the Moscow Institute of Physical Culture, 1956. Member of the CPSU, 1963. USSR champion, 1956, 1964 and 1967. World champion, 1958, and 1956–66 with her team. Olympic champion with her team, 1960. Individual silver medal, 1960.

Rathaus, Daniil Romanovich (Maksimovich)
1868–1937. Poet.
Studied law at Kiev University. Became popular as a romance writer in the 1890s with *Pesni Serdtsa* and other volumes of poetry. Many of his romances were set to music by Russian composers. After the October Revolution 1917, went abroad. Published a book of verse in Berlin. Died abroad.

Rattel, Nikolai Iosifovich
1875–1938. Major-general.
Graduated from the Academy of the General Staff, 1902. Took part in the Russo-Japanese war, 1904–05, and WWI as a major-general. Drafted into the Red Army, where he held high staff-officer positions until the mid-1920s. Thereafter, economic administrator.

Ratushinskaia, Irina Georgievna
1954–   . Poetess, dissident.
Born in Odessa. From a russified family of Polish gentry. Graduated in physics from Odessa University, 1976. Worked at the Odessa Pedagogical Institute, 1977. Married a young scientist, I. Gerashchenko, 1979, and moved to Kiev. Began writing poetry in her teens, but was unable to publish her work. Tried to emigrate, 1980, when she was already known as a poetess through samizdat. Arrested after taking part in a human rights demonstration in Moscow, 1981, but soon released. Re-arrested, 1982, and sentenced to 7 years imprisonment and 5 years exile. In labour camps in Mordovia. Became a cause célèbre in the West. After international pressure, released in Oct. 1986, having lost 42 lb in weight. Allowed to emigrate to the West. In May 1987, stripped of Soviet citizenship for 'deceitful propaganda intended to win the West's trust'. Travelled extensively in Europe and the USA. Author of *Vne Limita*, Germany, 1986, and *Ia Dozhivu*, NY, 1986.

Raukhverger, Mikhail Rafailovich
5.12.1901–   . Composer.
Born in Odessa. Composer of music for children's operas and ballets. Also worked in radio and film. Author of very popular operas and ballets, including *Krasnaia Shapochka*, 1947, and *Snezhnaia Koroleva*, 1965.

Razin, Evgenii Andreevich (before 1924 – Neklepaev)
1898–1964. Major-general.
Joined the Bolshevik Party, 1917, and the Red Army, 1918. Took part in the Civil War as a political commissar. Graduated from the Military Academy of the Red Army, 1924, and from the Institute of Red Professors, 1936. During WWII, in the Historical Department of the General Staff, 1942. Professor at the Academy of the General Staff until 1957. Author of historical works on WWII from the Stalinist point of view.

Razumnyi, Aleksandr Efimovich
1.5.1891–16.11.1972. Director, cameraman.
Graduated from the Odessa Art School, 1914. Entered the film industry, 1915. First film: *Zhizn' i Smert' Leitenanta Shmidta*, 1917. Adapted Gorkii's *Mother*, 1920. Chief cameraman at Lenin's funeral, 1924. Emigrated a year later. Made one film in Berlin, *Lishnie Liudi*, 1926. Returned to the USSR, 1930. From 1945, director of popular science films. Taught at the Proletkino Studio and the GIK (later the VGIK). In the 1950s worked at the Lithuanian Film Studio.

Razumovskii, Georgii Petrovich
19.1.1936–   . Politician.
Member of the CPSU, 1961. 1st secretary of the Krasnodar Kraikom, CPSU, 1983–85. Responsible for cadres affairs. Chief of the Department for Party Organizational Work of the Cen. Cttee. of the CPSU from Apr. 1985. Chairman of the Commission of Legislative Proposals of the USSR Supreme Soviet since 28 Nov. 1985. Member of the Cen. Cttee. of the CPSU from 1986. Elected to the Secretariat of the Cen. Cttee. on 6 Mar. 1986.

Rdultovskii, Vladimir Iosifovich
1876–1939. Gun ammunition designer.
Graduated from the Mikhailovskoe

Artillery School, 1902. Drafted into the Red Army, 1918. Head of an ammunition designers' team, 1925. Designed many types of Soviet gun ammunition, as well as equipment for ammunition production.

Rebikov, Vladimir Ivanovich
31.5.1866–4.8.1920. Composer, pianist.
Born in Krasnoiarsk. Pupil of N. Klenovskii in Moscow, and G. Müller in Berlin. Taught for some time in Berlin and Vienna. Lived in Odessa, 1894–98, and in Kishenev, 1898–1901. Founded branches of the Russkoe Muzykalnoe Obshchestvo. Lived mainly in Moscow, 1901–09. One of the early exponents of musical modernism in Russia. Author of 10 operas and several pieces in other genres. Died in Yalta.

Rediger, Aleksandr Fedorovich (Ruediger)
1854–1918. General, statesman.
Son of Theodor Ruediger, a military specialist. Graduated from the Academy of the General Staff, 1876. Took part in the Russo-Turkish war, 1877–78. Professor of military administration at the Academy of the General Staff, 1880. Deputy Minister of War of Bulgaria, 1882–83. Served in the Russian War Ministry, 1884–1905. Minister of War, 1905–09. His reforms of the Russian Army were implemented, 1905–1912.

Reformatskii, Aleksandr Nikolaevich
7.12.1864–27.12.1937. Chemist, scientist.
Born in the village of Borisoglebskoe, now Ivanovo Oblast'. Brother of the academician Sergei Reformatskii. Graduated from Kazan' University. Taught at Moscow University from 1889. In 1894, worked under V. Meyer in Heidelberg. Professor of the Moscow Collective Courses, 1898, then the Higher Women's Courses, 1898. Taught at the 2nd Moscow University, 1918, then at the Moscow Institute of Chemical Technology from 1930. Director of the Moscow Practical Academy. Professor of chemistry at the A. L. Shaniavskii People's University, 1901–19. Wrote many works on chemistry — *Neorganicheskaia Khimiia* (26 reprints from 1903) and *Organicheskaia*

Khimiia (7 reprints from 1914). Died in Moscow.

Reformatskii, Sergei Nikolaevich
1.4.1860–27.12.1934. Chemist, scientist, academician.
Born in the village of Borisoglebskoe, now Ivanovo Oblast'. Graduated from Kazan' University, 1882. Pupil of A. M. Zaitsev. Taught at the same university, 1882–89. In 1889–90, worked in Heidelberg at the V. Meyer and V. Ostwald Laboratory. Professor of Kiev University, 1891–1934. Professor at the Kiev Higher Women's Courses, 1906–19. Many scientific works, including *Nachalnyi Kurs Organicheskoi Khimii* (17 reprints from 1930). Chairman of the Physico-Chemical Society at Kiev University, 1910–16, 1920–33. Died in Moscow.

Regelson, Lev Lvovich
1939–   . Historian, physicist.
Born in Moscow. Graduated in physics from Moscow University. In the mid–1960s, became active in the Russian religious movement. Compiled an extensive history of the Russian Orthodox Church under communism, *Tragedia Russkoi Tserkvi*, published in Paris. Arrested, 1979. Admitted anti-Soviet activity. Released after trial. Gave up his samizdat activity.

Reilly, Sidney George (Rozenblum, Sigmund Grigor'evich)
24.3.1874–5.11.1925? Intelligence agent.
Probably born near Odessa (himself gave Ireland as his place of birth). Relative of the Duma member Leontii Bramson. Close to the SRs in his youth. Emigrated to South America, moved to Britain, and became a freelance agent for British intelligence. Returned to Russia before 1900. British-Japanese double agent in the Far East, became a Buddhist in China. Returned to Petersburg, friend of the Mongol guru, Badmaev, 1906. Became a well-known society figure, and a freelance agent of Russian intelligence. Allegedly gave the police information on Azef and Dzhugashvili (Stalin). Organized the first international aviation week in Petersburg. Moved

to Japan, 1914, then to the USA. After the Bolshevik take-over, involved in a series of attempts to topple the Soviet government, arriving in Russia, 1918, on a British mission with a Soviet passport given to him in London by Litvinov. Arrested by the British authorities in Murmansk, and freed only after personal intervention from a high-level member of the SIS, sent specially to Russia. Acquired a Cheka passport in the name of comrade Relinskii, and tried to organize the kidnapping of Dzerzhinskii and Lenin. After Dora Kaplan shot and wounded Lenin, a prize of 100,000 roubles was put on his head. Escaped to London. Sentenced to death in absentia at the Bruce Lockhart trial. Lived as a businessman in the USA. After his friend Savinkov was lured to the Soviet Union by the GPU, decided to return to his former attempts to fight the communist dictatorship, but fell into the same trap, set by the GPU cover organization Trest, operating as an underground anti-communist group. Crossed the Soviet-Finnish border on 25 Sep. 1925 with a passport in the name of N. Sternberg. All further information on him is inconclusive. A shooting incident was staged by Soviet border guards on 29 Sep. 1925, to create the impression of his death. In Sep. 1927, *Izvestia* wrote that he was executed in June 1927. In 1966, *Nedelia* wrote that, during his interrogations at the Lubianka, he gave valuable information and was thereafter executed, 5 Nov. 1925. According to some information, he was still alive in prison, but insane, in the mid–1940s. The exact circumstances of his life after arrest by the GPU and of his death remain a mystery.
See: R. H. Bruce Lockhart, *Memoirs of a British Agent*, London-NY, 1932.

Reisner, Larisa Mikhailovna
1895–1926. Revolutionary.
Daughter of a professor. Close to the Bolshevik leaders. Renowned as a famous beauty in Petersburg before WWI. Among her admirers was N. Gumilev. Married the revolutionary F. Raskol'nikov, who was later appointed Soviet Naval Minister, which in turn brought her the post of vice-minister of the Red Navy.

Accompanied her husband to the Soviet Embassy in Afghanistan. Left him for another sailor and revolutionary, Dybenko.

Reiss, Ignatii (Poretskii, Ignace; Krasny-Rotstadt, Joseph)
1899–9.1937. Intelligence agent, defector.
Born in Poland. Before the 1917 Revolution, involved in communist activity. Arrested and sentenced to 5 years imprisonment. After the October Revolution 1917, became a Cheka agent. Worked in Poland, Germany, Austria and other countries. Ordered to organize a Soviet spy network in Britain from Holland, 1927. In the 1930s, operated in France under the then head of Soviet espionage, M. Shpigelgliass. Ordered to return to the Soviet Union, July 1937. Defected and wrote an open letter denouncing the crimes of the Stalinist secret police. Went to Switzerland on a Czech passport. Lured by Shpigelgliass, with the help of his former girlfriend, to a rendezvous with a GPU assassination squad sent from Paris. His body was found with multiple gun wounds in a hired car on a road near Lausanne.

Reiter, Maks Andreevich
1886–1950. Col.-general.
On active service during WWI as a colonel. Joined the Red Army, 1919. Took part in the Civil War. Joined the Bolshevik Party, 1922. Graduated from the Frunze Military Academy, 1935. Took part in WWII. Commander of the South Urals military district, 1943–45. Head of the Vystrel Courses, 1946.

Reizen, Maria Romanovna
4.8.1892–25.5.1969. Ballerina.
Born in Moscow. Graduated from the Moscow Choreographic School, 1909. Pupil of V. D. Tikhomirov. With the Bolshoi Theatre, 1909–50. Appeared in the Ballets Russes in Paris, 1910–12. Taught young dancers, 1936–48. Taught at the Moscow Choreographic School, 1950–51. Died in Moscow.

Reizen, Mark Iosifovich
3.7.1895–197 ? Singer, bass.
Born at Zaitsevo near Lugansk.

Soloist at the Leningrad Opera, 1925–30. Soloist at the Bolshoi Theatre, 1930–54. Took part in the denigration of Chaliapin after his death ('betrayed his country', 'had nothing to offer of interest to art'), which earned him the contempt of and a boycott by his colleagues, despite the dangers of disagreement with the party line. Rewarded by 3 Stalin Prizes, 1941, 1949, 1951. From 1954, taught at the Moscow Gnesin Musical Pedagogical Institute. Wrote memoirs, *Stranitsy Vospominanii*, 1965.

Remizov, Aleksei Mikhailovich
6.7.1877–26.11.1957. Author, calligrapher.
Born in Moscow. As a student, arrested for revolutionary activity, exiled from Moscow in 1897. Spent 6 years in exile and prison. First literary work published in 1902. Developed an original style and approach based on the oral tradition. Had a great influence on Belyi, later Babel', Zamiatin, Pilniak and other modernists of the 1920s. Emigrated in 1921 to Berlin. Moved to Paris in 1923. Continued writing in his unique style to the end of his life. After WWII, in the wave of nostalgia, and with Stalin's promises of safety, took a Soviet passport, but refrained from returning to the Soviet Union. Lived in his last years in extreme poverty, relying on help from friends and fellow writers. One of the main protagonists of the modernist school in Russian literature. Extended his mystifying style to life (founder of Obezvelvolpal, the High and Mighty Order of the Great and Free House of Apes — almost every Russian writer of note received a title and diploma in Remizov's calligraphy). Throughout his life, an eccentric who turned his flat into something like a sorcerer's cave. Died in Paris.
Main works: *Collected Works*, 8 vol. Several autobiographical works dealing with the revolution and pre-revolutionary life in Russia, also fairy-tales and religious legends.

Rennenkampf, Pavel Karlovich
1854–1918. General.
Graduated from the Academy of the General Staff, 1882. Took part in the

Russo-Japanese war, 1904–05, as the commander of a Cossack division. Supressed revolutionary disturbances by soldiers returning from the Russo-Japanese war in Siberia, 1905–07. During WWI, commander of the 1st Army. His delay in helping Samsonov's army in East Prussia, according to some historians, contributed to the complete defeat of the Russians at Tannenberg, 1914. Arrested after the Bolshevik take-over and soon thereafter shot by the Cheka.

Repin, Il'ia Efimovich
5 8.1844–29.9.1930. Artist.
Portrait, genre and historical painter. Also worked in sculpture. Born in Chuguev, Khar'kov Oblast'. Son of a military settler. Studied at the Chuguev School of Military Topography. Pupil of the painter I. Bunakov. Continued his education at the Petersburg School of Graphic Art of the Society for the Encouragement of Artists, 1863, then at the Academy of Arts, Petersburg, 1864–71. Pupil of the painter I. Kramskoi. Studied at academies in Italy and Paris, 1873–76. From 1878, Peredvizhnik. Returned to his native Chuguev. From 1882, lived in Petersburg. Most of his paintings are held in the Russian Museum, Leningrad and the Tretiakov Gallery. Lived and died in Kuokkala, Finland (independent after 1917). In 1940, the Il'ia Repin Museum was set up in Chuguev, and in 1958, a monument was erected in Moscow in his honour. Exhibitions from 1865, with a major exhibition held in Moscow in 1958.

Rerberg, Georgii Ivanovich
28.9.1939– . Cameraman.
Cameraman on nearly all of A. S. Mikhalkov-Konchalovskii's films such as *Pervyi Uchitel'*, 1965, *Dvorianskoe Gnezdo*, 1969, and *Diadia Vania*, 1971. Cameraman on A. Tarkovskii's *Zerkalo* (The Mirror), 1975. Among his many other films are *Liubov' Orlova*, 1984, *Melodii Beloi Nochi*, a co-production with Japan, 1977, and *Otets Sergii*, 1978.

Rerberg, Ivan Ivanovich
4.10.1869–1932. Engineer, architect.
Born in Moscow. Graduated from the Petersburg Military Engineering

Academy, 1896. Taught at the Moscow School of Painting, Sculpture and Architecture, 1906–19. Architect of many public buildings — the Severnoe Strakhovoe Obshchestvo (Northern Insurance Society), 1910–11, the Kiev Railway Station, 1914–17, the School of Red Commanders (now the Presidium of the Supreme Soviet), 1932–34, the Central Telegraph on Gorkii Street — all in Moscow. Died in Moscow.
See: 'Pamiati Bolshogo Stroitelia', *Stroitelstvo Moskvy*, 1932, Nr. 10.

Revutskii, Lev Nikolaevich
20.2.1889–30.3.1977. Composer.
Born in the Poltava Gouvt. Trained at the N. Tutkovskii Music School. Pupil of N. Lysenko, and at the N. Lysenko School of Musical Drama, 1903–05. On graduating from university, 1907, entered the school of the Russkoe Muzykalnoe Obshchestvo. Pupil of S. Korotkevich (later of G. Khodorovskii). After the foundation of the Kiev Conservatory, 1913, studied composition under R. Glier. Began composing from 1908–09. Graduated from the Conservatory and University (Faculty of Law), 1916. Spent 2 years in the army, on the Riga front. Worked in Priluki as a piano soloist and accompanist. Taught at the Lysenko Musical Drama Institute, Kiev, from 1924. Member of the board of the Union of Composers of the Ukrainian SSR from 1932. Chairman, 1944–48. Taught at the Conservatory from 1933. Professor of Composition and History of Music at the Tashkent Conservatory from 1935. Returned to musical activities in Kiev. Doctor of the history of art, 1941. Member of the Ukrainian SSR Academy of Sciences from 1957. Composed in the classical tradition.

Rezanov, Aleksandr Gennad'evich
6.10.1948–   . Athlete.
Born in Aleksandrovsk, on the island of Sakhalin. Honoured Master of Sports (handball), 1976. With Zaporozh'e Burevestnik. Graduated from the Zaporozh'e branch of the Dnepropetrovsk Metallurgical Institute, 1975. Works as a metallurgical engineer. Olympic champion, 1976.

Rezantsev, Valerii Grigor'evich
8.10.1946–   . Athlete.
Born in Novomoskovsk, Tula Oblast'. Graduated from the Kazakhskii Institute of Physical Culture, 1969. Honoured Master of Sports (wrestling), 1970. Member of the CPSU, 1977. With Alma-Ata Dynamo. USSR champion, 1970–75. European champion, 1970 and 1973–74. World champion, 1970–75. Olympic champion, 1972 and 1976.

Riabchinskaia, Iulia Petrovna
21.1.1947–13.1.1973. Athlete.
Born in the village of Peshchanka, Vinnitsa Oblast'. Canoeist, won a gold medal at the 1972 Olympic Games in Munich. Died in Poti, Georgia, less than a year after her victory, as a result of taking dangerous anabolic steroids.

Riabikov, Vasilii Mikhailovich
1907–1974. Col.-general.
Joined the Bolshevik Party, 1925, and the Red Army, 1933. Graduated from the Naval Academy, 1937. 1st Deputy Minister of Armaments, 1939. After WWII, 1st Deputy Prime Minister of the RSFSR, and 1st Deputy Chairman of GOSPLAN. Non-voting member of the Cen. Cttee. of the CPSU, 1952, and full member, 1961.

Riabinkina, Elena L'vovna
21.8.1941–   . Ballerina.
Graduated from the Moscow Theatre School. Pupil of V. P. Vasil'ev. With the Bolshoi Theatre from 1959. Additional study under E. P. Gerdt and M. T. Semenova. Appeared in films. Took part in guest performances abroad.

Riabov, Aleksei Panteleimonovich
17.3.1899–18.12.1955. Composer, conductor.
Born in Khar'kov. Conductor in musical comedy theatres in Khar'kov from 1929, and Kiev from 1941. Artistic director of the Kiev Theatre of Musical Comedy from 1945. Author of some 20 operettas, including *Kolombina*, 1923, *Sorochinskaia Iarmarka*, 1936, *Svad'ba v Malinovke*, 1937, and *Krasnaia Kalina*, 1954. Also wrote chamber music and music for the theatre. Died in Kiev.

Riabushinskaia, Tatiana
23.5.1916–   . Ballerina.
Born in Moscow. Emigrated. Pupil of A. E. Volinin and M. F. Kshesinskaia. First appearance at the age of 13. Leading dancer with the Ballets Russes de Monte Carlo, 1932–36. Appeared with the Ballets Russes du Colonel de Basil, 1936–39, Ballet Theatre, Ballet des Champs Élysées, 1942–50, and others. Joined the David Lichine company. Leading dancer in the Balanchine ballet *Konkurentsiia*, 1932, then leading roles in ballets by L. F. Miasin, M. M. Fokin and others. Retired from the stage in the 1950s. Settled in California. Taught at the Lichine School.

Riabushinskii, Nikolai Pavlovich (Shinskii)
1876–1951. Businessman, arts patron.
Brother of P. Riabushinskii. A representative of one of the rich merchant families in Moscow which by their liberal patronage created the material base for the flowering of culture in Russia at the turn of the century. Among his many initiatives was the financing of the Symbolist magazine *Zolotoe Runo*.

Riabushinskii, Pavel Pavlovich
1871–after 1930. Politician, publisher.
Son of the textile millionaire, Pavel Riabushinskii (d. 1894). After his father's death, took over the family business. Brilliant businessman. Developed further the success of his father. His empire included banks, land and automobiles. In 1916, started the first Russian automobile workshops. Chairman of the Association of Cotton Industrialists from 1913 until Oct. 1917. Leader of the Progressive Party and publisher of its newspaper *Utro Rossii* (The Dawn of Russia). All of his factories and banks were nationalized by the Bolsheviks. Emigrated, and settled in Paris.

Riabyshev, Dmitrii Ivanovich
1894–1985. Lt.-general.
Private during WWI, and Bolshevik organizer. Joined the Red Army, 1918. Commander of a regiment and a brigade. Graduated from the Frunze Military Academy, 1935.

Commander of several armies during WWII. Deputy commander of several military districts, 1946–50.

Riadnov, Evgenii Karlovich (real name – Shults)
1853–19.9.1925. Singer.
Born on his father's estate in the village of Riadnovka, Khar'kov Gouvt. Appeared in theatres in Italy, France and Austria. Moved to Tiflis, 1880. Soloist at the Mariinskii Theatre, 1881–85. Taught in Tiflis from 1910. Educated a generation of singers including K. Maksakov and A. Inashvili. Died in Tiflis.

Riauzov, Sergei Nikolaevich
8.8.1905– . Composer.
Born in Moscow. Author of music for ballets, films, songs, choral music, and symphonies.

Riazanov, Aleksei Konstantinovich
1920– . Major-general.
Born in the village of Kochetovka, Tambov Oblast'. Graduated from the Chkalov Aviation School in Borisoglebsk, 1939, from the Frunze Military Academy, 1950, and the General Staff Academy, 1958. Served as a pilot, wing commander, and deputy commander of the 4th Fighter Regiment, 1941–45. Member of the CPSU, 1942. Flew 509 missions, and shot down 31 German planes personally, 16 in group combat. Senior posts in the Air Force from 1959. Member of the Central Apparatus of Soviet Air Defences (PVO). Senior posts in military districts, the General Staff and the PVO, 1950–75.

Riazanov, David Borisovich (Goldenbakh)
10.3.1870–21.1.1938. Revolutionary, historian.
Born in Odessa. Joined the revolutionary movement, 1887. Active in Odessa and Petersburg. Menshevik, 1903–17. Lecturer at the SD Party school at Longjumeau, 1911. First editor of the collected works of Marx and Engels (in the original German), 2 vols, published in Germany before 1916. After the October Revolution 1917, joined the Bolsheviks (for a short time leaving the party after Brest-Litovsk). Founder and director of the Marx-Engels Institute (the chief ideological institution of Marxism) in Moscow, 1921–31. Edited the collected works of Marx, Engels, Plekhanov, Hegel. Uncharacteristically for Bolshevik Party members, tried courageously to protect his employees from arrest during the Stalinist purges. Expelled from the party in 1931, dismissed, exiled (at first to Leningrad, later to Saratov). Arrested in 1937, and died in prison.

Riazanov, Eldar Aleksandrovich
18.11.1927– . Film director.
In 1944, entered the Directors' Faculty of the VGIK. Pupil of Grigorii Kozintsev and Sergei Eisenstein. One of the best comedy-makers in the Soviet Union. *Carnival Night*, made in 1956, starring Liudmila Gurchenko, became a Soviet classic. Other films: *The Girl Without an Address*, 1957; *How Robinson Was Created*, 1961; *The Hussar Ballad*, 1962, *The Zigzag of Success*, 1968; *The Old Rascals*, 1971; *The Amazing Adventures of Italians in Russia* (Soviet-Italian co-production, Dino De Laurentis, 1973); *The Irony of Fate*, 1975. People's Artist of the RSFSR, 1974.

Riazanov, Petr Borisovich
21.10.1899–11.10.1942. Composer, musicologist.
Born in Narva. Taught at music schools in Leningrad, including the Mussorgskii Music School. Professor at the Leningrad Conservatory. Collected and arranged folk songs. His pupils included N. Bogoslovskii, G. Sviridov, B. Maizel' and A. Machavariani. Wrote orchestral music, and songs using folk motives. Died in Tbilisi.

Riazanov, Vasilii Georgievich
1901–1951. Lt.-general.
Joined the Red Army and the Bolshevik Party, 1920. Graduated from the Zhukovskii Air Force Academy, 1935. High command posts in the Air Force during WWII. Distinguished himself at the battles for the Dniepr and the Vistula. Several high command posts in the Air Force after WWII.

Riazanovskii, Valentin
1884–? . Philologist, lawyer.
Educated in Kostroma. Graduated from Moscow University in 1908. Lecturer at the Demidov Lycée in Iaroslavl' in 1915. Professor at Tomsk University, 1918. Professor at Irkutsk University, 1920. Professor at Harbin University (China) in the law faculty, 1922–34. Lived in China until 1938. Moved to the USA in 1938.
Main works: *Customary Law of the Mongol Tribes*; *Fundamental Principles of Mongol Law*; *Customary Law of the Nomad Tribes of Siberia*; *Survey of Russian Culture*, 2 vol.; *The Development of Russian Scientific Thought*.

Rigert, David Adamovich
12.3.1947– . Athlete.
Born in the village of Nagornoe, Kokchetav Oblast'. Honoured Master of Sports (heavy athletics), 1971. With the Trud team from Shakhty, Rostov Oblast'. Member of the CPSU, 1977. Graduated from the Moscow Institute of Physical Culture, 1978. European champion, 1971–79. World champion, 1971–78. USSR champion, 1972–78. Olympic champion, 1976. Between 1971–79 world record-holder 63 times.
Source: A. Kolodnyi, 'Voskhozhdenie k P'edestalu', in *Tvoi Chempiony*, Issue 3, Moscow, 1977.

Riisman, Avgust Tynisovich (Ristmets)
28.2.1890–23.4.1926. Revolutionary.
Born in Estonia. Son of a worker. Trained as a teacher, 1908. Taught as a people's teacher in Revel (now Tallinn). Took part in WWI. Joined the communists in Estonia in 1919. Member of the Communist Party, 1920. Illegally crossed the border into Soviet Russia. From 1922–25, lived in Leningrad. Studied at Leningrad University, at the same time taught in schools in Estonia. Member of the Cen. Cttee. of the CP of Estonia from 1925. Main organizer of the Communist Congress in Tallinn. Arrested by the police, tried and executed.

Rikhter, Dmitrii Ivanovich
6.11.1848–2.7.1919. Statistician, economist.
Born in Moscow. Author of the

Geograficheskii Slovar' Rossii (Geographical Dictionary of Russia, 1909–11, 6 issues). Died in Pushkin.

Rikhter, Sviatoslav Teofilovich
20.3.1915–   . Pianist.
Born in Zhitomir into a musical family. Studied music as a child under his father, who was a pianist and organist. Worked at the Odessa Opera and Ballet Theatre, 1933–37. Pupil of G. Neigauz, 1937–47. Studied at the Moscow Conservatory. Solo concerts all over the USSR from 1940. From 1950, all over the world. Received his first award at the 3rd All-Union Competition of Concert Pianists, Moscow, 1945. Lives between Moscow and Tarusy, the writers and artists' village.

Rimskii-Korsakov, Andrei Nikolaevich
17.10.1878–23.5.1940. Musicologist.
Born in Petersburg. Elder son of Nikolai Rimskii-Korsakov. Editor-publisher of *Muzykal'nyi Sovremennik*, 1915–17. Head of the Music Score Department, and later the Music Manuscripts Department of the M. Saltykov-Shchedrin Public Library, Leningrad, from 1918 until his death. Author of many musical works, including some on his father.

Rimskii-Korsakov, Andrei Vladimirovich
29.8.1910–   . Specialist in acoustics.
Born in Petersburg. Grandson of Nikolai Rimskii-Korsakov. Graduated from Petersburg University. Doctor of physics and mathematical sciences. Co-inventor of the electrical instrument, the emiriton, together with A. Ivanov, V. Kreitser and V. Dzerzhkovich. Carried out research in the field of electrical musical instruments. Author (with N. D'iakonov) of *Muzykal'nye Instrumenty*, Moscow, 1952.

Rimskii-Korsakov, Georgii Mikhailovich
26.12.1901–   . Musicologist, composer.
Born in Petersburg. Grandson of Nikolai Rimskii-Korsakov. Lecturer at the Leningrad Conservatory, 1927

–62, in music acoustics and score-reading. Author of a symphony, cantatas, string quartets, and pieces for piano. Author of several works on acoustics.

Ritenbergs, Haral'd Al'fredovich
11.5.1932–   . Ballet dancer.
Born in Riga. Graduated from the Riga Choreographic School, 1952. Pupil of V.T. Blinov. With the Riga Theatre, 1950–77. Guest appearances abroad. Director of the Riga Choreographic School from 1978.

Riumin, Valerii Viktorovich
1939–   . Cosmonaut.
Graduated from the Moscow Forestry Institute, 1966. Joined the Soviet cosmonauts team. In the late 1970s and early 1980s, made 3 long space flights (185 days on Salyut 6-Soyuz, Apr.–Oct. 1980). Highly decorated (twice Hero of the Soviet Union).

Rodchenko, Aleksandr Mikhailovich
5.12.1891–3.12.1956. Photographer, artist.
Born in Petersburg. His father was a prop-maker in a theatre and came from a family of farm-workers, while his mother worked in a laundry. Attended the Kazan' art school, 1910–14, where he met his future wife, the artist Varvara Stepanova. In 1915, moved to the Stroganov Academy of Decorative Arts in Moscow, but disliked the teaching methods. Became interested in Cubo-futurism and began to make abstract drawings and paintings. Following the February and October Revolutions of 1917, ran workshops in decorative arts for the Visual Arts Section of the People's Commissariat for Enlightenment (IZO Narkompros) and began to exhibit regularly. In 1920, met Vladimir Mayakovsky, a meeting which led to friendship and collaboration. Became a member of the Institute of Artistic Culture (INKHUK), founded in Moscow by V. Kandinskii, and made his first photo-montages. In 1922, designed titles for Dziga Vertov's newsreels and began to use typography and graphic art in poster design and book jackets. Designed the cover and layout for *LEF*, the magazine founded

and edited by Mayakovsky, and made photo-montages to illustrate Mayakovsky's poem *Pro Eto* (About This), which was published in 1926. His collaboration with Mayakovsky was to last until the poet's death in 1930. Began experimenting with photography, at first to provide him with material for his collage and montage work. From 1924, took many portraits of his famous friends, including the now famous series on Mayakovsky. During 1925–26, worked as photo-reporter for several magazines and newspapers, and as designer for the films *The Journalist* (with Lev Kuleshov) and *Moscow in October* (with B. Barnet), and for several stage plays produced by Meyerhold. When *LEF* stopped publication in 1927, Mayakovsky started the monthly magazine *Novyi Lef*, for which Rodchenko continued to provide material. Took part in the 1928 exhibion 10 Years of Soviet Photography, which was held in Moscow, then in Leningrad. That year, became a recognised leader of the Oktiabr' group. Shortly afterwards, was accused of plagiarism of Western photography, and criticized for his formalism. After Mayakovsky's suicide, the VKHUTEMAS (the Art and Technical Workshop), in which Rodchenko had taught for 10 years, was disbanded. Once more he was accused of formalism in his *Pioneer* photographs and this led eventually to his expulsion from the October group in 1931 (the group disbanded soon afterwards). In 1933, together with his wife, designed the White Sea Canal issue of *USSR in Construction*, for which he had taken many photographs. Exhibited at the 1935 exhibition Masters of Soviet Photography, and also published some of his photographs in *Sovetskoe Foto*. In 1937, photographed athletics, the circus and the ballet, and in 1939, held an exhibition at the Writers' Club in Moscow. His design of posters and magazine layouts as well as his remarkable photography and photo-montages influenced several generations of photographers and artists throughout the world. During the 1930–40s taught at the Photographic Union. After WWII, lived with his wife in the centre of Moscow, forgotten by everybody. After his death, the famous collector Costakis visited his wife, and reported that the famous couple lived in great material

poverty and complete solitude.
Source: *Soviet Photography, 1917–40. The New Photojournalism*, edited by S. Morozov and Valerie Lloyd, London, 1984.

Rodimtsev, Aleksandr Il'ich
1905–1977. Col.-general.
Joined the Red Army, 1927, and the Bolshevik Party, 1929. Sent to Spain during the Spanish Civil War, 1936–39. Graduated from the Frunze Military Academy, 1939. Several high command posts during WWII. Became widely known during the Battle of Stalingrad. After WWII, military adviser and attaché in communist Albania. Several command posts in the Soviet forces, 1956–66.

Rodin, Aleksei Grigor'evich
1902–1955. Col.-general.
Joined the Red Army, 1920. Took part in the Civil War. Joined the Bolshevik Party, 1926. Graduated from the Academy of Mechanization of the Red Army, 1937. Commander of tank detachments. Took part in the Soviet-Finnish war, 1939–40. Commander of tank forces at various fronts during WWII. Head of Tank Military Training of the Soviet Armed Forces, 1949–54.

Rodnina, Irina Konstantinovna
12.9.1949–   . Athlete.
Born in Moscow. Honoured Master of Sports (figure skating), 1969. With the Central Sports Club of the Army. Graduated from the Moscow Institute of Physical Culture, 1974. Member of the CPSU, 1975. World and European champion, 1969–78. USSR champion, 1970–71, 1973–75, 1977, and 1968–72 with A. Ulanov. Olympic champion, 1976. Sports instructor. Her professional life has been well documented in the Soviet press.
See: A. Chaikovskii, *Irina Rodnina*, Moscow, 1977.

Rodos
1898?–1956? Colonel.
One of the chief investigators at the Lubianka. In the 1930s, in charge of the questioning and torturing of Kossior, Kosarev, Chubar' and others. Arrested after Beria's fall. In 1956, just before the XXth Party Congress, brought to Moscow to a plenary session of the Cen. Cttee. and ordered to describe his work in the 1930s. After the congress, he was shot (probably in 1956).

Rodygin, Evgenii Pavlovich
16.2.1925–   . Composer.
Born in Chusovaia, Perm' Gouvt. Moved to Sverdlovsk. Author of the famous song *Ural'skaia Riabinushka*. Also composed musicals.

Rodzianko, Mikhail Vladimirovich
21.2.1859–24.1.1924. Politician.
Born into a rich Ukrainian family. Educated at the Pages Corps. Served in the Chevalier Guards. One of the leaders of the October Party (Oktiabristy). Member of the State Council (Upper Chamber) 1906–07. Deputy of the 3rd and 4th Dumas, 1907–17. Chairman of the Duma, 1911–17. Cadet during WWI. After the February Revolution 1917, headed the provisional Cttee. of the State Duma, 1917. With General Denikin's army during the Civil War, 1918–20. In 1920, emigrated to Yugoslavia, where he died. Wrote his memoirs, *Krushenie Imperii*, 1927.

Roerich, Nikolai Konstantinovich
9.10.1874–13.12.1947. Artist, stage designer.
Born in St. Petersburg. A man of extremely wide interests and talents, and a most prolific painter of great originality. Painted over 7,000 pictures. Graduated from the University and from the Academy of Fine Arts in Petersburg. Started professional life as an archaeologist. His paintings were related to his archaeological, anthropological and esoteric interests. Best known for his stage designs for the Polovtsian Dances, a scene from Diaghilev's production of *Prince Igor* staged in 1909 during the Paris season. Another of his famous works was *Sacre du Printemps* at the Theatre du Chatelet in May 1913. From 1916, lived in Finland and other Scandinavian countries. From 1920–23, toured America with his pictures and enjoyed great success. Had a great influence on American anthroposophs who attached great mystical importance to his paintings. Meticulous historical research made his stage designs very significant and forceful. In 1923, went with his family on an anthropological expedition– to the East Altai, Mongolia and Tibet. From 1928, lived in the Himalayas at Kulu (some 60 miles north of Simla). Founded and directed his own Institute of Himalayan Research. Died at Kulu.

Roerich, Sviatoslav Nikolaevich
5.11.1904–   . Artist.
Born in St. Petersburg. Son of Nikolai Roerich. Studied architecture in London, then Harvard and Columbia universities. In 1923, visited India and has lived there since 1936. Visited the USSR in 1960 and 1974–75 in connection with his father's exhibitions. His pictures are held in India and in the Tretiakov Gallery.

Rogal'-Levitskii, Dmitrii Romanovich
14.7.1898–17.12.1962. Composer.
Born in the mining village of Uspenskii, Iakutia. Moved to Moscow where he studied at the Conservatory. Orchestrated many pieces by other composers such as Skriabin, Liszt and Chopin. Editor of the *State Hymn of the Soviet Union*. His pupils included A. Khachaturian, T. Khrennikov, R. Shchedrin and A. Eshpai. Author of *Sovremennyi Orkestr*, 4 vol., Moscow, 1953–56. Died in Moscow.

Roginskii, Sergei Vasil'evich
1901–1960. Lt.-general.
Joined the Red Army, 1920. Took part in the Civil War. Graduated from the Military Engineers' Academy, 1934, and from the Academy of the General Staff, 1939. Took part in WWII. Chief-of-staff of Engineering Forces of the Soviet Army, 1951–54.

Rogov, Aleksandr Nikolaevich
27.3.1956–   . Athlete.
Born in Moscow Oblast'. Honoured Master of Sports (rowing), 1976. With Moscow Spartak. Studied at the Moscow Oblast' Institute of Physical Culture. USSR champion and Olympic champion, 1976.

Rogov, Ivan Vasil'evich

1899–1949. Col.-general, political officer.

Joined the Bolshevik Party, 1918,and the Red Army, 1919. Took part in the Civil War. Political officer in naval border-guard forces. Head of the political department of the Soviet Navy, and Deputy Minister of the Navy, 1939. Member of the Cen. Cttee. of the Bolshevik Party, 1939–49. Took part in WWII in the Black Sea.

Roizman, Leonid Isakovich

4.1.1916– . Organist, pianist.

Born in Kiev. Pupil of A. Gedike and A. Gol'denveizer. Professor at the Moscow Conservatory from 1950. Also appeared as an organist from 1950. In charge of installing organs in many Soviet cities.

Works: *Organnaia Kul'tura Estonii*, Moscow, 1960; *Iz Istorii Organnoi Kul'tury*, Moscow, 1960.

Rokossovskii, Konstantin Konstantinovich

21.12.1896–3.8.1968. Marshal.

On active service during WWI as a sergeant. Joined the Red Army, 1918, and the Bolshevik Party, 1919. Took part in the Civil War as a cavalry division commander. Graduated from the Frunze Military Academy, 1929. During the purge of the military after Tukhachevskii's fall, arrested and imprisoned. At the beginning of WWII, when Stalin's Civil War favourites Voroshilov and Budennyi demonstrated their complete military incompetence, recalled with other officers from the Gulag and returned to high command positions. In charge of several highly successful Soviet operations. Gained the reputation of being one of the most efficient Red Army commanders during WWII. After the war, sent by Stalin to Poland, officially as Polish Minister of Defence and Deputy Prime Minister, but in fact as the Soviet viceroy. Given the title Marshal of Poland. Returned to the Soviet Union, 1956. Deputy Defence Minister until 1962.

Romanenko, Iurii

1944– . Cosmonaut.

Took off on 6 Feb. 1987 on a mission to the space station Mir. Spent 326 days in orbit. Returned to Earth on 29 Dec. 1987. Matched the space endurance record set by 3 other Soviet cosmonauts in 1984 (L. Kizim, V. Solov'ev and Ol. Atkov on Saliut 7), opening a new age in Soviet space research. Has shown that a man can work effectively for as long as 11 months in space. Became a national hero.

Romanenko, Prokofii Logvinovich

1897–1949. Col.-general.

Took part in WWII as a sub-lieutenant. Joined the Red Army, 1918. Joined the Bolshevik Party, 1920. During the Civil War, partisan commander and commander of a cavalry regiment. Graduated from the Frunze Military Academy, 1933. Took part in the Spanish Civil War and the Soviet-Finnish war. On active service during WWII. Commander of the Eastern Siberia military district, 1945–47.

Romanenko, Vitalii Petrovich

13.7.1926– . Athlete.

Born in Kiev Oblast'. Honoured Master of Sports (shooting), 1955. With the Kiev Armed Forces Club. Honorary Coach of the Ukrainian SSR, 1974. World and European champion, 1954–62. USSR champion, 1955–62. Olympic champion, 1956.

Romanov, Aleksei Osipovich

16.10.1904–3.11.1979. Sports official, medical official, editor.

Born in the village of Ekaterinograd-skaia, now Kabardino-Balkarskaia ASSR. Sports official from 1925. Graduated from the Moscow Institute of Physical Culture, 1930. Member of the CPSU, 1946. Chairman, then 1st Deputy Chairman of the All-Russian Sports Cttee. of the Council of Ministers of the RSFSR, 1951–58. Deputy Health Minister of the RSFSR, 1952–71. Member of the Olympic Cttee. of the USSR, 1951–79. Chairman of the Scientific Methodological Council of the USSR Sports Cttee., 1958–65. Referee (All-Union category), 1964. Honorary member of the Moscow Olympic Cttee., 1971–79. Editor-in-chief of *Teoriia i Praktika Fizicheskoi Kultury*. Author of many articles and books on physical culture and health. Died in Moscow.

Romanov, Boris Georgievich

22.3.1891–30.1.1957. Ballet dancer, choreographer.

Born in Petersburg. Graduated from the Petersburg Theatre School, 1909. Pupil of M. K. Obukhov. With the Mariinskii Theatre. Mainly character dancer. First productions as a choreographer at the Petersburg Liteinyi Theatre. Influenced by M. M. Fokin. His aesthetics were influenced by the Russian acmeist poets. Later stressed the classical tradition. Choreographer with the Mariinskii Theatre from 1914. After the October Revolution, took part in productions in various Petersburg theatres. At the head of the Russkii Romanticheskii Teatr, giving guest performances abroad, 1921–26. Emigrated. Choreographer with A. P. Pavlova's company, 1928–34. At the Colon Theatre, Buenos Aires, and with other theatres in Paris, Monte Carlo, Belgrade and Rome. With La Scala and Rome Opera, 1934, and the Metropolitan Opera, New York, 1938–42, and 1945–50. Taught in Buenos Aires, and at the School of Ballet Repertory, New York. Worked also for the Ballets Russes de Monte Carlo, and for Chicago Opera, 1956. Died in New York.

See: T. Mara, 'Boris Romanov', *Dance Magazine*, Mar. 1957.

Romanov, Grigorii Vasil'evich

7.2.1923– . Politician.

Son of a peasant. Served in the Soviet Army during WWII. Joined the Communist Party in 1944. Worked as a designer in 1946. Graduated from the Leningrad Shipbuilding Institute in 1953. Section head of the Design Bureau of Zhdanov Works, USSR Ministry of Shipbuilding, Leningrad, 1946–54. Party posts in Leningrad, 1955–70, including 1st secretary of Leningrad Oblast' Cttee. Long-standing party boss of Leningrad with a reputation of extreme toughness. Member of the Presidium of the USSR Supreme Soviet from 1971. Candidate member, 1973–76, and full member of the Politburo of the Cen. Cttee. of the CPSU from 1976. Took over control of defence after Marshal D. Ustinov's death in

1984, with the elderly Marshal Sokolov as nominal Minister of Defence. Was one of Gorbachev's main rivals. Involved in the general Brezhnevite malaise (used priceless Tsarist porcelain for a relative's wedding which resulted in some of the pieces being broken by drunken guests). Under Gorbachev, removed from all his posts, with rumours of his alcoholism and corruption emerging everywhere.

See: A. Avtorkhanov, *Ot Andropova k Gorbachevu*, Paris, 1986; M. Shatrov's article in *Ogonek*, Nr. 4, 1984.

Romanov, Panteleimon Sergeevich
5.8.1884–8.4.1938. Author.
Born in the village of Petrovskoe, now in Tula Oblast' into a well-to-do family. One of the best known writers of the 1920s, now almost forgotten. His *Polnoe Sobranie Sochinenii* was published in 1929–30.

Romanova, Maria Fedorovna (m. Ulanova)
22.1.1886–26.12.1954. Ballerina.
Born in Petersburg. Graduated from the Petersburg Theatre School, 1903. With the Mariinskii Theatre, 1910–24. Taught at the Petrograd Choreographic School from 1917. Taught and coached at the Kirov Theatre from 1930. Among her pupils was her daughter G. S. Ulanova. Died in Leningrad.

Romanovskaia, Elena Evgen'evna (b. Kozhemiakina)
24.5.1890–22.11.1947. Folklorist.
Born in Tsarskoe Selo. Lived in Uzbekistan and studied Uzbek folk music. Author of many works, including *Khorezmskaia Klassicheskaia Muzyka*, Tashkent, 1939, *Tashkentskaia Klassicheskaia Muzyka*, Tashkent, 1940, and *Uzbekskaia Instrumental'naia Muzyka*, Tashkent, 1948. Died in Tashkent.

Romanovskii, Vladimir Vatslavovich
21.6.1957–   . Athlete.
Born in Grodno Oblast', Belorussia. Honoured Master of Sports, (rowing), 1976. With the Central Sports Club of the Navy. USSR champion, 1976–77. Olympic champion, 1976.

Romanovskii, Vladimir Zakharovich
1896–1967. Col.-general.
On active service during WWI as a sergeant. Joined the Red Army, 1918. During the Civil War, commander of an armoured train. Joined the Bolshevik Party, 1920. Graduated from the Frunze Military Academy, 1935. Commander of several armies during WWII. Professor at the Frunze Academy, 1959.

Romashin, Anatolii Vladimirovich
1.1.1931–   . Actor.
Graduated from the MKHAT Studio School, 1959. Joined the Mayakovsky Theatre, Moscow. Entered the film industry, 1959. Made over 50 films. His major success was as Nicholas II in E. Klimov's *Agoniia*, 1981.

Romishevskii, Igor' Anatol'evich
25.3.1940–   . Athlete, sports and party official.
Born in Moscow Oblast'. Honoured Master of Sports (hockey), 1968. With the Central Sports Club of the Army. Member of the CPSU, 1968. Graduated from the Moscow Forestry Technical Institute, 1969. Coach. Member of the Cen. Cttee, of the Komsomol, 1970–74. Dean of the Faculty of Physical Education and Sport at the Moscow Physico-Technical Institute, 1974–79. Chairman of the Hockey Federation of the RSFSR from 1975. USSR champion, 1963–72. European champion, 1968–70. World champion, 1968–71. Olympic champion, 1968 and 1972.

Romm, Mikhail Il'ich
24.1.1901–1.11.1971. Film director.
Born in Irkutsk. His films include *Lenin v Oktiabre* (1937), and *Lenin v 1918 Godu* (1939), a classic example of Stalinist cinema. Served in the Red Army, 1918–21. Graduated from the Higher State Artistic and Technical Institute, 1925. Entered the film industry as a scriptwriter and assistant director. His remarkable first (silent) film, *Pyshka* (a free adaptation of a Maupassant short story), became a Soviet classic. Began to adapt his talent to the demands of the time. One of the first artists of note to publicly admit in 1956 that the whole period from the mid-1930s had little to do with art but more to do with propaganda. His *Nine Days of One Year*, 1962, was a remarkably fresh film which was warmly received. Died in Moscow.

Room, Abram Matveevich
28.6.1894–26.7.1976. Film director.
Born in Vilnius. Studied at the Petrograd Psychoneurological Institute, then at Saratov University. Director of Saratov Childrens' Theatre, 1919–23, then the Moscow Theatre of Revolution, 1923–24. Left theatre and turned to cinema. In 1925, filmed *Bukhta Smerti*, which became a classic. *Predatel*, 1926, and *Prividenie Ne Vozvrashchaetsia*, 1930, were interrupted in the middle of their production and shelved. *Strogii Iunosha* was also interrupted, and several people, including Iurii Olesha, the author of the script, were arrested. Made noteworthy adaptations of Aleksandr Kuprin's *Granatovyi Braslet*, and Anton Chekhov's *Tsvety Zapozdalye* (1965 and 1970). Taught at the VGIK (Moscow State Film School).

Rosenberg, Alfred
12.1.1893–16.10.1946. Politician, author.
Born in Reval (Tallinn), then in Russia. Of Baltic German descent. Studied engineering in Riga and architecture at Moscow University. Moved to France and later Germany after the October Revolution 1917. Joined the National Socialist (Nazi) Party, 1919. Became its main ideologue with the book *Myth of the 20th Century*, held in high regard by Hitler personally, who considered its mixture of racism, anti-Semitism and anti-Christianity profound, although it never gained any popularity even among the Nazi faithful. Kept his close spiritual affinity with Hitler, who made him the editor of the official party newspaper *Voelkischer Beobachter*, and during WWII, appointed him Minister for the Occupied Eastern Territories (Head of Ostministerium), 17 July 1941. Personally responsible for the application of the master race theory to the occupied territories in Eastern Europe and Russia, including appalling treatment of the civil population and mass deportations,

which soon aroused universal hatred and resistance. Main enemy of the Vlasov movement within Germany. After WWII, tried at Nuremburg, found guilty of war crimes and hanged.

Rosenberg, Valentina Maksimovna
17.10.1915–27.4.1977. Ballerina.
Born in Petrograd. Graduated from the Leningrad Choreographic School, 1931. Pupil of E. N. Geidenreikh, M. F. Romanova and M. T. Semenova. With the Leningrad Malyi Theatre, 1931–52. Died in Leningrad.

Roshchin, Anatolii Aleksandrovich
10.3.1932– . Athlete.
Born in Riazan' Oblast'. Member of the CPSU, 1962. Honoured Master of Sports (wrestling), 1963. With the Leningrad Armed Forces. Graduated from the Leningrad Institute of Physical Culture, 1965. USSR champion, 1962–71. World champion, 1963, 1969–70. European champion, 1966. Olympic champion, 1972.
See: D. Ivanov, *Eto i Est' Bor'ba. Anatolii Roshchin*, Moscow, 1975.

Rosin, Samuil Izrailevich
14.8.1890–10.1941. Poet.
Born in the village of Shumiachi, now Smolensk Oblast', into a working-class Jewish family. Worked as a manual labourer. First poetry published in 1918. Killed in the Battle of Moscow.
See: *Izbrannoe*, Moscow, 1958.

Rossi, Jacques
1908– . Intelligence officer, lexicographer.
Born in France. His father died before his birth. As a child, moved with his mother and stepfather to Warsaw. Received a linguistic education, mastering several European and Asiatic languages. Joined the illegal Communist Party of Poland, 1927. During the Spanish Civil War, sent as an intelligence officer to set up a secret radio station behind Franco's lines. After Stalin recalled his NKVD agents in Spain, and Orlov and Krivitskii had defected, Rossi returned to the USSR and was promptly sent to the Gulag camps. Prisoner from 1937–58, in exile in Central Asia, 1958–61. Managed to move to Poland, and later to emigrate to the USA. Lives in France. After his release from the Gulag, started to compile a reference book on the Gulag system, and after a quarter of a century of work, published it in London, creating a classic work of its kind. (*Spravochnik po Gulagu*, London, 1987).

Rossolimo, Grigorii Ivanovich
17.12.1860–29.9.1928. Psychiatrist.
Born in Odessa. Graduated from Moscow University in medicine, 1884. Pupil of A. I. Kozhevnikov. Co-student and close friend of Anton Chekhov. From 1890, head of the Clinic of Nervous Diseases at the A. A. Ostroumov Hospital. In 1911, resigned in protest against the activities of the Minister of Education L. A. Kasso. Founded his own clinic for childrens' nervous diseases, 1911. From 1917, taught at Moscow University. Director of a clinic and of the Kozhevnikov Institute of Neurology. After the October Revolution, chief psychiatrist at the RKKA. Died in Moscow.

Rostovtsev, Mikhail Ivanovich
10.11.1870–20.10.1952. Historian.
Born in Kiev. Studied at Kiev and Petersburg universities. Professor at Petersburg University, 1901–18. Historian of antiquity, one of the greatest world authorities in his field. Emigrated, 1918. Professor at Wisconsin University 1920–25, and at Yale University, 1925–44. Member of the academies of many countries. Died in New Haven, USA.

Rostropovich, Leopold Vitol'dovich
9.3.1892–31.7.1942. Cellist.
Born in Voronezh. Son of the cellist, Vitol'd Rostropovich (died 9.10.1913) and father of the cellist Mstislav Rostropovich. Pupil of A. Verzhbilovich. Gave concerts all over Russia. Taught in Voronezh, Saratov and Orenburg. Professor at the Azerbaidzhan Conservatory in Baku, 1925–31. From 1931, lived in Moscow. Author of many works for the cello. Died in Orenburg.

Rostropovich, Mstislav Leopoldovich
27.3.1927– . Cellist, conductor.
Born in Baku. Son of a musician. Graduated from Moscow Conservatory, 1946. Became internationally known as a soloist with the Moscow Philharmonic. In the early 1970s, gave refuge to A. Solzhenitsyn, which cost him his position and his country. Left the Soviet Union with his family and was stripped of Soviet citizenship in 1978. Became a household name in the West. Lives in London. Has homes in the USA, Paris, Aldeburgh and Lausanne. Married to the opera singer Galina Vishnevskaia. Queen Elizabeth II conferred on him an honorary knighthood in 1987 on his 60th birthday.

Rotmistrov, Pavel Alekseevich
1901–1982. Marshal.
Joined the Red Army and the Bolshevik Party, 1919. Took part in the Civil War. Graduated from the Frunze Military Academy, 1931. During the Soviet-Finnish war and WWII, commander of tank forces. After WWII, commander of Soviet tank forces in Germany, and later in the Far East. Graduated from the Academy of the General Staff, 1953, and became a professor at the same Academy. Head of the Academy of Tank Forces, 1958. Deputy Minister of Defence, 1964–68.

Rotshtein, Fedor Ivanovich (Rotstein, Theodore)
26.2.1871–30.8.1953. Historian, state official, diplomat.
Born in Kaunas. Social Democrat, 1901 (later Bolshevik). Lived in England as a political emigré, 1890–1920. Active in the British trade union movement and communist press. In 1911, joined the left wing of the Labour Party. One of the founders of *Call*, 1916. One of the founders of the British Communist Party, 1920. Returned to Soviet Russia. USSR representative in Iran, 1921–22. Member of the Collegium of the People's Commissariat for Foreign Affairs, 1923–30. One of the chief editors of the *Bolshaia Sovetskaia Entsiklopediia* (first edition, 1927–45). Wrote a history of the working class movement in Great Britain, 1925. Also *The Decline of British Industry, Its Cause and Remedy*, London, 1903. Died in Moscow.

Rovner, Arkadii Borisovich
1940–   . Writer.
Appeared in *Novyi Zhurnal, Apollon, Okkultizm I Ioga, Ekho* and *Gnozis*. His main work is the novel *Kalalatsy*, 1980. Has lived in New York since 1974.

Rozai, Georgii Al'fredovich
1887–4.1917. Ballet dancer.
Born in Tambov Gouvt. Graduated from the Petersburg Theatre School, 1907. Pupil of M. K. Obukhov. With the Mariinskii Theatre, 1907–15. Appeared in the Ballets Russes in Paris, 1909–11. Character and grotesque dancer. Appeared in the productions of M. Petipa. Died in Peterhof.

Rozanov, Ivan Nikanorovich
21.8.1874–22.11.1959. Linguist, author, bibliophile.
Born in Morshansk, now Tambov Oblast'. Brother of Matvei Rozanov. Graduated in history and philology from Moscow University, 1899. Professor of Moscow University, 1918. Head of the Department of the History of Books at the Historical Museum, Moscow, 1919–41. Worked at the Moscow Gorkii Institute of World Literature of the Academy of Sciences, 1935–53. From 1900 published some 300 works, including *Russkaia Lirika*, 1914, *Pesni Russkikh Poetov*, 1936 and *Russkie Pesni 19-go Veka*, 1944. His private library and collection of Russian poetry was unique. After his death, it was given to the Pushkin Museum, Moscow. Died in Moscow.

Rozanov, Matvei Nikanorovich
8.12.1858–20.10.1936. Author, linguist, academician.
Born in Moscow. Elder brother of Ivan Rozanov. Graduated from Moscow University, 1883. Professor, Moscow University, 1911–29. Wrote on Jean-Jacques Rousseau, A. Pushkin and his ties with Italian literature, and Jacob Lentz. Died in Moscow.

Rozanov, Mikhail Mikhailovich
25.10.1902–   . Author.
Born in Tambov Gouvt. Worked as a newspaper reporter in various Russian towns. Fled to Manchuria in 1928. Arrested during the Soviet-

Chinese war, and sentenced to 10 years in the labour camps. Inmate of the Solovki camps. Freed 21 June 1941 on the first day of the war in the USSR, and immediately taken into the work battalions run by the NKVD. (There are very few survivors from these battalions, since they were always used in the front-line.) Taken prisoner and became a POW in Germany, and after the war, a Displaced Person. Left Germany for the USA in 1949. Considered one of the best pre-Solzhenitsyn historians of the Gulag system. His *Zavoevateli Belykh Piaten* became a post-war bestseller among Russian readers outside the USSR. Wrote the 3-vol. *Solovetskii Kontslager v Monastyre* (Solovki Concentration Camp in a Monastery), USA, 1978–87. Lives in Buffalo, NY.

Rozanov, Sergei Vasil'evich
5.7.1870–31.8.1937. Clarinettist.
Born in Riazan'. Pupil of F. Tsimmerman. Professor at the Moscow Conservatory. Author of 2 clarinet manuals (1940 and 1951). Also made clarinets. Died in Moscow.

Rozanov, Vasilii Vasil'evich
2.5.1856–5.2.1919. Author, journalist.
Born in Vetluga, Kostroma Gouvt. Educated at high school in Simbirsk (Ulyanovsk) and Novgorod. Graduated from Moscow University, 1881. History and geography teacher at provincial high schools (Simbirsk, Elets, Viazma). As a student, married the former mistress of his idol Dostoevskii (Appolinaria Suslova), 1880. This disastrous marriage scarred him for life. Parted with his wife (who refused to agree to divorce), 1886, and started a new family life (illegally, as no church marriage was possible under the circumstances). Moved to Petersburg in 1893. From 1899, a regular contributor to the newspaper *Novoe Vremia*. Gained fame, bordering on notoriety, by his open contempt for all the traditional values of the intelligentsia (political dogmatism, left-wing conviction, atheism, faith in progress). At the same time, scandalized conservative circles by his pro-Old Testament and anti-Christian position (condemning the ascetic traditions of the Christian

church), and his stress on sexuality as the basis of all life. His religious attraction to Judaism and political anti-Semitism completed the confusion and insured that he offended just about everybody. Despite all this, he was widely read, due to his always unexpected, often profound, always aphoristic way of thinking. In his time, practically the only Russian thinker to appreciate the works of K. Leontiev, considered then unduly pessimistic and reactionary. Member of the Religous-Philosophical Society, 1902–3. Can be regarded as the Russian Freud (though his pansexism is founded on a different basis and is much less gloomy). Died of hunger in Zagorsk in the revolution. Main works: *Izbrannoe, Solitaria, Religia i Kultura, Priroda i Istoriia, Semeinyi Vopros v Rossii*, 2 vol., *Temnyi Lik, Ludi Lunnogo Sveta*.

Rozanov, Vladimir Nikolaevich
15.12.1872–16.10.1934. Surgeon.
Born in Moscow. Graduated in medicine from Moscow University, 1896. One of the organizers of the surgery department of the Soldatenkovskaia Hospital (now Botkin Hospital). Chief surgeon of the hospital, 1910. On 23 Apr. 1922, operated on V. Lenin (this was Lenin's second operation as a result of Dora Kaplan's attempt on his life, Aug. 1918). From 1929, chief surgeon of the Kremlin Hospital. Also taught at the Teaching Hospital. Diagnosed Stalin's paranoia in the early 1930s. Died in Moscow after an unexplained poisoning in a Moscow hotel.

Rozanova, Maria Aleksandrovna
17.8.1885–27.10.1957. Botanist.
Born in Moscow. Assistant and close collaborator of the academician Nikolai Vavilov. Graduated from the Bestuzhev Higher Women's Courses at Petrograd University, 1916. From 1933, professor. Chief of Section of the All-Union Institute of Plant-Growing of the Academy of Sciences. Taught at Leningrad University until 1944. Died in Leningrad.

Rozenberg, Fedor Aleksandrovich
1.3.1867–5.6.1934. Orientalist.
Born in Viliandi. Graduated from Petersburg University, 1889. Pupil of

K. G. Zaleman. Worked at the Asian Museum, 1902–31. From 1912, senior scientist-keeper. From 1930, worked at the Institute of Oriental Studies. Specialist on Iranian literature and culture. Wrote many articles on Iran and its art. Corresponding member of the Academy of Sciences. Died in Leningrad.

Rozenov, Emilii Karlovich
27.10.1861–17.6.1935. Pianist, music critic.
Born in Paris. Studied in Paris, Petersburg and Moscow. Concert pianist. Appeared in the music press. Wrote on Bach and other composers. Died in Moscow.

Rozenshil'd, Konstantin Konstantinovich
2.4.1898–1979? Musicologist.
Born in Warsaw (then in Russia). Taught at the Gnesin Music Pedagogical School, Moscow.
Works: *Istoriia Zarubezhnoi Muzyki do Serediny 18-go Veka*, Moscow, 1963; *Molodoi Debiussi i ego Sovremenniki*, Moscow, 1963; *Muzykal'noe Iskusstvo i Religiia*, Moscow, 1964.

Rozhavskaia, Iudif' Grigor'evna
12.11.1923– . Composer.
Born in Kiev. Wrote music for children's theatre and ballet. Author of the vocal symphony, *Snegurochka*, 1955, and the ballet *Korolevstvo Krivykh Zerkal*, 1955 (produced, 1965). Also wrote children's songs.

Rozhdestvenskaia, Natal'ia Petrovna
7.5.1900– . Singer.
Born in Nizhnii-Novgorod. Pupil of S. Druziakina. Soloist with All-Union Radio, Moscow, 1929–60.

Rozhdestvenskii, Gennadii Nikolaevich
4.5.1931– . Conductor.
Born in Moscow. Pupil of the conductor N. Anosov, and the famous pianist Lev Oborin. Graduated from the Moscow Conservatory, 1954. Began his conducting at the age of 18. Principal conductor, Bolshoi Theatre, 1965–70. Chief conductor, Moscow Chamber Opera, 1974. Chief conductor and artistic director, Great Symphony Orchestra

of Radio and Television of the USSR, 1961–74 and artistic director of Stockholm Philharmonic Orchestra from 1974. Chief conductor, BBC Symphony Orchestra, 1978–early 1980s. Guest conductor in Europe, Israel and the USA. Married to the concert pianist Victoria Postnikova.

Rozhdestvenskii, Robert Ivanovich
20.6.1932– . Poet.
Born in the village of Kosikha, Altai Krai. Son of an officer. Grew up in orphanages (possibly lost his parents during the war). Graduated from the Moscow Gorkii Literary Institute, 1956. Began writing at the end of the 1940s. First poetry published, 1950. Became famous in the early 1960s.

Rozhdestvenskii, Vasilii Vasil'evich
1884–1963. Artist.
Landscape painter. Studied at the Moscow School of Painting, Sculpture and Architecture, 1900–11, under A. Arkhipov, N. Kasatkin and K. Korovin. Exhibitions: Moscow Association of Artists, 1907, the Mir Iskusstva, 1911–12, 1917, 1922, the Bubnovyi Valet, 1913–14, 1927, Painting, Moscow, 1915, the 5th State Exhibition, Moscow 1918–19. Personal exhibitions: Moscow, 1935, 1940, 1945, 1957. Died in Moscow.

Rozhdestvenskii, Vsevolod Petrovich
2.7.1918– . Composer, conductor.
Born in Poltava. Music director of the Franko Theatre in Kiev from 1945. Composer of many musicals, and also pieces for the cinema.

Rozhin, Igor' Evgen'evich
30.9.1908– . Architect.
Born in Petersburg and graduated from the Leningrad VKHUTEIN, 1925–30. Pupil of V. Gelfreikh, L. Rudnev, I. Fomin and V. Shchuko. One of Stalin's architects and chief exponent of socialist realism in architecture. The metro stations Novokuznetskaia (1943) and Elektrozavodskaia (1946), the Soviet Embassy building in Warsaw (1954–56), are some of his many works. Taught at the Moscow Architectural Institute, 1935–64 and from 1972.

Rozhkov, Petr Frolovich
1900–1962. Major-general.
Joined the Red Army, 1919. Took part in the Civil War. Joined the Bolshevik Party, 1924. Graduated from the Dzerzhinskii Military Academy, 1934. Took part in the Khalkin Gol operations and the Soviet-Finnish war as an artillery officer. During WWII, mainly in anti-aircraft forces in the Leningrad area. After WWII, in anti-aircraft forces in the Far East. High command posts in the Soviet anti-aircraft forces until 1950.

Rozhnov, Vladimir Evgen'evich
1928– . Psychiatrist, state official.
Pupil of Professor Basov. Deputy chief of the Psychotherapy Department of the Institute of Doctors. Educated at the Academy of Medical Sciences. For more than 30 years, carried out research into the effect of psychotherapy and hypnosis on the human body. Wrote (with his wife) *Hypnosis and Medicine*, 1955, and *Hypnosis and Mystics*, 1974. Also interested in parapsychology; involved with the experiments being carried out by Sviaduch and Romen at a laboratory in Alma–Ata, Kazakhstan. Together with Dr Shcherbakova and Dr Raevskii, involved in experiments to test the ability of hypnosis to affect personality and to influence opinion. Involved in the case of Father Dimitrii Dudko and other religious politicals. Acted as Dr Andrei Sakharov's doctor in the Semashko Hospital in Gorkii, administering neuroleptics to him.

Rozin', Fritsis (Friedrich) Adamovich (Rozinsh; literary pseudonym – Azis)
19.3.1870–7.5.1919. Revolutionary, politician.
Founder of the Latvian Communist Party. Born in Latvia. Son of a peasant. Studied at Tartu University, 1891–97. Joined the revolutionary movement. In 1899, emigrated to England. Organizer of the Latvian social-democratic press. Translated the Communist Manifesto into Latvian. One of the organizers of the Latvian Social-Democratic Party, 1904, and member of its Cen. Cttee. Returned to Latvia, 1905. Delegate of the 5th Congress of the RSDRP, 1907. In 1908, arrested and sentenced

to hard labour. In 1913, exiled to Eastern Siberia. Escaped to the USA. Editor of the Latvian Social-Democratic (Bolshevik) newspaper *Worker*. Returned to Latvia, Oct. 1917. From Mar. 1918, Deputy People's Commissar of Nationalities of the RSFSR. Member of the VTSIK Presidium. In 1919, Commissar of Agriculture in Soviet Latvia. Died in Latvia.

Rozov, Viktor Sergeevich
21.8.1913– . Playwright, script-writer
Prominent playwright. Scripts include *The Cranes Are Flying*, which is now a Soviet modern classic, and *The Letter That Was Never Sent*, 1960. Worked for several theatres.

Rozovskii, Mark Grigor'evich
1937– . Playwright, stage director.
Born in Moscow. Began writing for *Iunost* and other magazines in the early 1960s. Staged classical adaptations and his own original plays at Moscow University Students' Theatre. His remarkable adaptation of Leo Tolstoy's *Kholstomer* (History of a Horse) in Georgii Tovstonogov's production was performed by the Leningrad Gorkii Theatre at the 1987 Edinburgh Festival with great success.

Rubakin, Nikolai Aleksandrovich
13.7.1862–23.11.1946. Author, bibliographer, book collector.
Born in Oranienbaum (now Lomonosov) into a rich merchant family. Graduated in physics and mathematics, then in law from Petersburg University. As a student, involved in revolutionary activity. Briefly arrested. In 1907, emigrated to Switzerland leaving his library (some 130,000 books) to the Russian League of Education. Sympathised with, but did not return to, the USSR. For nearly 30 years, closely connected with the Soviet government. Shortly before his death gave his Western library of some 200,000 books, as well as his valuable archive, to the Lenin Library, Moscow. From 1930, received an honorary pension from the Soviet government. Died in Lausanne, buried in Moscow.
See: A. N. Rubakin, *Rubakin, Lots-man Knizhnogo Moria*, Moscow, 1967.

Rubashvili, Vladimir
26.12.1940–4.2.1965. Wrestler.
Georgian athlete. Honoured Master of Sports (wrestling). Many times USSR and Georgian champion. Bronze medal-winner at the XVIIth Olympic Games. Died during training.

Rubin, Evgenii Mikhailovich
1929– . Lawyer, sports journalist.
Born in Moscow. Graduated from the Moscow Law Institute, 1952. Worked in the Soviet judicial system for 3 years. In 1955, turned to journalism, specializing in sport. Staff editor with *Sovetskii Sport* newspaper for 20 years. Left the USSR, 1978. Lives in New York. In 1980, co-founded (with S. Dovlatov and others) the weeklies *Novyi Amerikanets* and *Novaia Gazeta*, which he edited until Sep. 1983, when it became a daily under the name of *Novosti*. Editor-in-chief till Dec. 1983. Has contributed to several other Russian emigré publications.

Rubinstein, Ida L'vovna
1885–20.9.1960. Ballerina.
Born in Petersburg. Pupil of M. M. Fokin. Took part in Russian performances abroad. Appeared in Paris, 1909. Gifted mime artist. Appeared successfully in Petersburg, Paris and London in the *Dance of Salome* especially produced for her by Fokin, 1908. Directed her own company, 1909–11 and 1929–35, Several ballets were choreographed especially for her. Appeared in plays and films. Emigrated. Died in Vance, in the Alpes Maritimes (France).

Rubo, Frants Alekseevich
17.6.1856–13.3.1928. Artist.
Battle and monumental artist. Born in Odessa. Studied at the Odessa School of Graphic Art, 1865, then at the Munich Academy of Arts, 1878, under I. Brandt. Professor and dean of the battle painting department at the Academy of Arts, Petersburg, 1903–12. From 1913, lived mainly in Germany. Exhibitions: from 1882 until 1913 in Russia (Nizhnii Novgorod, Petersburg). Died in Munich.

Rudakov, Mikhail Vasil'evich
1905–1979. Lt.-general, political officer.
Joined the Red Army, 1923, and the Bolshevik Party, 1926. Graduated from the Lenin Military-Political Academy, 1938. Political officer during WWII. After the war, in charge of political control in the Personnel Department of the Armed Forces. After the Khrushchev thaw, demoted to political work in universities, 1956–69.

Rudenko, Bella Andreevna
18.8.1933– . Coloratura soprano.
Born in Bokovo-Antratsit in the Ukraine. Graduated from the Odessa Conservatory, 1956. First stage appearance in 1955 at the Odessa Theatre of Opera and Ballet. After 1956, moved to the Kiev Opera Theatre. Became a powerful lyrical coloratura soprano. From 1973, with the Bolshoi Theatre performing in such productions as *Ruslan and Liudmila* (as Liudmila), and *La Traviata* (as Violetta).

Rudenko, Mykola Danilovich
1920– . Dissident.
Joined the Komsomol, 1935. Took part in WWII. Became a well-known establishment writer in the Ukraine in the early 1960s. Later involved in the human rights movement. Expelled from the Ukrainian Union of Writers, May 1975. Sent to a psychiatric hospital on KGB orders, Feb. 1976, but soon released. One of the founders of the Ukrainian Helsinki Group, Nov. 1976. Arrested Feb. 1977, sentenced to 7 years in prison and 5 years in exile. Released under Gorbachev, emigrated, 1987.

Rudenko, Roman Andreevich
30.7.1907– . Lawyer, state official.
Born in the village of Nosovka, Chernigov Oblast'. Son of a peasant. Member of the CPSU from 1926. Educated at the Moscow Law School, then the Higher Law Courses at the Law Academy, 1941. Worked for the security services in the Ukraine from 1929. Ukrainian Chief Prosecutor, 1944–53. Chief Soviet Prosecutor at the Nuremberg war trials, 1945–46. USSR General Prosecutor from 1953.

Rudenko, Sergei Ignat'evich
1904– . Marshal.
Joined the Red Army, 1923, and the Bolshevik Party, 1928. Graduated from the Zhukovskii Air Force Academy, 1932. High command posts in the Air Force during WWII. Commander of airborne troops, 1948. Commander of Strategic Aviation, and Deputy Commander-in-chief of the Air Force, 1950–58. Non-voting member of the Cen. Cttee. of the CPSU, 1961–66. Head of the Air Force Academy, 1968–73.

Rudenkov, Vasilii Vasil'evich
7.5.1931– . Athlete.
Born in Gomel' Oblast', Belorussia. Graduated from a railway high school, 1948. Honoured Master of Sports (track and field athletics), 1960. With Moscow Dynamo. USSR champion, 1959–61. Olympic champion, 1960. Works as a sports instructor.

Rudnev, Nikolai Aleksandrovich
1894–1918. Revolutionary.
Joined the Bolshevik Party, 1917, and the Red Army, 1918. Took part in the Civil War, mainly near Khar'kov in the Ukraine. Fell in action against Wrangel near Tsaritsyn (later Stalingrad).

Rudnev, Semen Vasil'evich
1899–1943. Political officer, partisan.
During the Bolshevik take-over, took part in the storming of the Winter Palace, Nov. 1917. Took part in the Civil War. Joined the Bolshevik Party, 1917, and the Red Army, 1918. Graduated from the Military-Political Academy, 1929. During WWII, political commissar of partisan detachments in the Ukraine under Kovpak. Promoted to major-general, 1943. Fell in action.

Rudnev, Vadim Viktorovich
1879–1940. Politician, editor.
Active member of the SR Party. 1st mayor of Moscow after the fall of the monarchy. Emigrated after the October Revolution 1917. Editor of one of the most important Russian periodicals in the West—*Les Annales Contemporaines* (with Ilia Fondaminskii-Bunakov) in Paris. Died in France.

Rudov, Iurii Vasil'evich
17.1.1931– . Athlete.
Born in Taganrog. Honoured Master of Sports (fencing), 1960. With Moscow Dynamo. World champion, 1959, 1961 and 1963. USSR champion, 1960. Olympic champion, 1960.

Rudzutak, Ian Ernestovich
15.8.1887–29.7.1938. Revolutionary, politician.
Born in the village of Tsauni, Latvia, into a peasant family. From 1906, involved in revolutionary activity. In 1909, arrested and sentenced to 15 years hard labour (reduced to 10 years). Imprisoned in Riga Tsentral (Riga prison) and Butyrki prison, Moscow. Released after the February Revolution 1917. Participant in the October Revolution 1917. Chairman of the Sovnarkhoz (Council of the National Economy) and member of the Presidium of the VSNKH, 1917–20. Chairman of the Central Soviet of the Textile Industry. Member of the Cen. Cttee. Chairman of the Transport Trade Unions, 1920–21. Chairman of the Turkkomissiia, VTISK (Commission of Turkestan Affairs) and the Turkburo. Member of the Presidium and General Secretary of the Cen. Cttee. Chairman of the Cen. Cttee. of the Central Asia Bureau, 1922–24. Participant in the Genoa Conference, 1922. Secretary of the RK VKPB, 1923–24. Minister of Transport of the USSR, 1924–30. From 1928, chairman of the Cttee. of the Chemical Industry of the USSR. Delegate at the 9th and 17th party congresses. Member of the Cen. Auditing Cttee., and the VTSIK. Stalinist member of the Cen. Cttee. and of the Politburo (1926–32) of the Bolshevik Party, but later a victim of Stalin's purges. Perished in the Gulag.

Runov, Viktor Sergeevich
26.5.1907– . Composer, conductor.
Born in Petrovsk, Saratov Gouvt. Military conductor. Author of many military songs. Also wrote suites, cantatas, and rhapsodies.

Rupshene, Angele Stasio (Iankunaite)
27.6.1952– . Athlete.
Born in Vil'nius, Lithuania. Hon-oured Master of Sports (basketball), 1976. With Vil'nius Zhal'giris. Studied at the Vil'nius Pedagogical Institute. World champion, 1971 and 1975. European champion, 1972, 1976 and 1978. Olympic champion, 1976.

Rurua, Roman Vladimirovich
25.11.1942– . Athlete.
Born in a Georgian village. Honoured Master of Sports (wrestling), 1966. With Tbilisi Kolmeurne. Member of the CPSU, 1970. Graduated from the Georgian Polytechnical Institute, 1972. USSR champion, 1963–70. World champion, 1966–70. Olympic champion, 1968.

Rusak, Vladimir Stepanovich (Stepanov)
6.1949– . Deacon.
Born at Baranovichi, Belorussia. Graduated from the Zagorsk Theological Academy, 1977. Employed in the publishing department of the Moscow Patriarchate. Gathered a unique collection of documents on church-state relations in Russia after 1917. Wrote a history of the Russian Orthodox Church under Soviet rule. Part of this work has been published in the West. The other part was confiscated by the KGB. Arrested in Apr. 1986. Sentenced to 7 years in camps and 5 years exile. Released, 1988.

Rusanov, Valerian Alekseevich
22.1.1866–17.7.1918. Guitarist, composer.
Born in Moscow. Pupil of A. Solov'ev and A. Diubiuk. Editor-publisher of the magazine *Gitarist*, 1904–06. Composer of music for the guitar. Gave concerts all over Russia. Author of *Gitara i Gitaristy*, Moscow, 1899–1901. Died in Moscow.

Ruslanova, Lidia Andreevna
27.10.1900– . Singer.
Born in Saratov. Mordovian by nationality. Pupil of M. Medvedev. Leading singer of Russian folk songs. Attracted crowds to her concerts. Entertained Stalin and his foreign guests in the Kremlin Concert Hall. Sold millions of records.

Russkikh, Aleksandr Georgievich
1903– . Lt.-general, political officer.
Political officer during the Civil War, 1919–22. Graduated in law from Leningrad University, 1930. Took part in the Soviet-Finnish war and WWII. After WWII, deputy head of Soviet Military Administration in Germany. After Stalin's death, demoted to political officer at the Military Medical Academy, 1954–59.

Rustamov, Seid Ali ogly
13.5.1907– . Composer, conductor.
Born in Erevan'. Taught at the Baku Conservatory in the Tara Class. Chief conductor of the Azerbaidzhan Radio Orchestra. Author of operettas, songs, and music for ballets. Several Stalin Prizes.

Ruzgaite, Aliodia Vintsovna
24.6.1923– Ballerina.
Born in Kaunas. Pupil of A. Fedorova, V. Nemchinova, V. Kelbauskas. Graduated from the ballet school of the Kaunas Theatre, 1939, from the Faculty of Philology, Kaunas University, 1949, and from the Drama Faculty of the GITIS (State Institute of Dramatic Art), 1953. Appeared with the Vil'nius Theatre, 1942–68. Teacher of choreography at the Churlenis (Vil'nius) School of Arts and at the Vil'nius School of Culture. Author of *Khoreograficheskoe Iskusstvo*, 1960, and *Put' Litovskogo Baleta*, 1964.

Ruzhitskii, Konstantin Ivanovich, Archpriest
29.3.1888–17.11.1964. Russian Orthodox clergyman.
Born at Molchitsy in Volhynia. Son of a deacon. Educated at the Volhynia seminary in Zhitomir, 1912. Graduated from the Moscow Theological Academy, 1916. Priest in various parts of the Ukraine, 1916–45, and at the St. Vladimir Cathedral in Kiev, 1945, where he supervised the rebuilding of the war-damaged cathedral. Represented the Moscow church authorites at the L'vov Council, 1946, when on Stalin's orders, the Ukrainian Uniate Church (Greek Catholic) was officially incorporated into the Russian Ortho-dox Church (continuing to exist underground). Professor (Greek language and psychology) at the Kiev Seminary, 1948–49. Dean of the Moscow Theological Academy, 1951.

Ruzskii, Nikolai Vladimirovich
1854–1918. General.
Graduated from the Academy of the General Staff, 1881. Took part in the Russo-Turkish war, 1877–78. Chief-of-staff of the 2nd Manchurian Army during the Russo-Japanese war, 1904–05. During WWI, commander of the Northwestern, and Northern fronts. On good terms with the leaders of the Duma. Considered for a time to be a candidate for supreme power after the fall of the monarchy. At his HQ in Pskov in Feb. 1917, Tsar Nicholas signed his abdication after pressure from Ruzskii. Murdered by revolutionary soldiers in the Caucasus.

Rybak, Igor' Mikhailovich
2.12.1934– . Athlete.
Born in Khar'kov. Honoured Master of Sports (heavy athletics), 1957. With Khar'kov Avangard. Graduated from the Khar'kov Medical Institute, 1959. Member of the CPSU, 1963. Works as a doctor. Candidate of Medical Sciences. European champion, 1956. Olympic champion, 1956.

Rybakov, Anatolii Naumovich (Aronov)
14.1.1911– . Author.
Born in Chernigov. Son of an engineer. In 1934, graduated from the Moscow Institute of Railroad Engineers. Fought in WWII, 1941–45. His first children's book *The Dagger* was published in 1948 (filmed in 1958). Won a Stalin Prize in 1951 for his novels *The Drivers* and *Ekaterina Voronina* (a film adaptation of the latter was made in 1955). All his books published in the 1960s (*The Adventures of Krosh*, *The Innocent Games*, *The Unknown Soldier*) have been turned into films. Received the Vasil'ev Brothers Prize in 1973. Suddenly emerged as a major modern writer with *Children of the Arbat*, published by a Moscow literary magazine in 1987. The book gives a detailed picture of Kremlin intrigues in the early 1930s and implies that Stalin ordered the murder of his rival, Sergei Kirov, in 1934. Apparently he had started the novel in 1967 without any hope of ever publishing it in the Soviet Union. *Children of the Arbat* has been hailed by liberal literary circles as a work of major importance for its honest treatment of themes until recently barred by official censors. Visited London, 1988, in connection with the publication of the English translation of this book. Other books: *Kortik*, *Bronzovaia Ptitsa*, *Povesti*, *Voditeli*.

Rybakov, Sergei Gavrilovich
9.10.1867–28.12.1921. Music ethnographer.
Born in Samara. Author of *Tserkovnyi Zvon v Rossii*, St. Petersburg, 1896, *O Poeticheskom Tvorchestve Ural'skikh Musul'man*, St. Petersburg, 1895, and *Muzyka i Pesni Ural'skikh Musul'man*, St. Petersburg, 1897. Died in Moscow.

Rybakov, Vladimir Mechislavovich
1947– . Writer, journalist.
Born in France. As a child moved with his parents to the Soviet Union. Re-emigrated to France in 1972. His books, *Tiazhest'*, *Zheltye i Krasnye* and *Tavro*, which deal mostly with his experiences in the Soviet Army on the Chinese border, have been translated into French and English. Journalist with *La Pensée Russe* Paris, and later with the Posev Publishing House, Germany.

Rybalchenko, Stepan Dmitrievich
1903–1986. Col.-general.
Joined the Red Army, 1919. Took part in the Civil War. Graduated from the Frunze Military Academy, 1936. In the 1930s and during WWII, held command posts in the Air Force. After WWII, commander of the Air Force in the Far East. Professor at military education establishments, 1956–63.

Rybalko, Pavel Semenovich
1894–1948. Marshal.
On active service during WWI. Joined the Red Army and the Bolshevik Party, 1919. Took part in the Civil War as a political commis-

sar. Graduated from the Frunze Military Academy, 1934. Military attaché in Poland and China, 1937–40. During WWII, became famous as a tank army commander. Commander of Soviet Tank Forces, 1947.

Rybnov, Aleksandr Vasil'evich
1.9.1906– . Choir conductor.
Born in Moscow. Chief choir conductor of the Bolshoi Theatre, 1930–58. Stalin Prize, 1950.

Rykhliakova, Varvara Trofimovna
1871–1919. Ballerina.
Graduated from the Petersburg Theatre School. Pupil of Kh. P. Ioganson and E. Cecchetti. With the Mariinskii Theatre, 1890–1910. Appeared in ensembles with M. F. Kshesinskaia, O. I. Preobrazhenskaia and L. N. Egorova. Taught at the Petersburg Theatre School.

Rykov, Aleksei Ivanovich
25.2.1881–14.3.1938. Politician.
Born in Saratov. Joined the SD Party, 1899. After the split, joined the Bolsheviks. Participated in the 1905 Revolution. Went abroad (to Paris), 1910–11. Upon his return to Russia, arrested and exiled to Siberia. Released after the February Revolution 1917. Commissar of the Interior in the first Bolshevik government, Oct. 1917. Chairman of the Supreme Council of the National Economy, 1918–21. Member of the Politburo, 1923. Deputy chairman, later chairman of the Council of People's Commissars (head of the government) after Lenin's death, 1924. Stalin's ally at the beginning of the struggle for Lenin's succession, but after eliminating his other rivals (Trotsky, Zinovev, and Kamenev), Stalin turned on Rykov and Bukharin. Branded as a leader of the right opposition, and dismissed from his post, 1929. Arrested and expelled from the party, 1937. Convicted at a show trial, Mar. 1938, and executed. Rehabilitated under Gorbachev.

Rylov, Arkadii Aleksandrovich
29.1.1870–22.6.1939. Artist.
Landscape and historical painter. Born in the village of Istobenskoe, now Istobensk, Kirov Oblast'. Studied at the Shtiglits Central School of Technical Graphic Art, 1888–91, then at the Petersburg Academy of Arts, 1894–97 under A. Kuindzhi. Member of the Mir Iskusstva and the Union of Russian Artists. Exhibited from 1901. Died in Leningrad where, a year later, a posthumous exhibition of his work was held.

Ryl'skii, Iakov Anufrievich
25.10.1928– . Athlete.
Born in Eastern Kazakhstan. Honoured Master of Sports (fencing), 1961. With Moscow Dynamo. USSR champion, 1954–58. World champion, 1958, 1961, 1963 and 1965. Olympic champion, 1964.

Ryl'skii, Maksim Faddeevich
19.3.1895–24.7.1964. Poet.
Born in Kiev. Grew up in the family of the Ukrainian composer N. Lysenko. Specialist in Ukrainian folk music. Author of biographies of Lysenko, Gulak-Artemovskii and other Ukrainian composers. Some 300 of his poems have been set to music by various composers. Translated into Ukrainian the librettos of operas by such composers as Glinka, Verdi, Rossini, and Tchaikovskii. Wrote neoclassic poetry in the 1920s and socialist-realist verse after the 1930s. Chairman of the Ukrainian Union of Writers, 1943–46. Academician, 1958. Highly decorated, 3 Orders of Lenin. Died in Kiev.

Ryndin, Vadim Fedorovich
5.1.1902–9.4.1974. Stage designer.
Born in Moscow. Trained at the Free Applied Arts Workshop in Voronezh, 1918–22, and at the VKHUTEMAS, Moscow, 1922–24. Chief stage designer with the Kamernyi Theatre, the Vakhtangov Theatre, and the Moscow Drama Theatre. With the Bolshoi Theatre, 1953–74. Distinctive traits of his artistry include a harmony between structure and picturesqueness, and local colour. Died in Moscow. Author of *Kak Sozdaet'sia Khudozhestvennoe Oformlenie Spektaklia*, Moscow, 1962, and *Khudozhnik i Teatr*, Moscow, 1966. See: V Berezkin, *Vadim Ryndin*, Moscow, 1974.

Rynin, Nikolai Alekseevich
1877–1942. Space scientist.
Graduated from the Petersburg Communications Engineering Institute, 1901. Head of the Faculty of Air Communications at the same institute, 1920. Professor at the Civil Aviation Institute, 1930. One of the organizers of an early rocket research group in Leningrad, 1931. Early theoretical works on rockets and space flights.

Ryskal', Inna Valer'evna
15.6.1944– . Athlete.
Born in Baku, Azerbaidzhan. Honoured Master of Sports (volleyball), 1968. With Baku Neftchi. Graduated from the Azerbaidzhanian Institute of Physical Culture, 1968. Sports instructor. European champion, 1963, 1967 and 1971. Olympic champion, 1968 and 1972. World champion, 1970.

Ryzhenko, Natalia Ivanovna
1.3.1938– . Ballerina, choreographer.
Born in Moscow. Graduated from the Moscow Choreographic School. With the Bolshoi Theatre, 1956–77. Appeared in many parts. Debut as choreographer and stage designer, together with V. V. Smirnov-Golovanov, in 1968 in a TV ballet film. Several other joint productions of ballet films. Choreographed, together with Smirnov-Golovanov and M. M. Plisetskaia, the ballet *Anna Karenina* produced at the Bolshoi in 1972. Many other joint productions with Smirnov-Golovanov at the Stanislavskii and Nemirovich-Danchenko Theatre. Choreographer with the Odessa Theatre from 1977.

Ryzhkov, Nikolai Ivanovich
28.9.1929– . Politician.
Educated at Kramatorsk Technical School, 1950. Started work as a shop steward at the Ordzhonikidze heavy machinery plant in the Urals, where he rose through the ranks. Chief welder, 1959–65, chief engineer, 1965–70, director of the plant, 1970–71. Head of the Uralmash production association, 1971–75. 1st Deputy Minister of Heavy Machinery and Transport Equipment Construction, 1975. 1st deputy chairman of GOSPLAN, 1979–82. Member of the Cen. Cttee. of the CPSU, 1981,

secretary of the Cen. Cttee., 1982, head of a department of the Cen. Cttee., 1982–85. Member of the Politburo, Apr. 1985. Head of Soviet government (after the reluctant retirement of one of the last survivors of the Brezhnev era, Tikhonov), Sep. 1985. An active member of the Gorbachev leadership, connected with glasnost and perestroika.

Ryzhov, Aleksandr Ivanovich
1895–1950. Lt.-general.
Took part in WWI as a sub-lieutenant. Joined the Red Army, 1918. Took part in the Civil War. Graduated from the Academy of the General Staff, 1940. Commander of several armies during WWII.

Rzaev, Azer Guseinovich
15.7.1930–   . Violinist, composer.
Born in Baku. Prominent Azerbaidzhanian musician. Wrote a musical comedy, pieces for violin and piano, songs, romances and chamber music.

Rzaev, Gasan Guseinovich
2.6.1928–   . Composer.
Born in Baku. Brother of Azer Rzaev. Taught at the Baku Conservatory. Wrote orchestral music, and pieces for the theatre and variety stage.

Rzhevskii, Leonid Denisovich
8.8.1905–1986. Author, literary scholar.
Born in Latserdovka, near Rzhev. Son of an officer. Graduated in philology from Moscow University, 1930. Took part in WWII, taken prisoner by the Germans, 1941. After 1945, in DP camps in West Germany. One of the founders of the magazine *Grani*, published in Frankfurt. Moved to the USA. Taught Russian literature at American and Scandinavian universities. Wrote several novels and many articles and linguistic studies published in various Russian periodicals abroad.

S

Saadi, El'vira Fuadovna
2.1.1952–   . Athlete.
Born in Tashkent. Honoured Master of Sports (gymnastics), 1976. Graduated from the Uzbek Institute of Physical Culture, 1974. With Tashkent Dynamo, and from 1974, with Moscow Dynamo. USSR champion, 1972–73. Absolute champion of the USSR, 1973. World champion, 1974, Olympic champion, 1972 and 1976.

Saar, Mart Mikhkelevich
28.9.1882–28.10.1963. Composer, organist.
Born in Estonia. Taught in Yuriev (Tartu). Professor at the Tallinn Conservatory. Composer of over 400 choral works. Author of a book on musical theory, 1915. Died in Tallinn.

Sabaneev, Boris Leonidovich
13.2.1880–7.1.1918. Organist, musicologist.
Born in Moscow. Brother of the composer Leonid Sabaneev (b. 1881). Professor at the Moscow Conservatory. Famous organist. Died in an accident in Moscow.

Sabinina, Marina Dmitrievna
10.9.1917–   . Musicologist.
Born in Petrograd. Author of several books on D. Shostakovich, and the biography *Sergei Prokof'ev*, Moscow, 1957. Also wrote many articles for the music press.

Sabirova, Malika Abdurakhmanovna
22.5.1942–   . Ballerina.
Born in Dushanbe. Graduated from the Leningrad Choreographic School, 1961. Pupil of E. V. Shiripina, V. S. Kostrovitskaia, B. V. Shavrov and N. P. Bazarov. Debut with the Aini Theatre in a concert performance. With the same theatre as leading dancer from 1962. Prize-winner at the International Ballet Competition in Varna, 1964, and in Moscow, 1969. Took part in guest performances abroad.

Saburov, Aleksandr Nikolaevich
1908–1974. State security officer.
Joined the Bolshevik Party, 1932.

Officer of the NKVD, 1938. During WWII, commander of communist partisans near Orel and in Northern Ukraine. Hero of the Soviet Union, 1942. Major-general, 1943. From 1944, on regular NKVD and MVD service.

Saburova, Irina Evgen'evna
1905–1980. Author.
After the Civil War, lived in Latvia and wrote for the local Russian-language press in Riga. During WWII, moved to Germany, where she lived in DP camps. Became one of the most popular women writers of Russian literature in the West. Her novel, *Korabli Starogo Goroda*, about life in pre-war Riga, was translated into several languages. Lived near Munich, worked for Radio Liberty in the 1950s and 1960s. Died in Munich.

Sadovskii, Mikhail Aleksandrovich
6.11.1904–   . Physicist.
Graduated from the Leningrad Polytechnic Institute, 1928. Specialist in the physics and mechanics of explosions. Author of works on seismography.

Safin, Rennat Ibragimovich
29.7.1940–   . Athlete.
Born in the Tatar ASSR. Honoured Master of Sports (biathlon), 1969. With Leningrad Dynamo. Graduated from the Leningrad High School of Physical Culture, 1976. USSR champion, 1967, 1970–72, also in 1971 (20km race). World champion, 1969–71 and 1973. Olympic champion, 1972.

Safin, Shazam Sergeevich
7.4.1932–   . Athlete.
Born in Gor'kovskaia Oblast'. Honoured Master of Sports (wrestling), 1952. With the Moscow Armed Forces team. Graduated from the Moscow High School of Physical Culture, 1953. Olympic champion, 1952.

Safonov, Aleksandr Kononovich
1875–27.9.1919. Revolutionary.
Born in the village of Frolovskoe, near Kostroma. Son of a peasant. In

1888, a worker. From 1904, worked for the Bolsheviks at Iaroslavl' and Petersburg. Several short periods of exile. In 1908, one of the organizers of the local Moscow party organization of the RSDRP. Arrested and exiled to Eastern Siberia. During the February Revolution 1917, in Irkutsk, organized the Irkutsk Bolshevik Cttee. From Aug. 1917, in Moscow, member of the Rogozhskii Party Raikom. In 1919, with the 2nd Army on the Eastern front (against Kolchak), later with the 12th Army on the Western front. Killed at a Moscow party meeting by an anarchist bomb. Buried at the Kremlin wall on Red Square.

Safonov, Boris Feoktistovich
26.8.1915–30.5.1942. Pilot, lt.-colonel.
Born in the village of Siniavino, near Tula. Son of a worker. Joined the army, 1933. Graduated from the 1st Military Aviators School in 1934. In 1941, Commander of the 72nd Air Regiment, later the 2nd Air Regiment of the VVS (Military Air Forces) Northern Fleet. Over 300 personal flights. Shot down 22 German planes. Twice Hero of the Soviet Union. Killed in action near Murmansk trying to protect British sea convoys against German air attack.

Safonov, Vasilii Il'ich
6.2.1852–27.2.1918. Pianist, music teacher, conductor.
Born at Stanitsa Itsiurskaia, Terskii District. In 1880, graduated from the Petersburg Conservatory. Taught at the same conservatory, 1880–85. From 1885–1905, professor at the Moscow Conservatory. From 1889–1905, conductor of symphonic music concerts with the Moscow branch of the Russian Music Society. From 1906–09, conductor of a philharmonic orchestra and director of the National Conservatory in New York. Returned to Russia as a solo pianist (with L. Auer, K. Davydov and others). Promoter of Russian symphonic music. Among his pupils were A. Skriabin and N. Metner. Died in Kislovodsk in the Caucasus. His daughter became the common-law wife of Admiral Kolchak during the Civil War and wrote interesting memoirs about her father and Kolchak, published in the West.

Safronov, Vladimir Konstantinovich
29.12.1934–26.12.1979. Athlete.
Born in Irkutsk. Honoured Master of Sports (boxing), 1957. With the Moscow Armed Forces Team. Graduated from the Moscow Polygraphic Institute, 1963. Member of the CPSU, 1963. Olympic champion, 1956. USSR champion, 1958 and 1962. Died in Moscow.

Safronova, Liudmila Nikolaevna
9.9.1929– . Ballerina.
Born in Leningrad. Graduated from the Leningrad Choreographic School, 1947. Pupil of A. Vaganova. Leading dancer and teacher of classical dance with the Saratov Theatre. With the Malyi Theatre, Leningrad, from 1950. Teacher and coach with the Royal Institute of Arts in Pnom-Penh, 1969–70, and with the Cairo Ballet, 1970–75. Among her pupils were Sonia Sarkis, El'khem al-Amir and Eglel Gallan. Teacher at the Leningrad Choreographic School from 1975.

Sagdeev, Roald Zinnurovich
26.12.1932– . Head of the space research programme.
Born in Moscow. Graduated from Moscow University, 1955. Member of staff of the Institute of Atomic Energy, 1956–61. Head of Laboratory of the Institute of Nuclear Physics of the Siberian Branch of the USSR Academy of Sciences, 1961–70. Member of the USSR Academy of Sciences, 1968. Head of Laboratory of the Institute of High Temperature Physics of the USSR Academy of Sciences, 1970–73. Director of the Institute of Cosmic Exploration from 1973, and head of the Soviet Space Agency, 1987. In 1987, in California, illegally tried to buy a supercomputer that could have been used to destroy incoming missiles. According to American Customs, was prepared to pay $4 million (£2.4 million) for the computer. Apparently connected with the GRU (military intelligence). Resigned as head of the space research programme, 1988.

Saidashev, Salikh Zamaletdinovich
3.12.1900–16.12.1954. Composer, conductor.
Born in Kazan'. His songs, ballets and orchestral pieces dominated the Tatar musical scene. Chief conductor at several Kazan' theatres. Also wrote military marches, music for children's plays, and pieces for radio. Highly regarded by the music establishment. Died in Moscow.

Saifiddinov, Sharofiddin Sanginovich
24.8.1929– . Composer, music official.
Born in Dushanbe. Official Tadzhik composer and 1st Secretary of the Union of Tadzhik Composers. Composer of the opera *Pulat i Gul'ru* (produced in 1957). Also wrote musicals for Tadzhik theatres, symphonies, popular songs, and cantatas.

Sakandelidze, Zurab Aleksandrovich
9.8.1945– . Athlete.
Born in Kutaissi. Honoured Master of Sports (basketball), 1967. With Tbilisi Dynamo. Member of the CPSU, 1972. Graduated from the Georgian Polytechnical Institute, 1975. Works as an engineer. European champion, 1965–71. World champion, 1967. Olympic champion, 1972.

Sakharov, Aleksandr
1948– . Diplomat.
Worked in the Radio and TV Department of Social Information of the United Nations in New York from May 1980. Previously held several high positions in the Ministry of Foreign Affairs, Moscow. Defected with his wife and daughter in New York, Mar. 1981.

Sakharov, Andrei Dmitrievich
21.5.1921– . Physicist.
Born in Moscow. Graduated from Moscow University in 1942. Doctor of physical science, 1953. Member of the USSR Academy of Sciences. At the Lebedev Institute of Physics, 1945. As a nuclear scientist, played a crucial role in the development of the Soviet hydrogen bomb after WWII, involved in top-secret research and design. His articles on the use of nuclear energy for peaceful purposes

were published in the magazine *Atomnaia Energiia*. Work with nuclear power made him extremely conscious of the scientist's responsibility towards mankind. This led to him demanding a ban on all nuclear weapons, and so to his dismissal and early retirement. In the 1960s, helped by his second wife, Elena Bonner, Sakharov became involved with the dissident movement, demanding glasnost and defending human rights. Being by far the most prominent personality in dissident circles, gained wide recognition. One of the co-founders of the Committee for Human Rights in Moscow in 1970. Many of his appeals and open letters circulated in samizdat. Came under increasing pressure from the authorities and in the end was exiled to Gorkii, where he lived under the closest supervision of the KGB. Connection with the outside world was maintained by his wife, who lived in Moscow and was able to travel abroad for health reasons. In Dec. 1986, Sakharov received a surprise call from Gorbachev, and soon thereafter was allowed to return to Moscow. Took part in an international conference against nuclear arms in Moscow in 1987 and was received by Prime Minister Thatcher in the British Embassy in Moscow during her trip to the USSR, 1987. Declared his support for Gorbachev's attempts to reform Soviet society, at the same time demanding the release of all people imprisoned for their convictions. Nobel Peace Prize winner, 1975. The Sakharov Prize for the defence of human rights was established by the EEC in 1987. Visited the USA, 1988.
Main work: *Thoughts on Progress, Peaceful Co-existence and Intellectual Freedom*, 1968.

Sakharov, Igor' Konstantinovich
1902–1977. Colonel.
Son of a general. Took part in the Civil War, evacuated after the defeat of the Whites. In the 1920–30s, served in several armies in Latin America, and in the French Foreign Legion. During the Civil War in Spain, became a colonel in Franco's army. Decorated several times by Franco for bravery. During WWII, with K. Kromiadi, organized the first Rus-

sian anti-Stalinist detachments under the Germans near Pskov. Later joined the Vlasov movement. Commander of detachments of the ROA, which in 1945 fought against the Red Army near Frankfurt/Oder. Joined General Buniachenko on the march to Czechoslovakia, and took part in the liberation of Prague, May 1945. After WWII, lived in DP camps in Germany. Emigrated to Australia. Died in a car crash.

Sakharov, Vladimir
1945–   . Defector.
Son of a diplomat. Graduated from the Institute of International Relations (MGIMO), 1968. Worked as a Soviet diplomat and intelligence agent in Egypt, North Yemen and Kuwait. Transferred to Moscow Radio. Defected to the West, 1972. Settled in the USA. Lectured on the work of Soviet spies abroad.

Sakulin, Pavel Nikitich
1.9.1868–7.9.1930. Literary scholar.
Born in Voskresenskoe, Samara Gouvt., into a peasant family. Graduated from Moscow University, 1891. Lecturer in Russian literature at Moscow University, 1902–11, but resigned in protest against the intervention of the authorities in university life. His monograph on V. Odoevskii, 1913, is an encyclopaedia of Russian intellectual life in the 1820–30s. In the 1920s, tried, rather unsuccessfully, to combine serious research with Marxist dogma. Died in Leningrad, buried in Moscow. Interest in his work resurfaced in the 1960s after decades of neglect.

Sakva, Konstantin Konstantinovich
4.9.1912–   . Musicologist.
Born in Usman', Voronezh Gouvt. Author of many articles on music and composers. Editor-in-chief of Muzgiz Publishing House, Moscow, 1949–51 and 1956–63.

Salikhova, Roza Galiamovna
29.4.1944–   . Athlete.
Born in Nizhnii Tagil, Sverdlovskaia Oblast'. Honoured Master of Sports (volley-ball), 1969. With Moscow Dynamo. Graduated from the Moscow Oblast' Pedagogical Institute,

1971. Sports instructor. European champion, 1967 and 1971. Olympic champion, 1968 and 1972. World champion, 1970. USSR champion, 1970–73, 1975 and 1977.

Salina, Nadezhda Vasil'evna
11.9.1864–4.4.1956. Singer.
Born in Petersburg. Pupil of K. Everardi and Pauline Viardot. Daughter of the violinist Vasilii Salin. Soloist at the Moscow Private Opera, 1885–87. Soloist with the Bolshoi Theatre, 1888–1908. Professor at the Musical Drama School of the Moscow Philharmonic Society. Author of *Zhizn' i Stsena*, Leningrad-Moscow, 1941. Died in Moscow.

Salkazanova, Fatima
1941–   . Journalist, broadcaster.
Ossetin by nationality. Born in Moscow. At the age of 15, arrested for an article which she had sent to a newspaper. Spent 3 years in Norilsk camps with her mother, who was sentenced to 10 years. Married a Frenchman and emigrated to Paris in 1965. Graduated from the Sorbonne. Leading journalist with Radio Liberty in Paris.

Salkind, Michel (Zalkind, Mikhail Iakovlevich)
1890–1974. Film producer, impresario.
Born in Kiev. Son of a lawyer. Graduated from Kiev University. Director of the Kiev Opera. Impresario to many opera stars, including Sobinov and Chaliapin. Sent by the Provisional Government on a mission to Siberia, Oct. 1917. Arrested and sentenced to death by a revolutionary tribunal. Escaped. In the anarchy of the Civil War, appointed head of all horse transport. Met Lenin and Trotsky, 1920. Moved to Moscow, where he met Meyerhold. Emigrated, 1921. Producer of *The Joyless Street* (director, G. W. Pabst). Promoter of Greta Gustafson (later Greta Garbo). Agent for Aleksei Granovskii's Jewish Theatre, and its famous leading actor Solomon Mikhoels, during their European tour. Spent 3 days in Mexico with Mikhoels, then took the theatre on to the USA. Produced some 68 films, including *The Trial* (after Kafka), *The Life of Shelley*, and

Don Quixote (with Chaliapin). Left Germany, 1933, and moved to France, then in 1939, to Mexico, where he produced, with his son Aleksandr, some 14 films, including a comedy with Buster Keaton, and *The Gentle One* (after Dostoevskii). Returned to Paris, 1946. Met Abel Gance and produced his famous film *Austerlitz*, 1960, with a budget of 2.5 million dollars. After *The Life of Cervantes*, tried to produce *The Life of Lenin* but his script was turned down by his financial backers. In his later years, artistic adviser on his son's films (who later produced *The Three Musketeers, Superman 1* and *2*, and others). Died in a Paris hotel.

Salmanov, Grigorii Ivanovich
1922– . General.
Joined the Red Army, 1940. Took part in WWII. Graduated from the Frunze Military Academy, 1949, and from the Academy of the General Staff, 1964. Several high command posts in the army, including that of commander of the Kiev and Transbaikal military districts. Non-voting member of the Cen. Cttee. of the CPSU, 1971–76, and full member, 1981–86.

Sal'nikov, Sergei Sergeevich
13.9.1925– . Athlete, sports journalist.
Born in Krasnodar. Honoured Master of Sports (football), 1953. With Moscow Spartak. Graduated from the High School of Sports Instructors attached to the Moscow Institute of Physical Culture, 1955. Worked as a sports instructor. Graduated from Moscow University in journalism, 1960. Member of the CPSU, 1960. Sports commentator. USSR champion, 1954, 1956 and 1958. Olympic champion, 1956.

**Saminskii, Lazar' Semenovich
(Saminsky, Lazare)**
8.11.1882–30.6.1959. Composer, conductor, music scholar.
Born near Odessa. Studied music in Odessa, then in St. Petersburg. Moved to Tiflis, 1911. Appeared in Tiflis concert halls, 1911–18. Emigrated, 1918. Settled in the USA, 1920. Lived in New York. Founder of the annual Three Choirs Festival,

1936. Used Jewish choral and folk music as the basis for his own music. Author of symphonies, suites, choral music, and operas.
Works: *Ob Evreiskoi Muzyke*, St. Petersburg, 1914; *Music of the Ghetto and the Bible*, NY, 1934; *Living Music of the Americas*, NY, 1949.
Source: *Lazare Saminsky, Composer and Civic Worker*, NY, 1930.

Samoilo, Aleksandr Aleksandrovich
1869–1963. Lt.-general.
Graduated from the Academy of the General Staff, 1898. Staff officer during WWI in the General Staff and the Army HQ. Joined the Red Army, 1918. Staff officer during the Civil War at the Northern and Eastern fronts. In the 1920s, staff officer and military inspector. Professor at military educational establishments, 1926–48. Joined the Bolshevik Party, 1944.

Samoilova, Tat'iana Evgen'evna
4.5.1934– . Film actress.
Born in Leningrad. Daughter of the actor Evgenii Samoilov. Graduated from the Shchukin Drama School in 1958. Played in the Mayakovsky Theatre, then in the Film Actors' Theatre Studio. First film made in 1955. Her second film, *The Cranes Are Flying*, directed by Mikhail Kalatozov, made her famous all over the world. The film was shown at the Cannes Film Festival with tremendous success. This was followed by *An Unposted Letter*, also directed by Kalatozov. Played opposite the famous actor Innokentii Smoktunovskii. Starred in the Franco-Soviet co-production, *Leon Garros is Looking For His Friend*, 1961. Played Anna Karenina in Aleksandr Zarkhi's film of the same title, which was discussed for months in the Russian press. Her other films were less successful and she disappeared from the screen in the late 1970s.

Samokhin, Mikhail Ivanovich
1902– . Col.-general.
Joined the Red Army, 1924, and the Bolshevik Party, 1926. Educated at a pilots' school, 1931. Served as a pilot in the Baltic fleet. Took part in the Soviet-Finnish war, 1939–40. During WWII, commander of the air force of the Baltic fleet. After the war,

commander of the air force of several Soviet fleets, and of the anti-aircraft defence forces of the Navy. Deputy Commander of Soviet Anti-Aircraft Defence Forces, 1957–63.

Samokish, Nikolai Semenovich
25.10.1860–18.1.1944. Artist.
Born in Nezhin. Battle painter. Pupil of R. Tsybulskii in Nezhin. Studied at the Petersburg Academy of Arts, 1879–85, under B. Villevalde, and at the Paris Academy of Arts, 1885–86. Pupil of the battle painter E. Detail. Professor at the Petersburg Academy of Arts from 1912. Dean of the battle painting department from 1913. Book illustrator. Exhibited from 1887. Personal exhibitions: Khar'kov, Kiev, Simferopol', 1940, the Jubilee Exhibition, Moscow, 1941, Simferopol', 1957. Died in Simferopol'.

Samosud, Samuil Abramovich
14.5.1884–6.11.1964. Conductor.
Born in Tiflis. Conductor at the Mariinskii Theatre, Petrograd, 1917–19. Artistic director at the Leningrad Malyi Opera Theatre, 1918–36, the Bolshoi Theatre, 1936–43, and the Moscow Stanislavskii and Nemirovich Danchenko Musical Theatre, 1943–50. Highly decorated (Stalin Prize, 1941, 1947 and 1952). Died in Moscow.

Sampilov, Tsyrenzhap Sampilovich
1893–1953. Artist.
Battle and historical painter, also portrait, landscape and still-life painter, sculptor, book illustrator and stage designer. Studied in Chita at the Siberian Art-Industrial School of Painting and Graphics, 1914, then in the studio of the sculptor I. N. Zhukov, near Lake Baikal. Went to Moscow in 1927. Studied at the VKHUTEIN. Graduated, 1930. People's Artist of the Buriat-Mongol ASSR. First exhibition in Chita in 1920. Other exhibitions: Moscow, 1923, Ulan-Bator (Mongolia), 1926, Moscow, 1928, 1940, 1945, 1947, 1950. Personal exhibitions: 6 Artists in Kirzhach, 1940, (posthumously) Ulan-Ude, 1954.

Samson, Vilis Petrovich
1920– . Politician.
Organized communist partisan de-

tachments in German-occupied Latvia, 1942. Joined the Bolshevik Party, 1943. After WWII, taught Marxism at the Latvian Communist Party School. Graduated from the Academy of Social Sciences of the Cen. Cttee. of the CPSU, 1949. Minister of Education of the Latvian SSR, and Secretary of the Presidium of the Latvian Academy of Sciences. Chairman of the Scientific Editing Cttee. of Dictionaries and Encyclopaedias in Latvia, 1969.

Samsova, Galina (Samtsova)
17.3.1937–   . Ballet dancer.
Born in Stalingrad. Studied at the Kiev Choreographic School. Graduated in 1956. Dancer, then star at the Kiev Theatre of Opera and Ballet. Married the Canadian dancer and teacher A. Ursuliak. Moved with him to Canada, where she joined the Canadian National Ballet, 1961. Starred in many ballets all over the world, including the London Festival Ballet. In 1972, together with her second husband A. Prokovskii, set up the New London Ballet. From 1979, a star of the Royal Ballet, also a teacher and choreographer. Continued to dance throughout the 1970s. Now divorced from Prokovskii.

Samusenko, Tatiana Dmitrievna (Petrenko)
2.2.1938–   . Athlete.
Born in Minskaia Oblast'. Honoured Master of Sports (fencing), 1960. With Minsk Dynamo. Graduated from the Belorussian Polytechnical Institute, 1962. Works as a mechanical engineer. World champion, 1966, and with her team, 1963–67 and 1970. Olympic champion, 1960, 1968 and 1972. Member of the CPSU, 1976.

Sanadze, Tengiz Georgievich
30.3.1927–   . Ballet dancer.
Born in Tbilisi. Graduated from the Choreographic School of the Paliashvili Theatre. Joined that theatre on graduation. Produced ballets jointly with R. V. Dolidze and A. I. Tsereteli. Appeared in the company's guest performances abroad.

Sandalov, Leonid Mikhailovich
1900–   . Col.-general.
Joined the Red Army, 1919. Took part in the Civil War. Joined the Bolshevik Party, 1925. Graduated from the Frunze Military Academy, 1934, and the Academy of the General Staff, 1937. Staff officer during WWII.

Saneev, Viktor Danilovich
3.10.1945–   . Athlete.
Born in Sukhumi. Graduated from the Georgian Institute of Subtropical Management, 1967. Honoured Master of Sports (track and field athletics), 1968. With Tbilisi Dynamo. Works as an agronomist. Member of the CPSU, 1977. USSR champion, 1968–78. World record holder, 1968–71 and 1972–75. Olympic champion, 1968, 1972 and 1976. European champion, 1969 and 1974.

Sangovich, Iadviga Genrikhovna
11.12.1916–   . Ballerina.
Born in Petrograd. Graduated from the Moscow Choreographic School. With the Bolshoi Theatre, 1936–64. One of the best Soviet character dancers during the 1930s. Took part in guest performances abroad.

Sanin, Aleksandr Akimovich (real name – Shenberg)
1869–8.5.1956. Actor, director, impresario.
Graduated from Moscow University. Actor and director at the Aleksandrinskii and MKHAT theatres. His major film was *Polikushka*, 1919, which was released only in 1922. Adapted D. Merezhkovskii's *Petr i Aleksei* for the screen, 1918. Directed many productions of the Bolshoi Theatre. Emigrated. Made several films and produced plays in France and Germany.

Sapel'nikov, Vasilii Lvovich
2.11.1868–17.3.1941. Pianist.
Born in Odessa. Pupil of L. Brassin and S. Menter. Professor at the Moscow Conservatory, 1897–99. Moved to Odessa in 1916. Emigrated, 1922. Lived first in Germany, then in Italy. Author of operas and pieces for the piano. Died in San Remo, Italy.

Sapgir, Genrikh Ven'iaminovich
1928–   . Poet, author.
Born in Biisk. Became well-known in the USSR as a poet and for his children's books. His other work circulated in samizdat from the early 1960s. Contributed to the unofficial literary miscellany *Metropol*. Lives in Moscow.
Works: *Sonety Na Rubashkakh*, France, 1978.

Sapogov, Anatolii Aleksandrovich
6.2.1929–   . Ballet-dancer.
Born in Penza. Graduated from the Leningrad Choreographic School, 1950. Pupil of V. I. Ponomarev. With the Kirov Theatre, 1949–75. Character and grotesque dancer. Distinguished himself in modern repertoire.

Saradzhev, Konstantin Solomonovich (real name – Saradzhian)
9.10.1877–22.7.1954. Conductor.
Born in Derbent. Pupil of A. Nikish. Founder, with V. Derzhanovskii, of the Vechera Sovremennoi Musyki in Moscow, 1909. Professor at the Moscow Conservatory, 1922–35. His many famous pupils included Leo Ginzburg, B. Khaikin and M. Paverman. Chief conductor of the Erevan Opera and Ballet Theatre, 1935–40. Died in Erevan.

Saradzhishvili, Vano (Ivan Petrovich)
13.5.1879–11.11.1924. Singer.
Born in Signakhi, East Georgia. Pupil of I. Prianishnikov and A. Panaeva-Kartseva. From 1907, soloist with the Tiflis Opera Theatre. Toured all over the Caucasus and Russia. Appeared in several Georgian films. Died in Tiflis.

Sar'ian, Martiros Sergeevich
28.2.1880–5.5.1972. Artist.
Born in Nakhichevan'-na-Donu (now Rostov-on-Don). Landscape, still-life and portrait painter. Also stage designer. Studied at the Moscow School of Painting, Sculpture and Architecture, 1897–1903, under Leonid Pasternak, A. Korin, N. Kasatkin, A. Arkhipov and A. Vasnetsov. Pupil of K. Korovin and V. Vasnetsov, 1903–05. Exhibitions: Blue Rose, 1907, Zolotoe Runo, 1908–09, Union of Russian Artists, 1910–12, and from 1925, regularly in Azerbaidzhan and Armenia. Visited Turkey, Egypt

and Iran, 1910–13. Illustrated Armenian fairy-tales, 1933. Lived and died in Erevan, Armenia.

Sarycheva, Tatiana Filippovna
7.2.1949– . Athlete.
Born in New York. Daughter of a senior Soviet official serving in the USA. Honoured Master of Sports, (volleyball), 1970. With Moscow Lokomotiv. Sports instructor. Olympic champion, 1968 and 1972. World champion, 1970. European champion, 1971 and 1975. Graduated from the Moscow Institute of Physical Culture, 1978.

Sass, Anatolii Fomich
22.12.1935– . Athlete.
Born in Moscow. Honoured Master of Sports (rowing), 1968. With Moscow Spartak, 1965. USSR champion, 1967–68. Olympic champion, 1968 (with A. Timoshinin). Graduated from the Moscow Institute of Physical Culture, 1972.

Sat'ian, Aram Movsesovich (stage name – Satunts)
18.2.1913– . Composer.
Born in Mary, Turkmenia. Brother of Ashot Sat'ian. Author of the musical *Vostochnyi Dantist* (produced in 1944). Also wrote the symphonic poem *Zangezur*, 1947, and music for theatre, cinema and variety stage.

Sat'ian, Ashot Movsesovich
18.1.1906–30.9.1958. Composer, military conductor.
Born in Mary, Turkmenia. Brother of Aram Sat'ian. Author of the vocal symphony *Pesni Araratskoi Doliny*, 1952, and also marches and music for films. Died in Erevan.

Satpaev, Kanysh Imantaevich
11.4.1899– . Geologist.
Graduated from the Tomsk Technological Institute, 1926. President of the Kazakh Academy of Sciences, 1941. Discovered valuable ore deposits in his native Kazakhstan. Highly decorated (3 Orders of Lenin). Supervised geological work on the Dzhezkazgan ore deposits, which were extracted by slave-labour in the 1930–50s.

Sats, Natalia Il'inishna (Tukhachevskaia)
1903?– . Stage director.
Born in Irkutsk, Siberia. Daughter of the composer Il'ia Sats. In 1917, graduated from the Skriabin School of Music. One of the founders of the first theatre for children, the Mossovet Children's Theatre, 1918. From 1920–36, director and artistic director of the Moscow Children's Theatre. At the centre of Moscow cultural life during the 1930s. Wife of Marshal Mikhail Tukhachevskii. After her husband's arrest and execution, she too was arrested, tried in secret, and sent to a labour camp in Siberia as the 'wife of an enemy of the people'. Set free after Stalin's death in 1953. After 16 years in the prisons and camps, she returned broken and in poor health, but continued teaching and working in her theatre. Graduated in 1954 from the Moscow GITIS (Institute of Theatrical Art). Wrote several books: *Teatr Dlia Detei* (Theatre for Children), 1925, *Nash Put'*, 1932, *Deti Prikhodiat v Teatr*, 1961, and *Volshebnye Ochki*, 1965.

Savel'ev, Boris Vladimirovich
28.7.1896–1975? Composer, violinist.
Born in St. Petersburg. Wrote music for the ballet *Alladin i Volshebnaia Lampa*, also orchestral pieces, symphonies (*V Russkom Muzee*, 1960), suites, folk songs, and music for films.

Savel'ev, Sergei Petrovich
26.2.1948– . Athlete.
Born in Raichikhinsk on the Amur river, in the Far East. Graduated from the Khabarovsk Institute of Physical Culture, 1974. Honoured Master of Sports (skiing), 1976. With the Central Sports Club of the Army. USSR champion, 1973, 1976–78. Olympic champion, 1976 (30km race). World champion, 1978.

Savel'eva, Liudmila
24.1.1942– . Film actress.
Born during the Siege of Leningrad. Trained as a ballerina. Graduated from the Leningrad Vaganova Ballet School in 1960. Was discovered by Sergei Bondarchiuk and offered the role of Natasha in *War and Peace*. Spent 6 years making this film.

Became nationally and internationally known. Vittorio de Sica invited her to come to Italy to play in his film *The Sunflowers*, 1971. Other films: *The Seagull*, 1971, *The Flight*, 1971, and *The Headless Horseman*, 1973 (opposite Oleg Vidov).

Savelova, Zinaida Filippovna
12.11.1862–14.3.1943. Musicologist, bibliographer.
Born in Orel. Chief researcher, and bibliographer at the Moscow Conservatory Library from 1910. She refused to be evacuated without her books. Translated many books and articles on music and composers. Died in Moscow.

Savina, Iia
2.3.1936– . Film actress.
Born and grew up in Voronezh. Graduated from Moscow University, 1958. As a student, acted in an amateur drama studio. Discovered by Iosif Kheifits. Played the leading role in his *The Lady with the Little Dog*, 1960. Became nationally and internationally famous. Never repeated this success in other films. Combines her work in cinema with work at Moscow's Mossovet Theatre. Films: *Asia's Happiness* (1967, A. Mikhalkov-Konchalovskii); *Anna Karenina* (1968, A. Zharkhi); *A Day in the Life of Dr Kalinnikova* (1974, Titov); *A Lovers' Romance* (1975, A. Mikhalkov-Konchalovskii); *Krotkaia; Otkrytaia Kniga; Chastnaia Zhizn'*.

Savina, Nina
29.9.1915–1965. Canoeist.
Honoured Master of Sports (canoeing). Many times USSR champion. Bronze medal winner at the XVth Olympic Games.

Savinkov, Boris Viktorovich (penname – V. Ropshin)
31.1.1879–7.5.1925. Revolutionary, politician, author.
Born in Khar'kov. Member of the SR Party from 1903. One of the leaders of the terrorist wing of the SRs, 1903–06. Took part in the assassination of Pleve, Minister of the Interior, and Grand-Duke Sergei Aleksandrovich, Governor-General of Moscow. Arrested, sentenced to death,

escaped from prison in 1906. Temporarily left the SR Party in 1907. Published a novel about a terrorist's life *Kon' Bledni* (Pale Horse), in 1909. Emigrated, 1911. During WWI, served as a volunteer in the French Army. After the February Revolution in 1917, returned to Russia. Appointed Commissar of the Provisional Government at the HQ of the Russian Army. Later commissar of the South-Western front, and Deputy Defence Minister under Kerenskii. Link man between Kerenskii and the army. Played a crucial and controversial role in the Kornilov-Kerenskii negotiations which led to Kornilov's revolt and arrest. After the October Revolution 1917, took part in many anti-Bolshevik initiatives (the Krasnov offensive, the Organization of the Volunteer Army (Dobrovolcheskaia Armiia), and the Union for Defence of the Fatherland and Freedom). Head of the Russian Political Cttee. in Warsaw during the Soviet-Polish War, connected with anti-Bolshevik partisans (e.g. Bulak-Balakhovich). Tried to organize anti-Bolshevik underground activity in the USSR in 1921–23 from Poland. Lured to the USSR by Cheka agents masquerading as anti-Bolsheviks, arrested at the border while trying to cross it secretly, 16 Aug. 1924. At a show trial, made to declare disillusionment with the anti-Bolshevik struggle. Sentenced to death on 29 Aug. 1924, commuted to 10 years' imprisonment. Letters from prison addressed to known Russian emigrés and pleading for the end of the struggle against the Bolshevik authorities were published in his name. Died in a Moscow prison (fell from the 5th floor window of the GPU building). According to Soviet official sources, he had committed suicide. According to other versions, he was thrown from the window of his interrogator's office.
Main works: *Pale Horse*, 1909, *That Which Did Not Happen*, 1916, *Black Horse*, 1923, and *Book of Poems*, (posthumous) 1931.
See: Roman Gul, *General B.O.* (Savinkov), London, 1930.

Savitskaia, Svetlana Evgen'evna
1948–   . Cosmonaut.
Daughter of Marshal E. Savitskii. Graduated from the Moscow Ord-

zhonikidze Aviation Institute, 1972. Champion pilot (18 world records). Joined the Communist Party, 1975. Test pilot, 1976. Cosmonaut, 1980. First woman to step out into space, 25 July 1984 (3 hours 35 minutes test programme). Twice Hero of the Soviet Union.

Savitskii, Evgenii Iakovlevich
1910–   . Marshal.
Joined the Red Army, 1929, and the Bolshevik Party, 1931. Educated at a pilots' school, 1932. Fighter pilot during WWII, twice Hero of the Soviet Union. Commander of Soviet fighter forces, 1948. Graduated from the Academy of the General Staff, 1955. Non-voting member of the Cen. Cttee. of the CPSU, 1961–66. Deputy Commander-in-Chief of Soviet Anti-Aircraft Forces, 1966–1980.

Savitskii, Georgii Konstantinovich
1887–1949. Artist.
Landscape, portrait, animal and battle painter, and illustrator. Born in Penza. Studied at the N. Seliverstov Art School, 1902–05, under K. Savitskii, then at the Petersburg Academy of Arts, 1908–15, under G. Zaleman. Pupil of V. E. Makovskii. Exhibited from 1910. Personal exhibitions: Moscow, 1941, 1944, 1948, 1954; Leningrad, 1955. Died in Moscow.

Savitskii, Petr Nikolaevich
1895–   . Historian, economist, journalist, politician.
Born in Chernigov Gouvt. Graduated from Petersburg Polytechnic, 1917. During the Civil War, left Russia. Lived in Czechoslovakia. One of the leaders of the Eurasians, who reconsidered Russian history from the geopolitical point of view (stressing the Asiatic heritage, especially from the time of the Tatar domination). Professor of Russian language at Prague University. Director of the Eurasian publishing house, 1921–39. Dismissed under the German occupation, 1941. Headmaster of the Russian high school in Prague 1940–44. After the Soviet army entered Czechoslovakia at the end of WWII, deported to the Gulag, 1945. After Stalin's death, released

from the camps and returned to Czechoslovakia in 1956. Re-arrested in 1961 in Prague.
Main works: *Russia's Geographical Characteristics*, *Russia as a Separate Geographical Unity*, *The Struggle for the Eurasian Movement*.

Savitskii, Samuil
1955?–   . Sound engineer.
University graduate. Trained as a sound engineer. Worked for radio and TV. His last employment in the USSR was with the pop group Black Coffee. Went on tour abroad, and defected in Madrid.

Savranskii, Leonid Filippovich
28.4.1876–1969? Singer.
Born in Togancha, Kiev Gouvt. Pupil of M. Zotova. Soloist with the Bolshoi Theatre, 1914–46. Taught at the Moscow Conservatory from 1946. Professor, 1948–54. Irina Arkhipova was one of his many pupils.

Savshinskii, Samarii Il'ich
6.7.1891–1973? Pianist.
Born in Petersburg. Pupil of L. Nikolaev. Professor at the Leningrad Conservatory. Wrote a biography of his tutor *Leonid Nikolaev*, Leningrad-Moscow, 1950. Other works include *Pianist i Ego Rabota*, Leningrad, 1960.

Sazandar'ian, Tatevik Tigranovna
2.9.1916–   . Singer (mezzo-soprano).
Born in Zangezur. Pupil of S. Barkhudarian. From 1937, soloist with the Erevan Opera and Ballet Theatre. From 1961, taught at the Erevan Conservatory.

Sazonov, Sergei Dmitrievich
10.8.1860–25.12.1927. Diplomat.
In the Diplomatic Service from 1883. Secretary of the Russian Embassy at the Vatican, 1889–98. Ambassador at the Vatican, 1906–09. Brother-in-law of P. Stolypin. Minister of Foreign Affairs, 1910–16. Retired in the summer of 1916. During the Civil War, 1918–20, head of the foreign affairs department in General Denikin's government, later represented the government of Admiral Kolchak

at the Paris Peace Conference. Lived in Poland, keeping his pre-revolutionary estate. Died in Nice.

Sazonov, Vitalii
1947–6.9.1986. Artist.
Born in Siberia. Son of a Russian father and Ukrainian mother. Lived with his parents in Odessa from 1952. Studied at Odessa University in the Archaeology Department, 1966. First exhibition, 1967, in Odessa. Took part in a major unofficial exhibition in Moscow in Nov. 1975. Emigrated, 1981. Settled in Munich. Exhibition at the Ukrainian Free University, Munich, 1981. Other exhibitions in Cologne, Metz, Toronto, Chicago, Canberra, Sydney, and in Sweden and Switzerland. His last exhibition was in Frankfurt-on-Main. Died of a heart attack in his studio-flat.

Sedel'nikov, Fedor Semenovich
1902–1952. Vice-admiral.
Joined the Red Navy, 1921, and the Bolshevik Party, 1925. Graduated from the Naval Academy, 1933. Submarine commander in the 1930s. During WWII, Commander of the Caspian and the Amur Navies. Staff posts after WWII. Professor at the Academy of the General Staff, 1950.

Sediakin, Aleksandr Ignat'evich
26.11.1893–29.7.1938. Military commander.
Born in Petersburg. Son of a soldier. In 1915, graduated from the Irkutsk Military School. Took part in WWI. In 1917, joined the Bolsheviks. From 1918–20, commander of a Red Army brigade, deputy commander of the 13th Army and the 15th Sivash Rifle Division. Infantry inspector in Petrograd military district, 1920. Commander of the Southern Group of the 7th Army which suppressed the anti-Bolshevik Kronstadt revolt, 1921. Commander of troops in Karelia, Petrograd military region, and then Privolzhskii military district. From 1927, deputy head of the Chief Directorate of the Red Army. Inspector of infantry and tank troops. From 1931–32, head and commissar of the Dzerzhinskii Military-Technical Academy. In 1933–36, Deputy Chief-of-staff of the RKKA. From July 1937, commander of air-defence forces of

Baku military district. Arrested during the purge of the Red Army and after the execution of Marshal Tukhachevskii. Became a victim of the Gulag.

Sedova, Iulia Nikolaevna
21.3.1880–23.11.1969. Ballerina.
Born in Petersburg. Graduated from the Petersburg Theatre School. Pupil of E. Cecchetti. With the Mariinskii Theatre, 1898–1911 and 1914–16. Appeared in productions of M. I. Petipa. Successful character dancer. With the Moscow Bolshoi Theatre, 1904–05. Appeared in guest performances in Europe and the USA, 1911–14 (her partner was M. Mordkin). Emigrated. Lived in France from 1918. Worked as a choreographer and teacher. Directed a school of dancing in Nice. Died in Cannes.

Sedykh, Andrei (Tsvibak, Iakov Moiseevich)
1902–   . Journalist, editor, author.
Emigrated during the Civil War. Settled in Paris. Reporter on Miliukov's daily *Poslednie Novosti*. As Bunin's secretary, accompanied him to Stockholm in 1933 to receive the Nobel Prize for Literature. Moved to the USA, 1940. Co-editor, 1967, editor, 1973, of the New York daily *Novoe Russkoe Slovo* (now the oldest Russian newspaper anywhere in the world). Published short stories and memoirs.

Sedykh, Iurii Georgievich
11.5.1955–   . Athlete.
Born in Novocherkassk, Rostov Oblast'. Honoured Master of Sports (track and field athletics), 1976. With Kiev Burevestnik. Studied at the Kiev Institute of Physical Culture. USSR champion, 1976, 1978. Olympic champion, 1976 (hammer-throwing). European champion, 1978.

Seifullin, Saken (Sadvakas)
12.6.1894–1939. Author, editor, politician.
Born in a village in Kazakhstan. Studied at the Omsk Teachers' Seminary, 1913–16. First story published in 1910. During the February and October Revolutions 1917, a

Bolshevik official in Kazakhstan, member of the Akmolinsk Revkom. In 1918, taken prisoner by the Whites, but escaped. In 1919, a Communist Party worker in Akmolinsk. In 1920, in Orenburg. From 1922–25, chairman of the Sovnarkom of the Kazakh ASSR and full member of the VTSIK. From 1925–37, editor of *Trudovoi Kazakh* (Working Kazakh), then editor-in-chief of *Literary Front* (in the Kazakh language). Published poetry and novels. One of the first Soviet Kazakh writers. Arrested in 1938, perished in the Gulag.

Seifullina, Lidia Nikolaevna
3.4.1889–25.4.1954. Author.
Born near Cheliabinsk. In 1920, graduated from the Moscow Higher Pedagogical Courses. Short stories first published in 1917. After the arrest and execution of her husband, V. Pravdukhin, arrested herself as a 'wife of an enemy of the people'. In the Gulag, but survived. Released after Stalin's death. Died in Moscow. Author of *Virineia*, 1925 (staged and filmed in the 1960s), *Peregnoi*, 1922. *Pravonarushiteli*, 1922, and *Tania*, 1934. Considered to be one of the most interesting new proletarian women writers in Soviet literature.

Seina, Violetta
1961–   . Security services officer (KGB).
Employed by the UPDK (Directorate of Services to the Diplomatic Corps), the organization run by the KGB, which provides staff (secretaries, cooks, drivers, maids etc) for foreign organizations and individuals residing in the USSR. In early 1987, she was the cause of all coded radio communications between Washington and its Embassy in Moscow being stopped, following the alleged betrayal of secrets by 2 American marine guards, one of whom was her lover. According to a Pentagon official, she infiltrated the US Embassy in Moscow just before the Iceland summit in Oct. 1986, causing the worst security breach in American history. The Seina operation resulted in the elite, 28-man marine contingent which guarded the American Embassy in Moscow being

summoned home in disgrace for interrogation, with 2 of them facing espionage charges. Her method of operation was simple: she 'accidentally' met one of the marines, Lonetree, in a Moscow underground station in Sep. 1985. As the relationship developed, she was invited to Embassy parties, and soon persuaded Lonetree to let 'uncle Sasha' (the high-ranking KGB officer Aleksei Efimov) roam around the most secret corridors of the Embassy. Efimov was soon paying Lonetree to help him systematically collect codes, ciphers and photostats. The blueprints of the Embassy, along with the names, photographs and addresses of CIA Moscow contacts, were also taken away. She was eventually exposed by the young marine who could stand the pressure no longer. Lonetree was jailed in the USA for 30 years for trading secrets for sex and fined $5,000.

Sekar-Rozhanskii, Anton Vladislavovich (real name – Rozhanskii)
18.5.1863–28.1.1952. Singer.
Born in Vlotslavsk. Pupil of S. Gabel'. From 1896, soloist with the Moscow Private Opera. Professor at the Moscow Conservatory, 1914–19. Emigrated to Poland, 1920. Taught at the Warsaw Conservatory. Died in Lublin.

Seleznev, Petr Ianuar'evich
1897–1949. Politician.
Joined the Bolshevik Party, 1915. Party functionary. Before and during WWII, 1st Secretary of Krasnodar Kraikom. In charge of the communist partisan movement near Krasnodar during WWII. After the war, conducted the re-Stalinization of this Cossack region. Non-voting member of the Cen. Cttee. of the VKP, 1939.

Selitskii, Boris Sergeevich
22.9.1938– . Athlete.
Born in Leningrad. Honoured Master of Sports (heavy athletics), 1968. With Leningrad Lokomotiv. Graduated from the Leningrad Institute of Physical Culture, 1976. USSR champion, 1967. World and European champion, 1968. World record-holder, 1968–69. Olympic champion, 1968 (weight-lifting, 485 kg).

Seliutskii, Gennadii Naumovich
23.12.1937– . Ballet dancer.
Born in Petrozavodsk. Graduated from the Leningrad Choreographic School, 1956. Pupil of F. I. Balabina. With the Kirov Theatre. Took part in concert productions of the Chamber Ballet. Teacher at the Leningrad Choreographic School from 1963.

Seliverstova, Valentina Mikhailovna
24.12.1926– . Athlete.
Born in Omsk, Siberia. The only woman in the world to make 3,000 parachute jumps, including 49 world records. 3 times world champion (1954, 1964 and 1966) and 10 times USSR champion (1952–65). Has over 100 medals including 66 gold. Started as a coach in 1954. Graduated from the Omsk Institute of Physical Culture in 1958. World sports judge from 1966.

Sel'vinskii, Il'ia (Karl) Lvovich
24.10.1899–22.3.1968. Poet, playwright.
Born in Simferopol'. Graduated from Moscow University in social studies, 1923. First work published in 1915. One of the leaders of the constructivist movement. Most famous early work, *Ulialiaevshchina*, 1927. Also wrote plays in the 1930s (*Pao-Pao*, *Umka-Belyi Medved'*), which were not successful. Other books: *Pushtorg*, 1928, *Rytsar' Ioann*, 1937, and *Babek*, 1941. Died in Moscow.

Semashko, Nikolai Aleksandrovich
20.9.1874–18.5.1949. Medical official, politician.
Born in the village of Livenskoe, near Orel. Son of a village teacher. In 1891, entered the medical faculty of Moscow University. Joined the Bolshevik Party in 1893. Involved in revolutionary activity, arrested and exiled. Graduated from Kazan' University as a doctor in 1901. Doctor in Orel and Saratov Gouvts. From 1904, involved in party work in Nizhnii Novgorod. Participant in the 1905 Revolution. Arrested at the Sormovo factory. Emigrated to Geneva in 1906, where he met Lenin. Delegate at the Stuttgart Congress of the 2nd International, 1907, as the Geneva party representative. In 1908, moved to Paris. Secretary of the

Foreign Bureau of the SDs until 1910. In 1911, lectured at the party school at Lonjumeau. In 1912, took part in the 6th Prague All-Russia Conference of the RSDRP. In 1913, in Serbia and Bulgaria. Was interned there during WWI. In Sep. 1917, returned to Moscow. Delegate at the 6th Congress of the RSDRP. Active participant in the October coup, 1917. From July 1918–30, 1st Narkom (Minister) of Health of the USSR. Combined administrative duties with lecturing at Moscow University. From 1930–36, member of the Presidium. From 1945–49, director of the Institute of School Hygiene. One of the founders of the first Medical Library, 1918, and the House of Scientists, 1922. From 1927–36, editor-in-chief of the Soviet *Great Medical Encyclopaedia*. A clinic in Moscow bears his name. Died in Moscow.

Semeiko, Nikolai Illarionovich
1923–1945. Captain.
Joined the Red Army, 1940. Educated at a pilots' school, 1942. During WWII, became known as a fighter pilot, twice Hero of the Soviet Union. Shot down during a dog fight with German planes at the end of WWII.

Semenets, Vladimir Ivanovich
9.1.1950– . Athlete.
Born in Vol'sk, Saratov Oblast'. Honoured Master of Sports (cycling), 1972. From 1973, with Leningrad Dynamo. USSR champion, 1971–77. Olympic champion, 1972. Graduated from the Kiev Institute of Physical Culture. 1975.

Semeniaka, Liudmila Ivanovna
16.1.1952– . Ballerina.
Born in Leningrad. Graduated from the Leningrad Choreographic School, 1970. Pupil of N. V. Belikova. Joined the Kirov Theatre. With the Bolshoi Theatre from 1972. Perfected her art under G. S. Ulanova. A lyrico-dramatic dancer. Prize-winner at the International Ballet Competition in Tokyo, 1976. Anna Pavlova Prize, Paris, 1976.

Semenov, Grigorii Mikhailovich
25.9.1890–30.8.1946. Cossack commander.
Born in Siberia, near Chita, Baikal

District. Graduated from the Orenburg Military School in 1911. On active service during WWI. In July 1917, commissar of the Provisional Government in Siberia, one of the commanders of the anti-communist Cossack groups. Fought the Red Army in Siberia, 1917–20. In 1917 (Oct.–Dec.), organized a revolt against the Bolshevik government (Semenovskii Miatezh). In Aug. 1918, in alliance with Czechoslovak legions, set up a military government in Siberia (Provisional Siberian Government). Commander of a corps in Chita. At first, not recognized by Admiral Kolchak, later appointed by him Commander of Chita military district. In 1919, backed by the Japanese, proclaimed himself Ataman of the Transbaikail Cossack Army. After the defeat of Kolchak, took over power in Siberia and the Far East, but was defeated by the Red Army in 1920. Fled abroad, Sep. 1921. Lived in Korea, Japan and Northern China. In Sep. 1945, abducted by SMERSH in Manchuria. Tried and hanged.

Semenov, Iulian Semenovich
8.10.1931– . Author.
Graduated from the Moscow Institute of Oriental Studies, 1953. For some time, worked as a foreign correspondent and political commentator. Turned to full-time thriller writing and soon acquired the reputation of being the Soviet Ian Fleming. His writing is aimed at the Soviet mass market. Specializes in popular novels featuring the exploits of handsome, brave and honest Soviet intelligence agents, which feed rumours that his KGB connections are not confined to fiction only. His novels are officially heavily promoted, with nearly everything turned into films or TV serials which attract audiences of more than 200 million. First received fame for *Petrovka 38* (HQ of the criminal police, CID). Other books include: *Major Vikhr*, 1967, and *17 Mgnovenii Vesny*, 1969. His latest bestseller, *TASS Is Authorized to Announce*, 1979, was translated into English in 1987. Also available in English is the sequel, *International Knot*, John Calder, 1988.

Semenov, Viktor Aleksandrovich
16.2.1892–13.4.1944. Ballet dancer.
Graduated from the Petersburg Theatre School, 1912. Pupil of M. K. Obukhov. Joined the Mariinskii Theatre. Leading classical dancer. Taught at the Petersburg Theatre School. Later, coach with the ballet company of the Bolshoi Theatre, and teacher at the Moscow Choreographic School until 1936. Teacher with the A. V. Aleksandrov Song and Dance Ensemble of the Soviet Army, 1939–44. Died in Moscow.

Semenov, Viktor Vladimirovich
1937– . Cybernetics expert.
In 1960, graduated from the Bauman Higher Technical College (MVTU), the most elitist technical establishment in Moscow. Specialist in automatic control systems. Member of staff of the MVTU from 1960. Member of the CPSU, 1964. Lecturer from 1966. Doctor of technical science, 1971. Lives in Moscow. Author of *Technicheskaia Kibernetika. Teoria Avtomaticheskogo Regulirovaniia*, 4 vol., 1967–69.

Semenov, Vladilen Grigor'evich
12.11.1932– . Ballet dancer, choreographer.
Born in Samara. Graduated from the Leningrad Choreographic School. Pupil of V. I. Ponomarev. Leading dancer with the Kirov Theatre, 1950–72. Appeared in traditional concert productions. Teacher at the Leningrad Choreographic School from 1963. Artistic director of the Kirov Theatre Ballet Company, 1970–72. Choreographer and coach with the same theatre from 1970.

Semenov-Amurskii, Fedor Vasil'evich
1902–1980. Artist.
Non-conformist artist. Only twice exhibited by the Soviet cultural authorities: Moscow, 1967 and 1976. Died in Moscow. A major posthumous exhibition of his work was organized by I. Shelkovskii in the Chevalier Gallery, Paris, Sep. 1987.

Semenov-Tian'-Shan'skii, Petr Petrovich
21.6.1866–8.4.1942. Entomologist.
Born in St. Petersburg. Son of Petr

Semenov-Tian'-Shan'skii, the famous geographer. From 1885–89, studied at Petersburg University in the natural science faculty. In 1888–89, made his first expedition to Western Turkestan, near the Caspian Sea. From 1890, worked at the Zoological Museum of the St. Petersburg Academy of Sciences. Honorary member of the Russian Entomological Society, 1909. Many articles and books on Russian entomology. Also known as a translator of Horace. Died in Leningrad.

Semenova, Iuliiaka Larionovna
9.3.1952– . Athlete.
Born in Lithuania. Honoured Master of Sports (basketball), 1971. With Riga Daugava. Graduated from the Latvian Institute of Physical Culture, 1973. USSR champion, 1968–73, 1975–79. European champion, 1968, 1970, 1972, 1974, 1976 and 1978. World champion, 1971 and 1975. Olympic champion, 1976.

Semenova, Marina Timofeevna
12.6.1908– . Ballerina, ballet teacher.
Born in Petersburg. Graduated from the Leningrad Choreographic School. Pupil of A. Ia. Vaganova. As a student, appeared as a leading dancer in school concerts. Leading dancer with the Leningrad Opera from 1925–30. Distinguished for the width and elasticity of her leap. Tragic and comic parts were equally within her reach. Took part in the production of many of the early Soviet ballets. Though a classical dancer, adapted her genre to the demands made in the 1920s. Guest performances at the Paris Opera, 1936. Taught at the Moscow Choreographic School, 1954–60. Teacher and coach of the leading dancers of the Bolshoi Theatre from 1953. Taught in the Choreographic Department of the GITIS (State Institute of Dramatic Art) from 1964. Among her many pupils were N. Bessmertnova, M. Kondrat'eva and N. Timofeeva.

Semichastnyi, Vladimir Efimovich
1917– . Head of the KGB.
Started his career in the Komsomol. Close to Aleksandr Shelepin, and succeeded him as head of Komsomol,

and later as head of the KGB, Nov. 1961–Apr. 1967. His agreement to the replacement of Khrushchev sealed the latter's fate by depriving him of KGB support. Replaced by Andropov. Responsible for the vilification campaign against Boris Pasternak, when he was awarded the Nobel Prize for Literature for his novel *Doctor Zhivago*. Later, appointed 1st Party Secretary of Azerbaidzhan, where he is remembered as a ruthless Stalinist.

Semizorova, Nina L'vovna
15.10.1956– . Ballerina.
Born in Krivoi Rog. Graduated from the Kiev Choreographic School, 1975. With the Shevchenko Theatre, and the Bolshoi Theatre from 1978. 1st prize in the International Ballet Competition, Moscow, 1977. Took part in guest performances abroad.

Senderei, Samuil Zalmanovich
29.1.1905– . Composer.
Born in Mogilev. Author of a symphony, choral music, and songs based on Jewish folk motives. Worked for film and theatre.

Senderov, Valerii Anatolievich
1945– . Dissident.
Born in Moscow. Graduated from Moscow University. Mathematician. Took part in human rights campaigns. Political prisoner. Freed from the Gulag under Gorbachev, Feb. 1987. Continues his human rights activity. One of the best known Soviet dissidents in Moscow. Openly describes himself in Moscow as a member of the NTS. Reported to the outside world on many events of the late 1980s which were not raised in the official press, despite glasnost. One of the founders of the Moscow group of the International Human Rights Society. Attacked several times by the press.

Senilov, Vladimir Alekseevich
8.7.1875–18.9.1918. Composer.
Born in Viatka. Author of 3 operas, a symphony and music for cello and piano. Died in Petrograd.
See: *Apollon*, Nr. 12, 1910.

Sen'ko, Vasilii Vasil'evich
1921–1984. Colonel.
Joined the Red Army, 1940, and the Bolshevik Party, 1942. Gunner-bomber during WWII, highly decorated (twice Hero of the Soviet Union). Graduated from the Air Force Academy, 1952. Taught at pilots' schools after WWII.

Serafim (Batiukov)
1880–1942. Russian Orthodox clergyman.
Monk, 1922. Worked in a Moscow factory. Clandestinely a priest of the Catacomb Church, which split from the official church, condemning its submission to the atheist authorities. Went completely underground in 1928. Lived at Zagorsk, and continued to serve in a secret congregation at this Russian religious centre until his death.

Serafim (Chichagov), Metropolitan of Leningrad
9.6.1856–30.1.1938. Russian Orthodox clergyman.
Son of a nobleman. Graduated from the Pages Corps, 1875. Bishop of Sukhumi, 1905. Took the initiative in the canonization of Serafim of Sarov (who became one of the most venerated Russian saints). Archbishop of Bessarabia, 1912. Member of the Russian Church Council, 1917. Metropolitan of Leningrad, 1933. Retired in 1933, lived near Moscow. Highly regarded as a religious author.

Serafimovich, Aleksandr Serafimovich (Popov)
19.1.1863–19.1.1949. Author.
Born near Rostov. Son of a Cossack officer. Grew up in Russian Poland, later moved to stanitsa Ust'-Medveditskaia (in 1933 re-named Serafimovich). From 1883–87, studied at Petersburg University in the physico-mathematical faculty. In 1887, arrested, together with Aleksandr Ulianov (Lenin's brother). Exiled to Arkhangelsk Gouvt. In 1890, returned to the Don, and became close to the SDs. First short story published in 1889. In 1901, met M. Gorkii. Member of the Sreda literary group, wrote in the populist vein. Contributor to *Znanie*. In 1917, took part in the Bolshevik revolution.

Pravda correspondent during the Civil War, 1918–22. From 1926–29, editor of *Oktiabr'* magazine. Main work: *Zheleznyi Potok*, 1924, a socialist realist classic of the Civil War period. Died in Moscow.

Serebriakov, Konstantin Terent'evich
17.6.1852–1919. Singer.
Born in Tambov. Famous bass who reigned at the Mariinskii Theatre for 24 years. Retired in 1911.

Serebriakov, Pavel Alekseevich
28.2.1909– . Pianist.
Born in Tsaritsyn. Pupil of L. Nikolaev. Professor at the Leningrad Conservatory, 1938–51. From 1962, director of the Conservatory. Among his pupils were I. Laz'ko, E. Murina and G. Fedorova.

Serebriakova, Galina Iosifovna
20.12.1905–1980. Author.
Born in Kiev. Took part in the Civil War, 1918–22. Joined the Bolshevik Party at the age of 15. In 1925, graduated from Moscow University in medicine. First work published in 1925. Main work: *Prometei*, a 3-volume biographical novel about Karl Marx. In 1936, arrested and sent to the Gulag. Spent 20 years in prisons, camps and in exile. After Stalin's death, rehabilitated. Returned to Moscow in 1956. Remained a staunch communist.

Serebriakova, Zinaida Evgen'evna
12.12.1884–19.9.1967. Artist.
Born in the village of Neskuchnoe, now in Kursk Oblast'. Daughter of Evgenii Lanceray. In 1902, pupil at the Princess Tenisheva Workshops, also under O. Braz, 1903–05. Member of the Mir Iskusstva group. Emigrated to France in 1924. Lived in Paris. Continued working until her death.

Serebrianyi, Iosif Aleksandrovich
1907– . Artist.
Born in the Ukraine. Portrait, landscape and historical painter, also designer of film and political posters. Studied at the M. Guzhavin Art Studio, Poltava, 1922–24, then in the

Graphics Department of the Leningrad Artistic-Industrial College, 1924–27, and later at the VKHUTEIN, Leningrad, 1927–31, under V. Savitskii, V. Belianin and A. Rylov. Also a private pupil of V. E. Savitskii. From 1929, studied at the M. P. Bobyshev Stage Design Studio. Exhibited from 1925.

Seredina, Antonina Aleksandrovna
23.12.1929–   . Athlete.
Born in Kalininskaia Oblast'. Honoured Master of Sports (rowing), 1960. With Moscow Spartak. Member of the CPSU from 1953. USSR champion, 1958–68. European champion, 1959–67. Olympic champion, 1960. World champion, 1966 and 1968. Graduated from the Moscow Institute of Physical Culture, 1966.

Sergeev, Andrei Vasil'evich
1893–1933. Aviation commander.
Joined the Bolshevik Party, 1911. Sergeant during WWI. Took part in the storming of the Winter Palace, 1917. Participant in the Civil War. Joined the Red Army, 1918. Educated at a pilots' school, 1917. Organizer of the Red Air Force from 1917. Head of the Chief Administration of the Air Force of the Red Army, 1921–22. Aviation specialist in the Ministry of Foreign Trade, 1926. Deputy head of the Administration of Civilian Aviation, 1933. Died in an air crash.

Sergeev, Konstantin Mikhailovich
5.3.1910–   . Ballet dancer, choreographer.
Born in Petersburg. Attended evening classes at the Leningrad Choreographic School. Pupil of E. P. Snetkova, M. A. Kozhukhova and V. A. Semenova. Later studied at the school itself. Pupil of V. I. Ponomarev. Graduated, 1930. Appeared in the company of I. F. Kshesinskii in guest performances all over the country, 1928–29. Leading dancer with the Kirov Theatre, 1930–61. Mainly in the classical repertoire, in lyrico-romantic roles. Partner of Galina Ulanova in the 1930s and early 1940s. Choreographer with the Kirov Theatre, 1946–55 and 1960–70. Produced several ballets, his most notable production being *Cinderella*

at the Kirov Theatre, 1946. Stressed the dramatic and psychological element in ballet. Adapted classical ballet to demands for modernity. Artistic director of the Leningrad Choreographic School, 1938–40, and from 1973.

Sergeev, Nikolai Dmitrievich
1909–   . Admiral.
Joined the Red Navy, 1928, and the Bolshevik Party, 1930. Graduated from the Naval Academy, 1941. Naval staff officer during and after WWII. Chief-of-staff of the Soviet Navy, 1964–77.

Sergeev, Nikolai Grigor'evich
27.9.1876–23.5.1951. Ballet dancer.
Born in Petersburg. Graduated from the Petersburg Theatre School, 1894. Joined the Mariinskii Theatre. Producer from 1903. Leading dancer, 1904. Chief producer with the Marinskii Theatre ballet company from 1914. Taught at the Petersburg Theatre School, 1897–1917. Emigrated, 1918. Taught at Sadlers Wells Ballet, 1933–38. Moved to France. Died in Nice.

Sergeev, Viktor Ivanovich
5.4.1935–   . Ballet dancer.
Born in Leningrad. Studied at the choreographic studio attached to the Gorkii Palace of Culture, Leningrad, 1948–53. With the Kuibyshev Theatre from 1953. Produced dances for operatic and theatrical performances. Taught at the choreographic school attached to the Kuibyshev Theatre, 1960–64. Coach and choreographer with the international gymnastics team from 1961. From 1967, honorary coach of the gymnastics team of the RSFSR.

Sergeev-Tsentskii, Sergei Nikolaevich (Sergeev)
30.9.1875–3.12.1958. Author.
Born in the village of Preobrazhenskoe near Tambov. Son of a village teacher. In 1895, graduated from the Glukhov Teachers Institute. From 1905, lived in the Crimea. Travelled all over Russia and wrote books about his travels. First story published in 1898. Main work, *Sevastopolskaia Strada*, 1937–39, re-

ceived the Stalin Literary Prize, 1941. Academician, 1943. Also wrote plays. Died in Alushta in the Crimea. After his death, a museum was set up in Alushta in his honour.

Sergievskii, Maksim Vladimirovich
25.10.1892–20.6.1946. Philologist.
Born in Moscow. In 1916, graduated from Moscow University. International authority on gypsies and a specialist on the gypsy language. Professor of romance languages, 1925–46, at Moscow University. Member of the British Gypsy Lore Society. Many works on the subject. Died in Moscow.
Main work: *Istoria Frantsuzskogo Iazyka*, 1938.

Sergii (Stragorodskii, Ivan Nikolaevich), Patriarch of Moscow.
11.1.1867–15.5.1944. Russian Orthodox clergyman.
Born in Arzamas. Graduated from the Petersburg Theological Academy, 1890. Inspector at the academy, 1899–1901. Bishop of Iamburg, 1901. Bishop of Finland and Vyborg, 1905–17. Highly regarded as a scholar. Chairman of the religious-philosophical meetings at Petersburg. Bishop, then Metropolitan of Vladimir, 1917. Deputy locum tenens of Patriarch Tikhon, 1925. After the death in Tikhon, spent 6 months in prison during the winter of 1926–27. Published in July 1927 a declaration pledging loyalty to Soviet authorities. Became thereafter in the eyes of the authorities the preferred candidate for the leadership of the church. His declaration led to internal and external splits (Catacomb Church, Church in Exile) and remains controversial, representing a practical compromise to some, and capitulation before atheism to others. It remains, however, the basis of existence of the Moscow patriarchate. Metropolitan of Moscow and Kolomna, 1934. After a long wrangle, recognized within the church officially as the locum tenens of the Patriarch, 1937. Remained head of the church at the peak of the persecutions in the 1930s (only a handful of bishops remaining outside of prisons and camps). During WWII, stressed the patriotic character of the church. Took part in a

meeting with Stalin (together with the Metropolitans Aleksii and Niko-lai), 8 Sep. 1943. Immediately there-after, elected Patriarch of Moscow, thus restoring the patriarchate after almost 2 decades. Died in Moscow less than a year after this event, succeeded by Aleksii.

Serkebaev, Ermek Bekmukham-edovich
4.7.1926–   . Singer.
Born in Petropavlovsk. Pupil of A. Kurganov. From 1947, soloist with the Alma-Ata Opera Theatre. Sang in many films.

Serov, Georgii Valentinovich
1894–1929. Actor, film director.
Son of the famous painter, V. Serov. Actor with MKHAT. Pupil of Vakh-tangov. Emigrated after the revolu-tion. Settled in France, where he worked as a film director.

Serov, Ivan Aleksandrovich
1905–   . General, head of the KGB.
Son of a peasant from a village in the Vologda Oblast'. An active commu-nist locally from the age of 21. Joined the Red Army, 1923. Attended a military school, then the Military Academy. From 1939, in the NKVD. Until 1941, NKVD chief in the Ukraine, serving under Khrushchev (to whom he was close all his life). Personally responsible for the mass deportations and terror campaign in Western Ukraine, Western Belorussia and in Bessarabia before WWII. During and after WWII, 1st Deputy People's Commissar (Deputy Mini-ster) for State Security (NKGB), 1941–54. According to some sources, involved in the mass murders of Polish POWs at Katyn'. Supervised mass executions of prisoners in Soviet jails before the German advance. Organized mass deporta-tions from the Baltic republics (both before and after the German occupa-tion), and later, during WWII, the deportation of whole nations— Crimean Tatars, Kalmucks, Ingu-shis and Chechens accused of colla-boration with the Germans. After WWII, deputy head of SMERSH. From 1945–47, Deputy Supreme Commander of the Soviet Forces in Germany (in charge of the Sovietiza-tion of East Germany). In 1953, took part in the arrest of Beria and his closest associates. Mar. 1954, ap-pointed chairman of the KGB, succeeding as security chief Sergei Kruglov, who suffered a heart attack (or, according to some sources, committed suicide). Visited England in 1956 to prepare the ground for the visit of Khrushchev and Bulganin (the first such visit of Soviet leaders to the West). In charge of the suppression of the Hungarian Revo-lution, 1956. According to R. Med-vedev, only Serov's loyalty gave Khrushchev the chance to insist on a plenary session of the Cen. Cttee. in summer 1957, and to defeat Molotov, Kaganovich and Malenkov. In Dec. 1958, suddenly replaced as KGB chief by Shelepin on Khrushchev's orders and appointed chief of mili-tary intelligence (GRU). Remem-bered as one of the most sinister of Stalin's security chiefs. Removed from his post as GRU chief in 1963 in connection with the Penkovskii af-fair. According to UPI, expelled from the party under Brezhnev, spring 1965, for his crimes under Beria (and Khrushchev) in Stalin's time.

Serov, Vasilii Matveevich
29.12.1878–9.1918. Revolutionary.
Born in Khvalynsk, near Saratov. Son of a craftsman. In 1899, gradu-ated from the Kazan' Teachers' Institute. Teacher in Aktarsk. In 1902, moved to Petersburg. Corre-spondence course student at Peters-burg University. Involved there in revolutionary activity. Took an ac-tive part in the revolution, 1905–07. In 1907, deputy from the Bolshevik faction (Saratov constituency) at the 2nd State Duma. End of 1907, arrested for Bolshevik activity, sen-tenced to 5 years hard labour and exile to Eastern Siberia. Continued revolutionary activity in Eastern Siberia. Mar. 1917–Aug. 1918, chair-man of the Verkhneudinsk Soviet (Siberia). In Aug. 1918, taken prisoner near Chita by the Whites, tried and executed.

Serova, Valentina Semenovna (Bergman)
1846–6.1924. Composer, music critic, charity worker.
Born in Moscow. Wife of the composer Aleksandr Serov (1820–71), who taught her, and with whom she later collaborated. Mother of the artist Valentin Serov. Dedicated half of her time to collecting food and clothing for starving peasants. Also organized help for striking workers. Taught art to peasant children on her estate. Author of 5 operas, including *Uriel Dakosta* (produced in 1885), and *Il'ia Muromets* (produced in 1899). Also composed for the piano.

Seryshev, Stepan Mikhailovich
1889–1928. Military commander.
Joined the Bolshevik Party, 1917, and the Red Army, 1918. Quelled an anti-communist rebellion in Irkutsk, 1917. Organizer of Red partisans in Siberia during the Civil War. Com-mander of the Amur front, 1920–22. Military attaché in Japan, 1926–27.

Sevela, Efraim Evelevich
1928–   . Author.
Scriptwriter in the USSR. Emigrated to Israel, 1971. Moved to the USA, 1977. Became famous for his hu-morous short stories such as *Osta-novite Samolet, Ia Slezu*, and *Popugai Govoriashchii Na Idish*. Other books include *Legendy Invalidnoi Ulitsy*, *Zub Mudrosti*, and *Viking*. His subject is the fate of the small man in the street, described with Jewish humour.

Severianin, Igor Vasil'evich (Lotarev)
16.5.1887–20.12.1941. Poet.
Born in St. Petersburg. First poems published in 1904. Became very famous in 1913, when *Gromokipia-shchii Kubok* was published. Main (and the only significant) representa-tive of ego-futurism. Immensely popular for a short period, com-pletely eclipsed since. In contrast to the vulgar, pretentious verse which brought him fame in Russia, some of his poetry in exile reaches real depth and is marked by genuine feeling. Emigrated to Estonia after the October Revolution 1917. Translated foreign poets, including Baudelaire, Verlaine, Mickiewicz and some Es-tonians. Died in Tallinn, Estonia.

Severnyi, Andrei Borisovich
11.5.1913–4.4.1987. Astrophysicist.
Born in Tula. Graduated from Moscow University in 1935. Worked at the Shternberg Institute of Astronomy, 1938–46. In 1941, joined the CPSU. After the war, assigned to the Crimean Observatory. Pioneered research on the global oscillations of the sun. Discovered one which had a period of 160 minutes, the nature of which has not yet been satisfactorily explained. The new science of solar seismology was the result of this discovery. Made several visits to Britain and spoke good English. In 1964, elected vice-president of the International Astronomical Union. Main works: *The Stability and Oscillation of Gaseous Spheres and Stars*, 1948; *Magnetic Fields of the Sun and the Stars*, 1966.

Shabalin, Aleksandr Osipovich
1914–1982. Vice-admiral.
Joined the Red Navy, 1936. Took part in the Soviet-Finnish war, 1939–40. Became widely known as a navy captain during WWII. Twice Hero of the Soviet Union. Deputy Commander of the Frunze Naval Academy, 1969–75.

Shabanov, Vitalii Mikhailovich
1923– . General.
Joined the Red Army, 1941. Took part in WWII. Graduated from the Leningrad Air Force Academy, 1945. Joined the Bolshevik Party, 1947. Head of a laboratory and design office, 1949. Deputy Minister of the Radio Industry of the USSR, 1974–78. Deputy Minister of Defence, 1978. Non-voting member of the Cen. Cttee. of the CPSU, 1981, and full member, 1983.

Shabanova, Rafiga Makhmudovna
31.10.1943– . Athlete.
Born in Baku. With Baku Spartak. Graduated from the Azerbaidzhanian Institute of Physical Culture, 1968. Physical education teacher. Honoured Master of Sports (handball), 1976. Olympic champion, 1976.

Shadrin, Vladimir Nikolaevich
6.6.1948– . Athlete.
Born in Moscow. Honoured Master

of Sports (hockey), 1971. With Moscow Spartak. Graduated from the Moscow Gubkin Institute of Oil and Gas Industry, 1975. Mechanical engineer. Member of the CPSU, 1977. USSR champion, 1967, 1969 and 1976. European champion, 1970 and 1973–75. World champion, 1970–71 and 1973–75. Olympic champion, 1972 and 1976.

Shafarevich, Igor Rostislavovich
1923– . Mathematician.
Born in Zhitomir. Graduated in mathematics from Moscow University, 1940. Professor of Moscow University. Academician, 1958. Lenin Prize, 1959. From the late 1960s, active in the human rights movement, concentrating on the rights of believers. Close to Solzhenitsyn. Dismissed from his job, 1974. Wrote a study of Soviet laws relating to religion. Wrote a historical study on socialism through the ages, defining it as the death wish of mankind (*Sotsialism, kak Iavlenie Mirovoi Istorii*), published in France and translated into several languages.

Shafran, Daniil Borisovich
13.2.1923– . Cellist.
Born in Leningrad. Son of the cellist Boris Shafran (1896–). 1st prize at the All-Union Competition of Violinists and Cellists, 1937, and at the International Competition of Cellists in Prague, 1950.

Shafranov, Petr Grigor'evich
1901–1972. Col.-general.
Joined the Red Army, 1919. Took part in the Civil War. Graduated from the Dzerzhinskii Artillery Academy, 1934. Took part in WWII as an artillery commander, holding several high posts. Worked in the HQ of the Warsaw Pact Forces, 1959–66.

Shagin, Ivan Mikhailovich
1904–1982. Photographer.
Born in the Iaroslav Oblast'. Son of a peasant. At the age of 11, began working in a small shop in Moscow. Later earned a living as a sailor on a Volga steamer. In 1924, returned to Moscow and worked in co-operative enterprises, first as a labourer, then

as a salesman and instructor. In 1919, became interested in photography and began taking amateur pictures. By 1930, had become a professional photographer. Worked as a press photographer for the newspapers *Nasha Zhizn'* and *Kooperativnaia Zhizn'*, also for Selkhozgiz, the state agricultural publishing house. From 1933–1950, photo-reporter for *Komsomolskaia Pravda*. Also worked for the magazine *USSR in Construction*. During WWII, war correspondent for *Komsomolskaia Pravda*. Produced many illustrated books and picture reports for the Izogiz art publishing house, also for *Sovetskii Khudozhnik*, Progress Publishers, *Pravda* and the Novosty press agency. See: *Soviet Photography, 1917–40*, London, 1984.

Shaginian, Grant Amazaspovich
30.7.1923– . Athlete.
Born in Armenia. Honoured Master of Sports (gymnastics), 1951. Member of the CPSU, 1951. With Erevan Spartak. International referee from 1957. Honorary Coach of the Armenian SSR, 1961. Graduated from the Erevan Institute of Physical Culture, 1966. USSR champion, 1948–55. Absolute USSR champion, 1952. Olympic silver-medallist, 1952. World champion, 1954.

Shaginian, Marietta Sergeevna
2.4.1888–1982. Author.
Born in Moscow. Daughter of a physician. Graduated from the Higher Courses for Women, 1912. Began to write prose and poetry before WWI. Wrote criticism (on Z. Gippius and other Symbolists). Journalist with Caucasian newspapers, 1906–1919. After the October Revolution, became a conformist Soviet writer. Wrote a novel on the Ulianov family and published research on Lenin's parentage in the magazine *Novyi Mir*. Collected works, 6 volumes, published in Moscow, 1956–58.

Shaiket, Arkadii Samoilovich
1898–1959. Photo-journalist.
Born in the town of Nikolaev. Became a locksmith's apprentice. Moved to Moscow in 1918. In 1922, worked as a retoucher in a portrait photographer's studio. Learnt there

the basics of photography. Became a photo-journalist. Worked as a photographer for *Rabochaia Gazeta*, the largest circulation daily. From 1924, worked for the weekly illustrated magazine *Ogonek*. His photographs were included in the exhibition of 78 photographs of achievements which toured to Berlin, Vienna and Prague. Took part in a series of *USSR in Construction* and *Nashi Dostizheniia* (Our Achievements). War photographer during WWII.
See: *Soviet Photography, 1917-40*, London, 1984.

Shakhlin, Boris Anfiianovich
27.1.1932-   . Athlete.
Born in Ishim, Tumen' Oblast'. Honoured Master of Sports (gymnastics), 1955. With Kiev Burevestnik. Graduated from the Kiev Institute of Physical Culture, 1955. Member of the CPSU, 1964. International referee from 1968. Vice-president of the Technical Committee of the International Gymnastics Federation. USSR champion, 1955-62. European champion, 1955, 1963. World champion, 1958. Olympic champion, 1960. Author of *Moia Gimnastika*, Moscow, 1973.

Shakhovskaia, Galina Aleksandrovna (real name – Rzhepishevskaia)
20.2.1908-   . Choreographer.
Born in Moscow. Graduated from the Moscow Lunacharskii Technical School of Choreography, 1929, and from the State Theatre Experimental Workshops, 1930, as actor-director. From 1936, dancer and choreographer at the Variety Theatre. From 1940, choreographer, and from 1942 -65, chief choreographer at the Operetta Theatre. Also stages dances in theatre and film.

Shakhovskaia, Zinaida Alekseevna (Schakovskoy; m. Malewsky-Malevich; Jacques Croise), Princess
30.8.1906-   . Author, editor.
Born in Moscow. Left Russia with her parents during the Civil War. Educated at the American College for Girls in Turkey, 1921-23, and at the Monastere de Berlaymont, Brussels, 1923-25. Graduated from the College de France, Paris, 1925-26. Married the diplomat, Sviatoslav de

Malewsky-Malevich, 1926. Started to write in French in the 1920s. Participated in the brilliant literary life of Russian Paris between the wars. Close to Bunin and Nabokov. Correspondent for Belgian newspapers. During WWII, in Britain, involved in helping the Free French. War correspondent with the Allied forces in Italy, Greece, Germany and at the Nuremberg trials, 1945-47. After WWII, lived in Moscow as the wife of a Belgian diplomat, and described the country and the personalities she met, such as Zhukov and Khrushchev. Editor of the Parisian Russian-language newspaper *Russkaia Mysl'*, 1968-78. Received the Chevalier de la Legion d'Honneur and other awards. Author of several novels, volumes of memoirs and works on Russian history.

Shakhovskoi, Dmitrii Ivanovich, Prince
1861-1939. Politician.
Left-wing member of the Cadet Party. Member of the 1st Duma. After the February Revolution 1917, Minister of Social Security, May-July 1917. Emigrated.

Shakhurin, Aleksei Ivanovich
1904-1975. Col.-general.
Graduated from the Moscow Engineering Economics Institute, 1932. Joined the Red Army, 1934. In the late 1930s, 1st Secretary of Iaroslavl', later Gorkii obkom. Member of the Cen. Cttee. of the Bolshevik Party, 1939-46. Minister of the Aviation Industry of the USSR, 1940-46. Arrested after Stalin was told by his son, Vasilii, an air-force officer, that US planes were better than Soviet planes. Released after Stalin's death, 1953. Deputy Chairman of the Cttee. for the Foreign Economic Relations, 1953-59.

Shalaev, Stepan Alekseevich
1929-   . Politician.
Graduated from the Moscow Technical Institute of Forestry, 1951. Chief engineer in the forest industry in the Udmurt ASSR, 1951-53. Member of the CPSU, 1954. Director of various timber works in the Udmurt ASSR, Kalinin and Novgorod oblasts, 1955-62. Chairman of

the Cen. Cttee. of the Timber, Paper and Wood-Processing Industries Workers' Union, 1963-68. Secretary of the All-Union Central Council of Trade Unions, 1968-80. Deputy to the USSR Supreme Soviet from 1979. Member of the Presidium from Nov. 1982. USSR Minister of the Timber, Pulp and Paper and Wood Processing Industries, 1980-82. Candidate member of the Cen. Cttee. of the CPSU from 1981. Chairman of All-Union Cen. Council of Trade Unions, 1982. One of Gorbachev's supporters.

Shalamov, Varlam Tikhonovich
1907-17.1.1982. Author.
Born in Vologda. Son of an Orthodox priest, who was a missionary in the Aleutian Islands. Worked in a leather factory in Kuntsevo, 1924-25. Studied law at Moscow University, 1925-29. Accused of counter-revolutionary activity, and sentenced to 3 years of prison and 2 years in exile. Construction worker. Journalist in Moscow, 1933. Re-arrested and sent to the Gulag, 1937. 5 years in prison camps. Re-tried in 1943, and sentenced to 10 years. Released in 1953. Allowed to live in Moscow (possibly officially rehabilitated in 1956). Became widely known through his samizdat short stories, describing life in the Gulag camps. During his last years, some of his articles and poems were published in the official Soviet press. A collection of his best short stories, *Kolymskie Rasskazy*, was published in 1978 in England. Spent his last years in a home for invalids, completely blind and deaf, and developed a mental disease which affected his speech. 3 days before his death he was taken to a mental hospital. (4 years previously, when the first symptoms of the disease had appeared, his friends had been unable to convince the doctors to give him medical treatment). Remembered as one of the longest-serving inmates to survive the Gulag prisons and camps and the author who gave the most vivid descriptions of the Gulag horrors.

Shalimov, Viktor Ivanovich
20.4.1951-   . Athlete.
Born in Solnechnogorsk, Moscow Oblast'. Honoured Master of Sports

(hockey), 1975. With Moscow Spartak. Graduated from the Moscow Oblast' Institute of Physical Culture. World and European champion, 1975. Olympic champion, 1976. USSR champion, 1976.

Shamburkin, Viktor Nikolaevich
12.10.1931–   . Athlete.
Born in Leningrad. Member of the CPSU, 1959. Honoured Master of Sports (shooting), 1960. With Moscow DOSAAF. Graduated from the Leningrad Institute of Physical Culture, 1965. USSR champion, 1957–71. World record-holder, 1958–62. World champion, 1958. Olympic champion, 1960.

Shamrai, Galina Iakovlevna (Rud'ko)
5.10.1931–   . Athlete.
Born in Tashkent. Honoured Master of Sports (gymnastics), 1954. With Moscow Burevestnik. Graduated from the Moscow Pedagogical Institute, 1956. Schoolmaster. International referee from 1975. Olympic silver-medallist, 1952. World champion, 1954. USSR champion, 1955.

Shamshiev, Bolotbek Tolenovich
12.1.1941–   . Film director, actor.
Prominent Kirghizian director. Graduated from the VGIK as a director in 1964. His documentary *Manaschi*, 1966, won several international prizes. Began as an actor in L. Shepit'ko's *Heat*, which became a modern Soviet classic. Specializes in Kirghiz historical subjects and folk-legends. His best films include *The Gunshot at the Mountain Pass*, 1969, starring S. Chokmorov, and *The Curse*, also with S. Chokmorov, and dealing with opium smuggling in Kirghizia.

Shaparenko, Aleksandr Maksimovich
16.2.1946–   . Athlete.
Born in Sumskaia Oblast'. Honoured Master of Sports (rowing), 1966. From 1973, with the Kiev Army Sports Club. Graduated from the Kiev Institute of Physical Culture, 1974. Member of the CPSU, 1975. USSR champion, 1967–79. European champion, 1967, 1969. World champion, 1966, 1970, 1973, and 1977–79. Olympic silver-medallist (with V.

Morozov), 1968, and solo Olympic champion, 1972.

Shapiro, Maria Lazarevna
1901–1962. Journalist.
Lived with her parents in Blagoveshchensk. During the October Revolution 1917, moved to Harbin with the White Russians. Graduated from Harbin Law Institute. Worked as a journalist on Russian newspapers in China. After WWII, arrested in Harbin by SMERSH and sentenced for her journalistic work to 10 years in the Gulag camps. Released, 1955. Her memoirs on pre-war Russian life in Harbin and her experiences in the women's Gulag camps, *Zhenskii Kontslager*, which she wrote in a nursing home in Mordovia, were published in the West in the late 1970s and early 1980s.

Shapiro, Valentina
1948–   . Artist.
Born in Moscow. Studied art. In 1972, emigrated to Israel, where she became a very successful artist. Exhibited in Israel, and in Paris at the Katya Granoff Gallery. Moved to Paris, and then to Switzerland.

Shapkin, Timofei Timofeevich
1885–1943. Lt.-general.
During WWI, a Cossack NCO. Joined the Red Army, 1920. Took part in the Civil War as a regimental, and later brigade, commander. Highly decorated (3 Orders of the Red Banner). Graduated from the Frunze Military Academy, 1935. Joined the Bolshevik Party, 1938. Took part in WWII.

Shaporin, Iurii Aleksandrovich
8.11.1887–9.12.1966. Composer.
Born in Glukhov, in the Chernigov Gouvt. Began composing while at school, 1898–1906. As a student at Kiev University, studied composition. Changed to Petersburg University, and graduated from the Faculty of Law in 1912. Studied at the Petersburg Conservatory, 1913–18. Pupil of N. Sokolov, N. Cherepnin and M. Steinberg. In charge of the music department of the Bolshoi Theatre of Drama (now the Gorkii Academic Bolshoi Theatre), 1919–28. Musical director of the Pushkin

Theatre, 1928–34. Professor at the Moscow Conservatory from 1939. Frequent appearances abroad. Died in Moscow.

Shaposhnikov, Boris Mikhailovich
2.10.1882–26.3.1945. Marshal.
Graduated from the Academy of the General Staff, 1910. Took part in WWI as a colonel. Joined the Red Army, 1918. Throughout his life, regarded as a very competent staff officer. Commander of Leningrad and Moscow military districts, 1925–28. Chief-of-staff of the Red Army, 1928–31. Head of the Frunze Military Academy, 1932–35. Chief of the General Staff, 1937. Non-voting member of the Cen. Cttee. of the Bolshevik Party, 1939. Deputy Minister of Defence, 1940. Head of the Academy of the General Staff, 1943–45. Author of works on military theory.

Shaposhnikov, Il'ia Kalustovich
3.1.1896–17.1.1953. Composer.
Born in Rostov-on-Don. Author of the opera *Bakhchisaraiskii Fontan*, performed on radio in 1937. Also wrote 2 symphonies, musicals, suites, pieces for piano and orchestra, and songs for films. Died in Rostov-on-Don.

Sharanskaia, Avital' (Natasha)
(b. Shtieglitz)
1953–   . Wife of A. Sharanskii.
Met Sharanskii outside the Moscow synagogue in the autumn of 1973. Married him in June 1974, when he was already on the brink of arrest by the KGB. Emigrated to Israel from where she tirelessly campaigned for the release of her husband. Received by Prime Minister Thatcher, President Reagan, and many other world leaders. Eventually won her campaign. Lives with her husband in Israel.

Sharanskii, Natan (Sharansky, Anatolii)
1948–   . Jewish human rights campaigner.
Born in Stalino, now Donetsk, in the Ukraine. Son of a journalist. Studied at the Moscow Institute of Physics and Technology. In 1973, joined the

Jewish rights movement. Came into conflict with the KGB. Took up the cases of Jewish refuseniks, and passed a list of names to American helpers. Accused of espionage and high treason. Spent nearly a decade as a Gulag prisoner. Released thanks to the efforts of his wife Avital' (Natasha) and the pressure of world-wide public opinion. Lives in Israel, where he has become a national hero. Continues his fight for the release of those who are still imprisoned in the USSR for their convictions.
Memoirs: *Fear No Evil*, London and NY, July 1988.

Sharii, Valerii Petrovich
2.1.1947–   . Athlete.
Born in Minskaia Oblast'. Honoured Master of Sports (heavy athletics), 1975. With the Minsk Armed Forces Team. World record-holder, 1972–73, 1975–76. European champion, 1975–76. World champion, 1975–76. USSR champion, 1975, 1977–78. Olympic champion, 1976.

Sharokhin, Mikhail Nikolaevich
1898–1974. Col.-general.
Joined the Red Guards, 1917, and the Red Army, 1918. Took part in the Civil War. Joined the Bolshevik Party, 1920. Graduated from the Frunze Military Academy, 1936, and the Academy of the General Staff, 1939. Staff officer, and later, during WWII, army commander. Returned to staff work after the war. Head of Military Higher Education Establishments, 1953–57.

Sharov, Iurii Dmitrievich
22.4.1939–   . Athlete.
Born in Saratov. Honoured Master of Sports (fencing), 1964. With Saratov Burevestnik. Graduated from the Smolensk Institute of Physical Culture, 1962. Member of the CPSU, 1971. World champion, 1963–66, and 1969. USSR champion, 1964. Olympic champion, 1964.

Sharshun, Sergei Ivanovich
4.8.1888–24.11.1975. Artist, author, poet.
Born in Buguruslan in the Urals. Son of a Slovak settler. In 1908, moved to Moscow, where he studied art. Began as an impressionist. In 1912, moved to Paris, where he met Braque and Picasso. From 1916–17, lived and worked in Barcelona where he exhibited for the first time. Returned to Paris, 1920. At one time, joined the cubists, praised by Picasso. Very famous in the 1920s, but went completely out of fashion and was forgotten sometime after the 1930s. In old age, lived in great poverty. Rediscovered posthumously. Several exhibitions in Paris. Also rediscovered in the Soviet Union.
Works: *Dolgolikov* (a novel), *Nepriiatnye Rasskazy, Raketa, Bez Sebia.*

Shatalov, Vladimir Aleksandrovich
1927–   . Cosmonaut.
Graduated from a special air force school, 1945, from a military aviation college, 1949, and from the Air Force Academy, 1956. Served in the Soviet Air Force, 1949–63. Cosmonaut, 1963. Commander of Soiuz 4. Took part in the docking manoeuvre with Soiuz 5, and then landed 40 km. from Karaganda in Jan. 1969. Commander of Soiuz 8 (with A. S. Eliseev). Participated in a group flight of 3 spaceships, landing 145 km. north of Karaganda in Oct. 1969, and with Soiuz 10 in 1971. Senior space official, 1987. Head of the Cosmonaut Training Centre, 1988.

Shatilov, Konstantin Vasil'evich
5.11.1924–   . Ballet dancer. choreographer, teacher.
Born in Leningrad. Graduated from the Leningrad Choreographic School, 1947. Pupil of A. Pushkin and B. Shavrov. Joined the Kirov Theatre. Taught at the Leningrad Choreographic School, 1957–66, 1969–70 and from 1973. Director at the Cairo Ballet School, Egypt, 1966–69. Chief choreographer at the Novosibirsk Theatre, and chief coach at the Novosibirsk Choreographic School, 1970–73. Worked at the Berlin Opera, 1972.

Sha ov, Gennadii Ivanovich
27.5.1932–   . Athlete.
Born in Leningrad. Honoured Master of Sports (boxing), 1956. Graduated from Leningrad University in law, 1956. With Leningrad Burevestnik. Member of the CPSU, 1956. USSR champion, 1955–56 and 1958. European champion, 1955 and 1959. Olympic champion, 1956.

Shatov, Mikhail Vasil'evich (Kashtanov)
1917?–22.10.1980. Captain, author.
Took part in WWII. Taken prisoner by the Germans. Joined the Vlasov army, the ROA. Escaped from SMERSH. Lived in DP camps in Germany, 1945–49. Moved to the USA, 1950. Published his major work on the history of the Russian anti-Stalin movement during WWII, using over 2,000 sources (*Bibliografiia Dvizhenia Osvobozhdeniia Narodov Rossii* — Bibliography of the Liberation Movement of the Peoples of Russia, NY, 1961). One of the founders of the Congress of Russian Americans. Died in the USA.

Shatov, Vladimir Sergeevich
1887–1943. Revolutionary, politician.
Took part in the Bolshevik take-over in Petrograd, 1917. Commissar for the Defence of Railways near Petrograd during the Civil War, 1918–21. Minister of Defence and Minister of Railways of the Far Eastern Republic (Soviet buffer state), 1921–22. In the late 1920s and 1930s, in charge of railway construction (using Gulag inmates as slave labour) in Turkestan and Siberia. Later, Deputy Minister of Railways of the USSR.

Shatrov, Mikhail Filippovich (Marshak)
1932–   . Playwright.
Prominent playwright. Specialized in historico-revolutionary subjects. His first success in the early 1960s was *Imenem Revoliutsii*. His play *Shestoe Iulia*, 1964, was made into a film in 1968. *Tak Pobedim!* was produced by the Moscow Arts Theatre in 1982 (State Prize, 1983). Increased his output after Gorbachev took office, and became his close friend. Within 3 years wrote and produced 3 plays, *Diktatura Sovesti, Brestskii Mir* and *Dal'she... Dal'she... Dal'she (Further... Further... Further)* which depict the days before, during and soon after the October Revolution 1917, and feature the previously unmentionable personalities of Trotsky, Zinov'ev and Bukharin. The

premiere was attended by all members of the Politburo, headed by the General Secretary, Gorbachev. *Further*... appeared in Jan. 1988 in the magazine *Znamia*, and immediately became the cause of a great controversy in the press. One of the best-known playwrights in the Soviet Union at present.

Shatunovskaia, Lidia (m. Tumerman)
1906– . Theatre critic, author.
Born in Odessa. Graduated from the Moscow Theatre Institute. Theatre critic for various Moscow magazines. Wife of the physicist Lev Tumerman. After her husband's arrest in 1947, arrested also, as 'the wife of an enemy of the people'. Sentenced to 20 years in camps. Released after Stalin's death, 1954. Left the USSR, 1972. Settled in Israel. Wrote memoirs: *Zhizn V Kremle*, USA, 1982; *Istoriia Odnogo Aresta*, Israel, 1976; *Dom Na Naberezhnoi, Kontinent*, 1982.

Shaumian, Stepan Georgievich (Suren)
1878–1918. Revolutionary.
Joined the SD Party, 1900. Member of the Cen. Cttee. of the Bolshevik Party, 1917. Commissar for Caucasian Affairs, 1917. Chairman of the Soviet in Baku, 1917. One of the organizers of the Bolshevik take-over in the Caucasian region. Head of the local Baku government and Minister of Foreign Affairs, 1918. Among the 26 Baku commissars shot by SRs and the British. Later glorified as a martyr for the revolutionary cause. Became the subject of several films.

Shavelskii, Georgii, Protopresbyter
6.1.1871–10.2.1951. Russian Orthodox clergyman.
Born near Vitebsk. Educated at Vitebsk seminary. Priest, 1895. Graduated from Petersburg Theological Academy in 1902. Last Chief Almoner of the Russian Army and Fleet, 1911. Member of the Holy Synod, 1915–17. After the October Revolution 1917, emigrated to Bulgaria. Professor of theology in Sofia.
Works: *Memoirs*, 2 vols; *Orthodox Pastoral Work* (in Bulgarian).

Shavkaladze, Robert Mikhailovich
1.4.1933– . Athlete.
Born in Tbilisi. Graduated from the Georgian Institute of Physical Culture, 1955. Honoured Master of Sports (track and field athletics), 1960. With Tbilisi Dynamo. Graduated from Tbilisi University, 1961. Member of the CPSU, 1964. Olympic champion, 1960. USSR champion, 1964.

Shavrin, Iurii
1924–1974. Athlete.
Honoured Master of Sports (sailing). 12th place at the XVIth Olympic Games. 9th place at the XVIIIth Olympic Games. There have been several articles about him in the American and Canadian press suggesting that his death was caused by misuse of steroids.

Shavrov, Boris Vasil'evich
16.8.1900–26.10.1975. Ballet dancer, teacher.
Born in Petersburg. Graduated from the Petrograd Theatre School, 1918. Joined the Opera and Ballet Theatre (now the Kirov Theatre). On tour abroad with the ballerina E. Liuk, 1922–23. One of the greatest performers in duet dance. From 1929, taught at the Leningrad Choreographic School. Artistic director there, 1930–38. From 1946, coach at the Kirov Theatre. Among his pupils were Iu. Grigorovich and B. Bregvadze. Died in Leningrad.

Shavrov, Ivan Egorovich
1916– . General.
Joined the Red Army, 1935, and the Bolshevik Party, 1940. Graduated from the Red Army Mechanization Academy, 1941. Tank officer during WWII. Graduated from the Academy of the General Staff, 1948. Deputy commander of Soviet forces in Germany, 1957. Head of the Academy of the General Staff, 1973. Worked in the HQ of the Warsaw Pact Forces, 1978–84. Member of the Cen. Cttee. of the CPSU, 1971–76.

Shavrov, Vadim Mikhailovich
1924–1983. Church historian.
Born in Moscow. In his youth, a fanatical communist. Served in the Soviet Navy during WWII. Arrested, 1948 (in connection with the arrest of his father), sentenced to 10 years in the Gulag camps. Released, 1954. Entered Odessa seminary, 1955. Later became well-known in samizdat, writing on religious subjects. Gave a detailed description of his own conversion from militant atheist to Christian believer. Co-writer (with Krasnov-Levitin) of a 3-volume history of the Living Church schism in the Orthodox church (an attempt to subvert the church from within). Placed into a special psychiatric clinic, 1982. Released shortly before his death.

Shavyrin, Boris Ivanovich
1902–1965. Artillery designer.
Graduated from the elite Bauman Technical Institute in Moscow, 1930. Became the Soviet Union's best-known mortar designer. Highly decorated (4 State Prizes).

Shchadenko, Efim Afanas'evich
1885–1951. Col.-general.
Joined the Bolshevik Party, 1904, and the Red Army, 1918. During the Civil War, organized groups of Red Cossacks on the Don River. In the 1920s political officer at the Frunze Military Academy. Deputy Minister of Defence and Head of the Personnel Department for Leading Cadres of the Red Army (involved in the purges of the military), 1937. During WWII, Deputy Minister of Defence in charge of personnel and drafting into the armed forces. Member of the Cen. Cttee. of the Bolshevik Party, 1939–41. Demoted to non-voting member, 1941.

Shchapova, Elena Sergeevna (m. Limonova; de Carli)
1950– . Model.
Born in Moscow. Worked as a model for the Moscow fashion house Dom Modelei on Kuznetskii Most. One of the top fashion models and cover girls in the USSR. Married the poet Eduard Limonov. Left the USSR, 1975. Settled in the USA. Created a sensation as the first Russian model to pose in the nude for photographic publications. Began writing poems, some of which appeared in Russian emigré magazines. Divorced Limo-

nov, and married the Italian Count de Carli. Lives in Italy.

Shchedrin, Rodion Konstantinovich

16.12.1932–   . Composer, pianist. Born in Moscow. Son of the music historian K. Shchedrin. Husband of the ballerina Maia Plisetskaia. Entered the Moscow Choral School, 1944. His first, mainly choral, compositions date from that time. Entered the Moscow Conservatory, 1950. Pupil of I. Shaporin (composition) and I. Flier (piano). While an undergraduate, finished his music for the ballet *Konek Gorbunok*, 1958. This and the symphony composed in 1958 made his name. Wrote operas, ballet music, symphonies, cantatas and oratorios. One of the most interesting modern Soviet composers. Wrote the music for *Anna Karenina* in which his wife played the leading part. Taught at the Moscow Conservatory, 1965–69. Honorary member of the Bavarian Academy of Art.

Shcheglov, Afanasii Fedorovich

1912–   . General. Joined the Soviet Army, 1929. Graduated from the Frunze Military Academy, 1939. Joined the Bolshevik Party, 1939. Took part in the Soviet-Finnish war, 1939–40, and in WWII, on the Leningrad front. Graduated from the Academy of the General Staff, 1948. Deputy Commander of Anti-Aircraft Defence Forces, 1966–74. High posts at the HQ of the Warsaw Pact Forces, 1974–85.

Shchegolev, Pavel Eliseevich

1877–1931. Historian, literary scholar. Editor of the magazine *Byloe*. Well-known specialist on Pushkin and Lermontov. Emigrated after the revolution, 1917. Lived and died in Paris.

Shchelkin, Kirill Ivanovich

1911–1968. Scientist. Graduated from the Crimean Teachers' Institute, 1932. Moved to Moscow. Graduated from the Physico-Technical Institute, 1937. Professor at the Physical Engineering Institute in Moscow. Worked on the theories of burning and explosions. Highly decorated (5 State Prizes).

Shchelokov, Nikolai Anisimovich

26.11.1910–13.12.1984. State security official, general, politican. Born in Almaznaia in the Ukraine. Son of a worker. Member of the CPSU from the age of 21. Graduated from the Dnepropetrovsk Metallurgical Institute, 1933. Miner, 1936. Engineer. Deputy head of various metallurgical plants in the Ukraine until 1938. Served in the army, 1934–35 and 1941–46. Chairman of Dnepropetrovsk City Soviet, 1939–41. Deputy Minister of Local Industry, 1946–47. Worked for the Cen. Cttee. of the Ukrainian CP, 1947–51. 1st Deputy Chairman of the Council of Ministers of the Moldavian SSR, 1951–62. Deputy to 1954, member of the Economic Cttee., 1962–66. Chairman of the Trade and Public Services Cttee. of the Soviet of Nationalities of the USSR Supreme Soviet, 1966–68. Chairman of the Economic Soviet of the Moldavian SSR, 1957–58. Member of the Bureau, 1956–66. 2nd Secretary of the Cen. Cttee. of the Moldavian Council of Ministers, 1962–63. Member of the Industry Bureau of the Cen. Cttee. of the Moldavian CP, 1962–64. USSR Minister for the Maintenance of Public Order, 1966–68. Member of the Cen. Cttee. of the CPSU from Apr. 1968. USSR Minister of the Interior from Nov. 1968. until Dec. 1982. Promoted to general, Sep. 1976. For many years close to Brezhnev. After Brezhnev's death, fired from the Cen. Cttee. for speculating in foreign cars, Dec. 1982. Transferred to the Group of Inspectors-General of the Ministry of Defence, headed by the elderly Marshal Moskalenko. (His son, who occupied a senior position in the Cen. Cttee. of the Komsomol, was also fired.) According to Soviet press reports, committed suicide (shot himself) while under investigation. Died in Moscow.
See: A. Riadnov, 'Kucher Na Obluchke', *Posev*, No. 3, 1984.

Shchepkina-Kupernik, Tatiana Lvovna

1874–1952. Author, poet, translator. Became well-known in the early 20th century, mostly as a talented translator of Western European literature. Her original work was prolific, but rather shallow. One of the few representatives of the pre-revolutionary intelligentsia active throughout the Stalin years. Published her memoirs in 1928.

Shcherbachev, Vladimir Vladimirovich

24.1.1889–5.3.1952. Composer, pianist. Born in Warsaw. At the Petersburg Conservatory, 1908–14. Pupil of A. Liadov and M. Steinberg. Studied, concurrently, at the law and philological faculties of Petersburg University. First symphonic compositions, 1910–12. Musical director with Diaghilev's company of opera and ballet in London, Rome, Paris and Monte Carlo, 1911. Taught at the conservatory, 1912–14. Army service, 1914–18. Lecturer, director of the music department of the NARKOMPROS, 1918–22. Member of the Russian Institute of the History of Art, 1922–31. Pianist and musical director with the Petrograd Philharmonic Orchestra, musical director of the Peredvizhnoi Theatre, and professor of composition at the Leningrad Conservatory, 1924–31 and 1944–48. Taught theory at the Institute of History of Art and at the Central Technical School for Music, 1926–31. Professor of composition at the Tiflis Conservatory, 1931–32. Died in Leningrad.

Shcherbakov, Aleksandr Sergeevich

1901–1945. Politician. Joined the Bolshevik Party, 1918. Komsomol official, 1919. Took part in the Civil War. Graduated from Sverdlov Communist University, 1921–24. Party official, 1924. Graduated from the Institute of Red Professors, 1932. Joined the Staff of the Cen. Cttee. of the Bolshevik Party, 1932. Secretary of Leningrad, Irkutsk and Donetsk obkoms, 1936–38. 1st Secretary of the Moscow Party Cttee., 1938–45. Secretary of the Cen. Cttee. of the Bolshevik Party, 1941. Non-voting member of the Politburo, 1941. Head of the Political Administration of the Armed Forces, Deputy Minister of Defence, and Chief of Sovinformburo, June 1942.

Shcherbakov, Vladimir Ivanovich

1901–1981. Lt.-general. Joined the Red Army, 1919. Took

381

part in the Civil War. Joined the Bolshevik Party, 1926. Graduated from the Frunze Military Academy, 1938. Took part in the Soviet-Finnish war and WWII. After the war, commander of several military districts.

Shcherbitskii, Vladimir Vasil'evich
17.2.1918– . Politician.
Born in Verkhnedneprovsk, now Dnepropetrovsk Oblast'. Son of a worker. Komsomol worker, 1934–35. Graduated from the Dnepropetrovsk Institute of Chemical Technology, 1941. Member of the CPSU, 1941. High commands in the army, 1941–45. Engineer at a coke-chemical plant in Dneprodzerzhinsk, 1945–46. Secretary of the party cttee. at the same plant, 1946–48. Various senior party positions in Dneprodzerzhinsk, and in Dnepropetrovsk, 1948–61. Member of the Cen. Cttee. of the CPSU from 1961. Chairman of the Council of Ministers of the Ukrainian SSR, 1965–72. Elected to the Politburo on 9 Apr. 1971. 1st Secretary of the Cen. Cttee. of the Ukrainian CP from 25 May 1972. Member of the Presidium of the USSR Supreme Soviet from 20 Sep. 1972. The last surviving Brezhnevite during the Gorbachev years.

Shchetinkin, Petr Efimovich
1885–1927. Partisan, state security officer.
Took part in WWI as a captain. Highly decorated (4 St. George Medals). Joined the Bolshevik Party, 1918. Chief-of-staff of the Red Partisan Army in Siberia, 1919. Involved in the hunting down of the legendary White commander of Mongolian detachments, Baron Ungern-Sternberg, 1921. Chief-of-staff of Siberian military district border guards (GPU), 1922–26. Built up the state security network in communist Mongolia, 1926. Probably killed on the Soviet-Mongolian border.

Shchors, Nikolai Aleksandrovich
1895–1919. Military commander.
Took part in WWI as a sub-lieutenant. Joined the Bolshevik Party, and the Red Army, 1918. Organized Red partisan groups in Western Russia, near Novozybkov.

Fought in the Civil War as a divisional commander. Fell in action. Later glorified as a revolutionary hero. Became the subject of several films.

Shchukin, Aleksandr Nikolaevich
1900– . Radio scientist.
Graduated from the Leningrad Electrotechnical Institute, 1927. Professor of the Naval Academy in Leningrad, 1940. Chairman of the Research Council on Radiowaves of the Academy of Sciences. Specialist in short-wave communication.

Shchukin, Boris Vasil'evich
17.4.1894–7.10.1939. Actor.
Studied at the E. Vakhtangov Studio, 1920. Best known for his portrayal of Lenin in the films *Lenin v Oktiabre*, 1937, and *Lenin v 1918 Godu*, 1939. Also played Lenin on the stage in *Chelovek s Ruzh'em*.

Shchukin, Sergei Ivanovich
1876?–1936. Industrialist, art collector, patron of the arts.
The third of 6 sons of a well-known Moscow textile industrialist, from Old Believer background. One of the Russian merchant princes, who by their wealth and enthusiasm for the arts made the flowering of Russian culture in the early 20th century possible. One of the first people in Russia to appreciate the work of the modern French artists. Became a major patron and collector of Matisse, Cezanne, Picasso and Gaugin. 38 Matisses hung on the walls of his Grand Salon in Moscow in the former Trubeskoi Palace, opened to the public, 1908. By 1914, owned the largest private collection of Impressionists in the world (221 paintings). Relying only on his own instinct, searched out the work of rejected artists, boldly buying and seeking no advice. Turned his home into a public gallery and received anyone who was interested in seeing the work. Art authorities from many European capitals used to come to him in order to study the artists. Also a founder of the Institute of Philosophy at Moscow University. His collection was nationalized after the October Revolution 1917, but the treasure remained inaccessible to the public for

a long time in the vaults of the Pushkin Museum and other galleries, during the heyday of Stalinist obscurantism. Emigrated after the Bolshevik take-over. Died in France.

Shchusev, Aleksei Viktorovich
1873–1949. Architect.
Born in Petersburg, and studied at the Petersburg Academy of Arts. In 1910, academician. Became Stalin's chief architect (the Soviet Albert Speer), responsible for the Lenin Mausoleum in Moscow, 1925–30, the Marx-Engels Institute in Tiflis (Georgia), the theatre on Mayakovsky Square, the Hotel Moskva and the Komsomolskaia-Kol'tsevaia metro station. Father-figure of socialist realism in Soviet architecture. His early pre-Stalinist work is outstanding: for example, the Kazanskii Vokzal, one of the busiest central railway terminals in the USSR, constructed during 1913–26, in 17th-century style. Member of the USSR Academy of Architecture, 1939. All his Stalinist-period buildings combine classical and Georgian styles. Awarded the Stalin Prize.

Shebalin, Vissarion Iakovlevich
11.6.1902–28.5.1963. Composer.
Born in Omsk. Studied at the Omsk Music School, 1920–23, pupil of M. Nevitov. His first compositions date from that time. Entered Moscow Conservatory, 1923. Graduated with distinction, 1928. Pupil of N. Miaskovskii. Taught at the Moscow Technical School for Music, 1923, and at the conservatory from 1928. Lecturer from 1932. Professor from 1935. Directed the composition class at the Music School (known from 1944 as the Pedagogical Institute for Music). Doctor of the history of art, 1941. Professor at the Sverdlovsk Conservatory, 1941–42. Taught at the Institute for Military Conductors, 1948. Head of the same Institute from 1949–51. As a composer, followed the classical tradition, especially that of Taneev. Died in Moscow.

Shegal', Grigorii Mikhailovich
1889–1956. Artist.
Genre, landscape and historical painter. Studied at one of the art schools

of the Society for the Encouragement of Art, 1912–16, under Nikolai Roerich, A. Rylov and F. Bukhgolts, then at the Petersburg Academy of Arts, 1917–18, under B. Beliaev, I. Tvorozhnikov and A. Makovskii. Also at the VKHUTEMAS, Moscow, 1922–24, under A. Shevchenko. Exhibited from 1926 in Moscow. Personal exhibitions: 1935, 1949, Moscow; (posthumously) 1958, Moscow.

Sheina, Svetlana Konstantinovna
26.12.1918– . Ballerina.
Born in Odessa. Graduated from the Leningrad Choreographic School, 1938. Pupil of A. Vaganova and E. Gerdt. Dancer at the Leningrad Malyi Theatre. Choreographer there, 1959–76. Choreographer at the Cairo Theatre, Egypt, 1969–70. Choreographer at theatres in Moscow, Khar'kov and Tallinn. From 1976, teacher-consultant at the Wielki Theatre, Warsaw.

Sheinin, Lev Romanovich
1906–1967. State security official, author.
Member of the Communist Party, 1929. Senior investigator with the Prokuratura of the USSR, dealing especially with important political cases, 1934–50. According to some information, one of the main specialists in the staging of the political trials of the 1930s. Stalin Prize, 1950, but in the early 1950s, was himself arrested and imprisoned for a short time. Released after Stalin's death. Turned to writing. Became a well-known crime writer from the mid 1950s.

Shelepin, Aleksandr Nikolaevich
1918– . Head of the KGB.
Born in Voronezh. Studied at the Moscow Institute of History, Philosophy and Literature, 1936–39. Member of the CPSU, 1940. Early connection with the security services. 1st Secretary of the Cen. Cttee. of the Komsomol, 1952–58. Organized the 6th World Youth Festival in Moscow, 1957. Member of the Cen. Cttee. of the CPSU. Appointed chairman of the KGB, succeeding Serov, Dec. 1958. Sent R. Abel to spy in the USA and ordered the murder of the Ukrainian nationalist leader, Ban-

dera, in Munich. Replaced by Semichastnyi, Nov. 1961, and appointed head of Soviet Trade Unions. In 1975, went to Britain with a trade union delegation. The visit was met by large protest demonstrations of Ukrainians and Jews, and proved disastrous for his career. On his return to Moscow, lost his seat in the Politburo and any importance in Soviet political life.

Shelest, Alla Iakovlevna
26.2.1919– . Prima ballerina.
Born in Smolensk. Graduated from the Leningrad Choreographic School, 1937. Pupil of E. Gerdt. Dancer and soloist at the Kirov Theatre, 1937–63. Her speciality was dramatic roles. In the late 1940s, prima ballerina. Many appearances at the Kremlin Theatre. Entertained Soviet leaders and foreign VIPs at private concerts. Chief choreographer at the Kuibyshev Theatre, 1967–76. Worked at the Tartu Theatre, Estonia, 1975. Taught at the Leningrad Choreographic School and in the ballet department of the Leningrad Conservatory.

Shelkov, Valentin Ivanovich
23.9.1906– . Ballet dancer, teacher.
Born in Odessa. Graduated from the Leningrad Choreographic School, 1933. Pupil of A. Pushkin. Dancer at the Leningrad Malyi Theatre, 1933–34. Dancer and teacher at the Sverdlovsk Theatre, 1934–51. Taught at the same time at the Sverdlovsk Choreographic School. Teacher, then director at the Leningrad Choreographic School, 1951–76.

Shelkovskii, Igor Sergeevich
1937– . Editor, publisher, sculptor.
Born in Orenburg. Graduated from Moscow Art School. Active in the unofficial art movement in Moscow and Leningrad. Left the USSR, 1976. Settled in France. Publisher and editor of the art magazine *A-IA*. As a sculptor, has exhibited with other Russian artists, and on his own. Organizer of many exhibitions of Russian artists settled in France. Also known as a journalist and art critic. Lives near Paris in the

International Artists Centre, at Villedieu, Elancourt.

Shemiakin, Mikhail Mikhailovich (Chemiakin, Michel)
1943– . Artist, publisher.
Born in Moscow. Son of a senior military official. Lived with his parents in Dresden until 1957. Returned to Leningrad, where he studied art in several art schools. Expelled from all of them. Became a famous non-conformist artist. Led the clash between artists and the Soviet cultural authorities. Several arrests. At one time, locked up in a psychiatric hospital. Eventually left the Soviet Union in 1971. Lived in Paris, and became an instant commercial success. Financed a glossy art magazine, *Apollon-77*, in which he introduced many new names in art and literature. Moved to California in 1981. Very successful in the USA. Lives between Paris, Los Angeles and New York.

Shengelaia, Ariadna Vsevolodovna
13.1.1937– . Actress.
Graduated from the VGIK, 1960. Wife of the director Eldar Shengelaia. First film, 1957. Appeared in *Granatovyi Braslet*, 1965, *Belyi Karavan*, 1965, *Goya*, 1972, *Chudaki*, 1974, and *Uchenik Lekaria*, 1983.

Shengelaia, Eldar Nikolaevich
26.1.1933– . Film director.
Born in Georgia. Son of Nikolai Shengelaia, the father of Georgian cinematography, and Nata Vachnadze, one of the first Soviet Georgian screen stars. Graduated from the VGIK in 1958. Notable films: *The White Caravan*, 1964; *Mikela*, 1965; *An Extraordinary Exhibition*, 1968; *The Eccentrics*, 1974. Other films: *A Snowy Fairy Tale*, 1959; *Samanishvili's Step-Mother*, 1974. Leading director at Gruzia Film Studio.

Shengelaia, Georgii Nikolaevich
15.10.1937– . Film director.
Younger brother of Eldar Shengelaia. Graduated from the VGIK in 1966. His directorial debut was *Alaverdoba* (Gruzia Film Studio, 1966). As a student, acted in 3 films directed by

fellow Georgian directors. Became internationally known with *Pirosmani* (Gruzia Film Studio, 1969), the biographical story of the famous Georgian primitivist artist. Other films: *Melodies of the Veriiskii Suburb*, 1973; *Our Daily Water*, 1976. Married to the leading Georgian actress Sofiko Chiaureli.

Shengelaia, Nikolai Mikhailovich
19.8.1903–4.1.1943. Film director. Born in Georgia. Studied at Tbilisi University. In 1922, published some of his poems. Entered the film industry, 1924. Pupil and assistant to K. M. Mardzhanishvili on his film *Burevestniki*, 1925. Continued work on his tutor's films. Also worked with I. Perestiani and Iu. Zheliabuzhskii. First film, *Giulli*, 1927, with L. Push. In 1928, made *Eliso*, scripted with the help of S. Tretiakov. This was one of the first films about the history of the Caucasus, and became a classic of Georgian cinema. In the 1930s, his films were dull official commissions and not based on his own ideas (such as *26 Bakinskikh Komissarov*, 1933). Tried to film M. Sholokhov's *Podniataia Tselina*, 1933–34, but shooting was stopped. *Zolotistaia Dolina*, 1937 (Stalin Prize, 1941), glorified the collectivization campaign in Georgia. One of the first Georgian filmmakers in the Soviet period. Apparently very gifted, but had no chance to show off his talent. Now officially recognized as the father of the Georgian cinema.

Shenshin, Aleksandr Alekseevich
18.11.1890–18.2.1944. Composer. Born in Moscow. Trained singers for Moscow Radio and the Bolshoi Theatre. Wrote music for many theatre plays. Author of an opera, operettas, ballets, and symphonies. Conductor of the Moscow Children's Theatre. Died in Moscow.

Shepitko, Larissa Efimovna
6.1.1938–2.7.1979. Film director. Born in the Ukraine. Pupil of Dovzhenko. Graduated from the VGIK, 1963. Diploma feature film, *Heat*, 1961, made entirely in the Kirghizian steppes in temperatures of 120F (40-50C). Fell ill, but continued directing from a stretcher. The film

made her famous in the Soviet Union due in part to the fine camera-work of Iurii Sokol and the avant-garde music of Alfred Shnitke. Other films: *Wings*, 1966, and *You and I*, 1971. Visited the London Film Festival in 1977 with *The Ascent*, her last film. Married Elem Klimov. Died in a car crash in 1979 during the shooting of *Farewell*, based on a novel by V. Rasputin. The film was completed by Klimov. A sequel *Larissa* was made in her memory.

Sheremet'ev, Aleksandr Dmitrievich, Count
12.3.1859–3.12.1919. Music scholar, conductor, composer.
Born in St. Petersburg. Conductor of his own symphonic orchestra, 1882. In 1898, organized in Petersburg the Obshchedostupnye Simfonicheskie Kontserty (symphonic concerts for the general public). Conducted, along with M. Vladimirov, at these concerts. The Musical-Historical Society in Petersburg was named after him. From 1910–15, this society gave free concerts and lectures on the history of music. After Nov. 1917, left Petersburg for Finland. Died there on his estate near Terioki.

Sheremet'evskaia, Natal'ia Evgen'evna
23.2.1917–   . Ballerina, ballet critic.
Born in Petrograd. Graduated from the Leningrad Choreographic School, 1935, then from the theatre department of the GITIS, 1959. Dancer at the Leningrad Malyi Theatre, 1935–44. Dancer with the Ensemble of Folk Dance, 1945–49. From 1958, ballet critic. Ballet researcher at the Moscow Institute of the History of the Arts, 1964–77. Wrote many articles and books on the ballet.

Sheripov, Aslanbek Dzhemaldinovich
1897–1919. Revolutionary.
Organized the first Soviet in Chechnia. Commander of the Red Chechen partisans during the Civil War. Defended the town of Groznyi against the Whites. After his defeat, went underground. Arrested by the Whites and shot.

Sherman, Isai Ezrovich
11.6.1908–13.6.1972. Conductor. Born in Kiev. Graduated from the Leningrad Conservatory, 1931. Pupil of A. Gauk. Conductor at the Leningrad Malyi Theatre, 1930–37 and 1945–49. Conductor at the Kirov Theatre, 1937–45. From 1957–67, conductor in Kazan', Gorkii, and Petrozavodsk. Taught at the Leningrad, Kazan' and Gorkii conservatories. Died in Leningrad.

Shershenevich, Vadim Gabrielevich
1893–1942. Author, poet.
Imaginist poet. Belonged to the circle of S. Esenin, A. Mariengof, and R. Ivnev. For 4 years, worked as a bookseller with Sandro (Aleksandr) Kusikov. First a futurist, then an ego-futurist. Founder of the ego-futurist publication *Mezonin Poezii*, with Riurik Ivnev. First book of poetry, 1911. Poems include: *Carmina* and *Romanticheskaia Pudra*, 1913; *Avtomobil'naia Postup'*, 1916; *Loshad' Kak Loshad'*, 1920; *Zolotoi Kipiatok* (with A. Mariengof and S. Esenin), 1921; *Itak Itog*, 1926. Books include: *Futurizm Bez Maski*, 1913; *2 x 2 = 5. Listy Imaginista*, 1920; and *Komu Ia Zhmu Ruku*, 1924. Involved romantically with the actress Iulia Dizhur. Following a quarrel, she shot herself, after which he dedicated all his poems to her. Died in Barnaul from tuberculosis.

Shestakov, Nikolai Ivanovich
1883–1938. Artist.
Genre, landscape and portrait painter. Studied at the M. K. Iukhnevich School of Painting, Moscow, 1904–08. Pupil of A. Arkhipov and S. Maliutin, 1912–16. Exhibitions: Moscow, 1918–33. Member of The Mir Iskusstva, 1921. Died in Moscow.

Shestakova, Tatiana
1957–   . Actress.
Graduated from the Leningrad Theatre Institute, 1972. Worked at the Leningrad Theatre for Children until 1975, when she joined the Leningrad Comedy Theatre. In 1982, became a member of the Russian Drama Theatre. Played Sonya in Chekhov's *Uncle Vanya*, which brought her national recognition. At that time, joined the Malyi Theatre as

a guest actress in their productions of *The House* and *Brothers and Sisters*. Appeared in the lead in the Moscow Arts Theatre production of *The Meek*. Toured abroad from 1983. Played the part of the mother in E. Klimov's *Come and See*. Appeared in and co-produced *Stars in the Morning Sky* by A. Galin, which made a successful tour of Britain in 1988.

Shestov, Lev Isaakovich (Schwartzmann)

31.1.1895–20.11.1938. Philosopher. Born in Kovno. Son of a wealthy businessman. Graduated from Kiev University, 1915. Studied in Italy and Switzerland, 1915–18. One of the first to write on Nietzsche and Kierkegaard in Russia. Gained a reputation as an original existentialist thinker, opposed to the rationalism and positivism of the previous generation. Wrote on the impossibility of reconciling reason (Athens) with faith (Jerusalem), siding wholeheartedly with the second. Despite his irrationalist position, wrote in an elegant and very lucid style. Emigrated after the Civil War in 1920. Lived in Geneva, moved to Paris, 1921. Contributed to the Russian press abroad and to West European philosophical publications before WWII.
Main works: *Dostoevskii and Nietzsche*; *All Things are Possible*; *Potestas Clavium, Kierkegaard and Existentialism*; *Athens and Jerusalem*; *Sola Fide*; *Philosophy and Revelation*.

Shevardnadze, Eduard Amvros'evich

25.1.1928– . Politician. Georgian. Son of a teacher. Member of the Communist Party from 1948. Graduated from the Party School of the Cen. Cttee. in Georgia in 1951. Also graduated from the Kutaissi Pedagogical Institute, 1959. Various Komsomol posts including 2nd, later 1st, Secretary of the Cen. Cttee. of the Georgian Komsomol, 1956–57. Member of the Cen. Cttee. of the Georgian Communist Party, 1960. Candidate member of the Bureau of the Cen. Cttee. of the Georgian Communist Party, 1960–61. 1st Deputy Minister for Protection of Public Order in Georgia, 1961–65. Minister of Internal Affairs in Georgia, 1965–72. Known for his ruthless purges of the Georgian party bosses used to an easy life under the previous party boss, Mzhavanadze. 1st Secretary of the Tbilisi City Cttee. from July 1972. 1st Secretary of the Cen. Cttee. of Georgia CP, Sep. 1972. Member of the Cen. Cttee. of the CPSU from 1976. Non-voting member of the Politburo of the CPSU, Nov. 1978. Full member of the Politburo, July 1985. Soviet Foreign Minister, 1985.

Shevchenko, Aleksandr Vasil'evich

1882–1948. Artist.
Landscape painter. Studied at the Moscow Stroganov School of Graphic Art, 1897–07, then in Paris, 1905–06. Returned to Moscow and studied at the School of Painting, Sculpture and Architecture, 1908–10. Pupil of Konstantin Korovin. Exhibitions from 1906: Moscow Salon, 1910–11; The Union of Youth, 1912; Mishen', Moscow, 1913,; The Mir Iskusstva, 1913, 1917, 1921. After the October Revolution 1917, exhibited regularly until 1944. Personal exhibitions: together with Robert Falk and A. Nuremberg, Moscow, 1924, then again in Moscow, 1924, 1933 and 1944. Died in Moscow. Posthumous exhibition, Moscow, 1958.

Shevchenko, Arkadii Nikolaevich

1930– . Diplomat.
Born in the Ukraine. Son of a doctor. A former political adviser to the Soviet Foreign Minister, Andrei Gromyko, and his protegé. United Nations Assistant Secretary-General, when he defected to the United States in 1978. Caused a sensation by announcing that he had been work-. ing secretly for the CIA for 2 years. His Russian wife returned to Moscow and was found dead a month later in their Moscow flat. According to the Soviet Government, it was suicide. Wrote political memoirs, *Breaking With Moscow*. Gave a rare insight into the workings of Kremlin policy-making. Now lives in the United States with his new American wife, the editor Elaine Jackson.

Shevchuk, Ivan Pavlovich

1892–1942. Major-general.
Joined the Bolshevik Party, 1917. Organized Red partisan detachments in Siberia during the Civil War. Graduated from the Frunze Military Academy, 1933. Divisional commander during WWII. Fell in action.

Shidlovskii, Aleksandr Georgievich

1.2.1941– . Athlete.
Born in Moscow. Graduated from the Moscow Oblast' Pedagogical Institute, 1968. Honoured Master of Sports (water polo), 1970. With the Moscow Armed Forces Team. USSR champion, 1963–71. European champion, 1970. Olympic champion, 1972.

Shidlovskii, Sergei Illiodorovich

1861–1922. Politician.
Left-wing member of the Octobrist Party. Member of the 3rd and 4th Dumas. In the latter, he was a member of the Progressive Bloc. Emigrated after the 1917 Revolution. Died in Paris.

Shifrin, Avraam Isaakovich

1923– . Journalist, editor.
Born in Minsk. Took part in WWII. After the war, studied law. For some time, worked in the Soviet judicial system. Arrested, 1953. Sent to the Gulag. Released after 10 years in camps and 4 years of internal exile. Became involved in the Jewish national movement. Left the USSR, 1970. Lives in Israel. Author of a very detailed and thorough guide to Stalin's prisons and camps which has been translated into several languages. In Oct. 1987, testified at the John Demjanjuk trial in Israel. Said he had been recruited by the KGB while serving as a state prosecutor. Helped to compile false charges against Soviet citizens who had escaped to the West, in order to discredit them or request their extradition. Told how in 1953 he was convicted of spying for Israel and the US, and was given the death sentence, later commuted to life imprisonment. Told of the KGB ploy of writing to prominent people in the West in order to collect the signatures on their replies for forgeries.
Works: *The First Guidebook to the Prisons and Concentration Camps of the Soviet Union*, Switzerland, 1980; *Chetvertoe Izmerenie* (memoirs), Frankfurt, 1973.

Shik, Aleksandr Adolfovich
1901?–4.1968. Editor.
First editor of the theatre-music department of the first Russian newspaper in France after WWII, *La Pensée Russe*. Erudite in ballet, music and theatre. Died in Paris.

Shikanian, Dmitrii Azar'evich (Dmitriev)
24.11.1901– . Ballet dancer. conductor.
Born in Baku. Studied ballet at M. Perini and M. Mordkin's private ballet studios, 1917–22. Graduated from the Tbilisi Conservatory, 1922, and from the Conducting Department, 1938. Dancer and soloist at the Paliashvili Theatre, Tbilisi, 1921–29 and 1931–36. In 1930–31, with the Saratov Theatre, where he was a soloist. Conductor at the Paliashvili Theatre, 1936–41. Conductor at the Spendiarov Theatre, Erevan, 1941–57. Conductor at the Nal'chik Musical Theatre (Kabardino-Balkarskaia Republic), 1968–69. Also worked as a choreographer at all these theatres.

Shikin, Iosif Vasil'evich
1906–1973. Political officer.
Graduated from courses for political commissars, 1939, and joined the Red Army. Deputy head of the Political Administration of the Soviet Army, 1942, and head of the Administration, 1946–49. Head of the Lenin Military Political Academy, 1949–50. Worked in the Cen. Cttee. of the CPSU, 1950–61. Member of the Central Revision Commission of the Cen. Cttee., 1956–73. Ambassador in Albania, 1961–62.

Shilder, Andrei Nikolaevich
1861–1919. Artist.
Landscape painter. Pupil of Ivan Shishkin. Exhibited from 1884. Exhibitions: the Academy of Arts, St. Petersburg, 1883; TPKHV, 1884–1918; 1st Exhibition of Graphic Art of Russian Artists, St. Petersburg, 1890; MOLKH, 1894–95; All-Russian Exhibition, Nizhnii Novgorod, 1896; Exhibition of Original Graphic Art, St. Petersburg, 1898. Died in Iaroslavl'.

Shilin, Afanasii Petrovich
1924–1982. Lt.-general.
Joined the Red Army, 1942. Artillery officer, twice Hero of the Soviet Union, during WWII. Graduated from the Dzerzhinskii Artillery Academy, 1952, and from the Academy of the General Staff, 1966. After WWII, held several high posts in the Soviet artillery. Deputy chairman of DOSAAF, 1976.

Shilkov, Boris Arsen'evich
28.6.1927– . Athlete.
Born in Arkhangelsk. Honoured Master of Sports (skating), 1954. With Leningrad Trud, 1957. USSR champion, 1953–55. European champion, 1954. World champion, 1954. World record-holder, 1955–63 (5,000 metres). Olympic champion, 1956 (5,000 metres).

Shilovskii, Evgenii Aleksandrovich
1889–1952. Lt.-general.
On active service during WWI as a captain. Graduated from the Academy of the General Staff, 1917. Joined the Red Army, 1918. Took part in the Civil War. In the 1920s and 1930s, lecturer at the Frunze Military Academy and the Zhukovskii Air Force Academy. Professor at the Academy of the General Staff, 1941. Wrote on military history and tactics.

Shimanov, Gennadii Mikhailovich
1937– . Dissident.
Born in Moscow. Early involvement with the dissident movement in Moscow. Committed to a mental hospital, 1962. Became known through his articles in samizdat, representing an extreme Russian nationalist view, combining conservative and communist ideas.

Shingarev, Andrei Ivanovich
1869–1918. Politician.
Doctor by profession. Member of the Cadet Party. Member of the 2nd, 3rd and 4th Dumas. After the February Revolution 1917, Minister of Agriculture in the Provisional Government. Together with his colleague F. Kokoshkin, murdered by revolutionary sailors just before the opening session of the Constituent Assembly, in the Mariinskii Hospital, where they had been transferred from the Peter and Paul Fortress. The Bolshevik authorities sabotaged the search for the murderers which at the time created a nationwide sensation.

Shiriaev, Aleksandr Viktorovich
10.9.1867–25.4.1941. Ballet dancer, choreographer, teacher.
Born in Petersburg. Child-dancer at the Aleksandrinskii Theatre, 1877–81. Graduated from the Petersburg Theatre School, 1885. Pupil of M. Petipa, P. Karsavin and P. Gerdt. Character and grotesque dancer, also a great comedian. In 1902, leading dancer during the Russian Season in Monte Carlo. Choreographer at the Mariinskii Theatre and abroad. In 1905, fired from the Mariinskii Theatre, which caused a great protest from the other dancers and choreographers. In 1918, returned to the Mariinskii/Leningrad Opera and Ballet Theatre. The Training Theatre attached to the Kirov Theatre was renamed in his honour. Wrote, with A. Lopukhov and A. Bocharov, *Osnovy Kharakternogo Tantsa*, 1939. Died in Leningrad.

Shiriaev, Boris Nikolaevich
1889–1959. Journalist, author, educationalist.
Graduated from Moscow University. In the late 1920s and 1930s, twice condemned to death. Inmate of the Solovki concentration camp. During WWII, edited a Russian newspaper under German occupation in the North Caucasus. After WWII, in refugee camps in Italy. Among his books is a description of his life in Solovki (*Neugasimaia Lampada*), and memoirs of his life in Italy, where he earned his living by making dolls and selling them in the markets (*DP v Italii*). Died in Italy.

Shirinskii, Sergei Petrovich
18.7.1903– . Cellist.
Born in Ekaterinodar. Brother of the violinist Vasilii Shirinskii. Member of the Beethoven State Quartet from 1923. Professor at the Moscow Conservatory.

Shirinskii, Vasilii Petrovich
17.1.1901–16.8.1965. Violinist, conductor, composer.
Born in Ekaterinodar. Member of the Beethoven State Quartet from 1923 (2nd violin). Professor at the Moscow Conservatory. Author of operas, 6 quartets, 2 symphonies, and pieces for piano, and radio and theatre plays. Died in Mamontovka, near Moscow.

Shiripina, Elena Vasil'evna
8.11.1910– . Ballerina.
Born in Petersburg. Graduated from the Leningrad Choreographic School, 1926. Pupil of A. Vaganova. Until 1945, dancer and soloist at the Kirov Theatre. Taught at the Leningrad Choreographic School, 1944–68.

Shishakov, Nikolai Ivanovich
1925– . Artist.
Miniature painter. Studied at the Mstera Art School. Since 1950, has lived and worked in Mstera. Creator of miniature objets d'art, including *Skazka O Tsare Saltane* (The Fairy-Tale about Tsar Saltan) box.

Shishkin, Arkadii Vasil'evich
1899–after 1973. Photo-journalist.
Born in the village of Kukarka, Viatka. Son of the village carpenter. At the age of 10, apprenticed to the portrait photographer N. Rikhter in Kazan'. Later moved to Petrograd, where he trained as a film projectionist. Worked first as a projectionist, then as a copyist. After the October Revolution 1917, worked for a few months in a photographic studio in Ekaterinburg (now Sverdlovsk). In 1918, served in the Red Army. From 1923, worked as a photographer for local newspapers in Viatka (now Kirov). In 1924, won a photographic competition in the Moscow newspaper *Krestianskaia Gazeta*, which offered him a job. Soon became its leading full-time photo-reporter. During WWII, photographer for the political wing of an army division. At the end of the war, joined the *Krestianka* magazine. Personal exhibitions: Minsk, 1964, Ioshkar Ola, 1966, Kirov, 1967, Perm', 1967, Tambov, 1969, Moscow, 1969.

Shishmarev, Vladimir Fedorovich
1875–1957. Philologist, academician.
Author of *Lirika i Liriki Pozdnego Srednevekov'ia*, which was published in Russian in Paris, 1911. Editor of works by French poets in Paris. Became close to S. Taneev (he himself was a violinist). In all his works, insisted on the connection between poetry and music.

Shishov, Ivan Petrovich
8.10.1888–6.2.1947. Composer.
Born in Novocherkassk. Taught at the Moscow Conservatory, 1925–31. From 1930, editor at Muzgiz (State Music Publishing House). Author of 3 operas, including *Tupeinyi Khudozhnik* (produced in 1929), ballets, symphonies, musicals and songs. Died in Moscow.

Shishova, Liudmila Nikolaevna
1.6.1940– . Athlete.
Born in Gorkii. Master of Sports (fencing), 1958. Graduated from the Gorkii Medical Institute, 1969. Doctor. With Gorkii Spartak. Olympic champion, 1960.

Shitov, Sergei Fedorovich
1879–1942. Artist.
Genre, portrait and landscape painter. Born in Iaroslavl', where he attended the Amateur Art Classes, then studied at the Moscow School of Painting, Sculpture and Architecture, 1896–1903, under V. Serov. Taught in Iaroslavl' Art School. Exhibited from 1912. Exhibitions: Iaroslavl' Art School. Exhibited from 1912. Exhibitions: Iaroslavl' Art Society, 1912–15, Oblastnye Khudozhestvennye Exhibitions, 1937, 1939, 1940. Died in Iaroslavl'.

Shkadov, Ivan Nikolaevich
1913– . General.
Joined the Red Army, 1935. Took part in WWII as a tank detachment commander. Graduated from the Academy of the General Staff, 1959. Head of the group of Soviet advisers and chief consultant to the government of Cuba, 1964–66. Commander of the Northern Military Group, 1967–68. Head of the Administration of Military Schools at the Ministry of Defence, 1969. Chief of the Personnel

Department of the Ministry of Defence, 1972. Deputy Minister of Defence, responsible for personnel matters, 1982.

Shkafer, Vasilii Petrovich
1867–after 1937. Singer, opera director.
Born in Moscow. Pupil of Fedor Komissarzhevskii. From 1892, singer, and later soloist, with various private operas. Soloist with the Bolshoi Theatre from 1904, and the Mariinskii Theatre, 1906–09. Returned to Moscow. Opera director at the Bolshoi. Memoirs: *Sorok Let Na Stsene Russkoi Opery, 1890–1930*, Leningrad, 1936.

Shklovskii, Viktor Borisovich
24.1.1893–6.12.1984. Author, literary scholar.
Born in Petersburg. Son of a teacher. Studied at Petersburg University. Started his literary career as a futurist. In the 1920s, the main exponent of the formalist method in literary scholarship, defending the right to linguistic experiments. Put forward the alienation theory, later popularized in the West by Brecht. In the 1930s, had to capitulate before Stalinist conformism *(Pamiatnik Nauchnoi Oshibke*, 1930). Specialist in cinema theory. Wrote interesting memoirs on the turbulent art movements of the 1920s.

Shkol'nikova, Nelli Efimovna
8.7.1928– . Violinist.
Born in the village of Zolotonosha, Kiev Gouvt. Pupil of Iu. Iankelevich. 1st prize at the J. Thibaud International Competition of Violinists in Paris, 1953. Made solo concert appearances in Moscow and Leningrad.

Shkuro, Andrei Grigor'evich (Shkura)
7.2.1886–1947. Lt.-general.
Born in Ekaterinodar. Son of a Kuban Cossack colonel. Attended Moscow Cadet Corps, 1907. Graduated from the Nikolaevskoe Cavalry School in Petersburg, 1907. Served on the Persian border, 1908. During WWI, became known as a Cossack officer, sent with missions behind enemy lines on the Rumanian front.

After the October Revolution 1917, returned to his native Kuban, and during the Civil War, recruited a group of White Cossacks which waged a successful guerrilla war against the Reds. Later joined the Dobrovolcheskaia Armiia under General Denikin, and became a cavalry corps commander. Awarded the British Order of the Bath. Fought against Makhno and Budennyi. Took (and lost) Voronezh. Emigrated after the Civil War, 1920, worked as a Cossack show-rider in a circus. During WWII, joined the Cossack forces under German command. Opposed the joining of the Cossacks with General Vlasov's ROA. After the end of WWII, interned in Austria, and handed over by the British to the Soviet authorities. Condemned to death for high treason and executed (hanged) in Moscow with other former Civil War Cossack White commanders.
See: N. Tolstoy, *Victims of Yalta*, London, 1977.

Shlakhtin, Erast Erastovich
23.9.1886–3.12.1973. Colonel.
Graduated from the Don Cadet Corps, 1904, the Mikhailovskoe Artillery School, 1907, and from the Military Academy, 1913. During WWI, adjutant of the Ataman of all Cossack Armies, Grand Duke Boris Vladimirovich. During the Civil War, Chief-of-staff of the 3rd Don Cossack Division (White). Evacuated from the Crimea after the defeat of the Whites. Worked as a topographer in Yugoslavia. During WWII, adjutant of the 1st Regiment of the German Army's Russian Corps in Yugoslavia, fighting communist partisans. After WWII, in DP camps in Germany. Moved to France. Died at Hyeres (Var), France.

Shlein, Nikolai Pavlovich
1873–1952. Artist.
Genre, portrait and landscape artist. Studied at the Moscow School of Painting, Sculpture and Architecture, 1889–1919, under V. Serov, also at the Petersburg Academy of Arts, 1900–03, and later in Paris. Exhibited from 1892. Exhibitions: Spring Exhibitions at the Academy of Arts, 1897–1913, MOLKH, 1898–1910, MTKH, 1899, TPKHV, 1900–22,

Repin Society of Artists, Moscow, 1928. In Iaroslavl' from 1939. Personal jubilee exhibition, Moscow, 1940; 40-Years Work, Kostroma, 1941. Died in Kostroma where, a few months later, a posthumous exhibition of his work was held.

Shlemin, Ivan Timofeevich
1898–1969. Lt.-general.
Took part in WWI. Joined the Red Army, 1918, and the Bolshevik Party, 1920. Took part in the Civil War. Graduated from the Frunze Military Academy, 1925. Head of the Academy of the General Staff, 1937–40. Commander of several armies during WWII. After the war, Chief-of-staff of Land Forces, 1948. Professor at the Academy of the General Staff, 1954–62.

Shlezinger, Stanislav Fedorovich
1862–5.3.1917. Pianist, music scholar.
Born in Warsaw (then in Russia). Pupil of T. Leshetitskii. In 1888, founded and headed a music school in St. Petersburg. One of the pioneers of Russian piano methodics. Died in Petrograd. Author of *Sistematicheskii Khod Obucheniia Igre na Fortepiano*, St. Petersburg, 1898, and *Pianist-Metodist*, issues 1–24, St. Petersburg, 1902–06.

Shliapentokh, Vladimir
1947?– . Professor of sociology.
Emigrated from the Soviet Union in the 1970s. Settled in the USA. Staff lecturer at Michigan State University. Once conducted polls for *Pravda*, *Izvestia*, and other Soviet newspapers. His article about the ethnic disturbances in Armenia and Azerbaidzhan (written in collaboration with D. Shliapentokh) was run by the *Los Angeles Times* and the *International Herald Tribune* (5 Mar. 1988).

Shliapina, Galina Arkad'evna
20.12.1951– . Prima ballerina.
Born in Izhevsk. Graduated from the Perm' Choreographic School, 1970. Joined the Perm' Theatre. Soon attracted attention with her technique and artistry. Joined the Bolshoi Theatre. Became one of their star dancers and a prima ballerina. As

such, appeared in the production of *Swan Lake* which toured Britain in July-Aug. 1987, the first ever Anglo-Soviet collaboration combining the magnificence of Soviet ballet and the brilliance of British design.

Shliapnikov, Aleksandr Gavrilovich (Belenin)
1885–1937? Politician.
Son of a worker. Member of the SD Party from 1901. Organizer of workers in Petersburg. Lived in France after the 1905 Revolution. In 1915, on Lenin's request, set up the Russian Bureau of the Bolshevik Cen. Cttee. to run the party in Petrograd (together with Viacheslav Molotov). After the February Revolution 1917, member of the Executive Cttee. of the Petrograd Union of Metal Workers. One of the organizers of the October Revolution 1917. People's Commissar for Labour, later for Trade and Industry. Member of the Cen. Cttee. of the Bolshevik Party till 1922. Leading member of the first Soviet Government. Organizer and leader of the Workers Opposition group, 1920–22. Dismissed from the government. In 1930, had to publicly acknowledge his mistakes. In 1933, expelled from the party. After the murder of Sergei Kirov, arrested and sent to the Urals camps. Died in a Gulag camp. Exact date not known. Rehabilitated, 1988.

Shlugleit, Iegoshua Moiseevich
1875–1926? Artist.
Landscape painter. Born in Odessa. Studied at the Odessa Society of Fine Arts, then the Petersburg Society of Arts, 1895–1901. Pupil of Il'ia Repin. Began exhibiting in 1898. Exhibitions: Spring Exhibitions at the Academy of Arts, St. Petersburg, 1898–1902, 1904–12, 1914, MOLKH, 1901–04 1908–11, St. Petersburg Society of Artists, 1905–14, the Society of Water-Colour Artists, St. Petersburg, 1909, the Association of Artists, 1912, 1914. His last-known picture was purchased in 1927 by the Moscow Rumiantsev Museum (now part of the Tretiakov Gallery).

Shmelev, Ivan Sergeevich
21.9.1873–24.6.1950. Author.
Born in Moscow. Son of a merchant. Graduated in law from Moscow

University, 1898. Became widely-known for his novel *Chelovek iz Restorana*, published in *Znanie* in 1910 (a film of the same title was made later). In Russia and even more in emigration (he left in 1922 for Berlin, and then Paris), he became famous for his colourful and evocative descriptions of traditional Russian life, especially the life of merchants. In *Leto Gospodne* (1933–48), he gave a picture of the yearly cycle of Orthodox church festivals as they affected the life of the people. Wrote one of the most harrowing accounts of the Bolshevik terror in the Crimea, *Solntse Mertvykh*, 1923. (After the defeat of the Whites, his only son, a young officer with the Whites, was shot and he himself went into hiding in Alushta expecting the same fate). During WWII, published some stories in a German-sponsored Russian newspaper in Paris, which caused difficulties after the war. Later he was republished in the Soviet Union (*Povesti i Rasskazy*, Moscow, 1960), where, though not mentioned, he had not been forgotten, and managed to retain his popularity. A powerful, conservative publicist in the emigré press between the wars, his articles were republished in Paris under the title *Dusha Rodiny*, 1967. Died in Paris. Other books include: *Kulikovo Pole. Staryi Valaam*, Paris, 1958; *Inostranets*, Paris, 1963; *Svet Vechnyi*, Paris, 1968.

Shmelev, Vladimir Konstantinovich
31.8.1946–   . Athlete.
Born in Magadan. Honoured Master of Sports (pentathlon), 1972. With the Moscow Oblast' Armed Forces Team. Member of the CPSU, 1975. Graduated from the Moscow Institute of Physical Culture, 1976. USSR champion, 1971–75. Olympic champion, 1972, with his team. World champion, 1973–74, with his team.

Shmeman, Aleksandr Dmitrievich, Archpriest
13.9.1921–13.12.1983. Theologian, church historian, broadcaster.
Born in Reval, now Tallinn (Estonia). Moved to France in 1929. Graduated from the St. Sergius Theological Institute, Paris, 1945. Lecturer in church history at the same institute,

1945–51. Priest, 1946. Moved to the USA, 1951. Professor at Columbia University. Professor of church history and liturgics at St. Vladimir Academy, New York, from 1951. Dean of the Academy, 1962–83. Prominent in world-wide ecumenical work, and gained a wide audience in the USSR through his religious broadcasts.
Works: *The Historical Way of Orthodoxy*, and many books on liturgical subjects in Russian and in English.

Shmidt, Otto Iul'evich (Schmidt)
1891–1956. Geophysician.
Graduated from Kiev University, 1913. Professor at Moscow University, 1923–56. Editor-in-chief of the *Bolshaia Sovetskaia Entsiklopediia*, 1924–41. Director of the Arctic Institute, head of Glavsevmorput', vice-president of the Academy of Sciences, and director of the Institute of Geophysics, 1930. In the 1930s, head of several famous Soviet arctic expeditions (on ships and drifting ice). Also wrote on problems of higher algebra, such as theories of groups.

Shmurlo, Evgenii Frantsevich
1853–1934. Historian.
Professor at Derpt University. Correspondent of the Russian Academy of Sciences in Rome, 1903. Worked in the hitherto closed Vatican archives. Emigrated after the Bolshevik take-over, 1917. Settled in Prague, 1924. Founder of the Prague Historical Society. Very active in the cultural life of emigré Russians in Czechoslovakia.

Shmyrev, Minai Filippovich
1891–1964. Partisan.
Took part in WWI and the Civil War. Joined the Bolshevik Party, 1940. One of the first organizers of the communist partisan movement in German-occupied Belorussia, 1941. Commander of a partisan brigade near Vitebsk. Worked in the HQ of the partisan movement, 1942. After WWII, involved in the re-Stalinization of Vitebsk.

Shmyrova, Tatiana Ivanovna
28.9.1913–   . Ballerina, teacher.
Born in Sedlets, Poland. Graduated

from the Leningrad Choreographic School, 1930. Pupil of A. Vaganova. Dancer and soloist at the Kirov Theatre, 1930–59. Graduated in theatre history from the Leningrad Theatre Institute, 1954. PhD from the GITIS, 1957. From 1960, taught at the Leningrad Choreographic School. Author of many articles on ballet in the periodical press.

Shnitke, Alfred Garrievich
24.11.1934–   . Composer.
Born in Engels. Moved to Moscow. Teacher at the Moscow Conservatory. Specialist in electronic music. Author of songs, concertos, cantatas, suites and music for stage and screen. Probably the most outstanding modernist composer in the Soviet Union at present. Wrote an oratorio *The History of Doctor Faust* inviting the best-known Soviet pop singer, A. Pugacheva, to take part in it, scandalizing the Soviet musical establishment. Popular in Western avant-garde art circles.

Shollar, Liudmila Frantsevna (Vil'tzak, Liudmila Fedorovna)
15.3.1888–1978. Ballerina, teacher.
Graduated from the Petersburg Theatre School, 1906. Pupil of M. Fokin. Until 1921, dancer and soloist at the Mariinskii Theatre. Took part in Russian Seasons abroad, 1909–14. Worked closely with M. Fokin. From 1914–16, nurse at the front. Wounded twice. Emigrated in 1921. Lived in France, and then moved to the USA, 1936. Soloist with Diaghilev's Ballets Russes, 1921–25. From 1925–35, with the Colon Theatre in Buenos Aires. With the I. Rubenstein Company and others. With her husband, A. I. Vil'tzak, opened a ballet school in New York, which operated until the late 1940s. Until 1963, taught at the New York American Ballet School, and then at the Ballet Theatre. Taught in Washington, 1963–65, and from 1965 in San Francisco, where she died.

Sholokhov, Mikhail Aleksandrovich
1905–1984. Author, Nobel Prize laureate.
Born at Kruzhilino-na-Donu, now in Rostov Oblast'. In the period follow-

ing the October Revolution 1917, as a member of one of the so-called 'prodotriady', played an active part in the confiscation of grain supplies from peasants. After the Civil War, worked as a house painter and loader. In the mid 1920s, suddenly emerged as a major writer of Cossack stories: *Donskie Rasskazy*, 1925, and *Lazorevaia Step'*, 1926, followed by the magnificent novel in 4 volumes, *Tikhii Don* (And Quiet Flows the Don), 1928–34. Following the publication of the latter, he became a favourite of the official establishment, living in splendour in the Cossack village of Veshenskaia, and owning several houses, a luxury Moscow apartment, a private aeroplane, and herds of cattle imported from Scotland and Denmark. Joined the CPSU in 1932. Awarded the Stalin and Lenin Prizes, and in 1965, the Nobel Prize for Literature. A dogmatic communist, he had previously attacked B. Pasternak when he was given the same prize in 1958. Demanded the execution of A. Siniavskii and Iu. Daniel' during their trial in 1965, and was also openly hostile to A. Solzhenitsyn. The authorship of *Tikhii Don* has long been a matter of controversy: some believe that the real author was Fedor Kriukov, a widely-known writer of Don Cossack stories before the Civil War. They point out that when the first volume was published in 1928, Sholokhov was a barely-educated 23-year-old, and also that the style and fine detail of the first 2 volumes are nowhere to be found in his later works, such as *Podniataia Tselina* (Virgin Soil Upturned, 1st vol. 1931, 2nd vol. 1959), *Sud'ba Chelovska* (A Man's Life, 1956), and *Oni Srazhalis' Za Rodinu* (They Fought For Their Motherland, 1971). The original manuscript of *Tikhii Don* was never produced.
See: *Stremia 'Tikhogo Dona'*, YMCA, Paris, 1974. Jeanne Vronskaya, 'Big Literary Scandal Confronts Russ Over Authorship of *Don*', *Variety*, 11 Sept. 1974 and 10 Oct. 1974.

Shor, David Solomonovich
1867–1.4.1942. Pianist.
Born in Simferopol'. Pupil of V. Safonov. Founder of the Moscow Trio, and of the Beethoven Studio. Emigrated, 1925. Moved to Palestine, 1927. Died in Tel-Aviv.

Shor, Sarra Markovna
1897–1959. Artist.
Born in Kiev. Portrait, landscape and water-colour painter, and book illustrator. Also worked in etching and the graphic arts. Studied at the Kiev Art School, 1911–15, under F. Krichevskii and I. Makushenko, then at the Academy of Arts, 1915–16, under G. Zaleman and V. Makovskii. Exhibitions: The Four Arts, 1926–29. Moscow, 1927, Leningrad, 1932, Moscow, 1936, 1938–39, 1941, 1943, 1945, 1947, 1954 and 1957. Personal exhibition: Moscow, 1945.

Shorin, Mikhail Georgievich
15.9.1904–7.3.1965. Choir conductor.
Born in Kuchino, Moscow Gouvt. From 1929, conductor of various choirs. Chief choir conductor at the Bolshoi Theatre, 1944–58. Died in Moscow.

Shorin, Vasilii Ivanovich
1871–1938. Military commander.
Took part in the Russo-Japanese war, 1904–05. On active service during WWI as a colonel. Joined the Red Army, 1918. Active participant in the Civil War. Fought in the Caucasus, Siberia and Turkestan.

Shostakovich, Dmitrii Dmitrievich
25.9.1906–9.8.1975. Composer, pianist.
Brilliant composer, pianist and teacher. Pupil of A. K. Glazunov. Born in Petersburg. Received his first musical training from his mother when he was 9 years old. Studied at the I. Gliasser Music School, 1916–18. His earliest compositions date from that time. Entered the Petrograd Conservatory, 1919. Graduated, 1923, in piano, and in 1925, in composition. Apart from Glazunov, trained also by M. O. Shteinberg. His first opera, *Nos* (after Gogol'), was created in 1928, and staged in 1930. Wrote music for *Hamlet*, 1932. In 1934, composed the opera *Ekaterina Izmailova*, which was attacked by the Stalinist press, and banned shortly afterwards (he composed a second version in 1963). Professor from 1939. Directed the Composition Class at the Moscow Conservatory, 1939–48. Wrote music for *King Lear*, 1940. Taught at the Leningrad Conservatory until 1941, and from 1945–48. During WWII, worked in Kuibyshev. Moved to Moscow, 1943. During Zhdanov's cultural terror in 1948, was again attacked by the press, and all his performances and music were banned. Honorary member of the Academy of Santa Cecilia in Italy, and the Royal Academy of Music in Britain, 1958. Honorary Doctor of Oxford University, winner of the Sibelius Prize, and Commander of the French Order of Arts and Literature, 1958. Honorary member of the American Academy of Sciences, 1959. An innovator who remained nonetheless a follower of the classical Russian tradition. A film about him, based on S. Volkov's book *Testimony*, has been made by the British director Tony Palmer, with Ben Kingsley playing the leading role.

Shostakovich, Maksim Dmitrievich
10.5.1938–   . Conductor, pianist.
Born in Moscow. Son of Dmitrii Shostakovich. Performed his father's 2nd Piano Concerto to win a place at the Moscow Conservatory. In 1966, made his conducting debut his father's symphony *October*. Took 5th place in the Moscow Conductors' Competition. After his father's death in 1975, was almost constantly in conflict with the Soviet authorities, and felt the lack of his father's backing. Conductor of the Soviet Radio and Television Orchestra. On their Apr. 1981 tour of Germany, conducted his 19-year-old son Dmitrii's performance of his father's 2nd Piano Concerto. Defected with his son after the final concert in the Bavarian city of Fuerth. Settled in the USA, and has since performed all over the world.

Shostakovskii, Petr Adamovich
15.2.1851–4.1917. Pianist, conductor.
Pupil of A. Dreishok and T. Kullak. In 1878, founded a music school in Moscow, which in 1883 became the Music Dramatic School of the Moscow Philharmonic. Director of the Moscow Music Society and of its symphonic concerts. Died in Moscow.

Shpagin, Georgii Semenovich
1897–1952. Weapon designer.
Originally a metal-worker in a

weapons factory, became one of the best-known designers of Soviet machine-guns (the DT, DSHK, PPSH–41, and the OPSH).

Shpalikov, Gennadii Fedorovich
6.9.1937–1.11.1974. Scriptwriter.
Talented scriptwriter of the 1960s. Worked with every distinguished director. Graduated from the VGIK. All his scripts were the subject of long discussion in the Soviet press. Had a drink problem, developed a depressive disease and committed suicide.

Shragin, Boris Iosifovich
1926–   . Journalist.
Born in Viaz'ma. Graduated in philosophy (Marxism) from Moscow University. Wrote many articles on aesthetics for the Soviet press. Became involved in the Jewish rights movement. Expelled from the Communist Party, 1968. Emigrated, 1974. Settled in the USA. Wrote many polemical articles on Russian history, philosophy and literature.

Shteifon, Boris Aleksandrovich
1880?–30.4.1945. Lt.-general.
Took part in WWI. During the Civil War, fought with the Whites. Evacuated to Gallipoli with the remnants of the White armies. One of the military leaders in Gallipoli under the command of General Kutepov. Moved to Yugoslavia. During WWII, joined the Russian Corps, organized to fight the communist partisans, and after the arrest by the Germans of General Skorodumov, the founder of the corps, took over command under the new name of the Russian Guard Group, comprising 12,000 men. Fought Tito's partisans. Died of a heart attack. The Russian Guard Group surrendered to the British in Austria and was the only Russian anti-communist formation treated as regular POWs and not threatened by extradition to SMERSH.
See: N. Tolstoy, *Victims of Yalta*; also, memoirs of Corps members — *Russkii Korpus, USA*.

Shteiger, Anatolii Sergeevich
7.7.1907–1949. Poet, journalist.
Born in Kiev Gouvt. Emigrated with his parents in the 1920s. Lived in

Constantinople, Prague and Paris. Joined the mladorossy in the 1930s. Worked as a journalist during WWII in Switzerland fighting against the Nazis, who attacked him in their newspapers. Published the books *Etot Den'*, 1928, *Eta Zhizn'*, 1932, and *Neblagodarnost'*, 1936, all in Paris. Just before his death, finished his last book, *Dvazhdy Dva-Chetyre*, which was published in 1950 by S. K. Makovskii's Rifma, a small publishing house in Paris.

Shtein, Emmanuil Alekseevich (Sztein)
1934–   . Editor, chess journalist.
Born in Bialystok (Poland). During WWII, under Soviet occupation. Emigrated from the USSR to Poland, 1961. Involved in the Polish dissident movement. Arrested, 1966. Emigrated from Poland, 1968. Settled in America. Published an anthology of chess poetry, and a bibliography of Russian poetry abroad.

Shteinberg, Eduard Arkad'evich
1937–   . Artist.
Son of Arkadii A. Shteinberg, the artist, poet and translator. Changed profession several times, working as a labourer, warder, and even as a fisherman. In 1954, moved to the town of Tarusa, where many artists and writers lived. Started painting at that time. Met George Costakis, and the avant-garde Russian artists at his home-museum. His first solo exhibition of over 50 pictures was held in Moscow in 1978, and attracted much attention. Invited to exhibit in Germany, Switzerland, Italy, the USA and Sweden. Took part in the Hermitage exhibition in Moscow, 1987. A major exhibition of his work was held at the Claude Bernard Gallery, Paris, 1988.

Shteinberg, Iakov Vladimirovich
1880–1942. Photo-journalist.
Began working as a photo-reporter in 1902. Attracted attention with his pictures of daily events, which were among the most interesting from the early Russian photo-journalists. In 1913, a staff photographer for *Solntse Rossii*, one of the earliest Russian periodicals to utilize photographs, particularly genre pictures of

daily life and portraits of writers and artists by young photographers. Became a renowned photographer with his pictures of both the February and October Revolutions 1917. Also photographed the first volunteers to join the Red Army, Petrograd workers, soldiers and sailors. Some of these photographs were used by Rodchenko and his wife Stepanova in their album *The First Mounted Detachment*, 1917. During this period, worked as a reporter for the first Soviet illustrated magazines *Plamia* and *Iunyi Proletarii*. Responsible for 2 of the best-known pictures of Lenin. During the mid- and late 1920s, devoted himself to recording the events in industrial and cultural life. Head of the Society for Artistic and Technical Photography, founded in Petrograd in 1923, and in this capacity did much to win public recognition for photography. Exhibited in the large 1928 exhibition marking the 10th anniversary of Soviet rule. Left over 6,000 negatives which are held in the State Archive of Film and Photographic Documentation in Leningrad.
See: *Soviet Photography*, *1917–40*, London, 1984.

Shteinberg, Lev Petrovich
15.9.1870–16.1.1945. Conductor.
Born in Ekaterinoslav. Conductor of the Bolshoi Theatre from 1928 until his death. Professor at the Moscow Conservatory. Also wrote music for ballets, symphonies, and cantatas. Died in Moscow.

Shteinberg, Maksimilian Oseevich
4.7.1883–6.12.1946. Composer, teacher.
Born in Wil'no. Taught at the Petersburg Conservatory from 1908. One of his many pupils was D. Shostakovich. Wrote ballets, symphonies, a violin concerto, string quartets, and songs. Died in Leningrad.

Shteinpress, Boris Solomonovich
13.8.1908–   . Musicologist, editor.
Born in Berdiansk. Taught at the Moscow and Sverdlovsk conservatories until 1943. Senior music editor of the *Bolshaia Sovetskaia Entsiklopediia*, 1938–40 and 1943–59. Author

of many books including *K Istorii Tsyganskogo Peniia v Rossii*, Moscow, 1934.

Shtemenko, Sergei Matveevich

1907–1976. General.
Joined the Red Army, 1926, and the Bolshevik Party, 1930. Graduated from the Mechanization Academy of the Red Army, 1937, and from the Academy of the General Staff, 1940. During WWII, as Head of the Operations Department of the General Staff, worked closely with Stalin. Chief of the General Staff, 1948–52. Deputy Minister of Defence. Several other high posts in the General Staff. Non-voting member of the Cen. Cttee. of the CPSU, 1952–56. Chief of Staff at the Warsaw Pact HQ, 1968.

Shterenberg, Abram Petrovich

1894–1979. Photographer.
Born into the family of an artisan in the town of Zhitomir in the Ukraine. At the age of 15, began his photographic training, and soon became a professional photographer. In 1919, joined the Red Army. As a soldier, worked in B. Kapustianskii's photo atelier in Tashkent, Uzbekistan. Attended a school of art and design, and worked in the army's photographic department. In 1922, settled in Moscow, living with his brother David, a well-known painter. In the mid-1920s, began his career as a photo-journalist. Worked in the photographic service of the People's Commissariat for Transport, for the picture agencies Russfoto, Unifoto, Soiuzfoto and for the Photographic Artists Studio of the State Cinema Publishing House. Soon acquired the reputation of being a powerful portrait photographer. His photographs of writers and artists, both Russian and foreign, are unique. 50 of his pictures were displayed at the 1928 exhibition, 10 Years of Soviet Photography. Close to Rodchenko, Ignatovich and other fellow-members of the October group. After being accused of formalism, he stuck to news photography, but eventually returned to portraiture. As a news photographer, took pictures of parades and demonstrations in Red Square. One of the leading photographers covering the meeting between the Soviet icebreaker *Malygin* and the German airship Graf Zeppelin. Experimented also with landscape and still-life photography. During the 1930s, exhibited several times in Russia and abroad. During WWII, a corporal in the signals. In the post-war years, disappeared from public life, but continued to work for the Novosti press agency. His last 15 years were lived in isolation, totally forgotten.
See: *Soviet Photography, 1917–40*, London, 1984.

Shtern, Grigorii Mikhailovich (Stern)

1900–1941. Col.-general.
Regimental and brigade commissar during the Civil War. Military commander in Turkestan and Khorezm, 1923–25. Graduated from the Frunze Military Academy, 1929. Chief military adviser with the Republicans during the Civil War in Spain, 1937–38. Took part in military operations against the Japanese at Khalkin-Gol, and in the Soviet-Finnish war, 1939–40. Commander of the Far Eastern front, 1940–41. Member of the Cen. Cttee. of the Bolshevik Party, 1939–41.

Shtern, Lina Solomonovna

1878–1968. Academician.
Born in Libava, now Liepaia, Latvia. Daughter of a wealthy Jewish businessman. Graduated from Geneva University. Lived in Germany, Italy and France. Worked as a physiologist and biochemist in several European laboratories. After the October Revolution 1917, returned to the USSR. First woman academician at the USSR Academy of Sciences. Spent the years 1949–55 in the Gulag and in exile. Lived in Dzhambul, Kazakhstan. In 1987, Nauka publishing house in Moscow published her biography.

Shtern, Liudmila Iakovlevna

1937– . Human rights campaigner.
Born in Leningrad. Trained as a geologist. Involved in protests against the trial of A. Siniavskii and Iu. Daniel, and against the persecution of Dr. Andrei Sakharov. Harassed by the KGB, and forced to leave the USSR, 1975. Settled in the USA, where she has been active in the human rights movement, contributing to many Russian emigré periodicals.
Works: *Po Mestu Zhitel'stva*, NY, 1980; *Pod Znakom Chetyrekh*, USA, 1984.

Shternberg, Pavel Karlovich (Sternberg)

1865–1920. Revolutionary, astronomer.
Graduated from Moscow University, 1887. Joined the SD Party, 1905. Took part in the 1905 Revolution. Professor at Moscow University, 1914. Director of the Moscow Observatory, 1916–17. Active participant in the Bolshevik take-over in Moscow in Oct. 1917. Took part in the Civil War. Author of works on astronomy and gravimetry.

Shtiurmer, Boris (Stuermer)

1848–3.1917. Politician.
Prime Minister of the Russian government in 1916. Denounced by the Duma as pro-German, mainly because of his German name (no proof of any treason emerged after the revolution). Resigned in Nov. 1916. Arrested after the February Revolution, died in prison.

Shtogarenko, Andrei Iakovlevich

15.10.1902– . Composer.
Born in the Ekaterinoslavl' Gouvt. Graduated from the Khar'kov Institute for Music and Drama, 1936. Pupil of S. Bogatyrev. First compositions in 1931. From 1937, deputy chairman of the Khar'kov branch of the Union of Composers. First cantata performed in Moscow, 1943. Director of, and professor at, the Kiev Conservatory, 1954–68.

Shtokolov, Boris Timofeevich

19.3.1930– . Singer (bass).
Born in Kuznetsk. Soloist with the Sverdlovsk Opera and Ballet Theatre, 1954–59, and with the Kirov Opera and Ballet Theatre from 1959.

Shtranikh, Vladimir Fedorovich

1888–1961. Artist.
Genre and landscape painter, and graphic artist. Studied at the Moscow

Stroganov School of Graphic Arts, 1900–07, and at the Moscow School of Painting, Sculpture and Architecture, 1909–16. Pupil of Konstantin Korovin and A. Vasnetsov. Exhibited from 1909 until 1961. Personal exhibitions: the Shtranikh Mobile Exhibition, Smolensk, Kaliningrad, Riga, Iaroslavl', 1958.

Shtraukh, Maksim Maksimovich
24.2.1900–3.1.1974. Actor.
From 1921–24, actor at the 1st Theatre of Proletkult. Assisted S. Eisenstein in *Battleship Potemkin* and *Oktober*. Played in Eisenstein's *Stachka*. Later became a nationally-known face for his portrayal of Lenin in *Chelovek s Ruzh'em*, 1938, *Rasskazy o Lenine*, 1958, and *Lenin v Pol'she*, 1966.

Shtrimer, Aleksandr Iakovlevich
8.11.1888–1971? Cellist.
Born in Rostov-on-Don. Pupil of L. Abbiate. Professor at the Leningrad Conservatory. Trained a generation of cellists, including Daniil Shafran.

Shturman, Dora Moiseevna (b. Shtok; m. Tikhtina)
1923– . Author, historian.
Born in Khar'kov. Arrested in Alma-Ata in 1944 while still a student. Sentenced to 5 years in labour camps. In the 1960s, taught Russian language and literature, and published articles in the press. One of her numerous books, *Nash Novyi Mir*, under the pen-name of V. E. Bogdan, circulated in samizdat. Left the USSR, 1977. Settled in Israel. Major political writer, critic and sociologist in the Russian emigré press. Books: *Selskie Shkoly Na Ukraine 1948–62*, Israel, 1978; *Nash Novyi Mir*, Israel, 1981; *Mertvye Khvataiut Zhivykh*, London, 1982; *Zemlia Za Kholmom*, USA, 1983; *Sovetskii Soiuz V Zerkale Politicheskogo Anekdota* (with Sergei Tikhtin), London, 1985.

Shtykov, Terentii Fomich
1907–1964. Politician.
Educated at a technical school, 1927. Joined the Bolshevik Party, 1929. 2nd Secretary of the Leningrad obkom, 1938. Non-voting member of the Cen. Cttee. of the CPSU,

1939–52, and full member, 1956–61. Political officer during the Soviet-Finnish war and WWII. Continued his career as a political officer in the armed forces after WWII. Ambassador in North Korea, 1948–51. Party official, 1951–59. Ambassador in Hungary, 1959–60.

Shub, Esfir' Il'inishna (Shub, Esther)
16.3.1894–21.9.1959. Documentary film-maker.
Graduated from the Moscow Higher Women's Courses. Secretary of the theatrical section of the People's Commissariat of Education, 1919–21. Entered the film industry, 1922, as an editor. Worked as senior editor of feature films at Goskino (State Cinema) until 1942. Worked at the State Film Archive researching footage of life at the Winter Palace, following which she produced the film *Padenie Dinastii Romanovykh* (The Fall of the Romanov Dynasty), 1927, which has since became a valuable historical documentary. Using archive material, compiled other films: *Velikii Put'*, 1927, and *Rossiia Nikolaia II i Lev Tolstoy* (The Russia of Nicholas II and Leo Tolstoy), 1928. In the 1930s, made considerable efforts shooting propaganda films using archive material to support the party line. In 1934, worked in Turkey, producing *Turtsiia Na Pod'eme*. In 1939, with the documentary film-maker Roman Karmen, made a film about the Spanish Civil War from a Stalinist point of view. Memoirs: *Krupnym Planom*, Moscow, 1959.

Shubin, Ivan Filaretovich
1881–1937. Military commander.
Took part in WWI. Joined the Bolshevik Party, 1917, and the Red Army, 1918. During the Civil War, commander of a Red Cossack brigade. Highly decorated (3 Orders of the Red Banner). Liquidated by Stalin.

Shubina, Liudmila Egorovna
9.10.1948– . Athlete.
Born in Kazan'. Honoured Master of Sports (handball), 1976. With Baku Spartak. Graduated from the Azerbaidzhanian Institute of Physical Culture, 1977. Schoolteacher of

physical education. Olympic champion, 1976.

Shubina, Maria Timofeevna
8.5.1930– . Athlete.
Born in the Mordovskaia ASSR. Honoured Master of Sports (rowing), 1960. With Vladivostok Spartak. Graduated from the Kazan' Medical Institute, 1956. Doctor. World champion, 1958, 1963 and 1966. USSR champion, 1959–67, with various teams. Olympic champion, 1960. European champion, 1963, 1965 and 1967.

Shukhov, Boris Khabalovich
8.5.1947– . Athlete.
Born in Odessa Oblast'. Honoured Master of Sports (cycling), 1970. With the Kuibyshev Armed Forces Team. Graduated from Grozno University, 1976. Lecturer. Member of the CPSU, 1976. USSR champion, 1968 (25km race), and 1972. World champion, 1970. Olympic champion, 1972.

Shukshin, Vasilii Makarovich
25.7.1929–2.10.1974. Writer, scriptwriter, director, actor.
Born in Siberia. Worked for years as a fitter, served in the Navy, taught at evening classes. Graduated from the VGIK (State Film School, Moscow), 1960, as a director. Acted in *Dva Fedora*, *My Dvoe Muzhchin* (based on the A. Kuznetsov short story), *Alenka*, *Zhurnalist*, *Kalina Krasnaia*, and others. Became famous for his short stories in *Novyi Mir*. From 1960 until his death, one of the leading writers of derevenskaia proza. Tried to make a film about Sten'ka Razin, the legendary rebel and leader of the Don Cossacks, but the title of the story and film, *Ia Prishel Dat' Vam Voliu* (I Came to Give You Freedom), was too much for the authorities and it was never realised. His best (and last) film remains *Kalina Krasnaia* (The Red Snowball Tree), 1973, based on his own story, directed and acted by him. Died of a heart attack. His death was mourned as a national tragedy. Other works: *Sel'skie Zhiteli*, 1963, *Kharaktery*, 1973, *Liubaviny* (novel), 1965, and *Zhivet Takoi Paren'*, (script and film), 1964.

Shuleikin, Mikhail Vasil'evich
1884–1939. Radio engineer.
Graduated from the Petersburg Polytechnical Institute, 1908. Joined the Red Army, 1918, communication systems specialist. Academician, 1939. Specialist on antennae reception, broadcasting devices, and radio waves.

Shul'gin, Lev Vladimirovich
14.3.1890–1975? Composer.
Born in Taganrog. Editor of *Muzyka i Revoliutsiia*, 1926–28. Author of pieces for piano and choir. Composer of the famous revolutionary song *Zamuchen Tiazheloi Nevolei*, 1924.

Shul'gin, Vasilii Vital'evich
1878–1965. Politician.
Of Ukrainian parentage. Right-wing member of the Duma. Travelled with A. I. Guchkov to Pskov in Feb. 1917 in order to receive the abdication proclamation from Nicholas II (who was returning from the Army HQ in Mogilev to his family in Tsarskoe Selo). Soon became disillusioned with the February Revolution, and fled abroad after the October Revolution 1917. Lived in Yugoslavia, and continued his political activity (retaining his private estate in Western Ukraine, then Poland). In the 1930s, became the victim of skilful provocation by Soviet intelligence, which masterminded a special operation (Trest) masquerading as an underground monarchist organization. Travelled secretly (as he thought) to the USSR with agents of Trest, and after his return wrote a book, *Tri Stolitsy*, praising the strength of monarchist underground groups in the USSR. After the disclosure of the operation by the GPU, retired from politics. At the end of WWII, fell into the hands of SMERSH in Yugoslavia, was deported to the USSR and sent to the Gulag camps. Released during the Khrushchev thaw, 1956. Wrote memoirs, which were published in the Soviet Union in the 1960s. Also took part in the documentary film *Pered Sudom Istorii*, in which very valuable and rare excerpts from 1917 (Nicholas II after the abdication) and WWII (Vlasov) newsreels were incorporated.

Shul'man, Mikhail Borisovich
1907– . Party official, theatre manager.
Born in Odessa. In the late 1920s, worked in the Cheka. Joined the Communist Party, 1926. Moved to Moscow. Became the party secretary in Meyerhold's theatre. Official of the Political Section of the Red Army, close to Ia. B. Gamarnik. One of the organizers and the first director of the Red Army's Song and Dance Ensemble. Was on tour with the Ensemble in Paris when M. Tukhachevskii was arrested, and Gamarnik committed suicide. Shul'man was arrested upon his return to Russia in 1937. All his colleagues in the Political Section were shot (over 80 people). After torture, he had a nervous breakdown and was sent to Kazan's psychiatric hospital. Released in 1939, and sent to the Kolyma concentration camps, where he organized a secret group called the 'real communists'. Released, 1949. Went to L'vov. Re-arrested, 1950. Sentenced to 8 years in the camps. Spent his term in the Vorkuta concentration camps. Released and rehabilitated, 1955. Became a well-known circus expert, and a trainer of dolphins. Left the USSR, 1973. Lives in Israel.
Memoirs: *Butyrskii Dekameron*, 2 vols., Israel, 1979; *Vospominaniia: Vstrechi, Portrety*, Israel, 1984; *Odessa – Tel-Aviv. Radio-Liubov' Moia*, Israel, 1985.

Shults, Vadim Mikhailovich
1877–1928? Artist.
Landscape and water-colour painter. Studied at the Moscow School of Painting, Sculpture and Architecture, 1894–1900, under A. Arkhipov, N. Kasatkin and Leonid Pasternak, then at the Petersburg Academy of Arts, 1900–07. Pupil of Il'ia Repin. Began exhibiting from 1895. Exhibitions: TPKHV, 1905, 1917; MOLKH, 1906; the Society of Russian Water Colour Artists, St. Petersburg, 1907, 1910, 1912–13; St. Petersburg Society of Artists, 1910; Spring Exhibitions at the Academy of Arts, 1910, 1912–13, 1917; Iaroslavl' Art Society, 1913; the Association of Artists, 1914, 1916; 1st State Free Exhibition of Works of Art, Petrograd, 1919; AKHPP, Moscow, 1924. In 1926, the Iaroslavo-Rostovskii Art Museum received from the artist several paintings: *Naturshchitsa*; *Obnazhennaia Naturschhitsa* (31x20.5cm), and *Obnazhennaia Naturshchitsa* (39.5x34cm).

Shul'zhenko, Klavdia Ivanovna
24.3.1906– . Singer.
Born in Khar'kov. Pupil of N. Chemezov. Became extremely popular in the 1930–50s, drawing huge crowds to her concerts. Mainly a variety singer. Melodia, the official Soviet record company, produced millions of her records. Entertained Red Army soldiers and officers during WWII.

Shumakov, Aleksei Vasil'evich
7.9.1948– . Athlete.
Born in Krasnoiarskii Krai. Honoured Master of Sports (wrestling), 1976. With Krasnoiarsk Burevestnik. Graduated in engineering from the Krasnoiarsk Polytechnical Institute, 1971. Member of the CPSU, 1977. USSR champion, 1972. European champion, 1976. Olympic champion, 1976. World champion, 1977.

Shumavtsov, Aleksei Semenovich
1925–1942. Partisan.
During WWII, organized an underground Komsomol group near Kaluga. Arrested and shot by the Gestapo. Posthumously awarded the title of Hero of the Soviet Union (1957).

Shumilov, Mikhail Stepanovich
1895–1975. Col.-general.
Took part in WWI. Joined the Red Army and the Bolshevik Party, 1918. Graduated from the Vystrel Courses, 1929. Took part in the Civil War, the Soviet-Finnish war, and WWII. Gained fame during the Battle of Stalingrad. Graduated from the Academy of the General Staff, 1948. Commander of several military districts after WWII.

Shumskaia, Elizaveta Vladimirovna
12.4.1905– . Singer (soprano).
Born in Ivanovo. Pupil of D. Beliavskaia. Soloist with the Bolshoi Theatre from 1944 for nearly 30 years. Very often entertained VIPs at the Kremlin Concert Hall.

Shumuk, Danilo

1914– . Political prisoner.
During the 1930s, in his native Western Ukraine (then Poland), active in the underground communist movement. Imprisoned by the Polish authorities before WWII. During the Soviet occupation of Western Ukraine, 1939–41, became disillusioned with communism. Joined the Ukrainian Partisan Army (UPA), which led an underground struggle against Soviet rule. Arrested, 1945, during the return of the Red Army. Sentenced to death, commuted to life imprisonment. Veteran Gulag inmate. Released, 1967. Re-arrested, 1972, for his involvement with Ukrainian dissident groups, and sentenced to 10 years in prison and 5 years exile. Released under Gorbachev, 1987. Emigrated to Canada.

Shurukhin, Pavel Ivanovich

1912–1956. Major-general.
Joined the Red Army, 1931. Took part in the Soviet-Finnish war, 1939–40, and WWII. Twice Hero of the Soviet Union (for his courage during battles on the Dnepr and in the Carpathians).

Shutkov, Fedor Vasil'evich

15.2.1924– . Athlete.
Born in Moscow Oblast'. Honoured Master of Sports (sailing), 1960. With the Central Sports Club of the Navy. USSR champion, 1948–69. Olympic champion, 1960. European and North African champion, 1964.

Shuvalov, Viktor Grigor'evich

15.12.1923– . Athlete.
Born in the Mordovskaia ASSR. Honoured Master of Sports (hockey), 1953. With the Central Sports Club of the Army. Coach with DSO Spartak. Graduated from the Moscow State Institute of Physical Culture (GIFK), 1964, in the military department (training officers for special assignments). Probably with the security services. USSR champion, 1951–53 and 1955–56. European champion, 1954–56. World champion, 1954, 1956. Olympic champion, 1956.

Shvarts, Elena

1948– . Poetess.
Born in Leningrad. Active in the unofficial Leningrad subculture. Her verse circulates in samizdat, and is much admired by connoisseurs.

Shvedov, Dmitrii Nikolaevich

3.12.1899–1973? Composer, conductor.
Born in Moscow. From 1923, taught at the Leningrad Conservatory, and from 1931, at the Tbilisi Conservatory, in the class of opera singing. Author of the opera Revizor, 1934. Composer of songs, romances, and pieces for stage and screen.

Shvetsov, Arkadii Dmitrievich

1892–1953. Aircraft-engine designer.
Graduated from the Moscow Higher Technical School, 1921. Chief designer at an aviation works, 1934. Designed engines for many types of Soviet aircraft, such as the Iak, Tu, and Il. Four State Prizes.

Shvetsov, Vasilii Ivanovich

1898–1958. Col.-general.
Joined the Bolshevik Party, 1918, and the Red Army, 1919. Took part in the Civil War. Graduated from the Frunze Military Academy, 1929. Commander of several armies during WWII.

Shvetsova, Vera Nikolaevna

2.19.1929– . Ballerina, teacher.
Born in Cherepovets. Graduated from the Leningrad Choreographic School, 1948. Pupil of A. Vaganova. Dancer with the Leningrad Malyi Theatre, 1948–50, and the Spendiarov Theatre in Erevan, 1951–53. Soloist with the Riga Theatre, 1953–73. From 1961, taught at the Riga Choreographic School, and at the East Berlin Choreographic School, 1963–65.

Shviadas, Ionas Izidorovich

9.10.1908–15.10.1971. Composer.
Born in Libava, now Liepaia. Trained at the Klaipeda Music School. Graduated in 1929 (trumpet). Studied composition under M. Zhilevichius, S. Shimkus and A. Iokhov. Played with the Kaunas Conservatory, and taught the trumpet there, 1935–40. Founded and directed the State Ensemble for Song and Drama, 1940. Head of the Department of Folk Music Instruments at the Vilnius Conservatory, 1945. Collected Lithuanian folk songs over many years. Composed in many genres. Died in Vilnius.

Sibiriakov, Eduard Fedorovich

27.11.1941– . Athlete.
Born in Cheliabinsk. Honoured Master of Sports (volley-ball), 1969. With Odessa Burevestnik. Member of the CPSU from 1970. Graduated from the Zhukovskii Military Aviation Academy, 1972. Military pilot. World champion, 1962. Olympic champion, 1964 and 1968. USSR champion, 1966 and 1970. European champion, 1967.

Sibiriakov, Lev Mikhailovich (real name – Spivak)

1870–1938. Singer.
Born in Polovnoe, Volynskaia Gouvt. Pupil of S. Rossi. From 1902, soloist at the Mariinskii Theatre (bass). Emigrated to Poland. Professor at the Warsaw Conservatory. Died in Warsaw.

Sibirtsev, Vsevolod Mikhailovich

30.7.1893–5.1920. Revolutionary.
Born in Petersburg. Studied at the Petersburg Polytechnic. Became a Bolshevik at the age of 20. In 1917, junior officer with the 12th Army on the Western front. Participant of the 1st and 2nd All-Russia Congress of Soviets. Active participant in the October Revolution 1917. Worked at the Military Commission of the Petrograd Soviet. In Jan. 1918, sent to Vladivostok. In Mar. 1918, Secretary of the Executive Cttee. of the Vladivostok Soviet. Arrested by White Czechoslovaks in June 1918 (together with other Bolsheviks). Escaped, Aug. 1919. Editor of the underground Bolshevik newspaper Kommunist. Agitator in the army. In 1920, member of Military Council of the Provisional (Bolshevik) Government of Primorsk District. In Apr. 1920, arrested by the Japanese. Executed together with S. Lazo and A. Lutskii.

Sibor, Boris Iosifovich (real name– Livshits)
21.6.1880–29.7.1961. Violinist.
Born in Torzhok, Tver' Gouvt. Pupil of L. Auer. Soloist in the ballet orchestra of the Bolshoi Theatre. Professor at the Moscow Conservatory. Died in Nikolina Gora near Moscow. Author of *Tekhnicheskie Uprazhneniia Dlia Skripki*, 1910–28, Moscow.

Sidel'nikov, Aleksandr Nikolaevich
12.8.1950– . Athlete.
Born in Solnechnogorsk, Moscow Oblast'. Honoured Master of Sports (hockey), 1976. With Moscow Kryl'ia Sovetov. Studied at the Moscow Institute of Physical Culture. USSR champion, 1974. World and European champion, 1973–74. Olympic champion, 1976.

Sidiak, Viktor Aleksandrovich
24.11.1943– . Athlete.
Born in Kemerovskaia Oblast'. Member of the CPSU from 1966. Honoured Master of Sports (fencing), 1968. From 1969, with the Armed Forces in Minsk. Graduated from the Belorussian Institute of Physical Culture, 1973. World champion, 1969. Olympic champion, 1972, and, with his team, in 1968 and 1976. USSR champion, 1973 and 1978. In 1973, the International Fencing Federation named him the world's best fencer.

Sidorenkov, Genrikh Ivanovich
11.8.1931– . Athlete.
Born in Smolenskaia Oblast'. Honoured Master of Sports (hockey), 1956. With the Moscow Armed Forces. Graduated from the Moscow High School of Sports Instructors attached to the Institute of Physical Culture, 1964. Sports instructor. European champion, 1954–56 and 1958–60. World champion, 1954 and 1956. USSR champion, 1955–56, 1958 and 1960–61. Olympic champion, 1956.

Sidorov, Anatolii Makarovich
22.12.1942– . Ballet dancer.
Born in the village of Zubovo in the Vologodskaia Oblast'. Graduated from the Leningrad Choreographic School, 1962. Pupil of K. V. Shatilova. With the Malyi Theatre. First interpreter of the part of Ivanushka in *Kon'ek Gorbunok* (the Little Hunchbacked Horse) by R. Shchedrin, 1963, and of several other parts, 1966–75. Appeared in the classical repertoire. Teacher of the pas de deux at the Leningrad Choreographic School from 1970. Prize-winner at the ballet festival in Parma, Italy, 1962.

Sidorova, Valentina Vasil'evna (Burochkina)
4.5.1954– . Athlete.
Born in Moscow. Honoured Master of Sports (fencing), 1976. With Moscow Spartak. Studied at the Moscow Institute of Physical Culture. USSR champion, 1973–77. Olympic champion, 1976. World champion, 1977–78 and, with her team, in 1974–75 and 1977–79. In 1977 and 1979, the International Fencing Federation named her the world's best fencer.

Sidur, Vadim
1924–26.6.1986. Sculptor.
Born in Dnepropetrovsk. Took part in WWII. Was wounded and became an invalid at the age of 19. Graduated from the Moscow Stroganov Art School. Became famous in the early 1970s. In 1974, attacked by the weekly *Sovetskaia Rossia* for formalism. Member of the Moscow branch of the Union of Soviet Artists. After his death, left 500 sculptures in his basement studio. Suddenly rediscovered, after an article in *Literaturnaia Gazeta* by a non-professional authority on sculpture, the academician Vitalii Ginzburg. Recognition came posthumously after articles about him appeared in *Ogonek* and similar periodicals.

Siforov, Vladimir Ivanovich
1904– . Electronics scientist.
Graduated from the Leningrad Electrotechnical Institute, 1929. Joined the Red Army and the Bolshevik Party at the beginning of WWI. Professor at the Leningrad Aviation Engineers' Academy, 1941–53. Academician, 1953. Deputy Minister of Radio Technology of the USSR, 1954–55. Worked at the Institute of Radiotechnology and Electronics of the Academy of Sciences, 1954–66. Director of the Institute of Information Communication in the Academy, 1966.

Sikhver, Iaan Khansovich
1879–1918. Revolutionary.
Member of the Bolshevik Party, 1905. Took part in the 1905 Revolution. In 1917, tried unsuccessfully to organize an Estonian Red Guard. Chairman of the Revolutionary Military Council of Estonian soldiers in Petrograd, 1918. Member of the Provisional Estonian Revolutionary Cttee.

Sikorskii, Igor Ivanovich
25.5.1889–26.10.1972. Aircraft designer.
Born in Kiev. Studied at the Petersburg Naval School, 1903–06, and the Kiev Polytechnical Institute, 1907. One of the first designers of helicopters, 1908–11. The first aeroplane made to his design flew in 1910. Became a qualified pilot, 1911. Constructed the first large Russian aeroplanes (Grand, Russkii Vitiaz, Ilia Muromets), 1912–14. After the Bolshevik take-over, emigrated, 1919. Settled in the USA, and founded an aviation firm, 1923, which became an important part of the American aviation industry, especially in helicopter construction. Died in Easton, Connecticut, USA.

Silant'ev, Aleksandr Petrovich
1918– . Marshal.
Joined the Red Army, 1938. Fighter pilot during WWII. Graduated from the Air Force Academy, 1950, and the Academy of the General Staff, 1957. Chief-of-staff of the Air Force, 1969. Deputy Commander-in-chief of the Air Force, 1969–80.

Silich, Liubov' Nikolaevna
28.9.1908– . Stage designer.
Born in Moscow. Trained with the VKHUTEIN, 1924–30. Worked in Moscow theatres. Designed the Bolshoi Theatre's production of *Coppelia*, 1949. Designed the costumes for the same theatre's production of *The Sleeping Beauty*, 1952. Much work with the choreographic ensemble Berezka.

Siluan (Antonov, Simeon Ivanovich), starets
1872–24.9.1938. Russian Orthodox clergyman.
Son of a peasant. In his youth, served in the army. Became a monk at Athos in Greece, 1892. After that spent all his life in the Athos monasteries, attaining the reputation of a starets. Highly revered for his saintly life. A book on his life and teaching by Sofronii (Sakharov) was published in several languages in the 1940s and 1950s. Died and buried at Athos. Considered a candidate for canonization in the Russian Orthodox Church.

Simachev, Nikolai Romanovich
15.12.1927– . Ballet dancer, choreographer.
Born in Moscow. Graduated from the Moscow Choreographic School. Pupil of N. Tarasov. With the Bolshoi Theatre, 1946–68. Responsible, together with S. Vlasov, for a new production of *The Fire Bird*, 1964. Taught at the Moscow Choreographic School, 1949–56. Choreographer and coach with the Bolshoi Theatre from 1968.

Simanovskii, Nikolai Petrovich
16.2.1854–5.7.1922. Doctor, scientist.
Born near Saratov. Graduated from the Petersburg Military Medical Academy, 1878. Worked at the S.P. Botkin Clinic. Professor, 1886. In 1893, founded the first ear, nose and throat clinic in Russia. Established a scientific society of specialists in ENT diseases in Petersburg in 1903. Head of this society until his death. Responsible for the creation of the Russian school of ear, nose and throat specialists. Several works and lectures on the subject. Academician, 1907. Died in Petrograd.

Simashev, Fedor Petrovich
13.3.1945– . Athlete.
Born in the Tatar ASSR. Honoured Master of Sports (skiing), 1970. With Moscow Dynamo. Graduated from the Moscow Oblast' Pedagogical Institute. Schoolmaster from 1973. USSR champion, 1968–76. World champion, 1970. Olympic champion, 1972.

Simeonov, Konstantin Arsen'evich
20.6.1910– . Conductor.
Born in the village of Kaznakovo, Tver' Gouvt. Pupil of A. Gauk and I. Musin. Appeared as a symphonic conductor, 1936–60. From 1961, chief conductor of the Kiev Opera and Ballet Theatre.

Simforian, archimandrite
1900?–1.1981. Russian Orthodox clergyman.
Monk at the Valaam monastery on an island in the Ladoga Lake. After the Civil War, this territory belonged to Finland. During the Finnish-Soviet war, the monks were evacuated to Finland, taking their valuable library, icons and bells with them, 1940. One of the founders of the New Valaam monastery in Eastern Finland. Later, head of the monastery. Died and buried at New Valaam (Valamo). The last survivor of the brotherhood of Old Valaam.

Simoniak, Nikolai Pavlovich
1901–1956. Lt.-general.
Joined the Red Army, 1918, and the Bolshevik Party, 1920. Took part in the Civil War. Graduated from the Frunze Military Academy, 1936. Army commander during WWII.

Simonian, Nadezhda Simonovna
26.2.1922– . Composer.
Born in Rostov-on-Don. Wrote music for the ballet *Zhemchuzhina* (produced, 1965), and the cantata *Ozero Sevan*, 1949. Also wrote music for plays, films, circus and radio.

Simonian, Nikita Pogosovich
12.10.1926– . Athlete.
Born in Armavir. Honoured Master of Sports (football), 1954. Member of the CPSU from 1955. Graduated from the Moscow Institute of Physical Culture, 1963. Honoured Coach of the USSR from 1969. Honoured Sports Personality of the Armenian SSR, 1976. Senior coach of the USSR international football team, 1976–79. USSR champion, 1952–58. Olympic champion, 1956.

Simonov, Evgenii Rubenovich
21.6.1925– . Stage director.
Born in Moscow. Son of the famous director Ruben Simonov. In 1947, graduated from the Moscow Shchukin Theatre School where his father was professor. Assistant director, later director, and from 1969 chief director, at the Vakhtangov Theatre in Moscow, where his father had reigned for 20 years. Staged contemporary Soviet plays as well as Russian classical works and some foreign dramas. His own plays include *Aleksei Berezhnoi* (1962, Vakhtangov Theatre), and *John Reed* (1967, Malyi Theatre).

Simonov, Konstantin (Kirill) Mikhailovich
28.11.1915–1979. Author, journalist, poet.
Born in Petrograd. Grew up in Riazan and Saratov. His step-father taught at a military school, his mother was a typist. Correspondence student at an FZU (fabrichno-zavodskoe uchilishche) in 1930, while working as a fitter at the Universal mechanical plant. In 1931, moved with his family to Moscow. Fitter at an aviation plant. Technician at the Mezhrabpomfilm studio. Tried to publish in *Pravda* his first poem about the Belomorkanal, Stalin's pet project, built by Gulag prisoners. Was encouraged to work on the subject but did not succeed in publishing it because it was 'bad poetry'. Entered the Gorkii Literary Institute. His first poems were published in 1936 in *Molodaia Gvardia* and *Oktiabr'*. Graduated from the Institute, 1938. His next poem was inspired by the Soviet general Lukach (the author Mate-Zalka), who was killed in the Spanish Civil War. *Pravda* war correspondent in Mongolia, Finland and other parts of Europe. Joined the Communist Party in 1942. Became famous during WWII for his sincere lyrical poems *Zhdi menia i ia vernus', tolko ochen' zhdi*, and others. After WWII, journalist in China, the USA, Japan and other countries. Took part in many Stalinist propaganda campaigns. Wrote propaganda plays such as *Russkii Vopros*. Published war diaries. From 1946–50 and 1954–58, editor-in-chief of *Novyi Mir*. From 1950–53, editor-in-chief of *Literaturnaia Gazeta*. From 1946–59 and throughout the 1970s, secre-

tary of the Union of Writers. 2 novels *Zhivye i Mertvye* and *Soldatami Ne Rozhdaiutsia*, were filmed in the 1960s. From 1956–61, member of the Central Auditing Commission of the CPSU.

Simonov, Ruben Nikolaevich
1.4.1899–5.12.1968. Stage director, actor.
Born in Moscow. Studied law at Moscow University. In 1919, entered the Chaliapin Drama Studio. In 1920, moved to the 3rd MKHAT Studio. From 1922, actor at the Vakhtangov Theatre. From 1924, stage director at the same theatre. From 1939, chief director at the Vakhtangov Theatre. Notable productions: *Princess Turandot* (with a remarkable score by the composer Sizov), and *The Marriage* (after Chekhov). During the 1930s, forced to stage propaganda plays. Forbidden to stage the best foreign playwrights. Staged a few operas for the Bolshoi (*Abessalom I Eteri* and *Carmen*). After the war, headed the Armenian and Uzbek studios. From 1946, professor at the Shchukin Theatre School. Most remembered for his portrayal of Stalin in *Chelovek s Ruzh'em* (Man with a Rifle) in front of Stalin himself on 21 Jan. 1938 at the Bolshoi on the occasion of the anniversary of Lenin's death. According to his contemporaries, he was frozen by Stalin's gaze and lost his voice. Died in Moscow.
Source: Iurii Elagin, *Ukroshchenie Iskusstv* (Persecution of Arts), NY, 1952.

Simonov, Sergei Gavrilovich
1894– . Gun-designer.
Joined the Bolshevik Party, 1927. Head of a design bureau, 1929. Designed an automatic rifle, anti-tank gun and other weapons. 2 State Prizes in the 1940s.

Simonova, Nina Ivanovna
9.5.1922– . Ballerina.
Born in Moscow. Graduated from the Moscow Choreographic School. Pupil of M. Kozhukhova. With the Bolshoi Theatre, 1940–62. One of the best-known Soviet character dancers. In concert work until 1967.

Simov, Viktor Andreevich
14.4.1858–21.8.1935. Stage designer. Born in Moscow. Graduated from the Moscow School of Painting, Sculpture and Architecture in 1882. Pupil of V. Perov, I Prianishnikov and A. Savrasov. Joined the Peredvizhniki, and took part in their exhibitions: 1883, 1891 and 1893. Worked mainly at the Moscow Art Theatre, apart from the period 1912–25. Stage designer for *Tri Sestry, Vishnevyi Sad, Na Dne, Tsar Fedor Ioannovich*, and *Diadia Vania*. The period between 1912–25 in his official biography is unclear. Probably lived abroad. Died in Moscow.

Simovich, Roman Appolonovich
28.2.1901– . Composer.
Born in Galitsia. Taught at the L'vov Conservatory. Author of 5 symphonies, 1945–56. Also wrote chamber music.

Siniavskii, Andrei Donatovich (pen name – Abram Terts)
1925– . Author, critic.
Born in Moscow. Graduated from Moscow University, 1952. Became known as a critic, writing for a number of leading magazines. Author of a study (with A. Menshutin) of the poetry of the early period of Soviet literature, *Poezia Pervykh Let Revolutsii, 1917–20*. Together with his friend and collaborator Iulii Daniel, sent and published abroad (under the pseudonyms Abram Terts and Nikolai Arzhak) several satirical works, under the title *Fantasticheskii Mir Abrama Tertsa*, and later *Sud Idet* and *Liubimov'*. The Abram Terts stories mystified the literary world in the East and West for a number of years. Together with Daniel, he was the first famous literary dissident. Eventually exposed, and in Sep. 1965, became involved in a trial which created an international sensation, and which received well-documented coverage in the Western press. Became a world celebrity. Convicted for slandering the Soviet system and sentenced to 7 years hard labour. Protests against the trial marked the beginning of the modern dissident movement in the USSR. After serving his term, emigrated, 1973. His literary criticism of Russian classical literature, *Progulki s Push-*

kinym and *V Teni Gogolia*, published in the West, received a mixed reception. His works have been translated into many languages. Founded and edits his own magazine *Sintaksis*, together with his wife Maria Rozanova. Lives in a suburb of Paris. Professor at the Sorbonne.

Sinisalo, Gel'mer-Rainer Nestorovich
14.6.1920– . Composer.
Born in Zlatoust in Cheliabinskaia Oblast'. Trained at the Moscow Conservatory under V. Voloshinov. Author of symphonies and chamber music. Composed music for the first Karelian ballet *Sampo*, based on the Finnish epic *Kalevala*, produced at the Petrozavodskii Theatre of Musical Drama, 1959. Author of the ballet *Ia Pomniu Chudnoe Mgnoven'e* on themes from M. Glinka, produced at the Dzhalil' Theatre in Kazan', and the L'vov Theatre, 1962. Other ballets, 1963–74. State Prize of the Karelian ASSR, 1974.

Sisikin, Iurii Fedorovich
15.5.1937– . Athlete.
Born in Saratov. Honoured Master of Sports (fencing), 1960. With the Saratov Armed Forces from 1964. World champion, 1959, 1961–62 and 1965–66. Olympic champion, 1960 and 1964. Member of the CPSU from 1976.

Sitkovetskii, Iulian Grigor'evich
7.10.1925–23.2.1958. Violinist.
Born in Kiev. Pupil of A. Iampol'skii and D. Bertier. Second prize at the Wieniawski International Competition in Poznan, 1952, and at the Queen Elizabeth of Belgium International Competition in Brussels, 1955. The cause of his premature death is not explained in official Soviet sources.

Sitnikov, German Borisovich
6.8.1932– . Ballet dancer, choreographer.
Born in Sverdlovsk Oblast'. Graduated from the Moscow Choreographic School, 1951, and from the GITIS, 1975 (Department of Ballet Teachers). With the Bolshoi Theatre, 1951–73. Taught at the Moscow Choreographic School, 1952–55.

Produced the ballet *Plamia Parizha* in Ulan-Bator, 1971, on a theme by V. Vainonen. Choreographer and coach with the Bolshoi Theatre from 1973.

Sitnikov, Vasilii Iakovlevich
1915–1.12.1987. Artist, icon collector.
Born in the town of Lebedian'-on-Don. Son of a wealthy peasant who lost everything during the Civil War and the collectivization campaign. Began collecting Russian icons from the age of 13. His magnificent collection is now at the Moscow Rublev Museum. Graduated from a school of naval mechanics, 1934. Began painting at an early age. Studied and taught art. Arrested, 1941, after being denounced by his neighbours. Sent to the notorious Kazan' psychiatric hospital. Released, 1947. Lived a very unconventional lifestyle. Opened a private art school and attracted hundreds of pupils. The Sitnikov school also attracted the attention of the KGB. In 1959, became a famous, established artist. At an opening of an exhibition, when the Minister of Culture, Mikhailov, asked him to explain an abstract picture, he told him in front of a crowd, 'Why explain the meaning of art to a donkey? The donkey does not need art.' He was arrested. The cultural authorities were happy to let him leave the country when his pupils sent him an invitation to Israel and a visa. Lived in an Austrian mountain village for 5 years as a recluse, during which time he painted the huge masterpiece *Glory to Doctor Mayer*, a caricature on the Germans and Russians. In 1981, left Austria for New York. Received a great amount of attention from his pupils and the press. Died from a heart attack in New York.

Sivers, Rudolf Ferdinandovich
23.11.1892–8.12.1918. Military commander.
Born in Petersburg. Took part in WWI as a junior officer. In 1917, joined the Bolsheviks. One of the founders and editors of *Okopnaia Pravda*, the newspaper of the 12th Army. In July 1917, arrested by the Provisional Government. Released after 3 months. Active participant of the October Revolution, fighting Kerenskii's troops at Pulkovo. In Nov. 1917, fought against the army of ataman Kaledin. In Feb. 1918, took Rostov-on-Don from the Whites. Commander of the 5th Army. In July 1918, commander of the Osobaia Brigada (Special Brigade) with the 9th Army on the Southern front against the Cossack general Krasnov. Killed in action near the village of Zhelnovka. Buried at Marsovo Pole in Petrograd.

Sivko, Sergei
7.6.1940–10.11.1966. Athlete.
Honoured Master of Sports (boxing). Many times USSR champion. Silver medal winner at the XVIIth Olympic Games. Knocked down by a car while drunk.

Sivkov, Grigorii Flegontovich
1921– . Major-general.
Joined the Red Army, 1939. Fighter pilot during WWII, highly decorated (twice Hero of the Soviet Union). After WWII, test pilot. Graduated from the Zhukovskii Air Force Academy, 1952. Professor at the Zhukovskii Air Force Academy, 1972.

Sizenko, Evgenii Ivanovich
1931– . Politician.
Member of the CPSU, 1953. Graduated from the Moscow Timiriazev Agricultural Academy, 1954. Worked as an agronomist in Riazan Oblast'. Taught at the same academy, 1957–60. Senior administrative positions in Moscow Oblast', 1961–70. Secretary of Moscow Oblast' Cttee. of the CPSU, 1970–78. 1st Secretary of Briansk Oblast' Cttee. of the CPSU, 1978. Member of the Cen. Cttee. of the CPSU from 1981. 1st Deputy Chairman of Gosagroprom, the umbrella organization which oversees the Soviet agricultural industry, 1987.

Skal'be, Karlis
7.11.1879–14.4.1945. Author.
One of the major Latvian poets and writers. Worker, teacher, later journalist. First work published in 1896. At first wrote poetry: *Mechty Uznika* 1902; *Kogda Iabloni Tsvetut*, 1904; *Serdtse i Solntse*, 1911; *Vechernie Ogni*, 1927. Became known for his fairy-tales. In 1944, emigrated and settled in Sweden. Died in Stockholm.

Skibine, Georges (Skibin, Iurii Borisovich)
30.1.1920– . Ballet dancer, choreographer.
Born in Yasnaia Poliana. Pupil of Olga Preobrazhenskaia and Serge Lifar. Emigrated. Debut in Paris as a cabaret dancer. With the Ballet de Monte Carlo, 1938, the Original Ballet Russe, 1940, the Ballet Theatre, 1941–42, the company of A. Markova and A. Dolin, 1946, and the Grand Ballet du Marquis de Cuevas, 1947–56. Leading dancer in ballets by M. Fokin and L. Massine. Produced several ballets for the Cuevas company, 1948–55. Star of the Paris Opera, 1957–62, and chief choreographer with the company, 1958–61. Artistic director of the Harkness Ballet, New York, 1964–66. In these years produced *Bacchus and Ariadne* by Albert Roussel, 1964, *Fire Bird*, 1967, *Bandar Log*, 1969, and *Carmina Burana*, 1970.
Source: I. Lidova, 'Georges Skibine'. *Les Saisons de la Danse*, March, 1970.

Sklianskii, Efraim Markovich
12.8.1892–27.8.1925. Politician.
Born in Fastov. Joined the Communist Party in 1913. Studied at Kiev University, in the medical faculty, 1911–16. Propaganda worker for the Kiev RSDRP. From 1916, served in the army as a soldier, then a doctor. After the February Revolution 1917, member of the 5th Army Party Cttee. Member of the Petrograd Revolutionary Cttee. Commissar at the General Staff High Command, Mogilev. Deputy Minister of War, 1917–18. From Mar. 1918, member of the Senior Military Soviet of the RSFSR. From Apr. 1918–Mar. 1924, Deputy Chairman of the Revolutionary Military Soviet. Trotsky's right-hand man. Member of the Narkomzdrav Collegium, 1920–21. In Apr. 1924, demoted to the VSNKH as Chairman of Mossukno Trust. Found drowned during a business trip to the USA.

Skobelev, Matvei Ivanovich
1885–29.7.1938. Politician.
Born in Baku into a wealthy family. Menshevik, 1903. Emigrated, 1906–12. Deputy of the 4th Duma (Zakavkaz'e District), 1912. One of the leaders of the social democrat faction. After the February Revolution 1917, member of the Ispolkom and Deputy Chairman of the Petrograd Soviet. Labour Minister in the Provisional Government. After the October Revolution 1917, broke with the Mensheviks. Emigrated from Georgia to France. Cooperated with the Soviet Government in France. Representative of the Central Union in Paris, then in Brussels. In 1922, joined the Bolsheviks. From 1924, worked at the USSR Foreign Trade Mission. Returned to the USSR, and disappeared as a victim of the Gulag.

Skobeltsyn, Dmitrii Vladimirovich
24.11.1892–1977. Physicist, academician.
Born in Petersburg. Graduated from Petrograd University, 1915. Worked at the Polytechnical Institute, 1916–37, and the Physico-Technical Institute, 1925–29 and 1931–39 in Leningrad. From 1937, at the Physical Institute of the Academy of Sciences. Worked at the M. Skladovski-Curie Laboratory, Paris, 1929–31. Professor at Moscow University, 1940, and Rector of the same university until 1960. Published many works on nuclear physics. Academician, 1946. Died in Moscow.

Skoblikova, Lidia Pavlovna
8.3.1939– . Athlete.
Born in Zlatoust. Honoured Master of Sports (skating), 1960. Member of the CPSU from 1964. Graduated from the Cheliabinsk Pedagogical Institute, 1965. With Moscow Lokomotiv, 1968–71. Schoolmaster. From 1974, Dean of the Faculty of Physical Education at the Moscow Trade Unions Higher Party School. World and USSR champion at 25 world championships and 15 USSR championships. Won 40 gold medals. Olympic champion, 1960 (1,500 and 3,000 metres), and 1964 (500, 1,000, 1,500 and 3,00 metres).
Source: A. Kishkin, *Rasskaz ob Olimpiiskoi Chempionke*, Cheliabinsk, 1961.

Skoblin, Nikolai Vladimirovich
9.6.1893–1937? General.
Born at Nezhin in the Ukraine. Son of a colonel. Educated at the Chuguev Military School, 1914. Took part in WWI, decorated for bravery. During the Civil War, divisional commander in the Denikin army, later one of the best-known commanders with General Wrangel in the Crimea. Evacuated to Gallipoli after the defeat of the Whites. Married there the famous folk-singer N. Plevitskaia, 11 years his senior, and fell completely under her spell. Accompanied his wife on her triumphant tours all over the world in the 1920s. At the same time, tried to regain some of the glamour he had previously known as a commander of the crack division of the Whites, by intrigues in ex-officers' organizations, and by shady affairs with the secret services of various countries. According to some information, he was involved with the German secret service in the preparation of the fake Zinov'ev letter which led to the British Labour Party's defeat in the 1924 general election. Also, again with the German secret service, involved in arousing Stalin's suspicions against Marshal Tukhachevskii and his alleged connections with Germany, which led to the virtual liquidation of the leadership of the Red Army on Stalin's orders on the eve of WWII. More certain are facts pointing not to Germany, but to the Soviet Union. At some point during these years, he must have found out that his wife had become a Soviet agent, and agreed to cooperate while pretending to remain a loyal friend to his former co-fighters in the Civil War. Cooperated in the kidnapping of his former commander and personal friend General Kutepov in Paris, 1930. Managed to remain above suspicion and continued to associate with other former White officers. Repeated his service to the NKVD by luring Kutepov's successor, General Miller, to kidnapping and probably death, but this time was found out. Fled in 1937 after this incident (Plevitskaia was arrested and died in a French prison). Probably killed by his NKVD controllers.
See: B. Prianishnikov, *Nezrimaia Pautina*, USA, 1979.

Skobov, Iurii Georgievich
13.3.1949– . Athlete.
Born in Briansk Oblast'. Honoured Master of Sports (skiing), 1972. With Kirov Trud. Studied at the Kirov Pedagogical Institute. USSR champion, 1972–174. Olympic champion, 1972.

Skomorokhov, Nikolai Mikhailovich
1920– . Marshal.
Joined the Red Army, 1940. Educated at a pilots' school, 1942. Fighter pilot during WWII, twice Hero of the Soviet Union. Joined the CPSU, 1943. Credited with shooting down 46 enemy planes. Graduated from the Frunze Military Academy, 1949, and from the Academy of the General Staff, 1958. High command posts in the Soviet Air Force after WWII. Head of the Air Force Academy, 1973.

Skorikov, Grigorii Petrovich
1920– . Marshal.
Joined the Red Army, 1937. Educated at a pilots' school, 1942. Took part in WWII. Joined the Bolshevik Party, 1941. Graduated from the Frunze Military Academy, 1948, and from the Academy of the General Staff, 1957. 1st Deputy Chief-of-staff of the Air Force, 1971, and Chief-of-staff, 1978–85.

Skoropadskii, Pavel Petrovich
15.7.1873–26.4.1945. General, politician.
Born in Wiesbaden. Son of a landowner, descendant of an 18th century Ukrainian Cossack Hetman. Educated at the Pages Corps, 1893. Served in the Chevalier Guard Regiment (Konnogvardeiskii Polk). During WWI, Lt.-general, Commander of the 1st Cavalry Guard Division. In Aug. 1917, appointed Commander of the Ukrainian Corps by the Provisional Government. After the Bolshevik take-over 1917, appointed head of the army by the Ukrainian Rada, Oct. 1917. Under German occupation during WWI, elected in Kiev Hetman (head of state) of the Ukraine, 29 Apr. 1918. Unable to keep his position without German help, overthrown by left-wing Ukrainians under Petliura, 14 Dec. 1918. Emigrated to Germany. Died in Metten in Bavaria.

Skrinskii, Aleksandr Nikolaevich
15.1.1936–   . Nuclear scientist.
Born in Orenburg. Graduated from
Moscow State University, 1959.
Member of staff at the Institute of
Nuclear Physics of the Siberian
Branch of the USSR Academy of
Sciences from 1959. Professor at
Novosibirsk Univesity, 1967. Member of the USSR Academy of
Sciences, 1970. Lives between Moscow and Novosibirsk. Author of
Ispol'zovanie Sinkhrotronnogo Izluchenia Nakopitelia VEPP-3 Dlia Rentgenostrukturnykh Issledovanii, (Reports of the USSR Academy of Science, Nr 4), 1974.

Skripko, Nikolai Semenovich
1902–   . Marshal.
Joined the Red Army, 1919. Took
part in the Civil War as an artillery
officer. Joined the Air Force, 1927.
Commander of a regiment, and later
a division, 1938–40. Commmander
of the Strategic Bombers Corps,
1940. During WWII and afterwards,
held command positions in bomber
and transport detachments of the Air
Force. Member of the Central Revision Commission of the CPSU,
1961–66.

Skuibin, Vladimir Nikolaevich
3.6.1929–15.11.1963. Film director.
Born in Moscow. Studied at the
Shchepkin Theatre School. Graduated from the VGIK (Moscow State
Film School), 1955, as a director.
Films: *Na Grafskikh Razvalinakh*
(based on the Arkadii Gaidar story,
1957, with I. Bolgarin), *Zhestokost'*
(based on the P. Nilin story, 1959),
and *Chudotvornaia* (based on the V.
Tendriakov story, 1960). His last film
was *Sud* (1962, with A. Manasarova).
Died in Moscow from cancer.

Skuratov, Vladimir (Skouratoff)
12.2.1925–   . Ballet dancer.
Born in Paris. Pupil of O. I.
Preobrazhenskaia, B. Kniazeva and
A. Volinin. Leading dancer with the
Nouveaux Ballet de Monte Carlo,
1946, the Original Ballet Russe, 1947,
the Grand Ballet du Marquis de
Cuevas, 1952–57, and the London
Festival Ballet, 1959–60. With
Roland Petit's productions and also
with S. Lifar's production of *Shota
Rustaveli*. Also appeared with theatres in Strasbourg, 1967–69, and

Bordeaux, 1970.
Source: I. Percival, 'He can bring a
poor ballet to success', *Dance and
Dancers*, Dec. 1959.

Skurikhin, Anatolii Vasil'evich
1900–   . Photo-journalist.
Born in the town of Kotelnich (now
in Kirov Oblast'). As a teenager, an
enthusiastic amateur photographer.
His landscape pictures attracted the
attention of the editors of *Sovetfoto*.
In 1928, won several awards in a
photographic competition run by the
magazine. Moved to Moscow and
studied at the State Art and Technical
Workshops. Became a photoreporter. From 1930, worked on
Komsomolskaia Pravda and later on
Izvestia.

Skveri, Mikhail Petrovich
20.11.1856–13.10.1924. Revolutionary.
Born in Odessa of an Italian father
and Russian mother. His mother was
a peasant. Studied at the Odessa high
school. Left school at the age of 15.
Worked in an Odessa factory. Met E.
Zaslavskii, an active Bolshevik.
Member of the Iuzhnorossiiskii Soiuz Rabochikh. In Jan. 1876, arrested.
In 1877, exiled to Siberia (Tobolsk).
From 1884, again in Odessa on
probation. His Bolshevik activity
continued. In 1907, arrested. In 1917,
head of a department at Odessa
Public Library. Contributor to *Katorga I Ssylka* and other magazines.
Died in Odessa.

Skvirskii, Lev Solomonovich
1903–   . Lt.-general.
Joined the Red Army, 1920. Took
part in the Civil War. Joined the
Bolshevik Party, 1924. Graduated
from the Frunze Military Academy,
1935. Later professor at the Academy. Took part in the SovietFinnish war and WWII. Professor at
the Academy of the General Staff,
1951. Carried out scientific research
work for the General Staff, 1957–60.

**Skvortsov-Stepanov, Ivan Ivanovich
(real name – Skvortsov; pseudonym
– I. Stepanov)**
8.3.1870–8.10.1928. Historian, economist, politician.
Born in Bogorodsk (now Noginsk).

His father was a factory clerk. In
1890, graduated from the Moscow
Teachers Institute. Taught in Moscow. Revolutionary activity from
1891. In 1896, joined the SDs. Several
short arrests and exile. In 1905, a
party lecturer. Delegate at the 4th SD
Party Congress. In 1907 and 1911, a
Bolshevik candidate in the Duma.
From 1914–17, on party work in
Moscow. After the February Revolution 1917, editor of *Izvestia*. Member
of the editorial board of *Social
Democrat*. During the October Revolution 1917, member of the Moscow
Revolutionary Cttee. Member of the
first Soviet government (Minister of
Finance). Chairman of the editorial
board of Gosizdat (State Publishing
House). From 1927, deputy editor of
Pravda. From 1926–28, editor of
Leningradskaia Pravda. Member of
the Presidium of the Communist
Academy. Anti-Trotsky and against
the new opposition. Member of the
editorial board of the first edition of
the *Sovetskaia Entsiklopediia*. Translator and editor of *Das Kapital*. Died
in Sochi. Buried at the Kremlin wall
on Red Square.

Sladkov, Ivan Davydovich
23.3.1890–5.6.1922. Revolutionary.
Born in the village of Molodenok,
Tula Oblast'. Junior naval officer,
1910. Joined the Communist Party,
1917. Took part in the October
Revolution 1917. Bolshevik agitator
on the ship *Aleksandr II*. Bolshevik
agitator in the Baltic fleet. One of the
organizers of the revolt on the
Gangut battleship. Arrested, Dec.
1915, and sentenced to 7 years hard
labour. Set free, Feb. 1917. Member
of Petrograd and then Kronstadt
Soviets. During the October coup
1917, organized the take-over of the
Petrograd military port. Commissar
of the same port. From June 1919,
Commissar of the Krasnaia Gorka
and Seraia Loshad' forts. Commandant of many military districts,
1920. From 1 Apr. 1921, Commissar
of the Naval Forces of the Soviet
Republic. Died in Sebastopol.

Slashchev, Iakov Aleksandrovich
24.12.1885–11.1.1929. General.
Born in Petersburg. Son of an officer.
Educated at the Pavlovskoe Military

School in 1905. Graduated from the Academy of the General Staff in 1911. Commander of the Moscow Life Guards regiment in 1916. During the Civil War, with the Whites, became known for cruel repressions. After the failure of General Denikin's march on Moscow, held the Perekop (Northern entrance to the Crimea) for the Whites against overwhelming odds, enabling the Whites to rally in the Crimea under General Wrangel. Released from duty by Wrangel in Aug. 1920 (to recover from serious drug addiction). Evacuated to Turkey in 1920. Accepted the Soviet Government's amnesty, and with a group of officers returned to the Soviet Union in 1921. Used for propaganda purposes, advising his former military comrades to return (all who followed his advice were liquidated as soon as they crossed the border). Allowed to give tactical training to Red commanders in Moscow, 1921–29, under the close supervision of the secret police. Shot in Moscow by a person who claimed that a relative had been executed on his orders during the Civil War. Another version is that the assassin was sent by the secret police, because though sentenced to 5 years, he was soon released.

Slatin, Il'ia Il'ich
19.7.1845–1931. Pianist, conductor. Born in Belgorod. Pupil of A. Dreishok. In Khar'kov, in 1871, founded the music classes of the Russkoe Muzykal'noe Obshchestvo, which in 1883 became a music school. Also founded the Simfonicheskoe Sobranie which he headed, 1871–90. Conducted in many towns in Russia and in Europe. Died in Khar'kov.

Slavin, Lev Isaevich
27.10.1896–1984. Writer.
Born in Odessa. Took part in WWI and the Civil War. During WWII, war correspondent for *Krasnaia Zvezda* and *Izvestia*. His first story was published in 1922. Many of his books were filmed or staged: *Dva Boitsa*, 1943 (film); *Interventsiia*, 1932 (play); *Chastnaia Zhizn Petra Vinogradova*, 1935 (film); *Syn Mongolii*, 1936 (film); *Vozvrashchenie Maksima*, 1937, (film by Grigorii Kozintsev and Leonid Trauberg).

Slavina, Maria Aleksandrovna
1858–1951. Singer (mezzo-soprano). Pupil of N. Iretskaia and K. Everardi. Soloist at the Mariinskii Theatre, 1879–1917. Professor at the Petrograd Conservatory, 1919–20. Emigrated to France, 1920. Died in Paris.

Slavinskii, Evgenii Osipovich
24.1.1877–23.9.1950. Cameraman.
In 1908, worked for the Pathé brothers as a stills photographer. His first feature film as a cameraman was *Den' Venchaniia*, 1912. Filmed Lenin on many occasions. The film *V. I. Lenin*, 1949, was made from his material. His best feature films were *Bukhta Smerti*, 1926, and *Shvedskaia Spichka*, 1922, (released in 1926). Cameraman on V. Mayakovsky's film *Baryshnia i Khuligan*, 1918.

Slepnev, Mavrikii Trofimovich
1896–1965. Pilot.
Took part in WWI and the Civil War. Joined the Red Army, 1918. Pilot instructor in the 1920s. In the 1920s and 1930s, as a civilian pilot, made long-distance flights over unexplored territories in the Arctic, Far East and Central Asia. Took part in the rescue of the Cheliuskin expedition, 1934. Graduated from the Zhukovskii Air Force Academy, 1936. Commander of Zeppelin formations in the 1930s. Chief Inspector of Civil Aviation. Head of the Academy of Civil Aviation, 1939. On active service during WWII. At Naval Aviation HQ, 1944–45. Member of the TSIK of the USSR, 1935–37.

Slepushkin, Aleksandr Ivanovich
11.11.1870–30.3.1918. Harpist.
Pupil of V. Posse. From 1908, soloist in the Bolshoi Theatre Orchestra. Taught at the Moscow Conservatory. His pupils include M. Korchinskaia and N. Parfenov. Died in Moscow.

Sliunkov, Nikolai Nikitovich
26.4.1929–   . Politician.
Born in the village of Garadzets, Gomel' Oblast'. Son of a worker. Graduated from a mechanical-technical school. Worked as a foreman and shop superintendent. Deputy Chairman of the Trade Union Cttee. of the Minsk Tractor Plant, 1950–60.

In 1954, joined the Communist Party. Director of the Minsk Spare Parts Plant, 1960–65. Director of the Minsk Tractor Plant, 1965–72. Member of the Cen. Cttee. of the Belorussian CP, 1966–76. 1st Secretary of Minsk City Cttee., 1972–74. Deputy Chairman of the USSR GOSPLAN, 1974–83. 1st Secretary and member of the Bureau of the Cen. Cttee. of the Belorussian CP from 1983. Close associate of Gorbachev. Promoted to full membership of the Politburo. Regarded as an economic reformer, and a promoter of Gorbachev's glasnost policy. In charge of economic administration in Gorbachev's new team. Head of the commission of the Cen. Cttee. on economic and social policy, in charge of the economic decentralization programme, 1 Oct. 1988.

Sliusarenko, Zakhar Karpovich
1907–   . Lt.-general.
Joined the Bolshevik Party, 1929, and the Red Army, 1932. Educated at a tank forces school, 1934. Commander of tank detachments during WWII. Distinguished himself during the battle of the Vistula and the storming of Berlin, twice Hero of the Soviet Union. Commander of the Northern Military Group, 1960–65.

Slivinskii, Vladimir Richardovich
4.6.1894–7.8.1949. Singer.
Born in Moscow. Pupil of N. Raiskii. Soloist at the Leningrad Opera and Ballet Theatre (Kirov), 1924–30, and at the Bolshoi Theatre, 1930–38. Died in Moscow.

Slobodianiuk Podolian, Stefan Ivanovich (Solodovianiuk)
1876–1927. Artist.
Portrait and landscape painter. Studied at the Petersburg Academy of Arts, 1905–12, under V. Makovskii. Exhibitions: the Academy of Arts, Petersburg, 1907–11; Spring Exhibitions at the Academy of Arts, 1909–15; A. Kuindzhi Society, 1926–27; Art of the People of the USSR, Moscow, 1917–27. Died in Moscow.

Slobodkin, Iakov Pavlovich
11.8.1920–   . Cellist.
Born in Rostov-on-Don. Pupil of S.

Kozolupov and M. Iampol'skii. 4th prize at the All-Union Competition of Violinists and Cellists in Moscow, 1937. 2nd prize at the Wihan International Competition of Cellists in Prague, 1950. Teacher at the Moscow Conservatory.

Slonim, Mark L'vovich
1894–1976. Journalist, literary scholar.
Member of the SR Party. Elected member of the Constituent Assembly, 1917. Member of the Direktoriia in Ufa. Emigrated after the Civil War. Settled in Prague. Editor of the SR magazine *Volia Rossii* (which regularly published Tsvetaeva), 1921 –32. Moved to Paris, where he became chairman of the literary society Kochev'e. During WWII, in the USA. Later returned to Europe, taught Russian literature at Swiss universities. Died in Switzerland.

Slonimskii, Iurii Iosifovich
13.3.1902–23.4.1978. Ballet critic, scenario writer.
Born in Petersburg. Trained at the School of Russian Drama, Petrograd, 1918. Private lessons from 1918 from A. Sakselin, V. Vainonen and G. Balanchine, pupil at the Petersburg Ballet School. First ballet reviews published under the pseudonym Iu. Mamontov, while a student at the Faculty of Law at Petrograd University. Lectured on ballet from 1920. Collaborated with D. Shostakovich on the first scenario for the ballet *The Little Mermaid*, 1922–23. Researcher with the Leningrad Institute of Art History, 1922–24 and 1932–61. Taught at the Leningrad Choreographic School, 1932, Prepared in collaboration with others, the manual *Osnovy Kharakternogo Tantsa*, 1934. In collaboration with F. Lopukhov organized, for the first time in ballet history, a department for the training of choreographers. Lectured there on the analysis of ballet performance. Honorary Doctor of the Paris Dance Academy, 1959. Professor at the Choreographic Department of the Leningrad Conservatory from 1962. Consultant for productions of the Academic Theatre of Opera and Ballet, and productions of the experimental company Molodoi Ballet. Published works on the theory and practice of modern choreography. Author of over 400 articles, many in the collection *V Chest' Tantsa*, 1968. Influenced many young choreographers. Died in Leningrad.

Slonimskii, Nikolai Leonidovich (Slonimsky, Nicolas)
27.4.1894– . Musicologist, conductor, teacher, pianist.
Born in St. Petersburg. Studied at the Petersburg Conservatory. Close friend of the Merezhkovskiis and D.V. Filosofov. Emigrated, 1920. Settled in the USA, 1923. Lived first in Boston, then Los Angeles, and later in New York. Compiled *Music Since 1900*, 1937. Editor of Baker's *Biographical Dictionary of Musicians*, 1958 (with supplements, 1965, 1971). Editor of Thompson's music dictionaries, and of the American music section of the *Enyclopaedia Britannica* from 1958. Translated into English *50 Russkikh Pesen ot Glinki do Shostakovicha*, NY, 1951. Visited the USSR, 1962. Other works include *Music of Latin America*, Buenos Aires, 1945, *Lexicon of Musical Invective*, 1953, and *Perfect Pitch: a Life Story*, OUP, 1988. Appeared at the Almeida Theatre in London, July 1988.

Slonimskii, Sergei Mikhailovich
12.8.1932– . Composer, musicologist.
Graduated from the Leningrad Conservatory, composition class, 1955. Pupil of O. Evlakhov. Graduated from the piano class, 1956. Pupil of V. Nilsen. Author of musicological works and original compositions, and choreographic miniatures, such as *Prokhodiashchiaia Krasotka* and *Favn i Nimfa*, both 1964, *Tri Gratsii*, 1970, and a ballet scene for *Master i Margarita : Velikii bal u Satany* (not produced).

Slonov, Iurii Mikhailovich
14.7.1906– . Composer.
Born in Moscow. Son of Mikhail Slonov. Author of 5 operettas, over 300 songs, and works for theatre, cinema and radio. Lives in Moscow.

Slonov, Mikhail Akimovich
16.11.1869–11.2.1930. Composer.
Born in Khar'kov. Became close to S.

Rakhmaninov and F. Chaliapin. Edited a collection entitled *70 Arii i Romansov* (performed by Chaliapin). Recorded Chaliapin's performance *Nochen'ka i Dubinushka*. Wrote songs especially for Chaliapin, such as *Akh Ty Solntse Krasnoe* and *Proshchal'noe Slovo*. One of the first composers of revolutionary songs after 1917, including *Pervomaiskii Gimn*. Died in Moscow.

Slutskaia, Vera Kliment'evna (Bronislavovna, Berta)
17.9.1874–12.11.1917. Revolutionary.
Born near Tsarskoe Selo, now Pushkin, Leningrad Oblast', into a lower middle-class family. Trained as a dentist. Joined the revolutionary movement, 1898. Member of the BUND Party, 1901, and of the SD Party, 1902. Took part in the 1905–07 Revolution in Minsk and Petersburg. Joined the Bolsheviks, 1907. Delegate of the 5th Congress of the RSDRP, 1907. Party worker in Petersburg, 1913. Several arrests and exile, 1914. Member of the Petersburg Cttee., Feb. 1917. Delegate of the 6th Congress RSDRP. Took part in the October Revolution 1917. Killed during the Kerenskii-Krasnov revolt, Nov. 1917, while transporting medical supplies to the Reds.
See: *Zhenshchiny Russkoi Revolutsii*, Moscow, 1968.

Slutskii, Anton Iosifovich
1884–24.4.1918. Revolutionary.
Born in Warsaw. Joined the revolutionary movement, 1905. Several arrests and exiles. After the February Revolution 1917, party worker at the Obukhovskii Factory, Petrograd. Took part in the October Revolution 1917 in Petrograd. Delegate of the 6th Congress of the RSDRP. Member of the VTSIK. From Mar. 1918, Chairman of the Soviet of People's Commissars in the Crimea (Republic of Tavrida). Executed near Alushta by the Whites.

Slutskii, Boris Abramovich
7.5.1919– . Poet.
Born in Slaviansk. Graduated from the M. Gorkii Literary Institute, Moscow, 1941. Joined the Communist Party, 1943. Participant in WWII.

First book, *Pamiat'*, 1957. Became a famous poet in the late 1950s.
Works: *Vremia*, 1959; *Segodnia I Vchera*, 1961; *Godovaia Strelka*, 1971.
See: I. Erenburg, 'O Stikhakh Borisa Slutskogo' (About Boris Slutskii's Poetry), *Literaturnaia Gazeta*, 28 July 1956.

Slutskii, Evgenii Evgen'evich
19.4.1880–10.3.1948. Mathematician, economist.
Born in the village of Novoe, Iaroslavl' Oblast'. Studied at Kiev University, 1901–02, then at Munich Polytechnic, 1902–05. Graduated in law from Kiev University, 1911. Received a gold medal diploma. Taught at the Kiev Commercial Institute, 1913. Worked at the Central Statistics Directorate, 1926. Taught at Moscow University from 1934. Taught at the Mathematics Institute of the Academy of Sciences from 1938. Many scientific works. Died in Moscow.
See: A. Kolmogorov, *Evgenii Evgen'evich Slutskii, Uspekhi Matematicheskikh Nauk*, 1948.

Slutskii, Mikhail Iakovlevich
19.7.1907–23.6.1959. Documentary film-maker.
Graduated from the GIK (later the VGIK), 1932. Took part in filming Stalin's industrialization campaign and its achievements in the 1930s, working with Roman Karmen on these projects. 3 Stalin Prizes. Worked at the Ukrainian Documentary Studio, 1947–56. After Stalin's death, made a feature film with M. Bilinskii and K. Mints, *V Odin Prekrasnyi Den'*.

Smakha, Mikhail (Smaha, Mykola)
27.8.1938–25.3.1981. Athlete.
Ukrainian. Honoured Master of Sports (track and field athletics). Many times USSR and Ukrainian champion. Bronze medal-winner at the XIXth Olympic Games.

Smetanin
1947–1986. Diplomat, security officer.
Soviet security officer working as a diplomat in Portugal in the 1970s.

Arrested, tried in secret, and probably shot. As far as is known, accused of revealing the Soviet spy network in Portugal to the CIA. His wife Natalia, who was arrested with him, was sentenced to 5 years in the Gulag.

Smetanina, Raisa Petrovna
29.2.1952– . Athlete.
Born in the Komi ASSR. Honoured Master of Sports (skiing), 1976. With Syktyvkar Urozhai. Graduated from the Syktyvkar Pedagogical High School, 1970. Schoolmaster. USSR champion, 1974 and 1976–77 at various distances. World champion, 1974 and 1978. Olympic champion, 1976 (10 km race).

Smidovich, Petr Germogenovich
19.5.1874–16.4.1935. Revolutionary.
Born in Rogachev, now Gomel' Oblast', into a noble family. Studied at Moscow University. In 1894, expelled for revolutionary activity. Exiled to Tula. In 1895, went abroad. Graduated from the Paris Higher Electrotechnical School. Worked as an engineer in Belgium. Member of the Belgian Labour Party. In 1898, returned to Russia. Revolutionary in Petersburg. In 1900, arrested and deported. From 1902, an agent of Lenin's Iskra. Secretly returned to Russia, 1903. One of the organizers of Iskra's distribution and printing in Uman'. Member of the Sredne-Uralsk (1903), Severnyi (1904), and Baku and Tula (1905) RSDRP Cttees. From 1908, member of the Moscow RSDRP Cttee. Arrested and exiled to Vologda Gouvt., 1908. Party worker in Kaluga, then in Moscow, 1910. Senior party posts during the October Revolution 1917. 1918–19, member of MOSSOVET, then Sovnarkhoz. In 1920, member of the Soviet delegation during peace negotiations with Poland. Took part in the suppression of the Antonov and Kronstadt anti-Bolshevik revolts. Member of the VTSIK, 1921. Various party posts. Died in Moscow. Buried at the Kremlin wall on Red Square.

Smirnov, Aleksandr Fedorovich
12.8.1886–6.5.1969. Colonel.
Son of a nobleman. Infantry officer, 1907. Fought in WWI on the Rumanian front. Highly decorated for

bravery. Took part in the Civil War, fighting against the Red Army. Emigrated in the 1920s, and settled in Paris. Worked at the Citroen factory for 36 years. Chairman of the Russian emigré association, the Grenadier Society Abroad. Died in Paris.

Smirnov, Andrei Kirillovich
1895–1941. Lt.-general.
Took part in WWI as a lieutenant. Joined the Red Army, 1918. Took part in the Civil War as a regiment commander, 1921. Joined the Bolshevik Party, 1927. Graduated from the Frunze Military Academy, 1927. Head of the Administration of Higher Military Educational Establishments, and Inspector of Soviet Infantry. Commander of the Khar'kov military district. Army commander during WWII. Fell in action.

Smirnov, Boris Fedorovich
17.4.1912– . Musicologist, composer.
Born in St. Petersburg. Works: *Iskusstvo Vladimirskikh Rozhechnikov*, Moscow, 1959; *Skripichnye Narodnye Naigryshi*, Moscow 1961; *Iskusstvo Sel'skikh Garmonistov*, Moscow, 1962; *Muzykal'naia Kul'tura Mongolii*, Moscow, 1963.

Smirnov, Dmitrii Alekseevich
19.12.1882–27.4.1944. Singer.
Born in Moscow. Pupil of K. Krzhizhanovskii and A. Dodonov. Soloist at the Bolshoi Theatre, 1904–22. Emigrated, 1922. Gave concert tours of the USSR in 1926 and 1928. Died in Riga.

Smirnov, Dmitrii Nikolaevich
1848?–1928. Revolutionary.
Born in the village of Smolnitsy near Galich, Kostroma Gouvt., into a peasant family. Worker in Petersburg from 1861. In 1873, joined the narodniki. In 1874, arrested and tried in the famous 'Trial of the 193'. Acquitted but remained on the police blacklist. From 1876, member of illegal workers' cells, later member of the Northern Union of Russian Workers. Arrested at the end of 1876, and exiled. Emigrated to Bulgaria, 1885. Returned to Russia, 1890. Worker in Tula. Gave up revolutionary activity.

Smirnov, Efim Ivanovich
1904– . Politician, medical officer.
Graduated from the Medical Academy, 1932, and from the Frunze Military Academy, 1938. During WWII, head of the Medical-Sanitary Administration of the Armed Forces. After WWII, Minister of National Health, 1947–53. Editor of a special 35-volume series of reports on the medical service during WWII.

Smirnov, Georgii Lukich
1922– . Politician.
Started his career as an activist in the Komsomol, 1942, gradually moved to key party posts in the Cen. Cttee. apparatus, 1957–62. Member of the CPSU, 1943. Graduated from the Volgograd Pedagogical Institute, 1952, and from the CPSU Cen. Cttee. Academy of Social Sciences, 1957. Assistant professor, Doctor of Philosophical Sciences, 1971. Member of the editorial staff of the theoretical organ of the CPSU, *Kommunist*, 1962–65. Posts in the Cen. Cttee., 1965–69. Deputy chief of the Propaganda Department, 1969–74. 1st deputy chief, 1974. Candidate member of the Cen. Cttee., 1976. Gorbachev's aide from 1985. Head of the Marxism-Leninism Institute in Moscow.

Smirnov, Igor' Valentinovich
8.12.1926– . Choreographer.
Born in Saratov. Graduated from the Moscow Choreographic School, 1944 (pupil of N. Tarasov). Choreographer with the operatic studio of the Moscow Conservatory, 1944–99, and with the GITIS, 1951. Taught choreography in Romania, 1953–54, and in Japan, 1963–64. Chief choreographer with the Musical Theatre of the Karelian ASSR in Petrozavodsk, 1958–60, 1962 and 1964–67. With the Stanislavskii and Nemirovich-Danchenko Theatre, 1960–61. His productions in Petrozavodsk marked the introduction of a professional theatre of ballet in Karelia. Head of the choreography class at the Moscow Institute for Culture. Contributes to periodicals on questions of choreography. Author of *Tantsuet Kareliia*, 1977.

Smirnov, Il'ia Kornilovich
1887–1964. Lt.-general.
On active service during WWI. Joined the Red Army, 1918, and the Bolshevik Party, 1919. Graduated from the Frunze Military Academy, 1934. Took part in WWII on different fronts.

Smirnov, Ivan Fedorovich (party name – Lastochkin)
15.1.1885–4.1919. Revolutionary.
Born in Moscow. Tailor by profession. Joined the Bolsheviks in 1906. Party worker in Moscow, Samara (now Kuibyshev), Rostov-on-Don, Tsaritsyn (now Volgograd). From 1912, party worker in the Ukraine (Kiev, Khar'kov, Odessa). Organizer of illegal party cells. Several short arrests. In 1914, exiled to Siberia. After the February Revolution 1917, party post in Kiev. From 1918, illegal party work in Odessa. Chairman of an underground party cttee. in the Ukraine. One of the organizers of the Inostrannaia Kollegia in charge of agitation and propaganda among the armies of the Allies during the Civil War. Chairman of the Odessa Revkom. Member of the VTSIK. Arrested, Mar. 1919, by the Whites and executed in Odessa.

Smirnov, Konstantin Nikolaevich
1899–1981. Lt.-general.
Joined the Red Army, 1918. Took part in the Civil War. Educated at a pilots' school, 1921. High air force command posts before and during WWII. Commander of Airborne Troops, 1946–51.

Smirnov, Lev Nikolaevich
21.6.1911– . Party official, state security officer.
Born in Petersburg. Aged 23, joined the NKVD under Iagoda. Worked in State Security under Ezhov and Beria. Whether he graduated in law is unconfirmed. In 1945, joined the Communist Party. Sent to the Nuremberg Trials, 1945–46, as the USSR's Assistant to the Main Prosecutor. During the Tokyo Trials, 1946–48, acted in the same capacity. Deputy Chairman of the Supreme Court of the USSR, 1957–62. Chairman of the Supreme Court of the RSFSR, 1962–72. President of the Association of Soviet Lawyers from 1964. Member of the Council of the International Association of Lawyers Democrats at the same time (appointed by the Soviet Government). Highly decorated.

Smirnov, Nikolai Ivanovich
1917– . Admiral.
Joined the Red Navy, 1937. During WWII, submarine commander in the Pacific and the Black Sea. 1st Deputy Commander of the Black Sea fleet, 1960. Commander of the Pacific fleet, 1969. 1st Deputy Commander of the Navy, 1974. Non-voting member of the Cen. Cttee. of the CPSU, 1971–76.

Smirnov, Nikolai Konstantinovich
1902–1973. Vice-admiral.
Joined the Red Navy, 1923. Graduated from the Military Political Academy, 1933. Deputy head of the Political Administration of the Navy before WWII. Took part in WWII as a political officer in the Baltic fleet. Party functionary after the war.

Smirnov, Petr Aleksandrovich
1897–1938. Political officer.
Joined the Bolshevik Party, 1917, and the Red Army, 1918. Political commissar during the Civil War. Head of the Political Administration of the Baltic fleet, 1926–37, and of the Red Army, June 1937. Deputy Minister of Defence, Oct. 1937. Navy Minister, Jan. 1938. Liquidated by Stalin.

Smirnov, Viktor Viktorovich (Smirnov-Golovanov)
6.9.1934– . Choreographer, film director.
Born in Moscow. Graduated from the Moscow Choreographic School. Pupil of N. Tarasov. With the Bolshoi Theatre, 1953–74. Chief choreographer with the Odessa Theatre of Opera and Ballet. Debut as scenario-writer and choreographer, 1968. Produced, with N. Ryzhenko, the ballet film *Romeo and Juliet*, which was shown at International Festivals of Television Films in Monte Carlo and Adelaide. New productions of the classical ballets *The Sleeping Beauty* and *Don Quixote*

at the Odessa Theatre of Opera and Ballet.

Smirnov, Vitalii Georgievich
14.2.1935– . Sports and party official.
Born in Khabarovsk. Member of the CPSU from 1960. Chairman of the USSR Federation of Water Polo, 1962–70. Graduated from the Moscow Institute of Physical Culture, 1968, then from the Moscow Higher Party School of the Cen. Cttee., 1975. 1st Deputy Chairman of the USSR Sports Cttee., 1970–77. Deputy Chairman of the USSR Olympic Cttee. from 1970. Member of the Executive Cttee. of the Moscow Olympic Cttee. from 1974. Chairman of the Organizing Cttee. of Olimpiada-80 from 1975.

Smirnov-Sokolskii, Nikolai Pavlovich (real name – Smirnov)
17.3.1898–13.1.1962. Show-business artist, writer, bibliophile.
Born in Moscow. Studied at a commercial school. Worked as a bookseller, then as a reporter. From 1915, actor in summer theatres and in the Odeon Theatre of Miniatures in Moscow. Also remembered as a witty compère at various concert halls. Famous book collector. His private library contained rarities of the 18th century, underground and censored editions. Wrote on A. Radishchev and A. Pushkin. His books *Rasskazy O Knigakh*, Moscow, 1959, and *Moia Biblioteka*, 2 vols, Moscow, 1963, were best-sellers at the time of publication. Died in Moscow.

Smirnova, Elena Aleksandrovna
1888–15.1.1934. Ballerina.
Born in Petersburg. Wife of the ballet dancer B. Romanov. Appeared with the Mariinskii Theatre while still a student. Pupil of M. Fokin. With the Mariinskii Theatre, 1906–20. Made many guest appearances in Moscow, Siberia, and also in Paris, London, New York, and Tokyo. Took part in the first Russian Season in Paris, 1909. Emigrated. Lived abroad from 1920. Directed, with her husband, the Russian Romantic Ballet Company in Berlin. Taught in Buenos Aires from 1928. Died in Buenos Aires.

Smirnova, Margarita Vladimirovna (Giriavenko)
12.3.1933– . Ballerina.
Born in Moscow. Graduated from the Moscow Choreographic School. Pupil of M. Kozhukhova and G. Petrova. With the Bolshoi Theatre, 1951–71. Taught from 1954. Teacher and coach in Bucharest, at the Tokyo ballet school, in Tashkent, in Petrozavodsk, and in Kazan'. Lecturer in choreography at the Moscow Institute of Culture from 1967, and with the GITIS from 1979.

Smit-Falkner, Maria Natanovna (Smith-Falkner, Mary)
16.2.1878–7.3.1968. Economist.
Born in Taganrog, into a wealthy Jewish family. Her parents sent her to be educated in England. Graduated from London University as an economist in 1905. Married a Smith, then a Falkner. Divorced. Returned to Russia. In 1918, joined the Communist Party. From 1919, served in the Red Army on the Southern front. In 1921, taught at Moscow University, then at the Plekhanov Moscow Institute of People's Management, and later at the Oil Institute. Corresponding member of the USSR Academy of Sciences, 1939. Party administrative posts in GOSPLAN and at the Institute of Economics of the Academy of Sciences. Published many works on the international capitalist economy, and especially on Britain's capitalist system. Died in Moscow.

Smoktunovskii, Innokentii Mikhailovich
18.3.1925– . Film and theatre actor.
The most celebrated Russian actor in the Soviet Union for his roles of Hamlet and adaptations of Chekhov and Dostoevskii. Studied at the Studio of Krasnoiarsk Pushkin Theatre. A soldier during WWII. After the war, turned down by a theatre due to his 'lack of talent'. Worked in theatres in Norilsk in the Polar Circle, Makhach-Kala, Volgograd and Moscow. Became famous for his portrayal of Prince Myshkin in a stage adaptation of Dostoevskii's *Idiot*. First film role in Mikhail Rom's *The Murder in Dante Street* in 1956. Became famous in *An Unposted*

Letter, directed by Mikhail Kalatozov and starring Tatiana Samoilova. Films of note: *Nine Days of One Year* (director M. Romm, 1962), *Chaikovskii* (director Igor Talankin, 1970), *Crime and Punishment* (director Lev Kulidzhanov, 1970), *Uncle Vanya* (director Andron Mikhalkov-Konchalovskii, 1971), *A Lovers' Romance* (director Andron Mikhalkov-Konchalovskii, 1975). Became internationally known as the Russian Hamlet in the film of the same title made in 1964 by the distinguished director Grigorii Kozintsev. Has worked with every director of note. Vasiliev Brothers' State Prize, 1971. People's Artist of the USSR, 1974.

Smoleeva, Nina Nikolaevna
28.3.1948– . Athlete.
Born in Volkhov, Leningrad Oblast'. Honoured Master of Sports, (volleyball), 1968. From 1969, with Moscow Dynamo. Sports instructor. Graduated from the Moscow Oblast' Institute of Physical Culture, 1974. European champion, 1967, 1971 and 1975. World champion, 1970. Olympic champion, 1968 and 1972. USSR champion, 1970–73 and 1975–77.

Smolenskii, Vladimir Alekseevich
7.1901–8.11.1961. Poet.
Emigrated after the Civil War. Educated at the Russian High School in Paris. Became a well-known representative of the Parizhskaia Nota in the 1930s. Close to Z. Gippius and D. Merezhkovskii (Gippius's secretary). Collected works published in 1957. Died in France.

Smolich, Nikolai Vasil'evich
24.6.1888–31.7.1969. Stage director.
Born in St. Petersburg. Studied at Petersburg University, 1905–08. Actor at the Aleksandrinskii Theatre, 1911–17. Director from 1916. Director of the State Theatre of Opera and Ballet (Mariinskii) from 1922 (in 1935, the name was changed to the Kirov Opera and Ballet Theatre). Staged many Western classical operas – *La Traviata*, *Les Huguenots*, and *Faust*. Artistic director of the Leningrad Malyi Opera Theatre, 1924–30. Staged *Nos*, and *Lady Macbeth of Mtsensk (Katerina Izmailova)* by Dmitrii Shostakovich, 1934. Director, then chief director of the Bolshoi Theatre, 1930–36, 1947–48. Artistic

director and director of the Shevchenko Opera and Ballet Theatre, Kiev, 1938–47. Taught at the Moscow Conservatory, 1961–63. Died in Moscow.

Smol'tsov, Ivan Vasil'evich
5.9.1892–8.4.1968. Ballet dancer, choreographer.
Born in Moscow. Brother of the dancer V. V. Smol'tsov. Graduated from the Moscow Theatrical School. Pupil of N. Domashev. With the Bolshoi Theatre, 1910–53. One of the leading Soviet classical dancers. Taught at the Moscow Choreographic School from 1920. Among his pupils were Asaf Messerer and Mikhail Gabovich. Choreographer and coach with the Bolshoi Theatre from 1934. Produced, in collaboration with V. Kudriavtseva, the ballet *Giselle* at the Moscow ballet theatre Ostrov Tantsa, 1939. Conducted many performances with a branch of the Bolshoi Theatre during WWII. Died in Moscow.

Smol'tsov, Viktor Vasil'evich
8.2.1900–7.2.1976. Ballet dancer, choreographer.
Born in Moscow. Brother of the ballet dancer I. V. Smol'tsov. Graduated from the Moscow Choreographic School, 1918. Pupil of N. Domashev and V. Tikhomirov. Debut with the Bolshoi Theatre in *The Little Hunchbacked Horse*. Among his best roles were Petrushka, and Ivanushka in *The Little Hunchbacked Horse*. Large mime repertoire, including Don Quixote, and Friar Laurence in *Romeo and Juliet*. Partnered A. Balashova on a European tour, Anna Pavlova in Paris, 1922, and L. Bank in Paris, Berlin and Riga. Retained an academic style in classical dance. Taught at the Moscow Choreographic School from 1925, and at the Moscow Art Ballet under V. Kriger, 1931–32. Artistic director, choreographer and teacher in Baku, 1934–35.

Smorgacheva, Liudmila Ivanovna
29.11.1950–   . Ballerina.
Graduated from the Kiev Choreographic School. Pupil of Z. Serkova. With the Shevchenko Theatre. State Prize of the USSR, 1976. Prize winner at the International Ballet Competition, Tokyo, 1978.

Smushkevich, Iakov Vladimirovich
1902–1941. Lt.-general.
Joined the Red Army and the Bolshevik Party, 1918. Took part in the Civil War. Educated at a pilot's school, 1932. Fighter pilot in the Spanish Civil War, 1936–39. Later served at Khalkin Gol against the Japanese, 1939. Deputy Commander of the Air Force, 1937, and Commander, Nov. 1939. Non-voting member of the Cen. Cttee. of the VKP, 1939.

Smyslov, Vasilii Vasil'evich
24.3.1921–   . Chess player, grandmaster.
Born in Moscow. At the age of 17, chess champion of the City of Moscow. Second place in the 1948 World Championship. World champion in 1957–58. In 1988, ranked number 20 in the chess world.

Snechkus, Antanas Iuozovich
1903–1974. Politician.
Joined the Bolshevik Party, 1920. Underground leader of communists in independent Lithuania before WWII. 1st Secretary of the Cen. Cttee. of the Lithuanian CP, 1936–39 and 1940–74. During WWII, in charge of communist partisans in Lithuania. Non-voting member of the Cen. Cttee. of the CPSU, 1941, and full member, 1972. Responsible for introducing Stalinism in his homeland during the Soviet occupation before WWII, and the re-Stalinization after the war.

Snegirev, Gelii Ivanovich
1927–1978. Journalist, human rights campaigner.
Born in Khar'kov. Educated at the Khar'kov Theatre Institute. Worked in a Kiev newsreel studio. Involved in the human rights movement as a Ukrainian nationalist. Wrote memoirs describing the involvement of his mother in the purges in the Ukraine in the 1930s. Expelled from the party, 1977. Arrested, and died in prison of a heart attack.

Snesarev, Andrei Evgen'evich
13.12.1865–4.12.1937. Military commander, orientalist.
Born in Staraia Kalitva, Voronezh Oblast'. Son of an Orthodox priest. Graduated from Moscow University in mathematics, 1888, then from the Moscow Conservatory. Knew 14 languages. Graduated from Moscow Infantry School, 1890, then from the Academy of the General Staff, 1899. Served in Turkestan. Became interested in the Middle East and Far East. Wrote travel diaries on Afghanistan, Tibet and India. Served in the General Staff from 1904, taught military geography at military schools. Chief-of-staff of a Cossack Division from 1910. Commander of a regiment, brigade, then a division during WWI. In Sep. 1917, Lt.-general and Commander of the 9th Army Corps. In May 1918, joined the Red Army. Commander of the Northern-Caucasian military district, June-July 1918. From Mar. 1919, Commander of the Belorussian-Lithuanian Army. From Aug. 1919–July 1921, head of the Academy of the General Staff. From 1921–30, rector and professor at the Institute of Oriental Studies, Moscow. Professor at the Air Force Academy, 1924, and at the Military-Political Academy from 1926. Accused of being a member of a monarchist group. Victim of Stalin's purges. Shot in Moscow.

Snetkova, Evgenia Petrovna (Vecheslova)
4.7.1882–16.11.1961. Ballerina, ballet teacher.
Born in Petersburg. Graduated from the Petersburg Theatre School. Pupil of Enrico Cecchetti. With the Mariinskii Theatre from 1900. First appearance with the corps de ballet. Small solo roles before 1922. Taught classical dancing in private studios in Petrograd, and at A. Volynskii's School of Russian Ballet, 1917–20. Taught the junior classes at the Leningrad Choreographic School, 1920–51. Produced performances for the School theatre as well as concert performances. Among her pupils were G. Komleva, A. Osipenko, N. Dudinskaia, S. Koren', and K. Sergeev. Died in Leningrad.

Snezhnevskii, Andrei Vladimirovich
20.5.1904–   . Psychiatrist, state medical official.
Born in Kostroma. Graduated from

Kazan' University in psychiatry, 1925. Director and chief doctor at the V. Serbskii Institute of Criminal Psychiatry, Moscow, 1950–51. Dean of the Psychiatry Department of the Institute for the Improvement of Medical Qualifications, Moscow, 1951–64; at the same time Director of the Institute of Psychiatry of the Academy of Medical Sciences. In his official capacity, responsible for putting many sane people into psychiatric institutions for their political views. His connections with the KGB have been well documented by many Western and Russian researchers. Honorary member of the International Association of Psychiatrists from 1972 and at one time foreign member of the Royal College of Psychiatry (UK). Under international pressure and following many protests, resigned. Retired and lives in Moscow.

Sobchenko, Viacheslav Georgievich
18.4.1949–   . Athlete.
Born in Moscow. International Class Master of Sports (water polo), 1972. Graduated from the Likhachev Higher Technical School, 1973. From 1975, with the Central Sports Club of the Navy. Member of the CPSU from 1978. Olympic champion, 1972. USSR champion, 1975–78.

Sobennikov, Petr Petrovich
1894–1960. Lt.-general.
Joined the Red Army, 1918. Took part in the Civil War. Joined the Bolshevik Party, 1940. Several high command posts during WWII. Head of the Vystrel Courses, 1955–59.

Sobeshchanskaia, Anna Iosifovna
15.1.1842–5.12.1918. Ballerina, ballet teacher.
While a student at the Moscow Theatre School, appeared with the Bolshoi Theatre. Pupil of K. Blazis. Among her roles was that of the Gitana in Felipe Taglioni's eponymous production. In her later career, developed a realistic style. Appeared as Aspiccia in the *Pharao's Daughter* (choreography by Marius Petipa). Ended her stage career in 1879, and became a teacher of young ballerinas.

Sobinov, Leonid Vital'evich
7.6.1872–14.10.1934. Singer (tenor).
Born in Iaroslavl'. Son of an estate manager. Graduated in law from Moscow University, 1894. Practised as a lawyer, 1895–99. Started singing as a law student in the university chorus. Studied simultaneously at the musical-dramatic college of the Moscow Philharmonic Society, 1892–97. Actor with an Italian opera group. In 1897, made his debut at the Moscow Bolshoi in Rubenstein's *Demon*. Worked with the Mariinskii Opera House in St. Petersburg, at La Scala and all over Europe. 1917–18, director of the Bolshoi Theatre. One of the major talents of the Russian classical school of singing. Emigrated in 1919. Died in Riga. Was later reburied in Moscow.

Sobol', Aleksandr Mikhailovich
13.1.1909–   . Ballet dancer, choreographer, ballet teacher.
Born in Belostok. Graduated from the Lysenko Ballet Studio. Pupil of A. Vil'tzak and Ia. Romanovskii. Additional training at the Moscow Choreographic School, 1933. Pupil of V. Semenov and A. Monakhov. With the Lysenko Theatre, 1925–35, the Shevchenko Theatre, 1935–37 and 1939–45, the Bolshoi Theatre, 1937–39, and the Stanislavskii and Nemirovich-Danchenko Theatre, 1945–60. Produced *Swan Lake*, in collaboration with N. Konius, for the Warsaw Opera, 1961. Taught at the Warsaw Ballet School, 1960–63, and at the Moscow Choreographic School, 1964–68. Teacher and coach at the Bolshoi Theatre in Lodz, 1968–71 and 1973, and at the Musical Theatre in Szczecin, 1975–77.

Sobol, Andrei (Iulii Mikhailovich)
1888–7.6.1926. Author.
Involved in revolutionary activity from an early age. Member of the Socialist-Zionist Party, 1903–05. Participant in the 1905 Revolution. Sentenced to exile, 1906. In Siberia, joined the SRs, escaped abroad. Returned to Russia, 1914. Took part in literary polemics in the 1920s, at first insisting on the political responsibility of the writer, later stressing the writer's independence. Committed suicide.
Works: *Liudi Prokhozhie*, 1923; *Chel-*

ovek Za Bortom, 1924; *Sobranie Sochinenii*, 4 vols., Moscow–Leningrad, 1926.

Sobolev, Aleksandr Vasil'evich
1868–1920. Major-general.
Divisional commander during WWI. Joined the Red Army, 1918. During the Civil War, taken prisoner by the Whites and executed.

Sofinskii, Vsevolod Nikolaevich
1924–   . Diplomat, intelligence officer.
In the Diplomatic Service from 1963. Embassy counsellor (cultural affairs) at the USSR Embassy in London, 1963–69. Senior posts at the Ministry of Foreign Affairs, Moscow, 1969–71. Head of the Department of Cultural Relations with Foreign Countries, 1971–73. Head of the Press Department at the Ministry of Foreign Affairs, 1973–79. Ambassador to New Zealand and Tonga, also to Western Samoa from Jan. 1979. Expelled from New Zealand in 1982 having been caught by the Security Intelligence Service passing money to the Moscow-aligned Socialist Unity Party.

Sofronitskii, Vladimir Vladimirovich
8.5.1901–29.8.1961. Pianist.
Born in Petersburg. Studied in Warsaw under A. Mikhailovskii. Also studied at the Petrograd Conversatory under L. Nikolaev. Solo concerts in Leningrad, Moscow, Warsaw and Paris. Known for his 12 historical concerts. From 1936–42, professor at the Leningrad Conservatory. 1942–61, professor at the Moscow Conservatory. Died in Moscow.

Sofronov, Georgii Pavlovich
1893–1973. Lt.-general.
Joined the Bolshevik Party, 1917, and the Red Army, 1918. Took part in the Civil War. Graduated from the Frunze Military Academy, 1935. Several high command posts during WWII. Professor at the Academy of the General Staff, 1946–53.

Sokal'skii, Vladimir Ivanovich
6.5.1863–1919. Composer, pianist, music critic.
Born in Heidelberg. Nephew of the Ukrainian composer Petr Sokal'skii (1832–87). Appeared in the Khar'kov musical press under the pen-name

Don Diez, 1896–1911. Author of the children's opera *Repka*, produced in 1900. Also wrote symphonic music, suites, music for piano, and songs using Russian and Ukrainian lyrics. Died in Sevastopol.

Sokol'nikov, Grigorii Iakovlevich (real name – Brilliant)
1888–1939. Politician.
Bolshevik since 1905, but opposed Lenin's intolerance towards the Mensheviks. One of the first members of the Politburo, Feb. 1917. Responsible for the nationalization of the banks after Oct. 1917. Chairman of the third Soviet peace delegation in 1918, signed the Brest-Litovsk peace treaty with Germany. Political Commissar with the Red Army during the Civil War. People's Commissar of Finance, 1921–26. Took part in the new opposition at the end of the 1920s. In charge of the oil industry, 1926–29. Ambassador to Britain, 1929–32. In 1936, arrested, tried and sentenced to 10 years imprisonment. Re-arrested, tried and shot.

Sokolov, Arkadii Andreevich
26.4.1937– . Ballet critic.
Graduated from the Leningrad State Institute for Theatre, Music and Cinematography, 1967. Studied for a higher degree at the same institute, 1970. Began writing in 1963, mainly on problems of professional ballet and the art of folk dancing. Ballet critic for several newspapers, and author of several books.

Sokolov, Dmitrii Nikolaevich
1882?–after 1960. Lawyer.
In the autumn of 1918, appointed by Admiral Kolchak to investigate the circumstances of the murder of the Tsar and his family at Ekaterinburg. Produced a detailed report, later wrote a book on this subject. Emigrated after the Civil War.

Sokolov, Iurii K.
1935?–1982. Store manager.
In the 1970s, director of the Moscow Gastronom Number 1 on Gorkii Street (formerly the millionaire Eliseev's Food Store, nationalized after Oct. 1917). Arrested and accused of corruption and stealing food (caviar etc) worth millions of roubles. Also involved in gold and currency dealings. Executed after his sensational trial.

Sokolov, Nikolai Aleksandrovich (Kukryniksy)
1903– . Artist.
Born in Rybinsk. Studied at Rybinsk Gorproletkult Art Studio, 1920–23, and in the Graphics Faculty of the VKHUTEIN, Moscow, 1923–29. From 1924, member of the Kukryniksy (a trio of political artists whose other members are M. Kupriianov and P. Krylov), drawing political cartoons for newspapers and magazines. Also worked as a portrait and landscape painter. Exhibited with the Kukryniksy from 1932. Personal exhibitions from 1932 in Moscow, Bucharest and Sofia.

Sokolov, Nikolai Aleksandrovich
26.3.1859–27.3.1922. Composer.
Born in Petersburg. Taught at the Pevcheskaia Kapella, 1886–1921. From 1908, professor at the Petersburg Conservatory. Member of the Beliaevskii Kruzhok. Wrote 2 ballets based on H. C. Andersen stories. Also wrote pieces for piano and violin, and symphonies. Died in Petrograd.

Sokolov, Nikolai Dmitrievich
1870–1928. Lawyer, politician.
Member of the Menshevik Party. In Mar. 1917, secretary of the Executive Cttee. of the Petrograd Soviet. Edited the *Order No. 1*, which started the dissolution of the Russian Army by removing most discipline requirements. Appointed senator by the Provisional Government. Law adviser to the Soviet government after Oct. 1917.

Sokolov, Nikolai Sergeevich
25.6.1912– . Ballet dancer, producer.
Born in Krasnodar. Graduated from the Leningrad Choreographic School. Pupil of S. Petrov and V. Ponomarev. With the Tbilisi Theatre of Opera and Ballet, 1930–31, and the Malyi Theatre, Leningrad, 1931–62. Directed the ballet company of the Malyi Theatre, Leningrad, 1963–75.

Sokolov, Oleg Germanovich
5.10.1936– . Ballet dancer.
Born in Leningrad. Graduated from the Leningrad Choreographic School. Pupil of B. Shavrov. With the Kirov Theatre, 1954–76. Appeared in productions by V. Chabukiani, R. Zakharov and F. Lopukhov. Teacher at the Leningrad Choreographic School from 1964. State Prize, 1970.

Sokolov, Sasha (Aleksandr Vsevolodovich)
1943– . Author.
Born in Ottawa. Son of a Soviet diplomat. Graduated in journalism from Moscow University. In conflict with the Soviet authorities. Left the USSR in 1975 with his Austrian wife. Settled in Canada, later moved to the USA. Became famous after the publication of his first book, *Shkola Dlia Durakov* (Ardis, USA, 1976), which has since been translated into many languages. This and the follow-up, *Mezhdu Sobakoi i Volkom*, (Ardis, 1979), are both marked by their elegance of style. He is considered to be one of the new talents of modern Russian literature. Lives in Vermont, USA.

Sokolov, Sergei Aleksandrovich (Krechetov)
1876–1936. Author, publisher.
Member of symbolist circles before WWI, owner of the symbolist publishing house Grif, 1903–13. During WWI, at the front, taken prisoner by the Germans, in POW camps together with Tukhachevskii. During the Civil War, joined the Whites, worked in the propaganda department of Denikin's army, 1919. Emigrated, 1920, settled in Paris. Moved to Berlin, 1922, founded the publishing house Mednyi Vsadnik. After the Nazis came to power, fled to France. Died in Paris.

Sokolov, Sergei Leonidovich
1.7.1911– . Marshal.
Born in Evpatoria in the Crimea. Son of a clerk. Joined the army, 1932, and the Communist Party, 1937. Graduated from the Military Academy for Armoured and Mechanized Troops, 1947, then from the General Staff Military Academy, 1951. During WWII, chief-of-staff of a regi-

ment, commander of armoured and mechanized troops on the Karelian front. Chief-of-staff, then 1st deputy commander of various military districts, 1955–65. Commander of the Leningrad military district, 1965–67. Candidate member, 1966, full member of the Cen. Cttee., 1968. From 1967, 1st Deputy Minister of Defence. Marshal, 1968. From the end of 1984, Soviet Defence Minister and a non-voting member of the Politburo. In June 1987, removed and replaced by General Dimitrii Iazov after the violation of Soviet air space by the 19-year-old West German Matthias Rust, who landed his Cessna aircraft near the Kremlin.

Sokolov, Valer'ian Sergeevich
30.8.1946–   . Athlete.
Born in the Chuvash ASSR. Honoured Master of Sports (boxing), 1968. With Cheboksary Dynamo. Member of the CPSU from 1970. Graduated from the Chuvash Agricultural Institute, 1972. Mechanical engineer. USSR champion, 1968–69, 1971 and 1973. Olympic champion, 1968.

Sokolov, Vladislav Gennad'evich
28.12.1908–   . Choir conductor.
Born in Rybinsk, Iaroslavl' Gouvt. Pupil of G. Dmitrevskii. From 1936, conductor of the Children's Choir of the Institute of Artistic Education attached to the Academy of Pedagogical Sciences. Conductor of the Moscow State Choir from 1956. Professor at the Moscow Conservatory. Author of *Rabota s Khorom*, Moscow, 1959.

Sokolov-Mikitov, Ivan Sergeevich
29.5.1892–20.2.1975. Author, bibliophile.
Born near Kaluga. In 1916, published his first work. Emigrated after the 1917 Revolution. Lived in Germany and France. In 1922, returned to the Soviet Union. Known as a book collector. Died in Moscow. Author of *Chizhikova Lavra* (1926, about his life as an emigré), and *Detstvo*, 1931–53.
See: Roman Gul, *Ia Unes Rossiiu*, USA, 1984.

Sokolov-Skalia, Pavel Petrovich
3.7.1899–3.8.1961. Artist.
Born in Strel'na, near Leningrad. Studied at the Mashkov Art School in Moscow, 1914–18. Chairman of the Bytie Society, 1920. Graduated from the Moscow VKHUTEMAS, 1922. Member of the AKHRR from 1926. Taught at the Grekov Studio of War Painters, 1935–41. Artistic director of Okna TASS, 1941–45. Official artist. Performed many state political duties. Responsible for political propaganda in art. Stalin Prize in 1942. Member of the party from 1952.

Sokolova, Evgenia Pavlovna
1.12.1850–2.8.1925. Ballerina.
Born in Petersburg. As a student at the Petersburg Theatre School appeared with the Petersburg Bolshoi Theatre in ballets by Cesare Pugni. Pupil of L. Ivanov, M. Petipa and Kh. Ioganson. Appeared in the ballet *Amur Blagodetel'*, specially created for her by Marius Petipa. With the Mariinskii Theatre from 1869. First major role: Esmeralda, 1870. Left the stage, 1886. Chief coach with the ballet classes at the Mariinskii Theatre, 1902–04. Teacher and coach with the State Theatres, 1920–23. Among her pupils were Matilda Kshesinskaia, Anna Pavlova and Vera Trefilova. Died in Leningrad.

Sokolova, Marina Alekseevna
4.3.1939–   . Stage designer.
Born in Moscow. Graduated from the VGIK, 1963. Worked as an animator. Designed scenery and costumes for plays and operettas. Designed for various ballet theatres including the Kirov, the Malyi, the Stanislavskii and Nemirovich-Danchenko, and the Bolshoi.

Sokolovskii, Nikolai Nikolaevich
3.12.1865–24.1.1921. Violinist, composer.
Pupil of I. Grzhimali (violin). Taught violin at the Moscow Conservatory, 1890–1909. From 1906, professor at the Conservatory. Member of the Viola Quartet of the Moscow branch of the Russkoe Muzykal'noe Obshchestvo. Author of music for violin, and a harmonics manual. Died in Moscow.

Sokolovskii, Vasilii Danilovich
21.7.1897–10.5.1968. Marshal.
Born at Kozliki, near Grodno. Son of a peasant. Joined the Red Army, 1918. Took part in the Civil War as a regimental commander, brigade commander, and divisional chief-of-staff. Graduated from the Military Academy of the Red Army, 1921. Deputy Chief of the General Staff, Feb. 1941. During WWII, gained prominence as Commander of the Western front, 1943–44, and Deputy Commander of the 1st Belorussian front, Apr. 1945. Commander of Soviet Forces in Germany, 1946–49, and 1st Deputy Minister of Defence, 1949. Chief of the General Staff, 1952–60. Member of the Cen. Cttee. of the CPSU, 1952–61, and non-voting member of the Politburo, 1961–68. Highly decorated (8 Orders of Lenin). Died in Moscow. Buried at the Kremlin wall.

Sokolskii, Aleksandr Kuz'mich
1903–1979. Col.-general.
Joined the Red Army, 1921. During WWII, commander of artillery at different fronts. Graduated from the Academy of the General Staff, 1952.

Solin, Lev Lvovich (real name – Kaganovich)
21.5.1923–   . Composer.
Born in Kiev. Moved to Moscow, where he studied at the Conservatory. Author of choral music, including *Pesni o Stepane Razine*. Also composer of music for theatre plays.

Sollertinskii, Ivan Ivanovich
3.12.1902–11.2.1944. Music critic, music historian.
Born in Vitebsk. Lived in Petersburg from 1906. Graduated from Leningrad University in 1924. Worked at the Institute of the History of Art, 1929. Lecturer and critic. From 1929, with the Leningrad Philharmonic. Artistic director, 1940–44. Authority on Leningrad musical life during the 1920–30s. Died in Novosibirsk.

Solntseva, Iulia Ippolitovna
7.8.1901–   . Actress, director.
Graduated from the State Institute of Musical Drama, 1922. Her major acting part was *Aelita*, 1924. Other

films as an actress include *Papirosnitsa Iz Mossel'proma*, 1924, and *Zemlia*, 1930. Married A. Dovzhenko, and assisted him and co-directed his films until his death. Filmed, using Dovzhenko's scripts, *Poema o More*, 1958, and *Povest' Plamennykh Let*, 1961. In 1971, made a film about Dovzhenko, *Zolotye Vorota*.

Sologub, Fedor Kuz'mich (Teternikov)
1.3.1863–5.12.1927. Poet, author.
Born in Petersburg. Graduated from the Pedagogical Institute in 1882. Taught mathematics for 25 years at various schools. First poems published in 1884. One of the founders of the Russian symbolist movement in poetry and prose. Much admired by his contemporaries at first, but lost influence later. His pessimistic, dark mood, apparent from the beginning, turned to complete despair after the October Revolution. Died in Leningrad.
Main works: *Collected Poems*; *Melkii Bes* and *Tvorimaia Legenda* (novels).

Sologub, Nikolai Vladimirovich
1883–1937. Military commander.
Graduated from the Academy of the General Staff, 1910. Took part in WWI as a colonel. Joined the Red Army, 1918. During the Civil War, chief-of-staff at the Eastern front, and army commander, and chief-of-staff at the Western front, later became Commander of Armed Forces in the Ukraine and the Crimea. Head of the Air Force Academy, and Deputy Commander of the Air Force. Deputy head of the Frunze Military Academy, 1925. Professor at higher educational establishments of the Red Army.

Sologubov, Nikolai Mikhailovich
8.8.1924– . Athlete.
Born in Moscow. Honoured Master of Sports (hockey), 1956. With the Central Sports Club of the Army. USSR champion, 1950–64. European champion, 1955–63. World champion, 1956 and 1963. Olympic champion, 1956. Captain of the USSR international team, 1957–61.

Solomentsev, Mikhail Sergeevich
7.11.1913– . Politician.
Born in the Urals. Son of a peasant. Graduated from the Leningrad Polytechnical Institute. Began as a collective farm worker, 1930, then became a foreman, deputy head, chief engineer, and director of plants in Lipetsk, Cheliabinsk Oblast', and Cheliabinsk, 1940–54. Member of the CPSU, 1940. Probably worked in the armaments industry throughout WWII, since there is no evidence of his military service. During the post-war years, held senior party posts in industry and in the party apparatus. Member of the Cen. Cttee. of CPSU from 1961, secretary of the Cen. Cttee., 1966. Chairman of the RSFSR Council of Ministers, 1971–83. Chairman of the Party Control Cttee. of the Cen. Cttee. of the CPSU from June 1983. Elected to the Politburo on 26 Dec. 1983. Lost this position, 30 Sept. 1988.

Solonitsyn, Anatolii (Otto) Alekseevich
30.8.1934–11.6.1982. Actor.
Best known for his appearances in A. Tarkovskii's *Andrei Rublev*, *Solaris* and *Zerkalo*. Became famous after his powerful performance in *Andrei Rublev*. Played the important role of Dostoevskii in *26 Dnei Iz Zhizni Dostoevskogo*, which won a prize at the West Berlin Film Festival. Was a tense actor who lived on his nerves. This eventually caused his early death.

Soloukhin, Vladimir Alekseevich
14.6.1924– . Author, poet.
Born at Alepino, Vladimir Oblast'. Son of a peasant. Started to appear in print, 1946. Graduated from the Gorkii Literary Institute in Moscow, 1951. First book of poems, *Dozhd v Stepi*, 1953. Became widely known with his book *Vladimirskie Proselki*, 1957, describing his wanderings about the devastated and impoverished Russian countryside. One of the first writers after WWII to draw attention to the social and ecological disaster of modern rural life in Russia, became one of the most influential writers of the village style 'derevenshchiki'. In the 1960s, wrote about the necessity to preserve the national heritage (*Rodnaia Krasota*), which became the concern of a popular movement later. Author of

Pisma iz Russkogo Muzeia, 1966, and *Chernye Doski*, 1969. Wrote memoirs of village life before the kolkhozes, *Smekh za Levym Plechom*, published in Frankfurt, 1988.

Solov'ev, Iurii Filippovich
20.8.1925– . Politician.
Served in the Soviet Army, 1943–44. Graduated from the Leningrad Engineering Institute of Rail Transport, 1951. Began as a shift supervisor, and later became a section chief, chief engineer, and administration chief during the construction of the Leningrad subway, 1951–73. Member of the CPSU, 1955. Deputy Chairman of the Executive Cttee. of Leningrad City Soviet, 1973–74. Secretary of Leningrad Oblast' Cttee., 1974–75. Member of the Cen. Cttee. of the CPSU from 1976. 1st Secretary of Leningrad Gorkom, CPSU, 1978–84. USSR Minister for Industrial Construction, 1984–85. 1st Secretary of Leningrad Obkom, CPSU, from 6 July 1985. Elected to the Politburo on 6 Mar. 1986. Member of the Presidium of the USSR Supreme Soviet from 19 June 1986.

Solov'ev, Iurii Vladimirovich
10.8.1940–12.1.1977. Ballet dancer.
Born in Leningrad. Graduated from the Leningrad Choreographic School, 1958. Pupil of B. Shavrov. Joined the Kirov Theatre. Known for his huge leap, faultlessly accurate dancing technique, and masterly pas de deux. One of the best academic dancers. A gifted grotesque and comic dancer. Died in Leningrad.

Solov'ev, Nikolai Nikolaevich
27.7.1931– . Athlete.
Born in Ivanovskaia Oblast'. Honoured Master of Sports (wrestling), 1957. With Leningrad Trudovye Rezervy. Graduated from the Leningrad Institute of Physical Culture, 1961. USSR champion, 1955 and 1959. Olympic champion, 1956.

Solov'ev, Sergei Mikhailovich
1885–1942. Author.
Nephew of the philosopher V. Solov'ev. Close friend of A. Belyi and A. Blok. Published several volumes of verse. Translated classical and

Western literature into Russian. Became an Orthodox priest, and later converted to Catholicism. Wrote a full biography of his famous uncle.

Solov'ev, Vladimir Isaakovich
1942– . Journalist.
Born in Tashkent. Published many articles in Soviet periodicals, including *Novyi Mir* and *Iunost'*. With his wife E. Klepikova, announced the formation of the Soviet private press agency Solov'ev-Klepikova Press, 1977. Emigrated, 1977, and settled in the USA. With his wife, published a number of sensational Kremlinologist works in Russian and English (*Borba v Kremle: Ot Andropova do Gorbacheva*, USA, 1986).

Solov'ev-Sedoi, Vasilii Pavlovich
25.4.1907–2.12.1979. Composer.
Born in Petersburg. Improvised from the age of 10. After graduating from school, 1923, worked as an accompanist and improviser with clubs, studios of artistic gymnastics and for radio. Musical training at the Leningrad Central Technical School for Music, 1929–31. Pupil of P. Riazanov. At the Leningrad Conservatory from 1931, graduated, 1936. During WWII, at the head of the Iastrebok Theatre of Miniature at the Kalinin front, 1942. Participated in artistic productions at munition factories, 1943, and with divisions of the Krasnoznamennyi Baltic fleet, 1944–45. In Leningrad from 1944. Concentrated on composition with intervals for concerts of his own works and guest performances. Wrote operettas, music for ballets, and over 400 songs. Died in Leningrad.

Solovtsov, Anatolii Aleksandrovich (pen names – Groman, Groman-Solovtsov)
25.10.1898–28.10.1965. Musicologist.
Born in Moscow. Author of *N. A. Rimskii-Korsakov*, Moscow, 1948, *Pikovaia Dama Chaikovskogo*, Moscow, 1949, and *F. Shopen. Zhizn' i Tvorchestvo*, Moscow, 1949. Died in Moscow.

Solts, Aron Aleksandrovich
22.3.1872–30.4.1945. Politician, lawyer.
Born in Lithuania. Son of a merchant.

Member of the SD Party from 1898. Studied law at Petersburg University. Involved in revolutionary activity from 1895. In 1901, worked at Lenin's *Iskra*. Bolshevik agitator all over Russia. Several short arrests, and exiles to Siberia. In 1916, member of the Cen. Cttee. of the RSDRP, Moscow Bureau. After the February Revolution 1917, member of the Moscow Cttee. of the RSDRP. Staff member of *Pravda*. In 1918, left-wing communist. Worked for the Cen. Cttee. of the CPSU, 1920–34. From 1921, member of the High Court of the RSFSR, then USSR, later worked with the USSR Chief Prosecutor. Member of the International Control Commission of the Komintern.

Soltys, Adam Mechislavovich (Soltis)
4.7.1890–197? Composer.
Born in Lemberg (now L'vov). Son of the Polish composer, M. Soltys. Professor at the L'vov Conservatory in the post-war years. Composer of the ballet *L'vinoe Serdtse*, 1930. Also wrote 2 symphonies, tone poems, pieces for piano and violin, and songs based on Polish folklore.

Solzhenitsyn, Aleksandr Isaevich
11.12.1918– . Author, Nobel Prize laureate.
Born in Kislovodsk, Northern Caucasus. His father died before Aleksandr's birth. Brought up by his mother (the daughter of a rich farmer), who knew French and English well, and worked as a typist and stenographer. Educated at high school in Rostov-on-Don. Graduated from Rostov University in mathematics and physics, 1941. Artillery captain, 1941–45. Arrested in Feb. 1945 at the front in East Prussia by the NKVD for disparaging remarks about Stalin in his letters. Sentenced to 8 years imprisonment. Spent the first 5 years of his prison term employed as a mathematician in a special scientific research institute in Moscow (Sharashka) run by the MVD-MGB. Later gave a remarkable description of this establishment in his novel *V Kruge Pervom (The First Circle)*. Sent to a labour camp in Kazakhstan, 1950–53 (described in *Olen' i Shala-*

shovka – The Love Girl and the Innocent – and in *One Day in the Life of Ivan Denisovich*). Released after Stalin's death in Mar. 1953 with terminal cancer, prohibited to live anywhere except Central Asia. Described his illness in *Rakovyi Korpus* (The Cancer Ward). Settled in Kok-Terek, Kazakhstan, as a mathematics teacher, 1953–56, and made an amazing recovery. Receiving permission to move to Central Russia, returned to Riazan, resuming family ties with his first wife N. Reshetovskaia. His first story was published in the magazine *Novyi Mir* thanks to the efforts of its editor-in-chief Tvardovskii and the personal permission given by N. Khrushchev. *Ivan Denisovich* was the first public description of the tragedy of the Gulag camps in the USSR, which so deeply affected the life of the whole nation, and created a sensation in 1962. Became an over-night celebrity and a symbol of the demands for glasnost. By judicious use of his literary talent and practical ingenuity (described in *The Calf and the Oak*), gained enormous prestige and was able for years to successfully resist considerable pressure (constant persecution by the KGB, expulsion from the Writers Union, refusal to publish his works). His works and declarations (against censorship, for religious freedom and for a return to traditional cultural values) became well-known in samizdat, although after 1966 he was unable to publish anything officially in the USSR and even his previously published works were removed from libraries. Awarded the Nobel Prize for Literature in 1970. Not permitted to receive the prize officially, and refused the Swedish offer to get it clandestinely (in the end, received it in person at a full-scale ceremony in Stockholm when already living in the West). The pressure from the establishment and the KGB was matched by the deep sympathy which was felt for him among very wide circles in the USSR. Given refuge at the most difficult time by Mstislav Rostropovich and his wife, the opera singer Galina Vishnevskaia, at their dacha in Peredelkino. Received the widest cooperation from hundreds of his former Gulag inmates when gathering material for his sensational 3-volume *Gulag Archipelago*. Met a young

scientist Natalia Svetlova, and married her (after his estrangement from Reshetovskaia, who had been manipulated by the KGB). When the *Gulag Archipelago* began to appear abroad (Les Editeurs Reunis, Paris), expelled from the USSR (in handcuffs, on a special plane with a KGB guard) to Germany. Stayed with Heinrich Böll (a fellow Nobel Prizewinner), later moved to Zurich, where he completed research for *Lenin in Zurich.* In 1976, moved to the USA, where he settled with his family in the state of Vermont. A Laureate of the Templeton Prize for the Advancement of Religion. Seen by some in the West as a shrewd and difficult personality with right-wing and monarchist leanings, due to his sharp polemics against left-wing circles. In the 1980s, engaged in a multi-volume historical work *Krasnoe Koleso* (The Red Wheel) on life in Russia during WWI and the Revolution 1917, which he regards as the main work of his life. Also instrumental in starting a debate on post-WWII forcible repatriation of Russians, 1943–47, and the lifting of the anathema on Old Believers by the Russian Orthodox Church, practically healing the schism (Raskol). Despite many acrimonious controversies, generally regarded by enemies and friends alike as by far the most important figure of present times in Russian literature. Other works: *A Letter to the Leaders of the Soviet Union, Avgust 14* (August 1914), *Matrenin Dvor.* Several editions of his collected works published in France, USA and Germany.
See: M. Scammell, *Solzhenitsyn*, London, 1986.

Somov, Konstantin Andreevich
30.11.1869–6.5.1939. Artist.
Born in St. Petersburg. Son of Andrei Somov, editor of *Vestnik Iziashchnykh Iskusstv.* One of the founders of the Mir Iskusstva group. Studied at the St. Petersburg Academy of Arts, 1888–97, in 1894, under Repin. Also studied at the Paris Academy, 1897. Corresponding member of the Petersburg Academy of Arts, 1913. Professor, 1918. In 1923, emigrated to France. Influenced by modernist German and British graphical artists, also by the Rococo style and the Venetian school. Became very famous

for his erotic illustrations, such as *Kniga Markizy.* Died in Paris.

Sorge, Richard
4.10.1895–7.11.1944. Intelligence officer, journalist.
Grandson of a German Marxist, Friedrich Sorge (1828–1906), who at one time was Karl Marx's private secretary, and later one of the organizers of the Communist Club in New York. Son of an oil technician in Baku, where he was born. In 1910, the family returned to Germany. Served in the German Army during WWI. Met and became close to socialists at a hospital. From 1919, a member of the German Communist Party. Graduated in political science from Hamburg University, 1920. Editor of a party newspaper. For a short time, taught history at a school in Hamburg, but was more interested in teaching his pupils Marxism and communism. Dismissed for this activity. Became a coal miner. Tried to recruit fellow workers to the Communist Party. Dismissed again. In 1924, went to Moscow. Multilingual, highly organized and intelligent he was employed by various organizations, but the main occupation was his training at an intelligence school. Joined the Soviet Communist Party, 1925. Tried, unsuccessfully, to operate in London. Went to Los Angeles to establish a network of Soviet agents there. Returned to Moscow for more training, this time at a GRU school. Sent to Shanghai to collect information about Chiang Kai-shek's Nationalist Army. Returned to Germany and made the highest connections with both Abwehr and Gestapo senior officials. Became a member of the Nazi Party and at the same time an instant success with newspapers. Obtained a post in Tokyo as a correspondent for several influential newspapers. The German Press Association gave a reception in his honour, which Goebbels attended personally. In Tokyo, became an outstanding reporter. His dispatches appeared and were discussed everywhere in the German-speaking world. Became a press attaché at the German Embassy in Tokyo. But his main activity was to serve Stalin. Sent Moscow very valuable political and military information. Was first to give warning about Hitler's plan to

invade the Soviet Union on 21 June 1941, even supplying Stalin with the exact number of German divisions ready on the border. His warning was ignored. His private life in Tokyo was a series of society scandals. Embarrassed the German community with his many affairs with famous women. Eventually was entrapped by Japanese military counter-espionage, who introduced him to a cabaret dancer. Arrested in Oct. 1941. Sentenced to death in Sep. 1943. Executed a year later. The dancer was shot on a Tokyo street by a SMERSH agent soon afterwards. Under Khrushchev, made a Hero of the Soviet Union (5 Nov. 1964). Became a cult figure. A wide-screen film about his exploits was made by Mosfilm Studio, followed by many articles and several books. Glorified as an extraordinary Soviet agent. Buried in Tokyo.
See: Ronald Seth, *Encyclopaedia of Espionage*, London, 1972.

Sorgenfrei, Vilgelm (Wilhelm) Aleksandrovich
1882–1938. Journalist, poet.
Member of the intelligentsia in Petersburg before the 1917 Revolution. Friend of A. Blok. Victim of the Gulag.

Sorokin, Ivan Lukich
16.12.1884–1.11.1918. Revolutionary.
Born in Stanitsa Petropavlovskaia near Ekaterinodar (now Krasnodar). Son of a Kuban Cossack officer. Took part in WWI. Left-wing SR. In 1918, joined the Bolsheviks. Organized a revolutionary regiment consisting of Cossack officers. Chief Commander of the Northern Caucasus Army, Aug. 1918. Turned his army against the Bolsheviks. Arrested local communist leaders and shot them. Declared an outlaw, Oct. 1918. Started an uprising in Piatigorsk. Taken prisoner, and executed in Stavropol.

Sorokin, Pitirim Aleksandrovich
21.1.1899–10.2.1968. Sociologist.
Born in Vologda Gouvt. Son of a goldsmith. Deprived of his mother at 3 years of age, left home at 10. With his brother, became an itinerant

craftsman in Northern Russia, repairing crosses and cupolas of village churches. After receiving a grant, joined a village school. Studied at the Teachers' Seminary at Khrenovo, Kostroma Gouvt., 1903. Lay preacher from the age of 12. Joined the SRs at 16. After the 1905 Revolution, arrested for revolutionary activity. During his 4 months in prison, studied revolutionary literature. After his release, continued his revolutionary work in Ivanovo-Voznessensk. After a Cossack raid, which left dead on both sides, decided to give up political activity and concentrate on his education. Studied law at Petersburg University under Petrazhitskii. First scientific work on criminology, 1913. Graduated from Petersburg University, 1914. Edited the SR newspaper *Volia Naroda*, elected to the Constituent Assembly and the Soviet of Peasant Deputies, 1917. Secretary to A. Kerenskii. 3 days before the Constituent Assembly was due to meet, arrested by the Cheka. After his release, joined the anti-Bolshevik Soiuz Vozrozhdeniia Rossii. Went to the North to organize resistance to communism (with N. Chaikovskii), but, unable to get to Arkhangelsk, had to hide in the forests. In the winter, gave himself up to the Cheka, expecting to be executed. (His older brother, who was in the White Army, was executed, his younger brother died in a Bolshevik prison). Saved by Lenin's article, which stressed the need to preserve intellectuals of worker or peasant origin. Returned to Petrograd and scientific work, 1919. Published his 2-vol. *Sistema Sotsiologii*, circumventing censorship. During NEP, continued his teaching activity and his polemics with the Bolsheviks. Banned from teaching, 1921. Tried to publish a brochure on the horrors of hunger, seen during his trip to Samara, 1922. Expelled from Russia along with a group of famous intellectuals, 23 Sep. 1922. Moved from Berlin to Prague, where he edited the magazine *Krestianskaia Rossiia*, and published several sociological works. Invited by American sociologists to the USA, 1923. First professor of sociology at Harvard, 1930. Adopted American citizenship. One of the founders of American and world sociology. Founded and directed the Harvard Center for the Study of Creative Altruism, 1949. Retired from academic life, 1959. His numerous works on sociology, philosophy and morals were very influential worldwide. Died in Winchester, Massachusetts.

Sorokina, Maria Sergeevna
9.3.1911–21.12.1948. Ballerina.
Born in Moscow. Studied at the Moscow Choreographic School, 1923–25, then at the Lunacharskii Technical School, 1925–29. Pupil of A. Messerer. Joined the Moscow Drama Ballet under N. Gremina. With the Moscow Art Ballet (later amalgamated with the Nemirovich-Danchenko Theatre) from 1932. First interpreter of the role of the Miller's wife in *The Three-cornered Hat*, by N. Kholfin. Great dramatic talent. Last appearance in *Francesca da Rimini* (choreographer Kholfin). Died in Moscow.

Sorokina, Nina Ivanovna
13.5.1942– . Ballerina.
Born in Moscow. Graduated from the Moscow Choreographic School, 1961. Joined the Bolshoi Theatre. Known for her technical virtuosity, musicality and dramatic talent. Appeared in the productions of M. Plisetskaia. 1st prize at the International Competition of Ballet Dancers, Moscow, 1969. Prize at the international competition in Varna, 1966. Gold Star (with Iu. Vladimirov) at the Paris Festival of Dancing, 1970.

Sosnovtsev, Boris Andreevich
20.7.1921– . Composer.
Born in Samara. Taught at the Saratov Conservatory (theory of music and composition). Author of an opera, cantatas, a symphony, a sinfonietta, choral music, and romances. Wrote for the musical press.

Sosnovtseva, Nina Aleksandrovna
1928– . Artist.
Miniature painter. Studied at the Mstera Art School, and has worked in Mstera from 1947. Has created many miniature objets d'art including a Ruslan and Liudmila miniature box.

Sotnikov, Tikhon Ivanovich
6.10.1901– . Composer.
Born in Voronezh. Moved to Rostov-on-Don. Taught at numerous music schools, 1936–61. Author of an opera, 2 symphonies, cantatas, and music for the theatre and films. Author of *Muzyka Pesen Kazakov-Nekrasovtsev*, Rostov-on-Don, 1963.

Soutine, Chaim
1893–9.8.1943. Painter.
Born in Smilovitchi near Minsk. Son of a Jewish tailor. Started work as a tailor's apprentice. Moved to Minsk, 1907. Worked in a photographic studio. Studied at an art school in Vilnius, 1910. Moved to Paris, 1912. Volunteered for the French Army, 1914. Became known as a painter, 1916 (using the same art dealer as his friend Modigliani). In the 1920s, lived in the South of France. In the 1930s, resident in Paris. Became popular in America. During the German occupation, lived in hiding in various parts of France. Returned to Paris for an operation, but died soon after.

Sove, Boris Ivanovich
21.12.1899–15.8.1962. Linguistic scholar.
Born and educated in Vyborg. Studied at the Petrograd Technological Institute. Emigrated during the Civil War, settled in France. Studied at the Paris Theological Institute, 1925–28. Graduated from Oxford University, 1931. Professor of the Old Testament and Hebrew at the Paris Theological Institute, 1931. Moved to Finland, 1939. Librarian of the Slavonic department at Helsinki University Library, 1939–62. Translated Orthodox liturgical texts into Finnish.

Sovetnikov, Ivan Gerasimovich
1897–1957. Lt.-general.
On active service during WWI. Joined the Red Army, 1918. Took part in the Civil War. Sent to Spain during the Spanish Civil War, 1936–39. Joined the Bolshevik Party, 1939. Took part in WWII. Graduated from the Academy of the General Staff, 1949.

Soyer, Raphael (Soier, Rafail)
24.12.1899–4.11.1987. Artist.
Born in Borisoglebsk in the Ukraine. Son of a teacher of Hebrew. His twin brother Moses and younger brother Isaac are both artists. Emigrated to the USA with his parents in 1912. Settled in Manhattan. Became a realistic painter best known for his sombre and haunting portrayals of harried New Yorkers. During the 1930–40s, his main subject was tramps. In 1981, awarded the Gold Medal of the American Institute and Academy of Arts and Letters. Died in New York. Memoirs: *Diary of an Artist*, NY.

Spadavekkia, Antonio Emmanuilovich (Spadavecchia)
3.6.1907– . Composer.
Born in Odessa. Graduated from the Composition Class of the Moscow Conservatory. Pupil of V. I. Shebalin, 1937. Author of operas, orchestral works and chamber music, romances, and ballets on modern themes.

Spasokukotskii, Sergei Ivanovich
10.6.1870–17.11.1943. Surgeon.
Born in Kostroma. In 1893, graduated from Moscow University. In 1898, chief surgeon at Smolensk Hospital. In 1909, chief surgeon at Saratov Hospital. In 1912, director of a surgical clinic at Saratov University. In 1926, dean of the Surgical Department of the Moscow Pirogov 2nd Medical Institute. Created his own school of medicine. Died in Moscow.

Spasskii, Boris Vasil'evich
30.1.1937– . Chess player, grandmaster.
Born in Leningrad. In 1955, youth chess champion. Graduated from Leningrad University as a journalist, 1959. World chess champion in 1969. Kept his title for 3 years, then lost to Bobby Fisher. Left the Soviet Union. Married a French woman. Lives in Paris. Continues his career in chess.

Spektorskii, Evgenii Vasil'evich
1875–3.3.1951. Lawyer.
Specialist in philosophy and history of law. The last pre-revolutionary dean of Kiev University. Emigrated after the Bolshevik take-over. Taught in Belgrade, Prague and Lubliana. After WWII, in DP camps in West Germany. Settled in the USA. Taught at the St. Vladimir Theological Academy in New York. Died in America.

Spendiarov, Aleksandr Afanas'evich (real name – Spendiarian)
1.11.1871–7.5.1928. Composer.
Classical Armenian composer. Born in Kakhovka. In 1895, graduated from Moscow University as a lawyer. Studied the theory of composition, 1892–94. Studied under N. Rimskii-Korsakov in St. Petersburg, 1896–1900. Lived in the Crimea. Close to Glazunov. Author of many symphonies. Winner of Glinka Awards in 1908–10 and 1912. After the October Revolution 1917, conductor of a choir. From 1924, lived in Erevan, the capital of Armenia. Was at the centre of musical life in Armenia. After his death, his name was given to the Armenian Theatre of Opera and Ballet. Died in Erevan.

Speranskii, Georgii Nesterovich
20.2.1873–14.1.1969. Paediatrician.
Graduated from Moscow University, 1898. Professor, 1909. Founded the first hospital for infants in Moscow, 1910. Active in organizing child care in the USSR.

Speranskii, Nikolai Ivanovich
30.7.1877–5.3.1952. Singer (bass).
Born in Tambov. Pupil of K. Everardi. Soloist with the Moscow Private Opera, 1901–04, and with the Zimin Opera Theatre, Moscow, 1905–16. Founder of the Opera Theatre in Saratov, 1917, and of an opera group in Rostov-on-Don, 1920. Taught at the Saratov, Rostov and Baku conservatories, and at the Moscow Conservatory from 1932. From 1939, professor at the Moscow Conservatory. Taught at the Gnesin Music Pedagogical Institute, 1946–51. Trained a generation of singers including R. Mamedov (Biul'-Biul'). Died in Moscow.

Spesivtseva, Olga Aleksandrovna
18.7.1895– . Ballerina.
Born in Rostov-on-Don. Pupil of K. Kulichevskaia. Further training under E. Sokolova and M. Fokin. With the Mariinskii Theatre, 1913–24. Several appearances with Diaghilev's Ballet Russe abroad. Distinguishing traits: lightness and control of line. Especially dramatic in the role of Giselle. One of the last ballerinas of the romantic tradition and first of the expressionist school. Emigrated. With the Paris Opera, 1924–32. Appeared in ballets by M. Fokin (e.g. *The Fire Bird*) After leaving the Paris Opera, appeared with various companies in Australia and Argentina. In the USA from 1939.

Spiridon, (Kisliakov, Georgii Stepanovich) Archimandrite
1875–11.9.1930. Russian Orthodox clergyman.
Lived in Kiev. Known for his pastoral and welfare work. Wrote on religious subjects. Very popular in Kiev, especially among the poor. When he died, his coffin was carried to the cemetery by the city's beggars, for whom he had been the spiritual father for decades.

Spiridonova, Maria Aleksandrovna
28.10.1884–1941. Revolutionary.
Born at Tambov into a wealthy family. As a teenager, involved in revolutionary activity. Close to the SRs. Aged 19, according to revolutionary sources shot the tsarist general Luzhenovskii, who was in charge of quelling peasant uprisings during the 1905 Revolution. After the assassination, allegedly beaten up and raped by the general's Cossack guards. According to other sources, shot her lover in a jealous fit. Sentenced to death for the murder, commuted to life exile in Siberia. The case was widely used in revolutionary propaganda (by Lenin, among others) as an example of tsarist cruelty. Spent her years of exile in Nerchinsk. Released immediately after the February Revolution 1917, and returned to Petrograd. Became one of the leaders of the left-wing SRs. After the Brest-Litovsk Peace Treaty, one of the organizers of the anti-Bolshevik uprising in Moscow, July 1918. Initially very successful (the Cheka founder, Feliks Dzerzhinskii was taken prisoner, but soon released as a

fellow revolutionary), the uprising was eventually crushed by Latvian Cheka detachments. Officially given a very lenient sentence: one year in prison. In reality, was never free again, moving from one concentration-camp or prison to another, and living in exile under close secret-police supervision. In contrast to the publicity surrounding her before the revolution, her fate under communist rule was kept secret. In 1941, an inmate of the notorious Orel prison and shortly before the arrival of the German army, shot by NKVD guards (together with the other inmates; this was the standard practice of the NKVD in 'cleaning' up prisons before retreating). *The Sixth of July*, a film about her as a leader of the July 1918 anti-Bolshevik uprising, directed by Iurii Karasik in 1968 (Mosfilm) and starring Alla Demidova, makes no mention of her tragic end.

Spirin, Leonid Vasil'evich
21.6.1932–23.2.1982. Athlete.
Born in Moscow Oblast'. Honoured Master of Sports (track and field athletics), 1956. With Moscow Trud. Graduated from the Moscow Institute of Physical Culture, 1957. Coach. Olympic champion, 1956 (20km walk). USSR champion, 1958.

Sposobin, Igor Vladimirovich
3.5.1900–31.8.1954. Musicologist.
Born in Moscow. Professor at the Moscow Conservatory. Co-author of music manuals with S. Evseev, and V. Sokolov. Died in Moscow.
Works: *Muzykal'naia Forma*, Moscow, 1947; *Elementarnaia Teoriia Muzyki*, Moscow, 1951; *Prakticheskii Uchebnik Garmonii* (with the above-mentioned authors), Moscow, 1934–35.

Sprogis, Artur Karlovich
1904–1980. Intelligence officer.
Joined the Bolshevik Party, 1920. Sent to Spain as an NKVD officer during the Spanish Civil War. Graduated from the Frunze Military Academy, 1940. During WWII, head of a special school for intelligence agents, and of the HQ of communist partisans in Latvia. In charge of the communist underground in Latvia and Belorussia, 1943–44.

Sredin, Aleksandr Valentinovich
1872–1934. Artist.
Pupil of Konstantin Korovin and V. Serov in Moscow, and J. P. Lorain and J. J. Benjamin Constan in Paris. Portrait painter and interior designer. Exhibitions: MOLKH, 1898, 1903–06, 1910; MTKH, 1904–10, 1924; the New Society of Artists, 1906–08, 1910; the Union of Russian Artists, 1907–18, 1922–23; 2nd State Exhibition, Moscow, 1918–19; 22 Artists, Moscow, 1927; the Association of Artist – Realists, 1928.

Sreznevskii, Viacheslav Izmailovich
3.10.1849–1937. Photographer, scientist.
Born in St. Petersburg. Son of the philologist Izmail Sreznevskii. In 1870, graduated from Petersburg University. One of the founders and directors of the photographic department of the Russian Technological Society until 1916. Founder and editor of *Photograph* magazine, 1880–84. Author of the first reference guide on photography in Russia, 1883. One of the founders of, and later professor at, the Petrograd Higher Institute of Photography and Photo-Technique, 1918. Inventor of many Russian cameras. After the October Revolution 1917, disappeared from the scene. Probably emigrated.

Stakhanov, Aleksei Grigor'evich
3.1.1906–1977. Coal miner.
Born in the village of Lugovaia near Orel. In 1935, became a celebrity for pioneering a movement among workers and peasants to increase productivity. The Stakhanovtsy movement was glorified in the press, books and on film. In reality, it was a propaganda exercise. Where a few groups of workers were given the best equipment and favourable conditions, they produced much better results than other workers. After Stalin's death, the artificiality of the movement was admitted, and it was replaced by the so-called Brigady Sotsialisticheskogo Truda (Teams of Socialist Labour).

Stakhovich, Mikhail Aleksandrovich
1861–1923. Politician.
Member of the State Council. Member of the 1st and 2nd Dumas.

Leader of the nobility in Orel Gouvt. Russian Ambassador in Madrid. Remained at his post after the 1917 Revolution.

Stakhurskii, Mikhail Mikhailovich
1903–1971. Politician.
In the Red Army during the Civil War and WWII. Joined the Bolshevik Party, 1921. Graduated from the Dnepropetrovsk Agricultural Institute, 1937. After WWII, 1st Secretary of the Vinnitsa obkom and the Khabarovsk kraikom.

Stalin, Iosif Vissarionovich (Dzhugashvili, Soso; Stalin, Joseph; party name – Koba)
21.12.1879–5.3.1953. Politician, statesman.
Born in Gori, Georgia. Fourth child of a shoemaker and a washerwoman. Until the age of 11, did not speak Russian. Educated at the Gori church school, 1894. Entered the Tbilisi Orthodox Seminary. Started reading Darwin and Marx. Joined the revolutionary movement and the SD Party in 1898. Involved in revolutionary propaganda among railway workers in Georgia. Expelled from the seminary for revolutionary activity, 1899. Active local Caucasian Bolshevik. Masterminded 'expropriations' (bank robberies) for the revolutionary cause. In this capacity, noticed by Lenin, who called him 'the wonderful Georgian'. One of the organizers of the multi-million rouble robbery in Tiflis, June 1907. Arrested and convicted 6 times, but on 5 of these occasions, quickly reappeared in the Caucasus, a fact which later led to suspicions about his relations with the police (mentioned now even in the Soviet press). In 1903, married Ekaterina Svanidze, a young uneducated Georgian woman, who a year later gave birth to their only son, Iakov. (Ekaterina died from tuberculosis in 1907). Participated in the RSDRP Conference and Congresses, 1905–07. On Lenin's and Zinov'ev's insistence, coopted in absentia onto the Cen. Cttee. of the Bolshevik Party at the 12th Party Conference in Prague, Jan. 1912. At this time, took the Russian pseudonym Stalin (derived from the word steel). In Petersburg,

Stalin

Stalin

involved in the Bolshevik press (*Zvezda* and *Pravda*), 1912–13. Participant at the Cracow Party Conference, 1912. Wrote his first theoretical work (with Bukharin's help), *Marxism and the National Question*, 1913. Again arrested in Mar. 1913, and sent to the Turukhansk region in Siberia. Returned to Petrograd in Mar. 1917. Became active in the Petrograd party organization. Considered to be a moderate member of the party leadership. Member of the Bureau of the Cen. Cttee. and one of the editors of *Pravda*. Along with Kamenev, and later Zinov'ev, took a conciliatory line towards the Provisional Government. After the Bolshevik take-over, October 1917, appointed People's Commissar for Nationalities, 1917–23. During the Civil War, Political Commissar on several fronts, most prominent with Voroshilov at Tsaritsyn against General Wrangel. A similar role during the Soviet-Polish war ended in disaster and led to friction with the military commander M. Tukhachevskii, and the party military leader, Trotsky. In 1919, married Nadezhda Allilueva, daughter of a fellow revolutionary. From this marriage, there were two children – Svetlana and Vasilii. In Apr. 1922, appointed by Lenin General Secretary of the Cen. Cttee. of the Party. Held the post for over 30 years. At the time of his appointment, the post had a purely administrative and technical significance, as a coordination centre, but with his uncanny political instinct, he realized the possibilities of the position and used it as a base to build up a degree of immense personal power. Starting with many handicaps — elementary education, no personal or theoretical achievements in the party, a national-minority background — he nevertheless out-manoeuvered all his rivals and succeeded in destroying them spiritually and later also physically. Closely followed Lenin's line during the Brest-Litovsk crisis and the NEP period, building up the reputation of being sound and reliable, though grey and unimaginative. But after strokes had incapacitated Lenin, Stalin showed callous disregard for his sick former leader and comrade and rudely insulted N. Krupskaia, Lenin's wife. Shortly before his death, in his so-called *Testament* (the

existence of which has been denied in the Soviet Union for decades, but which has since been published), Lenin gave an unflattering description of Stalin, voicing grave warnings and practically recommending his removal. Lenin's advice was disregarded by his successors, to their own tragic cost. By adroit manoeuvering, allying himself with one group to defeat another and constantly changing alliances (with Zinov'ev and Kamenev against Trotsky, with Bukharin and Rykov against Zinov'ev and Kamenev, and later against Trotsky, and finally against Bukharin and Rykov), he made himself the undisputed master of the party. Outwitted all of Lenin's heirs, none of whom had considered him a serious threat until it was too late. (Trotsky had called him 'the most outstanding mediocrity'; see his *Portrety*, USA, 1984). Removed, vilified and killed his defeated rivals (Trotsky, Zinov'ev, Kamenev, Rykov, Bukharin and others). Using unprecedented terror tactics, he moved against the last important opponent of the totalitarian state — the independent farmer — launching his collectivization drive in 1929. This was linked to a largely successful industrialization campaign (5 year plans), assisted by the creation of a huge pool of slave labour, which was used on important industrial projects (hydroelectric dams, new industrial centres like Magnitogorsk, canals, labour camps in Siberia and Central Asia). Finally succeeded in transforming the Communist Party of the Soviet Union into a body completely obedient to him alone. His personality cult reached absurd proportions, showing utter disregard for morals and truth. Using the social aspirations of the new generation of communists, he succeeded in obliterating the Old Bolsheviks, and re-wrote party history in a drastic and primitive way (*The Short Course of the History of the VKPB*). His theoretical works were hailed as a great development in the history of Marxism and of all human thought in general. Considered himself an expert in linguistic theory (the subject of many jokes in the USSR), and a competent judge in all spheres of arts (literature, poetry, films, music). The practical result was a cultural desert, which created abroad the rather

misleading stereotype of Russia as a culturally-backward nation. Succeeded in almost liquidating the church as an organization after a ferocious atheistic campaign in the 1930s. After the assassination of his too-popular colleague and friend S. Kirov (a still officially unexplained incident, according to many researchers engineered by Stalin himself; see V. Antonov-Ovseenko, *Portret Tirana*, and A. Avtorkhanov, *Tekhnologia Vlasti*), unleashed a purge of the party and military elites (see R. Conquest, *The Great Terror*). Thousands of the most prominent names in the country were dragged into oblivion as a result of this campaign. Another still officially unexplained crime concerns the disappearance of several thousand POW Polish officers in the USSR on the eve of WWII at Katyn and other places (see I. Mackiewicz, *Katyn*). There is little doubt that they were executed by Beria's NKVD on Stalin's orders. Abroad, his image was heavily influenced by the conception of the USSR as an enemy of the quickly-growing menace of Hitler (see W. Laqueur, *The Fate of the Revolution*.) This made many in Western countries, especially among the intelligentsia, ready to doubt any evidence of Stalin's crimes and to swallow uncritically even the most absurd of his propaganda tricks. In reality, he tried everything to reach an understanding with Hitler (Molotov-Ribbentrop Pact, Soviet supplies to Nazi Germany, German-Soviet occupation of Poland, extradition of German communists from the USSR to Nazi Germany), and when it turned out to be impossible, was severely shocked by the German invasion, June 1941. But after an initial loss of nerve, he put up a determined resistance with his usual cruelty and shrewd political instinct, at once replacing Marxist slogans by patriotic ones. Later reached practically a concordat with the Orthodox Church and in all other ways encouraged hopes for radical changes after the war. At the same time, all Soviet POWs (including his own elder son Iakov) were officially proclaimed traitors. The same fate befell whole nations (Crimean Tatars, Volga Germans, Chechen-Ingush and others) which were deported by the NKVD with the utmost cruelty to

417

remote parts of the USSR. A massive partisan movement under the control of the NKVD and SMERSH waged war on the invader, but even more on anti-Stalin elements among the civilian population. After the first major victory over the Germans at Stalingrad (formerly Tsaritsin, now Volgograd), 1942–43, he assumed, in addition to his post as party leader, the posts of Head of Government, Chairman of the State Cttee. for Defence, Minister of Defence, and Supreme Commander. Assisted by able military leaders such as Zhukov and Rokossovskii, and with enormous material help from the West, and in particular the USA, he was able to turn the tables in the war against Nazi Germany, making a decisive contribution to the Allied victory in WWII. The summit meetings at Teheran, 1943, Yalta, 1945, and Potsdam, 1945, laid the foundations of the post-war period largely on his terms concerning Eastern Europe and the Far East. The immediate post-war years (years of the Iron Curtain in Europe, and the Cold War worldwide) saw him at the peak of his power in the Soviet Union, in the world communist movement and in world politics, while he personally retreated into paranoia, practically never leaving the Kremlin, sensing enemies and conspiracies everywhere. On the international scene, he started a characteristic vilification campaign against Tito (who had dared to oppose him), tried to starve West Berlin into submission, and began the Korean War, which ended in statemate after UN intervention. At the time of his death, he was preparing a new purge, The Doctors' Plot, and, according to some sources, a huge anti-Semitic campaign. Died at his country dacha at Kuntsevo near Moscow. He was the real creator of the Soviet Union as it was until the time when Gorbachev took over, and has left a legacy which may be extremely difficult to change. 3 years after his death, Khrushchev, in order to gain popularity inside the country, criticized Stalin in his secret report to the 20th Party Congress, Oct. 1956. Later, after further criticism, his body was removed from the Lenin Mausoleum and buried at the Kremlin wall. The evaluation of his legacy still remains the great division of Soviet society, evoking fear among many and hopes among some. His tremendous significance in 20th century history is, however, not in doubt. Works describing his impact and politics are too numerous to mention, but few people seem to have had a deep insight into his personality. A source highly recommended is Boris Bazhanov, *Vospominaniia Byvshego Secretaria Stalina* (Memoirs of Stalin's Former Secretary, 1923–28), France, 1980.

Stalin, Vasilii Iosifovich
1929–1969. General.
Younger (and favourite son) of Joseph Stalin from his second wife Nadezhda Allilueva. Born in Moscow. In the Soviet Air Force from the age of 20. Served in the Far East on the Chinese border. Died of alcoholism.

Stanishevskii, Iurii Aleksandrovich
28.10.1936– . Theatre critic, ballet historian.
Born in Khar'kov. Graduated from Khar'kov University, 1960. Entered for a further degree at the GITIS, 1963. Doctor of the history of art, 1974. Head of the History of Art, Folklore and Etnography. Author of books and articles, in Ukrainian, on the ballet.

Stanislavskaia, Maria Petrovna
1852–1921. Ballerina.
Graduated from the Petersburg Theatre School. With the Bolshoi Theatre, Moscow, 1872–88. Powerful technique, good plasticity. Among other roles, appeared in *Swan Lake*. Taught at the Moscow Theatre School. Among her pupils was Vera Karalli.

Stanislavskii, Konstantin Sergeevich (Alekseev)
17.1.1863–7.8.1938. Stage director, actor, teacher.
Born in Moscow. Son of a rich merchant, a patron of the arts. Acted in his family's private theatre, the Alekseevskii Kruzhok, which staged vaudevilles and operettas by foreign playwrights. In 1888, with stage director A. Fedotov and singer F. Komissarzhevskii, founded the Society of Art and Literature. In 1898, together with V. I. Nemirovich-Danchenko, founded the Moscow Arts Theatre (MKHAT). Created the Sistema Stanislavskogo method of acting, which became known throughout the world. Staged nearly all the Russian classics and some of the best foreign plays. In 1912, with L. Sulerzhitskii, organized the First Studio of MKHAT. After the October Revolution 1917, forced to stage propaganda plays written by new proletarian writers. Many actors and directors of the Stanislavskii Theatre emigrated. He became a target for attacks from the cultural authorities. In 1918, head of the Opera Studio at the Bolshoi Theatre. In 1935, founded the Opera-Dramatic Studio. Was proclaimed father of the socialist-realist method in stage production. The Sistema Stanislavskogo method of acting was grossly distorted by the official theoreticians of the Soviet theatre. Died in Moscow. After Stalin's death, the sistema was criticized in the Soviet press. His Moscow house was turned into a museum, while the MKHAT theatre was given his name.

Stanitsyn, Viktor Iakovlevich (real name – Geze)
2.5.1897–1976. Actor, stage director. Born in Ekaterinoslav (now Dnepropetrovsk). Studied at the Second MKHAT Studio. From 1924, actor with MKHAT. Became known for his classical roles. Played nearly all the Russian and foreign classics. In 1934, a stage director, combining acting and teaching at the Nemirovich-Danchenko School-Studio. Also in many films. 4 times State Prize winner (1947, 1949, 1951, 1952). K. Stanislavskii's Prize in 1974.

Stankevich, Anton Vladimirovich
25.6.1862–10.1919. Military commander.
Son of a nobleman. Born on the estate of Gubino, now kolkhoz Oktiabr, near Vitebsk. Graduated from the Wilno Infantry Military School, 1880. During WWI, commander of a regiment, then a brigade, later a division. During the October Revolution 1917, joined the Bolsheviks. In 1919, Commander of the 42nd and the 55th Rifle Divisions of

the 13th Army on the Southern front. Was taken prisoner at Zolotarevo near Orel by a White Army regiment and hanged as a traitor. Later reburied at the Kremlin wall on Red Square.

Stankevich, Vera Mikhailovna
6.1.1920– . Ballerina.
Born in Leningrad. Graduated from the Leningrad Choreographic School. Pupil of M. Romanova. With the Malyi Theatre, Leningrad. Took part in WWII. Afterwards had many leading roles. Notable for character and grotesque dancing. Teacher at the Leningrad Choreographic School from 1964, and at the Krupskaia Institute of Culture. Teacher and coach at the Malyi Theatre, Leningrad. Took part in organizing and teaching at the Iraq Ballet School in Baghdad, 1969–71.

Stankevich, Vladimir Benediktovich (Stanka, Vladas)
1884–1969. Politician.
Member of the Duma, secretary of the Trudovik faction. Army officer during WWI. Member of the Executive Cttee. of the Petrograd Soviet, 1917. Close to Kerenskii, who appointed him Chief of the Political Department of the Army and Navy Ministry. Went with him to the front in June 1917 before the ill-fated offensive. Emigrated after the Bolshevik take-over, Oct. 1917.

Starevich, Vladislav Aleksandrovich (Starewitz)
8.8.1882–1965. Puppet cinema director.
Born in Moscow. Father of Russian puppet cinema. One of the first film directors in Russia in this genre. Also did the camera-work on his films. Began experimenting in 1911. First 2 films in 1912: *Beautiful Lukanida*, and *Revenge of a Cameraman*. Other films include *Strekoza I Muravei* (1913, after Ivan Krylov), and *Noch' pered Rozhdestvom*, (1913, after Nikolai Gogol'). After the October Revolution 1917, emigrated to France. Lived in Paris and continued making unique films such as the famous *Reineke Lis*, 1939. Died in Paris.

Starikov, Filipp Nikanorovich
1896–1980. Lt.-general.
Joined the Red Army, 1918. Took part in WWI and the Civil War. Joined the Bolshevik Party, 1924. On active service during the Soviet-Finnish war and WWII. After WWII, professor at the Academy of the General Staff.

Starkopf, Anton
22.4.1889–30.12.1966. Sculptor and artist.
Born in Estonia. Studied with Azbe in Munich, 1911–12, then at the Russian Academy in Paris, 1912–14. Taught at the Tartu Higher Art School, Pallas, 1919–40 (one of its founders, and later a director). Taught at the Art Institute, 1944–50. Professor, 1947. 1945–48, director of the Art Institute. Considered a major Estonian artist and sculptor. Died in Tartu.

Starokadomskii, Leonid Mikhailovich
8.4.1875–27.1.1962. Doctor, scientist, arctic explorer.
Born in Saratov. Graduated from the Petersburg Military-Medical Academy in 1899. Senior doctor with a hydrographical expedition to the North Pole on the *Taimyr* and *Vaigach* ice-breakers, 1910–15. From 1932–34, Narkomvod with the North Polar Expedition. An island in the region of the Severnaia Zemlia archipelago, discovered in 1913, now bears his name. Died in Moscow.

Starokadomskii, Mikhail Leonidovich
13.6.1901–24.4.1954. Composer, organist.
Born in Brest-Litovsk. Pupil of N. Miaskovskii. Taught at the Moscow Conservatory. Author of an opera, 4 operettas, oratorios, music for piano and violin, songs, and music for the theatre, films and radio. Best-known for his neo-classical concerto for orchestra, and his organ concerto (rare in Soviet music). Died in Moscow.

Staronosov, Petr Nikolaevich
18.1.1893–18.11.1942. Artist, book illustrator.
Born in Moscow. Self-taught artist Illustrator of many popular maga-

zines such as *Znanie I Sila*, *Pioner*, *Krasnaia Niva* and *Vokrug Sveta*. Illustrated many books. Some work at the Tretiakov Gallery and the Pushkin Museum in Moscow. Became known for his illustrations of fairy-tales. Held many exhibitions. Died in Moscow.

Starostin, Aleksandr Petrovich
22.8.1903–1981. Soccer star, sports official.
Born in the village of Pogost, Iaroslavl' Oblast'. Second of 4 brothers, all soccer stars during the 1930s, and many times champions of the USSR. In the 1930s, captain of the USSR national football team. From 1950–70s, chairman and deputy chairman of the RSFSR Football Federation. Wrote memoirs, *The Captain's Story*, 1935.

Starostin, Andrei Petrovich
24.10.1906– . Soccer star, sports official.
Born in Moscow. Third of the 4 famous Starostin brothers. In the 1930s, played for the USSR national football team. Master of Sport in 1940. From 1959, deputy chairman of the USSR Football Federation. Wrote books about football: *Bol'shoi Futbol*, 1957, and *Povest O Futbole*, 1973.

Starostin, Nikolai Petrovich
26.2.1902– . Soccer star, sports official.
Born in Moscow, eldest of the 4 Starostin brothers. During the 1920–30s, played for the USSR national team. In 1934, Honorary Master of Sport in the USSR. From 1955–75 coach of the Spartak football team. Wrote *Zvezdy Bol'shogo Futbola*, 1957, about star footballers in the USSR.

Starostin, Petr Petrovich
29.8.1909– . Soccer star, sports personality.
Born in the village of Pogost near Iaroslavl'. Trained as an engineer. During the 1930s, played for the Spartak football team. Like his 3 elder brothers, was a famous sports personality.

Starshinov, Viacheslav Ivanovich
6.5.1940– . Athlete.
Born in Moscow. Honoured Master of Sports (hockey), 1963. With Moscow Spartak. Graduated from the Moscow Aviation Technological Institute, 1964. Member of the CPSU, 1969. USSR champion, 1962, 1967 and 1969. European champion, 1963–70. World champion, 1963–71. Olympic champion, 1964 and 1968. Captain of the USSR international team, 1969–71.

Stasevich, Abram Lvovich
10.1.1907– . Conductor.
Born in Simferopol'. Pupil of Leo Ginzburg. Author of a cantata, symphonic music, and romances. Music editor of S. Prokof'ev's oratorio *Ivan Groznyi*. His arrangement was also used in the 1961 film of *Ivan Groznyi*.

Stashinskii, Bogdan
4.11.1931– . SMERSH agent.
Born in a village near L'vov, West Ukraine (then Poland). Recruited by the NKVD-MVD in the early 1950s, trained and sent to West Germany to liquidate Lev Rebet, a Ukrainian nationalist leader. Murdered him by firing into his face an ampoule of prussic acid from a special disguised weapon which he had been trained to use at a SMERSH training school in Karlshorst, East Germany. The inquest verdict was death from natural causes, since the liquid left no trace. For this 'perfect murder' he earned promotion in the KGB and high decorations. Sent again to Munich in 1959 to trace and liquidate Stefan Bandera, another, more prominent, Ukrainian leader. Carried out the assassination in exactly the same way but the inquest was carried out very shortly after the murder and traces of the acid were found. Meanwhile, he met and married an East German girl, Inge Pohl. Told his life story to his wife, and under her influence decided to flee to the West (at that time they were living in Moscow). His wife was pregnant and he managed to convince the KGB to allow her to give birth in her native Berlin near her parents. She was allowed to go to Berlin, but without her husband. The child died soon after birth, and he was allowed to join his wife. Defected successfully to West Berlin and sur-

rendered himself to the Americans. Disclosed much valuable information, but was put on trial for the 2 murders. Sentenced to 8 years in prison but released on condition that he cooperated with West German and American intelligence. Now lives in the West under an assumed name. See: *The Stefan Bandera Assassination*, Ukrainian Press Information, Oct.–Nov. 1959.

Stashkov, Nikolai Ivanovich
1907–1943. Partisan commander.
Joined the Communist Party, 1931, and the Red Army, 1938. Appointed 1st secretary of the underground Dnepropetrovsk obkom during the German occupation of the Ukraine. Leader of the communist partisans in the Dnepropetrovsk area. Arrested by the Germans in 1942 and executed.

Stasov, Dmitrii Vasil'evich
1.2.1828–28.4.1918. Lawyer, public figure.
Brother of the famous music critic Vladimir Stasov, and son of the architect Vasilii Stasov. Born in St. Petersburg. Educated at the St. Petersburg School of Law, 1847. Until 1861, worked at the Senate. One of the country's liberal lawyers at the time of Alexander II's reforms. One of the organizers of the Law Reform, 1864. An organizer and director of the Russian Music Society, 1859. Sympathetic to revolutionary ideas. Helped to arrange the meeting between Chernyshevskii and Hertzen in London in 1859. One of the top lawyers of the 1860s. Defence lawyer in the famous political trials involving Nechaev, Ishutin and others. Also, defence lawyer in the 193 (terrorists) trial, the trial of 17, and that of Kovalskii. Watched by the secret police because of his sympathies with Russian terrorists. Several short arrests in 1861 and 1879. Involved in the revolutionary activity of his daughter Elena Stasova. Lenin found refuge in his flat, June-July 1917, after the defeat of the Bolsheviks' attempted coup, from the police of the Provisional Government. Wrote *Muzykal'nye Vospominaniia* (Russian Music Gazette) 1909, Nr 11–15, and about the trial of Karakozov (*Byloe*, 1906, Nr 4). Died in Petersburg.

Stasova, Elena Dmitrievna
15.10.1873–31.12.1966.
Revolutionary, politician.
Born in St. Petersburg. Daughter of Dmitrii Stasov. Member of the SD Party from 1898. Educated at a Petersburg high school. Together with Nadezhda Krupskaia, carried out Bolshevik agitation in schools for workers. In 1898, an agent of the Soiuz Bor'by Za Osvobozhdenie Rabochego Klassa. In 1901, began working as an agent of *Iskra*. Party work in Petersburg, Orel, Moscow, Smolensk, Kiev and other cities. From 1904–06, Secretary of the Northern Bureau of the Cen. Cttee. of the Petersburg RSDRP, then the Russian Bureau of the Cen. Cttee. of the RSDRP. In 1906, in Geneva worked for *Proletarii*. 1907–12, propagandist in Tbilisi. Many short arrests. Exile in Siberia, 1913–16. 1917–20, Secretary of the Cen. Cttee. of the Bolshevik Party. Took an active part in the October Revolution 1917. During the 1920s, held various party posts all over the country. From 1921, at the Comintern. From 1935–43, in the International Section of the Comintern. 1938–46, editor of *Inostrannaia Literatura* (English and French editions). Died in Moscow. Buried at the Kremlin wall.

Statkevich, Liudmila Stanislavovna
11.1.1923– . Ballerina.
Born in Leningrad. Graduated from the Leningrad Choreographic School, 1942. Pupil of A. Vaganova, A. Lopukhov and B. Shavrov. Joined the Kuibyshev Theatre as a leading dancer. Also taught at the theatre, 1960–64.

Statkun, Tamara Vital'evna
11.12.1954– . Ballerina.
Born in Leningrad. Graduated from Leningrad Choreographic School, 1971. Pupil of E. Shiripina. Joined the Malyi Theatre, Leningrad, and became a leading dancer there.

Stavskii, Vladimir Petrovich (Kirpichnikov)
12.8.1900–14.11.1943. Author.
Born in Penza. Bolshevik from an early age. Took part in the Civil War. Later wrote about the Civil War and approved of the collectivization

campaign. Secretary of RAPP, 1928–33. General Secretary of the Union of Writers, 1936–41. Editor of the magazine *Novyi Mir*, 1937–43. During WWII, front correspondent. Killed in action near Nevel.

Stechkin, Boris Sergeevich
1891–1969. Scientist.
Graduated from the Moscow Higher Technical Institute, 1918. Carried out pioneering work on the theory of jet engines in the 1920s. One of the founders of TSAGI, and professor at the Zhukovskii Air Force Academy until 1953. Academician, 1953. Laboratory director and head of the Institute of Motors of the Academy of Sciences, 1954. Authority on aerodynamics.

Steenberg, Sven
1905–   . Army interpreter, author.
Born in Riga, where he studied law. During WWII, as a German Army interpreter on the Eastern front, came into contact with many Russians associated with the ROA (Russian Liberation Army). Constantly in contact with both Germans and Russians who worked closely with General Vlasov from 1942–45. Businessman in West Germany in the post-war years. Provided remarkable inside information on the Vlasov story in his well-documented book *Vlasov*, NY, 1970.

Stefanovich, Mikhail Pavlovich
14.2.1898–1975? Singer, stage director.
Born in Kiev. From 1919, soloist at opera theatres all over Russia, and from 1933, director and artistic director of opera theatres in many cities. Artistic director and chief director of the Kiev Opera Theatre, 1947–54. Wrote about Ukrainian opera singers in the music press.

Steklov, Iurii Mikhailovich (Nevzorov, real name–Nakhamkis)
27.8.1873–15.9.1941. Revolutionary, journalist, historian.
Born in Odessa. Involved in revolutionary activity from 1888. A social-democrat after 1893. Bolshevik from 1903. Participated in the 1905 Revolution. Emigrated in 1910, and

lived in Paris. Lectured at the Longjumeau party school. Returned to Russia in 1914. After the February Revolution 1917, member of the Executive Cttee. of the Petrograd Soviet. Close to Trotsky. One of the editors of Gorkii's newspaper *Novaia Zhizn'* (New Life). Editor of *Izvestia*, 1917–25. One of the founders of the literary magazine *Novyi Mir*, 1925. Author of many works on socialist and revolutionary history such as *International*, 1864–1914, 2 vol. and biographies of Marx, Bakunin, and Chernyshevskii. Arrested in 1938. Died in Gulag camps.

Steklov, Vladimir Andreevich
9.1.1864–30.5.1926. Mathematician.
Born in Nizhnii Novgorod (now Gorkii). In 1887, graduated from the Khar'kov Technical Institute under A. Liapunov. From 1889–1906, taught mechanics at the same institute, from 1896 as a professor. 1902, doctor of mathematical sciences. From 1906, at Petersburg University. In 1921, founded the Physico-Mathematical Institute of the Academy of Sciences and remained its director until his death, when the Institute was renamed in his honour. Internationally-known mathematician. Visited the USA, and subsequently wrote *To America and Back, My Impressions*, 1925. Died in the Crimea. Buried in Moscow.

Stel'makh, Grigorii Davidovich
1900–1942. Major-general.
Joined the Red Army and the Bolshevik Party, 1919. Took part in the Civil War. Graduated from the Frunze Military Academy, 1926. Staff officer at different fronts during WWII. Fell in action.

Sten, Ian Ernestovich
1899–1937. Revolutionary.
Joined the Bolshevik Party, 1917. Took part in the Bolshevik take-over in Syzran'. Active participant in the Civil War. Graduated from the Institute of Red Professors, 1921. Worked in Agitprop, deputy director of the Institute of Marx and Engels, considered an important specialist in communist ideology in the 1920s. Dared publicly to point out Stalin's incompetence in Marxist theory.

Expelled from the party, 1932. Liquidated on Stalin's orders. Posthumously rehabilitated.

Stenberg, Enar Georgievich
29.6.1929–   . Stage designer.
Born in Moscow. Graduated from the Moscow Surikov Institute, 1956. Pupil of M. Kurilko. Designed for plays and operettas in Moscow from 1957. Created the sets and costumes for several ballets. Worked for the Moscow Classical Ballet, the Stanislavskii and Nemirovich-Danchenko Theatre, the Kirov Theatre, the Malyi Theatre and others.

Stenberg, Georgii Avgustovich
20.10.1900–14.10.1933. Artist.
Born in Moscow. Younger brother of Vladimir Stenberg. Worked with his brother specializing in political and film posters. Also designed and decorated many buildings and squares during political celebrations such as May Day and October Revolution Day. One of the first constructivists and a participant in the movement of industrial art. Graduated from the Moscow Stroganov School of Art and Industry and studied at the Free Art Shops, 1912–20. Member of INKHUK, and the Society of Young Artists (OBMOKH). Considered himself an artist-agitator. Died in Moscow.

Stenberg, Vladimir Avgusovich
4.4.1889–1982. Artist.
Born in Moscow. Brother of Georgii Stenberg. Studied at the Moscow Stroganov School of Art and Industry, 1912–17. Also at the Free Arts Shops, 1917–20. Artist and designer in charge of decorating political meetings and other national celebrations during the 1920s. Member of INKHUK, and the Society of Young Artists. One of the first constructivists, and participant in the movement of industrial art. Carried out many state orders such as producing political posters for meetings (nearly always with his younger brother Georgii). One of the first film-poster artists, also theatrical designer) for B. Brecht and others. Died in Moscow.

Stepanenko, Galina
1967–   . Ballet dancer.
Pupil of Sofia Nikolaevna Golovkina of the Bolshoi Theatre. Has received many international awards despite

her young age. Demonstrated her brilliant technique on stage during her 6-week British tour at the London Coliseum, 1987.

Stepanenko, Ivan Nikiforovich
1920– . Major-general.
Joined the Red Army, 1940. Educated at a pilots' school, 1941. Joined the Bolshevik Party, 1942. Fighter pilot during WWII. Graduated from the Frunze Military Academy, 1949, and from the Academy of the General Staff, 1957. Several high command posts in the Air Force.

Stepanian, Aro Levonovich
25.4.1897–9.1.1966. Composer.
Born in Elisavetpol' (now Kirovobad). Author of 5 operas, symphonies, sonatas, choral music, songs, and pieces for piano and violin. Died in Erevan.

Stepanian, Nelson Georgievich
1913–1944. Lt.-colonel.
Joined the Bolshevik Party, 1932, and the Red Navy, 1941. Instructor pilot before WWII. During WWII, fighter pilot in the Navy, carrying out many successful attacks on German ships. Died in action.

Stepanian, Ruben Gerasimovich
29.12.1902– . Conductor.
Born in Baku. Graduated from the Violin Class of the Erevan Conservatory, 1931 and the Class of Symphonic Conducting, 1936. First violin and assistant conductor, 1933–37. Conductor from 1937 (with some intervals), at the Spendiarov Theatre.

Stepanov, Aleksandr Sergeevich
4.9.1899–2.6.1963. Choir conductor.
Born in Elets, Orel Gouvt. Choir conductor at the Moscow Bolshoi Theatre's Opera Studio, 1921–25, the Bolshoi Theatre, 1930–37, and at the Stanislavskii and Nemirovich-Danchenko Music Theatre from 1938. Chief choir conductor there from 1950–59. Artistic director of the Respublikanskaia Russkaia Khorovaia Kapella, 1942–49. Died in Moscow.

Stepanov, Aleksei Stepanovich
6.5.1858–5.10.1923. Artist.
Born in Simferopol'. Genre and landscape painter, animalist and graphic artist. Studied at the Moscow School of Painting, Sculpture and Architecture, 1880–84, under V. Perov, A. Savrasov, I. Prianishnikov, V. Makovskii and V. Polenov. Member of the Peredvizhniki, 1891–1903. One of the founders of the Union of Russian Artists. Exhibited from 1880. Died in Moscow. Posthumous exhibitions: Moscow, 1941, 1948 and 1959 (in connection with the 100th anniversary of his birth).

Stepanov, Georgii Andreevich
1890–1957. Vice-admiral.
Joined the Red Navy, 1918. Took part in the Civil War (Onega). Chief-of-staff of the Black Sea fleet, 1924. Head of the Marine Engineers' Academy, 1939. During WWII, Commander of the White Sea fleet. Head of the Department of Higher Education of the Navy, 1944–53.

Stepanov, Vladimir Pavlovich
14.1.1890–27.6.1954. Choir conductor.
Taught at the Sinodal'noe Uchilishche, 1912–18. Conductor of the Synod choir, 1912–18. Chief choir conductor at the Bolshoi Theatre, 1926–36, and at the Kirov Opera Theatre, Leningrad, 1936–50. Taught at the Moscow and Leningrad conservatories. From 1946, professor of both. Died in Moscow.

Stepanskaia, Galina Andreevna
27.1.1949– . Athlete.
Born in Leningrad. Honoured Master of Sports (skating), 1976. With Leningrad Trud. Coach. Studied at the Leningrad Institute of Physical Culture. USSR champion, 1973–75. Absolute USSR champion, 1976–77. Olympic champion, 1976 (1,500 metres).

Stepashkin, Stanislav Ivanovich
1.9.1940– . Athlete.
Born in Moscow. Honoured Master of Sports (boxing), 1964. With the Moscow Armed Forces Club. Member of the CPSU from 1965. Graduated from the Moscow Insti-

tute of Physical Culture, 1967. USSR champion, 1963–65. European champion, 1963, 1965. Olympic champion, 1964.

Stepin', Aleksandr Karlovich (Stepin, or Stepin'sh, Artur)
24.5.1886–29.2.1920. Military commander.
Son of a Latvian peasant. Involved in Bolshevik activity in Latvia from 1905. From 1907, a soldier, then officer. Took part in WWI. After the February Revolution 1917, commander of a regiment. After the October Revolution 1917, served in the Moscow military region. In 1918, fought against White Cossacks near Kamyshin. Joined the Bolshevik Party in 1919. A commander at the Southern front. From 1919–20, Commander of the 9th Army fighting General Denikin. Died of typhoid.

Stepun, Fedor Avgustovich
19.2.1884–23.2.1965. Philosopher, author, literary and art critic.
Born in Moscow. Son of an estate manager. In childhood, moved to Kaluga Gouvt. Deeply influenced by contact with the Russian countryside and people. Educated in Moscow. Graduated from Heidelberg University, 1910. Editor of the international philosophical magazine *Logos* in Moscow, 1910–14. Toured all over Russia, lecturing on art, philosophy and literature. During WWI, artillery officer. After the February Revolution 1917, head of the Political Department at the War Ministry, close to Savinkov, but left his official position in Oct 1917. Appointed by Lunacharskii director of the State Experimental Theatre, 1920–22. Dismissed for not being in tune with proletarian culture. Expelled from the Soviet Union with a group of professors, 1922. Professor of sociology at Dresden University, 1926–37. Dismissed by the Nazis. After WWII, professor of Russian culture at Munich University, 1947. Contributed to many Russian publications abroad. Consistent defender of liberal values throughout his life.
Main works: *Zhizn i Tvorchestvo*; *Zapiski Praporshchika Artillerista*; *Russkaya Dusha i Revolutsiia*; *Byvshee i Nesbyvsheesia* (memoirs, 2 vols); *Theater und Film*; *Der Bolschewismus und die christliche Existenz*; *Vstrechi*.

Stetsenko, Iurii Nikolaevich
11.4.1945–   . Athlete.
Born in Kiev. Member of the CPSU
from 1967. Honoured Master of
Sports (rowing), 1970. With Kiev
Lokomotiv. Graduated from the
Kiev Institute of Physical Culture,
1976. USSR champion, 1964–65 and
1967–72. World champion, 1966 and
1970–71. Olympic champion, 1972
(1,000 metres).

Stetskii, A.I.
1896–1939. Politician.
Active member of the Communist
Party. Joined Bukharin in the
struggle for power, but later recanted
and for a time was promoted by
Stalin. Head of the Culture and
Propaganda Department of the Cen.
Cttee. of the Bolshevik Party. Member of the Organizing Cttee. of Soviet
Writers (nominally under Gorkii, but
in reality run by Stetskii). Liquidated
by Stalin.

Stiedry, Fritz
11.10.1883–1970? Conductor.
Austrian by nationality. Chief conductor of the Leningrad Philharmonic, 1933–37. Left the USSR
towards the end of 1937. Moved to
the USA.

**Stogorskii, Aleksandr Pavlovich (real
name – Piatigorskii)**
26.2.1910–   . Cellist.
Born in Ekaterinoslav. Brother of G.
Piatigorskii. Pupil of M. Iampol'skii.
Professor at the Moscow Gnesin
Music Pedagogical Institute. Editor
of the cello music of many Soviet
composers.

Stolbov, Pavel Afanas'evich
30.8.1929–   . Athlete.
Born in Voroshilovgradskaia Oblast'.
Member of the CPSU from 1959.
Honoured Master of Sports (gymnastics), 1961. With the Moscow
Armed Forces Club. Graduated
from the Moscow Oblast' Pedagogical Institute, 1962. School sports
teacher. International referee from
1970. Olympic champion, 1956.
USSR champion, 1956–63. Absolute
USSR champion, 1957. World champion, 1958. European champion,
1959. USSR Cup champion, 1959.

Stolerman, Samuil Aleksandrovich
21.12.1874–22.12.1949. Conductor.
Pupil of Vladimir Safonov. Chief
conductor at the Odessa Opera and
Ballet Theatre, 1927–44, and at the
Kiev Opera Theatre from 1944. Died
in Kiev.

Stoliarov, Grigorii Arnol'dovich
20.3.1892–14.9.1963. Conductor.
Born in Odessa. Chief conductor at
the Odessa Opera and Ballet Theatre,
1920–29. Professor at the Odessa
Conservatory, 1923–29. Chief conductor and professor at the conservatories in Moscow and Alma-Ata.
From 1954, chief conductor at the
Moscow Operetta Theatre. Died in
Moscow.

Stoliarskii, Petr Solomonovich
30.11.1871–29.4.1944. Violinist,
teacher, music professor.
Violin teacher whose pupils included
David Oistrakh, Emil Gilel's, N.
Milshtein and other internationally-
famous names. Born in Lipovtsy near
Vinnitsa in the Ukraine. Graduated
from the Odessa Music School in
1893. 1893–1919, violinist with the
Odessa Opera Theatre. From 1912,
started teaching children and founded his own music school. From
1919, taught at Odessa Conservatory.
Professor, 1923. One of the founders
of the Russian violin school. His
name is connected with the method
of early violin training of children.
Posthumously, his name was given to
his school, which is much sought
after by parents for their children.
Died in Sverdlovsk, where his school
had been evacuated during WWII.

Stolypin, Arkadii Petrovich
2.8.1903–   . Politician.
Born in Petersburg. Son of Prime
Minister P. Stolypin. Badly wounded
as a child when terrorists bombed his
father's house on Aptekarskii Island
near Petersburg, Aug. 1906. Orphaned, 1911. His sister was killed by
Red Guards during the Civil War in
the Ukraine, 1920. Fled abroad with
other members of his family. Educated at high school in Paris. Wrote a
book about his father, published in
Paris. Graduated from the St. Cyr
Military Academy before WWII.
Joined the Russian emigré youth

organization NTSNP (later NTS),
1935. Head of the NTS in France,
1942. Short arrest by the Gestapo.
Given the task of creating lines of
communication between the NTS
and the Allies. After WWII, active in
re-creating NTS groups in Western
Europe and protecting Russian refugees from Beria's SMERSH. With S.
Melgunov, published *Svobodnyi Golos* in Paris. Head of the foreign
relations department of the NTS in
Frankfurt in the 1950s. Head of the
NTS in France from the beginning of
the 1970s.

Storozhev, Nikita (Storojev)
1950–   . Singer.
Born in Kharbin. In 1955, returned to
the Soviet Union with his parents.
Educated at Sverdlovsk University
and Sverdlovsk Conservatory. Worked as a soloist (bass) at the Moscow
Bolshoi Theatre, 1977–81, and sang
in the Patriarchal Cathedral (Elok-
hovskii Sobor) in Moscow. Emigrated, 1981. Many performances all
over the world.

Strakhova, Marina Borisovna
23.2.1910–   . Ballet teacher.
Born in Petersburg. Graduated from
the evening classes of the Leningrad
Choreographic School. Pupil of M.
Romanova. Graduated from the
Pedagogical Department of the Choreographic School, 1940. Pupil of A.
Vaganova, A. Lopukhov and N.
Ivanovskii. Graduated from the
Pedagogical Department of the Leningrad Conservatory. Teacher and
specialist in method dancing at the
Leningrad Choreographic School
from 1940. Teacher in the Choreographic Department of the Lenin-
grad Conservatory from 1962.

Stravinskii, Igor Fedorovich
17.6.1882–6.4.1971. Composer, conductor.
Born in Oranienbaum (now Lomonosov). Son of the singer F. Stravinskii. Started playing piano at the age
of 9. At 18, mastered the theory of
composition. From 1900–05, studied
law at Petersburg University. In
1902, was discovered by Nikolai
Rimskii-Korsakov who became his
teacher and musical father. First
composition, *Fantasticheskoe Sker-*

tso, 1908. Worked for Diaghilev in Paris. Became internationally known for *Zhar-Ptitsa*, 1910, *Petrushka*, 1911, and *Vesna Sviashchennaia*, 1913. From 1910, lived between Paris, Switzerland and Russia, where he lived on his wife's estate. From 1914, settled in Switzerland. In 1920, moved to France, and in 1939, to the USA. In 1945, became an American citizen. Concerts all over Europe and America. In 1962, made a concert-tour of the USSR, where he was received ecstatically. Died in New York, later reburied in Venice near Diaghilev.

Strel'nikov, Nikolai Mikhailovich
14.5.1888–12.4.1939. Composer, conductor, music critic.
Born in Petersburg. Graduated from the Petersburg Law School, 1909. Studied composition under A. Zhitomirskii from 1909. Lectured and taught at the Narkompros from Oct. 1917. Contributed to the periodical *Zhisn' Iskusstva* from 1922. Directed the Concert Department of the Philharmonic 1921–22. Musical director and conductor with the Leningrad TIUZ (Teatr Iunogo Zritelia). Composed operas, also worked in other genres. His main activity was that of music critic. Died in Leningrad.

Strik-Strikfeldt, Vilfrid Karlovich (Strick-Strickfeldt, Wilfried)
23.7.1897–7.8.1977. Captain.
Born in Helgoland. Of German Baltic descent. Educated in Petersburg. Volunteered to join the Russian Army, 1915. Took part in WWI. During the Civil War, fought against the Red Army in the Baltic and near Petrograd. Before WWII, lived in Riga, where he worked for the Red Cross and aid organizations, helping Russian refugees. During WWII, in the German Army, specialist on Russian affairs. Close to the German military conspirators against Hitler (Stauffenberg and others). As the link man between the German Army and Vlasov, actively involved in creating the ROA. Wrote memoirs of his wartime experience, *Protiv Stalina I Gitlera* (Against Stalin and Hitler), Germany, 1981. Died in Oberstaufen in Bavaria.

Strizhenov, Oleg Aleksandrovich
10.8.1929– . Actor.
Became famous for his part as a young White officer in G. Chukhrai's film *Forty First* (Sorok Pervyi), 1956. Another important role was that of Prince Volkonskii in *Zvezda Plenitel'nogo Shchast'ia*, 1975.

Strod, Ivan Iakovlevich
1894–1938. Military commander.
Took part in WWI as a sub-lieutenant. Joined the Red Army, 1918. Active participant in the Civil War in the Far East. Highly decorated (3 Orders of the Red Banner). Graduated from the Vystrel Courses, 1926. Joined the Bolshevik Party, 1927. Victim of Stalin's purges of the military.

Strode, Irena Karlovna (Sirmbarde)
19.8.1921– . Ballerina, choreographer.
Born in Penza. From 1928–32, trained at A. Fedorova's ballet studio. Graduated from the ballet school attached to the National Opera, 1939. Pupil of E. Tangieva-Birzniek and K. Plutsis. Additional training at the Moscow Choreographic School, 1943–44. Pupil of M. Kozhukhova. With the Riga Theatre, 1944–57. Choreographer with the Song and Dance Ensemble of the Philharmony of the Latvian SSR. Took part in guest performances abroad. Taught at the ballet studio, 1945–48, and at the Riga Choreographic School from 1957. Among her pupils were V. Viltsin', L. Tuisova, G. Balyn', I. Dumpe and T. Repina.

Strokach, Timofei Amvrosievich
4.3.1903–15.8.1963. State security officer.
Born in the village of Belotserkovtsy, Primorskii Krai. Son of a peasant. In the Red Army from 1919. Fought during the Civil War, 1919–22, in the Far East. From 1923, on border guards service (GPU, NKVD). Member of the Communist Party, 1927. Veteran member of the Cen. Cttee. of the Communist Party of the Ukraine, 1938–59. From Oct. 1940, Deputy Minister of the Interior of the Ukrainian SSR. During WWII, with SMERSH, organizer of operations

against Germans and anti-Stalin Russians. In 1944, promoted to lieutenant-general. From 1946–56, Minister of the Interior of the Ukrainian SSR. From 1956, held a senior post in USSR Ministry of the Interior. Died in Kiev.

Struchkova, Raisa Stepanovna
5.10.1925– . Ballerina.
Born in Moscow. Graduated from the Moscow Choreographic School, 1944. Pupil of E. Gerdt. Joined the Bolshoi Theatre. One of the leading stars in the 1950–60s. Known for her excellent plasticity, perfect technique and dramatic gifts. Appeared in the ballet film *Khrustal'nyi Bashmachek* in the role of Cinderella, and in several television films. The TV film *Dushoi Ispolnennyi Polet* was dedicated to her. Took part in guest appearances abroad. Teacher of methodology in the Choreographic Department of the GITIS from 1967. Professor from 1978.

Strugatskii, Arkadii Natanovich
28.8.1925– . Author.
Born in Batumi. Elder of the 2 Strugatskii brothers. Graduated from the Moscow Military Institute of Foreign Languages, 1949. With his younger brother Boris, became famous for science fiction short stories and novels: *Strana Bagrovykh Tuch*, 1959, *Obitaemi Ostrov*, 1971, *Vtoroe Nashestvie Marsian*, 1967, *Piknik Na Obochine* and *Za Milliard Do Kontsa Sveta* (filmed under the title *Stalker* by A. Tarkovskii), *Ulitka Na Sklone* and *Skazka O Troike*, 1972, *Gadkie Lebedi*, 1972, *Les*, 1981. Many of their books have been translated into several languages. A. Tarkovskii's film based on their stories brought them international fame.

Strugatskii, Boris Natanovich
15.4.1933– . Author.
Born in Leningrad. Younger brother of Arkadii Strugatskii. Graduated from Leningrad University in physics and mathematics. Successful science fiction writer, working with his brother on science fiction novels.

Struve, Boris Aleksandrovich (real name – Struve-Kriudener)
3.3.1897–29.4.1949. Musicologist.
Born in Kolomna. Professor at the Leningrad Conservatory. Died in Leningrad.
Works: *Profilaktika Professional'nykh Zabolevanii Muzykantov,* Leningrad, 1935; *Protsess Formirovaniia Viol i Skripok,* Moscow, 1958.

Struve, Gleb Petrovich
2.5.1893–   . Literary scholar.
Born in Petersburg. Emigrated after the revolution. Educated in Prague. Moved to England. Lecturer at the School of Slavonic Studies, London. After WWII, moved to the USA. Professor of Russian literature at Columbia University, NY.
Main works: *Soviet Russian Literature,* 1944, *Russian Literature in Exile,* 1956. Edited, with Filippov, the collected works of Pasternak, Akhmatova, Gumilev, Kliuev, Zabolotskii, Voloshin, published in the USA.

Struve, Nikita Alekseevich
16.2.1931–   . Editor, literary scholar, publisher.
Born in Paris. Graduated from the Sorbonne. Professor at the University of Paris. Director of the Russian publishing house YMCA Press in Paris, which published many works by Russian philosophers and writers (including Solzhenitsyn) which at the time were not available elsewhere. Editor of the magazine *Vestnik RSHD.* Author of *Les Chretiens en URSS.*

Struve, Otto
12.8.1897–6.4.1963. Astronomer.
Born in Khar'kov. Descendent of a famous Russo-German family of astronomers. Graduated from Khar'kov University, 1919. Emigrated after the Civil War. Settled in the USA, 1920. Professor at Chicago University, 1932. Director of several American observatories (Green Bank, 1959–62). Vice-president, 1948–52, and president, 1952–55, of the International Astronomers' Union. International authority on stellar evolution. Died in Berkeley, California.

Struve, Petr Bernhardovich
26.1.1870–26.2.1944. Historian, economist, sociologist, politician, editor.
Born in Perm'. Son of the governor there. Graduated in law from Petersburg University, 1895. In his youth, an extreme revolutionary radical. One of the first Marxists in Russia and author of the first SD Manifesto. Went abroad and became editor of the left-of-centre newspaper *Osvobozhdenie,* published in Stuttgart, 1902. Member of the Cen. Cttee. of the Cadet Party, 1905. Member of the 2nd Duma. Editor of the influential magazine *Russkaia Mysl'.* A prominent member of the Vekhi, 1909 (authors who criticized the revolutionary zeal and abstract dogmatism of the intelligentsia). Moved to the right wing of the Cadets, later left the party. Became the best-known voice of right-wing liberal circles (condemned by Lenin as a traitor to the revolutionary cause). Opposed the October Revolution 1917. Joined the Whites, 1918–20. After the Civil War, emigrated. Lived in Belgrade and Paris. Among Russian emigrés, considered the most prominent representative of right-of-centre opinion (rivalling Miliukov on the left-of-centre). Lived mostly in Belgrade, 1928–42. Edited the newspaper *Vozrozhdenie* in Paris before WWII. Died in Paris.
Works: *The Social and Economic History of Russia,* Paris, 1952 (contains a bibliography of his works, over 600 titles).

Struve, Vasilii Vasil'evich
2.2.1889–15.9.1965. Historian, orientalist, academician.
Born in Petersburg. Graduated from Petersburg University in 1911. Pupil of B. Turaev and P. Kokovtsev. Studied at Berlin under A. Erman. From 1916, taught at Leningrad University. From 1918–33, head of the Egyptian Department of the Hermitage. 1937–40, director of the Institute of Ethnography, Academy of Sciences. In 1935, academician. From 1941–50, director of the Institute of Oriental Studies (Institut Vostokovedenia). Leading authority on Egypt. Author of many monographs, articles and books. Editor of historical magazines. One of the initiators of the *Sovetskaia Istoricheskaia Entsiklopediia* (Soviet Histo-

rical Encyclopaedia). Died in Leningrad.

Stuchenko, Andrei Trofimovich
1904–1972. General.
Joined the Red Army, 1921, and the Bolshevik Party, 1929. Graduated from the Frunze Military Academy, 1939. Took part in WWII. Commander of several military districts after the war. Non-voting member of the Cen Cttee. of the CPSU, 1961–71. Head of the Frunze Military Academy, 1968.

Stuchevskii, Ioakhim (Egoiakhin)
7.2.1891–197? Cellist, composer.
Born in Romny, in the Ukraine. Pupil of Iu. Klengel. Concert tours until 1909. Moved to Europe. Author of the 4-volume *Igra Na Violoncheli,* 1927. From 1938, lived in Tel-Aviv. Composer of chamber music, and music for cello using Jewish folk motives. Died in Israel.

Stukalin, Boris Ivanovich
1923–   . Politician.
Member of the CPSU from 1943. Graduated from the Voronezh Pedagogical Institute in 1950. Journalist. Edited a local Komsomol newspaper *Molodoi Kommunar,* 1952–56, then the party newspaper *Kommuna,* 1956–60. Head of the RSFSR Section at the Department of Agitation and Propaganda of the Cen. Cttee. of the CPSU, 1960–63. Chairman of the State Cttee. on Printing and Publishing with the Council of Ministers of the RSFSR, 1963–65. Deputy Editor of *Pravda,* 1965–70. Chairman of the USSR State Cttee. on Publishing, Polygraphy and the Book Trade, 1970–82. Member of the Cen. Cttee. from 1976. Head of the Propaganda Department of the Cen. Cttee. from 1982. Adviser to Eastern European governments on propaganda, church affairs and socialist influence on the young generation.

Stukolkina, Nina Mikhailovna
26.8.1905–   . Ballerina, choreographer.
Born in Tver' Gouvt. Graduated from the Petersburg Theatre School. Pupil of O. Preobrazhenskaia and E Gerdt. With the Kirov Theatre of

Opera and Ballet, 1922–57. Distinguishing traits: thoroughness of style and great plasticity. Taught at the Kirov Theatre, 1950–58, the Leningrad Comedy Theatre, 1960–64 and 1971–73, the Navoi Theatre, 1968–71, and the Chuvashskii Musical Theatre from 1978. Produced ballets for the Kirov Theatre, in collaboration with A. Andreev, for the Minsk and Navoi theatres, and for the Chuvashskii Musical Theatre. Joint author with A. Andreev of the book *Chetyre Ekzersisa*, 1972.

Stupnikov, Igor' Vasil'evich
27.8.1932–   . Theatre, ballet and literary critic.
Born in Leningrad. Studied for a higher degree in the Philology Department of Leningrad University, 1964. Graduated from the 1st Leningrad Institute of Foreign Languages, 1956. Lecturer at Leningrad University from 1972. Ballet critic from the 1960s. Author of *Molodye Artisty Leningradskogo Baleta*, Leningrad, 1968, and *Mastera Tantsa, Materialy k Istorii Leningradskogo Baleta, 1917–73*, (in collaboration with A. Degen), Leningrad, 1974.

Subbotin, Nikita Egorovich
1904–1968. Lt.-general.
Joined the Red Army, 1926, and the Bolshevik Party, 1929. Graduated from the Lenin Political Military Academy, 1941. Political officer in the army during WWII.

Sudakov, Gennadii Vladimirovich
20.2.1952–   . Ballet dancer.
Born in Saratov. Graduated from the Perm' Choreographic School. Pupil of Iu. Plakht. With the Perm' Theatre from 1971, and leading dancer with the Leningrad Malyi Theatre from 1977. State Prize, 1977.

Sudeikin, Sergei Iur'evich
19.3.1882–12.8.1946. Artist, theatrical designer.
Born in Smolensk. Trained at the Moscow School of Art and Architecture, 1897–1909, under K. Korovin, and at the Petersburg Academy of Arts, 1909–10. Began his career as a theatrical designer at the studio of

K. Stanislavskii and V. Meyerhold in Povarskaia Street, Moscow, and with the theatre of V. Komissarzhevskaia in Petersburg. Worked with producers such as F. Komissarzhevskii, A. Tairov, N. Evreinov and Iu. Ozarovskii. Drawn to stylized theatre. Emigrated to Paris in 1921. Moved to New York, 1923. In the USA, designed mainly for ballet in collaboration with the choreographers A. Bolm, G. Balanchine, B. Nizhinskaia, M. Mordkin and M. Fokin. Designed the ballet *Feia Kukol* (performed by Anna Pavlova's company in 1923). In New York, reached the Metropolitan Opera with *Petrushka*, 1925. Died near New York.

Sudets, Vladimir Aleksandrovich
1904–1981. Marshal.
Joined the Bolshevik Party, 1924, and the Red Army, 1925. Educated at a pilots' school, 1929. In the 1930s, sent to Mongolia. Took part in the Soviet-Finnish war, 1939–40. Bomber commands during WWII. Deputy Commander-in-chief of the Air Force, and Commander of Strategic Aviation after WWII. Commander-in-chief of Anti-Aircraft Defence Forces and Deputy Minister of Defence, 1957–66. Non-voting member of the Cen. Cttee. of the CPSU, 1961–66.

Sudoplatov, Pavel Anatol'evich
1900?–1953. State security officer.
Head of secret police troops. During WWII, in charge of the NKVD controllers of the communist partisans. His special department (in charge of assassinations and other terrorist actions), created in 1942, was incorporated in the state security ministry as an autonomous unit, 1946. Arrested and executed with other Beria aides, 1953.

Suk, Viacheslav Ivanovich
16.11.1861–12.1.1933. Conductor.
Born in Kladno, Czechoslovakia. In 1880, moved to Russia. Conductor at the Bolshoi Theatre, 1906–33. Responsible for nearly all of the Bolshoi's West European productions. From 1927, chief conductor at the Stanislavskii Opera Theatre. Appeared also as a symphonic conductor. Died in Moscow.

Sukhanov, Nikolai Nikolaevich (Gimmer)
1882–1940. Revolutionary.
Journalist and economist, specializing in agrarian questions before WWI. Member of the Menshevik Party. Close to Gorkii, worked on his newspaper *Novaia Zhizn'*. Very active in the February Revolution 1917 in Petrograd. Wrote extremely valuable memoirs of 1917, *Zapiski o Revoliutsii*, published in Berlin in the early 1920s. Arrested in 1931 by the NKVD, later released, then re-arrested, 1939. Either died after torture or was shot in the Gulag.

Sukharnova, Olga Leonidovna
14.2.1955–   . Athlete.
Born in Krasnoiarskii Krai. Honoured Master of Sports (basketball), 1956. With the Moscow Oblast' Spartak. Graduated from the Moscow Technological Institute, 1979. European champion, 1972, 1974, 1976 and 1978. World champion, 1975, Olympic champion, 1976. USSR champion, 1978.

Sukhishvili, Il'ia Il'ich
4.4.1907–   . Ballet dancer, choreographer.
Born in Tiflis. Trained at the studio of Georgian Folk Dance. Pupil of A. Aleksidze, and at ballet school under M. Perini, 1922–24. Debut in Georgian folk dances on the variety stage, 1924. With the Paliashvili Theatre (with intervals), 1926–45. Producer of and dancer in Georgian operatic dances. Concurrently produced Georgian dances at the Shevchenko Theatre, at the Stanislavskii and Nemirovich-Danchenko Theatre, and at the Leningrad Theatre of Musical Comedy. Gold medallist at the International Festival of Folk Dance, 1935. Soloist with the Song and Dance Ensemble under A. Aleksandrov, 1939–40. Leading dancer in and producer of Georgian dances with the Song and Dance Ensemble of the NKVD, 1939. Organizer (with N. Ramishvili) of the Ensemble of Georgian Folk Dance, and one of its leading dancers and its director and artistic director until 1954. Stalin Prize, 1949. Winner of the S. Rustaveli Georgian State Prize, 1973.

Sukhoi, Pavel Osipovich
1895–1975. Aircraft designer.
Graduated from the Moscow Higher Technical Institute, 1925. Designer at the TSAGI, 1925. Designed many types of Soviet aircraft (the Su-2 and others of the Su-series). Several State Prizes.

Sukhomlin, Aleksandr Vasil'evich
1900–1970. Lt.-general.
Joined the Red Army and the Bolshevik Party, 1918. Took part in the Civil War. Graduated from the Frunze Military Academy, 1927, and from the Academy of the General Staff, 1938. Professor at the Academy of the General Staff, 1940. Commander of several armies during WWII. After the war, taught at the Frunze Academy and the Academy of the General Staff. Carried out scientific research work for the General Staff, 1959–63.

Sukhomlinov, Vladimir Aleksandrovich
1848–1926. General, minister.
Graduated from the Academy of the General Staff, 1874. Took part in the Russo-Turkish war, 1877–78. Commander of a cavalry school, 1884, and of a cavalry division, 1897. General Governor in Kiev, Volhynia and Podolia, 1905–08. Head of the General Staff, 1908. Controversial Minister of War, 1909–15. Accused by Duma members of irregularities and treason, dismissed, but not tried during WWI. Retired from public affairs.

Sukhoruchkin, Fedor Vasil'evich
1901–1954. Lt.-general.
Joined the Red Army, 1922, and the Bolshevik Party, 1927. Commander of tank forces at different fronts during WWII, and afterwards.

Sukhorukov, Dmitrii Semenovich
1922– . General.
Joined the Red Army, 1939. Took part in WWII as an officer in the airborne troops. Joined the Bolshevik Party, 1944. Graduated from the Frunze Military Academy, 1958. Deputy Commander of Airborne Troops, 1969. Commander of the Central Group of Armies, 1976–79, and Commander of Soviet Airborne Troops, 1979.

Suleimanova, Giuzel' Galeevna
25.2.1927–14.4.1969. Ballerina.
Born in Ufa. Graduated from the Leningrad Choreographic School. Pupil of M. Romanova. With the Ufa Theatre from 1945. Leading dancer. Took part in guest performances abroad. Died in Ufa.

Surguchev, Il'ia Dmitrievich
27.2.1881–19.11.1956. Author.
Born in Stavropol. Graduated from Petersburg University's faculty of Eastern languages in 1907. First successful novel, *The Governor*, published in 1912. Popular playwright in the 1910s. After the October Revolution 1917, emigrated, 1920. Continued writing and publishing in Russian emigré publishing houses. Died in Paris.
Main works: *Collected Works*, 4 vol., *Stories*, 2 vol.

Surits, Elizaveta Iakovlevna
25.2.1923– . Ballet critic.
Born in Berlin. Graduated from the Theatrical Faculty of the GITIS, 1949. Editor at the Central Theatrical Library of the GITIS, 1949. Worked with the All-Union Research Institute for the History of the Arts. Entered for a higher degree in 1970. Author of books, and articles in anthologies, periodicals and encyclopaedias: 'New York City Ballet in Moscow', in *Teatr*, 1961, No. 3; *Anna Pavlova, 1881–1931*, Moscow, 1956; *Vse o Balete. Slovar'-spravochnik* (compiled from foreign articles on ballet), Moscow-Leningrad, 1966; 'Balet', *Bolshoi Teatr, SSSR, 1969–70*, Moscow, 1973; *Muzyka i Khoreografiia Sovremennago Baleta*, Leningrad, 1974; *Khoreograficheskoe Iskusstvo Dvadtsatykh Godov*, Moscow, 1979.

Susaikov, Ivan Zakharovich
1903–1962. Political officer.
Joined the Red Army, 1924, and the Bolshevik Party, 1925. Graduated from the Mechanization Academy of the Red Army, 1937. Before, during and after WWII, political functionary in the tank forces of the Soviet army.

Sushkov, Vladimir
1945?– . Politician.
Held a top position in the Ministry of Foreign Trade. Ran the department controlling exports and imports. Trained as an engineer. At the end of 1985, suddenly arrested with a group of others, including his wife Valentina. According to the Soviet news agency TASS, found guilty of taking bribes worth 127,000 roubles from unnamed foreign companies. Received a 13-year prison term, and his property was confiscated. Became the first senior official to suffer in the clamp-down on official corruption started after the death of Brezhnev in 1982.

Sushkova, Valentina
1952– . Party official.
Wife of Vladimir Sushkov. Occupied a senior position in the State Cttee. for Science and Technology. Her main occupation was as a hostess to foreign VIPs, clients of her once powerful husband. Accepted expensive gifts, jewellery, foreign currency and roubles for helping foreign companies to get a contract. Appeared in public places, always overdressed and was nicknamed the 'Golden Signora' for her passion for gold. Received an 11-year jail sentence with confiscation of her property, after her husband's arrest and conviction in 1985.

Suslin, Viktor
1937– . Composer.
Born in Miassy in the Urals. Started playing piano aged 4. Studied at a music school in Khar'kov. Pupil of Vsevolod Topilin. Continued his training at the Moscow Gnesin Institute. Pupil of Nikolai Peiko in the Composition Class, and of Anatolii Vedernikov in the Piano Class. Reader at Moscow Conservatory, 1972–74, at the same time giving solo piano concerts. His first composition received prizes, 1961 and 1969. Entered the avant-garde music group Astrei (with Sofia Gubaidulina and Viacheslav Artemov). His avant-garde compositions received recognition at the Rouen Festival of New Music, 1971. Harassed by the Union of Soviet Composers, and lost his job. For a short time, worked as a street cleaner in Moscow. Emigrated in 1981. Teaches music at the Lübeck Music School. Lives in Hamburg. Works for Sikorski Music Publishers in Hamburg as an editor of avant-garde Russian music.

427

Suslov, Boris Vasil'evich

15.10.1930–   . Ballet dancer.
Born in Kirghiz region. Graduated from the Frunze Choreographic School, 1952. First appearance with the Frunze Theatre, 1950. Soloist from 1952. Theatrical director and coach from 1974. Assistant director with the Frunze Theatre from 1977.

Suslov, Il'ia Petrovich

1933–   . Author, journalist.
Editor of the humour section of *Literaturnaia Gazeta*, 1967–73. In 1974, emigrated to the USA. His works include: *Proshlogodnii Sneg, Vremia I My*, 1976, *Rasskazy O Tovarishche Staline*, 1981, and *Vykhod K Moriiu*, 1982. Lives in Washington.

Suslov, Mikhail Andreevich

1902–1982. Politician.
Son of a peasant. Active in the Komsomol, 1918. At the age of 19 joined the Communist Party. Moved to party work, and sent to study at a Workers' Faculty in Moscow, then at the Plekhanov Institute of National Economy and the Economic Institute of Red Professorship. Top position on the Cttee. of Party Control in late 1920. Took an active part in the party purges, 1933–34. Became secretary of the Rostov Oblast' Party Cttee., 1937.1st Secretary of the Ordzhonikidze (now Stavropol) Krai Cttee. In 1941, member of the Cen. Cttee. High-ranking political officer in the NKVD during WWII. In 1944, restored Soviet rule in Lithuania, responsible there for mass arrests and deportations. In 1946, headed the Department of Agitation and Propaganda of the Cen. Cttee. of the CPSU. Remained in this post until his death. In 1948, took over the office of Cominform, specializing in foreign affairs, in particular in relationships with foreign communist parties. Editor-in-chief of *Pravda*, 1949–50. From 1954, chairman of the Foreign Affairs Cttee. of the Supreme Soviet. Member of the Cen. Cttee. Presidium in 1955. Chief ideologist of the Kremlin until his death. His job was to stop any attempts to challenge communist authorities in East European countries, and in the Soviet Union. At the end of his life, he was the most influential Stalinist in the Kremlin leadership.

Suslova, Appolinaria Prokof'evna

1840–1918. Author.
Insignificant writer, important in Russian literature by virtue of her personal connections with 2 literary giants, F. Dostoevskii and V. Rozanov. In the 1860s, as a young girl, represented the new type of emancipated woman. Became the lover of Dostoevskii, and a prototype of his infernal heroines. Published novels in the Dostoevskii magazines *Vremia* and *Epokha*. Much later, in the 1890s, married the young student V. Rozanov, who was at that time under Dostoevskii's spell. After the full disaster of this marriage became apparent, refused a divorce out of spite, forcing Rozanov into illegal family life with his new wife, and concentrating his mind on 2 subjects – sex and the cruelty of church laws on family life. Her description of her years with Dostoevskii was published posthumously, *Gody Blizosti s Dostoevskim*, 1928.

Suve, Enn Vil'khel'movich

27.22.1949–   . Choreographer.
Born in Raplaskii district, Estonia. Graduated from the Tallinn Choreographic School, 1959, and the Choreographic Department of the GITIS in 1964. Pupil of R. Zakharov. Joined the Estonia Theatre in 1966, and worked as chief choreographer there from 1969–73. Characteristic traits: use of traditional classical expression, sometimes mixed with stylization of national and genre dancing, and frequent use of the grotesque and humorous.

Suvorov, Anatolii Andreevich

1890–1943. Artist.
Engraver, etcher, book illustrator and lithographer. Studied at the Moscow Stroganov Central Art-Industrial School, 1901–14, under D. Shcherbinovskii, S. Vinogradov and K. Pervukhin. In 1910–11, sent by the Stroganov School to Italy to study xylography, etching and lithography, under I.N. Pavlov and N. I. Piskarev. First exhibition: Petersburg, 1913. Other exhibitions: The All-Union Art-Industrial Exhibition, Moscow, 1923, The 4 Arts, 1926, 10 Years of Russian Xylography, Leningrad, 1927, Moscow, 1927–28, Leningrad, 1932, Moscow, 1934, 1936, 1938–39, 1941–43. Killed during WWII.

Suvorov, Viktor

1948–   . GRU officer.
Worked in Soviet military intelligence. Took part in the invasion of Czechoslovakia, 1968. Defected to the West. Wrote a series of studies, published in English, on Soviet subversion tactics, military life and the special Soviet invasion forces Spetsnaz.

Svarog, Vasilii Semenovich

1883–1946. Artist, guitarist.
Famous painter. Also known as a remarkable guitarist. Wrote original music and arrangements for the guitar. Many of his paintings were also on musical themes. (He himself was painted playing the guitar by I. Repin).
Source: *Muzyka i Byt*, 1927 (Nr 3, 4, and 12 include articles by him).

Svechin, Aleksandr Andreevich

29.8.1878–29.7.1938. Military historian, major-general.
Born in Ekaterinoslav. Son of a general. In 1897, graduated from the Mikhailovskoe Artillery School. In 1903, graduated from the Academy of the General Staff. Took part in the Russo-Japanese war, 1904–05. In 1914, served at Army HQ. Commander of a regiment, 1915–17, and a division, 1917. In 1917, Chief-of-staff of the 5th Army. Moved to the Northern front. In Mar. 1918, joined the Red Army. From Nov. 1918, professor at the General Staff Academy (now Frunze Military Academy). From 1919, taught and wrote articles and books analyzing military operations. Liquidated by Stalin.
Main works: *Istoriia Voennogo Iskusstva*, Moscow, 1922–23. *Evoliutsiia Voennogo Iskusstva*, 2 vol., Moscow/Leningrad. 1927.

Svechin, Mikhail Andreevich

1876–1956. Lt.-general.
Born in Petersburg. Graduated from the 2nd Cadet Corps, and from the Nikolaevskoe Cavalry School, 1895. Graduated from the Academy of the General Staff, 1902. Took part in the Russo-Japanese war and the Civil War. Major-general, 1915. Chief-of-staff of a cavalry division. Commander of several regiments in the White Army. Commander of the 1st Cavalry Corps, appointed by Kornilov. Fought in the South and

evacuated with the remnants of the White Army, 1920. Chairman of the Nice branch of ROVS. Very popular figure in the Russian community in the South of France. Died in Nice.

Svechnikov, Mikhail Stepanovich
1882–1938. Military commander. Graduated from the Academy of the General Staff, 1911. On active service during WWI as a colonel. Joined the Red Army, 1918. Fought against the anti-communist Cossacks, Krasnov and Kaledin, during the Civil War. Commander of Red forces in West Finland, 1918. Deputy Commander-in-chief of the unsuccessful Red forces during the Finnish Civil War, 1918. In charge of organizing the Red Army in Petrograd in spring 1918. Commander of the Caspian and Caucasian fronts, 1919. Professor at the Military Academy, 1922. Victim of Stalin's purges of the military leadership.

Sven, Viktor Borisovich (Kulbitskii)
2.2.1897–24.10.1971. Author, journalist.
Born in Okhonovo. Son of a landowner. Educated at Smolensk High School. During the Civil War, joined the White Army. Taken prisoner by the Reds, 1919, sent to a concentration camp, and then to the Red Army. Became a Soviet journalist and Tass correspondent, 1925. Close to M. Prishvin. During WWII, moved to Germany. After the war, in DP camps in Germany. Published several books of short stories describing the people and natural life of Russia. In the 1950s and 1960s, worked at the Russian desk of Radio Liberty in Munich. Died in Munich.

Sverdlin, Lev Naumovich
16.11.1901–29.8.1969. Actor.
Studied at the Lunacharskii High School and at the GVYTM (State Theatre Workshops). Pupil of V. Meyerhold, and from 1926, actor in his theatre. Entered the film industry, 1925. His major role was in B. Barnet's film, *U Samogo Sinego Moria*, 1936. From 1943, worked at the Mayakovsky Theatre.

Sverdlov, Iakov Mikhailovich
3.6.1885–16.3.1919. Revolutionary, politician.
Born in Nizhnii Novgorod. Son of an engraver. Member of the SD Party from 1901. Became one of the most active Bolshevik propagandists in many Russian towns, especially on the Volga and in the Urals. During the 1905 Revolution, led the Bolsheviks in Ekaterinburg (now Sverdlovsk). Arrested and imprisoned, escaped, worked in the Moscow revolutionary underground. Until the 1917 Revolution, periods of exile (once with Stalin in Turukhansk) alternated with revolutionary work in different cities. Released from exile after the February Revolution 1917, active in Petrograd and Ekaterinburg. One of the organizers of the October Revolution 1917 (member of the Cen. Cttee. and Secretary of the Cen. Cttee. of the Bolshevik Party). Immediately after the Bolshevik take-over, appointed chairman of the All-Union Executive Committee (Head of State), 8 Nov. 1917. Chairman of the commission for the preparation of the first constitution of the RSFSR. One of the ablest and most active organizers among the Bolsheviks in the early period of Soviet power, highly valued by Lenin. Responsible (with Lenin) for the order to assassinate the Tsar and his family. According to the official version, died after a sudden illness. Buried at the Kremlin wall. According to Robert Massie, at the time there were persistent rumours that his sudden death at this young age was caused by an attack on him by a worker at a meeting in Moscow. A documentary clip showing his funeral was shown on Soviet TV, Nov. 1987, in connection with 70 years of the October Revolution. His head, clearly visible in the open coffin, was bandaged.

Sveshnikov, Aleksandr Vasil'evich
11.9.1890–1978? Conductor.
Born in Kolomna. Organizer and head of the All-Union Radio Vocal Ensemble, 1928–36. Artistic director of the Leningrad Academic Capella, 1937–41. Conductor of the State Choir of Russian Song from 1941. Founder and first director, from 1944, of the Moscow Choir School. From 1948, director of the Moscow Conservatory. Arranged many choral works.

Sveshnikov, German Aleksandrovich
15.5.1937– . Athlete.
Born in Gorkii. Honoured Master of Sports (fencing), 1960. With the Gorkii Armed Forces Team. Honoured Coach of the RSFSR, 1975. USSR champion, 1958–69. World champion, 1959–69. Olympic champion, 1960 and 1964.

Svetlanov, Evgenii Fedorovich
6.9.1928– . Composer, conductor.
Born in Moscow. Learned music from the age of 6. Graduated from the Gnesin Pedagogical Institute of Music, 1951. Graduated from the Moscow Conservatory, 1955. Pupil of Iu. Shaporin and A. Gauk. While a student, worked as assistant conductor with the Bolshoi Symphony Orchestra on All-Union Radio and Television. On the strength of a competition, was chosen as Conductor of Opera and Ballet by the Bolshoi Theatre. Chief conductor, 1963–65. Chief conductor and artistic director of the State Academic Symphony Orchestra of the USSR from 1965. Author of *Muzyka Segodnia*. Followed the classical tradition. Composed symphonies, chamber music, instrumental and vocal works. Many guest performances abroad. Guest conductor of the BBC Symphony Orchestra. Lives in Moscow and London.

Svetlov, Valerian Iakovlevich (real name – Ivchenko)
29.10.1860–1934. Ballet critic, editor.
Born in Petersburg. Began writing about ballet in the 1890s. Supported the innovations of M. M. Fokin. Member of the committee for the organization of Russian Seasons abroad, 1909. Editor of the periodical *Niva*, 1910–16. Emigrated. Lived in Paris from 1917 until his death.
Works: *Zhretsy. Teatral'nye Ocherki*, Petersburg, 1896; *O. O. Preobrazhenskaia*, Petersburg, 1902; *Terpsikhora*, Petersburg, 1906; *Sovremennyi Balet*, Petersburg, 1911; *Anna Pavlova*, Paris, 1922; *Tamara Karsavina*, London, 1922; *The Diaghileff Ballet in Paris*, London, 1929; *In Defence of Classical Art in Dance*, London, 1931; 'Quelques Idées sur le Modernisme', *Archives Internationales de la Danse*, Paris, 1933.

Svetoslavskii, Sergei Ivanovich
6.10.1857–19.9.1931. Artist.
Born in Kiev. Landscape and genre painter. Studied at the Moscow School of Painting, Sculpture and Architecture, 1875–83, under A. Savrasov. Member of the Peredvizhniki from 1891. Exhibitions: at the TPKHV, 1884–1900, and MOLKH, 1890–92, the All-Russian Exhibition, Nizhnii Novgorod, 1896, and the Mir Iskusstva, 1901–02. Died in Kiev.

Svetov, Feliks Grigor'evich
1927– . Author.
Born in Moscow. Son of the prominent Soviet historian Grigorii Fridliand, who perished in the Gulag camps in the 1930s. Graduated in philology from Moscow University. Published many articles and books from 1955. Expelled from the Union of Writers after protesting against the harassment of Dr. A. Sakharov, and the arrest of his own wife Z. Krakhmalnikova in 1982. His archive was confiscated by the KGB and he was arrested in Jan. 1985. Released from exile in Altai in 1987. Works: *Otverzi Mi Dveri*, Paris, 1978; 'Russkie Sud'by' (contributed to *Iz Pod Glyb* under the name of F. Korsakov); *Mat' Mariia: Poeziia, Sluzhenie, Krest, Nadezhda*, Paris, 1984.

Sviatopolk-Mirskii, Dmitrii Petrovich, Prince
1890–1939. Literary scholar.
Son of the liberal Minister of the Interior before WWI. Left Russia with his parents after the October Revolution 1917. Settled in England, lecturer in Russian literature at London University. Wrote the best history of Russian literature in the English language. Contributed to the Russian emigré press. Close to M. Tsvetaeva. Became a left-wing intellectual. Joined the British Communist Party, 1930. Returned to the Soviet Union, 1932. At first allowed to continue scholarly work, but soon denounced by Stalinist critics as a White Guard in 1935, after he dared to criticize Fadeev, a classic exponent of socialist realism. Arrested, 1937. Died in the Gulag.

Sviderskii, Frants Ivanovich
18.1.1877–13.5.1939. Revolutionary.
Born in Kukov (then Russian Poland). Revolutionary activity from 1897. From 1899, a socialist-democrat in Poland and Lithuania. Party work in Warsaw. Arrested, sentenced to death, commuted to hard labour for life on the island of Sakhalin. In 1905, escaped from Sakhalin to the USA. Joined the left wing of the American Socialist Party. From 1919, member of the Communist Party of the USA. Party worker at Detroit. In 1921, returned to Soviet Russia. Party work in 1922. His official biography finishes here. Probably a victim of the Gulag.

Svilova, Elizaveta Ignat'evna (m. Vertova)
5.9.1900–11.11.1975. Film editor.
In 1914, photo-editor at the Pathé Brothers Laboratory. Worked for the Moskinokomitet (Moscow Film Cttee.), 1918–27. Later at Goskino. Met and later married Dziga Vertov, and worked with him in the Film Archive. In the 1920s, member of the Kinoki group. Assistant and co-director to her husband. After his death, prepared a book, *Dziga Vertov v Vospominaniiakh Sovremennikov* which was published in Moscow a year after her own death.

Sviridov, Georgii Vasil'evich
16.12.1915– . Composer.
Born in Fatezh, near Kursk. In 1941, graduated from the Leningrad Conservatory composition class under P. Riazanov and Dmitrii Shostakovich. 1962–74, Secretary of the Union of Composers. Wrote musical compositions for poems by Sergei Esenin and Boris Pasternak, also composed music for films and theatre plays.

Sviridov, Vladimir Petrovich
1897–1963. Lt.-general.
On active service during WWI. Joined the Red Army, 1919. Took part in the Civil War. Graduated from the Frunze Military Academy, 1930, and the Academy of the General Staff, 1938. During WWII, commander of artillery forces at the Northern and Leningrad fronts. Deputy chairman of the Allied Control Commission in Hungary, 1945–48. Commander at the Central Group of Armies, 1949. After Stalin's death, demoted to deputy com-

mander of a military district, 1954–57.

Svirskii, Aleksei Ivanovich
8.10.1865–6.2.1942. Author.
Probably born in Zhitomir in the Ukraine into a poor Jewish working-class family. Lost his parents and became a homeless child wandering around the country. Began writing about his adventures in 1892. First story published in 1893 – *Rostovskie Trushchoby* (Rostov's Slums). *V Stenakh Tiur'my* (Inside a Prison) was about his imprisonment as a thief in 1894. *Evreiskie Rasskazy* and *Deti Ulitsy* were published in 1909. The heroes of his books are drunkards, thieves and prostitutes. Other books: *Istoriia Moei Zhizni* (Story of My Life), 1929–34, 2nd reprint in 1940. Died in Moscow.

Svirskii, Grigorii Tsezarevich
1921– . Author.
Born in Ufa. Graduated in philology from Moscow University. His first publication appeared in 1947. Published many articles, books and film scripts between 1956–66. Came into conflict with the authorities. In 1968, expelled from the Communist Party. In 1971, expelled from the Union of Writers. Left the USSR in 1972. Lived in Israel, moved to Canada. Books: *Zalozhniki*, France, 1974; *Na Lobnom Meste: Literatura Nravstvennogo Soprotivleniia, 1946–76*, London, 1979.

Svobodin, Aleksandr Petrovich (Liberté)
1925– . Literary and film critic, author.
Born in Moscow. Son of Pierre Liberté (pseudonym), a worker in the Comintern. His mother worked in Lenin's Secretariat. Graduated from Moscow University. Prominent literary critic. Appeared in print in the early 1960s. Member of the writers and film-makers' unions. Founder and member of the Board of the Union of Theatre Workers. Talked about glasnost and changes in all spheres of life in the USSR at the Soviet Playwrights Symposium in London, May 1988. Works: *Teatral'nye Povesti*, 1964; *Teatral'naia Ploshchad'*, 1981; *Mikhail Ul'ianov*, 1988; *Narodovol'tsy*, a play; and *Nas Venchali Ne v Tserkvi* (filmed by B. Tokarev); Also made

over 20 30-minute TV films about actors.

Sychkov, Fedot Vasil'evich
1870–1958. Artist.
Genre, portrait, landscape and water-colour painter. Studied at the Petersburg Academy of Arts, 1895–1900. Also with the artist P. Kovalevskii. Exhibted from 1904: Spring Exhibitions of the Academy of Arts, 1904–07, 1909–12, 1914–17; St. Petersburg Society of Artists, 1904–10, 1912–15, 1917, the Society of Water-Colour Artists, St. Petersburg, 1906–16; the Association of Artists, 1914–16. Personal exhibitions: Saransk, 1945, 1952, and Moscow 1952. Died in Saransk, in Mordovian ASSR.

Syrmus, Edvard (Sirmus, Edward)
10.7.1878–16.8.1940. Violinist.
Born in Estonia. Pupil of A. Marto, and L. Kape. Toured all over Europe at the turn of the century playing mainly in workers' clubs. According to Soviet sources, deported from England in 1919 for revolutionary activity. During WWI and the Civil War, toured the fronts. Lived in Europe, 1921–32 and 1933–36. From 1936, lived in the USSR. Died in Moscow.

Sysoev, Viacheslav Viacheslavovich (Syssoev)
30.10.1937–   . Cartoonist.
Born in Moscow. Self-taught artist. Specializes in sharp political cartoons on Soviet life, bureaucrats, foreign policy, and abuse of human rights. All this brought him into conflict with the Soviet authorities. Several short imprisonments. Became virtually hunted by the KGB. Went into hiding for 4 years. In 1980, detained at the notorious Ganushkin psychiatric hospital in Moscow in the special department for dissidents. However, his caricatures continued to be published in the West. Became a cause célèbre in France, with several artistic personalities signing letters of protest against his harassment. The Paris magazine *Canard Enchainé* published his drawing *The Monument to the Unknown Gulag*, which made him internationally famous, and which was later reproduced on the cover of Varlam Shalamov's *Kolyma*. The International Association for the Defence of Artists (AIDA) brought pressure to bear on the Soviet authorities, and he was at last released on 9 Feb. 1985, and restored as an artist in Moscow. Some of his cartoons (on China) have since been published in a Soviet magazine.
Works: *La Vie est devenue Meilleure* (album of caricatures), Paris: Alternative, 1980; *Silence, Hôpital*, autobiography, with illustrations by the author, Paris: Scarabee and Co, 1984.

Sysoev, Viktor Sergeevich
8.2.1915–   . Admiral.
Born in Barakovo, Riazan' Oblast'. Joined the Soviet Navy, 1937. Graduated from the Frunze Higher Naval School, 1939. Served on destroyers in the Black Sea, and with the Northern fleet, 1941–45. Member of the CPSU, 1942. Graduated from the Naval Academy, 1952. After the war, commander of a destroyer, and Chief-of-staff of the Black Sea fleet, 1955–60. Professor at the USSR Navy Academy, 1960–65. 1st Deputy Commander, 1965–68, and Commander of the Black Sea fleet, 1968–74. Head of the Naval Academy from Mar. 1974.

Sytin, Ivan Dmitrievich
5.2.1851–23.11.1934. Publisher, bookseller, editor.
Born at Gnezdnikovo near Soligalich. Son of a rural clerk. Worked in bookshops in Moscow. Started to print lubki (folk prints), 1876, and later published cheap books for readers in villages, 1877. Collaborated with L. Tolstoy and Chertkov (Posrednik publishing house), 1884. Gradually became one of the most important publishers in Russia in the 1890s. Published cheap mass-editions of Russian classics. Published encyclopaedias at the beginning of the 20th century – *Narodnaia*, 14 volumes, *Voennaia*, 18 volumes, *Detskaia*, 10 volumes – and published the magazine *Vokrug Sveta*, 1891, and the mass-circulation newspaper *Russkoe Slovo* (1 million copies). Had his own bookshops in 60 Russian cities. Dispossessed by the Bolsheviks, continued to work as a state employee in his former print shop. Memoirs, *Zhizn dlia Knigi*.

Sytin, Pavel Pavlovich
1870–1938. Major-general.
Graduated from the Academy of the General Staff, 1899. Took part in the Russo-Japanese war, 1904–05, and WWI as a major-general. During the 1917 Revolution, elected Corps Commander by his soldiers, and joined the Red Army with his corps. Took part in the Civil War. Soviet military attaché in independent Georgia, 1920–21. Professor at military educational establishments, 1922. Victim of Stalin's purges.

Szamuely, Tibor
1890–1919. Revolutionary.
Joined the Hungarian SD Party, 1908. During WWI, in the Austro-Hungarian Army. After 1915, POW in Russia. Became one of the most active organizers of Bolshevik sympathizers among the POWs. Took part in the quelling of the left-SRs revolt in Moscow, July 1918. Active organizer of international brigades of the Red Army during the Civil War, which were often used for Cheka duties. From Jan. 1919, one of the leaders of the Hungarian Soviet Republic, in charge of state security, and responsible for Red terror operations. Visited Soviet Russia in May 1919 in an unsuccessful attempt to secure help from Lenin. After the fall of Soviet power in Hungary, killed by Hungarian anti-communists.

T

Tabakov, Mikhail Innokent'evich
18.1.1877–9.3.1956. Trumpet-player.
Born in Odessa. Trumpet virtuoso. Soloist with the orchestra of the Bolshoi Theatre, 1898–1938. Professor at the Moscow Conservatory and the Gnesin Music-Pedagogical Institute. Author of *Progressivnaia Shkola dlia Truby*, 1946. Trained a generation of musicians, including T. Dokshitser and G. Orvod. Died in Moscow.

Tabidze, Titsian Iustinovich
21.3.1895–1937. Poet.
Born in the village of Shuamta in Georgia. Graduated from Moscow University, 1917. became close to the Russian symbolist poets. In his native Georgia organized a group of symbolist poets, The Blue Horns (Golubye Rogi), 1915. Edited the publication of this group, *Barrikady*.

Considered a classic author of Georgian poetry of the 20th century. A victim of the Gulag camps during the Stalin years. Rehabilitated posthumously.

Tagantsev, Nikolai Stepanovich
19.2.1843–21.3.1923. Lawyer, senator.
Born in Penza. Graduated from Petersburg University in law, 1867. Professor there, 1870. Member of the Senate. Foremost authority on criminal law before the revolution. Formulated the Criminal Code and compiled commentaries to it. Lifelong fighter against capital punishment. Editor of the prestigious legal magazine *Zhurnal Grazhdanskogo i Ugolovnago Prava*. Died in Leningrad.

Tagirov, Gai Khadzheevich
9.1.1907– . Ballet dancer, choreographer.
Born in Kemerovskaia Oblast'. Graduated from the Theatre School, 1928, from the Choreographic Studio in Kazan', 1929, and from the Moscow Choreographic School, 1938. Pupil of A. Chekrygin, A. Monakhov and P. Gusev. With the Kamala Tatar Theatre, 1928–33 (where he produced dances for the first time). Choreographer and teacher with the Dzhalil' Theatre, 1939–52. Chief choreographer with the Tatar State Ensemble of Song and Dance, 1952–70. Director, teacher and artistic director with the studio attached to the Dzhalil' Theatre. Teacher at the Kazan' Institute of Culture from 1970. Author of ballet scenarios and the book *Tatarskie Tantsy*, 1960.

Tairov, Aleksandr Iakovlevich (real name – Kornblit)
6.7.1885–25.9.1950. Stage director.
Born in Romny, in the Ukraine. Studied law at Petersburg University. At the same time, worked as an actor and director in theatres in various cities. In 1914 in Moscow founded the Kamernyi Teatr, which he ran for 32 years until he was dismissed as artistic director during an anticosmopolitan campaign. The Zhdanov cultural authorities let him stage some socialist-realist plays for 3 more years. In his main theatrical work *Zapiski Rezhissera* (Notes of a Stage Director), re-published in Moscow in 1970, stressed the mime element, which he considered the foundation of all theatrical art. At his studio attached to the Kamernyi Theatre, concentrated on juggling, acrobatics, fencing, breathing, gymnastics, movement, dancing and rhythm. Such principles were diametrically opposed to Stanislavskii's. Sets and lighting were of the utmost importance in all his productions. Later influenced by constructivism and cubism. In 1934, his production *Optimisticheskaia Tragediia* was attacked by the Soviet press for its formalism. He was made to work under party cttee. control and began adapting himself to socialist realism. Became less and less productive until eventually his theatre was closed in 1950. Died in Moscow.
See: Iurii Elagin, *Ukroshchenie Iskusstv*, NY: Chekhov Publ. House, 1952.

Tairov, Boris Aleksandrovich
29.11.1906– . Ballet dancer, choreographer.
Born in Odessa. Son of Aleksandr Tairov. Graduated from the Music and Drama Department of the Odessa Technical School. Pupil of V. Presniakov. With the Odessa Theatre, 1923–33, the Lysenko Theatre, 1933–34, and the Shevchenko Theatre, 1934–37. Teacher at the Kiev Choreographic Technical School from 1934. Choreographer with the Kiev Operetta Theatre, 1944–72. Composed scenarios for ballets. With the Kiev Institute of Drama, 1936–51, and with the studio attached to the Kiev Operetta Theatre from 1962.

Tairova, Alia Azizovna
5.8.1917– . Ballerina.
Born in Ashkhabad, Turkmenia. Graduated from the Baku Choreographic School, 1939. Additional training in the Pedagogical Department of the Moscow Choreographic School. First appearance in ballet at the Azizbekov Theatre, 1934–37, and then with the corps de ballet of the Akhuntov Theatre. Appeared also as a soloist. Many leading parts. Teacher from 1942. Taught at the Baku Choreographic School, 1945–47. Director of the same, 1947–78.

Taktakishvili, Otar Vasil'evich
27.7.1924– . Composer, conductor.
Born in Tbilisi. Early training at the Tbilisi Music School. At the Conservatory, 1942–49. Postgraduate work under S. Barkhudarian. While a student, worked as conductor of the Radio Choir, 1947–52. Conductor and artistic director with the State Choir, 1952–56. With leading symphonic and choral ensembles in performances of his own works from 1957. Teacher of composition at the Tbilisi Conservatory from 1959. Professor in 1966. His music was influenced in melody and rhythm by Georgian literature. Combined modern techniques with elements of folk music. Composed operas, 2 symphonies, oratorios, cantatas, and other vocal and instrumental pieces.

Taktakishvili, Shalva Mikhailovich
27.8.1900–18.7.1965. Composer.
Born in the village of Kvemo-Khviti, Georgia. Professor at the Tbilisi Conservatory. Author of operas, a ballet, symphonies, choral music, chamber music, romances and songs. Died in Tbilisi.

Tal', Mikhail Nekhem'evich
9.11.1936– . Chess player, grandmaster.
Born in Riga. Extremely talented chess player. World champion, 1957–58. Nicknamed the 'Riga Magician'. Despite his bad health, still considered one of the strongest chess players in the world. Plays for the Soviet Union team all over the world.

Talalikhin, Viktor Vasil'evich
1918–1941. Pilot.
Educated at a pilots' school, 1938. Became widely known for his skill in dog-fights during the first weeks of WWII. Shot down by German aircraft.

Talberg, Nikolai Dmitrievich
22.7.1886– . Historian, journalist.
Born in Korostyshev near Kiev. Son of a professor at Kiev University. Educated at the Kiev High School. Graduated from the Law School in Petersburg, 1907. Worked in the Ministry of the Interior, 1907–17. During the Civil War, active in underground monarchist organi-

zations. Joined the Ministry of the Interior of Hetman Skoropadskii in Kiev, recruiting many former Tsarist officers in the Ukraine. After the fall of Skoropadskii, emigrated to Bulgaria. Moved to Berlin. Between the wars, active in the Russian monarchist press and monarchist organizations in Western Europe. After WWII, in DP camps in Austria and Germany. Emigrated to the USA, 1950. Professor of the Orthodox seminary at Jordanville monastery, USA. Buried at the same monastery, Main works: *Istoriia Russkoi Tserkvi, Imperator Nikolai 1, Tragediia Russkogo Ofitserstva.*

Tal'iantsev, Nikolai Iakovlevich
1895–1946. Sculptor.
Studied privately at the studio of D. D. Pashkov, 1909–13, then at the art school of the Society for the Encouragement of the Arts, and privately at the V. V. Kozlov and L. A. Dietrikh Sculptors' Studio, 1913–16. Later, at the Leningrad Academy of Arts. Graduated, 1925. Exhibited from 1915 in Iaroslavl' and Leningrad.

Tal'ts, Iaan Augustovich
19.5.1944–   . Athlete.
Born in Estonia. Graduated from an agricultural high school in Estonia, 1963. Honoured Master of Sports (athletics), 1969. Member of the CPSU, 1973. USSR champion, 1967–68 and 1972. European champion, 1968–70 and 1972. World champion 1969–70 and 1972. Olympic champion, 1972.

Talyzin, Nikolai Vladimirovich
28.1.1929–   . Politician.
Electrical fitter, 1942–50. Graduated from the Moscow Electrical Engineering Institute of Communications, 1955. Senior posts at the State Scientific Research Institute of Radio Engineering, 1955–65. Member of the CPSU, 1960. Deputy USSR Minister, 1st Deputy Minister of Communications, 1965–75. Minister, 1975–80. Professor, 1975. Deputy Chairman of the USSR Council of Ministers and the USSR's Permanent Representative in Comecon, 1980–85. Member of the Cen. Cttee. of the CPSU from 1981. Member of the Politburo, 10 Oct. 1985. 1st Deputy Chairman of the USSR Council of Ministers from 14 Oct. 1985. Chairman of the USSR State Planning Cttee. (GOSPLAN) from 14 Oct. 1985. Chairman of the Commission for the Improvement of Management, Planning and the Economic Mechanism of the USSR Council of Ministers from Jan. 1986. Member of the Cen. Cttee. of the CPSU from 1981.

Tamara Khanum (real name – Petrosian, Tamara Artemovna)
29.3.1906–   . Ballerina, choreographer, singer.
Born in Fergana. Daughter of a worker. Stage debut, 1919. Pupil of A. Kamilov. Trained at the Lunacharskii Technical Theatre School, 1923–24. Appeared with the Sverdlov Russian Opera, Tashkent, 1921–25, and at the World Exhibition of Decorative Arts in Paris, 1925. Took part with M. Kari-Iakubov and others in the organization of the first Uzbek Theatre of Musical Drama, 1923, in Samarkand (at Tashkent from 1931). Worked there till 1934. Organized the ballet school attached to the Uzbek Theatre of Musical Drama (the Tamara Khanum Ballet School from 1935). Took part in the World Festival of Folk Dancing, London, 1935. With the Uzbek Philharmonic from 1936. Guest appearances in many towns in the USSR and abroad. Reformed the style of Uzbek female dancing, and created the genre of song-mime miniatures. Producer as well as dancer. Stalin Prize, 1941.

Tamarkina, Roza Vladimirovna
23.3.1920–5.8.1950. Pianist.
Born in Kiev. Pupil of A. Goldenveizer and K. Igumnov. 2nd prize at the Chopin International Competition, Warsaw, 1937. From 1946, taught at the Moscow Conservatory. The cause of her premature death is not given in Soviet sources.

Tamberg, Eino Martinovich
27.5.1930–   . Composer.
Born in Tallinn. Author of an opera, oratorio, suite, concerto, string quartet, pieces for piano, songs, and music for theatre and cinema.

Tamm, Igor' Evgen'evich
8.7.1895–12.4.1971. Physicist.
Graduated from Moscow University, 1918. Worked at Moscow University, 1924–41, and from 1954. Teacher of many physicists who later became well-known in Soviet science. Nobel Prize for physics, 1958. With A. Sakharov, proposed a new method of controlled thermonuclear reaction, 1950. Academician 1953.

Taran, Pavel Andreevich
1916–   . Lt.-general.
Joined the Red Army, 1937. Educated at a pilots' school, 1938. Took part in the Soviet-Finnish war, 1939–40. During WWII, commanded bomber groups, and acted as a pilot instructor. Graduated from the Academy of the General Staff, 1958. Worked at the Ministry of Defence, 1960–79.

Taranovskaia, Sof'ia Leonidovna
27.12.1928–   . Ballerina, teacher.
Probably born in China. Graduated from the O. King Ballet School in Shanghai. From 1949, soloist at the Sverdlovsk, then Cheliabinsk theatres. Many leading parts. Liricodramatical talent. Ballet teacher from the late 1960s.

Taranovskii, Fedor Vasil'evich
1875–1936. Law historian.
Graduated from Warsaw University. Professor at Warsaw and Petersburg universities. Emigrated after the Civil War. Professor at Belgrade University and member of the Royal Serbian Academy. Died in Belgrade.

Tarasenko, Ivan
1962–1987. Sculptor.
Ukrainian sculptor. Emigrated from the Soviet Union, 1981. Lived in Dyfed, Wales. Member of the Mutoid Waste Company. Victim of the King's Cross underground station fire disaster in London on 18 Nov. 1987.

Tarasov, Aleksandr Alekseevich
23.3.1927–   . Athlete.
Born in Moscow Oblast'. Honoured Master of Sports (pentathlon), 1957. With Leningrad Dynamo. Graduated from the School of Trainers attached to the Institute of Physical Culture, Leningrad, 1959. Member of the CPSU, 1963. Olympic champion, 1956. World champion, 1957–59. USSR champion, 1958.

Tarasov, Nikolai Ivanovich
19.2.1902–8.2.1975. Ballet dancer, choreographer, stage director.
Born in Moscow. Graduated from the Moscow Choreographic School, 1920. Pupil of N. Legat. With the Bolshoi Theatre, 1920–35, as one of its leading dancers. Taught at the Moscow Choreographic School, 1923 –60. Director and artistic director of the same, 1942–45, and artistic director, 1953–54. Taught at the Moscow Artistic Ballet under V. Kriger, 1929–30. Artistic director at the Variety and Ballet Technical School, 1933–37. From 1946, taught and supervised the future choreographers' class at GITIS. Professor there from 1962. Among his famous pupils were Iu. Zhdanov, A. Lapauri and M. Liepa. Author of a ballet manual, *Metodika Klassicheskogo Trenazha*, Moscow, 1940, with A. Chekrygin and V. Morits, and of *Klassicheskii Tanets*, 1971, Moscow. State Prize, 1975. With A. Vaganova, co-scriptwriter of *Metodika Klassicheskogo Tantsa*, 1947. Died in Moscow.

Tarasov, Vladimir
1947– . Jazz musician.
Born in Arkhangelsk. Self-taught musician. Played as lead drummer with a professional jazz band from the age of 14. Member of the Lithuanian Symphony Orchestra and the Lithuanian State Symphony Orchestra. Member of the Ganelin Trio, with whom he had a huge success on their British tour in 1984.

Tarasova, Alla Konstantinovna
6.2.1898–5.4.1973. Actress.
Dramatic actress. Emigrated in 1922. Appeared in the German film *Raskolnikov*, 1923. Returned to the USSR and became a leading actress at the MKHAT Theatre. Married her equally famous partner, Ivan Moskvin. Made many films. Played Anna Karenina in a 1953 version of Tolstoy's masterpiece.

Tarasova, Olga Georgievna
17.2.1927– . Ballerina, choreographer.
Born in Kiev. Graduated from the Moscow Choreographic School, 1946, and from the Ballet Department of the Moscow GITIS, 1957.

Character dancer. Soloist with the Bolshoi Theatre, 1946–66. With the Tokyo Ballet, 1966. Toured extensively in the USSR. With Lapauri, directed the ballet films *Podporuchik Kizhe*, 1968, and *Imia Tvoe*, 1970. From 1968, teacher at GITIS. Choreographer with many theatres after 1969.

Tarich, Iurii Viktorovich (real name – Alekseev)
24.1.1885–21.2.1967. Film director.
Studied at Moscow University, 1903–05. Became involved in revolutionary activity and exiled to Siberia, 1905–07. After his release, appeared as an actor in various theatres and started working as a scriptwriter in film studios. In 1926, made his best film, *Kryl'ia Kholopa*. Made many films subsequently, but none of any particular value.

Tariverdiev, Mikael Leonovich
15.8.1931– . Composer.
Born in Tbilisi. Moved to Moscow. Author of a ballet, a concerto for orchestra, and songs. Composer of very popular music for film and theatre.

Tarkhov, Nikolai (Tarkhoff, Nicolas)
10.1.1871–5.6.1930. Artist.
Born in Moscow. Son of a wealthy merchant. Studied in Moscow art schools. Met K. Korovin, 1897, and the circle of Young Muscovite Painters (P. Kuznetsov, P. Utkin, and A. Sredin). Travelled throughout Russia, including the Caucasus and Samarkand. Promoted by Korovin. Visited Paris, 1899. Exhibited his paintings at the World of Art and the Union of Russian Painters. Appointed to the studios of I. P. Laurens and L. O. Merson. Married in 1905 and had 4 children. From 1900, worked incessantly, painting many different subjects such as markets, street scenes, working people, and crowds. Died in Paris. A major exhibition of his work took place in 1981 at the Petit Palais.

Tarkovskii, Andrei Arsenievich
4.4.1932–29.12.1986. Film director.
Born in Moscow. Son of the poet Arsenii Tarkovskii. Graduated from the VGIK as a director in 1961. Studied under Mikhail Romm. His

first (short) film was *The Steam-Roller and the Violin* (1961, script by A. Mikhalkov-Konchalovskii, camera-work by V. Iusov). Won a prize at the New York Film Festival. First feature film, *Ivan's Childhood* (1962, camera-work again by V. Iusov). Became internationally known after *Andrei Rublev*, which was finished in 1966 but remained banned for some 5 years. The film was brought by sheer chance to the Cannes Film Festival in 1969 and received the International Critics' Prize. *Solaris* (1972), a science-fiction film, received another award at Cannes. *Mirror* (1975) and *Stalker* (1978) were shown in the Soviet Union for only a few weeks. All Tarkovskii's films were criticized and remained too obscure for the Russian public as well for the critics. Eventually managed to get work in Italy, where *Nostalgia* was made in 1983. In 1984, announced his defection and was subsequently stripped of his Soviet citizenship. Became a legend in the West and was showered with offers to make films from several countries. Tried his hand at stage production with *Boris Godunov* at Covent Garden. His last film, *The Sacrifice*, was made in Sweden in 1985, and received the jury's special grand prize at Cannes in May 1986. Was already ill with cancer when he was invited by Covent Garden to make a new production of *The Flying Dutchman*. Died of cancer in Paris. Posthumously widely acclaimed in the USSR, with a Tarkovskii Heritage Commission being set up in 1987. All his films are now released in the USSR and are widely praised.

Tarle, Evgenii Viktorovich
1875–1955. Historian.
Graduated from Kiev University, 1896. After 1917, professor at Petrograd, and later Moscow universities. Many historical works, especially on the Napoleonic epoch, and the 18th and 19th century in general. Several State Prizes.

Tarmak, Iuri Aaduvovich
21.7.1946– . Athlete.
Born in Tallinn. Estonian. Honoured Master of Sports (track and field athletics), 1972. With Leningrad Dynamo. Graduated in economics from Leningrad University, 1975. Member of the CPSU, 1975. Olympic champion, 1976.

Tarnopol'skii, Vladimir Moiseevich
9.3.1897–1942. Composer.
Born in Rostov-on-Don. Moved to Moscow. Studied at the Moscow Conservatory. Member of the Prokoll. Author of the opera *Pir Vo Vremia Chumy*, 1937. Wrote symphonies, pieces for the balalaika, romances, and music for plays. Died in the Battle of Stalingrad.

Tarsis, Valerii Iakovlevich
1906–1983. Author.
Born in Kiev. Graduated from Rostov University, 1929. Worked as an editor in the Khudozhestvennaia Literatura publishing house, wrote short stories, and worked as a translator. During WWII, newspaper correspondent at the front. Wounded, married his nurse (the niece of the Soviet aviation commander, Alksnis). Demanded permission to leave the USSR, 1961. Sent his unpublished works abroad, 1962, and was detained in the Kashchenko psychiatric hospital (one of the first cases of this method of persecution, rare under Khrushchev but becoming widespread under Brezhnev and Andropov). Expelled from the USSR in the late 1960s. Settled in Switzerland. Published his works abroad, but his initial success was not repeated. Died in Switzerland.
Main works: *Skazanie o Sinei Mukhe, Palata Nomer 7.*

Tartakov, Ioakim Viktorovich
1860–23.1.1923. Singer.
Born in Odessa. Pupil of K. Everardi. Soloist at the Mariinskii Theatre, 1882–84 and 1894–1923. From 1909, chief stage-director at the Mariinskii Theatre. Died in Petrograd.

Tatushin, Boris Georgievich
31.3.1933– . Athlete.
Born in Moscow. Master of Sports of the USSR (football). With Moscow Spartak. Coach. Graduated from the School of Trainers, 1968. USSR champion, 1953, 1956 and 1958. Olympic champion, 1956.

Taube, Aleksandr Aleksandrovich, Baron
1864–1919. Lt.-general.
Son of Baron A. Taube. Graduated from the Academy of the General Staff, 1891. On active service during WWI. Joined the Red Army, 1918. Took part in the Civil War as Chief-of-staff of the Red Army in Siberia. Taken prisoner by the Whites in Bodaibo, and sentenced to death. Died in prison.

Tavadze, Tamara Georgievna
25.7.1898–after 1970. Theatrical designer.
Born in Tiflis. Trained in Moscow at the Artists' Studio, 1916–17. At the Technical Arts Institute, 1922–28. Designed for ballet with the Paliashvili Theatre, 1920–22, and the Bolshoi Theatre, 1927–36. Honoured Artist of the Georgian SSR, 1962.

Tavrion (Batozskii), monk
1898–1978. Russian Orthodox clergyman.
Monk of the Orthodox Church. First arrest, 1925. Spent almost 30 years in prisons, in exile and in the Gulag. Widely revered for his saintly life by other inmates and later considered one of the great representatives of the starets tradition in modern times.

Tavrizian, Mikhail Arsen'evich
27.5.1907–17.10.1957. Conductor.
Born in Baku. Pupil of A. Gauk. Graduated from the Moscow Conservatory. From 1935, conductor, and from 1938, chief conductor at the Erevan Opera and Ballet Theatre. Died in Erevan.

Tediashvili, Levan Kitoevich
15.3.1948– . Athlete.
Born in Georgia. Honoured Master of Sports (wrestling), 1971. Graduated from the Georgian Institute of Physical Culture, 1971. From 1973, with the Tbilisi Armed Forces. Member of the CPSU from 1976. Sports teacher. USSR champion, 1971 and 1973–74. World champion, 1971 and 1973–75. Olympic champion, 1972 and 1976. European champion, 1974, 1976 and 1978.

Teffi, Nadezhda Aleksandrovna (Buchinskaia, Lokhvitskaia)
1872–1952. Author.
Became one of the best known and best loved humorists in Russia before WWI. Emigrated, 1920. Settled in France, where she continued to write her humorous stories, based on the often absurd life of penniless and confused refugees. Widely read by Russians all over the world between the wars. Published several collections of stories, and memoirs of the revolutionary period Died in poverty in Paris.

Telegin, Aleksei Dmitrievich
1900?–3.9.1980. Actor.
Emigrated after the Civil War. Settled in Paris. Became a well-known member of the Russian theatrical community in Paris, took part in stage productions by Evreinov, M. Chekhov and many others. Died in Paris.

Telegin, Konstantin Fedorovich
1899–1981. Lt.-general, state security official.
Joined the Red Army, 1918, and the Bolshevik Party, 1919. Took part in the Civil War. Graduated from the Military Political Academy, 1931. Political officer in NKVD troop detachments, 1936. Took part in the Soviet-Finnish war, 1939–40. High posts in the NKVD (state security), 1940–41. On active service as a political and secret police officer during WWII. Prominent member of the Soviet Military Administration in Germany, 1945–46. Deputy head of the Vystrel Courses, in charge of political work, 1955–56.

Temirkhanov, Iurii Khatuevich
10.12.1938– . Musical director, conductor.
By his own account, born around the corner from the Yusupov Palace in Leningrad (now a musicians' residence) where Rasputin was poisoned before being thrown into the Neva. Played the violin at the Tovstonogov Theatre, Leningrad. From 1977, musical director of the Kirov Opera Theatre, Leningrad. Staged 3 operas – *The Queen of Spades, Eugene Onegin* and *Boris Godunov* – known in Russia as the *Temirkhanovskie spektakli.* In July 1987, brought them to Covent Garden, where they were warmly received by both critics and public. Many guest appearances in the West.

Teodorovich, Ivan
1875–1937. Politician.
Member of the SD Party from 1902. 1st Commissar of Food Supply in the

Soviet government, Oct. 1917. Resigned, Dec. 1917. Took part in the Civil War, 1919–20. Worked at the Commissariat of Agriculture, 1920–28. General Secretary of the Peasant International, 1928–30.

Terapiano, Iurii Konstantinovich
21.10.1892–3.7.1980. Journalist, literary critic.
Born in Kerch in the Crimea. Studied law at Kiev University, 1916. Took part in WWI. Joined the White Army, 1919. Evacuated to Constantinople. Settled in Paris, 1925. Chairman of the union of young poets in Paris. One of the main exponents of the Parizhskaia Nota in Russian emigré poetry. For many years, literary critic of the newspaper *Russkaia Mysl'* in Paris. Edited an anthology of Russian emigré poetry, *Muza Diaspory*, 1960. Published memoirs, *Literaturnaia Zhizn Russkogo Parizha za Polveka*.

Terekhova, Margarita Borisovna
25.8.1942– . Film actress.
One of the best character actresses in Soviet cinema. Studied at Tashkent University's Faculty of Physics. Later, left for Moscow, where she was accepted by the Mossoviet Theatre Drama Studio. Graduated from there to become an actress in the Mossoviet Theatre. Her first film at Armenfilm (Armenia) was *Hello, It's Me* (1966, director F. Dovlatian). Her second film was a co-production with Bulgaria, *Running On the Waves*. Gained international recognition for her 2 roles in Andrei Tarkovskii's *The Mirror* (Mosfilm, 1975). Other films of note: *Monologue* (Lenfilm, 1972, director Il'ia Averbakh); *Moscow, My Love* (Mosfilm, co-production with Japan, 1974, director Aleksandr Mitta).

Terekhova, Tat'iana Gennad'evna (Berezhnaia)
21.1.1952– . Ballerina
Born in Leningrad. Graduated from the Leningrad Choreographic School, 1970. Pupil of E. Shiripina. Leading soloist with the Kirov Theatre. Winner of the Moscow International Ballet Competition, 1977.

Terelia, Iosif Mikhailovich
1943– . Dissident.
Human rights and nationalist activist in the Ukraine. Arrested 1962, sentenced to 4 years in prison. Escaped from Uzhgorod prison, 1963, caught and sentenced to 5 years. Escaped from the labour camp, 1965. Re-arrested, Mar. 1966 and sentenced to 8 years for Ukrainian nationalism. In 1972, certified insane by the Serbskii Institute. Imprisoned in psychiatric hospitals, 1972–76. Re-arrested 1976, soon released, but re-arrested, 1977, and again held in a psychiatric hospital. Known for his radical nationalism. Released and allowed to go abroad, Sep. 1987. Settled in Canada.

Terent'ev, Boris Mikhailovich
28.1.1913– . Composer.
Born in Odessa. Composer of popular songs, such as *Ia More Liubliu*, *Morskoe Serdtse* and *Gvardeiskaia Pol'ka*. Wrote several operettas, symphonies, romances, and songs for the variety stage, radio and theatre.

Terent'ev, Fedor Mikhailovich
4.10.1925–20.1.1963. Athlete.
Born in the village of Padany, Karelia. Honoured Master of Sports (skiing), 1956. With the Moscow Armed Forces. USSR champion, 1951–62, at various distances. Olympic champion, 1956. Died in Leningrad. Official sources do not give the reason for his premature death.

Tereshchenko, Mikhail Ivanovich
1888–1958. Businessman, politician.
Wealthy businessman from Kiev. Owner of sugar factories, and of the Sirin publishing house. Deputy Chairman (under Riabushinskii) of the Military-Industrial Cttee. Well-known ballet critic. Member of the Provisional Government. Finance Minister, Mar.–Apr. 1917. Minister of Foreign Affairs, May–Oct. 1917. Emigrated, 1918. Settled in England. Died in London.

Tereshchuk, Boris Pavlovich
18.3.1945– . Athlete.
Born in Kiev. International Class Master of Sports (volley-ball), 1968. With Kiev Lokomotiv. Graduated from the Ukrainian Agricultural Academy, 1973. Agrochemist. Member of the CPSU from 1973. USSR champion, 1967. Olympic champion, 1968. European champion, 1971.

Tereshkova, Valentina Vladimirovna (m. Nikolaeva)
6.3.1937– . Cosmonaut.
Born in the village of Maslennikovo, Iaroslavl'. Daughter of a kolkhoz farmer. Worked at the Iaroslavl' tyre factory, 1954, and at the Iaroslavl' textile factory, Krasnyi Perekop, 1955–60. Member of the local aviation club, making over 160 parachute jumps. Selected for a team of cosmonauts, 1962. First woman cosmonaut in orbit, 16–19 June 1963. Hero of the Soviet Union, 22 June 1963. Graduated from the Zhukovskii Military Aviation Academy, 1969. Visited many countries. President of the Cttee. of Soviet Women, 1968. Failed to be re-elected during the Gorbachev perestroika, 1986. Member of the 250-strong Soviet delegation which went to the town of Chautauqua, New York, in Aug. 1987 to talk to American leaders about putting an end to the Cold War. Member of the Cen. Cttee. of the CPSU, non-voting, 1971. A crater on the reverse side of the moon has been named after her. Married her fellow cosmonaut Nikolaev. Their daughter is the first child in history to have parents who are both cosmonauts.

Ter-Gevondian, Anushavan Grigor'evich
8.3.1887–6.6.1961. Composer.
Born in Tbilisi, Georgia. Wrote music for various Georgian and Armenian orchestras and ballet productions (*Nevesta Ognia*, 1934; *Anait*, 1940). With the Spendiarov Theatre in the post-war years. Worked closely with M. Moiseev. Died in Erevan.

Terlezki, Stefan
1932– . British politician, MP.
Born near the Carpathian Mountains in the Ukraine. Son of a Ukrainian trade-unionist. During WWII, in Germany, later emigrated to Britain. Married a Welsh woman and became Conservative MP for Cardiff West. M. Gorbachev, during his visit to Britain, invited Terlezki to visit his family, whom he had not seen for 42

years. His father's return visit on a 28-day tourist visa became national news in the UK.

Ter-Tatevosian, Dzhon Gurgenovich
14.9.1926–   . Composer.
Born in Erevan. Wrote 2 symphonies (1962 and 1965), music for string quartet, romances, and music for film and theatre.

Tesh, Sergei Nikolaevich
5.8.1899–   . Dormra player, conductor.
Born in Moscow. Pupil of G. Liubimov, and member of his Domra Quartet. Became a famous domrist. Later, conductor of a folk orchestra.

Teteriatnikov, Vladimir Mikhailovich
1938–   . Art historian.
Born in Moscow. Graduated from the Moscow Institute of the Fishing Industry and from postgraduate courses at the Moscow Institute of Art History and Theory. Until 1975, worked at the Rublev Museum, Moscow. Published articles in the press. Left the USSR, 1975, and settled in the USA. Writes about Russian art and icons. Lives in New York. Author of *Icons and Fakes*, NY, 1981, and 'Staroobriadtsy – Sozdateli Russkogo Narodnogo Iskusstva', *Novyi Zhurnal*, 1977, USA.

Teterin, Aleksandr Vasil'evich
1927–   . Diplomat.
Member of the Diplomatic Service from 1968. Embassy Councillor, 1968–71, then Embassy Councillor-Envoy at the USSR Embassy in Egypt, 1971–74. USSR Ambassador to Nigeria, 1974–78. Chief of the Consular Administration of the USSR Ministry of Foreign Affairs, 1978. USSR Ambassador to Norway, 1987.

Tevchenkov, Aleksandr Nikolaevich
1902–1975. Lt.-general, political officer.
Joined the Red Army, 1919, and the Bolshevik Party, 1920. Took part in the Civil War. On party-political work in the army, 1926. Graduated from the Military Political Academy, 1933. Political officer in different armies during WWII. Worked at the Ministry of Defence, and at the Lenin Military Political Academy, 1951–66.

Tiazhel'nikov, Evgenii Mikhailovich
1928–   . Politician, diplomat.
Born in Verkhniaia Sanarka, Cheliabinsk Oblast'. Son of a peasant. Graduated from the Cheliabinsk Pedagogical Institute, 1950. Lecturer. Member of the CPSU, 1951. Various Komsomol and party posts in Cheliabinsk. Rector of the Cheliabinsk Pedagogical Institute, 1961–64. Secretary of the Cheliabinsk Oblast' Cttee. of the CPSU, 1964–68. 1st Secretary and member of the Bureau of the Cen. Cttee. of the USSR Komsomol, 1968–77. Member of the Cen. Cttee. of the CPSU from 1971, and head of its Propaganda Department from 1977–82. Close to Brezhnev. Ambassador to Rumania under Andropov.

Tigranian, Armen Tigranovich
26.12.1879–10.2.1950. Composer, choir conductor.
Born in Aleksandropol'. From 1913 lived in Tbilisi. Author of the first Armenian folk opera *Anush*. Also wrote musicals and songs. Died in Tbilisi.

Tigranian, Nikogaios (Nikolai Faddeevich)
31.8.1856–17.2.1951. Music scholar, folklorist, composer.
Born in Aleksandropol' (now Leninakan). Went blind at the age of 9. Travelled widely all along the Caucasus, in Russia, and in Western Europe collecting folklore. Appeared as a pianist in Europe. One of the biggest collectors of Armenian, Georgian, Kurdish and Iranian folk songs. Made use of these folk motives in his own music. Died in Erevan.

Tigranov, Georgii Grigor'evich
25.3.1908–   . Musicologist.
Born in Petersburg. Professor at the Leningrad and Erevan conservatories.
Works: *Armianskii Muzykal'nyi Teatr*, 2 vols., Erevan, 1956–60; *A.A. Spendiarov*, Moscow, 1959; *K. Saradzhev. Zhizn' i Tvorchestvo*, Erevan, 1961.

Tikhomirnova, Irina Viktorovna
31.7.1917–   . Ballerina.
Born in Moscow. Graduated from the Moscow Choreographic School, 1936. Pupil of E. Gerdt. Leading dancer with the Bolshoi Theatre. State Prize, 1947. During WWII, entertained at the Baltic front. Concert soloist until 1962. In the 1960s, taught at the Moscow Choreographic School. Taught at the Théâtre de la Monnaie, Belgium, 1961. From 1970, with Moskontsert (Moscow Concert). Also appeared with foreign ballet groups.

Tikhomirov, Georgii Vladimirovich
27.12.1913–   . Composer.
Born in Moscow. Studied at the Moscow Conservatory. Author of music for folk orchestras, operas (including *Ivan Peresvetov*, 1954), and cantatas (including *Kreml'*, 1947).

Tikhomirov, Lev Aleksandrovich
19.1.1852–10.1923. Revolutionary, philosopher, historian.
Born in Gelendzhik in the Caucasus. Educated at Kerch' High School. Studied at Moscow University. Early involvement in narodnik revolutionary activity. Arrested 11 Nov. 1873. Spent 4 years in the Peter and Paul Fortress in St. Petersburg. Released, 1878. One of the leaders of the terrorist wing of Narodnaia Volia, member of its Executive Cttee., and editor of its newspapers. After the assassination of Alexander II in Mar. 1881, wrote to his successor, Alexander III, the famous ultimatum ('Letter from the Executive Cttee. of Narodnaia Volia'). Fled abroad, 1882, lived in Switzerland and France. Asked for pardon, 1888, which was granted. Returned to Russia. Lived in Novorossiisk, and later in Moscow. Became one of the most outstanding thinkers in the monarchist camp. His criticism of the revolutionaries was especially relevant because of his deep personal knowledge of their theories and practice. Editor of *Moskovskie Vedomosti*. In his later years, close to Stolypin. Died in Sergiev Posad (now Zagorsk).
Main works: *Monarkhicheskaia Gosudarstvennost'*; *Nachala i Kontsy*; *Konstitutionalisty v Epokhu 1881*

Goda; *Demokratiia Liberal'naia i Sotsial'naia*; *Edinolichnaia Vlast' Kak Printsip Gosudarstvennogo Stroeniia.*

Tikhomirov, Nikolai Ivanovich
1860–1930. Rocket scientist.
Rocket technology specialist. Founder and first director of the Soviet Union's Gasodynamic Laboratory, 1921. Designed the first Soviet rockets.

Tikhomirov, Vasilii Dmitrievich
29.3.1876–20.6.1956. Ballet dancer, choreographer, teacher.
Born in Moscow. Studied at the Moscow Theatre School, 1886–91. Pupil of I. Ermolov. Graduated from the Petersburg Theatre School, 1893. Pupil of P. Gerdt and P. Karsavin. Soloist from 1893, and choreographer from 1913 with the Bolshoi Theatre. Artistic director there, 1925–30. Permanent partner of E. Gel'tser. Taught at the Moscow Theatre School from 1896. Artistic director, 1917–31. Among his pupils were M. Mordkin and V. Kriger. Retired, 1935. Died in Moscow.

Tikhon (Belavin, Vasilii Ivanovich), Patriarch of Moscow
19.1.1865–7.4.1925. Russian Orthodox clergyman.
Born in Klin, near Toropets, Pskov Gouvt. Educated at Pskov seminary, 1878–83. Graduated from Petersburg Theological Academy in 1888. Monk, 1891. Archimandrite, 1892. Rector of Kholm seminary, 1892. Bishop of Lublin, 1898. Bishop of Alaska and the Aleutian Islands (responsible for the Russian Orthodox churches in the USA), 1899. Resided in San Francisco, later New York. Archbishop, 1905. Became widely known for his religious activity in the USA. After his return from America, Archbishop of Iaroslavl', 1907. Archbishop of Wilno and Lithuania. Evacuated to Moscow at the beginning of WWI, 1914. Member of the Holy Synod, 1914. Elected Archbishop, later Metropolitan of Moscow, 1917. Elected chairman of the Russian Church Council (Sobor), Aug. 1917. Patriarch of Moscow (third according to the votes taken at the Council, but among the 3 candidates elected by lot drawn under an icon in the Saviour Cathedral by a blind monk), 28 Oct. 1917. Had to resist enormous pressure from the communist authorities and the Living Church (radical priests with revolutionary slogans, used by the authorities to undermine the church). Arrested 16 May 1922. Released after the publication of a declaration in his name, promising loyalty to the Soviet government, 15 June 1923. His release brought an almost immediate collapse of the Living Church, abandoned both by believers and the authorities. Pressure from the state on the church continued and, according to most sources, hastened his death. Survived an assassination attempt by the Cheka. Died in Moscow. Retains a unique position as a church leader revered by all the divided factions of the Russian Orthodox Church in the USSR and abroad.

Tikhonov, Aleksandr Ivanovich
2.1.1947–   . Athlete.
Born in Cheliabinskaia Oblast'. Honoured Master of Sports (biathlon), 1968. With Novosibirsk Dynamo. Member of the CPSU from 1976. Olympic champion, 1968, 1972 and 1976. World champion, 1969–78.

Tikhonov, Aleksandr Nikolaevich (pen-name – Serebrov)
1880–1956. Editor, publisher.
Publisher-editor of the magazine *Letopis'* and the newspaper *Novaia Zhizn'*. Co-proprietor of the Parus Publishing House. After the October Revolution 1917, head of several publishing houses. Editor of *Federatsiia*. Close to Mayakovsky and Lili Brik.

Tikhonov, Nikolai Aleksandrovich
1905–   . Politician.
Son of an engineer. Worked as an assistant train driver and technician, 1924–30. Graduated from the Dnepropetrovsk Metallurgical Institute, 1930. Worked as an engineer and deputy chief engineer at various plants in Dnepropetrovsk and Pervouralsk, 1930–47. Director of a pipe factory in Nikopol, 1947–50. Head of the Main Board of the USSR Ministry of Ferrous Metallurgy, 1955–57. Chairman of Dnepropetrovsk Economic Council, 1957–60. Member of the Cen. Cttee. of the Ukrainian CP 1960–61. Deputy Chairman (with the rank of USSR Minister) of the State Economic Council of the USSR Council of Ministers, 1960–63. Candidate member, 1961–66, and full member of the Cen. Cttee. of the CPSU from 1966. Deputy Chairman of USSR GOSPLAN, 1963–65. Deputy Chairman of the USSR Council of Ministers, 1965–76. 1st Deputy Chairman of the USSR Council of Ministers, 1976–80. Candidate member of the Politburo, 1978–79. Member of the Cen. Cttee. from 1979. Head of Government (Chairman of the USSR Council of Ministers) when Gorbachev took office in Mar. 1985. Removed as one of the last of the Brezhnevite old guard in 1986. Officially retired for health reasons.

Tikhonov, Viacheslav Vasil'evich
8.2.1928–   . Film actor.
Born in Pavlovskii Posad, near Moscow. First film in 1948. Graduated from the VGIK (Moscow Film School), 1950. Actor of the Film Actor's Theatre Studio in Moscow. Popular film actor in the 1960s. Played mainly soldiers and sailors until he was discovered by Sergei Bondarchuk. Became a star in the Soviet Union for his role of Prince Andrei Bolkonskii in *War and Peace*, 1967. Played the leading part in the TV soap opera *Semnadtsat' Mgnovenii Vesny*, 1973. State Prize, 1976. Married the equally famous actress Nonna Mordiukova. Films include: *Maksimka*, 1953, *It Happened in Pen'kovo*, 1958, *Midshipman Panin*, 1960, *An Optimistic Tragedy*, 1963, *Egor Bulychev And Others*, 1973, *They Fought For Their Country*, 1975.

Tikhonravov, Mikhail Klavdievich
1900–1974. Space rocket designer.
Graduated from the Zhukovskii Air Force Academy, 1925. One of the designers of the first Soviet liquid-fuel rocket, 1963. Took part in the early stages of the design of space technology. Member of the International Astronautics Academy, 1968.

Timanova, Vera Viktorovna
18.2.1855–1942. Pianist.
Born in Ufa. Pupil of K. Tauzig and F. Liszt. Appeared as a concert pianist in Western Europe and Russia. From the 1890s, lived in Petersburg, where she gave several concerts. Taught at the E. Rapgof Music Courses. Died during the Siege of Leningrad.

Timashev, Nikolai Sergeevich
1886–1971? Sociologist.
Born in Petersburg. Educated at the Lycee, 1908. Graduated in law from Petersburg University. Professor of law, Petrograd Polytechnic, 1917. Involved in the Tagantsev affair (resistance to communism among the Petersburg intelligentsia). Fled to Finland, 1921. Professor of the Russian law faculty in Prague, 1923. Professor of Institut d'Etudes Slaves, Paris, 1928. Lecturer in sociology at Harvard University, 1936. Professor of sociology at Fordham University, 1940–57. Editor of the magazine *Novyi Zhurnal*, 1960. Published an introduction to the sociology of law in the USA.

Timireva, Anna Vasil'evna
(b. Safonova; m. Knipper)
1893–31.1.1975. Author, common-law wife of Kolchak.
Born in Kislovodsk. Moved with her parents in 1906 to Petersburg. Educated at a Petersburg secondary school in 1911. Studied painting. Married a naval officer, Timirev, 1911–18. During WWI, lived in the Baltic ports, and became acquainted with Admiral Kolchak. During the Civil War, met Kolchak again in Siberia, and became his constant companion. Insisted on being arrested with him in Jan. 1920. Released in Oct. 1920. Almost continuously from 1921 until Stalin's death in Mar. 1953, an inmate of various Gulag camps. Released from exile in 1954. Rehabilitated in 1960. Wrote interesting memoirs on her childhood in the family of the musicologist and conductor Safonov (her father) and on her life with Admiral Kolchak.

Timofeev, Grigorii Nikolaevich
16.6.1866–18.3.1919. Music writer.
Born in Petersburg. Author of biographies of Balakirev, F. Chopin and A. Aliab'ev. Also wrote for the music press.

Timofeev, Lev Mikhailovich
1936– . Journalist, economist.
Born in Moscow. Graduated from the Moscow Institute for Foreign Trade. Published many articles in the Soviet press. Some of his work circulated in samizdat. Published in the West a bitter attack on the results of the communist transformation of rural life, *Tekhnologia Chernogo Rynka ili Krestianskoie Iskusstvo Golodat'*, 1982. Arrested, 1985, sentenced to 6 years in camps and 5 years exile. Released under Gorbachev, Feb. 1987. Organized the *Glasnost Bulletin*, Moscow, with Grigoriants. Later published the magazine *Referendum* and organized the press club Glasnost. Took part in many unofficial seminars.

Timofeev, Nikolai Andreevich
8.5.1906– . Composer.
Born in Petersburg. Author of the operetta *Katerina, Soldatskaia Zhenka*, produced in 1940. Also wrote symphonies, songs for films, and music for the theatre.

Timofeev-Resovskii, Nikolai Vladimirovich
20.9.1900–1981. Biologist.
Graduated from Moscow University, 1925, and sent by the Institute of Experimental Biology to Germany. Involved in experimental research with German scientists. Ignored the order of the Soviet Embassy in Berlin to return to Moscow, 1937, and thus became a defector in Soviet law, a crime aggravated by his staying in Nazi Germany. At the end of WWII, abducted by SMERSH in Berlin. Brought to Lubianka prison in Moscow. Tried in secret, and sent to the Gulag. When the authorities realized his scientific value, they transferred him, in a state of almost total exhaustion, to a Moscow prison hospital. After his recovery, sent to the Urals to a sharashka (a special research institute for imprisoned scientists). Carried out research into the influence of radiation on human genes. Released after Stalin's death. Appointed head of Obninsk Labo-ratory of Medical Radiology, 1964–69. Constantly supervised by the KGB, refused permission to go abroad to attend international conferences. Mentioned by Solzhenitsyn in *Gulag Archipelago*, D. Granin in 'Zubr', *Novyi Mir*, 1–2, 1987, Zhores Medvedev in *The Medvedev Papers*, Macmillan, 1971, Raisa Berg in *Sukhovei*, Chalidse Publ., 1983.

Timofeeva, Nina Vladimirovna
11.6.1935– . Ballerina.
Born in Leningrad. Graduated from the Leningrad Choreographic School, 1953. Leading soloist with the Kirov Theatre. From 1956, with the Bolshoi Theatre. On many tours abroad during the 1960–70s. Performed in the ballet film *Solisty Bol'shogo Baleta*, 1980. Worked with Iu. Grigorovich.

Timoshenko, Semen Konstantinovich
18.2.1895–31.3.1970. Marshal.
Took part in WWI. Joined the Red Army, 1918, and the Bolshevik Party, 1919. Graduated from higher academical courses of the Red Army, 1927. High commands during the Soviet occupation of Western Ukraine, 1939, and the Soviet-Finnish war, 1939–40. Stalin's Minister of Defence at the beginning of WWII, 1940–41. Along with some other of Stalin's favourite veterans of the Civil War, demonstrated amazing incompetence. Moved to high but largely nominal commands, making room for the younger and more efficient generation of military leaders. Member of the Cen. Cttee. of the Communist Party, 1939–52, and non-voting member, 1952–1970. Commander of several military districts after WWII. Chairman of the War Veterans Cttee., 1962–70.

Timoshinin, Aleksandr Ivanovich
20.5.1948– . Athlete.
Born in Moscow. Honoured Master of Sports (rowing), 1968. From 1970, with the Moscow Armed Forces. Member of the CPSU from 1976. Graduated from the Moscow Institute of Physical Culture, 1977. Sports trainer. USSR champion, 1968–75. Olympic champion, 1968 (with A. Sass), and in 1972 (with G. Korshikov).

439

Timoshkina, Natal'ia Leonidovna (Sherstiuk)
25.5.1952–   . Athlete.
Born in Zhitomir Oblast'. Honoured Master of Sports (handball), 1976. With Kiev Spartak. Graduated from the Kiev Institute of Physical Culture. Sports teacher. USSR champion, 1969–75 and 1977–79. Olympic champion, 1976.

Tiniakov, Aleksandr Ivanovich (Odinokii)
1886–1922. Poet, journalist, Cheka official.
Lived in Kazan' before WWI. Minor poet. Joined the Cheka, first in Kazan', 1917, and later in Petrograd. In this role, received the attention of literary figures, who had previously refused to take notice of him.

Tiomkin, Dmitrii (Temkin)
10.5.1899–11.11.1979. Composer.
Born in Russia. Graduated from Petrograd University and from the Petrograd Conservatory. Emigrated to the USA, 1925. Became a leading film composer (*High Noon* and many other films). Settled in London. Died in the USA. Author of *Please Don't Hate Me*, Garden City, 1959.

Tishin, Boris
1929–1.9.1980. Athlete.
Born in Moscow. Honoured Master of Sports (boxing). Many times USSR and European champion. Bronze medal winner at the XVth Olympic Games.

Tisse, Eduard Kazimirovich
13.4.1897–18.11.1961. Cameraman.
Entered the film industry in 1914 after graduating from the Private School of Art and Photography in Liepaia. Took part in filming the events of WWI. Member of the All-Russia Photo Department, 1919–23. War cameraman during the Civil War. Filmed Lenin on many occasions, 1918–24, and later his footage was used in the film *Vladimir Il'ich Lenin*, 1948. For a short time in 1921, taught at the State Film School (VGIK). Met S. Eisenstein and began his long collaboration with him. Cameraman on *Stachka*, 1925, with V. Khvatov, followed by *Bronenosets*

Potemkin, 1925, *Oktiabr'*, 1927, and *Staroe i Novoe*,1929. Internationally recognized as a cameraman of remarkable talent. Accompanied S. Eisenstein and G. Aleksandrov on their tour of the USA and Europe, 1931–32. Shot Eisenstein's *Viva Mexico!* Other films include *Aleksandr Nevskii*, 1938, and *Ivan Groznyi* (Ivan the Terrible). His films are internationally recognized as masterpieces of the Soviet cinema.

Titov, Iurii Evlampievich
27.11.1935–   . Athlete, sports official.
Born in Omsk, Siberia. Honoured Master of Sports, 1956. Graduated from the Kiev Institute of Physical Culture, 1959. International referee from 1968. Deputy chairman of the USSR Federation of Sports Gymnastics from 1968. Member of the CPSU from 1969, and head of the Gymnastics Department of the Sports Cttee. of the USSR. President of the International Federation of Gymnastics from 1976. Olympic champion, 1956, and with his team in 1964. World, European and USSR champion, 1957–62.

Titov, Vladimir
1938–   . Human rights campaigner.
Former KGB lieutenant, who left the KGB in 1961 because of disillusionment with its methods. Became involved in the human rights campaign in the USSR, which soon led him into conflict with his former bosses. Spent 18 years in labour camps, 5 of them in a special mental hospital. Released in 1987. In an unprecedented campaign to publicize the plight of scores of sane Soviet political prisoners, gave a press conference to more than 30 Western journalists in a small private flat under the nose of the KGB. Gave a devastating account of how he was classified as schizophrenic for giving information to Western contacts about Soviet prison labour being used on various energy projects, including the pipeline linking Siberia to Western Europe. According to him, 20% of the 1,000 inmates of Soviet psychiatric institutions were perfectly healthy, and there only because of their beliefs. Described in

detail 18 such hospitals where sane people were treated by psychiatrists in military uniforms.
Source: *The Times*, Nov. 1987; *Khronika Press*, Frankfurt am Main, Nov. 1987.

Titov, Vladimir
1947–   . Cosmonaut, colonel.
One of 2 cosmonauts who ejected to safety from a rocket which caught fire during lift-off in 1983. In the same year, took part in a flight which ended prematurely after his spacecraft was unable to dock with the unmanned Saliut 7 station. As mission commander, with A. Levchenko and M. Manarov, he was launched in a Soiuz spacecraft on 21 Dec. 1987, on a third long-term mission to the orbiting station Mir.
Source: *Krasnaia Zvezda*, Dec. 1987

Titova, Liudmila Evgen'evna
26.3.1946–   . Athlete.
Born in Chita. Honoured Master of Sports (skating), 1968. With Moscow Zenit. Graduated from the Moscow Aviation Institute, 1972. USSR champion, 1967–72. Olympic champion, 1968 (500 metres). World record-holder, 1970–72.

Tits, Mikhail Dmitrievich
8.3.1898–1971? Composer.
Born in Petersburg, of Ukrainian parentage. Studied at the Petersburg Conservatory. Moved to Khar'kov. Professor at the Khar'kov Institute of Arts. Author of 2 operas (with Iu. Meitus, and V. Rybal'chenko), including his most famous – *Perekop* – produced in 1938. Also wrote chamber music, choral music, and arrangements of Ukrainian folk songs.

Tiukalov, Iurii Sergeevich
4.7.1930–   . Athlete.
Born in Leningrad. Honoured Master of Sports (rowing), 1952. With Leningrad Dynamo. Graduated from the Leningrad V. I. Mukhina Higher Artistic Industrial School, 1957. Artist-architect. USSR champion, 1948–62. Olympic champion, 1952 (solo), and 1956 (with A. Berkutov). European champion, 1954, 1956–59 and 1961.

Tiulenev, Ivan Vladimirovich
1892–1978. General.
On active service during WWI. Joined the Red Army and the Bolshevik Party, 1918. Took part in the Civil War as commander of a cavalry brigade. Graduated from the Military Academy of the Red Army, 1922. Deputy Inspector of Cavalry of the Red Army, 1936. Took part in the occupation of Eastern Poland, 1939. Commander of the Moscow military district, 1940. Commander of the Southern front, 1941, and the Transcaucasian front, 1942. Worked at the Ministry of Defence, 1946. Non-voting member of the Cen. Cttee of the VKP, 1941–52.

Tiulin, Iurii Nikolaevich
26.12.1893–1973? Musicologist, composer.
Born in Revel'. Moved to Leningrad. Professor at the Leningrad Conservatory. Author of cantatas, music for folk instruments, suites, and romances.
Works: *Uchebnik Garmonii*, Moscow, 1959; *Stroenie Muzykal'noi Rechi*, Leningrad, 1962.

Tiuneev, Boris Dmitrievich
15.10.1883–21.7.1934. Musicologist.
Born in Odessa. Professor at the Odessa Conservatory. Music editor of the *Russkaia Muzykal'naia Gazeta*, Petersburg, 1905–18. Wrote many articles for this paper. Returned to Odessa from Leningrad, where he had lived until 1930. Died in Odessa.

Tiurin, Oleg Grigor'evich
29.6.1937–   . Athlete.
Born in Leningradskaia Oblast'. Honoured Master of Sports (rowing), 1964. With the Central Sports Club of the Navy. Coach. Graduated from the Leningrad Institute of Physical Culture, 1969. USSR champion, 1963–65, 1967. European champion, 1964. Olympic champion, 1964 (with B. Dubrovskii).

Tiurina, Liubov' Nikolaevna (Evtushenko)
25.4.1943–   . Athlete.
Born in Moscow. Honoured Master of Sports (volley-ball), 1970. With Moscow Dynamo. Graduated from the Moscow Oblast' Institute of Physical Culture, 1976. USSR champion, 1967 and 1970–71. European champion, 1967 and 1971. World champion, 1970. Olympic champion, 1972.

Tkachenko, Ninel' Aleksandrovna
21.9.1928–   . Singer.
Born in Khar'kov. Pupil of T. Veske. From 1958, soloist at the Opera Studio attached to the Kiev Conservatory. Soloist at the L'vov Opera and Ballet Theatre, thereafter 1960–62, and at the Minsk Opera Theatre.

Tkachenko, Tamara Stepanovna
19.10.1909–   . Ballerina, teacher.
Born in Rostov-on-Don. Graduated from the Moscow Choreographic School, 1926. Pupil of V. Tikhomirov. Graduated from the same school as a teacher, 1940. Leading dancer, 1926–48. Character roles at the Bolshoi Theatre. Taught character dance at the Moscow Choreographic School, 1940–60. From 1946, taught folk dance at the GITIS. Professor there from 1970. Author of several books on folk dance.

Todorskii, Aleksandr Ivanovich
1894–1965. Military commander.
Joined the Bolshevik Party, 1918, and the Red Army, 1919. Took part in the Civil War as a divisional commander. Graduated from the Frunze Military Academy, 1927. Head of the Zhukovskii Air Force Academy, 1933–34. Spent many years in the Gulag. Later actively involved in the fight for rehabilitation of former Gulag victims. Lt.-general, 1955.

Tokaev, Grigorii Aleksandrovich (Tokaty, Gregory)
1910–   . Rocket and space scientist, professor, author.
Born in Ossetia in the Northern Caucasus. Son of a peasant. Moved to Leningrad, 1929. Educated, 1930, at the Rabfak (Rabochii fakul'tet) 2-year courses for young people from proletarian backgrounds. Regarded as a highly gifted mathematician. Entered and graduated from the elite MVTU in Moscow (the Bauman Higher Technical School), 1932. Graduated from the Zhukovskii Air Force Academy, 1937. Worked first as an aeronautical research engineer, and was soon promoted to head of the Aeronautics Laboratory, 1938–41. Worked on top-secret military projects throughout WWII, which automatically relieved him from active military service. At the same time, lecturer in aerodynamics and aircraft design at the MVTU, the Moscow Aviation Institute, and the Moscow Energetics Institute. One of the first Soviet rocket scientists, 1944. As such, and with the rank of lt.-colonel, sent to East Berlin to inspect captured German secrets, and probably interview captured German rocket-scientists. In 1947, defected to the British Zone and was flown to London. For the next 7 years, still distrusted by the British and the Americans, plunged into a condemnation of Stalin's USSR. Told how he was once arrested, beaten up and severely injured for telling anecdotes about Stalin and Molotov. Wrote 3 political books: *Stalin Means War*, 1951, *Betrayal of an Ideal*, 1954, and *Comrade X*, 1955, a personal account of the underground opposition to Stalin in the USSR. Gave a series of lectures to British students and specialists. Worked at several secret military establishments in Britain, 1948–52. Naturalized British citizen. Taught aeronautics at Imperial College in the late 1950s. Became involved in the Apollo programme, 1956–68. Reader in Aeronautics and Astronautics at the Northampton College of Advanced Technology, 1960–61. Head, 1961–75, and professor, 1967–75 at the same college, and at City University. Visiting professor at universities in the US, Nigeria, Iran, Turkey and Holland. Lives in England. Published several books in English on Soviet rockets and space research.

Tokarev, Fedor Vasil'evich
1871–1968. Weaponry designer.
Educated at a Cossack officers' school, 1900. After the October Revolution 1917, worked at the Tula Armaments Factory. In the 1920s and 1930s, designed a number of automatic rifles, machine guns and pistols (the MT, TT, and SVT). Joined the Bolshevik Party, 1940.

441

Tol'ba, Veniamin Savel'evich
12.11.1909– . Conductor.
Born in Khar'kov. Professor at the Kiev Conservatory, 1941–50. Conductor at the Kiev Opera and Ballet Theatre, 1953–60. Teacher at the Kiev Conservatory.

Tolbukhin, Fedor Ivanovich
16.6.1894–17.10.1949. Marshal.
On active service during WWI as a captain. Joined the Red Army, 1918. Took part in the Civil War. Graduated from the Frunze Military Academy, 1934. Became widely known as a successful army commander during WWII in the Caucasus, the Crimea, Stalingrad, and the Ukraine. Chairman of the Allied Control Commission in Bulgaria, 1944. Commander of the Southern Group of Armies, 1945–47.

Tolkunov, Lev Nikolaevich
1919– . Politician, journalist.
Studied at the Gorkii Institute of Literature. Member of staff, and later assistant chief editor and war correspondent for *Pravda*, 1936–46. Member of the CPSU, 1943. Graduated from the Higher Party School of the Cen. Cttee., 1946. Special correspondent for *Pravda*. Deputy executive secretary, then deputy head of the editorial board of *Za Prochnyi Mir, Za Narodnuiu Demokratiiu*, 1946–51. Deputy editor of *Pravda*, 1951–57. Worked for the Cen. Cttee., 1957–65. Chief editor of *Izvestia*, 1965–76. Deputy to the Foreign Affairs Cttee. of the Soviet of Nationalities of the USSR Supreme Soviet from 1966. Chairman of the news agency Novosti from 1976. Candidate member of the Cen. Cttee. from 1976.

Tolmachev, Nikolai Gur'evich
1895–1919. Political officer.
Joined the Bolshevik Party, 1913, and the Red Army, 1918. One of the first Bolshevik political commissars in the armed forces. Insisted on the creation of political (control) departments in all detachments of the Red Army and initiated the specialized education of political commissars. During a battle near Petrograd, when he was seriously wounded and surrounded by the Whites, he shot himself.

**Tolstaia, Aleksandra Lvovna
(Tolstoy, Countess Alexandra)**
1885–26.9.1979, Author, social worker.
Born at Yasnaya Poliana. Youngest daughter of Leo Tolstoy. Helped her father to escape from his estate and begin his last travels, which ended with his death at Astapovo. After the Revolution 1917, keeper of the L. Tolstoy Museum at Yasnaya Poliana. Left the USSR for Japan in the 1920s. Moved to the USA, and settled there. Created a farm and the foundation *Tolstovskii Fond*, which helped countless Russian refugees for many decades, financing resettlement programmes, old people's homes, orphanages and many other humanitarian aid projects. Wrote books about her father and published her memoirs. Regarded as the grand old lady of Russian emigrés in the West.

**Tolstaia, Sofia Andreevna (Bers;
Tolstoy, Countess Sofia)**
1847–4.11.1919. Wife of L. Tolstoy.
Became, and remained for many years, the devoted wife and helper of Tolstoy, raising a large family at Yasnaya Poliana as well as copying all her husband's manuscripts (as often as 20 times, during re-working), and running his large estate. Became the object of much attention after the estrangement of the couple in their old age and especially after L. Tolstoy secretly left home in Oct. 1910, and died soon thereafter at a railway station, refusing to see his wife. After his death, she sold the larger part of the estate to her daughter Aleksandra to be divided among the peasants. She retained the orchard, which was considered to be the largest in Europe. Buried at the church cemetery at Kochaki, near Yasnaya Poliana.

Tolstoi, Aleksei Nikolaevich, Count
1883–1945. Author.
Born into the family of one of the counts Tolstoi, though according to some information, an adopted son. Graduated from the Petersburg Technological Institute. Brought up in the family of his stepfather, Bostroëm. Started to write before WWI, as poet and prose writer, gaining fame with some of his stories on the subject of the impoverished

aristocracy such as *Khromoi Barin*. During WWI, correspondent for the newspaper *Russkie Vedomosti*. After the October Revolution 1917, emigrated. Lived in Berlin and Paris. Wrote a novel about the fate of White Russian emigrés (*Road to Calvary*). Soon realized that a refugee life meant only hardship, even for a known and relatively successful writer. Returned to the USSR in 1923, and began writing in the socialist realist style. As one of only a handful of Soviet writers with a European education and reputation among the new proletarian elite, was often used to represent Stalin's USSR at international conferences (The International Congress of Writers, Paris, 1935, the London Congress of Culture, 1937). Nicknamed 'Comrade Count', he became a prominent member of the official literary establishment, and practically a courtier at Stalin's court. Having started his novel about White emigrés in the West, managed to change it in midstream in such a way that subsequent volumes appeared in the USSR, and the work was awarded the Stalin Prize. Wrote historical novels in which, under the guise of Ivan the Terrible and Peter the Great, he glorified Stalin, and won 2 more Stalin Prizes. During WWII, prolific and effective member of the Soviet propaganda machine. Officially proclaimed a great writer, became in the Soviet Union a byword for limitless opportunism. Died in Moscow.
See: R. Gul, *Ia Unes Rossiiu*, 2 vol., USA, 1984.

Tolstoi, Dmitrii Alekseevich
20.1.1923– . Composer.
Born in Berlin. Son of Aleksei Tolstoi. Lived with his parents in Germany during their emigration. Returned with his parents to the USSR. Author of an opera (*Maskarad*, produced in 1957), ballets, including one based on his father's book *Aelita*, 1966, cantatas, symphonies, pieces for piano and violin, songs for films and music for the theatre. Lives in Moscow.

**Tolstoi, Sergei Lvovich, Count
(Tolstoy, Sergei)**
28.6.1863–23.12.1947. Composer.
Son of Lev Tolstoy. Born on his

father's estate, Yasnaya Poliana, Tula Gouvt. Worked at the State Institute of Music Science, Moscow, 1921–32. Author of collections of Indian songs and dances, and Scottish songs. Author of *Sputnik Etnografa*, Moscow, 1929 (with P. Zimin), and *Ocherki Bylogo*, Moscow, 1929. Lived out WWII at Yasnaya Poliana. Died in Moscow.

Tolstykh, Boris Leont'evich
1936–   . Politician.
Trained as an electronics engineer. Graduated from Voronezh State University, 1959. Worked as an engineer at the Voronezh Elektronika complex (one of the chief manufacturers of military aircraft and space technology). Directorgeneral at the same complex, 1977. Responsible for the production of the video-cassette recorder, the Elektronika VM-12. Instrumental in the complete modernization of the factory. Appointed Chairman of the USSR State Cttee. for Science and Technology. Deputy Chairman of the USSR Council of Ministers.

Tolubko, Vladimir Fedorovich
1914–   . Marshal.
Joined the Red Army, 1932, and the Bolshevik Party, 1939. Graduated from the Academy of Mechanization of the Red Army, 1941. Commander of tank detachments during WWII. Professor of the Academy of Mechanization, 1943. Graduated from the Academy of the General Staff, 1950. Head of military training in the Soviet military administration in Germany, 1956. 1st Deputy Commander of Strategic Rocket Forces, 1960. Commander of the Siberian military district, 1968, and of the Far Eastern military district, 1969. Commander-in-chief of Soviet Strategic Rocket Forces, 1972–85, and Deputy Minister of Defence. Non-voting member of the Cen. Cttee. of the CPSU, 1971, and full member, 1976.

Tomashov, Daniil Porfir'evich
23.12.1875–10.3.1926. Violin-maker.
Born in the village of Poloshkovo, Mogilev Gouvt. Pupil of P. Khilinskii. From 1906, lived in Moscow. Became a famous violin-maker. His violins received the Gold Medal at the Exhibition of Musical Instruments in Rome in 1911. Died in Moscow.

Tomilin, Viktor Konstantinovich
15.5.1908–9.12.1941. Composer.
Born in Berdichev in the Ukraine. Taught music at the Rimskii-Korsakov Music School, Leningrad. Author of symphonies, and music for films and theatre. Killed in the Battle of Nevskaia Dubrovka near Leningrad.

Tomin, Nikolai Dmitrievich
1886–1924. Military commander.
After the February Revolution 1917, elected Commander of the 1st Orenburg Cossack Division. Joined the Red Army, 1918. Commander of the Transbaikal Division, 1921–22. Commander of a cavalry brigade, 1922. Joined the Bolshevik Party, 1924. Killed in action against central Asian anti-communist partisans.

Tomin, Nikolai Nikolaevich
28.12.1948–   . Athlete.
Born in Zaporozh'e. Honoured Master of Sports (handball), 1976. With the Moscow Armed Forces. USSR champion, 1976–79. Olympic champion, 1976.

Tomskii, Aleksandr Romanovich
16.1.1905–27.9.1970. Ballet dancer, choreographer, teacher.
Born in Moscow. From 1922, with the Zimin Private Opera. Pupil of A. Messerer at the evening courses of the Moscow Choreographic School, 1923. With the Moscow Theatre of Operetta, 1927–29. With theatres in Sverdlovsk, 1929–32, and Perm', 1932–37. Choreographer at the Tashkent Opera and Ballet Theatre, 1937–41. With the Navoi Theatre, 1939. With the Moscow Stanislavskii and Nemirovich–Danchenko Theatre, 1941–48, and the Bolshoi Theatre, 1948–51. Leading dancer. Artistic ballet director with the Bolshoi Theatre, 1957–59, and the Leningrad Malyi and Stanislavskii and Nemirovich–Danchenko Theatre, 1959–64. Choreographer with various ballet theatres all over the USSR. Died in Milan while on a visit. Buried in Moscow.

Tomskii, Mikhail Pavlovich
1880–1936. Politician, trade unionist.
Head of the Soviet Trade Unions in the 1930s. Member of the Politburo. The only genuine worker among the Bolshevik ruling group. Close to Nikolai Bukharin. Became a victim of the Stalin purges together with Bukharin. Committed suicide.

Topman, August
10.7.1882–1970? Organist, conductor.
Born in Estliandskaia Gouvt. Pupil of L. Gomilius. Head of the Estonian School of Organists. Professor at the Tallinn Conservatory. Emerged as a prominent organist between the wars. Also conducted orchestras and choirs. Re-arranged Wagner pieces for the organ.
Source: L. Roizman, *Organnaia Kul'tura Estonii*, Moscow, 1960.

Topol', Eduard Vladimirovich
1938–   . Journalist, author.
Graduated from the Moscow VGIK (State Film School) as a scriptwriter. 7 feature films were made using his scripts. Left the USSR, 1978, and settled in the USA. Writes in collaboration with F. Neznanskii. Author of *Zhurnalist Dlia Brezhneva, Ili Smertelnye Igry*, Frankfurt, 1981.

Toradze, David Aleksandrovich
14.4.1922–   . Composer.
Born in Tiflis. Teacher at the Tbilisi Conservatory. Author of an opera, ballets, and choral music. Worked for the Georgia Film Studio, and for the theatre.

**Trail, Vera Aleksandrovna
(b. Guchkova; m. Suvchinskaia)**
1906–1987. Journalist.
Daughter of A. Guchkov. After 1917, emigrated with her parents. Married the musicologist Suvchinskii, a leader of the Eurasians in Prague, later member of a pro-Soviet organization in Paris (of which M. Tsvetaeva's husband S. Efron was also a member). After her divorce, married the British communist Trail (King's College, Cambridge) who volunteered to fight against Franco in Spain and was killed in action. Became an active member of the

French Communist Party. Visited the USSR several times, lived there in 1936. Close friend of Baroness M. Budberg. Played a part in the return to the USSR of Sviatopolk-Mirskii, who later died in a concentration camp. After the Soviet-German Pact, arrested in France, 1939. Released, 1941, and moved to London with the help of A. Halpern (husband of Salomea Andronikova). Settled in London, ran an au pair agency, and wrote novels and film reviews for *The Observer*. Spent her last years in Cambridge.

Trapeznikov, Sergei Pavlovich
1912– . Politician.
Son of a worker. Farmhand, worker in a sawmill, 1925–29. At the age of 18, joined the Communist Party. Komsomol and party worker in Penza Oblast' during the collectivization campaign, 1929–34. Various senior posts in party and propaganda departments of various governmental organizations, 1935–48. In 1946, graduated from the Moscow Teachers' Training Institute. Director of the Party School of the Cen. Cttee. of the Moldavian CP, 1948–56. Member of the Cen. Cttee. of the Moldavian CP, 1956. Invited to Moscow by Brezhnev. High position in the Cen. Cttee. of the CPSU. Deputy Rector of the Moscow Higher Party School on the Cen. Cttee., 1960–65. From 1966 until 1983, in charge of culture, science and education on the Cen. Ctee. His utterly reactionary role in Soviet cultural life has been openly acknowledged in the Soviet press only under Gorbachev, but throughout his 18-year rule Soviet scientists consistently used their right to a secret vote to reject his candidature as Academician, despite strong pressure from the Politburo. In 1983, Andropov quietly sent him into retirement.
See: Andrei Sakharov, 'Razmyshleniia o Progresse, Mirnom Suchestvovanii i Intelektualnoi Svobode' (Thoughts about Progress, Peaceful Co-existence and Intellectual Freedom), *Posev*, 1968. Also: A Riadnov, 'Kucher na Obluchke', *Posev*, Nr 3, 1984.

Trauberg, Il'ia Zakharovich
3.12.1905–18.12.1948. Film director.
Brother of Leonid Trauberg. Entered the film industry, 1927. His major work was the silent film *Goluboi Ekspress*, 1929, which in 1931 was turned into a sound film. Also worked as a scriptwriter and film critic.

Trauberg, Leonid Zakharovich
17.1.1902– . Film director.
Studied at the Studio of Comic Opera, Petrograd. In 1919, founded a theatre studio in Odessa. In the same year, with G. Kozintsev, founded the Fabrika Ekstsentricheskogo Aktera (FEKS), which became a training school for many actors. From 1924 until 1945, made several films with G. Kozintsev. Head of the Higher Directors' Courses in Moscow, 1962–68.

Trefilova, Vera Aleksandrovna (Ivanova)
8.10.1875–11.7.1943. Ballerina.
Born in Vladikavkaz. Graduated from the Petersburg Theatre School, 1894. With the Mariinskii Theatre until 1921. Took part in the Russian Seasons in Paris, 1907. Emigrated to Paris to join Diaghilev, 1921. With Diaghilev's Ballets Russes until 1926. Also taught ballet. Died in Paris.

Tregubov, Ivan Sergeevich
19.1.1930– . Athlete.
Born in the Mordovskaia ASSR. Honoured Master of Sports (hockey), 1956. With the Central Sports Club of the Army. Coach. USSR champion, 1955–61. European champion, 1955–59. World and Olympic champion, 1956.

Tret'iak, Ivan Moiseevich
1.2.1923– . General.
Born in the village of Malaia Popovka, Poltava Oblast', in the Ukraine. Member of the Soviet Army from 1939. Commander of a regiment during WWII. In 1943, joined the Communist Party. Fought on the Western and 2nd Baltic fronts. In 1946, chief-of-staff, then 1st deputy commander of a unit and commander of a unit until 1967. Commander of the Belorussian military district, 1967–76. Candidate member of the Cen. Cttee. of the CPSU from 1971, full member, 1976. Member of the Bureau of the Cen. Cttee. of the Belorussian CP, 1976. Commander of the Far Eastern military district from May 1976. Still in charge when a Soviet fighter shot down a Korean jumbo jet in 1983, killing all 249 people on board. After Marshal A. Koldunov's dismissal, as a result of the Mathias Rust affair, appointed new Chief of Soviet Air Defence Forces.

Tret'iak, Vladislav Aleksandrovich
25.4.1952– . Athlete.
Born in Moscow Oblast'. Honoured Master of Sports (hockey), 1971. With the Central Sports Club of the Army. Graduated from the Moscow Institute of Physical Culture, 1976. Member of the CPSU from 1976. Worked in the Cen. Cttee. of the Komsomol from 1974. USSR champion, 1970–79. European champion, 1970, 1973–75 and 1978–79. World champion, 1970–71, 1973–75 and 1978–79. Olympic champion, 1972 and 1976.

Tret'iakov, Sergei Mikhailovich
20.6.1892–9.8.1939. Playwright, poet, journalist.
Born at Kuldiga. Son of a teacher. Educated at Riga High School. Studied at Moscow University. In the Red Army during the Civil War. Classic of revolutionary propagandist theatre and poetry. Close to Mayakovsky, prominent member of LEF. Profoundly influenced Berthold Brecht, who considered himself his pupil. In the 1920s, author of the most famous plays of the moment (*Neporochnoe Zachatie*, *Slyshish Moskva*, *Zemlia Dybom*, *Khochu Rebenka*), many of them staged by Meyerhold. After a stay at Peking, where he taught Russian at the university, wrote his best known play, *Rychi Kitai*, a world classic of communist propaganda theatre (first performance, 23 Jan. 1926). Enjoyed the patronage of Trotsky. Victim of Stalin's purges, accused of espionage and shot.

Tret'iakov, Sergei Nikolaevich
1886?–16.6.1944. Businessman, politician, NKVD agent.
Born in Moscow. Member of the

famous Moscow merchant families (grandson of the founder of the Tretiakov Gallery, and of the millionaire Savva Mamontov). Chairman of the Moscow Stock Exchange. Chairman of the Economic Council of the Provisional Government, Sep.–Oct. 1917. In the Winter Palace during the attack by the Bolsheviks. Arrested with other ministers. Released in the spring of 1918. Emigrated through Khar'kov to Paris, summer–autumn 1918. Offered the post of Trade and Industry Minister by Admiral Kolchak. Went to Omsk, Sep. 1919. Later in Irkutsk, Deputy Prime Minister and Minister of Foreign Affairs (under Pepeliaev), but very soon thereafter had to flee abroad. Returned to Paris to his family. De facto head of the Trade and Industrial Union created by Russian businessmen abroad. After some shady business dealings, became engulfed in financial difficulties. Through a former colleague in the Siberian government, became enmeshed in NKVD operations. On his premises in Paris, meetings of Russian businessmen and other emigré organizations were conducted before WWII. He also let rooms to the organization of White Army veterans, ROVS. During WWII, the Gestapo discovered NKVD files in Minsk concerning a Soviet agent in Paris. A search revealed that the meeting-room in Tretiakov's house in Paris and the office of ROVS were bugged with wires connected to the former Soviet Embassy on Rue de Grenelle. Later it was found that he had hidden General Skoblin (who was involved in the kidnappings of General Kutepov and General Miller) in his flat after Skoblin had escaped from the ROVS headquarters. Arrested in France by the Gestapo, died in a Nazi concentration camp near Berlin.

Tret'iakova, Tatiana Petrovna (Poniaeva)
13.12.1946–   . Athlete.
Born in Moscow. Honoured Master of Sports (volley-ball), 1972. From 1974, with Moscow Dynamo. Coach. USSR champion, 1965–77. European champion, 1967 and 1971. Olympic champion, 1968 and 1972. World champion, 1970.

Triandafillov, Vladimir Kiriakovich
1894–1931. Military commander.
On active service during WWI. Joined the Red Army, 1918, and the Bolshevik Party, 1919. Took part in the Civil War. Graduated from the Academy of the Red Army, 1923. Deputy Chief-of-staff of the Red Army, 1923. Wrote on military history and military theory. Died in an aircrash.

Tributs, Vladimir Filippovich
1900–1977. Admiral.
Joined the Red Navy, 1918, and the Bolshevik Party, 1928. Took part in the Civil War. Navy captain in the 1930s. Commander of the Baltic fleet, 1939–47. Deputy Navy Commander-in-chief in the Far East, 1947. Head of the Hydrographic Service of the Navy, 1949, and professor at the Academy of the General Staff. Admiral-inspector of the Soviet Navy, 1957–60.

Trifon (Turkestanov, Boris Petrovich), Metropolitan
29.11.1861–14.6.1934. Russian Orthodox clergyman.
Born in Moscow. From a family of Georgian princes, the Turkestanishvili, who settled in Russia at the time of Peter the Great. His mother Naryshkina took him in his childhood to the Optina Pustyn' monastery, where he was blessed by the starets Amvrosii, whose spiritual pupil he became in 1887, after finishing at the Polivanov High School and studying at Moscow University. Monk at Optina Pustyn', 1889. Delivered the oration at starets Amvrosii's funeral, 1891, in Shamordino Convent. Graduated from the Moscow Theological Academy, 1895. Rector of Moscow Seminary, 1899. Bishop of Dmitrov, 1901–14. During WWI, with the Russian Army at the front as a regimental priest, awarded the Order of St. George, which was the highest award for bravery, and was a unique award for a clergyman. Wounded, retired to the New Jerusalem Monastery, 1915. Returned to the front, 1916. Elevated to archbishop in 1923 by Patriarch Tikhon, whose funeral oration he delivered in Apr. 1925. Metropolitan, 1931. Died in Moscow.

Trifonov, Iurii Valentinovich
1925–28.3.1981. Author.
Born in Moscow. Son of V. Trifonov, who was executed in 1938. Graduated from the Moscow Gorkii Literary Institute, 1949. Became famous for his novel *Studenty*, 1950. Other books: *Utolenie Zhazhdy*, 1963, (film, 1965); *Igry V Sumerkakh*, 1970; *Dolgoe Proshchanie*, 1971; *Drugaia Zhizn'*, 1975; *Dom Na Naberezhnoi*, 1976; *Starik*, 1979. Stalin Prize, 1951. His last novel *Vremia i Mesto*, published a few months before his death, was openly anti-Stalinist. Died in Moscow.

Trifonov, Valentin Andreevich
1888–1938. State security official.
Joined the Bolshevik Party, 1904. One of the organizers of the Red Guards in Petrograd, 1917. Joined the Red Army, 1918. Cheka official during the Civil War. Head of the Military Collegium of the Supreme Court of the USSR (in charge of political trials), 1923–25. Liquidated by Stalin.

Triolet, Elsa Iur'evna (b. Kagan, Mme Louis Aragon)
24.9.1896–16.6.1970. Author.
Born in Moscow. Younger sister of Lili Brik. Studied architecture in Moscow. Met V. Mayakovsky in the autumn of 1913, 6 months before her sister met him. In 1918, left for Paris. Married the officer André Triolet. Became an author, writing first in Russian, then in French. In 1928, met Louis Aragon, whom she married after her divorce. Lived with him until her death. Became a well-known French communist writer. Translated Mayakovsky into French. Died in France.

Trofimenko, Sergei Georgievich
1899–1953. Col.-general.
Joined the Bolshevik Party, 1918, and the Red Army, 1919. Graduated from the Frunze Military Academy, 1932, and from the Academy of the General Staff, 1937. Took part in the Soviet-Finnish war, 1939–40. During WWII, commander of several armies. After WWII, military district commander in Tbilisi, Belorussia, and the Northern Caucasus.

Trofimova, Nina Iur'evna
4.5.1953–   . Athlete.
Born in Novgorod. Honoured Master of Sports (rowing), 1973. With Novgorod Spartak. Studied at the Novgorod Pedagogical Institute. USSR champion, 1970–76. World champion, 1973. Olympic champion, 1976 (with G. Kreft, 500 metres).

Troianovskii, Boris Sergeevich
15.4.1883–12.6.1951. Musician.
Born in the village of Rugodevo, Pskov Gouvt. Virtuoso balalaika-player, who attracted huge crowds to his concerts. Also wrote original music for the balalaika, and arrangements of Russian folk songs. Died in Leningrad. Author of *Russkie Narodnye Pesni v Obrabotke Dlia Balalaiki*, Leningrad, 1953.

Trotskii, Lev Davidovich (Bronstein; Trotsky, Leon)
7.11.1879–20.8.1940. Revolutionary, politician.
Born at Ianovka near Elizavetgrad (Kirovograd) in the Ukraine. Son of an estate manager. Educated at Odessa High School. Early involvement in revolutionary activity. Arrested and exiled to Siberia, 1898. Became a member of the SD Party. Went abroad to London, and then to Switzerland, 1902. Worked with Lenin on *Iskra*. After the split of the SD Party, 1903, joined the anti-Lenin Menshevik faction. Returned to Russia, 1905. Main organizer (with Helphand-Parvus) of the 1905 Revolution in Petrograd, and creator of the rule of the Soviets (workers' councils). After the defeat of the revolution, exiled to Siberia, 1906. Went abroad, 1907. Living in Vienna, contributed to the Russian revolutionary and the West European socialist press. Proposed the concept of the permanent revolution (worldwide revolution). At the start of WWI, moved to Switzerland and later to the USA. Edited with Bukharin the Russian language journal *Novyi Mir* in New York. After the February Revolution 1917, on his return to Russia through England, arrested by the British authorities, but was released after protests by Miliukov (then Foreign Minister of the Provisional Government). In Petrograd again, became one of the main revolutionary organizers. Arrested after the unsuccessful Bolshevik coup in July 1917. Officially joined the Bolsheviks in Aug. 1917. Member of the Cen. Cttee. of the Bolshevik Party. Main organizer and practical leader of the October Revolution 1917. Appointed Commissar of Foreign Affairs in the first Soviet government. Conducted the Brest-Litovsk peace negotiations, baffling the Germans by first using the meeting for propaganda purposes, then proclaiming the 'no peace, no war' situation, and finally abandoning the talks (concluded later on Lenin's insistence without him). Resigned from his post and was appointed Commissar of War. Created the Red Army and achieved victory in the Civil War by his extremely effective actions: his use of unprecedented terror (special Cheka detachments, often Latvian, Chinese, or from revolutionary groups of prisoners of war, especially Hungarian), and his use of professional military cadres from the Imperial Army drafted into the Red Army, their complete loyalty insured by a double hostage system — firstly by a communist political commissar attached as a supervisor to every military commander and secondly by the hostage situation of the members of the officers' families. Disregarded criticism from party activists and communist partisans, who objected to this use of military specialists as wrong and dangerous on ideological and practical grounds. During the Civil War, had several misunderstandings with Stalin, which later cost him dearly. Continued his propagandist and journalistic vocation. Wrote the manifesto of the Comintern, 1919. Took an active part in cultural discussion, and played the role of a patron of revolutionary art. Brilliant orator, he overshadowed Lenin and completely overwhelmed Stalin, whom he in any case treated with open contempt, calling him 'the most outstanding mediocrity'. During the revolt of the Kronstadt sailors, did not hesitate to apply his methods of utter terror to his former revolutionary comrades. Nevertheless, during the struggle for Lenin's succession, was easily outmanoeuvered by Stalin in his various permutations with and against Zinov'ev, Kamenev and Bukharin. Proposed schemes of mass compulsion (labour armies and collectivization) which were successfully denounced by Stalin as extremist (and later realized by him in a modified form). Similarly his concept of 'permanent revolution' was defeated by Stalin's 'socialism in one country.' Removed from his post as Commissar of War, 1925, and from the Politburo, 1926. Expelled from the party with his followers, 1927, exiled to Alma-Ata, 1928, and banished from the USSR, 1929. Subjected to an unprecedented campaign of vilification by Stalin, presented as the source of all evil and a tool of fascism. Lived in exile in Turkey, 1929–33, and in France, 1933–35. After a short stay in Norway, moved to Mexico, 1936. Wrote on the Russian revolution and on Stalinism, and tried to organize the 4th International as a pure revolutionary movement, not corrupted by Stalinist bureaucracy. Killed by Mercador, a Spanish agent of Stalin, in his study in Coyoacan by an ice-pick blow to the skull. A non-person in the Soviet Union for many years, his historical significance is now beginning to be recognized in Soviet political science.

Troyat, Henry (Tarasov, Lev)
1.11.1911–   . Author.
Son of an Armenian merchant. Left Russia with his parents after the October Revolution 1917. Educated in France. Became a well-known French author. Wrote a series of successful biographical novels on Russian literary figures (Dostoevskii, Pushkin, Lermontov, Gogol). Member of the French Academy, 1959. Lives in Paris.

Trubetskoi, Evgenii Nikolaevich, Prince
23.9.1863–21.1.1920. Philosopher, art critic.
Born in Akhtyrka. Graduated from Moscow University. Founded the Psychological Society in Moscow. Taught at the Law Lycée in Iaroslavl' and at Kiev University. Professor at Moscow University, 1905–18. During the Civil War, with the White Armies. Died from typhoid at Novorossiisk, awaiting evacuation.
Main Works: *Filosofiia V. Solov'eva*, 2 vols, *Smysl Zhizni*, *Umozrenie v*

Kraskakh, Memoirs (posthumous, Sofia, 1921).

Trubetskoi, Grigorii Nikolaevich, Prince
27.9.1874–6.1.1930. Diplomat, politician.
Graduated from Moscow University. On Diplomatic Service in Vienna, Berlin, Constantinople, 1896–1906. Russian Ambassador to Serbia, 1914–15, at the crucial moment of the beginning of WWI. Member of the Russian Church Council, 1917–18. Member of the South Russian government under the Whites, 1919–20. Emigrated in 1920 to Austria. From 1923, lived in France. Memoirs: *Gody Smut i Nadezhd*, 1917–19, Montreal, 1981.

Trubetskoi, Nikolai Sergeevich, Prince
16.4.1890–25.6.1938. Philosopher, linguistic scholar.
Born in Moscow. Son of the rector of Moscow University. Graduated from that university, 1913, and lectured there. During the Civil War, at Rostov-on-Don. Left Russia after the Civil War. Taught at Sofia and Vienna universities. Gained a worldwide reputation for his philological research. Head of the Prague School of Linguists. Joined the Eurasian movement and contributed to their publications. Died in Vienna of a heart attack soon after the occupation of Austria by Nazi Germany. Main works: *Europe and Mankind*; *Problema Russkogo Samosoznaniia*; *Nasledie Chingiz Khana*; *The Morphological System of the Russian Language*; *The Foundations of Phonology*; *Grammar of Church Slavonic*.

Trubetskoi, Pavel (Paolo) Petrovich, Prince
1866–1938. Sculptor.
Born in Italy. Lived in Russia, 1897–1906. Professor of the Moscow School of Painting, Sculpture and Architecture. Renowned for his statuettes, such as Tolstoy on a horse, and many others. Created the modernist equestrian monument of Aleksander III in Petersburg (since 1937, in the courtyard of the State Russian Museum in Leningrad). Died in Italy.

Trubnikov, Kuz'ma Petrovich
1888–1974. Col.-general.
On active service during WWI. Joined the Red Army, 1918. Took part in the Civil War as a regimental, and later brigade commander. Graduated from the Vystrel Courses, 1925. During WWI, Deputy Commander of the Belorussian front. After WWII, Deputy Commander of the Northern Group of Armies.

Trufanov, Nikolai Ivanovich
1900–1982. Col.-general.
Joined the Red Army, 1919. Took part in the Civil War. Graduated from the Frunze Military Academy, 1939. On active service during the Soviet-Finnish war, 1939–40. Took part in WWII. After WWII, worked in the Soviet military administration in Germany, and later in the Far East. Deputy Commander of the Far Eastern military district, 1956–57. Soviet adviser in communist China, 1957–59.

Trukhin, Fedor Ivanovich
1899?–2.8.1946. Lt.-general.
From an aristocratic Russian family. As a young officer, became attracted to the revolution. Graduated from the Military Academy. Advanced rapidly in the Red Army. Chief-of-staff of the Baltic military district, 1941. Severely wounded and captured by the Germans in the summer of 1941. Declared his opposition to Stalin and made contact with the NTS (Narodno-Trudovoi Soiuz), an anti-communist group in the Wüstrau camp. Joined General Vlasov. Attempted to turn the Dabendorf School, where he was transferred, into an ideological centre for the Russian liberation movement, as well as a centre for selecting and training capable officers. Vlasov's deputy, he was appointed Chief-of-staff of the KONR (Komitet Osvobozhdeniia Narodov Rossii) armed forces, 1944. Made contact with the Americans on 5 May 1945, and received an ultimatum to surrender within 36 hours with his entire 2nd Division. Stopped in Przibram by Czech communist partisans, who took him into a building to a 'friendly reception'. Inside, handed over to SMERSH. Brought to the Lubianka prison in Moscow, tried in secret, and hanged with Vlasov and others on 2 Aug. 1946.

Tsalkalamanidze, Mirian Vasil'evich
20.4.1927– . Athlete.
Born in Georgia. Honoured Master of Sports (wrestling), 1956. With Tbilisi Trudovye Rezervy. Graduated from the Georgian Institute of Physical Culture, and from the Georgian Agricultural Institute. Engineer and sports instructor. Member of the CPSU, 1967. USSR champion, 1954, 1956. Olympic champion, 1956.

Tsander, Fridrikh Arturovich (Zander, Friedrich)
1887–1933. Rocket designer.
Graduated from the Riga Polytechnical Institute, 1914. Pioneer of rocket designing in the Soviet Union. Senior engineer in the design bureau of the Aviation Trust, 1926. Engineer in the Central Institute for Aircraft Motor Design, 1930–31. Designed the jet engines OR–1 and OR–2. One of the founders of GIRD (Gruppa Izuchenia Reaktivnogo Dvizheniia). Created the basis for the first Soviet rocket with a liquid-fuel jet engine.

Tsarman, Aleksandr Aleksandrovich
6.7.1873–28.1.1939. Ballet dancer, choreographer, composer.
Born in Moscow. Graduated from the Moscow Theatre School, 1890. Pupil of I. Khliustin. Joined the Bolshoi Theatre. From 1898, choreographer. Experimented with new dances. On 1 Jan. 1900, at the Blagorodnoe Sobranie Hall, showed the new dance *pas d'espagne* set to his own music. Composed music for folk dances. Taught dancing in Moscow schools. Died in Moscow.

Tseitlin, Aleksandr Davidovich
2.3.1906–23.5.1975. Conductor.
Born in Melitopol'. First violinist and conductor at the Bolshoi Theatre, 1936–59. Worked with A. Messerer. From 1960, taught at the GITIS. Died in Moscow.

Tseitlin, Lev Moiseevich
15.3.1881–9.1.1952. Violinist.
Born in Tiflis. Pupil of L. Auer. Professor at the Moscow Conser-

vatory. Founder in 1922 of Persimfans. Trained a generation of violinists including B. Gol'shtein and S. Furer. Died in Moscow.

Tsekhanovskii, Mikhail Mikhailovich
7.6.1889–22.6.1965. Film director, graphic artist.
Graduated from the Moscow School of Painting, Sculpture and Architecture. One of the first animators in the Soviet Union. Made the first animated film with sound, *Pochta*, 1929, followed by over 50 more in the same genre.

Tselkov, Oleg Nikolaevich
1934– . Artist.
Born in Moscow. Expelled from 2 art schools (Minsk and Leningrad) for refusing to follow the socialist realist method in his paintings. Graduated from the Leningrad Theatre Institute as a stage-designer. Active in unofficial artistic events in both capitals. Left the USSR, 1977. Lives in Paris, where he has exhibited on his own, and with other Russian artists.

Tseloval'nikov, Igor' Vasil'evich
2.1.1944– . Athlete.
Born in Erevan. Honoured Master of Sports (cycling), 1972. With the Khar'kov Armed Forces Team. Graduated in economics from Khar'kov University, 1969, and from the Leningrad Institute of Physical Culture, 1972. Economist and sports instructor. USSR champion, 1967, and 1971–74. Olympic champion, 1972.

Tsereteli, Iraklii Georgievich
1882–1959. Politician.
Menshevik leader. Member of the 2nd Duma. Exiled to Siberia. Returned after the February Revolution 1917. Like Kerenskii, became a link man between the rival powers of the government and the Soviet. Member of the Executive Cttee. of the Petrograd Soviet, and from May 1917, Minister of Mail and Telegraph Communications in the Provisional Government. Also member of the Contact Commission between the Petrograd Soviet and the government. Emigrated, 1923. Became one of the founders of the 2nd Inter-

national. Remained a staunch opponent of Bolshevism. After WWII, refused to join the group of Russian emigrés, led by Maklakov, who visited the Soviet Embassy in Paris to drink Stalin's health, 12 Feb. 1945. Thus there was no Social-Democrat present in the group (though there were a number of former right-wing politicians), a fact which has been later pointed out with glee by the *Sotcialisticheskii Vestnik* in New York, the only remaining socialist Russian paper in the world.

Tsereteli, Kora Davidovna
15.8.1930– . Film critic.
Graduated from the Institute of Foreign Languages, Tbilisi, 1952. Leading Georgian film critic. Author of many articles and books on the Georgian cinema.

Tsereteli, Tamara Semenovna
14.8.1900– . Singer (contralto).
Born in Chiaturi, Georgia. Famous variety singer, 1920–59. Attracted huge crowds to her concerts of gypsy songs. Appeared in films and on stage.

Tsesevich, Platon Ivanovich
7.12.1879–30.11.1958. Singer (bass).
Born in the village of Negdedich, Minsk Gouvt. Pupil of Ia. Liubin. Appeared in theatres all over Russia from 1904. Soloist at the Bolshoi Theatre, 1915–17. Emigrated, 1924. Returned to the USSR, 1933. Died in Moscow.

Tsfasman, Aleksandr Naumovich
14.12.1906– . Jazz pianist, composer.
Born in Aleksandrovsk, Zaporozh'e. Moved to Moscow. Studied at the Moscow Conservatory. Pupil of Feliks Blumenfeld. Influenced by black American jazz. Gave up the conservatory and organized a jazz band. Soon became a living legend, the king of Soviet jazz with his own orchestra, and a millionaire. Entertained both Stalin's circle and the NKVD. Voroshilov and Molotov, together with senior NKVD agents, were seen dancing at his concerts. His private life was that of a playboy. Travelled with his band only by first

class wagon-lit, reserved for foreign VIPs, and had numerous affairs with famous actresses, and drunken brawls. Once beat up a chief of militia in Tbilisi telling him, 'There is plenty of filth like you but there is only one Tsfasman'. Not only did he get away with this, but the next day the head of the Georgian police came to his hotel to apologize for the inconvenience, having already sent him 12 bottles of the best Georgian brandy. Acquired admirers among the most ferocious in the NKVD, including Ezhov himself. He himself wrote most of the songs for his orchestra, which in the 1930s appeared in several films.

Tsignadze, Vera Varlamovna
24.9.1926– . Ballerina.
Born in Baku. Graduated from the Baku Choreographic School, 1943. Joined the Akhundov Theatre in Baku. Moved to Tbilisi. Leading dancer at the Paliashvili Theatre in Tbilisi. Permanent partner of V. Chabukiani. State Prize, 1948. From 1969, taught at the Tbilisi Choreographic School. Winner at the International Ballet Festival, Budapest, 1969. Many tours abroad.

Tsimakuridze, David Mikhailovich
29.3.1925– . Athlete.
Born in Poti. Honoured Master of Sports (wrestling), 1951. With Tbilisi Burevestnik. Graduated from the Georgian Institute of Physical Culture, 1953. Member of the CPSU, 1954. Honorary Coach of the USSR, 1956. USSR champion, 1945–47, and 1949–52. Olympic champion, 1952.

Tsinev, Georgii Karpovich
1907– . KGB official, general.
Member of the CPSU, 1932. Graduated from the Dnepropetrovsk Metallurgical Institute, 1934, and the Military Academy of the General Staff, 1953. Began as a supervisor, and later became an engineer and acting deputy head of the Nizhnepetrovsk Liebknecht Works, 1934–39. Party posts in the Ukraine (possibly security posts), 1939–41. Commander of a regiment and an operative group, and deputy head of the political administration of the army. Probably with SMERSH, 1941–45. Deputy Head, Deputy High

Commander, and Chief-of-staff of the Soviet Section of the Allied Commission in Austria, 1945–51. Senior posts in the USSR Cttee. for State Security (KGB) from 1953. Deputy Chairman of the KGB, July, 1970. Member of the Central Auditing Committee, 1971–76. Candidate member of the Cen. Cttee. of the CPSU, 1976–81. Full member from 1982. Became 1st Deputy Chairman of the KGB after the mysterious death of S. Tsvigun in Jan. 1982. Regarded by observers as an experienced GRU officer.

Tsiolkovskii, Konstantin Eduardovich
1857–19.9.1935. Scientist, space researcher.
Born near Riazan'. Son of a forester. Became completely deaf at the age of 9, which isolated him from his surroundings and concentrated his mind on the problems of space and science. Mathematics teacher at provincial secondary schools (Borovsk, Kaluga), 1877–1927. Self-taught expert in astronomy, biology and chemistry. Pioneer of research into problems of aviation and space travel, suggesting metal airships and airplanes in the late 1890s, and the exploration of the expanses of the universe with jet-propelled instruments in 1903 (the theoretical idea of space-rockets). Regarded as the father of space exploration in the USSR, though his prophetic visions were only theoretical.

Tsiurupa, Aleksandr Dmitrievich
1870–1928. Politician.
Joined the SD Party, 1898. From Feb. 1918, Minister for Food Supplies. During the Civil War, in charge of supplies for the Red Army and of the activities of the Prodarmiia (detachments which confiscated food from the peasants). Deputy Prime Minister of the RSFSR, 1921, and of the USSR, 1922. Member of the Presidium of the VTSIK and TSIK of the USSR, 1922–28. Chairman of GOSPLAN USSR, 1923–25. Minister for Foreign and Internal Trade, 1925–26. Member of the Cen. Cttee. of the Bolshevik Party, 1923.

Tsomyk, Gerts Davidovich
1.6.1914– 　. Cellist.
Born in Mogilev. Pupil of K. Min'iar-

Beloruchev. 1st prize at the All-Union Competition of Musician-Soloists, Moscow, 1933. Never repeated this success. Professor at the Sverdlovsk Conservatory.

Tsukanova, Maria Nikitichna
1924–1945. Nurse.
Nurse with the marines in the Pacific fleet, 1942. Saved over 50 wounded in a battle against the Japanese in Korea. Taken prisoner and killed. Posthumously awarded the title Hero of the Soviet Union.

Tsutsunava, Aleksandr Razhdenovich
28.1.1881–25.10.1955. Film director.
Studied at Tbilisi University. From 1900, worked in theatres in Tbilisi and Kutaisi. Made the first Georgian full-length feature film, *Khristine*, 1916. His best film is probably *Naezdnik Iz Wild West*, 1925. All his films are about Georgia and the Georgian people. From 1947, chief director of the Paliashvili Opera and Ballet Theatre, Tbilisi.

Tsvetaev, Viacheslav Dmitrievich
1893–1950. Col.-general.
On active service during WWI as a lieutenant. Joined the Red Army, 1918. Took part in the Civil War as a divisional commander. Member of the Bolshevik Party, 1918–21, and again from 1943. Graduated from the Frunze Military Academy, 1927, and later professor at the same Academy. Several high command posts during WWII. Commander of the Southern Group of Armies, 1945. Head of the Frunze Military Academy, 1948–50.

Tsvetaeva, Marina Ivanovna
(m. Efron)
8.10.1892–31.8.1941. Poetess.
Born in Moscow, daughter of the professor of art history and founder of the Alexander III Museum (now the Pushkin Museum) in Moscow. Educated in Moscow, Switzerland and Germany. Studied at the Sorbonne in 1909. First book of poems published in 1910. Met Sergei Efron at the house of the poet Voloshin in the Crimea and married him in 1912. During WWI and the revolution, stayed in Moscow and was separated from her husband (who as a young

officer had joined the Whites). Wrote a cycle of poems in praise of the White Armies (*Lebedinyi Stan*), sometimes giving public recitals. Acclaimed as an original poetic voice. Emigrated in 1922 to join her husband (through Berlin to Prague). Moved to France in 1925, lived near Paris. Her modernist style coupled with a deep historic feeling, her helplessness in practical life and her proud conception of her own role as a poet put her outside all groups and made her life extremely difficult. Attacked from the right and from the left, often refused publication, lived in extreme poverty. Her husband, disillusioned with the Whites, became involved with the GPU. After the murder of a GPU defector, Ignatii Reiss, in Switzerland, in which he had taken part, he fled to the Soviet Union. Tsvetaeva's daughter Ariadna preceeded her father (she also had communist leanings at that time and worked for a communist paper in France). Completely broken, Tsvetaeva followed them to the USSR with her son. Allowed to live near Moscow, but her isolation was even deeper than in the West (her daughter was already in the Gulag and her husband had disappeared, probably executed). Refused permission to publish her works, branded as a White guard and counter-revolutionary. During WWII, evacuated to the small town of Elabuga (Tatar Autonomous Republic). After trying, unsuccessfully, to get a job as a cleaner, committed suicide by hanging herself. Her son was conscripted and soon thereafter died in action. Her daughter, and her sister Anastasia, who had remained in the USSR, survived and, during the post-Stalin thaw, were able to assist in the resurgence of interest in her work. Now recognized as the greatest poetess in Russian literature, equalled only by Akhmatova. Published in millions of copies both in the USSR and abroad.
Main works: *Stikhotvoreniia i Poemy*, Moscow; *Prose*, 2 vol., USA. See also: Ariadna Efron, *Pisma iz Ssylki*.

Tsvigun, Semen Kuzmich
1917–19.1.1981. Security services official, general.
Graduated from the Odessa Pedagogical Institute, 1937. With the

security services from 1939. Senior position with SMERSH during WWII. Deputy Minister of State Security and Deputy Chairman of the KGB in the Moldavian SSR from 1951. In 1955, moved to the Tadzhik SSR in the same position, and to the Azerbaidzhan SSR, 1963. From 1967, 1st Deputy Chairman of the USSR KGB. Non-voting member of the Cen. Cttee. of the CPSU, 1971, full member, 1981. General in the army. Brother-in-law of L. Brezhnev. The cause of his sudden death is still a mystery. Believed to have committed suicide (shot himself or took poison, because he had become a subject of investigation by the KGB leadership. During the Gorbachev glasnost period, mentioned in connection with the Brezhnev 'mafia'.

Tsybin, Vladimir Nikolaevich
23.7.1877–31.5.1949. Conductor, composer.
Born in Ivanovo-Voznesensk, Moscow Oblast'. Pupil of V. Krechman. Flute-player and soloist in the orchestras of the Bolshoi Theatre and the Mariinskii Theatre. From 1923, professor at the Moscow Conservatory. Author of *Osnovy Tekhniki Igry na Fleite*, Moscow, 1940. Died in Moscow.

Tsybulenko, Viktor Sergeevich
13.7.1930– . Athlete.
Born in Kievskaia Oblast'. Honoured Master of Sports (track and field athletics), 1956. Graduated from the Kiev Institute of Physical Culture, 1958. Member of the CPSU, 1968. USSR champion, 1952, 1955–57 and 1959. Olympic champion, 1960.

Tsygankov, Gennadii Dmitrievich
16.8.1947– . Athlete.
Born in Amurskaia Oblast'. Honoured Master of Sports (hockey), 1972. With the Central Sports Club of the Army. Graduated from a school for sports instructors, 1974. Member of the CPSU, 1976. USSR champion, 1970–73, 1975 and 1977–79. World champion, 1971, 1973–75 and 1978–79. Olympic champion, 1972 and 1976. European champion, 1973–75 and 1978–79.

Tsyganov, Viktor Viktorovich
1896–1944. Lt.-general.
On active service during WWI. Joined the Red Army, 1918. Took part in the Civil War. Graduated from the Frunze Military Academy, 1933. Commander of several armies during WWII.

Tsyriulnikov, Mikhail Sergeevich
1920– . Kremlin gynaecologist.
One of the highest-paid doctors in the Soviet Union in the 1960s. For 15 years, in charge of the Kremlin Maternity Hospital with a staff of 380, of whom 76 were top surgeons. Among his patients were the wives and daughters of members of the government, foreign diplomats' wives and the artistic élite, including the daughter of Premier Kosygin, Brezhnev's daughter Galina, Khrushchev's wife Nina, the first woman in space Valentina Tereshkova, the famous ballerina Plisetskaia, and the wife of A. Solzhenitsyn, Natalia Svetlova, (because of whom he was fired from his job). Emigrated in 1977 to Paris. Works there as a gynaecologist at the Hospital Port-Royal. Writes medical articles for the Russian emigré press.

Tubin, Eduard Iozepovich
18.6.1905– . Composer.
Born in Kallast, Tartu region. Studied composition at the Tartu Higher Music School. Pupil of Ch. Eller. Graduated in 1930. Until 1934, conductor with the Vanemuine Theatre and the Tartu Male Voice Choir Author of an opera, several symphonies, chamber and vocal pieces. After the annexation of Estonia by the USSR, left for Sweden. In the post-war years, worked with several Stockholm theatres.

Tukhachevskii, Mikhail Nikolaevich
16.2.1893–11.6.1937. Marshal.
From an aristocratic family of Polish origin. Graduated from the Aleksandrovskoe Military School, 1914. Joined the exclusive Semenovskii guards regiment. Lieutenant during WWI. Taken prisoner by the Germans, a POW at the Ingolstadt fortress (together with the French POW De Gaulle), escaped but recaptured. Returned to Russia after the Revolution 1917. Joined the Red Army, 1918. Showing brilliant military abilities, made an extraordinary rapid career. Commanded the Southern front and later the Caucasian and Western fronts, 1920–21. Led the Soviet invasion of Poland, which was halted just before Warsaw, mainly due to French help (from Weygand) and Wrangel's thrust from the Crimea. During the Polish campaign, had serious quarrels with Stalin (at the time a political commissar) which cost him dearly later. After the Civil War, in charge of the crushing of the revolt by the Kronstadt sailors and of the peasant revolt under Antonov in the Tambov region. Although a member of Bolshevik Party since 1918, did not personally show any interest in ideology (or anything else except his own career). In the 1920s, completely transformed the image of the Red Army from irregular revolutionary detachments to a well-drilled professional force. Very interested in modern technology, he was an early convert to the value of tank forces and mechanization. Also paid attention to the possibilities of rocket weapons. Earned the nickname of the 'Red Bonaparte'. Head of the Academy of the Red Army after the Civil War, and Commander of the Western Front, 1922–24. Chief-of-staff of the Red Army, 1925–28. Commander of the Leningrad military district, 1928. Deputy Defence Minister, Deputy Chairman of the Revolutionary Military Council of the USSR, and Head of Armaments of the Red Army, 1931. Non-voting member of the Cen. Cttee. of the VKP, 1934–37. 1st Deputy Defence Minister, and Head of Military Training, 1936. In Jan. 1936, appointed head of the Soviet delegation to the funeral of King George V in London. During this trip, also visited France and Germany. Came under suspicion from the secret police (NKVD). His fall led to an unprecedented bloodbath in the highest ranks of the Red Army, which was practically decapitated by Stalin on the eve of WWII. Although the underlying cause was Stalin's deep suspicion of all able and popular men, and his wish to settle old scores, there is evidence that the immediate cause of Tukhachevskii's fall was a complicated intrigue by Nazi Germany, where counterfeit documents had been prepared al-

legedly describing his anti-Soviet stance during his trip to Western Europe; the documents were leaked to Benes in Czechoslovakia, who immediately secretly shared this knowledge with Stalin. In May 1937, demoted to the post of Commander of the Volga military district. Soon recalled to Moscow in June 1937. On 10 June, it was officially reported that he had been arrested along with Iakir and Putna. On 11 June, it was announced that the investigation had been completed (now Soviet sources give this date as the day of his execution). The following day, Soviet newspapers announced that the 3 had been executed for high treason and conspiracy with military leaders of a foreign power. Rehabilitated during the Khrushchev campaign against Stalin's crimes. His considerable theoretical and practical contribution to the build-up of the Red Army is now fully acknowledged in the Soviet Union, although details of his tragic fate still remain shrouded in secrecy.

Tulikov, Serafim Sergeevich
7.7.1914–   Composer.
Born in Kaluga. Author of many political songs. Highly decorated, with several Stalin Prizes. Wrote over 200 songs, some for orchestra, and others for the variety stage. After Stalin's death, switched to songs for children, and operettas. His music was used in the film *Barankin, Bud' Chelovekom*, 1965.

Tumanian, Ovanes
1869–1923. Author.
His books became a basis for several Armenian operas: *Almast*, by A. Spendiarov, *Anush*, by A. Tigranian, and *Garnik Akhper*, by K. Zakarian. Several Armenian composers set his works to music.

Tumanina, Nadezhda Vasil'evna
14.9.1909–   . Musicologist.
Born in Voronezh. Taught at the Moscow Conservatory. Professor. Works: *Opernoe Tvorchestvo Chaikovskogo*, Moscow 1957 (with V. Protopopov); *Chaikovskii i Muzykal'nyi Teatr*, Moscow, 1961.

Tumanova, Tamara Vladimirovna (Toumanova)
1919–   . Prima ballerina.
Her parents emigrated through Siberia to China. Born in Shanghai. Grew up and studied ballet in Paris at the Olga Preobrazhenskaia Ballet School. From 1933 until 1938, star with the Ballet Russe de Monte Carlo. Appeared with the Original Ballet Russe, 1940, the Ballet Theatre, 1940–45, the Grand Ballet du Marquis de Cuevas, 1949, and the Festival Ballet, 1952–54. With the Paris Opera, 1947–50 and 1956. With La Scala, 1951–52 and 1956. Worked closely with George Balanchine, Leonid Miasin and Serge Lifar. Played Anna Pavlova in an American film.

Tumanskii, Sergei Konstantinovich
1901–1973. Aircraft engine designer.
Graduated from the Zhukovskii Air Force Academy, 1931. Deputy Chief Designer during WWII. Chief Designer, 1956. Academician, 1968. Designed engines for bombers, civilian airliners, training planes, supersonic fighter planes (including the MIG), and other aircraft.

Tupikov, Vasilii Ivanovich
1901–1941. Major-general.
Joined the Bolshevik Party, 1921, and the Red Army, 1922. Graduated from the Frunze Military Academy, 1933. Military attaché in Germany, 1940. At the beginning of WWII, returned to the USSR. Fell in action.

Tupolev, Aleksei Andreevich
20.5.1925–   . Aircraft designer.
Born in Moscow. Son of A. N. Tupolev. Graduated from the Moscow Aviation Institute, 1949. Designer of various supersonic jets (among them the TU–144, which he developed with his father in 1968). Member of the CPSU, 1959. USSR State Prize, 1967.

Tupolev, Andrei Nikolaevich
1888–12.1972. Aircraft designer.
Educated at Moscow Technical Institute. Pupil of the famous scientist N. Zhukovskii. One of the founders of the Aerodynamic Aircraft Design Bureau, 1916, (later the Central

Institute of Aerodynamics and Hydrodynamics). Has been involved in the design of about 100 different types of civil and military aircraft, including the ANT–25 in the 1930s and the modern planes, TU–104 and TU–114. During the purges, arrested and sent to the Gulag, 1939. For several years his name was not mentioned and his books were withdrawn from colleges and libraries. During WWII, along with other scientists, released from the camps to help the war effort. Completely rehabilitated in the 1960s.

Turchin, Valentin Fedorovich
1931–   . Mathematician.
Born near Podolsk. Graduated in physics from Moscow University. Became involved in the human rights movement. Close to Dr. A. Sakharov and other like-minded scientists. Dismissed from his job, 1974. Emigrated, 1977. Settled in the USA.

Turchina, Zinaida Mikhailovna
17.5.1946–   . Athlete.
Born in Kiev. Honoured Master of Sports (handball), 1972. Wtih Kiev Spartak. Graduated from the Kamenets-Podolskii Pedagogical Institute, 1972. USSR champion, 1969–79. Olympic champion, 1976.

Turenkov, Aleksei Evlampievich
21.1.1886–27.9.1958. Composer.
Born in Petersburg. Author of operas, including *Tsvetok Schast'ia*, produced in 1940, ballets, including *Lesnaia Skazka*, and music for string quartets, and for film and theatre.

Turin, Viktor Aleksandrovich
1895–1945. Film director.
Studied at the Theatre School, Petersburg. In 1912, went to the USA. Graduated from the Boston Institute of Technology. Worked in Hollywood as an actor and librettist. Returned to the USSR, 1922. Made some propaganda documentaries, then a feature film, *Nas Bylo Troe*, 1928. His major work was the documentary *Turksib*, about the Turkestan-Siberian Railway. His last film was *Bakintsy* (The People of Baku), 1938.

Turishcheva, Liudmila Ivanovna
7.10.1952– . Olympic champion.
Born in Groznyi. Honoured Master of Sports (gymnastics), 1970. From 1978, with Kiev Dynamo. Graduated from the Rostov Pedagogical Institute, 1974. Member of the CPSU from 1978. USSR champion 1970–75. USSR Cup winner, 1967–74. World champion, 1970 and 1974. European champion, 1971 and 1973. Absolute USSR champion, 1972 and 1974. Olympic champion, 1972, and with her team in 1968, 1972 and 1976. World Cup winner, 1975–76.
Source: V. Golubev, *Liudmila Turishcheva*, Moscow, 1977.

Tushnova, Veronika Mikhailovna
7.7.1915–7.7.1965. Poetess.
Born in Kazan'. Daughter of a professor. Graduated as a doctor, 1935. Began to write poetry in the late 1930s. During WWII, worked as a military doctor at the front. Wrote Stalinist poems, which she later disowned. Committed suicide by poisoning herself on her 50th birthday in Moscow. According to one source, this decision was taken when she found out that her former husband had been the author of many denunciations, and therefore guilty of many Gulag tragedies.

Tvardovskii, Aleksandr Trofimovich
21.6.1910–18.12.1971. Poet, editor.
Born at Zagor'e near Smolensk. Son of a peasant who became a victim of collectivization. Studied at the Smolensk Pedagogical Institute. Graduated from Moscow Institute of Philosophy and Literature, 1939. Joined the Communist Party, 1940. In the 1930s, wrote conventional poems, glorifying the collectivization. Became known for his long poem *Strana Muravia*, 1936, describing the doubts and aspirations of the farmers. War correspondent during the Soviet occupation of Western Ukraine and the Soviet-Finnish war. During WWII, became the most popular poet in the country, publishing throughout the war in verse the life story of a private soldier at the front. His simple, honest, humorous and patriotic character Vasilii (Vasia) Terkin became at once a folk hero. Published another long narrative in verse *Za dal'iu dal'*, 1950–60 (in-

cluding after Stalin's death, the first sombre reflections on his epoch). Became the outstanding editor of the magazine *Novyi Mir*, 1950–54 and 1958–70, putting it on a much higher level than the other Soviet periodicals. Created a sensation by launching the completely unknown ex-Gulag prisoner Solzhenitsyn, personally persuading Khrushchev to allow the publication of *Odin den Ivana Denisovicha* in *Novyi Mir*, 1964. Returning to his former folk hero, wrote a continuation of Vasilii Terkin as a bitter satire on Stalinism (*Vasilii Terkin na tom svete*), describing it as the kingdom of death, which his severely wounded hero visits and overcomes (published in *Izvestia*, 1963). During the years of Brezhnevite stagnation, fell victim to despair and alcoholism. Replaced as editor of *Novyi Mir*, 1970. Died soon thereafter. Buried at the Novodevich'e cemetery in Moscow. In 1988, Gorbachev donated the royalties from the foreign editions of his works to a foundation for the building of a memorial to Vasilii Terkin.

Tvorozhnikov, Ivan Ivanovich
1848–1919. Artist.
Genre and historical painter. Studied at the Petersburg Society for the Encouragement of the Arts, then the Academy of Arts, 1868–75. Exhibited from 1870. Exhibitions: the Academy of Arts, 1870, 1884, 1886, 1888–1892, 1894, and the TPKHV, 1917–18.

Tyrkova-Williams, Ariadna Vladimirovna
2.11.1869–12.1.1962. Author, politician.
Born in Okhta (Petersburg). Daughter of a land-owner. Grew up on the Vergezha estate near Novgorod. Educated at Petersburg High School. Childhood friend of N. Krupskaia, Lenin's future wife. Expelled from the high school (her brother helped organize the assassination of Alexander II). Married ship's engineer A. Borman, 1890. After her divorce, 1897, became known as a journalist, writing in many newspapers. Took up politics. Arrested, 1903, for smuggling revolutionary literature, sentenced to 2 years, but instead went abroad. Settled in Stuttgart with P.

Struve, worked in his newspaper *Osvobozhdenie*. Met the New Zealander Harold Williams, who was with Struve as *The Times* correspondent. Moved with Struve's paper to Paris, and returned after the 1905 Revolution to Russia. Became a member of the Cen. Cttee. of the Cadets (the only woman, nicknamed 'the only real man' in the Committee). Married H. Williams, who had become correspondent in Russia (and for a short time in Turkey) for British newspapers. Became a British citizen. During the Civil War, active supporter of the White Armies. Between the world wars, lived in London, where H. Williams was leader-writer and foreign editor of *The Times*. Actively opposed any communist influence. Tried to draw the attention of world opinion to slave labour in the USSR in the 1930s (unsuccessfully). During WWII, lived with her son in Southern France. After WWII, settled in the USA, 1951. Active in the Russian emigré press and in social work, especially in the resettling of Russian refugees of WWII. Author of *Zhizn' Pushkina* (The Life of Pushkin), 2 vols, Paris, 1929, and memoirs. Died in Washington.

Tyshchenko, Mikhail
1926–1981. Football player.
Famous Ukrainian football player. Honoured Master of Sports. Many times USSR, Ukrainian, and European champion. Gold medal winner at the XVIth Olympic Games.

Tyshkevich, Tamara Andreevna
31.3.1931– . Athlete.
Born in the village of Ikonki, Vitebskaia Oblast', Belorussia. Honoured Master of Sports (track and field athletics), 1956. With Leningrad Zenit. Sports instructor. Graduated from the Leningrad Institute of Physical Culture, 1962. USSR champion, 1956–57. Olympic champion, 1956.

U

Ubiivovk, Elena Konstantinovna
1918–1942. Partisan.
Student at Khar'kov University,

1937. Took part in partisan activity in German-occupied Ukraine, near Poltava. Engaged in intelligence work, arrested by the Gestapo and shot. Posthumously proclaimed a Hero of the Soviet Union after a very long delay (1965), allegedly because her heroic activity came to light through research conducted long after the war.

Uborevich, Ieronim Petrovich
1896–1937. Military commander.
Educated at the Konstantinovskoe Artillery School, 1916. Took part in WWI as a sub-lieutenant. After the Bolshevik take-over, organized the Red Guards in Bessarabia. During the Civil War, joined the Red Army, 1918. Commander of several armies. After the Civil War, army commander in the Ukraine and the Crimea, and Commander of the Eastern Siberian military district. Minister of War of the Far Eastern (buffer) Republic, and Commander-in-chief of the People's Revolutionary Army occupying the Far East, 1922. Commander of several military districts, including Moscow, in the late 1920s. Deputy Chairman of the Revolutionary Military Council of the USSR, and Head of Armaments, 1930–31. Non-voting member of the Cen. Cttee. of the VKP, 1930–37. Commander of the Belorussian military district, 1931–37. Liquidated by Stalin during the purge of the military leadership. Rehabilitated under Khrushchev.

Udolov, Ivan Vasil'evich
20.5.1924–16.10.1981. Athlete.
Born in Rostovskaia Oblast'. Honoured Master of Sports (weight-lifting), 1952. Graduated from the Rostov Technical School of Physical Culture, 1956. USSR champion, 1950–56. World record-holder, 1952–56. European champion, 1952–53. Gold medal winner, 1952. World champion, 1953.

Uglanov, N.A.
1886–1937. Politician.
Secretary of the Moscow party organization. Formerly a follower of the Stalinist line, joined N. Bukharin in 1928–29, and consequently, in 1930, lost his post. Later arrested and executed as a follower of Bukharin.

Uglov, Fedor Grigor'evich
5.10.1904–   . Surgeon, academician.
Born in Chuguevo, Irkutsk Oblast'. Graduated in medicine from Saratov University, 1929. Joined the Communist Party, 1931. Head of a department at the 1st Medical Institute, Leningrad, from 1950. At the same time, Director of the Scientific Research Institute of Pulmonology, 1967–72. Academician, 1967. Recipient of the Lenin Prize for developing surgical methods for the treatment of lung diseases, 1961. Author of many medical books. In 1987, took part in Gorbachev's anti-alcoholism campaign.

Ukolov, Dmitrii Matveevich
23.10.1929–   . Athlete.
Born in Tul'skaia Oblast'. Honoured Master of Sports (hockey), 1954. With the Central Sports Club of the Army. Driver by profession. USSR champion, 1950–60. European champion, 1954–59. World champion, 1954 and 1956. Olympic champion, 1956.

Ulanov, Aleksei Nikolaevich
4.11.1947–   . Athlete.
Born in Moscow. Honoured Master of Sports (figure skating), 1969. Graduated from the Moscow Institute of Physical Culture, 1974. European champion, 1969–72. World champion, 1969–72. USSR champion, 1970. USSR champion, 1971, with Irina Rodnina. Olympic champion, 1972. From 1975, soloist with the Leningrad ensemble, Ballet on Ice.

Ulanova, Galina Sergeevna
8.1.1910–   . Prima ballerina.
Born in Petersburg into a theatrical ballet family. Graduated from the Leningrad Choreographic School, 1928. Pupil of her mother, the ballerina M. F. Romanova. Also trained by A. Vaganova. Joined the Kirov Theatre in 1928. Moved to Moscow, 1944. Soloist with the Bolshoi Theatre, 1944–60. Became a household name. Gave many performances in the Kremlin Hall entertaining Stalin and his circle, and foreign VIPs. Dancer in the tradition of classical Russian ballet. Also a

great dramatic actress. Several State Prizes. In the late 1950s, started to train young ballet dancers. Among her many famous pupils were N. Timofeeva, E. Maksimova, V. Vasil'ev, L. Semeniaka and A. Kondratov. Made several tours in Europe and America and was admired by all the critics. Several books have been written about her life and career, including A. Kan, *Dni s Ulanovoi*, Moscow, 1963 (tr. from English); V. Golubov, *Tanets Galiny Ulanovoi*, Moscow, 1948; V. Bogdanov-Berezovskii, *Galina Sergeevna Ulanova*, Moscow, 1961.

Ulanovskaia, Nadezhda Markovna (Elaine)
1903–1986. GRU officer, author.
Born in Bershady, Ukraine. During the October Revolution, involved in Bolshevik activity in Odessa. Married a communist activist, A. Ulanovskii, who later became a prominent intelligence officer. Worked with her husband in Soviet spy networks in many countries, including Germany, China and the USA, in the 1930s, usually in charge of message transmission and coding. Controller of Whittaker Chambers in the USA before WWII. During the restructuring by Stalin of the Soviet agents' network in the 1930s, recalled to Moscow. Worked as a secretary of the Moscow Bureau of Foreign Correspondents (under close state security supervision). During WWII, assigned as interpreter to the Australian author G. Blunden, who later wrote a book based on conversations with her. Arrested, 1948, and sent to the Gulag for 15 years. (Her husband was arrested for protesting about her arrest. Her daughter Maia was also arrested and sentenced to 25 years in camps.) Released, 1956. Became a Jewish rights activist. Joined her children in Israel, 1975 (they had emigrated there earlier). Interesting memoirs published in Israel.
Works: *V Rossii i Zagranitsei*, 1977; *Istoria Odnoi Sem'i*, 1982; *Zhizn' i Smert' M. Iakubovicha*, 1983.

Ulanovskii, Aleksandr (Walter, Ulrich)
1894–1962? GRU officer.
Exiled to Siberia before WWI for revolutionary involvement. Lived in Siberia with Stalin. During the Civil

War, active communist organizer in Southern Russia. Organized communist partisan groups in the Crimea under the Whites. After the Civil War, joined military intelligence (GRU). Built up Soviet spy networks in Germany, China and the USA. Recalled to Moscow in the late 1930s. Arrested, 1948, sent to the Gulag. Released, 1956.

Ulianov, Mikhail Aleksandrovich
20.11.1927– . Actor, director.
Born in the Siberian village of Bergamak. Moved with his family to the town of Tara on the banks of the Irtysh River. In 1950, graduated from the Shchukin Drama School in Moscow. Actor at the Moscow Vakhtangov Theatre. Known more as a film actor. First film in 1953, *Egor Bulychev and Others*. Became famous in the Soviet Union for his part in *The Brothers Karamazov* (Mosfilm, 1969, director Ivan Pyriev). One of his most forceful performances was as the leading role in *The Chairman* (Mosfilm, 1965, director Aleksei Saltykov). Other films include: *Ekaterina Voronina*, 1957; *The Soldiers Were Marching*, 1959; *A Simple Story*, 1960; *The Baltic Sky*, 1961; *The Silence*, 1964; *The Flight*, 1971; *Liberation*, 1972. Artistic director of Moscow's Vakhtangov Theatre, 1987.

Ulianov, Nikolai Pavlovich
1875–1949. Artist.
Portrait and historical painter and stage designer. Studied at the Moscow School of Painting, Sculpture and Architecture, 1892–99, and later at the studio of Valentin Serov, 1899–1902. Exhibited from 1893. Exhibitions: Russian Portraits at the Tavricheskii Palace, St. Petersburg, 1905; Water-colour, Tempera, Drawing, Moscow, 1906; Leonardo da Vinci Society, Moscow, 1906; The Mir Iskusstva, 1906, 1911–13, 1915–17, 1921; The Zolotoe Runo, 1908–10; The Union of Russian Artists, 1910–13, 1923. Exhibited regularly until 1947 in Moscow and Leningrad. Personal exhibitions: Moscow, 1929, and posthumously in Moscow, 1951.

Umakhanov, Magomed-Salam Il'iasovich
1918– . Politician.
Member of the CPSU, 1939. Served in the Soviet Army, 1939–48. Graduated from the Higher Party School of the Cen. Cttee. of the CPSU, 1952. High party positions in Daghestan including Chairman of the Council of Ministers of the Daghestan ASSR, 1956–67. Member of the Cen. Cttee. of the CPSU from 1971. A Brezhnevite, he was sent into retirement by Andropov after Brezhnev's death.

Umarov, Makhmud
10.9.1924–25.12.1961. Athlete.
Honoured Master of Sports (shooting). Silver medal winner at the XVIth and XVIIth Olympic Games. Several articles appeared in the American and Canadian press suggesting that his death was caused by drugs.

Umerov, Bekir
1958– . Dissident.
Born in Uzbekistan. One of the leaders of the Crimean Tatars' movement for their return to their homeland in the Crimea. Graduated from the Ferghana Polytechnical Institute as an engineer. Came into conflict with the authorities in connection with the Tatar graduates who were not allowed to leave Uzbekistan. Although an Uzbek himself, took an active part in their movement. Arrested for the first time at the age of 16. As a teenager, sentenced to 6 months hard labour. Lost his job in 1985 because of his protests against the treatment of the Tatars. Member of the Tatar delegation to Moscow, 1987, and participant in the negotiations with President Andrei Gromyko.

Unbegaun, Boris Genrikhovich
1898–4.3.1973. Philologist.
Born in Moscow. Educated at a Moscow high school. Graduated from the Mikhailovskoe Artillery School, took part in WWI and the Civil War (on the side of the Whites). Evacuated from the Crimea after the defeat of Wrangel, and moved to Yugoslavia. Graduated from Lubljana University, and later from the Sorbonne. Librarian of the Institut d'Etudes Slaves in Paris. Compiled a catalogue of Russian periodicals in Paris libraries. Professor of Slavonic philology at Strasbourg before WWII. Deported by the German authorities to Buchenwald concentration camp. After his release, returned to Strasbourg University, and then moved to Brussels University. A special chair of comparative Slavonic philology was created for him at Oxford University, 1953–67. After his retirement from Oxford, lectured in the USA and Australia. Member of the Belgian and German academies. Died in New York.

Ungern von Sternberg, Roman Fedorovich
1886–1921. Lt.-general.
From a family of Baltic barons. On active service in the Russian army during WWI. After the October Revolution 1917, organized anti-communist military detachments in Eastern Siberia. During the Civil War, a close ally of ataman Semenov, Commander of the White Cossacks in Siberia. Became very familiar with the way of life, traditions and religion of the Central Asian people, whose ways and dress he adopted, becoming something like a local Mongol chieftain. De facto dictator of Mongolia, Feb. 1921. Defeated after his return with his forces to Russia, May-Aug. 1921. Captured by the Reds, sentenced to death and shot.

Unshlikht, Iosif Stanislavovich
1879–1938. Politician, state security officer.
Joined the SD Party, 1900. Took part in the 1905 Revolution (in Russian Poland). Active participant in the Bolshevik take-over, 1917, member of the Military Revolutionary Cttee. in Petrograd. One of the Cheka chiefs, Dec. 1917. During the Civil War, Minister of War of the Lithuanian-Belorussian Soviet Republic. Deputy chairman of Cheka and the GPU, Apr. 1921–1923. Head of Armaments of the Red Army, 1923, member of the Revolutionary Military Council. Member of the Revision Commission of the Bolshevik Party, 1924, non-voting member of the Cen. Cttee. of the VKP, 1925. Deputy chairman of the Revolutionary Military Council and Deputy Defence Minister, 1925–30. Deputy chairman of VSNKH, 1930–33, head of civil aviation administration, 1933–35, secretary of the Union Council of TSIK USSR, 1935. Arrested, 1937. Liquidated by Stalin.

Urbanovich, Galina Napoleonovna
5.9.1917- . Athlete, international referee.
Born in Baku. Honoured Master of Sports (gymnastics), 1946. Graduated from the Moscow Institute of Physical Culture, 1957. Honoured coach of the RSFSR, 1964. International referee, 1968. Sports instructor. USSR champion, 1939–52. Absolute USSR champion, 1943–48, and 1950. Olympic silver medallist, 1952.

Urbanskii, Evgenii Iakovlevich
27.2.1932–5.11.1965. Film actor.
Graduated from the MKHAT Studio School, 1957. Joined the Moscow Stanislavskii Drama Theatre. Entrusted with the leading role in Iu. Raizman's film *Kommunist*, 1958. Became a celebrity for his 2 films — *The Ballad of a Soldier* (director, G. Chukhrai), in which he played the minor but unforgettable part of a war-invalid, and *The Letter That Was Never Sent* (Neotpravlennoe Pis'mo), 1960 (directed by M. Kalatozov). Became a national hero when he appeared in Chukhrai's anti-Stalinist film *Chistoe Nebo* (The Clear Skies), 1961. Died on location while making the film *Direktor*, and was mourned throughout the country. In 1968, E. Stashevskaia-Naroditskaia made a film about him.

Urbel', Ida Arturovna
16.12.1900- . Choreographer, ballet teacher.
Born in Vil'iandi, Estonia. Trained, 1922–29, at private ballet studios in Tallinn and Riga. Graduated from the Paris National Association of Professors of Dance and Ballet Dancers, 1932. Choreographer at the Ugala Theatre in Vil'iandi, 1932–35. Choreographer at the Tartu Vanemuine Theatre, 1935–57, and chief choreographer, 1957–73. Also worked with Estonian folk dancers. Ran her own ballet studio in Vil'iandi 1929–35, and directed a ballet studio attached to the Vanemuine Theatre, 1935–57.

Uritskii, Moisei Solomonovich
1873–1918. State security chief.
Graduated in law from the Kiev University, 1897. Joined the SD Party, 1898. Menshevik after the split in the party. Changed over to the Bolsheviks in summer 1917, member of the Cen. Cttee. of the Bolshevik Party, July 1917. Active participant in the Bolshevik take-over, Oct. 1917, in Petrograd. Appointed head of the Petrograd Cheka, Mar. 1918. Assassinated (shot) by the SR student Leonid Kannegiesser, whose friend had been executed by the Cheka shortly before.

Urusevskii, Sergei Pavlovich
23.12.1908–12.11.1974. Cameraman.
Graduated from the Leningrad Art Industrial High School, 1929, and from the Institute of Applied Arts (formerly the VKHUTEIN), 1935. Pupil of V. A. Favorskii. Entered the film industry, 1935. First film — *Kak Possorilis' Ivan Ivanovich s Ivanom Nikiforovichem*, 1941. War cameraman, 1941–45. From 1946–55, cameraman on many dull Stalinist films. His big success was *The Forty First*, a film by G. Chukhrai in 1956, followed by M. Kalatozov's *The Cranes Are Flying*, 1957, which received international recognition. His next film, Kalatozov's *The Letter That Was Never Sent*, became the subject of discussion in the professional press for the next 2 years. In 1964, worked on *I Am Cuba*. An extremely gifted man, who was married to his camera. *Beg Inokhodtsa*, 1970, is only remembered for his dazzling photography.

Urusov, Sergei Dmitrievich, Prince
1867–after 1945. Politician.
Deputy Minister of the Interior just before the 1917 Revolution. Liberal politician and lawyer. Emigrated after the Bolshevik take-over, Nov. 1917.

Usmankhodzhaev, Inamzhon Buzrukovich
1930- . Politician.
Uzbek. Graduated from the Central Asian Polytechnical Institute in Tashkent, 1955. Joined the Communist Party in 1958. Worked as an engineer, and construction section chief of Ferganavodstroi Trust (irrigation project). Chief architect of Margilan city, 1955–60. Instructor on an Oblast' Cttee. of the Uzbek CP. Chairman of Syr-Daria City Executive Cttee. Secretary of Syr-Daria Oblast' Cttee. of the Uzbek CP, 1960–69. Instructor in a department of the Cen. Cttee. of the CPSU, 1969–72. Chairman of Namangan Oblast' Executive Cttee., 1972–74. 1st Secretary of Andizhan Oblast' Uzbek CP, 1974–78. Member of the Cen. Cttee. of the Uzbek CP, 1978. Chairman of the Presidium of the Supreme Soviet of the Uzbek SSR, 1978. Deputy Chairman of the Presidium of the USSR Supreme Soviet, 1979. Member of the Cen. Cttee. of the CPSU from 1981. 1st Secretary of Uzbek CP Cen. Cttee. From 1987, pursuing Gorbachev's policy of glasnost in Uzbekistan.

Usov, Anton Ivanovich
16.8.1895–1970? French-horn player.
Born in Stanitsa Mikhailovskaia, Don region. Pupil of F. Ekkert. From 1916, soloist at the Bolshoi Theatre, and later with PERSIMFANS, and the Great All-Union Radio Symphonic Orchestra. Professor at the Moscow Conservatory.

Uspenskii, Nikolai Dmitrievich
3.1.1900–23.7.1987. Liturgical scholar, musicologist.
Born near Novgorod. Son of a priest. Educated at the Novgorod Seminary. Graduated from the Petrograd Theological Institute, 1925. After the closure of the Theological Institute in 1928, started a new career as a musicologist. After WWII, professor at the Leningrad Conservatory and the re-opened Theological Academy. Wrote a history of Russian liturgical singing, 1957. Active participant in international Orthodox conferences and ecumenical work. Taught liturgics, church history, and church singing. Died in Leningrad.

Uspenskii, Petr Demianovich (Ouspensky)
1878–2.10.1947. Philosopher, author, occultist.
Born in Moscow. Son of an officer in the survey department of the government. Started work as a journalist and translator in Petersburg. Became known as an adherent of the theory of different levels of consciousness, according to which each of these

levels or orders have their own characteristics and laws, and only the lowest is capable of being observed by the physical senses. Travelled widely in Turkey, Greece, India, Ceylon and Egypt before WWI. Met the Caucasian mystic Gurdjieff in 1915 in Moscow, and later reinterpreted his occult ideas for Western society. During the Civil War, went to the Caucasus, again met Gurdjieff, emigrated to Turkey in 1921, invited to England by Lady Rothermere. His studies of the fourth dimension and such subjects as yoga, the tarot, dreams, hypnotism and eternal recurrence made an impact on sympathetic Western groups, especially between the wars. Brought Gurdjieff to England, and later helped him to set up a sort of guru community in France. Broke with Gurdjieff in 1924, and returned to his English disciples. His lectures just before WWII attracted up to a thousand people. Soon after the outbreak of the war, left London and moved to the USA. Tried to organize groups of disciples in America, without much success. Returned to England, 1947. Resumed his lectures, preaching new levels of self-awareness, but his declining health soon prevented this activity. After his death, his wife returned to America (where she died in 1963) and published his works popularizing the esoteric teachings of Gurdjieff. These writings gained a wide audience and remain influential in theosophical circles. All his documents and records are held at the library of the University of Yale.
Main works: *Tertium Organum*; *A New Model of the Universe*; *Letters from Russia 1919*; *In Search of the Miraculous*; *The Fourth Way*; *The Psychology of Man's Possible Evolution*; *The Strange Life of Ivan Osokin*; *Talks with the Devil*; *The Symbolism of the Tarot Cards; Conscience*.
See: J. H. Reyner, *Ouspensky. The Unsung Genius*, London, 1981.

Ustiian, Ivan Grigor'evich
1939– . Politician.
Moldavian. Son of a peasant. Member of the CPSU, 1961. Graduated from the Kishinev Agricultural Institute, 1965 and the CPSU Cen. Cttee.'s Academy of the Social Sciences, 1973. Senior party posts in Moldavia. Chairman of the Council of Ministers, Jan. 1981. Minister of Foreign Affairs of the Moldavian SSR, 1981. Member of the Bureau of the Cen. Cttee. of the Moldavian CP, Jan. 1981 until Dec. 1985. Replaced by Ivan Kalin. Officially retired for health reasons.

Ustinov, Dmitrii Fedorovich
30.10.1908–20.12.1984. Politician, marshal.
Born in Samara (now Kuibyshev). Son of a worker. At the age of 19, joined the Communist Party. Worked as a fitter and machine operator in various plants in Gorkii and Ivanovo Oblast's. Graduated as a mechanical engineer from the Leningrad Military Technical Institute, Naval Artillery Research Institute, 1934. Design engineer, chief designer, and director of the Bolshevik Arms Factory in Leningrad until 1941. Was made people's commissar of armaments at the age of 32. Responsible for armaments during WWII. In 1946, the post was changed to that of Minister of Armaments, a position he held until Stalin's death in Mar. 1953. Deputy in the USSR Supreme Soviet, 1946–50 and 1954. After WWII, played a decisive role in enlisting the knowledge of captured German scientists in building up the USSR's rocket forces. A driving force behind the Soviet space programme. Full member of the Cen. Cttee. of the CPSU, 1952. USSR Minister of the Defence Industry, 1953–57. Deputy Chairman, and 1st Deputy Chairman of the USSR Council of Ministers, 1963–65. Candidate member, 1965–76, and full member of the Politburo from 1976. A civilian until his appointment in Apr. 1976. Promoted to Marshal 3 months later. USSR Minister of Defence, 1976–Dec. 1984. Died in Moscow.

Ust'vol'skaia, Galina Ivanovna
17.6.1919– . Composer.
Born in Petrograd. Taught at the music school attached to the Leningrad Conservatory, and later at the Conservatory itself. Wrote pieces for symphony orchestra, cantatas, suites, and music for films.

Utesov, Leonid Osipovich
21.3.1895–9.3.1982. Singer, conductor.
Born in Odessa. In the 1930s, became an extremely famous jazz singer. Appeared in many films which were instant box office successes. Became a screen idol after his film *Veselye Rebiata*, 1934. Organized, and appeared as conductor and singer in his own jazz orchestra.
See: L. Utesov, *S Pesnei Po Zhizni*, Moscow, 1961.

Utkin, Iosif Pavlovich
1903–1944. Poet.
At the age of 24, became a famous poet. Many of his verses have been set to music by Soviet composers. Author of some of the first revolutionary songs, such as *Pesnia Dlia Osoboi Dal'nevostochnoi Armii* and *Nad Rodinoi Groznye Tuchi*. D. Shostakovich also used his poetry.

Uvarov, Aleksandr Nikolaevich
20.3.1922– . Athlete.
Born in Tul'skaia Oblast'. Honoured Master of Sports (hockey), 1954. With Moscow Dynamo. Plumber by profession. USSR champion, 1954. European champion, 1954–56. World champion, 1954, 1956. Olympic champion, 1956.

Uverov, Ivan Mikhailovich
1894–1953. Military commander.
On active service during WWI as a captain. Joined the Red Army, 1918. Took part in the Civil War as a regimental commander. Became widely known during the defence of Petrograd against the Whites, and during the march of the Red Army into Poland, 1920. Highly decorated (3 Orders of the Red Banner). Later became an economic administrator.

V

Vachnadze, Nato (Natalia Georgievna)
14.6.1904–14.6.1953. Film actress.
Born in Gurdzhaani, Georgia. The wife of Nikolai Shengelaia. Entered the film studios in 1923. Her best roles were in the silent cinema in Georgia in *Delo Tariela Mklavadze* and *Esma*, 1925. These were followed

by *Ovod*, 1928, *Zhivoi Trup*, 1929, and *Kvartaly Predmest'ia*, 1930. Acted in many Russian films. In the 1930s, forced to accept the parts of collective-farm women. In 1981, the N. Vachnadze Museum was opened in her birth-place.

Vaganova, Agrippina Iakovlevna
26.6.1879–5.11.1951. Ballet teacher. Born in Petersburg. Studied at the Petersburg Theatre School with P. Gerdt, O. Preobrazhenskaia and A. Oblakov, 1897. Danced with the corps de ballet of the Mariinskii Theatre, and soon became a soloist. Strict follower of the classical teaching of Marius Petipa and N. Legat. In 1916, gave up dancing and became a teacher at the Leningrad Choreography School, which was given her name after her death. Created at least 2 generations of top dancers, including such internationally-known names as Galina Ulanova, N. Dudinskaia, I. Kolpakova and Natalia Makarova. From 1931–37, artistic director of the Kirov Ballet Theatre, Leningrad. From 1946, professor. Died in Leningrad. Author of *The Basics of Classical Dance*, 1934.

Vagner, Vladimir Aleksandrovich (Wagner)
29.3.1849–8.3.1934. Psychologist. Professor of Petersburg University, 1906–1931. Founder of the Psychoneurological Institute in Petrograd. Specialist in bio-psychology. Author of *Bio-Psikhologiia*, 2 vol., 1910–13.

Vail, Petr Lvovich
1949–   . Journalist, human rights campaigner.
Born in Riga, Latvia. Trained as a journalist. Reporter with the Latvian *Sovetskaia Molodezh'*. In 1977, emigrated to the USA. Contributor to *Novoe Russkoe Slovo*, New York, *Novyi Amerikanetz*, *Kontinent*, *Vremia I My*, *Ekho*, and *Chast' Rechi*. Teaches Russian literature at American universities. Author (together with A. Genis) of *Sovremennaia Russkaia Proza*, USA, 1982.

Vainshtein, Mikhail Zakharovich
1928–   . Editor, journalist.
Born in Tula. Graduated from the Moscow Polygraphic Institute. Moved to Tbilisi. Editor of *Literaturnaia Gruziia*. Published numerous books and articles on the history of Russian and Georgian literature in the USSR. Left the USSR, 1977, and settled in Israel. Edited and published: Lev Lunts's *Rodina I Drugie Proizvedeniia*, Jerusalem 1981; Erenburg's *Staryi Skorniak I Drugie Proizvedenia*, Jerusalem, 1983; Semen Gekht's *Prostoi Rasskaz O Mertvetsakh I Drugie Proizvedeniia*, and A. Tsybulevskii's *Levkina Istoria I Drugie Proizvedeniia*.

Vaitsekhovskaia, Elena Sergeevna
1.3.1958–   . Athlete.
Born in L'vov. Honoured Master of Sports (diving), 1976. Student at the Moscow Institute of Physical Culture. USSR champion, 1974. Olympic champion, 1976.

Vakhonin, Aleksei Ivanovich
10.3.1935–   . Athlete.
Born in the village of Abagur, Kemerovo Oblast'. Honoured Master of Sports (heavy athletics), 1965. USSR champion, 1961–64, 1966–67. European champion, 1963, 1965–66. World champion, 1963–64, 1966. Olympic champion, 1964.

Vakhrameev, Ivan Ivanovich
15.10.1885–20.7.1965. Sailor, revolutionary.
Born in Iaroslavl'. Navy NCO, 1908–18. One of the communist organizers of the Baltic fleet during the October Revolution 1917. Retired as a colonel, 1949. Died in Leningrad.

Vakhtangov, Evgenii Bagrationovich
13.2.1883–29.5.1922. Actor, stage director.
Born in Vladikavkaz (now Ordzhonikidze). Son of a tobacco factory owner. Studied at Moscow University, 1903. Changed to a Moscow theatre school, and joined the Moscow Art Theatre, 1911. After the revolution, became an enthusiastic exponent of revolutionary art. Head of the Directors Section of the Theatrical Department of the Ministry of Education, 1919. Famous reformer of theatre art in the early 1920s. Founded his own studio within the Moscow Arts Theatre, which became the Vakhtangov Theatre, 1926. Died in Moscow.

Vakhterov, Vasilii Porfir'evich
25.1.1853–3.4.1924. Educationalist. Born in Arzamas. Graduated from the Theological Seminary in Nizhnii Novgorod. Inspector of elementary schools, 1881–96 (Smolensk, Moscow). Author of the standard pre-revolutionary ABC, 1898. One of the best-known organizers of general education in Russia before the revolution. Founder of the Union of Teachers, 1905. On bad terms with the authorities before the revolution because of his democratic convictions. Condemned the Bolshevik take-over from a liberal position. Lecturer at the Pedagogical Faculty of Moscow University, 1923–24. Died in Moscow.

Vakhtin, Boris Borisovich
1930–1981. Author, translator.
One of the leaders of the Leningrad literary group Gorozhane whose membership also included V. Maramzin, I. Efimov and S. Dovlatov. Circulated widely in samizdat. Published his short stories in *Ekho*. His novella *Dublenka* was published in *Metropol'*, 1979.
See: P. Vail, A. Genis, *Sovremennaia Russkaia Proza*, USA, 1982.

Vakhvakhishvili, Tamara Nikolaevna
4.1.1894–1970? Composer.
Born in Warsaw. Musical Director of the Sh. Rustaveli Theatre, Tbilisi, 1922–26, and of the K. Mardzhanishvili Theatre, Tbilisi, 1928–33. In Moscow from 1933. Author of ballets, mimes, musical comedy, a symphony and miscellaneous works. Author of 'Odinnadtsat' let s Mardzhanovym, Vypiski iz dnevnikov (1922–33)', *Teatr*, 1965, Nr 7.

Vaksberg, Arkadii Iosifovich
1932–   . Journalist.
In the 1960s, appeared in *Literaturnaia Gazeta* and the magazine *Iunost'*. Specialized in legal matters. Under Gorbachev, became a prominent legal expert-journalist, and an ardent campaigner for radical changes in the

Soviet legal system. Leading voice in the group of liberals who are helping in Gorbachev's perestroika.

Vaksel', Platon L'vovich
26.8.1844–1919. Musicologist, music critic.
Born in Strel'na, near Petersburg. Lived in Madeira and Portugal, 1862–70. Musical editor of the newspaper *Journal de St. Petersbourg*, 1880–97. First writer to give a survey of Portuguese music. Died in Petrograd.
Works: *Miguel de Glinka, Esboco Biografico*, Punchal, 1862; *Ricardo Wagner e Francisco Liszt*, Lisbon, 1875; *Abriss der Geschichte der Portugiesischen Musik*, Munich, Berlin, 1888.

Valentinov, Nikolai (Vol'skii, Nikolai Vladislavovich)
1879–early 1920s. Journalist, revolutionary.
Member of the SD Party, Bolshevik, 1902, Menshevik, 1904. Before WWI, lived abroad as a political emigré. Close to Lenin in Switzerland. Follower of Mach and Avenarius in philosophy. Returned to Russia after the revolution, 1917. Re-emigrated, 1930. Contributed to many Russian periodicals in the West. Wrote books on Lenin based on his personal experience and meticulous research (*Maloznakomyi Lenin*). Lived in France and later in the USA. One of the best researchers of the early period of Bolshevism.

Val'ter – Kiune, Ekaterina Adolfovna (Walter – Kühne)
13.5.1870–1930. Harpist.
Born in Petersburg. Pupil of Albert Tsabel' (1835–1910). Professor at the Petersburg Conservatory. One of her pupils was K. Erdeli. Appeared in concerts. Emigrated in 1917. Author of transcriptions for the harp. Died in Rostock, Germany.

Valts, Karl Fedorovich
1846–1929. Stage designer.
Born in Petersburg. Son of the chief machinist of the Mariinskii Theatre, F. Valts. From 1855, studied art design in Germany with O. Rahm and K. Gropius. From 1861 onwards, with the Bolshoi Theatre. Called the

'magician of the stage'. Stage designer for the Malyi Theatre, Moscow, and the Mariinskii Theatre, Petersburg. With the Ballets Russes during their first season in Paris. Memoirs: *65 Let V Teatre*, 1928.

Valukin, Evgenii Petrovich
19.8.1937–   . Ballet dancer, choreographer.
Born in Moscow. Graduated from the Moscow Choreographic School, 1958. Pupil of M. Gabovich. Dancer and soloist at the Bolshoi Theatre until 1978. Choreographer at the National Ballet School, Toronto, 1963–64, 1967, and 1974.

Vampilov, Aleksandr Valentinovich
1937–1972. Playwright.
First publication, *Dom Oknami v Pole*, 1964. Other works: *Proshchanie v Iune*, 1966, *Starshii Syn*, 1968, and *Proshlym Letom v Chulimske*, 1972. This last (The Last Summer in Chulimsk) became a soap opera on Soviet TV, and was staged in 1987 at the Riverside Studios, London. British critics called it 'North Enders' or 'Kremlin Street'.

Vanetsian, Aram Vramshapu (Vramovich)
1901–   . Artist.
Genre and portrait painter, also graphic artist and book illustrator. Studied at the Moscow Stroganov Central Art-Industrial School, 1915–17, then at the VKHUTEMAS, Moscow, 1918–23. Pupil of Robert Falk and Pavel Kuznetsov. Exhibitions from 1939, all in Moscow. Official portrait painter of military commanders and officers.

Vannikov, Boris Lvovich
7.9.1897–22.2.1962. Col.-general.
Born in Baku. Son of a worker. Took part in the Civil War in the Caucasus. In the 1920s, director of several machine building factories. From 1937, in the Ministry of Armaments. Minister (peoples commissar) of Munitions during WWII, 1942–46. Organized the immense war effort in this field. Highly decorated (6 Orders of Lenin). Died in Moscow. Buried at the Kremlin wall.

Varfolomei (Remov), Archbishop of Zagorsk
1886?–26.6.1936. Russian Orthodox clergyman.
After the closure of the St. Trinity Lavra (Zagorsk monastery), organized a secret seminary for the training of Orthodox priests. Arrested and shot by the NKVD.

Varlikh, Gugo Ivanovich (Varlich, Hugo)
1856–23.1.1922. Conductor.
Born in Kassel of Czech parents. In Petersburg from the early 1870s. Director of the Court Orchestra, Petersburg, 1888–1917. Died in Petrograd.

Varvatsi, Vladimir Nikolaevich (Komneno-Varvatsi)
1896–1922. Revolutionary, naval officer.
Graduated from the Naval Corps, 1917. Participated in the October Revolution in Petrograd, 1917. Joined the Red Navy, 1918. During the Civil War, Commander of the Red Navy on the Volga, the Dvina, and later in the White Sea. Commander of the Red Navy in the Baltic, 1920. Commander of the Eastern region of the Black Sea, 1921.

Vasiagin, Semen Petrovich
1910–   . Political officer.
Joined the Soviet Army and the Communist Party, 1932. Party-political work in the NKVD armed forces, 1933. Graduated from the Communist University in Moscow, 1937. All his life in high political commissar posts in various parts of the army. Chief of the political department of the land armed forces, 1967. Member of the Cen. Revision Commission of the CPSU, 1966–81.

Vasil'chikov, Georgii Illarionovich, Prince (Vassilchikov, George)
22.11.1919–   . Author, businessman.
Born in Beaulieu-sur-Mer, France. Son of Prince Illarion Sergeevich Vasil'chikov and Princess Lidia Viazemskaia. Educated in France and Lithuania. Studied at the universities of Rome and Berlin, and the École Libre des Sciences Politiques et

Sociales, Paris. Fled from Lithuania with his parents in 1940 after its annexation by the USSR. Lived in Rome, Berlin and Paris, 1941–46. Journalist on *Le Parisien Libéré* and with the Agence France Presse. In 1946–47, interpreter at the Nuremberg war trials. From 1947–77, interpreter, and later senior research assistant at the United Nations, first in New York, and later in Geneva. Has written numerous articles and books under various pen-names, as well as his own. Edited the *Berlin Diaries, 1940–45* of his sister Maria (Missie) Vassiltchikov. Lives in London and Rolle, Switzerland.

Vasil'chikov, Illarion Sergeevich, Prince (Vassilchikov)
15.4.1881–3.6.1969. Statesman.
Born in Tsarskoe Selo. Son of Prince Sergei Illarionovich Vasil'chikov. Graduated in law (with a gold medal) from St. Petersburg University. Sub-lieutenant in the Battalion of the Guard Fusiliers of the Imperial Family, 1905. In 1906, resigned and joined the 1st Department of the Imperial Senate. Member of the commission inspecting conditions in Turkestan (now Soviet Central Asia), on whose recommendation the now world-famous irrigation system of that area was set up. Aged 28, Marshal of the Nobility of the Government of Kovno, the youngest such appointee in Russian history. In 1912, elected as Member from Kovno to the 4th Duma, where he sat as a member of the Oktiabrist Party. In Feb. 1917, member of the Temporary Cttee. of the State Duma which, until the formation of the Provisional Government, was the de facto government of Russia. Appointed by the Provisional Government commissar for the re-organization of the Imperial Red Cross. Became a member of the new Governing Board of the Red Cross, a function which he retained until his death, after the Board transferred its seat abroad. Member of the Orthodox Church Council, 1917–18, which re-established the Patriarchate abolished by Peter the Great. Emigrated, 1919. Moved to Paris. Later returned to Lithuania, where his family estates were before the October Revolution 1917. Elected member of the National Congress, which in 1926 attempted

but failed to unify all Russian emigré organizations. Acted continuously as spokesman of the large Russian community in Lithuania. Fled Lithuania upon its annexation by the USSR in June 1940. Moved to Berlin, and later Baden-Baden. Gave Russian language lessons to staff officers of the French occupation forces in Germany. Dedicated his last years to Russian Orthodox Church affairs. Awarded the Order of St. Vladimir by Patriarch Aleksii. Died in Baden-Baden.

Vasil'chikov, Sergei Illarionovich, Prince (Vassilchikov)
5.8.1849–27.8.1926. Military commander.
Born in St. Petersburg. Son of Prince Illarion Illarionovich Vasil'chikov, Governor-general of Kiev and Podolia. Educated at the Corps des Pages, St. Petersburg. Sub-lieutenant in the Imperial Horse Guards, 1867. Appointed ADC General to Emperor Alexander II during the Russo-Turkish war, 1877–79. Commander of the Regiment of Dragoons of Nizhnii Novgorod, 1884–90. Commander of the Hussars of the Guard, 1890. GOC. of the Corps of the Guards, and the military district of St. Petersburg, 1901–07. Emigrated, 1919. Died in Versailles.

Vasil'chikova, Lidia Leonidovna, Princess (Princess Lydia Vassilchikov; b. Princess Lidia Viazemskaia)
10.6.1886–13.11.1948. Social worker, Red Cross worker.
Born in Tambov. Daughter of Prince Leonid Dimitrievich Viazemskii, ADC General to the emperors Alexander II, Alexander III and Nicholas II. Educated in St. Petersburg and at Oxford University. Married Prince Illarion Vasil'chikov, 1909. Founded and ran a hospital train at the front throughout WWI. Emigrated, 1919. Lived in France, Germany and Lithuania. Whilst in France, set up a highly successful amateur theatre company which she managed, and in which she also performed. In June 1940, escaped from Soviet-occupied Lithuania to Italy. In 1941, moved to Germany, where, following Hitler's invasion of the USSR, she established, despite Hitler's personal opposition, a world-

wide aid organization to provide food and clothing to starving Soviet POWs in the German camps. Died in an accident (run over by a car) in Paris.

Vasil'chikova, Maria Illarionovna (Princess Missie Vassilchikov; Mrs Peter Harnden)
11.1.1917–12.8.1978. Author.
Born in St. Petersburg. Daughter of Prince Illarion Sergeevich Vasil'chikov and Princess Lidia Viazemskaia. Educated in Paris. Moved to Lithuania with her parents, 1934. Secretary at the British Legation. In 1938, moved to Switzerland, then to Italy, and eventually to Germany. In Jan. 1940, settled in Berlin, where she first worked at the Drahtloser Dienst or DD (Wireless Service), the news service of the Reichs-Rundfunk Gesellschaft or RRG, and later with the Foreign Ministry's Information Department. Soon found herself on close terms with many of the key figures in the German anti-Nazi resistance, who were actively involved in the attempt on 20 July 1944 to assassinate Hitler. After vain attempts to help her arrested friends, many of whom were to die on the gallows, fled Berlin for Vienna, where she worked as a nurse in a military hospital. Shortly before the fall of Vienna to the Soviet armies, she was evacuated with the hospital to Western Austria. Married Captain Peter G. Harnden, a US Army Intelligence officer, later an internationally prominent architect. All through the war, she kept a secret diary, published in London in 1985 under the title *The Berlin Diaries, 1940–1945*, which immediately became an international bestseller. After the war, lived with her husband and 4 children in France and Spain. Died of leukaemia in London.

Vasilenko, Matvei Ivanovich
25.11.1888–1.7.1937. Military commander.
Born in the village of Podstavka in the Ukraine. Educated at the Tiflis Military School, 1909. Took part in WWI (captain). During the Civil War, army commander (against the Whites at Tsaritsyn and Kuban', against Poland, and against Ar-

459

menia). In the 1930s, Infantry Inspector of the Red Army. Victim of Stalin's purge of the Red Army.

Vasilenko, Sergei Nikiforovich
30.3.1872–11.3.1956. Composer, conductor.
Born in Moscow. While still at school, studied musical theory with A. Grechaninov. Graduated from the Faculty of Law of Moscow University, 1895, and from the Moscow Conservatory in 1901. Pupil of S. Taneev, M. Ippolitov-Ivanov and V. Safonov. While a student, conducted a student orchestra. Appeared in Moscow in private opera, 1903–04. Taught from 1906. Professor of instrumentation and composition at the Moscow Conservatory from 1907. Director, conductor and founder of the Istoricheskie Kontserty, for which he adapted ancient music. Continued his career as composer, conductor, teacher and lecturer after the October Revolution. For some time, influenced by impressionism and exotic themes. After the revolution, concentrated on folk music. Among his more than 200 pupils was M. Ashrafi. Died in Moscow.

Vasil'ev, Aleksandr Aleksandrovich
1867–1953. Historian.
Professor at Petrograd University and the Pedagogical Institute. Wrote a 2-volume *History of Byzantium*. Emigrated in the mid 1920s. Settled in the USA. Became professor at Wisconsin University. Died in America.

Vasil'ev, Dmitrii Dmitrievich
1943– . Journalist, photographer.
Became known in the late 1980s as a leader of the right-wing movement Pamiat', which he calls a 'national patriotic front'. Accused of anti-Semitism. Lives in Moscow.

Vasil'ev, Dmitrii Ivanovich
21.10.1900–5.1.1984. Director.
Graduated from the Chaikovskii Film School, 1927. Assistant to S. Eisenstein on *Aleksandr Nevskii*, 1938, and to V. Pudovkin on *Vo Imia Rodiny*, 1943, *Admiral Nakhimov*,

1947, and *Zhukovskii*, 1950. Co-director with M. Romm on *Lenin v Oktiabre*, 1937. Assistant to De Santis on *Oni Shli Na Vostok*, 1967, an Italian-Soviet co-production.

Vasil'ev, Nikolai Grigor'evich
1908–1943. State security officer.
Party member, 1929. Political Commissar in the army, 1930 (state security services). During WWII, NKVD controller of partisan detachments in the rear of the German occupying forces near Novgorod (Partizanskii krai). Killed in action.

Vasil'ev, Pavel Nikolaevich
25.12.1910–1937. Poet.
Born in Zaisan, Kazakhstan. Son of a Semirechenskii Cossack. Very popular in his time. Amazingly sincere poet in the sycophantic atmosphere of the 1930s. Arrested and disappeared in the Gulag, circumstances of death unknown. Poems re-published during the Khrushchev thaw in the late 1950s.

Vasil'ev, Petr Vasil'evich
1899– . Artist.
Born in Odessa. Studied at the Odessa Art School, 1914–26, under K. Kostandi, T. Dvornikov and D. Krainev. Portrait and genre painter. Exhibited from 1938. Performed a great deal of official political work including portraits of Lenin for governmental organisations. Took part in many official exhibitions.

Vasil'ev, Valerii Ivanovich
3.8.1949– . Athlete.
Born in Volkovo, Novgorod Oblast'. Honoured Master of Sports (ice hockey),1973. With Moscow Dynamo. European and world champion, 1970, 1973–75, 1978–79. Olympic champion, 1972, 1976.

Vasil'ev, Vladimir Viktorovich
18.4.1940– . Ballet dancer.
Born in Moscow. Graduated from the Moscow Choreographic School, 1958. A pupil of M. M. Gabovich. Joined the Bolshoi Theatre, and soon became one of their stars.

Vasil'ev – Buglai, Dmitrii Stepanovich
9.8.1888–15.10.1956. Composer.
Born in Moscow. One of the earliest writers of Soviet revolutionary songs. Master of choral music. Died in Moscow.

Vasil'ev-Iuzhin, Mikhail Ivanovich
10.11.1876–8.11.1937. Politician, state security official.
Born in Piatigorsk. Son of a worker. Joined the SD Party 1898. Took part in the 1905 Revolution. After the February Revolution 1917, Bolshevik leader in Saratov. From 1919, high posts in the Cheka, later State Prosecutor, and Deputy Chairman of the High Court of the USSR, 1924–37. Liquidated by Stalin.

Vasil'eva, Elizaveta Ivanovna (Dmitrieva, Cherubina de Gabriac)
12.4.1887–5.12.1928. Poetess.
Born in Petersburg. Daughter of a teacher. Educated as a teacher at Petersburg. Studied at the Sorbonne, 1908. On the advice of the poet M. Voloshin, sent her ultra-romantic poems under the pen-name of Cherubina de Gabriac to the best literary magazine of the day, *Apollon*, and became overnight an idolized celebrity. Cause of the last of the famous Russian literary duels (between Gumilev and Voloshin). When her real identity became known, cruelly humiliated by ridicule. Later wrote verse for children with Marshak in the 1920s. Worked as a librarian at the Academy of Sciences. Died in Tashkent.

Vasil'eva, Margarita Vasil'evna (Rozhdestvenskaia)
10.7.1889–13.2.1971. Ballerina.
Born in Moscow. Graduated from the Moscow Theatre School, 1906, with A. Gorskii. Soloist with the Bolshoi Theatre, 1906–41. Took part in the Ballets Russes seasons, 1909 and 1911, in Paris and London. From 1930–59, taught at the Bolshoi Theatre. From 1946, taught at the Moscow GITIS. Professor, 1962.

Vasil'eva, Raisa Rodionovna
1902–1938. Author.
Writer of children's books. Arrested in 1935 during the purge after the

Kirov murder. Sentenced to 5 years. Sent to the Vorkuta concentration camps, 1936 or 1937. According to some information, organized hunger strikes. Shot during the executions at Kirpichnyi Zavod.
See: *Pamiat 3*, Paris, 1980, p. 322.

Vasil'eva, Zinaida Anatol'evna
29.12.1913– . Ballerina, ballet teacher.
Born in Petersburg. Graduated from the Leningrad Choreographic School. A pupil of Agrippina Vaganova. From 1933, soloist with the Leningrad Malyi Theatre, and later with the Bolshoi Theatre. Leading dancer with the Minsk Theatre, 1937–49. Choreographer, 1950–61. Taught at the Novosibirsk and Odessa theatres. Taught classical dance at the Cairo Ballet School, 1962–65.

Vasilevskaia, Vanda L'vovna (Wasilewska, Wanda)
21.1.1905–29.7.1964. Author.
Born in Cracow. Daughter of a leader of the Polish Socialist Party. Polish communist. Graduated from Cracow University, 1927. Moved to Soviet-occupied L'vov, 1939. Became a Soviet citizen. During WWII, worked in the political administration of the Soviet armed forces. After the war, participated in disarmament propaganda campaigns. Her books were introduced into the school curriculum as compulsory reading. During the late 1950s–60s, completely forgotten. Died in Kiev.

Vasilevskii, Aleksandr Mikhailovich
30.9.1895–5.12.1977. Marshal.
Born in the village of Novaia Golchikha near Kostroma. Son of a village priest. Educated at the Alekseevskoe Military School, 1915. Took part in WWI (captain). During the Civil War, in the Red Army. Graduated from the Academy of the General Staff, 1937. One of the best staff officers during WWII. Member of the General Staff, Deputy Chief, May 1940, Head of the Operations Department, Aug. 1941, Chief of the General Staff, and Deputy Minister of Defence, June 1942. Coordinated most of the large operations of the Soviet Army during WWII (including Stalingrad, Kursk and others). Commander of the Belorussian front, Feb. 1945 (occupation of East Prussia, including Koenigsberg). Commander-in-chief of Soviet forces against the Japanese, June 1945. After WWII, again Chief of the General Staff and Deputy Minister of Defence, 1946. Minister of the Armed Forces, 1949–53. Deputy Minister of Defence 1953–57. Chairman of the War Veterans Cttee., 1956–57. Most of the strategic achievements ascribed to Stalin in WWII belonged in fact to Vasilevskii's tactical and staff work. Member of Cen. Cttee. of the CPSU, 1952–61. Highly decorated (7 Orders of Lenin).

Vasilii (Basil, Krivoshein, Vsevolod Aleksandrovich), Archbishop of Brussels and Belgium
30.7.1900–22.9.1985. Russian Orthodox clergyman.
Born in Petersburg. Son of the minister A. Krivoshein. Emigrated during the Civil War with members of his family. Lived in France. Graduated from the Sorbonne in 1921. Monk at Mount Athos in Greece, 1925–47. Gained a reputation as an authority on the ascetic teaching and patristics of the Orthodox Church. Moved to Oxford in 1951. Priest, 1951. Bishop of Volokolamsk (Moscow Patriarchate) with residence in Oxford. Active in the ecumenical movement. During his visits to the Soviet Union, made many independent declarations on the teaching and situation of the Russian Orthodox Church. Bishop of Brussels, 1960. Archbishop, 1960. Died in Leningrad.

Vasilii (Rodzianko, Vladimir Mikhailovich), Archbishop
1915– . Russian Orthodox clergyman.
Born in the Ukraine. Grandson of the chairman of the 4th Duma. Emigrated with his parents during the Civil War, 1919. Settled in Yugoslavia. Graduated in theology at Belgrade University. Became a priest of the Serbian Orthodox Church. After WWII, imprisoned by Tito, but later released. Moved to Great Britain. For many years, a priest in the Serbian Church in London. Editor of religious broadcasts for the BBC Russian Service, 1955. Moved to the USA. Archbishop of San Francisco (American Autocephalous Orthodox Church), 1981. Retired and moved to Washington. Broadcast on Radio Vatican in Russian. Made several visits to the USSR in the 1980s, including a pilgrimage in connection with the Millenium of Russian Christianity. Decorated for his work by the Patriarch of Moscow.

Vasin, Vladimir Alekseevich
9.1.1947– . Athlete.
Born in Moscow. Member of the CPSU, 1971. Honoured Master of Sports (diving), 1972. With Moscow Spartak. Graduated from Moscow University in economics, 1973. USSR champion, 1966, 1969, 1972. Olympic champion, 1972.

Vasnetsov, Appolinarii Mikhailovich
6.8.1856–23.1.1933. Artist.
Born in the village of Riabovo, now Kirov Oblast'. Studied under his brother Viktor Vasnetsov, V. Polenov and Il'ia Repin. Member of the Association of Peredvizhniki from 1899. One of the founding members of the Union of Russian Artists, 1903. Academician of the Petersburg Academy of Arts, 1900. Painter and graphic artist. Specialized in historical subjects from the 1890s. Stage designer (*Khovantshchina* by M. Mussorgskii, S. Mamontov's Private Russian Opera, and the Mariinskii Theatre). Taught at the Moscow School of Painting, Sculpture and Architecture, 1901–18. Head of the Commission for the Restoration of Old Moscow from 1918. Exhibitions: the Mir Iskusstva, 1899–1901; 36 Artists, 1901–03; SRKH, 1903–18, 1922–23. Personal exhibitions: 1929, 1933, 1950, 1956. Died in Moscow. His house in Moscow has since been turned into the Vasnetsov Museum.

Vasnetsov, Viktor Mikhailovich
15.5.1848–23.7.1926. Artist.
Born in the village of Lop'ial, now Kirov Oblast'. Studied at the Petersburg Art School, 1867–68, under I. Kramskoi, then at Petersburg Academy of Arts under P. Chistiakov, 1868–75. Member of the Association of Peredvizhniki from 1878. Went to France, 1876, and Italy, 1885. Lived in Petersburg and Moscow. Began as

461

an illustrator for mass-circulation magazines and popular publications. Illustrated Nikolai Gogol's *Taras Bulba*, 1874. Worked in the field of historical painting, also genre-painter of Russian fairy-tales, byliny, and religious themes, and stage designer (for S. Mamontov's Private Opera). Exhibitions: the Academy of Arts, 1869, 1873, 1881; TPKHV, 1874, 1876, 1878–84, 1889, 1897; All-Russian Exhibition, Moscow, 1882; MOLKH, 1891, 1909; the Mir Iskusstva, 1900; Russian Portraits in the Tavricheskii Palace, St. Petersburg, 1905. One-man exhibitions: 1899, and posthumously in 1927 and 1948. Died in Moscow, where a Vasnetsov Museum has since been set up.

Vatsietis, Ioakim Ioakimovich
23.11.1873–28.7.1938. General, state security official.
Born in Latvia. Son of an agricultural worker. Joined the Russian Army, 1891. Educated at the Wilno Infantry School, 1897. Graduated from the Academy of the General Staff, 1909. Colonel during WWI. After the October Revolution 1917, joined the Bolsheviks. Became one of the main organizers of the Latvian detachments which were Lenin's pretorian guard during the early years of Soviet rule. Suppressed the anti-communist Polish corps of Dowbor-Musnicki, Jan. 1918. Commander of the Latvian division, Apr. 1918. Defeated the left SRs' uprising in Moscow, July 1918. Supreme commander of the military forces of the republic, 1918–19. His detachments were among the few professional and totally ruthless forces of the Red Army in its early days who were employed at the front against the Whites and for terror operations against the population. After the Civil War, professor at the Military Academy of the Red Army, 1921 (lectured on military history). Liquidated by Stalin.

Vatutin, Nikolai Fedorovich
16.12.1901–15.4.1944. General.
Born in the village of Chepukhino, near Kursk. Son of a peasant, joined the Red Army, 1920. Took part in the Civil War. Graduated from the Frunze Military Academy, 1929, and the Academy of the General Staff,

1937. Became known during WWII as an able front commander. Died after being seriously wounded in a battle with anti-communist Ukrainian nationalists. Buried in Kiev.

Vaupshasov, Stanislav Alekseevich
27.7.1899–1976. Colonel, state security official.
Born in Gruzdzhiai in Lithuania. Joined the Red Army, 1918. In the early 1920s, communist partisan in Western Belorussia (then Poland). Returned to the Soviet Union, and became a Cheka and GPU official. During the Spanish Civil War, NKVD official in Spain, 1937–39. After his return to the USSR, continued his NKVD work. During WWII, sent as an NKVD controller of partisans to the rear of the German Army in Belorussia. Head of the partisan network near Minsk, 1942–44. One of the most successful NKVD agents dealing in terror during the war. Highly decorated (4 Orders of Lenin).

Vavilov, Nikolai Ivanovich
25.11.1887–26.1.1943. Biologist, botanist, geneticist.
Son of a businessman. Graduated from Moscow Agricultural Institute in 1911. Professor at the Institute, 1911–17. Professor at Saratov University, 1917. Head of the Botanical Institute, 1921–24. Director of this Institute, which was reorganized and renamed the Institute of Plant Breeding, Petrograd, 1924–40. Through numerous expeditions all over the world in the 1920s and 1930s, built up a unique collection of cultivated plants. Gained a world-wide reputation as the foremost authority in his field. Member of the Academy of Sciences, 1929, President of the Academy, 1929–35. Director of the Institute of Genetics of the USSR Academy of Sciences, 1930–40. President of the Soviet Geographical Society, 1931–40. Fellow of the Royal Society and other foreign scientific bodies. Opposed Lysenko's dictatorship in Soviet science and became its victim. Dismissed from all his posts, arrested in Aug. 1940, and sent to the Kolyma concentration camps. Died in a jail in Saratov. Buried in a common grave with other

prisoners. After Stalin's death, rehabilitated. His name was given to his former institute and a gold medal was created in his name, to be awarded for outstanding success in the development of Soviet agriculture.

Vavilov, Sergei Ivanovich
24.3.1891–25.1.1951. Scientist.
Born in Moscow. Son of a businessman. Brother of the geneticist N. Vavilov. Graduated from Moscow University, 1914. Taught physics at Moscow University, lecturer, 1918, professor, 1929–32. President of the Academy of Sciences of the USSR, 1945. One of the founders of the Znanie Society. Chief editor of the *Bolshaia Sovetskaia Entsiklopediia* 1949.

Vazem, Ekaterina Ottovna
25.1.1848–14.12.1937. Ballerina, ballet teacher.
Born in Moscow. Studied at the Petersburg Theatre School, 1857–67, with L. Ivanov, A. Bogdanov and E. Guge. Danced with a Petersburg ballet company until 1884. Became a leading ballerina. Taught at the Petersburg Theatre School, 1886–96. Among her famous pupils were Anna Pavlova, O. Preobrazhenskaia, M. Kshesinskaia and A. Vaganova. After the October Revolution 1917, taught privately. Memoirs: *Zapiski Balleriny Sankt Peterburgskogo Bolshogo Teatra, 1867–84*, Leningrad-Moscow. 1937.

Vazgen I (Baldzhian, L.K.), Catholicos of Armenia
1908–   . Head of the Armenian Church.
Born in Rumania. Priest of the Armenian Church in Rumania, 1943. Later head of the Armenian Church in Rumania and Bulgaria. Elected Patriarch-Catholicos of all Armenians, 29 Sep. 1955, becoming the 130th head of the church in the oldest Christian country in the world. Widely respected for his theological works and his diplomatic skills. Able to improve the position of the Church in Armenia. Lives at Echmiadzin.

Vedenin, Viacheslav Petrovich
1.10.1941– . Athlete.
Born in the village of Sloboda, Tula Oblast'. Honoured Master of Sports (skiing), 1970. Graduated from the Moscow Institute of Physical Culture, 1973. Member of the CPSU, 1974. With Moscow Dynamo. USSR champion, 1966–73. World champion, 1970 (30km race). Olympic champion, 1972 (30km race).

Vedernikov, Aleksei Stepanovich
1880–1919. Revolutionary.
Joined the SD Party, 1897. Took part in the 1905 Revolution in Moscow. During the October Revolution, directed the seizure of the post office and telegraph in Moscow. Commander of the Red Guards in Moscow after the Bolshevik take-over, 1917. Quelled an anti-communist uprising in Murom during the Civil War.

Vedro, Adolf
16.10.1890–27.9.1944. Composer.
Born in Narva. Professor at the Tallinn Conservatory. According to official sources, died in Khaapsalu under torture during the German occupation. Author of operas, concertos for piano, and choir music.

Veidle, Vladimir Vasil'evich (Weidle)
1.3.1895–1979. Philosopher, art historian.
Born in Petersburg. Graduated from Petersburg University in history, 1916. Lecturer there, 1916–18. Professor at Perm University, 1918–20. Taught history of art in Petrograd, 1920–24. Emigrated to France in 1924. Professor of Christian art at the St. Sergius Theological Institute, Paris, 1932–52. Taught at the Catholic University at Louvain, Belgium, after WWII. Broadcaster with Radio Liberty in Munich in the 1950s. Frequent contributor to Russian publications abroad.
Main works: *Russia Absent and Present, Les Abeilles d'Aristée, Bezymiannaia Strana, Svet Vechernii.*

Veinberga, Tatiana Eduardovna (Makno)
4.9.1943– . Athlete.
Born in Riga. Honoured Master of Sports (volley-ball), 1968. With Riga Daugava. Coach. Olympic champion, 1968.

Veisberg, Iulia Lazarevna
6.1.1880–4.3.1942. Composer.
Born in Orenburg. Wife of the musicologist A. N. Rimskii-Korsakov. Composed operas, symphonies, and works for voice and orchestra. Died during the Siege of Leningrad.

Vekman, Aleksandr Karlovich (Weckmann)
31.7.1884–10.4.1955. Vice-admiral.
Born in Kronstadt. Took part in WWI as a naval officer. Joined the Red Navy, 1919. Took part in the Civil War as a naval artillery officer. In the 1920s, commanded the Red Navy in the Black, Caspian and Baltic seas. Chairman of the cttee. for commissioning new navy ships from 1927. Retired 1947. Died in Leningrad.

Veleva-Mel'nik, Faina Grigor'evna
9.6.1945– . Athlete.
Born in the village of Bakota, Kamenets-Podolskii raion, Khmelnitskaia Oblast'. Graduated from the Erevan Institute of Physical Culture, 1969. Honoured Master of Sports (track and field athletics), 1971. From 1973, with Moscow Spartak. USSR champion, 1970, 1972–77. European champion, 1971, 1974. World record-holder, 1971–75. Olympic champion, 1972 (discus). Coach.

Vel'iaminov, Nikolai Aleksandrovich
1855–1920. Surgeon.
Graduated from Moscow University, 1877. On active military service during the Russo-Turkish war, 1877–78. Professor of the Military Medical Academy, 1894. Organized the Russian Red Cross during the Russo-Japanese war, 1904–05. Dean of the Military Medical Academy, 1910–12. Organized the ambulance service in Petersburg. During WWI, head of the medical service of the Imperial Guard.

Velichko, Konstantin Ivanovich
1856–1927. General.
Participated in the Russo-Turkish war, 1877–78. Graduated from the Engineering Academy, 1881. During the Russo-Japanese war, 1904–05, responsible for the fortifications of

Vladivostok and Port Arthur. Editor of the *Military Encyclopaedia*, 1910. During WWI, engineering inspector at Supreme HQ. After the October Revolution 1917, in the Red Army. Professor of engineering at military educational establishments.

Velikanova, Ksenia Mikhailovna (Asia)
1936–12.8.1987. Biologist, human rights campaigner.
Daughter of the academician M. A. Velikanov and sister of Tatiana Velikanova. Third child in a family of 7 children. Married Sergei Miuge, a scientist and former Gulag prisoner. Graduated from Moscow University as a biologist. Became involved in the human rights campaign. Died in Moscow of cancer. Buried at the Khovanskii Cemetery.

Velikanova, Tatiana Mikhailovna
3.2.1932– . Human rights campaigner.
Born in Moscow. Elder daughter of M. A. Velikanov (1879–1964). Graduated from Moscow University in mathematics and physics, 1954. Taught mathematics and physics at schools in Sverdlovsk Oblast'. Married the scientist K. I. Babitskii. Returned to Moscow, 1956. Researcher at a scientific institute. Published several scientific works. Became involved in the human rights movement after her husband's arrest during a demonstration against the Soviet invasion of Czechoslovakia, 1968. Member of the Initiative Group for the Defence of Human Rights from May 1969. Took part in the distribution of the samizdat *Khronika Tekushchikh Sobytii*. Arrested, Nov. 1979. Detained at Lefortovo prison, Moscow. Sentenced, Aug. 1980, to 4 years in the camps, and 5 years in exile. Her case received international publicity.

Velikhov, Evgenii Pavlovich
1935– . Physicist, state official.
Graduated from Moscow University in 1958. Doctor of Physico-Mathematical Science in 1964. Member of staff of the Institute of Atomic Energy from 1958. Head of the Laboratory, 1962–70. Deputy director, then director of a branch of the same institute from 1971. Joined

the Communist Party in 1971. Professor at Moscow University from 1973. Member of the USSR Academy of Sciences from 1974. Leading expert on space weapons. Adviser to the Kremlin. Accompanied Gorbachev on his visit to Britain. Vice-president of the USSR Academy of Sciences. Speaks perfect English.

Vengerov, Semen Afanas'evich
17.4.1855–14.9.1920. Literary scholar.
Born in Lubny. Graduated from Moscow and Yur'ev Universities, 1880. Prolific and enthusiastic commentator, historian and bibliographer of Russian classical literature. Compiled a *Biographical Dictionary of Russian Writers*, 6 vols, 1886–1904. Wrote monographs on many 19th century writers. Prepared the first full edition of the works of Belinskii in 13 vols. Editor of the literary section of the Brockhaus and Efron Encyclopaedia. Founder and first chairman of the Rossiiskaia Knizhnaia Palata (Russian Chamber of Books), 1917. Died in Moscow.

Vengerova, Izabella Afanas'evna
1.3.1877–7.11.1956. Pianist.
Born in Minsk. Sister of the literary critic S. Vengerov. Pupil of A. Esipova. Taught at the Petersburg Conservatory, 1907–21. Professor from 1913. Gave concerts in Russia and abroad. Emigrated. Professor at the Curtis Institute, Philadelphia, from 1924. Among her pupils were L. Bernstein, S. Barber and L. Foss. Died in New York.

Vengerovskii, Iurii Naumovich
26.10.1938–   . Athlete.
Born in Khar'kov. Honoured Master of Sports (volley-ball), 1965. Graduated from the Khar'kov Pedagogical Institute, 1962. Member of the CPSU, 1964. World champion, 1962. USSR champion, 1963. Olympic champion, 1964.

Veniamin (Kazanskii, Vasilii Pavlovich), Metropolitan of Petrograd
1874–13.8.1922. Russian Orthodox clergyman.
Born in Northern Russia. Graduated from Petersburg Theological Academy in 1897. Bishop of Gdovsk in 1909. Archbishop, later Metropolitan of Petrograd in 1917. Very popular among his congregation. In 1922, accused of refusing to surrender church valuables (allegedly needed to help people who were dying of hunger). This was the method used to strip the church of its considerable collection of gold and silver objects. At a show trial in Petrograd, found guilty, sentenced to death with a group of co-defendants, and shot. Remembered for the calm dignity he showed at his trial.

Veniamin (Voskresenskii, Vasilii Konstantinovich), Bishop of Tutaev
1871–5.10.1932. Russian Orthodox clergyman.
A graduate of Moscow Theological Academy. Bishop of Romanov, 1921. Bishop of Rybinsk, 1927. Known as a modern representative of the old Russian starets tradition. Bishop of Tutaev, 1930. During the collectivization campaign, arrested, 1930. Died near Krasnovodsk.

Verbitskaia, Anastasia Alekseevna
22.2.1861–1928. Author.
Born in Voronezh. Daughter of a landowner. At the turn of the century, an extremely fashionable author, discussing sex, family and the problems of women, subjects considered very daring at that time. Since then, largely forgotten.

Verderevskii, Dmitrii Nikolaevich
1873–1946. Admiral.
Born in Petersburg. Educated in the Naval Corps, 1893. Among the young reformers of the Navy after the defeat in the Russo-Japanese war. During WWI, in the Baltic fleet, head of a submarine division, 1916–17. Chief-of-staff of the Baltic fleet, Apr.–May 1917, and Commander, Jun. 1917. Fired, and court-martialled, July 1917, for refusing to help the Provisional Government during the Bolshevik revolt. After the defeat of the Kornilov revolt, appointed Naval Minister, Sep. 1917. Requested retirement on the day before the October Revolution, 6 Nov. 1917. Emigrated after the Bolshevik takeover. Lived in France. Member of masonic lodges. After WWII, changed to a pro-Soviet position, and became a Soviet citizen. Died in Paris.

Vereiskii, Georgii Semenovich
30.7.1886–18.12.1962. Artist.
Born in Proskurov (now Khmelnitskii). Portrait and landscape painter, graphic artist, lithographer and etcher. Started at the E. Shreider Studio, Khar'kov, 1900–04. Worked at the New Artistic Shop, Petersburg, 1912–15. Pupil of Mstislav Dobuzhinskii. Also studied under B. Kustodiev, E. Lanceray and A. Ostroumova-Lebedeva. Graduated in law from Petersburg University, 1912. Exhibitions: the Mir Iskusstva, 1915–18, 1924; 1st State Free Exhibition, Petrograd, 1919; 10 Years of Russian Xylography, Leningrad, 1927; Russian Graphic Art, 10 Years after the Revolution, Moscow, 1927. Personal exhibitions: Moscow, 1946, Leningrad-Moscow, 1962. Died in Leningrad.

Veresaev, Vikentii Vikent'evich (Smidovich)
4.1.1867–3.6.1945. Author.
Born in Tula. Studied medicine at Moscow and Derpt Universities. In the 1890s, a 'legal Marxist', a writer of novels about the intelligentsia and the hard life of the peasantry, close to Gorkii. Military doctor during the Russo-Japanese war, 1904–05. Head of the Publishing House of Writers in Moscow, 1911–18. After the revolution, wrote memoirs and biographies (Pushkin, Gogol). In his old age, translated Homer and was honoured as an old Marxist and revolutionary. Died in Moscow.

Vergelis, Aron Alterovich
7.5.1918–   . Journalist, poet.
Born in Liubar near Zhitomir. Soviet-Jewish poet writing in Yiddish. Member of the CPSU, 1955. Editor of the magazine *Sovietish Heimland*. Often called upon to deny any existence of anti-Semitism in the USSR.

Verkhovskaia-Girshfeld, Tatiana Mikhailovna
1895–1950? Artist.
Studied art at P. Kelin's school in

Moscow, 1913–14, then at the Moscow School of Painting, Sculpture and Architecture, 1914–19, under Konstantin Korovin, also at the State Free Art Shops, 1919–20. Portrait, genre, still-life and landscape painter, also stage designer, and water-colour artist. Exhibitions from 1917. Her last exhibition was held in Moscow in 1947.

Verkhovskii, Aleksandr Ivanovich
9.12.1886–19.8.1938. General.
Born in Petersburg. Educated in the Pages Corps. Graduated from the Academy of the General Staff, 1911. During the February Revolution 1917, served in the Crimea. Popular in left-wing circles. Elected Deputy Chairman of the Sevastopol Soviet. Commander of the Moscow military region, July-Sep. 1917. Major-general, 1917. Minister of War in the Provisional Government, 12 Sep. 1917. Demanded a separate peace for Russia. After his demand was rejected, sent on sick leave (practically resigned), 4 Nov. 1917. Arrested by the Bolsheviks as an SR, 1918. Joined the Red Army, 1919. High general staff posts during the Civil War. Thereafter professor at the Frunze Military Academy and other military educational establishments. Wrote on tactics and military history. Left memoirs which were published in 1959. Victim of Stalin's purge of the Red Army.

Vernadskii, Georgii Vladimirovich
20.8.1887–18.6.1973. Historian.
Graduated from Moscow University, 1910. Lecturer at Petrograd University, 1918–20. After the Civil War, left Russia, 1921. Lived in Prague, 1922–27. Head of Seminarium Kondakovium. Moved to the USA to teach at Yale University, 1927. The most prominent historian of the Eurasian movement (stressing the geopolitical concept of Russia as a special entity between Europe and Asia). Very influential at American universities, where his concepts made a lasting impression. Valuable research on Russia as part of the medieval Mongol Empire (Golden Horde). Retired, 1956. Died in the USA.
Main works: *An Outline of Russian History*; *Bohdan, Hetman of Ukraine*; *Ancient Russia*; *The Mongols and Russia*; *A History of Russia*; *Russian Historiography*.

Vershigora, Petr Petrovich
16.5.1905–27.3.1963. Major-general, author.
Born in a village in Moldavia. Son of a teacher. Graduated from the VGIK (State Film School), worked as an actor and film director in Kiev, 1938. During WWII, became a famous partisan leader in the Ukraine, 1942–45. After the war, professor at the Academy of the General Staff, 1947–54. Published several propagandist novels about partisan exploits during WWII, such as *Liudi s Chistoi Sovest'iu*. Stalin Prize, 1946. Died in Moscow.

Vershinin, Konstantin Andreevich
3.6.1900–1973. Marshal.
Born in the village of Borkino near Tver'. Son of a peasant. Joined the Red Army and the Communist Party, 1919. Graduated from the Zhukovskii Air Force Academy, 1932. Air Force Commander during WWII (in the South, and the Caucasus). Commander-in-chief of the Soviet Air Force, 1946–49. Commander-in-chief of the Air Defence System, 1953–54. Again Commander-in-chief of the Air Force, 1957–69. Deputy Minister of Defence. Member of the Cen. Cttee. of the CPSU, 1961–71.

Vershinin, Sergei Iakovlevich
1896–1970. Major-general, NKVD, SMERSH officer.
Joined the Red Army, 1919. Took part in the Civil War. Thereafter, served in the border guards of the NKVD. During WWII, head of the NKVD of the Karelo-Finnish SSR. Head of the partisans in Karelia, 1942–44. After WWII, charged with the task of hunting down anti-Stalin refugees in Europe (Representative of the Council of People's Commissars for the Repatriation of Soviet Citizens), 1945–47, an operation controlled by SMERSH.

Vershinina, Nina
1909– . Ballerina, ballet teacher.
Born in Moscow. Emigrated with her parents to China. Grew up in Shanghai and Paris. Received training with O. Preobrazhenskaia and Bronislava Nijinskaia in Paris. Worked with R. von Laban. Made her debut in 1929 with the Ida Rubenstein Company. In 1933, with Rene Blum's Ballets Russes de Monte Carlo, and afterwards with Colonel de Basil's Ballets Russes. In 1937–38, with the San Francisco Ballet. From 1939–41, with de Basil's Original Ballet Russe. In 1950, moved to Latin America. Taught in Rio de Janeiro and Buenos Aires. Organized her own ballet school in Copacabana.

Vertinskaia, Anastasia Aleksandrovna
19.7.1944– . Actress.
Daughter of the world-famous cabaret singer and poet Aleksandr Vertinskii, who returned to the Soviet Union during WWII after many years abroad. Graduated from the Shchukin Drama School in Moscow in 1967. Started her film career at the age of 16, when the director Ptushko offered her the leading role in his film *Crimson Sails* (an adaptation of Aleksandr Grin's story, 1961). Became famous for her part as Ophelia in *Hamlet*, directed by Grigorii Kozintsev in 1964. Played Princess Liza in Sergei Bondarchuk's *War and Peace*. Played Kitty in Aleksandr Zarkhi's *Anna Karenina*. Married Nikita Mikhalkov, the actor and director. Other films include: *The Human Amphibian*, 1961; *In Love*, 1969; *Cheer Up!*, 1969; *What Happened to Polynin*, 1971; *The Premature Man*, 1972.

Vertinskaia, Lidia Vladimirovna
14.4.1923– . Actress.
Born in Paris, where her parents had emigrated after October 1917. Married the millionaire singer Aleksandr Vertinskii in Paris. Their return to the USSR in the middle of WWII was well publicized in the Soviet press. Worked in theatre. Her film debut was in *Ptitsa Feniks-Sadko*, 1953. Other films include *Don Kikhot*, 1957, and *Korolevstvo Krivykh Zerkal*, 1963.

Vertinskaia, Marianna Aleksandrovna
28.7.1943– . Actress.
Daughter of Aleksandr Vertinskii. Graduated from the Moscow Shchu-

kin Theatre School, 1966. From 1962, appeared in films, such as *Mne Dvadtsat' Let*, 1965, *Smert' Pod Parusom*, 1977, and *Pena*, 1979.

Vertinskii, Aleksandr Nikolaevich
21.3.1889–21.5.1957. Cabaret singer, film actor, poet, composer.
Born in Kiev. Appeared in Pierrot costume with a repertoire of his own songs from 1915. Became an extremely famous variety and restaurant singer. Emigrated in 1919. Appeared in cabarets and restaurants all over the world. Became a millionaire. Returned to Stalin's Soviet Union during WWII. His return received great publicity aimed at White Russians all over the world. (Donated a train-load of medical supplies which were worth one million roubles and badly needed at the time of the war.) Brought with him his actress wife. Created an intimate musical genre and original form of diction. Received the Stalin Prize in 1951 for his participation in the propaganda film *Zagovor Obrechennykh* (Conspiracy of the Doomed). Set his own poems and those of Aleksandr Blok and Sergei Esenin to music. Had a great success every time he appeared on the stage, especially after Stalin's death, when his concerts became more frequent. Lived in Moscow. Performed in Leningrad. Remained faithful to his decadent style of performing which greatly annoyed the cultural establishment. Died in Moscow.

Vertov, Dziga (Kaufman, Denis Arkad'evich)
2.1.1896–12.2.1954. Documentary film maker.
Born in Belostok. One of the founders of the Soviet documentary cinema. Head of the News Service, 1917–21, coordinating the work of news cameramen. Founder and director of Kinopravda (Film Verité), 1922–25. One of the main theoreticians and author of the Kino-glaz (Cinema Eye) Manifesto. His best documentaries are *Kino-glaz* and *The Man With the Movie Camera*. Both films were criticized as being 'unrealistic' and 'distortions of present day life'. Many of his projects were rejected, and he was practically unable to work in his favourite genre.

Lived in Moscow, completely forgotten until his death. In the post-war period, nominally on the staff of the Moscow Documentary Film Studio, where from time to time he edited the cinema magazine *News of the Day*, but was unable to make films. Left diaries which read like an accusing voice from the grave, and are of great historical value. His films include: *Shagai Sovet*, 1926; *Shestaia Chast' Mira*, 1926; *Simfoniia Donbassa*, 1930; *Tri Pesni o Lenine*, 1934.

Veselovskii, Boris Borisovich
4.7.1880–28.5.1954. Historian, statistician.
Born in the village of Bobylevka, near Saratov. Historian of the pre-revolutionary local rural government system (the zemstvo). His 4-volume *Istoriia Zemstva za 40 Let* was published in 1909–11. After the October Revolution 1917, worked in the Tsentroarkhiv, GOSPLAN. Professor of Moscow University in the 1920–40s. Died in Moscow.

Vetokhin, Iurii Aleksandrovich
1928– . Computer programmer.
Born in Leningrad. Tried to escape to Turkey by swimming the Black Sea. Caught and placed in a mental institution, 1963. Later released. Took a cruise to Indonesia on a Soviet ship, and defected, 1979. Settled in the USA. Published his memoirs in America (*Sklonen k Pobegu*, USA, 1983).

Vidov, Oleg
1950– . Film actor.
Top box-office draw in the Soviet Union throughout the 1970s. Soviet audiences flocked to see him in fairy tales, romantic films and a 1972 cowboy film, *The Headless Horseman* (based on a Mayne Reed story), which sold some 300 million tickets. Despite this success, he was dissatisfied with his lack of creative control and went back to VGIK to study directing. Eventually made a critical film about the Soviet transport system, after which he was offered no leading roles. Defected from Yugoslavia and Austria to Rome, and eventually settled in Hollywood.

Vigdorova, Frida Abramovna
1915–1965. Author.
Born in Orsha. Graduated from the Moscow Teachers' Institute. Taught Russian literature in schools. First work published in 1938. During the post-war period, became known as a children's writer. Instrumental in helping the poet Iosif Brodskii, first by making notes of his sensational trial, then by passing them to the Western press and circulating them in samizdat. Her diary was published in the almanac *Vozdushnye Puti*, 1965.

Vigner, Leonid Ernestovich (Vigners)
9.11.1906– . Conductor.
Born in Moscow. Son of the music teacher Ernest Vigners (1850–1933). Pupil of E. Kuper and G. Shneefokht. Chief conductor with the Latvian Opera, 1944–49, and of the Latvian Symphony Orchestra and Collectives' Choir in Riga from 1949. Professor at the Latvian Conservatory.

Viktorov, Mikhail Vladimirovich
5.1.1894–8.1.1938. Naval officer.
Born in Iaroslavl'. Graduated from the Naval Corps, 1913. Served in the Baltic fleet during WWI. After the October Revolution, joined the Red Navy, and took part in the suppression of the Kronstadt sailors' revolt, 1921. Commander of the Baltic fleet, 1921, the Black Sea fleet, 1924, the Baltic fleet, 1926, and the Pacific fleet, 1932–37. Arrested and disappeared during Stalin's purges of the military. Probably executed.

Vikulov, Vladimir Ivanovich
20.7.1946– . Athlete.
Born in Moscow. Honoured Master of Sports (ice hockey), 1967. Member of the CPSU, 1971. Graduated from the Moscow Institute of Physical Culture, 1976. USSR champion, 1966–79. European champion, 1966–70, 1975. Olympic champion, 1968 and 1972. Considered one of the top ice hockey players in the world.

Vil', Elza (Elizaveta) Ivanovna
4.5.1882–1941. Ballerina.
Born in Petersburg. Graduated from the Petersburg Theatre School, 1900.

A pupil of E. Vazem and E. Cecchetti. With the Mariinskii Theatre, 1900–08. From 1908–13, with Anna Pavlova's company abroad. Died in Leningrad.

Vil'ev, Mikhail Anatol'evich
1893–1919. Astronomer.
Specialist in the history of astronomy and the movements of the moon and comets. Compiled a list of solar eclipses in Russia from the 10th–18th centuries. Died in Petrograd during the revolution.

Vil'iams, Petr Vladimirovich (Williams)
30.4.1902–1.12.1947. Stage designer.
Born in Moscow. Studied at the VKHUTEMAS under Petr Konchalovskii, 1918–23. Also a pupil of Konstantin Korovin. Stage designer with the Bolshoi Theatre from 1941. State Prizes 1943, 1945 and 1947. Died in Moscow.

Vilinskii, Nikolai Nikolaevich
2.5.1888–7.9.1956. Composer.
Born in the village of Golta, in Kherson Gouvt. Taught at the Odessa Conservatory from 1920. Professor from 1926. At the Tashkent Conservatory from 1941, and the Kiev Conservatory from 1944. Among his pupils were K. Dan'kevich and V. Femelidi. Author of a cantata, songs and romances. Died in Kiev.

Villuan, Vasilii Iul'evich
28.10.1850–15.9.1922.
Violinist, composer, conductor.
Born in Moscow. Nephew of the pianist A. Villuan. In 1873, organized and directed, till 1918, the music classes at the Nizhegorodskii section of the Russkoe Muzykal'noe Obshchestvo (Russian Music Society). Taught violin and piano. One of his many pupils was S. Liapunov. Died in Nizhnii Novgorod.

Vil'mont, Nikolai Nikolaevich (Wilmont, William)
7.3.1901–   . Literary scholar.
Born in Moscow. Graduated from the Moscow Briusov Literary Institute, 1926. Expert on German literature. Edited Russian-language editions of Goethe, Schiller, Thomas Mann and others. Translated German literature into Russian.

Vil'tzak, Anatolii Iosifovich
1896–1976? Ballet dancer, choreographer, teacher.
Born in Petersburg. Brother of the circus artist N.I. Vil'tzak, and husband of the ballerina Liudmila Shollar. Graduated from the Petersburg Theatre School, 1915. Dancer with the Mariinskii Theatre. Emigrated, 1921. With Diaghilev's Ballets Russes, 1921–25, and later with Ida Rubenstein's Ballet Russe de Monte Carlo, and the American Ballet. Worked closely with Bronislava Nijinskaia. Taught at various American ballet schools. Died in San Francisco.

Vil'tzak, Valentina Iosifovna
2.5.1900–11.9.1947. Ballerina, teacher.
Born in Ivanovo-Voznesensk. Sister of Anatolii Vil'tzak. Graduated from the Petersburg Theatre School, 1914. Pupil of Enrico Cecchetti. Ballerina with various theatres in Petrograd and Khar'kov, 1914–24. With the Sverdlovsk Theatre, 1924–34, and the Paliashvili Theatre, 1934–36. One of the organizers of the Tbilisi Choreographic School, 1935. Taught at the Tashkent Theatre, 1936–38, and the Navoi Theatre, 1944–47. Died in Tashkent.

Vinaver, Maksim Moiseevich
1862–1926. Lawyer, politician.
Born in Warsaw. Graduated from Warsaw University in 1886. Became a famous lawyer in Petersburg. One of the founders of and, with Miliukov, practically the leader of the Cadet Party. Member of the Cen. Cttee. of the Cadets. Member of the 1st Duma, signed the Vyborg Manifesto. Opposed the October Revolution 1917. Minister of Foreign Affairs in the Crimean government in 1919. Emigrated to France the same year. Lived in Paris. Throughout his life, in Russia and abroad, very active in various Jewish political, social and cultural organizations. His memoirs, *Nedavnee*, Paris, 1926, contain memorable portraits of pre-revolutionary Russian lawyers, judges and politicians. One of the best known and most highly respected representatives of the Jewish community in Russia before the revolution.

Vinnichenko, Vladimir Kirillovich
26.8.1880–1951. Politician, author.
Born near Kherson. Studied at Kiev University. Prolific author, close to populists, before WWI. Prominent left-of-centre Ukrainian politician during the revolutionary years. Member of the Ukrainian Central Rada. Head of the Directoria. Emigrated after the defeat of Ukrainian nationalist forces. Settled in France. Died in Paris.

Vinogradov, Aleksandr Iur'evich
10.11.1951–   . Athlete.
Born in Moscow. Honoured Master of Sports (canoe), 1976. Graduated from the Smolensk Institute of Physical Culture, 1974. Member of the CPSU, 1977. USSR and world champion, 1971–76. Olympic champion, 1976 (with S. Petrenko), in the 500 and 1,000 metres race.

Vinogradov, Aleksandr Pavlovich
21.8.1895–late 1970s. Scientist, academician.
Born in Petersburg. Graduated from Leningrad University, 1924. Director of the Vernadskii Institute of Geochemistry, 1947. Academician, 1953, and professor of Moscow University in the same year. Research in many fields of geochemistry, from biogeochemistry to cosmic geochemistry. Took part in the creation of the Soviet atomic industry. Supervised research on lunar dust brought back from the moon by Luna-16. Member of the academies of science of many countries. Honorary chairman of the International Association of Geochemistry and Cosmic Chemistry. Highly decorated (5 Orders of Lenin).

Vinogradov, Ivan Matveevich
14.9.1891–1971? Mathematician.
Born in the village of Miloliub, near Velikie Luki. Son of a village priest. Graduated from Petersburg University, 1914. Academician, 1929. Director of the Mathematical Institute of the Academy of Sciences, 1932. Authority on the analytical theory of

numbers. Fellow of the Royal Society, 1942. Considered one of the foremost modern mathematicians in the world.

Vinogradov, Konstantin Petrovich
3.6.1899– . Conductor.
Born in Moscow. Chief conductor with the Soviet Army's Krasnoznamennyi Ensemble of Song and Dance, 1946–65. Taught at the Gnesin Pedagogical Institute of Music. Arranged works for choral performance.

Vinogradov, Nikolai Ignat'evich
26.12.1905– . Admiral.
Born in the village of Surikha, near Nizhnii Novgorod. Graduated from the Naval Academy, 1939. Submarine commander before and during WWII. Admiral, 1954. Involved in the enormous Soviet build-up of submarine power in the post-WWII period.

Vinogradov, Oleg Mikhailovich
1.8.1937– . Choreographer.
Born in Leningrad. Graduated from the Leningrad Choreographic School, 1958. Pupil of A. Pushkin. Danced with the Novosibirsk Theatre. From 1963, assistant choreographer with the same theatre. Chief choreographer of the Leningrad Malyi Theatre, 1973–77. Choreographer, 1967–72, and chief choreographer, 1977 onwards, of the Kirov Ballet Theatre. Later became principal choreographer of the same theatre. Staged numerous ballet productions with his company at home and abroad.

Vinogradov, Pavel Gavrilovich (Vinogradov, Sir Paul)
30.11.1854–19.12.1925. Historian.
Born in Kostroma. Professor of Moscow University, 1884. Specialized in medieval history (especially British). Resigned, 1902, and moved to England. Professor at Oxford University, 1903. From 1908, again professor at Moscow University (keeping his Oxford professorship). Resigned from Moscow University, 1911, protesting against the dismissal of some of his colleagues. After the October Revolution 1917, emigrated

to Britain and became a British subject. Some of his research has created new perspectives in British medieval studies: *Villainage in England,* 1892, and *English Society in the 11th Century,* 1908. His collected papers were published in English in Oxford, 1928. Member of the academies of science of several countries. Died in Paris.

Vinogradov, Sergei Arsen'evich
13.7.1869–5.2.1938. Artist.
Born in the posad (village) of Bolshie Soli, Kostroma Gouvt. Studied at the Moscow School of Painting, Sculpture and Architecture, 1880–89, under V. Polenov. Member of the Peredvizhniki, and took part in their exhibitions, 1899–1901. Genre and landscape painter. One of the founding members of the Union of Russian Artists, 1903. In 1923, emigrated. Exhibitions: MOLKH, 1889–90, 1892–1901, 1908; MTKH, 1894–1905; 36 Artists, 1901–02, 1903; the Mir Iskusstva, 1901–03, 1906; SPKH, 1903–04, 1906–18. Personal exhibition: Riga, 1936–37. Died in Riga.

Vinogradov, Viktor Vladimirovich
12.1.1895–4.10.1969. Linguistics scholar.
Born in Zaraisk. Graduated from Petrograd University, 1917. Specialist in the Russian language. Professor of Leningrad University, 1920–29, and of Moscow University, 1945–69. Director of many centres of linguistic research. Took part in the compilation of the large modern dictionaries of the Russian language (*Ushakov,* 4 vols, 1935–40; *Academical Dictionary,* 17 vols, 1948–65; *Academical Dictionary,* 4 vols, 1957–61; *Dictionary of Pushkin's Language,* 4 vols, 1957–61). Member of the academies of science of many countries. Chairman of the International Cttee. of Slavists, 1957. Died in Moscow.

Vinogradova, Valentina Alekseevna (Kamenek)
17.5.1943– . Athlete.
Born in Moscow. Honoured Master of Sports (volley-ball), 1968. USSR champion, 1963, 1965–69. European champion, 1963, 1967. Olympic champion, 1968.

Vinogradskii, Sergei Nikolaevich
13.9.1856–24.2.1953. Microbiologist.
Born in Kiev. Graduated from Petersburg University, 1881. Founder and chairman of the Russian Microbiology Society, 1903. Emigrated after the Bolshevik take-over, 1922. Head of the Agrobiology Department of the Pasteur Institute in Paris, 1922–53. Member of the French Academy of Sciences and fellow of the Royal Society. Died in Paris.

Vinokur, Grigorii Osipovich (penname – L. Kirillov)
1896–1947. Linguist, literary critic.
In the 1920s, head of the Press Bureau of the Soviet Embassy in Riga. Contributor to *Novyi Put',* a newspaper in Riga financed by the Soviet Embassy. In 1922, publisher-editor of *Novyi Put'.* Among his best articles was a review of P.O. Iakobson's book *Noveishaia Russkaia Poeziia,* and a review of Mayakovsky's *150,000,000.*

Vinokurov, Aleksandr
1869–1944. Politician.
Active in the revolutionary movement from the 1890s. After the October Revolution 1917, Commissar for Social Security, 1918–21. President of the Soviet Supreme Court, 1924–38. Later worked in the public health system.

Vinokurov, Eduard Teodorovich
30.10.1942– . Athlete.
Born in Chimkentskaia Oblast'. Honoured Master of Sports (fencing), 1968. Graduated from the Higher School of Trainers at the Leningrad Institute of Physical Culture, 1966. Member of the CPSU, 1968. USSR champion, 1966. World champion, 1967–71, 1974–75. Olympic champion, 1968, 1976. Silver medal, 1972. Became an international referee.

Virsaladze, Simon Bagratovich
31.12.1908–13.1.1979. Stage designer.
Born in Tbilisi. Studied at the Tbilisi and Moscow academies of art, 1926 and 1928–31, and also at the Moscow VKHUTEIN, 1927. Worked as a stage designer with the Tbilisi Paliashvili Theatre, 1932–36. Chief designer with the same theatre, pro-

ducing stage designs for numerous ballet productions. Academician, 1975. USSR People's Artist, 1976. Lenin Prize, 1970. State Prize, 1949, 1951, 1977.

Virta, Nikolai Evgen'evich
19.12.1906– . Author.
Born in the village of Bolshaia Lazovka, near Tambov. Son of a village priest. Became known for his novels of the 1930s, which depicted the Antonov peasant revolt in Tambov from the official point of view (made into plays and operas by Khrennikov). War correspondent during WWII. Gained national attention with his novel on rural life, *Krutye Gory,* 1956, in which, despite his own dogmatic trend, he gave for the first time a more or less realistic picture of the devastation of Russian rural life caused by the policies of Stalin.

Vishnevskaia, Galina Petrovna (m. Rostropovich)
25.10.1926– . Soprano singer.
Born in Leningrad. Studied singing, and began performing in 1944 at the Leningrad Oblast' Operetta Theatre, then appeared with the Leningrad Philharmonic. In 1952, soloist with the Moscow Bolshoi Theatre. Was once the darling of Soviet audiences and the Soviet government. Married the internationally-known cellist-conductor Mstislav Rostropovich. Suffered persecution by the Soviet bureaucracy: for example, in 1962, prevented from appearing in a part written for her by Britten in his *War Requiem.* In the early 1970s, together with her husband, persecuted by the authorities for having offered refuge to A. Solzhenitsyn. Forced to leave the Soviet Union in 1974. In 1978, both were stripped of Soviet citizenship following interviews in which they were critical of the Soviet government. Has performed all over the world. Lives in France and the USA. Her memoirs, *Galina,* have been translated into many languages.

Vishnia, Ostap (Gubenko, Pavel Mikhailovich)
11.11.1889–28.9.1956. Author.
Born in Hrun', near Sumy. Studied at Kiev University, 1917. Became a

well-known and popular satirist in the 1920s. Collected works (*Usmishki,* 4 vols), 1930. Especially liked in his native Ukraine. His works have been translated into several other languages in the USSR. Arrested, 1934, and sent to Gulag camps. Released during WWII. His works began to reappear after Stalin's death. Died in Kiev.

Vishniak, Mark Veniaminovich (Markov Veniamin)
1883–1971. Politician, journalist.
Trained as a lawyer. Active in revolutionary circles, involved in terrorism. Exiled to the Crimea. Went abroad. After his return, began pleading in courts while still on the wanted list. Right-wing SR. Secretary of the Constituent Assembly in 1917. Emigrated after the October Revolution 1917. Lived in Paris. One of the editors of the magazine *Annales Contemporaines,* the most influential Russian magazine abroad between the world wars. During WWII, moved to the USA. Consultant on Russian affairs for *Time* magazine. Died in the USA. His memoirs (published in the USA) contain valuable information, especially on the Constituent Assembly.

Vishniakov, Aleksandr Aleksandrovich
1886?–6.9.1972. Lawyer.
Graduated in law from Petersburg University. Deputy attorney in Kutaisi from 1914. Emigrated, and lived in Marseilles. Well-known figure in the Russian community (head of the Refugee Cttee.). Played an active part in religious life there. Member of the Russian Professional Lawyers' Association until his death in Paris.

Vishnitzer, Mark Lvovich
1882–1955. Politician.
Well-known Russian-Jewish public figure before WWI. Contributor to the *Jewish Encyclopaedia,* publications of the Academy of Sciences, *Russkaia Mysl', Minuvshie Gody,* and others, 1907–1914. Emigrated to France, later moved to the USA. Chairman of the Union of Russian Jews in New York, 1951. Contributed to *Novyi Zhurnal.* Died in Tel Aviv.

Vitachek, Evgenii Frantsevich
29.4.1880–16.2.1946. Maker of stringed instruments.
Born in Czechoslovakia. Father of the composer Favii (Fabii) Vitachek. Moved to Russia in 1895. In Moscow from 1898. Keeper of the State Collection of Rare Musical Instruments. Died in Moscow. Author of *Ocherki po Istorii Postroeniia Smychkovykh Instrumentov,* Leningrad, 1952 (2nd ed., Moscow, 1964).

Vitalii (Maksimenko, Vasilii Ioannovich), Archbishop of Eastern America and Jersey
8.8.1873–21.3.1960. Russian Orthodox clergyman.
Born at Glafirovka, near Taganrog. Son of a deacon. Educated at Mariupol, and at the Kiev and Kazan' theological academies, 1900. Monk, 1900. Archimandrite at Pochaevskaia Lavra in Volhynia, 1903. After the October Revolution 1917, organized the move of the monks and their large printing press from Pochaev to Ladomirovo (Vladimirovo) in Transcarpathia (then Czechoslovakia). Re-started the publishing of religious books, 1926. During WWII, the Ladomirovo monastery was evacuated, first to Bratislava, then to Germany, to Switzerland, and later to the USA, 1946. Continued the traditions of the Pochaevskaia Lavra and the St. Hiob Press at the Trinity Monastery in Jordanville, New York, making it the main centre of the Russian Orthodox Church in Exile, with a seminary and icon-painting shop, and continuing typographical work, supplying the best-produced religious literature in Church Slavonic and Russian anywhere in the world for a large part of the 20th century. Buried at St. Vladimir Cathedral in Jackson, USA.

Vitalii (Ustinov, Rostislav Petrovich), Metropolitan of East America and Canada, Head of the Russian Orthodox Church in Exile
1910– . Russian Orthodox clergyman.
Born in Petersburg. Son of a naval officer. Evacuated with Wrangel's army from the Crimea to Constantinople after the Civil War. Educated at a cadet corps in Yugoslavia. Moved to France, 1923. Served in the French Army, 1934. Monk at the St.

Hiob monastery in Transcarpathia, 1939. During WWII, priest in Berlin, working among Russian POWs and refugees. After the war, in DP camps in Hamburg. Organized the resettlement of Russian refugees overseas. Priest of the Russian Church in Exile in London, 1947–51. Appointed Bishop to Brazil, 1951. Moved to Edmonton in Canada, 1955, and later appointed Bishop of Montreal. Elected Head of the Russian Church in Exile, Jan. 1986. Lives in Montreal.

Vitol, Iazep (Vitols, Iosif Ivanovich)
26.7.1863–24.4.1948. Composer, music critic.
Born in Valmiera, Latvia. Member of the Beliaevskii Kruzhok (Beliaev's Circle). Professor at the Petersburg Conservatory. Founder and director of the Latvian Conservatory. Professor there from 1919. Among his many famous pupils were N. Miaskovskii, S. Prokof'ev, V. Shcherbachev, Ia. Ivanov, M. Zarin', A. Skulte, and A. Zhilinskii. Author of cantatas, symphonies, works for violin with orchestra, and a string quartet. Died in Lübeck.

Vlad, Roman
29.12.1919–   . Composer, pianist, music critic.
Born in Chernovitsy, Bukovina. Pupil of A. Casella (1883–1947). Emigrated. In Rome from 1938. Artistic director of the Rome Philharmonic Academy, 1955–58, and of the festival Florentine May from 1964. President of the Italian Society for Contemporary Music from 1960. Adopted the dodecaphonic style. Author of choreographic works, cantatas, choral and orchestral works, chamber music, and music for theatre and film.
Literary works: *Modernità e Tradizione nella Musica Contemporanea*, Torino, 1955; *Storia della Dodecafonia*, Torino, 1958.

Vladimir (Bogoiavlenskii, Vasilii Nikiforovich), Metropolitan of Kiev and Galich
1.1.1848–25.1.1918. Russian Orthodox clergyman.
Born in Malye Morshki, Tambov Gouvt. Son of a priest. Graduated from Kiev Theological Academy, 1874. Monk, 1886. Bishop of Samara, 1891. Head of the Georgian Exarchate, 18 Oct. 1892. Metropolitan of Moscow, 1988 Metropolitan of Petersburg, 1912. Because of his disapproval of Rasputin, removed from the capital to the Ukraine. Metropolitan of Kiev, 1915. Murdered by Bolshevik sailors near the Kiev Cave Monastery. Considered to be the first of the modern martyrs of the Russian Orthodox Church.

Vladimir (Sabodan, Viktor Markianovich), Metropolitan of Rostov and Novocherkassk
23.11.1935–   . Russian Orthodox clergyman.
Born in Markovtsy, Khmelnitskaia Oblast', Ukraine. Son of a peasant. Studied at the Odessa seminary. Graduated from the Leningrad Theological Academy, 1962. Priest and monk, 1962. Taught at the Odessa seminary, later dean of the seminary. Bishop of Zvenigorod, 1966. Represented the Russian Orthodox Church in the World Council of Churches in Geneva. Bishop of Chernigov, 1969. Bishop of Dmitrov, dean of the Moscow Theological Academy, 1973. Archbishop, 1973. Metropolitan of Rostov and Novocherkassk, June 1982. Exarch of the Patriarch of Moscow in Western Europe, Mar. 1984.

Vladimir (Tikhonitskii, Viacheslav Mikhailovich), Metropolitan of the Russian Orthodox diocese in France
22.3.1873–18.12.1959. Russian Orthodox clergyman.
Born in Orlov, Viatka Gouvt. Son of a priest. Graduated from Viatka seminary, 1894. Graduated from Kazan' Theological Academy, 1898. Head of the church mission in Kirghizia, 1901. Bishop, 1907 (Grodno diocese). During WWI, evacuated to Moscow. Returned to Grodno, 1918. Archbishop, 1923. Expelled by the Polish authorities, 1924. Stayed in Prague, then moved to France. Archbishop in Nice, 1945–59. Head of the Russian Orthodox diocese (West European Exarchate of the Oecumenical Patriarch) in France, 1946–59. Died in Paris.
Works: *Slova i Poucheniia,* Paris.

Vladimir Kirillovich (Romanov), Grand-Duke
30.8.1917–   . Head of the Romanov family in exile.
Born in Borja, Finland. Son of Grand-Duke Kirill (Cyril), cousin of Nicholas II, and Princess Victoria Melita, daughter of Alfred, Duke of Edinburgh. Born during the flight of his parents from Russia after the February Revolution 1917. His father, a naval officer, was initially sympathetic to the revolution, but the Navy was very soon taken over by radical anarchist and Bolshevik sailors. Educated privately at a Russian high school in Paris. Studied at London University. His father was proclaimed head of the Romanov family and pretender to the throne (other Russian monarchists preferred Grand-Duke Nikolai Nikolaevich, a former commander-in-chief during WWI). Settled with parents at St. Briac-sur-Mer in Brittany. Worked as a factory worker in the Midlands (under the name Mikhailov, used previously by Peter the Great during his brief stay in England). At the beginning of WWII, managed to return to France. In 1944, stayed at his sister's home near Heidelberg (she was married to Prince Carl of Leiningen). Interned at Lichtenstein with a Russian monarchist regiment formed by the Germans, in May 1945. After WWII, lived in Madrid and St. Briac. His claim to the throne of Russia is disputed by some monarchists who regard his marriage to Princess Bagration-Mukhranskii as morganatic. His only daughter, Grand-Duchess Maria, married Prince Franz Wilhelm Hohenzollern in 1976. Lives between St. Briac and Paris.

Vladimirov, Ivan Alekseevich
10.1.1870–14.12.1947. Artist.
Born in Vilnius. Studied at the I. Trutnev Art School, Vilnius, and the Petersburg Academy of Arts, 1891–97, under B. Villevalde and A. Kivshenko. Pupil of F. Rubo and E. Detail in Paris. Battle-painter specializing in historical subjects. War artist/correspondent during the Russo-Japanese war, 1904–05, the Balkan Wars, 1912–13, and WWI, 1914–16. Exhibitions: St. Petersburg Society of Artists, 1894–96; Spring Exhibitions of the Academy of Arts,

1897–1917; TPKHV, 1916, 1918; A. Kuindzhi Society, 1926–27. Personal exhibition: The War Paintings of I. Vladimirov, 1915. Died in Leningrad.

Vladimirov, Mikhail Vladimirovich (Itsegson)

28.1.1870–13.10.1932. Conductor. Born in Porkhov, Pskovskaia Gouvt. Conductor in Petersburg with Count A.D. Sheremet'ev's orchestra of wind instruments from 1897, and with his symphony orchestra from 1900–10. The music school of the Baltic fleet was organized according to his plans in the early 1900s, and also the military music school for land forces in Petrograd, 1920. Taught at the Leningrad Conservatory and at military educational establishments. Died in Leningrad. Author of manuals for wind instruments, 1930, 1932.

Vladimirov Petr Nikolaevich

1893–26.11.1970. Ballet dancer, ballet teacher.
Born in Petersburg. Graduated from the Petersburg Theatre School, 1911. Pupil of Mikhail Fokin. Joined the Mariinskii Theatre. Danced with Diaghilev's Ballets Russes in the 1912, 1914 and 1921 seasons. With the Anna Pavlova Company, 1928–31. Taught at the American Ballet School, New York, 1934–67. Died in New York.

Vladimirova, Maria Vladimirovna

17.1.1879–8.11.1965. Singer.
Born in Astrakhan'. Sister of the singer V. Barsova. Professor at the Moscow Conservatory. Among her pupils were V. Barsova, E. Kruglikova and V. Kandelaki. Died in Moscow.

Vladimov, Georgii Nikolaevich (Volosevich)

19.2.1931– . Author.
Born in Khar'kov. His father was a POW in Germany during WWII. Graduated in law at Leningrad University, 1953. Became famous after the publication of his short story Bolshaia Ruda, 1961. One of the leading writers of the magazine Iunost during the 1960s. Other books include Tri Minuty Molchaniia (1969,

Posev, W. Germany) and Vernyi Ruslan, which for a long time circulated in samizdat before being published by Posev in 1975. Since then, it has been translated into several languages. Came into conflict with the Soviet authorities over the foreign publication of his works. Emigrated and worked for some time as an editor of the monthly magazine Grani.

Vladykin, Mikhail Alekseevich

1878–1948. Artist.
Born in Iaroslavl'. Studied at the Iaroslavl' Art School, 1897–1903, then at the Moscow School of Painting, Sculpture and Architecture, 1903–04, under V. Serov. Portrait and genre painter. Taught at the Iaroslavl' Art School. Exhibitions: Iaroslavl' Art Society, 1912–15; Iaroslavl' Society of Art Workers, 1929; Oblast' Art Exhibitions, Iaroslavl', 1929, 1937–45. Personal (jubilee) exhibition, Iaroslavl', 1936.

Vladykina, Anna Grigor'evna

1875–1941. Artist.
Born in Iaroslavl'. Studied first at the Iaroslavl' Art School, then at the Moscow Stroganov School of Graphical Technique, 1899–1905. Genre and landscape painter. Exhibitions: Iaroslavl' Art Society, 1912–15; Iaroslavl' Society of Art Workers, 1928–29; Oblast' Art Exhibitions, Iaroslavl', 1929, 1937, 1939, 1940.

Vlasenko, Lev Nikolaevich

24.12.1928– . Pianist.
Born in Tiflis. Pupil of Ia. Flier. 1st prize at the Liszt Competition in Budapest, 1956. 2nd prize at the P.I. Tchaikovskii Competition in Moscow, 1958. Teacher at the Moscow Conservatory.

Vlasov, Aleksandr Kondrat'evich

12.11.1911– . Cellist.
Born in Vil'no. Pupil of S. Kozolupov. 2nd prize at the All-Union Violin and Cello Competition in Moscow, 1937. Professor at the Gnesin Pedagogical Institute of Music. Author of pieces and adaptations for cello.

Vlasov, Aleksandr Vladimirovich

1932– . Politician, state security officer, party official.
As an instructor in the Cen. Cttee. of the CPSU, conducted a campaign against corruption in the Chechen-Ingush ASSR. 1st Secretary of the Checheno-Ingush obkom, 1975. 1st Secretary of the Rostov Party obkom, 1984. Minister of Internal Affairs of the USSR, Jan. 1986. Lt.-general, 1986. Chairman of the Council of Ministers of the RSFSR, 3 Oct. 1988. Non-voting member of the Politburo, Oct. 1988.

Vlasov, Andrei Andreevich

1.9.1900–2.8.1946. Lt.general, commander-in-chief of the ROA.
Born at Lomakino, a village near Nizhnii Novgorod. Son of a peasant. Started his education at a seminary. Joined the Red Army in 1919. Took part in the Civil War with the Reds. Assigned to the Chinese Mission in 1938–39 (military adviser to Chiang Kai-shek). Promoted to major-general, 1940. Promoted to lt.-general after the Battle of Moscow, Jan. 1942. Deputy commander of the North-West front intended to break the Leningrad siege. Captured by the Germans near Volkhov in 1942, and held in a POW camp. By this time he was completely disillusioned with Stalin's communism. Being in captivity, and out of reach of SMERSH and his peasant roots (the memory of the violence of the collectivization campaign which had resulted in the death of over 10 million peasants) led him to the decision to organize (with German help) a People's Army to fight Stalin. In June 1943, by Hitler's personal order, forbidden all activity, except purely propaganda exercises. In Oct. 1943, Hitler ordered the transfer of all Russian and other national units with the German Army to the Western front, depriving them of the role of an anti-communist force. Some of these units took part in atrocities during WWII. But Hitler's order was to a large extent sabotaged by German military commanders. Vlasov was strongly supported, however, by anti-Hitler German officers (Count Stauffenberg, Gehlen and others). In Sep. 1944, received by Himmler, who was initially completely against him but, realising that defeat was imminent,

and looking for any available manpower reserves, decided to use Vlasov's enormous prestige among the Russians under German occupation. On 28 Jan. 1945 in Prague, an agreement between the KONR (Committee of the Liberation of the People of Russia) and the German Reich was signed. The KONR published a programme of democratic reforms, the so-called Prague Manifesto. Vlasov was appointed commander-in-chief of the ROA (Russian Liberation Army). In Feb. 1945, the 1st Division of the ROA was formed. On 14 Apr. 1945, it went into action on the Oder front against the Red Army with limited success and moved south to Czechoslovakia. In May 1945, the ROA, answering a call for help from the Czechs, supported the uprising in Prague against the Germans, thus ensuring its success. This was the final military action of WWII in Europe. Immediately thereafter, Vlasov surrendered his army to the Americans and was handed over to SMERSH (according to the Yalta agreement between the Allies and Stalin). The ROA ceased to exist. The vlasovtsy (Vlasov's men) who didn't manage to escape were handed over to the Soviets by the Western Allies during 1945–47. Vlasov and his staff officers were taken to Moscow Lubianka prison, secretly tried for treason and hanged as traitors on 2 Aug. 1946 (reported in *Izvestia).* Vlasov's role during WWII remains a subject of controversy. While many agree with the official condemnation of him as a turn-coat and traitor, others see him as a tragic figure, or as a potential Russian De Gaulle.
Sources: N. Tolstoi, *Victims of Yalta*; A. Solzhenitsyn, *Gulag Archipelago* (in which the author states that he met many vlasovtsy in the camps); Konstantin Kromiadi, *Za Zemliu Za Voliu* (memoirs), USA, 1980; Sven Steenberg, *Vlasov*, NY, 1970; Rev. Aleksandr Kiselev, *Oblik Generala Vlasova*, USA, 1980; Nicholas Bethell, *The Last Secret,* London, 1976; Julius Epstein, *Operation Keelhaul,* USA, 1973; Colonel V. Pozdniakov, *Andrei Andreevich Vlasov*, USA, 1973; C. Andreev, *Vlasov and the Russian Liberation Movement*, 1987; J. Hoffman, *Die Geschichte der Wlassow-Armee,* Freiburg, 1984.

Vlasov, Boris
14.3.1913–2.11.1987. Shipping industrialist, businessman.
Born in Odessa. Son of a shipping and coal millionaire. After the October Revolution 1917, moved with his parents to Poland. Received an engineering degree from the Vienna Technische Hochschule. Worked for his father and took over the Vlasov Group after his death in 1961. Acquired the ex-troopship *Oxfordshire* to ship Australian government-assisted immigrants from Britain and Europe. Diversified into cruising through his firm Sitmar Cruises, using the ex-Cunard liners *Carinthia* and *Sylvania* (re-named *Fairsea* and *Fairwind*), operating out of Miami. Built up a tanker fleet. In the 1970s, ordered 5 oil tankers from Cammell Laird. In 1974, in conjunction with the Italian investment group Capitalfin, took over the British company Shipping and Industrial Holdings. Later took over control of Silver Line. Owned by that time 2,500,000 tons of bulk and general cargo ships, together with 4 cruise liners. Continued to prosper in shipping operations. During the 1970s, he was one of the largest owners of British flag tonnage. *The Times* in its obituary called him a 'figure of major stature in the troubled shipping industry'. Hated photographers and any kind of publicity. In his later years, became a virtual recluse. His last post was as head of the Nassau-based V Group of shipping companies. Described as a multilingual gentleman with a true European culture and an *âme slave* enigmatic to non-Slavs. Died in Japan.
Source: *The Times,* 4 Nov. 1987.

Vlasov, Iurii Petrovich
5.12.1935–   . Athlete, engineer, author.
Born in the village of Makeevka, Donetsk Oblast'. Graduated from the Zhukovskii Military Air-Force Academy, 1959. Military engineer. USSR champion, 1959–63. European champion, 1959–64. World champion, 1959, 1961–63. Olympic champion, 1960 (heavyweight: 537,5kg). Silver medal, 1964.
Works: *Sebia Preodolet'. Rasskazy1* Moscow, 1965; *Beloe Mgnovenie,* Moscow, 1972.

Vlasov, Stepan Grigor'evich
10.12.1854–1919. Singer (bass).
Born in the Cossack village of Gundorovskaia, in the Don Cossack district. Pupil of G. Galvani. Soloist with the Moscow Private Russian Opera, 1885–87. Soloist with the Bolshoi Theatre, 1887–1907. Taught in Moscow and Novocherkassk. Died during the Civil War.

Vlodzimirskii, Lev Emel'anovich
1910?–1953. State security official, lt.-general.
Of Polish parents. Moved to Moscow. Started to work in the GPU under Ezhov. Became one of the most notorious henchmen at the Lubianka prison. After Stalin's death and Beria's fall, arrested and shot.

Vodop'ianov, Mikhail Vasil'evich
1899–1980. Major-general.
Joined the Red Army, 1919. Took part in the Civil War. Educated at a pilots' school, 1929. Took part in the rescue of the Cheliuskin expedition, 1934. One of the first Heroes of the Soviet Union, 1934. First to land an aircraft at the North Pole, 1937. During WWII, on active service, major-general, 1943. Wrote memoirs.

Vodov, Sergei Akimovich
1898–17.5.1968. Editor.
During the Civil War, joined the White Army in Odessa, 1919. Evacuated after the defeat of the Whites. Settled in France. Secretary of the National Union of Young Russians in France before WWII. Editor of the Parisian Russian newspaper *Russkaia Mysl'* in the 1950–60s. Died from a heart attack in Munich.

Voiachek, Vladimir Ignat'evich
1876–1971. Lt.-general.
Graduated from the Medical Military Academy, 1899. Otolaryngologist. After the October Revolution, joined the Red Army, 1918. Appointed head of the Medical Military Academy, 1925. Later head of a department in the Academy, 1930. Consultant professor, 1956–68.

Voikov, Petr Lazarevich (Party names – Petrus', Intelligent)
1.8.1888–7.6.1927. Revolutionary, diplomat.
Born in Kerch'. Early involvement in

revolutionary activity. Emigrated, 1907. Menshevik, 1907–1917. Lived in Switzerland. Returned to Russia with Lenin, 1917. Joined the Bolsheviks, Aug. 1917. Member of the Executive Cttee. of the Ural oblsoviet, Jan.–Dec. 1918. Participated in the murder of the Tsar and his family and the burning of the corpses. Ambassador to Poland in the 1920s. Assassinated at the Warsaw railway station by the young White Russian Boris Koverda.

Voinovich, Vladimir Nikolaevich
1932–   . Author.
First published in the early 1960s. Became famous for his satirical books published abroad: *Zhizn' i Neobyknovennye Prikliuchenia Soldata Ivana Chonkina* (Paris: YMCA Press, 1976), *Ivan'kiada* (USA: Ardis, 1976), *Putem Vzaimnoi Perepiski* (YMCA, 1978), and *Pretendent Na Prestol* (YMCA). Emigrated in 1980. See: P. Vail, A. Genis, *Sovremennaia Russkaia Proza,* USA, 1982.

Volchetskaia, Elena Vladimirovna
4.12.1943–   . Athlete.
Born in Grodno. Graduated from the Grodno Pedagogical Institute, 1965. International Class Master of Sports in gymnastics, 1965. USSR champion, 1961–65. Olympic champion, 1964.

Voldemar, A.
1883–1942. Politician, historian.
Lecturer in history and ancient languages at Petersburg University and the Bestuzhev Courses, 1911–14. Professor at Perm' University, 1916. Took part in the Brest-Litovsk peace talks as an expert from the Ukrainian Rada. From Brest, went to Berlin and later became the first Lithuanian Prime Minister and Minister of Foreign Affairs. Lecturer at the Higher Education Courses in Kaunas (Lithuania), 1920. Professor of History at the new Lithuanian University, 1922. Again Prime Minister and Minister of Foreign Affairs of Lithuania, 1926–29. In 1934, after an attempted coup, sentenced to 8 years in prison, amnestied, 1938. After the Soviet occupation of Lithuania, arrested by the NKVD. Died in the Gulag.

Volf–Izrael, Evgenii Vladimirovich
7.8.1874–26.9.1956. Cellist.
Born in Petersburg. Pupil of A. Verzhbilovich. Soloist with the Mariinskii Theatre from 1908. Professor at the Leningrad Conservatory. Honorary Artist of the RSFSR. 1935. Died in Leningrad.

Volfson, Zeev Bentsionovich (Komarov, Boris)
1944–   . Ecologist, author.
Graduated in geography from Moscow University and from the Moscow VGIK (State Film School) as a scriptwriter. Worked as an ecologist. Collected information on destroyed Russian churches and monasteries, and smuggled it to the West. As the result, a fine informative album, *Razrushennye I Oskvernennye Khramy,* full of excellent photographic material, was published in Germany, 1981. Left the USSR, 1981. Lives and works in Jerusalem. Doctor of Jerusalem University. Another valuable book, *Unichtozhenie Prirody,* on ecological disasters in the Soviet Union, was published in 1978 in Germany under the pen-name Boris Komarov.

Volin, Boris Mikhailovich (Fradkin)
13.6.1886–15.2.1957. Politician, editor.
Born at Glubokoe, a village in Belorussia, son of a civil servant. Joined the Bolshevik Party in 1904. Active in Ekaterinoslav during the 1905 Revolution. Thereafter, several arrests and escapes. Emigrated to France in 1911, returned to Russia in 1913. Graduated in law from Moscow University in 1917. Involved in the Bolshevik take-over in Moscow after the October Revolution. One of the senior editors of *Pravda,* 1918. During the Civil War, a Bolshevik official in central Russia (Orel, Briansk, Kostroma), Deputy Minister of the Interior of the Ukrainian Socialist Republic. Deputy editor of *Izvestia,* 1925–26. Head of Glavlit, 1931–35, and a senior executive at the Ministry of Education. Director of the Department of Literature at the

Institute of Red Professors. Editor of the magazine *Class Struggle,* 1931–36. Head of several party schools, 1935. 1st Deputy Minister of Education of the RSFSR, 1936–38. Editor of *Istoricheskii Zhurnal* (Historical Journal), 1935–45. Member of the Marx-Lenin Institute from 1945. Died in Moscow.

Volinin, Aleksandr Emel'ianovich
4.9.1882–3.7.1955. Ballet dancer, teacher.
Born in Moscow. Graduated from the Moscow Choreographic School, 1901. Pupil of V. Tikhomirov and A. Gorskii. Danced with the Bolshoi Theatre until 1910. After that, toured abroad. From 1914–25, partnered Anna Pavlova. In 1925, opened a ballet school in Paris, and taught there until his death. Among his pupils were T. Riabushinskaia, I. Chauviré and A. Dolin. In 1946, choreographed *Giselle* for the Royal Danish Ballet. Died in Paris.

Volkonskii, Andrei Mikhailovich
14.2.1933–   . Composer, pianist, clavichord player.
Born in Geneva to Russian parents who later returned to the Soviet Union (his father was Prince M. Volkonskii). Author of cantatas, orchestral and piano music, a string quartet, vocal music, and music for theatre and films. Became a famous concert pianist in Moscow.

Volkonskii, Sergei Mikhailovich, Prince
16.5.1860–25.10.1937. Theatre manager.
Born on his family's estate at Faal, near Tallinn. Graduated in philology from Petersburg University. Director of the Imperial Theatres, 1899–1901. Promoted the Mir Iskusstva artists in their theatrical work. Hired A. Benois, K. Korovin, L. Bakst, V. Serov and E. Lanceray. Appointed A. Gorskii chief choreographer of the Bolshoi Theatre. Promoted M. Fokin, V. Nijinskii and I. Duncan. Emigrated after the October Revolution 1917. Died in the USA. Author of 'Russkii Balet V Parizhe', *Apollon,* 1913, and memoirs.

Volkov, Aleksandr Vasil'evich
1916– . Artist.
Genre and landscape painter. Graduated from the Moscow Art Institute, 1942. Studied under P. Pokarzhevskii and S. Gerasimov. Exhibitions: The All-Union Young Artists, Moscow, 1939, 1948; The All-Union Artists, 1947, 1949–51, 1957; Sovetskaia Rossia, Moscow, 1960.

Volkov, Efim Efimovich
1844–1920. Artist.
Studied at one of the art schools of the Society for the Encouragement of the Arts, 1866–67, and at the Petersburg Academy of Arts, 1867–70, as a free student. Landscape painter. Exhibitions: Academy of Arts, 1870, 1878; TPKHV, 1878–1918; All-Russian Exhibition, Moscow, 1882; MOLKH, 1891–92; All Russian Exhibition, Nizhnii Novgorod, 1896. Personal exhibition (together with V. Makovskii): St. Petersburg, 1902.

Volkov, Egor
1927–1.3.1988. Political prisoner.
During WWII, taken prisoner by the Germans and put into a Nazi concentration camp. After the war, repatriated, and sentenced to imprisonment in Gulag camps. After serving 2 terms of imprisonment, released but soon re-arrested, 1967, for trying to organize a strike. Spent over 20 years in psychiatric hospitals. Released, Nov. 1987, shortly before his death. Died in a hospital in the village of Poiarkovo, Amur Oblast'.

Volkov, Leonid Ivanovich
9.12.1934– . Athlete.
Born in Gorkii. Honoured Master of Sports (ice hockey), 1964. Graduated from the Moscow Oblast' Pedagogical Institute, 1969. USSR champion, 1958–65. World and European champion, 1964–65. Olympic champion, 1964.

Volkov, Solomon Moiseevich
1944– . Musicologist.
Born in Central Asia, near the Pamirs. Graduated from the Leningrad Conservatory. Published numerous articles in the press. Was at

one time close to Dmitrii Shostakovich and collected stories about his life. Left the USSR, 1976, and settled in the USA. His book *Testimony: The Memoirs of Dmitrii Shostakovich* was published in the USA in 1979, and has since been translated into several languages. A film of the book, also called *Testimony*, was made by Tony Palmer in 1988.

Volkov, Vladislav Nikolaevich
1935–1971. Cosmonaut.
Graduated from the Moscow Aviation Institute, 1959. Took part in 2 space flights. Died in an accident during his second return flight to Earth.

Vol'nov, Gennadii Georgievich
28.11.1939– . Athlete.
Born in Moscow. Member of the CPSU, 1964. Honoured Master of Sports (basket-ball), 1964. Graduated from the Moscow Institute of Physical Culture, 1971. USSR champion, 1959–69. European champion, 1959–69. World champion, 1967. Olympic champion, 1972. Silver medal, 1960, 1964. Bronze medal, 1968.

Volodarskii, V. (real name – Goldstein, Moisei Markovich
1891–20.6.1918. Politician.
Born in the village of Ostropol' in the Ukraine. Member of the SD Party. Emigrated before WWI. Member of the Socialist Party in the USA. Returned to Russia in 1917, and joined the Bolsheviks. Leader of the Petrograd Soviet, and Commissar in the Soviet government. Assassinated by the SRs. Buried at Marsovo Pole, Leningrad.

Volodin, Vladimir Sergeevich (real name – Ivanov)
20.7.1891–27.3.1958. Actor, operetta comedian.
Born in Moscow. With the Moscow Operetta Theatre, 1929–57. Appeared in many films. Received the Stalin Prize in 1951 for his part in the film *Kubanskie Kazaki*. Died in Moscow.

Volokhonskii, Anri Girshevich
1936– . Poet.
Born in Leningrad. Received a

technical education. Became known as a modernist poet in samizdat. Emigrated, 1973, and settled in Israel. Moved to Switzerland.

Voloshin, Maksimilian Aleksandrovich (Kirienko)
28.5.1877–11.8.1932. Poet, painter.
Born in Kiev. Son of a Ukrainian father and a German mother. In his youth, involved in revolutionary activity, exiled to Central Asia. Moved to Paris, studied at the Sorbonne. Visited many countries, especially in the Mediterranean region, and was deeply influenced by their nature and culture. Attracted to anthroposophy. First poems published in the 1900s. Personally acquainted with almost all of his literary contemporaries, but stood apart from movements and groups, retaining complete individuality. Fought the last of the famous literary duels in Russia (with N. Gumilev), and discovered Marina Tsvetaeva. Settled in Koktebel in the Crimea, turning his house at the seaside into a centre of literary life. During the Civil War, gave refuge to both Reds and Whites, sheltering them from each other. Wrote a deeply tragic cycle of poems on the revolution, the Civil War, and the terror of the 1920s. Also a literary critic, and a prolific and original landscape painter. One of the most colourful figures of the Silver Age of Russian literature. His collected works, in 2 volumes, were published in 1970s in the USA.

Vol'skii, Vasilii Timofeevich
1897–1946. Col.-general.
Joined the Bolshevik Party, 1918, and the Red Army, 1919. Graduated from the Frunze Military Academy, 1926. During WWII, commander of tank detachments in the Crimea and North Caucasus. Took part in the Battle of Stalingrad. Deputy Commander of Tank and Armour Divisions of the Red Army, 1943. Commander of the 5th Tank Army, 1944–45.

Vorob'ev, Arkadii Nikitich
3.10.1924– . Athlete, professor, sports official.
Born in the village of Mordovo,

Tambov Oblast'. Honoured Master of Sports (heavy-weight wrestling), 1952. Member of the CPSU, 1954. Graduated from the Sverdlovsk Medical Institute, 1957. Honoured Coach of the USSR from 1964. Professor, 1972. Rector at the Moscow Institute of Physical Culture from 1977. Many times world, European and USSR champion, 1950–61. Olympic champion, 1956 (462.5kg). Bronze medal, 1952. Author of *Tiazheloatleticheskii Sport*, Moscow, 1977.

Vorob'ev, Iakov Zinov'evich (Vasilii)
17.11.1885–9.1919. Revolutionary, state security official.
Born in Vasilkov near Kiev. Son of a medical orderly. Joined the Bolsheviks, 1907. Studied at the Odessa Dental School. Underground party work, several arrests. At the end of 1917, seized power for the Bolsheviks in Nizhnii Novgorod (now Gorkii). Head of the Cheka in Nizhnii Novgorod, Mar. 1918. On the way to Voronezh to establish Soviet power, fell into the hands of the Whites and was shot.

Vorob'ev, Klementii Iakovlevich
1866–1930. Statistician.
Before WWI, worked in the statistical departments of several zemstvos. After the October Revolution 1917, statistician in Omsk and Simbirsk. From 1925, statistician in the Central Statistical Administration (TSSU). Produced many valuable statistical studies, which now serve as original sources for the study of pre-revolutionary rural Russia.

Vorob'ev, Mikhail Petrovich
29.12.1896–12.6.1957. Marshal.
Born in Khasaviurt in Daghestan. Conscripted into the army, 1916. Joined the Red Army, 1918. Received a technical education after the Civil War. General Inspector of the Engineers before WWII. From 1942–52, Commander of the Engineering Forces of the Soviet Army. Died in Moscow.

Vorob'ev, Sergei Il'ich
1895–1983. Col.-general.
Joined the Bolshevik Party, 1918. In the Red Army, 1918–22, and again from 1923. Artillery officer during

the Civil War. Supply officer of the Baltic fleet, 1938. During WWII, Deputy Naval Minister. Head of the rear of the Soviet Navy, 1946. Retired, 1948.

Vorob'ev, Vladimir Petrovich
27.6.1876–31.10.1937. Medical scientist.
Born in Odessa. Graduated from Khar'kov University, 1903. Professor there, 1917. Specialist in anatomy, prepared an *Atlas of Human Anatomy*. One of the team of doctors who embalmed Lenin's body. Died in Khar'kov.

Voronin, Aleksandr Nikiforovich
23.5.1951– . Athlete.
Born in Cheliabinsk. Honoured Master of Sports (heavy-weight wrestling), 1976. Studied at the Prokop'evskii High School of Physical Culture. USSR champion, 1975, 1979. European champion, 1976–77, 1979. World champion, 1976–77. Olympic champion, 1976 (242, 5kg).

Voronin, Mikhail Iakovlevich
26.3.1945– . Athlete.
Born in Moscow. Honoured Master of Sports (gymnastics), 1966. Graduated from the Moscow Institute of Physical Culture, 1973. Honoured Coach of the RSFSR, 1973. Member of the CPSU, 1974. World champion, 1966. USSR champion, 1966–72. European champion, 1967–71. Olympic champion, 1968. Bronze medal, 1968.

Voronina, Zinaida Borisovna
10.12.1947– . Athlete.
Born in Ioshkar-Ola, Mari ASSR. Honoured Master of Sports (gymnastics), 1968. USSR champion, Olympic champion, and silver medal, 1968. World champion, 1970.

Voronkov, Vladimir Petrovich
20.3 1944– . Athlete.
Born in the village of Tugaevo, Chuvash ASSR. Honoured Master of Sports (skiing), 1970. Graduated from the Leningrad Institute of Physical Culture, 1976. USSR champion, 1968–71. World champion, 1970. Olympic champion, 1972.

Voronov, Gennadii Ivanovich
31.8.1910– . Politician.
Born in the village of Rameshki, near Tver'. Son of a teacher. Electrician, 1929. Educated at the Tomsk Industrial Institute, 1936, but later worked as a full-time party official (agitation and propaganda). 1st Secretary of Chita obkom, 1948–55. Member of the Cen. Cttee. of the CPSU, 1952. Deputy Agriculture Minister of the USSR, 1955–57. 1st Secretary of Orenburg obkom, 1957–61. Member of the Presidium, Oct. 1961. Prime Minister of the RSFSR, Nov. 1962. Member of the Politburo, Apr. 1966.

Voronov, Georgii
1888?–after 1945. Medical scientist.
Became internationally famous for his hormone experiments on monkeys as part of his research into rejuvenation. Started his work in Petrograd, continued later in Paris and in Switzerland. Attracted enormous attention in the 1920s and 1930s, completely forgotten since. Died in Switzerland.

Voronov, Nikolai Nikolaevich
5.5.1899–28.2.1968. Marshal.
Born in Petersburg. Joined the Red Army, 1918, served in the artillery. Graduated from Frunze Military Academy, 1930. Director of the 1st Leningrad Artillery School, 1934. Soviet military adviser to the Republicans in Spain during the Civil War, 1936–37. From 1937 till 1950, Head of Artillery of the Soviet Armed Forces. July 1941–Mar. 1943, Deputy Minister of Defence. President of the Artillery Academy, 1950–58. Responsible for the enormous build-up of Soviet artillery from the 1930s to 1950s. Head of operations during the Battle of Stalingrad. Highly decorated (6 Orders of Lenin, 4 Orders of the Red Banner). Died in Moscow, buried at the Kremlin wall.

Voronskii, Aleksandr Konstantinovich
31.8.1884–13.10.1943. Literary critic.
Born in the village of Khoroshavka, near Tambov. Son of a village priest. Expelled from the local seminary. Bolshevik from 1904. Before WWI, engaged in underground party work in many Russian towns. After the

October Revolution, became the editor of the first communist literary magazine, *Krasnaia Nov'*, 1921–27. Insisted on literary, rather than propagandistic, value in literature. Removed from the editorship (for Trotskyism), 1927. In 1924, founded the literary group Pereval, which was liquidated in the 1930s. Memoirs: *Za Zhivoi i Mertvoi Vodoi*, 1927. Victim of Stalin's purges. Rehabilitated posthumously during the Khrushchev thaw, 1956.

Vorontsov, Iulii Mikhailovich
1929–   . Diplomat.
Graduated from the MGIMO (Institute of International Relations), Moscow, 1952. Occupied top positions in the USSR Ministry of Foreign Affairs. Member of the Soviet Delegation to the United Nations, 1954–58 and 1963–65. Councillor at the USSR Embassy in the USA, 1966–70. USSR Ambassador to India, 1977. Member of the Cen. Cttee. of the CPSU from 1981. 1st Deputy Foreign Minister, 1987. Special responsibility for the arms control negotiations in Geneva, 1987. Ambassador in Afghanistan, 10 Oct. 1988.

Voroshilov, Kliment Efremovich
4.2.1881–2.12.1969. Marshal, politician.
Born in the village of Verkhnee, now Voroshilovgrad Oblast'. Son of a railway worker. Worked in metallurgical works and in repair shops in Southern Russia in 1968. Bolshevik from 1903. Chairman of Lugansk Soviet during the 1905 Revolution. Several times arrested and exiled, but managed to escape. Carried out underground party work during 1908–17. Chairman of Lugansk Soviet, and revolutionary city mayor of Lugansk after the October Revolution 1917. City Commissar in Petrograd, Nov. 1917. One of the organizers of the Red Army in the South, commander at Tsaritsyn (against General Wrangel). Minister of the Interior in the Ukraine, organizer of the 1st Cavalry Army (with Marshal Budennyi). Crushed the Kronstadt sailors' revolt in 1921–24. Commander of the Moscow military district, 1924–25. Minister of Army and Navy, chairman of the

Revolutionary Military Council, 1925–34. Allied with Stalin (a close friend since the Civil War) against the Red Army chief organizer Trotsky. People's Commissar of Defence, 1934–40. Main ally of Stalin during the purge of his fellow top military commanders in 1936–38. At the beginning of WWII, Deputy Prime Minister, chairman of the Committee for the Defence of the Fatherland, Commander of the South-West Army Group, Commander of the Leningrad front. Chief commander of the partisan movement (controlled by the NKVD). Participated in the Tehran conference between Stalin, Churchill and Roosevelt in 1943. After WWII, head of the Allied Control Commission of Hungary. Deputy Prime Minister from 1946 until Stalin's death in Mar. 1953. Chairman of the Presidium of the Supreme Soviet (nominal Head of State) from 1953 to 1960. A veteran member of the Cen. Cttee. of the CPSU from 1921 till 1961, and member of the Politburo from 1926 till 1952. Forced to retire in 1960 by Khruschev, officially on the grounds of ill health, in fact a victim of the power struggle within the party. Died in Moscow and buried at the Kremlin wall.

Vorotnikov, Vitalii Ivanovich
20.1.1926–   . Politician.
Controller, technician, deputy head and secretary of a party cttee., and chief controller of a plant (possibly in the aviation industry), 1942–44 and 1947–60. Member of the CPSU, 1947. Graduated from the Kuibyshev Aviation Institute, 1954. Senior party positions in Kuibyshev. Member of the Cen. Cttee. of the CPSU, 1971. USSR Ambassador to Cuba, 1979–82. 1st Secretary of Krasnodar Kraikom, CPSU, 1982–83. Chairman of the RSFSR Council of Ministers, 24 June 1983. Elected to the Politburo, 26 Dec. 1983.

Vorovskii, Vaclav Vatslavovich (Orlovskii, P.; Shvarts; Zhozefina; Favn)
27.10.1871–10.5.1923. Revolutionary, politician, literary critic.
Born in Moscow. Son of a Polish engineer. Before WWI, became known as an orthodox Marxist literary critic, praised by Lenin himself. Active

Bolshevik Party member, 1903, taking part in many party meetings and congresses. After the February Revolution 1917, appointed head of the Bolshevik office abroad (based in Stockholm). After Nov. 1917, Soviet Ambassador to Sweden, Denmark and Norway. Ambassador to Italy, 1921. Concluded the Soviet-Italian trade agreement, May 1922, and prepared the Soviet-German Rapallo Treaty, 1922. Secretary of the Soviet Delegation at the Genoa and Lausanne conferences, 1922–23. Shot by the White Russian Konradi in Lausanne. Buried at the Kremlin wall.

Vorozheikin, Grigorii Alekseevich
1895–1974. Marshal.
On active service during WWI. Joined the Red Army, 1918. Regimental commander in the Red Army during the Civil War. Graduated from the Zhukovskii Air Force Academy, 1933. During WWII, Commander of the Central Front Air Force, Chief-of-staff of the Soviet Air Force, and 1st Deputy Commander of the Soviet Air Force. Faculty Head at the Air Force Academy, 1953–59.

Voskov, Semen (Samuil) Petrovich
1889–1920. Revolutionary.
Born near Poltava, Ukraine. Worked as a carpenter. Took part in the 1905 Revolution in Poltava. Arrested, escaped, and went abroad in 1906. Organized revolutionary groups among Russian workers in the USA, one of the founders of the magazine *Novyi Mir*. After the February Revolution 1917, returned to Russia. Bolshevik Party representative at a large armaments factory in Sestroretsk. During the October Revolution 1917, supplied the Red Guard (Bolshevik workers' detachments) with arms. Participated in the siege of the Winter Palace 1917, and the arrest of the ministers of the Provisional Government. Took part in the quelling of the Krasnov revolt. Political commissar of the Red Army on many fronts during the Civil War. Died of typhoid at Taganrog.

Voskresenskii, Rafail Nikolaevich
1922–   . Artist.
Born in Iaroslavl'. Landscape paint-

er. Studied at the Iaroslavl' Art School, 1945–50, under V. Kartovich, G. Kozyrev and A. Churin. Member of the Union of Artists, Iaroslavl' branch. Exhibitions: Oblast' Art Exhibitions, Iaroslavl', 1953–59; Spring Exhibition of Iaroslavl' Artists, 1954; Works of Artists of Vladimir, Gorkii Ivanovo, Kalinin, Kostroma, Iaroslavl', Moscow, 1955; Works of Artists of the RSFSR, Moscow, 1955; Works of Iaroslavl' and Gorkii Oblast' Artists, Moscow, 1955–56; Iaroslavl' Artists, Iaroslavl', 1958.

Voskresenskii, Vladimir Il'ich
1946–1.1970. Poet, editor, journalist.
Born in Moscow. Studied at the Moscow Energetics Institute, but never had the chance to practice his profession. Some of his poems appeared in the Soviet press. Co-editor of 8 issues of the samizdat publications *Tetradi Sotsialisticheskoi Demokratii Russkoe Slovo* and *Feniks-66.*

Voslenskii, Mikhail Sergeevich
1920–   . Sociologist.
Born in Berdiansk. Graduated from Moscow University. In 1946, acted as a translator at the Nuremberg war trials. Professor at Moscow Lumumba University for students from Africa, Asia and the Middle East. Member of the Presidium of the USSR Academy of Sciences. Defected to the West, 1972. His book *Nomenklatura: Gospodstvuiu-shchii Klass Sovetskogo Soiuza*, London, 1984, has been translated into several languages. Expert on Kremlin politics.

Vostorgov, Ioann, priest
1872–23.8.1918. Russian Orthodox clergyman.
Widely known as a writer on religious subjects and as a preacher. Lived in Tiflis, later in Moscow. Priest of the church of St. Basil at the Red Square during the 1917 Revolution. Murdered during revolutionary anarchy.

Vostretsov, Stepan Sergeevich
1883–1932. Revolutionary, state security officer.
Joined the Red Army, 1918. Member

of the Bolshevik Party, 1920. Regimental commander during the Civil War. Head of Cheka detachments in Siberia, 1921. Commander of the army of the buffer Far Eastern Republic, 1922. During the Soviet-Chinese conflict, 1929, Commander of the Transbaikal troops.

Vostrukhov, Vladimir Ivanovich
1895–1971. Col. general.
During WWI on active service. Joined the Red Army, 1919, and took part in the Civil War. Regimental commander, 1921. Professor at the Vystrel Courses. During WWII, supply specialist. After WWII, Head of the Rear Administration and Supply Academy. Head of the Rear Administration of the Air Force, 1949–53.

Voznessenskii, A. Alekseevich
1900–1950. Politician.
Brother of the Soviet Deputy Prime Minister N.A. Voznessenskii. Minister of Education of the RSFSR. One of the victims of the Leningrad case: accused by the secret police of conspiring to separate Russia from the rest of the Soviet Union. Tried in secret, and probably shot.

Voznessenskii, Andrei Andreevich
12.5.1933–   . Poet.
Born in Moscow. Graduated from the Moscow Architectural Institute, 1957. Began appearing in print in the late 1950s, one of a group of promising young Soviet poets, including Evtushenko and Akhmadullina. Attracted to verbal experiments in the spirit of the 1920s (*Mastera*, 1959). Claimed for himself the tradition of the early Pasternak. Accused of formalism after the appearance of his collections of poems *Parabola,* 1960, and *Treugolnaia Grusha,* 1962. Very popular at mass poetry readings in the early 1960s. Gained success in Moscow and later in America with the musical (a genre new to the Soviet Union) *Iunona i Avos'*, dealing with the tragic love story of a Russian officer and the daughter of the Spanish governor of California in the early 19th century.

Voznessenskii, Nikolai Alekseevich
1.12.1903–30.9.1950. Politician.
Born in the village of Teploe near

Tula. Graduated from the Sverdlov Communist University, 1921. Studied, and later taught, at the Institute of Red Professors, 1928–31. Chairman of GOSPLAN, 1938. 1st Deputy Prime Minister of the USSR, 1941. Member of the Cen. Cttee. of the CPSU, 1938, and of the Politburo, 1947. Wrote a book entitled *The War Time Economy of the Soviet Union During the Patriotic War*, 1947. Lost his post in connection with the so-called Leningrad case, one of the most bizarre actions of Stalin and Beria. A purge of party officials was launched secretly after WWII under the pretext that they had conspired to bring about the separation of Russia from the USSR by making Leningrad the capital of the RSFSR. Thousands were arrested, tried in secret and condemned to the Gulag or execution. The main victims of this case were Voznessenskii and his brother, who were executed on Stalin's orders.

Vronskii, Evgenii Alekseevich
1883–1942. Singer (baritone).
Born in the village of Sorochinskoe, Samara Gouvt. Appeared in operas in Moscow, Odessa and Tbilisi. Professor at the Tbilisi Conservatory. Among his pupils were D. Andguladze, D. Badridze, D. Gamrekeli and N. Ovanisian. Died in Tbilisi.

Vronskii, Sergei Arkad'evich
3.9.1923–   . Cameraman.
Graduated from the VGIK as a cameraman, 1953. From 1955, one of the leading cameramen of the Mosfilm Studio. Among his works are *Brothers Karamazov*, 1969, *Tabor Ukhodit v Nebo*, 1976, and *Osennii Marafon*, 1979. State Prize, 1981. Lives in Moscow.

Vronskii, Vakhtang Ivanovich (Nadiradze)
10.9.1905–   . Choreographer.
Born in Tbilisi. Graduated from the Tbilisi Ballet School, 1923. Dancer, and later soloist with the Rostov-on-Don, Saratov, Baku and Tashkent theatres. From 1932, choreographer. With the Odessa Theatre, 1940–54, and the Shevchenko Theatre, 1954–69. Artistic director and chief choreographer of the Ukrainian Ballet on Ice, 1961–73.

Vuchetich, Evgenii Viktorovich
15.12.1908–1974. Sculptor.
Born in Ekaterinoslav (now Dnepropetrovsk). Studied at the Rostov Art School, 1926–30, and the Leningrad Academy of Arts, 1931–33. One of the main exponents of Stalinist socialist-realist art in sculpture. Constructed many of the largest Soviet memorials: the Soviet Army memorial in Berlin, the war memorial in Stalingrad (now Volgograd), the Dzerzhinskii statue in front of the Lubianka in Moscow, and others. Highly decorated (5 Stalin Prizes).

Vvedenskii, Aleksandr Ivanovich
1856–7.3. 1925. Philosopher.
Born in Tambov. Professor of Petersburg University, 1890. Chairman of the Philosophical Society in Petersburg, 1899. Follower of Kant. In the 1920s, continued to criticize Marxist views.

Vvedenskii, Aleksandr Ivanovich
19.1.1904–1941. Poet.
Born in Petersburg. Studied at Petrograd University. Co-founder of the OBERIU absurdist literary circle. Published verse for children in the official press. Arrested, 1932. In prison for one year. Moved to Khar'kov, 1936. Re-arrested, 1941. Died in prison, circumstances unknown. Interest in him re-awakened in the 1970s. His collected works, in 2 vols, have been published in the USA.

Vygodskii, Nikolai Iakovlevich
3.4.1900–1939. Organist, pianist.
Born in Petersburg. Taught at the Moscow Conservatory. Arrested in 1935 and sent to the Gulag. Died in the camps. The exact place and date of his death are not known. Rehabilitated after his death. Author of musical compositions, transcriptions of organ pieces for piano and articles on musical subjects.
Source: *Sovetskaia Muzyka*, 1960, Nr. 12.

Vyrupaev, Konstantin Grigor'evich
2.10.1930–   . Athlete.
Born in Irkutsk. Honoured Master of Sports (wrestling), 1956. Member of the CPSU, 1962. Graduated from the Omsk Institute of Physical Culture, 1968. Honoured Coach of the RSFSR, 1968. Olympic champion, 1956. Bronze medal, 1960.

Vysheslavtsev, Boris Petrovich
1877–1954. Philosopher, sociologist.
Born in Moscow. Son of a lawyer. Graduated from Moscow University in law, 1899. Studied philosophy at Marburg University. Professor at Moscow University, 1917. Dismissed by the communist authorities, expelled with a group of professors in 1922. Lived in Paris, lectured at the St. Sergius Theological Institute in Paris before WWII. After WWII, moved to Switzerland. In his philosophical and sociological works, criticized the prominence of Marx and Freud in modern thought, considering them responsible for the impoverishment of cultural and spiritual life.
Main works: *Etika Sublimirovannogo Erosa*; *Krizis Promyshlennogo Obshchestva*; *Filosofskaia Nishcheta Marksizma*; *Vechnoe v Russkoi Filosofii*.

Vyshinskii, Andrei Ianuar'evich
10.12.1883–22.11.1954. State prosecutor, politician.
Born in Odessa. Member of the SD Party (Menshevik) from 1903. Graduated from Kiev University in law, 1913. Joined the Bolshevik Party, 1920. Rector of Moscow University 1925–28. Worked at the Ministry of Education of the RSFSR, 1928–31. Published manuals on law (*Kurs Ogolovnogo Processa*, 1927). From 1931, worked in the Soviet legal system. State prosecutor, 1935–39, gaining notoriety by his appalling behaviour at the Stalinist show trials of the period, publicly humiliating some of the best-known leaders of the state and party, and making quite unbelievable accusations. Rewarded by being appointed member of the Gen. Cttee. of the party, 1939. Put his experience into theoretical form in *Teoriia Sudebnykh Dokazatelstv v Sovetskom Prave*, 1941. Later worked in high government and diplomatic posts – Deputy Prime Minister of the USSR, 1939–44, Deputy Foreign Minister, 1940–49, Foreign Minister 1949–53. From Stalin's death, Mar. 1953, again Deputy Foreign Minister, and Soviet representative at the UN, 1953–54. When de-Stalinization was begin-

ning to gain ground, died suddenly in New York of a heart attack.

Vysotskii, Vladimir Semenovich
1938–1980. Poet, actor, ballad singer.
Born in Moscow. Studied at the Moscow Construction Engineering Institute. Graduated from the Moscow MKHAT Actors' School. From 1964, worked as an actor in the Moscow Taganka Theatre. Gained fame for his singing and poetry. His songs circulated in magnitizdat (private tape recordings) all over the Soviet Union, though during his lifetime, no official records of his were issued. As an actor, received recognition in the role of Hamlet. Acted in many productions. His name guaranteed box-office success. Also acted in many films. Married the French actress Marina Vlady (Poliakova-Baidarova). Towards the end of his short life, became a pop-idol (and victim of alcoholism). The authorities disliked him for his nonconformism, but he was privately admired even by KGB men. Immensely popular for the last 10 years of his life. Died in Moscow. His death was mourned throughout Russia, with many thousands turning up for his funeral. After his death, his recorded songs and books of his verse became available. Now recognized as the voice of protest during the years of Brezhnevite stagnation.

W

Walter (Swierczewski, Karol)
22.2.1897–28.3.1947. Revolutionary, party official, general.
Born in Warsaw. Son of a worker. During WWI, evacuated to Moscow. During the October Revolution 1917, member of the Red Guard. Member of the Bolshevik Party from 1918. During the Civil War, fought in the Red Army on different fronts. Graduated from Frunze Military Academy in 1927. During the Spanish Civil War, volunteered to fight for the Republicans. Commander of the International Brigade. During WWII, served in the Soviet Army and organized communist sympathizers among Polish POWs. Member of the Cen. Cttee. of the Polish Communist Party. Organized the Polish Army in

the USSR in Sep. 1944, which fought alongside the Soviet Army against the Germans. Deputy Defence Minister of the Polish (communist) government, Feb. 1946, helped to bring communists to power in Poland with Soviet assistance. Killed by Polish anti-communists in Baligrod, Southern Poland.

Weinbaum, Mark Efimovich
1900?–19.3.1973. Editor.
For many decades, editor of the New York Russian newspaper *Novoe Russkoe Slovo*. (As no pre-1917 newspaper survived in the Soviet Union, this New York newspaper, founded in the early 20th century, is now the oldest existing Russian newspaper in the world. Apart from serving the Russian community in the USA, it is read in many other countries.) Maintained a consistently liberal and anti-communist line. Also for many years chairman of the Literaturnyi Fond, an aid organization for Russian writers in exile.

Wilkitskii, Boris Andreevich
3.4.1885–6.3.1961. Hydrographer, explorer.
Born at Pulkovo, near Petersburg. Son of the founder of the Russian Hydrographic Administration and polar explorer. Graduated from the Naval Academy in Petersburg, 1908. Took part in the Russo-Japanese war, 1904–05. Head of an expedition to the Northern Siberian coast, 1913–15. Discovered Severnaia Zemlia, Wilkitskii Island, Malyi Taimyr, and Starokadomskii Island. The strait between the Taimyr peninsula and Severnaia Zemlia was named after him. During the Civil War, with the Whites in Arkhangelsk. Emigrated to Britain, 1920. Later worked for many years as a hydrographer in the Belgian Congo. Died in Brussels.

Wolff, Marc
1891–11.1987. Lawyer.
Born in Peterhof. A witness of the events of Bloody Sunday during the 1905 Revolution. Studied at Heidelberg and London. Graduated from Petersburg University in law. His career started at the Petrograd Bar. Lawyer during the first days of the October Revolution 1917. Emigrated in 1920. Settled in London. Called to the English Bar in 1926. Retired in

1976. His daughter Tatiana Wolff is an authority on Pushkin.

Wrangel, Aleksei (Alexis) Petrovich, Baron
1923–   . Author, authority on horsemanship.
Born in Yugoslavia. Son of Baron General Petr Nikolaevich Wrangel. Educated in England and the United States. Sportsman, rider and authority on horsemanship. Lives in Ireland. Author of *The End of Chivalry*, USA, 1982. Also wrote a remarkable book about his father: *Russia's White Crusader, General Wrangel*, USA, 1987.

Wrangel, Petr Nikolaevich, Baron
15.8.1878–25.4.1928. General.
Born into a Baltic aristocratic family of Swedish origin. Graduated from Petrograd Mining Institute in 1901. Joined a cavalry regiment as a private in 1901. Volunteered to serve at the front during the Russo-Japanese war, 1905 (Trans-Baikal Cossacks). Graduated from the Academy of the General Staff in 1910. During WWI, commander of a cavalry corps. After the October Revolution 1917, went to the Crimea, arrested by the Bolsheviks, narrowly escaped execution. Joined the Dobrovolcheskaia Army (Whites) in Aug. 1918. Commander of the Caucasian Army (Cossack cavalry), led an offensive to the East (Volga), and took and later lost Tsaritsyn (later Stalingrad, where Stalin was the Political Commissar of the Reds commanded by Voroshilov during these operations). After a quarrel with General Denikin, dismissed and sent abroad (Constantinople). When, after the defeat of Denikin, the rest of his army was evacuated to the Crimea, called back and elected commander-in-chief (confirmed by Denikin's last order). Tried to reorganize the White forces (the Volunteer Army was renamed the Russian Army). Carried out a land reform, with the transfer of land to the peasants, and tried to conclude an alliance with Poland (rejected by Pilsudski). After initial success leading his armies out of the Crimea into Northern Tauria, defeated by the Red Army, which was able to concentrate on his forces after peace was signed with Poland. Organized a large-scale evacuation of his forces

and civilian refugees (over 150,000) to Turkey, which was at that time under Allied control. Abroad, created a closely-knit organization of White Civil War veterans (ROVS – Russkii Obshchevoinskii Soiuz) in 1924. Died in Brussels, buried in the Russian cathedral in Belgrade. Left a detailed history of the Civil War.
See: *Vospominaniia* (Memoirs), 3rd ed., Frankfurt, 1969.

Z

Zabelina, Aleksandra Ivanovna
11.3.1937–   . Athlete.
Born in Moscow. Honoured Master of Sports (fencing), 1960. With Moscow Dynamo. Graduated from the Moscow Historical Archives Institute, 1970. USSR champion, 1957–59, 1962, 1968, 1972. World champion, 1957, 1967. Olympic champion with her team in 1960, 1968 and 1972.
See: I. Obraztsov, 'Piatnadtsat' Let Spustia' from the collection *Tvoi Chempiony*, Moscow, 1977.

Zabolotskii, Anatolii Dmitrievich
16.9.1935–   . Cameraman.
Graduated from the VGIK, 1959. Worked at the Belarus', and then the Tallinn film studios. Moved to Mosfilm. Worked with V. Shukshin on *Pechki-Lavochki*, 1972, and *Kalina Krasnaia*, 1964.

Zabolotskii, Nikolai Alekseevich
7.5.1903–14.10.1958. Poet.
Born in Kazan'. Studied in Moscow and Leningrad. Began as a writer for children. Later gained a reputation for his modernist poetry (influenced by Khlebnikov): *Stolbtsy*, 1929, and *Torzhestvo Zemledeliia*, 1933. Combined a pantheistic approach to nature with primitivist stylistic experiments. Arrested, 1938, sent to the Gulag in Siberia, and later to exile in Kazakhstan. His long poem *Rubruk v Mongolii* was published posthumously, 1960. Translated the masterpiece of Georgian literature by S. Rustaveli, *Vitiaz v Tigrovoi Shkure*.

Zagladin, Vadim Valentinovich
1927–   . Politician.
In 1949, graduated from the Moscow

State Institute of International Relations (MGIMO). Candidate of Historical Sciences. Lecturer at the MGIMO, 1953–4. Joined the Communist Party in 1955. Editor of *Novoe Vremia* (political weekly), 1957–60. From 1954–64, editor of *Problemy Mira i Sotsializma*. Member of the Apparatus of the Cen. Cttee. of the CPSU, 1964–67. Deputy from 1967–75, then 1st Deputy Head of the International Department of the Cen. Cttee. Member of the Cen. Auditing Commission, 1971–76. Candidate member of the Cen. Cttee., 1976–81, full member, 1981. Under Gorbachev, Deputy Chief of the Cen. Cttee.'s Department for Relations with Foreign Communist Parties.

Zagurskii, Boris Ivanovich
8.8.1901– . Musicologist, music administrator.
Born in Mogilevskaia Gouvt. Director of the Leningrad Malyi Opera, 1951–61. Author of *Kratkii Ocherk Istorii Leningradskoi Konservatorii*, Leningrad, 1933, and *M.I.Glinka. Ocherk*, Leningrad, 1940.

Zaikov, Lev Nikolaevich
3.4.1923– . Politician.
Worked as a metal worker, group chief, foreman, deputy shop superintendent, shop superintendent, and plant production chief, 1941–61 (possibly in the military industry, since there is no evidence of military service during WWII). Senior administrative posts, 1946–76. Member of the CPSU, 1957. Graduated from the Leningrad Economical Engineering Institute, 1963. Member of the Cen. Cttee. of the CPSU from 1981. 1st Secretary of Leningrad obkom, CPSU, 1983–85. Secretary of the Cen. Cttee. from 1 July 1985. Elected to the Politburo on 6 Mar. 1986. 1st Secretary of the Moscow City Party cttee. (after the dismissal of Boris Eltsyn), 1987.

Zaionchkovskii, Andrei Medardovich
1862–1926. General, military historian.
Graduated from the Academy of the General Staff, 1888. Took part in the Russo-Japanese war, 1904–05, and WWI. Joined the Red Army, 1919. Army Chief-of-staff during the Civil War. Professor at the Military Academy of the Red Army, 1922. Author of works on the history of the Crimean War and WWI.

Zaitsev, Aleksandr Gennad'evich
16.6.1952– . Athlete.
Born in Leningrad. Honoured Master of Sports (figure-skating), 1973. With the Central Sports Club of the Army. Graduated from the Leningrad Institute of Physical Culture, 1974. Member of the CPSU from 1976. USSR champion, 1973–77. Partner of Irina Rodnina. World and European champion, 1973–78. Olympic champion, 1976.

Zaitsev, Boris Konstantinovich
29.1.1881–28.1.1972. Author.
Born in Orel. Son of a factory manager. Educated at Kaluga. Studied at Moscow University and at the Moscow Mining Institute. First appeared in print, 1901. Became a member of the Sereda circle in Moscow. A lyrical writer in the Turgenev and Chekhov traditions, soon attracted attention by his short stories and novels. Military service during WWI. Despite his gentle nature, became a resolute opponent of Bolshevism. During the revolutionary years, organized the Writers' Shop in Moscow, where writers could sell their books. First president of the Russian Writers' Union, 1921. Allowed to go abroad for health reasons, 1922. Lived in Berlin, travelled in Italy, settled in France, 1924. Chairman of the Union of Russian Writers and Journalists in Paris. Wrote novels (*Zolotoi Uzor, Golubaia Zvezda, Dom v Passy*) and biographies (Zhukovskii, Turgenev, Chekhov). Close to Bunin, after whose death he remained for many years the most outstanding survivor of classical Russian literature abroad. Translated Dante and Flaubert into Russian. Contributed to many Russian periodicals abroad. Memoirs published after WWII. Died in Paris.

Zaitsev, Boris Mikhailovich
23.3.1937– . Athlete.
Born in Moscow. Honoured Master of Sports (ice-hockey), 1964. With Moscow Dynamo. Graduated from the Moscow Oblast' Institute of Physical Culture, 1969. World and European champion, 1963–64. Olympic champion, 1964.

Zaitsev, Egor Viacheslavovich
1961– . Fashion designer.
Born in Moscow. Son of a famous fashion designer. Followed in the footsteps of his father. Known for his designs in sporting clothing, shoes and equipment.

Zaitsev, Iurii Konstantinovich
17.1.1951– . Athlete.
Born in the village of Pobedino, Sakhalin Oblast'. Honoured Master of Sports (heavy athletics), 1976. With Temirtau Enbek. Student at the Karaganda Pedagogical Institute. USSR champion, 1976. World champion, 1976 and 1978. Olympic champion, 1976. European champion, 1978 and 1979.

Zaitsev, Ivan Matveevich
1878–1934. General.
Chief-of-staff of the Cossack Ataman Dutov. Took part in the Civil War, fighting with Admiral Kolchak against the Red Army. Fled to China. Returned from China in 1927 under an amnesty proclaimed by the Soviet government. A few months later, arrested and sent to the Solovki concentration camp. Managed to escape and return to China. Published in Shanghai one of the first reports on life in the Solovki camp, *Solovki, Kommunisticheskaia Katorga*, 1931 (a valuable source, especially on the fate of the large group of bishops concentrated there at that time).

Zaitsev, Mikhail Mitrofanovich
1923– . General.
Joined the Soviet Army, 1941. Member of the CPSU from 1943. Graduated from the Military Academy of Tank Troops in 1954, then from the Military Academy of the General Staff in 1965. Commander of various units until 1972. 1st Deputy Commander of Troops in the Belorussian military district, 1972–76. Member of the Cen. Cttee. of the Belorussian CP, 1976–81. Commander of Soviet Troops in East Germany from 1980. Full member of the

Cen. Cttee. of the CPSU from 1981. A key figure in the changing face of the Soviet forces pitted against Nato. One of the new breed of Soviet generals, surrounding himself with a group of young educated officers who have welcomed his encouragement of initiative.

Zaitsev, Oleg Alekseevich
4.8.1939– . Athlete.
Born in Moscow. Honoured Master of Sports (ice-hockey), 1966. With the Central Sports Club of the Army as a coach. Graduated from the Moscow Oblast' Institute of Physical Culture, 1969. Member of the CPSU from 1969. USSR champion, 1963–66, 1968. World and European champion, 1964, 1966–68. Olympic champion, 1964 and 1968.

Zaitsev, Viacheslav (Slava)
1937– . Fashion designer.
Born at Ivanovo. Educated at the Moscow Textile Institute, 1956. Chief designer to the All-Union Fashion House, 1965. Exclusive fashion designer of the rich and powerful in the Soviet Union. His clients include the wives of Kremlin officials, artistic personalities, members of the Diplomatic Corps, and other VIPs. Very talented and in touch with Western fashion. Raisa Gorbachev's personal designer and fashion adviser as well as a good friend. Regularly shows his collection of haute couture at the Ministry of Light Industry, where he is officially employed. Has been criticized by conservative elements in the Soviet government who believe that his clothes are fit for theatre or a show, but not for life. Calls his art the 'renaissance of Russian fashion'. Has also designed shoes, jewellery, kitchen utensils, and furniture. Paints in the cubist style. Teaches design at Soviet professional schools. Licensed his designs for sale in the USA. The first Soviet fashion designer to take part in international fashion shows.

Zak, Iakov Israilevich
20.11.1913– . Pianist.
Born in Odessa. Pupil of Genrikh Neigauz. Professor at the Moscow Conservatory. 1st prize at the International Chopin Competition, Warsaw, 1937. Among his pupils were R. Mirvis, N. Petrov and A. Cherkassov.

Zakharchenko-Schulz, Maria Vladimirovna (Lysova, Mikhno)
9.12.1893–6.1927. Anti-communist revolutionary.
Daughter of a landowner. Educated at the Smolny Institute in Petersburg. Took part in WWI as a volunteer. In 1917, returned to her native Penza. Organized a group of active opponents of the communist regime. Took part in the Civil War in the White Armies, evacuated from the Crimea after Wrangel's defeat. One of the main members of a small White-Russian terrorist group organized in the 1920s by General Kutepov. Made several secret trips to the Soviet Union, trying to harass the GPU, but was soon enmeshed in the GPU net Trest masquerading as an underground monarchist organization. Killed by GPU troops on the border, while trying to return from the Soviet Union to Poland.

Zakharov, Georgii Fedorovich
1897–1957. General.
Took part in WWI and the Civil War. In the Red Army from 1919. Graduated from the Frunze Military Academy, 1933. Distinguished service during WWII (Deputy Commander of the Stalingrad front, later in the North Caucasus, Ukraine and Belorussia). After WWII, head of the Vystrel Courses and active in the military training system.

Zakharov, Matvei Vasil'evich
1898–31.1.1972. Marshal.
Joined the Communist Party, 1917. Took part in the storming of the Winter Palace during the October Revolution 1917. In the Red Army during the Civil War. Graduated from the Frunze Military Academy, 1928. On active service during WWII, first against Germany, and later Japan. After WWII, Deputy Chief of the General Staff, Head of the Academy of the General Staff, and Commander of Soviet Occupation Forces in Germany. Chief of the General Staff, 1960–71, and 1st Deputy Minister of Defence of the USSR.

Zakharov, Semen Egorovich
1906–1986. Admiral, political officer.
Joined the Communist Party, 1926.

Joined the Soviet armed forces, 1932. Graduated from the Lenin Military Political Academy, 1938. Made a career as a Stalinist political officer in the Navy, and as political controller of personnel in the Ministry of Defence. Under Stalin, member of the Cen. Cttee. of the CPSU, 1939–52. Demoted to non-voting member, 1952–56.

Zakharov, Vasilii Georgievich
1934– . Politician.
Graduated from Leningrad State University, 1957. Lecturer at the Tomsk Polytechnical Institute, then at the Leningrad Technological Institute. Member of the CPSU from 1964. Minister of Culture of the USSR, Mar. 1986 (replacing the veteran Brezhnevite Demichev).

Zakharov, Vladimir Grigor'evich
18.10.1901–13.7.1955. Composer, conductor.
Born in the Donbas. Studied at the Taganrog Music School from 1916, then at the Rostov Conservatory, 1922–27. Pupil of N. Kheifets. Taught theory at the Music School. In Moscow from 1929. Worked in radio till 1933. Directed the Piatnitskii Russian People's Choir from 1932 till his death. His most important work was influenced by choral music and was almost entirely centred on song. Died in Moscow.

Zakharova, Galina Petrovna
22.3.1947– . Athlete.
Born in Kiev. With Kiev Spartak. Graduated from the Kamenets-Podolskii Pedagogical Institute, 1973. Honoured Master of Sports (handball), 1976. USSR champion, 1969–76. Olympic champion, 1976.

Zakharova, Konkordia Ivanovna (Ezhova, Tsederbaum)
1878–1939. Revolutionary, politician.
Joined the SD movement in the 1890s. Later became a Menshevik. Wife of S. Ezhov (Tsederbaum). Exiled several times before 1917. Secretary of the Cen. Cttee. of the Mensheviks, 1921. In the 1920s–30s, arrested several times and exiled with her husband. Last arrest in 1937. Died in a concentration camp.

Zakharova, Nadezhda Dmitrievna
9.2.1945– . Athlete.
Born in the village of Golovanovo, Pskov Oblast'. Honoured Master of Sports (basketball), 1973. With Leningrad Spartak. Member of the CPSU from 1975. Works as a sports instructor. European champion, 1968–76. World champion, 1971 and 1975. USSR champion, 1974. Olympic champion, 1976.

Zakhvataev, Nikanor Dmitrievich
1898–1963. Col.-general.
Took part in WWI and the Civil War. Joined the Red Army, 1918. Member of the Communist Party, 1925. Graduated from the Frunze Military Academy, 1935, and from the Academy of the General Staff, 1939. Thereafter, professor at the Academy of the General Staff. Several high posts during WWII. After the Hungarian uprising, sent to direct the re-Sovietization of the Hungarian Army, 1957–60.

Zalesskii, Mikhail Nikolaevich
4.6.1905–22.3.1979. Journalist.
Born in Simferopol'. Volunteered for the White Army aged 14. In 1920, sent off by General Wrangel to continue his education together with other teenage soldiers. With the Donskoi Cadet Corps, evacuated to Yugoslavia. Studied at Zagreb University. In the 1930s, member of the NTS. On dangerous assignments during WWII in occupied Soviet territories. In the post-war years, worked at the Institute for the Study of the USSR in Munich. Moved to the USA, 1949, and settled in San Francisco. Head of the NTS there until his death. Member of the Cossacks Union and the Cadets Association. In 1978, published a book of poems, *Slava Kazach'ia*. Wrote for *Russkaia Zhizn'*. Book reviewer for *Posev*. Died in San Francisco.

Zalygin, Sergei Pavlovich
6.12.1913– . Author, editor.
Born in the village of Durasovka, Bashkir ASSR. Graduated from the Omsk Agricultural Institute in 1939. Worked as an engineer, hydro-technologist, and hydrologist in the Siberian branch of the USSR Academy of Sciences. Began writing when he was a student. First work published in 1936. Editor-in-chief of *Novyi Mir*, 1987. The first non-party editor-in-chief in state-controlled publishing. Encouraged by Gorbachev's policy of glasnost, started publishing previously banned literary works. Published in *Novyi Mir* Pasternak's famous long-banned *Doctor Zhivago*, 1988. In Oct. 1988, made an (unsuccessful) attempt to publish Solzhenitsyn.
Main works include: *Rasskazy* (Stories), 1941; *Tropy Altaia* (Altay's Paths), 1962; *Na Irtyshe* (On the Irtysh), 1964; *Solenaia Pad'* (The Salty Ravine), 2 vol., 1967–68.

Zamiatin, Evgenii Ivanovich
20.1.1884–10.3.1937. Author.
Born in Lebedian', near Lipetsk. Educated at Voronezh High School, 1902. Trained as a shipbuilder at the Petersburg Technological Institute. Took part in the 1905 Revolution. First appeared in print, 1908. Became widely known with his novel *Uezdnoe*, 1913, satirizing Russian provincial life. Before the 1917 Revolution, member of the Bolshevik Party. During WWI, sent as a naval engineer to England, Mar. 1916, to inspect ice-breakers ordered for the Russian Navy. Returned, Sep. 1917. Wrote a satire on England, *Ostrovitiane*, 1918. After the Revolution 1917, one of the most influential modern writers in Russia. Active as a writer and lecturer on Russian literature during the revolutionary years. Became profoundly disillusioned, and wrote about the return to caveman existence, coining the famous phrase 'I am afraid Russian literature has only one future – its past'. In 1920, wrote the anti-utopian novel *We* (My), which was never published in the USSR (English translation published in the USA, 1924, French publication, 1929), and which may have given Orwell the idea for *1984*. Became completely isolated after that, and wrote a personal appeal to Stalin for permission to emigrate, 1931. Was allowed to go abroad, 1932. Settled in France. Defended the position of the writer as an eternal heretic. Died in France.

Zamiatin, Leonid Mitrofanovich
1922– . Politician, diplomat.
Graduated from the Moscow Ordzhonikidze Institute of Aircraft Construction, 1944. In the same year, joined the Communist Party. Entered the Diplomatic Service, 1946. Councillor with the Soviet Delegation to the UN, 1954–57. USSR Deputy Representative at the Preparatory Cttee., then at the Council of the International Atomic Energy Agency, 1959–60. Deputy head, 1960–63, and head of the American Department, 1962. Head of the Press Department of the USSR Ministry of Foreign Affairs, 1962–70. Director-general of the news agency TASS until 1978. Member of the Cen. Auditing Cttee., 1971–76. Member of the Cen. Cttee. of the CPSU from 1976. Chief of the Cen. Cttee's Department for International Information from 1978. Ambassador to the UK, 1987.

Zamotailova, Tamara Alekseevna (Liukhina)
11.5.1939– . Athlete.
Born in Voronezh. Graduated in engineering from Voronezh University, 1963. Honoured Master of Sports (gymnastics), 1971. International referee, 1975. Olympic champion, 1960 and 1964. Bronze medal, 1960. USSR champion, 1961.

Zander, Lev Aleksandrovich
19.2.1893–17.12.1964. Theologian.
Born in Petersburg. Educated at the Lycée. Graduated from Petersburg University, 1913. Studied in Heidelberg, 1913–14. On active service during WWI, 1914–17. Professor of philosophy in Perm', later Vladivostok, during the Civil War, 1919–20. Emigrated to China, 1922. Moved to Czechoslovakia, 1923. Professor at the Sergius Theological Institute in Paris. An active participant in the world-wide oecumenical movement from its beginning. Involved in the cultural and youth work of Russian emigrés in France and other countries. Died in Paris.
Main works: *Leont'ev i Progress*; *Dostoyevsky, God and the World*; *Evangelisches und orthodoxes Christentum*; *Vision and Action*; *Images greques*.

Zaporozhets, Aleksandr Ivanovich
1899–1959. Lt.-general, political officer.
Joined the Red Army, 1918. Member of the Communist Party, 1919. Political Commissar during the Civil War. Head of the political administration of the army, 1940. Deputy Minister of Defence, 1941. One of Stalin's political controllers of the armed forces. After WWII, continued his career as a political officer.

Zarin', Marger Ottovich
24.5.1910–   . Composer, writer.
Born in Latvia. Accepted at the age of 13 into the Junior Department of the Riga Conservatory. Soon entered the Pedagogical Institute. Taught for some time in schools. Returned to the Conservatory. Pupil of I. Vitol, A. Daugul and P. Iozuus, 1929–33. First compositions, 1936. Composed mainly operas. First oratorios in the history of Latvian music. Wrote over 30 literary works in Latvian.

Zarubin, Viktor Ivanovich
1866–1928. Artist.
Studied at the P. Julian Academy, Paris, 1893–96, under J. Lefeuvre and T. Fleuri, then at the Higher Art School of the Petersburg Academy of Arts, 1896–98, under A. Kuindzhi. Graduated in physics and mathematics from Khar'kov University. Landscape and water-colour painter. Exhibitions: Petersburg Academy of Arts, 1897–1912, 1914–15; St. Petersburg Society of Artists, 1905; the Society of Russian Water Colour Painters, St. Petersburg, 1907, 1910–13, 1915–16; the Association of Artists, 1912–16; TPKHV 1915–18; 1st State Free Art Exhibition, Petrograd, 1919; AKHRR, 7th and 8th Exhibitions, Moscow, 1925, 1926; the Kuindzhi Society Exhibition, 1927.

Zarubina, Zoia
1920–   . Interpreter, translator, professor.
Stalin's personal secretary for foreign affairs. Also worked with other senior governmental figures in the Kremlin from the late 1940s. Accompanied Stalin to the Yalta and Potsdam conferences. Speaks perfect English. On 31 May 1988, spoke on BBC television live from Moscow about her work for Stalin, life under Gorbachev, and especially about the new role of women in Soviet society.

Zarudnaia, Varvara Mikhailovna (Zarudnaia-Ivanova)
17.12.1857–14.3.1939. Singer (soprano).
Born in Ekaterinoslav. Wife of the composer Mikhail Ippolitov-Ivanov. Pupil of Camillo Everardi. With the Tiflis Opera, 1883–93. Professor at the Moscow Conservatory, 1893–1924. Among her pupils was Vera Petrova-Zvantseva. Died in Moscow.

Zashchipina, Natal'ia Aleksandrovna (Natasha)
14.1.1939–   . Actress.
Child actress. Became nationally known after her first film *Zhila-Byla Devochka*, 1944. Then appeared in *Slon i Verovochka*, 1946. Made several children's films but few of any merit in her adult life.

Zaslavskaia, Tatiana Ivanovna
9.9.1927–   . Economist.
Born in Kiev. Graduated from Moscow University in economics, 1950. Senior economist at the Moscow Institute of Economics of the Academy of Sciences from 1950. Head of the department of social problems at the Institute of Economics and Organization of Industrial Production (IZIOPP) of the Siberian branch of the USSR Academy of Sciences in Novosibirsk. One of the key economic advisers to M. Gorbachev.

Zaslavskii, David Iosifovich
13.1.1880–28.3.1965. Journalist.
Born in Kiev. Member of the social democratic movement from 1900. Started to work in the press in 1904. Member of the Cen. Cttee. of the BUND, 1917–18. Contributed to *Pravda* from 1928. Member of the CPSU from 1934. For decades, one of the main exponents of the official line of the party and prominent in all vilification campaigns (led the attack on B. Pasternak after he was awarded the Nobel Prize for *Dr Zhivago*). Became almost a symbol of the party hack. Died in Moscow.

Zaslonov, Konstantin Sergeevich
1910–1942. Partisan commander.
Organized partisan groups in German-occupied territory in Belorussia, 1941. Commander of the partisan movement near Orsha, 1942. Fell in action.

Zass, Aleksandr
1888–1962. Circus artist.
Born in Wilno (now Vilnius). Son of a Jewish father and Russian mother. Entered the circus and soon became a strongman, nicknamed the Iron Samson. His usual advertising stunt when he arrived in a new town was to have a car run over him. His most famous stunt was inspired by a real event in his life, when he had had to carry a horse on his shoulders. In his act he made this even more complicated by wading knee-deep through water while carrying the 375kg. horse. He was called up for active service when WWI broke out. Repeated his stunt under enemy fire when his horse was shot in the leg. After the war, as a private, moved to England, and performed all over Europe. Worked in the circus until his death. In his 70s, he was still able to walk into the arena carrying a special shoulder-pole, on the ends of which sat 2 enormous lions. His strength was the more remarkable taking into consideration his height (a mere 167cm.) and his weight (only 80kg.).

Zasulich, Vera Ivanovna
8.8.1849–8.5.1919. Revolutionary.
Born in Mikhailovka near Gzhatsk. Daughter of a nobleman. Early involvement in revolutionary activity. Arrested in connection with the Nechaev Affair, 1869–70 (which served as the basis for Dostoevskii's *The Possessed*). After her release, returned to revolutionary activity. On 24 Jan. 1878, shot the Petersburg police chief Trepov, seriously wounding him in the face, in protest against the flogging of an imprisoned revolutionary. Her trial became a cause célèbre when the jury found her not guilty. After her release, fled abroad and settled in Switzerland, 1880. Together with Plekhanov, founded the first Marxist group, Osvobozhdenie Truda, 1883. Illegally visited Petersburg, 1899–1900, and met

Lenin. Later worked abroad with Lenin on several revolutionary publications (*Iskra* and others), which left in her a distaste of Lenin's methods of work and of his personality. During the split of the SD Party, 1903, joined the Mensheviks. Returned to Russia, 1905. Denounced the Bolshevik take-over in Oct. 1917, and soon thereafter died in Petrograd, completely disillusioned with her former revolutionary comrades.

Zataevich, Aleksandr Viktorovich
20.3.1869–6.12.1936. Composer, ethnographer.
Born in Orlovskaia Gouvt. Author of piano pieces and romances. Literary works: collections of Kirghiz songs – *1000 Pesen Kirgizskogo (Kazakhskogo) Naroda*, Orenburg, 1925; *500 Kazakhskikh Pesen i Kiu'ev*, Alma-Ata, 1931; *250 Kirgizskikh Instrumental'nykh p'es i Napevov*, Moscow, 1934. Died in Moscow.

Zatonskii, Vladimir Petrovich
1888–1938. Politician.
Graduated from Kiev University, 1912. Joined the Bolsheviks, 1917. Active in establishing communist rule in the Ukraine. Took part in the Civil War. Head of the political administration of the Red Ukrainian Armed Forces, 1924–25, Secretary of the Cen. Cttee. of the Bolshevik Party in the Ukraine, 1925. Minister of Education of the Ukrainian SSR, 1933–38. Arrested and disappeared during Stalin's purges. Presumably shot, or died in the Gulag.

Zaveniagin, Avraamii Pavlovich
1901–1956. Politician, state security official.
Joined the Bolsheviks, 1917. Deputy Minister of Heavy Industry, 1937. Head of the construction of the Norilsk Metallurgical Combine, 1938. In this capacity, head of the infamous Norilsk concentration camps. Deputy Minister of the Interior, 1941–50. Deputy Minister of Medium Machine Engineering, 1953–54. Deputy Prime Minister of the USSR, 1955.

Zavetnovskii, Viktor Aleksandrovich
14.11.1875–16.5.1950. Violinist.
Born in Petersburg. Pupil of P.

Krasnokutskii. Organizer and director of a string quartet, 1907. Soloist and conductor with the Symphony Orchestra of the Leningrad Philharmonic (formerly the Court Orchestra), 1910–45. Teacher of the violinist Galina Barinova. Died in Leningrad.

Zbrueva, Evgenia Ivanovna
5.1.1868–20.10.1936. Singer (contralto).
Born in Moscow. Daughter of the singer and composer Petr Bulakhov. Pupil of Elizaveta Lavrovskaia. Soloist with the Bolshoi Theatre, Moscow, 1894–1905, and with the Mariinskii Theatre, Petersburg, from 1905. Professor at the Petrograd Conservatory, 1915–17. Author of *Vospominaniia, Muzykal'noe Nasledstvo*, Moscow, 1962. Died in Moscow.

Zdanevich, Il'ia Mikhailovich (Iliazd)
1894–1975. Poet, artist, publisher.
Born in Tiflis, Georgia. His Polish father was a teacher of French, his mother was Georgian. As a young man, corresponded with Marinetti. Graduated from Petrograd University, 1917. One of the first Russian futurists in Petrograd and Tiflis (Tbilisi). Left for Constantinople, 1920, and for Paris, 1921. Became a Dadaist. One of the founders of the poetic group Cherez. Organized poetry readings by V. Mayakovsky and A. Kusikov in Paris. Published books of modernist poetry and stunning typography. Over a period of 34 years, published 22 such books. The exhibition Iliazd and the Illustrated Book (18 June–18 Aug. 1987) in New York attracted a lot of attention. Died in Paris.

Zednik, Vladimir Iosifovich
7.5.1885–10.3.1962. Violin maker.
Born in the village of Seliduby in Volynskaia Gouvt. Moved to Petersburg. Became a famous violin maker after the 1917 Revolution. Many Soviet musicians play his violins. Died in Leningrad.

Zeidman, Boris Isaakovich
10.2.1908– . Composer.
Born in Petersburg. Professor from 1939. Taught at the Baku Conser-

vatory. Among his pupils were F. Amirov, A. Badalbeili, S. Gadzhibekov and Dzh. Dzhangirov. Taught at the Tashkent Conservatory from 1957. Author of operas (e.g. *Gore ot Uma*), a dramatic symphony, concertos for piano and orchestra, for alto, for bassoon, and for cello, 2 quartets, pieces for choir, romances, and music for plays and films.

Zel'dovich, Iakov Borisovich
8.3.1914–2.12.1987. Physicist.
Born in Minsk. Graduated from Leningrad University. Leading physicist. Made immense contributions in the fields of the physics of explosions, elementary particles and astrophysics. Involved in a number of military projects. Professor at Moscow University. Highly decorated (3 Orders of Lenin). Member of many foreign scientific institutions. Cambridge University awarded him an honorary doctorate. Tried in his later years to emigrate, but was twice prevented. Died in Moscow.

Zelenaia, Rina Vasil'evna (Ekaterina)
7.11.1902– . Actress.
Became very famous for her voice as a child. Acted on radio, in the theatre and in films. Graduated from a theatrical school, Moscow, 1919. Began as an actress in Petrograd theatres, performing in such plays as *Ne Rydai* and *Balaganchik*. Moved to Moscow, where she appeared at the Satire, and Variety and Miniatures Theatres. Entered the film industry, 1931. Became a very popular comedienne. Films include: *Putevka v Zhizn*, 1931; *Podkidysh* and *Svetlyi Put'*, 1940; and *Inostranka* and *Tri Tolstiaka*, 1966. Very popular with Soviet children.

Zelenin, Eduard (Zelenine, Edouard)
1938– . Artist.
Born in Novokuznetsk, Kemerovskaia Oblast'. Studied at the Sverdlovsk Art School, 1954. Moved to Leningrad, 1958. Studied at the Repin Academy of Arts. Expelled from the Academy for formalism. Returned to his birthplace, where he worked in various jobs. Moved to Moscow. Played an active part in the non-conformist art movement. Clashed with the Soviet cultural

authorities, and was expelled from the USSR. Moved to Paris, 1975. Many exhibitions all over Europe. Visited Moscow, Oct. 1988. Received a lot of attention from fellow artists.

Zelenoi, Aleksandr Pavlovich
1872–1922. Vice-admiral.
Graduated from the Naval Corps, 1892. Took part in WWI as a vice-admiral, 1917. Joined the revolutionary forces, 1918. Appointed Head of the Red Naval Forces in the Baltic, 1918–20.

Zelinskii, Nikolai Dmitrievich
1861–1953. Scientist.
Graduated from Odessa University, 1884. Thereafter, spent practically all of his life as a professor at Moscow University, 1893–1953. Member of the Academy of Sciences of the USSR, 1929. Founded the Institute of Organic Chemistry of the Academy of Sciences, 1934. Authority on petrochemical research with a worldwide reputation.

Zel'ma, Georgii Anatol'evich
1906–1984. Photographer.
Born in Tashkent, Uzbekistan. In 1921, moved with his family to Moscow. Started taking amateur pictures with an old Kodak camera. Apprentice at the Russfoto Agency which supplied pictures to the foreign press. In 1924, sent by Russfoto back to his native Tashkent to become their Central Asian photo-correspondent. His knowledge of the Uzbek language meant that the Agency was provided with detailed captions and picture reports. From the late 1920s until the war, worked for various Moscow newspapers and magazines including *USSR in Construction*, *Krasnaia Zvezda*, *Izvestia* and the Soiuzfoto Picture Agency. Commissioned by Roman Karmen, the famous documentary maker, to produce stories entitled *The USSR From the Air* and *Ten Years of the Iakut Soviet Socialist Republic*. Both stories were published in *USSR in Construction*. With Maks Alpert, produced a special issue about the chemical works in Solikamsk. During WWII, correspondent for *Izvestia*. After the war, worked for the magazine *Sovetskaia Zhenshchina*.

See: *Soviet Photography, 1917–40*, London, 1984.

Zemliachka, Rozalia Samoilovna (b. Salkind; m. Samoilova; party names – Demon, Osipov)
1.4.1876–21.1.1947. Revolutionary, Cheka official.
Born in Kiev. Member of the SD Party from 1896. Co-opted onto the Cen. Cttee. of the SD Party in 1903. Active participant in the 1905 Revolution in Moscow. Several arrests. Secretary of the party organization in Baku, 1909. Emigrated from Russia, but returned during WWI. During the Civil War, head of the political departments of the 8th and 13th Armies. After Wrangel's defeat, Secretary of the Crimean party obkom, Nov. 1920. Responsible (with Bela Kun) for the blood-bath in the Crimea in the aftermath of the Civil War. In the early 1920s, Secretary of Zamoskvoretsk raikom in Moscow. Held many high party posts. Member of the Cen. Cttee. of the CP, 1939. Deputy Prime Minister of the USSR, 1939–43. Died in Moscow, buried at the Kremlin wall.

Zemtsov, Il'ia Grigor'evich
1938– . Sociologist, author.
Born in Baku. Published several sociological works in the Soviet Union. Became involved with the Jewish rights movement. Emigrated, 1973. Settled in Israel. Director of the Jerusalem International Research Center on Contemporary Society. Published research on Iu. Andropov, on the social life of the Soviet ruling class (*Chastnaia Zhizn' Sovetskoi Elity*, London, 1986) and other contemporary Soviet subjects.

Zenkevich, Boris Aleksandrovich
1888–1962? Artist.
In 1911, living as a political emigré in Liège, studied privately under F. Marechal, then at the studio of I.P. Pokhitonov. Later studied at the Saratov Bogoliubov Art School, 1917, then in the Saratov Higher Art Shops, 1918, under A. Savinov. Genre and landscape painter and graphic artist. Exhibitions in Saratov from 1919. Other exhibitions: Moscow, 1925–26, 1929; Moscow, 1927 (two exhibitions); Leningrad, 1932;

Moscow, 1933; Moscow-Leningrad, 1933; Kiev, 1934; Moscow, 1939, 1941, 1943, 1945, 1947, 1951–52, 1954, 1957. Personal exhibition with A. Lentulov and N. Chernyshev, Moscow, 1940.

Zenkovskii, Vasilii Vasil'evich, Archpriest
4.7.1881–5.8.1962. Philosopher, psychologist, theologian.
Born at Proskurov. Son of a headmaster. Graduated from Kiev University, 1909. Professor of psychology at Kiev University, 1915–1919. Under Hetman Skoropadsky during the Civil War, Ukrainian Minister of Culture and Religious Affairs. Left Russia in 1919. Professor of philosophy and theology at Belgrade University, 1920–3. Director of the Pedagogical Institute in Prague, 1923–6. Professor of philosophy at the St. Sergius Theological Institute in Paris, 1926–62. Priest, 1942. Doctor of theology, 1948. One of the best-known representatives of Russian Orthodoxy in the West. Active in youth work among Russian emigrés. Author of a standard 2 vol. work on Russian philosophy. Died in Paris.
Main works: *Psikhologiia Rebenka*; *Russkie Mysliteli i Evropa*; *Istoriia Russkoi Filosofii*, 2 vols; *Apologetica*; *Osnovy Khristianskoi Filosofii*; *Gogol*.

Zenzinov, Vladimir Mikhailovich
1880–20.10.1953. Politician.
Born in Moscow. Son of a merchant. Educated at German universities, 1904. Joined the Moscow committee of the SRs, 1905. Joined the terrorist group of the SRs, 1906. Member of the Cen. Cttee of the SR Party, 1909. Member of the Executive Cttee of the Petrograd Soviet, 1917. Editor of the SR newspaper *Delo Naroda*. Active opponent of the Bolshevik take-over, 1917. Member of the Ufa Directoria, 1918. Emigrated, 1920. Settled in France. Representative of the SRs abroad. Close to Kerenskii, worked in his newspaper *Dni* in Paris. Member of the editorial board of *Sovremennye Zapiski*, Paris, until his death. Suppressed the publication of the 4th chapter of Nabokov's *Dar*, a parody on N. Chernyshevskii. Wrote memoirs. Moved to the USA, and died in New York.

Zernov, Mikhail Stepanovich
1857–1938. Doctor.
Well-known Moscow doctor. Founded the sanatorium at Essentuki in the Caucasus, which became the favourite rest home of the Moscow intelligentsia. His children later became well-known figures in the Russian emigré communities in Britain and France.

Zernov, Nikolai Mikhailovich
9.10.1898–25.8.1980. Theologian, church historian.
Born in Moscow. Studied medicine in Moscow, 1917. After the Civil War, emigrated, 1920. Graduated from Belgrade University in Theology, 1925. PhD, Oxford, 1932. Lecturer in Eastern Orthodox culture at Oxford University, 1947. Active in the Orthodox youth movement and in the oecumenical movement. Doctor of Theology at Oxford University, 1966. Died in Oxford.
Main Works: *St. Sergius–Builder of Russia*; *The Church of the Eastern Christians*; *The Ecumenical Church and Russian Orthodoxy*; *The Russian Religious Renaissance of the 20th Century*; *Na Perelome*; *Za Rubezhom*.

Zerov, Mykola
1890–1941. Poet, literary critic.
Considered to be the founder of modern Ukrainian literary scholarship. Taught literature at Kiev University in the 1920s and 1930s. Arrested, 1935. Died as a Gulag camp inmate.

Zhabotinskii, Leonid Ivanovich
28.1.1938– . Athlete.
Born in the village of Uspenka, Sumskaia Oblast'. Honoured Master of Sports (weight-lifting), 1964. Graduated from the Khar'kov Pedagogical Institute, 1964. Member of the CPSU, 1964. World record-holder, 1963–70. USSR champion, 1964–69. World champion, 1964–66 and 1968. Olympic champion, 1964 (572,5kg). European champion, 1966 and 1968. Author of *Stal' i Serdtse*, Moscow, 1969.

Zhadov, Aleksei Semenovich
1901–1977. General.
Joined the Red Army, 1919. Took part in the Civil War. Joined the Communist Party, 1921. Graduated from the Frunze Military Academy, 1934. During WWII, Commander of the Airborne Troops Corps. After the war held several high commands, including head of the Frunze Military Academy.

Zhalakiavichus, Vytautas
14.4.1930– . Film director.
First Soviet Lithuanian director at the Lithuanian Film Studio, which was set up in 1949. He directed his first film, *Drowned*, in 1956, while still a student. Graduated from the VGIK as a director in 1958. Moved to Mosfilm in the early 1970s. Specializes in political subjects – mainly the establishment of Soviet rule in Lithuania, and WWII. Films include *No One Wanted to Die*, 1965, *That Sweet Word Freedom*, 1973, and *The Accident*, 1974.

Zharmukhamedov, Alzhan Musurbekovich
2.10.1944– . Athlete.
Born near Tashkent, Uzbek SSR. Graduated from the Uzbek Institute of Physical Culture, 1967. Honoured Master of Sports (basketball), 1979. With the Moscow Military Forces team. European champion, 1967, 1971 and 1979. USSR champion, 1970–74, 1976–79. Olympic champion, 1972. Bronze medal, 1976.

Zharov, Aleksandr Alekseevich
1904–1984. Poet.
Joined the Communist Party in 1920. Became an established poet. Author of propaganda verse, including verse for children. His words have been set to music for voice and orchestra by various composers.

Zharov, Sergei Alekseevich
20.3.1896–1984. Conductor, choir master.
Cossack officer during WWI. Evacuated with the Whites after the Civil War. In the Balkans with his former comrades-in-arms created the Don Cossack Choir, which soon became world-famous. Toured Europe and America with great success. A diminutive, boyish figure, he created a strong impression with his firm command of the giant singers in Cossack uniform. Before WWII, took his choir to the United States, and made America their home. After WWII, started touring again, and was especially popular in Germany and France. Died in America.

Zhavoronkov, Semen Federovich
1899–1967. Marshal.
Joined the Bolshevik Party, 1917. Took part in the Civil War. Graduated from the Military Political Academy, 1926, and from the Zhukovskii Air Force Academy, 1936. Commander of the Pacific Fleet Air Force, 1938–39. Commander of the Soviet Navy Air Force, 1939, and during WWII. Head of the Civil Aviation Administration, 1949–57, and 1st Deputy Head of Civil Aviation, 1957–59.

Zhdanov, Andrei Aleksandrovich
26.2.1896–31.8.1948. Politician.
Born in Mariupol (now Zhdanov). Joined the Bolsheviks, 1915. Revolutionary propagandist in the reserve regiments in the rear of the army during WWI. Chairman of the first Soviet in Shadrinsk, Mar. 1917. Political commissar with the Reds during the Civil War. Later, party boss in the provinces (Tver', Nizhnii Novgorod). Member of the Cen. Cttee. of the Bolshevik Party during the collectivization, 1930. Secretary of the Cen. Cttee., member of Orgburo, 1934. Replaced Kirov after his assassination as the party boss in Leningrad. Member of the Politburo, 1939. One of the most trusted aides of Stalin. During WWII, involved in the defence of Leningrad against the Germans. After the war, attacked prominent writers (Zoshchenko, Akhmatova). As Stalin's controller of culture, initiated the most obscurantist period in Soviet history ('zhdanovshchina'). Died in Moscow.

Zhdanov, Viktor Mikhailovich
13.2.1914– . Virologist.
Born in the Ukraine. Graduated from the Khar'kov Medical Institute 1936. Member of the CPSU from 1941. Head of Laboratory and Director of the Institute of Microbiology and Epidemiology in Khar'kov, 1946–50. Head of Laboratory of

the Institute of Virology of the USSR Academy of Medical Sciences from 1951, and later head of the whole institute. Member of the USSR Academy of Sciences from 1960. In charge of a team of medical scientists working on AIDS.

Zhdanovich, Viktor Frantsevich
27.1.1938– . Athlete.
Born in Leningrad. Honoured Master of Sports (fencing), 1960. With Leningrad Burevestnik. Graduated from the Leningrad Institute of Physical Culture, 1963. USSR champion, 1959. World champion, 1959–63. Olympic champion, 1960 and 1964.
See: *Leningradtsy-Olimpiitsy,* Leningrad, 1973.

Zhebelev, Sergei Aleksandrovich
22.9.1867–28.12.1941. Historian, archaeologist.
Born in Petersburg. Specialist in classical antiquity. Graduated from Petersburg University, 1890. Professor at the University, 1904–27. Wrote a classical introduction to archaeology, 2 vols, 1923, and many monographs on historical and archeological subjects. Translated Plato, Aristotle, and other classical thinkers. Directed archaeological research near the north coast of the Black Sea. Academician, 1927. Died of hunger during the Siege of Leningrad.

Zhedrinskii, Vladimir Ivanovich
1890?–1974. Stage designer.
Emigrated after the Civil War. Settled in Yugoslavia. Moved to France, 1952. Chief designer at the Nice Opera House, he transformed the theatre into an art centre with a world-wide reputation.

Zhelezniak, Iakov Il'ich
10.4.1941– . Athlete.
Born in Odessa. Honoured Master of Sports (shooting), 1972. With Odessa Dynamo. Graduated from the Odessa Pedagogical Institute, 1969. World, European and USSR champion, 1965–77. World record-holder, 1972–74. Olympic champion, 1972.
See: A. Bashkatov, *Ia. Zhelezniak,* Moscow, 1976.

Zhelezniakov, Anatolii Grigor'evich (Zhelezniak)
1895–1919. Sailor, revolutionary.
Sailor in the Baltic fleet. During 1917, one of the revolutionary leaders of the sailors. At first an anarchist, later joined the Bolsheviks, and became one of the organizers of the Red sailors as the main military force of the Bolshevik take-over in Oct. 1917. Took part in the storming of the Winter Palace, Oct. 1917. Best remembered for his role as the Commander of the Bolshevik Guard of the Constituent Assembly, who closed the first and only session of the Assembly by declaring that 'the guard is tired'. During the Civil War, fought in the Ukraine (on ships and armoured trains). Mortally wounded near Verkhovtsevo station.

Zheliabuzhskii, Iurii Andreevich
24.12.1888–18.4.1955. Cameraman, director, scriptwriter.
Graduated from the Higher Technical School. Entered the film industry, 1915. Filmed the events of both the February and October Revolutions. Filmed Lenin and other political figures on many occasions. His first film was *Novoe Plat'e Korolia,* 1919. Turned to directing in the same year. Specialized in agit films, such as *Deti-Tsvety Zhizni* and *Gidrotorf.* Best known for his remarkable photography in *Polikushka,* 1922. From propaganda films he turned to fairy tales, including *Morozko,* 1924, and *Papirosnitsa ot Mossel'proma,* 1924. Made the wonderful film *Kollezhskii Registrator,* 1925, based on A. Pushkin's short story. Switched to animated films, and headed an animation studio from 1927. Taught at the VGIK, becoming a professor there.

Zhelobinskii, Valerii Viktorovich
27.1.1913–13.8.1946. Composer.
Born in Tambov. Author of operas, e.g. *Kamarinskii Muzhik* (1933), operettas, symphonies, concertos for piano and for violin with orchestra, instrumental pieces, romances, and music for plays and films. Died in Leningrad.

Zheludkov, Sergei Alekseevich
1910–1984. Russian Orthodox clergyman.
Born in Moscow. Priest, 1946.

Graduated from the Leningrad Seminary, 1954. Took part in samizdat activity, writing articles on religious subjects. One of the best-known religious dissidents in the 1960–70s.

Zhemchuzhina, Polina Semenovna (Molotova)
1896–1967. Politician.
Member of the Communist Party, 1918. Worked in the Ukraine. In the early 1920s, delegate to a Moscow conference of women's departments of party cttees. Met and married Molotov. Became the best friend of Stalin's wife, Nadezhda Allilueva. After 16 Nov. 1932, when Allilueva was found shot, Molotov and Ordzhonikidze were the first to be called to the scene with their wives. In the 1930s, Deputy Minister of the Food Industry, Minister of the Fishing Industry, Head of Glavparfiumer (perfume industry). During WWII, one of the leaders of the Anti-Fascist Committee of Soviet Jews. Had many conversations with Golda Meir when the latter came to Moscow as the Israeli Ambassador (the USSR being the first country to recognize Israel). In 1949, during the anti-Semitic campaign against cosmopolitism, she was arrested, while Molotov was replaced by Vyshinskii as foreign minister. Sent into exile, but in Jan. 1953, included in a group of 'Zionist conspirators', and tortured. After Stalin's death, released by Beria, who called her a 'true communist'. According to Stalin's daughter Svetlana, who visited the Molotovs in the early 1960s, she enthusiastically remembered Stalin as being the man who had saved the Soviet Union from the fifth column, and placed all her hope on the cultural revolution of Mao Tse-tung which was at that time in full swing. Died in Moscow.

Zhemchuzhnaia, Evgenia Gavrilovna (b. Sokolova)
1900–1982. Librarian.
Wife of the film director V.L. Zhemchuzhnyi. In Mar. 1925, met Osip Brik who had come to her library to research into I. Turgenev. Started an intimate relationship with him which lasted until his death 18 years later.

Zherebtsova-Andreeva, Anna Grigor'evna

25.9.1868–1944/45? Singer (mezzo-soprano).

Born in Grodno. Pupil of Natalia Iretskaia. Professor at the Petersburg Conservatory. Emigrated in 1922. Taught in Riga later in her life. Died in Riga.

Zherve, Boris Borisovich

1878–1934. Naval expert.

On active service in the Navy during the Russo-Japanese war, 1904–05, and WWI. Graduated from the Naval Academy, 1913. Joined the Red Navy, 1918. Professor, and later head of the Naval Academy, 1928–34. Author of works on naval history and theory.

Zhigalov, Aleksei

1915–1962. Athlete.

Honoured Master of Sports (diving). Many times USSR champion. 8th place at the XVth Olympic Games.

Zhigalova, Liubov'

1925–1978. Athlete.

Honoured Master of Sports (diving). Many times USSR champion. 6th place at the XVth and XVIth Olympic Games.

Zhiganov, Nazib Gaiazovich

15.1.1911– . Composer.

Born in Uralsk. Was orphaned, and grew up in children's homes. Musical training at the Kazan' Music Polytechnic, 1928–30, at the Music School attached to the Moscow Conservatory, 1931–35, and at the Moscow Conservatory, 1935–38. Pupil of Litinskii. Artistic director of the Tatar Theatre, 1939. One of the founders of the Kazan' Conservatory, and its director from 1945. Lecturer from 1947. Professor, 1953. His works are mainly operatic.

Zhigarev, Pavel Fedorovich

1900–1963. Marshal.

Joined the Red Army, 1919, and the Bolshevik Party, 1920. Graduated from the Zhukovskii Air Force Academy, 1932. Commander of the Soviet pilots in China, 1937–38. Head of the Training Department of the Air Force, 1938. In 1941, Commander of the Soviet Air Force, which was almost annihilated by the surprise German attack. Transferred to the Far East, 1942. Commander of the Strategic Bomber Force, 1948–49. Again Commander of the Soviet Air Force, 1949, and from 1953, Deputy Minister of Defence. Head of the Civil Aviation Administration, 1957, and head of the Anti-Aircraft Forces Academy, 1959.

Zhigilii, Liudmila Vasil'evna (Borozna)

2.4.1954– . Athlete.

Born in Leningrad. International Class Master of Sports (volleyball), 1972. Played for Leningrad Spartak. From 1975, with Moscow Dynamo. Works as an instructor at a training centre. Olympic champion, 1972. USSR champion, 1977.

Zhilenkov, Georgii Nikolaevich

1909–1946. General, politician.

Grew up in state orphanages. Rose to become a senior party functionary. Active Communist Party member. Before WWII, secretary of one of the Moscow party raikoms. Brigade Commissar in the 32nd Army. Near Smolensk, encircled by Germans and taken prisoner. Soon disguising himself as a private soldier, volunteered for a German unit as a Hilfswilliger, employed as a munitions driver. Did not reveal his true identity until he was about to be shot with a group of other Hiwis on suspicion of sabotage. Sent to Lotzen special camp, and later to Berlin, where he met General Vlasov's men. One of the first organizers of Russian anti-Stalin military units with the German Army during WWII. Joined General Vlasov and the ROA. Mainly active as a political and propaganda expert. Was suspected of being a Soviet agent by some of his comrades, who approached Vlasov's chief-of-staff, Kromiadi, with the suggestion of liquidating him. In 1945, handed over to SMERSH by the Americans in Germany. Imprisoned at Lubianka, sentenced to death and hanged.

Zhilinskii, Arvid Ianovich

1905– . Composer, pianist.

Born in Latvia. Lecturer at the Riga Conservatory. Author of an operetta, an opera, ballets, songs, choral works, and music for plays and films.

Zhilinskii, Boris Leonidovich

29.5.1890–18.10.1961. Pianist.

Born in Wil'no. Pupil of Sergei Liapunov and Karl Kipp. Close to Milii Balakirev. Soloist with the All-Union Radio, Moscow, in the postwar years. Died in Moscow.

Zhilinskii, Dimitrii

1934– . Artist.

His painting *1937* caused a furore in the summer of 1987 at the opening of an exhibition by members of the Soviet Academy of Arts, an important artistic event held once every 5 years in the huge state art gallery on the banks of the Moskva River. The painting – one of nearly 1,400 exhibits – depicts the artist's father standing pathetically in his underclothes with his arms in the air as 3 uniformed members of the secret police, the NKVD, hunt through his personal belongings and his family look on helplessly in fear and despair.

Zhilinskii, Iakov Grigor'evich

1853–1918. General.

Graduated from the General Staff Academy, 1883. Took part in the Russo-Japanese war, 1904–05. Chief of the General Staff, 1911–14. At the beginning of WWI, Commander of the North Western front. Widely held responsible for the Russian defeat by Hindenburg in East Prussia in 1914. Representative of the Russian Army HQ at the Allied Council in Paris, 1915–16.

Zhinovich, Iosif Iosifovich

14.5.1907– . Composer, cymbal player, conductor.

Born in Minsk Gouvt. Artistic director of the Belorussian Orchestra of Folk Instruments. Lecturer at the Minsk Conservatory. Author of works for folk instrument orchestras, a cymbal quartet, arrangements of folk songs, and a cymbals manual.

Zhirkov, Mark Nikolaevich

13.3.1892–15.4.1951. Composer.

Born in Viliuisk. Organizer of the

Iakut National Choir. Author of music for the Iakutsk Theatre, and of the first Iakutsk operas and ballets in co-operation with G. Litinskii. Died in Iakutsk.

Zhitomirskii, Aleksandr Matveevich
23.5.1881–16.12.1937. Composer.
Born in Kherson. Professor at the Leningrad Conservatory. Among his pupils were A. Balanchivadze and A. Gauk. Author of symphonic poems, a concerto for violin and orchestra, a string quartet, pieces for violin and cello with piano, romances, and arrangements of Jewish folk songs. Died in Leningrad.

Zhitomirskii, Daniel' Vladimirovich
22.12.1906– . Musicologist.
Born in Pavlograd. Taught at the Moscow Conservatory, 1930–48, and at the Gorkii Conservatory from 1956. Lecturer from 1936. Author of *Balety P. Chaikovskogo*, Moscow-Leningrad, 1950, *Robert i Klara Schuman v Rossii*, Moscow, 1962, and *Robert Schuman*, Moscow, 1964.

Zhivotov, Aleksei Semenovich
14.11.1904–27.8.1964. Composer.
Born in Kazan'. Known for his cycle of romances. Author of suites, a symphonic cycle, and music for plays and films.

Zhloba, Dmitrii Petrovich
1887–1938. Revolutionary, military commander.
Active in the 1905 Revolution, organizing communist workers in Nikolaev. Took part in the Bolshevik take-over in Moscow, Oct. 1917. During the Civil War, became a famous commander of the Red Cavalry, fighting the Cossacks of the White Armies. Victim of Stalin's purges.

Zhluktov, Viktor Vasil'evich
29.1.1954– . Athlete.
Born in Kramatorsk, Donetsk Oblast'. Honoured Master of Sports (ice-hockey), 1978. With the Central Sports Club of the Army. Student at the Moscow Aviation Institute. USSR champion, 1975–79. Olympic champion, 1976. World and European champion, 1978–79.

Zhmudskii, Vladimir Vladimirovich
23.1.1947– . Athlete.
Born in the village of Dubliany, L'vov Oblast'. From 1969, with the Central Sports Club of the Navy. Honoured Master of Sports (waterpolo), 1972. With Kiev Dynamo. Student at L'vov Institute of Physical Culture. European champion, 1966. USSR champion, 1970–78. Olympic champion, 1972.

Zhordania, Noi (Noah)
1864–1953. Politician.
Prominent Menshevik. During the Civil War, head of the government of independent Georgia, 1918–20. When the Red Army entered Georgia, emigrated to France, 1921. Wrote memoirs, published in the USA.

Zhordania, Vakhtang
1944– . Conductor.
Born in Tbilisi of a Georgian father and a Russian mother. Graduated from the Tbilisi Conservatory as a pianist, then from the Leningrad Conservatory as a conductor. Pupil of Evgenii Mravinskii, and his assistant for 3 years. Chief conductor of the Saratov Philharmonic, then for 6 years chief conductor of the Khar'kov Symphony Orchestra. Defected to the West in 1983, together with Viktoria Mullova, through Finland and Sweden. Has performed all over the world since then.

Zhubanov, Akhmet Kuianovich
29.4.1906– . Composer, musicologist, conductor.
Born in Aktiubinskaia Gouvt. Kazakh by nationality. Professor, and head of department, at the Alma-Ata Conservatory. Doctor of art history. Organizer of the People's Orchestra, 1934 (renamed the Kurmangazy Orchestra in 1944). Member of the Kazakh Academy of Sciences, 1946. Author of operas, tone poems on Kazakh themes, pieces for piano and for Kazakh folk instruments, songs, and music for plays and films. Literary works: *Struny Stoletii, Ocherki Zhizni i Tvorcheskoi Deiatel'nosti Kazakhskikh Narodnykh Kompozitorov*, Alma-Ata, 1958; *Solov'i Stoletii*, Alma-Ata, 1963 (in the Kazakh language).

Zhubanova, Gaziza Akhmetovna
2.12.1927– . Composer.
Born on a collective farm in the Aktiubinskii Oblast'. Daughter of the composer A. Zhubanov. Trained at the Gnesin Music School, 1945–49. Entered the Moscow Conservatory, 1949. Pupil of Iu. Shaporin. Graduated, 1954. Further training under the same teacher. Her work has an epic quality, and shows some folk influences. Director of the Alma-Ata Conservatory from 1975. Lecturer from 1975. Professor from 1978. Wrote operas, music for ballets, oratorios, works for children's choirs, cantatas and other pieces.

Zhuk, Isaak Abramovich
16.12.1902– . Violinist.
Born in Poltava. Pupil of Abram Iampol'skii. Father of the violinist, Valentin Zhuk. Conductor of the Bolshoi Theatre String Quartet from 1930, and of the State Symphony Orchestra of the USSR from 1952. Organized and directed the Bolshoi Theatre String Quartet from 1931.

Zhuk, Valentin Isaakovich
28.6.1934– . Violinist.
Born in Moscow. Son of the violinist Isaak Zhuk. Pupil of Abram Iampol'skii. 5th prize at the International Tchaikovskii Competition, 1958, 2nd prize at the Paganini Competition, 1963, and 2nd prize at the J. Thibaud Competition, 1961.

Zhukov, Aleksei Vladimirovich
31.12.1908–19.4.1967. Ballet teacher.
Born in Moscow. Graduated from the Moscow Theatre School, 1927. Dancer at the Bolshoi Theatre until 1951. Taught at the Moscow Choreographic School from 1932. Founder and head of ballet schools in Cairo, Egypt, 1958–63, and Phnom Penh, Cambodia, from 1966 until his death. Buried in Moscow.

Zhukov, Gavriil Vasil'evich
1899–1957. Vice-admiral.
Joined the Red Navy, 1918. Took part in the Civil War. During WWII, one of the main defenders of Odessa and Sevastopol. Head of the Black Sea Naval School, 1948–51.

489

Zhukov, Georgii Konstantinovich
1.12.1896–18.6.1974. Marshal.
Joined the Red Army, 1918. Took part in the Civil War. Commander of a cavalry regiment, 1923. Graduated from higher military courses for Red Army commanders, 1930. Became widely known as the commander of the Soviet forces which fought the Japanese at Khalkin Gol, 1939. Chief of the General Staff and Deputy Minister of Defence, Jan.–July 1941. When, at the start of WWII, the Soviet stars of the Civil War, Voroshilov, Budennyi and Timoshenko, demonstrated their complete incompetence, he became the most prominent of the younger generation who were put in charge of the army by Stalin. Appointed Commander of the Leningrad front and the Western Forces. In command at the time of the first serious German setback during the winter of 1941–42 before Moscow. Coordinated most of the Soviet Union's successful operations (the Battle of Stalingrad, the breaking of the Leningrad blockade, the Battle of Kursk, and the Battle of the Dnepr). Commander of the 1st Ukrainian Front, May–Mar. 1944. Commander of the 1st Belorussian front, Nov. 1944. Led the Soviet advance on Berlin, 1945. Became the best-known and most popular Soviet commander of WWII, despite his ruthless methods (such as clearing minefields by ordering his infantry through them). Soviet representative at the capitulation ceremony of the German armed forces, and 1st Commander of the Soviet Occupation Forces in Germany, 1945. Commander of Ground Forces and Deputy Minister of Defence, 1946. Soon after WWII, his personal archive was confiscated by the NKVD and Beria tried to get confessions from arrested Red Army officers implicating Zhukov in order to arrest him. Stalin, jealous of his popularity, transferred him to obscure posts as military district commander, 1946–53. After Stalin's death, again Deputy Minister of Defence, 1953. Instrumental in using the influence of the army to prevent Beria taking power. Rewarded by his appointment to the post of Minister of Defence, and with membership of the Cen. Cttee. of the CPSU, 1953–57. Helped Krushchev to defeat Molotov, Malenkov and Kaganovich in the struggle for power, but soon thereafter, while on a trip to Yugoslavia, suddenly dismissed by Khrushchev, who was afraid of his influence, and who accused him of 'Bonapartist tendencies', 1957. Received many Soviet and foreign honours and decorations (4 times Hero of the Soviet Union). Wrote memoirs of WWII, showing his great personal respect for Stalin as Supreme Commander, and his complete approval of Stalinist methods of leadership.

Zhukov, Leonid Alekseevich
20.4.1890–3.11.1951. Ballet dancer.
Born in Moscow. Graduated from the Moscow Theatre School, 1909. Soloist with the Bolshoi Theatre. One of its leading dancers during the 1920–30s. From 1923, combined his dancing with choreography. Choreographed, danced and taught in various ballet theatres all over the Soviet Union. Made several silent ballet films. Died in Moscow.

Zhukov, Pavel Semenovich
1870–1942. Photographer.
Born in Simbirsk. After secondary school, moved to Petersburg and became apprenticed to the then well-known photographer Konstantin Shapiro. Became a portrait photographer. The studio he worked in enjoyed the patronage of the Petersburg Academy of Arts, and as a young photographer, he was given the opportunity of visiting the Petersburg College of Arts and the Academy of Arts in Rome. Before the Revolution, took a series of portraits of distinguished personalities from Russian literature and art. Photographed Tolstoy, Chekhov, Kuprin, Tchaikovskii, Rubinstein, and others. Also took many photographs in factories, theatres, shops, and on the streets of Petersburg. After the October Revolution, appointed chief photographer of the political administration of the Petrograd military district. Documented many events and VIPs. In 1920, transferred to Moscow to photograph leading political and social figures, such as Kalinin, Lunacharskii and Chicherin. Responsible for one of the best known pictures of Lenin. During the 1930s, photographed 5-year-plan projects around the country. Died during the Leningrad blockade. A large part of his collection is held in the State Archive in Leningrad.
See: *Soviet Photography, 1917–40*, London, 1984.

Zhukovskaia, Glafira Viacheslavovna
8.5.1898–1978. Singer (soprano).
Born in Samara. Pupil of E. Konstantinov. Soloist with the Zimin Opera, 1923–25, and soloist with the Bolshoi Theatre, Moscow, 1925–48.

Zhukovskii, German L'vovich
13.11.1913– . Composer.
Born in Volynskaia Gouvt. Author of operas (e.g. *Pervaia Vesna*, 1960), ballets (e.g. *Rostislava*, 1955), a vocal-symphonic poem, pieces for piano, and violin and piano, choral works and music for films.

Zhukovskii, Nikolai Egorovich
17.1.1847–17.3.1921. Scientist, mathematician, aviation expert.
Born in the village of Orekhovo near Vladimir. Son of a railway engineer. Graduated from Moscow University in 1868. Professor of theoretical mechanics at the University from 1885. Professor at the Moscow Higher School of Engineering. President of the Moscow Mathematical Society, 1905. One of the foremost authorities in the world on aerohydrodynamics. Before WWI, worked on the theoretical problems of aeronautics, ballistics and hydromechanics. Organized the Aerohydrodynamic Institute, 1918, and in the early 1920s, the Aviation Engineering Academy. His work formed the basis of Soviet aviation design and industry. Died in Moscow.
Main works: *Collected works*, 9 vols, Moscow-Leningrad, 1935–37.

Zhukovskii, Stanislav Iulianovich
1873–1944. Artist.
Studied at the Moscow School of Painting, Sculpture and Architecture, 1892–98, under N. Kasatkin, K. Savitskii, S. Korovin, L. Pasternak, A. Arkhipov and I. Levitan. Landscape painter. Interior designer.
Exhibitions: Moscow School of Painting, Sculpture and Architecture, 1893–99; MTKH, 1895–96; MOLKH,

1895–1901; TPKHV, 1896–1918; Mir Iskusstva, 1902–03; the Union of Russian Artists, 1904–05, 1906–18, 1922–23; 2nd State Exhibition, Moscow, 1918–19. Personal exhibition: Moscow, 1921.

Zhurakovskii, Anatolii Evgen'evich

4.3.1897–10.10.1939. Russian Orthodox clergyman.
Born in Moscow. Son of a teacher. Educated at Tiflis and Kiev. Close to V. Zen'kovskii. Studied at Kiev University. During WWI, teacher at the front. Priest, 1920. Wrote religious works, took part in disputes with atheists in the 1920s in Kiev. Actively condemned the schisms of the 1920s in the church (Living Church, autocephaly). Arrested, 1923, held at Butyrki prison in Moscow, exiled to Krasnokokshaisk (Yoshkar Ola). Returned to Kiev, 1924. Joined the Iosiflane movement (who rejected Metropolitan Sergii's submission to the demands of the atheist government). Moved to Leningrad. Arrested, 1 Oct. 1930. Sentenced to death, commuted to 10 years in the Gulag. Inmate of Solovki, and construction worker on the Belomor Canal. For his open religious convictions he was again imprisoned and sentenced to 10 more years of Gulag. Died of exhaustion and tuberculosis. His letters and memoirs were published in France in the 1980s.

Zhurakovskii, Gennadii Evgen'evich

23.8.1894–10.3.1955. Teacher.
Brother of A.E. Zhurakovskii. Influenced by L. Tolstoy. Graduated from Kiev University. Taught at Kiev, and later in the 1930s, in Moscow. Specialist on the history of pedagogics, and also on the pedagogical works of Tolstoy, Pirogov and Makarenko.

Zhuravlenko, Pavel Maksimovich

11.7.1887–28.6.1948. Singer (bass).
Born in the Ukraine. Pupil of A. Sekar-Rozhanskii. Soloist with the Theatre of Musical Drama, 1912–18. With the Mariinskii Theatre from 1918, and concurrently with the Malyi Theatre. Died in Leningrad.

Zhuravlev, Pavel Nikolaevich

1887–1920. Partisan leader.
Organizer of Red partisans in Siberia, fighting the Cossack ataman Semenov. United the guerrilla groups into a partisan army, 1919. Fell in action.

Ziloti, Aleksandr Il'ich

9.10.1863–8.12.1945. Conductor, pianist.
Pupil of F. Liszt. Organized and conducted symphonic concerts in Moscow from 1903, and later in Petersburg. Teacher of S. Rakhmaninov. Appointed head of the (former) Imperial Theatres after the 1917 Revolution, but soon dismissed by Lunacharskii. Emigrated, 1919. Taught music in New York, 1924–42. Works: *Moi Vospominaniia o Liste*, 1911; *Vospominaniia i Pisma*, 1963.

Zimin, Aleksandr Nikolaevich

1904–1937. Politician.
Prominent Menshevik. Arrested 1921, re-arrested, 1922. Imprisoned in Moscow, exiled. Escaped, 1922. Underground party activity in Southern Russia (Khar'kov, Rostov), 1922. Re-arrested, 1923. Exiled to the Solovki concentration camp, and later to Narym, Siberia. Arrested for the last time in 1937, and probably shot the same year.

Zimin, Evgenii Vladimirovich

6.8.1947– . Athlete.
Born in Moscow. Honoured Master of Sports (hockey), 1968. With Moscow Spartak. Works as a coach. USSR champion, 1967 and 1969. European champion, 1968–69. World champion, 1968–69 and 1971. Olympic champion, 1968 and 1972.

Zimin, Petr Nikolaevich

16.5.1890– . Acoustics and musical instruments specialist.
Born in Chernigov. Worked at the GIMN (the State Institute of Musical Science). Author of *Fortepiano v ego Proshlom i Nastoiashchem*, Moscow, 1934. Also (with Sergei Tolstoi) *Sputnik Etnografa*, Moscow, 1929.

Zimin, Sergei Ivanovich

3.7.1875–26.8.1942. Impresario.
Born in Orekhovo-Zuevo. Son of a wealthy merchant. Organizer and owner of a private opera in Kuskovo near Moscow, 1904. Arranged performances in the Solodovnikov Theatre from 1908. Gave the opportunity to many young talents to prove themselves. Died in Moscow.

Zimmermann, Julius Heinrich

22.9.1851–25.4.1922. Music publisher, musical instrument manufacturer.
Born in Sternberg, Germany. Lived in St. Petersburg. In 1876, founded in St. Petersburg the famous music publishing house Zimmermann. In 1882, opened a Moscow branch, which was followed by branches in Leipzig in 1886, London in 1897, and Riga in 1903. His factory of musical instruments became world-famous. After the October Revolution 1917, lost everything and returned to Germany. Died in Berlin. His Frankfurt-on-Main branch still operates.

Zinger, Viktor Aleksandrovich

29.10.1941– . Athlete.
Born in the village of Davydovo, Riazan' Oblast'. Honoured Master of Sports (hockey), 1967. With Moscow Spartak. Graduated from the Moscow Institute of Physical Culture, 1973. World and European champion, 1965–69. USSR champion, 1967, 1969 and 1976. Olympic champion, 1968.

Zinov'ev, Aleksandr Aleksandrovich

1922– . Satirical author, dissident.
Born in Pakhtino, near Kostroma. During WWII, member of the Soviet Air Force. Graduated from Moscow University in philosophy (Marxism). Published works on philosophy in the Soviet official press. Became involved in the human rights movement. His satirical work *Ziiaiushchie Vysoty* was published abroad and created a world-wide sensation, 1976. Emigrated, 1978. Settled in West Germany. Published a number of other satirical works, giving colourful descriptions of the absurdities of communist society. Described himself as a 'homo sovieticus', and had deep insights into his chosen subject.

Zinov'ev, Grigorii Evseevich (Apfelbaum, Radomyslskii)

1883–1936. Politician.
Born in Elizavetgrad. Member of the

Social Democratic (Labour) Party from 1901. Emigrated in 1902. In 1903, met Lenin and became his closest collaborator abroad until 1917. Lived in Bern, returned to Russia, again went abroad in 1905. Returned after the 1905 Revolution. In 1907, member of the Cen. Cttee. of the Bolshevik Party. Arrested in 1908. After a few months, released, emigrated again. From 1908, co-editor of all Lenin's publications. After the start of WWI, with Lenin in Galicia (Austro-Hungary) and in Switzerland. Took part in the Kienthal and Zimmerwald conferences. During WWI, the Cen. Cttee. of the Bolshevik Party was virtually in the hands of Lenin and Zinov'ev. Returned with Lenin on the sealed train through Germany in 1917. After the unsuccessful Bolshevik revolt in July 1917, went into hiding with Lenin at Razliv. With Kamenev, opposed Lenin's plan to seize power in Oct. 1917. After Oct. 1917, Chairman of the Petrograd Soviet. After the Soviet government moved to Moscow in Mar. 1918, remained in Petrograd as practically the dictator of the city and all Northwestern Russia. Responsible for the first wave of terror in Petrograd in 1918–19. Candidate member of the Politburo in 1919 and full member from 1921–26. Head of the Comintern. During the Kronstadt revolt, panicked and was saved by Trotsky and Tukhachevskii. Helped Stalin to defeat Trotsky in 1923–24. Tried (with Kamenev) to seize power, but was defeated by Stalin and Bukharin in 1925. Made a new unsuccessful attempt to seize power (with Trotsky). Lost all his posts and influence in 1926. Several times (on Stalin's orders) expelled from the party, and re-admitted. Became the chief accused at the famous show trials in 1935 and 1936. Sentenced to death, and executed. One of Lenin's closest collaborators among the old Bolshevik guard. Remembered mostly for his rule of terror in Petrograd after the 1917 Revolution, his fiery speeches at international conferences of the Comintern in the 1920s, and his pathetic appearance at the Stalinist show trials in the 1930s. Rehabilitated under Gorbachev, 1988.

Ziv, Mikhail Pavlovich
25.5.1921– . Composer.
Born in Moscow. Author of an operetta, an oratorio, symphonies and suites. Also wrote the music for the famous film *Chistoe Nebo* (by G. Chukhrai), and for other films and plays.

Zlatogorova, Bronislava Iakovlevna
20.5.1905– . Singer (mezzo-soprano).
Born in Kiev Gouvt. Pupil of A. Sperling and Elena Murav'eva. Soloist with the Bolshoi Theatre, 1929–53.

Zlatovratskii, Aleksandr Nikolaevich
1878–1959. Sculptor.
Pupil of Sergei Konenkov, 1895–1900. Studied at the Petersburg Academy of Arts, 1900–05, under G. Zaleman and V. Beklemishev. Exhibitions: Moscow Association of Artists, 1908, 1911; State Modern Sculpture, Moscow, 1926; ORS, 1927, 1929, 1931; Leningrad, 1932; Moscow, 1933; Moscow Sculptors, 1937; Moscow, 1939–40, 1945, 1953. Died in Moscow.

Zof, Viacheslav Ivanovich
1889–1937. Revolutionary, politician.
Member of the Bolshevik Party, 1913. In the summer of 1917, helped Lenin to go underground after the unsuccessful Bolshevik revolt in July. During the Civil War, Bolshevik organizer in the Baltic fleet. Head of the revolutionary naval forces, 1924–26. Chairman of the Soviet Trade Shipping Administration (Sovtorgflot), 1927. Deputy Minister of Water Transport, 1930–31. Liquidated by Stalin.

Zolotarev, Vasilii Andreevich
7.3.1872–25.5.1964. Composer.
Born in Taganrog. Professor. Taught at the Moscow and Kuban' conservatories, 1909–1918, at the Odessa and Kiev Institutes of Musical Drama, the Sverdlovsk Technical School for Music, and the Minsk Conservatory, 1933–41. Among his pupils were Z.L. Polovinkin, K. Dan'kevich, A. Svechnikov, A. Bogatyrev, M. Kroshner, V. Efimov, D. Lukas and M. Vainberg. Author of 3 operas, a ballet, 7 symphonies, rhapsodies, suites, 6 string quartets, cantatas, choral works and romances. Died in Moscow.

Zonina, Ekaterina Nikolaevna
1919– . Artist.
Miniature-painter. Studied at the Mstera Professional-Technical Art School. From 1937, has lived and worked in Mstera. Exhibitions: Vladimir, 1947–49, Moscow, 1949.

Zoshchenko, Mikhail Mikhailovich
10.8.1895–22.7.1958. Author, humorist.
Born in Petersburg of Ukrainian parentage. While a law student at Petrograd University during WWI, volunteered for the army. Enrolled at Pavlovskoe Military School. Infantry-lt. in 1915, wounded and poisoned by gas at the front in July 1916. Retired from the army in Mar. 1917 as a captain. Lived in Petrograd during both revolutions 1917. Joined the Red Army in 1918, but left it in 1920. Member of the literary group the Serapion Brothers. During NEP in the 1920s, became widely known as a humorist. First book, *Rasskazy Nazara Il'icha*, 1922. In his short stories, he depicted the confused and defenceless man in the street, up against the revolution and all its twists, and trying to move along with the times, as well as the emerging New Class. During WWII, evacuated to Kazakhstan with other writers. In the post-war campaign against modernism, became a target of vicious attacks initiated by Zhdanov. Expelled from the Writers Union (together with A. Akhmatova). His works appeared in print again only after Stalin's death during the thaw in 1956. Died in Leningrad. Enormously popular among readers in the USSR.
Works: *Pered Voskhodom Solntsa*; *Rasskazy*.

Zozulia, Fedor Vladimirovich
1907–1964. Admiral.
Joined the Red Navy, 1925. Member of the Communist Party, 1938. Graduated from the Navy Academy, 1938. Several staff positions in the Caspian and Baltic fleets before and during WWII. Chief-of-staff of the Navy, 1958–64, and 1st Deputy Commander of Naval Forces.

Zubkov, Ivan Ivanovich
1883–1938. Artist.
Miniature painter. A Palekh master. A member of the team which decorated the Leningrad Pioneer Palace. Exhibitions: The Art of Palekh, Moscow, 1932; Folk Art, Moscow, 1937. Worked in papier-maché. Made many Palekh miniature objets d'art.

Zubovich, Boris, Baron
(de Zoubovitch, Bob)
1899– . Film director, cameraman.
Born in Russia. Both his parents came from the Baltic provinces. Studied film-making in Moscow. Left Russia, 1923 and moved to France. Settled in Paris. Cameraman for 20th Century Fox, 1944–45. Took part in the filming of the liberation of Paris, 1944. Turned to directing and became a famous animator. His puppet films – Le Briquet Magique and Au Clair de la Lune – are regarded as masterpieces of French cinema. Operated some 300 puppets. Opened his own puppet film studio in the 1960s. Lives near Paris.

Zurov, Leonid Fedorovich
1902–1971. Author.
Born near Pskov. Emigrated after the Civil War. Considered to be a promising young writer in the 1920s and 1930s. Lived together with his fiancée, the writer Galina Kuznetsova, with Ivan Bunin in the south of France. After WWII, contributor to the Parisian Soviet newspaper Sovetskii Patriot. Contributed to several Russian emigré publications, including Novyi Zhurnal. Died in Paris in a psychiatric asylum.

Zverev, Anatolii Timofeevich
1931–8.12.1986. Artist.
In the 1970s, became a famous non-conformist artist. Took part in the so-called Bulldozer Exhibition. Exhibited in Moscow, Leningrad, Paris and Amsterdam. Died in Moscow. A major posthumous exhibition, held in Sept. 1988 in Tbilisi (Georgia), attracted considerable attention.

Zverev, Vasilii Ivanovich
20.7.1904– . Composer.
Born in Moscow. Author of sonatas, suites, pieces for wind instruments, works for choir, and romances.

Zybina, Galina Ivanovna
22.1.1931– . Athlete.
Born in Leningrad. Honoured Master of Sports (track and field athletics), 1952. Graduated from the Leningrad Pedagogical Institute, 1957. From 1960, with Leningrad Trud, USSR champion, 1952 and 1957 (javelin-throwing). World record-holder, 1952–59. European champion, 1954. Olympic champion, 1952 (shot-putting). Silver medal, 1956.

Zybtsev, Aleksei Lukich
19.6.1908– . Pianist.
Born in Voronezh. Pupil of Konstantin Igumnov. Professor at the Moscow Conservatory (classical chamber ensemble).

Zygin, Aleksei Ivanovich
1896–1943. Lt. general.
Took part in WWI and the Civil War. Graduated from the Vystrel Courses, 1928. During WWII, Commander of the 58th, 39th and 4th Guards. Fell in action.

Zykov, Meletii Aleksandrovich
1902?–1944. Journalist.
Born in Odessa. Son of a Jewish merchant. In the 1920s, member of the intellectual élite, knew Lenin and other Bolshevik leaders. In the early 1930s, married the daughter of Bubnov, the Minister of Education. Promoted from chief-editor of a provincial newspaper in Uzbekistan to N. Bukharin's Izvestia. After the execution of Bubnov and Bukharin, arrested and sent to the Gulag for 3 years. In 1940, released, and in June 1941 sent to the front as a political commissar. Taken prisoner by the Germans. Joined General Vlasov and became the editor of his paper Zaria, and his main specialist in ideology and propaganda. Became probably the only Jew in Nazi Germany with a communist past and Marxist leanings to hold a high official position. As a convinced liberal socialist, was much disliked by old emigrés. Never directly confirmed his Jewish origins, nor did he deny them. Because of this, a group of Vlasov's men had to guard him round the clock from the Gestapo. Recognized by both friends and enemies as a brilliant intellectual. Eventually kidnapped by the Nazi secret police, the SD, and disappeared. It is suspected that he was denounced by one of his old emigré enemies. Either shot, or died in a German concentration camp. No official investigation into his disappearance was ever carried out.

Revolutionaries, politicians, state officials, diplomats, party functionaries

A

Adamashin, A.L.
Adamovich, E.N.
Adzhemov, M.S.*
Afanas'ev, I.
Afanas'ev, S.A.
Afanas'ev, V.G.
Afanas'eva, A.S.
Aganbegian, A.G.   See also: Economists
Aksel'rod, P.B.*
Aleksandrov, A.P.
Aleksandrov, I.G.   See also: Economists
Alekseev, N.N.*
Aleksinskii, G.A.*
Aliev, G.A.R.
Alliluev, S.I.
Allilueva, N.S.
Andreev, A.A.
Andreeva, Z.A.
Andropov, I.V.
Antipov, N.K.
Antonov-Ovseenko, V.A.
Anvelt, I.I.
Aptekman, O.V.
Arbatov, G.A.
Argunov, A.A.*
Aristov, A.B.
Arkhipov, I.V.
Armand, I.T.
Aronson, G.I.*
Arosev, A.I.
Artem, F.A.
Ashenbrenner, M.I.
Astankova, E.V.
Astrov, N.I.*
Averichkin, F.S.
Avksent'ev N.D.*

B

Badaev, A.E.
Baibakov, N.K.
Bakaev, V.G.
Bakhirev, V.V.
Bakhmetev, B.A.*
Baranov, P.I.
Barmin, A.G.*
Baron, K.I.*
Basanavicius, J.*
Bazovskii, V.N.
Begma, V.A.
Beliaev, M.A.
Beliaev, N.I.
Beloborodov, A.G.   See also: State
   security, Red commanders
Belonogov, A.
Berdnikova, A.V.
Berens, E.A.
Berg, A.I.
Beria, L.P.   See also: State security
Berzin, I.A.
Bessmertnykh, A.A.
Biriukova, A.P.
Bobrinskii, A.A.*   See also: Aristocracy
Bobrinskii, V.A.*   See also: Aristocracy
Bobrovskaia, C.S.
Bodiul, I.I.
Bogatyrchuk, F.P.*   See also: Vlasov
Bogoliubov, K.M.
Bogomolov, D.V.

Bonch-Bruevich, V.D.
Borodin, M.M.
Bramson, L.M.
Breshko-Breshkovskaia, E.K.*
Brezhnev, I.L.
Brezhnev, L.I.
Briukhanov, N.P.
Bronskii, M.
Bublikov, A.A.
Bubnov, A.S.
Bukharin, N.I.
Bulach, T.O.
Bulatov, V.S.
Bulganin, N.A.
Burtsev, V.L.*
Butaev, K.S.
Bychkova, A.N.

C

Chaianov, A.V.   See also: Economists
Chaikovskii, N.V.*
Chaplin, B.N.
Chaplin, N.P.
Chernenko, K.U.
Chernov, V.M.*
Chernyshev, V.E.
Chicherin, G.U.
Chkheidze, N.S.*
Chkhenkeli, A.I.*

D

Dalin, D.I.*
Dan, F.I.*
Dan, L.O.*
Deich, L.G.
Demichev, P.N.
Demirchian, K.S.
Denike, I.P.*
Dinkov, V.A.
Dobrynin, A.F.
Dolgikh, V.I.
Dolgorukov, P.D.*   See also:
   Aristocracy
Donskoi, D.D.
Dubinin, I.V.
Dymshits, V.E.

E

El'kin, B.I.*
El'tsin, B.N.
Eliutin, V.P.
Emel'ianov, N.A.
Enukidze, A.S.
Ermash, F.T.
Evdokimov, G.E.
Ezhov, S.O.

F

Falin, V.M.
Fedorov, A.F.
Fedorov, M.M.*
Figner, V.N.
Filonenko, M.M.*
Finogenov, P.V.
Fondaminskii, I.I.*
Frolov, V.
Furtseva, E.A.

G

Gamarnik, I.B.
Ganetskii, I.S.
Gapurov, M.
Garvy, P.A.*
Gaven, I.P.
Gedymin-Tiudesheva, P.I.
Gegechkori, E.P.*
Geidarov, A.
Gerasimov, G.
Gessen, I.V.*
Gessen, V.M.*
Gikalo, N.F.
Glebov-Avilov, N.P.
Gnedin, E.A.
Gol'din, S.B.*
Gol'dman, L.I.   See also: Economists
Goloded, N.M.   See also: State security
Goloshchekin, F.I.
Golovin, F.A.
Goncharskaia, S.S
Gorbachev, M.S.
Gorbunov, N.P.
Goremykin, I.L.
Gorev, B.I.
Gostev, B.I.
Gots, A.R.
Grigorovich, I.K.*
Grishin, V.V.
Groman, V.G.   See also: Economists
Gromyko, A.A. junior
Gromyko, A.A.
Gubkin, I.M.   See also: Scientists
Guchkov, A.I.*
Gusev, F.T.
Gusev, S.I.
Gvozdev, K.A.

H

Halpern, A.I.*
Helfand, A.L.*
Hrushevskii, M.S.

I

Iakovlev, A.N.
Iakubovich, M.
Iaroslavskii, E.M.
Ioffe, A.A.
Ionov, I.I.
Iordanskii, N.I.   See also: Authors
Iurenev, K.K.
Izmailov, N.F.
Izvol'skii, A.P.*

K

Kachin, D.I.
Kaganovich, L.M.
Kalin, I.P.
Kalinin, M.I.
Kalinin, P.Z.
Kamenev, L.B.
Kamkov, B.D.
Kaplan, F.
Karelin, V.A.*
Karotamm, N.G.
Karpov, V.
Karpovich, P.V.
Katushev, K.F.
Kazem-Bek*   See also: Clergy

* An asterisk denotes someone who emigrated at sometime in his or her life.

Kerenskii, A.F.*
Kerzhentsev, P.M.
Keskula, A.E.*
Kevorkov, B.S.
Kharchev, K.M.
Khatisov, A.I.*
Khitrun, L.I.
Khokhlov, I.S.
Khrushchev, N.S.
Khrustalev-Nosar', G.S.
Khudaiberdyev, N.D.
Kirichenko, A.I.
Kirov, S.M.
Kliuchnikov, I.V.
Kokoshkin F.F.
Kokovtsov, V.N.*   See also: Aristocracy
Kol'bin, G.V.
Kolegaev, A.
Kollontai, A.M.
Kol'tsov, M.E.   See also: Authors,
   journalists
Konovalov, A.I.*
Kornienko, G.M.
Korniets, L.R.
Kornilov, A.A*
Korotchenko, D.S.
Korsun, N.G.
Kosior, S.V.
Kostelovskaia, M.M.
Kosygin, A.N.
Kotel'nikov, V.A.
Kotliarevskii, S.A.
Kovalev, A.G.
Kozlov, F.R.
Kozlovskii, M.I.
Krasin, L.B.
Krasnoshchekov, A.M.   See also:
   Economists
Kravchenko, V.A.*
Krivoshein, A.V.*
Kropotkin, P.A.   See also: Aristocracy
Krupskaia, N.K.
Krylenko, N.V.
Krym, S.S.*
Krymov, A.M.
Kubikov, I.N.
Kugushev, V.A.   See also: Aristocracy
Kuibyshev, N.V.
Kuibyshev, V.V.
Kulishova, A.M.*
Kunaev, D.A.
Kuskova, E.D.*
Kvitsinskii, I.

L

Larin, I.   See also: Economists
Larionov, A.A.
Lashevich, M.M.
Lazimir, P.E.
Lenin, V.I.
Liakhovich, K.I.
Liashko, A.P.
Liber, M.I.
Ligachev, E.K.
Likhachev, I.A.
Likhtenshtadt, V.O.
Litvin-Sedoi, A.I.
Litvinov, M.M.
Liubimov, I.E.
Livshuts, A.*
Loginov, V.P,
Lomeiko, V.

Lomonosov, I.V.
Lomov-Opokov, G.I.
Luk'ianov, A.I.
Lunacharskii, A.V.
Lvov, G.E.*   See also: Aristocracy

M

Maevskii, V.A.   See also: Authors
Maiskii, I.M.
Makeev, N.V.*
Makhal'skii, V.K.   See also: Economists
Maklakov, V.A.*
Malantovich, P.N.
Malenkov, G.M.
Malevskii-Malevich, S.S.*
Mal'tsev, N.A.
Manuil'skii, D.Z.
Marchlewskii, I.I.*
Markov, N.E.
Martens, L.K.   See also: Authors,
   editors
Martov, L.*
Martynov, A.S.
Masherov, P.M.
Masliukov, I.D.
Medunov, S.F.
Medvedev, V.A.
Mekhlis, L.Z.
Miasnikov, A.F.
Miasnikov, G.I.
Mikhailov, V.M.
Mikoian, A.I.
Miliukov, P.N.*
Miliutin, V.
Mironov, F.K.
Molotov, V.M.
Morozov, N.A.   See also: Scientists
Mozhaev, P.
Mukashev, S.
Mukhlevich, R.A.
Murakhovskii, V.S.
Mzhavanadze, V.P.

N

Nabiev, R.N.
Nabokov, K.D.*
Nabokov, V.D.*
Naiashkov, I.S.
Nakhimson, S.M.
Natanson, M.A.
Naumov, A.N.*
Navashin, D.S.*
Nekrasov, N.V.
Nevskii, V.I.
Nikiforov, V.M.
Nikonov, V.P.
Nogin, V.
Novgorodtseva, K.T.

O

Obolenskii, V.A.*   See also: Aristocracy
Odinets, D.M.
Olitskaia, E.L.
Ordzhonikidze, G.K.
Osinskii, N.

P

Pal'chinskii, P.A.
Panina, S.V.*

Paskutskii, N.A.
Pavlov, S.P.
Pel'she, A.I.
Pepeliaev, V.N.
Pereverzev, P.N.*
Peshekhonov, A.V.*
Peterson, K.A.
Petrazhitskii, L.I.*
Petrosiants, A.M.
Petrovskii, G.I.
Petrovskii, V.F.
Petrunkevich, I.I.*
Piatakov, G.L.
Piatnitskii, I.A.
Plekhanov, G.V.   See also: Philosophers
Podbel'skii, V.N.
Podvoiskii, N.I.
Pogozheva, L.P.
Polovtsev, P.A.*
Ponomarenko, P.K.
Popov, D.M.
Popudrenko, N.N.
Posern, B.P.
Postnikov, S.P.*
Postyshev, P.P.
Potemkin, V.P.
Potresov, A.N.*
Primakov, E.M.   See also: Economists
Prokopovich, S.N.*   See also:
   Economists
Promyslov, V.F.
Proshian, P.P.
Protopopov, A.D.

R

Radek, K.B.   See also: Authors,
   journalists, editors
Randpere, V.*
Raskol'nikov, F.*
Razumovskii, G.P.
Reisner, L.M.
Riazanov, D.B.
Riisman, A.T.*   See also: Foreigners
   involved in Russian affairs
Rodzianko, M.V.*
Romanov, G.V.
Rotshtein, F.I.   See also: Authors,
   journalists, editors
Rozin', F.A.*   See also: Foreigners
   involved in Russian affairs
Rudenko, R.A.
Rudnev, N.A.
Rudnev, V.V.*
Rudzutak, I.E.
Rykov, A.I.
Ryzhkov, N.I.

S

Sagdeev, R.Z.   See also: Scientists
Sakharov, A.*
Sakharov, V.*
Samson, V.P.
Savinkov, B.V.   See also: Authors
Savitskii, P.N.*   See also: Economists
Sazonov, S.D.*
Seleznev, P.I.
Semashko, N.A.
Serov, V.M.
Shakhovskoi, D.I.*   See also:
   Aristocracy
Shalaev, S.A.

State security: CHEKA, GPU, OGPU, NKVD, MVD, MGB, KGB, GRU, SMERSH, agents-provocateurs, spies

State security

Grundman, E.I.
Guzenko, I.

I

Iagoda, G.G.
Iakovlev, I.K.
Ignat'ev, S.D.
Iurchenko, V.

K

Karatsiupa, N.F.
Kedrov, M.S.
Khenkin, K.V.   See also: Authors
Khokhlov, N.
Komarovskii, A.N.
Korzh, V.Z.
Kotel'nikov, V.S.
Krapivianskii, N.G.
Ksenofontov, I.K.
Kun, B.   See also: Foreigners involved
   in Russian affairs
Kurskii, D.I.
Kuz'min, N.N.
Kuznetsov, N.I.

L

Lamanov, I.I.
Lapin, A.I.
Latsis, M.I.
Leskov, A.N.
Levchenko, S.
Liushkov, G.S.
Lobov, S.
Lopukhin, A.A.
Lukach, M.Z.

M

Mal'kov, P.D.
Manevich, L.E.
Maslennikov, I.I.
Matrosov, V.A.

Matveev, A.P.
Menzhinskii, V.R.
Merkulov, V.N.
Molodtsov, V.A.

N

Naumov, M.I.
Nichkov, V.V.

O

Opperput, A.
Orlovskii, K.P.
Ostriakov, N.A.

P

Pavlunovskii, I.P.
Pen'kovskii, O.
Peters, I.K.
Philby, K.   See also: Foreigners involved
   in Russian affairs
Plevitskaia, N.V.   See also: Musicians,
   singers
Polenov, V.S.
Pontecorvo, B.M.   See also: Foreigners
   involved in Russian affairs
Prokopiuk, N.A.
Pugo, B.K.

R

Rakutin, K.I.
Reilly, S.G.
Reiss, I.
Rodos
Rossi, J.

S

Saburov, A.N.
Seina, V.
Semichastnyi, V.
Serov, I.A.

Shchelokov, N.A.
Shchetinkin, P.E.
Sheinin, L.R.   See also: Authors
Shelepin, A.N.   See also: Politicians
Skoblin, N.V.   See also: White military
   commanders
Smetanin
Sofinskii, V.N.
Sorge, R.   See also: Foreigners involved
   in Russian affairs
Sprogis, A.K.
Stashinskii, B.
Strokach, T.I.
Sudoplatov, P.
Suvorov, V.

T

Tal'berg, N.D.   See also: Authors
Telegin, K.F.
Tiniakov, A.I.   See also: Authors
Tretiakov, S.N.   See also: Politicians
Trifonov, V.A.
Tsinev, G.K.
Tsvigun, S.K.

U

Unshlikht, I.S.   See also: Politicians
Uritskii, M.S.

V

Vasiagin, S.P.
Vatsietis, I.I.
Vaupshasov, S.A.
Vershinin, S.I.
Vlasov, A.
Vlodzimirskii, L.E.
Vorob'ev, I.Z.
Vostretsov, S.S.

Z

Zaveniagin, A.P.   See also: Politicians
Zemliachka, R.S.   See also: Politicians

Military (general)

Agal'tsov, F.A.
Aganov, S.K.
Akhromeev, S.F.
Alafuzov, V.A.
Aleksandrov, A.
Alekseev, N.N.
Alekseev, R.E.
Aleshin, I.I.
Anisimov, N.P.
Antipenko, N.A.
Antonov, A.I.

B

Babadzhanian, A.K.
Badanov, V.M.
Bagramian, I.K.
Barinov, A.I.
Barsukov, E.Z.
Basistyi, N.E.
Batitskii, P.F.
Batov, P.I.
Bazhanov, I.P.
Beloborodov, A.P.

Belokoskov, V.E.
Belousov, L.G.
Belov, A.I.
Belov, K.
Belov, P.A.
Beregovoi, G.T.
Berzarin, N.E.
Biriuzov, S.S.
Blagonravov, A.A.
Bogatkin, V.N.
Bogdanov, S.I.
Bokov, F.E.
Bonch-Bruevich, M.D.
Borzov, I.I.
Budennyi, S.M.   See also: Red military
   commanders
Bugaev, B.P.

C

Chelnokov, N.V.
Cherepanov, A.I.
Cherevichenko, I.T.
Cherniakhovskii, I.D.

Cherniavin, V.N.
Cherokov, V.S.
Chibisov, N.E.
Chistiakov, I.M.
Chistiakov, M.N.
Chkalov, V.P.
Chuikov, V.I.

D

Degtiarev, G.E.
Demen't'ev, P.V.
Doronin, I.V.
Dovator, L.M.
Dragunskii, D.A.
Drozd, V.P.
Dubinda, P.K.
Dubovoi, I.N.
Dzhugashvili, I.I.

E

Efimov, A.N.
Efimov, P.I.

Efremov, M.G.
Egorov, G.M.
Egorov, M.A.
Eideman, R.P.
Eliseev, I.D.
Epishev, A.A.
Eremenko, A.I.
Ermachenkov, V.V.
Ermakov, A.N.
Evert, A.E.
Evstigneev, K.A.

F

Fabritsius, I.F.
Falaleev, F.I.
Fediuninskii, I.I.
Fed'ko, I.F.
Fedorenko, I.N.
Fedorov, E.P.
Fedorov, M.I.
Fesin, I.I.
Filatov, N.M.
Filatov, P.M.
Fil'chenkov, N.D.
Filipchenko, A.V.
Flerov, I.A.
Fomichev, M.G.
Fomin, N.S.
Frolov, A.S.
Frolov, V.A.

G

Gagarin, I.A.
Galler, L.M.
Gamarnik. I.B.   See also: Politicians
Gastello, N.F.
Gekker, A.I.
Gelovani, A.V.
Gel'vikh, P.A.
Gerasimenko, V.F.
Gerasimov, A.V.
Getman, A.L.
Gittis, V.M.
Glazunov, V.A.
Gluzdovskii, V.A.
Golenkin, F.I.
Golikov, F.I.
Golikov, L.A.
Golovanov, A.E.
Golovko, A.G.
Gorbatov, A.V.
Gordov, V.N.
Gorelenko, F.D.
Gorshkov, S.G.
Govorov, L.A.
Grave, I.P.
Grechkin, A.A.
Grechko, A.A.
Gren, I.I.
Grendal', V.D.
Griaznov, I.K.
Grigorenko, P.G.   See also: Human
  rights campaigners
Grishin, I.T.
Gritsevets, S.I.
Gromadin, M.S.
Gromov, B.
Gromov, M.M.
Gudymenko, P.E.
Gulaev, N.D.
Gusakovskii, I.I.

Gusev, N.I.
Gussein-zade, M.K.
Gutor, A.E.

I

Iakir, I.E.
Iakovlev, N.D.
Iakovlev, V.F.
Iakubovskii, I.I.
Iazov, D.T.
Ignat'ev, A.A.   See also: Aristocracy
Isakov, I.S.
Iumashev, A.B.
Iumashev, I.S.

K

Kachalov, V.I.
Kamanin, N.P.
Kamera, I.P.
Kamkov, F.V.
Kantaria, M.V.
Karbyshev, D.M.
Karioffi, G.S.
Kasatonov, V.A.
Kashcheeva, V.S.
Kashirin, N.D.
Katukov, M.E.
Kazakov, K.P.
Kazakov, M.I.
Kazakov, V.I.
Kazei, M.I.
Khadeev, A.A.
Kharkhanian, G.D.
Khalepskii, I.A.
Kharchenko, V.K.
Kharitonov, F.M.
Kharitonov, P.T.
Khetagurov, G.I.
Khlebnikov, N.M.
Kholostiakov, G.N.
Khomenko, V.A.
Khorun, I.I.
Khoruzhaia, V.Z.
Khozin, M.S.
Khrenov, A.F.
Khriukin, T.T.
Khrulev, A.V.
Khudiakov, S.A.
Khvesin, T.S.
Kirponos, M.P.
Kirsanov, P.S.
Kizhevatov, A.M.
Klembovskii, V.N.
Kleshcheev, A.E.
Klochkov-Diev, V.G.
Klubov, A.F.
Kniagnitskii, P.E.
Koldunov, A.I.
Kolpakchi, V.I.
Komarov, V.N.
Konev, I.S.
Konstantinov, A.U.
Korzhenevich, F.K.
Koshevoi, O.V.
Koshevoi, P.K.
Kosmodem'ianskaia, Z.A.
Kostenko, F.I.
Kostiaev, F.V.
Kotliar, L.Z.
Kovalenok, V.V
Krainiukov, K.V.

Krasil'nikov, S.N.
Krasnopevtsev, S.A.
Krasovskii, S.A.
Kravchenko, A.G.
Kravchenko, G.P.
Kreizer I.G.
Krivda, F.F.
Krylov, N.I.
Kukel', V.A.
Kulakov, N.M.
Kuleshov, P.N.
Kulik, G.I.
Kulikov, V.G.
Kurasov, V.V.
Kurkotkin, S.K.
Kurochkin, P.A.
Kuropatkin, A.N.
Kutakhov, P.S.
Kutiakov, I.S.
Kuznetsov, F.F.
Kuznetsov, F.I.
Kuznetsov, N.A.
Kuznetsov, N.G.

L

Laiok, V.M.
Lashchenko, P.N.
Lazarevich, V.S.
Lebedev, P.P.
Leliushenko, D.D.
Leonov, A.A.
Leonov, A.I.
Leonov, D.S.
Levandovskii, M.K.
Levanevskii, S.A.
Levchenko, G.I.
Liashchenko, N.G.
Liudnikov, I.I.
Lizichev, A.D.
Lobov, S.M.
Loginov, E.F.
Loktionov, A.D.
Lopatin, A.I.
Lopatin, A.V.
Losik, O.A.
Luganskii, S.D.
Lukin, M.F.
Lushev, D.G.

M

Makarov, V.E.
Maksimov, A.S.
Maksimov, I.P.
Malandin, G.K.
Malin, V.N.
Malinin, M.S.
Malinovskii, R.I.
Mal'tsev, E.E.
Malyshev, V.A.
Mamonov, S.K.
Manikovskii, A.A.
Mares'ev, A.P.
Margelov, V.F.
Mariakhin, S.S.
Martynov, E.I.
Matrosov, A.M.
Mel'nikaite, M.I.
Meretskov, K.A.
Mezheninov, S.A.
Mikhailov, M.E.

Military (general)

Molokov, V.S.
Moskalenko, K.S.

N

Nagornyi, N.N.
Naumenko, N.F.
Nedelin, M.I.
Nemitz, A.V.
Nevskii, G.G.
Neznamov, A.A.
Nikolaev, A.A.
Nikolaev, A.G.
Nikolai Nikolaevich (Romanov), Grand
  Duke   See also: Aristocracy
Novikov, A.A.
Novikov, N.A.
Novitskii, F.F.
Novitskii, V.F.

O

Odintsov, G.F.
Odintsov, M.P.
Ogarkov, N.V.
Oktiabr'skaia, M.V.
Oktiabr'skii, F.S.
Orlov, V.M.

P

Panfilov, I.V.
Panteleev, I.A.
Pantserzhanskii, E.S.
Parshin, G.M.
Parskii, D.P.
Pavlichenko, L.M.
Pavlov, D.G.
Pavlov, I.F.
Pavlov, P.A.
Pavlovskii, I.G.
Pen'kovskii, V.A.
Peredel'skii, G.E.
Peresypkin, I.T.
Perkhorovich, F.I.
Petin, N.N.
Petrov, I.E.
Petrov, V.I.
Pokrovskii, A.P.
Pokryshev, P.A.
Pokryshkin, A.I.
Pol'bin, I.S.
Poletaev, F.A.
Polivanova, M.S.
Poluboiarov, P.P.
Polynin, F.P.
Popkov, V.I.
Poplavskii, S.G.
Popov, M.M.
Porik, V.V.
Portnova, Z.
Preobrazhenskii, E.N.
Proshliakov, A.I.
Pshennikov, P.S.
Pstygo, I.I.
Psurtsev, N.D.
Pugachev, S.A.
Purkaev, M.A.
Putna, V.K.

R

Radzievskii, A.I.

Rakov, V.I.
Rall, I.F.
Raskova, M.M.
Razin, E.A.
Rediger, A.F.
Reiter, M.A.
Rennenkampf, P.K.
Riabikov, V.M.
Riabyshev, D.I.
Riazanov, A.K.
Riazanov, V.G.
Riumin, V.V.
Rodimtsev, A.I.
Rodin, A.G.
Roginskii, S.V.
Rogov, I.V.
Rokossovskii, K.K.
Romanenko, I.
Romanenko, P.L.
Romanovskii, V.Z.
Rotmistrov, P.A.
Rozhkov, P.F.
Rudakov, M.V.
Rudenko, S.I.
Rudnev, S.V.
Russkikh, A.G.
Rybal'chenko, S.D.
Rybalko, P.S.
Ryzhov, A.I.

S

Safonov, B.F.
Salmanov, G.I.
Samoilo, A.A.
Samokhin, M.I.
Sandalov, L.M.
Savitskaia, S.E.
Savitskii, E.I.
Sedel'nikov, F.S.
Semeiko, N.I.
Sen'ko, V.V.
Sergeev, A.V.
Sergeev, N.D.
Seryshev, S.M.
Shabalin, A.O.
Shabanov, V.M.
Shafranov, P.F.
Shakhurin, A.I.
Shapkin, T.T.
Shaposhnikov, B.M.
Sharokhin, M.N.
Shatalov, V.A.
Shavrov, I.E.
Shchadenko, E.A.
Shcheglov, A.F.
Shcherbakov, V.I.
Shevchuk, I.P.
Shilin, A.P.
Shilovskii, E.A.
Shkadov, I.N.
Shlemin, I.T.
Shmyrev, M.F.
Shorin, V.I.
Shtemenko, S.M.
Shtern, G.M.
Shubin, I.V.
Shumavtsov, A.S.
Shumilov, M.S.
Shurukhin, P.I.
Shvetsov, V.I.
Silant'ev, A.P.
Simoniak, N.P.

Sivkov, G.F.
Skomorokhov, N.M.
Skorikov, G.P.
Skripko, N.S.
Skvirskii, L.S.
Slashchev, I.A.
Slepnev, M.T.
Sliusarenko, Z.K.
Smirnov, A.S.
Smirnov, A.K.
Smirnov, I.K.
Smirnov, K.N.
Smirnov, N.I.
Smirnov, N.K.
Smirnov, P.A.
Smushkevich, I.V.
Snesarev, A.E.
Sobennikov, P.P.
Sofronov, G.P.
Sokolov, S.L.
Sokolovskii, V.D.
Sokol'skii, A.K.
Sologub, N.V.
Sorokin, I.L.
Sovetnikov, I.G.
Stalin, V.I.
Starikov, F.N.
Stashkov, N.I.
Stel'makh, G.D.
Stepanenko, I.N.
Stepanian, N.G.
Strod, I.I.
Stuchenko, A.T.
Subbotin, N.E.
Sudets, V.A.
Sukhomlin, A.V.
Sukhomlinov, V.A.   See also: Politicians
Sukhoruchkin, F.V.
Sukhorukov, D.S.
Susaikov, I.Z.
Svechin, A.A.
Svechnikov, M.S.
Sviridov, V.P.
Sysoev, V.S.
Sytin, P.P.

T

Talalikhin, V.V.
Taran, P.A.
Tereshkova, V.V.
Tevchenkov, A.N.
Timoshenko, S.K.
Titov, V.
Todorskii, A.I.
Tolbukhin, F.I.
Tolubko, V.F.
Tret'iak, I.M.
Triandafillov, V.K.
Tributs, V.F.
Trofimenko, S.G.
Trubnikov, K.P.
Trufanov, N.I.
Tsvetaev, V.D.
Tupikov, V.I.

U

Ubiivovk, E.K.
Ustinov, D.F.
Uverov, I.M.

V

Vakhrameev, I.I.
Vannikov, B.L.
Vasil'chikov, S.I.   See also: Aristocracy
Vasilevskii, A.M.
Vasil'ev, N.G.
Vatutin, N.F.
Vekman, A.K.
Velichko, K.I.
Verderevskii, D.N.
Verkhovskii, A.I.   See also: Politicians
Vershigora, P.O.   See also: Authors
Vershinin, K.A.
Vinogradov, N.I.
Vlasov, A.A.   See also: Vlasov's ROA

Vodop'ianov, M.V.
Voiachek, V.I.
Volkov, V.N.
Vol'skii, V.T.
Vorob'ev, M.P.
Vorob'ev, S.I.
Voronov,, N.N.
Vorozheikin, G.A.
Vostrukhov, V.I.

Z

Zaionchkovskii, A.M.
Zaitsev, M.M.

Zakharov, G.F.
Zakharov, M.V.
Zakharov, S.E.
Zakhvataev, N.D.
Zaporozhets, A.I.
Zaslonov, K.S.
Zelenoi, A.P.
Zhadov, A.S.
Zhavoronkov, S.F.
Zhigarev, P.F.
Zhilinskii, I.G.
Zhukov, G.K.
Zhukov, G.V.
Zozolia, F.V.
Zygin, A.I.

Red military commanders

A

Alksnis, I.I.
Altfater, V.M.
Anokhin, P.F.
Azin, V.M.

B

Baltiiskii, A.A.
Baryshnikov, V.A.
Bazilevich, G.D.
Beloborodov, A.G.   See also: State
   security, politicians
Belov, I.P.
Berzin, R.I.
Blinov, M.F.
Bliukher, V.K.
Bozhenko, V.N.
Bratoliubov, I.A.
Brusilov, A.A.
Budennyi, S.M.   See also: Military
   (general)
Buinakskii, I.D.

C

Chapaev, V.I.
Cheremisov, V.A.

D

Dakhadaev, M.A.
Dumenko, B.M.
Dundich, T.
Dushenov, K.I.
Dybenko, P.E.
Dzhangil'din, A.T.

E

Egor'ev, V.N.
Egorov, A.I.
Eikhe, G.K.

F

Frunze, M.V.
Furmanov, D.A.   See also: Authors

G

Gorbachev, B.S.

Gorodovikov, O.I.   See also: State
   security

I

Imanov, A.

K

Kakhovskaia, I.K.
Kakurin, N.E.
Kalandarishvili, N.A.
Kamenev, S.S.
Kamo, S.A.
Kazanskii, E.S.
Kikvidze, V.I.
Kireev, G.P.
Kliuev, L.L.
Kochubei, I.A.
Kork, A.I.
Kotovskii, G.I.
Kotsiubinskii, I.M.
Kovpak, S.A.
Kovtiukh, E.I.
Kravchenko, A.D.
Krivoshlykov, M.V.

L

Lazo, S.G.

M

Mamontov, E.M.
Markin, N.G.
Matveev, I.I.
Mezheraup, P.K.
Mikhnevich, N.P.
Murav'ev, M.A.

N

Nikiforova, M.

O

Odintsov, S.I.

P

Parkhomenko, A.I.

Pavlov, A.V.
Podtelkov, F.G.
Polivanov, A.A.
Poluian, I.V.
Polupanov, A.V.
Primakov, V.M.

S

Safonov, A.K.
Sediakin, A.I.
Shaumian, S.G.
Shchors, N.A.
Sheripov, A.D.
Sibirtsev, V.M.
Sikhver, I.K.
Sivers, R.F.
Smirnov, I.F.
Sobolev, A.V.
Stankevich, A.V.
Stepin', A.K.

T

Taube, A.A.
Tolmachev, N.G.
Tomin, N.D.
Tukhachevskii, M.N.

U

Uborevich, I.P.

V

Varvatsi, V.N.
Vasilenko, M.I.
Vedernikov, A.S.
Viktorov, M.N.
Voroshilov, K.E.   See also:
   Politicians

Z

Zhelezniakov, A.G.
Zhloba, D.P.
Zhuravlev, P.N.

White and nationalist military commanders

Alekseev, M.V.
Annenkov, B.V.
Antonov, A.S.
Arkhangel'skii, A.P.

B

Bandera, S.A.
Bermont-Avalov, P.R.
Bicherakhov, G.F.
Bicherakhov, L.F.
Bogaevskii, A.P.
Bulak-Balakhovich, S.N.

D

Denikin, A.I.
Drozdovskii, M.G.
Dukhonin, N.N.
Dutov, A.I.

G

Girei-Klych   See also: Vlasov's ROA,
    aristocracy
Golovin, N.N.   See also: Vlasov's ROA
Gotsinskii, N.
Grigor'ev, N.A.

I

Iudenich, N.N.
Ivanov, N.I.

K

Kaledin, A.M.
Kappel', V.O.
Khabalov, S.S.
Kharzhevskii, V.G.
Khorvat, D.L.
Kolchak, A.V.
Konovalets, E.
Kornilov, L.G.
Krasnov, P.V.   See also: Vlasov's ROA,
    authors
Kutepov, A.P.
Kuz'min-Karavaev, V.D.

L

Laidoner, I.I.
Lieven, A.P.   See also: Aristocracy

M

Makhno, N.I.
Malyshev, I.M.
Mamontov, K.K.
Markov, S.L.
Miller, E.K.

N

Nepenin, A.I.

P

Pepeliaev, A.N.
Petliura, S.V.
Piatnitsin, A.A.
Polkovnikov, G.P.
Pozdeev, K.R.

R

Ruzskii, N.V.

S

Semenov, G.M.
Shkuro, A.G.   See also: Vlasov's ROA

Shlakhtin, E.E.   See also: Vlasov's ROA
Skoblin, N.V.   See also: State security
Skoropadskii, P.P.   See also: Politicians
Smirnov, A.F.
Svechin, M.A.

U

Ungern von Sternberg

W

Wrangel, P.N.   *See also: Aristocracy

Z

Zaitsev, I.M.

Vlasov's ROA, WWII & similar anti-communist units

A

Aldan, A.G.
Artem'ev, V.P.
Azar, V.N.

B

Bogatyrchuk, F.P.   See: Politicans
Boiarskii, V.I.
Buniachenko, S.K.

G

Girei-Klych   See also: Aristocracy,
    white military commanders
Golovin, N.N.   See also: White military
    commanders

K

Kaminskii, B.
Kazantsev, A.S.   See also: Authors
Kononov, I.N.
Krasnov, N.N.

Krasnov, P.N.   See also: White military
    commanders, authors
Kromiadi, G.K.

L

Legostaev, F.M.   See also: Scientists

M

Mal'tsev, V.I.
Malyshkin, V..F

N

Naumenko, V.G.

P

Pozdniakov, V.V.   See also: Authors

S

Shatov, M.V.

Shkuro, A.G.   See also: White military
    commanders
Shlakhtin, E.E.   See also: White military
    commanders
Shteifon, B.A.
Shumuk, D.   See also: Human rights
    campaigners
Strik-Strikfeldt, W.K.   See also:
    Foreigners involved in Russian affairs

T

Trukhin, F.I.

V

Vlasov, A.A.   See also: Military
    (general)

Z

Zhilenkov, G.N.   See also: Politicians
Zykov, M.A.   See also: Authors, editors

Authors, poets, journalists, critics

A

Abovin-Egides, P.M.*
Abramov, F.A.
Adamov, A.G.
Adamovich, G.V.*
Adrianov, S.A.
Agurskii, M.S.*
Aigi, G.N.*
Aikhenvald, I.A.*
Aikhenvald, I.I.*
Aini
Aitmatov, C.
Akhmadullina, B.A.
Akhmatova, A.A.
Aksenov, V.P.*
Aldanov, M.A.*
Aldan-Semenov, A.I.
Alekseev, G.V.
Alekseev, M.N.
Aleshkovskii, I.E.*
Allilueva, S.I.*
Alpatov, M.V.
Amal'rik, A.A.*
Amfiteatrov, A.V.*
Andreas-Salome, L.*
Andreev, D.L.
Andreev, L.N.*
Andreev, V.L.
Andreevskii, S.A.
Anikst, A.A.
Antonov, D.A.*
Antonov-Ovseenko, A.V.
Anuchin, D.N.
Ardamatskii, V.I.
Arkanov, A.M.
Arsen'ev, K.K.
Arsen'ev, V.K.
Artsybashev, M.P.*
Arvatov, B.I.
Aseev, N.N.
Aspasia*
Averbakh, L.L.
Averchenko, A.T.*
Avtorkhanov, A.G.*

B

Babel', I.E.
Bachaev, M.*
Bagritskii, E.G.
Bakhrakh, A.V.*
Balmont, K.D.*
Baltrushaitis, I.K.*
Baltsvinik, M.A.
Balukhatyi, S.D.
Barabanov, E.V.
Barkhudarov, S.G.
Barkova, A.A.
Baumvol, R.L.*
Bazhan, M.
Bazhanov, B.*
Bazhov, P.P.
Bek, A.A.
Belinkov, A.V.*
Belinkova, N.A.*
Belotserkovskii, V.V.*
Belov, V.I.
Belyi, A.
Belykh, G.G.
Berberova, N.N.

Bergelson, D.R.
Berggolts, O.F.
Berkhin, V.
Berkov, P.N.
Bernstam, M.N.*
Betaki, V.P.*
Bezmenov, I.A.*
Bezymenskii, A.I.
Bialik, K.N.*
Bianki, V.V.
Bill-Belotserkovskii, V.N.
Biriukov, P.I.*
Bisk, A.A.*
Bitov, A.G.
Bitov, O.G.
Bliakhin, P.A.
Blok, A.A.
Boborykin, P.D.*
Bobrov, S.P.
Bobyshev, D.V.*
Bogatyrev, K.P.
Bokov, N.K.
Bokov, V.F.
Borovik, A.G.
Borovik, G.A.
Breitbart, E.A.*
Briusov, V.I.
Brodskii, I.A.*
Bukovskii, V.K.*
Bulgakov, V.F.
Bunin, I.A.*
Burenin, V.P.
Burliuk, D.D.*
Bykov, V.V.

C

Chalidze, V.N.*
Chebyshev, N.N.*
Chernyi, S.*
Chertok, S.M.*
Chinnov, I.V.*
Chornovil, V.M.
Chuguev, V.T.*
Chukovskaia, L.K.
Chukovskii, K.I.
Chulkov, G.I.
Churilin, T.V.

D

Daniel', I.M.
Danzas, I.N.*
Dar, D.I.*
Delone, V.N.*
Demin, M.E.*
Diushen, B.V.
Dolmatovskii, E.A.
Dombrovskii, I.O.
Doroshevich, V.M.
Dostoevskaia, A.G.
Dovlatov, S.D.*
Drozdov, A.M.
Drozhzhin, S.D.
Dudintsev, V.D.
Dzhalil', M.M.
Dzhambul, D.
Dzhanzugurov, I.

E

Efimov, I.M.*
Efron, A.S.*
Efron, S.*
Erenburg, I.G.
Ermilov, V.V.
Erofeev, V.
Esenin, S.A.
Etkind, E.G.*
Evtushenko, E.A.

F

Fadeev, A.A.
Fat'ianov, A.I.
Fedin, K.A.
Fedoseev, A.P.*
Fefer, I.S.
Filippov, B.A.*
Filosofov, D.V.
Forshteter, M.A.*
Furmanov, D.A.

G

Gaidar, A.P.
Galich, A.A.*
Galin, A.
Gal'perin, I.A.*
Ganina, M.A.
Gastev, A.K.
Gazdanov, G.I.*
Geller, M.I.*
German, B.V.*
Gershenzon, M.O.
Giliarovskii, V.A.
Ginzburg, E.S.
Gippius, Z.N.*
Gladilin, A.T.*
Gofshtein, D.N.
Gol'dshtein, M.E.*
Gol'dshtein, P.I.*
Gollerbakh, E.F.*
Golodnyi, M.S.
Golovach, P.R.
Golubinov, S.*
Gorbachev, G.E.
Gorbanevskaia, N.E.*
Gor'kii, M.
Gorodetskii, S.M.
Granin, D.A.
Grebenshchikov, G.D.*
Grin, A.S.
Grossman, L.P.
Grossman, V.S.
Gubarev, V.S.
Gul', R.B.*
Gumilev, N.S.
Gusev, N.N.
Gusev, V.M.
Gusev-Orenburgskii, S.I.*

I

Iakobson, A.A.*
Iakovlev, E.V.
Iashin, A.I.
Iashvili, P.D.
Ignatovich, B.V.
Il'f, I.A.

Rozovskii, M.F.
Rubin, E.M.*
Rybakov, A.N.
Rybakov, V.M.*
Ryl'skii, M.F.
Rzhevskii, L.D.*

S

Saburova, I.E.*
Salkazanova, F.*
Sapgir, G.V.
Savinkov, B.N.
Sedykh, S.*
Seifullin, S.
Seifullina, L.N.
Sel'vinskii, I.L.
Semenov, I.S.
Serafimovich, A.S.
Serebriakova, G.I.
Sergeev-Tsentskii, S.N.
Sevela, E.E.*
Severianin, I.V.
Shafarevich, I.R.
Shakhovskaia, Z.A.*
Shalamov, V.T.
Shapiro, M.L.
Shchepkina-Kupernik, T.L.
Sheinin, L.R.
Shelkovskii, I.S.*
Shershenevich, V.G.
Shifrin, A.I.*
Shik, A.A.*
Shiriaev, B.N.*
Shklovskii, V.B.
Shmelev, I.S.*
Sholokhov, M.A.
Shragin, B.I.*
Shteiger, A.S.*
Shtein, E.A.*
Shturman, D.*
Shukshin, V.M.
Shul'man, M.B.*
Shvarts, E.
Simonov, K.M.
Siniavskii, A.D.*
Skal'be, K.*
Slavin, L.I.
Slonim, M.L.
Slutskii, B.A.
Smirnov-Sokol'skii, N.P.
Smolenskii, V.A.*

Sobol', A.
Sokolov, S.*
Sokolov, S.A.*
Sokolov-Mikitov, I.S.
Sologub, F.K.
Soloukhin, V.A.
Solov'ev, S.M.
Solov'ev, V.I.*
Solzhenitsyn, A.I.*
Sorgenfrei, V.A.
Stavskii, V.P.
Steenberg, S.*
Steklov, I.M.
Stepun, F.A.*
Strugatskii, A.N.
Strugatskii, B.N.
Surguchev, I.D.*
Suslov, I.P.*
Sven, V.B.*
Svetov, F.G.
Svirskii, A.I.
Svirskii, G.T.*
Svobodin, A.P.

T

Tabidze, T.I.
Tal'berg, N.D.*
Tarsis, V.I.*
Teffi, N.A.*
Terapiano, I.K.*
Timofeev, L.M.
Tiniakov, A.I.
Tokaev, G.A.*
Tolstoi, A.N.
Topol', E.V.*
Trail, V.*
Trifonov, I.V.
Triolé, E.*
Trubetskoi, N.S.*
Tsvetaeva, M.I.
Tumanian, O.
Tushnova, V.M.
Tvardovskii, A.T.
Tyrkova-Williams, A.V.*

U

Uspenskii, P.D.*
Utkin, I.P.

V

Vainshtein, M.Z.*
Vaksberg, A.I.
Vasil'chikov, M.*
Vasil'ev, P.N.
Vasil'eva, R.R.
Vasilevskaia, V.L.
Veresaev, V.V.
Vergelis, A.A.
Vernadskii, G.V.*
Vershigora, P.O.
Vertinskii, A.N.
Vigdorova, F.A.
Vinokur, G.O.
Virta, N.E.
Vishnia, O.
Vishniak, M.V.*
Vladimov, G.N.*
Vlasov, I.P-
Vodov, S.A.*
Voinovich, V.N.*
Volfson, Z.B.*
Volin, B.M.
Volkov, S.M.*
Volokhonskii, A.G.*
Voloshin, M.A.
Voronskii, A.K.
Voskresenskii, V.I.
Voznessenskii, A.A.
Vvedenskii, A.I.
Vysotskii, V.S.

W

Weinbaum, M.E.*
Wrangel, A.P.*

Z

Zabolotskii, N.A.
Zaitsev, B.K.*
Zalesskii, M.N.*
Zalygin, P.P.
Zamiatin, E.I.*
Zaslavskii, D.I.
Zdanevich, I.*
Zemtsov, I.G.*
Zerov, M.
Zharov, A.A.
Zinov'ev, A.A.*
Zoshchenko, M.M.
Zurov, L.F.*
Zykov, M.A.*

Musicians, composers, conductors, singers (including musicologists, music critics and makers of musical instruments)

A

Adzhemov, K.K.
Agababov, S.A.
Akhron, I.I.*
Akhsharumov, D.V.
Akimenko, F.S.*
Akimova, S.V.
Al'chevskii, I.A.
Aleksandrov, A.N.
Aleksandrov, A.V.*
Aleksandrov, B.A.
Aleksandrovich, M.D.*

Alekseev, M.P.
Amiranashvili, P.V.
Andreev, P.Z.
Andreev, V.V.
Andzhaparidze, Z.I.
Anokhin, A.V.
Anosov, N.P.
Arakishvili, D.I.
Aranovich, I.M.
Arends, A.F.
Arkhangel'skii, A.A.
Arkhipova, I.K.
Arkhuzen, R.I.

Arutiunian, A.G.
Asaf'ev, B.V.
Ashkenazi, V.*
Ashrafi, M.A.

B

Babadzhanian, A.A.
Badridze, D.G.
Bakaleinikov, V.R.*
Baklanov, G.A.*
Balanchivadze, A.M.
Balanchivadze, M.A.

505

L

Labinskii, A.M.
Ladukhin, N.M.
Lagidze, R.I.
Lamm, P.A.
Lapshin, I.I.*
Laptev, K.A.
Laurushas, V.A.
Lavrov, N.S.
Lavrova, T.N.
Lavrovskaia, E.A.
Lazareva, R.F.
Lebedeva, A.R.
Lebedeva, E.I.
Lebedinskii, L.N.
Ledenev, R.S.
Leman, A.S.
Lemba, A.G.
Lemeshev, S.I.
Lenskii, A.S.
Leontovich, N.D.
Lepnurm, K.L.
Leshchenko, P.*
Lesman, I.A.
Levasheva, O.E.
Levashov, V.S.
Levi, N.N.
Levik, B.V.
Levik, S.I.
Levin, F.A.
Levin, I.A.*
Levina, Z.A.
Levitin, I.A.
Liadova, L.A.
Liapunov, S.M.*
Liapunova, A.S.
Liatoshinskii, B.N.
Lifshitsaite, N.
Lineva, E.E.
Lipaev, I.V.
Lipkovskaia, L.I.*
Lisitsian, P.G.
Lisitsin, M.A.
Listopadov, A.M.
Listov, K.I.
Litinskii, G.I.
Litvin, F.V.*
Litvinenko-Vol'gemut, M.I.
Liuban, I.I.
Liuboshits, A.S.
Liudkevich, S.F.
Liudmilin, A.A.
Livanova, T.N.
Lobachev, G.G.
Lobkovskii, A.M.
Lodii, Z.P.
Lokshin, A.L.
Lokshin, D.L.
Lubentsov, V.N.
Lufer, A.M.
Lukas, D.M.
Lukin, F.M.
Lur'e, A.S.*

M

Machavariani, A.D.
Magidenko, M.I.
Magomaev, M.M.
Maikapar, S.M.
Mailian, A.S.
Maizel', B.S.

Makarov, E.P.
Makarov-Rakitin, K.D.
Makarova-Shevchenko, V.V.
Maksakov, M.K.
Maksakova, M.P.
Maksimov, S.M.
Maldybaev, A.
Malinin, E.V.
Mal'ko, N.A.*
Markevich, I.B.*
Maslennikova, I.I.
Maslennikova, L.I.
Maslov, F.I.
Maslovskaia, S.D.
Massalitinov, K.I.
Matova, A.K.
Matsiutin, K.E.
Mazel', L.A.
Medvedev, M.E.
Medyn', Iakov G.
Medyn', Ianis G.*
Medyn', Iazep G.
Meichik, M.N.
Meitus, I.S.
Melikian, P.O.
Melikian, S.A.
Melik-Pashaev, A.S.
Melngailis, E.I.
Metner, N.K.*
Miaskovskii, N.I.
Miasnikova, L.V.
Mikhailov, K.N.
Mikhailov, M.D.
Mikhailov, N.N.
Miliutin, G.S.
Mil'man, M.V.
Mil'ner, M.A.
Milorava, S.E.
Mil'shtein, I.I.
Mil'shtein, N.M.*
Min'iar-Beloruchev, K.A.
Minkh, N.G.
Miroshnichenko, E.S.
Mirtskhulava, D.L.
Mirzoian, E.M.
Mishuga, A.F.*
Mlodek, R.M.
Mlynarskii, E.*
Mogilevskii, A.I.*
Mokrousov, B.A.
Molchanov, K.V.
Moldobasanov, K.
Monakhov, N.F.
Morfessi, I.I.*
Morozov, G.A.
Morozov, I.V.
Moshkov, B.P.
Mostras, K.G.
Mozzhukhin, A.I.*
Mravinskii, E.A.
Mshvelidze, S.M.
Mukhatov, V.
Mukhtarova, F.S.
Mullova, V.*
Muradeli, V.I.
Muradian, M.O.
Muravlev, A.A.
Musin, I.A.

N

Nabokov, N.D.*
Nadezhdin, B.B.

Nadirov, I.N.
Nalbandian, I.R.
Nasonov, V.T.
Nasyrova, K.
Natanson, V.A.
Nauialis, I.*
Nazarov, N.M.
Nazarov, N.V.
Nebol'sin, V.V.
Nechaev, V.V.
Necheporenko, P.I.
Neigauz, G.G.
Neigauz, S.G.
Nelepp, G.M.
Nest'ev, I.V.
Nezhdanova, A.V.
Niiazi, N.Z.
Nikolaev, Aleksandr Aleksandrovich
Nikolaev, Aleksandr Andreevich
Nikolaev, L.V.
Nikolaeva, T.P.
Nikol'skii, I.S.
Niman, F.A.
Nizhankovskii, O.I.
Nizhnikova, T.N.
Normet, L.
Nortsov, P.M.
Nosov, G.N.
Novikov, A.G.
Novikov, A.P.
Novikova, K.M.

O

Oborin, L.N.
Obukhov, N.*
Obukhova, N.A.
Oganesian, E.S.
Ognivtsev, A.P.
Ogolevets, A.S.
Ogonbaev, A.
Oistrakh, D.F.
Oistrakh, I.D.
Okaemov, A.I.
Okudzhava, B.S.
Olenin, A.A.
Olenin, P.S.
Olenina d'Alheim, M.A.
Onnore, I.I.
Orbelian, K.A.
Ordzhonikidze, G.S.
Orfenov, A.I.
Orlanskii-Titorenko, I.F.
Orlov, A.I.
Orlov, N.A.*
Orlova, A.A.
Orlova, E.M.
Orvid, G.A.
Osipov, N.P.
Ossovskii, A.V.
Ostrovskii, A.I.
Ots, G.K.
Ovanisian, N.M.
Ovchinnikov, V.
Ozerov, N.N.

P

Pakhman, V.*
Pakhmutova, A.N.
Paliashvili, I.P.
Paliashvili, Z.P.
Palitsyn, I.O.

Musicians, etc.

Stepanian, A.L.
Stepanian, R.G.
Stepanov, A.S.
Stepanov, V.P.
Stepanova, E.A.
Stiedry, F.*
Stogorskii, A.P.
Stolerman, S.A.
Stoliarov, G.A.
Stoliarskii, P.S.
Storozhev, N.*
Stravinskii, I.F.*
Strel'nikov, N.M.
Struve, B.A.
Stuchevskii, I.*
Suk, V.I.
Suslin, V.*
Svarog, V.S.
Sveshnikov, A.V.
Svetlanov, E.F.
Sviridov, G.V.
Syrmus, E.

T

Tabakov, M.I.
Taktakishvili, O.V.
Taktakishvili, S.M.
Tamarkina, R.V.
Tamberg, E.M.
Tarasov, V.
Tariverdiev, M.L.
Tarnopol'skii, V.M.
Tartakov, I.V.
Tavrizian, M.A.
Temirkhanov, I.K.
Terent'ev, B.M.
Ter-Gevondian, A.G.
Ter-Tatevosian, D.G.
Tesh, S.N.
Tigranian, A.T.
Tigranian, N.
Tigranov, G.G.
Timanova, V.V.
Timofeev, G.N.
Timofeev, N.A.
Tiomkin, D.*
Tits, M.D.
Tiulin, I.N.

Tiuneev, B.D.
Tkachenko, N.A.
Tol'ba, V.S.
Tolstoi, D.A.
Tolstoi, S.L.
Tomashev, D.P.
Tomilin, V.K.
Topman, A.
Trambitskii, V.N.
Troianovskii, B.S.
Tseitlin, A.D.
Tseitlin, L.M.
Tsereteli, T.S.
Tsesevich, P.I.
Tsfasman, A.N.
Tsomyk, G.D.
Tsybin, V.N.
Tubin, E.*
Tulikov, S.S.
Tumanina, N.V.
Turenkov, A.E.

U

Usov, A.I.
Uspenskii, N.D.
Uspenskii, V.A.
Utesov, L.O.

V

Vakhvakhishvili, T.N.
Vaksel', P.L.
Valter-Kiune, E.A.*
Varlikh, G.I.
Vasilenko, S.N.
Vasil'ev-Buglai, D.S.
Vedro, A.
Veisberg, I.L.
Vengerova, I.A.*
Vertinskii, A.N.
Vigner, L.E.
Vilinskii, N.N.
Villuan, V.I.
Vinogradov, K.P.
Vishnevskaia, G.P.*
Vitachek, E.F.
Vitol', I.*
Vlad, R.*

Vladimirov, M.V.
Vladimirova, M.V.
Vlasenko, L.N.
Vlasov, A.K.
Vlasov, S.G.
Volf-Izrael, E.V.
Volkonskii, A.M.
Volkov, S.M.*
Vronskii, E.A.
Vygodskii, N.I.
Vysotskii, V.S.

Z

Zagurskii, B.I.
Zak, I.I.
Zakharov, V.G.
Zarin', M.O.
Zarudnaia, V.M.
Zataevich, A.V.
Zavetnovskii, V.A.
Zbrueva, E.I.
Zednik, V.I.
Zeidman, B.I.
Zharov, S.A.*
Zhelobinskii, V.V.
Zherebtsova-Andreeva, A.G.
Zhiganov, N.G.
Zhilinskii, B.L.
Zhinovich, I.I.
Zhirkov, M.N.
Zhitomirskii, A.M.
Zhitomirskii, D.V.
Zhordania, V.
Zhubanov, A.K.
Zhubanova, G.A.
Zhuk, I.A.
Zhuk, V.I.
Zhukovskaia, G.V.
Zhukovskii, G.I.
Zhuravlenko, P.M.
Ziloti, A.I.*
Zimin, P.N.
Zimin, S.I.
Zimmermann, J.H.*
Ziv, M.P.
Zlatogorova, B.I.
Zolotarev, V.A.
Zybtsev, A.L.

Artists, designers, architects

A

Aladzhalov, M.K.
Aliakrinskii, P.A.
Amashukeli, G.*
Andreenko, M.F.*
Anisfeld, B.I.*
Annenkov, I.P.*
Anrep, B.V.*
Antonian, M.M.
Arkhipenko, A.*
Arkhipov, A.E.
Arnshtam, A.M.*

B

Baksheev, V.N.
Bakst, L.S.*

Baranov, V.M.
Bart, V.S.
Batiukov, I.P.
Benois, A.N.*
Benois, N.*
Benois, N.A.*
Berggolts, R.A.
Berman, E.*
Bialynitskii-Birulia, V.K.
Bilibin, I.I.
Bobyshov, M.P.
Bochkov, F.N.
Bogaevskii, K.F.
Bogdanov, I.P.
Bogdanov-Bel'skii, N.P.
Bokarev, K.S.
Bol'shakov, V.V.
Boskin, M.V.

Braz, I.E.
Brodskii, I.I.
Bruni, L.A.
Bulatov, E.
Burliuk, D.D.*
Bychkov, V.P.

C

Chagall, M.*
Chakhotin, P.*
Chekhonin, S.V.*
Chekhov, S.M.
Chekrygin, V.N.
Chemodurov, E.G.
Chistiakov, P.P.

Artists, etc.

Savitskii, G.K.
Sazonov, V.*
Semenov-Amurskii, F.V.
Serebriakova, Z.E.*
Serebrianyi, I.A.
Shapiro, V.*
Sharshun, S.I.*
Shchusev, A.V.
Shegal', G.M.
Shelkovskii, I.S.*
Shemiakin, M.M.*
Shestakov, N.I.
Shevchenko, A.V.
Shil'der, A.N.
Shishakov, N.I.
Shitov, S.F.
Shlein, N.P.
Shlugleit, I.M.
Shor, S.M.
Shteinberg, E.
Shtranikh, V.F.
Shul'ts, V.M.
Sidur, V.
Silich, L.N.
Simov, V.A.
Sitnikov, V.I.*
Slobodianiuk-Podolian, S.I.
Sokolov, N.A.
Sokolov-Skalia, P.P.
Sokolova, M.A.
Somov, K.A.*

Sosnovtseva, N.A.
Soutine, C.*
Soyer, R.*
Sredin, A.V.
Starkopf, A.
Staronosov, P.N.
Stenberg, E.G.
Stenberg, G.A.
Stepanov, A.S.
Suvorov, A.A.
Svarog, V.S.
Svetoslavskii, S.I.
Sychkov, F.V.
Sysoev, V.V.

T

Tal'iantsev, N.I.
Tarasenko, I.*
Tarkhov, N.*
Tavadze, T.G.
Trubetskoi, P.P.*
Tselkov, O.N.*
Tvorozhnikov, I.I.

U

Ul'ianov, N.P.

V

Valts, K.F.
Vanetsian, A.V.
Vasil'ev, P.V.
Vasnetsov, A.M.
Vasnetsov, V.M.
Vereiskii, G.S.
Verkhovskaia-Girshfel'd, T.M.
Vil'iams, P.V.
Vinogradov, S.A.*
Virsaladze, S.B.
Vladimirov, I.A.
Vladykin, M.A.
Vladykina, A.G.
Volkov, A.V.
Volkov, E.E.
Voskresenskii, R.N.
Vuchetich, E.V.

Z

Zarubin, V.I.
Zelenin, E.*
Zenkevich, B.A.
Zhedrinskii, V.I.
Zhilinskii, D.
Zhukovskii, S.I.
Zlatovratskii, A.N.
Zonina, E.N.
Zubkov, I.I.
Zverev, A.T.

The Ballet

A

Anisimova, N.A.
Astaf'eva, S.A.*
Asylmuratova, A.
Avdeenko, A.A.

B

Bakhrushin, I.A.
Balanchine, G.*
Baronova, I.*
Baryshnikov, M.*
Basil*
Bel'skii, I.D.
Berezka, D.*
Berezov, N.P.*
Berezova, A.A.
Bessmertnova, N.I.
Blok, L.D.
Bogatyrev, A.I.
Bolm, A.R.*
Borzov, A.A.
Bovt, V.T.

C

Chabukiani, E.V.
Chabukiani, T.M.
Chabukiani, V.M.
Changa, E.I.
Chekrygin, A.I.
Chekrygin, I.I.
Chernova, A.M.
Chernova, N.I.
Chernysheva, L.P.*

Chichinadze, A.D.
Chikvaidze, E.G.
Chistiakova, V.V.
Chkalova, N.N.
Chudinov, S.V.
Chudinov, V.A.
Chuzhoi, A.*

D

Danilova, A.D.*
Derevianko, V.I.*
Diaghilev, S.P.*
Dorinskaia, A.A.
Drozdova, M.S.
Dudinskaia, N.M.

E

Eduardova, E.P.
Eglevskii, A.*
Egorova, L.N.*
Eifman, B.I.
Ekston, A.M.
El'iash, N.I.
Elvin, V.*

F

Fadeechev, N.B.
Farmaniants, G.K.
Fedicheva, K.I.*
Fedorova, O.V.
Fedorova, S.V.*
Fenster, B.A.

Filippovskii, N.N.
Fokin, M.M.*
Fokina, V.P.*
Fominykh, L.N.
Froman, M.P.*

G

Gabovich, M.M.
Geiten, L.N.
Gel'tser, E.V.
Gerdt, E.P.
Godunov, A.*
Goleizovskii, K.I.
Golovkina, S.N.
Gorskii, A.A.
Grigor'ev, S.L.*
Grigorovich, I.N.
Grishkevich, M.N.
Gusev, P.A.

I

Iagudin, S.K.
Iakobson, L.V.
Iushkevich, I.*
Ivanovskii, N.P.

K

Karalli, V.A.*
Karsavin, P.K.
Karsavina, T.P.*
Khamzin, A.S.
Khanamirian, V.G.

Khliustin, I.N.*
Khokhlova, O.*
Khomutov, P.I.
Khudekov, S.N.
Kiaksht, G.G.*
Kiaksht, L.G.*
Kirsanova, N.*
Kniazev, B.*
Kokhno, B.*
Kolpakova, I.A.
Kondratov, I.G.
Konius, N.G.
Koren', S.G.
Kozlov, F.M.*
Kozlov, L.*
Kremshevskaia, G.D.
Kriger, V.V.
Kshessinskaia, M.F.
Kshessinskii, F.I.
Kulichevskaia, K.M.*
Kurgapkina, N.A.

L

Lapauri, A.A.
Lashchilin, L.A.
Lavrovskii, L.M.
Lavrovskii, M.L.
Legat, N.G.*
Leont'ev, L.S.
Lepeshinskaia, O.V.
Levashev, V.A.
Levinson, A.I.*
Lido, S.P.
Liepa, M.R.E.
Lifar, S.M.*
Lisitsian, S.S.
Litvinenko, V.K.
Liukom, E.M.
Lopukhov, F.N.
Lopukhova, E.V.
Lopukhova, L.V.*
Lukashova, I.P.
Lvov-Anokhin, B.A.

M

Makarova, N.*
Makletsova, K.P.*
Maksimova, E.S.
Mamedov, M.D.
Mamedova, S.G.
Martynov, G.R.
Mei, V.P.
Messerer, A.M.
Messerer, S.M.*
Mezentseva, G.S.
Mikhailov, M.M.
Mikhailichenko, I.G.
Mikhal'chenko, A.A.
Mitaishvili, L.I.
Mnatsakanian, E.G.
Moisseev, I.A.
Moisseev, M.F.
Moisseeva, O.N.
Mordkin, M.M.*
Morkovina, L.P.
Mosolova, V.I.
Muller, K.A.
Mungalova, O.P.
Muradian, Z.M.

N

Nadezhdina, N.S.
Nelidova, L.R.*
Nemchinova, V.N.*
Nikitina, T.P.
Nisnevich, A.G.
Nizhinskaia, B.F.*
Nizhinskaia, K.V.*
Nizhinskii, V.F.
Novikov, L.L.*
Nureev, R.G.*

O

Oblakov, A.A.
Obukhov, A.N.*
Obukhova, E.K.
Olbrei, R.I.*
Orlikovskii, V.*
Orlov, A.A.
Orlovskaia, N.N.
Osipenko, A.I.
Ozolin', A.K.

P

Panov, V.M.*
Panova, G.*
Papko, I.V.
Parsegov, V.V.
Pavlova, A.P.*
Pel'tser, N.V.
Pereiaslavets, V.*
Petipa, M.M.*
Petrov, P.N.*
Petrova, G.P.
Petrova, N.A.
Pirozhnaia, G.N.
Pisarev, A.A.
Plisetskaia, M.M.
Plisetskii, A.M.
Ponomarev, V.I.*
Pospekhin, L.A.
Preobrazhenskaia, O.I.*
Preobrazhenskii, V.A.
Presniakov, V.I.
Pushkin, A.I.

R

Radina, L.P.
Radunskii, A.I.
Ramishvili, N.S.
Ramonova, T.E.
Rassadin, K.A.
Reizen, M.R.
Riabinkina, E.L.
Riabushinskaia, T.*
Ritenbergs, H.A.
Romanov, B.G.*
Romanova, M.F.
Rozai, G.A.
Rozenberg, V.M.
Rubinstein, I.L.*
Ruzgaite, A.V.
Rykhliakova, V.T.
Ryzhenko, N.I.

S

Sabirova, M.A.
Safronova, L.N.
Samsova, G.*

Sanadze, T.G.
Sangovich, I.G.
Sapogov, A.A.
Sedova, I.N.*
Seliutskii, G.N.
Semeniaka, L.I.
Semenov, V.A.
Semenov, V.G.
Semenova, M.T.
Semizorov, N.L.
Sergeev, K.M.
Sergeev, N.G.*
Sergeev, V.I.
Shakhovskaia, G.A.
Shatilov, K.V.
Shavrov, B.V.
Sheina, S.K.
Shelest, A.I.
Shelkov, V.I.
Sheremet'evskaia, N.E.
Shikanian, D.A.
Shiriaev, A.V.
Shiripina, E.V.
Shliapina, G.A.
Shmyrova, T.I.
Shollar, L.F.*
Shvetsova, V.N.
Sidorov, A.M.
Simachev, N.R.
Simonova, N.I.
Sitnikov, G.B.
Skibin, G.*
Skuratov, V.*
Slonimskii, I.I.
Smirnov, I.V.
Smirnov, V.V.
Smirnova, E.A.*
Smirnova, M.V.
Smol'tsov, I.V.
Smol'tsov, V.V.
Smorgacheva, L.I.
Snetkova, E.P.
Sobeshchanskaia, A.I.
Sobol', A.M.
Sokolov, A.A.
Sokolov, N.S.
Sokolov, O.G.
Sokolova, E.P.
Sollertinskii, I.I.
Solov'ev, I.V.
Sorokina, M.S.
Sorokina, N.I.
Spesivtseva, O.A.*
Stanishevskii, I.A.
Stanislavskaia, M.P.
Stankevich, V.M.
Stankevich, L.S.
Statkun, T.V.
Stepanenko, G.
Strakhova, M.B.
Strode, I.K.
Struchkova, R.S.
Stukolkina, N.M.
Stupnikov, I.V.
Sudakov, G.V.
Sukhishvili, I.I.
Surits, E.I.
Suslov, B.V.
Suve, E.V.
Svetlov, V.I.*

The ballet

T

Tagirov, G.K.
Tairov, B.A.
Tairova, A.A.
Tamara Khanum
Taranovskaia, S.L.
Tarasov, N.I.
Tarasova, O.G.
Terekhova, T.G.
Tikhomirnova, I.V.
Tikhomirov, V.D.
Timofeeva, N.V.
Tkachenko, T.S.
Tomskii, A.R.
Trefilova, V.A.*

Tsarman, A.A.
Tsignadze, V.V.
Tumanova, T.V.*

U

Ulanova, G.S.
Urbel', I.A.

V

Vaganova, A.I.
Valukin, E.P.
Vasil'ev, V.V.
Vasil'eva, M.V.
Vasil'eva, Z.A.

Vazem, E.O.
Vershinina, N.*
Vil', E.I.
Vil'tzak, A.I.*
Vil'tzak, V.I.
Vinogradov, O.M.
Vladimirov, P.N.*
Volinin, A.E.*
Vronskii, V.I.

Z

Zhukov, A.V.
Zhukov, L.A.

Film, theatre & circus

A

Abesadze, O.D.
Abuladze, T.E.
Adomaitis, R.V.
Agadzhanova-Shutko, N.F.
Agishev, O.A.
Aleksandrov, G.V.
Al'pert, M.V.
Andreev, B.F.
Andreeva, M.F.
Araminas, A.
Arinbasarova, N.U.

B

Banionis, D.I.
Baranovskaia, V.F.
Barnet, B.V.
Batalov, A.V.
Batalov, N.P.
Bauer, E.F.
Bek-Nazarov, A.I.
Birman, N.B.
Blok, L.D.
Bogin, M.
Bondarchuk, S.F.
Borodai, M.M.
Bulla, V.K.
Buriatse, B.
Burliaev, N.P.
Bykov, R.A.

C

Chaikovskii, B.V.
Chardynin, P.I.
Cherkassov, N.K.
Cherviakov, E.V.
Chiaureli, S.M.
Chibisov, K.V.
Chkheidze, R.D.
Chokmorov, S.
Chukhrai, G.N.
Churikova, I.M.

D

Daneliia, G.N.
Demidova, A.S.
Demutskii, D.P.
Diebabov, D.G.
Dikii, A.D.

Dodin, L.
Donskoi, M.S.
Dovzhenko, A.P.
Durov, A.A.
Durova, E.R.
Dzigan, E.L.

E

Efremov, O.N.
Efros, A.V.
Eisenstein, S.M.
Ekk, N.V.
Erdman, N.R.
Ermler, F.M.
Ershov, I.V.
Evstigneev, E.A.

F

Faiko, A.M.
Fait, A.A.
Fedorova, V.
Fedorova, Z.A.
Fedoseeva-Shutko, L.N.
Fogel', V.P.
Frelikh, O.N.
Fridliand, S.O.

G

Gabriadze, R.L.
Gaidai, L.I.
Garin, E.P.
Gazhiu, V.
Gedris, M.V.
Gelovani, M.I.
Gerasimov, S.A.
Glebova-Sudeikina, O.A.
Gogoberidze, L.L.
Golovnia, A.D.
Gubarev, V.S.
Gureikin, S.A.
Gzovskaia, O.V.

H

Hurok, S.

I

Iakovlev, I.V.

Iakovlev, V.G.
Iaron, G.M.
Iarvet, I.E.
Ignatovich, B.V.
Il'enko, I.G.
Il'inskii, I.V.
Ioseliani, O.D.
Isarov, B.I.
Ishmukhamedov, E.M.
Iudin, K.K.
Iurenev, R.N.
Iurskii, S.I.
Iusov, V.I.
Iutkevich, S.I.
Ivanov-Barkov, E.A.
Ivanovskii, A.V.
Ivanov-Vano, I.P.
Ivashov, V.S.
Izvitskaia, I.V.

K

Kaidanovskii, A.L.
Kalatozishvili, G.M.
Kalatozov, M.K.
Kaliagin, A.A.
Kandel', F.S.
Kandelaki, G.I.
Kapler, A.I.
Kapralov, G.A.
Karasik, I.I.
Karmen, R.L.
Kaufman, M.A.
Kavaleridze, I.P.
Keosaian, E.G.
Khalip, I.N.
Khanzhonkov, A.A.
Kheifits, I.E.
Khitruk, F.S.
Khokhlova, A.S.
Kholodnaia, V.V.
Khutsiev, M.M.
Kikabidze, V.K.
Kirienko, Z.M.
Klepikov, I.N.
Kliachkin, R.
Klimenko, I.V.
Klimov, E.G.
Kmit, L.A.
Kniazhinskii, A.L.
Kobakhidze, M.G.
Kokochashvili, M.A.

Kommissarzhevskii, F.F.
Kostrichkin, A.A.
Koval'-Samborskii, I.I.
Kozintsev, G.M.
Kozlovskii, N.F.
Kramarov, S.
Kriuchkov, N.A.
Ktorov, A.P.
Kugel', A.R.
Kuleshov, L.V.
Kupchenko, I.P.
Kurbas, L.
Kuz'mina, E.A.
Kuznetsov, K.A.
Kvasha, I.V.

L

Lapikov, I.G.
Lapitskii, I.M.
Lavrov, K.I.
Lemberg, A.G.
Lemberg, G.M.
Leonov, E.P.
Levitskii, A.A.
Lilina, M.P.
Lisenko, N.A.
Litvak, A.
Liubimov, G.P.
Liubimov, I.P.
Livanov, V.B.
Lopushanskii, K.
Losskii, V.A.
Lotianu, E.V.
Luspekaev, D.B.

M

Maksakov, M.K.
Maksimov, V.V.
Malinovskaia, V.S.
Mamoulian, R.
Managadze, N.S.
Managadze, S.I.
Marchevskii, A.
Mardzhanov, K.A.
Maretskaia, V.P.
Martinson, S.A.
Maslennikov, I.F.
Massalitinova, V.O.
Medvedev, A.N.
Medvedkin, A.I.
Men'shov, V.V.
Meshkhiev, D.D.
Messerer, B.A.
Meyerhold, V.E.
Miasnikov, G.A.
Michurin, G.M.
Mikhalkov, N.S.
Mikhalkov-Konchalovskii, A.S.
Mikhoels, S.M.
Mitta, A.N.
Moskvin, A.N.
Moskvin, I.M.
Movshenson, A.G.
Mozzhukhin, I.I.

N

Nappel'baum, M.S.
Nardov, V.L.
Nazvanov, M.M.
Nekrasov, A.

Nemirovich-Danchenko, V.I.
Nikitin, F.M.
Nirod, F.F.
Norshtein, I.B.
Novitskii, P.K.

O

Obolenskii, L.L.
Okeev, T.
Okhlopkov, N.P.
Orlova, L.P.
Orlova, V.G.
Osyka, L.M.
Otsup, P.A.
Ozerov, I.N.

P

Paatashvili, L.G.
Panfilov, G.A.
Panso, V.K.
Papanov, A.D.
Papazian, V.K.
Paradzhanov, S.I.
Pashennaia, V.N.
Pel'tser, T.T.
Perestiani, I.N.
Petrenko, A.V.
Petritskii, A.A.
Petrov, N.M.
Petrov-Bytov, P.P.
Petrusov, G.G.
Pevtsov, I.N.
Pipinashvili, K.K.
Pisarevskii, D.S.
Pokrovskii, B.A.
Poloka, G.I.
Polonskaia, V.V.
Polonskii, V.A.
Popov, A.D.
Popov, O.K.
Preobrazhenskaia, O.I.
Protazanov, I.A.
Provorov, F.F.
Ptushko, A.L.
Pudovkin, V.I.

R

Raikh, Z.N.
Raikin, A.I.
Raizman, I.I.
Rassadin, S.B.
Razumnyi, A.E.
Rerberg, G.I.
Riazanov, E.A.
Rodchenko, A.M.
Romashin, A.V.
Romm, M.I.
Room, A.M.

S

Salkind, M.I.
Samoilova, T.E.
Sanin, A.A.
Sats, N.I.
Savel'eva, L.M.
Savvina, I.S.
Serov, G.V.
Shagin, I.M.

Shaiket, A.S.
Shamshiev, B.T.
Shatrov, M.F.
Shatunovskaia, L.
Shchukin, B.V.
Shengelaia, A.V.
Shengelaia, E.N.
Shengelaia, G.N.
Shengelaia, N.M.
Shepit'ko, L.E.
Shestakova, T.
Shishkin, A.V.
Shpalikov, G.F.
Shteinberg, I.V.
Shterenberg, A.P.
Shtraukh, M.M.
Shub, E.I.
Shukshin, V.M.
Simonov, E.R.
Simonov, R.N.
Skurikhin, A.V.
Slavinskii, E.O.
Slutskii, M.I.
Smoktunovskii, I.M.
Smolich, N.V.
Sokolova, M.A.
Solntseva, I.I.
Solonitsyn, A.A.
Sreznevskii, V.I.
Stanislavskii, K.S.
Stanitsyn, V.I.
Starevich, V.A.
Strizhenov, O.A.
Sverdlin, L.N.
Svilova, E.I.

T

Tairov, A.I.
Tarasova, A.K.
Tarich, I.V.
Tarkovskii, A.A.
Telegin, A.D.
Terekhova, M.B.
Tikhonov, V.V.
Tisse, E.K.
Trauberg, I.Z.
Trauberg, L.Z.
Tretiakov, S.M.
Tsekhanovskii, M.M.
Tsereteli, K.D.
Tsutsunava, A.R.
Turin, V.A.

U

Ul'ianov, M.A.
Urbanskii, E.I.
Urusevskii, S.P.

V

Vachnadze, N.G.
Vakhtangov, E.B.
Vampilov, A.V.
Vasil'ev, D.I.
Vertinskaia, A.A.
Vertinskaia, L.V.
Vertinskaia, M.A.
Vertinskii, A.N.
Vertov, D.
Vidov, O.
Volkonskii, S.M.

515

Film, etc.

Vronskii, S.A.
Vysotskii, V.S.

Z

Zabolotskii, A.D.

Zashchipina, N.A.
Zass, A.
Zelenaia, R.V.
Zel'ma, G.A.
Zhalakiavichus, V.

Zheliabuzhskii, I.A.
Zhemchuzhnaia, E.G.
Zhukov, P.S.
Zubovich, B.

Scientists (including doctors)

A

Afanas'ev, G.D.
Ageev, N.V.
Agoshkov, M.I.
Alekin, O.A.
Aleksandrov, A.D.
Aleksandrov, A.P.
Aleksandrov, P.S.
Alekseev, A.E.
Alekseevskii, N.E.
Alferov, Z.I.
Alikhanian, A.I.
Alikhanov, A.I.
Alimarin, I.P.
Ambartsumian, V.A.
Amiraslanov, A.A.
Andreev, N.N.
Andrianov, K.A.
Anichkov, N.N.
Anokhin, P.K.
Anoshchenko, N.D.
Anrep, G.V.
Antonov, O.K.
Arbuzov, A.E.
Arbuzov, V.A.
Artobolevskii, I.I.
Artsimovich, L.A.
Asratian, E.A.
Astaurov. B.L.
Avsiuk, G.A.

B

Babakin, G.N.
Bakulev, A.N.
Balandin, A.A.
Baranskii, N.N.
Bartini, R.L.
Basov, N.G.
Bei-Bienko, G.I.
Belavskii, S.I.
Beliaev, S.T.
Beliakov, R.A.
Belousov, V.V.
Belov, N.V.
Belozerskii, A.N.
Berg, L.S.
Beritashvili, I.S.
Bernshtein, S.N.
Bezredka, A.M.
Bitsadze, A.V.
Blokhintsev, D.I.
Blonskii, P.P.
Bochvar, A.A.
Bogdanov, A.A.
Bogoliubov, N.N.
Bogomolets, A.A.
Bogorov, V.G.
Bokii, G.B.
Bol'shakov, K.A.

Bonch-Bruevich, M.A.
Braunshtein, A.E.
Brekhovskikh, L.M.
Brodskii, A.I.
Bronshtein, M.P.
Bruevich, N.G.
Bruk, I.S.
Budker, G.I.
Budnikov, P.P.
Burdenko, N.N.

C

Chaplygin, S.A.
Chazov, E.I.
Chelomei, V.N.
Cherniaev, I.I.
Chernigovskii, V.N.
Chernov, D.K.
Chichibabin, A.E.
Chinakal, N.A.
Chugaev, L.A.
Chukhanov, Z.F.
Chukhrov, F.V.

D

Danilov, S.N.
Degtiarev, V.A.
Delone, B.N.
Demidov, G.G.
Deriagin, G.V.
Deviatkov, N.D.
Dikushin, V.I.
Dobrzhanskii, F.G.
Dolgoplosk, B.A.
Dollezhal, N.A.
Dorodnitsyn, A.A.
Dubinin, M.M.
Dubinin, N.P.
Dukhov, N.L.
Dumanskii, A.V.
Dzhanelidze, I.I.
Dzhelepov, B.S.

E

Eikhfeld, I.G.
Elanskii, N.N.
Emanuel, N.M.
Emel'ianov, V.S.
Engelgardt, V.A.

F

Fabergé, A.K.
Federov, E.K.
Fedorov, E.E.
Fedorov, S.
Fedorov, S.F.
Fedorov, V.G.

Ferdman, D.L.
Fersman, A.E.
Fesenkov, V.G.
Filatov, V.P.
Flerov, G.N.
Florensov, N.A.
Fok, V.A.
Fotiadi, E.E.
Frank, I.M.
Frumkin, A.N.

G

Galin, L.A.
Gazenko, O.G.
Gel'fand, I.M.
Gel'fond, A.O.
Ginzburg, V.L.
Girgolav, S.S.
Glushko, V.P.
Glushkov, V.M.
Gluzman, S.F.
Gorskii, I.I.
Grabin, V.G.
Grashchenkov, N.I.
Grave, D.A.
Gross, E.F.
Gubkin, I.M.
Gurevich, M.I.

I

Iakovlev, A.S.
Iangel', M.K.
Iankovich, L.D.
Iliukhin, S.V.
Imshenetskii, A.A.
Ioffe, A.F.
Ipat'ev, V.N.
Isaev, A.M.
Ishlinskii, A.I.
Iur'ev, B.N.
Ivanov, I.I.
Ivanov, L.A.

K

Kalashnikov, M.T.
Kalesnik, S.V.
Kalina, A.
Kamov, N.I.
Kantorovich, L.V.
Kapitsa, A.P.
Kapitsa, P.L.
Kargin, V.A.
Karpinskii, A.P.
Kazanskii, B.A.
Kazarnovskii, I.A.
Keldysh, L.V.
Keldysh, M.V.
Keldysh, V.M.

Scientists

W

Wilkitskii, B.A.

Z

Zel'dovich, I.B.

Zelinskii, N.D.
Zhdanov, V.M.
Zhukovskii, N.E.

Sport

Abdulbekov, Z.A.
Akimov, A.I.
Aleksandrov, B.V.
Aleksandrov, V.V.
Alekseeva, G.S.
Almetov, A.D.
Amosova, Z.S.
Andrianov, K.A.
Andrianov, N.E.
Anikin, N.P.
Anpilogov, A.S.
Antropov, O.P.
Antson, A.A.
Asatiani, N.P.
Astakhova, P.G.
Avilov, N.V.

B

Babich, E.M.
Babinov, S.P.
Bakatin, A.
Bal'boshin, N.F.
Baldycheva, N.V.
Barabash, T.B.
Baranova, L.V.
Barkalov, A.S.
Barysheva, O.F.
Bashashkin, A.V.
Bazhukov, N.S.
Beliaev, V.I.
Beliakov, V.T.
Belousov, V.P.
Belov, A.A.
Belov, S.A.
Belova, E.D.
Berdiaev, I.K.
Berkutov, A.N.
Biakov, I.I.
Blinov, I.I.
Blinov, V.M.
Bobrov, V.M.
Bocharova, N.A.
Bogdan, I.G.
Bogdanov, A.I.
Boiarskikh, K.S.
Bokun, G.
Boloshev, A.A.
Bolotnikov, P.G.
Bondarchuk, A.P.
Boreiko, V.V.
Borisov, V.F.
Borzov, V.F.
Botev, G.G.
Bragina, L.I.
Brumel', V.N.
Bugaenkov, I.V.
Bulatov, V.
Buldakov, I.
Buldakova, L.S.
Burda, L.V.
Burobin, N.A.
Burtsev, M.I.
Bushuev, V.G.

Butovskii, A.D.
Bykov, A.M.

C

Chaplygin, V.A.
Chasiunas, V.A.
Cherepovich, A.
Chernyshev, E.V.
Chesnokov, I.B.
Chikviladze, P.
Chimishkian, R.A.
Chirkova, S.M.
Chizhova, N.V.
Chochishvili, S.S.
Chukanov, A.A.
Chukarin, V.I.
Chukhrai, S.A.
Chuzhikov, N.F.

D

Danilova, P.A.
Daunen, T.V.
Davydov, V.S.
Degtiarev, A.V.
Dement'eva, E.G.
Deriugin, I.K.
Didenko, V.A.
Dmitriev, R.M.
Dolgushin, A.I.
Dreval', A.K.
Dubrovskii, V.I.
Duiunova, V.I.
Dyrdyra, V.F.
Dzeneladze, R.
Dzhugeli, M.N.

E

Edeshko, I.I.
Egorova, L.B.
Elizarov, A.M.
Emel'ianov, V.
Engibarian, V.N.
Eshinov, V.N.

F

Fediukin, A.V.
Fedorov, V.
Feriabnikova, N.V.
Filatov, I.N.
Filatov, S.I.
Filatova, M.E.
Firsov, A.V.

G

Ganzhenko, V.S.
Gassii, V.D.
Gazov, A.V.
Giliazova, N.F.
Glushchenko, T.G.
Golovanov, O.S.
Golovanov, V.S.

Golubichnyi, V.S.
Gorbachev, N.S.
Gorbiatkova, N.
Gorokhova, G.E.
Gorokhovskaia, M.K.
Gorshkov, A.G.
Grigor'ev, O.G.
Grishin, A.K.
Grishin, E.R.
Gromova, L.P.
Grozdova, S.K.
Guliaev, V.V.
Gundartsev, V.I.
Gurevich, B.M.
Gurevich, M.M.
Guryshev, A.M.
Gusakova, M.I.
Gusev, A.V.
Gushchin, A.P.

I

Iakushev, A.S.
Iakushev, V.P.
Iarygin, I.S.
Iashin, L.I.
Il'in, A.M.
Il'in, I.P.
Il'in, V.P.
Ionov, A.S.
Ionov, V.N.
Isaev, A.K.
Ishchenko, M.A.
Iukha, S.
Iumin, V.S.
Ivanitskii, A.V.
Ivanov, E.G.
Ivanov, N.P.
Ivanov, V.N.
Ivanov, V.T.
Ivanova, L.G.

K

Kabanov, A.S.
Kacharava, V.S.
Kalachikhin, V.A.
Kalinchuk, E.I.
Kalita, I.A.
Kaminskii, V.V.
Kapitonov, V.A.
Kapustin, S.A.
Karaseva, O.D.
Karavaev, O.N.
Karlova, L.A.
Karmanov, V.
Kartoziia, G.A.
Kazakov, R.A.
Kazankina, T.V.
Kharin, P.P.
Kharlamov, V.B.
Khimich, A.I.
Khisamutdinov, S.S.
Kidiaev, I.K.
Kiknadze, A.

Kim, N.V.
Kirzhinov, M.N.
Kizimov, I.M.
Klepikov, A.G.
Klim, R.I.
Klimenko, V.I.
Klimov, I.M.
Klimova, N.G.
Kniazeva, O.N.
Kochergina, T.I.
Kol'chin, P.K.
Kol'china, A.P.
Kol'chinskii, A.L.
Kolesnikov, N.A.
Kolesov, A.I.
Komnatov, G.V.
Konev, A.
Konovalenko, V.S.
Konstantinov, V.V.
Korbut, O.V.
Koridze, A.G.
Korkiia, M.S.
Korol', P.K.
Korol'kov, E.V.
Korshikov, G.E.
Koshel', A.V.
Koshevaia, M.V.
Kosichkin, V.I.
Kosykh, G.G.
Kotkas, I.I.
Kovalenko, S.I.
Kovalenko, V.A.
Kratasiuk, V.I.
Kravchenko, V.I.
Kravtsov, V.N.
Krepkina, V.S.
Kriss, G.I.
Krovopuskov, V.A.
Kruglov, N.K.
Krylov, I.N.
Kuchevskii, A.I.
Kuchinskaia, N.A.
Kudreva, N.A.
Kulakova, G.A.
Kulikov, E.N.
Kurentsov, V.G.
Kurviakova, R.V.
Kurynov, A.P.
Kuryshko, E.S.
Kushnerik, S.G.
Kuts, V.P.
Kuzin, V.E.
Kuzin, V.S.
Kuz'kin, V.G.
Kuznetsov, B.D.
Kuznetsov, B.G.
Kuznetsov, M.N.

L

Lagutin, B.N.
Lagutin, I.V.
Lapinskii, E.V.
Latse, R.
Latynina, L.S.
Lazakovich, T.V.
Lednev, P.S.
Lemeshev, V.I.
Leonkin, D.M.
Leont'eva, G.A.
Liapkin, I.E.
Likhachev, V.N.
Lilov, B.

Litoshenko, M.P.
Liugailo, S.A.
Lobanov, I.T.
Lobova, N.R.
Loktev, K.B.
Lomakin, T.F.
Luk'ianov, A.V.
Lusis, I.V.
Lutchenko, V.I.
Lysenko, L.I.

M

Maiorov, B.A.
Maiorov, E.A.
Makarenko, S.L.
Maksimov, V.S.
Mal'tsev, A.N.
Malyshev, I.A.
Mamatov, V.F.
Mamedbekov, R.
Manina, T.I.
Mankin, V.G.
Maslenkin, A.E.
Matushevas, V.L.
Matveev, B.
Mavlikhanov, U.A.
Medved', A.V.
Mekokishvili, A.S.
Mekshilo, E.P.
Melan'in, V.M.
Mel'nikov, B.B.
Mel'nikov, N.A.
Midler, M.P.
Mikhailov, B.P.
Mikhailov, I.M.
Mikhailovskaia, L.N.
Mikhal'chuk, V.I.
Minaev, E.G.
Minaicheva, G.I.
Mironova, Z.S.
Mishakov, E.D.
Mkrtychan, G.M.
Moisseev, I.I.
Mokeev, A.A.
Mondzolevskii, G.G.
Morozov, V.I. (1940–   )
Morozov, V.I. (1952–   )
Mukhacheva, L.A.
Mukhin, L.
Muratov, V.I.
Muratova, S.I.
Murauskas, R.

N

Nadyrova, T.P.
Nagornyi, S.V.
Nalbandian, S.R.
Nazlymov, V.A.
Nenenene, A.I.
Nesterova, K.I.
Netto, I.A.
Nevzorov, V.M.
Nikanchikov, A.
Nikiforov, V.V.
Nikolaev, V.V.
Nikolaeva, M.N.
Nikonova, V.G.
Novak, G.
Novikov, I.A.
Novikov, I.T.
Novikov, S.P.

Novikov, V.

O

Odinokova, L.I.
Ogon'kov, M.P.
Oliunina, A.S.
Ol'khova, N.A.
Oshchepkov, S.M.
Osipov, L.M.
Ovechkina, T.N.
Ozolina, E.A.

P

Pakhomova, L.A.
Panchuk, L.M.
Panin-Kolomenkin, N.A.
Pantiukhov, I.B.
Parfenov, A.I.
Pashkov, A.K.
Pavlovskii, A.
Petrenko, S.V.
Petrik, L.L.
Petrov, A.
Petrov, E.A.
Petrov, V.V.
Petukhov, S.A.
Petushkova, E.V.
Piatkas, K.
Pikkuus, A.N.
Pinaeva, L.I.
Pinegin, T.A.
Pinigin, P.P.
Pliukhfel'der, R.V.
Poiarkov, I.M.
Polivoda, A.I.
Polupanov, V.A.
Ponomareva, N.A.
Popenchenko, V.V.
Poradnik, L.K.
Pozdniak, D.I.
Press, I.N.
Press, T.N.
Prozumenshchikova, G.N.
Prudskova, V.A.
Puchkov, N.G.
Punkin, I.G.
Puzanov, N.V.

R

Ragulin, A.P.
Rakita, M.S.
Rastvorova, V.K.
Rezanov, A.G.
Rezantsev, V.G.
Riabchinskaia, I.P.
Rigert, D.A.
Rodnina, I.K.
Rogov, A.N.
Romanenko, V.P.
Romanov, A.O.
Romanovskii, V.V.
Romishevskii, I.A.
Roshchin, A.A.
Rubashvili, V.
Rudenkov, V.V.
Rudov, I.V.
Rupshene, A.S.
Rurua, R.V.
Rybak, I.M.
Ryl'skii, I.A.
Ryskal', I.V.

Sport

S

Saadi, E.F.
Safin, R.I.
Safin, S.S.
Safronov, V.K.
Sakandelidze, Z.A.
Salikhova, R.G.
Sal'nikov, S.S.
Samusenko, T.D.
Saneev, V.D.
Sarycheva, T.F.
Sass, A.F.
Savel'ev, S.P.
Savina, N.
Sedykh, I.G.
Selitskii, B.S.
Seliverstova, V.M.
Semenets, V.I.
Semenova, I.L.
Seredina, A.A.
Shabanova, R.M.
Shadrin, V.N.
Shaginian, G.A.
Shakhlin, B.A.
Shalimov, V.I.
Shamburkin, V.N.
Shamrai, G.I.
Shaparenko, A.M.
Sharii, V.P.
Sharov, I.D.
Shatkov, G.I.
Shavkaladze, R.M.
Shavrin, I.
Shidlovskii, A.G.
Shilkov, B.A.
Shishova, L.N.
Shmelev, V.K.
Shubina, L.E.
Shubina, M.T.
Shukhov, B.K.
Shutkov, F.V.
Shuvalov, V.G.
Sidel'nikov, A.N.
Sidiak, V.A.
Sidorenkov, G.I.
Sidorova, V.V.
Simashev, F.P.
Simonian, N.P.
Sisikin, I.F.
Sivko, S.
Skoblikova, L.P.
Skobov, I.G.
Smakha, M.

Smetanina, R.P.
Smirnov, V.G.
Smoleeva, N.N.
Sobchenko, V.G.
Sokolov, V.S.
Sologubov, N.M.
Solov'ev, N.N.
Spirin, L.V.
Starostin, Aleksandr, P.
Starostin, Andrei P.
Starostin, N.P.
Starostin, P.P.
Starshinov, V.I.
Stepanskaia, G.A.
Stepashkin, S.I.
Stetsenko, I.N.
Stolbov, P.A.
Sukharnova, O.L.
Sveshnikov, G.A.

T

Tal'ts, I.A.
Tarasov, A.A.
Tarmak, I.A.
Tatushin, B.G.
Tediashvili, L.K.
Terent'ev, F.M.
Tereshchuk, B.P.
Tikhonov, A.I.
Timoshinin, A.I.
Timoshkina, N.L.
Tishin, B.
Titov, I.E.
Titova, L.E.
Tiukalov, I.S.
Tiurin, O.G.
Tiurina, L.N.
Tomin, N.N.
Tregubov, I.S.
Tret'iak, V.A.
Tret'iakova, T.P.
Trofimova, N.I.
Tsalkalamanidze, M.V.
Tseloval'nikov, I.V.
Tsimakuridze, D.M.
Tsybulenko, V.S.
Tsygankov, G.D.
Turchina, Z.M.
Turishcheva, L.I.
Tyshchenko, M.
Tyshkevich, T.A.

U

Udolov, I.V.
Ukolov, D.M.
Ulanov, A.N.
Umarov, M.
Urbanovich, G.N.
Uvarov, A.N.

V

Vaitsekhovskaia, E.S.
Vakhonin, A.I.
Vasil'ev, V.I.
Vasin, V.A.
Vedenin, V.P.
Veinberga, T.E.
Veleva-Mel'nik, F.G.
Vengerovskii, I.N.
Vikulov, V.I.
Vinogradov, A.I.
Vinogradova, V.A.
Vinokurov, E.T.
Vlasov, I.P.
Volchetskaia, E.V.
Volkov, L.I.
Vol'nov, G.G.
Vorob'ev, A.N.
Voronin, A.N.
Voronin, M.I.
Voronina, Z.B.
Voronkov, V.P.
Vyrupaev, K.G.

Z

Zabelina, A.I.
Zaitsev, A.G.
Zaitsev, B.M.
Zaitsev, I.K.
Zaitsev, O.A.
Zakharova, G.P.
Zakharova, N.D.
Zamotailova, T.A.
Zhabotinskii, L.I.
Zharmukhamedov, A.M.
Zhdanovich, V.F.
Zhelezniak, I.I.
Zhigalov, A.
Zhigalova, L.
Zhigilii, L.V.
Zhluktov, V.V.
Zhmudskii, V.V.
Zimin, E.V.
Zinger, V.A.
Zybina, G.I.

Philosophers

A

Aksel'rod, L.I.
Aleksandrov, G.F.
Andreev, D.L.
Arsen'ev, N.S.
Askol'dov, S.A.
Asmus, V.F.

B

Berdiaev, N.A.
Bobrov, E.A.
Bogdanov, A.A.
Bogolepov, A.A.
Bulgakov, S.N.

C

Chelpanov, G.I.
Chizhevskii, D.I.

D

Deborin, A.M.

E

Ekzempliarskii, V.I.

F

Fedotov, G.P.

Florenskii, P.A.
Frank, S.L.
Fudel, S.L.

I

Il'in, I.A.
Il'in, V.N.

K

Karsavin, L.P.
Kartashev, A.V.
Kudriavtsev, P.P.

L
Lappo-Danilevskii, A.S.
Levitskii, S.A.
Lopatin, L.M.
Losev, A.F.
Losskii, N.O.
Lundberg, E.G.

M
Merezhkovskii, D.S.
Murav'ev, V.N.

N
Novgorodtsev, P.I.

P
Plekhanov, G.V.
Pomerants, G.S.

R
Radlov, E.L.

S
Shestov, L.I.
Spektorskii, E.V.
Stepun, F.A.
Svetov, F.G.

T
Tikhomirov, L.A.

Trubetskoi, E.N.
Trubetskoi, N.S.

U
Uspenskii, P.D.

V
Vysheslavtsev, B.P.

W
Weidle, V.V.

Z
Zander, L.A.
Zenkovskii, V.V.

Economists

A
Aganbegian, A.G.
Aleksandrov, I.G.
Antsiferov, A.N.

B
Bervi-Flerovskii, V.V.
Birman, I.I.
Bogdanov, A.A.
Bogoraz, I.A.
Brutskus, B.D.

C
Chaianov, A.V.
Czugunow-Schmitt, N.T.

D
Danielson, N.F.

G
Gol'dman, L.I.
Grinevitskii, V.I.
Groman, V.G.

I
Isaev, A.A.

K
Khodskii, L.V.
Kipen, G.A.
Kondrat'ev, N.D.
Krasnoshchekov, A.M.

L
Larin, I.

M
Makhal'skii, V.K.
Manuilov, A.A.

P
Posnikov, A.S.
Preobrazhenskii, E.A.
Primakov, E.M.
Prokopovich, S.N.

R
Rikhter, D.I.

S
Savitskii, P.N.
Skvortsov-Stepanov, I.I.
Slutskii, E.E.
Smit-Falkner, M.N.
Struve, P.B.

Z
Zaslavskaia, T.I.

Clergy (including church historians)

A
Afanasii (Sakharov)
Agafangel (Preobrazhenskii, A.L.)
Akakii*
Aleksandr
Aleksii (Ridiger, A.N.)
Aleksii (Simanskii, S.V.)
Anastasii (Gribanovskii)*
Antonii (Bartoshevich, A.G.)*
Antonii (Blum, A.B.)*
Antonii (Grabbe)*
Antonii (Khrapovitskii, A.P.)*
Anatolii (Gisiuk, A.G.)
Andronik (Nikol'skii, V.)
Arsenii (Zhadanovskii)

B
Bensin, V.M.*

C
Constantine (Zaitsev, K.)*

D
Damaskin (Tsedrik)*
Danzas, I.N.*
Dudko, D.S.

E
Efrem*
Ermogen (Golubov, A.S.)
Evgenii (Zernov, S.)
Evlogii (Georgievskii, V.S.)*
Evlogii (Smirnov, I.V.)

F
Famar (Mardzhanova, T.A.)
Feodor*
Feodora (Pilipchuk, N.V.)*
Filaret (Philaret; Voznessenskii, G.N.)*
Florenskii, P.A.
Florovskii, G.V.

G
Germogen (Dolganov)
Glagolev, A.
Glazunova, O.N. (Mother Aleksandra)
Gleb (Smirnov, I.I.)
Grigorii*
Gurii (Egorov, V.M.)

Clergy

H

Hackel, S.A.

I

Iakunin, G.P.
Illarion (Troitskii, V.A.)
Innokentii (Petrov, I.A.)*
Ioann (Alekseev, I.A.)*
Ioann (Maksimovich, M.B.)*
Ioann (Shakhovskoi, D.A.)*
Ioann (Snychev, I.M.)
Iosif (Petrovykh, I.S.)
Irinei (Bekish, I.)*
Iuvenalii (Maslovskii, E.A.)

K

Kallistrat (Tsintsadze, K.M.)
Kazem-bek See also: Politicians
Khariton*
Kirill
Konstantinov, D.*
Krug, G.I.*
Kuz'min-Karavaev, D.V.

L

Lavr*
Leontii (Turkevich, L.)*
Luka (Voino-Iasenetskii, V.F.)

M

Magdalina (Grabbe, N.P.)

Makarii*
Mansurov, S.P.
Manuil (Lemeshevskii, V.V.)
Maria (Pilenko, E.I.*
Meerson-Aksenov, M.G.*
Men', A.
Meyendorff, I.F.*
Mikhail (Ermakov)
Mitrofan (Krasnopol'skii, D.)

N

Nafanail (Lvov, V.)
Nikodim (Rotov, B.)
Nikolai (Iarushevich, B.D.)

P

Pavlin (Kroshechkin, P.K.)
Pelikh, T.T.
Petr (Polianskii, P.F.)
Petr (Zverev, V.)
Pimen (Izvekov, S.M.)
Platon (Kulbush, Kzelbut, P.P.)
Polozov, I.S.
Pol'skii, M.

R

Regel'son, L.L.
Rusak, V.S.
Ruzhitskii, K.I.

S

Seraphim (Batiukov)
Seraphim (Chichagov)
Sergii (Stragorodskii, I.N.)
Shavel'skii, G.*
Shavrov, V.M.
Shmeman, A.D.*
Siluan (Antonov, S.I.)*
Simforian*
Solov'ev, S.M.
Spiridon (Kisliakov, G.S.)

T

Tavrion (Batozskii)
Tikhon (Belavin, V.I.)
Trifon (Turkestanov, B.P.)

V

Varfolomei (Remov)
Vasilii (Krivoshein, V.A.)
Vasilii (Rodzianko, V.M.)*
Ven'iamin (Kazanskii, V.P.)
Ven'iamin (Voskressenskii, V.K.)
Vitalii (Maksimenko, V.I.)*
Vitalii (Ustinov, R.P.)*
Vladimir (Bogoiavlenskii, V.N.)
Vladimir (Tikhonitskii, V.M.)*
Zernov, N.M.*
Zheludkov, S.A.
Zhurakovskii, A.E.

Human rights campaigners

A

Abovin-Egides, P.M.
Agurskii, M.S.
Aikhenvald, I.A.
Airikian, P.
Akhmetov, N.
Alekseeva, L.M.
Amal'rik, A.A.
Antonov-Ovseenko, A.V.
Astra, G.

B

Begun, I.
Belov, I.S.
Bernshtam, M.S.
Bogatyrev, K.P.
Bogoraz, I.A.
Bogoraz, L.I.
Bonner, R.
Borisov, V.I.
Borodin, L.I.
Brailovskii, V.
Bukovskii, V.K.
Burzhuademov, K.

C

Chalidze, V.N.
Chertkova, A.
Chornovil, V.M.

D

Delone, V.N.
Demidov, G.G.
Dereviankin, A.
Dzhemilev, R.

E

Egides, P.M.
Esenin-Vol'pin, A.S.
Evdokimov, B.D.

F

Fainberg, V.I.
Fefelov, V.A.

G

Gabai, I.I.
Galanskov, I.T.
Germaniuk, U.S.
Gershuni, V.L.
Ginzburg, A.I.
Gluzman, S.F.
Gol'dshtein, P.I.
Gorbanevskaia, N.E.
Grigorenko, P.G.
Grigor'iants, S.
Grinberg, G.B.

I

Iakir, P.I.

K

Khartov, A.
Khodorovich, T.S.
Kistiakovskii, A.A.
Koriagin, A.
Krakhmal'nikova, Z.A.
Krasin, V.A.
Kukobaka, M.I.
Kvachadze, E.I.

L

Litvinov, P.M.
Liubarskii, K.A.

M

Madison, T.
Malakhovskaia, N.L.
Mamonova, T.A.
Marchenko, A.T.
Maslov, S.I.
Mitiunov, I.
Moroz, V.I.
Murzhenko, A.G.

O

Ogadzhanian, S.
Ogurtsov, I.V.
Orlov, I.F.

P

Pliushch, L.I.
Pod'iampol'skii, G.S.
Podrabinek, A.P.

R

Regel'son, L.L.

Rudenko, M.D.
Rusak, V.S.

S

Sakharov, A.D.
Senderov, V.
Sharanskaia, A.
Sharanskii, A.
Shimanov, G.M.
Shtein, E.A.
Shtern, L.I.
Shumuk, D.
Snegirev, G.I.

T

Terelia, I.M.
Titov, V.

U

Umerov, B.

V

Velikanova, K.M.
Velikanova, T.M.
Volkov, E.

Aristocracy

A

Aleksandr Mikhailovich (Romanov),
   Grand Duke
Aleksandra Fedorovna (Romanova),
   last Empress of Russia
Aleksei, Tsarevich, last heir

B

Bobrinskii, A.A., Count
Bobrinskii, V.A., Count

D

Dolgorukov, P.D. Prince

E

Elena Vladimirovna (Romanova),
   Grand Duchess

G

Girei-Klych, Sultan, Prince
Golitsyn, G.V., Prince

I

Ignat'ev, A.A., Count

K

Kirill Vladimirovich (Romanov),
   Grand Duke
Kokovtsov, V.N., Count
Kropotkin, P.A., Prince
Ksenia Aleksandrovna (Romanova)
   Grand Duchess
Kugushev, V.A., Prince
Kutuzov-Tolstoy, M., Count

L

Leonida, Grand Duchess
Lieven, Aleksandr Pavlovich, Prince
Lieven, Anatolii Pavlovich, Prince
Lieven, D.M., Princess
Lieven, D.A., Prince
Lieven, L.P., Prince
Lieven, P.P., Prince
Lobanov-Rostovskii, N.D., Prince
Lvov, G.E., Prince

M

Maria Fedorovna (Romanova),
   Empress of Russia
Mikhail Aleksandrovich (Romanov),
   Grand Duke
Moutafian, H., Princess

N

Nikolai II, last Russian Tsar
Nikolai Mikhailovich (Romanov),
   Grand Duke
Nikolai Nikolaevich (Romanov),
   Grand Duke

O

Obolenskii, S.S., Prince
Obolenskii, V.A., Prince
Olga Aleksandrovna (Romanova),
   Grand Duchess
Olga Nikolaevna (Romanova),
   Grand Duchess

P

Palei, V.P., Prince

S

Shakhovskaia, Z.A., Princess
Shakhovskoi, D.I., Prince
Sheremet'ev, A.D., Count
Sviatopolk-Mirskii, D.P., Prince

T

Tolstaia, A.L., Countess
Tolstaia, S.A., Countess
Trubetskoi, E.N., Prince
Trubetskoi, G.N., Prince
Trubetskoi, N.S., Prince
Trubetskoi, P.P., Prince

U

Urusov, S.D., Prince

V

Vasil'chikov, G.I., Prince
Vasil'chikov, I.S., Prince
Vasil'chikov, S.I., Prince
Vasil'chikova, L.L., Princess
Vasil'chikova, M., Princess
Vladimir Kirillovich (Romanov),
   Grand Duke
Volkonskii, S.M., Prince

W

Wrangel, A.P., Baron
Wrangel, P.N., Baron

Z

Zubovich, B., Baron

Foreigners involved in Russian affairs

A

Anders, W.
Antikainen, T.

C

Czapski, J.

D

Dowbor-Musnicki, J.

F

Falz-Fein, F.E.

G

Gachev, D.I.
Gavro, L.
Guenther, J. von

I

Ibaruri, R.

K

Kun, B.

L

Labourbe, J.M.

M

Madelung, A.
Mannerheim, K.G.E.
Middleton, S., Lady

Foreigners

P

Paleologue, M.
Philby, K.
Pontecorvo, B.M.

R

Rahya, E.
Riisman, A.T.

Rozin', F.A.

S

Sorge, R.
Steenberg, S.
Stiedry, F.
Strik-Strikfeldt, W.K.

Szamuely, T.

W

Walter, K.

Z

Zimmermann, J.H.

Miscellaneous

A

Agreneva-Slavianskaia, O.K.
Alekhin, A.A.
Alianskii, S.M.
Alloi, V.E.
Amarantov, B.
Andolenko, S.P.
Andreev, N.E.
Angelina, D.N.
Antsiferov, A.N.

B

Bagrov, L.S.
Bakhrushin, A.A.
Bark, P.L.
Basova, I.B.
Batiushkov, F.P.
Beilis, M.
Belinder, S.
Belokon', V.
Bel'skii, V.I.
Berezovskii, V.A.
Berg, R.L.
Bestuzhev-Lada, I.
Birman, I.I.
Bogdanova, N.S.
Bogdanovich, P.N.
Bogoraz, V.G.
Borisov, V.M.
Botvinik, M.M.
Brazhnikov, M.V.
Brezhneva, G.L.
Brik, L.I.
Brutskus, B.D.
Bulatovich, A.K.
Bulich, S.K.
Buryshkin, V.
Buryshkin, P.A.

C

Chuvanov, M.I.
Costakis, G.
Czugunow, T.K.

D

Dali, G.
Davitashvili, E.I.
Deterding, L.P.
Dostoevskii, F.F.

E

Evel'son, E.A.

F

Fabergé, K.G.
Felshtinskii, I.G.
Frenkin, M.S.

G

Golovatyi, F.P.
Golstein, A.V. (Holstein)
Gorbacheva, R.M.
Goricheva, T.M.
Gorlov, A.M.
Grekov, B.D.
Grigor'ev, A.D.
Grinkrug, L.A.
Grinkrug, M.A.
Gruzenberg, O.O.
Grzhebin, Z.I.
Gumilev, L.N.
Gurdzhiev, G.I.
Gurko, V.I.
Gurvitch, G.D.

H

Hackel, A.A.
Herzen, N.A.

I

Iakovleva, T.A.
Ianov, A.L.
Iashchenko, A.S.
Iokhelson, V.I.
Iskov, I.P.
Ivanov-Razumnik, R.V.
Izotov, N.A.

K

Kalmanovich, S.
Kamenetskii, B.E.
Kameneva, O.D.
Kaminskaia, D.I.
Kandinskaia, N.
Kannegiser, L.A.
Karpov, A.E.
Karskii, E.F.
Kasparov, G.K.
Kauzov, S.
Khodorovich, T.S.
Khudenko, I.
Kizewetter, A.A.
Klado, N.L.
Koni, A.F.
Korchnoi, V.L.
Kosminskii, E.A.

Kovalevskii, E.P.
Kovalevskii, P.E.
Koverda, B.S.
Krasin, V.A.
Kriukova, A.M.
Kriukova, M.S.
Krivoshein, I.A.
Krylov, V.P.
Kutuzov-Tolstoy, M.
Kuz'menko, G.A.
Kuznetsova-Budanova, A.K.
Kvitka, K.V.

L

Lamanova, N.P.
Lappo, I.I.
Larina, A.M.
Lavut, P.I.
Leger, N.
Lesnoi, S.I.
Liapunov, B.M.
Liatskii, E.A.
Likhachev, D.S.
Likhachev, N.P.
Lisovskii, N.M.
Lysenko, V.K.

M

Makarenko, A.S.
Makarenko, M.I.
Mamontov, S.I.
Margulies, M.S.
Martino, B.B.
Men'shagin, B.G.
Miller, M.A.
Minorskii, V.F.
Mints, I.I.
Mogilat, E.T.
Mollo, V.
Morozov, I.V.
Morozov, P.
Murav'ev, N.K.

N

Negretov, P.I.
Novitskaia, M.G.

O

Obnorskii, S.P.
Obolenskii, D.D.
Oldenburg, S.F.
Olenicheva, A.M.
Otto, A.F.
Ovechkina, N.